CAROL

W9-BDR-262

FIELDING'S CARIBBEAN

"That true otherness made up of delicate contacts, marvelous adjustments with the world, could not be attained from just one point; the outstretched hand had to find response in another hand stretched out from the beyond, from the other part."

from *Hopscotch*, a novel by Julio Cortazar

Fielding's
Caribbean
1982

by Margaret Zellers

Fielding Publications
105 Madison Avenue, New York, N.Y. 10016
In association with
William Morrow & Company, Inc.,
Publishers: New York

ISBN 0-688-00662-0

Printed in the United States of America

About the Author

Margaret Zellers is an inveterate traveler, but the Caribbean has long been her "second home," the place she chooses to settle when sun and sea seem to be the only things to sink in. Since graduation from Connecticut College, New London, she has been involved with traveling and writing for a living. Her first job, with a small advertising agency specializing in travel accounts, led to employment by the United States Virgin Islands government as director of their United States Information Office, with the responsibility of establishing and operating the area's first off-island tourism information office. Prior to that time, she has been involved with tourism efforts for the governments of Trinidad & Tobago, Barbados, pre-Castro Cuba, and the Dominican Republic. As a professional writer, Ms. Zellers apprenticed with the late Sydney Clark, named Dean of American Travel Writers by his colleagues and author of *All the Best in* . . . countries all over the world. Ms. Zellers worked on the books for the Mediterranean, Europe (including detailed books on specific countries), and the Caribbean. In 1973, Ms. Zellers took over as author, researcher, and area editor of *Fodor's Guide to the Caribbean, Bahamas and Bermuda,* a position she relinquished with the 1978 edition in order to write an entirely new Fielding's Caribbean which was first published for 1979.

Margaret Zellers was the first major travel guidebook author to acknowledge that local politics should be of interest to vacationers. Her "Political Picture," a factual assessment of the domestic politics for each island covered in the book, provides needed information and "The Caribbean Equation," an evaluation of the compatibility of visitors and domestic Caribbean communities, is widely respected, having been adapted for metropolitan U.S. newspapers and national magazines.

This edition of *Fielding's Caribbean* is the distillation of many years of travel in and around the Caribbean. It includes detailed information about well-known places including Cuba as well as the "unknown" islands of Anguilla, Terre de Haut, Canouan, Carriacou, Culebra, Jost Van Dyke, Bequia, Barbuda, and other small and special islands.

v

Other books by the author include:

Fielding's Sightseeing Guide to Europe—Off the Beaten Path (William Morrow & Company, Inc.)
Austria—The Inn Way (Geomedia Productions)
Switzerland—The Inn Way (Geomedia Productions)
Caribbean—The Inn Way (Geomedia Productions)
Bahamas—The Inn Way (Geomedia Productions)

Foreword

The Caribbean encourages three kinds of writing. The first is out-right fiction, and the novels make good vacation traveling companions. The second is starry-eyed travel writing, full of superlatives and well-chosen adjectives that describe the inevitable sun, sand, and sea. The third is political. This book is an effort to balance the last two subjects: travel and politics.

It's important to have the facts, not only about rooms, rates, and island activities, but also about what's happening in the country, to the people who live there. It's important to have the facts which relate to those of us who want to go to a Caribbean country for a week or two of relaxation, of swimming, sailing, scuba diving, or snorkeling, or of just being lazy in the sun with a good book. Is that dream possible? Yes. Without hesitation.

During the past year you may have read some of the comments about the Caribbean's politics and economics. There are many who know that some of the headlines have been misleading. There are others who are pleased to see some factual reporting finally come out of the Caribbean area—because the reporting seems to have focused U.S. government attention on an area too long neglected. Perhaps the attention can lead to action that will help our neighbors to the south. There are others who wish that the reporting could be more balanced so that the many constructive and important projects that have taken place in the Caribbean could have at least equal coverage.

By reading the specific island's "Political Picture" in the following chapters, studying the "Touring Tips," and hotel and restaurant commentary, you can decide which of the islands is right for you. Timid travelers will be more content in some places than in others; experienced travelers sensitive to the problems facing Third World countries will find interesting vacation pursuits on all islands.

"The Caribbean Equation" that follows (in the Introduction) may seem unusual text for a travel book, but awareness is the key to comfortable travel today. My concern is not so much what there is to do on an island as how we outsiders can best enjoy ourselves and, at the same time, do so with the greatest benefit to the places we are visiting. Only mutually rewarding visitor-host relationships are worth pursuing. Comments about the areas I have traveled for this edition reflect my assessment of just how well that essential goal is accomplished.

This 1982 edition of *Fielding's Caribbean* has been researched since sometime in the 1950s, when I made my first visit south. That visit left me with the first, and vital, impact. The edition you are holding, however, includes thoughts on the newest facts and trends in the Caribbean and involves more than 20 trips to Caribbean countries since the last edition went to press. The result is an interweaving of observations on an area I have known through the years.

During that time, there have been many who have helped me to understand what was, for me, at first, a foreign land. I am not a West Indian, but I empathize with the West Indian's challenges in today's Caribbean—and I thank many of my Caribbean colleagues and friends for making this book possible by sharing their thoughts and their cultures, and by showing me their sincere efforts to create a climate that is comfortable for visitors.

Especially I thank the people of the Caribbean—the lady in the Beetham market who showed me how to make sorrel and the one in Kingstown who gave me a lesson in spices; the fisherman on the beach at Turtle Bay who explained how he mended his nets and the lady selling flying fish at Oistins who shared her favorite way to cook the small fish; the friend in St. George's who entertained me in the 200-year-old family homestead and another who whisked me through the market at Fort-de-France before we went home to brew up blaff and dine with the family.

The travel world acknowledges that it was Temple Fielding who gave most travelers the courage to take suitcase in hand to set off for places unknown. It is his tradition that was an inspiration for this book.

My particular voyage through the writing of this book would not have been possible without the unfailing support of several people. First and foremost, my own family deserves heartfelt thanks for providing surcease from the piles of manuscript pages, and for the special thoughts that come forth when three generations share their Caribbean experiences. For patience beyond totaling, and for unflagging encouragement, thanks go to Morrow senior editor Eunice Riedel and my copy editor Naomi Black; and without the tireless typing of Ann Janovich, this book would never have gotten to the publisher.

My wish for all of you who seek hints for a happy Caribbean holiday in the pages that follow is that you will enjoy many wonderful experiences and relaxing times in the Caribbean, and that you will find in these islands at least some of the portion of joy that I have known. Happy vacation!

How This Book Is Researched—and Why

Helping you know what to look for, pointing out ways to find what's best for you, and helping you feel comfortable with your decision/investment in a Caribbean vacation is waht this book is all about. The government tourist offices, listed at the start of each chapter, can give you lists and current prices. This book is written to give you personal comments about all the places seen and settled in, in your behalf.

There are lobbies for travel agents, and one purpose of the American Society of Travel Agents is to get a better break for the agent. The airlines and steamship lines have their groups and associations who lobby for a better break for the company, and probably for carriers in general. Only the traveler has no lobby—and it's essential, therefore, that travelers be wary and wise, doing homework *before* traveling, and being aware *when* traveling, to get a better break with today's complex pricing and procedures. At the moment, although travelers are heading into the Caribbean from North America and Europe in unprecedented numbers, there is no consumer protection group for Caribbean travelers. This book is written to serve that purpose: to give you, the traveler, the benefit of a reporter's observations during constant and spontaneous travel through the Caribbean.

Coverage, while striving to be objective, is honest—and not completely impartial. In a few instances, for the benefit of readers, I have had to access (and criticize) a "friend," be it a hotel that has gone sour, in my opinion, an island that has sold its soul for cash, or a building that, although built with the best intentions, is not well designed for the function it serves. I have the interests of the traveler/consumer at heart, since I am one, but I also have a sincere dedication to working toward a Caribbean tourism that is compatible with the wishes of the West Indians who live in this area. Things seen and experienced during travels go into the observations and tips passed along to you. The experiences are my own; secondhand comments are noted as such.

Caribbean colleagues know that I roam on my own. They have seen me on the streets of their towns, at their airports, in the lobbies of their hotels, and seated in dining rooms, restaurants, and inns, as they go about their daily business while I am conducting mine. This book is the result of many years of wandering around the Caribbean, looking into all corners, climbing peaks and ashore at beaches. It is essential that opinions and facts give a reasonable and just comparison of facilities. The only way I can do that is to go to each place myself.

All of the places covered in this book have been personally visited— and several times. It is possible to get information from government representatives and public relations firms, and facts are checked with these offices, but there is nothing to compare with firsthand impressions. This Caribbean guide has been researched and written entirely by the author. The personal opinions expressed throughout the book are mine. Acceptance of favors from island governments and hotels has involved *only* practical help with getting from here to there, to see as much as possible on behalf of you who invest in this book. On occasion, travel assistance has meant lending me a car, or helping with arrangements to rent one at height of season (when there are no cars available). Other times it has meant flying around in a friend's airplane, or going by motorboat or sailboat, or making arrangements to charter a plane to cover distances quickly. At no time have I taken, or would I consider taking, money or favors for inclusion or praise in this guide or for comment in any of my work / writing.

As you can appreciate, it would be the rare (unfortunate) person who has worked with an area for more than 20 years and not made some good and lasting personal friends. My friendship with the people in the Caribbean is one thing, however; my business of writing and reporting is another. My responsibility is that of a reporter, stating the facts as I see them and bringing to my viewpoint as much information and background about the situation as I can possibly obtain by advance research and interviews. Sources are Caribbean friends and acquaintances as well as others who are involved with the area.

I subscribe to the Code of Ethics of the Society of American Travel Writers, of which I am a member. In addition, I am a longtime member of and enthusiastic participant in the Caribbean Tourism Association and the Caribbean Hotel Association. These organizations provide the opportunity to learn what the island areas see as their problems, and what they are doing to correct them. They also provide an arena for meeting with island officials and residents to modify some of the areas that we, as tourists and outsiders, see as problems. It is for these reasons that I serve as Director for Allied Members on the Board of the Caribbean Hotel Association.

Comments, observations, and suggestions are welcomed from all readers. I will do my best to reply to inquiries addressed to me as author of *Fielding's Caribbean,* in care of my publisher, William Morrow & Company, Inc., 105 Madison Avenue, New York, NY 10016.

Contents

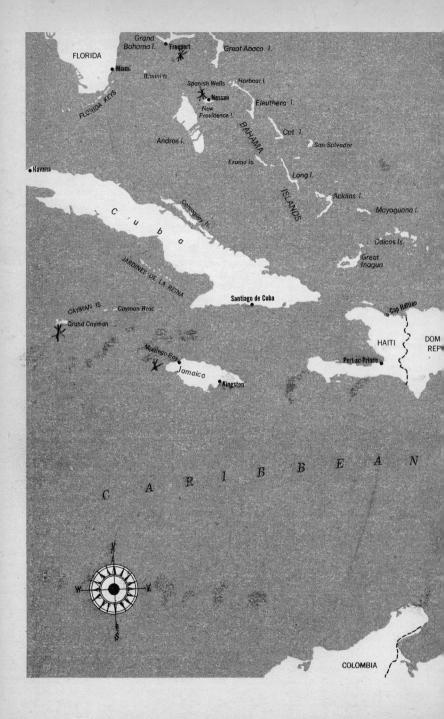

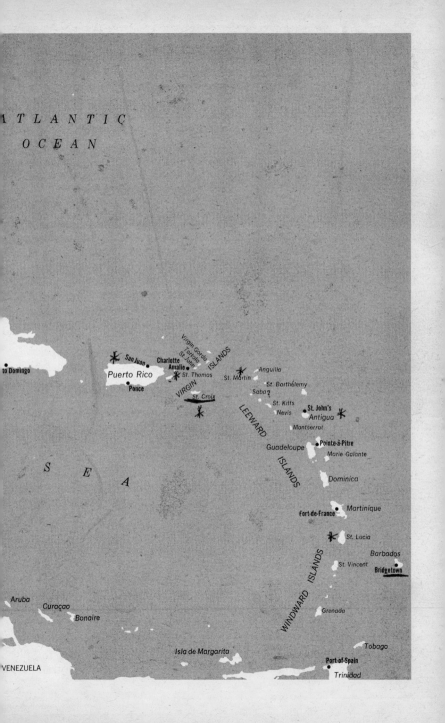

Introduction

THE CARIBBEAN EQUATION 1982

∙∙

"The Caribbean Equation," a current assessment of the expectations of vacationers and the realities of life in the Caribbean countries, first appeared in the 1981 edition of this guide. Constant
travels throughout the area, and interviews with political leaders as
well as with prominent members of the opposition and with local
businessmen, have contributed to the thoughts expressed in this
1982 Caribbean Equation. Portions of the following editorial have
appeared in the *Chicago Tribune* travel section, the *New York
Times* special Caribbean-Bahamas section, and in *ASTA Travel
News,* a magazine distributed to members of the American Society
of Travel Agents.

∙∙

Vacationers invest their hard-earned cash in what is promised as a
"dream vacation." Caribbean nationals of Third World countries
are demanding their right to the basic necessities of life. Can these
two forces be balanced? What is the solution to the "Caribbean
Equation"?

"It is our true policy to steer clear of permanent allegiances with
any portion of the foreign world." The comment is George Washington's, in his Farewell Address delivered on September 17, 1796.
Why is it, then, that we in the U.S. have such a difficult time accepting that our colleagues in the Caribbean are interested in development plans that may not complement our own? Are we so
unsure of our own free-enterprise system that we cannot tolerate
comparisons with other systems? Or is it that we have ignored our
responsibilities to help our friends to the south and now notice—
possibly too late—that Fidel Castro has sent out more effective
emissaries than we have?

It is only in recent months that Caribbean nations have come to
be perceived as having concerns similar to those of the Central

American countries. It is the Communist connection, emanating from Castro's Cuba, that has focused attention on the area. There is a danger, however, that some of the crucial economic and social problems that have been affecting the Caribbean islands for the past 20 years and more are being overlooked in the flurry of concern about "communism."

Except for the recent spray effect out of Communist Cuba, the islands of the Caribbean—those communities that form the slats of a picket fence that bulges eastward between the U.S. and South America and are washed by the eastern swells of the Caribbean Sea—have little more than poverty in common with the Central American countries. For the most part, they don't share a language, or even much of their heritage.

However, we in the U.S. should not underestimate the camaraderie of Third World countries, especially among those with geographical proximity. Although the friendships now being forged may be new ones (as between Cuba, which traditionally has preferred to think of itself as a Latin America country, and the small Caribbean island country of Grenada), they are based on a mutual need for a fast solution to the problems of poverty, food production, and adequate social services (hospitals, schools, etc.) and a mutual distrust of the superpowers.

Mr. Jean Holder, Executive Director of the Barbados-based Caribbean Tourism Research and Development Centre, has pointed out that *"We are 20 million people mostly on small islands, 12 under 200 square miles, some barren, stretched over a sea of 1,049,000 square miles, and living next door to the world's largest consumer society. We speak between 4 and 6 languages if you include patois and Papiamento, which divide us. We inherited a preference to look outward to Europe and North America, a distaste for regional cooperation, and a distrust of our Caribbean neighbors."*

Caribbean nationals attribute their present alignment not so much to political philosophy as to the fact that they have desperate and immediate needs that sometimes appear to have been addressed effectively by Communist Cuba.

"It is not very meaningful in the circumstances of our country to claim to adapt any particular 'ism,' for our problems require solutions which come from a variety of ideological sources," Dominica's eloquent Prime Minister Eugenia Charles said at a meeting in St. Maarten last fall.

"I am of the view that the broad mass of people of the Eastern Caribbean are not concerned with ideological models per se," Prime Minister Charles noted. "They are seeking a change in their low level of living. They are demanding the basic necessities of life and, increasingly, they are turning to serious-minded, experienced leaders to assist them in this."

George Odlum, the charismatic former deputy prime minister of St. Lucia, who formed his own political party in May '81, has sometimes been criticized for his Communist/Socialist friendships. Odlum has said, "If you talk to the man on the street in St. Lucia, he knows—and cares—nothing about Russia, America, capitalism, or communism. The urgency of the ideological way is not important. His main struggle is food."

At the first hint of need, Cuba has sent technicians, doctors, and educators (but seldom money, which is in short supply in Cuba). "Exporting the revolution" is one of the basic tenets of Marxism, and in the eyes of Caribbean countries, where new leaders are faced with awesome poverty and other problems, fast action by Cuban emissaries has created the impression that something significant is being done. Many Caribbean leaders, desperate for *some* visible activity in their fight for a better life for their people, overlook the ideological "assistance."

Thus, the aid to Jamaica by Cuban doctors and technicians resulted in visible health and building benefits that scored points for former Prime Minister Manley's government. Hospitals received improved services, schools were built, microdams were constructed for agriculture in the countryside. No one seemed to care much—at first—about the ideology that was planted along with the visible structures. (Election results in October 1980, however, proved that a people nurtured with democracy and free enterprise were loath to give it up.)

In Grenada, the new government of Maurice Bishop was able, within a few months, to point with pride to the start of a new airport within convenient distance of the capital of St. George's. Little matter that stacks of U.S. and Canadian-financed feasibility studies had "proved" that an airport on that terrain would be unsuitable. Grenadians believed (and still believe) that their present Pearls Airport, in the northern quarter of the country, over an hour's ride from the capital, was a serious handicap to development of industry and tourism.

The Grenadians will now have the airport they want and the credit goes to Cuba. Some speculate that Cuba's interest was encouraged by the opportunity for Communist control of the surrounding sea. (It is worth noting that, while Cuba is considered responsible for the new airport, the country has, in fact, supplied only construction equipment and personnel for which the impoverished Grenadian government must pay all operating expenses.

Venezuela has stepped in to provide asphalt and aid has come from other quarters, but Cuba continues to get most of the credit and a bond has thereby been built.)

Similar stories can be told, perhaps in less dramatic terms, for other Caribbean island countries. Regrettably, it took Cuban inroads in Jamaica and support for Grenada to spark a reaction from the U.S. government and private enterprise. The Reagan administration's focus on the problems in El Salvador, a Central American country that faces the Pacific Ocean, temporarily diverted attention from the Caribbean island communities, but the U.S. government is studying a long-term aid program, in association with Germany, and other European countries, as well as with Venezuela.

Tourism remains crucial for the countries of the Caribbean. Most have little else as a source of hard currency or employment. Trinidad has oil, Jamaica has bauxite, the Dominican Republic has nickel and other ores, but for most Caribbean islands the main crop is sugar—and tourists. Even the Commonwealth of Puerto Rico, where a very effective Operation Bootstrap has created an industrial economy, admits that tourism is a major factor in its economy.

When tourism "turns off," island economies are in big trouble. St. Croix in the U.S. Virgin Islands knows that; Jamaica knows that; even the Bahamas, while not in the Caribbean Sea, shares the problems inevitable when tourism "dries up."

"We want you. We welcome you and we benefit from seeing you in our islands," Jamaica's Minister of Tourism, Eric A. Abrahams, told a gathering of travel personnel at a meeting early this year.

His statement to the travel trade echoed the more encompassing words spoken frequently by Prime Minister, Edward Seaga, whose Jamaica Labour Party was elected by overwhelming margin in October 1980. Prime Minister Seaga's party defeated the People's National Party whose leader, Michael Manley, had espoused "democratic socialism." The PNP's friendship with Castro's Cuba, and its flirtation with Communism are well known.

Abrahams made references to his Jamaica Labour party government as one "born out of a political party that went to the polls on October 20, 1980 on some of the most fundamental issues facing poor countries today."

"What emerged out of that election was a clear message that the people of Jamaica have decided, after a long and painful experiment, that the route we will go is the route of the western democratic system and the free enterprise method of economic development."

"We have chosen that road not to cast us into any subservient role. We have chosen that road because of a stark realization that what we need to lift the level of the people of our country, more than anything else, is foreign inflows of money, foreign inflows of capital and foreign inflows of technology. And we don't believe that there is much prospect of us finding those inflows from the eastern European countries."

"There is very little difference," Abrahams noted, "between men irrespective of their political views as to goals. The goals are improvement and development."

Jamaica's dramatic turn from a course that appeared to lead to Communism may well turn the tide in the Caribbean island countries. Certainly all Caribbean countries are aware of the impressive election victory of the Jamaica Labour Party, and of the fact that free elections by the people of Jamaica resulted in that change. (The island of Dominica had had an equally impressive but less heralded turn of government a few months earlier when Dominican lawyer Eugenia Charles became Prime Minister, following the overwhelming victory of her Dominica Freedom Party over the imcumbent. Prime Minister Charles had been outspoken in her support of a democratic free enterprise system as the only profitable route for Dominica's future.)

Less than 20 years ago, there were 3 independent countries among the islands of the Caribbean. Cuba, the Dominican Republic, and Haiti had independent, albeit fragile, governments. In 1962, Jamaica and Trinidad & Tobago became independent, having pulled out from the fledgling West Indies Federation (of British Caribbean colonies) so weakening that organization that it dissolved a few years later.

Today there are 13 independent countries in the Caribbean, and Antigua is the fourteenth on November 1, 1981. It is reasonable to expect that most British-affiliated islands will become independent within a few years and the Netherlands Antilles also plan for independence. Many of the new nations have absorbing hard currency problems, in addition to unemployment, inadequate social services, and an infrastructure of roads and public utilities that can be described as archaic at best.

"Tourism plays a much more significant role than its contribution to the economy indicates," Puerto Rico's governor Carlos Romero Barcelo said in an interview in mid-March. "Tourism doesn't contribute that much to our gross state product, but the people who come to Puerto Rico and know Puerto Rico can help improve our image."

According to an official from the Puerto Rico Tourism Company, set up for the supervising and promotion of tourism, "about 8% of the work force is in tourism—about 60,000 jobs, and $600 million comes into the economy from toursim." In addition, as a benefit to the people of Puerto Rico, the competitive air fares that are available for tourists to Puerto Rico also help subsidize the air fares for Puerto Ricans.

On Barbados, where tourism has increased ten fold in the past 17 years, and the number of visitors hit record levels last year, the Barbados Board of Tourism has a program called "Make A Friend For Barbados." It is a community level program which involves not only the Ministry of Tourism, but also the Government Information Service, the Ministry of Education and Culture, the University of the West Indies Extra Mural Division, the Barbados Hotel Association, and workers' organizations.

Caribbean countries (or states) where tourism is still a fledgling business, but aspirations are great, are also devoting time and energies to "Tourism Week" programs. Antigua, St. Vincent, St. Kitts, and Trinidad & Tobago are among those islands that hold community programs in the late fall, and involve not only the hotels, but also the school children and the community in events that include seminars and cooking competitions.

Tourism as an avalanche of outsiders is relatively new to the Caribbean area, and many places were totally unprepared. Although hotel structures, built by professional (and off-island) international entrepreneurs, rose relatively rapidly on the best beaches of many Caribbean countries, little had been done about training of staff for those sophisticated properties. Village communities were overwhelmed by bikinied vacationers (they still are in many cases), and local sensitivities have been bruised.

By far the most effective catalyst to U.S.-Caribbean cooperation in recent months has been Caribbean/Central American Action, the Washington-based group that has undergone several name changes to reach its present acronym of CCAA. With a board of directors that includes an impressive array of U.S. corporate executives and Caribbean community leaders, CCAA has encouraged the increasingly important annual Conference of the Caribbean, held in Miami, and arranged the linking of U.S. Chambers of Commerce with Caribbean island chambers.

Founded in 1980, the organization defines its goal as not directly funding or administering projects, but "serving as a leveraging mechanism." It can look to a substantial record of projects created and/or helped along by its influence.

Through regional organizations—the Caribbean Tourism Association, the Caribbean Hotel Association, the Eastern Caribbean Tourism Association (whose energies are devoted to a half-dozen British-affiliated islands)—progress is being made. Bridges for inter-island communication have been built, and ideas are being shared. The Caribbean community is defining its goals, and implementing them. Tourism programs are being strengthened while alternative industries are being explored and developed. Opportunities for visitors to participate in local activities, be they Rotary Club meetings, Garden Club functions, talks at schools, contributions to island libraries and hospitals, or simply visits with island residents in their homes, are vast. Vacationers need only to express an interest.

While the people in the islands concentrate on being good hosts, many vacationers are preparing to be good guests. The Caribbean Equation—that delicate balance between carefree vacationers and care-burdened residents—requires sensitivity to all elements for a solution. The paradise image can become reality as many visitors know. One need only sail these seas, play these golf courses, fish these waters, wander through tropical forests and gardens, and share experiences with these people.

The Caribbean has changed over the past 20 years, and it is still changing. The same can be said of visitors. It seems reasonable to expect that, given the basic elements of the Caribbean communities (including their God-given virtues) and the basic elements for holiday plans, a solution is possible for the mutual advantage of both sides. A well-prepared visitor is a more sensitive tourist, and appealing to the senses is what this area is all about.

YOUR VACATION AND . . .

Safety: Comprehensive surveys about travel patterns seem to focus on "safety" as a major concern for most vacationers, and few areas have been as battered by "bad" headlines as have the islands of the Caribbean. One reason, I believe, is not that crime is any worse in these islands than it is in the rest of today's complicated world, but that many nonisland residents have grown up with a "paradise" image that is only reluctantly juxtaposed with reality. These islands *do* look like your dream island, be it Robinson Crusoe's retreat, or "Fantasy Island," or those glorious promotion pictures you see. And the Caribbean countries can be like that, and usually are. But they are also developing nations, and the interweaving of "haves" and "have-nots" is difficult at best, volatile at worst. Tourists are definitely "haves," whether you think of yourselves in that category or not. The fact is, anyone basking in the sun on a Caribbean beach has paid a substantial sum to be there and, with hotel rates, to stay there. The value of the clothes in one suitcase equals far more than a month's wages for a lot of people of the Caribbean, and in fact, is closer to the equivalent of the income for a year in some places. Add to that the cameras, sports equipment, and extra trappings—and you certainly see a "have."

All island governments are conscious of the need to protect not only you, but also their own people. Yes. You will be safe in the usual vacation hotels, and probably anywhere else you choose to go. However, I believe that anyone traveling anywhere in the world these days should do so conscientiously. I would advise leaving your expensive jewelry at home, keeping rental cars locked when you park them, avoiding dark and desolate back streets, keeping card-deck-sized folds of bills out of sight, using safe deposit boxes for extra cash and valuables, keeping million dollar camera equipment out of sight when not in use (and carry it with you on the airplane, don't check it with your baggage), and generally avoiding "rich" behavior unless it is so much a part of you that to do so will change your personality (and in that case, stay at one of the special enclaves for the rich that do still exist in the Caribbean and elsewhere).

Sensational headlines color the fabric of journalism. Assuming that the facts are correct (which they sometimes are not), chances are that the embellishments are part of a reporter's aspirations for recognition, or a media "hype" to sell magazines and newspapers. I wandered untroubled in Jamaica at the time of the Kingston headlines about violence, in Grenada when the Cuban "technicians" arrived with their machinery for the new airport, in St. Croix at times of headline-making crimes, and I was not bothered in any way. Ironically, for some, it seems to be much more "fun" to talk about the "problems in paradise" than to talk about how soft the sand was underfoot or how soothing the sea was, although the sand and sea are what make the memories.

Timid travelers will probably be happiest at the resorts with all the facilities within reach. You can take guided tours where you will have the security of the group. The rest of us will continue to live as we do at home, driving around in cars to sample restaurants, shop, and see the sights that sound interesting.

Throughout the island-by-island reporting that follows, I have included comments about the "Political Picture" which should prepare you for headlines in the local newspapers and any rhetoric you may hear while visiting the islands. I have also noted, with "Author's Observations" and comments throughout the text, the few places where I feel adventuresome travelers would be happier than timid tourists.

If you have any qualms about your vacation choice and "Is it safe?" please contact me, c/o William Morrow & Company, 105 Madison Avenue, New York, NY 10016, and I will give you the "latest facts" as I have them from my own constant Caribbean travels on your behalf and that of other readers.

Clothes—or lack of: Travel light with all baggage—mental as well as physical—when you head for the Caribbean. Clothes no longer make the man—or woman. In many places, except for the expensive and chic resorts mentioned throughout the book, fancy togs are taken more as a statement of the wearer's insecurities than as a fashion parade, and their obvious mark of affluence makes the wearer fair game for high charges. After all, if you can spend that much on clothes, surely you can give a little more for tips.

Summer is the season—all year around. Lightweight cotton is best (nylon and synthetics are hot), and some summer-weight jacket or sweater will be comfortable for evenings, mountain resorts, or restaurants with Caribbean-style air-conditioning (which, from my experience, is icebox-cold). While I don't recommend a daily uniform of cut-off blue jeans for everyone, they and the denim skirt are acceptable outfits, even in the French islands, where you will find that French resort fashions are de rigueur for the French folk who live and visit here. Swinging skirts, tight shirts open at the neck, and tight pants—if you can wear them well—are the fashion. On French beaches, nothing goes. Topless bathing is acceptable at hotels in the French West Indies and nudist beaches are proliferating, but if you are of the snicker-and-giggle school, forget about it. Those who choose to go where nothing goes usually do so with élan, and those who can't handle it look sophomoric.

When a resort perpetuates the dress-for-dinner ritual, it is noted when singled out for discussion in the individual chapters, but there is no island (although there *are* a few places on a couple of islands) where you MUST wear jacket-and-tie or gala long skirt. Summer travel gear is generally even more relaxed than winter wear, partly because that is the low-cost time to head south, although it is also the season when the flowers that bloom are priceless.

Barbados chose, a few years ago, to treat the tasteless dress of its vacationers with humor. A series of posters appeared all over the island—and especially at the points of abuse—with messages like these:

> We love to see you shopping m'am
> So please do help yourself
> But we'd rather the goodies on display
> Were all upon the shelf.

and

> Oh what a glorious figure
> Oh what a succulent peach
> But please don't wiggle it all around town
> Save it for the beach.

Although the Board of Tourism in Barbados is the only one I know in the Caribbean to have taken an official stand, the Minister of Tourism for Fiji asked his tourist board to "take steps to encourage visitors to dress more modestly." The result was to advise the cruise lines to suggest that passengers wear "appropriate attire."

A few coverups need not hamper the carefree cavorting you've come to the Caribbean for, but some clothes for heading into town or for island touring (or tiptoeing off the confines of your tourist hotel) are only a courtesy to your hosts.

Headlines have been made about incidents on island beaches, but consider the impact of a bare body, stretched out on powdery sand, on an island fisherman who has followed his family tradition of hauling his boat and mending his nets on that beach for the past hundred years or so. The remote beach you have found to free your soul and unshackle yourself may be the same remote beach (with sensuous surroundings) that tempts the new (and often jobless) generation to hang around these places—with the occasional result of rape or worse.

The wardrobe difference between beaches (and bathing suits) and cities (with coverup) is magnified in the Caribbean countries with a Latin tradition. In downtown San Juan, Puerto Rico, for example, short shorts and bare-back dresses have been seen only in the past decade or so—and are usually on tourists. This island, with its Spanish heritage still firmly intact in many of the villages, has the old-time European respect for public places, and certainly for churches. The same is true in the Dominican Republic, in the old part of the city of Santo Domingo. Businessmen in both these areas and in many other places throughout the Caribbean have doffed their jacket and tie (the mark of a respectable businessman) only in the past few years, and some are donning them again. Even without jacket and tie island citizens dress with dignity when they go to their cities and with appropriate pomp when they are meeting with politicians.

Special considerations for clothes have been discussed, when necessary, within each chapter. Check the "Customs of the Country" section.

I've often headed into the Caribbean for a week or more with one small suitcase (carry-on size), filled with one cotton skirt (in addition to the one I wear on the plane), 2 short-sleeved shirts, 1 long-sleeved shirt (plus the one I wear), one or two cotton dresses suitable for evening, plus bathing suits, beach cover-up, underwear, and sleepwear. Add to that something for sailing (long pants to ward off too much sun), plus sunglasses, suntan lotion, and personal cosmetics, and you're all set. For men, 2 pairs of trousers (khaki pants can double for evening), 2 shirts for daytime plus two (wear one on the plane) for evening, with bathing suits, underwear, etc., and a jacket you might wear on the plane will suffice.

Special social occasions may require something spectacular and convention cavorting has some clothing requirements that won't be on the vacation-visitor list. Coping with those situations is a matter of personal preference.

Two final tips: Take only "easy-care" clothes—things that don't require ironing, dry-cleaning, etc. And pack a bathing suit with your carry-on luggage. If your suitcase is "lost," at least you can sit on the beach while you wait for it to show up.

Customs: Duty-free allocations for U.S. citizens are $300 worth of duty-free merchandise, plus one quart of liquor, and gifts under $25 can be mailed home to your family and friends as often as your pocketbook can stand it. However, the catch with the "unsolicited gift, valued under $25" (and the packages must be so marked) is that if you are sending several to each member of one family living in the same house, and the packages all arrive on the same day, duty will have to be paid. I do not know how you can control the delivery date, but perhaps you can figure out some way. As to the liquor allotment, you *can* bring in more than your one quart allotment, but duty will be assessed according to a schedule listed in a booklet you can get through your local customs office. *Be sure* to check the regulations of your state on the importation of liquor. Some states do not allow the one quart import duty free even though the U.S. customs will let you have it.

Since most of the Caribbean countries qualify as underdeveloped countries, many items made in those countries are not dutiable. This notation on the customs bill is open to a lot of abuse, and I advise you to get a booklet called "GSP and the Traveler," available free from your local U.S. Customs Office. (GSP, incidentally, stands for General System Preference in a convolution of tag names that only a bureaucrat would dream up.) Antiques (anything more than 100 years old) can be brought through customs with no problem, but get a certificate stating year of origin from the person or store where you purchase the item. The original customs booklet, "Know Before you Go," has been reissued with the current information and should also be read thoroughly to avoid customs problems on reentry.

The United States Virgin islands (comprising St. Croix, St. John, and St. Thomas) have a unique status, partially the result of the turnover treaty negotiated with Denmark in 1917 when the U.S. government bought the islands, but these days mostly the result of heavy lobbying in Washington to keep a benefit that had become a boon to local shopkeepers and a mainstay of the tourism-oriented Virgin Islands economy. When you have spent 24 hours in the United States Virgin Islands, you may bring back to your hometown $600 worth of merchandise duty free and one gallon of liquor (purchased at duty-free prices). If you do not spend the total of $600 on purchases you plan to take with you, you may mail the additional merchandise with a value up to the $600 allotment to yourself *but* be sure to ask the shopkeeper for two copies of form 255. Put one copy on the package and keep the other copy for yourself, to take to customs when the package arrives in case there is any question. In addition, items made in the Virgin Islands (which can include an impressive cache of jewelry, leather goods, clothes, etc.) are not dutiable, so they may be brought in in any amount.

Documents for traveling in the Caribbean are minimal. Except for Cuba, you need no visa. For proof of citizenship, which you *will* be required to show, there's nothing to compare with your passport. Passports are not required by all Caribbean countries/islands, but they are, without doubt, the easiest means of clearing immigration without difficulties and, even more important (sometimes) than your arrival in the Caribbean, your return home to U.S. cities is often expedited *if* you have a valid U.S. passport in hand. Your passport, your immigration card (which will be provided on the plane if you have not been given one when you check in at the airport), and a return or ongoing ticket are the only documents needed for most of your Caribbean travels. If you have not invested the $15, which with 2¼" × 2¼" full-face photographs and a copy of your birth certificate, will get you a passport, then bring along voter's registration or a copy of your birth certificate to prove citizenship.

For Cuba, you will need a visa from the Cubans for entry into their country. Tour operators who have put together package tours have an arrangement with Cubatur where they submit the names of all participants in advance of departure so that visas are waiting at the arrival airport. If you enter Cuba on your own, be sure you have made arrangements for your Cuban visa (through the Cuban-interest section at the Czechoslovakian embassy in Washington) prior to departure from home. There are no U.S. government restrictions on travel to Cuba.

Haiti and the Dominican Republic require Tourist Cards. They can be purchased at the airline counter when you check in, or at the appropriate desk when you arrive in the country.

A word to the wise: Formalities for leaving any Caribbean country involves paying a departure tax (of varying amounts, depending on the country/island) and return of the carbon copy of the immigration form which you presented (in duplicate) on arrival.

■■

Drinking water is not the problem it once was in the countries of the Caribbean, but is a scarce commodity everywhere. Even the most modern places—San Juan, Puerto Rico; Montego Bay, Jamaica; St. Thomas, U.S.V.I.—have water problems, not with purity, just with quantity. Saltwater conversion plants are obsolete as soon as they are completed; wells are exhausted in many instances, and even where the freshwater table is high, the pipes and pumps to get the water to where it is needed for consumption are often not up to the task. You will never perish from thirst (and there's always local beer to drink), but you may turn on the faucet to have a trickle or nothing come out—even at luxury resorts. On one recent visit, I found this message on a card in my room;

WATER SERVED ONLY ON REQUEST
Let's All Help Conserve Water.
We can save 200,000 gallons daily in area restaurants.
THE WATER SHORTAGE IS REAL.
An 8-ounce glass of water requires another 16 ounces to wash it . . . a total of 3 glassfuls of water for every one served.
Every 100 racks of glasses we wash equals 15.2 kilowatt hours of electricity.
To raise every 1000 gallons of water 180° in temperature (for

sanitary purposes) requires 15.3 therms of gas or 437.4 kilowatt hours of electricity.

Your $150 or $200 per day does not entitle you to leave the faucet running for the water to get cool, or to take hour-long showers. Fresh water is scarce, even though you are surrounded by some of the world's most spectacular seas. Any water served to you in restaurants will be potable, but you'll be doing the islands a kindness if you refuse water you know you won't drink. In their enthusiasm to be good hosts, some hotels on islands with *real* water problems think that filling your water glass is a gesture of hospitality when, in fact, it's a waste. It would be cheaper for them to fill your glass with rum, and kinder for you to turn the glass over when you sit at table, if you're not fast enough to keep the water from being poured.

Electric current on almost all of the islands is sometimes on—and sometimes off. Do not head south armed with your electric razor, hair dryer, heat curlers, facial steamer, electric toothbrush, etc. and expect them to work on all islands. My advice is to return to the simple life—even to letting your wet hair dry in warm sun and trade winds. If you *must* take your electric appliances with you, also take a converter for most places. Although you will find standard U.S. current in most hotels in the U.S. Virgins and in Puerto Rico and in a handful of other places, even on those islands, when you are at a simpler spot, the electricity may run on another current— and it may (probably will) fail completely on occasion. Overloaded electrical conduits are as much a fact of island life as saltwater conversion plants that are too small for the burgeoning demands. Instead of taking all your modern American appliances, pack a flashlight, several books of matches, and some candles, along with your toothbrush and manual razor. They'll be far more useful (and lighter to carry) than all your modern trappings. Places where you are paying a premium are places where you can expect your appliances to work, but even then, check with management at Coco Point on Barbuda, Petit St. Vincent in the Grenadines, Peter Island off Tortola in the British Virgin Islands, and all the other places I have mentioned in the "Authors Awards for the Best—Top Luxury" (see below).

Language: Do not assume that when English is spoken, it is *your* English. Every English-speaking island has its own dialect, each distinct from the other, although outsiders cannot usually distinguish one from the other. The people you meet on the streets and working in and around the hotels will be far more familiar with their own colloquial sayings and speech short cuts than they will be with yours. Funny jokes with double meaning or quick quips over the breakfast table usually leave a young waitress or waiter completely befuddled. While you are slapping your thighs with glee, they will probably be talking in muffled tones with their fellow staff members about how crazy you are.

When you are asking for something special and your waiter or waitress smiles and says "yes," don't assume that means you will get what you think you have asked for. "Yes" in reply to "Do you have scrambled eggs?" means, simply, that they do have them—there's nothing in what you have asked to suggest that you want some. The same can be true with telephone calls: "Yes" in reply to "Is Ebenezer there?" means, simply, that he is at home—but the person who answered may not know that you would like to speak to him. So it goes in the Caribbean, where local customs are different from those in your hometown.

There are a lot of words in common parlance throughout the Caribbean—and Caribbean is one of them,—that have a special ring to the ear. Your pronunciation marks you immediately as "friend or foe," if not literally then certainly as one who has (or has not) taken the time to find out how things are called in the Caribbean. No one expects outsiders to be fluent in the local language, and by mimicking the intonation—and inserting an occasional "mon," we only sound like the complete outsiders we are. Of course, English is not the local language at all in the French-speaking islands (Martinique, St. Martin, Guadeloupe and her dependencies, plus Haiti), where speaking French is essential if you want to wander out of tourist troughs; or in Puerto Rico, the Dominican Republic, and Venezuela's Margarita, where Spanish is spoken. Speaking "pure" French or Spanish will be sufficient to be understood in the areas just mentioned, even if the local dialect is not "pure."

For words to watch, let's start with Caribbean—which is Ça-RIB-be-an or Ca-rib-BE-an, no one knows (or cares) for sure. Anyone who corrects you is being presumptuous since the proper pronunciation is "according to whom." The British usually accent the "rib" and on islands where independence factors are strong and British rule not popular, some trendy folk choose the other pronunciation. I know of no move to standardize the pronunciation, but there is some feeling among the new movers of the Caribbean that the area *is* the Caribbean, not the West Indies, because factors from all the countries that fringe the Caribbean sea are coming into play in the development of this region. South America (Venezuela especially), Mexico, and certainly Cuba have their effect on the emerging nations of the Caribbean. Cuba considers itself a Latin American country, and not a West Indian island—although the country *is* part of the West Indies as we know it.

Pronunciation of island names seems to confuse many travelers, so here's the list of the unusual pronunciation of some of the islands covered in this book:

Antigua: An-TEA-ga

Barbuda: Bar-BOO-da

Barbados: Bar-BA-dos—not "the Barbados" (it's only one island)

Bequia: BECK-way

Canouan: CAN-oo-wan

Carriacou: Carry-A-coo

Grenada: Gre-NAY-da (the other pronunciation is a city in Spain; and the country's best known beach L'Anse aux Epines is pronounced vaguely Lanse-eh-pan)

Guadeloupe: GUA-de-loop, and the dependencies are known as Les Saintes, pronounced Lay-San, with the island of Terre de Haut pronounced Tair-de-oh, all slurred together.

Jost Van Dyke: Yost Van Dyke

Nevis: NEE-vis (People who live here are Nevisians.)

Petit Saint Vincent: Petty Saint Vincent

St. Bathélemy: Commonly called Saint Barths, so spelled with the French abbreviation, but pronounced San Barts

St.Croix: Saint Croy

The special vocabulary in the Caribbean is immediately obvious to the sensitive traveler. However, since most of the local languages are spoken, not written, it is impossible for visitors—and often for long-stay outsiders—to pick up more than a sprinkling of local speech and expressions. There are some words that are commonly used throughout the Caribbean, and have been used—with no further explanation—throughout the text. At the risk of repeating the obvious for the experienced Caribbean travelers, here's what I mean when I use the word:

bohio—actually the thatched "hut" that the first settlers lived in, but used now to refer to the old-style small country homes in Cuba and other countries, as well as for the thatched shade "trees" on Caribbean beaches.

guayabera—the loose, straight, long-sleeved shirt that has been a "uniform" at the best occasions at Mexico's Acapulco for decades, as well as in Cuba. The shirt has now become the fashion for men, and on most Caribbean islands/countries, can go to most evening events.

MAP—Modified American Plan, which means breakfasts and dinners included in your hotel rate. One hotel has a MMAP, which is Mini-Modified American Plan, providing a salad lunch.

EP—European Plan, no meals.

package tour: a tour of several days sold at an all-inclusive price, sometimes (but not always) including air fare. Be sure to read the small print carefully to be sure just what the one price *does* include.

wholesaler and/or tour operator: the person/firm that negotiates special prices with hotels for blocks of rooms, and special rates with airlines for blocks of seats, or with cruise lines for blocks of cabins, to put together the package tour. The wholesaler usually receives 15% to 20% from the hotel (and sometimes other concessions); your hometown travel agent will get a 10% to 15% commission on your room/tour *from the hotel or wholesaler.*

peak season: from December 16 through April 15 or thereabouts for most Caribbean hotels. That is the time of top rates (the rates drop substantially—for exactly the same facilities, weather, and food—on April 16!)

shoulder season: In the Caribbean, the term refers to April-May and to September-October and sometimes November, and usually means good-value vacations.

off-season: the summer months. The term came into usage when Caribbean travelers were those who fled the cold winter climate. These days the "off-season" can be the busiest season for some areas, but the rates are lower than in winter months, sometimes as much as 40% less. Dates are usually April 16 through December 15.

Money matters are covered specifically within each chapter, as the facts pertain to the destination. In addition, throughout the discussions about restaurants and facilities, bouquets and brickbats have been thrown when value is good or not so good respectively. Keep in mind one obvious fact: the places of and in the Caribbean are in the tourism business because they want to make money—and how much value you get for the money you spend depends on you and the amount of research/homework you are willing to do. Start with the premise that there is profit in any business that survives in the Caribbean—and that profit is being made on you, the tourist. In some countries (Jamaica and Cuba are two) you will have to spend

U.S. dollars in special stores and for your hotel bills. In all countries, you will get better exchange rate for your money at the banks; and many stores and hotels charge a premium for their cash changing services, as is the practice all over the world. You will usually get a better exchange rate with traveler's checks than you will with U.S. dollars when you change money from U.S. currency to local. For those who intend to get off the beaten paths of tourism, having sufficient cash in the currency of the country is a courtesy to your hosts. People with "Mom and Pop" operations in small villages in the French West Indies, the hills of Dominica, or the back roads on St. Kitts, Trinidad, Tobago, and elsewhere cannot and should not be expected to know the present exchange rate—and how to handle U.S. $20 or more. You are welcome to come into the local rum shop or small store, but you will be obvious enough as an outsider; splashing down a pile of U.S. dollar bills, or even worse, a pile of local currency you haven't taken the time to figure out, is at best an inconvenience and at worst an affront.

Mail: The addresses for all hotels are included in parenthesis after the name. Mail to the properties should always include the name of the island, and the area—either W.I. (West Indies), or N.A. (Netherlands Antilles), or F.W.I. (French West Indies), or B.V.I. (British Virgin Islands), and in the case of the Caymans and Montserrat, B.W.I. (British West Indies). Only Puerto Rico and the United States Virgin Islands are covered under U.S. domestic postage rates, where a regular letter at press time costs 18¢ with rates expected to rise this year; airmail postage is not necessary since mail in the U.S. goes by air anyway. *For all other countries/islands in the Caribbean,* postage is 35¢ for the first half-ounce and 35¢ for each additional half-ounce. Reconfirm rates with your local post office. For all but the U.S. Virgin Islands and Puerto Rico, expect mail—even by air—to take at least a week, and sometimes as long as a month! If it takes less, consider yourself lucky, and if time is crucial, use telephone or telex, both of which are effective, and usually efficient, even to Cuba.

Package tours seem to be the trend of the present and future in the Caribbean. Beware of the package tour that is a package in price only. All offerings deserve careful scrutiny if you want to be sure of what you are really buying. In the present age of zealous lawyers and a public that fights for its rights, hotels and carriers are paying a lot of attention to the wording of their sales promotion literature. You should too.

The advantages of the package holiday (which means an air fare and hotel room all-inclusive holiday, offered at a lump price, usually for 7 nights and usually with some "extras") are that you know what you will be paying, in theory at least. There is an advertised flat price, *but* the responsibility rests with you, perhaps using your travel agent as interpreter, to figure out the value of just what is included. You will have a seat on an airplane, usually at the lowest possible rate (because the package assures the airline of filling a block of seats), and the same holds true for the hotel.

Disadvantages of some package holidays, for those of you who like to explore on your own, is that you are wedged in with a lot of other bodies—and many of those bodies are hell-bent for a fun holiday, with an exuberance that might not be natural to you. However, on some package plans you will never know who else is vacationing on "your" package unless you happen to get into a conversation at the hotel. For those of you who prefer small hotels and inns, where you can settle into an island way of life—and not a superficial way of life geared up for "The Tourist"—package tours only make sense if you find one that uses a small property.

Rates: When you find a bargain rate, expect very simple accommodations. Although there are a few places where the rates are still reasonable, most Caribbean hotels are raising rates. I deplore the practice that finds too many hotels raising their rates sky-high, for minimum facilities, on the assumption that the unsuspecting tourist will pay top dollar for God-given sunshine and sea. And in fact, that's just what's happening. As long as people will pay the high prices, the hotels will continue to charge them. I'm about to advocate a "beef boycott" against beefed-up prices in the Caribbean, and have noted the hotels in the text that I think are overpriced.

A lot of entrepreneurs are capitalizing on the chatter about "high prices" and are raising their rates, whether their costs have gone up commensurate with the rise or not, to "keep up with the times." Several hoteliers have asked me, during my roaming through the islands, what the other places are charging—indicating that their raises will be pegged to what the others are doing, and not to their actual costs.

Brace yourself to be "ripped off" if you must stay at the top-price places. Although a precious few *do,* in my opinion, give value for top dollar (Caneel Bay on St. John, Little Dix on Virgin Gorda, Casa de Campo in the Dominican Republic, Jamaica Inn at Ocho Rios, Petit St. Vincent in the Grenadines, Coco Point Lodge on Barbuda, Colony Club, Coral Reef—and perhaps Sandy Lane—on Barbados), many do not. I also recognize that what *I* am willing to pay for may not be what is important for you. For that reason, when hotels have been discussed, I have attempted to *report,* not editorialize, about the facts as I see them. This is a guide only; the final decision rests with you.

If you want to get what you pay for, settle for a small hotel and/or a simpler island. Among those to investigate are Anguilla, Terre de Haut off Guadeloupe, some places on Haiti, and the Dominican Republic, the lesser-known hotels on St. Vincent, some hotels on St. Kitts, and places on Bequia. There are also good values with the housekeeping facilities noted in the special section following the hotel listing in each of the following chapters.

As a single traveler, I take exception to my own decision to include only "winter rate for 2" either with or without meals, depending on the prevailing plan, or the best option. However in order to avoid making this book a clutter of numbers, the "winter rate for 2" was chosen as the standard, to be used by you as a guide to how prices compare from one resort to another and from one destination to another. This book is not a rate sheet. In the old days, when I did my first guidebook, the government tourist offices— when they existed at all—did not always have rates available. It was essential then to include the rates in books. Today all Caribbean countries/islands print hotel rate sheets, usually seasonally (summer/off-season and winter/high-season). In addition, many hotels have representatives and U.S. booking offices that quote exact rates. My choice of "rate for 2 this winter is about . . ." is only to give indication of range. As we go to press, some hotels have not yet decided their winter rates; most government offices do not have the total list for winter '81–'82. Addresses are given, and a letter to the hotel can provide the rate, if you choose not to turn the matter over to your travel agent and take his word for it.

Hotel rates usually change on April 16 and on December 15 throughout most of the Caribbean area. The highest rates are in the winter months, presumably because that's when the Northerners want to flee the cold. There are many of us who prefer the summer months, when the flowering trees are in full brilliant bloom, when the trade winds constantly blow (but not with the force of winter), and when the beaches and hotels are busy but not frantic. The fact is that the rates for the same room can be as much as 50% lower, and will certainly be 20% to 30% less.

Last-minute plans: There's always room for one more. If visions of stretching out on a sea-swept beach are all that keep you going, hang onto your dream—even when headlines holler that hotels and airplanes are full. There are ways to find your place in the sun, even at height of season, if you're willing to be flexible. You may head for some island or hotel you've never heard about, on an airline whose name hasn't become a household word, but the spirit of the Caribbean has always been one of spontaniety, and the sunshine is assured. Past seasons have seen unprecedented numbers of people heading to the Cayman Islands, Barbados, Sint Maarten, and, more recently, St. Barths, but there's still space somewhere for you.

Here are some tried and true ways to find both a room at the last minute on some sunny island and a route for getting there:

1. *Secure space on the plane.* Flexibility is the key. If you live near a major-city airport, going out to "stand-by" for a plane the computer says is "full" often yields a seat south. Most flights have at least a couple of "no-shows" and, if you're ready to go, you can sit in one of those seats. On the other hand, there are ways to be sure you have a reservation—even when everyone says "impossible." Flying at off-peak travel times often yields a better rate, as well as a chance for space. Even when your travel agent says "no space," you may find seats—if you're willing to invest some time in telephone calls. Most airlines serving Caribbean countries have toll-free numbers for reservations. Dial (800) 555-1212 to ask for the toll-free number from your area for *any* airline heading to a Caribbean destination. If you're reasonably flexible on where and when you go, chances are you will get seats, and it's important to secure your space on flights down to the islands and back *before* you start on your hotel space.

2. *Find a hotel.* It is not as awesome as it may seem. There are several non-traditional routes for finding a bed near a beach, even at height of season. Most Caribbean hotels have reservations representatives in U.S. cities. Call the government tourist office (see individual chapters) for your first choice island (the one you've been able to "reach" by plane) and ask for a list of hotel representatives with U.S. telephone numbers. Many of the reps also have 800 numbers; the same system used for finding an 800 number for airlines works for the hotel representatives.

Chances are that you'll secure a room through the rep, but—if that fails—here's another route: telephone the hotel association on the island in question. Most Caribbean countries have active and effective hotel associations. A telephone call or cable to the island may seem expensive, but if you can find a room for your vacation, the investment is worth the effort. Ask for a room, specify dates, and ask for a collect telex or cable reply for confirmation. If you have your heart set on a special hotel, often a direct call to that hotel can yield a room. You may catch the front desk just when they have received a cancellation. Otherwise, take your chances on the hotel, with the knowledge that you are heading south for sunshine—and that can be found on any number of beaches.

The following list includes telephone and numbers for members of the Caribbean Hotel Association and each office can be reached by dialing direct, as listed:

Antiqua—(809) 462-20374
Aruba—011-599-82-1566/3423
Barbados—(809) 426-5041
Bonaire—011-599-78448
British Virgin Islands—(809) 49-43119
Cayman Islands—Ask for Overseas Operator and Cayman Islands 9-4341
Curaçao—011-599-92-5000
Dominican Republic (809) 682-5479
Grenada—Ask for Overseas Operator and Grenada 4475
Chambre Syndicale Des Hotels De Tourisme De La Guadeloupe—011-596-826452
Haiti—011-509-72-5486
Jamaica—(809) 926-3635
Chambre Syndicale Des Hotels De Tourisme De La Martinique—011-596-712780
Puerto Rico—(809) 723-4262 & 725-2944
St. Kitts–Nevis—(809) 465-2695
St. Lucia—(809) 455-2479/8232
St. Maarten—011-599-52334/2333/3588
St. Vincent—(809) 457-1072
Trinidad & Togabo—Ask for Overseas Operator and Trinidad 43065
St. Croix—(809) 733-7117
St. Thomas/St. John—(809) 774-6835

3. *Contact your travel agent,* with the request that you be booked on one of the tours heading south. A quick flick through the Sunday travel section of your nearest metropolitan newspaper can yield the current listing of what's available. Vacationing this way is a little like taking a prize from the grab bag; you won't know what you've paid for until you "open the package," but at least you can go somewhere warm and sunny.

THE AUTHOR'S AWARDS FOR THE BEST

Everyone has his/her own idea of what makes a perfect holiday. I cringe when asked about my favorite resort or island. Often the person asking *really* wants to know what would be *his* or *her* favorite island—and that might not be what I am looking for when I head south. On the other hand, I do have some favorite oases—and they are mentioned in each chapter in the section noted as "Author's Awards." For quick reference, however, the following list has been assembled for those who know little or nothing about the Caribbean and who don't have time to plow through this entire book to find out which place really appeals to them. The choices are entirely my own, and if qualification is needed, it's given. All places mentioned are covered in some detail in the text. Refer to the island/country for further information.

Top luxury (pampered and perfect holidays)
>   Caneel Bay Plantation, St. John, U.S.V.I.
>   Casa de Campo, La Romana, Dominican Republic
>   Cobbler's Cove, Barbados, W.I.
>   Coco Point Lodge, Barbuda, W.I.
>   Curtain Bluff, Antigua, W.I.
>   Jamaica Inn, Ocho Rios, Jamaica, W.I.
>   La Samanna, St. Martin, French West Indies
>   Little Dix, Virgin Gorda, British Virgin Islands
>   Petit St. Vincent, Grenadine Islands, W.I.
>   Round Hill, Jamaica, W.I.

Simple surroundings for barefoot and boating types (camping comes later)
>   Anchorage Hotel, Dominica, W.I.
>   Anse Chastanet, St. Lucia, W.I.
>   Coconut Beach, St. Vincent, W.I.
>   Coconut Hill, Montserrat, B.W.I.
>   Frangipani, Bequia, St. Vincent, W.I.
>   Island Inn, Barbados, W.I.
>   Olde Yard Inn, Virgin Gorda, British Virgin Islands
>   Parador Hacienda Juanita, Maricao, Puerto Rico
>   Punta Aloe, Culebra, Puerto Rico
>   Rest Haven Inn, Nevis, W.I.

Family vacations, if your budget and your children are big
>   Bakoua, Pointe du Bout, Martinique, F.W.I.
>   Buccaneer, St. Croix, U.S.V.I.
>   Casa de Campo, La Romana, Dominican Republic

Cerromar and Dorado Beach Hotels, Dorado, Puerto Rico
Club Méditerranée operations on Guadeloupe and Martinique
Haiti, if you are an adventuresome family
Hilton Hotels (with family plan)
Marriott Beach Resort, Barbados, W.I.
Palmas del Mar, Humacao, Puerto Rico

Family vacations, if budget and children are small
Antigua apartment or cottage
Barbados apartment rentals
Camping (see below)
Jamaica villa, with maid/cook/nursemaid
Martinique's Hotel de la Marina (if you're fluent in French)
Montserrat home rental
Puerto Rico's Cerromar and Dorado beach, summer and holiday camp programs
Puerto Rico's Hilton hotels for summer, camp programs, and Christmas holiday
St. Thomas condominium
Tobago cottage

Inns with personality
Admiral's Inn, Antigua, W.I.
Arnos Vale, Tobago, W.I.
Casa del Frances, on Vieques, Puerto Rico
Castelets, St. Barthélemy, French West Indies
Nisbet Plantation, Nevis, W.I.
Splendid, Haiti
Sprat Hall, St. Croix, U.S.V.I.
Sundowner, Negril, Jamaica, W.I.
Vue Pointe, Montserrat, W.I.
Young Island, St. Vincent, W.I.

Camping, with sites and without
Brewer's Bay Campground, Tortola, British Virgin Islands (bare sites)
Cinnamon Bay Campgrounds, St. John, U.S.V.I. (cabins and tents)
Guadeloupe camping cars for rent-and-roam
Maho Bay Camp, St. John, U.S.V.I. (cabins)
Martinique (campsites at the southeast, near Le Marin and Macabou, and on the south at St. Luce and Ste. Anne)

Parc Naturel de Guadeloupe (some cleared sites; bring equipment)

Puerto Rico Centros Vacacionales (with simple structures at beachside settings)

Best beaches

Anguilla's coves, almost any of the 30 or more

Aruba's Palm Beach (hotels and a lot of people)

Barbuda's shores

British Virgin Islands' Sandy Cay (no one but you and other yachts)

Culebra's remote coves

Grand Cayman's Seven Mile Beach (hotels and some people)

Most of the Grenadines, but especially the Tobago Cays

St. John's Cinnamon Bay, Honeymoon Bay, Trunk Bay, and others

St. Martin's Baie Longue, where La Samanna Hotel is located

St. Thomas's Magens Bay (sand sometimes washes out)

Tobago's Courland Bay (long, with golden sand)

Scuba and snorkeling

Bonaire

Cayman Islands

Guadeloupe, from hotel concessions

Martinique, across the harbor from Fort de France at Point du Bout

Puerto Rico, east-end islands of Icacos, Culebra, and others

St. Croix, for the concessions at Christiansted harbor

St. Kitts's Ocean Terrace Inn

St. Thomas, especially Villa Olga, also known as St. Thomas Diving Resort

Tortola, for the operations out of Aqua Centres and others

Virgin Gorda, for Dive B.V.I. concessions

Nature walks and birding, with notation

Barbuda (frigate rookery and other birds)

Bonaire (flamingo nesting)

Cuba's Isle of Youth (Pines), Cayo Lago, Zapata Peninsula

Dominica's National Park

Guadeloupe's Parc Naturel

Puerto Rico's Monos Island

St. Lucia's Mount Gimie area (near Soufrière) and elsewhere

Tobago's terrain, and Bird of Paradise Island

Trinidad's Caroni Swamp and Asa Wright Nature Center
St. John, U.S.V.I., National Park

Gambling

Antigua (casino at Castle Harbour)
Aruba (casinos)
Barbados (slot machines in some hotels)
Bonaire (casino at Hotel Bonaire)
Curaçao (casinos)
Dominican Republic (casinos in Santo Domingo)
Haiti (Port au Prince casinos, plus slot machines)
St. Kitts (casino at the Royal St. Kitts)
Sint Maarten (casinos)
Puerto Rico (casinos)

Good value hints

Summer season (April 16–December 15), when rates are lowest
"Housekeeping Holidays." See each chapter listing.
7-night, all-inclusive holidays (check Jamaica, Club Meds in the French West Indies, some Puerto Rico hotels), where air fare is included with a paid-in-advance price
Charter a yacht and sail it yourself.
Fly by night (and/or investigate midweek fares).
Double up; two can usually get a better room rate.
Take a cruise at reasonable cost, and don't go shopping.
Stay at small, West Indian-style hotels on lesser-known islands.
Snack at lunch and splurge for dinner.
Read the small print and know *exactly* what you've paid for.

Anguilla

Anguilla Department of Tourism, Wallblake House, *The Valley, Anguilla, W.I.; P.O. Box 7835, Orlando, FL 32854; c/o CTA, 20 East 46th St., New York, NY 10017; 4 Broad Street Place, London EC2M 7HE, England.*

US $1 = EC $2.65
Unless otherwise noted, $ refers to U.S. currency.

"It's different from all the rest," Mr. Rivera told me as we shared Bob Rogers's cab from the airport. From the airport to where was my problem; finding the people he wanted to see for his business (based in Puerto Rico) was Mr. Rivera's, and—miraculously—our missions overlapped. And he was right with his first comment.

Not only did my plane, which was airborne from the tarmac on Sint Maarten's Juliana airstrip in 15 seconds and high in the sky in 22, fly over the width of Sint Maarten/St. Martin in exactly 2 minutes, but it landed 7 minutes and 56 seconds later on the strip at Anguilla, about as far as you can get, these days, from the crass commercialism of the Dutch part of Sint Maarten. (The return flight took 5 minutes 45 seconds, and if you wonder how I knew all that, I had the seat next to the pilot.)

As I strolled away from the plane, one of the island's several Mr. Gumbs strolled in my pace. "When you goin' back?" he said. I told him and offered to take back something with me—knowing how difficult and delayed the official mail service is. "Oh, no," he said. "I'm just gonna reconfirm your flight," and off he buzzed to his office, like the Mad Hatter looking at his watch in *Alice in Wonderland,* to do just that.

So much for arrival in Anguilla. That welcome and a stamp in my passport was all that was involved. "Since Christmas they do this road," Bob Rogers volunteered as we drove along the "main road" to the Valley, the sprawl of small West Indian buildings that groups only in its name. The reason they were working, some six months after their start, was to bury a high-tension wire in a trough at the side of the road. Why here and not the rest of the island, where telephone and electric wires are stringing across majestic views for the first time, is a question I have yet to have answered, but at the rate they're going, it looked to me as though the project was destroying the only island road worthy of the name.

Anguilla is a special place. Although tourism is in its infancy, there's a Department of Tourism, set up originally through the British government's Foreign and Commonwealth Office. And the policies of the Anguillan government, where people are independent and very secure—even though their island is small—are strict. One of the high rollers from the casino life in Sint Maarten was turned down for a hotel building permit. "We're not in a hurry. We can afford to be choosy," I was told. And that, I venture to say, is a remarkable achievement for an island in a region that has sold its soul, for the most part, to tourism.

When we stood on the deck and watched Endari's sister head off in a private motorboat for the opposite (and very clear) shore on St. Martin at Marigot, Endari told me that she had been to Saba, St. Kitts, Statia, and Sint Maarten—all the places we addicted wanderers yearn to see—but was about to make her first trip to New York in a month or two. When she had expressed yearning to go with her sister to St. Martin, her sister took her small baby in her arms, looked up, and said "I wish I was she here and she goin'." And that's the way I felt when, later in my travels, I was wished farewell at the Anguillan airport as I left.

■■■

POLITICAL PICTURE: Anguilla officially became a British Dependent Territory on December 20, 1980, marking the event on January 11, 1981, with a week of festivities. Although Anguilla had been grouped with St. Kitts and Nevis in 1967 as one Associated State destined to become one independent Caribbean country, the uncomfortable "alliance" was splintered when Anguilla was granted special status (in response to petitions from its 6000 nationals) on February 10, 1976.

The almost 10 years of the 3-island Associated State status was a period of relative turmoil for Anguillans. Anyone who remembers the press coverage in 1969 may recall the interest shown when British paratroopers landed on the beaches of Anguilla to "keep the peace." The confrontation was between Anguillans and Kittitians, or more especially due to the government policies of the late premier of St. Kitts-Nevis and at that time also of Anguilla, Robert

Bradshaw. For a number of reasons, one of them being that Anguillans believed they were not getting their fair share of British government appropriations or a fair shake with government policies, Anguillans petitioned to the British government to split from St. Kitts-Nevis and go it alone.

Former Chief Minister Emil Gumbs was the only member of his Anguillan National Alliance party to win public office in the elections held on May 28, 1980, and Ronald Webster who had been instrumental in the island's change of status in 1976 was voted Chief Minister. His Anguilla United Movement won 6 of the 7 elected seats in the legislature of 12 members, and elections held in June 1981, in response to a call for a vote of confidence, were won by Webster.

■■

CUSTOMS OF THE COUNTRY: The 6000 Anguillans are independent folk, staunchly proud of their island home and self-sufficient in their survival. For most of their history, Anguillans have tilled their own plots of land and built their own homes to live in. Most of the 35 square miles are small, private land-holdings, and for that reason, communities are not clusters of houses. Communities are named but not knotted together. Most Anguillans make their own living growing food for their meals on their own sun-parched plots or scooping it from the sea. An occasional cow or goat grazes, but life is simple.

This is certainly no place for your fancy togs and expensive trappings. It's a place to collect your soul, or contemplate, and enjoy good company (either what you meet or what you bring with you).

I've been told that Anguilla won't change much, even with the advent of tourism. Why should Anguillans be impressed by offers of a lot of money for their land, I was asked. "After all, Anguillans have heard it all before. They have been listening to it for 300 years." Here's hoping they're strong enough to resist the pressures of the '80s, and keep controls on their very unique island.

■■

MONEY MATTERS: Although the official currency is the Eastern Caribbean dollar, pegged to the U.S. dollar at about $2.60 EC to $1 US, United States currency is used throughout the island. If you want to transact in Eastern Caribbean currency, get your dollars at the bank. There is no place at the airport to change money, and it will be difficult to get Eastern Caribbean currency either in Sint Maarten (Dutch or French) or St. Thomas (American).

■■■

ARRIVAL can be by boat (sail or motor) or by plane, usually from nearby Sint Maarten, from either the Dutch or French airports. There is also service on small charter planes out of St. Thomas and some service from St. Kitts, several miles south. (Check for status of service from St. Kitts.)

The small breeze-swept terminal is a box that's been scrubbed up and painted as part of the tourism program. Arrival formalities are the same as on other, bigger islands (proof of citizenship with your passport is the best), but the friendly welcome is testimony to the fact that tourism hasn't stepped with a firm foot.

Boat service from French St. Martin's Marigot Harbor comes across to Blowing Point, and you can charter a yacht for a day sail out of Sint Maarten/St. Martin if that's all the time you have.

■■■

TOURING TIPS: Take taxis for your first time around, not only because roads aren't posted (there's no way to get lost—you simply keep finding places) but because the legends and lore you can pick up are worth the ride. There's no public bus service on the island, so if you do rent a car from Connor's Car Rental (or someone else the Tourist Office can suggest) plan to pick up people you pass. They'd do the same for you if they were driving. Connor's going rate for a Datsun automatic or a Toyota Corolla standard was $30 by the day or $150 by the week, with unlimited mileage (but how far can you go?). Gas is extra, and you can make arrangements by writing Maurice Connor, South Hill, Anguilla, W.I.— or phone him from the U.S. at (809) 497-2433 or when you arrive at 433.

Anguilla Travel Services is the island's first full-fledged travel agency. New owners of Cul de Sac have set up complete touring services with telex and telephone contact with the outside world, and provide local links that can "produce" boats for excursions, touring assistance, etc. Check at the time of your travels if having on-the-spot assistance seems important.

■■■

HOTELS on Anguilla are gradually growing on long sandy strands, following a clearly defined pattern that allows for plenty of self-expression—as long as the architect's drawings subscribed to some firm aesthetic requirements set down by the local government. During the survey for this edition, hotels in the works at the time of my last 2 years' visits were *still* "in the works." As we go to press, there are still only a handful of places to stay, with a total of about 80 rooms. Current plans will add another 100-or-so rooms. Mass tourism is a long way (at least as far as the flight to Sint Maarten) from Anguilla.

One way for communication is through the local Tourist Office, by cable to "Anggovt," by telex to 301 ADMIN AXA LA., or by direct-dial telephone from the U.S. to (809) 497-2451, which is the Tourist Office.

Hotels add a 10% service charge; there is also a 5% government tax.

AUTHOR'S OBSERVATION: Anguilla is poised on the edge of a plunge into big time tourism. It's probably a good thing that progress has been s-l-o-w, but, since fast talkers are tiptoeing around this island, plans are grandiose at least in conversation. I'll be surprised if much of the big talk has materialized during the life of this 1982 edition, but I've put some of the projects on the following pages so that you'll know what to ask about.

✤ **Anguilla Holiday Spa** (Mead's Bay, Anguilla, W.I.; about 50 rooms) is also called the "health farm." Assurances that the place "will be open by November '81" are taken as a grain of salt, but plans include sauna, exercise rooms, and activities geared to putting personal pieces back together (perhaps with minor adjustments). (If you want to splurge while you're leading the spartan spa life, take comfort in knowing that the elegant Malliouhana Beach Hotel is nearby.)

✤ **Corito Cottages** (South Shore, Anguilla, W.I.) speckle the shoreline (and beach) with a half-dozen places to stay. Lena Lloyd has refurnished the 2- and 3-bedroom cottages, and work on the pool improves its looks. The beach, dredged from offshore sands, is a sometime thing (depending on the seas), but the spectacular view is constant.

✤ **Cul de Sac** (Blowing Point, Anguilla, W.I.; 8 rooms) is coming into the "big time," with tourism professionals Stephanie Sawyer and Anguillan Clive Carder in charge. The complete overhaul that took place in 1981 resulted in 6 airy-and-comfortable studio apartments, plus travel services, pleasant restaurant (with good food) and a seaside setting that is guaranteed to soothe. The place captures a prime perch at shore's edge, with a view to St. Martin; it's a short walk to the cement slab that doubles as the dock for the ferry from that island's French capital of Marigot. The original building that was Ruth Goodnow's home had a few extra guest rooms for "friends," and the new owners continue the friendly homelike atmosphere. Rates for this winter figure to about $80 per apartment per night, meals extra. (You can cook "at home" or enjoy the *Cul de Sac* restaurant.) Beaches are not too far away, but you'll need a car for spur-of-the-moment exploring.

✛ **Malliouhana Beach Hotel** (Mead's Bay, Anguilla, W.I.; a few villas) makes the most of a superb location, but Robin and Sue Ricketts are wise enough, after several false starts, to talk about an opening date in the season of '82–'83. Fact is that two elegant, "I'd like to live here," villas were open and furnished as examples of what's to come by spring of '81. Marble, make-up mirrors, comfortable furnishings with no cost spared are part of the package. The two 2-story villas can be rented, if you go to the source (The Ricketts) and no one has gotten there first. The 20-room hotel, the rest of the "60 to 70 villas," and water in the swimming pool were in the future when I researched for this edition, but check. Mead's Bay is gorgeous, and the project is top quality.

✛ **Merrywing Resort** (Road Bay area, Anguilla, W.I.; 200 rooms planned) expects to be partially opened "by Christmas," but I suspect it may be Christmas of '82. Some of the resort facilities, which will be free-standing units as well as some clusters, may be open for this winter, but there was a long way to go when I looked. Timesharing and condominium-concept are both under discussion, but so are a lot of other facts for this place. The location—like almost any piece of shore on this island—is great.

✛ **Rendezvous Bay Hotel** (Rendezvous Bay, Anguilla, W.I.; 23 rooms) should have, as its alias, Gumbs's Retreat. Jeremiah Gumbs is a very special person, an Anguillan, and your host. Lydia Gumbs refers to her husband as a "very strong personality, but very helpful and human." He will do anything for you, including arrange for a fresh lobster to be progged from the nearby rocks so you can have it grilled for dinner. He's been running this hotel, built as a home, for the past 20 years, and the bougainvillea and other tropical plants, sugarbirds and assorted Anguillans feel as at home here as you will, if an island place with the imprint of its owners appeals to you. Your meals are family style, at 8 a.m. (for breakfast), at 12:30 and at 6:30—and the generator goes off about 10 p.m. (sometimes before that), when you presumably go to sleep. You can read by flashlight (bring your own) or by candlelight, but otherwise it's starlight or moonlight only. There's no phone, no steady electricity, and no time for any phoniness. Rooms are in a motel-style unit, with hot and cold water, modern-looking plumbing, and twin beds. Furnishings are sparse, but this is a back-to-nature set, where your daytime can be spent swimming at Rendezvous, a l-o-n-g stretch of talcum powder sand that runs off to the right of the rooms as you face the sea, or shelling, reading, writing, painting, or just puttering around. The tennis court split when an earthquake hit Antigua a few years ago, so the bounce on the ball is erratic, to say the least. (And to play you'll have to bring your own equipment, which isn't worth carrying down for this court.)

▪▪

HOUSEKEEPING HOLIDAYS are perfect on Anguilla, if you're self-sufficient and like plenty of quiet time. The selection of self-catering villas is expanding as I write, but the current scattering for rent include a few villas furnished with island antiques (from this and nearby islands) and some that are attractively furnished.

✜ **Caribbean Home Rentals** (Box 710, Palm Beach, FL 33480) has several properties for rent on Anguilla. The leader of the lot is a 3-bedroom, 3-bath house at Sandy Hill, on the south coast, with its own tennis court, but there are also listings for studio apartments and other homes.

✜ **Chinchary,** 2 apartments in one structure within a stroll from Sea Feathers and Loblolly, gives each renter utmost privacy, with separate entrances but the same view. The smaller apartment is "under" the bigger apartment, since it is tucked against the hill. The top apartment has 2 bedrooms, for $325 per week; the 1-bedroom unit rents for $225.

✜ **Coves of Anguilla** (Little Harbour, Anguilla, W.I.; 10 units with 10 more coming) was coming into reality but had come to an unexplained halt when I visited for this coverage. The site is spectacular, on the shore. The project is ambitious, with an impressive main building with arches and view over the sea. The individual units, which will flourish when the planting around them does, are cement structures of an interesting design that allows for a terrace, patio with privacy, and a huge porthole through which you can peep at your neighbor's cottage (but not at your neighbors directly, unless they are outside their walls). The bedroom is at the back of the unit; the sitting area—and terrace/patio—have prime view. There's reportedly excellent snorkeling at the rocks and rills around the shoreline, and plans for water sports when the complement of guests warrants. No rates are available as we go to press, and the official name may be different from the working title, but if you address the property as Coves of Anguilla at Little Harbour, or write care of the Tourist Office, the mail will eventually reach this place.

✤ **Dolphins,** (Sandy Hill, Box 105, Anguilla, W.I.), a 2-bedroom home with kitchen with view and comfortable furnishings, is on a hill, with the beach below. Owned by Mrs. Berkeley Howard, the quality is high and the surroundings sufficient for a carefree vacation for people who want peace, quiet, and a perfect view. Rates are $400 per week for the house, in winter.

✤ **Easy Corner Cottages** (c/o Maurice Connor, South Hill, Anguilla, W.I.) can be rented by day, week, or month, after negotiations with Mr. Connor (the same man who has the car rental business). The cottages I've looked at are furnished for outdoor or beachside living, and come in 2- or 3-bedroom versions. Rentals range from about $40 per day to $450 for a month, and most of the buildings are boxy cement, with flat roof and some variety of porch for open-to-breezes relaxation.

✤ **Loblolly** (Sandy Hill, Box 81, Anguilla, W.I.), 2 apartments in one building, has impressive antiques in the dining area, four-posters in the bedroom, and owner Jack Wigley's father, the barrister, hanging on the wall over the sideboard. Just what you'd expect for an English country house under the sun, Loblolly's tenants have Sea Feathers' for neighbors. Rates are $400 for a winter week; $200 from April 15 through December 14.

✤ **Rainbow Reef,** planned by David Burgland, is four 2-bedroom, 1-bath cottages at the shore. The cottages have a light-and-airy feeling, with basket chairs suspended from the porch ceiling and a kitchen that would be fun (even on vacation) for cooking.

✤ **Sea Feathers** (Sandy Hill, Box 81, Anguilla, W.I.) is an ideal "home" with 2 bedrooms, within walking distance of Jack Wigley's

Loblolly and his sister-in-law's Dolphin. With "all the comforts of home," you can have a carefree, sun-filled holiday here. Weekly rentals figure to about $450 in winter, less between April 15 and December 15.

✛ **Seahorse Apartments** (Blowing Point, Anguilla, W.I.), between Rendezvous Bay and Cul de Sac, on the shore with a view to St. Martin, are 2 in number. Both apartments have twin beds in the one bedroom and hot and cold water in the modern bathroom. The barbecue grill at beachside is your "stove" for dinners of fresh lobster or other local fish that you can get from the Anguillan fishermen when they return at end of day. Rates hover around $40 per day for the apartment, or $250 per week for 2, and Morris and Joan Paley will help you get your bearings and advise on the best snorkel and swimming areas.

✛ **Skiffles,** on a ridge with a view of Sandy Isle and Prickly Pear, is 5 apartments, upstairs and downstairs, some 2-bedroom (renting at about $695 a week this winter) and others 1-bedroom (at about $550 per winter week. John Graff's staff will arrange to stock your food in advance, for starter meals until you get your bearings (and your favorite food sources). There's a freshwater pool, a luxury on this desert-dry island surrounded by salt sea.

✛ **Webster Cottages** at Sea Feathers Bay are owned by the Chief Minister, Ronald Webster. The 8 apartments are 1-bedroom, 1-bath overlooking the beach. Although buildings are "in a row," the newness is softened somewhat by courtyards—and congenial neighbors.

■■

RESTAURANTS revolve around lobster and fish. If you must have steak, the best advice is to bring it frozen from home and cook it at your own house, or count on cuts that might be a little below the best your hometown butcher supplies. After all, most island supplies come through several freezer sessions, first to get to Sint Maarten stores, and then to get over to Anguilla. The fish is fresh from the sea, and the local lobsters—with a squeeze of lime and some melted butter—are the best you can get (and probably what you are eating when you order lobster on many of the other islands where local supplies have been depleted). Count on things to be casual, and the cooking to be the basic best.

Barrell Stay, with a beach bar and a barbecue pit where lobster is grilled while you wait, opened in spring '81. Bob Mazza fled Boston, and his partner Jean Celis is from Belgium. Together, with the help of the French chef that was here at least for the first few months, this place is one to try.

Lucy's Harbour View, on a hillside overlooking Sandy Ground, has a porch set for counter-style dining, facing the view of the seaside village, and an inside room with a handful of tables. The food is the reason for coming here. The thought of Lucy's chunks of fried potatoes make my mouth water as I write (and they come as part of your lobster dinner). My lobster was so big it couldn't fit on my plate, but it was superb! Look at the spontaneous paintings on the wall. They're the art of a Frenchman friend of Lucy's. Check to see if there's a special party going on while you're on Anguilla, or talk about arranging one yourself. The Harbour View excels when the small place is full of congenial people, and the tables are candlelit and flower-filled. The food is worth the visit any time.

Smitty's on the beach at Island Harbour is a bathing-suit, swim-while-you-wait kind of place. There are stools that pull up to the bar, under the thatched roof, and tables sprinkled around, with option to sit facing the sea view and the sandy cove or the other souls that have settled in here with you. Seafood is the food for the stomach; friendship is the food for the soul. Both thrive on the casual, comfortable atmosphere that finds the fishing boats lined up a safe distance from the waves' lap, after the day's catch is hauled.

■■■

PLACES WORTH FINDING are limited, and if you don't bother to get to any of them, your holiday can still be "perfect." This is a "no pressure" place. All the sights are natural, except for **Wallblake House,** the plantation house that is undergoing gradual restoration as it functions as the headquarters of the Department of Tourism. David Carty, Anguillan-born history buff, has assembled a thorough paper about Wallblake House. From it I learned that although the house you look at may not be the one that stood here in the 18th century, there are some foundation stones that date to 1787, and that's its claim to fame. The legends that languish around the house are almost as interesting as the architecture and the impressive restoration. There are tales of murder in the cellar, of destruction during the French invasion in 1796, of lavish living in the sugar heyday of Anguilla, and of family intrigue, with bachelor brothers and unknown wives of other brothers, and, most recently, the lonely years of Miss Mary Blake, who lived here until 1976, when she died, willing the property to the Catholic Church. (Be sure to note the elaborate decor of the new church—you can't miss it—next door.)

As to other places worth finding, I was told that the son of the former Chief Secretary and a friend walked around the shore—beach and rocks—of the island in 2 days. It might have taken less time, but they stopped en route and camped for a night—at the edge of their world. You might try that, but go with a local guide and stop at the Wallblake House tourism office for details before you start off.

One of the prize "things" worth seeing, in the minds of the Anguillans, is the *War Spite* that anchors in the cove at Sandy Ground. Built in 1906, the venerable wood schooner makes regular twice-monthly sailings to Sombrero Island, site of a lighthouse manned by Anguillans, a 4-hour sail to the east, but the real reason that Anguillans love their *War Spite* is that the ship smuggled in supplies during the islanders' rebellion against St. Kitts.

■■■

SPORTS center on the sea, and usually involve a local fisherman who may take you out in his boat. Because of beach abuse by visiting yachts and concern for pollution of the island, there's a plan afoot to issue cruise permits to yachts not registered in Anguilla in hopes that it will do away with the piles of refuse left by the crew and guests from yachts cruising out of St. Martin/Sint Maarten.

Anguillans are known for their prowess at sea. To witness one of the special August Monday races at Mead's Bay is a special treat. Be sure to ask about any event for the deep-hulled, hand-built racing craft, with their triangular handsewn sails.

There are no organized facilities for scuba, but bring your snorkel mask and fins. These seas are spectacular.

■■■

TREASURES AND TRIFLES will be handmade items that are newly cultivated crafts, sponsored through the Department of Tourism and made by schoolchildren and others who have been encouraged to follow basic designs. Otherwise, for free, you can pick up shells on the beach. There's a man who makes small island sloops (and plenty of people who make the life-size version sailed by fishermen for work and in a racing model with deep draught). Ask at Wallblake House for any new craftsmen who have been discovered and/or encouraged. They're looking for talent and have been fairly effective in ferreting it out, from my experience.

Antigua

Antigua *Department of Tourism, High St., St. John's, Antigua, W.I.; Suite 311, 610 Fifth Ave., New York, NY 10020; 60 St. Clair Ave. E., Toronto, Ontario, Canada M4T 1N5; 15 Thayer St., London SW1 W9TJ, England.*

US $1 = EC $2.65
Unless otherwise noted, $ refers to U.S. currency.

When they stepped out of my car at a crossroads in St. John's, I wished them a good evening. "The same in return, dear," I was told, and the "smock ladies" set off in their separate directions. My route was taking me along the northwest coast, just at the border of the fringe of hotels that has been sewn on the sands of Dickenson Bay, and the ladies I had carried into town are part of the commuter traffic that gets to work any way it can. There is no public bus service along this tourist-traveled route, so hitchhiking is faster than walking.

The smock ladies, as I call them, are an enterprising work force who sell by day and sew by night. They take their wares to the source for sales, to the beaches where the tourists fry in the sun. Dimity dresses, simply (but effectively) stitched, dance in the tradewinds from their makeshift clotheslines. And the chorus of smooth sales talk syncopates with the sound of the sea.

Some, like Clara, come to your lounge chair, swinging a basket full of images of herself. Colorful in their fabric-scrap dresses, the small dolls can be made to order for you or you can buy from the basket (which is best). One that I bought (for $4) was made for an English woman, but "when I came to give it and get money, she had none. I walked down to her husband as she said [a 20-minute walk to Buccaneer Cove], but he was too boozed-up to pay." No sale as planned for Clara.

Antiguans travel—everywhere and every way, usually on foot, and often with cargo. A woman I passed carried her transistor radio on her head, and a man on a moped wore a "hat" of a hand of bananas. A half-pint youngster with more than a whole pint of water on his head swayed across the road as I traveled along the south coast. He and a ribbon of friends had gone to the public spigot to bring home water, in any vessel that could carry some, for the household chores ahead.

Life on this island, as in most Caribbean countries, is a beguiling mix of time-honored traditions and modern commerce, a study in contrasts between most of the 75,000 Antiguans and all of the tourists, a potential confrontation between "haves" and "have-nots."

Miller met me on one of my visits, and stayed with me through a peripatetic travel day. He had driven his Ford Gran Torino from his home at 5:30 a.m., to wait at the airport in hopes of a fare. When I arrived at 9:30 or so, I was his first job. The car I rode in was immaculate, and in flawless condition. Miller had bought it in St. Croix, wrecked—but he had painted and repaired it, and, with EC$1500 for duty and EC$1000 for paint, the cost compared to a new one was at least possible. (Duty on a new car would be around EC$3800, he said, and the cost of the car prohibitive. Even tires can range between EC$100 and EC$300, "but the cheap ones wear out.")

With his cab, Miller supports 7 children and his wife; they all depend on him, even the 22-year-old who resents the help from his father but does nothing on his own. Jobs are hard to find for most, and the government policies that encourage tourism count on employment—for building, maintaining, and servicing the properties—as one of the major assets. Hard currency for troubled national coffers is another.

Tourism is the main crop of the island. Sugar had been phased out, but with the exchange purchase of a revitalized sugar mill (the big, old Antiguan mill has been exchanged for a more practical. smaller-but-used Barbados mill), the crop will be planted again. Sugar is intended to sweeten the government budget, although it will take a lot more than sugar to bring Antigua's economy to a viable economic level.

AUTHOR'S OBSERVATION: With the establishment of a United States Consulate in Antigua in spring 1980, perhaps reasonable and practical assistance can be offered. The potential of Antigua is obvious; so are the problems, and as the Associated States steps into independence within the duration of this edition it is essential that financial security on some level be reached so that Antiguans will have the opportunity to develop their country along avenues they choose.

■■

POLITICAL PICTURE: Antigua's Independence Day is November 1, 1981. Elections called for April 25, 1980 returned Prime Minister Vere Bird's party to office by an overwhelming majority and he had promised independence as part of his plan. Of the 17 parliamentary seats, Bird's party captured 13, the opposition party (Progressive Labour Movement) now holds 3 seats, and Eric Burton, running as an independent, has one seat. The Marxist Caribbean Liberation Movement, whose secretary resigned in the months just prior to election, failed to claim any seat.

Premier Vere Bird has been a prominent person in Antigua's government since his early days as a labor leader in the 1940s. He became the leader of the Antigua Labour Party in 1956, and led the government in full ministerial government in 1961, as well as into Associated Statehood in 1967. His opposition leader, George Walter, captured the office of premier when the Progressive Labour Party won the elections of 1971. Walter's term lasted only until 1976, by which time the Bird forces had gained control to win the election that year.

Challenges for the Bird government have been many and will continue through independence. Among the problems that must be faced with independence is fiscal viability. In Antigua, where deficit financing has been a fact of life since '71–'72 during the previous government's tenure, providing jobs is crucial to the economy and tourism plays a major role. Local income taxing was abandoned a few years ago because it cost too much to collect and the revenues received were not worth the bother. The rent achieved on an arrangement that started in January 1978 with the U.S. government for bases that have been in Antigua since World War II contribues to island coffers. Tourism revenues, although substantially increased during the boom season last year, are very fickle—as Jamaica and St. Croix have learned in the past.

As with many formerly British Caribbean countries, the Marxist/Leninist youth demand a hearing, especially now that they have formed their Marxist Caribbean Liberation Movement. An effective and integrated tourism is crucial in this country, as in all the Caribbean countries, not only for its obvious hard currency assets, but also for increased understanding between Antiguans and their visitors.

■■■

CUSTOMS OF THE COUNTRY are changing. Once firmly British, some relics from that heritage remain: a love of cricket, a passion for football (soccer) and an occasional tea; but you'll find that the enthusiasms of emerging nations everywhere are those, also, of Antigua. Whites are the minority; tourists are obvious—and not always beloved for their personalities but recognized for their dollar value. There's a price on your head, and it's as high as the traffic will bear. (In some cases, noted below, I think it is higher.)

There's no place for pretense here—unless it happens to be the enclave at Mill Reef or at the sands of Morris Bay. Most places are casual, fun-loving spots.

Power "outages" are a fact of Antiguan life as on most island communities, and the addition of new generators would help the situation, but they are slow in "appearing." Many hotels have added generators or fixed up the ones they have had all along, but don't be surprised if you are simply "in the dark" when the lights go out. In this country, as on some other Caribbean islands, keeping a small flashlight as part of your at-hand equipment makes a lot of sense if you are going out for dinner or want to find your way easily back to your room after social hour.

Clothes are casual, sometimes sloppy, around the very inexpensive nautical nooks (but even that area is sprucing up with the restorations at English Harbour). Downtown Antigua is still a local haven, where the latest fashions in resort clothes look very out of place and complete cover-up (no bathing suits or beach attire) is expected. Beachwear in town is a shock to local sensibilities. Summer season dress is more casual than winter at resorts. Even the most elegant nook of them all, Curtain Bluff, does not require jacket and tie at dinner when the summer season sets in, but jackets are usually worn by men dining here in winter, as well as by those dining at Anchorage, Blue Waters, and Half Moon. Shirt-jacs, guayaberas or whatever you call the straight, loose shirts of the southlands, are presentable for men at most evening events, but I have noticed a trend to jacket and tie as we move through the early '80s. Women dress up because they like to, not because custom demands.

AUTHOR'S OBSERVATION: There seems to be a slight improvement in the attitude of the cab drivers, waiters, and others involved with the day-to-day tourism. I have been critical, in past editions, of stony glances and high prices in Antigua, especially around the north coast hotels where most of the tourists congregate, and there are still some occasions when I feel that I am appreciated more for my dollars than for myself. A local tourism campaign could go a long way toward explaining tourism to a community that depends on it.

■■

MONEY MATTERS: Confusion sets in because the Eastern Caribbean dollar is local currency (EC$), but the tourist veneer on which you'll slide around on this island is strictly US$. Prices at some places are given in both currencies, figured at about US$1 to EC$2.60. Hotel rates are quoted in US$ for all the resort properties, even those with an obvious increase in European visitors. Only if you are wandering around on your own, in casual West Indian style, will you encounter Eastern Caribbean prices—at some restaurants, a few small hotels, and in some of the Antiguan-oriented stores, but since all places are open to everyone, prices are also given in EC$ for local residents. The tourist's Antigua can be expensive, not only with the hotel rates that are clearly marked, but also because it is almost impossible to move from your room without shedding at least an additional $30, and more often $60.

■■

ARRIVAL at Coolidge Airport on Antigua will be vastly improved when the new terminal opens. Started in October '79, the building *may* be opened on Independence Day, but will be used in '82 if progress continues apace. When you step out of your air-conditioned plane, you'll be wrapped in that blanket of warm and soothing Caribbean air.

After you've walked across the tarmac and around the circuitous route to immigration, you will need proof of citizenship (passport is best), your immigration card filled out (do this on the plane), and the answers to a few perfunctory questions about how long you intend to stay, where you are staying, and why you have come to Antigua.

In my opinion, a smile from the immigration officials would go a long way toward making the visitors feel welcomed. The stony faces and murmured comments do little to inspire a happy, holiday atmosphere.

Except when the European charter groups and other groups of travelers converge on Coolidge Airport, facilities can pretty well accommodate the traffic. The only bottleneck is the luggage area where all bags, etc. are stacked at one narrow space and everyone converges to grab his/her own to be the first through customs. Customs for vacationers does not usually involve much more than the comment that you are on vacation, and a quick glimpse by the customs inspector to prove that your luggage is, in fact, filled with bathing suits and tropical garb. There are times when the officials are more thorough, since it's their responsibility to see that everything on which duty should be paid is properly identified. (The "duty pay" desk is by the customs tables.)

The Antigua Tourist Board has an information desk which is sometimes staffed. If someone is behind the desk, stop by while you're waiting to claim your luggage to ask for a map, about the taxi fares, and about any special activities going on while you're in town. Otherwise pick up some folders and ask someone else (anyone) about taxi fares.

Once outside the customs area, you will be besieged with taxi drivers *or* you will find none around. I have yet to arrive to have the man in charge take the initiative about getting me a taxi, so ask if there's no one in evidence. This is also the best time to reconfirm your return reservation at the nearby airline desks. It is difficult, I have found, to get confirmation by telephone. Inquire now, also, about any short trips—perhaps to Montserrat or Barbuda—that you may want to make from an Antiguan base. (The staff at the LIAT counter can give you routes and rates.)

Departure facilities are perfunctory: a half-hearted search of your luggage when you enter the "departure lounge," and the opportunity to sit outside (if the "old" terminal is still in use) for some last-minute sunshine when you've finished your sweep past the small shops/booths.

The selection of shops at the "departure lounge" area, after you have gone through immigration, seemed cluttered when I passed through on recent travels. Merchandise is *strictly* for people leaving the island, liquor was not much of a bargain, and I found staff uninterested, bordering on rude. OK, in my opinion, if you must have some gift for a close friend you'd forgotten until now, but not worth any investment otherwise.

Cruise ships that tie up at the Deep Water Pier, on the right arm of the harbor of St. John's, deposit their passengers at a shopping center built especially with tourists in mind. The top shops (Coco and the couple of others) are represented with a small selection, and if you want to make the 10-minute hot walk along the cement road into the capital, follow the pavement toward the two towers of St. John's Cathedral, clearly visible a bit to your right.

■■

TOURING TIPS: Taxi rates are rising so rapidly that it is almost impossible to predict just how high they will be by the time you arrive. And taxi drivers on Antigua know all the ropes. Those who have been in business for a while have made their commitment to one union or another, and thereby comes their station: The airport taxis are the United Taxi Association, the hotel taxis are the National Association, and a splinter group takes care of the cruise passengers who land at the St. John's Deep Water Pier. The ride from the airport to Dickenson Bay (Halcyon Cove, Anchorage, Buccaneer Cove, and Antigua Village) jumped from $4.50 when I made the run in mid-1978 to $8.50 in 1980 to $10 more recently. Granted, gas, sold by the imperial gallon, rose from EC$2.40 to EC$5 during that time, and heavy duties on cars and car parts are burdensome, but it's obvious that taxi drivers will charge as much as the traffic will bear (and more, if you have not taken the time to find out the going rate for your route). Taxi touring does, however, give you the advantage of knowing where you're going, plus some commentary about what you are seeing. Most roads are unmarked. There is no good map that I've found, and for first-timers, the taxi drivers do know how to find some of the best beaches—Ffres, Yawls Beach, Dieppe Bay, and Dark Wood, for example—and where to pick up the cold drinks to take there with your picnic. If you take a cab from your hotel, chances are that the driver will be "yours" for the length of your stay, if not by choice then because he's waiting at the door when you step out—and the rest of the hotel staff know (or have been told) that you belong to him. Unless, of course, he's taken you around and doesn't want you again.

The rental car is another convoluted saga. There are more rental car outlets than I can count (or keep track of), but there's only one that gets my recommendation for your business. Get your car at Antigua Car Rentals, based at the Barrymore Hotel near St. John's. The firm is businesslike, will accept your credit card for any major company, and gives you service. Cars are clean and in good working order, and the printed rates are those you pay—no funny business. Motorbikes are also available through Antigua Car Rentals as well as other firms. Avis is their U.S. link

My experience with some of the other individual "entrepreneurs" has not been ideal. At height of season—and even in

May—if your rental agent thinks he can get away with it, prices are top rate. When you arrive, if you want to pick up a car and haven't made plans ask about rental at the airport. Plans at press time are uncertain (Lapps rents cars at the "old" terminal); as are the opening date—and facilities—in the new terminal.

All car rental operators charge $4 for your Antiguan license, which is good for a year. You can purchase your own for EC$10 in St. John's at the Inland Revenue Office on the second floor over the Post Office or at the police station near the airport. There has been no charge for mileage, but you're on your own for gas. There are plenty of gas stations, but if power fails not too many can pump gas. If you're lucky, you'll be near one of the hand-turned pumps when that happens and you need filling up. If you have no qualms about getting lost, renting a car can be convenient, especially if you want to roam from dawn through dusk to dark of night.

■■■

HOTELS ON ANTIGUA range from top luxury to rock-bottom, no private bath, humble quarters. Few places in the Caribbean have a longer list of simple spots, but before you race to make a reservation at any one of them, note that many Antiguan guesthouses may be simpler than anything you know at home. Providing a sun-warmed haven for snow-fleeing northerners began in the '40s, with the opening of Mill Reef Club, a private enclave that was pacesetter for the Caribbean luxury (open only to those who are "introduced" by a Mill Reef home owner). A few luxury places still thrive on Antigua's shores, but the majority of the island's hotels are casual, comfortable (not luxury) places where the camaraderie is as warm as the mix of guests allows. The island is shaped like a scallop shell crinkled at the edges, and the sprinkling of hotels have settled at the crinkles. There's nothing—not even many roads—in the middle. Getting from "here" to "there" may not look like much of a journey on the map, but you can be sure that routes will weave and dip—and take time, especially if you get lost as first-timers usually do.

When you're making plans, read the fine print on folders carefully. You will always be expected to pay the 5% government hotel tax, and a 10% (at least) service charge, but there may be more—and it all adds up. If costs count, head south as soon as the rates drop (which for some places is after April 1, for others April 15—but always ask). The weather does not change the day the rates do; in fact, from my observations, the weather in summer is as spectacularly sunny as the winter months. If you're on a breeze-swept beach, the slight rise in humidity doesn't affect you at all.

Author's awards for Antiguan hotels with special ambiance go to Curtain Bluff for distilling the resort life to a perfect recipe; to Blue Waters for maintaining a cozy, small-inn atmosphere in a place that has all resort facilities; to the apartments at the Copper and Lumber Store in English Harbour, where painstaking restoration puts you in 17th-century surroundings with 20th-century comforts; and to Spanish Main, a small and simple personality inn.

✢ **Admiral's Inn** (English Harbour, Box 103, St. John's, Antigua, W.I.; 14 rooms) is in the heart of one of the Caribbean's most historic ports (the place the British navy called home for its Eastern Caribbean fleet from 1707 to 1854). The simple rooms and attractive main-floor public rooms have succeeded in incorporating history and hospitality. This is no place for fussy travelers, or for those who have to have their toes in the sand to be happy, but self-sufficient, casual types with a boating interest can wallow here happily. All of the rooms are personality places, with size dictated by wood walls and halls. Overhead fans do most of the cooling. Room 1 has a four-poster double bed that adds to the antique atmosphere. Room 7 is one of the third-floor garret rooms, with a dormer window view over the harbor. The annex, in a building dating from 1775, when it was built as the provisional warehouse for Nelson's troops, holds 5 modern rooms. The single-story brick building, adapted for modern comforts, was also the "Condemned Articles Store" in its early history. It is a short walk from the terrace dining area and old beam bar. You'll pass the pillars that held the roof for the boathouse and sail loft, as you stroll along the path. Behind the bar there's a plan of Nelson's ship, H.M.S. *Boreas,* in a frame of lignum vitae (an island wood that is impervious to termites) which was originally a door frame from one of the inn's entrances. The ground floor of the inn was used in Nelson's day for storing pitch, and the building is made from ballast bricks brought in ships from England. This is a world apart, where the winter rates for 2 will hover around $60 for room, no meals; 2 meals daily per person brings the winter double over $100, depending on your room. Count on another 10% included for service and a $24 taxi fare for the 45-minute drive from the airport. (Your trip to St. John's will cost about $20; trips to nearby beaches are free and the inn is closed for September.)

✣ **Anchorage Hotel** (Dickenson Bay, Antigua, W.I.; 99 rooms) opts to provide "the Good Life" in tropical surroundings seaside. One of the first hotel complexes in Antigua when it opened in 1957, the Anchorage has added rooms and flourishes to keep up with the times. Visitors can wallow in the sea, setting out from a room in one of the blue rondavels (2 rooms per 2-peaked unit except for room 65 which makes a whole rondavel of its own), or from the green 2-story motel-style block behind. The check-in desk to the left of the entrance is your source for whatever information is not available at the activities desk. Options for daytime include offerings from the water-sports complex, to the right as you face the sea, and all the activities of Code's Halcyon Cove, which you can scuff to through the sand along the shore to the right, or Antigua Village and Buccaneer Cove, along the sand to the left. At Anchorage, dining is alfresco, with entertainment some evenings in season and food, from my experience, is good, well-served and "international." Check for opening in summer months. It's been the habit here to close for whatever refurbishing is necessary. Count on an international mix that includes European travelers who have come on an all-inclusive tour to Anchorage. Thatched bohios keep the sun off when you stretch out on the beach after your early morning jog or a swift game of tennis. (The courts are night-lighted; lessons have been priced at $17.50 per ½ hour; tennis balls are $6 per can.) Count on paying about $200 for 2, with 2 meals daily per person, for a hub where you'll be about 10 minutes' drive from downtown St. John's, and about 20 minutes ($10) from the airport.

✣ **Antigua Beach** (Hodges Bay, Antigua; 36 rooms) has kept the carpeting vacuumed and the rest of the extensive '78 redecoration in good shape so that tour groups and others who settle in on this hillside hotel about 10 minutes from the airport (and about $5 taxi fare) seem to enjoy it. Pat Gonzalves sank a reported $179,000 into renovation after he bought the property from the Crowe family, and he spends a lot of time on the property to be sure it's all maintained. Every area has had a complete overhaul. Extensive redecoration is aimed at providing an action-oriented place, with several sociable hubs. Antigua Beach is a mix of old and new. The rooms have wall-to-wall carpeting, balcony view either inland or toward the sea (ask for 26 to 35, or 5, 6, or 7 for sea view) and modern bath (where my shower head sent the spurts in all directions). Standard room rates are $70 to $100 for 2 in winter, and package tour rates are your best bet, but read the small print carefully to be sure that there *are* some things included in the rate you're paying. Evening entertainment is planned in season; a jukebox in the bar and Muzak through the loudspeakers masks the sounds of palm fronds rustling in the wind around the pool and surf rolling on the shore of the beach, about a 5-minute walk down the hill; golf is across the road at the course on Country Club Road.

✤ **Antigua Mill Hotel** (Box 319, Coolidge, Antigua, W.I.; 33 rooms) celebrated its metamorphosis on December 12, 1979. Perched on a hilltop, this transformed hotel may soon become an island favorite. Brian Gonzalves, active member of the Caribbean Hotel Association and part of the owning family of Antigua Beach, announced the name change and new look for the former Sugar Mill Hotel. All rooms have been refurbished, the small pool has been painted and cleaned up, an atmosphere conducive to a friendly inn has been created. As the nearest hotel to the airport, this small spot is destined to pick up a lot of overnight traffic (if the reputation for good value holidays doesn't fill the place with longer-staying visitors). A car could be helpful for getting around, but taxis can come here "on the double" from the airport if you want to go to town or beach. Count on rates to be about $65 for 2 this winter, meals extra.

✤ **Atlantic Beach** (Box 569, Crosbies, Antigua, W.I.; 24 rooms including 13 efficiency units) opts for casual surroundings, and a compatible young group who know (and need) good value. The pool is postage-stamp size; the small beach is often encased in seaweed, but there is a casual air around the place that appeals to young Canadians who come in on group tours and Americans who can find out about this place. Rooms are in a 2-story unit facing the sea, with terrace (with gate) or balcony, depending on your floor. The efficiency units have small but adequate stove (gas) and refrigerator. When the housekeeping gets to be too much, you can head for the dining room for conversation and food. Rates for rooms are about $135 for 2 with 2 meals per person daily. No charge for children under 3; apartments rent for $280 to $602 for 2 for a winter week.

✤ **Antigua Horizons** (Long Bay, Antigua, W.I.; 37 rooms) shares the beach with guests from Long Bay (who walk across the neck of land to reach the powdery sand from the shore of the neighboring bay). New management in '81 (with the arrival of the Stringers) means improvements—including a pool, a boat for waterskiing, and lawn tennis courts. Public rooms for this spot cluster beachside; guests go off to overnight in a 2-story block of rooms perched at the rocky end of the bay, or in the Horizons East that's by the tennis court a few steps from the hub. The several rooms that make up the convening area are open-air, casual, and comfortable. A room for 2 will run about $150, breakfasts and dinners daily. Your only option for eating out, without a long drive, is Long Bay, down the road.

✢ **Barrymore** (Fort Road, St. John's, Antigua, W.I.; 23 rooms) is a good bet if you know and like West Indian hotels. The buildings have been on the scene for 15 years or so, but the feeling around this place, that the LeBarries operate as an extension of their home, is Old-World West Indian. Businessmen and independent travelers with an interest in something more than the beach are lured by the low rates (about $40 per night in winter for 2) and by the opportunity to rent a car from on-premises Antigua Car Rentals. Known by experienced Caribbean travelers for its memorable West Indian and continental-style cooking, the Barrymore opened a new restaurant, **DuBarry's,** which is worth noting. There's a pool for use of guests, with a half-moon of dining tables at one end for good West Indian food in alfresco surroundings. Rooms, in blue-painted stucco shells, are scattered around the grounds, huddling around the main drive and stretching as far as the pool. Accommodations are simple, but clean and comfortable, with some nooks air-conditioned (most are not); all have private bath. You'll have to drive to a beach, with the nearest less than 5 minutes away.

✢ **Blue Waters Beach** (Soldier Bay, Antigua, W.I.; 48 rooms) is a special place, set in flourishing and well-tended gardens at shoreside. The hotel cups its own beach, about 20 minutes from the airport ($10), and another 15 from downtown St. John's, to which management thoughtfully provides hotel bus service (in at 9, out by 12, at $2 per head). Taxi rate is $7-and-rising per car. The road that weaves to this shoreside spot curves past the one tennis court to leave you at the lushly bowered front entrance. When you step through, you're in a place where Antiguan Osmund Kelsick captured a small-inn ambiance. At height-of-season winter, guests who don't want to be chaise-to-chaise with fellow guests can walk up and over the point (with its gazebo for sunset watching) and onto another less-trafficked strand, at present reached through a neighbor's property—but plans are to build steps down and across to the bench. The rest of the time there's plenty of sand for all. The pool claims part of the lawn, where the rest of the lounge chairs lie, but

find one of the hammocks, strung from convenient palms at places
that are perfect for pondering. Rooms are in 2-story wings stretching out on both sides of the sand-rimmed bay from the main building. It seems to me that the older (smaller) rooms have a cozier
feeling, but some prefer the bigger (newer) rooms to the right as
you face the sea. Blue Waters thrives on a strong return business
from October through March, testimony to the fact that this place
gives what it claims to have. After the usual mid-May to July 4th
closing for refurbishing, summer traffic is often package-plan vacationers, many from Britain as well as North America (Canada and
U.S.). Kudos have been given for the Sunday brunch. It's set up on
the stone terrace, with guests spilling out and around the grounds.
Other meal features are the Tuesday steak and lobster barbecue
and the Friday West Indian spread, all offered for the usual $15 or
so. Standard dinner menus include swordfish, turkey, rainbow
trout—with an omelet option, with all but the eggs flown in from
the Blue Waters supply house in New York. Rooms are air-conditioned, facing the sea, with the deluxe (queen-sized beds and bigger balcony/patio) to the right, the standard and moderate to the
left; all are comfortable and regularly painted and spruced up—and
nice nooks to call home for your holiday at winter daily rates of $94
for 2 standard; $132 deluxe, meals extra. If you add on the $24 meal
plan, you can have full American-style breakfast, plus afternoon tea
(English style) and dinner. Package plans are offered, but read the
small print carefully. On the honeymoon special, although some of
the items included are available at no charge to all guests, those
couples who pay almost $1000 for 7 nights, from December 16 to
April 15, 1982, can get round-trip transportation between airport
and hotel (usual cost is about $15 per person), plus champagne at
one breakfast or dinner in the room, wine with dinner one evening,
a complimentary shopping trip to St. John's, plus a bottle of Antiguan rum to take home and, of course, the option for all the hotel's
water sports, shuffleboard, table tennis, etc. (Check for the lower
summer rate honeymoon package, and for the family plan offered
winter and summer. The hotel usually closes for refurbishing from
mid-May through June.)

✝ **Callaloo** (Morris Bay, Box 676, Antigua, W.I.; 16 rooms) cuddles
close to the sea at Morris Bay, a short walk along the beach from the
luxury of Curtain Bluff. Cottages here are in 4 bands, 4 rooms in
each, with the central buildings a short walk across a natural sandy
area (sea-grape leaves and other relics of nature clutter the sand).
The social hub is special: brick-walled cozy bar area, in a Monop-

oly-house shaped building, with weathered-wood touches. Joseph Dubary tends the bar. The powdery beach gets swiped out by the sea, depending on the weather—so you may have to walk down a bit for calmer swimming. The cement terrace with aluminum plastic-wrapped sunning furniture is a comfortable spot to rest. There's a reading area, a separate dining hub next to the bar, and a $16 round-trip taxi fare to St. John's (the airport is about $17 one way). There's a hammock tucked under the trees, and a congenial, comfortable small-inn atmosphere. The only discordant note is the chicken-wire fence that outlines the main hub of the property, but perhaps when the tennis court is completed (sometime in '79 or later), a substitute can be found for fencing in—or fencing out. Rates for 2 in winter run about $100, everything but room extra.

✟ **Castle Harbour Inn and Casino** (Box 466, Queen Elizabeth's Rd., St. John's, Antigua, W.I.; 50 rooms) captures the hilltop overlooking the capital. When the place was Michael's Mount, it languished, and it still does, unless you are part of one of the occasional gambling junkets that fly down for a Caribbean-and-chips package. Winding up to the hilltop, you'll pass the guardhouse (often closed). From 5 to 7 p.m. bargain drinks are served at the bar, reached when you open the doors to the air-conditioned *Beef & Brew*. Keep moving if you like your Caribbean sun-spattered: There are outside tables through the side door, near the pool, and for my vacation dollar they're a far preferable place to sit than the neatly appointed inside (dark) dining room and bar. Rooms are in a curve of motel-style units, each with a view, adequate modern furnishings, and (of course) private bath, but you're inland, away from the beach. From all reports, food is only subsistence level. Although there is some action most nights if there's a group at the hotel or if one is expected, one night when I was there the answer was "negatory" by the barman—which I realized was no entertainment. Good for those who like the casino life, with a casual, Caribbean twist. Inquire about gambling junkets if this sounds like your kind of place. The printed room rate runs from $56 to $120 (for suites), for 2, meals extra. You're overlooking St. John's (too far to walk), and about $10 taxi fare from the airport—a 15-minute ride away.

✟ **Catamaran Hotel** (Box 958, Falmouth, Antigua, W.I.; 11 rooms) is splashed at seaside on a cove that was favored by historic yachts. When imposition of docking fees cleared out the freeloaders from English Harbour, many curved around to this neighboring bay. The rooms are in several pink stucco buildings (one wood exception is #7) that ribbon the shore. Numbers 3, 4, 5, and 6 share a cement-slab terrace area. All rooms are *very* simple, prone to the mildew that is the scourge of so many seaside places, and favored by boating types to whom price and camaraderie are more important than pristine housekeeping. I wasn't impressed by the tedious linoleum peeling up from the floors of the dining room, but the brick wall makes a good backdrop for the family-style meals. There's a worn hammock strung up near the small strip of sand that sends you swimming in the harbor. Deep-sea fishing, sailing, and other waterborne events are arranged at the front desk. Hugh Bailey is the man to find if you have questions. You'll be paying about $54 for 2 this winter, with another $25 or so each if you want meals.

✤ **Code's Halcyon Cove** (Dickenson Bay, Antigua, W.I.; 158 rooms) hops with action, prompted by European and American tour groups who call this place home, and by a long list of water sports, tennis, motorbikes, volleyball, horseback riding, jogging, etc. that gives the action-oriented plenty to keep them occupied. The former Hyatt link was broken as of March 1, 1980. London-based Hotel Management International took up the management reins and added the "Code's." Plans to put a casino (Antigua's second) in the new building at the entrance were underway as we go to press. Check for status if gambling is important for your holiday pleasure. Halcyon Cove is a percolating resort that has bubbled at beachside to include pool, beach, several 2-story units, a Warri Bar perched on stilts reached by a boardwalk over the sea, a water sports shack with all the options (waterskiing, scuba, snorkel trips, sails, fishing, etc.), and tennis courts where recent seasons have seen lessons priced at $10 per half hour. Activities include fitness classes, volleyball, ping-pong, jogging on the beach, horseback riding, and anything else guests and the activities director dream up. Shops provide surcease from sun, and as good a range of buyables as those you'll find in St. John's, a 15-minute taxi ride southwest. There are branches of the Shipwreck Shop (books, records, straw work, tourist items, etc.), Coco Shop (resort wear, pottery, bikinis and other bathing suits, and T-shirts, priced at $6 and $9, depending on size and saying). When selecting rooms, note that 101 and up are along the shore, with another 3-story unit behind them. The second and third floors are over the housekeeping area, where view is blocked by the 101 unit and the maids and friends gather to talk and laugh incessantly; 133 up to 156 cup the pool, with the 133 series closest to both pool and sea. The new blocks of rooms, completed for season of '79–'80, are the first ones you see to your left as you come down the drive. They stretch, in a Y-shape, from the beach to the branches of the Y which reach to the road; the check-in and reception area and some shops are on the right (inland) side of the road as you approach. If the whole beachside action hub gets to be too much for you, take the 4-passenger funicular (if it's running, which it often is not) up to the *Panorama Restaurant,* on the top of the hill. You'll want to head here anyway for the Saturday night limbo session, if your previous Caribbean capers haven't hardened you to that nimble feat. Halcyon Cove is good for casual, congenial types who won't mind the wastepapers that huddle at the base of planting, the Halcyon cars that the employees enjoy driving on various missions at and around the beach, and the paint that needs touching up around the buildings. Inquire about special rates for honeymoons, sports holidays, groups, and business affiliation. The regular daily rate for 2 in winter will run from $130 to $160, breakfasts and dinners included. (In addition to the full roster of activities offered by the Halcyon, you have the option of walking down the beach to Anchorage Hotel or past that, to the once secluded, still special Buccaneer Cove.)

✤ **Curtain Bluff** (Box 288, Old Road, Antigua, W.I.; 50 rooms) captures the crown, once again, for the top resort on Antigua. Top rate is worth it here if it is anywhere. When Howard Hulford built Curtain Bluff, for the season of '62, he started a precedent with his then 27 rooms that earned him the Caribbean Hotelier of the Year award for 1979. (The award is bestowed for atmosphere, staff training, and community involvement.) Like the rare wine that Howard keeps hidden in his wine cellar, this resort has improved with the years. The staff is loyal—or they're not around—and the key crew who keep this inn shipshape are a congenial crowd that keep things moving behind the scenes so that they don't seem to be moving at all. You'll certainly meet Ed and Anne Sheerin, and probably Howard and Chelle Hulford who have returned after a consulting job to Cotton Bay on Eleuthera in the Bahamas. The 2-story buildings sprinkled along the shore with the surf give each guest a good room, with a spectacular view, constant sea breeze, and comfortable furnishings that are set on imported Italian tile floors. Spacious bathrooms, meticulously cleaned, feature fluffy towels, a luxury long gone in most resorts. Daytime diversions are sea-oriented, with snorkeling, scuba diving, and Sunfish sailing compliments of the management. Only the day sail tallies up an extra charge, and that seems worth every penny of the $30 lunch-and-lolling cruise. Tennis courts get constant action, especially during early January Pro-Am Tennis Weeks. There's a putting green by the complex of roofs and walls that makes up the main hub of check-in area, indoor and terrace bar (where complimentary appetizers are served from 7 to 7:30), and the bright and airy lounge area that leads into the 2 dining terraces, both flecked with turquoise and wrought-iron chairs set off by white walls. The Sitones perform, as they have for almost all the 18 years this place has been open, with tunes of the '40s and '50s, and some more recent strains. Dinner is worth waiting for; Swiss chef Ruedi Portmann does his best to turn the usual into something special, which gets even better when you order one of the wines. His West Indian bouillabaisse won top award at the 1978 Caribbean Kitchen Competition, but it seems to me that a lot of his recipes could have, if they'd also been entered. The beaches are 2 long strands, one with surf and prevailing breeze, the other a powdery stretch that leads past neighbor Callaloo. Rates for winter of '81–'82 are in the $200s for 2, 2 meals (and cocktail appetizers) daily.

✤ **Galley Bay Surf Club** (Box 305, St. John's, Antigua, W.I.; 24 villas and 8 rooms) survives with a special recipe that has been served in the same style since the late '50s, when Edee Holbert opened the place. The beach is the main diversion. Your overnight nest can be beachside or in a rustic Robinson Crusoe cabin, back from the beach and built in bamboo and thatch (but hot). The 2 sections connect with a patio, giving you a bedroom in one wing, the bath and dressing room in the other, and complete privacy even though there are others nested in the same Garden of Eden. Furnishings, in keeping with the structure, are rattan. The beachfront rooms are a better bet, in my opinion, with pastel-painted walls, private terrace, and comfortable, beach-oriented furnishings. The beach-and-sea view is the best wall decoration; it's on the "wall" that leads to the terrace. For evening entertainment, if you want more than the moon and the stars, there is dinner—which will take you an hour or more after its 8 p.m. start. It can be followed with a local band that plays several times weekly during winter season, usually on the barbecue nights. Count on summer season to be slow-moving, if it's moving at all. There are riding trails for you to trot around, accompanied by the hotel's recommended horseman, who is a personality worth knowing. There's a "small hotel" feeling here. The house count can be over 50 when all rooms are filled. Count on paying

$114 to $124 for 2, meals extra, this winter, and know that you can
have the gorgeous stretch of powdery sand almost all to yourself
except at the height of season.

✤ **Halcyon Reef** (Box 63, Marmora Bay, Antigua, W.I.; 100 rooms)
was born as a privately owned casino hotel and brought up as a Holiday Inn. The government took over ownership/management in the
early '80s and the place hops along at a lively pace when the house
is full. Otherwise, if you check in here on your own, you're a long
way from the action and may get lonely. You'll be paying over $150
for 2, breakfasts and dinners daily, this winter. Facilities offer typical sun and sea diversions: pool, beach, tennis courts, shops, disco,
coffee shop, sailing. The casino was uprooted by the government a
few years ago to be transplanted at Castle Harbour Hotel, overlooking St. John's. The pool is surrounded by dining and bar areas, with
the dance floor nearby. Two-story buildings of modern rooms
stretch out under pagoda-style roofs that you can pick out on approach (and from the drive to Half Moon, across Willoughby Bay).
There's evening entertainment in season, a couple of shops with a
small selection, and a $17 taxi fare to reach this isolated spot from
the airport. Your nearest neighbors are the clutch of hotels around
English Harbour (The Inn, Galleon Beach, Admiral's Inn, Falmouth Beach Apts., and Catamaran), but you'll need a car to get
there. If you have some friends eager for a night on the town, put
on your jeans and head up the hill (by car) to the local nightclub
Hide Out, which may be too island-style for the novice West Indian
visitor.

✤ **Half Moon Bay** (Half Moon Bay, Box 144, Antigua, W.I.; 100
rooms) has very real on-premises pluses, including the beach (if
the heavy seas haven't reduced it to a sliver), a few holes of golf "to
be enjoyed, not endured," tennis courts, and water sports included
with your room rate. Proximity to Mill Reef was the major lure
when the inn was built, but today it's reason enough to come to this
coast. The appointments (white with royal-blue accents) are uniformly attractive, even when worn in spots, and the hefty wicker
couches and chairs that speckle the second tier of sitting area, set
off from the sea by salt-sprayed windows, are sturdy and comfortable. Staff seems cheery, from my observation, especially reservations manager Evelyn Burns, who worked her way, in 7 years, from
receptionist to her present responsible spot. Several rooms have
been refurbished so all are now in good shape. Separated into north

wing, middle wing, south wing, and new wing—with the new wing
the most spacious accommodations (and end-room suites)—guests
in the least expensive rooms have smaller nooks and the best value.
All rooms have sunning terrace; all guests have access to all facilities. Tennis enthusiasts can participate in the Antigua Tennis
Open, a week-long Pro-Am tournament that takes place at several
hotels the first week in January, with finals at Curtain Bluff. Half
Moon also is the locale for the Bozell and Jacobs Half Moon Bay
Tennis Week, with professional players in the round-robin spring
tournament. Inquire about special package plans (honeymooners,
tennis, golf, water sports, family), but plan on paying $210 for the
oceanfront deluxe double, with the oceanfront suites topping out at
$270 for 2, breakfasts and dinners daily.

✤ **The Inn** (Box 87, English Harbour, Antigua, W.I.; 30 rooms)
continues to idle slowly and steadily, with all the confidence a true
British retreat out of limelight can command. When you walk up to
the check-in desk, to the left of the open arched door, you will know
you are in an established resort. The fabric covering the comfortable couches is one step away from British drawing room chintz;
the furnishings are substantial wood, including the trestle tables
that punctuate the dining area; the bar, with wood walls, harks
back to a British pub, and the sun streams through the windows as
you overlook one of the classic Caribbean views—English Harbour.
The terrace speaks for itself. The main hub happens to occupy the
prize position for a picture-perfect view overlooking the restoration
(only Clarence House shares such a vantage point, and its view is
from a lower perch). Saunter (or ride in the inn's complimentary
car) down to the beach on the curving road that sweeps to the sea.
The handful of hilltop havens number no more than a half dozen,
and on the beach, #8, #9, #28, and #29 are single-story dwellings,
with 3 buildings each with 6 rooms (3 up, 3 beach level) to fill the
number gap. The beach bar, popular for lunch and lingering in the
shade, gives a perfect view of yachts bobbing at anchor. You can
slide into the sea at the slightest provocation, and will pay about
$125, meals extra, for the privilege. The range runs the reverse of
the terrain; hill rooms are least expensive, beach are next, and
beach superior are tops. Your nearest neighbor within walking distance is Galleon Beach, a stroll down the beach. The restoration at
English Harbour is across the bay, by boat or by car around the
curve. Count on $17 by taxi from the airport, and almost $15 to get
to St. John's.

✤ **Jolly Beach Hotel** (Box 315, St. John's, Antigua, W.I.; 400 rooms) jumped into the burgeoning Antiguan combine being assembled by European tour operator Alfred Erhart, who added the huge complex of rooms next door to the original 70-plus room hotel. Jolly Beach, now "topless," was born on the white and powdery sands in 1962. Now a haven for European sun-seekers who arrive on Universal Air Tour package holidays, Jolly Beach is on one of Antigua's spectacular strands of sand—and gives you night-lighted tennis courts, shuffleboard, an alfresco dining area, and "hundreds" of German, Swiss, and other European guests to enjoy. There's entertainment, and a twin-bedded nook to call home. Rooms in the original Jolly Beach hotel are far preferable to the small, boxy, utilitarian new units, in my opinion. The airport is a 25-minute ride ($15 taxi) across the island, but St. John's is 6 miles' ($10) drive to the north if you can't find all you want at the shops, or from the sand salesladies on the hotel grounds.

✤ **Long Bay** (Box 442, Long Bay Beach, Antigua, W.I.; 20 rooms) is a special small inn with the personality of its owners, lingering on the shore, at the end of a bounce-and-weave drive that takes almost half an hour from the airport ($15). This place incorporates all the atmosphere of the old West Indian buildings it was constructed to represent. Sea breeze sweeps through the property that the Lafauries built to their own taste. Boats tie up at the hotel's pier (and are available for guest fishing and sailing). Stone walls, woven rugs, a dart board, and plenty of secondhand books add to the homey atmosphere. Your room will be in a 2-story unit shore (but not beach) side, with #36 to #45 on the upper level to get the best breeze. The beach is a short walk to shared shores with Antigua Horizons. (The strand is long enough so that mingling is not mandatory.) Stone arches, and an eye for color (lots of bright pink accents with sun-faded yellow walls) make this place blend in with the bougainvillea. Check for the slow months when it may close, but book ahead for height-of-winter season if you want to be with a chummy, compatible group who are paying $140 for 2, breakfasts and dinners daily. Check for the scuba dive package if that sport interests you; otherwise count on owners Jacques and Jackie Lafaurie to keep life lively (and ask Jackie about her very special appliqués with island themes).

✤ **Meylock Inn** (All Saint's Road, St. John's, Antigua, W.I.; 13 rooms) is mentioned because it appears on the official Tourist

Board list and bargain-hunting vacationers should know that this place is in a hot pocket on the outskirts of the capital. The pool can be refreshing, but count on very simple rooms well known to commercial travelers but not by repeaters among the resort crowd. Winter rate for 2 is about $40, meals extra (and probably elsewhere).

✤ **Runaway Beach** (Runaway Bay, Antigua, W.I.; 15 rooms plus some villas) received a complete face-lift and some new villas along the beachfront, where winter rates will be for 2, no meals. The older rooms are 2 per unit, in cement boxes along the beach—which is nice strand if the seas have not gobbled up a portion. (If they have, it will be returned later, but perhaps after you've left.) The "road" to get to Runaway is paved part of the way past Barrymore's Hotel, but then dissolves into a bumpy dirt track weaving inland, near the shore. You'll be happy here if you *really* want to get away from it all, and Manager Florence Suttie is the person in charge. The price may be right, but you'll have to have a car—or pay a taxi driver—for mobility. I've been told that food has improved, but that offerings are far from gourmet style. Count on casual comfort more than pampering, but if you want to be on a beach, this warrants some thought.

✤ **Spanish Main** (East St., St. John's, Antigua, W.I.; 15 rooms) occupies a glorious old West Indian house, facing the Recreation Grounds at the inland fringe of the commerce of St. John's. Collectors of West Indian wood frame homes should head here, at least for a meal (make reservations and count on good food)—if not to settle into the simple rooms, some with private bath, that rent for about $40 for 2, per day, meals extra in a winter month. You have no pool or beach, but there's plenty of casual West Indian atmosphere, and the option to walk around the streets of St. John's at whim. For sea life, you'll have to take a taxi to Dickenson Bay, where you can find all the holiday action offered at Halcyon Cove and its neighbor Anchorage, or the beach bar at the Buccaneer Cove. A good buy for budget-minded who don't require a beach/resort life at the first footfall. The Brankers offer very simple, genuine hospitality here. (No air conditioning.)

✤ **Stevendale** (Fort Road, St. John's, Antigua, W.I.; 20 rooms) is a motel, next door to Barrymore and less expensive (as it should be). Not much for a vacation in my opinion, but it might be OK for penny-pinching business folk. (Even then, my vote would go to Spanish Main.) Rates here are about $40 for 2, sharing a stark room, no meals. Rooms are air-conditioned because the hot boxes have to be; there's not much air access.

✤ **White Sands** (Hodges Bay, Box 115, Antigua, W.I.; 40 rooms) has Halcyon Cove's former manager at the helm. When Garvin McKie took over this place he spruced things up, but the inn still wears its resort life with a casual, comfortable air. Along Hodges Bay Road (which I think is the most interesting residential shoreline drive in Antigua), the hotel has a homey feeling. Guests overnight in one of 3 strips of rooms: those near the pool, those near the garden, and those across the road at the patch of sand that is the beach. Miguel's Water Sports makes arrangements for the ride to Prickly Pear and other outings by boat. The whole complex (dart board, plus chairs, back-of-the-house open-air dining room) is casual but not sloppy, with a natural warmth that makes it appeal to "real" folks and family types—be they British, Canadians, or from the U.S. Garden and beach rooms figure in the $60s for 2, $100-plus including 2 meals daily per person, in winter months. Special events are barbecues, afternoon tea, and a ride into St. John's about 4 miles west. (The airport is a $7, 10-minute ride.)

> **A**UTHOR'S OBSERVATION: News from the rest of the world is hard to come by on this island. Vacationers leap at old newspapers brought by arriving tourists, and local folk have a hard time finding out what's going on on the neighboring island. There's no "real" newspaper. If knowing what's going on is important to you, bring your own small transistor and hope it is strong enough to pick up the beams from elsewhere. And whatever else you bring, be sure to hold onto the newspaper you have the opportunity to buy before you get on the plane south. Other guests will dive for it like a pelican for fish.

▪▪▪

HOUSEKEEPING HOLIDAYS ON ANTIGUA are for the beach-and-book crowd. Most accommodations are simple, functional, and more than adequate, but few have the luxury flourishes you may have gotten used to finding on some other Caribbean islands. Although you can find some foods on the shelves of the local markets, your best bet is to arrive with a well-packed box from home, or head to the hotels for your main meal of the day. Local fish can be bought through the management at many places, and certainly from the fish market at downtown St. John's. For fresh fruits and vegetables, and the mouth-watering Black Antigua pineapple (with smaller diamonds and a skinnier shape than the fat Hawaiian version), barter with the ladies in the St. John's market.

✤ **Antigua Village,** (Dickenson Bay, Antigua, 100 condominium units) Built on the beach in late '79, the apartments are now ready for rental (and sale). Managed by Peter Brine, the units are in 2-story clusters, nesting on the sand at what can be a narrow part of the beach that stretches along to Anchorage in one direction and Buccaneer Cove in the other. Good for independent types who want housekeeping, Antigua Village rates and dates are available through Peter Brine, c/o Buccaneer Cove.

✤ **Buccaneer Cove** (Box 804, Dickenson Bay, Antigua; 12 housekeeping units) gives beachcombers a place to call home, with a hub for sea-oriented conviviality when you want it. The band of sand at Dickenson Bay also is the sea route for guests at Anchorage, Antigua Village, and Code's Halcyon Cove and can be like Fifth Avenue on a spring day in the height of Antigua's winter season. Only its locale, at the southwest end of the strand, keeps Buccaneer Cove from being inundated by beach-strollers. The rotten road, that may have been paved by the time you visit, is another deterrent to wanderers; and the swamp at the "back door" is not too attractive, although reportedly "mosquito free." Having said all that, I recommend the place heartily—for anyone who likes the independence of a kitchen, and the convenience of a bar/restaurant area beachside, where you can get mixed drinks while you look at the view and the eclectic collection strung in the fishnets that attempt to camouflage the ceiling. There's a small commissary where you can buy liquor and other basics for your "home." Lunch is served daily, but the focal point is the Bar-B-Cue at lunch and dinnertime, when you cook your own Antiguan lobster (frozen in foil when puchased, but steamed succulent and served with a baked potato) and dance to the local band. This complex, managed by James Pullar, is ideal for casual, easy beachside living. Count on paying $50 to $100 per day for 2, depending on size and location of "your" unit. The beach is good and you can find diversions at Anchorage and Halcyon Cove by walking the sandy shore; or you can head out to sea for one of the *Servabo* cruises—an all-day sail (with lunch at $30), a cocktail cruise (check the day, expect to pay about $15)— or go deep-sea fishing. A good bet for a priceless vacation if you want seaside atmosphere with an option for independent action.

✦ **Caribbean Home Rentals** (Box 710, Palm Beach, FL 33480) has several listings around the island, with offerings that range from studio apartments to multi-room units and independent free-standing houses and villas. Winter rentals range from about $350 to $600 per week, for modest to spacious-but-not luxury places built for casual, Caribbean style life.

✦ **Cape Coast Cottages** (Jolly Beach, Antigua, W.I.; 7 units) share the glorious strand of white sand with the big-and-burgeoning Jolly Beach Hotel. As a quiet place to call home, this place offers a lot—including the activity of the big hotel which is just a stroll along the sand. Special holidays include car rental. Have your travel agent contact Sojourn Tours in New York. Week-long per-cottage rates are $350 to $600, with daily rates, meals extra, at $50 to $87 depending on whether you take the 1-bedroom or 2-bedroom version.

✦ **Copper & Lumber Store** (Box 1283, English Harbour, Antigua; 12 apts.) opened on December 1, 1977, with living quarters, and is the best bet for anyone with a historical interest but no requirement for being on a beach. Your modern apartment (either duplex or spacious double) will have an 18-century feeling with all the modern comforts. I could move right in to any one of the 12 apartments, which have a combination of wood, brick walls, and comfort that makes it easy to think of these nests as "home." Whether you bed into *Dread Thought, Boreas, Collingwood, Agamemnon,* or any of the 5 apartments that face the harbor, or *Britannia,* with its view over the harbor and yachts bobbing at anchor, Patricia Hodge will be your hostess. Able and affable (with a couple of years working in the Canada office for the Antigua Tourist Board), Patsy will help you get your bearings. Choice of rooms includes the twin-bedded units, with kitchen and living room (*Britannia* has a balcony); and the duplex units, comfortable for 4, with one bedroom upstairs with sink, and the main living area easily set up as the second bedroom. Rates range from $400 for a winter week for 4, down to $350 for the best 2-person units, and $250 for the perfectably acceptable "type C" 2-person place. No beach or pool.

✦ **Falmouth Harbour Beach Apartments** (c/o Admiral's Inn, Box 103, English Harbour, Antigua; 15 apartments) sit seaside on the protected cove of Falmouth Bay, within a stroll from English Harbour but well away from any historic atmosphere and high prices. All units have wood-slat terrace or porch (depending on first or second floor), with adequate modern appurtenances, including spatulas, whisks, egg beaters, and the like. Emphasis here is on do-it-yourself, with casual atmosphere that can keep you in your bathing suit or less for 24 hours a day. Good-value rates hover around $60 per day for 2, all meals, taxes, and 10% gratuities extra. You can walk around to Admiral's Inn for dinner or cook at home. Sailboats moor offshore (or pull up on the beach when size allows), so if the sea is your interest, you can settle in here at a good price. Amy gets raves for excellence as the manager from frequent guests.

✤ **Galleon Beach** (Freeman's Bay, Box 554, Antigua; 18 units) gives you the best of everything—a beach, a haven for good food and camaraderie, and the option to do what you want to—using your own cottages as your base. The 5 units along the beach are my favorites. Each has a bedroom, a living room with sofas that can make into 2 more beds, and a connecting kitchen—all spread along the beach with a sea view (and screens over louvers). The 13 hillside units are set up for 4, with 2 bedrooms, hillside view and breeze (an easy walk to the beach), and enough space around to merit privacy. Pat and Jack Henderson opened this place in 1971 or so, and have held the helm since. Their personalities are what make the guests come back, even when they have to take a $10 taxi ride to get here. (Rental cars are a good idea if you want mobility.) Yachts bob at anchor offshore; English Harbour is the next cove west; and The Inn, with its beachside bar/restaurant and the more elegant hilltop perch, is next door, a short drive or a long walk. Count on parting with $55 for the beach for 2, $80 for a hillside octagon for 4; and make your reservations early if you want a midwinter week or more. Dinner served at the attractive casual shoreside gathering area runs $10, and Pat Henderson claims the cook is tops. There's island entertainment some nights, conversation with other guests the rest of the time. A perfect place to relax and revive in uncluttered comfort. Ideal for independent travelers.

■■

RESTAURANTS ON ANTIGUA have traditionally been at the hotels. Only in recent seasons, when some hotels changed from prices that included breakfast and dinner, have some good small places opened.

AUTHOR'S AWARDS go to Spanish Main for serving interesting food in truly West Indian surroundings, to Admiral's Inn as much for its 18th-century setting as for the food (which I think is adequate but not spectacular), and to Roots which is making a name for itself with residents and the handful of visitors that find it.

Blue Waters Sunday brunch is worth a reservation if you're in that area north of St. John's (or better yet at the hotel itself). I've heard good things about the spread—not only from the owner (who also boasts about the Tuesday lobster/steak barbecue and the Friday West Indian buffet which you might look into), but from guests.

Curtain Bluff's evening atmosphere is entirely different from daytime tone although the same dining room is used, and the wine cellar you think you see through the iron grate with its Maine brass lock is phony. (The real stuff—with good vintages—is cellared around the corner in a temperature-controlled room that sifts through 3500 bottles in a season.) Chef Ruedi Portmann has been with the place for more than a decade, and although you'll find some of the main courses similar to what you'd order in a good restaurant at home, the special desserts are glorious. His West Indian Bouillabaisse won top prize in the 1978 Caribbean Kitchen Competition with Craig Claiborne and Pierre Franey as judges.

Anchorage Hotel has both atmosphere (with the sight and sound of the surf to enjoy while you dine) and good food. If you're not staying here, make a reservation for a special occasion.   **Dubarry's,** at the Barrymore Hotel on the outskirts of St. John's, is a new addition this season. Always known among island regulars for their excellent island food, the LeBarrie family has created special surroundings for what has always been special cuisine.

Bar-B-Cue at Buccaneer Cove on Dickenson Bay is a casual, beachside place where you can cook your own lobster, steak, or hamburger (or give it to the girl who tends the charcoal fire, if you'd rather stretch out on the beach while you wait). Major entrees are accompanied with baked potato and butter, and—for my money—an ice cold beer is the perfect beverage. Jamaica's Red Stripe was being offered, and rum punches can be ordered from Buccaneer Cove's bar. Wine is served in deference to the many Europeans and others who prefer wine with meals. Lobsters were catching $8.95 when I dined; 8-oz steak was $7.95, and a ubiquitous cheeseburger was $1.75. Noonday meals call for bathing suit attire; evening is slightly (but not much) more formal.

Shorty's on the Beach, also on Dickenson Bay in the shadow of Halcyon Cove, is another good snack-for-lunch spot.

The Place, on the main road from Dickenson Bay into St. John's, across from the Barrymore Hotel, was opened by a Swiss in the season of '78–'79. His reputation for interesting food in comfortable surroundings gives him a good following, especially among the many Europeans who are vacationing in Antigua.

Cockleshell, a seafood place not far from Runaway Beach, down the road to the shore past Barrymore, is worth finding for its grilled fish specialties. A casual, comfortable beachside place where the sea sounds can provide background music, Cockleshell is best by daylight.

Le Bistro, on the north coast, not far from most of the hotels, is probably the most elegant dining option. With cuisine that takes its tone from France (but does its cooking Antiguan style), the restaurant is pleasant—and expensive. Plan to make reservations on winter evenings when the place is popular.

Roots, on the corner of Moravian School Lane and St. George's Street in downtown St. John's, has entertainment Thursday, Friday, and Saturday, and is worth a reservation at other times for the Antiguan atmosphere—and good food. Lunchtime draws the biggest crowd among Antiguans who have to be in town and tourists who want to be.

The **Spanish Main,** in an old West Indian house on East Street, bordering the park, serves good food in pleasant surroundings, and is well worth making a dinner reservation when you are going to be in (or can get to) St. John's.

Also in the city/capital, **Brother B's** has made a name for itself for *very* informal island surroundings with hearty West Indian food. (This is no place for a dress-up evening.) Other casual spots to consider, for typical West Indian surroundings, are the **Oasis** and **China Garden,** both in simple West Indian houses (China Garden is on the second floor), and loved by locals.

■■■

PLACES WORTH FINDING are related to the island's history as the major port for British naval activity in the 19-century Caribbean. The restoration at English Harbour is worth the better part of a day, perhaps tied in with a prowl around the ruins at Shirley Heights and a visit to Fort Berkeley and to Clarence House. When a taxi driver offers to take you to Fig Tree Hill, demur unless you are fascinated by a wiggly road that slides to the shore through a banana plantation (a banana is known by the locals as a "fig" and thereby comes the name). The ride is a pretty one, but it will take you all of 15 minutes. If you are heading to Curtain Bluff, it's worth taking the road that goes along Fig Tree Drive, but the route is not, in my opinion, worth a special trip.

English Harbour was used by Admiral Horatio Nelson as the main base for the British fleet in the 18th and early 19th centuries, English Harbour, also called **Nelson's Dockyard,** still has many of the original buildings intact. Some, such as the Admiral's Inn and the Copper & Lumber Store, have been restored and rebuilt to accommodate overnight guests. Admiral's Inn was the "Lead Cellar," where pitch was stored in barrels, with the Engineer's Office on the upper floors (where the guest rooms are now located). The Copper & Lumber Store was completely gutted, to be rebuilt in tasteful old style over its cisterns, which were used to hold 50 tons of fresh water in Nelson's day.

The **Guard House,** at the right of the entrance to the Dockyard, is where you will be encouraged to pay your $1 entrance fee (and where you can mail postcards in the small post office). Farther along on your right is the **Admiral's House,** now a museum on its main floor and, in fact, never the admiral's house in spite of its name. (The admiral is supposed to have quartered in a house, now gone, on the site of the present Naval Officers' Quarters.) Inside the museum, the collection ranges from amusing to interesting, with a half dozen rooms open to the sea breeze and lined with pictures, early charts, and some cabinets with Arawak Indian relics found on Antigua. There's a model of *Arabella,* a schooner built in the 1840s, and another big model in the back room, plus a 4-poster canopy bed in the other back room that looks comfortable enough to climb into. Clay pipes found at Shirley Heights are in a cabinet, and I found the photographs of the Dockyard at a 1952 party fascinating. (A sweep through the museum can take as little as 15 minutes; what's outside seems more interesting to me.)

AUTHOR'S OBSERVATION: Avoid this place on a day when a cruise ship docks at St. John's, or get here early or late to avoid the crowd that swarms over the Dockyard. (If you're on the cruise ship, either ask your driver to speed here first, and get in and get out before the crowd, or make this your last stop before racing back to the ship.) With a lot of tourists wandering around, it's difficult to capture the 18th and 19th centuries.

A person worth finding is Desmond Nicholson, who may be over at his family charter boat business office in the small building near the dock. Desmond used to guide Thursday afternoon archeology walks around some of the former Arawak sites. Although he's given up on a regular routine, if you have a particular interest in the island's archeology, he's your best source for information.

The **Galley,** in which the shop is located, was the cookhouse used by the 19th-century crew from ships being worked on at the dockyard; the **Naval Officers' Quarters,** constructed in 1815, is destined to be a museum or some useful building as soon as funds can be raised to restore the building. The stone ground floor is part of a 600-ton cistern.

According to the small booklet, *The Romance of English Harbour,* the first reference to English Harbour was in a letter of December 9, 1671, when Sir Charles Wheler, Governor of the Leeward Islands, urged the Crown to consider English Harbour as a place for the British fleet because of its deep and huge pocket. By 1704, the Harbour was the home for the fleet, which set out from here on raids and forays over the next 100 years, the years of constant seesawing of power between British, Spanish, French, and Netherlands explorers, settlers, and pirates. By 1725 the dockyard was fitted out as a place for repairs, with the first dockyard across the harbor from the present site, at St. Helena, the shoreside spot now occupied by the Antigua Slipway, Ltd. (who incorporated some of the original slipway equipment into their modern lifts).

In the 1780s, when Admirals Rodney and Hood were battling for supremacy of the Caribbean seas, English Harbour was "filled" with the big ships that came in for work following battles. Rodney set out from here for the Battle of the Saints, fought off Dominica (when he captured the French Admiral Comte de Grasse); and Admiral Nelson set off from here, in more leisurely times, to court (and marry) Fanny Nisbet, who lived on nearby Nevis.

Clarence House, on the opposite hill, overlooking the harbour, was built in 1787, to be occupied by H.R.H. Prince William Henry, then Duke of Clarence, later King William IV. (The Duke of Clarence was commander of H. M. S. *Pegasus,* at the time when Captain Nelson was stationed here in command of H. M. S. *Boreas*). Clarence House, used by the present governor of Antigua as his weekend home, is open to the public on other occasions. If the narrow gate is open, drive through and give the caretaker a small stipend for the talk he offers about the furnishings (some supplied by the National Trust) as he takes you around. Clarence House was used by Princess Margaret during her honeymoon with Antony Armstrong-Jones, and more recently was the site for a luncheon for Queen Elizabeth and Prince Philip when they visited Antigua on

October 28, 1977. The building got a new roof after the hurricane of 1950 blew the older one off, but otherwise the structure is much the same as when it was built in the late 1780s.

Shirley Heights's ruins are interesting for prowling and view, as is **Fort Berkeley,** one of the 2 "posts" for the chain that was hung across English Harbour to keep unwanted ships out. The other end of that chain was strung from what was called Horseshoe Battery, part of Fort Charlotte, which is no longer standing.

AUTHOR'S OBSERVATION: Most of the restoration at English Harbour was undertaken by The Friends of English Harbour, a nonprofit organization dedicated to the authentic restoration of the area. Membership is open to all. You can write Box 1283, English Harbour, Antigua, W.I., for details, or just mail off your check for EC$80 Subscribing Patron, EC$120 Life Friend, or EC$5 Annual Subscription.

Other places worth finding after you've paid homage to St. John's Cathedral in the capital, are off the island. You can spend the day on **Montserrat** by flying over (15 minutes) in the morning and back in late afternoon. Check at LIAT (Leeward Islands Air Transport) for any day-tour package rate that will include a taxi tour. If one is still available (as it has been at times in recent years) it's a good deal. Otherwise the regular round-trip fare is about EC$66, plus a taxi tour and lunch either at Coconut Hill in Plymouth or 15 minutes outside town at Vue Pointe by beach or pool. You can also fly LIAT to **Barbuda** for the day, to lunch at Coco Point Lodge (beautiful beach), or to **St. Kitts** for the day, with lunch at Fairview Inn. In all cases, the day will run about $100 per person.

■■

SPORTS are sea-oriented, with Antigua Sailing Week the traditional focus for yachts that converge from U.S. ports and around the Caribbean. Held at the end of April or early May, depending on Easter, the events spoke out from English Harbour, a source for yacht charter at all times of the year.

Nicholson Yachts has operated from its English Harbour base since Commander V.E.B. Nicholson sailed his family into a nearby cove on New Year's Eve, 1949, after crossing the Atlantic. He stayed, first taking day charters from Mill Reef on the family yacht and gradually acting as "captain" of a fleet of yachts for charter.

These days son Rodney operates the firm that acts as land touch-stone for a fleet of some 80 yachts cruising the Caribbean.

Most hotels also acknowledged the lure of the sea, even for non-sailors. A day-sail has become part of the hotel activities, even when the yacht is not anchored offshore. Prize character craft, for my $30, is the 63-ton *Servabo,* a Brixham trawler that made its way across the Atlantic a few years ago and bases itself (scenically) off the shores of Dickenson Bay. The Barbecue Cruise (daily except Sun & W), heads out from Buccaneer Cove at 9:30 and fills your day with snorkeling, shelling, rope swinging, calypso, dancing, rum punches, a feast of a barbecue, and plenty of sunshine (take a long-sleeved shirt and some sun screen). The ship's 1000 square feet of deck can hold a crowd, which she usually takes in season. You'll have more space and just as much fun at the shoulder season when the ship may not go out daily, but will go out a couple of times per week.

During recent seasons, most of the beachside hotels have made arrangements for guests on some luxury yacht that anchors offshore or that can be boarded at a nearby cove. The *Cavalier* was anchored off Dickenson Bay on one recent visit, and a 7-hour sail on this 2-masted schooner cost close to $30 per person (children ½ price). Cocktail cruises depart at 2 in the afternoon, to return about 5, and usually include a sail and snorkel, with rum punch ($12.50). Luncheon cruises, which take all day (10–5:30, $30), are sun-scorchers. Those who want to learn to sail should check on location. Curtain Bluff has its own yacht for day-sails for its guests.

Fishing stories will circulate about the 183-pound blue marlin hauled in on September 2, 1977, by Reg Donawa, skipper of the *Caramel,* and his mate John Potter. The 37-foot sport-fishing boat goes out on half-day runs for about $90, with full day at $150, for 6 people, equipment provided. Check at English Harbour's Nelson Dockyard for the schedule and count on a good couple of hours rolling and pitching on the sea even if you don't come back with a fish. Deep-sea fishing is also arranged through Tojo's shop at Dickenson Bay, next to the Anchorage and Halcyon Hotels.

Scuba has gone local, with Tojo's on Dickenson bay offering a re-sort course. A 1-tank dive costs about $20; lessons start at $35 for 3½ hours. Trips are scheduled, but as the schedule tends to be flexible when the winter rush is passed, check at the Halcyon base late in the day before you want to head out. Check in well before departure time to be fitted for your equipment, if you're experienced. Novices will have pool time for instruction before they go out to dive. Introductory courses are given twice weekly (usually

Sun and Th at 1 p.m., at Halcyon Cove pool). Night dives with the pros run about $35 per person in group of 4, with equipment provided.

Tennis takes its cue from the Antigua Open, the Pro-Am tournament that takes place the first week in January (after the holiday crowd has gone home, and before the winter group arrives). Curtain Bluff and Half Moon are the host hotels (tournament information is available from both). Half Moon also has its Women's Tournament in early April, with visiting pro and amateur players. Places with courts in addition to Half Moon (5) and Curtain Bluff (3) are Blue Waters (1), Halcyon Beach (2), Anchorage (2), Jolly Beach (2), and Holiday Inn (2). There is a court near Antigua Beach, but not on the grounds, and it was either being resurfaced, or totally out of play, when I surveyed in early summer '79.

Golfers head to Cedar Valley Course, where the full 18 offer "an interesting game." Some hotels assist with transportation to the course, which is near St. John's, at the northern nub of the island. Antigua Beach uses the few holes of Gambles course, with the entrance just outside the hotel's driveway. The course is acceptable for exercise, but not as well maintained as the Cedar Valley 18. Half Moon has a few holes.

Horseback riding is arranged through Halcyon Cove and other Dickenson Bay hotels' activities desks. The horses lost their grazing ground when Halcyon added its new rooms. Although they were tethered to a post, with option only for parched dirt in their orbit when I checked for this edition, I was relieved to see the horses being walked to greener pastures at day's end. I hope their situation will have improved when you decide to ride. If you're at a hotel on another cove you will have to add the cost of a taxi to the cost of the ride. Figure about $15 per person for a couple of hours.

■■

TREASURES AND TRIFLES: "Sweetie" was what Katie called me as she wrapped the flour-sack skirt around my waist (over the wraparound skirt I had worn into St. John's) to show me how "perfect" it was for me. I didn't buy it, even for $6, but if you're in the market for flour-sack clothes or simple-and-colorful sundresses, St. John's shops have their share. Straight skirts also run about $6, less for small sizes, but the basic sack these days comes from Canada. Katie sits near her table stand, set up at the entrance of Kensington Court. If Katie's not here when you are, someone else is sure to be. It's a prize location, especially when Darcy's Steel Band starts playing around noontime, when the courtyard begins to fill with weary shoppers eager for a rum drink and to be revitalized by the peppy band. (You can buy records for a steep $10.)

Although most of the "official" shops are located around the streets of St. John's, with branches at the shopping plaza near the Deep Water Pier, recent seasons have seen a rapidly increasing crop of sand salesladies who patrol any of the beaches where there are apt to be tourists who will buy. The usual item for sale is sundresses, some of them quite nice (and certainly cool and simple) for between $14 and $20, depending on your bargaining power and the hour of the day. (You'll do better with US$ than with EC$.)

Shipwreck Shop, at the left of the Kensington entrance in St. John's, is full of "flotsam and jetsam." The selection of Penguin books is about the best on the island, and although most of the West Indian authors I used to buy from this shop were missing on my most recent visit, the racks did carry a full selection of Trinidadian V. S. Naipaul as well as some works by Dominican-born Jeans Rhys (who lived most of her adult life in Paris). In acknowledgment of his truisms, there seems to be a paperback revival of Herman Wouk's *Don't Stop the Carnival,* a classic about the traumas of island life (which include building and operating a hotel). Otherwise, Shipwreck stock is mediocre: flour-sack shirts and skirts, plastic "island" trinkets, beads and inexpensive shell jewelry, and a 5-&-10 assortment where the numbers now refer to $. Among items to look at twice are Arawak pottery (simple dishes, etc. made in Antigua), straw placemats, and the ubiquitous sugarbird, captured in coconut shell at the edge of a dish (also coconut shell) you can use at home for nuts or ashes.

St. Mary's Street has long been the main drag for shoppers, but merchandise looked tired on my recent visit. The selection varied between loose caftans, etc. of cloth with African or other lively patterns, some madras skirts with matching pocketbooks, and cloth by the yard. From St. John's harbor inland along St. Mary's, you'll find on your left Kensington Court and on your right **Cornelia's** (madras bags $10 and a selection of resort clothes), **Nubia** ("clothing for the alive," with floating caftans and imaginative evening designs), **Coco Shop,** the **Calabash,** and the **Pink Mongoose,** the last 2 across from each other in small wood houses-turned-shops. All 3 have a few of the traditional tourist items: typical, proper resort wear (long skirts, straight skirts, hats for sun—and at Coco Shop, some of the clothes made by Caribee on Nevis, with the name of the seamstress and what to me seems to be a sky-high price on the label).

In the rectangular shape that the Antigua Department of Tourism shades with blue on its map you'll find most of the shops and local travel agencies, all within a stroll of each other. Two non-shop spots that might interest the island enthusiast are the local market, south on Market Street just beyond **Everybody's Bookstore** (where you can pick up some interesting titles), and the Antigua library, upstairs over the court building diagonally across from the post office near the waterfront. The back room of the library has some interesting old books about Antigua's early history.

The Studio, in a magnificent old house across from Government House, on Cross Street, is worth your time, if you are going to make "one stop in town." Heike Petersen arrived in Antigua in 1964 and took over this place to make and show her island fashions not long afterward. Her designs are interesting, the use of fabric inspired; and if you see something you like but want it in another fabric, that can be arranged with a little time. (From St. Mary's Street, with the water at your back, walk inland to Cross Street, turn left and walk about 3 blocks.) The Studio staff encourages "escorts" to come in and sip while you wander.

Kel-print, George Kelsick's shop where Temple Street crosses St. Mary Street, offers some original prints on fabric worked into resort clothes. Quality seems to me to have dissipated with the years. The product for purchase these days is T-shirts, "printed to any design" and costing about $6.

Near English Harbour, at the turnoff from the Inn and Clarence House Road, **Webson's Straw Mart** has some interesting work, which the sign hanging at the corner of the house claims is made by the blind. At **The Galley Shop** inside English Harbour, you'll find warri boards, some clothes, hats, and other items. The selection is more interesting than at many places, but the best item to buy may be the booklet about the history of English Harbour because the purchase price helps the cause of the restoration.

A few hotels have shops/boutiques. Halcyon has branches of the Shipwreck Shop and Coco Shop. The most interesting boutiques are those at Curtain Bluff or at the Half Moon, where a branch of Calabash carries quality items.

Java Wraps boutique at Buccaneer Cove is worth the walk along the sand to find, if you don't drive directly to BC. In addition to the pleasing combinations of Caribbean colors incorporated into the Java designs (available by the yard and sewn for seaside wear), the shop carries the work of Dominic, an artisan well worth finding at his studio in the hills behind Dickenson Bay resorts. (Ask for directions, but call ahead to be sure that Dominic is "at home" and receiving visitors.)

Warri is an Antiguan passion. If you look quickly, you'll note that almost every cluster of Antiguans hunched over "something" is a cluster of players and kibitzers of a game of warri. (Note the group of taxi drivers at the airport grass-patch waiting area, if you've missed the game in play elsewhere.) The boards are multipocketed. The best boards are hand-carved (and hard to find). Modern versions are in many shops, and the board is good for hors d'oeuvres when you get home if you give up on the game of warri.

According to a sheet of rules handed to me at Callaloo, and provided by the "West Indian and West African warri champion, Nicholas A. Fuller," *warri* means 'house' in a great many African dialects, and the game came to the West Indies from the Gold Coast of Africa with the slaves. The word *warri* refers to the hollows on the board, and the counters are nickars, a small nut from the Guilandina plant.

"Each player starts with 4 nickars in each house on his side of the board—24 nickars on each side—and the object of the game is to capture 25 of them. The opening player takes all of the nickars out of any one of *his* houses and sows, or drops one into each successive house in a counterclockwise direction. The only way to capture the opponent's nickars is to *end* in one of his houses where there are only one or two nickars. Thus, if the last nickar drops in an enemy house to make a final count of 2 or 3 there, these nickars are captured and placed in the player's prison (one of the hollows at the ends of the board).

"If the warri from which the player starts contains more than 12 nickars, the sowing of them will naturally make more than one complete cycle of the board, in which case the emptied starting house is omitted and left empty.

"The nickars of any unbroken sequence of 2's or 3's behind the plundered house on the opponent's side are also taken.

"Each player takes one turn. When an opponent's warries are empty, a player must if possible put nickars into them. If he cannot do so, the game is over and all the nickars left on the board are his."

BARBUDA, about 27 miles northeast of its overseer Antigua, was described by Philip Deane in his *Caribbean Vacations*, researched and published almost 15 years ago, as "60 square miles of flat scrub with a good deal of game." Things haven't changed much—and the pronunciation certainly hasn't. It's Bar-*boo*-da—and not in any way related to Bermuda or Barbados. There are rumors of new hotels being built on this sand-rimmed island, which you can see clearly as you fly south to Antigua for your small-plane connection (15-minute flight) to Barbuda, but no realities—except for an exceptional resort that has claimed its point for almost 15 years.

✤ **Coco Point Lodge** (Box 90, St. John's, Antigua, W.I.) is the one and only, and worthy of its special status. The string of buildings that make up Coco Point stretch along a spectacular sandy shore, sprinkling the guests on the span at the spot of their choice. Some cluster; some don't. Each room has sea view, private bath, adequate (but certainly not lavish) furnishings, and a calculated carefree manner that gives you a feeling of security. In addition to the 10 "hotel-style" rooms in the main boxy building there is an assortment of cottages, with new ones being added now and then. At the moment, there are 4 houses with central living areas and a choice of 2, 3, or 4 bedrooms; there are 3 cottages without central living area but with 3 bedrooms, and there are other units present and planned. Palms punctuate the grounds on the point that the resort claims for its guests, but don't count on a lot of lush foliage. You *can* count on lots of beach—and several opportunities for boating (Sunfish or a 43-foot motor sailer), scuba diving, snorkeling—and shooting when management says you can. Don't bother with a lot of hunting equipment, and don't be disappointed if "the season" is not on. Hunting is the way the Barbudians get their food, and the Lodge senses its responsibility to keep the fauna flourishing. Bonefishing draws guests who cast at the flats, and those who want to head out for big game fish do so on the fully equipped 43-foot motor sailer. There's a landing strip on the resort's grounds for your own small plane or one of the Lodge's twin-engine Beechcraft Bonanzas, or perhaps the scheduled LIAT flight, which lands at the official Barbuda airport, about 15 minutes' drive from here. The tone at this place is set by calculated casual attire worn by people who can afford much more. The Lodge closes tight from May 1 through November, and space is tight the rest of the time—even at rates of $225 to $375 for 2, which covers everything including your drinks. (Special season rates from April 1 to April 30 and from December 1 to December 10 are a good value. Inquire for details.) Regular season rates from December 11 to March 31 range from $300 to $450 for 2. Stateside details for this spot are available from Robin Woodward, 52 Vanderbilt Ave., New York, NY, 10017.

Aruba

Aruba Tourist Bureau, A. Shuttestraat 2, Oranje-stad, Aruba, N.A.; Aruba Tourist Bureau, 1270 Ave. of the Americas, Suite 2212, New York, NY 10020; 2980 Biscayne Blvd., Miami, FL 33137; and Oficina de Turismo de Aruba, Edificio Centro Capriles (Local C-29), Plaza Venezuela, Caracas, Venezuela.

US $1 = NAf 1.77
Unless otherwise noted, $ refers to U.S. currency.

When Cobo Kock was a boy, he fished. And when he was 13 he started to work for Lago-Exxon, the refinery which opened in 1929 on the southeast shore of Dutch Aruba. He retired, after 36 years, with a treasured ring with two diamonds. His bright eyes were thick with glasses and his sight was weakening, but his love for Aruba and his natural warmth were stronger than Aruba's steady tradewinds that bend the divi-divi trees, permanently, in submission to the wind.

Jacobo Kock was a night watchman at the Aruba Caribbean Hotel when I met him. At 1 a.m. or later, when you leave the casinos and the nightclubs, either at this hotel or any one of the several (Sheraton, Holiday Inn, Americana, Concorde) that are cheek by jowl and a stroll along the beach from here, you might see his counterpart at the door. When Jacobo Kock was pensioned from Lago, he was offered a job as a night guard and, for me at least, Jacobo Kock doubled as "good will ambassador."

We talked for almost an hour one night, and when I passed again the next night, he gave me a gift—a book about the Netherlands Antilles with an inscription which I treasure. He offered to take me to meet some of his friends in his town of San Nicolas, out of the mainstream that finds tourist hotels and shops on beaches around the main town of Oranjestad. I never made that trip with him, but we talked about his hometown, which I visited later, and about life in Aruba.

There was more rain on Aruba in Jacobo Kock's boy days. There were cows on the island—for milk and meat. Now most of the meat comes from Ecuador, and produce from Venezuela and tourists from North and South America. The desertlike island is known for its constant sun, its casinos—and the trade winds that bend the divi-divi trees. Palm Beach, he said, had no people then. Today in daytime it's a parade of people, all shapes and sizes and colors in all kinds of dress—and undress. But at 6:30 p.m. you can still be "the only one" walking along Palm Beach. Most people have headed to the bars and casinos.

The mechanization of the Lago-Exxon complex, where Jacobo Kock had worked, put many Arubans out of work (and sent many other Netherlands Antilleans back to their home islands in the late '60s and '70s. Tourism came into focus as a source for employment, for spending money and possible savings for most Arubans. But, in the early 1970s, when North America was responding to its recession, the Aruban economy felt the effects of a fickle tourism, a tourism that had been pinned to tour operators who forced high prices and to United States travelers who turned elsewhere—or stayed home. Lean years encouraged self-appraisal. Tourism officials faced facts, defined their markets, diversified (to South America and Europe) and discussed a few basic facts of the business with domestic union officials, the schoolchildren, and all who could and would be involved with tourism. Things have changed since those troubled times, and they've changed a lot. Tallies for 1980 reached 190,000 visitors, and resort hotels reported a 79.8% average annual occupancy (which is considered good). Although the economy is undeniably tied to tourism, there is dignity involved in the industry. Opportunities have been provided for Arubans to participate at responsible levels, in administration and in training. The country has made a commitment to tourism.

Aruba is one of the Netherlands Antilles, one of the ABC islands (with Bonaire and Curaçao) in the south, a few miles off the shore of Venezuela's Peninsula de Paraguana. The 61,000 Arubans live on 72 square miles of sandy, dry land that is shaped like an arrowhead jettisoned from the tip of Colombia's Peninsula de la Guajira directly toward the coast of Venezuela. Influences from the Spanish culture that the country first knew are still strong, in the customs and in the language. A regional dialect (with Bonaire and Curaçao) of Papiamento, is an unusual tongue (for outsiders) assembled from Spanish, Portuguese, Dutch, English, and French with an overlay of Aruban independence.

AUTHOR'S OBSERVATION: Twentieth-century tourism threatened to overwhelm any indigenous culture with a rash of hamburgers, hot dogs, transistor radios, high-rise hotels, and other symbols of Americanization. Recent efforts to rebuild and sustain local customs and traditions have resulted in the Cas di Cultura (Cultural Center) for folkloric shows and ballet performances, a weekly **Watapana Festival** held in Oranjestad Tuesday evenings from mid-April until mid-December, and the end of February/early March (weekend before Lent) Carnival with elaborate costumes and street parades. A museum in Fort Zoutman is underway, and Papiamento is taught in schools and encouraged as the national language. The efforts by concerned Arubans have resulted in increased national pride, and, incidentally, a more interesting island for visitors.

■■■

POLITICAL PICTURE: Aruba, Bonaire, Curaçao, Sint Maarten, Saba, and Sint Eustatius make up the Netherlands Antilles, governed as one member of the Kingdom of the Netherlands since 1954. The individual islands have control of their internal affairs, with the center of the 6-island united government at Curaçao. Catching the fever that is in the political climate in the world today, Aruba made strong efforts to break away from its sister islands a few years ago, to declare itself independent and a separate country. Financial security of sorts (which comes from its oil refineries) and national pride fueled the fire of independence, but the government in The Hague refused to negotiate with Aruba alone—and behind-the-scenes activities to unite the half-dozen islands proved successful, at least temporarily. Independence is expected, but the time and the terms are still being discussed (with "within 13 years" being one tentative date). Meanwhile, Aruba has 8 delegates to the Staten, a body of 22 members that convenes in Curaçao. Aruba also has its own Island Council which governs the day-to-day affairs of the island. Elections are held every four years, with the MEP (Movimento Electorial de Pueblo) party in control, and Betico Croes, a staunch supporter of Aruban independence alone, is the party leader.

■■■

CUSTOMS OF THE COUNTRY have become so Americanized in the last two decades that it is difficult to find the indigenous ones. Although it is easy for visitors to get lost in a sea of casinos and cavorting at the shore, some awareness of the natural conservatism of the Arubans is essential for sensitive travels around the island. Although anything goes on the beaches, only proper street wear is acceptable for shopping and/or dining sprees in Oranjestad.

The coat-and-tie days are mostly gone, except for important domestic events held at homes or the public places revered by the Arubans. However, respect among the "old guard" is a fact of life, and visitors are expected to dress neatly for meals in restaurants. Men usually wear the guayabera or the local equivalent of the loose-fitting, neatly tailored shirt-jac; women do not wear long skirts as often as in the past, but dressing up in the evening—in elegant (but not necessarily expensive) pants and a suitable top, or in a calf-length dress or skirt and blouse—is the custom. Sandals are perfect footwear for island life, but the influence of South American visitors has put a Latin (dark-colored clothes are best) look to many dining spots.

Be sure to inquire about any special holidays and festivals while you are on the island. Participation will be a unique experience.

Dutch will be spoken at local gatherings. It—and Papiamento—are the national languages, but English is spoken by almost everyone. Expect to find some Dutch customs, especially those that have been translated to other Dutch-affiliated warm countries such as Indonesia (which gives Aruba its rijstaffel, or multi-dish rice table, an eating ceremony). Many holidays are those known in the Netherlands (Queen's Birthday, etc.), and Dutch cheeses, Bols gin, Heineken beer, and other Dutch products fill stores—and will fill you, if you choose.

■■

MONEY MATTERS: The official currency is the Netherlands Antilles florin or guilder (the words are interchangeable), noted as NAf and pegged to the U.S. dollar, *not* the Netherlands guilder. The rate is about US$1 to NAf1.77. U.S. currency is in common use "everywhere," including shops, restaurants, and hotels. You will not have to change to local currency for any reason I can think; even the local buses take American coins.

■■

ARRIVAL AT ARUBA'S Princess Beatrix Airport (named for the present Queen of the Netherlands) may surprise you, unless you know Dutch efficiency and expect modern facilities. Anyone familiar with the small and boxy airports of some of the British affiliated islands to the north will be stunned. This vast terminal was opened with fanfare in spring of '76 (and is the only airport in the Caribbean where I have arrived and my luggage did not—which, incidentally, was not the fault of the airport). Your immigration procedures will be efficient—and fastest if you have your plane-given immigration card carefully filled out and in hand with your passport (the best identification, although anything that *proves* place of birth will do). The local language is either Dutch or Papiamento, the Netherlands Antilles local tongue. Although most people at the airport are also fluent in English, they may not hear it as quickly as you speak it, and will speak slowly and distinctly with their own colloquialisms themselves.

Once you've collected your luggage and wrested it from the porter who was probably "at the ready" to sweep it from the conveyor belt (and will expect his healthy tip which he hopes will be $1 or more), you can face the taxi stand.

AUTHOR'S OBSERVATION: Aruban taxi fares are high, but that's your only route for getting from the airport to your hotel unless you are part of a group tour where arrangements have been made for a DePalm bus. Expect to pay at least $9 for a car for 4 going to Palm Beach hotels, even though the drive is only about 20 minutes. Once you're ensconced at your beachside hotel, consider the public yellow bus that runs a regular route threading the west shore to Oranjestad for 50¢.

When you leave, count on the departure tax of $5.75, and know that you can do your last-minute lingering, after immigration clearance, in an air-conditioned modern waiting area that is fringed with specialty shops offering "duty-free" items.

■■

TOURING TIPS: Count on your taxi from airport to hotel to tally up at a high price. That's been a fact of life here for the past several seasons, but the pumped-up gas prices make the tariff even higher.

To the Palm Beach hotels (all the high-rise, casino varieties) the fare will be almost $10 for a 20-minute ride. Taxis are not metered, but fares are set by government regulation. Be sure to inquire about the fare *before* you start your journey. It's a good idea to ask, before you leave the airport—and before you leave your hotel for some restaurant or touring—what the fare should be. Then ask again before you get into the cab.

Once you're on locale, one day with a rental car will show you all you'll need to see on this island where, in my opinion, the best sights are on the beach or under the waters just off those sandy shores. Car rental companies include the big names (Hertz, Avis, National, Budget) at rates that hover close to $30 per day for the smallest car (a Mazda or Toyota) and over $50 per day for an LTD station wagon. Weekly rates range from Budget's at over $100 to Avis for its Chevrolet Impala at $240 per week. Best bets, as on most islands, are the local firms that aren't aligned with the big companies. Look into Jansen's Dodge Lancer or Inter-Rent's Volkswagen. In most cases mileage is extra, as is gas—and insurance carries a daily fee of about $5, with the maximum weekly charge about $25.

If all you want to do is stroll around Oranjestad for a couple of hours, wait on the main road that runs past all the Palm Beach hotels for the yellow bus that takes Arubans and some of the rest of us into town for a pittance in local currency or 50 cents US. Ask at your hotel's front desk for the approximate schedule, but there are frequent bus services during daylight hours.

■■

HOTELS ON ARUBA baffle me, as far as describing them for you is concerned. Since nothing from the old days exists today, everything is high-rise and handsome, standing in 2 flanks—one honor guard of 6 properties on Palm Beach, where you can review the troops by walking down the beach, and another group at parade rest, on nearby Druif (Eagle) beach, closer to town. There are 2200 hotel rooms. All are modern, all have full American-style amenities, all have special package tour rates that make the daily rate seem obscene. Casinos clatter at all the big properties. As far as walls and halls are concerned, repeaters have their favorite (perhaps where the casino has befriended them) and I have mine—which is based on a period of ups and downs that we've shared. Major hotels are beachside, on the west coast; I heartily recommended a stroll along the beach, with your favorite twilight potion—and friend—to watch the sun set. It's one of the few times during the height of season when you can have the beach almost to yourself.

> **A**UTHOR'S OBSERVATION: There are only a few of us who are crazy enough to pay what is known in the travel trade as "the rack rate." That's the rate I have given when I've looked at individual hotels below, and it is astronomical for most hotels this winter. One reason it is so high is the increased costs, but another (and I suspect a more significant) reason is that the "rack rate" bears the brunt of the commissions, etc. that the hotel gives to those middlemen in the travel industry known as wholesalers, packagers, and travel agents. I suspect that the hotels actually clear less than half of the huge sum on most of their rooms, and I urge you, if you want to go to Aruba, to ask your travel agent to find you "the best deal." Hotel rooms are pretty similar.

In addition to your room rate, all hotels add the 5% government room tax. A 10% service charge is levied on your total bill. In most cases, you are encouraged (by staff if not by management) to sweeten bar tabs and the like, if you have any lingering conversations or ask for anything that involves more than a walk across the room.

> **A**UTHOR'S AWARD go again this year to the Aruba Caribbean, for keeping up with the times and for instilling in its staff a feeling of hospitality that benefits visitors; and to Manchebo Beach Resort, one of the very special properties of Grete and Ike Cohen. He was acknowledged as the Caribbean's Hotelier of the Year at the first awards ceremony in June 1978.

✛ **Airosa** (Palm Beach 33, Box 62, Oranjestad, Aruba, N.A.; 18 rooms) acts with poetic license when it puts itself on Palm Beach. It's actually near the area, and well worth considering if you want a simple air-conditioned place with reasonable rates. Each room has the basics, including private bath. The going rate this winter will probably be $40 for a room with kitchenette which 2 can share. You're not far from the public yellow bus route that passes all the Palm Beach biggies, on the way to Oranjestad.

✤**Americana Aruba** (Palm Beach, Aruba, N.A.; 200 rooms) picked a prize name that puts it first (almost) on any listing, in a country where "everything" begins with A. The property is *not* first on my list, although you will have the protective cover of being with the Pick Hotel chain for U.S. contact and reservations. The hotel started siphoning guests in the season of '75, setting them in one of the air-conditioned tower rooms, most with a sea view. The hotel wedges inland from its powdery beach activity (lounges, sports shack, and plenty of sand and sea) and fills its lobby and lounge area with shops, snack places, and fancy supper clubs. *Casino de Casino* speaks twice for itself, and offers the big-time expecteds. *Le Club Lounge* is for dancing in the dark; *Stellaris* is the super-priced supper club, with music from 7 to 11 p.m. except Mondays, and the *Villa Fiorita Terrace* is simple, sun-spattered, with an air-conditioned option if you don't want the sea breezes. Check for special packages, which come in profusion: honeymoon, sports, casino, etc., including the "Free Spree" summer special that lists all hotels. There are many ways to avoid paying the astronomical winter tariff for 2 that reaches well over $150, *everything* extra.

✤ **Aruba Beach Club** (Druif Beach, Aruba, N.A.; 133 suites) was finally born in June '77 after incubating on the beach over a couple of years while management/owners decided just what the financing was going to be. All that is of little matter to most who settle into the spacious new rooms (all air-conditioned, some with sea view) in this U-shaped building that has *not* opted to stand tall, but does offer all resort facilities: tennis, 2 pools (one reserved for adults), 3 restaurants, shops—and a beautiful beach. There's a minimarket—and a $15 per day charge for the right to use the kitchen facilities that are in your room. (Your choices are to pay about $25 for the breakfast and dinner plan at the hotel, or to go out for every meal and pay as you go.) You're about 10 minutes from the string of high rises that fence Palm Beach, and about 10 in the other direction for the capital of Oranjestad. The property is Aruban owned (Raymond Maduro is the name to know) and operated on the club-sharing plan. You can either stay in someone else's unit while they are not "at home" or buy one of your own. I'll back up the claims of the management that they won't often have to perform with the free drinks they offer you when/if it rains for more than 2 hours during the day (enough to ruin your sunning), or on the night they plan the weekly free manager's cocktail party. (If it rains that

night, Manager Frank Conway invites you, as his guest, to a party
the next night after your night in the rain.) Fact is that Aruba's sun
is so dependable daily that you are vacationing on a desert isle. The
problem with rain is that there's not enough of it—for the people
who live here, at least. Rates for winter for a regular spacious double runs up from $100 to sky-high for the room—with a 1-room
super suite at $200, a 2-room suite at $300 and the royal suite at
about $400 *per day,* for the rooms only! But summer-season spe-
cials have included the 7-night "Free Spree" with bonus features
and other special rates. (Even the printed summer rate, at about
$50 to $80 for 2, is OK).

✣ **Aruba Caribbean Hotel & Casino** (Palm Beach, Aruba, N.A.; 220
rooms) angles from the beach, giving you a choice of about 100
rooms in the main building (the first to stand on this beach), and
the rest in the newer block which rose on top of the single-story
wing of suites in the mid-'60s. These ground-level rooms are some
of the hotel's most convenient and most reasonable. The lower
floors of the garden wing have the best (lowest) rate. What you sacrifice in high-up view you more than make up for with convenience
of being able to go out your patio door and onto the beach. When
you arrive, a porte cochere leads to the lobby that maintains an
open, airy feeling (Spritzer & Fuhrmann branch is here). Elevators take you tower high, or down to the lower level (if you don't
want to walk down the stairs) to the shops, coffee shop, *Le Petit
Bistro* (see Restaurants), beach, and pool. Tennis courts are
around to the right as you face the sea at the lower level; the *Casino*
is convenient, naturally, off the lobby and across the hall from the
Bali bar, a dark, air-conditioned boite that begins to wake up about
6 p.m. and sometimes has dancing after dinner. *Cactus Needle*
snack bar is a spot at the beach, where once, in a fit of pique, before
I knew about Aruba's ever-constant wind, I moaned in dismay
"Does it *always* blow like this?" and got the answer "In September,
more or less." The *Klompen Club* is the nightclub, along the rabbit
run that connects the first-built tower with the now thriving annex.
The *Fisherman's Terrace* tempts me more than any of the other
dining spots in this hotel (except *Le Bistro*), with its seafood dinners and option for alfresco dining. Count on paying from $90 for a
garden room through $160 for your room for 2, with the suites sky-
rocketing from Junior through Master to Executive which soar to
(and perhaps beyond) $235 this season.

✣ **Aruba Concorde Hotel/Casino** (Palm Beach, Aruba, N.A.; 490
rooms) captured the 17-story tower (and some of the predecessor's

problems) that had been rising on the south end of the western shore's Palm Beach. The structure pierced the skyline as a private hotel, and then a Hyatt, to open as part of the Hoteles Concorde Venezuelan chain. (A sister resort also opened in December '77 on the Venezuelan island of Margarita.) The place is palatial, and kudos should be heaped on the interior decorator for putting a firm personality into the anonymous tower of "identical" rooms that threatened to be just like all the others. But I found the problems started when large groups converged at the dining rooms where service is s-l-o-w and food average. Before you get to your room, there's a shopping arcade guaranteed to pry your last dollar out of your hand, but you can fall into a chair to get solace from the sea view from the *Cadushi* coffee shop, before lifting to your launch pad, which will be air-conditioned, furnished in Caribbean colors, with color TV (sometimes in Papiamento, often in Dutch, Spanish, or English—and not working. There have been problems with the TV). You'll find a small refrigerator and a direct-dial telephone that usually works. For general use, there's a sauna, solarium, gymnasium—with masseuse available by appointment—and a wind tunnel at the entrance (the result of a design flaw) that makes the taxi to lobby a challenge. There are night-lighted tennis courts, 2 swimming pools, and a long and lovely stretch of sand shared with the other high-rise hotel guests. Obviously, conventions are encouraged here as elsewhere along Palm Beach: The hotel will have to have them to survive. Count on groups (and resulting confusion), or a very quiet lobby. Even package tour rates will have a hard time luring enough people to keep this place at top occupancy, but the casino tables can be yours no matter who else is in the house. *Disco Dixies Nightclub,* restaurants (*Cadushi* and *La Serre* Italian-style) and all the usual for a modern hotel are here—with plenty of Spanish spoken. Rates this winter are $100 and up for 2, everything extra. Inquire about special package tours (and read the small print *carefully* to be sure you are getting the bargain you think you are buying). Hopefully the problems noted when researching for this edition will be resolved by the time you visit. All had to do with maintenance and housekeeping.

✟ **Aruba Sheraton Hotel & Casino** (Palm Beach, Aruba, N.A.; 202 rooms) clamped onto its patch of powdery beach about the same time the Holiday Inn grabbed its. Once checked in, you can walk through a gardened link with the Aruba Caribbean, or, in the opposite direction, to the Concorde, but when you are here, you have a huge air-conditioned lobby and a group of air-conditioned dining halls where once you're closed inside, you could be anywhere. The only thing Aruban about the main "international" dining room is the Dutch link that comes with its being called the *Rembrandt Room*. Shops include beauty and coffee, sundries, etc. The poolside terrace is my choice for snacking, not because of the food (which is in the usual high-rise habit), but because it gives you a chance to thaw out from the air conditioning, which I found chilling. You can sit in the sun or saunter to the pool and beach. The casino is glamorous, with the usual games of chance; rooms are the modern mass-production that you expect in a chain reaction. Two-bedroom suites are the top of the price list, at more than $250 for rooms only; standard doubles race upward from about $120, but here (as at all the other hotels), you should inquire from your travel agent about "deals" offered with package tours. Tennis courts are on premises (and blocked so that wind doesn't always sweep you off the court).

✤ **Divi Divi Beach Hotel** (Druif Beach, Aruba, N.A.; 148 rooms) dots the coast on a span that it used to call its own, before sister resort Tamarijn, plus Manchebo Beach and the newest member, the Aruba Beach Club, moved in to share the sandy spot. I admit that I liked this place better when it was smaller, when there was a real inn feeling that is hard to find in Aruba. Perhaps Resident Manager Roger Coster can reinstate that. The newest rooms, in addition to making the business more profitable for the shareholders (I hope), give more people the chance to stay at one of the 3 places in Aruba that I think has a definable personality (Manchebo Beach and Talk of the Town are the other 2). Divi Divi puts you on its *Pelican Terrace* for a sea view, and inside, in the *Pelican Cafe,* for air-conditioned surroundings where French-style food is served. The *Red Parrot* is the other dining room, with food you'll find familiar to your American palate. The Sunday buffet is a lavish feast, Monday's beach party is full of guests who have become regulars and the newcomers (and outsiders from other hotels) that join them, but my favorite is the Wednesday seafood buffet that used to feature steak and crab legs (and I hope still does). Check for possible change of days, but count on some evening action in season to make up for the lack of casino. Summer season is slower, but there are still some events planned. There's a pool to supplement the beach that sometimes gets filtered by smashing seas so that it becomes a narrower strand, and tennis courts. A casual, comfortable homey kind of place where your room for 2 will cost from $80 to $150 this season.

✤ **Holiday Inn Aruba and Kings International Casino** (Palm Beach, Aruba, N.A.; 390 rooms) reminds me of an amusement park. There's something going on somewhere all the time. If the action's not anywhere else, count on plenty at the casino, which is *huge*. The *Salon Internacional* is the "gourmet" dining room, and nothing special in my opinion; *Palm Beach* room is the supper club, best when the Folklore group performs (usually Sunday). The *Bonbini Koffie Huis*, despite its cute name, is a commercial coffeehouse, standard HI style—with portions in plastic containers, and printed placemats. The beach is the northern end of the span that's shared with, in order, the new hotel that's being built this season, Americana, Aruba Caribbean, Sheraton, and Concorde, with *plenty* of room for all. (Those of us who think it is "crowded" are comparing it to the perfect, unpeopled stretch of 15 years ago or more.) One of the special evening events is the Friday night Carnival with buffet, music, and punctuation from Aruba's Carnival costumes. Your rooms are etched into a trio of boxes, with all the modern standards of Holiday Inn operations worldwide. This inn is part of the American branch (as opposed to the Canadian) in the Caribbean. Room rates range from about $90 to $150. (Your bill will splash well over that mark by the time you add meals, extras, tips, and taxes.) Inquire about package tours.

✤ **Manchebo Beach Resort Hotel** (Manchebo Beach, Aruba, N.A.; 72 rooms) is on Manchebo Beach, a wide span of sand. The swirl of the sea sweeps the sand to the eastern/southern shores, and used to leave rocky bones. Fortunes have been spent on hauling sand back. The view is great, the pool is smaller than many new ones and therefore has its own personality, and the *French Steak House* serves some of the best beef in town. (See Talk of the Town below to learn why.) The *Patio* is the alfresco dining spot, for breakfast, lunch, and fondue bourguignonne for dinner. Atmosphere here is comfortably casual (coat and tie are not demanded for dinner), and the small shop has island specialties (including the *paranda* mentioned when we look at Treasures and Trifles). Count on surroundings to be simply comfortable, and the rate to be about $100 tops for 2, with 2 meals daily on the related premises for $20 per person extra (related resorts are Talk of the Town and Surfside).

✤ **Talk of the Town Resort Hotel** (Oranjestad, Aruba, N.A.; 62 rooms) is a legend. Why would a nondescript building on the outskirts of the town, fronting a cement slab and the street, and a drive from the nearest beach be the "talk of the town" and a lot of other towns as well? Because this place conveys the spirit of an unparalleled host. When Ike Cohen was awarded the first Caribbean Hotelier of the Year Award at the Caribbean Tourist Conference-2, held in Puerto Rico in June 1978, the entire room of colleagues rose to their feet with applause. Ike Cohen came to Aruba in 1951 after wartime horrors in Holland, continuing to travel 17,000 miles around the United States before settling in Jacksonville, Florida. His construction business thrived, and he added a pool company and a laundromat before he left it all to return to Aruba. In 1966 he took over the former Strand, which was then an office building for a chemical company, and tore most of it down. The Coral Strand opened in its place, with the Talk of the Town restaurant, which became famous for good food at a time when there was very little to be had in the Caribbean. Ike and Grete Cohen hung the name over the hotel in 1971, and added the *Surfside Restaurant* in 1972, going on to bigger and better things, but always maintaining the concern for people, especially employees and the people of Aruba, as well as perfection of Ike's chosen field. That's why Ike and Grete Cohen have the spectacular conch shell trophy awarded by Robinson's, Inc., a printing company in Florida and sponsors of the award. Your rooms will be comfortable (a couple have kitchenettes), but don't count on sea view. There's a pool that is a welcome sight to any businesspeople who stay here and put in a day's work in Oranjestad, a congenial bar, and the candlelit dining room that gave this place its focus, plus the people that made—and maintain—the reputation. Ike Cohen charges fair rates, in view of what the Palm Beach scalpers are up to, with a daily double at $80 and up for 2, meals extra. (You can take the public bus to all of Palm Beach, or ride the hotel's courtesy car that connects to Manchebo's beach.)

✣ **Tamarijn Beach Hotel** (Druif Beach, Aruba, N.A.; 210 rooms) took its cue from its successful older sister, Divi Divi. The grove of about 11 white-stucco, brick-tile-roofed units range around the shore, sending their overnighters into the main building's *Kunuku Kitchen* for breakfast and lunch, and into *Jambo* to enjoy hearty Aruban fare in attractive surroundings (goat stew, sopito, and keshy yena supplement the expected steak and chicken). There's a pool-plus-beach, and 2 tennis courts for daytime action; nightlife concentrates on evening activities planned here and/or at the Divi Divi and other hotels at Druif Beach. The Thursday night Folkloric evening is worth including in your vacation week! Improvements in the second-floor rooms have changed the "peephole" window into sliding glass doors that open out to "your" balcony with sea view. The "front" door has become the back door, off the back of the room walkway, and your new front door leads to your terrace. As you walk in the front of the hotel the lobby is on your right, with the new activities room and library on the left, speckled with over-stuffed furniture in clubhouse beige and brown. Rates for winter figure from $90 to $140 for 2, meals extra. If you sign on for the MMAP (major MAP), you'll get a salad bar lunch plus breakfast and dinners daily. (Others pay $5 for the salad bar.)

■■
HOUSEKEEPING HOLIDAYS ON ARUBA may not work out to be the saving you think they are, although they will be a lot less expensive than the high-rise hotels. An added expense for most places will be a rental car, since few homes for rent are within walking distance of the beach—and beach is the reason for coming to Aruba (unless you huddle in the casino, in which case, investigate a hotel-casino package tour). Houses are usually boxy, cement, modern U.S. development style. I have not found much in the way of indigenous Aruban architecture. Straight lines, simple efficiency, and lots of stucco are the usual recipe, but you can count on places being clean and facilities adequate. Most places that need air conditioning have it, but inquire if it's crucial to your hot-weather happiness.

Although you can get food on location, you'll pay the same high prices that Arubans have to pay. Negotiating with the schooners that tie up at the Oranjestad wharf will give you good vegetables and fruits from Venezuela. Someone living locally can put you onto the best place to buy your fish (or the best person to buy it from). But if you need steaks like the ones you know at home, bring them with you. Canned goods, imported from the mother country, and offering the range of the European Common Market are an interesting array, and Indonesian spices can be plucked from market shelves.

AUTHOR'S OBSERVATION: If you want to eat at home but don't feel like cooking, head for Mido Restaurant (Dwarsstraat 5, off Nassaustraat in town) for Indonesian, Chinese, or fish dishes, or to some of the other Chinese places to get a takeout meal.

In addition to the efficiency apartments at the Aruba Beach Club on Druif Beach, investigate the following:

✤ **Edward's Seaview Apartments** (Malmokweg 19, Oranjestad, Aruba, N.A.; 4 apts.) put you about 400 yards from the beach. Surroundings are not fancy, but your apartment will have air conditioning, a private entrance, hot-water bath, and a good rate at about $250 for a winter week in one room, and $300 for 2 rooms.

✤ **Mr. C. D. Irausquin** (L.G. Smith Blvd. 526, Hadikoerari, Aruba, N.A.; apartments and rooms) offers independence (and good value) within the orbit of the big Palm Beach hotels. A rental car will give you mobility, although you can survive with the public bus service which runs along this road. The Hadikoerari area (also spelled Hadikurari) is at the north end of Palm Beach.

✤ **Cosy Corner Bungalows** (Hooiberg 26B, Box 512, Oranjestad, Aruba, N.A.; 3 houses) are an assortment of houses. You can walk to the heart of the shopping area from some houses and although your house may be in the hot town, it will probably be air-conditioned, with kitchen—and terrace to pick up whatever breezes do sweep down this street. The choices have one, 2, and 3 bedrooms, renting for daily rates of about $30, $40, and $50 per day with weekly or longer rates negotiated.

✤ **Mrs. Irene Norde** (Dadelstraat 23, Oranjestad, Aruba, N.A.) also has a furnished apartment for rent, on the outskirts of the capital. She charges about $300 per month when the apartment is available and also may be able to suggest rooms for rent at about $15 per person per day. You'll have to be self-sufficient for getting around, but that seems a small inconvenience when you compare this rate to what you're charged at the high-rise hotels thumbtacked to Palm Beach—and you can go to any of those places for the day or an extravagant night on the town.

✤ **The Vistalmar** (Bucutiweg 28, Oranjestad, Aruba, N.A.; 8 apts) is a businesslike operation that is the result of the talent of Alby and Kathlyn Yarzagaray, creators of this efficient, attractive innlike vacation base. Their careful attention to detail assures that your time in any one of the recently built apartments, in two wings with beach view, will be relaxed and easy. Check for rates which will probably be in the $50 daily, $280 weekly, range this winter. Bedrooms are air-conditioned, kitchens well-equipped, and your living quarters rattan punctuated.

■■■

RESTAURANTS ON ARUBA are a mélange of character places (boats, mills, etc.) and air-conditioned enclosed emporiums, with a splash of terrace alfresco opportunities to round out the picture. All the hotels have several dining options (coffee shop, snack places, elegant and expensive air-conditioned) mentioned in the hotel coverage. Most are not, in my opinion, worth mentioning again here. Food features cater to the American palate (hamburgers, club sandwiches, hot dogs, steaks), with an occasional foray into French cuisine. In recent seasons Aruban specialties have been added at some places to the Indonesian and Chinese that have always been popular.

AUTHOR'S AWARD goes to Talk of the Town, the place that proves just how talented Ike Cohen really is and that thrives on his considerable skills, and to Basi Ruti, for surviving as a beachside bistro in the bastion of the biggies.

Bali is a flat-bottom character craft permanently moored at Oranjestad Harbor. It's hokey, but fun—and the Bali bunch have been doing their thing, first with a smaller Bali and now with this BIG one, for over a decade. Open for lunch and dinner, Bali specializes in Indonesian rijsttafel, the rice table of the multiple hot and spicy dishes that must be on your menu at least once during your Aruban visit. Frankly, I cannot imagine staggering through the rest of the day after a lunch here; a dinner feast takes the better part of the evening—with the 20 dishes artistically prepared. Perhaps if you settle for a sate ("kebab" of pork cubes) or a red snapper, lunch would be acceptable, but that seems to me to miss the point at this port. Count on about $20 per person for a full rijsttafel, and come with a group if you can.

Basi Ruti, clinging to its piece of Palm Beach shore between the Americana and the Holiday Inn, is *very* beachside simple and may be gone by the time you visit. Its owners have yielded to pressure for yet another high-rise hotel, and one will be built on this site in 1982. In Basi Ruti as I have known it, wine bottles hang from the ceiling, Italian food is served, and there's not too much that can go wrong with spaghetti on the shore.

De Olde Molen, on the inland side of the Palm Beach road, is a real 1804 mill from Friesland, northern Netherlands. Its surprise at being here, on a hot patch of sand far from the motherland, practically shows on its facade, and may be one of the reasons why I've found the inside service fluttering with the speed of a windmill's sails in the Caribbean tradewinds. I can't vouch for the food (cooks change frequently), but the menu seems to have settled on standard steak and fish, and there's not too much that can be done to murder those unless the original produce is not top quality. The surroundings are fun—and this is one place that encourages dress-up evenings. It's open only for dinners, from 6 on.

La Dolce Vita, on Nassaustraat downtown, gets rave notices from local folk and wise visitors for its Italian food. The atmosphere is strictly Italian from the old country, and the food is a better than usual sample of that offered in Italy (which means more than just spaghetti).

Le Petit Bistro, in the base of the Aruba Caribbean (twirl down the stairs off the lobby and you are practically at its door), is spectacular. It gets my vote for French fare on Aruba—but you will pay Paris prices. The ceremony with service is lavish, the surroundings are elegant (and air-conditioned), and the place closes for some time during the summer season, so check if dining here is crucial to your holiday pleasure. The menu is French—in French, with translation below. Cheeses are a specialty, but it's flambés that get the attention. The wine cellar is complete, with labels high-price. You will easily part with $40 per person if you dine with dignity here.

Talk of the Town, at its unpretentious setting cuddling close to town on the main road from the resort areas, has been the talk of the town since 1964 when Ike and Grete Cohen opened their restaurant at the Coral Strand Hotel (see TOT Hotel coverage). Long before I had laid eyes on the place or tasted the food that was winning culinary kudos, I had heard about what the Cohens had accomplished here in an era that was *not* noted for excellent island food! At the moment, in addition to this restaurant, Cohen eating enterprises include the **Surfside** restaurant, across the road on the shore (where Aruban food is featured as well as sunset view), and Manchebo Beach Hotel's **French Steak House,** with its beachside bistro setting. Even when you take off, you will be testing Cohen cooking. They do the food service for the big commercial airlines. As for this spot, you will be stunned when you see it: Surroundings are simple. You dine in an uninteresting air-conditioned "box" with no view, but your meal by candlelight will be truly special— whether it be steak, lobster, or the chef's special. The National Restaurant Association bestowed its Great Menu Award in 1970; Ike Cohen is a member of the Chaîne des Rôtisseurs; and his award from his colleagues in the Caribbean was discussed above with the TOT hotel. It's popular for business lunches; most vacationers come for dinner, some arriving early enough to take advantage of the half-price-for-drinks happy hour that starts at 5:30, and lingering to lope around the dance floor from 10 p.m. to 3 a.m.! (There's also entertainment most evenings at Surfside.)

Chinese food thrives in the Caribbean—and especially here. For an oriental evening meal, try **Dragon Phoenix** on a side street in Oranjestad, the **Mido** on Dwarsstraat, just off Nassaustratt in Oranjestad (if there are 4 in your group, try the rijsttafel for 4), and **Bahia del Mar** near San Nicolas when you're touring the island.

■■■

PLACES WORTH FINDING ON ARUBA are minimal, in my opinion. For first-timers, a swing around the island—past the divi-divi trees, bent (as you may be also) to the prevailing trade winds, prickly stands of aloe, and plenty of hot, sandy desertland—reveals the second town of San Nicolas and the almost completely automated Lago-Exxon refinery (with golf course). My bet is that you will be as glad to get back to the beach in front of your hotel as I am to stay there. (Divi-divi trees, incidentally, bend to the southwest; you can use them as your compass.)

ORANJESTAD, the capital, takes its name from the Netherlands' House of Orange, and took its first importance from the fact that the wiley Dutch knew the value of a fort for protection from invasions. They built **Fort Zoutman,** named after a famous Dutch rear admiral who made a Caribbean name for himself in the many English-Dutch 18th-century forays. The site at Paardenbaai was a new location, far west on the south coast from where the previous commander had lived (near San Nicolas at Commandeursbaai). All gathered around the fort, and as houses fermented near the walls, the town grew—just in time to be named for the House of Orange in the early 1800s. The fort's William III Tower takes its name from the regent, since the lamp that made it a lighthouse was first lit on the King's birthday. The museum planned for the for may be open by the time of your visit. Check if you are interested in Aruba's history.

Head for the **waterfront** for wandering. The sloops and ships that tie up along the cement strip sell from their decks. Although you may not be in the market for vegetables from Venezuela, it is interesting to see what the local folks buy (while the boats' crews buy the luxury items that they can sell at high price, often on the black market, back home in Venezuela).

Too many visitors spend more time hunting and peeking for bargains and weaving around the sidewalks and streets than they do looking up, off, and around. Take some time to notice the few old buildings that house some of the shops. Oranjestad will never compete with Curaçao's Willemstad for "picture perfect Amsterdam in the sun," but it does have an occasional magic of its own.

Natural Bridge has been carved by the sea on the north coast where entertainment some afternoons is to watch the shark feeding. Safely pinpointed on the rugged windward side of the island, as far as you can get from where the tourists swim, the shark feeding is the time when refuse from the slaughterhouse is thrown off the rocks—and the water that always swirls with surf occasionally churn with Jaws activity. Lovely, if you like that sort of thing.

Mount Yamanota, between Santa Cruz and San Nicolas, east of the middle of the island, is Aruba's high point. It reaches 617 feet, which is pretty high on this hot, flat, sandy 72-square-mile sliver of land, 17 miles off the north coast of Venezuela. Getting to the top has got to be the hottest activity on Aruba. I have never climbed it, and I suspect that most of the people who talk with authority about the great view from the top of this peak, or the lower (541 ft.) Hooiberg (Haystack) near Oranjestad, have never climbed it either. You must bake—no, fry—on this hike with no greenery to hide under, but if this is your kind of challenge put on your hiking shoes and head up. You won't be the first.

Lago Oil & Transport Company, Ltd., a wholly owned subsidiary of Exxon, is largely responsible for the expansion of San Nicolas (and the cutback in employees due to automation is largely responsible for the fact that a lot of San Nicolas residents now drive taxis, or travel a long way to work at the Palm Beach and Druif Beach hotels, if they're lucky enough to get a job). The refinery is a sight to see. It opened on August 12, 1924, and has been stretching and adapting ever since. It now includes activity as a transshipment port for VLCCs (Very Large Crude Carriers). Bruno Tour buses leave from the Holiday Inn on Palm Beach (Tu and Th at noon) for an afternoon tour of the refinery. Check to see if the bus stops also at your hotel and if not, hike up the beach or otherwise get yourself to the Holiday Inn.

■■

SPORTS ON ARUBA use the sea for their arena and all the water sports are centered in *De Palm*. The firm has its headquarters at

L. G. Smith Blvd. 142 (write Box 656), but it's difficult to walk around the lobby of your towering hotel or on its beach without tripping over the local concession. If you can muster the strength to struggle from your lounge chair on that eye-blinking ribbon of striking white powder sand, you can head out for scuba, snorkeling, water-skiing, Sunfish sailing, or big-boat yachting.

Deep-sea fishing from the hotels costs about $180 for a half day and $260 for a full day, but 6 people (who bring a packed lunch) can make a gala day of it; beer and soft drinks are included "free" with your tackle and bait.

Snorkeling is best on reefs out from shore, with 2 departures daily (about 11 and at 2), unless you have a group that wants to charter the boat and guide to go at your own time. Usual rate is about $10 per snorkeler. If you don't want to snorkel, but want to see where your pals are going, the cost is about $5.

Scuba instruction starts in your hotel pool, with other novices who signed up when you did. Cost for in-pool instruction and one dive is about $35 per person, but the trips to the reefs for experienced divers are $25 per person, minimum of 2, or—if there are several of you—the boat will go when you want to, at a fee you negotiate. Usual departures are at 11 and 2. If the trip is not leaving from your hotel (due to a light house count) you can stroll down the beach to one of the other bastions to sign on with their group. No matter where you start from, you go to the reefs or wrecks, and there are two main features with the latter. The *Antilia*, a German freighter whose captain bailed out as soon as World War II was declared, is one. The captain crept ashore on the Dutch island to surrender after he submerged his ship in about 66 feet of sand off the shore. (According to one oft-told tale, the crew then went over to Bonaire for the duration of the war.) The other wreck is the *Pedernales,* an oil tanker that happened to be trafficking between Venezuela and Aruba in May 1941. She was split at the seams by a German sub, and when her sinking site put her in a major shipping lane, her bottom was dragged to a shallow spot where she was used for target practice by U.S. marines. Now the coral that grows on her sides and the fish that hover around make the wreck fascinating for underwater viewing.

Sailing is not much, except for the sea. There are no small islands to sail to for picnics, and Venezuela is 17 miles away—too long for a leisurely over-and-back. Sunfish sprout from Palm Beach, in front of or near the big hotels. To pull one out for a sail, count on about $15 per hour, including the service charge. For a lesson, add $5. Bigger boats for sunset cruising and a day at sea are usually at anchor off Holiday Inn, the Sheraton, or other Palm Beach hotels. *Aquaventure* and *Seaventure,* two trimarans, give you Dutch cheese and something to drink for $12.50 for 2 hours.

Golf is limited to the dry and dusty Aruba Golf Course, formerly the exclusive domain of the Lago-Exxon top staff, where "greens fees" for sand "greens," are about $5 per day, caddies are $2 for 9, and clubs rent for $3. There's a mini-golf course at the Holiday Inn.

Tennis courts speckle most of the Palm Beach hotels and Tramarijn on Druif.

■■■

TREASURES AND TRIFLES ON ARUBA are dropped on your doorstep, at the boutiques in your hotel where you'll find a selection of luxury imports at fair prices, plus booklets and Aruban items to buy. Major credit cards are accepted at most stores and most of the goods are strictly for tourist consumption, from my observation, and the island entrepreneur seems to be the ubiquitous De Wit, with stores on Main Street (Aruba Boekhandel), in San Nicolas (Aruba Post), and at the Aruba Caribbean, Divi Divi, Tamarijn, Aruba Sheraton, and Manchebo Beach. In addition to having a fair selection of moderately priced Aruban items, De Wit is publisher and/or distributor for several small fact-packed books about the Netherlands Antilles.

De Wits Aruba Boekhandel (bookshop) on Nassaustraat 94 is your source for beach reading as well as for books about the Netherlands Antilles. If you would like a completely unintelligible (to most of us) Papiamento textbook, here's your source. The shop carries an awesome selection of miscellany which has got to confuse the buyer, and will certainly provide constant treasure hunting for you.

Finding things made in Aruba is sometimes difficult, although the island prickles with aloe vera, a spiky small plant whose leaf gel is used in most sun-care potions and many cosmetics. There are some local fashions, notably the floating *paranda* for women, sold at the boutique at Manchebo Beach. The caftan is yards of colorful fabric, sewn enough to keep you together in something you can wear around the house or for an elegant evening. Tamarijn Beach has been holding an **Artisan's Fair** on Tuesday evenings, encouraging local folk to show their work—and you to part with your cash. The idea is a good one, and products displayed seem to be improving. It's worth making the dinner reservation to be here on the terrace for the evening if you are interested in local wares.

The **Workshop Art Gallery** on Oranjestraat 3, just off Nassaustraat heading toward the waterfront, specializes in things made in

Aruba. The selection varies, from *very* simple shell crafts to some interesting handwork. If you buy one of the Kwihi tables (the slab of wood with interesting grain) be sure to ship it home with you. Delays and problems seem to result otherwise. Forget about having one "made to order" no matter what is promised; the anguish will not be worth the price. **Casa del Mimbre** has Colombian specialties, ponchos known to the Colombians as ruanas, and colorful (and sometimes quality) South American items.

Aruban entrepreneurs choose to stuff the shelves of their shops with the Waterford and Baccarat crystal, English bone china, linens, and luxuries of yesteryear. If you're in the market for that kind of elegant item the shops that line Nassaustraat and filter out its side streets have some of the Caribbean's choicest selections. **Fanny's** (Nassaustraat 7) carries a small and special selection of the highlights, plus pipes and perfumes; **Lucor Jewelry** (on Oranje-straat, just off Nassaustraat) has some interesting local jewelry, plus a lot of "tourist trash"; and **Bon Bini Bazar** may yield something if you like shopping in crowded surroundings.

For perfumes and colognes, **Penha** and **El Louvre** are the names to know and the **New Amsterdam Store** (at the start of Nassaustraat) is the place for one-stop shopping in air-conditioned comfort. Its couple of floors hold counters stacked with watches, jewelry (including island charms), linens (and drip-dry embroidered table-cloths), plus clothes (some French) for women. The souvenir counter carries a complete collection, with some items priced so that it's reasonable to buy 10 and take care of everyone. The future's fashions are featured at **Aquarius,** where the walls and halls took on an avant-garde look a few years ago that now has its count-erpart in most modern shopping centers. All the hangy/clingy clothes are here, plus some new French fashions. Joggers, jumpers, and tennis court leapers should stop at **Sportshop Antiliano,** owned by European athletes Harry and Ciska Janssen, both of whom are competitive sports folk. Adidas is here, as well as Slazenger, Head, Yamaha, and the rest of those known to those who play the name game. Prices are less than hometown department stores, and rival those of your best cut-rate corner. Bikinis and maillots can be found here, if you want a new suit.

Spritzer & Fuhrmann corner the marketplace, with their 4 stores where Hendrikstraat makes a T with Nassaustraat. For row upon row, and floor after floor of unbelievable luxury, head here to shop in air-cooled comfort. The firm has come a long way from its watch-repair beginnings. For those who want to dip into the well of com-merce, these shops are IT. When you shop here, your only decision is how much you buy. What you buy has already been divined by the Spritzer & Fuhrmann's buyers; prices *may* represent a bargain for you, but do represent a prosperous business for the owners. If the sun keeps you beached, you can buy at the branches in the lobby of the Aruba Caribbean or at Divi Divi. Failing that, fling your last few dollars at the airport branch of Spritzer & Fuhrmann. (If you're interested in the S & F legend, look at the Curaçao Treasures and Trifles comment.) Other shops noted for their luxury jewelry and interesting designs are **Kan** and **Berlinski,** each with two shops, one of which is on Nassaustraat. (Berlinski's second shop is near the parking plaza at Hendrikstraat; Kan's main store is slightly out of the pocket of shops, about where Kruisweg comes into Nassaustraat.)

AUTHOR'S OBSERVATION: Although shops are officially open 8-12 and 2-6, Monday through Saturday, be sure to check on the afternoon hours. Some shops close Tuesday afternoons, a few on Saturday, and some small places button up completely if business is light (sometimes in spring or fall) and the staff needs a holiday. Check also on Aruban holidays.

Barbados

Barbados Board of Tourism, Box 242, Prescod Blvd.
& Harbour Rd., Bridgetown, Barbados, W.I. 800 Second Ave., New
York, NY 10017; 11 King St. West, Suite 1108, Toronto, Ontario.
M5H 1A3, Canada; 199 South Knowles Ave., Winter Park, FL
32789; Suite 1105, 666 Sherbrooke St. West, Montreal, Quebec,
Canada H3A 1E7; c/o Barbados High Commission, 6 Upper Bel-
grave St., London SW1 X8AZ, England.

US $1 = Bds $2.
Unless otherwise noted, $ refers to U.S. currency.

The green suitcase she carried on her head had a distinctly imported air about it, but the composure was entirely Barbadian. And
when "pandora's box" opened, out spilled beach smocks and sun
dresses in colors as vibrant as those of the bougainvillaea, hibiscus,
and other blooms that punctuate the green foliage nearby. Before
long the sundresses were grafted onto the fringe of a beach umbrella that became the sales stall.

The beach purveyors hold a daily parade from wherever their
ride drops them off to the nearest shore that is freckled with visitors. The Hilton beach and those along the west coast, dusting the
high-priced hotels, are the favorite launching pads for a day's sales,
although "tourists don't buy like they used to," I was told.

Cyril saunters along the sand swinging his attaché case, opening
it at the slightest flick of interest from a prospective buyer (and
even when there's no interest at all), and expects to sell the bracelets, pendants, and other coral and shell trinkets in his case for anywhere from $10 to $15 apiece. The final price, and whose dollars,
depends on bartering ability.

The dollars that the beach vendors quote are Barbados dollars,
stabilized at about 50¢ U.S. to Bds$1, but most of their sign lan-

guage sales to Europeans (whose English doesn't cope too well with bartering) are in U.S. dollars. Most of those dollars are seldom tallied into official tourism income, although a day's wages—on a good day—can be substantial.

Not much more than 20 years ago, before the crop of vendors began to grow on the beaches, there was a lady who used to come along the south shore road early in the morning, singing "Fly-eeng Feesh" to the accompaniment of the wooden-wheeled cart that carried them. And hand-hewn boats made up the fleet that was pushed through the rough seas until fishermen could set sail before the first light of dawn to catch those fish. In the center of Bridgetown, there was a much-photographed Barbadian face, topped with a towering cauldron of boiled bark juice known as mauby, the Coca-Cola of Barbados. Today the mauby is often in bottles, the fishing fleet is motorized, and the flying fish is bought from baskets at the shore, wherever the fleet comes in. But the changes in this country over the past 20 years are far more awesome than these few vignettes would indicate.

Although the island is only 21 miles long by 14 miles wide at its fattest part, people who lived in a west shore village years ago seldom got to the east. If you were born around Holetown, you stayed there. Someone in your family went out to fish for food, and perhaps someone knew that the town was named Jamestown when a landing party from the *Olive Blossom* stepped ashore long enough to pound a cross into the ground, and to carve "James, King of England and this island" on a tree. That was 1605, and it was 20 years later, after the king had granted the island to the Earl of Marlborough, that a settling party established a community. (And it was 2 years after that that Marlborough lost his colony to the Earl of Carlisle, and a settlement started at Carlisle Bay, where they built a bridge—at Bridgetown.) This island has always been British—until 1966 when it became independent.

British history weaves into the pattern of Barbados life like khuskhus into a basket. These days, it's hard to separate the pieces from the whole. When Rupert Granger drove me around on one of my visits, he talked about his work as a boy on the roads, pickaxing and pounding stones into pebbles to make the solid track we traveled along. Such strands have threaded this island for enough decades to make it possible for Amos Kidder Fiske in his *West Indies* (1899) to write about the parishes (there are 11) and the vestries that ran them and the fact that "the highways are kept in excellent condition."

As you follow along these "highways," which are good roads today, you weave past sugarcane, brought to the island by Dutch Jews from Brazil in the 17th century. Barbados planters claimed to be the first to establish large plantations, and they were so all-encompassing and managed so thoroughly that when the slaves were freed in 1834, they had no place to go. They stayed at work on the plantations, tilling plots that were theirs to hold.

You can drive up to Chimborazo in the north midsection of the island and see what life must have been like in those days. The community still keeps pretty much to itself; the plantation house, now a private home, perches on a windswept hill, with a spectacular view over undulating fields to the sea. The plantation isn't working as it used to now, and neither is the one at Drax Hall, where Sir William Drax implemented a process he had learned in Brazil in the 1640s. That was when sugarcane took over tobacco as the island's main crop. And it was in the 1960s that tourism took over sugar; when sugar prices began to drop, the tourism prices began to rise. The lady from Oistins still sells her flying fish, but she sits with her basket by the beach and road, and you drive to her to buy it.

■■

POLITICAL PICTURE: Barbados held national elections on June 19, 1981, and returned incumbent Prime Minister J.M.G.M. "Tom" Adams to another 5-year term. Adam had been elected Prime Minister in 1976, and he shares second generation political expertise with his countrymen. (His father, Sir Grantley Adams, for whom the country's airport is named, was an imposing and enlightened architect of Caribbean policies in the 1950s.) Former Prime Minister Errol Barrow, in office at the time of the country's step into independence on November 30, 1966, is leader of the opposition. The country's government is patterned on the British system. The Barbados House of Assembly, the Lower House, with 24 elected members, is one of the 2 houses in the Barbados Parliament. The other is the Senate, known as the Upper House, with 21 nominated members. The country is justifiably proud of its 97% literacy rate for a population that is usually tallied at 250,000.

The Barbados Industrial Development Corporation is active and effective with encouraging foreign investment in the country. A series of industrial parks put work places in residential areas and spread the income-producing jobs around the 166 square miles of the pear-shaped country. The 1980 figures tallied the gross domestic product at $814 million, with a per capita income figured at about $3,000—among the highest in the Caribbean countries.

The Offshore Banking Act, implemented in 1979 has encouraged banking in Barbados from foreign sources, and the Caribbean Development Bank has supplemented the incentives offered by the IDC by making loans for such high priority tourism projects as the Heywoods Holiday Village project, a multimillion dollar project for 27.8 acres on the country's northwest coast. Tourism is a major employer in this once agricultural country, and its value as a source for hard currency and for increased understanding of the Barbadian way of life is recognized by both major political parties and most of the Barbadians. Tourism receipts for 1979, the last full year of record at press time, is Bds$369.7 million, and official figures estimated that stay-over visitors (as apart from cruise-ship passengers) spent an average of Bds$966.2 per person. More than 370,000 visitors came to stay on Barbados in 1980, and totals including cruise passengers reached over 500,000. Political stability, with two strong parties dedicated to reasonable improvement of the life for Barbadians, has created a comfortable holiday home for vacationers.

AUTHOR'S OBSERVATION: This country does a better job, overall, than any other I know in the Caribbean for promotion of a tourism that is compatible with the interests and lifestyle for nationals. However, in the past 2 years, I have noticed incidents of "fat cat" attitudes that I find unbecoming in people who are happy to take my money and interested in having me return. The Barbados Board of Tourism and the Barbados Hotel Association are aware of the potential problem; I hope that clear focus on the importance of hospitality will help to improve the local attitude toward tourism.

■■

CUSTOMS OF THE COUNTRY hang on the British framework. Although the years since independence in 1966 have led toward development of a distinctly Barbadian way of doing things, the conservative "old English" habits have been instilled even in the new policies. Tea is often part of the daily ritual at some of the established hotels. When the Police Band plays at the gazebo, the ceremony will have a familiar ring to anyone who has visited the Mother Country, and if you are fortunate enough to see one of the holiday parades, the mounted horse guard is spectacular precision at its best (with tidy uniforms to match). The horse guard can also be witnessed, in practice and performance, at special events sometimes at Garrison Savannah. Check when you arrive.

Cricket is a national passion, especially since Barbados has birthed 4 of the top cricket players—Sir Garfield Sobers, Sir Frank Worrell, John Goddard, and Everton Weeks. From June to January, a crop of small transistors grow from Barbadian ears, and conversation can only take place when a cricket score does not. Matches can be witnessed at Garrison Savannah and at almost any patch of sand, or island field, when enough kids can be gathered together to field a team. The "uniform" may be bathing suits, or nothing.

Two Barbadian events that should be part of any perceptive person's holiday are participation in the "Evening on Us" program, where you are invited to a Barbadian home for an informal social occasion, and attendance at the performance of "1627 and All That," an entertainment staged at the Barbados Museum at the Garrison near Bridgetown.

The people of the country are called Barbadians. The term *Bajan,* although also used by some, seems to me to be less common these days, perhaps because it was used constantly by the British in the old days. *Bim* is the affectionate name for the country.

Clothes are conservative, not only on residents who will dress up to go into Bridgetown, and to church, but also on most visitors. Splashy resort wear is OK for the luxury hotels, and for special social fetes around the island, but for most roaming around, conservative, neat and comfortable dress is appreciated by the residents who take pride in calling this place home. A rash of topless men and bathing-suited women in the streets of Bridgetown and at supermarkets and other shops prompted a Barbadian-sponsored poster campaign a couple of years ago with amusing-but-pertinent rhymes.

Special Note: The June Crop Over Festival seems to have strayed from its original "fun for all" concept, according to reports from some island residents. What was planned as a good, old-time festival with folk dancing, maypole dances, traditional foods, and other events turned into, in isolated incidents, "confusion" in some quarters. Check with the Barbados Tourst Board for an honest appraisal of whether or not this traditional event would be something you'd enjoy.

MONEY MATTERS: When in doubt, ask whether the price you are being quoted is U.S. or Barbadian $, because US$1 equals about Bds$2, and know that the taxi fare you pay from the airport (or pier) to your hotel will be in Barbados dollars. Change your currency at the bank (open 8–1 M–Th, 8–1, 3–5:30 F; there is a branch bank at the airport before immigration), where you will get the best rate. Hotels here, as everywhere else in the tourist-oriented world, charge a premium for their exchange services. While the extra nibble they take may not be much on a $20 traveler's check, it can add up to a substantial sum on a big bill. Most bills will be presented in Barbadian currency. Credit cards are accepted at many hotels, restaurants, and stores, but if you spend cash, taking time to change your money to local currency is a way to show your willingness to "fit in."

ARRIVAL IN BARBADOS is a joy, especially when compared with arrival at many other Caribbean airports. Grantley Adams International Airport is a big, full-service facility with spokes to Europe as well as to the U.S., Canada, South America, and the rest of the Caribbean. The new terminal, opened in 1979, is bright, airy, modern, and efficient—with the only snag the long lines that move slowly to and through the immigration formalities. The staff at the Barbados Tourism and Hotel Association booth (where you can make hotel reservations if you arrive without any) are marvelous. I have used the on-the-spot reservation service countless times, and have found the staff efficient, helpful, and welcoming no matter what hour I have asked for help. The booth is a few steps from the airport branch of the Barbados National Bank, the place for you to change your money to local currency.

When you pass through customs (perfunctory if you seem to have only tourist trappings), you are "out the door" and at the taxi stand. Find the starter and tell him where you want to go. During travels for this edition, there were lags in the formerly efficient system that involved the starter giving you a slip of paper with the fare, in Barbados dollars. I hope efficiency will have returned. (The ride into Bridgetown area was about Bds$20, but fares may have risen again by the time you visit.)

If you are making side trips (to Grenada, St. Vincent, Dominica, or elsewhere), reconfirming your flights while at the airport on arrival is a system that has a lot to recommend it. It's not easy to reach airline personnel—any airline—by telephone.

Departure is relatively pleasant, but be prepared for l-o-n-g and slow check-in lines if you are heading out on a big plane flight. Even though your island traveling may tempt you to ignore the warning to check in more than one hour before flight time, do what you are told! If you don't appear in plenty of time, your seat may be given to a stand-by passenger, especially if you are flying one of the commuter airlines where seats are at a premium and wise island travelers know they can "always" get a last-minute seat.

There are attractive shops, with good merchandise (including Barbados Mount Gay rum and other liquor), at the airport. But know in advance that the walk from the air terminal to the plane on the tarmac can seem interminable if you are ladened with packages. The "in-bond" shopping pick-up desk is convenient (near the exit doors for flight departure), and the system works in Barbados. (See "Treasures and Trifles" comment.)

■■■

TOURING TIPS: Taxis are ready and willing to take you where you want to go and to wait while you dine, swim, tour, or whatever. Be sure to ask the going rate for the kind of tour or other journey you want *before* you get into a cab. The procedure at the airport (where the starter should give you a slip of paper with your fare written) has been mentioned above. For special excursions, negotiate your rate. Be sure you both understand whose dollars you are talking about, and pay that fee only when you get out of the car—for your sake and that of the next tourist.

AUTHOR'S   OBSERVATION: Be sure to track down (through the Tourist Board offices) a copy of *Welcome to Barbados,* a road map with most places of interest clearly marked. In addition to showing location of almost 200 places to stay, the handy folder details information about historic sites.

Rental cars are the best way to get around if you want to cover the island but be forewarned that car rental firms in Barbados are a law unto themselves. Tourism has made them "fat cats" in some cases, and it is not beyond the personnel to make you know that they are doing *you* a big favor by letting you use a car—at top dollar. I have had good luck (and good service) from a small, east coast firm called Stout's, operating out of a gas station east of the airport (and not too far from Marriott's Sam Lord's Castle hotel). The car was a mini-moke, and the personnel pleasant. From Sunny Isle Rentals, wedged into a backyard off the main southeast coast road (amid most of the hotels), I secured a new Subaru (and bordering-on-surly "service"). The woman who wrote out my rental agreement was "crisply efficient" at best, and the owner treated me like a stock car racing driver out to destroy his new Subaru. The car worked well. Roads are good, and usually direct, even when sign-posting means more to locals than it will to you with whatever map you have. If you want a car in winter, make a reservation for it when you reserve your hotel room, and hold onto your confirmation slip. Cars are at a premium in this land of tourism. Some hotels have their own fleet of mokes or other autos; others use rental firms with whom they have some deal.

Mini-mokes have moved onto Barbados with invasion force. One good thing about them is that they don't use much gas; one item to note is that anyone with a bad back should beware. The ride is not the world's smoothest.

Public buses are usually packed at commuter's hours (from 8 to 9:30 in the morning, around lunch time, and from 3:30 to 6 p.m.), but the service that runs along the south and west coasts can be an excursion, and an inexpensive way to get to Bridgetown or to other hotels for lunch or a day at the beach if you are not staying near one. Most buses are relatively modern; all are labeled with their destination, and bus drivers are helpful with directions if you can't figure out the place names.

■■

HOTELS around Barbados cover the complete range, not surprising when you consider that this spot has been in the resort business since the 17th century. One of the Tourist Board manuals claims that 17th-century "businessmen during their stay on the island lodged at the Ice 'Houses' and Boarding Houses." Life is more realistic these days. The "ice" is provided by air conditioners in some of the modern boxes built in a way that failed to take advantage of the prevailing tradewinds, or in pockets where the breeze can't burrow through. The low-rise luxury of the St. James coast is starting to spread to other areas of the island, but this west coast area still does its best. Even the chains that link this area with well-known American names (Hilton, Marriott, Holiday Inn) incorporate a Barbadian style into their hotel life and architecture. Choices of where to stay defy count. Each time I think I have a tally, someone mentions another small inn, or plans for a big one, but it's safe to say that there are well over 300 nooks to nest in on this island, with facilities ranging from wood-walled, old-building simple near the sea to stucco-cell, air-conditioned, on it—and everything in between. You can cook for yourself, or have a place where someone else can cook for you in your kitchen; you can stay at a homelike guesthouse or a high-rise action-packed hub. The mentions below are the places I know, firsthand, from roaming through and around them on my own, notebook in hand, often without any acknowledgment to or from the owners/managers, to whom I seem to be "just another tourist." Each Barbados foray yields new finds, but here are comments for this year.

AUTHOR'S OBSERVATION: Special package plans provide the special value they claim, and the "Best of Barbados" summer vacation plan once again gets my award for giving the most for the best price. Check into it if you're a value-conscious traveler.

Rates for the height of winter season hit alpine peaks, but there are prices in the valley as well—and many of those places put you close enough to the high-rise luxury so that the aura rubs off but the price doesn't. Summer rates, even without the "Best of Barbados" plan, are a shadow of the winter ones, sometimes half, usually at least ⅓ off the winter high. Most places change mid-April, to leap up again mid-December.

Added to your posted room tally is an 8% Barbadian government tax, and often a 10% service charge. Check to see if the hotel thinks a little sweetener for service is appropriate; from my experience, most of the staff does, even if management advises "no."

AUTHOR'S AWARDS go to Cobbler's Cove for creating an elegant enclave away from the crowds; to the Hilton for blending Barbadian life and international conveniences; to Island Inn, a simple small hotel with the courage to be a haven of natural hospitality; and to Ocean View, a bit of "old world" Barbados with a spectacular sea view.

✛ **Arawak Inn** (Inch Marlow, Christ Church Parish; 22 rooms) is an enclave of the good life, about 10 minutes' drive from the airport, on a road which doubles back around the end of the runaway and heads toward the coast. Popular with European visitors and a handful of others (some who come with group flights), the Arawak is a sort of oasis—out of the mainstream of Barbados tourist life, but with all the assets of a seaside location including a small beach which depends on the sea for its sand. The sea breezes that blow through your room (incessantly, on my visit), can be swirled by an overhead electric fan if they are not strenuous enough on their own. These same cooling breezes have taken their toll on some of the bathroom fittings and other metal that can be affected by salt air. The baked-brick tile floors, combined with the white walls and accent colors, give an airy, comfortable—and Mediterranean—feeling. There's some activity around the bar area, and the open-air dining area (where breakfast is served) near the pool. The 10-mile drive into Bridgetown can take an hour or more, depending on traffic and interim touring plans, but it is a 25-minute "straight shoot." Arrangements for pony trekking and windsurfing can be set up; tennis courts are here. The place is picture-perfect, with tennis court, pool, and well-groomed gardens that punctuate the white walls with flowers. Tiled paths link up white stucco nests with the public areas. Some units have a very practical kitchen and a private sunning terrace and many are now part of a condominium plan. Arawak has the potential for pampered and perfect holidays at rates of about $100 for 2 this winter, room only.

✛ **Bagshot House** (St. Lawrence, Christ Church, Barbados; 16 rooms) is one of the gems that helps this country have a stable tourism. Opened in 1946, this inn is maintained by Eileen Robinson as though it were a home—which it is, for a devoted following who return year after year and wouldn't think of going anywhere else. Anyone lucky enough to be a houseguest can enjoy French Toast (or several other selections) on the terrace with the sea view. Wedged onto the burgeoning south shore, Bagshot repeaters seem impervious to the constant traffic noises. The rooms are all beach-oriented, but if you want a beach view, say so. Not all rooms have it. When you bed in here you'll be about 20 minutes from the airport, and another 15 into Bridgetown. About $100 will cover 2, 2 meals daily per person this winter.

✤ **Barbados Beach Village** (Fitts Village, St. James, Barbados; 46 rooms plus 42 apts.) is a "best coast" biggy, sometimes used for groups who've been pulled together through Trust Houses Forte's efforts. The place is action-packed at height of winter season, when guests fill the lounge chairs by the pool, escaping to the expanse of beach if they want some privacy. Rooms are tucked in and around lush planting, with twin-bedded, modern rooms and luxury suites giving you a terrace or balcony to sit on as the sun goes down (or any other time). Some units come with kitchenettes so you can cook to keep costs down. Radio and air conditioning are always flourishes. The sofa in the suites turns into a double bed if you have understanding friends or small children. The water sports concession sets up activities, taking you out to sea in the small boat that moors nearby and sending you across the road and north for golf and tennis. An informal, casual holiday—the type favored by the English groups who can afford to come here—is what this place features. Dressing up (but not too much) for dinner is appreciated, especially on the evenings when there's special entertainment—which there is most of the time in winter, and when the group warrants at other times. Rates for 2 will range between $150 and $200, breakfasts and dinners daily. Special sports are an additional charge.

✤ **Caribbee** (Hastings, Barbados; 53 rooms plus 36 apts.) nests on the south coast, in the tightly threaded string of shoreline hostelries that housed the turn-of-the-century travelers. Caribbee has been revamped several times to keep up with the modern trends and to give a good-value holiday in sometimes crowded surroundings. Wedged onto a speck of shore, clinging to the main road into Bridgetown (about 5 minutes' drive), the hotel puts you at the hub of hotel action. Facilities are made for groups and middle-income travelers, who pay about $70 for 2, meals extra. There are plenty of dining choices (other hotels, if all else fails) within walking distance. Count on a pool at shoreside and entertainment most evenings in season. Not for anyone who demands elegance, the simply furnished air-conditioned rooms with bath are adequate but not lavish. For those who want housekeeping, inquire about the apartments on the inland side of the road.

✤ **Cobblers Cove** (Road View, St. Peter, Barbados, W.I.; 38 suites) captures a prize piece of west coast property half-an-hour's drive north of Bridgetown and turns it into a special oasis for people who prefer luxury. Taking the cue from the elegant, Barbadian comfort of the main house (pale pink paint on the stucco, white trim, and enough crenellations on the roofline to add importance), the rooms are in several 2-story, 4-room units hidden in lush foliage on a parcel of beach-fringed land. White interiors in the rooms are accented with bright colors, and a patio (or terrace, depending on your level) gives some rooms sea view and all rooms an airy feeling. The center of resort life is the pool with its terrace (a favorite snacking and sipping spot), the lounge area (with bar) to the right of the entrance, and the open-to-breezes patio for dining (where space is shared with inquisitive birds as well as compatible guests). A lovely stretch of sand is flecked with boats with colorful sails (and salesmen skippers who proffer an hour or two at sea) and punctuated with the fishing workboats that depart from the Speightstown area (just north of the hotel) and return with fish you can order from the daily menu. Count on elegant touches, fellow well-heeled guests from Britain and Europe as well as U.S. addresses, and a winter rate that will hover around $200 for 2, breakfasts and dinners daily. (Inquire about better values at other than peak season, and expect a slightly lower rate for the garden rooms. Beachfront is highest.)

✤ **Coconut Creek Club Hotel** (St. James, Barbados; 45 rooms plus 3 apts.) perches on the rocks and claims about a dozen new rooms this season, assuming they're finished in time. There's a band of sand that snuggles up to the coral cliffs but the main gathering areas are on the rocks, in the English pub bar, complete with beamed ceiling, dart board, and piano. Unusual stucco walls and wood-trim decor make the modern architecture seem cozy and comfortable. Pick a poolside spot for the sunset views as you settle into this west coast spot, about 6 miles north of Bridgetown and just south of Buccaneer Bay. Rooms range from oceanfront "superior" with the highest prices (about $160 for 2, 2 meals daily per person in winter), to poolside "standard," to the 3 very special apartments with efficiency units that are my choice for an independent vacation. Everything is air-conditioned, but most rooms don't have to be (I shut it off, savoring heat and sea sounds). Owen and Jean Ellison do their best as omnipresent host and hostess, and that is *very* good. If you have a problem, find them—but one of the reasons they are so accessible is that most people don't. Check on the special package "for honeymooners," that gives you bargain rate on 7-nights in an air-conditioned deluxe oceanfront room, with breakfast and dinner with wine, cocktail party, and twin T-shirts, plus a color print of the hotel.

✤ **Colony Club** (St. James, Barbados; 76 rooms) captures a top spot on the roster for low-lying, high-quality comfort in serene surroundings about 6 miles north, up the west coast. Way back in 1959 this place tucked its guests into 20 comfortable rooms and charged them from $18 to $28 per person for the privilege (and all 3 meals, plus tea). The tempo and price tag have changed in 20 years. Tally for 2 will range from $160 to over $200 this winter, with no lunch, but with taxes, tips, and the other 2 meals included. This isn't a spot to come to if you're counting pennies, but if you want some of the best that Barbados offers, it's here—in the decor that incorporates the flowers growing around the grounds into appropriate arrangements on antique tables, in comfortable rooms, air-conditioned in deference to those who insist (but you won't need it), and in elegant dinners with the option, for those who stay a week or more, to dine around at a group of related hotels. There's a pool and a long span of golden sand, and water sports are arranged. Even with the 76 rooms, management has maintained a small and elegant feeling. The winter crowd is the wealthier set, who not only can but do spend more than a couple of days here.

✤ **Coral Reef** (St. James, Barbados; 75 rooms) coddles its guests in comfortable surroundings that have been "settling in" since the first 10 rooms opened in 1951. By '55 it offered 25 rooms. Now that the room count is 74, it's noteworthy that the tone has kept up with the times, making minimal adjustments to modern travel tempo. One of a trio (with relatives Sandpiper Inn and Settlers Beach Hotel), Coral Reef encourages guests to mix and match so that the responsibility is on you to fit in and have fun. Surroundings are country-house cozy, with public room punctuated with stuffed furniture that's pleasant to sink into when you want to be in the shade. The spectacular flower arrangements set off by white walls in rooms and halls are worth a lingering look as you walk to the open-air, wrought-iron furnished breakfast and lunching area. There's a pool, spectacular sandy beach (that you can walk along to see neighboring hotels) with edges lapped by a gentle sea, and options for water sports, plus tennis. Thatched bohios beachside are sun shelters. The bowered precincts of Coral Reef claim a spot at the top of my roster of Barbadian retreats. Rooms are luxury, air-conditioned with a sea-breeze option, and places you won't mind calling home for as long as you can plan to stay. Inquire about special summer week-long plans that give you something extra for the rate you pay, and count on paying the steepest tariff at Christmastime, when you'll be paying $200 to $300 for 2, depending on your room (and whether or not you can get in at any price). Breakfasts and dinners are included in the rate.

✤ **Crane Beach Hotel** (St. Philip Parish, Barbados; 17 rooms) is a very special place that is being metamorphosed into a spectacular small hotel with elegant rooms. Julian Masters and his ever-patient French-born wife have lavished millions on what is almost a stage set of the opulent, elegant plantation life and Peter McKeaver has assumed the challenge of management. In 1860 the hotel's guests were island planters who vacationed on this shore when they wanted some bracing sea air and a change from the rolling inland terrain. Today, several modernities later, there are spectacular views and awesome history. The furnishings are plantation-style island antiques (or good copies), with some of the priceless early prints of Barbadian maps from Julian Masters's private collection hanging on some walls. White paint keeps the wood looking clean and neat, and the pool just outside the front door provides a focal point for those who don't want to plunge into the surf from the pink-sand beach below. The mealtime offerings include local lobster and other seafood plucked from the Caribbean, and these are best when accompanied with good wine. For bedding down, there are country-style double bedrooms, apartments, and deluxe suites. The deluxe suites in the south wing have coral-stone walls, louvered windows, pinewood floors with island-woven rugs, and antique furnishings. Each has a living room, kitchenette, terrace, balcony or sundeck, and a double bedroom with private bath. If you want to sleep in a four-poster bed, specify when you make your reservations. Not all rooms have them. One of the ground-floor suites is known as "Friendly Hall," and one of the first-floor suites is called "The Tower." Figure the $75 to $150 for 2 well spent; meals are extra.

✤ **Discovery Bay Inn** (Box 429, St. James, Barbados; 84 rooms) dotted the shores of St. James in the early '70s when its big air-conditioned rooms, with patios and telephone, opened around the pool. Part of a trio, Discovery Bay is at the midway point, just south of Holetown (and Colony Club) and north of Tamarind Cove. The option of moving from one to the other for meals puts some variety into your stay (and staples), but most guests paying the $160 to $200-plus winter rate stay put. It's just too much trouble to pry yourself from your own seaview terrace. There's a beach below, if you like to walk in the sand—or swim from it. Water sports, tennis, golf, and island tours can all be arranged through the activities desk, but there's nothing here but sand, sea, and pleasant surroundings.

✤ **Eastry House** (St. Peter, Barbados; 34 rooms) offers elegance, and an opportunity to understand what living in Barbados is all about. The big former plantation house sits on the hillside, inland from the west coast shore, overlooking spectacular verdant gardens with lush foliage (and monkeys in the woods, when I last looked). The rooms vary. Some are in the main house, others in separate cottages (newer buildings) around the grounds, and from all you walk down the hill to the beach. A hotel car will take you to the piece of shore the hotel claims as its own, but you may want your own rental car for mobility if you book here. Opened in 1959, the palatial home with its starlight dining terrace stood for all the elegance everyone wanted. Today, with addition of pool and other perquisites, the place is charging from $100 to $125 for 2, room only. Gordon Carlstrom gave this place a complete overhaul a few years ago and, after marriage to Pat, a Barbadian, this country "home" gives its guests a special kind of hospitality best known to the country's nationals. Count on finding comfortably furnished rooms punctuated with little luxuries. The beach house continues the expected elegance, with an imposing building at the shore for luncheon and some special occasions—in addition to sunning and swimming.

✤ **Flamboyant** (Hastings, Christ Church Parish, Barbados, W.I.; 9 rooms plus 8 apts.) claims mention here mostly because Barbadian Brian Cheeseman and his German-born wife, Isolde, have created a memorable small restaurant on the main floor of an imposing traditional home amidst the commercial clutter that runs along the southeast shore, near Bridgetown. The few rooms for overnight are simply furnished, but the price is right (at $15 for 2) and the hospitality is sincere. The 1- and 2-bedroom apartments in a separate building on the property rent for about $35 per day for 2.

✤ **Greensleeves Apartel** (St. Peter, Barbados; 16 rooms) decorates an inland arm that branches off the main west coast road, north of Holetown, about 20 minutes north of Bridgetown. When Nicolas Teller's interests built this place, elegance was the key. He's now sold out, but luxury lives on. The "apartments" are air-conditioned, with kitchen and spacious rooms with modern furnishings set up so you can stash your luxury loot in your own wall safe. Most of the units are part of a condominium plan, but you can be here when the owners are not. Cupping the central pool, 5 buildings have 1- and 2-bedroom apartments, each with balcony that overlooks the action—whatever it is. Ideal for a congenial group of friends, the apartment living may be too cozy if you don't feel like fitting in. Apartments in the back and biggest building will be the quietest. On the road-and-sea side of the pool, the elegant (expensive) dining room, with *huge* menu, lures people with plenty of cash (or good American Express credit cards) for the evening meal. The rest of the time, you'll have this complex pretty much to yourself and your fellow guests. There's a beach bar across the road, on a span of sand that's favored by those who want to be in the sea when they're on an island surrounded by it. For active sports and other entertainment, you'll have to go elsewhere. If you want mobility, figure a rental car into the price of your holiday. You'll need it, at least for a couple of days. For all this exclusivity, you'll be paying $260 or more for 2—room, taxes, and tips *only*. (All your meals, and everything else, are extra.)

✛ **Half Moon** (St. Lawrence, Barbados; 5 rooms; 26 apts.) sits on the sand on the busy south coast, planting its guests in 1- and 2-bedroom apartments, and some luxury suites around the pool and the sea (don't count on much of a beach right in front, but there is some sand along the shore). Informality is the keynote, with guests gathering for barbecue and buffet evenings and cooking at home most of the rest of the time. You're at the hub of holiday activities, with all water sports, dining spots, small shops and full services within an easy walk. One of the better bets, if you want to be independent and care about costs. For 2, the winter rate comes in at close to $80, everything extra.

✛ **Hilton International Barbados** (Box 510, St. Michael, Bridgetown, Barbados, W.I.; 192 rooms) hove into view on Needham's Point, a promontory, previously the exclusive property on an imposing fort and a photogenic lighthouse. The lighthouse hides not far from the garden wing and the beach, seemingly content to stand idle (except for a short stint a few years ago as a cave climber's practice pad when Scandinavian Ole Sorenson wrapped a line around the top and clambered up the side in preparation for his explorations of now-famous Harrison Caves). Fort Charles is integrated into the hotel activities, as the scenic site for special events (elegant cocktail parties, private Barbadian social functions and a weekly fete for hotel guests, for example). I have temporarily "tented" in this property at intervals since the first visitors walked through in November 1966, in celebration of the country's independence, and can safely report that the intriguing mixture, unequalled anywhere else on this island, of Barbadian traditions and personalities and modern international hotel guests and flourishes has never been better integrated than now, under the watchful eye of General Manager Ken Kennedy. You can thank people like Noel Wilkenson (who has been called "the best headwaiter in the Caribbean" by one not-too-impartial observer) and Colette, Gaylord, Don, Basil and others whose faces you'll quickly recognize after a few days "at home" here. My own propensity for small inns with personality makes high praise for a chain reaction even more significant, but this is a hotel with a heart—and I like it. Rooms in the arcaded 4-story coral-block building (with elevators that work when the power does) rim a center foliage-filled court that gives credence to the tropical ambiance that you come south to find (and provides surcease from relentless sun). Rooms are spacious, coral-walled, and comfortable, with view of either Caribbean Sea or Carlisle Bay. Top-rate corner suites are bigger than most Barbadian homes and 2-story buildings of garden rooms are set near the shore. Count on breakfast to be "the usual" (if Colette brings your French Toast, it has sugar on it), in the Terrace Cafe where waiting lines can be tedious if the hotel is filled and you choose to breakfast when everyone else does. Danish and coffee are served at the beach bar, a favorite daytime gathering spot, after 10 a.m. Days can be as active as you choose, with goat races on Sundays and donkey polo, tours of the property, bicycle rides, and craft classes as possibilities for other times. Tennis courts get good play at other than peak-sun times; there's a pool if you prefer it to salt water sea; and the soft sand that blankets the area in front of the hotel provides plenty of open space for you to be on your own, if you can fend off the beach vendors who are polite but persistent. Count on European and South American influences among your fellow guests, and know that when you bed in here you'll be at a source for the best that Barbados can offer. Winter room rates stretch from $100 to $150, everything but your bed-and-bath extra, but look into the seasonal special package holidays such as the "Best of Barbados," even better value at the Barbados Hilton with the addition of Hilton's own "Pleasure Chest" promotion. A selection from the best Barbados shops half-circles the entry way, with a Cave Shepherd branch for crystal, porcelain, and other luxury items and boutiques with clothes unique to Barbados.

✣ **Holiday Inn Barbados** (St. Michael, Barbados; 131 rooms, 7 suites) hatched on the sand at the site of the former Aquatic Club after the season of '68. Ever since, it's been spilling its guests onto the busy strand that stretches from here south to the Barbados Hilton (a stroll that can take you a leisurely 20 minutes, past the *Pebbles* beachside snack spot and the concessions for water sports). You'll find the Holiday Inn style in the air-conditioned dining room (*Carlisle*), or on the *Calypso Quay*—my choice for dinner and drinks if you want to dine here. It occupies a stilted perch in the sea, reached by boardwalk from shore, a short stroll from the piped music and constant action of the hotel hub. A West Indian floor show is part of the planned entertainment some evenings, with a manager's cocktail party providing a place to meet and greet your fellow guests. You can count on someone to be at the Holiday Inn at almost any time. Its proximity to Bridgetown (about 5 minutes' taxi ride) ensures the presence of well-heeled business travelers who want to sink into the sea after they've settled their business affairs in town. Shops on and around the grounds can take care of all your gifts for home if you don't want to head to the often hot heart of Bridgetown. Guests can leap into the pool, sign on for water sports, or make arrangements at the activities desk for tennis, golf, and horseback riding, all offered elsewhere for a fee (to which you'll have to add your taxi fare). Count on paying $105 to $120 for 2, meals extra, but ask about special package tours—in season and out.

✣ **Island Inn** (Garrison, Barbados; 26 rooms) is a favorite of mine, but it won't be ideal for everyone. Frank Odle, former director of Barbados tourism at head office in Bridgetown, is the man on the spot, and the Odle family is involved in ownership of this special inn. More than 20 years ago, when Alan Martyr ran this place as an extension of his home, the pace was set—and the homelike atmosphere hasn't changed, except for some sprucing up to keep up with the times. Barbadian Martin Donawa took over this place at the end of '77, and immediately perked up the nearby restaurant (*Brown Sugar*), now a separate business venture. *Peter the Fisherman* is the on-premise place to eat—and it is good and favored for excellent Barbadian food (order Flying Fish) and good ice cream. There's no beach (but there's one down the road, at Holiday

Inn or Hilton); there's no pool, but who needs it? What there is is excellent value, comfortable (but not necessarily cozy) surroundings, and an island atmosphere that survives all the crass commercialism that crowds in around it. Rooms are air-conditioned now (they weren't when I first stayed here), and all have private bath (another relatively new addition that has meant some small rooms when the wall had to make way for the plumbing). Shapes and sizes of rooms and baths depend on the room's location in the buildings (few baths have tubs). Room #15 sleeps 4, 2 in an alcove. A good bet for value-conscious travelers who don't need all the resort flourishes, Island Inn charges about $46 for 2 this winter, meals extra. Most of the rooms run along the hall behind the check-in desk, and, across the patio, behind the bar, but 4 rooms are in what used to be the manager's cottage at the back. (Wood walls are thin, and the place is lively many evenings when the band plays. This is no place for light sleepers).

✤ **Marriott's Sam Lord's Castle** (St. Philip, Barbados; 259 rooms) mingles into its lush planting so that the buildings almost melt into the landscape including the newest cluster-with-pool (which could be a separate hotel on any other tract of land). This is Sam Lord's city. The U.S. chain moved into Barbados with all systems "go" in 1972 and has been moving and improving ever since. From the traditional core of Sam Lord's Castle, locale for special invitation Castle Dinners and piano concerts and worth visiting for its own venerable past and antique furniture, the resort sprawls out in all directions. The variety of accommodations *must* have something to please everyone, and I suspect too many vacationers get wedged in here and never leave to see the rest of the island. (Rent a car for at least one day to see what else is around the rim and in the hinterland of one of the Caribbean's most stable and interesting islands.) The layout, in general terms, is this: Once you go through the gates (where you'll have to pay a fee if you are not an overnight visitor), there are shops. Keep going to the right to find one pool, pool restaurant, and a spot to overlook the beach. If you keep straight on, you'll reach the main white house (Sam Lord's) with the check-in desk; walk through the house and down the garden mall to the beach. Picture what this place must have been like when Sam hung lanterns on the shore to lure loaded caravels to the reefs where they wallowed while his team set out to plunder. The swinging lanterns, tradition says, led ships' captains to believe they were headed for Bridgetown, not the rocks they wrecked on. As you stand on Sam Lord's porch, the newest rooms are in blocks to your left—in very attractive 2-story units with 2 pools, plus restaurants (where service was appallingly slow and food mediocre, on my visit). Separate villas are scattered around the grounds. A breakfast buffet is served at the *Main Brace Bar,* to the left of Sam Lord's as you face the sea, and busy at height of season when you and everyone else lines up for the first meal of the day. The food at breakfast and other mealtimes continues to be commercial U.S. "average," in my opinion, except for the Bajan Night buffet, but surroundings are pleasant. There are tennis courts in 2 locales, water sports facilities, 3 pools (north near the new rooms; south near the first-built tennis courts and shoreside *Cobbler's Reef* bar and restaurant), plus beach activities (goat races and their ilk) to keep the action lively. There's regular evening entertainment in winter months, and most of the time, when house count warrants, in summer. This is a rambling chain resort that gives you all the Caribbean action options, at winter rates for 2 from about $115 to $150 meals *extra.* Check about package plans, especially in summer, that will bring the rate to more reasonable levels.

✣ **Miramar** (St. James, Barbados; 90 rooms) made its name in the early days of Barbadian tourism, when Oliver Messel's decor was fitted with Victor Marson's flair for an elegant resort (a flair he'd proved on this island, first at Ocean View, then at the old Sam Lord's and finally with his "own" spot here). The place in the old days had only a dozen rooms, all of them in the style of an elegant island home—which this place was for the precious few who found it. Then some rooms were added, then some more, then a boxy block for more—and now the original atmosphere is hard to find. Miramar still meanders along its shoreside spot, north of Holetown (and Colony and Coral Reef), and some of the old-timers who find it like it. For the young at heart who head here with a group of friends, the grounds are conducive to having a good holiday: beach, pool, tennis courts, water sports—and horseback riding and golf easily arranged nearby. Depending on your room, you'll be paying from $130 to $250, 2 meals daily, per person for the privilege of playing here this winter. Check for the honeymoon and other special rates sometimes offered in summer season; otherwise plan to be part of a steady winter repeat business that sometimes makes the place seem like a private club.

Miramar's restaurant specializes in elegant service (at high prices, with wine if you want it), with hotel-style West Indian food offered on every evening's menu along with the expected steaks and chops. Judy Stone is in charge.

✛ **Ocean View** (Hastings, Barbados; 39 rooms) occupies a patch of shore on the south coast, as it has "since time began," or at least since the start of modern Barbados tourism. This place is very special, clinging to the traditions, and some of the antique furniture (punctuated with spectacular flower arrangements). The seaside dining room is revered by Barbadians, who come here for their business lunches and for some of the island's best Barbadian food, served with the sea breeze. Typical of a turn-of-the-century hotel, Ocean View survives—and thrives—by adapting as little as possible, but enough to please. Your room will be wood-walled (you might be able to hear your neighbors), but the plumbing will work and the view—if you have a seaview room—will be spectacular. The rate is right, if you don't mind being crowded into a narrow band of land between sea and the main (very busy) road leading along the south coast west of Bridgetown, 2 miles away. One of my old-time favorites, this is no place for someone who needs the plastic modern mold. A good buy at $70 or so for 2, this winter, with breakfast and dinners daily. (Top rate seaview room is about $150.)

✛ **Paradise Beach Hotel** (St. Michael, Barbados; 182 rooms) puts all the elements for a happy beachside holiday into an action-packed complex on a west coast shore, not far from Bridgetown. Part of British-based Cunard Trafalgar's family, the hotel can be your land base for a week ashore before or after a Cunard island cruise. The hotel has grown in 20 years, from what was a simple beachside club well known to British and Barbadian families as the sandiest spot near the city to a huge conglomerate that has tried to be all things to all people. As a start, there is a cluster of rooms around a beachside pool near the area where the water sports folk set off for their scuba lessons. Then, on the other (north) side of the dining area and open-to-the-air terrace that is sometimes used for starlight dancing, there is another band of rooms. And the newest band of seaview rooms opened with flourishes at the same time as the new lobby and lounge area, in January 1981. In the back, up in the hills, are *more* rooms, plus the 5 tennis courts (some lighted for night play). The new bright color accents and plastic props make for an airy, open feeling and the beach is still the main emphasis; there's lots of action in and around it. Appealing to well-heeled people with children, and the young at heart, this is no place for those who seek solitude or are searching for the pampered and perfect life. There are special honeymoon, scuba, tennis, and family package tour weeks, as well as group rates and the packages put together with

owner Cunard-Trafalgar's ships. Check with your travel agent, or
pay the standard $150 to $250 for 2 this winter, meals and entertainment extra.

✤ **Regency Cove** (Hastings, Barbados; 66 rooms) rambles around
both sides of the road, with accommodations that fill a piece of the
shore south of Bridgetown. Bought by Barbadian-connected
owners, the hotel had Ms. Hinds as manager when I stopped by in
mid-'81. Complete refurbishing, after a period of being closed, assures attention to problem spots in this resort that sits on both sides
of the road and was once 2 separate hotels. The several stories of
the seaside building have rooms with water view; the inland rooms
(air-conditioned because they have to be; no view) are at the pool.
Winter rates are in the $75 range, meals extra.

✤ **Sandpiper Inn** (Long Bay, St. Philip, Barbados; 12 rooms plus 11
apts.) is a '70s child, built in a style that proved successful for sister
resort Coral Reef, although without its time-honored established
elegance. This is a West Indian hotel, with stucco walls and shake-
shingle roofs and wood-beamed balconies stretching along the second story and settling into terraces on the first. Rooms are simple,
neat, clean, and comfortable—there's nothing sparse about them,
but you won't find overstuffed furniture. Clustered around the
small, free-form pool and garden area, the hotel sends its guests
onto the beach during the day, for sailing and water sports, and
provides entertainment some evenings in season. (It's always up
the road at Coral Reef.) Rates ramble from $175 to $220 for 2 in
winter, 2 meals daily per person with the price $10 more per room
over the Christmas holidays. Inquire about special honeymoon and
other package week-long rates for special times in the year. A good
bet if you like small spots with an inn feeling.

✤ **Sandy Lane** (St. James, Barbados; 124 rooms) stepped into the
limelight the minute its welcoming staircase, with the traditional
curved railings, was ready for the first guests in 1961. The 67 rooms
that opened that season were sumptuous, in the best plantation
tradition—known by Sir Ronald Tree and wife Marietta (an American Boston Peabody who was for several years the U.S. delegate to
the U.N. Commission on Human Rights). Happy Ward was the architect. The splendid hotel he put together has survived the changing trends and a new tourist mix that brought this place into more
commercial spheres. Just as the white-glove, big-hat-for-tea group
have gone, so has the aura changed. What you find now is a stage

set of a bygone era adapted to modern use, and no one can criticize the elegant atmosphere of the dining terrace, facing the sea and candlelit at night. With the moon and the stars (and an occasional steel band) for accents, this is one of the most elegant spots on the elegant west coast of St. James, in spite of the commercial cast that Trust Houses Forte have put into the mix. "Everyone" has heard of Sandy Lane, but few of those folks stay here now. The guest list has leveled off to some who *want* to be at the name place, and others who've been here before and don't mind paying about $350 for 2 to have 2 meals daily and a room with a view. There are boutiques in one of the garden level rims of the main building, plus restaurant choices, pool to play in, strand of sand, and the golf course across the road.

✣ **Settlers Beach Hotel** (St. James, Barbados; 22 apts.) scatters its guests in several 2-story blocks of rooms, ranging around the gardened grounds on the fashionable west coast. Part of the trio that includes Coral Reef and Sandpiper, this complex, with its peaked roof wining and dining area blissfully open to the seaside breezes, is priced high—at about $180 for 2, tips, taxes, and room *only*. Meals will run about $7 or so for lunch and $25 or more for dinner, if you splurge at all—and breakfast tallies up another $5-plus depending on how much you eat. Sports are arranged, but there's nothing on your gardened 4 acres except sea, sand, pool, place to gather, and some air-conditioned surroundings.

✣ **Silver Beach** (Rockley, Barbados; 23 rooms) shows what can be done when you get off the high-priced luxury coast. With winter rates that reach to $60 for 2, 2 meals daily included, the hotel has simple rooms on a side street, back from the popular (and pleasant) south coast Rockley Beach, and offers one of the good values in Barbados. Not for anyone who wants fancy resort treatment, this is a place for real people who want real value—and enough of them do to make an interesting mix of guests. It's appealing to teachers and other professional types who like simple surroundings; the air-conditioned rooms scattered through the house all have private bath and telephone. You can walk to good dining spots, if you want some variety, and are on the public bus route for a 2½-mile excursion into Bridgetown.

✣ **Southern Palms** (St. Lawrence, Barbados; 72 rooms, plus 21 apts.) added new facilities during the early months of 1980. The place still specializes in constant action, often enjoyed by the group tours that come in hunks from cold climes in winter months. When it's full—or almost full—there's not enough room to notice some of the scruffy things I've found on slow-season prowls, but there are plenty of pluses here for nonfussy travelers. Entertainment focuses on the 2 pools, 3 spots to snack, and casual guests. The arched ground level of some buildings is topped by straight-strutted balconies; one of the convening places—the *Khus-Khus* bar and restaurant—has huge dunce-cap thatched roofs, and even they don't spike up at the same (or even compatible, to me) angles; the pool is a T—with very short arms. Only the beach is what you expect, when it hasn't been washed out with the surf. The hotel's own folder says "the decor of Southern Palms is unique"—and I'll agree with that. Housekeeping, on my recent sweep through, left something to be desired, but I suppose maids and others may have trouble finding out where the corners *are,* and which way to turn to get to them. Rooms continue the same eclectic style, but you can count on bed, air conditioning, private bath, perhaps a balcony (if you want one, ask for it—not all rooms have one). My preference for rooms is the 1-91 block with 2 units along the beach. For 2, winter rates range from $95 to $140, taxes and tips included, but *no* meals. Varied in entertainment and architecture, Southern Palms appeals to groups (who come in at special rates), to young at heart who want a lot of action (and can pay for it), and to people who thrive on cluttered surroundings.

✤ **Tamarind Cove** (Box 429, Paynes Bay, St. James, Barbados; 50 units) took its place on the west coast shore line up in March 1970, with claims of entertaining royalty, and certainly looking the part. Guests gambol on a white sand beach, part of that shared with neighbor Buccaneer Bay, or wallow in the pool, if they haven't set out under sail on a yacht that offers time at sea. The spacious doubles are spelled by an assortment of 1- or 2-bedroom suites, cupped around the pool and palm-punctuated garden areas, upstairs or down. Room service is available "24 hours a day," but place your breakfast order the night ahead if you care about it arriving exactly when you say it should. Dinner choices range from the menu here—vol au vent, roast beef, coquilles St. James (sic)—to whatever is on the carte up the coast at Colony, Coral Reef, Discovery Bay, and Sandpiper, all part of a dine-around planned to offer guests some variety. Hang around here on Thursdays for the barbecue and Barbadian floor show. Free service is provided for the 7-mile jaunt down the coast to Bridgetown (M-Sat, in at 9:30, out at 12:30). All water sports can be arranged at the beach. There's a tennis pro, and polo and the riding stables, plus Sandy Lane's golf, are not far along the coast. Plan on paying from $145 daily for the standard room to $260 for the 2-bedroom penthouse, for 2, 2 meals daily per person this winter.

✚ **Tides Inn** (Gibbs, St. Peter, Barbados; 10 rooms) is at the northern part of Barbados, on the west coast where the Caribbean sea is calm. Opened in 1958, the inn was completely refurbished in 1969 and again, with new ownership, in 1981. John Tyrell from California does his utmost to see that you are comfortable. Most guests enjoy the fact that there are no special activities and that the dining room is for their use only or for their guests, whom they may invite after notifying the management so that there are the right number of places set for the houseparty-style dinner. You can (and most do) have breakfast in your room, on your own patio. The beach is about 2 or 3 minutes' walk from Tides Inn, but some guests stay right at home for their sunbathing. This is a conservative, quiet place known and loved by many who come here regularly. Rates are from $70 to $86 for 2, 2 meals daily per person, this winter.

✚ **Treasure Beach Hotel** (St. James, Barbados; 24 suites and 3 studios) wiggled in between Sandy Lane and Tamarind Cove on the east coast beach area in the season of '77. The first 17 units proved that attractive units at good value will be the key for Charles Ward's property, where you have a pool, the beach, and easy access to Sandy Lane's golf course and tennis courts, and the next 10 assured it. (He tallied up 24 years at Paradise Beach, so he knows how to change with a resort.) Plan on parting with from $90 to $150 for 2, room only, this winter, but know that you will be on the "in" coast of Barbados, in one of the better value places. The studios are the farthest from the beach (and alongside the main coastal road so you'll hear the traffic instead of the surf), but they carry the best rate and you can spend your days on the beach.

■■

HOUSEKEEPING HOLIDAYS are best on Barbados. The country has been offering this kind of holiday—with quality, in quantity— for longer than any other Caribbean island I know. British set the pace, coming here for winters before, during, and soon after the turn of the century. Those who can afford it still do. The gap has been taken up (and the rapidly increasing roster of new places with housekeeping options filled up) by Canadians and people from the U.S. Not only the cost-conscious take advantage of the housekeeping options. An independent holiday, with your "own home," appeals to many who spend a month or more and don't want to be bound by a hotel dining room menu.

A Barbadian colleague told me that there are "more than 150 central offices for rental apartments," so the list below may seem paltry. As is the case with this entire volume, places included are those I know and have prowled around on your behalf. Places mentioned are a representative list of what's available, but there are more—many more.

Because the housekeeping pattern has been tried and proved true there are plenty of places to buy your staples as well as special island foods. Fresh fish is no problem to find, either from the peddlers who still proffer their catch from baskets on the beach, or from the special markets at Bridgetown and in some of the fishing villages. Try Oistins, where the flying fish fleet that used to set out under sail now motors through the waves to their catch.

Maids/cooks are available, if they aren't included in your rate, at about $50 per 5 half-days, or $15 per "day."

✤ **Asta Apartments** (Palm Beach, Hastings, Christ Church, Barbados, W.I.; 60 apts.) arrived a couple of years ago, on a curve of the same beach that stretches to Needham's Point and the Hilton. Ideal for self-sufficient types who enjoy the comforts of modern surroundings, a pool-punctuated courtyard that opens onto the beach, and the independence of being able to cook "at home." A small snack area on premises offers relief from household chores, and several good restaurants (*Flamboyant, Brown Sugar, Ocean View,* and others) are within walking distance. The road that spurs to Asta is off the main southeast Coast drive; within less than 10 minutes you can be in downtown Bridgetown by public bus if you choose that transportation. Count on rates from $50 to $75 for 2 this winter and inquire about the bigger apartments if you want more space than a pleasant studio allows. All rooms have terrace or balcony, depending on which of the 3 levels you are on.

✤ **Blue Horizon Beach Apartments** (Rockley Beach, Barbados; 118 apts.) lets you slip into the sea while the dinner is cooking. You're right on a small and busy strand of sand, shared with *all* the hotels that hover over and around this patch. Water sports are set up through the management from a pavilion at the beach, and Manager Malcolm Worme will answer any questions you may have about what's where and why. You'll be on your own for meals, which you can cook in the kitchen part of your 1- or 2-bedroom unit, and can count on paying $60 to $75 daily, depending on the size of your unit, for 2. Although you are in the busy apartment/hotel section of the country, you and everyone else may choose to be here because it's convenient to town (by public bus or car in about 10 minutes), and at the beach. You can walk to several spots for a dinner cooked by someone else.

✠ **Bresmay Apartment Hotel** (St. Lawrence Gap, Barbados; 50 apts.) broke into the holiday roster in season of '75 with 20 units and has grown to meet demand. Tom Anderson sends his guests onto Dover Beach from studio and larger apartments facing the sea but not right on it. (There's a pool at your "front door.") Although meals are served at the *Dinner Bell* (on the inland side of the street), and drinks at the *Dover Beach Bar,* many renters prefer to home-cook at least part of the time, and wander around to the other eateries that speckle this shore (Pisces and Luigi's among them). Rates for your winter rental for 2 range from $55 to $65 daily, but ask about long-term rates.

✠ **Buccaneer Bay** (St. James, Barbados; 36 units) beached itself on a sandy cove, not too far from Bridgetown and near enough to all the elegant luxury spots to make them possibilities for dining and dancing. This 2-story place is one of Barbados's best bets, not only because Margo Bennett runs "her" inn like her own home, but also because most of the air-conditioned rooms give you a sea view and a fully equipped kitchen to use or not as you please. The terrace tucked into the heart of the complex is ideal for sitting and sunning while you snack on something or have a lunch or dinner, but you can repair to your room for complete privacy if that sounds like your kind of vacation. The bus runs along the main shore road outside, connecting you at bargain rates to the string of hotels to the north and to Bridgetown, 6 miles south. Entertainment is planned some evenings in season, but don't count on much in spring and fall. Summer picks up with participation in the "Best of Barbados" program. A winter twosome will pay about $90 per day for oceanfront, $75 for non, for 2, with meals (2 per day per person) an additional $25 each.

✠ **Cacrabank** (Worthing, Christ Church, Barbados, W.I.; 22 apts.) captures a legendary name, but a new building edges up to the inland shore of Rockley Beach. (The original Cacrabank was one of the country's earliest hotels, a popular place in the 1950s and before.) Apartments range from standard to deluxe, and from studio to 1-bedroom. All have patio or porch facing toward the sea, and surroundings are neat, clean, and pleasant. Location on the flourishing southeast coast assures restaurants, stock-up markets, and activities within easy walk. Bridgetown is about 10 minutes by public bus or taxi. No need for a rental car, except for excursions. A good bet at $55 to about $70 for 2 this winter, for room only.

✤ **Golden Beach** (Palm Beach, Hastings, Christ Church, Barbados, W.I.; 26 apts.) gets high marks for providing comfortable studio and bigger apartments at great value. The 3-story building faces the sea and is angled around a small-but-adequate pool edged by a sun-sitting terrace. First floor rooms give you walk out access to the sand; top level offers more privacy. All are on the same span of sand that stretches, with one ankle-wade patch around a point, to Needham's Point and the Hilton. Next door to Asta Apartments, this small spot is another that gives good value at daily rates from $55 to about $70 for 2. Inquire about discounts for longer stays.

✤ **Golden Sands Apartment Hotel** (Maxwell Road, Christ Church, Barbados, W.I.; 27 apts.) is on the south coast, amid a crop of hotels, apartment hotels, restaurants, shops and entertainment spots, but when you settle on your balcony here, the seaview seems serene. With a L-shaped construction around the pool, most rooms have some privacy for balcony-sitters. Studios have a "pullman" kitchen on one wall of the room, and neat, clean appointments that make for comfortable, trouble-free living. Count on rates of $65 for 2 to $100 for a 1-bedroom unit that can sleep 4 comfortably this winter, and book well in advance if you're thinking about peak-season February.

✤ **Maresol Beach Apartments** (St. Lawrence Gap, Barbados; 31 apts.) were among the first places to set up housekeeping, and they're still among the best. More than 20 years ago, the several beachside 2-storied buildings, each with an apartment up and an apartment down, were committed for winter months at a time, year after year. Today, with additional apartments not only at the beach but alao in the back, across the road on the island side there's sometimes space for newcomers, even at height of season, but plan ahead if you want to be where those in the know go. The small mini-market next to the check-in desk gives you staples and liquor at supermarket prices; the rest of your goods you can get in town— or from the fish market. Maid service is included in your rate; compassionate nannies are available for the children or grandchildren (who are encouraged at other than peak Feb and March), and you'll find secretary Audrey Trotman a helpful and willing source of information. You'll pay from $45 to $70 daily (ask about long-term rates) for your winter rate, with exact price depending on size and location (beachfront are best, of course). A car will help for island touring, but you can walk to plenty of dining depots, and can take the bus into Bridgetown; the beach that stretches out before you offers some action options.

✤ **Margate Gardens** (Hastings, Barbados; 26 apts.) makes the most of a mix that's been brewing for about 10 years. It opened in 1970; the studio, 1- and 2-bedroom units are in boxy, barrackslike 3-story buildings. This haven of hospitality hides in planting that helps soften the otherwise boring buildings. Furnishings are simple but adequate. The place is perfect for beach-oriented holidays. You'll spend most of your time in your bathing suit by the pool or a few steps away from your "home" at the hotel's own beach or at the active Rockley Beach, where most of the hotels in the area pour their guests. When Rex Allamby told me that the place is owned and operated by Barbadians "whose families have lived here for over 300 years," he added that "new guests are introduced to others and given help and advice on what to do and where to go." What more could you ask for? From on-the-spot observations, it seems to me that anyone who thrives on no-nonsense surroundings, with good value in neat, clean, comfortable apartments, will find this a spot to return to. Rates for an apartment for 2 will run $50 to $80 daily, taxes and meals extra. The 2-bedroom unit (good for families) is close to $400. Your air conditioner and a daily sweep-out are included in your rate; cook/maid service is available for about $30 per week—and most of the maids are part of the reason this place is so special; they're as much a part of the vacation mix as the beach, pool, management, and fellow guests.

✤ **Monteray Apartments** (St. Lawrence Gap, Barbados; 21 apts.) sits next door to the Maresol apartments that are on the inland side of the road. With the option of walking across the street to the beach, guests can also slide into the small pool around which some of the apartments stretch. Opened in the late 1960s, Monteray has added some units and now offers *Heidi's Restaurant* (open to the public) for good food at reasonable rates in very pleasant surroundings. (Walk past the front desk in the living-room style lobby, to the back of the house where you'll find the bar and the restaurant.) Guests who bed in here can walk to a variety of hotels and special restaurants (even *Pisces* and *Witch Doctor* are not too far to walk) for meals and entertainment. Rates run $45 daily with better deals for long term. Meals are extra.

✤ **Robins Nest** (Long Bay, St. Philip, Barbados; 18 apts.) can be yours for a reasonable price. However, you're near the airport. This spot is often used by people who want to be in the orbit of the "village" that is the Marriott resort. The Wasons' home-turned-inn sits just outside the gates and has appended a couple of apartments (1-bedroom and studio) for those who want to do some light housekeeping. A mini-market on the premises provides staples, but more extensive menus can be planned with items bought from bigger markets near Bridgetown. Surroundings are simple and Robin's Nest is not ideal for those who insist on beach, but it has a pool. Tariff runs $40 to $60 for 2 this winter, meals extra.

✤ **Rockley Resort & Beach Club** (Rockley Beach, Christ Church, Barbados, W.I.; 288 apts.) rose from the shores along the southwest coast in December 1977 with the first of what is almost 300 apartments with full residential facilities. New and comfortable, the apartments give renters a pool (there are several around the grounds), plus the option for the beach and several casual eating spots. The newest cluster of apartments is owned by the Royal Trust Corp. of Canada and is woven into the Resort Condominium International time-sharing plan with the World Wide Vacation Exchange. Those who purchase one of the condominium weeks (for a starting price of $2600) can trade one of the weeks for time at another WWVE unit in some other country. Not only are the low-rise buildings that make up this complex an attractive addition to the area, but Rockley's Elizabeth Johnson, a Barbadian, provides able assistance from her office on the compound. She is the person to find on the spot if you have a question. Count on winter rates to be $110 to $130—all meals extra—with the option of cooking at home to keep costs reasonable.

✤ **Sandhurst Apartment Hotel** (St. Lawrence Gap, Barbados; 21 units) settles into the side-by-side settlement at a bulge on the shore known as St. Lawrence Gap. If you claim one of these air-conditioned units, you'll be sharing space at the sandy strand with a lot of other apartment renters who have chosen this site, about 15 minutes' drive west of Bridgetown. Hotel services are offered (housekeeping, sheets changed, etc.), and there are gardens on "your" side of the road. Some of the rooms have beach view, but the setting for all is simple. The price may be right, at about $100 per day for 2, meals extra this winter.

✤ **Sandridge** (St. Peter, Barbados; 52 apts.) snapped up a spot of shoreline and plastered it with an uninteresting 2-story shoe-box building honeycombed with copy-cat apartments furnished in modern motel style. For all that, plus pool, bar, mini-market on the premises (with shelves stocked with staples at skyrocketing prices), you pay $75 to $100 for 2 in height of winter—and that's what makes it worth talking about. The accommodations are adequate, modern, and usually clean, and the price is right—especially for the premium-rate, fashionable west coast where you're within a bus or car ride from the best of the lot. Worth considering if simple surroundings with an efficiency kitchenette in the heart of the high-rate district is what you're looking for.

✤ **Sandy Beach** (Worthing, Christ Church, Barbados; 89 units) bubbled from a prize piece of property, with some of the best names of Barbados responsible for the resort that opened officially in March 1980. John Goddard, chairman of the Sandy Beach Board of Directors, is involved in almost every facet of Barbadian development (Goddard's retail stores, plus rum, printing, banking, and the Chamber of Commerce), thereby putting the stamp of stability on this venture. General Manager Alfred Taylor was born (in Barbados) to a hotel family and has been active in hotel management here and in St. Lucia. The 86 suites, 50 2-bedroom units, and 39 1-bedroom units are scattered around grounds that include a swimming pool and offer a nearby beach with watersports facilities. In addition to a host of restaurants not far from the complex, there are the *Greenhouse* and the *Sand Bar Lounge* for on-the-spot conviviality. Count on rates to start at about $130 for 2 to share the smallest unit with more spacious surroundings for $175. More dollars warrant more space—and you'll need more dollars for meals and any sports and/or other entertainment.

✤ **Sichris Apartments** (Rockley, Christ Church, Barbados, W.I.; 24 apts.) settles near the beach at Rockley (across the road), amid the platoon of places for self-catering on the south coast. The 2-story units cup the pool, where tables are set up for mealtime if you want to "eat out" within a few steps of your room. Other dining options are within walking distance, as is the minimart for food supplies. The 1-bedroom units present a porch-face to the pool area, and the stucco walls that provide privacy also enclose your place (and tend to make the interior rooms dark). All are air-conditioned; rates this winter are $75 for 2.

✤ **Sunset Crest Resort** (St. James, Barbados; 750 apts.) doesn't really fit into the hotel *or* the housekeeping holiday rosters. This "resort" that ranges over 120 acres was planned as a housing development in the boom years just before the bust of the early '70s, when everyone expected everyone else to jump at the chance to buy a second home on every island—and rent them all to tourists in their absence. The plan works well—if you want an independent holiday in an informal "housing development" on the inland side of the shore-rimming road running along the west coast, north of Bridgetown. You are just south of Holetown, and near neighbor to elegant Sandy Lane. When you base here you are often with Canadian groups who take this place for back-to-back charters for chunks of the year. Sunset Crest is really a second city, with 1-, 2-, and 3-bedroom cement box "villas" focused on a center with supermarkets, drugstore, beauty shop, banks, department store—and a recreation area with clubhouse and 2 large pools (neither one large enough for everyone at height of season, from my observation, unless you like a crowd), several night-lighted tennis courts, a pitch-and-putt golf course that is a good shot away from the formal Sandy Lane course (which you may play for a fee), plus some planned evening activities that include barbecue, steel band, and the usual. You'll need a car if you want to get off the compound, but you can walk around if you're content to stay on the grounds. For a winter week, a family of 4 can plan to part with about $500 for a villa; daily rate is about $65, room only.

✤ **Sunshine Beach Apartments** (Hastings, Christ Church, Barbados; 15 apts.) is Dolly Bayley's place, perched on the shore with steps that lead into the sea if the waves have lapped out the beach. The 10 units vary in shape and size (studios, one-bedroom and 2-bedroom) with #9 the prize, for its balcony and shoreside setting. Not all rooms have sea view, so if that's essential for your vacation happiness, ask. Ask also about renting a mini-moke. They're available on the premises through family-affiliated Sunshine Rentals at the usual $120 per week, but the Bayleys let you rent your car for a day or two if it fits in with their rental schedule. Jan and Neville Bayley, daughter-in-law and son, are also active in the family enterprise. Rates this winter range around $50 daily (with reductions for longer stay), for the studio to the 2-bedroom apartment, with the usual 10% service charge and 8% government tax added on.

✣ **Welcome Inn** (Maxwell Coast Road, Barbados, W.I.; 110 apts.) sounds small, but isn't. The place seems huge, and is often filled with European and other groups of travelers who settle at the sand on the east end of the crop of hotels and apartments that line the south coast almost nonstop from Bridgetown to this place, 15 minutes' drive from the capital. A 6-story honeycomb holds most of the apartments (where your kitchen is an efficiency on one wall of your room), and action is at the separate building near the shore. There are restaurant facilities, beach activities, and all the accoutrements of a hotel, but you have the opportunity to cook for yourself when you're paying $85 to $100 this winter for 2. Ask about package tours using this hotel as a base.

✣ **Woodville Apartments** (Hastings, Christ Church, Barbados, W.I.; 28 apts.) settle on a piece of shore, giving you the chance to look to sea (instead of at all the vacation buildings that spread out around this spot). A large 2-bedroom apartment with seaview rents for about $550 for a winter week; studios are almost $400 per week. Surroundings are neat, clean, and pool-punctuated.

✣ **Worthing Court Apartments** (Worthing, Christ Church, Barbados, W.I.; 24 apts.) give you independence across the road from a beautiful beach. Six 1-bedroom units and 18 studios make up the complex, and pool plus terrace and small bar provide gathering spots. Rates are $55 to $65 for 2.

■■

RESTAURANTS around Barbados range from places in old homes with a lot of atmosphere to beachside places with little or none, with the whole roster of hotels—some of them with excellent restaurants—in the middle. Prices will be high (about $40 per person for a full meal with wine and flourishes) at the top spots, higher than they should be at some of the middle-range places, and very low if you are lured by local West Indian food and lucky enough to find a place that serves some. Surroundings at the best spots are eminently civilized, a hangover from the days of British rule that has become so much a fact of Barbadian life that everyone enjoys what used to be the exclusive province of the country club set (often whites only).

Brown Sugar, next to the Island Inn, just south of Bridgetown not far from Hilton and Holiday inns, is a good bet for good food in lovely surroundings, amid hanging plant-filled baskets, in a restored West Indian wooden house. Prices have risen rapidly, and Barbadian businessmen who used to fill this place at lunchtime are balking at the cost of the buffet, but it's still a prize place to sample substantial Barbadian food. High marks for good value, and an excellent meal with West Indian specialties.

Bagatelle, out Highway 2A (which runs north from Bridgetown, not along the coast, but the next main road inland, taking the left fork as you head north), bets its atmosphere on the Great House it inhabits, which owners claim dates from 1665. The atmosphere is terrific; prices are high, but somehow I don't mind because the surroundings are so special. The place seemed to be resting on its *Gourmet* magazine laurels ("The food is a tour de force") when I visited recently, but that's a better bed of compliments than most Barbadian places put their reputation on.

Flamboyant, in a spruced-up old house on the inland side of the main road through Hastings toward Bridgetown, is a casual place for good food. Brian and Isolde Cheeseman have planted tables on the front porch (the best place, from my experience, because if there's a breeze, you can enjoy it), as well as inside, and serve an interesting assortment of local and German accented (if not authentic) recipes.

Chateau Creole, is a hideaway on a spur off the main coastal road. Specialties include a mouth-watering stuffed whitefish (for Bds$34), Lobster Cantonese, Fire and Ice (an anchovie and egg paste served with pink-gin schnapps), and Senegalese soup. Waitresses in creole costume and the creole decor set the tone for this country house where the pleasantest dining is on the terrace on a moonlit evening.

Le Bistro, upstairs, on Prince William Henry Street, near the Careenage in the heart of Bridgetown, is a popular (and attractive) lunch spot if you are in town for shopping or looking around. Sandwiches spell gourmet attempts on a menu that changes specialties, and Le Bistro serves all the standard drinks.

Luciano's has a lovely setting, with house and gardens in the hotel-filled Hastings area, but I had a disastrous dinner the night I sampled service here. The local fish was so saturated in garlic that it was difficult for me to find another flavor—then or two days later. Perhaps you'll have better luck, and the place *looks* nice.

Ocean View Hotel, on the hotel-clotted shore road that leads southwest of Bridgetown, serves standard Barbadian food, which is exceptional if you like West Indian cooking. Surroundings are simple, seaside; the sea eggs and other specialties served when they are in season are the best I've tasted on the island. This place is a must for me, and might be for you.

Pisces, one of a trio of recommendables in and near the St. Lawrence areas, draws first place for my money. The fish from which it takes its name are served as specialties, all kinds, most of them fresh from the Barbados sea (and some of them "frozen fresh," I fear). Caribbean lobster is progged (and propelled by charter plane) from nearby seas. Atmosphere is pleasant, prices are the usual high, but when you stop here, on the sea side of the west end bend of the road, you will have a pleasant evening. (Call for reservations.)

Plantation Restaurant, following the tradition of turning former homes into dining nooks, is just in from the main shore-rimming road on the grounds of Caribbean Pepperpot and with a social section that is known as Stables, a pub/disco with a Bds$15 admission fee. Plantation's tables can be on the porch or in the house, and food is Barbadian French style.

Witch Doctor, owned by Dr. Donowa, is on the inland side, across from Pisces, and is popular with local folk as well as tourists who are smart enough to make a reservation. Island foods are specialties, but you can find beef and chicken here too.

Luigi's, in Dover, at the other "end" of the shoreline road, when it turns inland again, is the third. Italian? Of course, and good food is served on checkered tablecloths with candles in bottles for atmosphere.

AUTHOR'S OBSERVATION: When the Adams administration approved slot machines (locally known as fruit machines) in 1976, a few well-tended machines began to grow in lobbies of hotels and other commercial spots. When the rash threatened to become a plague, the "gambling" venture got some scrutiny. It seems to be under careful control in spite of the fact that many machines are located in the small rum shops, and are for local addiction.

■■■

PLACES WORTH FINDING around Barbados are mostly natural, unless you have a special interest in early West Indian/Barbadian history (in which case, note the museums, etc. below). A rental car for a day can cover most of the island's scenic highlights. Shaped like an avocado, Barbados wears a blanket of sugarcane from December until cane cutting season in late May or June. When the cane is tall, you can drive across the midsection of the island without being able to see anything but a wall of green fronds, reminiscent—for those who have driven in England—of the narrow roads in the southwest.

AUTHOR'S OBSERVATION: Driving (on the left) around Barbados is easy, if terrifying. In spite of the people, cars, buses, donkey carts, goats, etc. that share your road, driving yourself is the best way to travel if you want instant mobility and the best value (taxis are expensive), and don't mind getting lost. Places have names, but many of them are noted only in the hearts of the Barbadians. Signs, when they appear at all, will carry village names that you may not be able to find on the map you have.

The main "highways" spoke out from Bridgetown, with Highway 1 running along the west coast. Highway 7 curves south to run east along the coast, and 2 through 6, some of them with A branches, stretch out through the countryside like the fingers on your hand. Some fingers are webbed, but don't count on it. You may have to backtrack to get where you want to go, if you care. Gas is expensive, but most cars get good mileage and have fixed daily rental charges that put the total day on your expense account at well below what you would pay for a take-and-wait taxi. Your Barbadian license costs Bds$10; transact for it at the airport—otherwise, you'll have to go to the Bridgetown Police Station.

BRIDGETOWN is bustling and more geared to shopping than to sightseeing. There was a time, not too long ago, when you could share space on the town streets with the 2-wheeled jaunty carts drawn by donkeys. They were the main means of transportation, and many of the country people came to town that way. The Careenage was also intriguing in those days, when the island-built sloops and schooners were hauled for repairs, to be tipped on their sides with ballast and pulleys. Modern commerce has changed some of the traditions, and where it has not, the cars block the view and the heat that rises from paved-and-clogged streets takes most of the fun out of the escapade. Exception: If there is a parade or festival that follows the marching route from Garrison Savannah to Trafalgar Square, stand along the route. The mixture of pageantry and people is not to be missed.

Trafalgar Square is worth a glimpse, which is all you'll have time to give it as you whisk by in a car. If you stand nearby to look longer, be sure to keep looking left and right so you don't get run over. Nelson cruised around this area, from his base at Antigua's English Harbour, and was well known to Barbadians, who erected the monument to him in 1813. He had visited in port, aboard his *Victory*, not long before his death, notice of which reached Barbados on December 13, 1805. Old-time Barbadians used to make a big thing about the fact that this Trafalgar Square was dedicated before the one in London, but today ties to England—and to Nelson—are not on the top of most people's minds. The square and its importance to the island's early history are relics of another era.

George Washington's brother's house is talked about, as is the former President's smallpox attack endured while here, but that's about all there is to either event. The actual house of Lawrence Washington is a matter of speculation.

Garrison Savannah off the main road, just south of Bridgetown, is the playing field, the heart of the cricket matches, the weekend race track and site for any other big sports event in Barbados. This is *very* pertinent to modern Barbados, and if you want to witness the country at its most enthusiastic, arrive when a cricket match is being played between Barbados and any visiting country. Horse races are held here (Feb, March, May, Aug, & Nov). The 50-acre parade ground has been used for training and marches since the first British soldiers were stationed in Barbados in the late 1600s. When British troops officially withdrew in 1906, the fields continued to be used for some ceremonial events, but are at their liveliest when there's a sports event (any taxi driver can tell you what's going on if your hotel desk doesn't seem too sure).

AUTHOR'S OBSERVATION: Make the Barbados *Advocate* part of your daily diet. Not only is the paper one of the Caribbean's best, but the events information is interesting for visitors. You are welcome to attend anything listed— from band concert at Hastings to flower show, tea, or open-house tour. Special evening entertainment is also advertised, and mention in the *Advocate* is sometimes the best way to find out what is going on. Buying *The Bajan*, a magazine printed in Barbados, can also shed light on island activities, not only in Barbados but also on some of the neighboring specks.

St. Ann's Fort, the rust-red building at the fringe of the Savannah, was completed in 1703. The clock tower, completed almost 100 years later, survived the 1831 hurricane that wiped out most of the underpinnings and the buildings around it and still is the point to find if you're having trouble locating the Savannah.

Harrison Caves can be fascinating, if you happen to arrive at other than cruise passenger time. Located near Welchman Hall Gully, the Caves should be officially open by the time you visit (although they were only open for special appointments when I walked through). The ambitious project includes cement walking tracks which are intended as the roadway for electric carts that will take visitors on guided tours. Lights have been discreetly hidden, but are pointed toward the most intriguing stalagmites and stalactites. Fascinating—if you like that kind of thing.

Welchman's Hall Gully, almost in the middle of the island, east of Holetown (open daily; check at the south entrance; small fee; buy pamphlet), is a worthy goal if you are interested in tropical flora and in walking along wooded paths to find representative samples. The Barbados National Trust took over maintenance (and promotion) of this plot in 1960, and they do their utmost (often with volunteer workers) to make the grounds as interesting as possible. The original concept of the owner of this plantation was to plant as many indigenous shrubs and trees as could be found on Barbados and neighboring islands, concentrating on spice and fruit trees at the start. That was in the last half of the 1800s, when J. W. Carrington owned the plot. The work of the National Trust has concentrated on refurbishing the existing plants and adding representative worthy types. The entire excursion can take anyone with an interest at least half a day; you can wander along paths past carefully marked (and tended) flora. In sharp contrast to the usual day at the beach, this is a place for an afternoon walk on the day when you rent a car to explore the island.

AUTHOR'S OBSERVATION: Novice travelers to the West Indies should be forewarned that Barbadian taxi drivers, as a group, are a very savvy lot. They know how to "work" tourists; it behooves us to know how to "handle" taxi drivers. If you don't do your homework (know approximate fares and routes *before* you get in the cab), they might do it for you—at your expense.

Bathsheba coast is for nature lovers, and those who like salt spray as they saunter along a surf-pounded beach. This rugged northeast coast is spectacular, in my opinion, and far more worth a lingering wander than a lot of the 36 sights printed on the back of the Barbados Board of Tourism map (or the list of 50 Edward Stone assembled). What you find here is up to you, but the coast is a far cry from any of the calculated conventional nesting areas that cover most of the west coast. (It is an area favored by the old-time Barbadian families for *their* holiday weekends and weeks when they take leave from the busy life of Bridgetown.)

Andromeda Gardens, not far from Tent Bay on the Bathsheba coast (take Highway 3 from Bridgetown) should be seen at the start of your time in Barbados if you have any interest in the plants that surround you. The Bannochies have done a spectacular job of planting and pruning, so that orchids, oleanders, and varieties of hibiscus mix and mingle with the omnipresent bougainvillea, heliconia, and a host of other brilliant blooms. All set off by ferns and other greenery as well as waterfalls and guide commentary, if you ask for it.

House Tours are an annual event, sponsored by the Barbados National Trust. They are held in height of season late February, early March. Check for details prior to arrival if you are interested in peeking at private life in Barbados. If there is no planned tour, you can still go to restored homes that have been opened as small museums.

Drax Hall is "the oldest plantation house in Bardados." Records show it was started by James Drax in 1650, and it has remained in the family since that time. There are antiques from Europe, as well as some interesting Barbadian furniture and appointments, typical of what was used in the elegant homes of plantation owners.

Villa Nova (M–F, 10–4; small fee) opened to the public in 1976, after the present owners had purchased it from the late Lord Avon, better known as Sir Anthony Eden. The plantation house was built in 1834, and Queen Elizabeth stayed here during a visit when Eden was owner. The furnishings are a varied lot, many of them interesting antiques showing Barbadian adaptations of styles popular in Europe in the early 1800s.

St. Nicholas Abbey (M–F, 10–3; Bds $5) is "one of the oldest Plantation Mansions in Barbados," having been built between 1650 and 1660. The Jacobean Plantation house is a treasure, even without a glimpse at the antique-filled interior. But if Lt. Col. Stephen Cave (owner) is around when you visit, you are in for an afternoon you won't soon forget. Plan some time to walk around the grounds.

(Fees charged for entrance to each of the above house-museums go toward the projects of the Barbados National Trust, a prime mover for restoration of Barbadian treasures just before many homes and areas were about to be taken over or torn down to make way for '70s commerce.)

■■

SPORTS are beach- and sea-oriented. *All* beaches are public here. Even the most chichi resort cannot keep you (or anyone else) off its beach, but you may have to pay a high fee for the use of a lounge chair or a drink at the bar. Roads reach most beaches—the powdery, sandy ones on the calm west coast and the beaches pounded by rugged Atlantic surf that rolls in from Africa to the east coast. Only North Point is beachless and desolate (its terrain is rugged rock that looks like a moonscape).

Scuba has been the province of *Les Wotten* and *Willie's Watersports* (both still operating) for many years (they started the deep diving options here), and recent seasons have seen several newcomers in the seas. Some are affiliated with one or more hotels; others—such as *Marine Dive Tours* located at the Sea Life Aquarium along the St. Lawrence Gap shoreline near Pisces restaurant and the Blue Caribbean apartments—are complete concessions within a short walk of several hotels and apartment clusters. *Scuba Safari* operates near the Holiday Inn. *Blue Reef* at Miramar and *The Dive Shop* team at St. Michael also head out with professional scuba lessons and guides.

Snorkeling is enjoyed by many right off the St. James coast.

Jolly Roger is Clyde Turney's successful 2 ship fleet for fun. (Both boats are known as Jolly Roger and they take on a full complement of lively guests for a 4-hour cruise along the shore (about $15 for steak barbecue lunch plus rum punch, and pick up and delivery to your hotel). One of the boats is a 106-foot cargo ship that became a pirate craft after a metamorphosis in late 1977, to break into the season in early '78. Included in the summer "Best of Barbados" package tour, the trip should be part of your own plans even if you haven't bought that summer bargain week. It's fun, focused on savoring sun and sea (and plenty of punch). (In case you think the name comes from pirate fame, the folks who own her claim that it is adapted from French—"la jolie rougere," translated as the pretty red one, referring to the character craft's trademark red sails.) Special arrangements can be made for sunset cruising, which may be on a regular schedule if you're here at height of season.

Captain Patch, a slightly more sober but otherwise similar pirate ship, also cruises off the western coast with a complement of social sailors. Your hotel activities desk can give you all the details.

Golfers head to the Sandy Lane course, convenient on the west coast, with 18 holes ranging over 6986 yards or to the Rockley course, opened in January '81, at Sandy Lane. There are golf carts as well as Class A and Class B caddies. If you're here for the winter, look into the monthly membership which hovers around Bds$200. Clubs and carts can be rented; the pro is around, usually from 8:30 a.m. to 11:30 p.m., if you want him.

Tennis has come a long way from the whites on grass courts of yesteryear. There are still grass courts at Garrison near Bridgetown, but other courts (at Miramar, Hilton, Paradise Beach, Sandy Lane, Marriott Sam Lord's resort, and other hotels) are the usual U.S. known surfaces. Court time ranges from $5 per hour to $20, depending on location and demand, with lessons available at most of the resorts, and with some places putting tennis package rates on their program for summer. (It's worthwhile inquiring, if you are a tennis enthusiast. Although Barbados hotels have lagged behind some of the imaginative programs of resorts on Jamaica, there are good tennis week values at Marriott, Hilton, and Paradise Beach.)

■■■

TREASURES AND TRIFLES are balanced between things for tourists and items needed and purchased by people who live here. The 2 are not, as is the case in some islands, mutually exclusive. Top department stores compare with the best of their kind in many mainland cities, with imports from England and other places sharing shelf space with more and more things made locally, or in other Caribbean countries.

AUTHOR'S OBSERVATION: One purchase that is useful, attractive, and helpful to a local cause is the illustrated map-with-commentary printed through the Barbados National Trust and available at Cloister Bookshop on Hincks Street in Bridgetown, and at other outlets.

In general, the boutiques and resort-wear shops are at hubs at Holetown and Speightstown on the west coast, where branches of some of the big shops are supplemented (even surpassed) by boutiques with colorful fashions. Prices are high, but happily, so is quality. Even at Pelican Village (see below) and the few random shops around Bridgetown and along the beaches, I find quality has standardized and is better than it had been. Curving around the entrance to the Barbados Hilton there are some good shops, and unusual boutiques, and there's a cluster near the Holiday Inn. Marriott also has its mart. Along the south coast, mingling with the grocery stores and mini-marts favored by those who are "cooking at home" in one of the apartment/efficiency units that fill the Hastings-Worthing-Dover-St. Lawrence area, there are some shops for summer clothes. A branch of the **Barbados Handicraft Shop** is prominent at Dover (selling mats, hats, baskets, T-shirts, and other locally made items).

Note well: the "in-bond" shopping system. Officially, when the plan started years ago, purchasers who were leaving the island could buy in-bond for delivery to plane or ship, at a tax-free purchase price. If you buy far enough in advance of your departure (2 days, at least), airport delivery *should* be problem-free.

Cave Shepherd & Co., Ltd. on Broad Street, the main street of Bridgetown, is more like your downtown favorite department store (which it is for many Barbadians) than the typical tourist trap or jazzed-up boutique you may be used to finding in too many resort islands. However, hidden in the bolts of fabric and pots and pans are shelf after shelf of "good buys for visitors," most of them in the special "duty free" area where the items you expect to find (crystal, china, porcelain figures, baskets, liquor, perfume) are lined up waiting to be plucked and paid for. When I first knew this store, it was a simple West Indian emporium, the best of what existed at that time, but nothing fancy. Today, with a modern facade and an air-conditioned interior, the downtown shop stocks "all the best" from all over the world: linens, cashmeres, suits, jackets, Jantzen swimwear (if you've forgotten your bathing suit), Moroccan leathergoods, and even stereo equipment and radios (but I didn't find them at any bargain price). There's jewelry among the whole range of top department store offerings. Cave Shepherd concedes first place to none. If you want one-stop shopping (and a chance to sip and sup while so doing), head here—and plan to dine on Bajan flying fish and rice at the simple, subsistence-level Ideal Restaurant & Bar at the top floor. Cave Shepherd has branches around the island at Sunset Crest development, up the west coast; a store near Sandy Lane; a boutique-type spot at Holetown, north of Coral Reef and Colony; and in the Hastings area, opposite the Caribbee Hotel. If you have some extra cash at the last minute, Cave Shepherd can take care of it in their airport shops.

Harrison's is #1 on Broad Street—and, since 1878, when it was first opened in Bridgetown, with many Barbadians. With a new lump for luxury import buying at the corner near the intriguing older facade, the emporium offers a complete range of department store merchandise in its air-conditioned interior. Head for the duty-free area (which is not the entire shop) if you want export items (china, crystal, watches, jewelry, cameras, liquor, etc.), but wander around the other floors for some of the imports that you may not find at home but which are offered for Barbadian residents. Some of the clothes, fabrics, and accessories available for Barbadian use may set a new trend in your hometown (and things will be priced for the local market; exchanging currency to Barbadian $ at the bank will get the best price).

Da Costa & Musson Ltd., labeled "Da Costa" on its forehead facing Broad Street, has been in business since 1868, and its 19th-century facade keeps that era intact. Not so in the interior. That's all 20th-century, of the 1970s, after a complete renovation a little more than 100 years after its "birth." You'll find a good selection of British imports (especially the St. Michael brand found in London's Marks & Spencer), and an expanded selection of items of interest for visitors. Some of them can be shipped "in-bond" to your departure point (cruise ship pier, or airport), but frankly, unless the savings are considerable, pay the over-the-counter price and be done with it. All the paperwork for that other process takes a lot of time, plus the time you spend looking for your merchandise when you have other things on your mind at the airport or dock.

Pelican Village is an assortment of merchandise focused for the tourist. When the first crop of shops assembled under the peak roofs near the end of the Deep Water Pier (so that tourists could fall off the ship and into the shelves of the shops), merchandise was mostly handmade, lovingly if not professionally inspired. There's a high degree of professionalism in some of the work, especially that of Courtney Devonish, who has expanded his métier from the clay that he learned to mold as a boy to include fascinating wood sculpture. His shop, **C.O.D. Pottery,** is not far from the Government Handicraft Center, just outside the Pelican Village complex. **ArmBer Shop** (#24) is a good place for ready-made sundresses. Armin and Beryl (husband and wife) can make clothes to order, given a few days. Interesting shells are for sale at the **Marine Shop** (#25), and at **Sunny Isle** (#27) investigate the current crop of colorful string dolls, doorstops, mobiles, and handmade puppets with cork legs and winning personalities (for Bds$16).

Best of Barbados, at the Sandpiper Inn on the west coast, carries the most complete collection of Jill Walker prints, which will peer at you from all sides, in several shops around the island. However, after you've seen something of this country, you will realize that she has captured a lot of the local color. Quality of the prints for framing, her screen prints on children's clothes, and whatever craftwork she next gets into will be above the local average.

Batik Caribe, with studios at St. Vincent, has outlets around the country, most of them at tourist hubs. Look for Batik at Sam Lord's, the Hilton, Gulf House on Broad Street in Bridgetown, and at Na Desie Apartment Hotel, across from Sunset Crest #1 on the west coast. The colorful fabrics are stitched into resort wear or sold by the yard for wraps and/or stitching yourself.

Bonaire

Bonaire Tourist Bureau, Breedestraat, Kralendijk, Bonaire, N.A.; Bonaire Tourist Information Office, 1466 Broadway, New York, NY 10036; 67 Yonge St., Suite 828, Toronto, Ont. M5E 1J8.

US $1 = NAf1.77.
Unless otherwise noted, U.S. equivalents are figured at this rate.

When Ady Everts points to his "watch" and it says 25 feet, you're still going down. You feel like smiling, but that's hard to do when you're sprouting scuba gear and are awestruck by the scene unfolding all around you. And to think that there are a lot of people at home paying $3 to sit in a movie theater for kicks!

The staghorn coral and parade of fish that help light up the liquid atmosphere around Bonaire are a fact of life. They've been swirling for centuries around this coral reef that rises high enough—and stretches long enough—to hold houses, road, an airport, and a couple of small hotels. But you are still living on a reef . . . and you're the most recent intruder.

The underwater landscape has been growing forever, and the flamingos that fly here every day from an unknown nightly nesting spot have a longer tenancy than we do. They have a say over what changes are made on this island, and there are others who speak for the sea fans, the elkhorn coral, and the strands of growth in the majestic underwater arboretum.

Ady Everts is one of them. He's the first native Bonairean to receive the gold-plated certificate that makes him a certified YMCA scuba instructor. He's completed more than 2000 dives and is now certificated to give instruction in the 5 languages he speaks, as translator for the underwater world he probably never suspected when he was a young boy on Bonaire. Captain Don led him down to the depths—and at the same time to the heights—of this very special island he calls home. And now he can do the same for you, and perhaps more importantly, for others who live on this gem called Bonaire, whose true value too many never suspect.

■■
POLITICAL PICTURE: As one of the ABC islands (with Aruba and Curaçao) of the Netherlands Antilles, Bonaire has shared in the guidance and aid from the mother country. The 8400 people that live on this 112-square-mile, boomerang-shaped coral outcropping elect one representative to the 22-member Staten that meets in Curaçao to discuss policies and regulations for the 6 islands of the Netherlands Antilles. The local government, however, is strictly a Bonairean affair, with elections held every 4 years, and the present government is firmly ensconced until the next elections in 1981.

Tourism is the main hard-currency source for the island, and the development has been slow-but-sure, with a steady increase in North American visitors over the past several years. Annual visitors number about 25,000, and most of them head for the sea. It's the scuba and underwater exploring plus a 17,000-acre National Park known for its birding, that make this island special.

■■
CUSTOMS OF BONAIRE are Caribbean in a Dutch framework. Because the island (in size and population) is not large, local customs are akin to those in many small rural towns. Life for Bonaireans is conservative, and—although casual dress is common for everyone—visitors should cover up their beach attire when going into the small town of Kralendijk. At official government functions, guests will dress up, but that is about the only time you will see male residents in coat and tie, or women in long dresses (and even that does not always happen these days). Since this is a warm and sunny, beach-oriented outdoor place, casual clothes can go almost everywhere.

■■
MONEY is U.S. dollars insofar as visitors are concerned. Although the local currency is the Netherlands Antilles florin or guilder, pegged to the U.S. dollar at a rate of US$1 equals NAf 1.77 (and not pegged to the currency of its mother country), your hotel bill and other tourist expenses will be presented (and pay is expected) in dollars.

AUTHOR'S OBSERVATION: Vacationers interested in good values should inquire (from the Tourist Board office or your travel agent) about the "Free Spree" package holidays that start April 16, and are available through December 15. Based on a 7-night holiday, the Bonaire version of the ABC's "Free Spree" gives you funny money as a discount on a portion of your stay, and the money is accepted for car rental, dive lessons, and some other items available locally.

■■■

ARRIVAL ON BONAIRE is a study in Caribbean contrasts. The new airport terminal, financed from European Common Market funds and opened in 1979, is a spectacular modern building, with the tradewinds providing the air cooling when they sweep around 3 open "sides." The $5-million investment in runway extension was completed, and ALM Antillean Airlines flies nonstop from Miami in about 2½ hours at some times of the year. (You have every reason to wonder, as island officials must also, where the 400-plus passengers that could fill a 747 are going to sleep on an island that, even with this season's expansion, will have well under 400 rooms!) Smaller planes still provide the regular service, with frequent links between Aruba, Curaçao, and Bonaire, as well as from South American cities (especially Caracas).

Count on immigration routine to be perfunctory. You will be asked to show your immigration card (filled out on the plane) and your proof of birthplace/citizenship (passport is best, although not required; driver's license is *not* sufficient; voter's registration is).

AUTHOR'S OBSERVATION: As with Aruba and parts of Curaçao, the tradewinds blow over Bonaire *constantly*. Although the wind is warm, it is incessant—and any woman with a carefully lacquered hairdo should bring a helmet; pipe-smoking men should have hatch covers.

■■■

TOURING TIPS: Most of the interesting touring on this island is offshore. To get to the hotel base (where you'll find the boats to take you out for scuba or fishing), taxis wait for airport arrivals. Rental cars are available (specify when you make your hotel reservation), if you want to be mobile, but except for the flamingo nesting area and a couple of other island sights, most of the daily routine centers at the hotels or at Kralendijk, and you can walk the distance between hotels and town.

■■■

HOTELS ON BONAIRE are scuba-centered, and although people without underwater enthusiasm have been known to book rooms, chances are they are dedicated to the casual life that accompanies that crowd or to pursuit of the flamingos and other birds plus the special qualities that nature gives to this island. (There are those, of course, who bed in here while doing business with the International Salt Company, BOPEC oil company, and other island firms, plus many who just come for the prospect of silence and sea.) No matter where you book, you will be one of less than 700 tourists on the island, even if every place is booked to capacity. As noted above, there are fewer than 400 hotel rooms.

In anticipation of a burgeoning tourism, the island's officials have supported a project for hotel training that puts a U.N. instructor in charge of classes held in the community center. The students do on-the-spot training in the hotels. Consider this when you wait patiently for your meal to be served, or for other hotel service. What the staff may lack in speed, they make up for in smiles.

Twosomes should inquire about special honeymoon package holidays available from June 1 through December 15. The prices are good, the extra gifts and bonuses may seem fun, and no one asks to see your marriage license.

In addition to the charges on your hotel bill, you will find a 5% government room tax and a 10% or 15% service charge that takes care of all gratuities.

✤ **Flamingo Beach Hotel** (Kralendijk, Bonaire, N.A.; 114 rooms, including 9 cottages) flowers on the west coast, just south of town and a short leap from the airport. Its scuba resort personality and family connection with Aruba's Divi Divi and Tamarijn Beach has put its birth in the '40s as a prisoner-of-war camp far in its past. The place has a casual, comfortable ambiance, helped along by the constant enthusiasm of the scuba crowd that capers along after Alice and Peter Hughes, who operate their Angel of the Islands/Dive Bonaire scuba trips from here. On its own small beach, about 10 minutes' walk from town, the hotel hangs its restaurant and some of the newer rooms *over* the ocean. The original 1-story block still stands, but has had a complete face lift so that those who knew it "when" would never recognize it now. Some of the rooms are in the cottages and the bulk are in the newer 2-story units. Architecture is reminiscent of that at Aruba's Tamarijn Beach, with white stucco, Moorish-looking arches and the feeling of a casual resort with class. There is a patch of sand at the shore, but count on the pool plus a swirling Jacuzzi to keep the temperature under control. (For the Hughes' water-sports offerings, see Sports below.) Rates this winter will range from about $60 to $85 for 2, room and taxes, but add on another $20-plus per day per person for meals at the hotel, or plan to spend about that if you want to breakfast here and dine around.

✤ **Habitat** (Kralendijk, Bonaire, N.A.; 11 bungalows) hovers seaside, harboring casual, beach-bent types who want a shoreside commune kind of place. Life is casual and sea-centered, and people who stay here respond to that kind of life. There's nothing fancy at the Habitat; those who choose to "go formal" for the evening—which means put on a clean shirt, or skirt—can walk over to neighboring Hotel Bonaire, to put on their sandals before walking through the door. The specialty is scuba, with Captain Don as major domo—and his personality is in constant control. (Ask about his hydroponic "farming" if you are interested in another facet of his life.) The 11 bungalows used to be Bonaire Bungalows, taken over by Capt. Don in '76. They have 2 bedrooms, simply furnished kitchen, cement slab patio, and "sit down and order" casual restaurant where your limited choice will cost about $10 for dinner (breakfast is $3). Rates per cottage depend on the number of people, ranging from about $50 for 2 to over $70 for 6, but no matter how many you are, if you like the barefoot and boating life, consider this a good value. (Meals can be signed for in advance at Hotel Bonaire for $20 per person, for breakfast and dinner daily, but my advice is to *book* Hotel Bonaire if you're the kind who wants to be sure of your meals; otherwise sign on for a special meal or 2 after you arrive.)

✤ **Hotel Bonaire & Casino** (Kralendijk, Bonaire, N.A.; 145 rooms) added some new rooms in summer of '79 and they are the best bets if you insist on spic-and-span surroundings. The place hugs the sandy shore, about 2½ miles north of town. The red-tiled 2-story buildings stretch out from the main building. Some rooms have sea view and all are comfortable. Some were enlarged to accommodate more than 2 when the government took over the property in the mid-'70s, to try their hand at running it. Executive House is the management firm, and they've instigated promotion programs that bode well for this property. There are tennis courts near the beach and windsurfer and sailing lessons are offered for hotel guests— free! The marina next to the hotel gives vacationers another outlook on daily life. Facilities funded by the European Common Market include a restaurant and complete services. The port is fast becoming a favorite for yachts from Venezuela and Curaçao, as well as from other islands. The small and usually quiet casino is no competition for the lively action-packed spots on Aruba, but it's more than enough (in my opinion) for an island that cares more about nature and the sea. The swimming pool is set seaside, with the 2 bars nearby and a restaurant. Rates for 2 this winter range from about $75 for a 2nd-floor standard room, up to $95 for the slightly larger, 1st-floor superior. Count on $20 or more per day per person for 2 meals daily, and special low rates for children. (Children under 12 stay free in parents' room.) Captain Don handles the water-sports operation here (but *not* for children under 12).

✛ **Hotel Rochaline** (Breedestraat, Kralendijk, Bonaire, N.A.; 22 rooms) gives you the best value on the island, if you are enough of a Caribbean convert to care more about a comfortable, simply furnished air-conditioned room with sea-view balcony (small) than about being on a beach. The price is right—up to $50 per day for 2 for the "superior" room and less for a standard spot—but don't expect any fancy tourist flourishes geared for a demanding U.S. market. The small hotel is clean, neat, and in the center of things, not far from the northern cruise ship pier. This is no place for a first honeymoon, but it has its price advantages. (The supplement for 2 meals daily is $12, but my advice is to pay by the meal. You'll probably breakfast here, but there are other places to try for dinners.)

■■

RESTAURANTS ON BONAIRE are a small handful that speckle the area from Hotel Bonaire south to Flamingo Beach Hotel, with a couple of stops in town. With the increased air service, and more demanding tourists, the quality and presentation of food has improved. It's possible to get a good meal (and pay a good price) at both hotels, and the Chinese offerings have been touted by some who consider themselves experts. Seafood can be fresh from surrounding seas. Steaks are flown in and rijsttafel is a specialty one night a week (usually Tuesday, but check) at Flamingo Beach. Hotel Bonaire's best bet is the Bonairean night when funchi joins the local list of foods served.

Bonaire's Yacht Club has a restaurant that I found more memorable for its view than its food. It is popular with residents, yachtsmen from here and other ports, and with some of the scuba set who find it.

The Palace, on the fringe of Kralendijk, is a new restaurant worth trying.

Other spots to try are **Zeezicht** (Seaview) at the waterfront and famous for its fish platter, and the **China Garden** (on Breedestraat, in a former home), or **Great China** (also on Breedestraat in nondescript surroundings) for the fried noodles and the usual. If you're not staying here, stop by when you're in town to see what the special for the evening will be and to make your reservation so they'll have food enough for you. Check the status of the restaurant at the new marina; if it is open, it should be good and certainly the view will be. **Nadia,** in Nikiboko at Emerencianastraat has ice cream—and Chinese food sometimes.

■■

PLACES WORTH FINDING ON BONAIRE are in the sea for most who head to this island, but naturalists and birders have plenty to keep them occupied around the 112 square miles of this boomerang-shaped island. Man-made sights are few, and not nearly as interesting in my opinion as what nature has given to this special spot, namely flamingos, other birds, and incomparable sights under the sea that have some professionals referring to this area as one of the three best scuba areas in the world.

KRALENDIJK, the small capital, is 2 streets wide, with a few arms reaching inland; it is the hub of the island's "developed" area, which is the west coast. Except for the shops, there's not much of visitor interest in town. Even the boxy stucco buildings, most of them air-conditioned for staff survival, are not much to look at; there's a small selection of the Dutch architecture adapted to the Caribbean climate that you see in Willemstad, Curaçao, or even Aruba's Oranjestad. **Instituto Folklore Bonaire** on Helmundweg, in the fort (M, W, F 8–12, Sat 9–1) is worth some time, when you are in town, to look at the artifacts collected from Bonaire homes and grounds. In addition to a few utensils and some diagrams and comments about the earliest Indian settlers, there are some interesting musical instruments and a few costumes. (This isn't worth a special trip, but can occupy a half hour between shops.) The **Fish Market,** in the "Greek Temple" at the waterfront, should be visited in the morning for the best look at the catch.

Slave huts, on the southwest coast, are small and, although it may be interesting to see where the workers rested (2 per hut) while they worked on the salt flats, the area is hot and stark—with acres of shallow ponds of the Antilles International Salt Company stretching out to evaporate in the sun. The Willemstoren Lighthouse marks the island's southernmost tip. If you miss seeing it, don't consider your vacation ruined, but do try to catch the flamingos if you're vacationing here between December and May when they fledge.

BOPEC is the Bonaire Petroleum Corporation, a joint operation of Long Island, N.Y.'s Northville Industries and Paktank of Rotterdam. It created a furor among caring conservationists when it was proposed for Bonairean shores, but local politicians assuaged the protestors with promises that all precautions would be taken to keep the transfer of European, Mideast, and African oil to U.S. tankers a purely pipe-processed operation. No sea dumping or pipe splitting, they claim. And up to now, I'm told, there has been "no pollution."

Washington National Park at the northwestern nub of the island, and the **Lac Bay** area in the southeast are favorite areas for birders. The National Park started with about 5000 acres of rugged, arid land with scrub, cactus, and divi-divi trees, plus a waterhole that draws interesting birds and now has been expanded to about 13,-000 acres in a preservation scheme that should be emulated by other islands. Conservationists should track down a copy of *Field Guide of the Washington National Park,* published by the Netherlands Antilles National Parks Foundation. The small museum at the entrance to the park has a meager collection, and not much in the way of background on the exhibits, but it is worth a stop if you're up this way.

AUTHOR'S OBSERVATION: Bring your binoculars to Bonaire, for birds at Washington National Park, but especially for the flamingos at the Pekelmeer colony in the south, near the salt flats.

■■■

SPORTS ON BONAIRE are sea-centered. The water gives you a dependable visibility of 150 to 200 feet; you can get to a lot of interesting places without a boat; the water's warm enough to **scuba** without a wet suit, and there's very little current and few shark or barracuda. Add to that the fact that pros have put all their expertise into teaching you how to scuba, and you have ideal surroundings to learn—practically by osmosis.

Bonaire Scuba Center, with Bonarians Ady Everts and Eddie Statia in charge, started operations in Febrary 1981, although both men have "grown up" in waters off the shores of their home-island and probably know the special spots better than anyone else. Operating from a base at the Hotel Bonaire beach, the Center has full facilities and enough equipment for up to 80 divers. Stateside contact is through Bonaire Tours, Box 775, Morgan NJ 08879.

Aquaventure and Captain Don are known to anyone who is anyone in the underwater world. (Anyone who hasn't heard the name will know it after about 5 minutes on this island.) Don Stewart is king of Bonaire's underwater caverns, but many may not know that when Captain Don came ashore on Bonaire on May 21, 1962, he intended to continue to Antigua, and more verdant island dreams. The life he found underwater here far exceeded anything he hoped to find above the ground on other islands, so he stayed. At that point, the "invaders" who had landed on Bonaire were few, and the patch of land he clung to after 9 years at sea became his leap-off ledge for underwater explorations that have helped the Bonaireans realize the riches of the reefs that surround them. It is thanks largely to the pioneering (and perseverance) of Don Stewart that the scuba clan have recognized Bonaire as one of the world's top 3 diving resorts. His *Aquaventure* operation is based at the Hotel Bonaire, with the special *Habitat,* his "total resort" for divers where even table talk is dive-centered, a short walk from the Hotel Bonaire. A team takes beginners as well as experienced divers to the sites that rim Bonaire. (Special Hotel Bonaire program for children takes them snorkeling and scuba diving while parents head out to the depths. Captain Don has no time for children under 12.) Aquaventure's dive packages range from about $90 for basic equipment (tank, bac-pac, weights, belt, storage box for gear for 6 days) and 6 guided reef trips with 6 air fills, to $127 for 6 dive trips and unlimited air fills, and about $160 for equipment and unlimited dives and air fills. Details on scuba tours are available through Aquaventure, Box 127 Gedney Station, White Plains, NY 10605.

Peter and Alice Hughes are owners and operators of *Dive Bonaire, Inc.,* which uses *Angel of the Islands* as an alias. Their base is at Flamingo Beach Hotel. Peter Hughes had been diving and teaching in Trinidad, Roatán (Honduras), and Tobago before coming to Bonaire to set up the now defunct Teach-Tour operation. The Scotsman stayed, and his firm's facilities include the necessary tanks, regulators, fins, snorkels, etc., plus flat-top boats, a 31-foot cruiser for longer hauls, and a 60-foot sailboat for picnics and cruising as well as diving. Angel of the Islands 7-night tours are offered at all-inclusive prices, with transfers between airport and hotel, 2 meals daily, and either a 6-dive package ($326 each of 2), a 10-dive package ($377 each of 2), or an unlimited dive package ($407 each of 2). There's even an offering for nondivers, which is priced less, at under $250 per person. A certification course costs about $150 for a minimum of 4 people and must be arranged for in advance; masks, fins, and snorkels for a day will run about $10, and may work out to be a lot less trouble than bringing your own with you if you're not addicted to your own "uniform." The Hugheses' equipment is good, and in good condition.

Bonaire's diving opportunities are endless, and can be as easy as surveying the growth and life around the piers at the harbor of Kralendijk to heading out to Klein Bonaire, the small island that sits in the harbor, or making unscheduled dives at whim right from your hotel. Since the island *is* a coral reef, surrounded by more reefs, you can see plenty by walking in from shore.

Deep-sea fishing can be arranged out of either hotel, or through the Bonaire Yacht Club, and sailors can board *Gypsy Girl*, a 50-foot sloop that sails out of Hotel Bonaire. Hotel Flamingo has a glass-bottom boat so that even non-swimmers can see the underwater sights. Windsurfers join the other small craft (Sunfish equivalents) on the shores of the two main hotels.

Sailing regattas have been held for the past couple of years in October. Started as a race for traditional island sloops, the event may become annual. Check with the tourist office if you're interested.

Other sports on Bonaire are limited to tennis at Hotel Bonaire, or on the 2 town courts. The sea is all—unless you include birding as a sport, in which case there are about 130 species to track, and the spectacular flock of flamingos, bright pink from the special algae they feed on in the salt flats. The flamingos are in residence year round. Fall, winter, and spring are the best time for other birds.

■■■

TREASURES AND TRIFLES ON BONAIRE are sea-centered, and most of them are untouchable. The sights you capture with your (or a rented) underwater camera will be the best tokens of your trip to Bonaire, but if you want the more commercial items usually found in tourist resorts, you'll have to meander around Kralendijk or make a quick sweep through the selection at your hotel's boutique.

Spritzer & Fuhrmann on Breedestraat (the continuation of J. A. Abraham Boulevard) has 2 shops that stock watches, jewelry, and other luxury items often at prices slightly higher than those you have heard about in Curaçao and Aruba. Aruba's **Berlinski** has a branch here, and **Kan** is the third of the luxury trio. Do not expect the same extensive selection you might have seen in Aruba or Curaçao (or could see on a day's flight and shopping excursion to either island), but there will be something to spend your money on. If you have your heart set on a special item, start your shopping early enough so that the store staff have time to have a selection flown over from one of the other shops.

Fundashon Arte Industria Bonairiano, on J. A. Abraham Boulevard in town, is the local source for arts and crafts. While the assortment includes childlike shellwork, there are also a few locally made caftans, some black coral jewelry, and wraparound skirts made from fabric with island designs. The project was helped by a U.N. group devoted to encouraging, and training in, handicrafts.

Cambes, one of the few local industries, makes shirts and uniforms. Although you probably won't be in the market for one of the uniforms, some of the sport shirts and leisure clothes are worth a look. Ask about the "factory outlet" shop.

Stop at the **Kralendijk Supermarket** or **Lidia's** if you're interested in local and Indonesian spices, which can be bought off the shelf along with other European Common Market (and of course Netherlands) imports.

British Virgin Islands

British Virgin Islands Tourist Board, Box 134, Road Town, Tortola, British Virgin Islands; information also available from John Scott Fones, 515 Madison Ave., New York, N.Y. 10022; 801 York Mills Rd., Suite 201, Don Mills, Ont., M3B 1X7; West India Committee, 48 Albermarle St., London W1X 4AR England.

U.S. currency is legal tender in the British Virgins.

There's a place out on Cooper Island with a faded hammock, limp until I hung in it, suspended between two posts. The doors are hinged at the top, and when all seven of them are open with struts stuck in the holes in the low stone wall, they make the sunroof—and open the whole front of the hillside house to the tradewinds and the view. Spectacular!

I knew when I dove off the boat and swam to shore that this would be my place. The people who had lived here left a couple of weeks ago. The Worcestershire sauce, pepper, and even a lemon were still here . . . and so were the cat, one white rooster, and a fleet of scampering island lizards, those acrobats that range in size from one inch to 3 and are omnipresent on rocks, sills, walls, and windows throughout the Caribbean.

Whatever cares had come over with me on the boat slipped away when I dove into that water. It was clear as a new polished aquamarine and soft as a dive in a dream. The temperature? Perfect. The usual 80 or so that makes you think about nothing more strenuous than watching the view, or sticking your toes in the sand, or sipping a rum punch, little caring when the inevitable sail will appear on the horizon to glide across your view.

It's easy, when you look out to sails on the sea, to ponder about the days of the 17th and 18th centuries, when Spanish, Dutch, French, and English ships sailed through the Anegada Passage to what we know as Sir Francis Drake Channel. The Spanish paused on Virgin Gorda to work the copper mines until they ran out; the English claimed Tortola, early enough for the Earl of Cumberland to use it as his starting point for an assault on Puerto Rico in 1596. And the English held these islands long enough to be hassled by the Dutch who swept northwest from Sint Maarten to claim the area for a while. The English stepped in again, and eventually permanently, to pepper the Danes who had taken, and were tilling, neighboring St. John, now one of the U.S. Virgin Islands.

When Frederick Ernest Donovan reminisced about his boy days on Tortola, it wasn't wars he talked about, but the daily life he remembered wasn't much different from those days. In February 1974, when he was reflecting over his 100 years, he talked about what it was like to ride horseback from one end of Tortola to the other, carrying the accordion that he played at weddings. He was born at Carrot Bay, on the north shore toward the western end, and he met his wife Mary, when he played at a wedding at Fat Hogs Bay. He lived at Carrot Bay, farming like his family before him, until he died—leaving about 50 children, grandchildren, and great-grandchildren, some of them in the United States, some in Canada, some in England—and some at home.

Frederick Donovan's "formal" schooling came from whatever he picked up when the Methodist minister came through town, but he knew a lot. Quakers and Methodists were the main settlers in those days, and their system of free farming predated freedom for the slaves, granted officially in 1834—but granted by some before that. He even sailed to St. Thomas in the handmade boat he had bent himself, to sell the produce he grew on his own plot at the waterfront of an island where demand was greater.

Antwin George, who drives a cab, used to work in the cane fields on St. Croix. He says that is "one of the hardest jobs I ever worked, and so less money," but he and his brother saved to buy a pickup truck which would be one of the first motor vehicles on Tortola. They brought it over on a small boat—and if you've seen an island-built schooner, sturdy and seaworthy, you can imagine what the truck looked like strapped to the deck. He had to sell some cattle to pay the duty because he didn't have enough money after the $150 investment in the truck. The people at the East End "had their heart in their mout, thinkin' I goin' drive it into the sea," but Antwin George did not. He stepped in the cab of his truck, started the engine, and drove away—leaving his friends staring in disbelief.

There were about 3 cabs when Antwin George started driving his second car, a station wagon, a couple of decades ago; now there are

150—and the airport at Beef Island is busy when the Air BVI flights sweep in. Cab driving is one of the few well-paying jobs; working in tourism industries (perhaps at the hotels or with some of the charter boat firms that fill the harbor at Road Town with their fleets) is another.

Life is a little better now than it was when Frederick Donovan, or even Antwin George, was young, but there's still a long way to go—and most of the young British Virgin Islanders are in a hurry. They, too, take time out, however, to enjoy their equivalent of my Cooper Island. It doesn't cost them anything and the sea and the sun are an integral part of daily life in these 60-odd islands.

■■

POLITICAL PICTURE is refreshingly stable by comparison to some Caribbean countries. In these times when calling an appendage a "colony" is unfashionable, the British Virgin Islands are referred to as a territory and they have a system that encourages self-government. Fact is the governor is appointed by the British Queen. Governors work through the Foreign and Commonwealth Office, and the islands' Governor is James A. Davidson, appointed to his post in November 1978. Elections for Chief Minister, the leader of the islands' government, took place in fall '79, and H. Lavity Stoutt, a former Chief Minister, was returned to office. The former CM, Willard Wheatley, is still active in government. Since all the top B.V.I. political leaders have some awareness of the profit (and problems) of tourism, it seems safe to predict that there will be no drastic changes here—perhaps a rise in tourism taxes to take a toll from visitors who take their tan from these shores. But the pace for development of these islands (set for quality places, not quantity) seems to have become a steady one.

■■

CUSTOMS OF THE COUNTRY are casual. The 10,000 official British Virgin Islanders on these several isles are in daily control of their government and therefore, also, of the tourism development. In the "old days," most had gone to find work elsewhere, but with the surge of tourism development (all well-organized and sifted over several islands), many have returned. Efforts have been made in recent years to revitalize the August Festival, and enthusiasm among residents runs high. Parades are part of the fun, but music, some of it "imported" from other islands, makes the movement as the bands weave along their route through Road Town.

Tourism training in the schools became part of a crusade carried on by local citizens, many of whom are involved with small hotels. The efforts helped attitudes. Some of the students who participated in a B.V.I. Hotel Association project of "running" an island hotel and being its guests went on to employment in the inns that were part of the experiment. This kind of dual cooperation bodes well for islanders' involvement in the tourism industry that is the main financial source for this group of islands—as well as for most of the Caribbean.

Clothes will be casual. Little Dix still encourages jacket (no tie) for special winter evenings, but most hotels (including Peter Island) yield to open shirt and neat, but not excessively dressy, evening attire no matter what the time of year. Yachting types wear their usual throughout the season (in these areas known to "boat bums," some of it can be pretty seedy).

AUTHOR'S OBSERVATION: Be sure to get a copy (or better yet, buy a subscription for $9 U.S. per year, 6 issues) of *The Welcome,* published by the Caribbean Printing Company, Ltd., Box 133, Road Town, Tortola, British Virgin Islands, W.I. It is fact-filled, and an essential source for information if you plan to vacation in the B.V.I. (Single copies are available free from the information offices.)

Hotel rates and other B.V.I. costs have risen substantially again this winter, partly because many import and electricity costs have also risen, but mostly because hotels have been close to 100% full for the past couple of seasons. The best bet for budget watchers is to wait until the rate drop on April 16, when the same room that rents for sky-high tariffs in winter will go for about 40% less. The lower rates, and special incentives for families, are in effect until December 15. Weather, as Caribbean-o-philes know, is almost the same, winter and summer.

AUTHOR'S OBSERVATION: The B.V.I. policy of getting more from the tourists who *do* come rather than building more for the tourists that *might* come is admirable, if, in fact, the visitors get their money's worth. At this point, in my opinion, you do, if a simple beach-and-sea holiday is what you have in mind.

▪▪

MONEY MATTERS focus only on how fast it goes. U.S. currency is used in the British Virgin Islands, where their own currency—issued a couple of years ago—is sold only for commemorative value. It's not legal currency. Everything costs—and usually a lot. Don't count on finding many bargains in an economy that is priced for tourists who are expected to pay a big chunk of the tab for the islands' financing.

▪▪

ARRIVAL will be relatively easy, at least compared to what it used to be. Air BVI flies from Puerto Rico to Tortola with DC3s. Prinair also links San Juan, St. Thomas, St. Maarten, and other destinations of its network, with Tortola's Beef Island airport, and Dorado Wings and Coral Air fly interisland (out of Puerto Rico) as well. You have a choice, by air, of landing on Beef Island, satellite of Tortola and strung to it with the narrow Queen Elizabeth Bridge, which she herself dedicated on a visit in '66, or on Virgin Gorda, at the Rockefeller-sponsored airport built to accommodate guests at that island's first hotel, Little Dix Bay. The Air BVI, Dorado Wings, and charter planes that land these days bring guests for all Virgin Gorda hotels.

If you prefer to arrive by boat, regular ferry service operates between the waterfront at St. Thomas, neighboring U.S.V.I., and both Road Town and West End on Tortola. *Be sure* you read the schedule carefully so that you know your B.V.I. arrival (or departure) port; the two towns are about 20 minutes' drive apart and West End is only a cluster of a couple of small buildings. The crossing takes about an hour on either "Native Son," operated by Tortolans, or the "Bomba Charger," a St. Thomian-based operation. "Bomba Charger" added a new wave to its service in mid-March '81 when it started service, twice weekly, from St. Thomas' harbor to West End, Tortola, to continue on to Jost Van Dyke island and return to West End before going back to St. Thomas on same-day service. Check to see if this service has been supplemented.

Having said all that, arrivals are casual affairs—with your most formal entry at the Beef Island airport, the official B.V.I. entry point. There will be customs officials also at the ramp at West End for the ferries, at Soper's Hole for charter boats, and at Virgin Gorda's strip as well as at West End on Tortola if you arrive by boat from St. Thomas. You will be expected to have citizenship identification (passport is best) and return ticket; ritual will be perfunctory, but

official, and it can seem to take "forever" when routines move at island pace.

When you leave, departure tax is $2.50 by plane; $1.50 by sea.

■■■

TOURING TIPS: Count on boats and flippers on your feet to be
the best ways of touring the spectacular sea that surrounds these
shores (and offers the most intriguing touring options). There are
taxis for land touring (Antwin George has a thriving business, with
multi-passenger small buses plus cars, and there are many other
taxi drivers) on Tortola. Andy Flax and Speedy's Adventures connect Tortola and Virgin Gorda by boat. Speedy also has a road link
on Virgin Gorda, with taxis and small boxy buses for bounding
around these roads. Both Tortola and Virgin Gorda have the well-
known names (Avis, National, Budget) for rental cars. If you insist
upon having one when you winter here, be sure to make your request when you make your reservation. Cars are limited. Some
hotels have their own cars for rent, but cars are not always available
at peak season. Know *before* you get behind the wheel that driving
is on the left, roads sometimes "dissolve" into dirt tracks, potholes
are part of what keeps the speed limit low, and hairpin turns and
vertical slants keep drivers alert (or should).

In Road Town, Tortola, Travel Plan Tours is a full-fledged travel
agent, competent at handling local and long-distance reservations.
On Virgin Gorda, take your travel plans to Virgin Gorda Tours.

There are more yachts for charter in this area than anywhere
else in the Caribbean. (Some say the world.) Check the SPORTS
section for details on charter companies I have known to be reliable
experts.

Most of your touring on these islands is going to be to find a
beach or get to another island; there's not a lot in the way of sights
to see—except for nature's best.

■■■

HOTELS in the British Virgins are personality places. Only 2 properties—Little Dix on Virgin Gorda and Prospect Reef at Road Town
on Tortola—have more than 50 rooms; all the rest are small and
special places where the personality of the owner pervades the
place. Husband and wife teams own and/or manage 20 of the islands' 30 properties. These island inns are places to relax. There's
no such thing as gala nightlife in the nightclub sense; if that's what
you're looking for, go elsewhere. What you can find here is a slow-
moving pace that puts you in, on, and under the sea with little or no

effort. Island inns are tucked on half a dozen British Virgins, some linked only by boat to the nearest bigger island. Although accommodations at some spots are amazingly grand (air-conditioned in some cases, modern with private bath in all), the lights can go out during an island power failure, the supply of fresh water (most of which comes from the rain caught in cisterns built for that purpose) may be limited, and if you're cooking on your own, the best foodstuffs may be the local fish fresh from the sea and what you bring from home to stock your larder yourself.

All hotel bills, which are often high to start with, will carry the 5% government hotel tax, and may also add a 10% to 15% service charge. Be sure to ask if that is all that is expected; usually a sweetener is welcomed.

AUTHOR'S AWARDS go to the Bitter End on Virgin Gorda for creating (and maintaining) a marvelous island outpost; Mariner Inn at Road Town for hospitality to the boating set—both sailors and surveyors—seaside; and to Guana Island Club for turning its entire 850-acre island into an elegant oasis for 30 workworn guests.

Note: In the hotel listings that follow, properties are listed alphabetically within their island's section. The two main islands—Tortola and Virgin Gorda—have the largest concentration of hotels, although the hotels are scattered around each island. In addition, several properties occupy all, most, or at least a significant piece of property on a small island or cay. These resorts are grouped as "Resort Islands near Tortola" and follow the Tortola hotel listing.

■■

TORTOLA is the seat for the B.V.I. government. Most of the small hotels are either in or within walking distance of Road Town or on the northwest coast beaches.

✤ **Brandywine Bay Club** (Road Town, Tortola; 7 units) began life as a "for members only" club set up on the shore, between the Beef Island airstrip and Road Town. The elegant white stucco buildings, capped with red tile roofs, sit serene on the shore, confident in the knowledge that behind the greenery that borders the sea there are 2 tennis courts and an elegant patio area where "your kind" will alight at the cocktail hour (and perhaps at other times of the day). Each "cottage," connected to its neighbor, is a duplex unit, with 2 bedrooms each with private bath and view on the top floor, over the comfortable living area with tile floor, colorful furnishings and a view over the deck to the islands beyond. Full kitchen facilities turn this place into your own island home. A presumptuous Greek-style pillared temple sets the tone, provides a climbing goal, and commands the perfect view; the rest of the Club's atmosphere is a little more down to earth, although rates are sky high—at about $195 for 2, no meals. Rates for 4 hover around $250, but no credit cards are accepted. Your travel agent can make your reservations (even though the place is referred to as a "club") through David Mitchell.

✤ **CSY Yacht Club** (Box 157, Road Town, Tortola; 8 rooms), wedged between shore and road, is a hive of sailing activity year round. As one of 3 island hubs for Caribbean Sailing Yacht operations (the other 2 are in the Bay Islands of Honduras and at St. Vincent for the Grenadines), the nautical outlook is assured. Accommodations are spartan, with lookouts to sea through the spars of yachts waiting to be chartered. The second-story open-air dining room serves casual fare while you wait for your ship to come in. Not everyone's idea of a cushy holiday, this one appeals to the penny-pinching nautical set who fork out $50 for 2, breakfast included. If you like the barefoot and boating folk, consider this home port.

✤ **Fort Burt** (Box 139W, Road Town, Tortola; 7 rooms, 1 cottage) was closed May '78, and, reopened several months later with Wendy Ketchum in charge. The current operation is in keeping with the legends connected with this spot. When I first knew Fort Burt, it was a simple place, typical of the British Virgins (and, in fact, most of the Caribbean, at that time), operated by Chris and Millie Hammersley. In addition to Millie Hammersley's monkey (a traveling companion who joined her on major excursions to Puerto Rico and elsewhere), the characters of the place included the owners. A favorite tale is one of Millie setting off in a feeble boat with a picnic lunch which she spread out, along with herself, in the lobby of the then-new, and always luxurious, Caneel Bay Plantation on nearby St. John. When asked what she was doing, she replied that she was only doing what Caneel Bay guests did at her hotel when they came to Tortola on day trips. From that point on, Caneel Bay guests—and anyone else who wanted to come to Fort Burt—bought their lunch from Millie's kitchen at Fort Burt. When Paulina Dean, a du Pont heiress, bought the property in 1967, she renovated extensively, pouring money over all, and changing what had been a simple, character place into a nub of luxury. Since then this place has wavered, but Wendy Ketchum seems to have set a pace for lively, carefree congeniality, with disco activity some evenings. The view from rooms and terrace is superb. The vertical driveway that stands at the edge of the coast-rimming road is awesome— even for Tortolan cab drivers—but it is mercifully short; you can easily walk it (and into town), even if slowly. Check for status if you plan a visit this winter, and count on the handful of rooms to be comfortable, but a shadow of their former elegance. With the disco, this is no place for light sleepers or early-to-bed folk.

✛ **Long Bay** (Box 433, Road Town, Tortola; 44 rooms) nestles on the north side of Tortola, about 25 minutes' drive from Road Town and just under an hour's drive to the airport. Best-bet rooms—and those that carry the top tariff—are the 12 beachfront rooms, allocated 2 per cottage, that opened for January '79. Other rooms—superior, suite, or cottage—are up the hillside, and none has a balcony worth the name. The 7 2-bedroom cottages are twin-bedded and have a tub with shower in the bathroom; the living area has a sea view; both of the suite arrangements have shower only, with the superior status awarded because there is air conditioning, sitting room, and a dressing area next to the bathroom. Plain old suites are simple enough, not air-conditioned, and the closest to the beach so that the view is not as good, but the walk to the source is shorter. Families enjoy the cottages. All the suites have efficiencies, but if you let Mary Ford know ahead of time, arrangements can be made for dinner at the main house or at the beach, near the tennis court. The place is favored by professional folk, who like the beachside quiet, with an option for some sport and some good conversation, and a chance to dip in the pool near the beach if the sea seems too much of a challenge. Rates for the cottages are about $90 for 4, meals extra. Suites are about $60 for 2; beach units are $70 for 2. Be prepared for that soft sand on the beach to lead into sole-testing coral just below the sea level. (And to pay a $2.50 charge to swim here if you're not an overnight guest).

✛ **Mariner Inn** (Box 139, Road Town, Tortola; 39 rooms plus 2 suites) is a personal favorite, partly because of the special warm welcome offered by Ginny and Charlie Cary, their "right hands," Betty and Bob Jackson, and Richard Tilly, the on-the-spot manager. The place appeared at water's edge in late 1977, with a 2-story block of 24 rooms for nautical types to use, either before they set out to sea on one of the yachts chartered from the Carys' "Moorings," or while they stayed on land to listen to sailors' lore. Success led to additional rooms in '79. Fully equipped with chart rooms, lockers, commissary, and showers, the purpose is obviously the sea. Most furnishings in the rooms and elsewhere were made in Tortola; the atmosphere is true West Indian, with an open-air traditional feeling in spite of the newness. (All rooms have kitchenette and nautical view). Entertainment (local bands and barbecues) some evenings keeps the pool-bar alfresco restaurant area lively. *Underwater Safaris* offers full scuba services from its quarters at the inn. The per person (all equipment) cost for a 3-day course is $250. At $65 for 2, meals extra, this inn is a good buy when you include the spontaneous hospitality of "the captains" and their able crew.

✚ **Prospect Reef Resort** (Box 104, Road Town, Tortola; 131 rooms) percolates on the flatlands at the sea, west of Road Town, just below Fort Burt Hotel's hillside notch. It opened in the season of '75 with 35 units of the "more than 100" planned. Villas have a center courtyard, cottages have a circular stairway to the living area, studios have a sea view. The newest rooms are hotel-style units, a couple of them air-conditioned, but most with the usual overhead fan (which is more than adequate to circulate the air). All the multiroom units have "shut-off doors" for individual room rental, and that's what gives this place its baffling range (from $80 to $100 per day for 2, meals extra, this winter). (Best bet seems to be the housekeeping unit, with a $2 per day tableware and kitchenware charge, but not the $20 per day breakfast and dinner supplement.) Prospect Reef is saved from looking as big as it is by pleasant architecture, with low-rise buildings meandering around grounds punctuated with pools, lagoon, and planting, plus the marina. *The Prospect Restaurant,* in an upstairs dining room with sea view (and louvered windows to allow a sea-breeze cooling), offers reasonable fare (fish, when fresh, is recommended) at high prices. The marina-side drink-and-dine spot is more casual. The complex offers 6 Laykold night-lighted tennis courts, plus Paraquita Bay, about a 10-minute drive east, for small boat sailing and windsurfing out of the dock at Fort Discovery. Big boats (sail and motor) moor at the small marina at the foot of the restaurant, bar, shops, and water sports center. Some of the yachts are privately owned; others are available for day charter or deep-sea fishing. Check at the water sports desk. There's even a small beach area, but the best known beaches are a 15-minute drive to the north shore. Prospect Reef's competent and congenial director is Tortolan Elihu Rhymer, who splits his "48-hour day" with Air BVI (he's President) and being Chairman of the

Tourist Board. Check with him if there are any questions that need the top-notch answer, or with General Manager James Mason who's the man on daily duty.

✠ **Sebastians on the Beach** (Box 441, Road Town, Tortola; 29 rooms) stands at Apple Bay, waiting for beachcombers who will be content to overnight in the pink stucco box of 20 beachside rooms, the newest rooms by the main building, or the less expensive digs in the older unit (main house), also on the other side of the road. If you catch a similarity with this name and the better-known restaurant called Sebastians on the waterfront in St. Thomas, you've made an island connection. Jerry Sebastian was an island legend in the 1950s when escapees and island types flocked to his restaurant-on-stilts, precursor of the one which stands on that spot today. When Kay Sebastian, one of a succession of Jerry Sebastian's wives, opened this place on Tortola in 1966, she planned an elegant outpost, with fine china, crystal and food. It's slipped some with the years, to become a casual clubby spot that some find comfortable. Michael and Ursula Mikoleiczik tend to your needs and their housekeeping. Furnishings are beach-simple; the beach is about all anyone here cares about. The pocket of sand by the room units is the favored gathering spot for most guests who are paying $50 for 2, meals extra.

✠ **Smuggler's Cove** (Box 4, West End, Tortola; 4 rooms beachside, plus 3 cottages on the hill) will stay a smuggler's retreat until the road improves. The bounce-and-jounce route makes it seem much more remote than its actual distance from West End, but the powdery cove of white sand and the offshore snorkeling make the ride worth it for some of us and some devoted fisherfolk head this way for the two fishing boats run by son Matt. EP rates for doubles are about $60, and the hillside haven with 3 bedrooms goes for a tidy $90 daily in winter, meals extra. You'll need a car at this outpost if you want to communicate with the rest of the world.

✠ **Sugar Mill Estate Hotel** (Box 425, Road Town, Tortola; 21 rooms) operates more like a house party than a hotel. Owners Leonard and Joan Kushins have hammered, hacked, and honed a West Indian house that had been cut into thirds and floated around from Road Town some 60 years ago, plus the ruins of a sugar mill, into a congenial inn that gets repeaters. Made by hand, and maintained by a lot of careful coddling of guests, the place has a real West Indian personality. Rising up the slopes from what they've called a "snorkel beach" and spent a lot of money "building" to basking size, the hotel has rooms equipped with efficiencies. The first rooms were the 4 suites, and then the redwood honeymoon cottage was added. The 12 studio apartments behind the pool came next. The old stone sugar mill, at seaside, has been scrubbed and hung with Haitian paintings to present a good mood for Caribbean candlelight nights. The patch of sand, with its "Sand Bar," was an addition in early summer of '78. Although it won't take the place of some of the B.V.I.'s natural strands, it does provide a sandy spot to dunk from, but watch the coral on entering. Rates of about $62 to $75 for 2 are sliced in half for summer vacationers. Meals are extra, and although you can cook them yourself, chances are you'll leave that chore to Mrs. Scatliffe, whose recipes will linger with you long after your tan has gone.

✣ **Treasure Isle Hotel** (Box 68, Road Town, Tortola; 40 rooms) sits up from the shoreline at the east end of Road Town, overlooking the harbor—and the 27-foot Olympic *Solings* Steve Colgate uses for his Tortola division of his Offshore Sailing School. Setting his "Learn-to Sail" course at this land base with the summer season of '78, Steve Colgate continues the program he started in 1964 and now operates from several bases along the East Coast, U.S. (City Island, New York, and Sarasota, Florida, are two.) The Colgate crowd pay about $600 for each of 2 sharing a room, for a winter week (7 nights) of the "Learn to Sail." Breakfasts, transfers between airport and hotel, and, of course, the daily lessons, plus some bonus parties are included. Other meals (and air fare) are extra. (Info from Offshore Sailing Schools, 820 Second Ave., New York, NY 10017.) The hotel has rooms for other guests also, but sailing will be the popular table talk. From this port, you can wander down the hill and across the road to Mariner Inn, or along the road into Road Town to visit Village Cay Marina and other spots around town. Twenty-five of the rooms at Treasure Isle have a sea view from the air-conditioned perch, and a small balcony; biggest rooms are the 15 suites. There's a pool, cupped by a casual wicker-and-planted bar area and the dining room.

✣ **Village Cay Marina** (Road Town, Tortola; 48 units) grows at the northeast end of town, on a piece of land reclaimed from the sea a few years ago. Anyone who knew this area in the old days will have a hard time imagining all the nautical activity that takes place here now. Slow to start, the attractive, seaside units with a nautical emphasis are the hub of what is becoming a haven for sea souls. All the

facilities are new, plumbing works, some of the air conditioning
does also. But I marvel at what went on in the mind of the architect
who gave the prime sea-view spots to the office and store space,
putting the windows from most rooms facing walls or otherwise
uninteresting sights. The sometimes small, always simply furnished rooms put you at the heart of a lot of boating life, and a short
walk from the shops at the center of town. (Some of the best shops
are now here at the Cay, however). There's a seaside dining room,
with lookout to the boat slips, so that the view is spectacular. (The
bar styles itself an English pub.) Count on spending about $60 for
2 in winter, for the place that many yachts call home port.

✢ **Brewer's Bay Campground** (Box 185, Road Town, Tortola; 15 prepared sites, 10 bare sites) proves what the Rockefeller system is all
about, but the drive to get here is often perilous (depending on
washouts and the condition of "your" car). This project was started
in 1976 by local sons who had worked at the 29th U.S. National
Park campsites on neighboring St. John. Without the government
sponsorship, but with a lot of assistance and suggestions from the
officials, Noel Callwood and some partners opened up the campsites
on the north shore of Tortola in the season of '75. He and his wife
Josephine now oversee the operation. These sites have almost as
long a waiting list as those on St. John. If you are interested, contact the mail drop well ahead of intended camping time—and be
prepared to pay $12 for 2 for a prepared tent site, $2.50 each additional person, or $4 for a bare site that will take care of up to 6 peo-
ple. While housekeeping and grounds maintenance may not be up
to the St. John's park standards, the view, sea, beach, and natural
attributes are spectacular. Getting here is the challenge, and will
probably involve a taxi ($6) from the airport at Beef Island, served
by Air BVI, Dorado Wings, Coral Air, and Prinair from Puerto Rico.
Your alternative is to come to Road Town on the boat out of Charlotte Amalie, St. Thomas. (Be sure to reconfirm your return flight
when you arrive; it's a real project to try to reconfirm from the
campsites.)

▪▪

RESORT ISLANDS NEAR TORTOLA are within easy boat trip
from Tortolan shores. In some cases, it is feasible to plan for dinner
on Tortola, and boat home by moonlight. In all cases, a day on the
big island can be a nice diversion.

✢ **Drake's Anchorage** (Box 32, Mosquito Island, Virgin Gorda,
B.V.I.; 10 villas) lures yachts and sea-loving types. With the mid-

1979 reopening, 2 new and luxurious units sprouted on Lime Tree Beach. A windmill helped provide the island's electricity and solar panels were put in place for heating water. Vegetables and fruits for the daily meals have always been grown on the island, but the emphasis has been renewed (and the former units refurbished). Remote and special, as this place has been since Boston-based MIT professor Edward Fredkin bought the long-term lease in '69, Drake's Anchorage can provide an ideal getaway island for frustrated Robinson Crusoe types. Count on about $1,500 per week, with maid but no meals, for 4 for the luxury cottages this winter; daily rate for 2 is about $150 with all meals included for a room in one of the other units, each of which is suitable for 4.

✠ **Guana Island Club** (Box 32, Road Town, Tortola; 5 houses) gets its name from the rock "iguana head" that pokes out of a cliff on the southwest side. (Guana Island is a small island north of the east end of Tortola.) Residents James Lake and James Parke rowed from the island to Tortola to attend Quaker meetings, but that was a couple of centuries ago. Beth and Louis Bigelow rowed across when they decided to call this home in 1935, just before they organized Guana Island Club as a trust. They had arrived the first time by the boat that came across from Tortola, after they sighted the Guana and decided it was the Shangri-la they had been searching for during the previous 6 months of travels in the Pacific and Caribbean. You will be met by motor launch, and although everyone reached the hill-capping club by donkey up to about 17 years ago, today there's a Land Rover to take you to your cottage (as well as the donkeys, if you prefer one). The Bigelows built the first cottage while they lived in a tent on this 850-acre island, most of which still remains in its natural state, with tropical plants, as a bird sanctuary. Many of the 30 guests that fit into the 5 houses have been coming back for years, with children and grandchildren. Ownership by international lawyer Henry Jarecki hasn't changed the atmosphere and Mary Randall is your on-the-spot guide and hostess. There's no noisy, late-night entertainment; when the records run out, it's time for bed—unless a band happens to be playing, but that's an occasional thing. Hiking and swimming from any of the island's sandy coves are the usual daytime diversions (except for books), but there are tennis courts, a 5-hole "course" for golfers' practice, and plenty of places to set out to sea—for fishing, sailing, or just plain sunning. Guana Island Club's guests pay $195 daily for 2 in winter, all meals included—or you can rent the entire island at certain times of the year for $1500 per day or $8000 per week.

✤ **Last Resort** (Box 530, Long Look, Tortola; 6 rooms) occupies all of the speck that is Bellamy Cay, off the end of Beef Island, not far from the airstrip or from Marina Cay. It seemed "down at the heels" when checks were made for this edition, but this outpost has never been a "spit-and-polish" haven anyway. So nautical is this mooring that one of the options is a combination land-and-sea vacation priced at about $550 per couple per week in winter, 20% less in summer. Straight room rate for 2 with all meals is $60, with children under 12 at half price. Atmosphere is barefoot casual.

✤ **Marina Cay** (Box 76, Road Town, Tortola; 16 rooms) is on its own 6-acre island north of Beef Island, which is linked to Tortola by a short bridge. The inn is still in a state of flux, a status it's known for too long, as we go to press. New owners are hoped for. The place provided the anecdotes and setting for *Our Virgin Island*, a book sometimes found in paperback, written more than 25 years ago by Robb White. Modernizations (but not too many) make for more comforts, with rooms in a chain of airy A-frames that saunter along the shoreline below the main house on the hill. Dining is alfresco, at the main house or at the shoreside thatched shack favored by seafaring folk who anchor offshore and row in for dinner. The focus is water sports, with a completely equipped scuba shop that new owners would have to maintain. Bring books and let the cares seep out; there's nothing fussy here, and there's plenty to revive sagging spirits if you like the casual life—at rates that are higher than they might be because of the demand for spots like this. Count on something in the $100 orbit for 2, 2 meals daily, in winter.

✤ **Peter Island Hotel and Yacht Harbour** (Box 211, Road Town, Tortola; 32 rooms, plus a couple of lavish houses) was purchased in December '78 by Amway Corporation of Ada, Michigan. This special resort perches on its own island, on a cove that used to be uninhabited and was a favorite anchoring area for friends of mine from St. Thomas. Now it's too elegant for casual cavorting, with a nose-high pace set by modern decor, food, and staff.

There are about 1000 acres to the whole island, but some 500 of them are now in the Amway bag, having been purchased from Peter Island Estate-Peder Smedvig, Ltd. The late Torloff Smedvig acquired the property in 1968. In a feat unequaled in the Caribbean, he brought in the prefabricated parts, on his own ships from Norway. With West Indian workmen, led by 20 Norwegian foremen who had never set foot on Caribbean soil before (picture that), the place was assembled on the shoreline like some gigantic children's toy, to open in fall 1971. Rates settled at close to $300 for 2 this winter. The pace for pricey elegance has been set by those who come to Scandinavian modern surroundings (antiseptic A-frames with lots of wood and view, plus refrigerator, telephone, radio, television outlet, and overhead fans) to play under the sun. For action options, you play tennis, ride horseback, or sail (or talk with wealthy charters who slide into the Peter Island slips), all included in your daily room rate. The outpost elegance is reached by relatively easy connections (at least for this part of the world). The hotel's sturdy and enclosed boats ply the sound several times daily (and nightly) from Caribbean Sailing Yacht's depot near Road Town on Tortola. The trip takes about 30 minutes.

✤ **Sandy Ground** (Box 594, West End, Tortola; 8 homes) is the name for a piece of property on the island of Jost Van Dyke (in spite of the mail address). The island—3 square miles of it—is virgin territory. The homes scamper up from a white sand beach, giving you complete privacy, peace, and quiet. The place is yours—for fees that range from $300 upwards per week in winter. Since all houses are privately owned, each has the personality of its owner—and the overall management of Robert Grunzinger, who is the on-premises man. Biggest problem will be food acquisitions, but the Grunzinger management will stock your larder if you let them know the kinds of food you want (assuming it's available locally). There's no place but the sea on Jost Van Dyke, so bring meats well packed from home, and pick up the rest either in St. Thomas (best bet, with its supermarkets) or Tortola (Rite Way has good supplies) on your way through. To get here, you used to have to let the manager know in advance so he can race over to West End to pick you up by boat. You *still* have to do that on some days, but "Bomba Charger," a 100-passenger boat, added Little Harbour as a stop twice weekly in March '81, and may expand the service. Check. (Rental of small boats, scuba equipment, and arrangements for deep-sea fishing can be set up, but don't count on speed.)

▪▪▪
VIRGIN GORDA, the fat Virgin, got a second chance (after a first chance with discovery of gold in the 17th century) when Laurance Rockfeller sailed past in the mid-1950s. Soon after, his Little Dix

Bay was started. These days vacationers can find several small spots on this bigger-than-you-think island.

✦ **Biras Creek** (Box 54, North Sound, Virgin Gorda; 30 suites) caps a small hill, and slides down its sides to North Sound. The 150-acre estate is the province of a Norwegian shipping magnate who followed the lead of compatriot Torloff Smedvig (Peter Island). Biras Creek wears a tiara that is the main building (dining room; small shop with suntan lotions, etc.; bar and spectacular views). There's a swimming pool for cottage users who don't want to do more than step off their terrace, but the real beach is a short and tropical garden walk to Deep Bay for the beach bar in a beached boat and some minor activities. Tennis courts and the bird sanctuary supplement the snorkeling, scuba, and sailing activities. You'll be bedded down, once you've completed the expedition to reach this spot, in one of the 15 2-suite units that curve along the shore. Revered as an outpost with elegance by those hardy enough to make the big-plane-plus-small-plane-plus-boat-plus-car-plus-boat-plus-walk trip to get there. The Thonnings (she oversees the cooking; he manages with Scandinavian charm and West Indian understanding) did their island-inn teething at an even remoter spot, to which some of us beat a path, on a speck off Grenada. Winter single rates are breathtaking at $205, with 2 meals included. It pays to be one of 2 for a $245 tariff (and to eat a lot).

✦ **Bitter End Yacht Club** (John O'Point, North Sound, Virgin Gorda; 13 rooms in cottages) *is* at the bitter end; it shares the bay with Biras Creek, involves the same dip-and-dash route to get here, and is favored by well-heeled nautical types who don't mind paying a double room rate that hovers around $150 per day to get all meals and an option to use the hotel's fleet of 31 sailboats and windsurfers. A better deal can be worked out if your local yacht club goes as a group, and you barter on price to take over the entire spot—traveling at group rates on planes, etc. Smart sailors cruise in, to anchor offshore and spin yarns around the bar where they can pay for drinks only. They're the entertainment. Rooms are in simple but comfortable cottages that scamper up the hillside, with the 4 newest at the shoreline. Special day outing, in recent seasons, gives you a glimpse of the place from and returning to your choice of airport, harbor, or VG hotel, with a launch leaving from Gun Creek about 10:30 for a lively/boating/sunny day that departs The Bitter End about 3 p.m. The total tally last season was a well-spent $20, including your lunch, a swim and shower, plus the transportation. When Robin Lee sailed into this bay in 1966, he stayed to help Basil Symonette and others build the place. As he reports in *The Dove* (Harper and Row, 1972), "they have found a really lovely spot and they've hauled in all the material they need." Don and Janis Neal, the present managers, still haul in all the material they need—including guests.

✠ **Fischer's Cove Beach** (Box 60, The Valley, Virgin Gorda; 8 cottages and 12 rooms) is famous for its island food, especially the lobster dinners. Native son Anderson Flax returned home to Virgin Gorda in the early '60s, after a stint as a mechanic on neighboring St. Thomas. Recognizing the budding tourism complex that had been planted by Rockresorts, Andy Flax opened his Andy's by the Sea, a small bar popular with the workers and with the few tourists who reached Virgin Gorda in those days. The place grew on the choice sand-rimmed cove that had been given to him by his grandfather and began to serve local food in simple surroundings. Eventually to add cottages for guests who knew and wanted good value. (In the meantime, Andy stocked and started Virgin Gorda Tours Association, the island's first organized taxi business, and met and married his Antiguan-born wife, Norma.) The couple work hard to keep this shoreside place in shape, and the addition of 12 new rooms (6 on 6) turned the property into a real hotel. Rooms and facilities are comfortable for a casual holiday. The rates ($60 for 2 or about $350 for 2 for a week) make it a good deal for a place within walking distance of the Little Dix Marina.

✠ **Guavaberry-Spring Bay Vacation Homes** (Box 20, Virgin Gorda; 10 homes) has the look and the feel of a woodsy camp, except that your wood frame hexagonal home will be well furnished, and the weather and welcome by Charles and Betty Roy will be warm. The beach is down the walk, the tumble of gigantic rocks known locally as "The Baths" are not far away, and there are gigantic boulders next to the main house. When I first looked in on the Roys, the count was "five homes, but we hope to have seven," and they are now up to 10, with most of them filled with repeaters who know and love the place. *Flamboyant,* which was owned by a couple from Schenectady, N.Y., on one look-in, has 3 wood dunce-cap roofs, with the kitchen and living room under the middle one and a bedroom at each end, the entire mass giving a hospitable airy feeling. Highly recommended for independent housekeeping types who can stock up happily at the Virgin Gorda marina supermarket (or can bring canned goods and meat in a box from home). Small commissary on premises for emergency rations. You'll pay upwards of $400 per week for the 1-bedroom and close to $500 per week for the 2-bedroom houses. (Special honeymoon holidays.)

✤ **Little Dix Bay** (Box 70, Virgin Gorda; 82 rooms) has been nicknamed the British Virgin Islands Red Cross. The Little Dix development not only pumped a reported $2.5 million into the B.V.I. economy, but the resort also recognizes its responsibility to its guests—and to the people of the island where it "lives"—to provide what is expected (which means having its own desalinization plant, building roads, giving good wages, etc.). The newest unit of 16 rooms (opened June 1980) prove that this place doesn't rest on its laurels. Things have come a long way since Laurance Rockefeller cruised by on his yacht and spotted this sandy shore in the early 1950s. At that time, the island had no telephone, no power supply, no doctor, no paved roads, and no adequate schooling or jobs for the couple of hundred people who lived here. When the first boards and building blocks appeared on the beach in 1961, they set up a commotion that was to reverberate through nearby Peter Island (where the late Torloff Smedvig would pick up the cue for his Peter Island resort) and at a neck of land near North Sound, where another well-heeled Norwegian company, Mowinckle Shipping, would build Biras Creek. Little Dix opened in 1964, built mostly by British Virgin Islanders who learned their skills on the job, from foremen and others stationed here to build the resort. The staff, many of whom had had their first jobs at St. John's sister resort, Caneel Bay, returned to the British Virgins for a job in their own country. Access roads have been built, generators have been installed, and a shopping center was developed a couple of seasons after the hotel opened, at what is now known as the Virgin Gorda Yacht Harbour, also sparked and sponsored by the Rockresort group.

Visitors arriving here today, with time to complain about possible slow service, flickering lights, and an occasional water shortage, should pause to reflect on the miracle that this complex is here at all. Rates are high, but when you consider what is offered, if any place is worth paying over $250 per day for 2, breakfasts and dinners included, this place is. Now under management of Joel Jennings, a longtime Rockresorter who left the clan long enough to take some time at his own resort consulting business, Little Dix is a luxury retreat. Rooms are in viewful units tucked in clusters along flower-trimmed paths that meander along the beach with the newest units those down by the tennis courts. The main gathering spot (restaurant, bar, near the beach) is open to sea breezes, with a loose-fitting thatch cap to keep the sun off. Your room will be made of purpleheart wood, colorful fabrics, and all modern comforts, including air conditioning in some units. (I have always found the overhead fan more than enough motivation for stirring the soft breezes.) There is a complete tennis complex (5 courts), with pro around in peak season months, plus water sports easily arranged here and at the Yacht Harbour. Day boating excursions are offered through the activities desk; small shops are on premises for immediate purchases, and you have about 500 acres to meander around, book or binoculars in hand. The pace by day is leisurely, quiet, sun-and-sea-filled; entertainment some evenings is as rambunctious as a barbecue and steel band, but count on turning in early unless you bring a lively group from home, or happen to find one here.

Arrival at Little Dix is easiest and fastest by the small planes of Dorado Wings to the Virgin Gorda airstrip from Puerto Rico, but I think the boat arrival is best—to the Yacht Harbour from Road Town or St. Thomas. All that air-taxi-boat-taxi connecting makes you slow down enough to appreciate the imagination, effort, and money that went into creating this resort. If you vacation at other than peak season winter, check for the special spring, summer, and fall package holidays that link Little Dix with Caneel and sometimes with time on a yacht, for a split week or two.

✤ **Ocean View Hotel** (Box 66, Virgin Gorda; 12 rooms) is run by a member of the "big" family on Virgin Gorda, the O'Neals, and has made a name for itself among those who know good island food. Rooms are neat, clean, and simple and carry the most modest rates of Virgin Gorda's listed properties ($60 for 2, 2 meals daily). Sad to say, the ocean view that gave the place its name was obscured by the very successful, ever-expanding Virgin Gorda Yacht Harbour across the road, but since that may be source for entertainment at this "no beach" spot, that's not all bad.

✤ **Olde Yard Inn** (Box 10, The Valley, Virgin Gorda; 10 rooms) is the Devine place on Virgin Gorda, a small spot run by Joe and Ellen. Picture a library, packed with rare books and first editions, classical music with a dinner of fresh caught langouste (as the local lobster is called), and tropical tradewinds to air-cool your room, all for about $75 for 2, breakfast and dinner included. The Olde Yard Inn is casual, with classical overtones. There's nothing elaborate about the rooms or dress requirements, but there's plenty worth talking about after you've climbed 1500-foot Gorda Peak looking for wild orchids or been scuba diving or snorkeling, eyeing the parrot fish. The rooms are twin-bedded, very simple, but being out in the sunshine, with tradewinds wafting around, is the reason to come here anyway.

■■

ANEGADA, a flat slab of land about 20 miles to the northeast of Tortola and north of Virgin Gorda, is rimmed with white powdery sand beaches and wears a bracelet of rugged reefs that have caught enough ships through the centuries to have some of the most exciting scuba areas in the British Virgins. The 200 residents on the island, however, believe in the motto "once burned, twice shy." The first great dream for Anegada was in the late 1960s, when Englishman Kenneth Bates offered the British Virgin Islands government great schemes for development. Roads were started to lead to the hotels, elegant resorts, and second homes that would be built on land bought cheap from Anegadians or negotiated with the government. The plan dissolved in 1968, leaving plenty of Anegadians bitter and suspicious. When another developer appeared in the 1970s, promising "tourist and residential buildings, community facilities and the basic concepts for the use and development of part of the island which would offer every opportunity for local participation" plus "recommendations on the protection of the environment including flora and fauna, birds and fish and on the introduction of various small, specialized industries such as a turtle breeding unit," Anegadians were ready to take another chance. Conservation and interests of the residents (both fashionable ideas of the times) had been included in the programs, and the president of the company made a good-faith donation of $10,000 toward local causes (while someone else went around collecting $500 per house to be connected to the island's power system, which had been installed by the benevolent company). The only problem with this plan was that the perpetrator was Jean Doucet, president of Sterling Bank and Trust, the conglomerate with interests also in the Bahamas, which established in Grand Cayman under that colony's 1966 tax haven laws—and went broke in the mid-1970s, leaving Anegada (and all Sterling's other projects) deprived and once more destitute.

For this season, Anegada continues to offer what it always has had: a sunny flat island with a small community, the Settlement, and one 12-room inn, **The Reefs,** operated by Lowell and Vivian Wheatley, with simple accommodations that cost about $50 for 2, meals extra, in winter. Fishing folk, and those who know and love the sea and simple surroundings, can settle in happily here—especially if Lowell speeds you out for a sport-fishing day. Sailors who are not experts in these seas stay away; the reefs make the approach "perilous." All Island Air and small plane charter flights land at the strip near the Settlement. A taxi will take you along the south coast to The Reefs.

■■

RESTAURANTS: So-called international dining in the British Virgins is expensive, partly because almost everything is imported and partly because, I suspect, that's what owners/managers think the traffic will bear. The food served at some of the island inns is excellent, attractively served in tantalizing tropical settings, *but* the logistics of getting from one place to another make sampling all the best places "impossible." It's highly unlikely, unless you've booked for an overnight or more, that you'll be dining spur-of-the-moment at Biras Creek, for example. It's a long poke from anywhere except Bitter End Yacht Club, which shares its bay and is best linked by boat. Always make reservations; since most restaurants are small, head count is crucial. Dress is informal at most B.V.I. spots, with Little Dix and Peter Island the dressiest of the lot. All places encourage neat but not formal attire. (Biras Creek was compelled to modify their "dress informal" with the comment that "gentlemen are asked to wear long trousers for dinner." Presumably the women know what to wear.)

On *TORTOLA*, if you are in the Road Town area (and that can include Peter Island, linked by boat to the CYS dock), it's feasible to think about dining around the pool at **Mariner Inn,** where local fish and lobster are menu standards (at $10 and up), and there's entertainment most winter evenings. Robber Dick's at Village Cay Marina is another popular place, with seaview tables. **Sir Francis Drake Pub** offers simple (and reasonably priced) chicken and chips seaside, in nautical surroundings around the "other" side of Road Town (at the shore near hilltop Fort Burt). **Ali Baba** has an unusual menu including shish kabob (the usual, with beef) and shish tawok (same thing, but chicken) plus a kebeh, which is a wheatburger with nuts, onions, and beef. Steak, chicken, and shepherd's pie also appear on the menu, but be sure to ask about the daily special.

Don't miss **The Ample Hamper,** in one of its two locations (village Cay Marina and near the Moorings) but expect to find awesomely high prices for selected offerings. Not only can you stock your yacht from prepared "provisioning information" they've assembled, but you can get Mrs. Thomas's guava jelly (a good gift for folks at home) and a lot of tasty English imports (honey, tea, Fortnum & Mason marmalades) for take-home gifts. Rite Way supermarket offers more extensive selection of staples (and liquor) at close to reasonable prices. The best bet if you have the place to enjoy it, is the take-out food of **Carib Casserole,** where you can buy beef curry, sweet and sour pork, pineapple chicken in rum sauce— and hot Trinidadian roti, a meat-filled tart made fresh on Fridays (and available frozen at other times). Carib Casseroles are sold from their kitchen east of the post office, on the inland side of Main Street at their small and neat shop where they also serve lunch and dinner.

For fancy dining, Peter Island's **House of Peter** has departed from its Scandinavian specialties with the sale of the property, and now features beef Wellington, local fish and lobster, and entrecôte prepared by an English chef and costing you a healthy $20 from Sunday through Friday and $25 on Saturday for the full meal. **Prospect Reef** fell short of the accolades given it just after opening by *Gourmet* magazine, but food has improved, although it seems *very* expensive, with very slow service which I never mind unless the food isn't worth the wait. The menu reads well, but my suggestion is to stick with some simple fish, which should be fresh and good. The Sunday Barbecue buffet at **Prospect Restaurant** is a spectacular spread, and may be the best bet here. (**Drop Inn Bar,** on ground level at the small marina, has far more atmosphere than the upstairs dining room.)

On the north shore, it's relatively easy to cover the distance between Sebastians, Long Bay, and Sugar Mill if you have a car. Special dinners are worth reserving at **Sugar Mill,** *in* the sugar mill ruins that have been attractively refurbished, where you can sample some interesting island recipes with cook's flair and at Long Bay where the setting is also special. (The drive between Road Town and the north shore spots takes about 25 minutes.) Places that are better for lunch, partially because you can see where you are (and the views are spectacular) but also because getting to and from them after nightfall turns into a big project, are **Marina Cay,** on its own small speck off the east end of Tortola-Beef Island, and the **Last Resort,** another speck in the same vicinity where food was below average and service was *very* slow, even for an island atmosphere you expect will be low key.

On *VIRGIN GORDA,* Little Dix, Olde Yard Inn and Fischer's Cove are easy to reach, each from the other. My preference goes to **Olde Yard Inn,** for atmosphere and an interesting menu that shows the ingenuity and ability of the Devines. Try the local lobster, or the chef's choice of local fish, both of which are fresh and good. **Fischer's Cove** is good for simple surroundings with an island, sea-side view and West Indian food. **Little Dix** is a big resort, in comparison to the other 2 small and special places. You can expect elegant surroundings for your professional dinner, and hamburgers, sandwiches, and the usual fare for lunch by the beach. (Guests at Guavaberry Spring Bay and Ocean View can easily get to these 3 spots.)

Biras Creek, the best of the lot on this island, is a boat ride from wherever you are, unless you are staying here. Libby Thonning has made a practice of finding English cordon-bleu-trained lady chefs during her summer travels on the Continent. They follow her tried-and-true lead with recipes, but I'm sad to report that respected sleuths have sent word that "food was ordinary" when they sampled. Perhaps that was cook's night out; my samplings have been consistently good.

On *JOST VAN DYKE,* **Foxy's,** on the beach, is a legend to sailors, and to a lot of other boating folk who row to the beach to walk along the sands to sing at Foxy's place. As a boy, Foxy Callwood traded some of the cattle he tended for a boat and took to the sea. But he didn't sail too far in those days; he returned to his own shores to open a small bar, near enough to the church to draw complaints. His calypso bar moved, in deference to the church, to a piece of his father's property, on the shore at Great Harbour, where he added a kitchen and a London-born, Australian-raised wife whom he met on a sailing trip to Europe (to Greece and Italy) in the early '70s. The atmosphere at Foxy's has changed since the early, spontaneous days. Life is more complicated, and so is Foxy's—but the beachside spot is still *very* casual, sometimes with local calypso music, and occasionally with some simple food served at the tables on the beach. If a "way out" personality place appeals, cruise into the bay to see what's going on.

Foxy's seems to have sparked a quartet of simple spots, **Claude's Big Stop** on White Bay; **Harris Place** (near the *Bomba Charger* dock); **Abe's** at Little Harbour; and **Ira's,** where a fish dinner runs about $7 and the captain gets a welcoming drink (while you pay for yours, unless you are the captain).

■■■

PLACES WORTH FINDING are nature's best: coves, cays, and the Caribbean. There's nothing on land that's worth making the extra effort to get to, as far as I'm concerned. The **Baths of Virgin Gorda** have been too much talked about. They're great if you "discover" them on your own, but to make the Baths into a sightseeing excursion is to do them a great injustice. When you're on Virgin Gorda and in the mood for it, head here to wallow around the pools that have formed in grottoes created by the tumble of gigantic boulders. Otherwise, skip it—you won't have missed much, and you can use your spare time to follow your own whims, which is what the British Virgins are all about.

My idea of a place worth finding in this unique series of special spots is whatever I can reach by boat from the place I'm starting from, and that can be a cozy cove for a picnic lunch, another small inn on another small island, or the lively marinas at Road Town or at Virgin Gorda Yacht Harbour at North Sound, Virgin Gorda.

Even St. Thomas can be a place worth finding, if you sign on to go over in the morning on the *Bomba Charger,* or the *Native Son,* both ferry boats that run between Road Town or West End (both on Tortola), and Charlotte Amalie, St. Thomas, or between West End, Tortola, and St. Thomas. Be *sure* to check the schedule to find out if the boat you plan to take for return deposits you at the town you expect to reach—West End or Road Town. They're about 45 minutes' drive apart.

■■■

SPORTS are all wet—either on, in, or under the sea. The British Virgin Islands give you the most options for the best facilities for sailing, scuba diving, and certainly snorkeling. Even windsurfing, a late '70s option at the harbor in Road Town, Tortola, as well as Prospect Reef's enclosed lagoon northeast of town and at Bitter End on Virgin Gorda, is sweeping hardy souls across the seas with ever increasing enthusiasm. Sailfish, Sunfish, and other small boats sit on the sands at many shores (any shores that aren't so windblown that novice sailing is suicide).

Sailing on your own boat, either bare boat (you and your pals) or with skipper and crew, is best in this area. There's no place in the Caribbean that has a better cluster of small islands with powdery coves. The entire spectrum of British Virgins spreads out before you, if you start from St. Thomas to sail across the channel to St. John to work your way northeast (into the prevailing wind) from there. You can also set sail at Road Town, to take the prevailing winds for your first venture out of the harbor (after the intensive skipper's meeting that is part of the best charters). Boats are also available at the Virgin Gorda Yacht Harbour on Virgin Gorda.

The Moorings, Ginny and Charles Cary's venture operating out of their Mariner Inn at Wickham Cay II on the east shore of Road

Harbour is the best charter operation in the entire Caribbean, in my opinion. Charterers' briefings are professional, no-nonsense sessions, and boats are in top condition. The Carys' operation specializes in comfortable Custom 46s as part of a fleet of about 70 yachts including sloops and ketches, all fiberglass, all in top condition. All boats go in for check-up at the end of every cruise. If you have a problem on the high seas, you have the route to call—and have been advised of the spots where you're out of radio range. The Carys are pros. They sailed to this spot several years ago and continue to supervise their own operation here and in St. Lucia with conscientious daily attention. (U.S. contact for The Moorings, Ltd., is Box 50059, New Orleans, LA 70150.)

Caribbean Sailing Yachts, familiarly known as CSY, slipped into port a decade ago, from the original base at St. Thomas's east end. The boating complex at Baughers Bay gives you a couple of rooms for overnighting before and after cruising, plus a boat in the slip off the deck at your feet when you're ready to take to the high seas. 10 39-foot sloops, 22 34-foot sloops, and 30 44-foot cutters were listed as the fleet for this season. Started by a Tenafly, New Jersey, sailor/dentist, John van Ost, and now captained by son Bob, the fleet is part of a triple based operation that finds CSY Yachts cruising from ports in the Bay Islands off Honduras as well as into the Grenadines, usually on skippered charters from CSY port at St. Vincent. (The U.S. base is reached through Box 491, Tenafly, NJ 07670.)

Tortola Yacht Charters, acting as agents for several small boats and owning a few of its own Heritage 38s and Morgan 41s, specializes in special groups, often from U.S.-based yacht clubs, who chartered the fleet at a package price including air fare with a week on a boat. If you have a group that's interested, contact the office at 1 Hale Lane, Darien, CT 06820. (Check also at The Moorings and CSY to see how the rates compare.) TYC absorbed the Latitude Charter operation and moved its island base from Village Cay to Nanny Cay. Briefings have been, according to recent surveys, more casual than these seas (and most sailors) warrant.

Your land base will have details on all the daily charters, good for picnic and snorkel cruising, even for nonsailors. Among the ships that have set sail in seasons past, the *Galatea II,* a 35-foot motorsailor built in Finland in '72 has been one of the most dependable. For about $30 each for 4 people, you can enjoy open bar, full lunch, and a leisurely day, setting off from Prospect Reef Marina at Road Town. Captain Bill Draper, alias Santa Claus, was setting out from Prospect Reef when I last saw him, but you can find him on location by asking around—or in advance by writing to Box 240, Road Town, Tortola, B.V.I.

Tony and Jackie Snell set sail in their trimaran *Great Eagle,* usually moored at their Last Resort, on a cay off the northeast end of Beef Island and Tortola. Write Box 530, Long Look, Tortola, B.V.I., if you want to make your plans in advance. (Their day-sail rate is the usual $30 per person, lunch included). For other yachts that do (or might) go out, check at the Village Cay Marina where most of the captained yachts seem to base.

Scuba divers should head straight for *Bert Kilbride,* who with his newest Jaki, takes divers out to terrain he was among the first—if not *the* first in recent times—to explore. Divers can get full equipment, or you can bring your own and service it at the Virgin Gorda Yacht Harbour offices of *Dive BVI, Ltd.* There is new scuba enthusiasm at Peter Island Hotel off Road Town, Tortola, where *Kilbride's Underwater Tours* has a shop. *Aquatic Centre* has branches at The Moorings, Village Cay, and Prospect Reef, all in the orbit of Road Town. There are other firms, but these are ones I can vouch for—all professionals, all ethical, and all well equipped. (Rates will be standardized, restraint of trade or not.)

■■

TREASURES AND TRIFLES will not take you long to track down, unless you dive for (and find) sunken treasure. On the streets of Road Town, the few small shops with anything of interest for visitors center on Main Street, one road in from the newer Wickham's Cay Road, which lines the shore (on reclaimed land). **Bobbie's** usually yields something worth wearing, if you're in the market for expensive resort clothes. Her selection is not large, but given a little time you can have one of her styles made up in your chosen fabric. If you happen to hit a sale (June or fall), prices will be reasonable. Otherwise, I find them high for a "simple island frock" sewn by a local seamstress in a style you could do at home.

Flaxcraft and Handcraft has some interesting items next door, as long as you're in the neighborhood, and across the road, nearer the so-called Plaza, which is a wide cement slab with some planting between Main Street and the shore, find **Caribbean Handprints** and **Past and Presents.** The first-named has screened fabrics, in bright island colors and designs, in shirts, skirts, small-fry togs, hats, handbags, and an assortment of other items. All styles and clothes are Lilly-look-alikes, if you are in the market for that traditional Florida-Country Club class. P & P has an eclectic collection of old items, some called "antiques," but looking like they came from the attic of the owner or one of her friends. I haven't found much in here, but I always look.

Cockle Shop has the Tortola newspaper (which you can also pick up at the printing office across the road), some books about the islands, and a range of items including a small selection of china (commemorative plates), and place mats.

If you're in the market for a canvas bag, ask around to see if Pam Kinross is still in business. Some of her work was being carried at the **Sea Urchin,** in the group of shops below Fort Burt, but for items made to order (in the size and color you want), you'll have to talk directly to Pam.

Samarkand, one of a half dozen shops and a pub on the shore below Fort Burt Hotel, has some interesting handmade jewelry, expensive but innovative, using black coral and some other island bits with silver and sturdier stuff.

Inquire about two locally made products: BVI Native Seasoning with West Indian spices and a salt-in-the-sea source from sun-dried flats harvested at Salt Island ($1.50 for a 4-oz. shakerful), and Pusser's Rum (from British pronunciation of "purser's") which reportedly sells in the U.S. for $14.95 a fifth. Check at Ample Hamper and elsewhere for Mrs. Thomas's guava jelly. All three items (salt, rum, and jelly) make good gifts from the BVI.

On Virgin Gorda, the Yacht Harbour is the hub for most of the shops. Some shops started with Little Dix sponsorship, in the early days when it was all. In recent seasons, a separate clutch of bookstores, handcraft places, and clothes shops opened. Some of the merchandise is above average (and so is price), depending on what your shopping situation is at home. (If you are near a commercial city, you'll find the offerings paltry here.)

Liquor and perfumes are good, but not usually exceptional buys. The British Virgins do not claim "freeport" or "duty-free" shopping, although liquor prices are better bargains than you'll find at home (and at a few of the puffed-up priced Thomas shops). You'll do even better if you pass through the neighboring American Virgins so that you can take advantage of the special one-gallon allotment and the supermarket prices, in that place that made its name (and a fortune) on duty-free liquor, etc.

Cayman Islands

Cayman Islands Department of Tourism, P.O. Box 67, George Town, Grand Cayman, B.W.I.; 420 Lexington Ave., New York, NY 10017; 250 Catalonia Ave., Suite 604, Coral Gables, FL 33134; 333 N. Michigan Ave., Suite 1521, Chicago, IL 60601; 9999 Richmond Ave., Suite 131, Houston, TX 77042; 3440 Wilshire Blvd., Suite 1202, Los Angeles, CA 90010; 11 Adelaide St. W., Suite 406; Toronto, Ont., Canada M5H 1L9.

US $1 = CI $.80
Unless otherwise noted, $ refers to U.S. currency.

The sign said "open day and night," but the place wasn't. The pink stucco building wasn't hard to find, if you followed the West Bay Road, turned at the Esso Station, and stayed on the paved road as Alain had said. I had borrowed a friend's car to find Reynolds', because I heard they served the best Caymanian food on the island. I wanted to talk with Mrs. Reynolds about when I could come to try some—inconspicuously, before the "kids arrived about 12" as they do every weekend night.

"Mrs. Reynolds" turned out to be Mrs. Wright. She came smiling to the locked screen door when one of her children who had crept around the edge of the house went back to tell her I was there. Mrs. Wright does the cooking—and I could come as early as 6:30. She would have something cooked by then—probably some local fish—and then there would be chicken, and some vegetables the way only she can cook them. Her 16-year-old son Cleve had just won third out of 98 in a teenage island-wide running contest, the Annual Road Relay that the *Caymanian Compass* heralded as "the big athletic event of the year." It's a 24-mile relay, with 5 baton changes, and it started at 7 in the morning at Gun Bay. Cleve was first for his school.

Mrs. Wright was so proud that she sent her 4-year-old Joy, my announcer, out to the back room to bring out the trophy. It was beautiful—and Mrs. Wright didn't seem to mind that I had disturbed her when her door was locked and she obviously wasn't "open day and night."

On the car radio, as I drove on after making my reservation, they announced the birthday greetings—and the details about a village fair at the West Bay Community Center the next day. Life in the Cayman Islands is like many small towns, in spite of an impressive tourism and offshore banking overlay of sophistication. For most Caymanians, life is led in the shadow of a visitor community that is expected to number 200,000 by the time this year's figures are tallied. The local population of 16,600 on Grand Cayman (plus 1603 on Cayman Brac and 74 on Little Cayman) is vitally involved with the service industries, but day-to-day life goes on "as usual."

When you scuff in the powder along Seven Mile Beach, none of that seems to matter. Nothing matters . . . except that you get up early enough to be the first to find a sea star, a prize for being up before the shell collectors who parade down the beach in a hunt-and-peck order that is surpassed by the pace of the joggers. The joggers usually start later, but they finish first. It's a sort of tortoise-and-hare story, which seems appropriate on this island that began its recorded life as a source for turtles. So many of them used to wallow in the seas around the Caymans that ships heading back to Europe from settlements in Jamaica used to stop on the shores of Cayman Brac to pick up a supply for the crossing. This was in the earliest years; a record on June 26, 1655, notes that a ship headed to "the Kie of Manus to get some turtle for our sick people."

The name later became Kiemanus, and sometimes Caimanos, and by 1622, Caiman Isles—and still people came for the turtles. Today turtles take second place. They're being cultivated at the refinanced West Bay venture called Cayman Turtle Farm. Fishermen through the centuries captured the entire Cayman crop, and went farther afield, throughout the Caribbean and near the shores of Cuba, to return with turtles—and some say the mosquitoes that are the scourge of Cayman life.

But it's the beaches that bring people here today, and the tax haven status that makes offshore banking attractive. Both lures are the foundations on which the local economy is building.

■■■

POLITICAL PICTURE: It's easy to forget that the Caymans spent most of their history under the sheltering palms (and Parliamentary procedure) of Jamaica. It wasn't until Jamaica opted for independence, in 1962, that the Caymans had to choose their own future, and they appear to have chosen wisely, going about it quietly and well as a British Crown Colony. The Governor of the Cayman Islands is appointed by the Queen of England and is key member of the Legislative Assembly, comprised of 15 members with 12 elected by Caymanians.

Decision a few years ago to become an offshore banking center has resulted in a substantial investment by moneyed people, not only in the banks established in Grand Cayman, but also in building and other ventures. The Cayman Islands now claim to be the third largest offshore banking center in the world. There are no direct taxes on real estate or profits, although recent steps by the local government seem to lead toward some token building for Caymanian residents when developments are approved for visitors and prospective part-time residents (as with condominimus). Special incentives have been implemented for developing areas away from popular Seven Mile Beach on the main island, and for starting major projects on Cayman Brac and Little Cayman. There is no end in sight for the burgeoning development. The Caymans talk about having only 8 unemployed people, other than disabled and otherwise folk, out of the population of about 17,000.

With an economy booming, as this one is, the always stable political climate seems assured of continued success. This allows Caymanians to enjoy one of the highest standards of living in the Caribbean.

■■

CUSTOMS OF THE COUNTRY: The British links are firmly forged, although the Caymanian personality is distinctly its own. Life is "proper," pleasingly so; the swinging night life (or day life) known on neighboring Jamaica is a long way from these islands—even from Grand Cayman, where most of the hotels are located.

AUTHOR'S OBSERVATION: A modern custom worth considering if you like to join in local fun-and-frolic is the annual Pirate's Week, held during the last week in October. Parades, picnics, and pranks are all part of the fun, with costume parties obviously featuring pirate traditions. Check with the Department of Tourism, and make reservations as far ahead as possible (for airline and hotel space) at what is becoming a special island spectacular.

Local politicians make a fall ritual of discussing and deciding upon the opening hours for bars. Religious fervor is strong, and traditional enough to keep the lock on the doors on Sundays in some places. The solution as we go to press is to allow hotels, restaurants, and the airport lounge to be open from 1 p.m. to midnight on Sundays. Monday to Friday hours are 9 a.m. to 1 a.m., but only to midnight on Saturday. (Cayman Islands drinking and voting age is 18.)

Until 1972, the only people with Caymanian status were those with a Caymanian parent. Just being born here didn't count; your family had to have been here practically since Bodden or Ebanks, both of whom have been here "forever." (The Caymans' telephone book shows some 130 Ebankses and almost 100 Boddens, not to mention the towns and shops that carry the names.) Laws were modified in 1972 to allow foreigners to become Caymanian "by grant," if approved by the Caymanian Protection Board after they have been resident for at least 5 years. People who had been on the island for 5 years prior to the passing of the 1972 law could obtain Caymanian status by right, after they had applied to proper authorities.

Clocks run on Eastern Standard Time year round. East coast winter travelers who are on Eastern Daylight Time will find their watches an hour behind Cayman Islands time. Airline schedules are listed in local times.

Clothes are calculatedly casual. You won't see many of the sloppy hippie styles around Grand Cayman. Fishing and water sports attire is de rigueur during the days and salt in your hair is acceptable in the evenings. The most casual spots are those south of George Town and away from the Seven Mile Beach. Along the beach, guests at the high-priced hotels dress up in the traditional Caribbean style, complete with long skirts on ladies and even a few madras jackets on men. Neat, straight shirts with no tie are acceptable in many restaurants, but when you head to the Caribbean Club, the Swiss Inn, the Grand Old House, and a couple of the better places, don your best. (There are some good stores in town for resort clothes, but the selection is not extensive.)

Complete and compact information is supplied in the Cayman Islands Tourist Board's regularly updated "Rate Sheet and Fact Folder" and the "Holiday Guide." The local newssheet is the *Caymanian Compass,* published Tuesdays and Fridays and sold locally for CI$.25. For information about it, write Box 173, Grand Cayman. The *Cayman Times,* a slick weekly sheet, is CI$.25 from Box 686. Don't make a move without a subscription to intriguing, attractive, interesting *Nor'Wester Magazine,* Box 243, Grand Cayman. (Inquire about special Christmas gift rates for the best subscription price.) If you're contemplating investment, the *Cayman Islands Handbook* has most of what you'll need to know.

AUTHOR'S OBSERVATIONS: The Cayman Islands have been plagued in past seasons by pesky mosquitoes and other small nibblers known on other islands as "no see'ums." Since I am not a Caymanian year-round resident, I have to rely on the advice of my colleagues who are—and who assure me that the pincher-problem has been taken care of. My advice is to pack a proper portion of a bug repellent you find works for you; better safe than sorry. In support of my colleagues' comments, I will admit that, except after a quick rain shower on particularly muggy days (which are rare), the problem does seem to be under control—at least for the properties along regularly fogged and otherwise controlled West Bay Beach. If you are heading to Cayman Brac or Little Cayman, be prepared for mosquitoes.

MONEY MATTERS: The local currency is Caymanian dollars, and most signs are posted in that currency. Before you are fooled into thinking that food and other prices are low, note well that CI$1 equals US$1.25; the "lower" prices are not lower for you. United States dollars are accepted. If you want to change money, you will get the best rates from the taxi drivers.

AUTHOR'S OBSERVATION: The Cayman Islands economy is based on the banking business and on tourism, and tourism brings the bodies that help create the jobs. It seems to me that *everything* is geared to prying as many of your dollars from you as possible.

A Caymanian license to drive a car costs CI$2.40; your room tax per day on your hotel is 5%; departure tax at the airport is $4; taxis are expensive and most hotels charge extra for everything. Bar prices will vary, depending on what the management thinks the traffic will bear. Jamaican Red Stripe beer can run from $1 at a Caymanian place to $2.50 at the Grand Caymanian pool bar. All these extra tolls are extracted so politely and discreetly that it's hard to realize just how much you've paid until the final tally. Count on the extras to add up.

■■■

ARRIVAL: On Grand Cayman, the atmosphere at Owen Roberts Airport is tropical, with British efficiency. As you wait in line to go through one of the immigration lines, you can note that you need a license to sell goods in the Caymans (there's a poster so saying on an airport wall). And you should know that there are heavy penalties for bringing illegal drugs into the Caymans. You must have a return or continuing ticket, so the officials know you are not planning to be a drag on the community. When you have shown identification (passport is best), walk on and wait for your luggage. Taxis stand outside the airport entrance and from my experience are a cut above the taxis that hover around most Caribbean airport entrances. I've found reception warm, service pleasant, conversation enlightening—and the fee high—but somehow that seems acceptable when the service is willing.

Cayman Airways Limited is the local carrier, and as of December 1, 1977, locally owned. For ground services in Miami, the airline has its own staff manning an attractive and efficient check-in counter. (A comment seems in order for those of you who are not familiar with the jogging track that is the Miami Airport. Designed by someone who obviously seldom takes connecting flights, this airport is the world's worst, in my opinion, for getting from your arrival ramp to wherever you have to be next. Count on walking miles, and count on having to walk against the on-coming traffic, which has been worse than a major city metropolitan rush-hour when I've been plowing through this airport. If you can avoid Miami, do so.) CAL's application for additional services to Grand Cayman, approved in late '78, resulted in frequent (and popular) flights from Houston. Republic Airlines also flies to Grand Cayman daily from Miami, but check for additional services by the time you vacation. There are also charters.

Cayman Airways links Cayman Brac and Little Cayman to Grand Cayman. Through reservations can booked from your hometown. Red Carpet Airways flies from St. Petersburg through Grand Cayman to Cayman Brac several times weekly and sometimes flies from Tampa to Cayman Brac, where the Gerald Smith Airport runway was extended to take 727s and 737s in the season of '77–'78. Executive Air Services, a small charter service flying to Cayman Brac and Little Cayman, began operations February 1, 1978. Flight-seeing tours of Grand Cayman can be arranged, as can flights to Swan

Island, Jamaica, and Costa Rica. Find Skip
to discuss special plans.

Cayman Airways and Air Jamaica link King
man.

> **A**UTHOR'S OBSERVATION: Miami Airpo
> ing area that has proved ideal for my winter c   er
> luggage that did not need to vacation in the wa   ayman
> climate. The checkroom is near the Eastern Airlines com-
> plex at one end of the airport, and is an easy stop on the
> return trip if you are heading back to cold northern cli-
> mates.

■■■

TOURING TIPS: Since you can walk the entire length of West
Bay, otherwise known as Seven Mile Beach, either in the sand or
along the road, there's no pressure to rent a car unless you "must"
drive around the island. The local bus makes the run along the
beach-paralleling road, if your feet get tired.

Cico Car Rentals, with offices just outside the Grand Caymanian
Holiday Inn and at other convenient locations, will make arrangements for a rental car (at rates that hover above $30 per day, in-
cluding mileage). There are several other firms (Ace/Hertz, Budget, Coconut Car Rental, and National among them), but none of
them can arrange for your car to be delivered to the airport. The
local taxi association has that business all tied up. When you get
your car (probably after you check into your hotel), you can drive
around and can return the car to the airport. Rates are lower at
some firms during the summer, and except for peak season winter
months, shopping around for rates may pay off; in February and
March and at other peak times (Christmas holidays, for example)
you're lucky to get a car at any price—and rental firms make the
most of it. You'll need to invest $3, plus show your valid hometown
license, for a Caymanian driver's permit. Be prepared to drive on
the left, even when you're driving a U.S. car (with wheel on the
left).

Hondas can be rented from Caribbean Motors Ltd. Since Grand
Cayman is almost flat, the cycles and mopeds are OK if you don't
mind the heat. Mopeds are the least expensive, at about CI$15 per
day; the Sports 90 rents for about CI$20, and there are special
weekly rates that are more reasonable. You'll start with a full tank
of gas, and there's no extra charge for mileage.

AUTHOR'S OBSERVATION: Don't make a move without getting your copy of the *Tourist Weekly*, published by the Cayman Free Press and a fact-filled newssheet that will tell you the latest places to eat, shop, scuba dive, dance, etc.

▪▪

HOTELS ON GRAND CAYMAN: This island has no peer for offering quality accommodations on what I believe is the most attractive commercial beach in the Caribbean. I say commercial, because the hotels are here, but in a quiet, unobtrusive way—and there's nothing else that mars the scenery. Cayman Islands' officials appear to have taken more than one page (that of colonial status) from the successful resort book of Bermuda. All buildings are low-profile, set back from the beach, small in feeling if not in room count (although most are small in that also). No building can be taller than "a royal palm," which figures here to be 4 stories—tops. Even the Holiday Inn, which is choosing to use its first name (Grand Caymanian) as it gets older and wiser, is not your typical plastic package.

AUTHOR'S OBSERVATION: If you look through a handful of folders for hotels on Grand Cayman, the beach shown on 99% of them is the same beach—the l-o-n-g powdery ribbon that stretches along West Bay, and is known as "Seven Mile Beach" or "West Bay Beach." This is the beach that is pictured with nothing or a loving couple on it. That is the way it *can* be, but it probably won't be like that right in front of your hotel if you choose the multibodied beach at the Grand Caymanian Holiday Inn or a patch in front of Royal Palms and some of the other livelier hotels.

Of the almost 30 properties that string along Seven Mile Beach, at least half of them give you the option to cook (or be cooked for) at home. That's one way of keeping prices reasonable, and another way of getting you out and around. The hotels that stand at parade rest along the powdery strand of Seven Mile Beach are, from George Town heading north: Cocoplum, Cayman Sands, and Seagull, next door to Royal Palms. Then comes Coral Caymanian, the pink-and-elegant West Indian Club, Seascape, the Beach Club Colony, and the Caribbean Club. Pan Cayman House and Beachcomber are next, and after a gap of open space, there's the Grand Caymanian Holiday Inn (at the halfway point on the beach). Continuing north, you can walk to Galleon Beach with the new villas next door, then Surfside with some space for the public before you reach Harbour Heights, which nestles next to Coral Reef, White Sands Cottages, and Tarquynn Manor. Christopher Columbus and London House are next in the line-up. A short walk beyond Dulcal Cottages will bring you to Victoria House, Silver Sands, Dolphin Point, and Anchorage, and the end of the front line. Spanish Bay Reef is a nonwalkable distance farther north. Tortuga Club is about as far as you can get to the east end, and at least an hour from this area. Rum Point is beyond Cayman Kai at the midshore point along the north coast—and also about 45 minutes from George Town and airport and the newest developments (at Barkers, for example) can be down dry-and-dusty dirt roads, best traveled in a jeep. There's a 5% government tax on accommodations, and many places add a 10% to 15% service charge. Always ask, if it is not obvious.

Author's Awards for a classy, British/Caymanian style holiday with the old-time elegance preserved goes to West Indian Club, where your maid cooks your meals in your kitchen; and to Caribbean Club, which quietly carries on its luxury life with cuisine to match the clientele's demands.

✛ **Beach Club Colony** (Box 903, West Bay Beach, Grand Cayman, B.W.I.; 41 rooms) split off some of its rooms with a legal transaction in early '79, and added some newer nooks. Rooms are sectioned off as beachfront, oceanfront, and patio outlooks, with prices sliding down (but not far) from top rate "ocean" at about $100 per day for 2, no meals. Inquire about the "Slow Vacation" summer week-long holiday. Scuba and snorkel enthusiasts should head for the sports shack, beachside, where you can rent equipment, sign up for lessons, rent one of the pink-sail Sunfish to skim the seas, or sign on for the spaghetti supper cruise that heads out, weather willing. The screened-in dining area I found depressing on a warm sunny noontime when I wanted lunch near the beach, but that problem was solved later in the season when the beachside patio area started serving meals.

✛ **Caribbean Club** (Box 504, West Bay Beach, Grand Cayman, B.W.I; 18 villas), classiest of the lot, especially if you can cozy into

one of the 6 villas facing the sea, coddles its well-heeled guests—
who are paying $130 for 2, meals extra—for that 1-bedroom ocean-
front villa. If you don't mind being just off the beach (behind the
oceanfront villas) the rate will drop to $100 for 2, and if you choose
to stay here, you shouldn't be worrying about the $s. Caribbean
Club dining is in a class by itself, far above the usual island fare.
Inquire about winter "package" rates that give a slight break for 3-
night or 7-night stays.

✣ **Casa Bertmar** (Box 637, Grand Cayman, B.W.I.; 18 rooms) bets
its burgeoning success on the scuba interests of its owner, Kent Eldemire. This is a casual, sea-oriented enclave where guests are
included in a family-style atmosphere that allows for easy
conversation and comfortable clothes. Making the most of a Robinson Crusoe spirit that includes serious sensitivity to the sea, Casa
Bertmar is not for pampered folk who must have everything perfect.
This is for "real folks" who want to be surrounded by kindred spirits. Count on paying $85 to $90 for room for 2, with 2 meals daily
per person included. Threesomes will pay close to $100, but inquire
about special dive vacations where novices as well as pros can see
the special areas with the experts.

✣ **Cayman Diving Lodge** (Box 894, Grand Cayman, B.W.I.; 18
rooms) has a new lease on life. After decades as a legendary spot,
under "lock and key" of Bob Soto (who seldom used either lock or
key), the lodge was purchased by Erich Heindl and Gerry Hytha.
Their European backgrounds, and their affiliation with a Florida
firm that specializes in plans for vacationing Europeans on this side
of the Atlantic, assures a cosmopolitan climate for their refurbished
lodge. All rooms now have private bath, and—although the atmosphere is still casual, comfortable, and sea-oriented according to a
stage set by Bob Soto—there's a new dining room and bar, and a
complete revamp of all diving equipment (which now includes full
underwater photography equipment). A 6-night diving package
week starts at close to $300 (until December 15), and will be about
$450 for winter season. There are also 3-night diving holidays (with
2 meals daily and diving equipment), as well as one-night options.

✣ **Cayman Islander** (Box 509, Grand Cayman, B.W.I.; 43 rooms)
puts you within walking distance of (but not on) the beach, and
settles smart cost-conscious travelers who want new surroundings into rabbit-run units wrapped around a pool and courtyard.

Rates for 2, all meals extra, hover around $60 this winter, and those who nest here are next to Pagoda Restaurant and the movie theater and not far from a number of other good dining spots.

✣ **Cayman Kai** (Box 1112, North Side, Grand Cayman, B.W.I.; 26 apartments) claims isolation as an attribute. You're a good 45 minutes' drive from George Town and the airport, but everything you could want (except a lot of action) is right here. There's even a "Kaimissary" for you to stock up, but don't count on the latest cuts of filet. If you want them, bring some from home (hometown meat man can pack them from his cold storage; they'll survive very well until you get them into your Cayman Kai refrigerator). The single-story units (condominiums all) are like rickrack on the shore, with the ones closest to the beach the best for my vacationing $. Brace yourself for the sand flies, the scourge of all beachfront in the Caymans at sunset and other times. Your unit will be screened, but the pesky things get through sometimes. Come prepared with your favorite gnat spray. The main building holds the gathering area, fronted by a pool. The Kai Dive Shop provides the full range of water sports facilities (scuba lessons, dives, snorkeling, etc.). There are 26 sea lodges, some with porches and all with Costa Rican hammocks on the porch and kitchen facilities so you can be completely independent. The units with a living room in the middle are ideal for 2 couples, but the 20 villas, including the beach houses, are the best bet at $160 in winter for a 2-bedroom, 2-bath unit (no meals). During recent summer seasons, honeymooners and scuba divers (who can get all equipment at the Dive Shop for exploring some 2 dozen sites) have been able to take advantage of good-value package rates for 7 nights and 3 nights. Tennis courts were added to the lure of the 1.5-mile beach during the '76–'77 season. Find Gene De Marco if you have any questions when you get here.

✣ **Coral Caymanian** (Box 1093, West Bay Beach, Grand Cayman, B.W.I.; 18 rooms) offers a good buy if you are *not at all fussy* and want to be at the shoreline. Sometimes referred to as "the little brother" of the Royal Palms, oceanfront room rates here hover near $75 for 2 in winter, standards lower, efficiencies higher. Self-sufficient types who border on being beachcombers may find life here likable.

✣ **Galleon Beach** (Box 71, West Bay Beach, Grand Cayman, B.W.I.; 33 rooms) has been scrubbed and painted, with more than $400,-

ooo lavished on its premises. It stretches out beachside, just north of the Grand Caymanian Holiday Inn, with tennis courts, lighted for night play, between the 2 hotels. Beg (and pay the price for) one of the odd-numbered rooms in the 500 or 600 series if you want to be sure of sound surroundings. They face the beach, with 600s upstairs. The alternatives face the road and a building, which is no view at all. Rates range from $65 to $105 for 2, with all meals extra. You have a choice of spending your dollars at the *Man o' War* room (seafood) or cooking your own steak (paying dearly for the privilege) at *Cap'n Morgan's Steak Galley*. This is one of the first places to stay on Grand Cayman, and it, once again, had a "new" manager last season. Hopefully Handel Wittacher will be around when you get there.

✠ **Grand Caymanian Holiday Inn** (Box 904, Grand Cayman, B.W.I.; 210 rooms) has had extensive refurbishing, and more rooms added, for a burgeoning vacation business. This place has a loose link with the international Holiday Inn clan. Count on the instant reservations network, where your confirmation is as far away as your telephone, and on the matches, menus, ice buckets, and soap, but don't count on the finger-snapping service and the plastic modernities familiar to the big-time mainland operations. The Humphreys from Memphis, Tennessee, own this house. Marc Redt came in as manager in early '79, and he's the man to find if you have any problems.

You won't find the big plastic sign or the standard trappings. You will find some lively groups having a good time. The Grand Caymanian gives its guests the options of walking miles to left or right on the beach, where the hotel sits at the midpoint. Bob Soto's Diving Shop takes care of the water sports; a snack shop takes care of the poolside hamburgers and other grilled specialties, plus salads and the like—at prices that are more than you think they are (they're quoted in CI$). There's a thatch-fringed bar on an "island" reached by bridges in the middle of the pool, and a beach-level dining room where breakfast and indoor lunch are served. Elegant dinners, with a menu that was more impressive than the food when I dined, are served in *Chez Jacques*, island-renowned for gourmet meals. The action hub for local folk and the young at heart from here and far is the *Wreck of the Ten Sails* bar and disco, where Barefoot and his band hold forth in enthusiatic country-western-with-a-calypso-beat style. As dark a pocket as you'll find in any U.S. city, it pulsates and pounds with island tempos, limbo dances, and an alternating live and record show. (No cover for GCHI guests.)

In addition to beach, pool, shuffleboard, and 4 night-lighted tennis courts, the hotel is home for a branch of *CICO* car rentals (where you can also sign up for an oriental massage by calling a number posted on the wall). The biggest and brassiest of the Caymanian hotels also has the most action. And for that you pay from $84 to $104 for 2 for an oceanfront room (worth the extra if you thrive on sea view); standard rooms start at $88 for 2, all meals extra (add about $22 per person for 2 meals daily). Inquire for special scuba, tennis, and family plans that give better value.

Rooms follow the Holiday Inn pattern for size, shape, and facilities, but the wear and tear which was being corrected while I was in residence is typically Caribbean. In the lobby, you will find a handful of shops, a real estate office, and helpful staff behind the front desk.

✣ **Harbour Heights** (Box 688, West Bay Beach, Grand Cayman, B.W.I; 45 units) is one of the bigger complexes on West Bay, clearly seen from quite a distance on any sand-scuffing stroll. The 3 sections are linked to L-shape, facing the beach. The 2-bedroom, 2-bath units would be easy to call home, and the price may be right if you have a couple of friends to divide the $120 per day. (Maid service is included, and the rate drops to almost half in summer.) Department store summertime modern decorates the rooms, but you have the option to step off the carpet and onto your small balcony to look out to sea.

✣ **Royal Palms** (Box 490, West Bay Beach, Grand Cayman, B.W.I; 62 rooms plus 42 suites) grows at the George Town (south) end of the strand; some of the palms are acceptable, others still suffer from the sea breeze. Rooms that "U" around the pool can be hot (even though air-conditioned) and noisy; the suites are in a separate and new building, originally built as condominiums and most of them sold that way. Rates for the regular rooms range from $74 to $104 this winter, with one-bedroom apartments at $96, no meals. They are "subject to a surcharge" of $15 per day over Christmas holidays, presumably because demand is so great that management can squeeze more out of those who pay what sounds to me like "key money" to get a room. Bruce Copland, who had been the property's manager since 1975, moved up to a development post for the parent company in early '79, and the present manager Brian Shiels, spends time taking care of guests' needs (and staff and service problems). Steady breezes, sun, and sea-oriented guests mean a casual atmosphere at this spot. Rooms in the original buildings have a tendency to look well worn; sea breezes take their toll on painted cement walls and halls. The comfortable pub bar in the main building (with restaurant and check-in) draws the business folk who choose this place for its proximity to town and its recreation facilities. Shops on premises stock the larders for the suites' efficiencies, and the beachside small bar mingles guests and residents, taxi drivers included. Families (and small children) love the pool; the beach belongs to all. F.L.A.G. sets up your scuba and other watersports.

✢ **Spanish Bay Reef Diving Resort** (Box 800, Spanish Bay, Grand Cayman, B.W.I.; 27 rooms), one of the Cayman's top diving resorts until 1980 when it went into receivership, was sold at a precedent-setting auction in early '81, for a record $950,000. The buyer, APCO, is a Cayman-registered company whose principles are from Utah. Plans for the property have not been announced as we go to press, but continuation as a diving resort under the new name of Bay Reef is inevitable for this place. It's only 5-minutes by boat from one of the Cayman's top attractions for divers, the North Wall. Perched at the northwestern tip of the island, Bay Reef has attractive facilities. Coral stone and wood have been mixed-and-matched to create a congregating area; dining room with outdoor terrace, director's chairs of blue canvas and wood, and a huge, modern, efficient kitchen are at lower level, which you reach by curling down the circular stairs if you've entered at reception level, or by walking in through the terrace if you approach on the waterside. On the reception level, there's a bar area. Rooms are comfortably casual: wood walls, modern bathrooms, high ceilings with overhead fans. Rooms 5, 6, 7, and 8 are close enough to the sea for you to hear the surf pound through the night. There's a free-form pool, but no beach. You're on the rocks here, with some of the Cayman Islands' most interesting reefs not far offshore.

✢ **Sunset House** (Box 479, George Town, Grand Cayman, B.W.I.; 38 rooms) welcomes beachcombers of all ages to its congenial seaside hub just a short walk south of town. Scuba centers here, in the minds of many who have known Hebe Connors since she set up for guests in 1958. (The Briggses are her son and daughter-in-law.) The $190,000 spent on adding rooms and sprucing the place up makes it look better than ever. If "casual" is what you come south for, head toward the sea behind the blue-fronted West Indian wooden house that is the reception area and pull up a stool at "My

Bar." Smart and price-wise folk interested in long-term rental have found this place, where winter tariff gives you an efficiency for a reasonable $65 for 2; an apartment will run about $100 for 2 and a straight (and simple) room comes with 2 meals daily for $90 to $100. Air conditioners in all rooms; you'll see why. Some have "no" outlook (or air circulation). Investigate the special summer dive package rates that give you a week for about $400 per person, 2 sharing a room.

✦ **Tortuga Club** (Box 496, East End, Grand Cayman, B.W.I.; 14 rooms) has taken some time to settle in with new owners. The time-tested staff that tutored with former owner Suzy Bergstrom manages to keep things running, and Frank Connolly, a long-time member of the Tortuga "family," takes care of the day-to-day operation. The tennis court sees some action, but most activity is sea-centered, with dive master O. J. Holden setting the style. Santa Cruz Investments Co. of California took the place in tow in mid-'77 after purchase from Eric and Suzy Bergstrom, who had built it from scratch and called it home for 15 years. Roads for the 45-minute drive from George Town and/or the airport are better than they used to be, but it's still a long poke from intown activities. When you're here, it's the sea that beckons, and when you're done with that, chances are you'll get strung up in one of the hammocks or work your way into the conversation at the bar. Motel-style rooms stretch out along the shore, and while there's nothing lavish, the twin-bedded nooks are comfortable, sea-oriented, and stocked with instant coffee or tea to brew and sip at whim. Ask about special scuba and water sports package summer rates that include dives and equipment with a rate that hovers around $120 for 2 daily, 2 meals per day per person included. Special rates also for 5–12-year-olds for scuba and water sports as well as overnighting. Your winter rate will reach about $115 to $130 for 2 this season, with breakfasts and dinners daily. Tortuga Beach Villas, 23 2-bedroom units, are planned for use sometime in 1982.

■■

HOUSEKEEPING HOLIDAYS are popular with more than half the visitors to the Cayman Islands. Once you decide whether you want rustic, beach-oriented surroundings or congenial, clublike camaraderie, the decision is only half made. There are countless places (some included when I've commented on hotels because management is comparable to what's expected at hotels), most of them along Seven Mile Beach but some scattered around the other shores and villages of Grand Cayman, as well as a few on Cayman Brac and Little Cayman.

There's no longer any need to lug a lot of home-bought foods with you when you head to Grand Cayman, as recommended in previous editions. New food operations and better shipping procedures find supermarket shelves full most of the time, and good fish and casseroles can be bought from local folk. Prices are still sky-high (and getting higher as they are everywhere), but at least the merchandise is available. If you have some favorite items, bringing them is not a bad idea, but you won't have to go hungry without them. The *Red Rabbit,* at the Red Bay Plaza, can make up nibbles for parties, and has cabinets full of spectacular delicatessen items (including a lot of European imports in tins). Staples can be stocked from *Cayman Foods* on the Bodden Town road outside of George Town. For turtle meat and other delicacies (including steaks), try *Jacques Scott. Kentucky Fried Chicken* at the Merren Shopping Center on North Church Street is open until 10 p.m. Sunday through Thursday, and until midnight on Friday and Saturday, so you won't have to starve even if you decide not to splurge at one of the restaurants. *Macdonalds* is a place for hamburgers and snacks at Kirk Plaza in George Town. Commissaries at some of the condominium/apartment complexes take care of basics, a fact that is especially important if you've selected one of the places that is away from the mainstream Seven Mile Beach area.

AUTHOR'S OBSERVATION: Family business is big business for the Caymans. Borrowing a page from Bermuda, and now worth a book of its own, Grand Cayman offers "wholesome" beachside pleasures perfect for all ages, at all seasons. Summer rates are ideal for families; inquire about special family plans that many places offer.

✛ **Christopher Columbus** (Box 1091, West Bay Beach, Grand Cayman, B.W.I.; 25 apts.) is more than the Caribbean's first tourist. As Joe and Judy Hugget know, Christopher Columbus is also a $2-million-plus investment on a long sandy strand that is Grand Cayman's tourist playpen. The cement slab that cups the "largest pool on the island" sits between you and that famous beach, but it will take a mere couple of minutes to walk into the sea for your morning swim. The 3-story units stretch out so that most rooms have sea (and pool) view. Although all apartments are for sale as condominiums, you may be able to call one of them home if your schedule slides into the away-from-the-island time of the owners. Most luxurious set-up is the penthouse, for which you'll pay $165 per day this winter (but you can split that for 6 people). A regular 3-bedroom apartment (19 of them) rents for $145 and can hold 6 friendly people in comfort; the 10 2-bedroom units rent for $105, depending on the size and the view. Summer rates will settle at little more than half the winter tallies.

✤ **Cayman Sands Village** (Box 307, West Bay, Grand Cayman, B.W.I.; 13 villas) percolates at the sandy shore, not far from George Town. (You can easily walk into town.) When Valma Hew took over as manager, she brought the expertise of a Caymanian native to her post. She's one of the best sources for information about island food and some of the less-touted local events. Stretching along the sand and back from the shore near the Royal Palms, Cayman Sands is "distinctive" with its dunce-cap roofs, lined up like a class of errant children. Each of the villas has 2 separate bedrooms (no air conditioning) with private bath, plus living room and full kitchen. (One bedroom has double bed; one twins.) Ideal for families, or 2 understanding couples, the rate for 2 will be close to $100 this winter.

✤ **Coral Bay Village** (Box 1535, Spotts Bay, Grand Cayman, B.W.I.; 21 apts.) was wise enough to settle at the south shore, away from the band of development that is sending sun-worshipers onto Seven Mile Beach. With its own strand of powdery sand just outside the door, Coral Bay gives its guests simple-but-adequate accommodations in units built in the past couple of years (with some new for this season). The 2-story structures offer top-floor residents a better view, but ground-floor guests can walk straight out to sea. Each has 2 bedrooms, bath, and full kitchen. Rates are reasonable at $150 for 4 people, with maid/cook included. You'll want a car for mobility.

✤ **Lime Tree Bay** (Box 1557, Grand Cayman, B.W.I.; 43 apartments) is the governor's neighbor. (He has the beachfront property.) You turn inland and go through the gates on West Bay road to an expansive, tasteful development that offers one of the best holidays around. The white stucco units with their Mediterranean-style "brick" tile roofs are not just another condominium setup. This place has gone all out to provide the best, and does it creditably well, even in its fledgling seasons. The clubhouse, the conversa-

tional core for the development, is a low, houselike structure near
the pool—with sauna, card room, laundry room and a proclivity to
be let for private parties by members who have more friends than
they can fit into their studio, 1-bedroom, 2-bedroom, or townhouse
apartments. All places are fully furnished, usually by the owners
and often extremely elegantly, with an iron gate enclosing your
patio for privacy but not destruction of view, if you're not on the
second level. Other accoutrements include 2 night-lighted tennis
courts, putting green, shuffleboard, and boat dock for entrance into
the lagoon and eventual setting out to sea. The quality is much
higher than the prices. The Townhouse is tops at $170 per day, but
4 can comfortably call this home; studios are a modest $70 for 2.
Maid service is part of your price; food is not. Seven Mile Beach is
across the road.

✣ **London House** (Box 1356, West Bay Beach, Grand Cayman,
B.W.I.; 20 apts.) leaped into the season of '79 in time to scoop up
enough business to give it a season of repeat visitors by the second
year of business. An integral part of the personality of this place is
the long-and-lovely band of sand that stretches along the front of
the property all the way down to the outskirts of George Town, a
good span for joggers. The new, sea-view apartments are efficiently
equipped with full kitchen facilities, plus living room with dining
area and comfortable bedrooms. Balconies and patios (depending
on whether you're on the first or second floor) have a view over the
freshwater pool and sea. Ask for a room away from the pool if you're
bothered by other people's exuberance. Plans for making London
House a family place have been helped along with beach parties
and other activities when the complement of guests warrants as
well as with special summer family plan rates. If you're thinking
about this spot for a honeymoon, be sure to ask about the special
candlelight dinner, included in some of the package plans, at one of
the best local restaurants. The 2-bedroom apartments (16 of them)
can easily handle a family, but reserve early for the one-bedroom
units. There are only 3, and they go fast in season. Rates are $85 for
2 in summer ($10 each additional person) per day, with a limit of 4
in the one-bedroom and 6 in the 2-bedroom units. Winter rates are
planned for an awesome $195 to $215 for 2, reflecting the popularity of a well-run place. (Management knows better than anyone on
the island, the combination of tenacity, patience, and push that is
essential for running a "relaxed" resort on this tropical retreat.)

✢ **Pan-Cayman House** (Box 440, West Bay Beach, Grand Cayman, B.W.I.; 10 apartments) places high priority on giving people peace and quiet, with action options only a few feet away along the length of Seven Mile Beach. Separated from the Caribbean Club by Turtle Run, a palatial private home discreetly camouflaged by branches from beachside trees that bend to the white sand, Pan-Cayman House has its own homey atmosphere distilled in more than 10 years of hospitality by the Eberhardts (Bill and Lorraine). All rooms, upstairs or sand level, have a sea view—and if you want to be able to walk from your living room out to the sea with no steps up or down, request the ground level and brace yourself for footfall overhead. Furnishings are geared to simple living, with nothing that will be ruined if you sit around in your bathing suit. (Management advised me that too many of you who read this thought I meant *wet* bathing suits. I didn't; please don't—but you certainly can wallow around your place in your bathing suit—dry.) Count on your casual Caribbean surroundings to be very comfortable (not beachcomber "casual"), and the modern kitchen equipment to work (unless the island's power supply is erratic, in which case you will be in the same plight as everyone in town). A couple of thatched bohios perk from the sand to provide some shade, much-needed after an hour or two or sunning. Winter crowd usually includes some of the owners, but you're welcome to pay the $145 for 2 to join them if there's space. The 3-bedroom units, suitable for sleeping 6, are about $190, everything extra except maid service. If you want to vacation in September or October, investigate the special rate that lets 2 pay about $70, and 3 or 4 pay $80, for a 2-bedroom apartment. Good deal!

✢ **Seagull** (Box 1349, West Bay Beach, Cayman Islands, B.W.I.; 32 apts.) landed on this shore in late '79, when the first 12 units (each with 1 bedroom, bath, and kitchen) opened up on a wedge of land between Royal Palms and Cayman Sands. George Town is an easy walk in one direction, and all of Seven Mile Beach stretches north so that early mornings jogs or leisurely strolls can be some of your entertainment options. (Royal Palms' nightlife is right next door if you want hotel entertainment.) Rentals for 2 figure to about $110 per day this winter, and about half that up until November 30.

✢ **Seascape** (Box 170, West Bay Beach, Cayman Islands, B.W.I.; 8 villas) offers one of the best bets on the beach. Each of the villas is folded into the foliage between West Indian Club and Beach Club Colony, with the latter property a sort-of-sister in the earlier days. Seascape became an entity unto itself a couple of seasons ago, but is so closely mingled with some of the Beach Club Colony rooms that only the paint job distinguishes one from the other. Many of the units are on long-term rental so inquire about short-term (one week) rates if this place appeals.

✣ **Silver Sands** (Box 502, West Bay Beach; Grand Cayman, B.W.I.; 36 apts.) opened with 6 apartments ready and the rest rising from the sands just beyond Victoria House at the north end of Seven Mile Beach, just before the sign announcing the small West Bay Village, and the town cemetery. There's a freshwater pool for dunking if you don't fancy the miles of Caribbean sea that spread out before you across the sands; tennis courts are the only on-premises entertainment, other than conversation with guests. Plan on paying in the $120 range for 2 in a 2-bedroom unit; the rate with nothing included jumps to $155 if you are 3 or 4, and the 3-bedroom apartments suitable for families with 6 are $195.

✣ **Tarquynn Manor** (Box 1362, West Bay Beach, Grand Cayman; 20 units) is "exhibit A" of what I mean when I talk about cutting inns to the Bermuda pattern. Opened for business in 1977, the 20 units that greeted the first guests were crisp, colorful, and furnished with quality appliances in the kitchen. The 2-bedroom units have a living-room area, terrace that looks to sea, and a coveted privacy. (One bedroom is seaside, the other inland.) Canadian developer Don Butler planned this place, with a new-for-the-Caymans at that time plan of having apartments look out to the sea and their own view, with the "back door" facing the center courtyard. To settle in here, you'll be paying about $99 to $186 this winter, with summer rates almost $30 less, everything extra. All units are air-conditioned, most have twin beds in one bedroom and queen- or king-size in the other. These comfortable nooks are all privately owned on the condominium concept.

✣ **Victoria House** (Box 636, West Bay Beach, Grand Cayman, B.W.I.; 25 units) air-conditioned its apartments and lures some folks south with good-value long-term rentals during summer months. Furnishings are modern, nothing spectacular but certainly new, colorful, and more than adequate, and your fully electric kitchen has refrigerator and freezer. Studios and 1-bedroom units are perfect for 2, and perhaps for 3; but if you're 4 or more, search out a 2-bedroom unit or the penthouse rooms, in spite of the climb. The front office (which is on the left side as you face the property) is a fountain of information, with a bulletin board that posts the best and newest eating places (with their menus and often a guest comment or two). Tennis courts are on the roadside, and in almost constant use. When you're here, you're at the north end of Seven Mile Beach, within bicycling distance of the village of West Bay and a long sandy stroll of 4 miles or more to the hotels near George Town. (Good winter value at $60 for 2 in a studio, when the penthouse rents for $105 for 4; extra person charge is $8; better rates for longer stays.)

✣ **West Indian Club** (Box 703, West Bay Beach, Grand Cayman, B.W.I.; 9 units) leads my list of places to stay on Grand Cayman, if you want elegant surroundings with the convenience of your own maid and apartment. Royal palms stand at parade rest, lining the drive to the entrance of the pseudo-plantation-style pink building. The whole "stage set" is almost absurd when you realize that only 9 apartments are here, but the atmosphere that Austrian Rudi Selzer and his wife (and the property's manager) Joanne maintain inside is immediately reassuring. It's lovely—and nothing has been forgotten by the owners, whose apartment you will use (at a fee) in their absence. You have to stay at least a week, which won't seem nearly long enough when you settle in. The one-bedroom apartments run $150 per day, the 2-bedroom units are about $200, and the small efficiency (which is very pleasant) is $95. WIC runs its high season on its own terms with almost always a full house, and no stay less than 7 nights. There's a thatched bohio on the beach for sun shelter, with wood and plank seats for guest-gathering and one hammock in the middle. The whole expanse of Seven Mile Beach awaits (Royal Palms is one frog leap to the south).

✣ **Windsor House Apartment** (Box 487, George Town, Grand Cayman, B.W.I.; a 2-bedroom apartment for 4) is an ideal opportunity to see what Caymanian life is like. The owners live in the main house, connected to the 2-bedroom apartment, but you're on your own, with your own linen, cutlery, kitchen, and completely furnished flat. On the shore (no beach), you can walk into George Town to pick up the West Bay bus for any span of sand on spectacular Seven Mile Beach. Mr. and Mrs. Bernard St. Aubyn have no children, so they ask that you leave yours at home when you rent their apartment (for $25 daily in summer, $30 in winter). Best buy, if it sounds like your kind of place.

✚ **Villas of Galleon Beach,** (Box 71, West Bay Beach, Grand Cayman, B.W.I.; 74 units), elegant, expensive, and new to the '79 season, are slanted to offer maximum sea view, and to break up the marching order along the beach. The angular architecture is a welcome break, and so are the 30 one- and 2-bedroom suites that make up this place. If your idea of a holiday in the sun doesn't include workmen on premises with pick, shovel, and plastering tools, check on the status of the new units that are to be ready for spring of '80. Caymanian Carolyn Whittaker is resident manager, and she can tell you about all the facilities of the Galleon Beach Hotel, which are yours to use as resident at the villas. There's a dive shop nestled near the Villas at the beach, and other facilities a sandy stroll away. Count on paying about $150 for 2 for a one-bedroom villa and $225 for 4 to share the 2-bedroom villas this winter. (Summer rates, until December 15 and as a guide for summer of '81, are $105 for 2 in the one-bedroom unit; $125 for 4 in the 2.)

■■

RESTAURANTS have never been the main reason for coming to the Cayman Islands. If your palate is tuned to the gourmet cuisine of France, you'll find what's here is strictly subsistence level—and expensive for that. However, if your taste test includes visual as well as victuals, there's something to be said for about a half-dozen places. Reservations are advisable if you are counting on dining at a specific hour at places like Grand Old House, the Swiss Inn, Lobster Pot, Yorkshire Pudding, and Reynolds. Most restaurants add a 15% gratuity; you are not expected to do more.

AUTHOR'S AWARDS go to the Grand Old House, for its atmosphere more than for the food (which is good, but expensive) and to Mrs. Wright at Reynolds who serves the best island meal in some of the pleasantest simple surroundings (see below).

Almond Tree, under a heavy thatch roof near George Town at the south end of West Bay, is unusual. Lunches, and dinners are served with arts and crafts, and piña coladas are the specialty. This one makes up in enthusiasm of Lenny and Kathleen Loyd what it may lack in culinary expertise. The south seas atmosphere appeals to the barefoot and boating types. Your dinner, with a choice of meat, fish, and chicken entrees, will cost only $9, which is modest for this much food on this island. On Friday nights, entertainment is an underwater slide show.

Capt'n Morgan's has its following of folk who are content to pay $12 and up to cook their own steak, and munch it with warm garlic bread and a salad, at the Galleon Beach Hotel. Dinners offered daily, with the option to step next door to hear the latest calypsos (even though the Barefoot Man who made the name for this place left for the Grand Caymanian Holiday Inn).

Caruso's, at the inland end of Coconut Place shopping block, across from West Indian Club, Royal Palms, etc., serves moderately priced Italian food (lasagna, veal parmigiana, ravioli, etc.) with "French bread," salad, and beverage for $4! A miracle, even when you have to put up with drab surroundings. (They've done the best they could with the air-conditioned cement box they rented for the restaurant.) Open for lunch and dinner daily except Tuesday, Caruso's offers one of the best values if you want filling food. A carafe of wine costs $2.

Chez Jacques, at the Grand Caymanian HI, gets rave notices from some folk who are known to know and like good food, well served. Famed French offerings appear with island adaptations, but for a "big night out," this may be a place to try.

Grand Old House has an ideal setting, south of George Town. It was built as the Petra Plantation Great House. Now its porches are speckled with tables for those who want to dine with the sea breezes (inside rooms are also set up). Waitresses are dressed "plantation style," and are barefoot, but you are expected to wear shoes—and your good-to-best clothes. The place *is* informal, but in controlled Caymanian style—not sloppy-casual. The food? Well, when they say "island specialties," they mean fish (that often does not come from the island, but from Florida, etc.). The "foreign cuisine" leaves Phyllis and Tim Kelly with a long list of possibilities—including steak, chicken, and the usual. The surroundings are lovely, and it's worth making a reservation (closed Sun; music on Mon, Wed, & Sat in season). You're not encouraged to arrive for cocktails only, but you can have drinks—and wine (expensive)—with your meals.

Lighthouse, past Bodden Town in Breakers (and a place for on a day you've rented a car), serves interesting seafood specialties in way-out surroundings. Call Peggy Burgos (originally from Canada) if you want to find out what's special—and that can included special dinners on holidays. Reservations are essential for dinnertime; you can take a chance for lunch.

Lobster Pot acquired new owners to pull it out of the doldrums in the '77-'78 season. The location, upstairs and seaside near Bob Soto's scuba center, sets the tone—which is not fancy, but is pricey for the seafood meals, simply served. The food IS good, if you like local fish and lobster; my salad was nothing special (since the ingredients are all imported—except for an occasional local tomato—the result of a hydroponic farming experiment). Mervin and Clemens oversee this operation. For casual surroundings seaside, try it.

Pagoda, at the fringe of George Town and the start of Seven Mile Beach (south end), is great for fried won ton and other Chinese specials.

Ports-of-Call put its reputation on the lobster (good and expensive), but those in the know settle for the fish-and-chips which is the best buy at about $5. Purchase of this place, in early '81, by a group of long-time (and enthusiastic) Caymanian residents with other involvements in the islands' tourism plan, assures a fun-filled place. Count on some entertainment—and at least a $10 tab.

Reynolds, just up the street when you turn off the main road at the gas station, is THE place for the local kids on Friday and Saturday nights, when they arrive at 12 P.M. or later, after they've been to the movies or whatever. The rest of us might be happier arriving about 8, but it's a good idea to stop by early in the day to talk with Mrs. Wright about what she's serving and what time you should arrive. This one is simple, but you'll get good local food—with hot-sauce bottles on the formica table, and a breeze blowing through the room.

Swiss Inn, on the inland side of the road in the former Inter-Bank building, is EXPENSIVE, and I think too much so for what's offered. However, it is the only Swiss-style service in the Caymans—and that is expensive even in Switzerland. The Swiss inn feeling has to come from the stucco walls, studded with dark wood beams, and the air-conditioning that makes the "weather" about the same as Switzerland in winter. For a dressy evening, with as close as the island offers to gourmet food, try this—but bring a sweater, and a lot of money ($25 per person barely covers the basics).

Mrs. Borden's Pizza Hut (open M-Sat 4 p.m.-12 p.m.; Sun 4 p.m.-10 p.m.) was recommended to me as one of the great places to eat. Got the picture? The food *is* good—if you like pizzas—and I was surprised to find just how good it did taste after a day in the sun.

You'll need a car to get here; it's north of West Bay, on the east side near North Sound, at Batabano.

Yorkshire Pudding, within easy distance of the Seven Mile Beach hotels (it's on the inland side of the road), takes a page from London's best, and gives diners roast beef, lamb, and other British (and imported) staples. About 85 folks fill the publike place at height of season (reservations are advised), and ask manager David Moir for recommendations about the evening's best. Plan to pay $25 per person to enjoy this place.

So limited are your choices for special dining on the Caymans that I'm compelled to mention **Kentucky Fried Chicken,** which you can take across the street to Seven Mile Beach to munch (open M-Sat 11 a.m. to midnight; Sun noon-10 p.m.). The **Silver Sands Cafe** for ice cream and hefty sandwiches (open 9 a.m.-10 p.m.); and the **19th Hole,** connected to an 18-hole miniature golf course, for snacks including chicken, hamburgers, and pizza, plus beer. All are across the road from the hotels that line West Bay/Seven Mile Beach, about midway on the coast.

Best bets for mingling with the local folk in events that are off the "typical tourist" routes are **Pedro's Castle** (you'll need a car, or a lot of money and an understanding taxi driver), for the Saturday afternoon buffet and dancing, and **Galleon Beach**'s barbecue on Sunday afternoons.

Hotels with special mealtime offerings worth noting are include the **Tortuga Club,** where the menu changes, but where the atmosphere is dependably island outpost. It's a 45-minute drive from George Town.

■■

PLACES WORTH FINDING include the 325 wrecks that are submerged in the seas, festering with coral and embellished with colorful fish. The underwater sights off the North Wall, which is the result of a ridge of Cuba's Sierra Maestra some 200 miles away, make the seas off the northwestern shore fascinating when they're calm enough for scuba. The reefs at West Bay are almost always ideal (although not as exciting, according to some experts). Little Drop-Off, a relatively easy swim about 100 yards from shore, hides a submerged schooner, and trims its gnarled stern with purple sea fans, tube sponges, coral, and fish. Off George Town, the wreck of the 375-foot *Balboa* is "buried" in about 35 feet of water, the *Oro Verde,* sunk with ceremony in spring '80, has its collection of special fish, and although Kent Eldemire of Casa Bertmar is one of several who bemoans the ravages of oil tanker anchors as they scrape (and ruin) the sea floor, there's still a lot worth seeing.

> **A**UTHOR'S OBSERVATION: Strict diving regulations—and controls on the motorboats and big ships that anchor around here—are essential. The burgeoning tourism, if uncontrolled, will eventually deplete the natural resources that are the island's only real attraction.

Land attractions are led by **Seven Mile Beach,** the long strand of sand I keep talking about. In my opinion, the only other place worth finding is primarily of interest to ecologists and others fascinated with the life history of the green turtle. **Cayman Turtle Farm,** formerly known as Mariculture, was rescued from receivership in 1976 when the government agreed to accept 50,000 shares of the company in lieu of duties on the transfer documents of the sale. German money was poured into the withering enterprise. Special customs agreements need to be worked out with United States mainland ecologists. At press time, customs will confiscate your turtle purchases. CTF owners are *still* trying to convince U.S. officials that these turtles are harvested from a farm where they are being cultivated, and not from the rapidly diminishing supply in the open seas. The business seems to be making a go of it, and as though in appreciation, the first of the female turtles raised in the compound crawled up onto the fabricated beach in mid-1975 to lay her first batch of eggs. The following year, 29 turtles laid 15,186 eggs, and the hatch rate was recorded at over 88%. The tour guide who will take you around the expanding premises will tell you that there are almost 60,000 turtles, most of whom live in 40 tanks ranging from 30 to 70 feet in diameter, and that the water changes in the large tanks every hour and in the small tanks every 5 minutes. The place is fascinating if you are interested in the life cycle of the turtle and in the process that has evolved here for its cultivation and harvesting for the world market. (The turtle steaks you can eat in restaurants around town probably come from here.)

An easy way to see one of the best "places worth seeing"—the sea—is aboard *Queen Anne's Revenge.* Launched for lunch cruising and capering in the spring of '79, the pirate ship provides an entertaining day aboard ship and also has dinner cruises. Check for the times of day and cocktail cruising, both figured at about $25 per person if you sign up on the spot, at the dock in George Town, or through your hotel's activities desk or person.

■■■

SPORTS: **Scuba,** snorkeling, and water sports are the main reason
for coming to the Caymans and *Sport Diver, Undercurrent,* and
Skin Diver magazines regularly extoll the virtues.

> **A**UTHOR'S OBSERVATION: *Dive Cayman,* a book by is-
> land diver and photographer Nancy Sefton, is well worth
> purchasing prior to your arrival here for diving. Cost is
> $10, and orders can be place with Undersea Photo Supply
> of Cayman, Ltd., Box 1151, Grand Cayman, B.W.I.

Only Bonaire rivals this island for top-notch facilities and a single
focus, but the options for entertainment for hours *above* water are
much greater here. (St. Thomas has top-notch facilities and a lot of
other things on its mind.)

F.L.A.G., at the Royal Palms Hotel, offers a resort course at $40.
Check with Chet King, chief of the dive-instructors, for details—
and times for the course which will permit you to go to 30-feet
below.

Spanish Bay Reef, once the top source for scuba holidays, has
been through a closed-and-now-open-with-new-owners situation
over the past couple of years. Check for status when you go down.
The new operators hadn't been on premises long enough for me to
evaluate when this edition went to press.

Bob Soto is a time-honored Cayman name for diving and although Bob sold his interest, the firm is still one of the Caymans'
best. There are several shops, including ones at the Grand Caymanian on West Bay and at North Church Street next to the Lobster Pot restaurant and branches at Beach Club Colony and Cayman Islander. Rates for a morning 2-tank dive are about $27.50
with tanks, belt, and other equipment; a 1-tank dive in the afternoon is about $20; night dive is $25 for 2 hours; 3 hours in the pool
for beginners is the starting session, and only 6 novices go out at a
time, with 2 instructors. A "resort course," to allow you to go from
beginner to diver-with-supervision, costs $62.50. In addition to ar-
ranging for the lessons (contracted for, and paid for, in U.S. $), the
shop at the Grand Caymanian has a selection of T-shirts, fins,
masks, fish cards to wear around your neck so you can recognize
what you're seeing, and the interesting *Guide to Corals & Fishes* by
Idaz and Gerry Greenbert (published by Seahawk Press and sold
for $8). It's plastic, and perfect for underwater reading.

Casa Bertmar, south of George Town on the west coast, has a 6-night vacation plan. All diving equipment is included in the rate, which comes in at about $360 per person, 2 sharing, in winter. (Breakfast and dinners and a 2-tank boat dive are included in your rate.)

Surfside Water Sports, with its thatched pavillion nested in the "middle" of Galleon Beach's complex, also offers the full roster, with a scuba resort course at $62.50, the 6-day full scuba certification course with boat trips and equipment included at $250. You can learn to sail for $8 per half hour, and then rent a boat with a pal for $15 and more an hour.

Cayman Diver, an 83-foot custom diver, charges around $800 for a week aboard, for cruising around all the Caymans. The dive boat, with room for 12 divers plus the 6 crew, has comfortable accommodations and new ownership, as of early 1981 when Gerry Jones became co-owner and skipper. His background includes an American Airlines affiliation and a long-time love of scuba. Sea and See Travel, 680 Beach Street, Suite 340, Wharfside, San Francisco, CA has details.

Deep-sea fishing has its enthusiasts, especially since Daddy's Girl started bringing in record catches of marlin and wahoo. Most hotels can put you in touch with top fishing boat charterers, as can the water sports concessions and shops. For those who enjoy a day at sea, the North Sound picnic excursions are worth investigating. Bone-fishing is reportedly great off Little Cayman's flats, and the freshwater fish from Tarpon Lake tempt anglers based on LC.

It seems fair to say that in the Caymans, at least, you can do anything you want to with sea and sand, at a price.

Tennis is taking over for the land-based folk (especially since there *is* no other sport for this season, although golf may be a reality by next). The Cayman Tennis Open takes place over 3 weekends in March, and outsiders are welcome to participate—but you have to be around for the 3 weekends. There are about 30 asphalt-type courts on Grand Cayman, and a baker's dozen of courts along West Bay Beach. All of them can be played, some at a price. Check with the Grand Caymanian and Galleon Beach for the biggest clump of courts; others can be found at Victoria House, Silver Sands, Cayman Kai, and Beach Club Colony, and there's a court, also, out at Tortuga Club.

Golf may be a possibility for the '82–'83 season, but if this place is like most islands, inevitable delays will put practical (and challenging) play closer to the mid-'80s. The ambitious golf-condominium-marina project is called *Tamarind Golf and Country Club* and is on the inland side of the road along West Bay (Seven Mile) beach, near the Beach Club Colony. Plans for the 9-hole course revolve around the success of special soil and Bermuda grass, and are being masterminded by W. L. Overdorf. ARAMCO Ltd. of Canada is the property developer.

■■

TREASURES AND TRIFLES: George Town is bubbling with boxy banks, all gleaming new and most of them the result of a change in laws in 1966 that gave the Cayman Islands tax haven status. The capital is not a quaint West Indian town in any sense of the word; it is bustling (by comparison to what it was before the 1966 legislation), new, and built for commerce. There are few bargains for shoppers, but there are shelves loaded with the usual imported china and crystal. Shops to find are **Caymania II** with "duty-free" bargains that aren't really, **Mica Boutique** for clothes, across from **Black Coral** (jewelry) and **Arabus** (men's and women's clothes). Up the road a few paces are **Topaz Jewelers** (some interesting expensive black coral and tortoiseshell work), **The Jewelry Factory** (specialists in working local stones, shells, and coral), and the **Diamond Mine** (interesting quality jewelry and jewels). Turn right, with your back to the sea, and you will find a lot more banks, and a hub with supermarket and **Cayman Drug Store.** Around the corner, heading back toward the sea, you'll find **Treasure Cove** (with a branch in the Grand Caymanian, and a larger selection of Wedgwood and other imported china and crystal here), plus the **Grand Cayman Craft Market** (which isn't much, from my observation) and **English Shoppe, Ltd.** (with the imports you'd expect to find). The English Shoppe is next to Cayman Arms, at the shore, with **Brenda's** (bathing suits, summer clothes, some from U.S.) across the way.

Best bet for local art (some good, some average, some terrible—in my opinion) and Haitian imports is **Hole-in-the-Wall.**

One unique spot to window shop is the **Cayman Turtle Farm's Jewelry Shop,** but know that, as of this writing, purchases may be confiscated by U.S. customs. Since most turtles are listed on U.S. customs sheets as "endangered species," customs inspectors have been instructed to confiscate items made from turtle shell. It will be hard/impossible to convince them that your purchase is made from cultivated (and therefore *not* endangered) turtles.

The Other Caymans

Cayman Brac and Little Cayman were the first sighted and settled, according to the commentary by George S. S. Hirst in his *Notes on the History of The Cayman Islands,* written in 1090 when he was commissioner. "On the tenth day of May, 1503, Christopher Columbus returning from his fourth and last voyage from the Central America Coast discovered the Lesser Cayman Islands, which on account of the prodigious number of turtle seen both in the sea and on the shores, he called Las Tortugas." Hirst adds that "very shortly after their discovery he drove his weather beaten and sinking caravels into the harbour at St. Ann's Bay Jamaica," but not without noting in his log that his ships had passed between what could only be the Lesser Caymans. He could see two islands—and these are only 7 miles apart; Grand Cayman is about 60 miles west.

No one paid much attention to the islands during the early years of settlement—and no one did until the past year or two—but in the meantime, Jamaicans fleeing various oppressions (mostly Cromwellian), settled in Cayman Brac and Little Cayman, eventually bringing with them some slaves to till the soil. Jamaican ships stopped here to pick up turtles for the transatlantic crossing, not only because they were plentiful, but also because they could survive at sea until they were needed for dinner when they provided the much needed protein for sea-weary travelers.

Hirst continues, in his tedious notes, to point out that "we know that when the second settlers went to the Lesser Caymans in 1833, they found great quantities of Alligators and Iguanas." The second settlers to whom he refers are assumed to be Barbadians, 1000 of whom came north with Sir Thomas Modyford, supposedly destined for Jamaica. And the Little Cayman reef passage known locally as "Muddyfoots" is supposed, by Hirst, to have come from the name of Sir Thomas Modyford, although descendants of the second colonization say it was called by that name long before their ancestors arrived.

Historic details probably won't matter nearly as much as the current local lore when you are vacationing on either one of these specks. Both are geared only for outdoor, explorer types who search for an outpost for some kind of solitude and don't demand any fancy flourishes with the holiday tab. If that's what you're after, here are some spots to try.

■■

HOTELS ON CAYMAN BRAC: Count on a seaside emphasis
(with fishing and scuba for daytime entertainment) and a
pressure-free vacation.

✛ **Brac Reef Hotel** (Cayman Brac, B.W.I.; 31 rooms) burst on the
shore with the season of '78–'79 and sends its special guests out to
sea for scuba, snorkeling, and other water sports (including fishing) and around the island's roads on bicycles. The small hotel's
motel-style rooms, in a 2-story ribbon, aren't anything fancy, but
they are adequate, and fancy folk should head elsewhere anyway.
The "history," I've been told of this place, is that "Tom Sevik came
on vacation from Chicago, fell in love with Elsie Ebanks, married
her—and stayed." See what kind of place this is? Rates for winter,
with 2 meals daily per person, are from $65 to $75, meals extra,
for 2.

✛ **Buccaneer's Inn** (Box 68, Cayman Brac, B.W.I.; 34 rooms) began
life as a dream cottage for 2. When the dream dissolved (Anton
Foster's fiancee left), the cottage was rented for guests, to open as
the Buccaneer's Inn in 1955. New rooms and new management
were added in 1973, when the Scott brothers bought the inn from
their grandfather, Captain Bertie (father of the disappointed Foster), and Marita Parchment is manager at press time. This is an inn
for people who like their sun and sea pure, without a lot of extra
trappings. More like a comfortable camp than a resort hotel, the inn
provides all the basic comforts, but counts on its guests to be self-
sufficient about prowling around the island for caves or birdwatching or heading out to sea for fishing. You can stand in the shallow
flats for bone fishing, taking your cue from your guide who will
probably use minnows for bait (and will toss the fish back in after
the day's sport is over). Cecily Ebanks acts as driver and tour guide
on weekends and Tuesdays, when the 28-passenger bus takes
guests on a swing around the north and south coasts; for the rest of
the time, the inn's planned entertainment focuses on beach barbecues, picnics, boat trips to Little Cayman, an occasional dance, and
a swim in the saltwater pool. Rates range between $95 and $115 for
2, all meals, depending on the luxury of your room, but ask about
special diving weeks with all-inclusive good-value rates. The 10
rooms added in 1976 are "deluxe," with 2 double beds, wall-to-wall
carpeting, bath and shower, and a screened porch that is worth the
extra sum (to deter the sand flies).

■■■

HOTELS ON LITTLE CAYMAN: are well known only to a select few. Although historians claim that the Lesser Caymans were first settled in the 1600s, this 10-mile-by-2-mile island is really an outpost. Reached by boat or small planes from Cayman Brac or by the Executive Air Services charter from Grand Cayman—on an "independent" schedule that hopefully goes about when you want to, the island has "big time" potential with Cayman Airways Service, daily except Tuesdays.

✤ **Caymanus Inn** (Little Cayman, B.W.I.; about 12 units) did a flip-flop with potential fame when new owners came in—for a few months. As of this writing, the place is used mostly for "overflow" from Kingston Bight, with rumors of purchase plans. If things develop as it looks like they might, something big will undoubtedly happen here. If you're planning your visit for late '81, it's worth checking on any changes.

✤ **Dillon Cottages** (Little Cayman, B.W.I.; 2 cottages with 8 beds) offer simple, sea-oriented surroundings for folks who want a place on a remote island to use as a scuba or snorkel base. Weekly rates have been about $280 for 4 in winter, $250 in summer, and you either cook for yourself or go to Kingston Bight for a "big night out." The cottages are near the airstrip.

✤ **Kingston Bight Lodge** (Little Cayman, B.W.I.; 12 rooms with talk of 4 more for this season) is strictly for fishing folk, or those who want to be around fishing folk. Tarpon fishing in the lake, bone fishing on the flats, or deep-sea fishing for marlin, wahoo, or tuna are the name of the game here. Small groups funnel into this place through Little Cayman Adventures and Red Carpet Airlines, both Florida-based; some souls are adventuresome enough to take the whole complex over, paying something less than the standard all year for 2 of about $90, all meals, taxes, and the airport transfers included. Contact one of the Boddens for details (either Jody or Frank).

✤ **Southern Cross Club** (Little Cayman, B.W.I.) is private, but you can inquire about availability of rooms at this south shore spot with a sea center of interest.

A Caymanian aficionado advises me that the best route for on-the-spot facts for Little Cayman is to call the public telephone (8-2214) and ask your question from anyone who answers!

Cuba

Instituto de Turismo Nacional e Internacional, Cubatur, Calle 23, No. 156, Vedado, Habana, Cuba. There is no official representative for Cubatur in the United States. Your travel agent can contact tour operators with Cuba package holidays.

US $1.30 = 1 Cuban peso
Unless otherwise noted, $ refers to U.S. currency

Although tourism from North America to Cuba has yet to develop into the hard currency source that the Cubans had expected, and the relationship between Cuba and the United States is fragile at press time, Cuba is included in this edition for two reasons. First: the effect of Cuba (its emissaries and its Communism) is felt—either by acceptance, rejection, or hopeful curiosity—throughout the Caribbean. Second: U.S. citizens have little opportunity to read about the facts of daily life in Castro's Communist Cuba, although news coverage of the mass exodus in April and May of 1980 was thorough. This chapter constitutes no particular endorsement of Cuba as a tourist destination. By reporting on the country with the same standards of professional travel journalism that have been applied to all the Caribbean countries covered in this edition, I hope to give readers the opportunity to know a little more about a country that is seldom covered in the U.S. press, except at times of head-line-making crisis.

The fact is that Cuba does have some of the Caribbean's best beaches, the country does offer unique opportunities for scuba diving, and the hotel facilities are certainly as good as, and in some cases better than, those offered in many Caribbean countries. It is also a fact, in my opinion, that the climate in a Communist country is not conducive to carefree holidays in the sun. Those of you who choose to spend a holiday in Cuba undoubtedly have other, more personal reasons for visiting this troubled nation. And, for those of you who do plan to visit, what follows is an assessment of the country as I have seen it during several visits following my first visit to "modern" Cuba in August 1976.

AUTHOR'S OBSERVATION: Throughout the chapter, the capital of the country has been spelled Habana. That is the Cuban spelling, and in recognition of Cuba's current attempts to stand on its own it seems only logical to spell the capital city the way the residents—not the outsiders—spell it. The familiar "v" is the result of the English speaking world's pronounciation of the Spanish "b."

■■

POLITICAL PICTURE: When revolutionary forces, led by Fidel Castro, overthrew the government of Fulgencio Batista on January 1, 1959, a socialist system was implemented. The debacle of the Bay of Pigs (Playa Girón) on April 17, 1961, is referred to by Cubans as the "primera derrota del imperialismo en América"—the first defeat of American imperialism. The U.S. trade embargo implemented in 1961 gave Cuba cause to turn to its new ally, Russia, for aid which was willingly offered—along with a Soviet military presence in Cuba. The Communism of today's Cuba has grown through the years since the Revolution and is financed at a figure now mentioned as $12 million per day in economic aid from Russia. Castro's charisma is immediately obvious within Cuba, and is being felt, also, elsewhere in the Third World where Cuban technicians, doctors, and army forces are active. While economic problems plague Cuba's own government, the country is taking an ever-increasing role throughout the Caribbean. Africa, Central America, and Latin America with assistance to revolutionary forces, and medical and technical aid.

Castro's eminence in Cuba is secure, shored up not only by his own personality but, perhaps more effectively, by Russian involvement noted, in an October 15, 1979 issue of *U.S. News & World Report,* as a brigade of 2600 Russians, with 40 tanks and 60 armored cars, 10,000 military and civilian technicians and advisers, Soviet pilots flying air-defense over Cuba, a modern submarine base with at least one attack submarine at the south-coast port of Cienfuegos, MIG 23 fighter-bombers, surface-to-air missiles, electronic intelligence monitoring the U.S., and military transport planes capable of moving forces on short notice.

In addition, as part of periodic maneuvers by the Soviet Navy, a

4-ship squadron cruised Caribbean waters for a month in spring of 1981. It was reported as "the first Soviet naval force to visit Cuba in 18 months," and it included a tanker, 2 guided missile destroyers and a guided missile cruiser.

The 9.5-million Cubans receive free schooling, medical care, old age care, and other benefits from the system. The average salary is about 200 pesos per month, but there is little on which to spend the earnings. Material goods are limited; Cuban cigars are made for export and are not available for residents except with special permission; and rum—sold in Tourist Shops for 2.50 pesos—costs about 25 pesos in the neighborhood stores.

On the 21st anniversary of the Cuban Revolution, the economy was in serious trouble, with the price for the country's one crop, sugar, falling and a devastating disease affecting the cane in the growing seasons of '79. A modified economic plan for 1980 projected a 3% growth (the target for '78 had been 7.4% and for '79 6%, with the actual growth in '79 at about 5%). The Soviet subsidies come mainly in the form of preferred sugar prices which are paid in Communist currency, and a preferential price for Soviet oil (which is expected to go up, although not as high as the OPEC pricing).

With the "freedom flotilla" carrying more than 120,000 Cubans to the United States in the spring of 1980, Cuba has rid its country of some of the malcontents (as well as invalids and prisoners). As one Cuban youth noted, "In Cuba today . . . everyone has learned that if you play the game you have no problems."

■■■

CUSTOMS OF THE COUNTRY: *Señor* and *Señora* have gone with the Revolution. Everyone now is a *compañero* or *compañera,* as you will hear over loudspeakers and in conversation as you travel around the country. The appellation is roughly equivalent to "comrade," and acknowledges complete equality. *Adiós,* with its inherent reference to God (since it is roughly equivalent to "Go with God,") has given way to *hasta la vista.*

There is no class system based on wealth; power has been substituted instead. There is obvious respect (or calculated homage) for the people working a level above someone and a warmth with one's colleagues that seems more official than spontaneous. Since the system requires regular assessment of a person's work by his or her colleagues, and advancement in a profession depends on good recommendations, there is little allowance for personal "fits of pique." (That extends even to visiting writers: I have found my Cuban colleagues baffled, but always courteous, with some of my urgent requests, such as a last-minute rush through Morro Castle or an intensive survey of Santiago to report for this and previous editions.)

Many Cubans are proud of the accomplishments of the Revolution. The new schools, housing, hospitals, old-age homes, roads, factories, etc. speak for themselves; the work that has created them is the result of Herculean efforts, mostly by laborers who learned on the job from "foremen" who were learning with them. I was frequently reminded that qualified professionals left the country at the time of the Revolution, leaving those few who stayed behind to teach others while they did the job themselves (this is especially true of the country's doctors).

The resentment against the United States Government is strong, but in ways you may find difficult to understand, does not include the American people. You will find a cordial, even warm, welcome, but you can also expect to find political slogans on billboards and on signs in museums devoted to anti-imperialist comment. A Cuban colleague who had worked for an American company prior to the Revolution, but stayed in Cuba to work for the Revolution, was strong in her comments about a big country that would "cripple" a small one with the blockade of 1961.

Clothes do not make the man in Cuba; his contribution to Communism does. The Eastern Europeans who have been Cuba's main tourists for the past several years have not set much of a pace for fashion, and any display of wealth or high fashion is distinctly out of place in today's Cuba. Cuban women are issued, by government rations, coupons that can be exchanged for one pair of good shoes, one pair of everyday shoes, one meter of good fabric or 1½ meters of basic fabric, one blouse, and one skirt *per year*. In addition, with another kind of coupon, she can buy a bra, panties, stockings, and a few cosmetics when they are available. Coupons issued for men allow them to buy a sport shirt, dress shirt, perhaps a guayabera (the straight shirt with tucks that has been the uniform for men in Mexico and many other Latin American countries), a modestly priced pair of trousers, one pair of shoes, and a pair of work boots, also per year. Children are issued school uniforms, 2 per year, in addition to their small clothes allotment. Although this rationing system may change, there won't be drastic improvements in the near future. American tourists arriving with fat, big suitcases are ostentatious. For a week of travel, a plain skirt with shirts for women, with something slightly dressier for evening (a street-length dress is more in keeping with Cuban austerity than any resort finery), plus bathing suits for pool and beach, and sandals or walking shoes is enough. Men would be most comfortable in plain colored trousers, short-sleeved shirts, and a guayabera or lightweight jacket. Shorts should not be worn on the streets of Habana. Blue jeans are acceptable, but they should be neat.

■■

MONEY MATTERS: Although the Cuban peso is officially at par with the U.S. dollar, the exchange rate given at hotels and banks keeps a hefty chunk from $20. You will get 15.4 pesos in return, and they will go quickly. Although there is no tipping in this socialist/communist country, Cuban residents find they have to tip to get service, and tips will not be refused if you leave the change from the bills on the tray or table.

When you change money, you will be given a white slip on which all your money transactions should be recorded. Although from my experience, no one asks about the slip, you will get a discount if you use it in some bars and restaurants. At the Tourist Shops in hotels, only hard currency (U.S. dollars) may be used for purchases. At bars, restaurants, and other shops, when there is merchandise to buy, you will need pesos. Change your dollars into pesos (which are also marked with the $ sign) at the hotel exchange desk.

■■

ARRIVAL: The 100 sea miles between Cuba and Key West were crossed countless times during the "freedom flotilla" in spring of 1980, but more conventional methods of travel between Cuba and the U.S. are handled by American Air Ways Charters, Inc. 1840 W. 49 St. Suite 229, Hialeah, FL 33012, and other tour operators who put together package visits at all-inclusive rates. It is also possible to go to Cuba through Jamaica (flights from Kingston) and through Mexico. Cuba-Mex S.A. has offices in Merida, Cancún, and Mexico City.

The airport arrival usually involves waiting in line while immigration officials go through their government procedures. Your tour operator should have provided officials with a list of all names on the group and usually, if that is done, things move expeditiously. Habana's José Martí Airport is new and built with the expectation of increased arrivals. (The 17-km ride into downtown Habana takes about 25 minutes.) When you pass through immigration, you will proceed to luggage pickup and a thorough customs inspection. On the plane you will fill out your Declaración Jurada de Equipajes (baggage declaration) and should list cameras, radios, and other equipment. Departing passengers will find check-in relatively easy.

There's an air-conditioned bar area *before* you go through immigration. Once you have been processed through the exit formalities (show your passport; forfeit your immigration card), you will wait in an area with a couple of Tourist Shops where you can buy cigars, rum, and other Cuban-made items (including T-shirts).

Several Cuban cities have modern airport facilities. All are served by regular schedules on Cubana; some (Varadero, Holguín, Santiago, and others) are used for charter flights from U.S. cities and other destinations. Although Habana's José Martí is now the major airport, I suspect that airports for other cities will develop as tourist depots, if and when the efforts of Cubatur make some progress in efforts to distribute the visitor impact.

■■■

TOURING TIPS: In the Habana area, taxis are prevalent. They line up at your hotel, and you can take them into the center city or anywhere else you want to go. The dispatcher will ask where you want to go and will make arrangements for a car. There's also public bus service that you can take from Varadero hotels into the center city, but most visitors to Cuba will be part of group tours. In that case, your touring will be on air-conditioned bus, both for sightseeing and for getting around the country.

Traveling to other regions around Cuba can be arranged with Cubatur officials. If there is a special place you want to visit, make your request well in advance of your arrival in Cuba (through your tour operator), and have a good reason for wanting to get there. Cubana flights around the country *can* be arranged, as I found out from my own experience, but it takes time because seats are in demand, flights are limited, and Cuban officials want to be sure about your reason for the special request.

Freedom to travel "at will" is not part of the Cuban lifestyle these days, and the American's spontaneous movement does not fit easily into the system. With time and good will, almost anything can be arranged, but it may take days to set up what you consider to be a simple itinerary. My advice is to adapt your plans to the planned tours available; they have been set up to cover the places most visitors want to see.

■■■

HOTELS IN HABANA have been standing tall for a couple of decades. Most of them were born with American capital and ingenuity, and have known the "gilt-and-glamour" days of pre-Revolutionary Habana. When the programs and politics of Fidel Castro Ruz began to fill the airwaves and pages of print, vacancies filled the room charts of the hotels. Many closed; a few were put to other uses (the Capri housed the sugar workers on a holiday earned by their work on a harvest in the early 1960s), and all were left to their own devices while the country concentrated on the crucial programs for education, health, agricultural development, old-age care and other social programs.

When the first cracks appeared in the wall that had been built between Cuba and the U.S., government funds went into refurbishing. Today the top 5 Habana properties are first-class, if you can overlook some cosmetic problems with worn carpets and drapes, battered walls, corroded aluminum bathroom fixtures, and other signs of 20 years of no-care and steady wear. These problems will be remedied when funds permit, but today's visitors can be sure of clean rooms, clean linen (even though it may be flimsy by U.S. standards), and a very willing staff. If your air conditioner does not work, someone will come along to fix it. If the Russian lightbulb blows out, it will be replaced. The Kleenex box in the bathroom may be threaded with a roll of toilet paper, but efforts are obvious to make the best of what's there.

A UTHOR'S OBSERVATION: Visitors who must have sudsing soap should bring their own. If you must have a fluffy towel, pack one—and leave it with a Cuban friend. If you use a washcloth, bring that also. There are none available.

At this writing, your room rate will have been negotiated by the tour operator who packages the tour you take. Most travelers to Cuba at this time will pay one sum for the week-long, or longer, stay. If you are going to Cuba on independent business, inquire when you request your visa about individual hotel rates. From my experience, they vary—apparently according to what the traffic will bear.

✛ **Capri** (21 and N Streets, Vedado; 216 rooms) is one of the city's top hotels, used by the government to house visiting guests and by those who want to stay at Habana's best. Most head straight for the top—to the 17th floor, where you weave your way through an unmarked door to the small air-conditioned bar with "windows" that look out on flipping feet and diving bodies as they wallow in the water of the pool you can reach by the 18th floor. Providing one of the most spectacular views of Habana, the 18th floor is a special spot for those who want to be assured of a good breeze with their pool and sunshine view. The buffet offered in the *Dorado Restaurant* on the 4th floor is one of the city's best, with a good selection of fresh fruits and Cuban specialties. Hotel guests head here for breakfast as well as for other meals. When house count doesn't fill the dining room, reservations are accepted from Cuban residents, who must check at the front desk for space and entry permit. The colorful and competent stage show in the *Cabaret* during one of my visits almost reached the caliber of pre-Revolutionary Cuba. Costumes were professional, dancing and entertainment colorful and lively—and well-larded with the expected Revolutionary messages and themes as well as with a peppy version of "Steam Heat" and a swooning rendition of "I Did It My Way" (in Spanish). (Before the Revolution, the casino operation was in the hands of George Raft, until it sifted through his fingers to Florida operators, and then was closed by Fidel's regime.)

The shop on the main lobby level is for Cubans and tourists, with tobacco, some Cuban rum, records, dolls, and other nationally made items as well as copies of the weekly newspaper *Granma*, in Spanish and English. Capri's version of the Bazaar will replace the present Tourist Shop on the lower level.

✠ **Deauville** (Galiano Avenue and Malecón; 143 rooms) is downtown, about 5 blocks from the Prado. The 15-story traditional hotel, opened in the late 50s, was granted a casino license just before they became obsolete. Favored by Russians and other Eastern Europeans, the hotel is convenient to the downtown area, but is dark and dingy. I found none of the light and airy visitor aura that is beginning to creep into the lobbies of the Vedado hotels and the Riviera. The Tourist Shop on the second level is a cut below the Tourist Shops in the other hotels mentioned, and far inferior to the Bazaar in the Habana Libre.

✠ **Habana Libre** (23rd and L Streets, Vedado; 630 rooms) held the title of the top convention hotel in the Caribbean's resort world when Hilton International managed the property on which Cuba's Union of Caterers spent some $26,000,000 pre-Revolutionary dollars. After a complete refurbishing, which pruned and plucked the plants that fill the main-floor lobby, the hotel is again one of the city's best. The hotel's facilities are first-class and will be better when government coffers can afford new carpets and some overdue wall scrubbing. The Bazaar that opened in May 1978 can compete with the best freeport shops, depending on the recent shipments. At opening time, the imports sold to tourists included Cannon sheets, guayaberas, perfumes, liquors and Cuban rum, cigars, and handicrafts. Some of the older staff have stayed aboard since before the Revolution. Their English is excellent; their enthusiasm for American visitors warm and obvious. Head up the winding stair-case for the pool-level bar, where canned music peps things up while you sip your *mojito* or Cuban beer along with the Cubans and other folks who gather here. The 25th-floor *Sierra Maestra Restaurant* offers the ubiquitous Cuban buffet, including a huge selection of sweet desserts. Count on your room to be a carryover from what you know to be the Hilton style, but be prepared for malfunctions of air conditioners and a new look for some of the furnishings that re-place those that haven't survived the 20 years (but you'll find that some items have—even with some signs of wear.)

✤ **Hotel Nacional** (O and 21st Streets, Vedado; 525 rooms) has weathered all the storms since its opening in 1929–1930. The pink palace still has its name etched on its "forehead," and stands, im-pressive, on its viewful bluff overlooking the Malecón and the sea. Used mostly by Eastern European and Mexican groups in the sea-son of 1978, the hotel is a city landmark with palatial aura. Note the tiles that border the main lobby, and the Moorish/Spanish-style ceilings overhead. Around the fringe of the lobby, you'll find the money-changing booth, a small shop for Cubans and tourists, check-in desk, and the like. The bright-blue public telephones on the wall by the entrance are the only discordant note in a lobby that has maintained its own venerable personality throughout all. (Take a lingering look at the gleaming brass Cutler Mail Chute, Correos de Cuba, made in Rochester, N.Y., and still claiming its prominent spot between the elevators.) More urgent matters have taken prec-edence over well-manicured lawns, but as you saunter around the back lawn that overlooks the Malecón, you can see remnants of the pitch-and-putt golf course and can note the marble compass rose set into a circle between two cannons, all of them pointing to the north.

Bathers didn't seem fazed by the murky pool when I watched them cavorting, and the cabanas that rim the outside edge are well used. There's one hot tennis court to the right as you enter the hotel. (And the second pool, at the "back" of the property, was empty when I saw it.) *La Veranda* is the nicest nook for dining, with view over the unfilled pool, and a garden. Next door is the en-trance to *Arboleda* dining room. Ask for Manuel, who has been with the hotel for 25 years and speaks good English. Menu offerings ran from 25¢ for juice, through the soup course to estofado (pork) at $4.50, filet mignon at $6.50 and up. The *Cabaret* starts at 9 p.m., and the dark, air-conditioned *Sirena* piano bar on the lower level, down the stairs from the lobby, is open from noon until late in the evening, for your rum or beer. (There's also a bar by the pool.)

A new bazaar, comparable to the one that opened in May 1978 at the Habana Libre, was expected for the Nacional, but during my ramblings, the best goods were found in the limited but acceptable selection at the Tourist Gift Shop to the right of the entrance, past the elevators and turning right down the hall. (Dolls, records, shirts, imported scotch, etc. as well as Cuban rum, shell pictures, some ceramics, hats, and some jewelry.)

✠ **Habana Riviera** (Malecón and Paseo Streets, Vedado; 360 rooms) was Miami rackets' boss Meyer Lansky's ill-timed plunge into the money market of Habana. The high-rise hotel about 5 minutes' taxi ride from the downtown area opened with fanfare in 1959, at the time of the Revolution. One of the first to be refurbished, the 16-story hotel offers first-class accommodations, with new lamps and fixtures in some rooms, and modern American-made plumbing that works (despite difficulties of getting parts for repair). Air conditioners and carpets show some signs of wear, but the overall impression here is of a good Revolutionary hotel. The former casino has become the *L'Aiglon Restaurant* and there are dancing and floor shows in the *International Cabaret* and *Copa Room*. The dining room (buffets) is at the end of the lobby; the pool is on the second level, and the Tourist Shop and post office are one floor below the lobby.

▪▪

HOTELS AROUND THE COUNTRY (for Santiago de Cuba and Varadero, see pages 242 and 254 respectively): **SANTA MARÍA,** a resort area built since the Revolution at a beach on the north shore, east of Habana, has several hotels.

✠ **Marazul** (188 rooms) at Santa María, was one of the first in the government's plan announced in the mid-1970s to build 59 new hotels. This one opened, on a long stretch of white powder sand, in mid-1976, with an ultramodern look, helped along with white plaster walls, colorful accents, and several levels with plenty of open space to take advantage of the breezes that blow through the main areas. The lobby has plants for accents; the big dining room (where the long tables are filled with a complete buffet at mealtime) is air-conditioned. There is a big swimming pool (not as big as the "mirror" resort, Pasacaballo, at the south coast's Cienfuegos, but the southern resort does not have the white sand beach you find here). There are the usual public rooms, Tourist Shop (with T-shirts, rum, cigars, dolls, records, and an inventory that increases as time and talent allow), snackbar, bar and activities desk. Rooms are clean, neat, twin-bedded, with private bath and modern plumbing, as you'd expect in any modern first-class hotel. You can take a taxi into downtown Habana for about 8 pesos for the half-hour ride.

✛ **Villa Megano** (49 villas, 25 of them suitable for 4) is also at Santa María. It shares the beach of Marazul and is a cottage-type resort built on a hillside, with some of the feeling, a colleague commented, of Las Brisas in Mexico's Acapulco.

✛ **Playa Hermosa** (several homes with a total of 117 beds) is nearby on the north coast. The complex is available for international visitors, if some tour operator sets it up. You can walk to the beach from your 1-, 2- or 3-bedroom house.

✛ **Bacuranao** (58 cottages) is on the north shore just before you reach Santa María. The hotel is a sprawl of single-story, small and simple units. During my first visit, the property was being used for Russian and other Eastern European vacationers; signs were in Russian as well as Spanish and French, the last a hangover from a one-season use of the property by Club Méditerrannée (which has no resort in Cuba at this time and a hedonist ideology that conflicts with the austerity imposed by Communism). The property hugs a small bay on which some people row boats or rubber rafts. There's a pavilion at one edge of the bay for drinks and dining. A store offers the usual Tourist Shop items. The hotel has been used for Canadian charters during the past couple of winters.

✛ **Trópico** (49 villas, 25 of them suitable for 4) is the last resort on the north coast beaches in Habana Province. When I first saw the property in August 1976, Juan Manuel Martínez Tinguano was in charge of the property, in thanks for help he gave to Fidel during the Revolution. The property was "built for the people" in 1959 and is used by Canadian groups on some winter charters. A notice posted on a board near the bar/dining room area urged visitors not to wear shorts in museums, and advised that bikes rent for 50 centavos per hour, tennis rackets rented for one peso per hour, and archery, basketball, badminton, and billiards were available as entertainment, in addition to rental of rowboats, sailboats, and fishing equipment, and scuba lessons. Plans for groups include a rum-tasting party at the beach and a Cuba night, as with all the resort area hotels where visitors stay for a couple of nights or longer. Rooms at Trópico are simple but adequate, with emphasis on the beach, pool, and outdoor informal life.

✙ **Mayabe Hotel** (20 minutes outside Holguín; 40 rooms) nests on the top of a wooded hill, overlooking the plains and lake. Opened in 1972, the mountain resort lures guests who enjoy wooded walks, riding horseback, dancing to the band that plays at the alfresco music area on evenings when the house count warrants a band, and spending leisure hours in the wood-beam restaurant where beer is served in handmade pottery mugs. The bamboo and wood construction of the main building (and the check-in area where there is a television set surrounded by chairs) supports the country atmosphere. There's another bar beyond the pool (new for July 26, 1978), with a penned donkey that is a favorite for guests. (The donkey drinks beer.) Americans will see some similarity to small inns in U.S. mountain resorts. There are 20 "old" rooms, with private bath and tepid water, and 20 new rooms built in the same style for opening in July 1978.

✙ **Hotel Guardalavaca** (Guardalavaca; 225 rooms) is one of the modern hotels, built for resort life for groups of Eastern European or North American visitors in winter as well as for Cubans during the summer months. A completely planned resort, the hotel houses guests in three 2-story white stucco buildings with air-conditioned rooms, some with balconies and refrigerator unit, all with private bath. Wood chairs are painted white, with bright-colored cushions, and the Canadian-made hand dryer in the ladies' room almost blew me out the door. The big dining room has tables for 4 or more, air-conditioned (to freezing cold, as is the case in many Cuban dining rooms). The bar (for rum and beer) serves inside and poolside from one bar, with stools on the pool side, and comfortable chairs in the room with a red and blue colorful plexiglass wall. Hector Gomes Torres, the second in command, advised me that June, July, and August are "almost full" with domestic tourism; December and January were "almost full with 5 international groups and 2 Canadian groups." Guests come on charters from Sweden, Finland, Spain, both Germanies, Russia, Martinique, and other places.

There was an inventory list on the back of the door of #202 (and I suspect, also, in other rooms). #202 is a big triple with refrigerator, small table with 4 stools, TV, shower with plenty of towels (beach towels printed with "Havana Club" and "Cuba"). The lobby Tourist Shop had T-shirts, plus the usual rum, cigars, and handmade items.

The beach, where I swam and played with 2 small Cuban children, is spectacular—a long strand of white powder gradually sloping to the sea, with rental boats (pedal, sail, row) at one end of the beach and a concession for food and rental of the separate bungalows in a nearby area that Cubans may use for their vacations at the other end of the beach. Bohios along the sand protect from the sun, if you can't find one of the several sea grape trees to call home for a day. The beach is a short stroll from the hotel.

✣ **Hotel Jagua** (Cienfuegos; 137 rooms), imposing on the shoreside where boats depart for excursions around the harbor and by water to Hotel Pasacaballo, was finished in 1959 and "opened by the Revolution in 1960." The palatial building was started by Batista's brothers, to be a private home. Its vast halls and elegant main-floor rooms are now used as the lobby for the hotel, with an air-conditioned (cold) dining room at the back on the right, and a pool in the patio. The lunch I had here, served in the best Cuban tradition by a man who had been an expert in his profession before the Revolution and now teaches young people aspiring to be good waiters and maîtres, was a fresh fruit plate (with watermelon, papaya, pineapple) followed by fresh red snapper, fried bananas, rice, and an avocado and cucumber salad, with the usual sweet dessert and thick coffee.

✣ **Hotel Pasacaballo** (across the harbor entrance from Castillo de Jagua, Cienfuegos; 188 rooms) is a mirror image of the Marazul at Santa María, on the north coast just outside Habana. Completed in August 1976, the hotel is modern in every respect, typical of the new properties around Cuba that have an almost Scandinavian feeling, helped along by white walls, several open and airy plant-trimmed patios, and colorful accents. The swimming pool is *huge*, Olympic size or more, stretching out at the "back" of the hotel, with a poolside bar and lounge chairs. There are bicycles for rent, a Tourist Shop, 3 bars, beauty parlor, "nautical activities" arranged, and a magnificent view framed in the windows of the freezing cold air-conditioned dining room serving the usual Cuban fare, often accompanied by elegantly poured beer. There's a coffee shop on the lower level for snacks. Room 517, my home on one visit, is reached from lobby level by a Hitachi (Japanese) elevator, and has a pool view, plus comfortable (narrow) bed, private modern bath, and all the accoutrements of a first-class modern hotel.

✤ **Rancho Luna** (near Cienfuegos; 225 rooms) is about 5 minutes' drive from Pasacaballo, with the Escambray mountains in the background. Its location on the beach makes it a favorite with Cuban and Eastern European visitors. The one-story units stretch out along the south shore.

✤ **Playa Ancon,** about 15 km (20 minutes' drive) from Trinidad, on the south coast, has a few beach hotels. One, with no pool, is the same style as Pasacaballo; another, Costasur (72 rooms) has pool, beachside location and some tourist amenities.

✤ **Guamá Tourist Village** (Zapata Peninsula; 44 bungalows) takes its name from an Indian hero who fought the Spaniards. Reached by a 45-minute boat trip through La Laguna del Tesoro (Treasure Lake), the resort was started in 1960, opened in 1961, and is the result of Cuban ingenuity in dredging islands out of a crocodile-infested lagoon. (The crocodiles are now caged and cultivated at what you will be shown as a tourist site, where you take the boat for Guamá). Your thatched hut, built in Taino Indian style, will be on one of 7 small islands. Before you picture a primitive spot, know that every unit has modern plumbing, air-cooling, comfortable beds, and the option to row your bungalow's rowboat to the main dining and dancing area or to walk along the boardwalks that weave around, linking the islands in the lagoon. Gaining a reputation for excellent fishing, Guamá is a unique resort—the only one of its kind in the Caribbean. There's an Indian Museum, with life-sized bronze-colored Taino Indians standing around in frozen action poses, on one of the islands. (The Indians are the work of Rita Longa.) You can row to the museum or go on the motor launch that brings you to the village. (The name of "my" boat on my first trip was "Alcatraz.") To the east of the Zapata Peninsula is Playa Girón, known to Cubans as the "primera derrota del imperialismo en América," and to Americans as the Bay of Pigs.

■■

RESTAURANTS IN HABANA:　If the changes I have noted since my first visit to Communist Cuba in August 1976 continue as the pace for Cuban restaurants, you can count on improvements on the scene described below. Things are moving fast in this country, especially when the project concerns tourist facilities, acknowledged (but not yet realized) as a source for hard currency. A few of the menus reflect the flair and flourishes known with cuisine elsewhere. The basic ingredients are Cuban. Offerings include excellent fish, some good pork, and stewed and other types of beef. Eggs are always available, as is rice. Although 7 ounces of chicken or pork every 10 days is the rationed allotment for Cubans, buffet tables at tourist hotels (Libre, Riviera, Capri, Nacional in Habana) are heaped with an assortment of cold and hot dishes, plus fresh fruit and Cuban-sweet desserts and cheese. Although visitors may tire of continuous buffets, the procedure is as much for the Cubans who splurge on a meal out as it is for the visitors—as you will note by the mealtime enthusiasm of your Cubatur guides.

When you present your white currency paper with payment of bills in many bars and restaurants, you will receive a tourist discount. The procedure applies also for the costs over and above the minimum charge at cabarets and floor shows.

Cuban beer is the common mealtime beverage (note the care with which it's poured); wine is often available by the glass, but don't expect it to be French import, unless you're prepared to pay plenty. It's more likely to be Portuguese or from Communist countries.

The Cuban art of restaurant service is reappearing. In the top restaurants, the service will be as close to the "white glove" treatment of yesteryear as you'll find anywhere in the Caribbean. Cuban pride in perfect performance is part of the mealtime ritual.

La Floridita on Calle Obispo at Monserrate is heartily touted as a Hemingway haven. This is the place where he is supposed to have lingered with the bartenders to help perfect the daiquiri, served everywhere in modern Cuba in foamy frozen splendor. Before the Revolution, Floridita was one of two grand restaurants (Zaragozana, which moved to Old San Juan, Puerto Rico, was the other). Some of the bartenders who worked here in the Hemingway era are still around, but the current Cuban claims that the Floridita is "at the level of the American Bar of Paris, the Savoy of London or El Plaza of Buenos Aires" seem a bit ambitious to me, and hark back to the earlier era when an old issue of *Esquire* (with the clipping framed on the wall) called the place one of the 7 great bars. At present, the white plastic covers on the bar stools look a little too new, the tables set like animals on a merry-go-round around the pillar in the back room are not always full, and there's a lack of joy that was never a part of this place before. Those were the days when a writer could call this "an institution of unique integrity in a city where catering to tourists has corrupted the spirit and meaning of a truly honest bar," and note that "at the Floridita, man's spirit may be elevated by conversation and companionship not entered into betrayal by his baser instincts." The potential for a "truly great bar" is here, but at the moment you'll have to content yourself with recollections of Hemingway, helped along by a lingering look at his bust in a corner. The service at Floridita is some of Cuba's best; you can count on spending the equivalent of $15 per person for a full meal.

La Torre, at Calle 17 between M and N streets, on the top of the apartment building that blocks the sunset view for guests at the Hotel Capri, is one of Cuba's top spots. When I returned to Cuba for my first post-Revolution visit in August 1976, this was the first place I dined—and the service even then, when Cuba was making its initial steps to reenter the world tourism market, was exceptional. This is a "luxury" spot where you can easily part with 100 pesos for a full dinner for 2, complete with view over the night lights of the city and service that's up to the best. The street-level entrance is somber and the elevator ride reminiscent of that in an office building, but the sparkling lights of Habana lend a festive evening aura.

El Emperador, also at Calle 17 between M and N, but on street level next door to the entrance for La Torre, is smaller, more intimate, with an atmosphere that is helped along by wandering guitar players (when they're performing). Prices are not quite as high as the top-floor La Torre.

El Patio, at the Cathedral Plaza on the corner near San Ignacio and Empedrado, was the former home of Marqués Aguas Claras (as you can note on the shield at the left of the entrance). Choices for lingering include the front terrace, on the historic Plaza, and the tables around the fountain in the center courtyard. There are small, private air-conditioned dining rooms for special dinners. (Reserve by calling ahead.) Dinners will run about 4.50 pesos for fish (pescado), but spaghetti costs a modest 2.60 to 3.80 pesos depending on the sauce. Chicken (pollo) runs about 6, and your juice will be about a peso.

Bodeguita del Medio a few doors down, on Emperado off Cathedral Plaza, is a classic—and another Hemingway favorite. According to the legend as told to me, the chair that hangs upside down in the back room corner is the one that Leandro García, the first writer to mention Bodeguita, used to sit on, but another story claims that a peasant who used to come into the place asked that his chair be reserved when he went to heaven. The saloon doors that open onto the street swing into the bar that backs up to the cluttered kitchen where country food is prepared. Several small and crowded rooms are like closets without doors, and the atmosphere is like no place else I know. Although some of the clippings of yesteryear (a *Harper's Bazaar* fashion article showing ladies floating around in a "moth dress," and clippings from *Life* magazine) have been replaced by political slogans about Panama, Angola, Ethiopia, and the current Cuban communist causes, the place still stands as a statement of the times. (This is one lingering place you can count on to be packed with people.)

Las Ruinas, in Lenin Park 15 miles south of the city, is the restaurant where Fidel often entertains visiting dignitaries. Surroundings are elegant, ultramodern, and built to incorporate the ruins of walls of an old sugar mill. There's a piano, on which '40s tunes are played during dining hours, and Tiffany lamps hang at appropriate places. Note especially the 5 stained-glass panels, done by Rene Puertocarrero. Furniture harks to the 19th century, with ferns softening the austerity of a very modern new building. There is no reason to expect less than the best Cuban service and food here; you are paying for it. Dinner for 2 can cost the equivalent of $100, with wine and all flourishes, including cigars.

Sloppy Joe's, on a side street in the old city, is a shadow of its former self. When American visitors return in bulk to Cuba, the place may come to life again as we flock to see the 40s photos of Rudy Vallee, Alice Faye, Ray Milland, Sophie Tucker, Rosalind Russell, Cesar Romero and Tyrone Power, among others. All were habitués of Sloppy Joe's during their visits to pre-Revolution Habana, and their photos and comments are plastered all over pillars and walls. The bar, when I visited, was empty—with a few bottles of Cuban rum in liquor cabinets once bursting with the best of the imported brands. This is a stand-up, informal place that thrives on crowds of people, but seems pitiful in their absence.

Coppelia ice cream parlor is the place to find for Cuban-watching and for delicious ice cream. There's a Coppelia parlor not far from the Habana Libre and the Hotel Capri.

■■■

PLACES WORTH FINDING in Habana are touchstones for more than 4 centuries. The tour you take to reach Cuba will undoubtedly have sightseeing in Habana as part of its program, but during free time, you can walk, bus, or take a taxi (they wait outside the hotels) to the Cathedral Plaza, to Plaza de Armas, or to the Prado, the mall that stretches from what had been the Capitol to the Malecón. These are the 3 main hubs for touring in old Habana.

La Habana's full name is San Cristóbal de la Habana. After 2 attempts to found a city to the west, the present site became the start of the city in 1519. Llave del Nuevo Mundo (the key of the New World) was the nickname given to the early city, because of its prize location for control of the Florida and Yucatan peninsulas. The key on the seal of Habana symbolizes this fact.

All museums are closed on Mondays. Be sure to check for specific opening hours. Times change, and although most places are open sometime on Sunday, some museums open only in the morning, others only in the afternoon.

Castillo del Morro (Morro Castle), on the eastern point of the harbor entrance, is one of the city's most photographed sights. The restaurant, museum, and tourist facilities opened for July 26, 1978. On my visit to this former prison (used for Castro's political prisoners), just after it was changed from prison to public restaurant, I stepped over the scaffolding, walked through the potential shops and restaurants, and photographed the spectacular view across the mouth of the harbor to the city of Habana, as the first foreign journalist to visit the fort just prior to the time it was to be open for visitors. Morro Castle was built in 1589, as one of the 2 terminals from which the heavy chain was hung across the harbor each evening (Castillo de la Punta was the other terminal).

Castillo de la Punta (Castle of the Point) houses exhibitions of arms from early times, in addition to having a restaurant and other tourist facilities.

AUTHOR'S OBSERVATION: Check at your hotel's tour desk to see if the boat ride past La Fuerza, El Morro, La Punta, La Cabaña, and La Chorrera is still operating. The excursion departs from Base Náutica near the 1830 Restaurant at Desembocadura del río Almendares, west of the downtown area. *Piraña,* a motorboat similar to Hemingway's *Pilar,* and the first of a series of fishing boats built by the Cuban government, takes a minimum of 8 people at 5 pesos per person, for a tour that departs at 9:30, 11, 3, or 4:30. You will probably have to assemble your group, but the excursion will be well worth the investment. La Habana presents a very different picture from the sea.

Museo de la Ciudad de la Habana, in the former palace of the Captains-General, on Plaza de Armas, is an opportunity to step back into another era. The minute you pass the entrance and look at the courtyard with its statue of Columbus, you are removed from Habana of the 1970s. I was told that the palace was built in 1557, was a convent, and was rebuilt as a palace in the 18th century. The huge rooms, the balconied center courtyard, and the wide staircase (with a piano on one level) attest to an earlier elegant era. Note especially the paintings of the 1800s (portraits of prominent Spaniards, and one William O'Ryan). As I wandered through in 1976, a woman guard in one of the rooms asked me if I was French. No, I replied, "United States." Her face broke into smiles, she quietly clapped her hands. "Oh," she said, "that is so good." The exhibits palled by comparison to the welcome, but on subsequent visits I appreciate the visual background in Cuban history.

The city of Habana was established in 1519 at the small church across from Museo de la Ciudad, on the site of what is now El Templeto. Diego Columbus's statue stands in the front of the building; the pineapples on the pillars are the symbol of hospitality, and the Greek temple known as El Templeto was completed in 1828. Inside is a famous painting showing the first mass held in the New World, but getting to see the painting is difficult. The building is usually closed.

At the park between the Museo and El Templeto, there is a statue of Don Carlos Manuel de Céspedes, the "father of Cuba" as president of the new Cuba in 1868.

Museo de Arte Colonial de la Habana, the Museum of Colonial Art of Habana was reopened on the Plaza de la Catedral in 1969. If only to get inside one of the oldest buildings around the 16th-century plaza you should find an hour or 2 to wander through the colonial rooms, to look at the silver water pitchers, with bowls, that served as elegant sinks for early settlers, the parasols and mantillas, the urns and vases of earlier times.

This area around the Cathedral Plaza is one of the most picturesque in old Habana. A cafe table at El Patio restaurant provides a perfect place for a lingering look. (The famed Bodequita del Medio, a Hemingway favorite, is around the corner along San Ignacio.)

Fraternity Park, the Latin American park, where 21 countries planted mahogany trees in soil brought from their homelands, is at one side of the big capitol building which you will recognize because it looks like the Capitol in Washington, D.C. The former seat of the government is now the Academy of Sciences. In the capitol building is **Museo Felipe Poey,** with special sections devoted to minerals, natural science, a planetarium and archeological finds in Cuba, in addition to areas used for special exhibitions. (During my 1976 visit, the building's interior, and the lawns outside were filled with Russian heavy machinery and weapons for war.) The name "Capitolio" is still etched on the imposing building's "forehead." To the right of the former capitol, the Habana Theater performs downstairs in what had been a private club for wealthy Spanish in the 19th century. (The Plaza Hotel and the Hotel England, now remodeled for Cuban travelers, are in this area.)

Along the Prado, leading to the Malecón and the site of one of Habana's liveliest carnivals, there are lampposts and urns that "were made from the remains of Spanish ships."

As you stand at the Malecón, looking up the Prado, the Museum of the Revolution is on your left.

Museo de la Revolución, in Batista's former palace, is testimony to the feats of the revolutionaries. Exhibits fill the several stories of the building, and tanks and other war vehicles are on the lawns outside. During one visit, I noted Fidel's comments that the "Yankees took our economy, they took our best lands, our minds . . . they exploited our public services, they took the biggest part of our lands . . ." It was explained to me that "Fidel has to be hard on the United States and imperialism to break the dependence, to make the people work to accomplish the impossible." For Americans unfamiliar with the feeling in Cuba today, the messages in the museum may be hard to take. From the soldiers and tanks at the front gates to and through the exhibits of the Bay of Pigs, past Fidel's comments against Yankee imperialism, the museum stands as a school about the Revolution for young Cubans, and a reminder for the rest of us.

On the inland side of the Museum of the Revolution, there is an exhibition area showing the *Granma*, the humble ship in which Fidel made his landing on the south coast of Cuba, when he headed into the Sierra Maestra with the guerrillas.

Museo Nacional, in the Palacio de Bellas Artes, is worth as much time as you can give it. The ramps that lead to the various levels make it easy (if long) to walk to the top for the most current Cuban art, all of it representing Revolutionary themes that are popular in Cuba today. Ancient Greek, Roman, and European art is at other levels, with some interesting examples of early Cuban art and the portraits and scenes that were popular in the 18th and 19th centuries.

Not far from the railroad station, you can see one of the few remaining bits of the old city walls, most of which were destroyed in August 1863. The wall around the old city was started on February 6, 1674, and completed by the 1790s.

Casa Natal de José Martí, across from the central railroad station, has several small rooms lined with photographs and documents from the life of the man regarded as the "Apostle" of Cuban freedom. José Martí, always regarded as a hero by the Cuban people, has now been adopted by the Revolution as one of its heroes. Martí traveled to Key West and Tampa, Florida, to raise money for his revolution against the Spaniards; Fidel followed his route when he traveled to Cuban communities in the United States to raise money for his Revolution in the early years.

Museo de Artes Decorativas (decorative arts; Calle 17 e/e y D, Vedado) should not be missed by anyone with an interest in colonial Cuban history. The former home in which the collections of china and furniture are displayed is worth a visit for itself. Be sure to take time to look at the ceilings, walls, decoration around the windows and doors, and the elegant touches that have been refurbished before the museum was reopened after the Revolution.

Museo Histórico de Guanabacoa, about 30 minutes' drive outside Habana in the suburban hills at Guanabacoa, is a folk museum, with exhibits (photographs and documents) about the early weed women and rituals of the Indians.

Parque Lenin, a favorite recreation area for Cubans, is about 15 miles south of Habana. In addition to an amphitheater for 2400 people, opportunities for horseback riding, and sports areas, there is a tourist train that runs all around the park, to the delight of Cuban children and parents. (Las Ruinas, the elegant restaurant is in Lenin Park.)

The Hemingway myth is alive and well in Habana and its surroundings. Not only is the Floridita, the restaurant/bar where Hemingway is said to have encouraged the development of the daiquiri, open and serving at Calle Obispo, but around the corner from the Habana cathedral on the Old Plaza that was the center of 16th-century life, the Bodequita del Medio Cafe hangs a Hemingway Fishing Tournament poster on the wall right inside its saloon-style doors.

Finca Vigía, Hemingway's home at San Francisco de Paula, 30 minutes' drive out of Habana, is a museum. You can peer through the windows, but may not enter or photograph the interior. The Cubans say that Mary Hemingway donated the home; Mary Hemingway has been quoted as saying she did not. However, it's still here—and Hemingway's beloved fishing boat, *Pilar,* is sitting on struts in the "front yard."

Ernest Hemingway bought his house in 1936, and lined the drive with palms. As you look through the windows, you can see homey chintz-covered couches and chairs, half-finished bottles of liquor, and one place where Hemingway used to write—atop his bookcase, with a view through the window. His favorite records, scattered around, seemed to include Russian folk songs, Cole Porter, Artie Shaw, and the William Tell Overture. In the bedroom, there's another typewriter, propped up on a fat *Who's Who in America*. His study has tiled floors, and a camel saddle, plus driftwood and other personal treasures, and in the dining room, the mahogany trestle table is surrounded by Spanish-style chunky chairs. Etched hurricane globes were on the table when I looked in. After peeking at Hemingway relics, wind around to the lookout area, atop one of the outbuildings. The view over the plains between the village and Habana is awe-inspiring.

The house, and other Hemingway spots, including Cojimar, the fishing village where he kept his boat, and which he used as the setting for *The Old Man and the Sea,* are part of a Hemingway Tour, set up and promoted by Cubatur.

If you go by road between Santiago and Holquín, you will pass **COBRE,** a village about ½ hour out of Santiago, where the **Church of Our Lady of Charity** holds the statue of the patron saint of Cuba that washed up on the sea. The Revolution has allowed the church to stand, and the village to thrive on it, out of respect for the legend.

HOLGUÍN, about 2 hours' drive from Santiago, is not much of a sightseeing goal, but it is to be an entirely new city, planned by the Revolution to replace the existing old city. Lenin Hospital in Holguín is one of the biggest in the country, and the town is on its way to becoming an industrial hub (cane-cutting and lifting machinery is made here). The modern airport is destined to become the funnel for vacationers to reach Guardalavaca, a new resort on one of the country's several powdery beaches, although it can also be used for military purposes.

Banes, about 45 minutes' drive from Guardalavaca, is Batista's hometown, the "birthplace of the tyrant," I was told. The **Museo Regional de Arqueología Indocubana** (Indo-Cuban museum), in an air-conditioned building that was constructed by the Banco Continental (which I was told was an American bank), holds a modest but meaningful collection of relics from the Indo-Cuban cultures. Opened in 1965, the museum shows the migration of the Arawaks, and mortars and pestles as well as other implements believed to have belonged to the Ciboney tribe (spelled Siboney elsewhere). Daggers found near tombs and maps showing where the earliest Indians lived in Cuba are also exhibits, but it was the drawings of

Taino Indian life by J. Martínez, done in '73, that made the daily habits clear (with artist's license, but I suppose his imagination is as good as anyone's). Note the facial expressions on the handles broken from early Indian vessels, and the other cases that hold ceremonial cups. There are 2 canoe paddles in a case by the stairway: One is a copy of a Maisi paddle from Baracoa (the original is in a museum in the U.S.); the other is from the Bahamas and here for an unexplained reason. Photos of burial sites at Yaguajay are displayed, and necklaces—old and modern, all restrung—are hung from pins in a cabinet on the wall.

CIENFUEGOS, in one of Cuba's pouch harbors on the south coast, is developing as a major port, with emphasis on industry. It is also the home port for Cuba's Russian submarines and other military equipment. It was the site of the country's first fertilizer plant, built after the Revolution, and has an oil refinery in addition to being "home" for 12 sugar mills, a 600 bed hospital, a 30,000-person regional sports stadium (with complete housing for the teams), and an open classroom experimental school (no walls). The bay of this city, known as the Pearl of Cuba by those who live here, is 10 miles long. The town is named for Don José Cienfuegos, one of the captains-general during the 18th century, when the Spanish built a fort here to defend the area from the British. Although the harbor is one of the south coast's largest, poking deep into the land, the town was not settled until 1819 when Frenchman Louis de Clouet led a small group from New Orleans which had recently been purchased by the United States. "The rich families used to live" on a tongue of land known as Punta Gorda before the Revolution. When I saw this city in August 1976, there were hundreds of red and blue Fords at one of the port depots, newly arrived from Argentina to be used as taxis and government cars. **Palacio Valle,** and some of the other former homes along the seaside boulevard near the Hotel Jagua are now museums, full of "chandeliers and furniture for the people."

TRINIDAD, almost in the middle of Cuba's south coast, is a national monument. It was also the scene of fierce fighting during the Revolution, when guerrillas swept into town on raids from the surrounding Escambray mountains. Today, Villa de la Santísima Trinidad (Town of the Most Holy Trinity) is a tourist attraction as a city-museum that is one of the best preserved examples of 17th- and 18th-century stone houses with the familiar Spanish-style iron grates. On separate occasions, I was told that some of the stone (I suspect ballast bricks) came from Philadelphia, or from Boston, on trading ships in the early centuries of the rum triangle. Regardless of the U.S. connection, the city is the third oldest in the country, after Baracoa (1511) and Bayamo (1513). It was a thriving city in 1585, when Diego Velázquez was Governor (He established this city in 1514, about the same time as Santiago de Cuba). At one time in recent history 37,000 people lived in this city that is about 400 kms from Habana, but during my first visit in August '76, the only visible residents were a few old people who peeked from their doorways to look at an obvious outsider, and some children, hands full of what I know elsewhere in the Caribbean as "gnips," but which are called *mamacillo* here, a fleshy grapelike fruit the size of a golf ball and a favorite of young and old.

As I munched on gnips, bought from a teenager on horseback, I wandered the cobbled streets, lined with beige-to-pink stone buildings in almost perfect examples of 17th-century building: tiled roofs, iron grills caging the windows, intricate lintels over the doors. The entire city is a museum worth seeing (in spite of the heat of the town).

Most tours will plan a visit to the **Brunet Palace,** at the "top" of town, near La Iglesia de la Candelaria de la Popa, which was started in 1726. Inside the palace, the riches of colonial Cuba have been preserved. You can wander past elegant furniture, religious paintings, jewelry and jewel cases, and elegant chandeliers. Note the peaked wood ceilings (built so the heat would rise) and the arched doorways to allow for the breeze. Some of the typical Cuban adaptations of European styles are obvious in the furniture, with wood frames filled with woven reed backs and seats so that breezes could circulate. Tiled floors are also impressive. The home was built in the 1750s, in the Spanish style adapted for West Indian living, with open patios. As you walk around town, ask your guide to point out the houses of the Malibran Segartes and Ortiz families, also good examples of colonial homes of wealthy settlers. The former Convent of Santa Ana has become a school of the Revolution.

THE ISLE OF PINES, according to Amos Kidder Fiske in *The West Indies* (1899), "remained uninhabited until 1828, when a military section was established there. In recent years, it has become a health resort for consumptives." Sydney Clark notes, in his *All The Best in the Caribbean 1959,* that "at the conclusion of the Spanish-American War the U.S. acquired the island, or so it was thought, from Spain. More than 10,000 Americans settled there, foreseeing a rosy future for this American island, and many of them invested heavily in real estate and in building developments. But in 1926, the United States Congress, guided and goaded by the enlightened legal mind of Elihu Root, decided that the island was and is an obvious satellite of Cuba and not, like Puerto Rico, an annexable tidbit of territory. The ambitious plan of American settlers and promoters collapsed and this lovely isle of pines and grapefruit and cool trade winds and buried pirate treasure fell into a prolonged sleep. Finally Cuba realized that she had an uncorked gold mine of holiday treasure and began to bestir herself to develop it. This trend has reached its spectacular climax, so far, in the new hotel. The Cuban government built and owns this superlative resort and it would be hard to exaggerate its beauty or its luxurious refinements." All that was written at the time of the Revolution, during which the Isle of Pines gained local fame as the place where Fidel served the 20 months before his release from his 15-year sentence, imposed at the hospital-turned-court in Santiago, in 1953.

Today the Isle of Pines is locally known as the Isle of Youth, in recognition of the 11,000 students who work and are schooled here.

El Colony (Isle of Pines; 90 rooms) has been a hotel since the 1950s, but in those days it didn't look like this one does. Completely modernized (by workmen who I suspect were political prisoners, when I visited the Isle of Pines in '78 to see the "new" hotel in progress), the Colony has been used as a base for *Scuba Cuba* holidays, packaged and promoted by American Air Ways Charters (toll free phone is 800–327–7711; Florida phone is 305–558–9281). With all the modern touches—rooms with view, pool, mealtime buffets and beach oriented holidays—water sports enthusiasts have the opportunity to enjoy some exciting underwater sights.

■■

SPORTS: Fishing has always been a Cuban favorite. During my first visit after the Revolution, in August 1976, I went to sea on the prototype of what has become a Cuban fishing boat, used for the Hemingway International Tournament, which was reinstituted for the first time after the Revolution, in May 1978. The *Piraña*, as the fishing boat is called, has fighting chairs and a flying bridge in a style reminiscent of Hemingway's fishing boat, the 38-foot *Pilar*. United States, Venezuelan, Soviet, and Cuban teams participated in the Hemingway Tournament, which took place in about 20 miles of sea off Habana. The 60 boats ranged in size from 31 to 65 feet. Excitement and anticipation filled the air in Varadero the days before the American yachts were to arrive to fill the up-until-then empty slips at the Yacht Club. The flock of reporters and fishermen who came to participate in the event temporarily overwhelmed the

Cuban hosts who headed from Habana offices to the docks at Varadero to be sure that all entry procedures were followed and that things moved along expeditiously. The event was a resounding success; resulting publicity in sport pages of U.S. papers presented another side to life in Cuba from that then filling the front pages (with the Africa tangles).

Guamá Tourist Village, at the Zapata peninsula, has been home for groups organized for birding tours and fishing excursions. The Isle of Pines and its small sand-rimmed Cayo Lago are being developed for water sports.

Scuba is developing in Cuba following professional standards. Some of the areas have been explored by American divers. Developments are underway (see above) with more planned for the Isle of Pines, off Trinidad, where the drop-off is not too far from the coast, and at some areas near Varadero where arrangements are made through your hotel to depart from the Base Náutica, the Yacht Club. There is a man at Intur in charge of the "activity of scuba diving at a national level," and you can be sure—as with other projects that are offical policies of Cuba's Communist government—the development will be orderly and for group tours.

Spear fishing is restricted in most areas, according to the government's conservation plans. At some areas, such as Cayo Lago off the Isle of Pines, where there is plenty of fish and lobster, spear fishing is permitted. There are strictly imposed seasons for lobster progging, so that the supply has time to regenerate, thus avoiding the depletion of stock that has pushed prices sky-high and made local langouste scarce in many places elsewhere in the Caribbean.

Birdwatching follows suggestions made by American birder George Harrison, who spotted 95 species in the Zapata Swamp and noted 25 endemic birds. Tours will house participants at the Zapata area as well as in the mountains.

Physical fitness programs are part of the regimentation and training for youths in the Revolution. Special sports complexes have been built in many cities around the country and the sports facilities and the housing are used to accommodate visiting teams for sports holidays. Eastern European groups and other countries sympathetic to Cuba's Communism are already using these facilities.

■■

TREASURES AND TRIFLES are not an integral part of the Cuban economy these days. Stores for Cubans have sparse merchandise, and what is there is rationed. There are special stores for tourists in all the tourist hotels. In May 1978 the first "freeport" **Bazaar**

opened at the Habana Libre, to be followed by similar shops in other hotels housing international visitors. The average Cuban cannot buy in the Tourist Shops. You will find Eastern European crystal, Russian and Eastern European radios and other electronic equipment, Cuban rum and cigars, as well as some simple handicrafts, and a few other imports when shipments can be arranged. If Cubatur's plans continue, you can expect to find more in the Tourist Shops than I saw when I visited. You will find Cuban T-shirts, labeled "Tea-shirt" in one case I noticed where the shirts were made in China. Inquire especially about modern Cuban artwork, both ceramics and paintings.

Cuba 64, in old Habana, not far from the Cathedral Plaza, is a shop with a collection of handicrafts, some good, some novice quality. Plans are to upgrade the quality of the crafts, but no matter what is on display, the surroundings—an old colonial house—are attractive and worth the visit.

■■
SANTIAGO DE CUBA is known as the "hot spot" of the country—partly because of the weather in this east end valley bowl, partly because of the sentiments of the *mambises,* the field workers whose uprisings against the Spanish provided the strength for the eventual overthrow of the colonial power, and partly because this is where the Revolution got its start.

Erna Fergusson, in her *Cuba,* published in 1946, points out that the city was popular with North Americans, who used to enjoy riding "out to San Juan Hill, where Teddy Roosevelt charged; El Caney, where the Rough Riders landed; Daiquirí, of mixed memories [the beach that gave rise to the famous Barcardí rum drink which U.S. Navy claims to have named], and Santiago itself, where our General William Shafter accepted the surrender of Spain's General Toral." Fergusson notes that "Santigueros will never forgive or forget that the United States and not Cuban troops marched in to conquer the city, and it was a Yank and not a Cuban who took the Spaniard's sword. Indeed the whole episode of surrender and occupation [in the Spanish-American War] was marked by our national genius for doing things wrong. Our officers even neglected to invite Cuban generals to participate in the surrender ceremonies." Her comments were written in 1946; I heard some of the same comments from my Cubatur guides during my visit.

Santiago de Cuba is at the southeast end of the country, almost 2 hours' Cubana flight from Habana and about 13 hours' drive on the new 8-lane highway that will eventually stretch from one end of the country to the other and already goes most of the way between the capital and the country's third oldest city.

■■

HOTELS IN SANTIAGO have their own personalities. Where you stay will depend on where Cubatur puts you (or the group you are traveling with).

✛ **Casa Grande** (Plaza de la Catedral, Santiago; 62 rooms) sits on the corner of the Plaza, diagonally across from the cathedral. Rooms are big, furnishings tired, but the hotel is used by some Eastern European groups and by businessmen. The 5th-floor open-air cabaret has music most evenings, and the hotel has the aura of ages past. Historic but lacking all the modern conveniences, Casa Granda (sic) was described by Erna Fergusson, in her book *Cuba* (1946), as "Santiago's great tourist hotel, the Casa Granda, and that is not a misspelling of Grande, but the name of a family. Casa Granda's big time was when Grace Line Steamers put in regularly, bringing North Americans."

✛ **Balcón del Caribe** (near El Morro Fort, Santiago; 78 rooms) sits atop a cliff at the shore. The 2-story blocks of rooms opened for the first guests in May 1978, who could sit by the pool for entertainment. Plans to have a fishing pier and nightclub had not been realized when I visited, but San Pedro del Mar, which opened in the '40s and is a popular open air nightclub for music with beer or rum, is a short walk from the hotel.

✛ **La Gran Piedra,** a mountain resort about an hour's ride in special mountain bus, is said to have a spectacular view. Some tours include a visit to this outpost.

✛ **Las Américas** (Santiago; 68 rooms) was one of the first new hotels, built in the early '70s. It is home for many groups who pass through town, but the lack of pool or any cooling-off place other than the dining rooms makes it a step below the Hotel Versalles. Rooms are simply but adequately furnished; they stretch out in a 2-story box just off the main road.

✛ **Hotel Versalles** (Santiago; 60 rooms) sits on a hillside, off the main road between the airport and the center of the city. The hotel has an African atmosphere created with dark wood and raffia Cuban country-style furniture and an open, airy feeling. Rooms are in single-story units that stretch off from the center lobby building, with its TV set for entertainment, and the counter that serves as tourist shop. There's a good-sized pool, with cabanas at one end and the poolside bar down a few steps at the other end where you can get a good view overlooking Santiago. The air-conditioned dining room under some of the living units was super-cooled during my visit (you almost need a sweater); the food was typical of the Santiago area and excellent. The fact that my shower was missing its spray head and the soap did not suds made no difference in basic comforts. If you have a reservation here you are at the best.

■■

PLACES WORTH FINDING IN SANTIAGO DE CUBA are legion. Not only does the city's role in the Revolution merit at least a half dozen important places, but there are museums for colonial furniture plus parks and cemeteries that shed light on the Cuban revolutionary spirit.

Bosca de los Héroes, not far from Las Américas hotel, is a monument to Che Guevara. It's on the spot where Che spoke to the Santiago people for the last time. The pebbled path that you meander up to reach the angular monument on the small rise represents the rivers in the mountains of Bolivia. The trees that have been planted on the site symbolize the woods in which he was lost, and the marble slabs that make up the monument are from Bayamón. Images and names of people important to the Revolution are etched into the planes and panels, but you have to get close to the blocks to read the inscriptions. The names are of those who went with Che to Bolivia.

Fort Yarayo, built in 1868 for defense from the pirates, seems small and misplaced at its location on the outskirts of old Santiago. At that time, however, the sea filled this area.

Santa Ifigenia Cemetery stretches for miles. A hot spot in a hot city, the cemetery's main appeal is to those on a Revolution pilgrimage. The José Martí tomb, to the left as you face the main entrance, is lined with stones onto which some of his sayings are etched. There are 28 stones: 14 leading to the tomb and 14 behind it. Among the thoughts are those he voiced at Cajobayo when he said, "He who thinks of himself does not love his country." At Playitas, "The people are mixed with the blood of the men." At Mijial, "There is no sermon like life itself." At Río Guayabo, "The government should be born out of the people." At Palenque, "When a people divide, they kill themselves." And at Cabezedas de Ciguatos, "Liberty is the definitive religion." José Martí, considered a fighter for all Latin

America, died on April 11, 1895. His tomb was started in 1949, and not dedicated until 1951. The 6 women standing around the outside of the dome represent the 6 provinces of his time, and are marked on the inside by the 6 shields of those provinces, which were Camagüey (with cattle raising), Oriente (with fruit), Pinar del Río, Habana (bee and key), Matanzas, and Las Villas. As you look through to the flag-covered box below, note that the sun always hits the tomb because, as was explained to me, "he did not want to be in the dark." I was also told that he wanted fresh flowers and a flag on his tomb (the flowers were missing when I visited).

If you enter through the main gate at the cemetery, you will find the tomb of Carlos Manuel de Céspedes, the father of the country, straight ahead on the left. (Between the José Martí Monument and the de Céspedes tomb, there's a monument for Thomas Estrada Palma whom, I was told, "sold Cuba out" to the Americans. He lived 1835–1908.)

The Bacardís you pass as you wander around are of the rum family. Emilio Bacardí, who was mayor of Santiago in the early 1900s, was a fighter for independence and is acclaimed in today's Cuba for the museum in his name in downtown Santiago.

José Martí district, community of prefab cement buildings on the outskirts of town, was the Soviet Union's response to the damage of Hurricane Flora, which swept through this area in 1968. The Soviets dedicated the factory in which all the cement slabs were made. 45,000 people live in the community which has 3 primary schools, 2 secondary schools; 6 day-care centers and a "Friendship School," where each classroom has a country's name. Students spend time studying everything about the country (in May 1978, there was no United States room). By 1980, I was advised, "José Martí will be the new Santiago." At the time of my visit, it was hot, dry—and still building.

Santiago University, a modern complex of buildings between the José Martí district and the center of Santiago, was opened on October 10, 1947. At the time it "was built by a private society," to open with 5 areas of study available to those who paid to attend. The university was recognized by the government in 1951, offers 26 courses of study, and is crowned with a sign that says "Viva el Internacionalismo Proletario."

Ateneo Armondo Maestre, perched on a hill not far from Hotel Versalles, on the outskirts of the city, is the modern sports center. If there's anything going on, see if you can attend. Sports events will be entertaining, but the place was at its best during one of my visits when the *Sierra Maestra* (local newspaper) was having its special cultural festival. Cuba's top bands and musical groups performed every evening for one week in early May 1978, in the first of what is hoped will become an annual cultural festival.

Granjita Siboney, about 20 minutes' drive from downtown Santiago, along a route that is marked with monuments to revolutionary heroes, is a farmhouse museum. There are 6 monuments on the left and 20 on the right as you drive out to the farm; each monument has its own personality and purpose. A couple of them are shelters for the bus stop. The route was dedicated in 1973, on the 20th anniversary of the assault on the Moncada barracks (July 26, 1953). Abel Santamaría rented the property as a chicken farm, building the coops along the street to cover the cars and weapons that the Revolutionaries were assembling on the site. Your guide will point out the well in which the guns were hidden. It was at this spot that the plans were laid for the assault on the Moncada barracks. The place has been a museum since 1964 and in the several small rooms, you can see pictures of Cuba at the time of the Moncada, including a picture of a U.S. Marine urinating on the statue of José Martí, Fidel arguing in front of the U.S. Embassy, and a young Raúl leading a strike at the university. There are issues of *El Acusador* of July 1952, the underground newspaper, with articles about the times. While you look at all this, birds chirp outside. The chicken farm tells a story far different from its outside appearance.

Moncada Garrison has become a symbol of the Revolution, as the place Fidel, Abel Santamaría, and Raúl planned to attack (for arms) when they were captured in 1953. Fidel and Raúl were tried, found guilty, and sent to prison on the Isle of Pines. The attack on the arsenal of the barracks was planned to gather arms for the Revolution, but Fidel was apprehended as he approached the barracks in his car. It was carnival week, and the arms they had sought to capture had been moved to make sleeping quarters for additional troops, brought into Santiago de Cuba to keep the merrymaking residents under control. After 2 hours of fighting, Fidel ordered withdrawal; Raúl also withdrew from his base at the Palace of Justice. The Garrison is now a school, with the wing to the left as you face the vast sun-bleached yellow fort housing a museum over the former arsenal (which is now an infirmary for the schoolchildren). There's a model of the barracks and the nearby buildings showing the Batista officers' club (now the office of the Department of Education), Colonel Chaviano's house (now the offices for the TV station) and officers' and soldiers' houses, now used by families. The Military Hospital has become the School of Dentistry. In the first room to the right homage is paid to the Heroes of Independence:

Carlos Manuel Céspedes, Ignacio Agramonte, Antonio Maceo, Máximo Gómez, and José Martí, all of whom waged their wars against the Spaniards. The explosion of the *Maine* in Habana's harbor, during the turn-of-the-century war of independence from Spain "was the excuse of the United States to enter the war," I was told. "They made intervention in Cuba for 3 years." The life and activities of Julio Antonio Mella, founder of the Communist Party in Cuba in 1925, are presented in another room where I also noted that 1940 to 1950 was a "time of prostitution, gambling, assassination of leaders, and longshoremen leaders in Cuba," and "the corruption in Cuba was very great." At this time, Fidel represented workers as well as students. My guide explained that "Moncada was the only way to solve the problems of the country; Fidel showed us how bad things really were," and as you walk through the exhibits, you can note the points he made. There are photographs of revolutionaries, captured and dead. My guide noted that there were no bullet holes or blood on the uniforms although the soldiers were found dead—in the Moncada courtyard (where I could hear the children reciting lessons at the school as I looked to see where the dead men had lain). The truck in which Fidel was brought to the provisional prison, in what is now the memorial to Abel Santamaría, is in another courtyard. As you look closely at the display cabinets, you can note the "ammunition," *cocteles molotov* made from Pepsi bottles and olive oil bottles among them. Around the walls are pictures of Fidel and other revolutionaries. There is a picture of Fidel, after 22 months on the Isle of Pines (now being turned into a scuba resort); pictures of meetings with Melba Hernández and Haydée Santamaría (Abel's sister), the 2 women who were in the mountains with Fidel (Melba is now Cuban ambassador to Vietnam and Haydée also has a high government position). There are pictures of training in Mexico, and "gathering funds for the new struggle," as well as some *Granma* landing uniforms, those worn when, on December 2, 1956, troops landed at the Golfo de Guacanayabo to head into the Sierra Maestra. A map in one room shows the routes of troops from the *Granma* landing, and copies of the underground newspapers, plus the routes of Che Guevara and Camilo Cienfuegos, who were charged with "giving the war from the east to the west" of Cuba, i.e., bringing the war to Habana and beyond. That project took about 2 months, from August 21, 1958 to October 7, 1958, and culminates in pictures of Fidel in Habana, talking to the people in the square around the statue of Máximo Gómez, a Dominican who fought for Cuban independence (the square is where

Batista's former palace has become the Museum of the Revolution). Wounded and marred faces and bodies surround you on all sides as you look at the exhibit cases. There are pictures of Celia Sánchez, a revolutionary who is now Secretary of Cuba's Communist Party, and whips and wrenches, "instruments of torture used by Batista's soldiers" against the revolutionaries. Playa Girón, the Bay of Pigs (1961), is presented as "the first defeat of imperialism in Latin America," and exhibits from this point on concentrate on Fidel's literacy campaign—to send the young to the fields to learn from and to teach the farmers. Che is shown at the U.N., and the walls are sprinkled with pictures of children in day-care centers. The last room (to the left as you face the entrance of the museum) shows the "solidarity of the Latin American peoples," with big pictures of Angela Davis, Jamaica's former Prime Minister Michael Manley meeting with Fidel, Panama's Omar Torrijos meeting with Fidel, Fidel with Chile's Allende (with a "Go home Gringoes" sign in the foreground), and Tanya's picture, as well as pictures about Cuban ties with Puerto Rico, Bolivia, Barbados, Guyana. The Latin America solidarity theme is carried to "solidarity with the rest of the world," showing the Soviet Union representatives with Fidel and meetings in Africa—with Neto and Arafat, as well as pictures of Fidel in Czechoslovakia.

Museo Abel Santamaría, behind the Moncada Garrison, is a memorial museum, opened in 1975, at the former Saturnino Lora Hospital. During the attack on the Moncada Garrison, this is where Abel Santamaría, the man who bought and stocked the "chicken farm" at Siboney, waited with his men to play their part in the 3-pronged attack. The messenger sent to tell them that Fidel had surrendered never reached them, and the group was captured in the hospital. Rooms used "to hospitalize paying patients" are pointed out by the guide. "As was typical in those days, these patients were better cared for," I was told. The walls that separated private patients' rooms have been knocked out. As you wander from one to the next, you are bombarded with photos supporting Fidel's progress with his 5 projects: Tierra, Vivienda, Desempleo, Industria, and Salud (land, housing, unemployment, industry, health). Photos showing neon lights of the Savoy Bar Club, Johnny's Bar Club, and all the evils of old Habana share space with photos of old and young in abject poverty. Photos of Esso and Texaco gas pumps are prominent on one wall, along with a "Land of Sugar" ad by U.S. Rainbow candy wafers seem hopelessly out of place in a room that shows children sitting on the floors in schoolrooms, old people in decaying buildings, and all the evils the Revolution lists from 1929 to 1958. Juxtaposed with coming-out pictures of Cuban debutantes are the wide eyes of starving children, bellies distended, plight obvious.

The focal point of the museum is the room where Fidel was tried, a room which had been the teaching room "for 20 or so nurses" in 1953. On October 16, 1953, the teaching room was used to "carry out the trial of Fidel who had already confessed to being involved in the Moncada Garrison attack." The trial began in the Palace of Justice (now the offices of the *Tribuno Provincial Popular*), "but in the third session Fidel was taken out and prevented from trial." From here Fidel was sentenced to 15 years, and taken to the Isle of Pines. My guide explained that Santiago justice used a trick (saying that Abelardo Crespo Arias, an important witness, was too ill to be moved from the hospital) to turn the trial of Fidel into a private one. Fidel was his own defense—and his chair and the chair of the unused defense provided by the Batista state are pointed out. Comment was made about the grandeur of the furniture—"typical of that used by the bourgeoisie." This is the room where Fidel gave the famous speech that included the much quoted phrase, "Condenadme no importa, La Historia me absolverá" (Condemning me is not important, history will absolve me). When I inquired about the pink paint that covers all the hospital furniture, I was advised that that is new—the furniture used by the bourgeoisie was white. The memorial garden and monument to Abel Santamaría was established in late 1978.

Casa de Frank y Joseu País, on a side street in the old part of Santiago, is a small but potent museum where a dozen neatly uniformed schoolchildren waited with wide eyes and no sign of impatience while I was given an English translation on the exhibits within the 4 humble rooms. This was the home of Frank País García, a revolutionary who organized the underground in Santiago to meet Fidel in the Sierra Maestra mountains after his *Granma* boat landing at the shores of the Golfo de Guacanayabo. The name and face of Frank País are prominent in Santiago and throughout the country. His death at 22, and his contribution to the Revolution, make him a hero, praised by Fidel and revered by the Santiagueros. Frank País died in 1957, captured and killed on the street as he left an underground meeting at a colleague's house. "Typical of his personality, he sent the others out before him; he alone was captured and killed," I was told. Each year, on the anniversary of his death, hundreds follow the path of his coffin. On the day of his burial, his casket was covered with the Cuban flag and the 26 July flag; the 26 July song and the national anthem are sung during the march, as they were sung at his funeral.

Frank País García was born December 7, 1935; he lived in this house with his 2 brothers (Joseu was also a revolutionary; the third brother, still living, was not mentioned much). His father was a Baptist preacher; his mother died in 1977. The exhibits throughout the small house hold his school records (he was a brilliant student who went on to become a teacher, a profession he left when underground activities took too much of his time); he was beloved by his friends (and by fellow Cubans). Frank País met with Fidel twice in his life—once in Mexico after Fidel left the Isle of Pines, and the second time in the Sierra Maestra, when his well-trained revolutionary forces joined those of Fidel.

Knowing Spanish is essential for full understanding of the young man whose love for his country was so strong that he was to write to his jealous girlfriend that, yes, in fact, he did have another. In a letter paraphrased for me, he said, "You have seen her, although without understanding her well. She has a white and blue striped skirt and on her head she has a red cap with a white star. Do you understand this? She occupies my mind, soul, actions . . . for me there is no one else but her." So great was the love of Frank País for his country that he hid the arms he captured for the underground activities in the air spaces around the wood beams of his bedroom. He was arrested for protesting policies of the government; he attacked hunters' clubs for the arms to train the guerrilla forces that were to wage the Revolution. In the courtyard of the small and humble home, a garden has been planted with flowers that the young Frank used to plant and others, flowers and trees, that have significance for the Revolution.

Casa Antonio Maceo, a small house on another side street not far from the main plaza, holds pictures and charts significant to Spanish Revolutionary Cuba (which Fidel says is the start of the Revolution he is carrying out). Some time spent here will make it immediately obvious why Antonio Maceo is revered in today's Cuba. Maceo was a revolutionary who took part in 800 battles in the Ten Years' War (1868–1878) and 119 in the 1985 War, and was wounded 29 times. His accomplishments in leading troops over 1900 kms from Santiago to Habana, from October 22, 1895 to January 22, 1896, are noted and documented on a map to the right as you enter the house.

The point is made in another exhibit that in 1884 both Cuba and Puerto Rico were "oppressed by the Spanish colonial yoke." Both made a pact to achieve independence, and when Antonio Maceo saw that Cuba's independence was near at hand, he promised, I was told, "when Cuba is independent, I will ask the government's permission to make Puerto Rico free. I would not like to turn in my spade leaving slaves in that part of America." Antonio Maceo was killed in 1896. He was a mulatto, "conscious of the racism of his time." Look around at the 19th-century house in which he was born. It has the original ceiling, and the original bricks are on the floor of the small room to the left of the entrance. In the small garden in the back you can note the U.S. printing machine, Washington Press, R. Hoe & Co., New York 1864 #2556, on which the revolutionary *El Cubano Libre* was printed.

One exhibit is devoted to Maceo's mother, who fought in the war, and his 18 brothers—6 by his father's first wife, and 4 with his mother Maria's first marriage, with 9 in the marriage that brought Antonio. Maceo's wife was also a fighter, who founded a woman's fund-raising organization in Kingston, Jamaica (the Sisters of Maria Maceo) in the 1880s.

Museo de Clandestinidad, in the former police station which was captured by Frank País on November 30, 1956, faces a plaza that is the site of one of Santiago's most traditional festivals, the Fiesta del Tivoli, a May festival with costumes and customs of earlier days. Dances and food are part of the festivities, but the exhibits in the museum project a serious time in Cuban history. (The 2nd-floor breeze-swept balconies provide one of the best overviews of old and new Santiago.) Among the exhibits which focus on Frank País and his underground activities are photographs of the meeting of Frank and Fidel in the Sierra Maestra. *New York Times* reporter Ted Matthews's account (Sunday, February 27, 1957) of the meeting in the Sierra Maestra—the first word the people had that Fidel was still alive—is displayed, as well as the report by UPI reporter Francis MacCarthy headlined "Muerto Fidel Castro afirma la United Press," which I was advised by my guide—the sister of one of the martyrs—was done to mislead the Cuban people. There are photographs of *Granma,* the boat used for the landing (the name now of Cuba's Communist paper) and a display of the instructions by Fidel to the Santiagueros about how to proceed after he and his men had taken the city in the name of the Revolution. In one of the display cases are the Cuban flag, *cocteles molotov* made with Hatuey beer bottles, the green uniform that was worn for the first time with the 26 de Julio red armband in the uprising of November 30, an assortment of medicines, pipe bombs, Esso can bombs, and other items used in the 25 months of struggle that resulted in Fidel

Castro's leadership of Cuba. (While I pondered all this, children laughed and played in the school that is part of the new building, attractively rebuilt in the old colonial style.)

Museo Emilio Barcardí (Tu-Sat 8 a.m.-10 p.m.; Sun 10-4 p.m., M 2-8 p.m.) in downtown Santiago, "was founded by Emilio Bacardí Moreau in 1899, opened in this location in October 1927, reestablished in 1964 under the National Council of Culture of the Revolution, and reopened for the people in 1968." Bacardí, a member of the rum family, was mayor of Santiago around 1900 and a supporter of independence. (His tomb is pointed out in Santa Ifigenia Cemetery.) The main exhibits on the street level are about the Indian heritage, showing the early settlements of the Tainos and the Siboneys (sometimes spelled Ciboney). The maces and capes of conquistadors are displayed, as well as 16th-century banners—and a wooden Santiago (St. James) on his white horse, prancing in the middle of the revolutionary exhibits. The 1810–1898 years of *autonomismo* are shown in dark halls "because there was no light on life" in those years, I was told. In the room covering 1868 to 1878, the Ten Years' War, it was pointed out to me that "Fidel says he fought the same revolution—that the revolution never stopped from that time." Personal effects of leaders are displayed—their plates, tiles, any small thing pertaining to the lives of any of the leaders, including Céspedes. There is also another printing press used for the revolutionary paper *El Cubano Libre*. Mambises (field worker) goods, their shoes made from palm fronds, hide bags, etc., are displayed in recognition of the contribution of the field workers to the Revolution. A display of 2 colonial cannons and countless machetes, hung at impressive intervals—fencelike around the cannons—makes its own statement. Other rooms show comments about Cuba by American officials—Breckenridge, the Platt Amendment, etc.

Upstairs offers a change from the revolutionary lessons, with displays of modern Cuban art as well as some of the original items in the Bacardí collection. Look for some of the Cuban artists: Baldomera Fuentes (1809–1877), Joaquín Cuadras (1843–1875), Manuel Vincens; and the portraits by Frederico Martínez (1828–1920). José Joaquín Tejada (1867–1943) was a Santiago painter. It's also worth inquiring about the huge painting showing Cortez in armor on landing in Cuba, painted by Juan Emilio Hernández Giro (1882–1953).

Mueble Colonial, the home of Diego Velázquez, on the main plaza diagonally across from the Cathedral, is the oldest house in Cuba, and one of the oldest in Latin America. It was built for Velázquez, the Spanish explorer who settled Santiago, in the early 1500s. Intricate wood-beam-and-paint ceilings, wood-screened windows with window seats where the dwellers could watch the world outside without being seen, and impressive sconces (with Russian light-bulbs) set the tone. The house was opened as a museum in 1971 to show furniture and architecture, room by room, from the 16th century through the early 20th century. In the earliest rooms there are trunks, heavy Spanish furniture, and a painting of Diego Velázquez. Note the heavy wood wardrobe that served as closet, and the table set with ceramic plates, assembled from pieces found near this site. The Cuban bedstead and chairs in the 17th-century room show the influence of Spain; the rest of the furniture in this room is genuinely Spanish. The tapestry representing the end of the 17th century may have been made in Cuba but is certainly woven with gold thread. (The room dividers are for the museum use; at the time of Velázquez, all the living was in one big, long room.) In the 19th-century room, all the furniture was made in Cuba, with the exception of a marble-top table. Spanish, French, and English influences are obvious, and Cuban silver is used in the plates and urns in the cabinet, although some of the pieces were worked in Germany. The gold storage area, uncovered during the recent excavations and remodeling, will be pointed out. It is on the far side of the courtyard, straight ahead from the entrance.

A second home has been acquired as part of the museum. It is entered from the Diego Velázquez home by walking through the carriage courtyard (look right, to the carriage doors that open out to the side street). There is Cuban furniture in most of the rooms, with styles similar to those known in Europe, except for the cane backs in chairs and settees for air circulation. In the Victorian room, the heavy sleigh bed was made in Santiago. "The father of the country slept in this bed"—and that is Manuel de Céspedes. I learned in the 20th-century room that the "bourgeoisie imported furniture from all over the world because they wanted to be in fashion" and "then is broken the development of Cuban furniture" which had filled the rooms from the earlier centuries. "The bourgeoisie show in this way how strong they are," I heard as I looked around the room filled with incredibly ornate Victoriana that looks absurd in any society. (The pièce de résistance was a pair of urns, with figures of Uncle Tom characters.)

Castillo del Morro, the fort at one side of the entrance to the harbor at Santiago de Cuba, is a 20-minute drive from the downtown area, past the new hotel (Balcón del Caribe) and the '40s-built San Pedro del Mar, a nightclub/dance place by the sea. The fort was built by the Spanish from 1630 to 1642. When Santiago was the capital of Cuba, this was the hub of activity, the fortress from which the pirates and others were bombarded, and the repository for arms and goods. It was past this fort that Cortez sailed on his way to Mexico, that Francisco Pizarro headed to conquer Peru, that Gonzalo Jiménez went to found Colombia, and that Juan Ponce de León headed to Puerto Rico before he went on to Florida; and it was inside these walls, according to one of the pamphlets printed and distributed by Cubatur, that "many of the patriots of our war for independence were imprisoned and executed. . . ."

In May 1978 goats grazed around the grounds, unconcerned by the planks and other signs of the restoration underway. The fort is now a museum, restaurant, and recreation area, well worth the drive out to see the view along the way as well as the pink cast to the stones, the massive walls, the drawbridge over which you enter, and the museum. (The original town was east of El Morro. The mosquitoes drove them to the present location.)

■■■

VARADERO is a 45-km long peninsula, "discovered in 1920 by French millionaire Irénée Dupont [sic]," who is in fact an American millionaire. The peninsula, with its powdery sand beach that runs almost 12 miles, was the playground of the very rich. In its pre-Revolution heyday, the villas that prickled the shore were second (or third) homes for wealthy Cubans and Americans. After the Revolution, when the government was spreading the wealth, the home owners were given their choice of residence. Some Cubans chose to live in their Varadero homes and "give the other property to the government." Americans left. Today, the former private homes of Varadero have been grouped as hotels, with a new central building, usually at the beach, for restaurant, bar, and recreation area. The government plan for Varadero, I was told, is to move the residents to the new city of Santa Marta, built on the cell system inland from the beach, and to turn all of Varadero into a tourist complex. Since the Revolution, cluster living is the Communist goal, but people have not been moved from their homes "until they want to go to the new residential communities."

■■■

HOTELS IN VARADERO: The Internacional, the Oasis, and Kawama I, were built as hotels before the Revolution. They have been refurbished; other hotels have been created on the cluster-of-former-homes policy. There are some new buildings, but most of the resort emphasis since the Revolution has been on creating more dining facilities at the hotels, adding activities, and improving the nightclub shows. A bus runs the gamut of hotels for a 5-peso fare, and a tourist "train" wiggles along the route at the height of the winter season (and perhaps at other times). To help bring the picture of Varadero hotels into focus, here's the list of the main properties from west to east along the beach (and bus route): Oasis, Barsena, (the airport), Kawama, Tortuga, Barlovento, Sotavento, Los Cocos, Tropical, Caribe, Los Delfines, Quatro Palmas, Arenas Blancas, Marazul, Internacional, Cabanas (or Villas) del Sol, and then through the du Pont gates to the former homes now known as Villa Cuba, and the du Pont mansion, now called Las Américas.

Since most Americans will be visiting Varadero as part of a group tour, the hotel base will depend on the tour operators' negotiations with Cubatur. You can roam from hotel to hotel, however, either by walking along the beach, taking the bus, or hiring a taxi—if you can find one. All hotels stretch along the beach, or just inland from the shore, so no further address is given in the comment below.

✢ **Arenas Blancas** (150 rooms), a resort of formerly private houses, now grouped, is one of the better hotels because the homes were elegant. "These people really knew how to live," a Cuban commented as we walked through one of the units. Arenas has its restaurant and entertainment area in a large former home, built in Spanish colonial style, with plenty of tile and elegant flourishes, with a huge clay water urn, called a *tinajón*, in the gardened courtyard. The houses scattered around the linking lawns hold most of the 150 bedrooms; the main house has the ping-pong table, Tourist Shop, and a place to play chess, dominoes, or whatever.

✢ **Cabanas del Sol** (145 rooms in villas) changed its name to Villas del Sol, "which sounds more elegant," but the property is villas with 2 or 3 bedrooms, with the option for bicycling, "nautical activities," and other resort activities arranged through the Cubatur representative. (The property abuts the houses grouped as Villa Cuba, at the east end of the strip.)

✢ **Caribe** (180 rooms) is a recently built 3-story hotel used mostly by Eastern European and Russian groups. Its public areas are around the central pool, which fits into the pocket of the U-shape. The beach runs along the "top" of the U. When I looked at the property, the game room was the scene of a boisterous game of pool, but there were pinball machines waiting for play.

✤ **Internacional** (162 rooms), at the middle of the stretch of accommodations, was a popular modern hotel when it was built in the years before the Revolution. Some of the bedrooms are big, with marble baths; most are comfortable, not lavish, and some have sea view. Used primarily by groups from Canada in winter, the public facilities at the hotel include the pool (site for beginners' scuba lessons), the restaurants, with an inside air-conditioned room and a terrace in the sun used in the winter months when the international tourist season is underway, a Tourist Shop, a game room with children's activities, Cubatur activities desk (where you can sign up for tours), and that great expanse of beach just off the terrace. (The small statues of Columbus on one side and Queen Isabella wishing him farewell on the other seemed out of place to me, in today's Cuba.) The nightclub at the Internacional has the area's top show, excellent when I saw it in '76 and reportedly better now that performers have had a couple more years to perfect their skills.

✤ **Kawama I** (64 rooms), gets its number to separate it from the newer Kawama II; its name comes from the name for the west end of the beach row. The first Kawama was a pre-Revolution hotel, adapted to the modern concept. The stone building with brick-colored tile roof is the original hotel; the newer section has been added since the Revolution, with 2-story units scattered over the grounds. There's a lot of variety in architecture, since some of the units were homes in the original hotel orbit, but there's a congenial Caribbean hotel feeling at the thatched-roofed shelter that serves as a beachside bar. If you are not staying here, drop by for a Cuban beer midafternoon.

✤ **Kawama II** is another group of beach villas, newly built to capture some of those who wanted to stay at Kawama I. There's not as much atmosphere with the newer villas, which looked to me like hot cement boxes.

✤ **Marazul** (58 rooms) uses the Internacional Hotel for its restaurant. The modern 2-story turquoise buildings run inland from the beach area and are filled with simple rooms, most with private bath, some with small refrigerator and stove. Marazul is popular with Cubans, who come here for a good-value summer vacation, cooking some meals to keep costs down.

✤ **Oasis** (130 rooms), one of the pre-Revolution hotels, perches at the western end of the string, on a beach that will not seem like much after you've scuffed through the powder of the main strand. This end of the beach has some seaweed and rocks underfoot offshore, and seems to be subject to the vagaries of wind and surf. The hotel, however, maintains some of the small-hotel feeling that gives a place personality. Rooms are adequate (nothing great), and the patio that is sometimes the dance floor on starry evenings has a small bohio for serving beer and rum drinks by the beach. There's the usual restaurant, Tourist Shop, and game room for guests who base here. I was advised that the hotel "is used as a transit hotel"; further questioning revealed that it was a place where groups who are spending only one or 2 nights, or overflow groups, are lodged.

✤ **Tortuga,** another "transit" hotel, is former homes and small villas which in their pre-Revolution life might have been middle-class vacation homes. By comparison to the villas used as part of Villa Cuba, for example, these places are small and boxy.

✤ **Villa Cuba** (80 rooms) is several former homes on the short streets that stretch straight back from the beach, at the eastern end of the peninsula, not too far from Las Américas, the former du Pont mansion. Most of the former privately owned furniture has been removed, either by the former owners or by the government, to be replaced with functional tables, chairs, beds and bureaus. Although each house has its own kitchen, meals are rarely served "at home" unless a Cuban family or group of friends has rented the entire villa (one reason may be that food rationing makes meals difficult). There is a central area at the beach for meals and entertainment.

■■

RESTAURANTS IN VARADERO are developing as the tourist business warrants. As of this writing, the restaurants at the hotels (notably the air-conditioned dining room at the Internacional) offer acceptable fare, but there is a trio of places to try for full meals and a couple of spots to find for leisurely lingering when you want to get out of the sun.

Albacoa is my top choice for seafood. Not only are the surroundings atmospherically simple, with fishnets, shells made into lampshades, and blue and white decor, but there's the opportunity to dine on the seaside deck, in the sunshine that is the reason I like to come to Varadero. Count on about 10 pesos per person for a seafood meal with appetizer—and try to get a table near the huge sea grape tree that shades the deck.

Castel Nuovo, in a former home on the inland side of the road that runs along the shore, just after you cross the bridge to the resort area, was recommended for excellent food in air-conditioned surroundings. I have not eaten here, but was told that cuisine is similar to that offered at Las Américas, at prices to match.

Las Américas is touted (not advertised, in this communist country) with the comment "The du Pont family used to spend their winters here in unbelievable luxury. Why don't you come for lunch?" And you should. The service aspires to be Cuba's best, even when you fill the only table in one of the several small dining rooms that now occupy the library and parlors on the main floor. The menu lists a complete range of fish, pork, eggs, and seafood—and my sampling was excellent, when I dined in the former library (amid shelves of English books that included Rose Macaulay's *Staying with Friends, and America Conquers Britain* by Ludwell Denney. *Let Them Live* and *Smile Please* stood next to *Sugar Facts & Figures 1952* and *Webster's Collegiate Dictionary*). The view out the window of the spectacular sea glimmering under warm sun was sharp contrast to the elegance of my surroundings. A full-course lunch or dinner can run about 10 pesos per person, with the entrees hovering around 5 pesos. Before or after your meal, weave your way down the stairs to the right as you enter to the downstairs bar that now occupies the former du Pont wine cellar. Your Cuban beer or rum will be quaffed in surroundings that have known the world's best wines.

Kastellito, a small house on the beach near the center of the town of Varadero, serves drinks and snacks on its porches. Because the house had character, this small spot has more atmosphere than most. It's a good place for late afternoon sipping while the sun goes down.

Coppelia ice cream is available at the center of town, near Ocho Mil Baquillas (8000 lockers), which is the government-built underground parking area with—you guessed it—8000 lockers where Cubans who come out for a swim can park their belongings. (Note the small turn-of-the-century hotel near the park on the inland side of the road. This and some of the other old Varadero buildings may be refurbished as restaurants or small hotels. Plans as I write are undecided.)

Cueva del Pirata, east of Las Américas, is the area's most interesting nightspot, in my opinion. Definitely for tourists, the Pirate's Cave does have real atmosphere. It is *inside* a cave, complete with nooks for sitting and sipping in niches in the rocks; waiters dress like pirates. (I could do without the huge phony spiders and trunks of gold that are tucked into other spots.) There's a floor show, and a deafening din when the music plays (rock surroundings don't offer ideal acoustics). Your tour may include a night here, but if not, take a cab to see what the place is all about.

■■■

PLACES WORTH FINDING IN VARADERO are linked with the sea or nature (as with the Bellamar caves near Matanzas). Most of the hotels have a tour desk, where a Cubatur representative will make arrangements for you to go scuba diving (15 pesos for 4 hours), on a glass-bottom boat ride (2.50 pesos), on an all-day boat safari with picnic lunch (15 pesos), to Guamá on the south coast by bus (15 pesos), to Habana, including lunch and tours (11 pesos), or on an overnight excursion to Habana, including the show at Tropicana (40 pesos).

Las Américas: A tour of the home and grounds of the former estate of Irénée du Pont is the top attraction in the Varadero area when you want to get off the beach. The private lake that was the du Pont "swimming pool" has been outfitted with a bar on stilts in the center, and pedal boats and rowboats you can hire to reach it. The golf course that ranges around the grounds needs a lot of work, which it may get when the people of the Revolution find they have enough leisure time to play golf. Right now all are too busy building the Revolution to take care of maintaining a golf course or to have the time to play it. The mansion, with its red plush, heavy wood pieces in the rooms on the main floor, still has some of the du Pont furniture, "which the du Ponts chose to leave here." Note the heavy wood ceilings, the marble floors, the huge open doorways—and the rings and rods from which heavy pull drapes used to hang. On the second floor you will see the bedrooms of the family; notice a glass-topped table with 1928 photographs of life as the du Ponts knew it—when they were building their mansion, and when they entertained the first guests. Much is made of Mr. du Pont's hobby of raising iguanas and using them for "iguana fights." There are a dozen or more photographs of the wealthy wandering around in their tropical white suits, and sometimes in more casual (always proper) attire. The only caption left intact on one of the iguana pictures reads "The competitor [no name] crouching to receive the attack." The house was built at a reported cost of 600,000 pesos; Mr. du Pont acquired the property "on the pretense of starting a hemp plantation"; he used it to entertain his friends and as a vacation home for his family of 5 girls and 1 boy. (Paint is peeling in the daughter's room and I noticed that Mr. du Pont's bedroom has the best view and breeze.) Be sure to go up to the top floor "cocktail terrace," which offers a breathtaking view in surroundings that seem Moorish.

Curaçao

Curaçao Tourist Bureau, Plaza Piar, Willemstad, Curaçao, N.A; 685 Fifth Ave., New York, NY 10022.

US $1 = NAf 1.77
Unless otherwise noted, all references are to US dollars.

There are those who used to climb the 1213-foot Christoffel in the early sunrise of Easter to pluck orchids from the top. At least so I've been told, but I've never talked with anyone who has done it. And when you drive to Westpunt, past the spikes of Turk's Cap cactus that punctuate the dry and dusty terrain, and the weird divi-divi trees, bent in a permanent bow—perhaps toward you, but certainly to the whim of the ever constant trade winds that soothe the sun-parched island from the northeast—it's difficult to imagine the devotion that would send one off to conquer "mountains" in the rising heat of the day. It was much cooler, when I headed out this way, to dive deep into the wine cellar of Landhuis Jan Kok, where cold Amstel, brewed locally from distilled seawater, was served.

The landhuizen of Curaçao's kunuku (as the countryside is called) are seldom seen; these houses are lived in and only a few are open to the general public, although you can pass by and look from the outside at almost 100 houses around the island. They have been built in the open style known in the Netherlands—where people show their best facade to those who may pass by. It was a sign of status in the mother country to have your city building standing tall since the street frontage, highly taxed, was regulated. That may apply in downtown Willemstad, but in the kunuku, the Netherlands custom of keeping the parlor curtains parted so that the outside world knows you have a nice home is more the way of life.

Curaçao of the kunuku, spelled also cunucu (a Papiamento word for country), is another world, far removed from the Curaçao of commerce that most see in and around Willemstad. The customs are consistently Dutch, adapted to the Caribbean. There are sandy shores when you head northwest out into the countryside of this 40-mile-long sliver that sits some 40 miles off the coast of Venezuela. When the Spaniards settled here in the 1500s, following the island's discovery by Alonso de Ojeda, a Spanish navigator, it was gold people were looking for—and freedom from harassment. Curaçao's comfort for the world's weary is nothing new; the island has welcomed Catholics, Jews, Protestants, Moslems, famous people such as Simón Bolívar, who hid out here twice during his wars for the liberation of South America, infamous people who have changed with their professions, plus many—like us—who come to rest for a while and revive.

POLITICAL PICTURE: The three Dutch islands in the south, Aruba, Bonaire, and Curaçao (known as the ABC islands), off the coast of Venezuela, plus the three Dutch islands in the northern Caribbean (Sint Maarten, Saba, Sint Eustatius) make up the Netherlands Antilles, acting as one member of the Kingdom of the Netherlands, with the seat of government at Willemstad, Curaçao. The 6 islands have complete control over their internal affairs, a fact made possible by tourism, oil refineries, and the coffers of the mother country.

Although each of the half-dozen islands feels today's pressure for independence on its own terms, all now seem to realize—especially after the problems that Surinam has faced since its independence a few years ago—that the responsibilities of being independent put awesome burdens on fragile economies. Once-imminent plans for independence as a group seem to have been postponed indefinitely.

Curaçao is the seat of the Netherlands Antilles government, and has 12 delegates of the 22 member Staten, the legislative council of parliament. (Members are elected every 4 years.) In addition, there is a 6-island Executive Council and an Advisory Council. For domestic government, each island has its own legislative and executive hierarchy which is called the Island Council.

Curaçao was first claimed by the Spanish, but was captured by the Dutch in 1623, in retaliation for having been driven from Sint Maarten, which they ultimately settled (successfully) in 1631.

CUSTOMS OF THE COUNTRY are officially Dutch, but Curaçao's long-time affiliation with the United States makes this island's customs seem "American." Look for the few vestiges of Netherlands traditions in the countryside, at festivals and dance performances sponsored by community groups, and when you have the opportunity to visit with any Curaçaon families. Dutch is the official mother tongue, but Papiamento, that verbal stew that is spoken in the ABCs (and spread to the northern Dutch triumvirate when workers who had come south to work in the oil refineries headed back north to their home islands) is now being taught in schools as well as being spoken by the old-timers.

In spite of this island's obvious involvement with tourism, visitors are advised to consider local sensibilities and cover up the beach attire for forays into town and sightseeing around the island. The basic Dutch conservatism is still a fact of many Netherlands Antilles' personalities.

■■■

MONEY MATTERS will revolve around how fast it goes. U.S. dollars are accepted, eagerly, everywhere. There will be no need to convert U.S. dollars into the local Netherlands Antilles florin or guilder (the words are used interchangeably), noted as NAf or simply fl. and *not* pegged to the guilder used in the Netherlands. Commerce is so tied to the United States, that the Netherlands Antilles guilder is pegged to the U.S. dollar at about NAf 1.77 to US $1. It is almost impossible to find a restaurant, shop, or other public place that is not used to dealing in dollars.

■■■

ARRIVAL ON CURAÇAO at Dr. Albert Plesman Luchthaven (airport), which was expanded and refitted to celebrate Curaçao's 300th birthday in 1975, will be a surprise to anyone expecting the quaint and quiet airports known on other Caribbean islands. This terminal is big, modern, and a merchandise mart that is worthy of being on an island that has more shops per square foot in its downtown area than any Caribbean port, with the possible exception of St. Thomas. ALM, American, and other international airlines wing in here regularly, funneling portions of their flight-payers into the covey of hotels that fleck the area around Willemstad.

Immigration officials are businesslike, without much time for happy-go-lucky vacationing types with quick comments. The object of your line standing is obviously to present immigration card and proof of citizenship (passport is best; voter's registration will do; driver's license is not proof enough, since it does not show where you were born). Baggage claim is an air-conditioned distance from the immigration formalities, and the taxis are gathered at the door to take you and luggage as soon as you step into the sometimes overwhelming heat outside.

Departure, once through immigration and customs, and after paying the $5.75 (10 NAf) departure tax, puts you at a shopping mall with a clutch of Netherlands imports (cheese and other items from across the sea). Some products carry good prices, all of them are good quality—and some of the best buys to bring home. Leave room in your carry-on luggage for last-minute purchases.

AUTHOR'S OBSERVATION: Inquire from the Curaçao Tourist Bureau and your travel agent about special all-inclusive week-long holiday plans. In recent seasons, interesting special interest holidays have been sold through tour operators. For example, special Passover programs focused on services at the Mikve Israel-Emanuel Synagogue which dates from 1732.

▪▪

TOURING TIPS: If you've invested in the "Bon Bini/Free Spree," Curaçao's version of the "Free Spree" offered in the ABC islands, where you get some extras with your airfare and room for a week-long stay, the short sightseeing tour may be worth the time. There *are* some interesting and historic sights in Willemstad, but my experience with the tour is that the reporting is so mechanical that the highlights are easily missed. If you're interested in the island's history, a visit to the tourist office can give you the basic printed information and an update on any new restorations or special buildings open to the public. Otherwise, rent a car for a day (that's all you'll need to cover the island) and drive around. If you decide to fly to Aruba or Bonaire for the day, be sure to check your ALM ticket envelope. Avis was offering a promotion that gives a car rental discount, providing your Avis car rental isn't already discounted in some way (or included in your "Bon Bini/Free Spree" plan).

Most Curaçao hotels offer complimentary transportation into Willemstad so, if you can adjust your plan to their schedule, there's no need for taxi expense for that jaunt.

▪▪

HOTELS ON CURAÇAO geared for vacationers number half a dozen, with another 8 or so used mainly by commercial (business) traffic. Not one of them sits on a beach worth the name, but most have worked sincerely to give you other things instead. The sun is over all, and the sea surrounds—even when you do your swimming in a pool. Curaçao's hotels have faced, and dealt squarely with, a rash of labor problems that added an unwanted ingredient in past seasons already sprinkled with serious difficulties. During the early '70s economic recession that got the blame for keeping many North American tourists at home, Curaçao's hotels set about solving some problems. In some cases, when private owners pulled out, the government got into the hotel business. Fuel costs forced some Miami-based cruise ships to reconsider carrying passengers this far south, but Caribbean-based cruise lines continue to come. Although Curaçao's tourism count from North America was down in '78, the Venezuelan business looked as though it could (and would) increase. Final figures for '79–'80, and also '80–'81, proved to be an overall increase in total visitors.

You'll find a lot of Spanish spoken here, as well as Dutch, English, and Papiamento. Officials are studying ways to make life more interesting for vacationers who come to this sun-struck island that has banked its past tourism fortunes on a picture-perfect town filled with "duty-free"' shops and hotels with lively casinos. As it stands this season, you will pay moderate to high rates, compared to those of other Caribbean islands. Always ask about special package tours, and expect to pay 5% government tax and 10% service charge.

A UTHOR'S AWARD goes to the Hilton International Curaçao for keeping a hand on the tourism tempo and giving guests enough activities to make the investment worth it.

✢ **Arthur Frommer Hotel** (Box 2179, Willemstad, Curaçao, N.A.; 100 rooms plus 47 2-bedroom villas) put its emphasis on informality and good-value surroundings when the doors opened here in the mid-'60s. In spite of the price-rise trend (to which this place has also succumbed), the value is still the best on the island—especially if you are content to bed into one of the 2-bedroom villas and do your own cooking for some meals. Surroundings include the Hilton, which shares the shores of Piscaderabaai. Inquire about special package-tour rates, and the possibility of scuba holidays using the villas for overnighting. There's a pool at the gathering area near the patch of sand that passes as a beach. *King Arthur's*

Pub is the drinking and dining depot, with option to go next door to the Hilton or take a 10-minute ride into Willemstad (hotel provides transportation for shoppers). The tall, good-looking man you'll see walking around checking and greeting is genial manager Frank Maynard, Curaçao's representative to the Caribbean Hotel Association and the man to find if you have any questions that the rest of the staff can't handle for you. This is an informal spot, good for family holidays (especially with the villas) or for a couple of couples who want to share with the housekeeping. The villa units offer more comfortable and independent surroundings, in my opinion, than the regular hotel rooms which were getting a needed painting and sprucing up when I looked in. Count on paying over $100 for 2 for your room; meals, tips and taxes extra, this season.

✤ **Avila Beach Hotel** (Box 79, Willemstad, Curaçao, N.A.; 45 rooms) perches on the shore, and makes the most of its scrap of shoreline for guests who want to dunk in the sea. This is the nearest sandy strand to the town of Willemstad; there's no pool. Nic and Jette Moeller have a prize property here, if you like small hotels with local flavor. The *Schooner Bar* on the beach is a nice place for a respite from in-town shopping. The most interesting part of the hotel, in my opinion, is the original section, which was the governor's palace a couple of centuries ago. The 3-floor hotel (no elevator) now provides modern accommodations that can be ideal for families, especially if you want to put your small ones in charge of one of the sitters that the management can provide (at a fee, of course). Count on rates to be about $60 for 2, all meals extra, this winter. The food at *Avila's Belle Terrace* competes with the view for comment. Located in the oldest part of the hotel (the original mansion), it has additions that spill down to almost sea level for the cocktail area. Menu offerings during the past seasons have featured barbecues, special beef fondue nights, a buffet in European/Scandinavian style, and some interesting Dutch dishes (including that intriguing-but-heavy Edam cheese stuffed with chicken, etc., that goes by the name of keshi yena). Skin diving and scuba can be arranged through the activities desk.

✤ **CP Curaçao Plaza** (Box 229, Willemstad, Curaçao, N.A.; 254 rooms) commands the prize location. You can sit at the pool and smile at the captain on the deck of one of the ships that glide past the historic Water Fort, part of Fort Amsterdam. He can see you clearly, because your poolside perch is inches away from the fort's parapet and a channel marker. When Inter-Continental built the first part of this hotel in 1957, it plucked the best possible Willemstad shore site for a luxury hotel. You are a short stroll from all the shops and right at the heart of the island's action, in the stage set that is 17th-century Willemstad. Although the original part of the hotel nestled into the existing fort and nearby land, the 15-story tower, with its hermetically sealed air-conditioned rooms, sticks out like the proverbial sore thumb in the middle of a geometric maze of roofs. It is a blatant statement to commercialism that gives those who book a dinner at the tower-top restaurant the best overview of town. Labor problems and other difficulties resulted in the dissolution of the IHC-Hotelmij "El Curacao" N.V. link—and Canadian Pacific Hotels, Ltd. of Toronto, Canada, stepped into the breach, sprinkling a healthy portion of more than $1 million face-lifting fund over the property. Refurbished rooms stand ready to welcome you. Canadians come here, of course, and there are a lot of others who want to take advantage of being at the heart of things, in surroundings that include a poolside bar and sunning area (where service was *slow* when I sat here), the lobby level *Cava de Neptune* nightclub with a glass panel that lets you peak at bodies in the pool, and the usual complement of specialty restaurants—topped off by the tower and its *Penthouse* dining room. The casino captures a convenient spot just off and up from the lobby. A room for 2 this winter will be about $100, everything extra.

✟ **Hilton International Curaçao** (Box 2133, Willemstad, Curaçao, N.A.; 200 rooms) captures top spot for overnighting in Curaçao. Not only is the hotel attractive, with seaside view that gives it a patch of sand more presentable than most in the city area, but it is also an action-packed hub (tennis, water sports, classes) that takes its cue from Hilton's Caribbean policy of putting a heart in the high rise. The hotel gobbled up the old Piscadera Bay Club, a favorite for many who knew this island in the '40s and early '50s, but it has more than made up for the old tradition by injecting a lot of Curaçao in the present place. The Pirate's Party is a special fete that draws residents as well as tourists who make plans to be here for that night at least. Buffet is local foods prepared by the Hilton chef, and entertainment includes folkloric dances. The *Tambu Nightclub* is the center of "formal" nightlife, with dancing every night in winter and the casino with all the games nearby. The *Pisca Terrace and Grill*, the coffee shop, has sea view and sunning options. Check for the night of the rijsttafel in the *Willemstad Room*; the rice table with 20-plus specialties is set up with all condiments, and although it *is* hotel style (and misses some of the authenticity of the real thing), it is an acceptable copy of the Indonesian tradition. You can get up at dawn to join the Dolphin Club (Friday mornings) to earn a certificate for leaping and jogging before the champagne breakfast (that is your reward) after your exercise, or you can head straight to the pool or beach for a swim after a night at the casino. Shops fill the arcades where you'll connect with a taxi to take you for the 10-minute ride into town. Special classes about local customs, and even Papiamento, are part of the program, especially during winter season and when the house count warrants. Look into the "Pleasure Chest" promotion (April 16–December 15) for week-long package tour rates that give you a lot more than your room for your money. Boat trips, rum parties, transportation to shops, tennis clinic, and other extras are included for your flat fee. Otherwise, 2 will pay $90 or more for winter room this season, with all meals, taxes, tips, and whatever you do in the way of watersports and/or tennis extra.

✤ **Holiday Beach** (Box 2178, Willemstad, Curaçao, N.A.; 200 rooms plus 20 shorefront cabanas) hatched on the shore in the late '60s as a Holiday Inn, clutching a patch of man-made beach between its 2 wings of 2 double-bed air-conditioned rooms. The place had a complete scrub up and clean out a couple of years ago, but it was close to needing another when I looked. Some rooms have balcony, all have sea view, with pool, tennis court, and a hotel activities desk to take care of touring. The public rooms and lobby are big and boxy (and air-conditioned). The casino is just off the lobby with shopping arcades nearby, and the former practice of letting union employees gamble "on credit" has been stopped. The place used to perk with off-duty employees losing money they could not hope to make. You can walk to the Otrabanda side of the pontoon bridge to stroll to Willemstad shops (if you don't mind the heat—the walk is on hot pavement, with plenty of heat rising). Taxis or the hotel's shuttle bus can take you into town in about 5 minutes; it's 5 minutes in the other direction to the Hilton or Frommer hotels. This hotel is used by groups and by conventions, and the lobby is active if the house count is high. The sand that spreads out before you sinks into a waist-level sea that's good for dunking but nothing to tempt Olympic swimmers. (And count on unceasing trade *winds* when you're outside.) Rates this winter are pegged at about $90 for 2, all meals, tips, and taxes extra.

✤ **Princess Beach** (Martin Luther King Blvd., Curaçao, N.A.; 140 rooms) pulled through its previous life as the Flamboyant Sands, née Flamboyant, a small family spot on an acceptable (for Curaçao) stretch of sand about 15 minutes' drive from downtown Willemstad. (Hotel provides regular shuttle to supplement at-whim taxis.) New life came with a new name of Princess Isles, which has now been modified to Princess Beach. As to what to expect? It's hard to say, but the property has a prize location, with some sand to sit on, seaside (where the tradewinds *blow*), and a pool as an alternative for swimming. The cement-sided pool has a sea view. Almost half a million was spent on refurbishing and sprucing up, which included a shopping mall and glamour in the casino that is counted upon to fatten fortunes—not necessarily yours, but probably the owners'. Tennis courts and water sports occupy sunshine hours. What you stay in while you partake of the "round-the-clock" entertainment that is offered is a clutch of 2-story blocks of rooms; the best (for my money) are those with sea view. Count on winter rates of close to $100 for 2, but ask about special package tours.

RESTAURANTS ON CURAÇAO: Curaçaoans have a Dutch tradition in their kitchens, especially in the kunuku (pronounced coo-NOO-coo, meaning country). Some restaurants now offer that tradition to you. If you want to know exactly what you're eating when you order by an unpronounceable Papiamento or Dutch name, buy *This Is the Way We Cook*, a clever cookbook by 2 American residents, Helen Dovale and Jewell Fenzi (the CP Drugstore at Curaçao Plaza used to carry it). Among foods you're apt to find these days are sopito (a fish and coconut soup), funchi (cornmeal with flavorings), zult (pickled pigs ears), keshi yena (a shell of Edam cheese stuffed with Caribbean shrimp, beef, or chicken and sundry spices) and sancocho di gallinja (a chicken stew, country style). On tables in the authentic spots, the hot sauce has the power to lift the lid from the jar, and your larynx from your throat. It may hide in an innocuous little bottle or it may be found in the familiar Indonesian spice wrapper that hints of what's inside. Indonesian rijsttafel is another feast, transported here centuries ago by the Dutch settlers who knew the 20-plus tasty and spice-filled dishes from the tables of their colonies in the East.

In the past, hotels catering to American tourists assumed that all visitors wanted Curaçao-style hamburgers, french fries, peanut butter, and steak, and you can find Big Mac and Kentucky Fried if you want it. Today, however, better-than-average Curaçaoan restaurants are emerging.

Bellevue, a local spot with strictly Curaçaoan cuisine and waitresses in traditional and colorful costumes, is a place for adventuresome diners who want to sample domestic food. Okra gumbo, under a Papiamento alias of giambo, is best with hot sauce, and soppi juana uses that prehistoric-looking animal, the iguana, for its meat. A casual place where dining is under a thatch-roof, Bellevue can be fun with a few friends.

Bistro Le Clochard, in Rif Fort on Otrabanda looking across Santa Anna Bay to the Curaçao Plaza Hotel, serves "cuisine Suisse et Française" for discriminating palates, taking the cue from the hotel school (in Switzerland) training of Curaçao-born owner/chef Freddy Berends. (His wife, Iris, is Swiss.) Lunch hours, in spite of the continental cuisine, are Dutch-rigid (from 12 to 2), with dinner service starting at 6:30 and carrying on until midnight. Comfort is the key word for clothes and cosmopolitan for the cuisine. Count on a steep tally at dinner hours, especially if you care about wine. (The bistro is a short walk from the depot where guests from out-of-town hotels are deposited by hotel-provided transportation.)

Bistro La Hacienda, across from the Princess Beach Hotel, hides an excellent cook in the kitchen and parades an awesome list of local foods in front of diners who claim a table in this country-style house. Keshi yena comes stuffed with a beef mixture (and is a *hearty* meal), but there are those who favor the veal. Menu standards include steak, chicken, and fish cooked Curaçao style (which is sauced and spicy). Count on parting with over $10 for a full dinner; lunch is served for less, but weekdays only.

De Taveerne, inland on the east side of Santa Anna Bay, in a residential part of Willemstad, would be worth visiting as a museum-of-sorts, even if Jerry and Christine Wielinga, and chef Kolenbracher (from the mother country), didn't serve such good food. The care that has been lavished on the decor of Landhuis Groot Davelaar is obvious to anyone intrigued by Curaçao's traditions. Reservations are essential (sometimes a day in advance) for the 52-seat cellar restaurant in the octagonal house; there's only one seating per evening.

Fort Nassau was Fort Republic when it was completed by the Dutch in 1797 and was closed for a couple of years in the mid-1970s while management/owners and staff worked out a few things. The problems with keeping things running in recent times are nothing compared to the rotating claims for ownership of this fort in the early days. The British claimed the fort in 1807, and named it Fort George, but when treaties in 1816 turned the island back to the Dutch the name became Fort Orange Nassau. Used by American antiaircraft crews in World War II, the fort opened as a restaurant in the 1950s. The fort provides a viewful dining spot overlooking Santa Anna Bay to the north and the harbor to the south. It is a traditional cruise passenger goal, so it's to be avoided on cruise ship days, unless you like crowds. When you're ensconced at a table it's difficult to see much more than what's around you—surroundings that have been seasoned with antiques or copies to give a publike feeling. If you're part of a rollicking group or want to have your own party inquire about renting the Stuyvesant Room, punctuated with heavy "oak" chairs and tables, with Delft and pewter touches (and air-conditioned to the freezing point when I looked in). The Battery terrace is the viewing spot, where cocktails are sometimes served. As we go to press, restaurant facilities are in a state of flux once again, so check when you arrive in Curaçao for current status. The view is worth a drive up to this perch anyway. If you're driving yourself, weave through Punda on De Ruyterkade, past the new market, turning left at the stoplight but *not* at the road to go up to go over the Queen Juliana Bridge. A second left on Pareraweg to turn left on Versaillesweg will thread you up the hill (a taxi is a lot easier than drive-yourself if you're bad on directions).

Fort Waakzaamheid Tavern, across the bay from Fort Amsterdam, not far off the Otrabanda ramp from the Queen Juliana Bridge, fits itself out in historic fashion and gives a fascinating view of Willemstad with its meals. In a country tavern atmosphere, you can dine on steaks, fish served local style, and sandwiches (lunchtime), quaffing a locally brewed Amstel beer with it all. Open lunch and dinner (daily except Tu), the tavern does its best to re-create some of the features of its past, preserving the aura of tavern life, but adapted for modern times. I found the staff and surroundings congenial and the price right at about $5 for lunch; figure $10 and up for dinner.

Golden Star, at Socratesstraat 2, where Dr. Maalweg meets Dr. Hugenholtzweg, just inland from the coast road leading southeast from Santa Anna Bay, is a dinerlike simple setting for some well prepared local food. When you see *bestia chiqui,* know it is goat stew; *chicharrón de pollo* is a popular chicken and onion dish. Interesting and earnest; if you want local food, leave the cooking to the Burkes. They're the best in the business. (Steak is also served, but not featured.)

Holland Club Restaurant, on the 3rd floor, over the Indonesia, is entered from Windstraat, easily overlooked between Handelskade and Heerenstraat. Seafood is a specialty in an air-conditioned box of a room that does its best to re-create a Dutch farmer's atmosphere.

There's no way you can realize what's upstairs from the inauspicious entrance off the street, so head up to take a look to see if you want to sign on for dinner. There are some acceptable Dutch specialties, with Curaçaoan adaptations, and you will find the ubiquitous (and not too good, from my taste testing) steak. Frankly, I prefer places with sunlight and sea breezes, but this place has its local businessman following. Closed Sun.

Indonesia is one flight up from Windstraat, putting you at eye level with the captain on the deck of the ships coming into the channel. The surroundings are typical of Indonesian restaurants in Holland as well as here, with simple-verging-on-seamy surroundings, and very special food. Not for timid tummies, the food here will delight those who want their spices *hot* and their rice dishes and sates in quantity. Nasi bami and nasi goreng, one-person rice plates, served with kropek (shrimp and cassava bread), are available also. Open lunch and dinner, closed Sun; this was one of the strongholds for coat-and-tie diners, so check on current status if that matters.

Landhuis Jan Kok opened a few years ago as a wine cellar, and after an interlude with closed doors, is now open as a special restaurant. Worth a visit almost as much for the opportunity to enjoy landhuis surroundings (and to sit on the porch where breezes cool) as for the food, this is a good place for lunch or an afternoon cool-off drink on the day you're touring the island. Lively entertainment (music) has been scheduled most weekends, but call in advance to be sure that continues through this season (and to find out what kind of food is served).

La Parrillada, east of the harbor and inland, at Cas Coraweg 78, claimed an Argentinian connection at some time in its past and has new management as of early April '81. I haven't eaten here since that date, but my guess is that if you've traveled in that country and come here expecting Argentinian beef, you'll be disappointed. I found the grilling à la parrilla to be better on atmosphere than on beef when I visited. Popular with the local folk, and casual (no jacket or tie) for all, the steakhouse used to give you antipasto from a cart and an option for shrimp and lobster (all frozen and flown in) as well as some local fish. Check to see about menu this season and if it's still closed Tuesday.

La Bistroëlle gets rave notices from some readers, and I agree. Recent visits have provided memorable food and surroundings. (Look at the photos of old Curaçao on the walls.) The location, behind a shopping center in the residential area east of the harbor well outside downtown Willemstad, at Zeelandia and Schottegatweg Oost, is anything but festive, and if you come here by cab, be sure to make arrangements for a pickup time.

Le Recif, wedged into the walls of Rif Fort on Otrabanda with a view over the channel entrance to Santa Anna Bay, serves seafood from 12 to 2 p.m. and also at evening hours. Don't expect only fresh-caught fish. The single-subject menu here includes herring in sour cream and smoked salmon, neither of them available offshore. The snapper fillet and stewed conch are relatively local, although consigned to a freezer due to the exigencies of sporadic guest count. Even if you visit here only for the *Soppitoe* (the special Curaçao fish chowder), this nook is well worth the visit (and money spent) if you are a fish eater.

The Wine Cellar, in a portion of a historic house in Willemstad, makes a name for itself mostly for its wine list, which carries on for "pages" with offerings from Germany, Italy, and the French Alsace area. The familiar Zeller Schwarze Katz sells for 17 Nfl., which figures to about $10. Your meals are mostly steak and beef. An entrecote (steak) runs about $9, with a filet for close to $10, but count on this for a leisurely evening, and come casual. Dutchman Nico Cornelisse is your host and his haven holds about 40 people maximum. The place opens about 6 p.m., and is closed Sunday.

Peach Garden (Schottegatweg Oost 177) has been praised in the past for its Chinese cuisine, but frankly, if my time were limited on a holiday in Curaçao, this would not be at the top of my list. **Chungking** (Wilhelminaplein 1) is a lot more convenient. **The Great Wall,** in boxy air-conditioned surroundings at the Centro Commercial Antilia, is also good.

■■

PLACES WORTH FINDING ON CURAÇAO are right in the heart of Willemstad. In one day you can see anything worth seeing around the mostly flat, parched, hot island, beaches and landhuizen included. There is only one chocolate-kiss hill—and that is called St. Christoffel; it's under 1300 feet and can be seen if you take the time to drive to Westpunt. It's in the northwest (and can also be seen from your plane window at take off).

WILLEMSTAD is enchanting, even though its sun-bleached pastel facades and Amsterdam-style stepped roofs cup crass commercialism. The town is photogenic, historic, and well maintained, partly because of a strong historical group, and partly because everyone here is well aware that the town of Willemstad is about all Curaçao has going for it at this point as far as something of tourist interest is concerned. It was named for King Willem II in 1647, during the early years of the Dutch settlement, and its port claims to be the fifth busiest in the world! Whether the oft-told legend about the faded pastel of the buildings is true or not, the soft colors help the aura that makes this town worth looking at today. (The story is that an early governor ordered the blinding white buildings painted pastel because the white hurt his eyes!)

Mikve Israel-Emanuel Synagogue, on Columbusstraat at Kerkstraat, claims 300 years of history. With its Beth Haim Cemetery, the museum, and the baths that were uncovered in the courtyard during excavations in 1976, it is the prize touring attraction for many visitors to Curaçao. The building at #26 Kuiperstraat was the rabbi's residence, but it has been incorporated into the museum (open 9–11:45; 2:30–4:45 M–F, closed Sat and Sun. If a cruise ship is in port on Sundays, the museum opens in the morning).

Bolívar House, opened a couple of years ago as a museum, holds an interesting collection of the South American liberator's memorabilia.

Queen Emma Pontoon Bridge started as a toll bridge when it spanned the river in 1888. It's free today, and still in use as a footbridge, because it provides the fastest link between Otrabanda and Punda, the two "halves" of the city. Vehicles have to head out, up, and over the blatant 193-foot Queen Juliana Bridge (see below). The pontoon bridge and the floating schooner market that survives at harborside in spite of the new, huge, modern market that was built to improve local shopping conditions, are places worth finding in town. (The new market, where housewives shop, is air-conditioned under the vast cement cap that curves into the harbor off De Ruyterkade near the Post Office.)

Queen Juliana Bridge can't be missed—even if you want to miss it. The $30-million fixed span that sits over Curaçao like some outsized buckle was finally dedicated on April 30, 1974—after a few false starts that had the 2 sides stretching toward the center (red parenthesis in the sky as you looked up from downtown) missing their center segment. Long after the bridge was completed, traffic had to wait for the access roads that would make it possible to head up and over this 4-lane highway to cross the 270-foot wide channel between Punda and Otrabanda. The goal was to undo the hair-pulling, horn-honking traffic snarl that Queen Emma caused. The rainbow-shaped bridge took 13 years to build and was talked about for more than 45. First discussions about the need for a new route started in 1929; the bridge was finally in use in mid-1974. The approach on the Punda side leads past the American Consulate, housed in a building that was given by the Dutch in thanks for assistance and protection offered to this island during the World Wars.

The spoon shape of **Curaçao's harbor** is the center of sightseeing. In the bowl, there can be as many as 14 oil tankers, plus countless other ships for repair, and around the edges you can see the spurts of fire from the refinery. (Note this view at night from the top of the Curaçao Plaza Hotel or the Fort Nassau restaurant for the most awesome effect.) The port of Willemstad has been called the western hemisphere's largest dry-docking facilities, and although few people are positive about the present-and-growing status of Cuba's south-coast Cienfuegos, this port is certainly plenty big. More than a dozen ships can be docked and serviced at one time, and you can see several tied up at the harbor docks at almost any season.

On the day you rent a car, head for Westpunt to find any of the Curaçao "beaches" and ask at the tourist office before you set out to find if any of the Landhuis are open. **Landhuis Jan Kok** is a delightful country goal, for a Bols gin or an Amstel locally brewed beer; it's an old house furnished with country antiques. **Landhuis Ascension** on the northwest side of Curaçao, in Banda Bou, is a social center for the Royal (Dutch) Navy. It's open on the first Sunday of the month (for services and sightseeing), but may be visited with special permission at other times. **Landhuis Santa Maria** is well worth visiting for handcrafts made by the handicapped, as well as for a look at the landhuis and its gardens. (In Willemstad, the Curaçao Museum is in a historic house as are De Taveerne restaurant and the retreat for the Sisters of Charity, Landhuis Habaai.) There are at least 15 of the old houses, Bottelier, Klein, Sint Joris, and Santa Kruz among them, that are interesting enough to slow down to look at from the outside, even if you aren't encouraged to wander around.

■■■
SPORTS ON CURAÇAO center on the sea for most visitors because of the sun, but residents are interested in the local baseball teams and soccer/football matches as well as tennis (which can be played at most hotels). **Scuba** is spectacular, they say, though the constant shipping activity has clouded some of the areas that used to be prime spots. While Curaçao can't compete with Bonaire for scuba, or Aruba for beaches, it does offer scuba package plans (see your

travel agent, or check at the Curaçao Tourist Board). Be sure to inquire about special good values during summer (up to December 15), when beginners and advanced instruction is included in one all-inclusive fee. For scuba and other **water sports,** head for the Hilton, where Piscadera Watersports is the place to check up on what's where. Not only does this shop offer the fullest range available in Curaçao, but I found its staff a cut above the others when I was asking questions. Princess Beach has a scuba diving concession, and, after pool lessons, boats provide excursions to good off-shore areas. **Deep-sea fishing** trips can be arranged, and there are some small boats for rent by the half-day or day for a **cruise** around St. Michels Bay. Scuba equipment, and arrangements for lessons (to start in the pool, and then set out in the boat for offshore interesting reefs) can be negotiated at the marina. It is easy to dive from shore, since the island is coral rock and the reefs are around it. Dr. Hans Haas made the first sports dive off Curaçao in 1939, where the Curaçao Hilton now stands. The classic wreck for this area is the Dutch ship Orange Nassau, easily reached with guide and group.

Golfers have no choice: The Shell 3400-yard par 36 course at Emmastad is it, and the greens are sand, but the fairways are "grass." It's not worth lugging your clubs this far; rental will be about $6,- with caddy at at $2 for 9. Open for visitors Tu–F, 8–4.

Tennis courts are touted, but except for the Hilton's courts, they're not much to write home about. Holiday Beach has 2, Princess Beach, Arthur Frommer, and the Country Inn each have one, and the Curaçao Sport Club's 4 are the most interesting if you want to play with some residents. There's a charge for all night-lighted courts over and above the daytime charge levied on nonhotel guests. In response to local enthusiasm for the sport, and as a brilliant publicity effort, Curaçao hosted some of the games for the Copa Marlboro del Caribe Tennis Tournament in January 1980. Part of the program was lessons for local folk by visiting pros.

Horseback riding is a marvelous way to get a new look at Curaçao. J. M. Pinedoe rents horses at his Rancho Allegre at Gr. Michiel. Both English and Western saddles are offered, as well as guides to lead you on lopes around the plantations of sandy Curaçao. (This will be a hot but fascinating couple of hours. By all means, come prepared with long shirt, hat, and plenty of sun screen.) Plan for an early morning sunup ride or a ride late afternoon (4-6) to get the full flavor of desert, Caribbean style. Make arrangements a day in advance, and be sure to settle the matter of cab if you do not have a car to drive yourself.

■■■

TREASURES AND TRIFLES ON CURAÇAO are tucked into all the nooks of the streets and plazas of a 5-block area in downtown Willemstad. Under the eaves of the 17th-century Dutch houses are some excellent buys—and some bargains that are not. The warning repeated throughout this book, when discussions center around "duty-free" and "free-port" shopping, applies here also. As far as cameras, binoculars, radios, tape decks, stereo equipment, etc. are concerned, be sure you know your hometown price. You may find that there's very little difference in the price you pay in Curaçao and what your local discount store can give because it buys in bulk. Camera lenses have proved to be very good buys in past seasons, but know exactly what you want and be sure that what you are looking at is the item you need—and not just a look-alike.

AUTHOR'S OBSERVATION: Shops and merchandise vary. For on-the-spot information, before you set out in the bazaar-filled town, ask for (and read carefully) the yellow *Curaçao Holiday*. It's fact-filled, and issued monthly so its information is "current."

El Louvre on Breedestraat 3, at the corner of Columbusstraat, is one place to survey for camera purchases; then look also at **Oduber and Kan,** also on Breedestraat, but across the street toward the pontoon bridge, and at **Boolchands Kohinoor,** at Heerenstraat 4 B. These 3 will give you a good idea of what's available.

As far as clothes are concerned, I do not see much in the way of bargains these days, but there are a lot of trendy fashions, some of them reasonably priced. **Aquarius,** at Breedestraat 11, is one place where the mod design of the store is almost more interesting than some of the fashions. If you are in the market for snug-fitting pants and Italian, French, or English clothes, look around here to find Cardin, Courrèges, Ted Lapidus, and others. Accessories are especially interesting—belts, scarves, jewelry, etc. Another store for Dior, Cardin, Oleg Cassini, and their ilk is **Jet Set** on Kerkstraat. (It does not close at lunchtime.) London's Marks & Spencer line is carried at **La Fortuna** on Heerenstraat, and you can buy Burbury and Aquascutum at **Cosmopolitan** next door on Heerenstraat.

Two stores to try for one-stop shopping are the **Yellow House** for perfumes and **New Amsterdam,** a typical department store that is stuffed with imports from everywhere and will be glad to charge any of them on whatever credit card you carry. Both stores are on Breedestraat. (The street-level shopping window of Yellow House is "standard" but look up at the 2nd floor for a glimpse at the past, with arched windows and interesting roofline trim.)

Spritzer & Fuhrmann's legend began in Willemstad, when Austrian watchmaker Charles Fuhrmann left the ship he had intended to take to South America and stayed in Curaçao in 1927. Not long after, a fellow watchmaking Austrian, Wolf Spritzer, also arrived in Curaçao, and the 2 opened a small watch repair shop in Willemstad. The natural interest in jewels and gold led to expansion into jewelry, and the jewelry caught the eye (and wallets) of servicemen stationed in Curaçao in the '40s. Business began and thrived when the postwar cruises sent people south in search of treasures and tans. Spritzer & Fuhrmann began its store splitting that now gives the enterprise some 30 outlets, with 550 employees, 90% of them Antillean. Some of the staff have been with the firm 40 years or more since the first store opened; others are newcomers like many of the shoppers, and the systems that are set up for sale are comparable to the most efficient in your hometown store. No "Mom and Pop" operation this! In the main stores, you will look, perhaps touch (with a salesperson standing by), and select, to have your purchase and your cash swept away to the special cash department. The system can be s-l-o-w if the store is crowded, so allow for your Spritzer & Fuhrmann purchases to be a total experience—or buy from one of the small boutiques that now speckle the best hotels and the airport departure lounges on Aruba, Curaçao, and Sint Maarten. You have a choice of 6 Spritzer & Fuhrmann stores in Willemstad, with the main building and 4 others on Breedestraat, and another around the corner on Heerenstraat. (Not incidentally, the S & F specialties are watches and clocks, jewelry, crystal, bone china, many imported luxury items, and spectacular and very special jewelry that commands—and gets—top price.)

Gallery RG, at 20 Keukenstratt, on the 2nd floor of a small 18th-century house in the "middle" of the shopping area, continues a tradition well known on the narrow, cobbled streets of Amsterdam. This is an exceptional art gallery, the enterprise of Egberdien van Rossum, who has gathered exceptional art, some of it local but most of it from elsewhere, for purchase, and viewing. Depending on the exhibit when you are in Curaçao, you may view gouaches, ceramics, wall hangings, sculpture, and perhaps some paintings. The gallery is sometimes closed, when the owners are on buying trips, so write ahead (Box 489, Willemstad, Curaçao, N.A.) if you want to be sure the place will be open and showing.

Recent sprucing up of Willemstad's shopping area has led to plazas, welcome resting places where you can sit at an umbrellaed cafe table while you tally your purchases and plan what to buy next. Gomezplein is one such spot.

Salas, at Salina, on the outskirts of town, is the place to head for if you are interested in books, newspapers (*The New York Times*), and magazines, in addition to a nice print of Curaçao's Handelskade (the waterfront) and the cookbook *This Is the Way We Cook*, mentioned under Restaurants above.

Van Dorp, with 4 shops on the island, also handles the daily news from its store on Breedestraat. Located near the waterfront end of the street, Van Dorp's selection of paperbacks includes the Penguin books, and the miscellany available can take care of most of the trinket needs for the remembrances for the folks back home.

Chalet Gourmet, on Kerkstraat 18 near the synagogue, is the place to find if you're in the mood for imported cheeses, caviar, truffles, Dutch or Swiss chocolate, and a large selection of other delectables. (And if you forget to make a stop downtown, the firm conveniently has a shop at the airport. Check to be sure it will be open if you are counting on it for last-minute purchases before flight departure.)

Landhuis Santa Marta, on Piscaderabaai, is the craft workshop for the handicapped. When you buy here, you can find one-of-a-kind items—and help a local industry.

Shops in Willemstad are open 8–12, 2–6, M-Sat, and some stay open even during the lunchtime. US$ are welcomed everywhere, and you can get your change in U.S. currency also. Credit cards are accepted in most stores.

Dominica

Dominica Tourist Board, Box 73, Roseau, Dominica, W.I.; Caribbean Tourist Association, 20 East 46th St., New York, NY 10017.

US $1 = EC $2.60
Unless otherwise noted, $ refers to U.S. currency.

Ilodalik hung on the window of the car like Kilroy over the fence. His jet black eyes peered at me while rivulets poured down the sides of his nose and cascaded from his eyebrows. The quick rain had sent most of his Carib friends into the shed, with the handful of French tourists who had been my partners for the expedition from nearby Martinique. They were learning how to make a gommier canoe—carved by the Caribs from one felled tree trunk. Ilodalik talked with me. I sat, dry in the cab of the truck that was our touring vehicle for the Dominica Safari. He told me about his friend Solomon, and his home in the Carib reservation, near the village of Sinicou, in the northeastern mountains of Dominica (pronounced Dom-i-NEE-ka).

He was soaked to the skin, but it didn't seem to matter since skin was most of what he wore. A tattered pair of shorts, a thatch of jet black hair, and a wide and flickering smile made up the rest of his outfit. And he knew that the quick deluge that had greeted our band of visitors is typical of Dominica's weather. The verdant island boasts 365 waterfalls and regular showers that make this destination one of the Caribbean's most fertile, rugged, and fascinating for botanists. Although the entire arrowhead shape rumples with flora and fauna, the Dominica National Park provides protection for the endangered Jacquot and Sisserou parrots, and for others of the 135 species of birds that flutter around Dominica.

Ilodalik is a 10-year-old Carib Indian, a descendant of the tribe that gave the Caribbean its name, and one of the group of Dominicans who make up the Caribbean's most noteworthy community of Caribs. (There is another settlement in the northern part of St. Vincent.)

This island was "given" to the Caribs by the French and the English in the treaty of Aix-la-Chapelle in 1748, when they were so busy battling over all the neighboring islands that they didn't have time for this one. It was the French who started nibbling first, after they had secured Guadeloupe about 25 miles off the north point of Dominica, and Martinique, almost the same distance off the southern point. The British then moved in in full force to claim the island as English in the early years of the war of 1756–1763. The band of French settlers permitted to remain were instrumental in a brief period under the French flag from 1778, but Rodney claimed Dominica again and secured it with a treaty in 1783.

But Ilodalik doesn't know all this—or care. All he knows is that he and all his friends scamper down the hillsides whenever they hear a car. If it is one of the groups of French tourists who come from Martinique for the day, they leap and dance along behind, catching the candy thrown by the tourists from the jeeps that jog along the rutted roads.

The reserve he lives in had only a bush track between Atkinson and Castle Bruce when I first knew it. It is now on one of the island's tour routes; a wide swath was cut along the Atlantic shoreline, to be paved—perhaps—when repairs from the damage from the recent hurricanes are finally completed on the 22 miles of coastal road. The "boundaries" of the reserve date to 1903, when the British government defined about 3700 acres around Salybia as a place for the Caribs to live. The area still has its own government, with a Carib chief elected every 5 years (and, if my figuring's correct, an election is due in '79). The chief has 5 councillors who aid in keeping laws. One prohibits outsiders from building houses in the reserve; another gives a Carib whatever uninhabited land he builds on and tills, and a few more declare that, although a Carib man can bring in a foreign wife (she may be as foreign as from Roseau), if a Carib woman marries outside the reservation, she must leave.

What is a cultural phenomenon for outsiders has been a problem in Dominica. Moves by some politicians are aimed at incorporating the Caribs into the community and claiming their land for the country. It is some of the country's richest. The Geest industry banana boxing plant at Salybia is one of the country's most productive.

Ilodalik and his brothers are a minority in Dominica, and they face the problems of minorities everywhere: inadequate schools, lack of health care, no good roads, no piped-in water (the rivers are all-purpose), and other problems not unique to Dominica's Carib reservations. You'll see few animals in the reservation, or around the rest of Dominica, for that matter; the diet is starch, breadfruit 3 times a day when it's in season, and yams, unless someone has been hunting manicou or agouti, or catching fish.

A new surge of "cultural awareness," sparked by the fact that the Dominican blacks are looking to their roots, has revived Carib interest in woven baskets, some of them so tight they can hold water, and making pirogues, as the canoes carved and burned from a single trunk of the gommier tree are called.

The men in Ilodalik's town play cricket and dominoes when they gather; the women (who outnumber the men) tend the children, plenty of them, and the fields. The Caribs are not much different from most of the rest of the Dominicans; they live off the land, and work when they can—for wages that I have heard tallied at about $100 as annual income.

As I drove away from the meeting with Ilodalik, his rain-stained bright-eyed face filling my mind, I heard the gentle clatter of what I looked to see was a sardine can—made into a wagon and pulled on a string by another small boy. I later learned that a family of 6 probably shared those sardines for lunch.

■■

POLITICAL PICTURE: The election of Prime Minister Mary Eugenia Charles and her Freedom Party in June 1980 proved fortuitous for the country. Prime Minister Charles is one of the Caribbean's most dynamic leaders. Her realistic approach to solutions for her country's problems, and also for the problems facing other Caribbean (and Third World) communities is an asset for the region. At conferences in Caribbean countries as well as at the annual Caribbean Conference held in Miami each fall, Prime Minister Charles has been straightforward and positive about the role of private enterprise. "We owe it to the people of the Caribbean to prove that parliamentary democracy works—and not state capitalism," which is the process advocated by Communist Cuba. "Private investment has played, is playing and must continue to play an important role in the economy of the islands," Prime Minister Charles said to a group of businessmen assembled in Sint Maarten in November 1980.

In her own country, Prime Minister Charles, whose background includes early schooling in Dominica, study of law in Toronto and

London and, although she planned to stay in Britain, a return to Dominica in 1949 to attend to family matters, has made herculean strides toward stability. In 1970, the Prime Minister was instrumental in forming the Dominica Freedom Party, and she played an active role in the opposition government during the years prior to Dominica's independence (on November 3, 1978) and the tumultuous years of government under former Prime Ministers Patrick John and Oliver J. Seraphin.

The regime of Patrick John was rife with allegations of corruption, and there are reports of attempted sale of Dominican passports to people of questionable background for as much as $10,000. In spring of 1981, following apprehension by the FBI of 10 alleged mercenaries intent on overthrowing the government of Dominica, Patrick John was put on trial for treason. Links were reported between former Prime Minister Patrick John and the mercenaries, who were apprehended in New Orleans at the start of their intended cruise to Dominica aboard a chartered yacht. The group of mercenaries included white members of neo-Nazi and Ku Klux Klan groups, an irony for a country whose 80,000 citizens are mostly descendants of black Africans; earlier episodes involving Patrick John, whose background as a schoolteacher who was active in labor union activities, pushed him into prominence as leader of his fledgling nation, linked him and other members of his government with "conspiring to help South Africa."

Prime Minister Charles' ability to pursue major aid for her country with the U.S., French, and other government groups, is doubly impressive in the light of the unusual problems she has faced with fragments from Dominica's radical political elements. When the 289-square mile island of Dominica became independent on November 3, 1978, there were fireworks, calypsoes, a lowering of the Union Jack and a raising of Dominica's new flag with the Sisserou parrot, and a visit from Princess Margaret, who flew in from her hideaway on the island of Mustique in the Grenadines. She was representing her sister, the Queen of England, and bid the assembled crowd "goodbye and God bless you all," as she turned over an independence gift and soon thereafter left the island.

After the tumultuous post-independence years that included 2 hurricanes, 3 changes of government, and 1 revolution-in-the-Caribbean-island-sense, Prime Minister Eugenia Charles' stable leadership is welcomed relief. The people of Dominica, always willing to work hard, are now concentrating on building a firm foundation for a free enterprise system that will provide benefits and an improved standard of living for Dominicans. This country is one of the Caribbean's most unusual, and most worthy of a conscientious traveler's time (and money).

■■

CUSTOMS OF THE COUNTRY are a curious combination these days. There are those of the traditional agricultural society, where most of the people have worked on plantations: bananas, limes, other citrus fruits, spices, and almost everything except sugar, which has never been big on this island. And there are some remnants of French and British customs. The 2 powers squabbled over this island, even though it was declared off-limits by both for most of the 18th century, and the Caribs have been here long before— and after—right up to today, in fact, when a small colony still exists in the northeastern area, not too far from Melville Hall airport. The Caribs have their own customs, but too many tourists simply look at the community as a curiosity piece, take pictures, and travel on. Chances are that you will have little to do with the true (and complex) Carib customs.

Most of the people of Dominica are field-workers who lead simple uncluttered lives. In recent years, Dominicans have attained self-rule; the old plantocracy is a thing of the past, if not in actual fact, then certainly in the minds of today's Dominicans. "More for those who have less" is the goal of government; well-heeled tourists parading around town (or anywhere else) in their colorful tropical garb from the pages of *Vogue* and its ilk are remarkably out of place.

Dominica is more pioneer country than Caribbean resort. The customs are those of a newly emerging nation: changing. The majority of Dominica's 73,000 population have an average annual income of less than $100 per year.

AUTHOR'S OBSERVATION: Dominica's needs are great. Tourism is one of the few possibilities for hard currency, and greater understanding, but this is not a "typical tourist" place. The sincere needs of the people can be met, partially, by clothing, books, canned foods and other items that are in limited supply—in spite of the airlift of aid that followed the hurricane holocaust. If you want to bring something to give to the children whose pictures you will be tempted to take, bring some colorful, simple children's books on well-chosen subjects.

Clothes for Dominica should include hiking boots, jeans, and sweaters for the mountains, where it can be cool, and waterproof

slicker for rain. You'll want a bathing suit, and something for informal evening wear, but this is not a "lot of luggage" place. This is a
West Indian island where you are encouraged to fit in, not parade
like a peacock.

■■
MONEY MATTERS revolve around the Eastern Caribbean currency, at about EC$2.60 to US$1. Transact for some EC$ *before* you
arrive on Dominica. On more than one of my island excursions, it
has been impossible to change money at the airport. This may be
solved with the new terminal, with its expanded services, although
money-change places are not always open. Come prepared with
some EC cash for purchases you may want to make when you stop
en route to Roseau (or wherever you're going). U.S. dollars mark
you as an obvious outsider (although hotels are glad to have them),
and U.S. small change has no value. Credit cards and personal
checks will not be much help either; you will need cash.

■■
ARRIVAL at Melville Hall airport puts you just about as far as you
can get from Roseau. Taxi fares are rising (since only tourists use
them), so figure about $15 for your almost-2-hour ride weaving and
jolting along the rutted mountain roads to Roseau, on the southwest corner. Hotels at other island locales will cost less; all rates
should be posted at the airport, but ask before you get into a car so
that both you and your driver know the fare and in whose dollars. In
summer of 1978, the new terminal building was opened; facilities
are a great improvement over the old building, but you still may not
find a phone that works or a taxi that is ready to take you where you
want to go if you arrive on your own on the spur of the moment
from nearby Guadeloupe or Martinique.

British government plans for a 2400-foot runway at Canefield,
about 5 miles from downtown Roseau, will be a great boon for business arrivals and others who want to spend some time in or near the
capital. The airstrip should be open by the time you visit, thanks to
British government's preparation and French paving.

■■
TOURING TIPS: This is not a place for the fainthearted or the
carsick crowd. Roads are rutted and weaving, and will be a long
way from what you have in your hometown, assuming you live in a
reasonably settled metropolitan area. Take a taxi, even though rates
are rising rapidly due to gas costs and local taxes, plus duties on

cars and parts. Plan far enough ahead, if you can, to ask your hotel to have a taxi meet you at the airport. Otherwise, travel as I usually do and ask the going rate for your ride before you leave the air terminal and take a cab at the door. The ride to Roseau is a winding, curving, back-breaking journey of almost 2 hours; the road to Portsmouth is a joy by comparison, but most of the hotels—and most of the reason you'll be coming to Dominica—will be at Roseau, on the southwest coast.

Check for the jeep tours if you don't have other arrangements for seeing the hinterland of this country. Whatever price they charge (and it is posted) will be worth the investment since you will get local lore as well as someone who knows the roads. I found the patter a bit canned on one earlier visit, but if you haven't heard any of the talk before, and this is your only way to learn, the day will be worth your time.

For canoe trips up the rivers, check with the Armours at Anchorage Hotel in Roseau.

■■■

HOTELS in Dominica are personality places, and personalities changed drastically with the devastation of August '79. As we go to press, only Anchorage, Sisserou, and Springfield Estates are in full operation, but comments about some of the other properties remain in this edition since they may well be open (rebuilt in some cases) by the time you plan to visit. Check with the Dominica Tourist Office (by overseas telephone at (809) 445-2351, which can be direct dialed from the U.S. and other places). For adventuresome travelers and people who enjoy knowing the real Caribbean (without a real beach), Dominica's inns offer great variety. Do not expect typical resort accoutrements. Long dresses and black tie have gone with most of the British customs; this is an everyman island where clothes do *not* make the man; ability to adapt does.

AUTHOR'S AWARD for hospitality goes to Anchorage Hotel, where Janice and Carl Armour share their Dominican lore as well as their home-turned-inn with you.

✤ **Anchorage Hotel** (Box 34, Roseau, Dominica, W.I.; 30 rooms) cups the shore, a couple of miles south of Roseau. Janice and Carl Armour's home has been expanded to include a 3-story block of rooms overlooking the small pool at the edge of the shore, plus a 2-story string of 8 rooms at the north side of the pool and main house.

All are comfortably, not lavishly, furnished, some with air conditioning and small balcony or patio. Sometimes used by visitors from Guadeloupe, Martinique, Barbados, and other nearby islands as a base for day touring and short overnight stays, the inn does well for a week or longer if you are an adventurous traveler. Not only do the Armours operate jeep safari tours and river rides, but they can also send you out to sea for fishing, arrange for a knowledgeable Dominican to take you hiking in the National Park, or set up any activity to follow your special interests. The cook's preparation of home-grown produce give menus here a special flavor. The Anchorage is ideal for anyone with a sincere interest in this unique island. Winter rates are from $82 to almost $90 for 2, breakfasts and dinners daily, and you'll want to plan to dine here. Although you are at the edge of Roseau, you will have weathered a rugged 2-hour, bouncing and weaving ride to get here. Leave all fancy togs at home; this is a casual, natural place.

✣ **Asta Hotel** (Box 82, Roseau, Dominica, W.I.; 16 rooms) is for bargain hunters who will pay no more than $40 for an air-conditioned room for 2, with 2 meals daily per person in winter. No special tourist facilities offered. Rooms are sparsely furnished in a boxy, balconied building at 13 Victoria Street, the main street at the inland side of Roseau. Popular with West Indian visitors who know good value.

✣ **Castaways** (Box 5, Roseau, Dominica, W.I.; 28 rooms) became the home "dorm" for Dominica's fledgling medical school when it started in April 1979, and rooms have been full of aspiring doctors who have paid substantial sums to come here prior to acceptance (they hope) at a U.S. medical school. At some time Castaways expects to operate again as a hotel, and you can expect good sized rooms, attractively furnished, with the usual amenities, plus balcony view. Your beach will be black/gray volcanic sand, which is all that Dominica has when it has any sandy coves at all. Sports facilities from the hotel can include spearfishing (outlawed on many other islands), plus scuba diving, sailing, and sport fishing. The 13 miles to Roseau may not sound like much, but it's a back-breaking ride for almost an hour on the island's rugged roads. The trip from the airport is another hour, so when you are here, you're here. For this season the med school still claims the property.

✣ **Castle Comfort** (Box 63, Roseau, Dominica, W.I.; 6 rooms) is operated as though it were (and it is) Dorothy Perryman's home.

The houselike building is simply furnished, with basics that probably will be 2 twin beds in your white-walled room. The seaside slab of cement is ideal for sitting at sunset (but hot at other times), and the dining room draws a sprinkling of visitors from British, European, and American towns. Ideal for anyone who must be in town for business, Castle Comfort is only a few minutes' easy drive from any place you'll want to be in Roseau (and the usual almost 2-hour harrowing ride from the north and the airport). Rates are about $50 for 2, with 2 Dominican-style meals per person daily.

✤ **Emerald Guest House** (Emerald Plantation, Box 20, Roseau, Dominica, W.I.; 8 cabins) is a rough-cut jewel in the middle of the lush terrain of Dominica. The A-frames that have been built in this tropical clearing give you a marvelous outpost, with the flair of Swiss management. Peter Kaufmann, who identified himself as a "former Swiss TV/movie maker," and Gina have set up a movie set of sorts. Ideal for a Tarzan and Jane who want some comforts, the wood cabins give all the basics around a social "center" that includes a pool, food service with some flair and exceptional local produce, and the opportunity to wander along footpaths through the verdant "jungle" or to sign on with Peter for one of the "safari" excursions he will organize if you're interested. For all of this, you'll be paying about $15 per person this winter, and chances are most of your fellow guests will be Europeans.

✤ **Fort Young** (Box 8, Roseau, Dominica, W.I.) was shattered by the hurricanes but is rebuilding with all new facilities. The former hotel was built inside the walls of the 18th-century fort. Check for its status in mid to late '82.

✤ **Island House** (Box 44, Roseau, Dominica, W.I.) with its several Gauguin-style cottages and foot bridges succumbed to winds and rains. It was ruined, but check for status when you look into places to stay. Resilience is a very real quality among Dominican hoteliers, and plans were to rebuild.

✤ **Layou River Hotel** (Layou Valley, Box 34, Roseau, Doninica, W.I.; 48 rooms) shares a link with Anchorage, and the Armours—whose more adventuresome guests settle in to this spot to enjoy nature at its best. The cement and stucco buildings with angular roofs nestle into lush foliage, wrapping guests in air-conditioned comfort (and constant hum). Popular with Europeans and others who enjoy tramping through the Dominican wilderness and adventures around the Layou River, the hotel provides music for dancing on Saturday nights (when house count warrants), special Dominican performers for plays and folklore (also depending on house count), and chances for horseback riding through the wilderness, tours through the jungle, and the opportunity to walk (or take the hotel transportation) about a mile to the shoreline and a beach-of-sorts. There's a pool on premises, and the natural pool formed by the river near the shoreline. You're about half an hour from Roseau, and an hour or so from the airport when you settle in here. Ideal for nature lovers, this is no place for lone travelers—unless you *really* want to be alone. Count on rates of about $88 for 2, breakfast and dinners daily.

✝ **Papillotte** (Box 67, Roseau, Dominica, W.I.; 5 rooms) offers "another world," a retreat from commercial realities and a haven for those who seek comfort in surroundings that include majestic waterfalls, lush tropical growth, and warm hospitality. The place that Cuthbert and Anne Grey Bapsiste have put together gives you comfortable rooms, with basic, island-made furniture, and awesome views. With mineral baths, a craft center (with some reasonable work, using local vines and grasses, as well as some wood carvings) and places for river dips and sunbathing all nearby, the fact that the 4-mile distance from Roseau figures to at least a 20-minute-drive doesn't make any difference. Food is reportedly excellent (although I have not tried it), and the surroundings will spellbind nature lovers. Count on less than $50 per day, for a room for 2 and 2 meals daily.

✝ **Reigate Hall Hotel** (Box 200, Roseau, Dominica, W.I.; 12 rooms) hides in the hills on the fringe of Roseau, with a view over the bay and a 5-minute-ride for the 1-mile-distance. The opening of Reigate gives visitors an opportunity to enjoy traditional, tropical West Indian hospitality in relatively new surroundings where basic comforts are assured. Adventuresome vacationers, who do not require sand to scuff through a few steps from the room, will enjoy the weekly bridge evenings, the sauna, the Dominican food that is spelled by roti (that crepelike catchall for curried fillings that is famous in Trinidad) at lunchtime, and the delightful-for-dunking swimming pool. Figure on about $65 this winter for 2, with 2 meals daily per person included.

✝ **Riviere La Croix Estate Hotel** (Box 100, Roseau, Dominica, W.I.) stood storklike with the front part on stilts amid Dominica's jungled terrain. It, too, did not survive winds and rain, but its verdant locale and the clearing that had been made for the hotel provided a base for rebuilding. Check for status.

✤ **Sisserou** (Box 156, Castle Comfort, Dominica, W.I.; 20 rooms) fluttered its wings in the early '70s and then went to sleep for a while to wake up for a flourishing business just before the hurricanes hit. Built for the season of '72–'73, the hotel had a brief reign as part of a French combine, and now is going it alone, filling a need for modern accommodations with easy access to Roseau for businessmen. It was refurbished after the hurricanes (which it survived much better than the mountain hotels). Its name, as you may have realized, is that of the Dominican parrot immortalized on the new nation's flag and seen sometimes in the hinterlands. This Sisserou nests about a mile from Roseau, at the shore with a sort-of-beach. (As stated elsewhere, beach aficionados will not be ecstatic about any of Dominica's beaches. Sand is usually black-to-gray volcanic sand which, while fascinating, is not the powdery talcum that dreams—and advertising campaigns—are made of.) Rooms have air-conditioning units, motel-style furnishings, and a patio or terrace with sea view. Count on rates to range around $50, for 2 including breakfasts this winter.

✤ **Springfield Plantation** (Box 41, Roseau, Dominica, W.I.; 5 rooms plus 4 cottages) survived and claims a quarter century of innkeeping. Mr. John Archbold, owner of the plantation, is the grandson of John Dustin Archbold, who followed John D. Rockefeller as chairman of the board of Standard Oil and became the first president of Standard Oil of New Jersey after the antitrust laws were passed. After 9 years in England, his mother, Ann Archbold Saunderson (who had spent her honeymoon on safari in Africa in 1902) packed up the 4 children, and left her husband and the Saunderson name to move to Bar Harbor, Maine. When John Archbold graduated from Princeton in 1934, he boarded a schooner and headed south, to land at and fall in love with Dominica. Several plantation acquisitions later, Archbold found himself in the innkeeping business, with the 4-bedroom Victorian plantation house at Springfield Estate. In 1972, just before the bottom fell out of the banana and citrus market, and waves of independence hit Dominican shores, Springfield Plantation had expanded to 15 rooms in this and other buildings. And about that time, taking the cue from Laurance Rockefeller's National Park grant of land on St. John in the U.S. Virgins, Archbold deeded 1200 acres of his Middleham Estate to the

Dominican government through the island's Nature Conservancy. The property is part of the Dominica National Park, whose entrance is 2 miles from Springfield Plantation. Botanists, scholars, and those on independent nature studies who stay here can know that they will be well fed on island specialties. Miss Millie Toussaint is the one who set the cooking precedent, and for your sake I hope she's still cooking when you get here. Ronald Lander was manager when I last checked. Rates for your stay will run from $60 to $90 for 2, 2 meals daily, for winter rooms, and somewhere under $70 for a week, with rate varying according to your choice of cottage or apartment.

Springfield Guest House, the original plantation house, perches on a bend of the old Imperial Road, at about 1163 feet, with a view of the sea and a steep slope at each "ear." Guests in the main house bedrooms (private bath with each) and the apartments use the sitting room with fireplace, and can rock on the veranda. There's a protected river pool near the house, and a small pool at Samaan (separate house with 2 double bedrooms and bath, plus living room and bedroom on the first floor). Bee House, a bamboo cottage, has 2 double bedrooms, plus kitchen, dining room, terrace with sea view (maid service provided), and Mount Joy is a full house, with pool in its garden, above Springfield House along the Imperial Road. Guests here have 4 bedrooms, with living room, kitchen, and veranda.

■■■

RESTAURANTS are usually the province of the hotels, with each having its own special way of cooking the local foods. (Taxes and shipping problems make importing difficult, so don't count on steak and french fries here.) You will be offered crapaud, otherwise known as "mountain chicken," and actually the huge frogs that live in the woods of Dominica. *They are delicious,* almost any way they are prepared, so order them if you see them on the menu. Sweetwater crayfish, land crab, fresh fish including tritri, fried plantain (a variety of banana), pawpaw (otherwise known as papaya), mangoes, christophine (a potatolike vegetable), and breadfruit are all offered in season. Pumpkin and callaloo are 2 favorite soups. (The latter is like spinach.)

Chances are you will dine where you overnight, unless you lunch at one of the other hotels when you're touring around. If you are in Roseau for lunch or dinner, check **La Robe** for Creole food. When I dined there Tony and Erica Burnett ran the place, and the food was excellent. **Papillote** should not be missed, if you have a car (or have made arrangements with a patient taxi driver who will wait while you dine), and reservations at **Springfield Plantation,** if you haven't chosen to stay here, will yield a memorable time. Plan for Springfield at mid-day to get full advantage of the surroundings or go up mid-afternoon for a swim (ask ahead for permission) and stay for dinner. (Same should be said for Papillote, since the falls are best, obviously, when you can see them!)

■■

PLACES WORTH FINDING: Begin at the airport. Before you've reached where you thought you were going, you will have passed most of them. Dominica's sights are natural ones, and are ideal for bird-watchers, hikers, and botanists. Some of the jungle areas are so thick that Eric Lamb, the man who started Dominica Safaris, the precursor of the jeep safari jaunts that the Armours and others offer, said "it would take a man a lifetime to clear a path through the wilderness. Some 300 rivers crisscross the steep terrain and no one knows how many waterfalls may exist in the seldom-visited interior." There are 3 hotels at the fringe of an area designated as a National Park (in a country whose entirety is one): Riviere La Croix, Island House, and Springfield Plantation.

Morne Trois Pitons National Park, with the office headquarters at Victoria Street (Dominica National Park Office, Box 148, Roseau, Dominica) is a chunk of 16,000 acres (25 square miles) in the south-central part of Dominica which was established in July 1975 by an Act of the Legislature as the first part of what is intended to be an expanding National Park network. Rangers work at clearing paths, and have made great progress on the **Emerald Pool Nature Trail** (which is almost too developed, especially if you come in as part of a big group). The Canadian Nature Federation assisted with the project, which involved funding through several international agencies including the Canadian International Development Agency (CIDA).

Other places in the park are the **Boiling Lake,** discovered in 1922, and the **Valley of Desolation,** combined goals of a 3½-hour hike that everyone refers to as "strenuous" and I have not taken. Island House is used as the starting point.

In conversations about Dominica with friends who live there, and with information gathered from my own explorations on several visits, I learned that the interior of Dominica has as many as 60 different tree species within a 10-acre plot and is the only place where either the Sisserou or the Imperial parrot (*Amazona arausica*), both endangered species, can be found. A reproduction of the Sisserou parrot flanks the Dominican coat of arms. Bird-watchers may also be interested in some other of the 135 species including the pigeons, doves, hummingbirds, swifts, fly-catchers, chicken-hawks, and bananaquits.

Friends have also pointed out that the usual touring spots, in addition to the Carib Indian Reservation and the Emerald Pool, are the **ruins of Fort Shirley** at the Cabrits, a cliff spot north of Portsmouth on Price Rupert Bay; **Trafalgar Twin Waterfalls,** where there's a hydroelectric station, east of Roseau; and the **Sulphur Springs** (which didn't fascinate me).

■■

SPORTS are for the rugged individualist on this island, despite the fact that there are boat tours, fishing programs, hiking forays, and other adventures planned and provided with guide by Anchorage Tours (the ubiquitous Armours).

Sailing is usually on a charter yacht, coming here from some place else. If you're the captain, you can check with customs and the Roseau jetty before you motor about a mile south to anchor at Anchorage, where the Armours have put in rudimentary facilities for overnight (in hopes that you'll dine at their hotel and stock up from their commissary).

Scuba diving has gained encomiums from the pros who know these Caribbean waters well. Neglected in favor of some of the better-known spots (Bonaire and the Caymans, for example), Dominica came to the attention of those who like to pioneer areas just after hurricanes, which often shift the bottom sands and uncover formerly hidden wrecks. An astounding collection of 17th- and 18th-century ships reportedly lie off Dominican shores, and many of them are yet to be discovered. Check with Janice and Carl Armour about sources for the current scuba sightings.

Boating trips up the coast from Roseau to Portsmouth are another Anchorage option, with a canoe trip up Indian River after your 3-hour excursion. The charge for a minimum of 4 is $80 ($20 per person).

Fishing, waterskiing, and zipping offshore in a **motorboat** can be arranged out of Anchorage for $20 per hour, but don't count on all the flourishes for deep-sea fishing vessels here. Life is marvelously simple, remember?

Hiking is best with a guide, either through the National Park (check with the Roseau office for guides) or through Anchorage Hotel, where the Armours can arrange for someone to accompany you.

Safari Tours, in Land Rovers, can be called sport by some. Certainly the excursion is not for the carsick crowd, unless well laced with your most effective Dramamine equivalent (but then, if you're *that* kind of traveler, you will never have survived the ride from the airport to anywhere within a few hundred feet of there.) Prices for the land safaris, which are primarily scenic and interesting if you like to photograph waterfalls, verdant greenery, and nature at its tropical best, run about $20 per person, minimum of 4 per jeep. If you're based at Roseau, some of the mid- and north section excursions are almost $50.

■■■

TREASURES AND TRIFLES are limited. This is not a typical tourist island with freeport shops and the like. What has been made for tourists is priced for tourists, and because there are not too many of us in Dominica, the price is sometimes high on the old "bird in the hand" theory. The basket and handicraft shops sprinkled along the road through the Carib Reservation on the east coast do have some interesting intricately woven work, but when you ask the price (which is seldom marked) it will be priced for you—and you are a lot richer (or so the owner thinks) than he is. (There's no doubt about your income versus that of the basket weavers, but as for the entrepreneurs who are setting up the shops? In relative terms, I'm not so sure.)

In Roseau, the best woven grass rugs—and they are interesting and a long-time favorite purchase—are at **Tropicrafts,** started almost 50 years ago by Sister Berine as the Convent Industrial School. The sisters are still active in overseeing the work of those who weave the rosettes and other sections at home, as well as those who stitch the final rug together on the floor of the vast hall that is home for Tropicrafts. (Rugs can sometimes be made to order, but you will do better if you can find something in stock that is close to what you want. Be sure to measure your porch or room before you leave for Dominica.)

Caribana Handcrafts at 31 Cork Street in Roseau "offers you the best of everything" according to its small folder, but what it stocks its shelves and rooms with are hats, mats, and woven items similar to those found at Tropicrafts.

Check the **Workshop for the Blind,** at the north edge of Roseau, for other handmade items. Prices here are worth every penny. If you buy some of the local coconut oil for sunning, *beware.* It's only for already tanned skin; novices will burn!

Dominican Republic

Secretaría de Estado de Turismo, Avenida César Nicolás Penson, Esq. Rosa Duarte, Apartado 497, Santo Domingo, República Dominicano; Centro Dominicano de Información Turística, Arzobispo Meriño 156, Santo Domingo, República Dominicana. Dominican Tourist Information Center, 485 Madison Ave., New York, NY 10022.

US $1 = RD $1 (Dominican peso)
Unless otherwise noted, $ refers to U.S. currency.

Maria made her grand entrance, gliding across the tiled patio, her terrycloth "train" sweeping the edge of the pool. It didn't seem to matter that her bathing suit was wet. Her arena was the courtyard of what had been the home of prominent 16th-century residents and is now a 20th-century hotel in the colonial restoration area of Santo Domingo. Maria is 8, but her bearing was reminiscent of another Maria—Doña Maria de Toledo y Rojas, a niece of Spain's King Ferdinand and the wife of Diego Colón, son of the Christopher Colón whom most English-speaking people know better as Columbus.

Santo Domingo makes the past come alive, not only in the performances of its children, but most vividly in the restoration of its 16th-century buildings that stand in a convenient cluster on the banks of the Ozama River in the center of the city. Columbus stands, as he has since the French cast him in bronze in 1837, on the biggest square, Plaza Colón, outside the Cathedral of Santa Maria la Menor. This is the cathedral that claims to hold the bones of Columbus and does hold a complement of devoted Dominican Catholics on Sundays and at other special times for services. (At least 4 other places also claim to hold the Columbus remains—the result of a nameplate switch intended to foil the rampaging Sir Francis Drake. This has puzzled historians for centuries.)

Don Francisco Billini, who as archbishop of the cathedral in 1877 discovered the bones of Columbus (who had discovered what is now the Dominican Republic on December 5, 1492) stands on marble in another of Santo Domingo's refurbished squares. Juan Pablo Duarte, considered by Dominicans to be the father of the country, stands in a third. (Duarte met with a group of patriots and started a movement for independence from Haiti, successful in 1844.)

Today's Juans, Franciscos, Diegos, and Marias face a life quite different from that of their ancestors. About 5 million Dominicans share the island of Hispaniola with the country of Haiti, on a two-thirds/one-third split that gives the Dominican Republic not only the larger but also the richer portion of land. Everything grows here, including tourism—and children. Sugar is the democratic republic's dominant income producer; nickel is next and tourism, while a distant third, is the hope of the future—if not for income, then certainly for understanding and employment.

When the car paused at a stoplight, three young boys rushed to the windshield and vigorously slobbered a wet cloth over the dusty surface. They glanced at the driver—and at me, but continued their work. The reward, if they are fast (and convincing) enough, might be 25 centavos (or a U.S. quarter).

When we sipped an icy *El Presidente* beer at one of the cafes along the Malecón, as the seaside boulevard in the city is known, two bright-eyed "salesmen" draped themselves at the entrance gate and almost silently slipped their carved ashtrays and other small items-for-sale over the wall for us to see. A flicker of interest on our part brought an avalanche of items from theirs, but a decision not to buy was greeted with the same enthusiasm as the sales pitch was presented. It's all in a day's work, and jobs are hard to find.

This sunny island is about 150 miles southeast of Cuba and 54 miles from the western end of Puerto Rico. It has links with both, and a multfaceted lifestyle that includes not only the city-of-salesmen and special sights but also the elegance of one of the Caribbean's most impressive resort communities about 2 hours out of the city, along the south coast to the east.

On the north coast, at Puerto Plata, several resorts are underway not far from the first, and ill-fated, settlement Columbus called Isabella. Already the town of Sosúa is a popular small resort for wealthy Dominicans and for other Spanish-speaking visitors who have bought, or can rent, homes. To Dominicans, Sosúa is better known for its excellent meat and cheese, available from streetside stores near the farms where Jewish settlers set up new businesses in the 1930s.

Farther east is the peninsula of Samaná, known to sportsmen who come here to hunt and fish in rugged, natural terrain, where a settlement of runaway slaves from the northeast coast of the United States still talk in the English of the 1800s. Santiago, in the middle of the country, on the route between Santo Domingo and Puerto Plata by air or road, is one of the oldest towns in the Dominican Republic. It doesn't look like much now, but when you see the plaza you'll know that with a little time and a lot of money, it could. The city was founded in 1504, and named for St. James in honor of an order of knights in Spain. Its real name is Santiago de los Caballeros, and its real wealth is agriculture. The fertile valley of the Yaque river is prime land for all crops; tobacco was the one in the 1800s when some thought that Santiago should replace Santo Domingo as the country's capital. But Santo Domingo prevailed—and is the place to feel the pulse of the past, the present, and probably the future of this country.

■■

POLITICAL PICTURE: The Dominican Republic will have elections on May 16, 1982, with the country's President to assume office on August 16, 1982. Visitors should expect to see political slogans and posters appearing on walls, posts, and palm tree trunks around the country—and especially in the cities.

Ties between Dominicans, Puerto Ricans, and Cubans are not only those of language and a Spanish heritage, but also of blood. Many families have relatives in one or both of the other islands, and that has been the case since the 1500s, when the Spanish colonized the three islands.

In the 1980s, when Third World countries are grouped together with "links" that are less substantial than those between the Dominican Republic, Cuba, and Puerto Rico, it should come as no surprise that there is Communist interest in the Dominican Republic (although I am assured by Dominican colleagues that it is "minimal").

United States-Dominican Republic relations have not always been smooth. The 30 years of the dictatorship of Generalíssimo Rafael Leonidas Trujillo Molino ended with his murder in 1961. A country that had had little experience with free elections went through a period of turmoil until 1966. During that time (in April 1965) the United States Marines were sent in "to restore order," in an action that is still being used by some Dominicans to show that the United States has designs on the country. The unfortunate timing of a visit by a United States Navy ship, intended as a "good will gesture," in April 1981 fanned the flames of anti-American sentiment and a few protest demonstrations took place. (Most appeared to have been instigated by the *Partido Comunist Dominicano* whose "Ferera Yanguis" (Out Yankees) posters "decorated" the walls of Santo Domingo, Romana and other cities.)

In spite of these isolated demonstrations, there is a wellspring of affection for Americans, and a strong sense of pride among many Dominicans who have worked hard during the 20 years since the end of Trujillo's oppressive regime, to build a strong middle class in a country where a "middle class" was almost non-existent. (There have been great extremes between wealth and poverty in the Dominican Republic, as in most Latin countries—and in many of the Caribbean island countries.)

One key element for the resolution of the political "confusion" that followed the death of Trujillo was the election of Joaquín Balaguer in 1966. Balaguer governed his country for three 4-year terms, bringing a measure of prosperity and creating a "middle class." He lost the election of May 16, 1978, to Antonio Guzmán, a 67-year old cattle rancher. Talk at that time revolved around the fact that José Francisco Peña Gómez, General Secretary of the *Partido Revolucionario Dominicano,* known for his leftist leanings, was active behind the scene. In fact, PRD candidate Guzmán, as President of the country, has taken a firmer stand against Cuban links than his predecessor Balaguer whose *Partido Reformista* was far to the right and attempted to come to the middle road with cultural and sporting exchanges with Cuba during his administration.

Democratic free elections resulting in a change of government marked Dominican politics for the first time in the elections of 1968. When Balaguer's military seized the ballot boxes in the middle of the elections (when indications were that Balaguer was losing), a flurry of protest arose. After some delay, balloting continued and, when the final count was tallied at the end of May 1968, Antonio Guzmán had been elected President. Not long thereafter, ex-President Balaguer left for Spain.

Balaguer returned to the Dominican Republic in April 1981 and it is expected that he will lead his *Partido Reformista* in the '82 elections. Although Guzmán declared in mid-1981 that he would not run for another term, his influence will continue. His colleague (and, some say, mentor) Peña Gómez will continue to be active, whether he takes a front line seat or continues to work behind the scene.

■■

CUSTOMS OF THE COUNTRY: This is a Latin country, in every way. Old-time Dominican families still treat daughters with the strict discipline of old Spain. Well-to-do Dominican families live the elegant life that visitors can witness at Casa de Campo. That may seem like an anachronism in today's world, but it is a fact here.

Dinner hour is late—9 p.m. or later—and places will be open for full meal service well after midnight. Siesta is still observed, if not for the nap time, then certainly for the closing of shops, museums, and offices. Traffic into and out of the city will be one clue to the importance of the long and lingering lunch hour.

Dominican coffee is a treat for those of us who like strong black coffee. I deplore the fact that many new hotels serve a watered-down version, calculated to "please" American palates. If you want the real thing, you will have to ask for Dominican coffee in places like the Sheraton coffee shop and some of the other U.S. chain hotels. If you want the watered-down American coffee, you'll have to ask for *it* in the Dominican restaurants, or bring your own small jar of instant coffee and ask for hot water.

Clothes in the city are conservative. Business suits are proper for business calls; dark dresses—with sleeves and backs if you are going into the cathedral—are suitable for women. Resort clothes are limited to Casa de Campo and to the north coast's Playa Dorada where the peacock parade is popular. If you want to attempt to fit into the country, dress with cool and understated elegance. That's what well-dressed Dominicans do.

■■

MONEY MATTERS: The Dominican peso is officially at par with the U.S. dollar, but it is worthless outside the country—and sometimes within it. Pesos will be useful, and a lot less conspicuous, for transactions if you are traveling off the usual tourist routes. When you are bargaining (common practice in all but the most elegant stores), the dollar gets a better price. Around the Old City, especially in the cathedral area, there are plenty of people ready to do black market business in dollar exchange. It is illegal, but accomplished. (Outside the gates of major hotels in the city a proliferation of money changers will offer you a better-than-par rate for your U.S. dollars. Although some "street banks" will take traveler's checks, most of the men eager for dollars will only give their variable rate— sometimes as much as 1.30 pesos per dollar—for cash. Be sure to count.)

You can convert dollars to pesos at your hotel, but you will have a difficult time doing the reverse. When you pay your bill in dollars, you will probably get your change in pesos. For that reason, and for last-minute transactions, be sure you have plenty of dollar bills. Taxi drivers and others will give you change in pesos that you will have a hard time getting rid of at the airport when you leave. Everyone—including airline personnel—gives you a blank stare and that "I can't do anything" shrug of the shoulders. At the duty-free shops, after you clear immigration, only dollars will buy.

▪▪

ARRIVAL at Aeropuerto Internacional de Las Américas is confusing at best, chaos at worst even with the substantial new addition. At peak winter, when several big planes ooze passengers at about the same time, the airport can be like a crowded subway. Brace yourself, especially if you do not speak Spanish (because almost everyone else does). The building is modern, attractive, and airy if you can see over the heads of the crowds. After tiptoeing across the tarmac, you will get to the big room for immigration, to be followed by luggage claim and customs. My advice is to head first to the Dominican rum display and gas up. Then, if you have not already bought your Tourist Card (sold by most airlines when you buy your ticket to the Dominican Republic), you will part with $5 U.S.—officials will not accept Dominican pesos if you happen to have some from previous travels, and that should tell you something about the value of the peso. That done, stand in the immigration line, where your passport is the best identification, although voter's registration and anything that shows where you were born is sufficient.

Customs is thorough, silent, and simple if you are not bringing anything but your own tourist trappings with you. A gooey sticker will be slapped on every piece of luggage, to be pulled off less than 2 minutes later—at the door when you exit. Porters are readily available, and difficult to divert if you happen to be a carry-on traveler, as I am. This is one of the few places where porters are present, and pleasant.

Brace yourself for the surge of people—taxi drivers as well as Dominicans waiting for friends and relatives—just outside the terminal doors. Plow through, hire a taxi (if you are not being met and/or haven't rented a car), and head for the shore-rimming highway into Santo Domingo or out to Romana.

▪▪

TOURING TIPS: Getting around the Santo Domingo area is easy and can be very inexpensive if you're adventuresome and/or speak

Spanish. Buses travel the routes from the Old City to the outskirts, bordering the hotels where you're apt to be staying. The bus ride costs 15¢. Taxi rates are rising and already reach $125 for a tour to Puerto Plata from Santo Domingo and $75 to La Romana. In addition, you can hail one of the cars that run jitney service along regular routes, and pay a modest cost for seat-in-car. Ask at your hotel about these routes, to be sure you're standing at the right spot to hail a cab.

Count on spending about $25 for your taxi ride from the airport into the city, unless you've made some other arrangement. The ride takes about 40 minutes and goes along a seaside highway built in Trujillo's era. (Hurricanes in 1979 severely damaged the planting, and the effects can still be seen.)

Rental cars are available, and rates vary according to the company and the kind of car. At the airport, Avis, National, Hertz, and Via (Ford) Rent-a-Car signs are prominent (you'll note them while you wait for your luggage), but outside—in addition to these four—there are at least 10 small booths, including Nelly Rent-a-Car, City, Budget, Dial, Merengue, Caribe—and most take Master Charge, Diner's Club, American Express, and BankAmericard. It will take a while for you to clear the papers for your car, and speaking Spanish will prove invaluable, not only for a rate, but also for standard negotiations.

One of the best bets, and a plan that has proved popular, according to tour operators and Dominican tourism officials, is a fly/drive holiday with a car rental included in your hotel room rate. (Your travel agent or the Dominican Tourist Information Center can give you details).

AUTHOR'S OBSERVATION: You'll be more comfortable if you speak Spanish and/or are a mechanic if you're renting a car for drives into the hinterlands. Car maintenance in the Dominican Republic leaves a lot to be desired, and the mañana attitude when it's *your* car that has broken down may ruin your vacation.

Roads are poorly marked if they are marked at all, and the official-looking maps lack a lot of minor and new roads. Getting from Santo Domingo to La Romana won't be much of a problem, once you get yourself out of the city traffic. The route is almost straight, along good roads following or just inland from the south shore. From Santo Domingo to Puerto Plata is a straight north-south shoot, but allow some time for a stop in Santiago, at least to look around, and be prepared for traffic as you approach Santo Domingo on the return run. The market stands that set up along the roadside (and serve good, strong Dominican coffee) are favorite halting spots for Dominicans, who buy fresh produce there.

There is bus service (operated by private companies) between Santo Domingo and Puerto Plata. The ride, on air-conditioned buses, takes about 3 hours 15 minutes and costs $5. Small-plane service flies between Santo Domingo and Puerto Plata, La Romana, Samaná, and other Dominican airstrips on regular service and on charter. *Avionca* is a charter airline flying a Turbo–Centurion II and other small-and-special planes.

There are bus tours of the Santo Domingo area. If you've never been here before, this is one of the few places in the Caribbean where I think a bus tour is helpful, not only to help you get your bearings, but also to get some of the background on this historic and fascinating country. I've often ridden in the coaches of Amber Tours, and although I thought the patter was a bit too practiced my last time around, that may also be because I've heard it several times before. Amber does a good job, with air-conditioned buses. Vimenca Tours also operates a local service. If your package holiday doesn't include a tour, and your travel agent hasn't sold you one, check with the hotel activities desk. They can certainly set you up.

Cruise ship passengers are poured into minibuses for guided tours around Puerto Plata. Frankly, there's not all that much to see. You can do about as well, better if you're an independent traveler and speak some Spanish, by walking as far as the market and taking a taxi if you want to go to the beach. Most of the cruise-bus tour service was organized by Mike Ronan, who came to the country as a Peace Corps worker and stayed to become an entrepreneur. His firm is known as Agencia de Viajes Cafemba; Lilly Tours and Via Tours are also tour operators.

■■

HOTELS IN SANTO DOMINGO provide close to 2500 rooms for overnighting, and most of them are modern, new, and in high-rise containers that offer choices of restaurants, nightclubs, saunas, shops, and pools (to make up for the city's lack of beach), plus access to an international array of good restaurants rivaled in the Caribbean only by Puerto Rico's San Juan area. There are a few small and inexpensive places where Americans-without-Spanish can comfortably stay, but speaking Spanish will be a tremendous asset no matter where you bed in. The high-rise hostelries will not carry price tags as sky-high as their Puerto Rican counterparts, and as of the moment, you get a lot for your money insofar as hotel rooms are concerned.

New life has come to the Dominican Hotel Association, with membership in the Caribbean Hotel Association and some policies underway to assist travelers and set some standards for island services. If you have a problem with your facilities, the place to register your complaint in writing, preferably in Spanish, is at the Asociación Nacional de Hoteles y Restaurantes, Inc., El Conde No. 451— Zona Postal 1; Santo Domingo, Rep. Dominicana.

Aᴜᴛʜᴏʀ'S AWARDS: Casa de Campo is still the tops on my tally. Management makes the most of the estate atmosphere, giving those of us who pay for the privilege a pampered and almost perfect life. For Santo Domingo shelter, Hotel Santo Domingo's surroundings are superb. Northcoast nooks in the Puerto Plata orbit are led by the Jack Tar Resort, the first of the buildings at the planned community at Playa Dorada.

✢ **El Embajador** (Avenida Sarasota, Santo Domingo, D.R.; 316 rooms) is owned by a Chinese group and the *Jardín de Jade,* a high-quality Chinese restaurant, is one of the best reasons I know for passing by. Thorough renovations and refurbishing bring this hotel up to first-class status. The hotel is a high-rise building in a sea of high-rise apartment buildings that turned this way-out spot into one of the city's prime residential areas. The land on which the apartments have risen once belonged to the Inter-Continental Hotel Corp., but became Dominican government property in lieu of payment of taxes. During Trujillo days, this place was *it*. The lobby has a bright, new look, with entrances to Jardín de Jade or to the casino, in brand-new quarters to the left, beyond the check-in area. The pool is big enough for serious swimmers, and outdoor tables give the bar area a nice cafe feeling. Rates this season start at $35 for 2, everything extra. Tennis courts and restaurants plus a couple of shops on location and some new restaurants (*La Trattoria* is one) in nearby buildings. The Old City is a $7 taxi ride away; the hotel stands alone on the outskirts of the city.

✢ **Hotel Jaragua** (Avenida Independencia, Santo Domingo, D.R.; 212 rooms) is best known to most tourists for its casino and *Lafuente* nightclub. The lobby has been full of lingerers and oglers when I've seen it and the place looks to me like it gets a lot of commercial action. I don't recommend it unless you know what you're getting into. I'd stick with the next-door Sheraton, and come over here for the show. Room rates are listed at about $35 for 2. (Tennis courts, 2 pools and bohío bar are popular with residents who use this place as a country club.)

✤ **Lina** (Máximo Gómez at 27 de Febrero, Santo Domingo, D.R.; 70 rooms) lards the well-known restaurant with several layers of rooms in a multi-story building with motel-modern overtones. Before Sheraton, and the Hotel Santo Domingo arrived on the scene, many Americans nested here in air-conditioned, adequately furnished rectangles. Some still do, if price and tradition are their main reasons. Rates are reasonable at $45 for 2, and you have a kitchenette in your room for quick meals so you can splurge on dinner downstairs. (For restaurant comment, see below.)

✤ **Hostal Nicolás de Ovando** (Calle Las Damas 53, Old Santo Domingo, D.R.; 60 rooms) brings the past alive. Staying here is like living in a stage set of the 16th or 17th century. A Caribbean gem equaled in brilliance only by El Convento in Puerto Rico's Old San Juan, this unique hostel is on the site chosen by Nicolás de Ovando, in the 16th century as the locale for the city, on the east bank of the Ozama River. He lived here from 1502 to 1509. The Office of Cultural Patrimony took over the property and the neighboring historic house of Francisco Dávila (built in the first years of the 16th century) to scrape off the abuses of ages, gut the interior, and restore what had become 3 houses (numbers 9, 11, and 13) along the venerable Calle Las Damas (street of the ladies), where the ladies of the court of Diego Colón (Columbus) used to live. In the process of restoration, several architectural feats of the early 16th century have been preserved: 5 of the original windows with their frames of worked stone, and some elements of what is obviously Isabellian lattice designs. The Dávila house is an example of a fortified house, with its own tower overlooking the Ozama. Together the properties were known as *Casona*, a small inn at a crossroads on the outskirts of the city.

The hotel is operated by Hoteles Luz Internacional (Interhotel) in the best Spanish-Dominican tradition. Service may be slow, but staff is willing and attentive. The small pool in one of the courtyards is surrounded by tables, an oasis in what can be a hot center city. Rooms are air-conditioned, furnished in copies of Spanish antiques, and reminiscent of the best of Spain's paradores (the chain of country inns). The Hostal's *Extremadura* dining room is one of the best eateries in town. The paella is a feast, the atmosphere romantic and enchanting, the prices high. An ideal spot for anyone who enjoys restoration of past glories, and a requirement (for at least a meal) if you want to claim you have been to the Dominican Republic. Rates this winter are about $50 for 2, but inquire about special packages.

✤ **Naco** (Tiradentes 22, Santo Domingo, D.R.; 104 rooms) is known for its casino. It nests near Vesuvio II restaurant and is another of the businessman's hotels that gives good rates, adequate air-conditioned surroundings, and the chance to speak Spanish. The plus, of course, is the casino—one of 4 (Sheraton, Jaragua, and Embajador are the others). Room rate for 2 is about $40. This one I'd recommend only for people who know what they're getting into. There's a pool, plus a nearby shopping center popular with residents.

✤ **Napolitano** (Ave. G. Washington, Santo Domingo, D.R.; 72 rooms) nests not far from the Sheraton on the busy Malecón, as the shore-rimming boulevard is known. With a roadside, open air bistro/cafe that is a favorite with residents, Napolitano has activity—even if it's only people-watching—at most hours of the day and night. Rooms are modern, reasonably comfortable with the expected hotel/motel furnishings and the place is popular with Latin businessmen. Speaking Spanish will enhance your time here, but if convenience is paramount for your in-the-city hotel, and price is a consideration, the Napolitano is worth considering. Winter rates for 2 figure to about $35, room only.

✤ **Ocean Inn** (Ave. G. Washington, Santo Domingo, D.R.; 60 rooms) opts for a shoreline spot, on the inland side of the sea-rimming road known locally as the Malecón. One of a handful of middle-sized, modern hotels, the Ocean Inn has neat and clean rooms, and is within a short walk of several popular restaurants, as well as being near the Jaragua and the Sheraton (for gala nightlife and casinos). One of the best values (and more comfortable if you speak Spanish), Ocean Inn's seaview rooms rent for about $30 for 2 this winter.

✤ **Hotel San Geronimo** (Avenida Independencia 205, Santo Domingo, D.R.; 72 rooms) is a pleasant and comfortable businessman's hotel with small check-in area, pool-plus-restaurant up one flight (elevator or stairs), and boxy rooms that must be air-conditioned for survival. You're one block inland from the seaside Malecón and its restaurants; the public bus will take you into downtown Santo Domingo for 15¢. Built by Leonard Porcella and his brothers, the hotel has 18 suites that are the choicest rooms, with view over the lower buildings between it and the sea. Speaking Spanish will make a big difference in your welcome. Rates are about $30 for 2, meals extra, if you make your own reservations; your travel agent will add on his commission (usually 15%) if he makes the booking for you.

✤ **Hotel Santo Domingo** (Avenida Independencia at Abraham Lincoln, Santo Domingo, D.R.; 365 rooms) has all the elegance of a palatial Dominican home. It is a city hotel with a very special feeling. When the ochre paint that marked the main hotel at its opening was wrapped around the former Hispaniola across the street, the two properties became one. The former Hispaniola, with its own restaurants, pool, and pulsating disco, is known as the Santo Domingo North. It's used by groups, and for the hotel's "standard" rooms. When you step out of the car at the entry portico of the main hotel and walk past the arched-and-open bar area through the doors to the enclosed, air-conditioned "lobby," you'll sense that this place is different. And it is not only the Dominican marble floors, the hand-fired tiles, and the lattice screens that make it so. The atmosphere comes from a combination of Oscar de la Renta colors and choice of fabrics with William Cox designs, and lofty air-filled courtyards with awnings at the edges and tropical plants throughout. There's no place like this Gulf + Western "palace" for an in-the-city hotel with options for elegant resort life. The main hotel's rooms are in two 5-story rectangles, joined at one "corner," and framing courtyards. Most have a sea view even if it is only a glimpse; others have a garden view. All have modern, colorful furnishings, and 45 of the total house count are mini-suites with balconies. The elegant Presidential Suite occupies a pool-and-sea view corner on the top floor. In addition to the swimming pool, with sundeck chairs and *Las Brisas* snack bar, there are tennis courts and shops, plus sauna and health club (with a masseuse whose hours are hard to define; if it's important to you, check on arrival and make a regular appointment). Although it's difficult to leave the comfortable chairs at *La Cabuya* bar near the lobby, with its overhead fans, Sydney Greenstreet air, and waitresses frocked by Oscar de la Renta, there's a piano bar at the back of the house, near the *Alcázar* restaurant, with entrance off the courtyard or through the restaurant to enter the pitch-black, air-conditioned entertainment area (popular with well-to-do Dominicans). Even the essential coffee shop has a special aura here; *El Cafetal* offers tables in the courtyard (under cover) facing a fountain, or inside in air-conditioning. Dinner is served here by candlelight, providing more reasonable fare than the Alcázar.

Santo Domingo North has a history that goes back to the days of *Paz* (peace), which is what this place was called when Argentine dictator Juan Peron lived here in temporary exile. It had a complete face lift, and an Oscar de La Renta/William Cox "wardrobe," when it became part of the Gulf + Western family, however. Prime rooms for those who want to be near the pool are the garden suites, some of which are on long-term rental to Dominicans.

During visits for this edition, I was sad to notice a lethargy on the part of some of the staff. Front desk attention was less than enthusiastic, and the winning smiles that I found a key to the hospitality when this hotel opened have given way, in a few cases, to the "so you're a tourist" attitude that is sometimes expected in other Caribbean islands. (This was a problem I noticed in the city hotels; it had not spread to the country places.) I'd advise you to be prepared for *slow* service—and if you get impatient because the staff doesn't seem to care or even to understand, pause to reflect that, when the main Hotel Santo Domingo opened in 1976, it was the first luxury hotel in Santo Domingo, and the only such place that many of the Spanish-speaking staff, most of them new to the hotel business, had seen. Corporación de Hoteles, S.A., a Gulf + Western subsidiary, had accomplished miracles with this and their Casa de Campo property. Both are pacesetters for tourism comforts not only in the Dominican Republic but elsewhere in the Caribbean. When here, you'll be in "another world," about 45 minutes from the airport, 15 minutes (and a $6 taxi ride) from historic downtown Santo Domingo, and you'll pay from about $60 (for the North Wing) to $100 for 2, room only, with the Presidential Suite at about $250 per day.

✠ **Plaza Dominicana Holiday Inn** (Avenida Anacaona, Mirador del Sur, Santo Domingo; 316 rooms) opened with fanfare as Loews in April 1977. Loew's pulled out in early '78 and, after flip-flop with management, Inns of Americas took over July 1, 1980 to start operation as a Holiday Inn. Despite the looks of the U.S.-modern sparkling white high rise—with 218 bedrooms with 2 double beds, 46 with king-sized beds, 12 bed-sitting rooms, 18 suites, 18 parlors, and 2 V.I.P. suites—do not expect too much. A casino is "in the works." Time (and more tourists) have smoothed some of the rough edges, but there is a lot of work to be done. I wish Holiday Inns success in doing it. Employees need help. What's second nature to you is not—even now—to them. Add to that the fact that their language is Spanish, and we often shriek at them in garbled English, and you may understand the problem. Take it slow. Relax and enjoy the Olympic-size pool with underwater bar stools and poolside bohíos and occasional entertainment; the 8 tennis courts; the health club with sauna and masseurs; an early-morning jog around the spectacular Paseo de los Indios, a 5-mile park just outside the hotel's gates, where you'll find well-tended and perfectly safe acres along the shore. (There's no beach, only rugged rocks and pounding surf.) The Old City is a half-hour $8 taxi ride east. Dining can be with colorful, modern Dominican market decor at *El Mercado* coffee shop, where it's easier to get hamburgers than Dominican food, or at the elegant *La Casa*—a replica of a colonial Dominican mansion which gives you a choice of dining in El Patio where a fountain splashes. There's a bar, La Sala (as the drawing room is called), or the tiled kitchen known as La Cocina, where asados (grilled specialties) are popular. *L'Azoteca,* the nightclub on the top floor, has flickers of popularity and can be lively if the crowd is. Daily winter rates rise from $70 for 2, meals extra. The extras, including the 5% room tax and tips, can quickly add up, and you'll find that meals and drinks can tally to more than the room, so don't be fooled by the low room cost. Check for special tours and rates.

✝ **Sheraton Santo Domingo** (Avenida George Washington 361, Santo Domingo, D.R.; 260 rooms) is an action-oriented chain reaction convenient to all the downtown Santo Domingo sights and restaurants. Sprouting 11 stories within a 15-minute stroll from Colonial Santo Domingo, the Lama brothers' Sheraton is far more than just a chain reaction. Manuel Baquero and Milan Lora were the architects who dreamed up this place, at present standing at only half its intended size. Insofar as we who sleep here are concerned, there are 7 junior suites, 14 one-bedroom suites, a presidential suite which makes up in view and size what it may lack in flourishes, 11 rooms with sofa beds that connect with standard rooms or suites, 5 rooms with "Murphy beds" for salesmen who presumably sleep where they sell, and 4 rooms equipped for handicapped. Each of the nooks has standard Sheraton requirements, plus 2 queen-sized beds and a view of the Caribbean, which you can look at but not touch unless you leap over the Malecón and the perilous rocks. Rooms are air-conditioned, have small balconies, wall-to-wall carpeting, dial telephones (that work, from my experience) and a color TV. HOWEVER, here as elsewhere, be patient with the staff. This is not a finger-snapping-service place, no matter how hard German-born manager Joe Jessen tries, and if he succeeds, he will have taken the soul out of the Dominicans.

When you finish touring the downtown historic area, you can fall into the swimming pool, step into the steam room (for men and for women), or leap around the tennis courts (4 lighted for night play).

And for dining and after dark options, you have the elegant, expensive 146-seat *Antoine's*, or the smaller area with the front terrace, up one level from the street so that you can see the sea, or the *Omni*, down-under disco that pulsates and pounds the eardrums until dawn ($5 cover). The Omni casino is now in full swing, with all the expected gamblers' options. *La Terraza* coffee shop has a few tables outside, but most seats are in air-conditioned primary-colorful surroundings (with the usual U.S. eating options which were nothing to rave about when I sampled). The air-conditioned bar, up a few steps from the check-in desks at the lobby level, has a fascinating metal panel under glass. (You'll have to make a point of looking at it; the place is dark and U.S.-city style.)

A high-rise giant that has to have special package holidays and groups to survive, this hotel will also appeal to businessmen who have to be near the city for calls. Ask about package rates that give a better bargain than the $70 or more for 2, meals extra, winter rate.

■■

HOTELS IN LA ROMANA, the resort area on the southeast coast:

✢ **Casa de Campo** (Box 140, La Romana, D.R.; 300-plus units) comes as close as any place to being the "perfect resort." It's the only resort in the Caribbean that has all the elements for the life of luxury. Corporacion de Hoteles, S.A., the Gulf + Western subsidiary that operates Hotel Santo Domingo, is the overseer here, and President Carlos Pellerano puts his Dominican heritage and previous top international hotel chain experience to good use to assure that you have a "dream vacation." Planned for ultimate luxury (and that includes elegant villas where you stay while enjoying polo, tennis, golf, trail riding, deep-sea fishing, sailing, or just plain sun basking), Casa de Campo is the Caribbean's leader—in looks and in facilities.

The staff, most of whom started in the hotel business when this place opened in the mid-1970s, are pleasant, helpful, and omnipresent. Although speaking Spanish helps for lengthy conversations, speaking slowly with basic English can achieve the looked-for results in most cases. You can count on amiable and capable pros for tennis and for golf (look for Juan Rios and Jon Bloom at the tennis courts, and Adeonis Castillo at the golf shop), and a daily check at the activities desk can fill your time (and empty your pockets) with a steady list of activities. (All activities can be billed to your room.)

The entire resort stretches over some 7000 acres. Oscar and Françoise de la Renta have their home here, near the 14th green; Charles Bluhdorn, Gulf + Western's president, claims a home, and the list gets longer with monied folk from South America, Europe, the U.S., and the Middle East. In the minds of many of the world's wealthy, Casa de Campo is IT.

Your choice of lodgings includes the casitas near the main building; 1-, 2-, and 3-bedroom golf villas on the fringes of both of the two 18-hole, Pete Dye-designed courses; and the tennis villas, up the hill at La Terraza near the 13 tennis courts, pro shop, pool, and snack bar. The same flair for incorporating the Caribbean into a comfortable interior design that marks the Hotel Santo Domingo makes Casa de Campo magic. *La Tropicana* dining room (where service operates on Dominican time—slowly) is fringed with terrace tables, with a handful tossed inside for those who insist that their tropcial evenings be air-conditioned. In April 1981, *El Patio Brasserie* opened, to serve meals and snacks all day and well into the nighttime for those who want less than banquet fare. *El Lago Grill,* near the golf shop and an easy stroll (or shuttle bus connection) from the main hub, serves meals buffet style, with grilled specialties for dinner in surroundings transformed by candlelight. (The real plus for this resort, however, is all the splendor at Altos de Chavón, described under *Places Worth Finding* and reached by shuttle bus in about 15 minutes ride from the main entrance of Casa de Campo.)

The one drawback (and it's easy to forget there is one) is the beach, a limited curve of golden sand at Las Minitas, reached by shuttle bus; horse-drawn carriage; or car in about 10 minutes' ride. The beach isn't much to rave about, if you know other Caribbean beaches (or even other strands—such as that at nearby Club Dominicus—in this country), but it is a span of sand with sea (plus bar, snack place, and water sports facilities) that seems to draw a crowd of people. Rates this winter for a room at Casa range between $145 and $170 for a room for 2, with suites and villas renting for expected sky-high prices. Although winter season rates are set in keeping with the super luxury you'll find here, summer season specials make holidays possible for most who are willing to save for a special experience. The drive from the airport to Casa de Campo takes almost 2 hours (reservations for your return can be confirmed at the hotel's transportation desk); some people fly in on their own—or a charter—plane.

✣ **Club Dominicus** (Trinitaria 69, La Romana, D.R.; 60 cottages plus 8 rooms in 2 villas) sits on one of the country's most beautiful beaches, but flip-flops with management arrangements make it difficult to predict what you'll find this season. Inquire—from several sources—if it matters. The coral stone cottages each have a pini pini wood frame, thatch roof, a tiled pedestal in the center of the room (for your "giant, comfortable bed or water bed with overhead Indian canopy"), and a waterfall shower. The villas can seem elegant, with small pool for sharing with the guests in the other 3 rooms (4 rooms per villa). Among the facilities that surround the cottages are tennis courts, small sailboats, snorkeling equipment, a library with self-help books, and a patch of meditation pads, with golf and deep-sea fishing available at extra charge. The complex is a half-hour drive from the main road between Casa de Campo and the town of La Romana. You're way out when you're here, but if you like beach-oriented holidays at a place with flexible management, this may be for you. Plans for this season have not been decided as we go to press. Check for more details.

■■

RESTAURANTS in and near La Romana are many. Vacationers have not only the hotel restaurants at Casa de Campo (*Tropicana, El Lago Grill, El Patio Brasserie* at the main hotel area, plus snack places at *Las Minitas beach* and *La Terrasa tennis village*), but the interesting choices also include:

Les Canaris, in the town of La Romana, about 10 minutes drive from Casa de Campo, has maintained the special surroundings that Charles Chevillot created when he opened this restaurant almost 6 years ago. He has now moved his island base (a relative of his popular New York city restaurants) to French St. Martin, and his successors haven't quite reached his pinnacle of perfection insofar as cuisine is concerned. The food is French-style, with sometimes delicate and sometimes super-rich sauces accompanying most dishes. (One disgruntled diner complained that it was "impossible" to get a plain steak, but I'm sure the chef would say that if you want a plain steak you should try someplace else.) Costumed staff help set the tone for the restored, traditionally Dominican wooden house, and dining can be on one of the porches or inside (which can be warm). Don't count pesos the night you dine here; $25 per person is a "bargain" for these special surroundings—and wine with your meal.

Among the restaurants at Altos de Chavón, look for:

Cafe del Sol, beyond the church and up the wide staircase to the right, on the plaza, is a favorite for snacks and drinks at any time of the day or night. Known for its pizza and sandwich plates, the cafe also serves crepes, ice cream concoctions, and a delicious fruit punch. A table on the patio, overlooking the plaza, is a prize spot on a pleasant evening (which is most Dominican evenings); there's limited space inside for those who want to be confined near the kitchen.

Casa del Rio, in spectacular surroundings that are floodlit at night, is the fish restaurant, but it is much more. A table at window-side in the terrace dining room almost suspends you over the river, and the view by nightlight is awesome. Paella and fresh fish are specialties, and reservations are recommended in peak season. The walk to reach here takes you past most of the sights of the village, but the reward for finding this place will be a memory that will last forever. Dominican earthenware is used for table service, and the tone is set by the stone walls and wood tables and chairs. Worth enjoying for atmosphere as much as for the food, which was excellent when I dined here, Casa del Rio is a "must."

Los Chinos is a place that I predict will quickly outgrow its compact surroundings in a nook just inside the gates of the 16th-century style village. Wood slat chairs painted bright red are a nice feature, but the support board of the table makes it impossible to pull up and put legs under. The food, prepared under the tutelage of an industrious Oriental who works in the hot kitchen, was exceptionally good one time when I dined (and mediocre another). The sweet and sour pork was just the right combination of tastes and crispness, and rice dishes proved excellent also. Prices were moderate; 2 could dine for about $10.

La Fonda, in a "back street" just off the plaza, is a charming hideaway serving interesting Dominican food. You can count on finding black bean soup and some slivered beef specialties that are accompanied with mashed local vegetables. Some dishes are spicier than others, and the fish dishes (especially shrimp when it's on the menu) are highly recommended. Pottery, country home cooking utensils, and tiles are part of the decor for tableware as well as wall covers. Count on about $10 per person for dinner, if you watch what you eat; closer to $20 if you go all out.

La Piazzetta, the Italian restaurant just to the left of the entrance walk (and a few steps from Los Chinos), is gorgeous to look at, but since my meal gave me indigestion for days I'd be careful in ordering. The Fetuccine Alfredo was my troublesome choice, but perhaps you'll have better luck. The atmosphere is elegant, with a building that incorporates touches from what one expects in an old Italian home: tiles, peasant cooking utensils and other touches affixed to the walls, and food service on attractive pottery with an interesting carafe for the house wine (and an awesomely expensive, and not too imaginative wine list). All right for show but not my first choice for good food, La Piazzetta is worth investigating prior to making your reservation. Count on the place to be pricey, at about $15 minimum per person.

●●●
HOTEL IN PUNTA CANA, on the east end;

✣ **Club Méditerranée** (Punta Cana, Dominican Republic; 600 beds) cavorts at the eastern shore of the country, about 150 miles from Santo Domingo, for the season of '81, with gala opening in April 1981. The property absorbs the site of former Punta Cana resort, a small-and-quiet hideaway for New York labor negotiator Theodore Kheel and friends. The former spot was razed in favor of the cement block and stucco buildings that now dot this remote shore. This place is parched, and since planting had to be blasted into coral rock, it will take foliage some time to gather flourishes. You can count on plenty of action, akin to that offered by Club Meds on other islands (Guadeloupe, Martinique and, more recently, Haiti) and the prepaid week, with beads for on-the-spot cash, will lure the guests that fill the cluster of 3-story buildings. An addition for this property is an 8th-night free, at Hotel Santo Domingo for a visit to the Colonial city. Even with the airplane shuttle service that connects with flights that come into Santo Domingo's Las Americas Airport, this Club is a l-o-n-g way from anything else. Excursions planned for Club Med guests include a visit to Santiago, Constanza, Sabana del Mar and other places. You can count on paying $625 for each of 2 sharing a room, for height of season this winter, and inquire about the shoulder and other break-in-the-rate weeks when costs are less.

●●●
HOUSEKEEPING HOLIDAYS are Spanish-Dominican style, and speaking Spanish certainly helps with the day-to-day necessities.

Some of the lodgings are new, modern, fully furnished apartments and villas, part of the condominium development schemes where units are available for rent in owner's absence. Other places are small, simple, and geared to an outdoor life that stands on no ceremony and isn't affected if the stove does not work (presumably because you can eat out or cook on a grill). There's not much in the Santo Domingo area, but most of what's available will be listed through ARAH, a Dominican rental service with offices at 194 Avenida 27 de Febrero, Santo Domingo, D.R. It's also a good idea to check with the American Chamber of Commerce offices at the Hotel Santo Domingo. They will be able to give you names of realtors used to working with Americans and may know of some homes or apartments for rent. The U.S. Embassy is on Avenida César Nicolás Penson, not far from the Plaza de la Cultura. *Caribbean Home Rentals* (Box 710, Palm Beach, FL 33480) lists properties at Sosua, and plans to add apartments and homes in other parts of the country. Contact them for details including prices and terms.

Many of the villas at Casa de Campo on the southeast coast are available for long-term rental. You have your choice of golf or tennis villas. Contact Casa de Campo management.

✣ **Palmas del Mar** (Playa Juan Dolio, southeast coast of Dominican Republic; 26 units) is a perfect place for a self-sufficient beach holiday in Spanish surroundings. Clustered around a couple of tennis courts, with a special pavilion for dancing (on the nights there is music), the beachside apartments are designed by Manuel Del Monte, best known to some of us for his tireless work on the restored area of the Old City of Santo Domingo. About an hour's drive from Santo Domingo (and almost that, farther east, from La Romana and Casa de Campo, and the recreation of a Spanish village at Altos de Chavon), Palmas del Mar can be ideal for those who want a quiet place with options to cook at home. There's a small market on premises for basics, and fish comes from the local fisherman. A handful of Dominican-style restaurants freckle the sides of the main road, not far from this beachside place, but don't count on a lot of planned activity here. Rates this winter for the 2-bedroom units, with full kitchen and living area (complete with TV), are about $80 per day and 4 can live here comfortably.

✣ **Punta Garza** (Playa Juan Dolio, Aptdo. Postal 1340, D.R.; 46 units) nests next to the beach, about an hour's drive from Santo Domingo, along the south coast. With a management link with El Embajador, the cluster of apartments is sometimes included as the beachtime partner of a week's holiday. The 2-story white stucco buildings are capped with red tile roofs in a style that is becoming Dominican (and has always been Mediterranean). Count on finding adequate furnishings, a beach-oriented atmosphere, and a few casual cafe-style restaurants in this popular beach area. Rates for a unit range around $50 in winter.

✣ **Villas del Mar** (Playa Juan Dolio, D.R.; 52 rooms) are scattered along the shore, down a dirt road spur off the main "coastal" road which weaves inland a bit at this section. For a beach-focused holiday, amid Spanish-speaking, Dominican families who come out from Santo Domingo on weekends, this place offers comfortable surroundings. Don't count on a lot of entertainment, unless you are with a group of friends. Rates for winter are about $20 for 2, meals—which you cook—are extra.

✣ **Villa Canes** (Playa Juan Dolio, D.R.; 20 apts) joins the rest of the shoreside places for the season of '81–'82. The new units have modern kitchen equipment, comfortable furnishings, and a beach orientation, as you'd expect. Count on rates to be under $50 for 2, with casual restaurants—and the beach—nearby.

■■■

RESTAURANTS IN SANTO DOMINGO are some of the Caribbean's best, and prices, compared to what people are paying elsewhere, are in the reasonable-to-expensive realm. Because the Dominican Republic is one of the few Caribbean countries where almost everything can be grown, raised, or caught locally (good vegetables, rice, coffee, beef, and, of course, chickens and fish), most of the meals will be excellent—with specialties prepared according to tried and true recipes of qualified chefs. Dominicans love good food and quality surroundings and expect to pay for them. In fact, there's a tendency here, as in many Latin countries, to equate high price with high quality. (One hotel manager told me of his previous stint in Rio, where the Chivas Regal wasn't selling too well at $150 per bottle; the price was put at $225 when the bottle was put on the table. The scotch went like hotcakes; everyone who could afford it wanted to be seen with a bottle on his table.)

AUTHOR'S AWARDS for Santo Domingo dining go again to La Bahía, for the best seafood in casual, comfortable surroundings, and to Lina's, long the acknowledged leader, and still so—as you'll readily admit if you order the Zarzuela.

You can still find very inexpensive, excellent food in small places in the countryside where the Dominican country people eat, but prices in Santo Domingo's well-known restaurants and at the tourist-and-otherwise popular places around the country will figure to at least $10 per person for a full meal.

In sharp contrast to the situation on many Caribbean islands, the luxury restaurants in the hotels are exceptionally good here. Hotel Santo Domingo's *Alcázar,* Hostal Nicolás de Ovando's *Extremadura,* Sheraton *Antoine's,* and Plaza Dominicana's *La Casa* are excellent, and unusually attractive.

La Bahía, on the Malecón near the Old City, is the best bet for a casual place with top-notch seafood. This inauspicious-looking spot, on a corner near the port in Santo is a Dominican (and my) favorite restaurant. Tourist-type Americans are a rare commodity, but Dominican couples and families fill this place almost every evening (but not until 9 or later). Wood chairs with rush seats get pulled up to simple tables, and discreet people-watching is a pasttime, if you're not lucky enough to have your own group of lively conversationalists. Camarones (shrimp) are superb; lambi (conch) is good, and the price is right—at about $5 per entree. This is a place to settle in for seafood Dominican style.

La Mesón de la Cava, better known as a nightclub near the Embajador Hotel, on Avenida Mirador del Sur, is also worth a dinner. Ottico Ricart, owner and chef overseer does some of the cooking himself, but your primary reason for coming here will not be only food. The place is 50 feet below the road; you pirouette down a perilous staircase that looks like it leads from a manhole cover. You can cuddle in a corner of the caves, or settle for a traditional table for 2 or more. Touristy? Yes, but well done and worth the investment in time and money.

Fonda de la Atarazana, across the road from the Alcázar in downtown Santo Domingo, is worth a stop for a cool beverage off the courtyard and a look out the window of the second-floor restaurant. If you get the right table, you'll be at eye level with Diego Columbus's home, a spectacular sight when it's night-lighted, but a good view anytime. Portions and food were heavy (country Dominican) when I tried this spot, but it's worth a visit for ambiance, and for convenience when you're touring the Old City.

Il Buco, next door to El Bodegon on Arzobispo Meriño (and not far from the Centro Dominicano de Información Tourística) is well worth an evening reservation. The owner came "back to the city" after a few years at the Gulf + Western Casa de Campo complex and opened his special restaurant on the site of what had been La Casa Verde. Specialties include the homemade pasta, well-cooked fish, and delicious desserts displayed on a trolley that is wheeled to your table. Be sure to attempt the antipasto assortment. The place is open for lunch and very popular in the evening with Dominicans (who like to dine late). Decor, with brick walls and stucco arches, gives an old-world feeling, very fitting for a place that is a short walk from the city's historic cathedral and other buildings. Plan for a leisurely Dominican-style meal here, and know that you will part with $15 per person for a meal with full flourishes, accompanied by wine.

Lina's Restaurant at the hotel on Avenida Máximo Gómez was better when it was small, but it is still *the* place to go, even though prices have settled at $10 realm for a meal, and surroundings have been enclosed and air-conditioned. Lina Aguado was a Spanish woman whom Trujillo brought to Santo Domingo to be his special cook. She left the generalíssimo's employ to open her own restaurant, which is now in the hands of her nephew Armando Alvarez. Zarzuela (seafood, including shrimp, lobster, bits of small clams, with Pernod in the sauce) is worth making the trip to Santo Domingo, and if you like garlic, the Mero à la Vasca (bass, Basque-style) is good.

Vesuvio erupts in two versions. Try **I,** on the Malecón since 1953, and still one of the best places to dine. Dominicans enjoying a casual night out settle into the al fresco tables near the entrance to the air-conditioned (and COLD) inner sanctum, which is a favorite for family celebrations. If you plan ahead, you can have a feast of suckling pig, but otherwise settle for one of the Italian specialties (fettucine at about $4, antipasto priced by the item, and homemade manicotti) or the steaks and seafood that are still the most popular items on the menu. The appetizer cart can provide a meal in itself, but ask Enzo Bonarelli, your host, for his suggestion for the evening special. Obviously the Italian fare is dependable. With the à la carte menu, you can find an entree and skip out leaving less than $10. (Closed Wed.)

Pizzeria, a Vesuvio relative, has opened next door, also on the Malecón, to offer simple, snack-style Italian food (including, obviously, pizza).

Jardín de Jade, at the Embajador Hotel, makes a name for itself with special Chinese dinners (which you can order by number of people in your party) and elegant surroundings, especially when you make a reservation in advance. Peking duck slivers appear in feather-light crepes, assembled in "packages" by your table's waiter. A 9-course dinner for 6 people (ordered that way) is under $50; 4 people dine well for under $30.

El Bodegón, at Arzobispo Meriño 152, in the Old City at the corner of the Plaza, not far from the cathedral, is an air-conditioned pocket of dining pleasure, with tile floors, dark-wood accents, and a comfortable atmosphere for enjoying award-winning meals. Try the cassoulet à la Gascona (lamb and pork stew with sausage) at $8, Zarzuela de Mariscos at $12 or, if you're budget-watching, spaghetti at about $5. Pato al higo (duck) and Mero à la Vasca (bass with garlic sauce) are specialties.

D'Agostini (Avenida Máximo Gómez 9) is no place for budget watchers. Management reportedly has a bottle of Château Latour 1967 in the wine cellar, available for $3,500, and a permanent wine stock valued at $100,000. Owner Natalino d'Agostini bought 12 cases of wine at $6,000 per case in 1976, and had one left by early 1977. Among his customers are the Hotel Santo Domingo. Atmosphere, service, and food are elegant and EXPENSIVE, but $60 for wine with dinner seems to be "nothing" to some Dominicans. (Some of D'Agostini's best customers are wealthy San Juañeros who have followed him here from his hometown across the sea at the Rich Port.)

Da Ciro (corner of Avenida Independencia and Pasteur) opened in the mid-1970s in what had been the Herrera Báez family home. Singing waiters and Italian songs supplement the extensive menu. Good food. Try the tagliolino Paglia et Fieno (straw and hay). Good fun if you have a scintillating group of companions, but a good bet even alone. Count on the usual steep dinner tariff, but you get plenty of atmosphere here.

da' Cirito is the pizza-style (lower cost) sister of Da Ciro, and popular with some for the conversation-and-snack times.

Maricris Terrace Restaurant on the Malecón got its start as a place where stern Dominican parents allowed their teenage children to go for a night on the town because it was run by Maria Christina de Arvelo, a friend of many of the parents. Fame spread, wisely so, and now the rest of us can settle in, to enjoy some really good Dominican food. Try Asopao de Pollo (a kind of rice chicken soup) with salad and Quesillo de Leche (a kind of baked custard) as dessert. Prices are low by Dominican standards.

The terrace of **Napolitana Hotel,** where you can get small pizzas as well as other snacks, is one of several places along Malecón where you can join Dominicans for the late-evening hours. **El Cas-**

tillo, on the sea-side of Malecón, is another (be sure to sit outside). Horse-drawn carriages are part of the parade that passes along the shore-rimming road, and you'll find the open-to-breezes places busy until the early hours of dawn. **El Paradiso,** next to Bahia on the Malecón on the city end of the shore-rimming road, has a rustic atmosphere and some snacks that are good when they alternate with sips of Dominican El Presidente beer. Sample the platos tipicos which include modongo (tripe—which appears on the menu as "beef stripe") or the bollito de yucca, a cheese and ground yucca root finger-sized nibble that is deep fried and delicious—if you like that kind of thing. Strictly casual, cafe-style is the atmosphere.

Peter's, a small place on the Malecón, and the better-known **Karin's** are places to try if you want a hearty German meal, supplemented with the local traditional Presidente or newer Corona beer.

For easy and relatively inexpensive city dining, there are always the hotel coffee shops (with Dominicana's *El Mercado* and the Sheraton's *Terraza* two to try), but don't count on any good Dominican food here. The few offerings on the menu are Americanized beyond recognition, and you'll do better with something you know is American—a club sandwich, or fruit or avocado salad, for example. If your stomach can stand it (and mine has often) buy chicharones, pastelitos, or empanadas from the street vendors or the cafes along the Malecón. The first is fried and crispy pork rind; the second and third are little and big pastries made from yucca flour and filled with spicy ground meat. The oranges and pineapples you'll see for sale from carts, especially in the country, are always juicy and delicious.

Good local rums are Bermudez, Sibonney, and Brugal, all readily available and a lot less expensive than scotch or other imported alcohol, which carries high duty.

■■■
PLACES WORTH FINDING: Colonial Santo Domingo leads the list, with the Cathedral, Casas Reales, and Casa de Colón three "requirements." When Miguel Diaz thought he had killed the servant of Don Bartolomé Colón (Columbus), Christopher's brother, he fled from the settlement in the north, and made his way to the south coast, where he met and fell in love with an Indian princess who lived with her tribe on the banks of the Ozama. When he became despondent with longing for his friends, she urged him to go north and bring some of them back. He did, only to find that he had not, in fact, killed the servant and was not a criminal. He then waxed enthusiastic about his home in the south, and the

gold mines at Jaina nearby. According to Samuel Hazard's report in his writings in 1873, Don Bartolomé confirmed the fact of the mines, checked with his brother for approval, and moved the whole north coast town of Isabela south to settle New Isabela on the banks of the Ozama. Columbus is thought to have visited when he returned from Spain in August 1498; the name change came either in honor of the day (Sunday) when the town was founded or of the father of Columbus, whose name was Domingo.

Soon after Nicolás de Ovando succeeded as governor in 1502, a hurricane wiped out the town, which he ordered rebuilt on the "other" side of the river, where it now stands. Hazard quotes Oviedo, a 16th-century historian, as saying that "as touching the buildings, there is no city in Spain, not even Barcelona, so much to be preferred as San Domingo. The houses for the most part are stone—the situation is much better than Barcelona, by reason that the streets are much larger and wider, and without comparison straighter and more direct, being laid out with cord, compass and measure. In the midst of the city is the fortress and castle, and such houses so fair and large that they may well receive any lord or noble of Spain with his train and family, and especially is this true of that of Don Diego Columbus."

Santo Domingo's Colonial City represents a $10 million investment on the part of the Dominican government, but its value is far greater to anyone interested in history. Not as authentic as Old San Juan, Puerto Rico (where the 16th- and 17th-century buildings remained to be restored), the building of the Old City of Santo Domingo has been modern, based on the old design.

Casa de Colón, also known as the Alcázar, is the house where Diego Colón (Columbus) lived with his bride (Dona María de Toledo y Rojas, a niece of King Ferdinand). The house is furnished as it might have been when they lived there in the 1500s. Most of the antiques have been donated by Spanish interests, and the handiwork (note the ceilings and tiled floors) was under the tutelage of Juan Guzman who worked with Manuel Del Monte Urraca. The tiles amid the terra cotta on the floors show a lion (Ferdinand) and a castle (Isabella). The 3 tapestries are especially valuable. Although they are of the 17th century, they depict the Columbus story. Note especially the 16th-century kitchen with tiles, and two wood benches by the fireplace. Food was carried up the narrow spiral stairs which you can climb to reach the 2nd floor dining rooms. One room is for the children, the other more formal for adults. There are ivory-encrusted desks and other furniture in the main hall, which was used for receptions; and the view from the balconies over the Ozama can be impressive. (Squint to overlook the modern boxcars, etc.) Despite what you may be told, the Alcázar is newly built, with stones mined from an area similar to that which was used for the original building. The government invested more than $1,000,000 in the palace they opened with fanfare on Columbus Day 1957. (And another RD$2 million has been invested recently in paving the Colonial City.) King Juan Carlos and his Queen Sophia were feted here at an elegant reception during their visit in 1975, following placement of additional gifts from Spain and completion of some of the work on the nearby areas—La Atarazana, Calle Las Damas, and the cathedral.

La Atarazana is where the conquistadors and others used to bring their ships for supplies and repair. It is the first arsenal in the New World, where arms and military equipment were stored and troops were trained. Today, after tireless work by the Oficina de Patrimonio Cultural, and its former director Manuel Del Monte Urraca, who trained with others in Spain, Atarazana is catacombed with shops and small restaurants, and will eventually have some small hotels. Nader's Art Gallery is in what was a Spanish convent. Although the appearance of the area is true to the 16th century all the construction is new, using old walls and arches when they were worthy and solid, with electric wires underground and brick walks unknown to the early settlers.

Samuel Hazard comments that "the walls of the older houses are very solidly constructed either of stone or . . . mampostería . . . glutinous earth . . . mixed with lime, and sometimes . . . with powdered stone; frames of plans are then made . . . and filled with layers of this composition, sand and lime being added. The whole is then moistened with water, well pounded and kneaded, and allowed to dry, the mould being withdrawn, leaves a firm solid wall, which, on exposure to the air, becomes hard as stone. Even the walls of the city are built in this way." And then he adds that "with the exception of the old churches, there are few really imposing buildings in the city."

As you walk from the Alcázar, along Calle Las Damas past Hostal Nicholás de Ovando, think what this street must have been like in the 16th century, when it was the official twilight promenade for the ladies of the court. If you plan your stroll for late afternoon, notice the pink cast to the walls as the sun goes down.

Casas Reales (Tu-F 9-12, 3-6; Sat 10-6; RD$.50 adults, RD$.25 children; English-speaking guides available, booklet in English for RD $3.50), on the west side of the street (the right, as you walk south with the Alcázar at your back), is a restoration in the 16th-

century style of what was the Palacio de la Real Audiencia y Chan-
cillería de Indias y el Palacio de los Gobernadores y Capitanes Gen-
erales de la Isla Española (Palace of the Royal Audience of the
Indies and the Palace of the Governors and Captains-General of
Santo Domingo). The name of Casas Reales has been noted in the
earliest documents of the city, when it was mentioned that the governor and the captains-general lived on the upper floor of the northwestern part of the building; the rest of the upper floor was occupied by the room for the royal audience, while the treasury and the
counting house were on street level. If you don't do more than look
at the large map of the world Columbus knew, showing his voyages
in colored lights (in room 1), the visit is worth it, but the furniture
is impressive and the entire restoration and museum give an excellent picture of the trappings and interests of life in the 16th and
17th centuries. In room 3 are exhibits of mining, agriculture, live-
stock, and the uses of tobacco in the Dominican economy; then you
walk through what were the stables and the powder magazine to
the carriage houses, past statues of A. de Suazo and Nicolás de
Ovando to reach the coin room. Created as a landmark on October
18, 1973, the museum was opened May 31, 1976, when King Juan
Carlos of Spain visited the country.

Casa de Bastidas (Tu-Sun 9-12, 3-6), on the east side of Calle Las
Damas, was the home of Rodrigo de Bastidas, mayor of Santo Domingo. It opened in late 1977 as a museum for treasures found on
sunken ships. Note the trees that flourish in the courtyard you walk
through to reach the small museum.

Farther along the Calle Las Damas, on the river side of the street,
you will pass **Fortaleza Ozama,** restored as a park, and the **Torre del
Homenaje,** dedicated to Queen Isabella in 1507 and home for Diego
Colón while his palace was being built. Sir Francis Drake burned
the tower when he pillaged the city in 1586. Modern day notoriety
comes with the fact that the tower was the hovel where political
prisoners were tossed during the reign (1930–1961) of Generalissimo Rafael Leonidas Trujillo. Turn right at the tower to stroll past
the bishop's houses to the cathedral.

"The Cathedral, the most interesting building in Santo Domingo,
is in its interior a grand old church, with pillars and arches and
crypts and altars innumerable; and as we view its vast extent we
can readily believe the accounts of the various historians, who give
such glowing relations of its splendours in ancient days. Its exterior
bears the marks of its great antiquity upon its form, not only in the
weather stained walls, but in the quaint architecture," Samuel
Hazard commented following his visit in the 1870s. The same is

true today. Built in the style of a Roman church, between 1512 and 1540 from stone by workmen who left for richer Mexico and other Central American cities before they finished the job, the cathedral was embellished with gold and silver which has been snitched by subsequent city occupants, "principally . . . during the occupation of the French," Samuel Hazard claims.

As you enter through the side gates, you walk into a small chapel where Sir Francis Drake is said to have slung his hammock to sleep—waking long enough to rob, pillage, and threaten the Spaniards and to chop off both hands of the bishop's statue, which stands nearby. Drake called this room home for his tumultuous 24-day stay in 1586, when he tried to barter with Diego Colón for the safety of the town and ended up burning most of it down. A very nice "ántikee," I was told by one guide, is the baroque Virgin, which dates from 1774. Look at the cherubs over one of the portals; their mouths form do, re, mi, fa, sol, la, ti—and then you have to go back to "do." The choir used to stand above them. Below them, on the side of the arch, the 3 crosses mark the spot for political asylum. In the old days, if a prisoner could reach and touch this spot, he would be given freedom and escorted out of the city.

The bones of Columbus, you will be told without hesitation, are in an elaborate tomb at the west entrance. The fact is no one knows for sure where the actual bones are located. Hazard mentions that in 1783 Frenchman Moreau de Saint-Mery found a lead coffin which he claimed held Columbus's bones. He was probably right— but they could have been the bones of Bartolomé, Diego, or Christopher, since all were eventually buried together. For decades, Cuba claimed the bones (a claim no longer accepted), and you can visit an elaborate tomb holding "the bones" in Seville, Spain. The most recent theory is that some of the bones of Columbus are in Seville, and some in the Dominican Republic, the result of a hurried excavation of ruined tombs in Santo Domingo in 1795, when only part of the dust of Columbus family remains was scooped up to be reburied in Cuba, whence it made its way eventually to Seville. (Thomas Dozier's article, "The Controversy on the Whereabouts of Columbus' Body," in an issue of the *Smithsonian* Magazine gives an interesting perspective on the saga.) No matter where the bones actually are, once a year, on October 12, a procession of the president, the mayor, and the bishop comes here to unlock three caskets—bronze holding crystal holding lead which is supposed to hold "the bones of Columbus." Note the friezes around the base of the tomb; they depict 4 important episodes in the life of Columbus. When you step outside to look at the face of the cathedral, note the frescoes, which are said to date from 1586, and the statues that re-place bronze ones Sir Francis Drake gets credit for taking. In 1512 the bell was put in the bell tower and the 5 bells there today still ring at regular daily intervals.

The plazas surrounding the cathedral have been fringed with some tourist shops and are the arena for the "hey, lady" sidewalk salesmen and the black-market money men. If you are on your own, sit for a few minutes in the park at the foot of the statue of Co-lumbus (who is supposed to be pointing to the New World—north—but in fact is pointing right at the Hipotecaria Universal S.A. with the Bank of America on its right). A devoted Indian maiden languishes at the base, carefully putting the final touches to Columbus's name with a quill.

Casa del Cordón, so named because of the cord of the order of Saint Francis over its main door, is a bank, but it is a bank with a conscience. The building is faithfully restored as it might have looked when it was built in 1503 for Don Francisco de Garay. Diego Colón and his wife Maria lived here when the Torre del Homenaje was damaged and before the Alcázar was completed. This is the house to which the ladies of Santo Domingo came to donate their jewels in hopes of staving off the rampage of Sir Francis Drake, who was then swaggering around town. The restored Casa del Cordón was reopened on March 16, 1974; trained guides will willingly show you around the boardroom and the executive offices so that you can see how a 16th-century building has been adapted to 20th-century commerce.

Dirección Nacional de Parques maintains several open spaces in and around Santo Domingo. The **Parque Litoral del Sur** fringes the Malecón (Avenida George Washington) between the Hotel Santo Domingo and the center of the Colonial City, with a sidewalk prom-enade for most of that distance, but guests at the Dominicana will look over **Paseo de Los Indios** and the **Parque Mirador del Sur,** an ideal (and perfectly safe) jogging or bicycling area that stretches out in front of the hotel. You can take the train around the grounds for 20¢. The several restaurants and play areas scattered around the park are favorite gathering spots for Dominicans when they have some leisure time; the grounds are very well kept and benches are prevalent.

Parque Zoológico Nacional, at the northern rim of the city in an area overlooking the Rio Isabela, moved to its present site a couple of years ago. Universitaria Nacional Pedro Henríquez Ureña ad-ministers the park, which has a lake for aquatic birds and an aviary for exotic and native birds as well as an African plain where the ani-

mals roam and a children's zoo. There's a train that tours the park
(40¢ adults, 15¢ children). Especially for children, the **Parque de
Atracciónes Infantiles** is on the site of the former zoo and botanical
garden, between Avenida Bolívar and César Nicolás Penson in the
center of the city. In additon to the animal exhibits, there are caves
to prowl around and special rides including a ferris wheel and
ponies.

Jardín Botánico Nacional Dr. Rafael M. Moscoso (Tu-Sun 9-12, 2-5;
closed M; 25¢ adults, 15¢ children; $1 boat; $5 carriage, 50¢ train,
25¢ children) is not too far from the zoo, in the Galá area of the city.
You can tour the grounds by horse carriage, as well as by train and
boat. There are more than 200 varieties of palm trees, in addition to
a Japanese garden area and a research section which includes diagrams of the country, and special laboratories (speaking Spanish
makes a difference, if you are serious about some research).

Parque Los Tres Ojos, off the Autopista de Las Américas on the
way to Boca Chica and the airport, is on most tours. It is actually 4
"eyes" or caves, that were mentioned in early histories of the city. If
you are interested in stalagmites and stalactites you might enjoy
the "eyes." Follow the tours through and around the pools. There's
a lot of climbing involved, so this is not an excursion for people with
weak knees or weak hearts. Those people can content themselves
with bargaining for some of the handmade items that will be offered
the minute you step off your bus at the grounds. (If you want to
glimpse Los Tres Ojos, allow an extra hour to do so on your trip to
the airport.)

Plaza de la Cultura is an impressive combination of modern buildings on the outskirts of downtown Santo Domingo, in an area that
once was property of Generalissimo Trujillo. **Muse del Hombre Dominicana** (check for opening hours, which change) should be on
top of the list of out-of-the-sun diversions for anyone with an interest in Caribbean history. Dioramas, maps, and displays of artifacts
found in excavations around the Dominican Republic and elsewhere in the Caribbean are attractively presented. Knowing Spanish helps if you want to know details; there are very few notices
printed in English, and from my experience, even the guide's commentary is not complete. The **Teatro Nacional** is the hub of the symphony and opera life. Special performances by visiting artists are a
highlight of the impressive season, which focuses mostly on Dominican artists. Check with the social director at your hotel or with
the Dominican Information Center near the cathedral in the Colonial City for details about obtaining tickets. (If you really care about

attending something, find out as soon as possible after you check into your hotel what performances are planned while you are in town.) In addition to the Museum of Dominican Man and the National Theater, the **Museum of Natural History,** the **Museum of Fine Arts,** and the **Public Library** are here—with the "Wind Rose Fountain" that looks like a dandelion gone to seed in the middle of the mall and mango trees around the grounds. (The U.S. Embassy is nestled nearby, in splendor among the Central Bank and government offices, including the Dominican IRS.)

Altos de Chavón is well worth a visit, even if you are based in Santo Domingo and have to devote the entire day to it. (It's almost 2 hours drive each way from the city; guests at Gulf + Western's Casa de Campo can hop aboard the hotel's shuttle bus and be at the remarkable area in a carefree 15 minutes or so.) Altos ("the heights") is a newly constructed 16th-century Spanish-style village, built on the high banks of the Chavón River, just east of the town of La Romana. The awesome creation is a labor of love, partly initiated by the necessity for Gulf + Western to invest some of its profits from what has been called "the largest sugar mill-and-plantation in the world" in the country of origin, it can be enjoyed by anyone with the wherewithal to get to the riverbank. The first building to rise on the site of the new-old village was the small church, dedicated to the Polish patron saint, St. Stanislas. Cobbled courtyards were underway, and the church was almost finished when I first visited the project; now—only a few years after the concept was first discussed—there are interesting handcraft boutiques (with some items made by the artists who live in the village), art galleries with work by Dominican artists for sale, and a roster of cafes and restaurants that doubled during one of my visits, in April 1981. Don't miss the *Museum,* a regional museum of Taino Indian history and artifacts. Even if you have a natural aversion to museums, make time for this one. This displays are attractive, and the doses of history are punctuated with interesting artifacts and reprints of pictures supplemented with drawings and diagrams. Even my 15-year-old nephew, whose enthusiasm for museums does not rival his interest in golf and tennis, found the displays intriguing and palatably educational. Some of the displays are in an open-to-breezes foyer; the core is in an air-conditioned "deep freeze" and contains valuable finds including jewelry and cooking implements from the earliest Indian settlers.

(For commentary on the restaurants, see page 309.) A schedule of special events (jazz and other musical performances, in addition to pageants, art shows, and opportunities for special dinners) is available through Casa de Campo resort. Even if there's nothing special planned, Altos de Chavon deserves your touring time.

■■■

SPORTS: **Tennis** has taken over here, as everywhere. When Plaza Dominicana got in swing in early 1977, one top sales point was the 8 championship tennis courts, with complimentary court fees and resident pro. Summer tennis package holidays are part of the promotion. Sheraton also has courts, with plans for more, and you can count on courts at Hotel Santo Domingo. Mecca for tennis enthusiasts is La Terraza Tennis Village, part of Casa de Campo. The 13 courts are used for tournament play, as well as for lessons and the complex with its tennis focus offers pool, snack place, tennis shop, and plenty of tennis talk. Special tennis package holidays are offered. There's a court or 2 at Montemar Hotel at Puerto Plata on the north coast, but I don't think they're much (and certainly not worth making a trip to play) and courts at the Playa Dorada complex that are pro caliber.

Golf came clearly into focus when Pete Dye's *Cajuiles I* opened at Casa de Campo on the southeast coast, with its 7 shoreside holes as part of the challenging 6,774-yard course. Now there's a second 18 at *Cajuiles II,* inland and abutting the first course. Golf carts, pro, and clubhouse are all here, in full country club fashion. In season, there can be a wait for starting times. Costs are high, but quality's here. Greens fees are $10 in winter; carts are another $16, and a caddy is about $5 for 18 holes. From a Santo Domingo base, there's the Santo Domingo Country Club's 18, available for guests who make reservations for play (through your hotel social director) 24 hours in advance. Your alternative is to drive 2 hours each way to play at Casa de Campo, or to go north, where the 18-hole Robert Trent Jones course at Playa Dorada has been ready for play since late '78, and is top caliber.

Scuba diving is possible, but the D.R. is not the best place to learn. Pool lessons are similar to those offered at other Caribbean resorts, but the offshore exploration is recommended only for experienced divers. La Caleta Reef and the reefs off Playa Palenque, where you can dive around ancient cannons, are two places that Scuba firms take their clients. (Check to see who is operating, and with what credentials, if you're interested in diving.) If you are experienced and hire a guide, Cabo Francés Viejo, Río San Juan, and Playa Magante can be challenging and interesting. In Santo Domingo, check with your hotel activities desk for prices and details about scuba excursions, and resort or regular certification courses. At Casa de Campo the activities desk has details. (Catalina Island offshore has some good snorkeling rocks and reefs.)

Fishermen should zero in on Casa de Campo for access to the fleet of Bertram 35s. The Club Náutico de Santo Domingo's Boca de Yuma Fishing International usually takes place in May. Now in its 15th year, the tournament includes only white and blue marlins, sailfish, and tuna for points—and speaking Spanish is a definite plus if you want to have any fun with this one. *Prieto Tours* (offices at Centro Comercial Nacional on Avenida 27 de Febrero) offers deep-sea fishing aboard the *Cristiana III,* a Bertram 28. Six people can charter for an 8-hour day out of Boca Chica for under $350, transportation, beer and soft drinks, box lunch, and experienced captain and mate included. Half-day is about $200.

Horseback riding is well organized at *Cajuiles Dude Ranch* at La Romana (arrangements made through Casa de Campo activities desk, or if you want to make a day of it, through Hotel Santo Domingo, including a 2-hour ride each way from Santo Domingo to La Romana and back). Paso Fino horses came to the Dominican Republic in 1493, when 25 of them limped off the ships of Columbus. From here, they went to Puerto Rico with Martín de Salazar in 1509, to Cuba with Diego de Velásquez in 1511, and to Mexico with Cortez in 1518. There are regional shows of Paso Finos around the country, with the *Feria Ganadera* (National Cattle Fair) usually held in February on the Malecón at Ciudad Ganadera. Since this is where many of the Paso Finos are stabled, you can see the horses almost any afternoon between 4 and 6 when the owners and trainers ride them.

Polo was the national passion during the Trujillo years, and there are still staunch supporters. Polo matches have been revived with all the elegant flourishes at the field at Casa de Campo. Here you can watch (or play) from September through May. There are also matches at the polo field, Sierra Prieta, from January through April, Saturday and Sundays, in Santo Domingo.

■■

TREASURES AND TRIFLES: Treasures are emerging—and being designed—amid what had become a landslide of simple, sloppy, overpriced tourist items that included a lot of amber that wasn't. Among the true treasures you can find today are the items at **Planarte,** an arm of the Fundación Dominicana de Desarrollo, Inc. (Dominican Development Foundation), which works with country folk in the development of crafts in leather and ceramics.

In their shop near the center of the Old City you can find well-made sandals at about $5, picture frames in leather, handbags, and several small pottery items that are easy to pack for the folks back home.

There are interesting items, also, at **El Círculo de Colecionistas,** just off Calle de las Damas on Calle Mercedes (check to see if the courtyard bistro has reopened). Items available here include attractive coasters with historic maps and prints as design, some limited-edition maps and prints for wall hangings, plus other quality items. Other Dominican work to look for includes some tortoiseshell items (which, since the U.S. government lists tortoise as an endangered species, are illegal to bring back to the U.S.), some good quality handmade furniture, baskets and macrame work if you like it, and some of the "sculptured" stone birds and other items that children make. These last make up in effort what they may lack in art. Altos de Chavón, 2 hours' drive along the south coast from the city, is a 1980s creation of a 16th-century Spanish-Dominican village that is devoted to handcrafts and paintings. Although not as overwhelming (yet) as Haiti's street vendors, the Santo Domingueños who flock around you in the Colonial City and at any tourist attraction can be tiresome. If you stop to look, be prepared to have young, supersalesmen come from every corner.

The Bishop's Basket at Avenida Independencia and Danae has good quality handicrafts, sold in a shop that is sponsored by the Episcopal Church. **La Plaza** at the cathedral is strictly a tourist shop, but the quality of shell work, larimar, and amber seems better here than at some of the other places. The **Columbus Gift Shop** at the Alcázar is another such spot.

For furniture, ask to find **Manuel Cáceres's** work. He took the cue from the furniture designs Oscar de la Renta innovated for the Gulf & Western hotels, and uses Creole techniques when he works with pine, horn, conch, plantain fiber, agave, sisal, and palm tree thatch. Some of the chairs, stools and tables are small enough to bring home without too much trouble, but do not ship furniture if you aren't prepared for a lot of problems. The process takes forever, and you may never see your treasure.

If you are short on reading matter, and can't find anything interesting in the hotel shops, stop at **El Greco** on Avenida Tiradentes to look through their selection of English-language paperbacks. Track down a copy of *Santo Domingo Past & Present, with a Glance at Hayti,* written in 1873 by American Samuel Hazard and one of the Colección de Cultura Dominicana printed in Spain by the Sociedad

Dominicana de Bibliófilos if you are interested in early Dominican history.

When you consider buying amber, be sure you are not looking at plastic. (A test is to light a match and hold it under the piece. If a black smudge starts to develop, and the piece begins to melt—it's plastic.) Amber is a lemon to brown-colored petrified resin from a coniferous tree that has long since gone. Amber was burned as incense at the time of Moses; Greeks rubbed it with fur to make it magnetic; Phoenicians and Syrians prized it; Columbus noted in his diary on December 16, 1492, that he received some as a gift from the Quisqueya Indian chief; 17th-century German guilds count amber cutters in their numbers; and man has used it as an amulet for sore throats (and Moroccans are supposed to have worn it for safety). In China and Korea it means good luck—and in 1800 it was discovered in the Dominican Republic. In the past 35 years, the mines near the Cordillera Septentrional in the west, and in the north between Puerto Plata and Santiago de los Caballeros have yielded plenty of amber. So much that some people, notably Antonio Prats Ventos, a Dominican sculptor, are using huge pieces as the block from which artistic shapes are worked. The real McCoy is here. Be sure that's what you are buying, if that's what you are paying the high price for.

Two shops that are dependable (and to which everyone goes) are: **Mendez Artesania,** S.A. (José Reyes and Arzobispo Nouel). Miguel Mendez is the one who "discovered" the blue stone, Larimar, which he named for his daughter Larissa, and the sea. The second shop is **Maria Ambar** (Calle Duarte 9), a small place in a residential community where you can find high quality that is worth the high price. If you want to design your own jewelry, capable staff can give suggestions.

Duarte Street is one of the top shopping areas, IF you like to bargain, and to rummage through a lot of not-so-good to find a few treasures. Shopkeepers are Arabs, Chinese, Spanish—and sharp. If you want clothes made, bring a picture and allow a couple of days for fashions to be made and fitted. Check the social hostess at your hotel for the names of the people she knows, trusts, and can badger into finishing in a hurry if you are having troubles with your own authority.

El Conde Street, most of the length of it, is another major shopping avenue, but you have to know what you are buying. The street is a short walk from the cathedral plaza, in the Colonial City.

El Mercado Modelo (the market) was a lot more fun when it was *el mercado* for the local people. These days, with the toutings of tourism officials (and people like me who write about it), it is a hybrid. Some of the best buys are still the local items (clay braziers for grilling fish, spices, market baskets), but in addition, you will have no trouble picking up a mahogany rocker (broken down and cardboard-cartoned for easy shipment home) and will be pestered by purveyors of all manner of merchandise they think you need. Buy—and bargain—carefully. It is easy to be taken for the tourist you are. Among the shops you'll find equipped to deal in almost-English are Domingo Antonio Castillo's **La Simpatía** (*stand 58*), the familia Jiménez shop (*stand 1*), **Matilde Diaz's** spot (*stands 3 or 5*), the **Santa Ana** of Andres Faria de Perez, and **La Delicia** (*stand 70*), operated by Jose Mejía. They, and many others, will lure you from your wanderings at least to listen to their sales pitch if not to buy.

La Atarazana shops are strictly for tourists, but the merchandise has been culled from some of the commercial best available. (Many find the shopping here, even at higher prices, less of a hassle than at El Mercado.) Located in the attractive mall, built to look as though it might be an old shopping area, the shops across the road from the Alcázar are actually on the site of an arsenal, where the pillage from rich ports in the conquistadors' Caribbean was stored. Among the shops to look for are **Nader's Art Gallery** (buy carefully; I thought there was a lot of high-priced junk here), open 9-12:30, 3-7 except Sun), **Artecentro** at #13, where crafts by the handicapped at the Centro de Rehabilitación are sold (when you buy here, you're contributing to more than just your own supply of souvenirs), and the **Zodiac** at #17 and **Columbus Gift Shop** at #27, both with amber, black coral, and pink conch shell jewelry (some junk, I think, and a few good pieces) as well as other standard Dominican crafts. By decree 3050, duty-free status was granted to Atarazana shops, creating the fourth duty-free shopping area in Santo Domingo.

Other duty-free shops, most of them featuring liquor bargains, plus the usual perfume and a few cameras and other items are at the Embajador Hotel (a small area), the Centro de los Heroes, which was the first duty-free shopping area and is a mass of overwhelming commerce where only U.S. dollars will do for transactions, and Las Américas International Airport at the departure lounge, which you reach after going through immigration. Deals offered at the special sales can be excellent (a quart of J & B for $6.65, a half-gallon of Cutty Sark for $10.50, 1/5 Dry Sack sherry for $3, and a huge bottle of Courvoisier 3 star for $19). *However,* remember that you can only bring back a quota duty free, and duty and IRS tax on rum is high ($4.29 for 2 extra bottles). Other airport offerings are silver and gold chains, watches, cameras, Sony radios and Kodak equipment. Do your preparatory shopping in your hometown camera store to be sure that you are, in fact, getting the bargain you think you are. An interesting gift for a gourmet friend could be the oranges or figs bottled in Armagnac. As with all the Free Port areas, you can only purchase with U.S. dollars; getting more of them is the purpose, as far as the Dominican government is concerned.

Altos de Chavón, the new creation of a 16th-century Spanish village in the style of historic Santo Domingo, is a masterpiece, well worth the 2-hour drive from Santo Domingo. The Altos is a must if you are staying out at Casa de Campo. Started in 1977 as a dream of the Bludhorns—he's president of Gulf + Western—the village is authentic to the line, design, and stones used in its chapel, the cobbled plaza, the houses, and the shops. Intended as a village where artisans can live and ply their crafts (which are sold from their "doorsteps"), Altos de Chavón has excellent and varied restaurants and shops with Dominican-made pottery, macrame sandals and bags, leatherwork, woodcarving, clothes (mostly for women), and artwork.

■■

PUERTO PLATA is the main port on the north coast. Samuel Hazard points out that "as far back as 1499 the town is spoken of as a flourishing place, and it is even said that Columbus, in one of his later voyages, himself traced the plan of the town, which was afterwards, in 1502, constructed by the orders of Ovando the Governor, who, in order to connect it with the interior, built a fine road. . . . In those days it was a lively place, being the port at which were embarked the products of the mines and the sugar from Santiago and La Vega—the Spanish merchantmen coming here in great numbers for cargoes. The port was originally discovered by Columbus in his first voyage and being overlooked by the high mountain . . . the top of which appeared at sea so white to the Spaniards, they thought it covered with snow, as it glistened like snow or silver. Being undeceived as to the snow, they called the port, from this circumstance, Silver Port (Puerto Plata)."

Hazard didn't think much of Puerto Plata when he visited in the early 1870s, but the town is the heart of a major tourism development program that is finally getting underway to be ready for vacationers in the 1980s. By the mid-1500s, pirates had already ravaged the town and in 1606 the Spanish government destroyed it, to stop illegal trafficking with foreign powers. By the mid-1700s, the town gained some fame again when it became a free port, and by 1822, new homes began to appear on the grid streets as coffee plantations developed on the hillsides around the city. Most of the interesting wood buildings, with their overhanging second-story balconies, date from this time (Hotel Castilla, for one); but too many have fallen, or been torn down, in favor of the boxy cement buildings that pass in this town as "modern." Puerto Plata still sleeps, despite its prominence as a cruise port (*Boheme, Skyward, Song of Norway, Caribe,* and *Romanza* have docked at Puerto Plata in recent seasons and more than 300 yachts anchor here during island cruising).

■■

HOTELS IN PUERTO PLATA are coming along slowly, and that seems to be the best way for this north-coast spot. The developments that are on the drawing boards are ambitious and of high quality—and it takes time to find people with enough money to afford to build them (most are planned on the condominium-for-rent-in-owner's-absence concept). Look for some north-coast action this season, especially at Playa Dorada, where the golf course was open for play for free for '79 and early '80 because caddies and course were ready long before there were places for people to stay. There are not a lot of rooms, or much in the way of planned entertainment (except at the Jack Tar Resort), but there is a town—and there are beaches and the golf course, plus cruise ships that make regular stops on runs from Miami.

✥ **Hotel Castilla** (John F. Kennedy 34, Puerto Plata; 16 rooms) provides a pocket of Sydney Greenstreet-style surroundings on a corner in downtown Puerto Plata. It was a surprise when I first discovered this place (then marked by a garish "Hotel Castilla" plastic sign, obviously compliments of Pepsi Cola), and I was enchanted: It's still an oasis in a hot Dominican town, but ownership has changed and so has some of the style. Things are very casual, rooms are simple—and maybe you won't mind when you realize that the overnight tally is under $20 for 2, for the room with bath, about $9 without. New Zealander John Morris opened the place, which he'd pulled together from odds and ends scavenged from shore and country villages. John Ashill, owner-in-residence after Morris, came to Puerto Plata from New York, via Europe (Spain, he said). Among the additions with Ashill ownership are the Casa Castilla, a small shop next door, carrying handmade items (see Treasures and Trifles comment below).

✠ **Jack Tar Resort** (Playa Dorada, Puerto Plata, D.R.; 208 rooms) is a newcomer with a long history. Part of the ambitious development plans for the north coast, this Dallas, Texas firm has a 3-year lease to operate the resort of elegant Playa Dorada. With several white stucco, terra-cotta-roofed villas scattered around the grounds, separated from the beach with sea-grape trees and a wedge of the golf course, the resort has a residential feeling. The hotel hub is a huge thatched bohío and stucco-walled area where restaurants, night-club, pools, shops, and all the action facilities are centralized. It's an easy walk from all the villas and from the 40 2-story units on the inland side of the pool. The Robert Trent Jones golf course has been ready for play for a couple of years, and those wise enough to head here before the hotel opened in mid-1980 could play free on the perfectly manicured course. Reasonable, package-plan, resort-pegged rates were instituted on opening day. All rooms have Dominican art, created by people in Puerto Plata area who attended a special art school. Spend some time looking at all the furnishings and trim on the buildings; it's Dominican, made by hand, elegant, interesting, and worth purchasing if you can find a local source for some of the furnishings. Jack Tar Resort is one of the Caribbean's best deals this winter, if you buy a package-plan. Daily rates for 2 are about $200, with some meals and use of all sports facilities included.

✠ **Hotel Montemar** (Avenida Circunvalación del Norte, Puerto Plata; 44 rooms plus 6 2-bedroom bungalows) operates on the Hotel School training property. For those who want a reasonably priced base, outside the usual American hotel bases, this is a pleasant, Dominican-style small hotel. Count on motel-style modern rooms in the main stucco block, and simple facilities in the bungalows. Colorful fabric, painting and repairing of furniture, and other cosmetic changes did a lot to improve the place after my first visit a couple of years ago. Linked to the Dominican Hotel School, and jointly operated by the Hotel School, the Central Bank, and the University of Santiago, the hotel is a model that the Dominican tourism family has a vital interest in making work. You'll have the option of basking in hot sun beside the on-premises pool, leaping around on one of 2 hot, asphalt tennis courts, or strolling about 5 minutes to the beach at the end of the road (where the turnaround is marked by a copy of Michelangelo's statue of David for reasons I have yet to have explained). The hotel's dining room (air-conditioned and enclosed) is carpeted, with white cloths, red napkins punctuating the tables, and acid green and royal blue accents on furnishings. The open-to-breezes cafeteria near the pool serves snacks and drinks, and food is good, Dominican fare, well-served. Count on paying slightly over $30 for 2 for room only, meals, taxes and tips extra.

■■

HOUSEKEEPING HOLIDAYS options around Puerto Plata are varied. Life can be almost-luxury, if you rent one of the new condominium units, or very casual in one of the shoreside bungalows that have been around for several seasons. Food will be fresh fish, which you can negotiate for with the local fishermen, or produce bought at the open-air market under a very modern shelter on a back street in Puerto Plata. Excellent kosher beef is cured and sold at Sosúa, from stands you will see by the side of the road (in front of the substantial business ventures that supply meat products for the rest of the country).

For self-sufficient types who like to fit into the ways of the country, the apartments and villas in Sosúa, east of Puerto Plata, are excellent values. The town is popular with Dominicans in summer and at Easter holidays, but you can have the place pretty much to yourselves during winter weeks. Contact Los Charamicos and La Sosúa Mar, both at Sosúa, D.R. (write in Spanish).

Check for rental of villas at Playa Dorada and Costambar. See the comment on Hotel Montemar for thoughts on those bungalows, and check with the Dominican Tourist Information Center for any properties they may have listed.

✤ **Playa Cofresi** (Santiago Highway, Puerto Plata; 53 rooms in several bungalows) offers simple cottages facing the sea and is very popular with Dominicans on weekends, when prices are higher than midweek. Rates during the week for a 2-bedroom sparsely furnished, boxy-stucco unit are $25 per day, meals and taxes extra; the 3-bedroom unit is $30, and both are $5 more on weekends. (If your travel agent books this for you, expect him to add on his commission, which is not included in the rates I've listed.) The villas are set back from the shore, and can be HOT. There's no air conditioning, but the overhead fans keep the air moving; kitchen facilities are limited to a hot plate and a good refrigerator. The place is casual, with a shoreside pool and pounding surf (the north shore is almost always *windy*). The *Sombrero* restaurant is casual (pizza, fish plates, etc.) but does not allow patrons in bathing suits. Rafael and German Silverio, who own this place, have the palatial residences that are perched on the hillside; they live much better than you will—but they're also paying a lot more than $20 for the privilege.

■■■

PLACES WORTH FINDING in Puerto Plata are many, but there are a few spots you'll want to avoid. The **Fort of San Felipe** will be a stop on your minibus tour from the ship. Skip it, unless you're addicted to typical tours. Buttons, coins, and cannon balls are displayed in the few rooms inside, and you'll have to double in half to crawl through the low doors that separate the small rooms. Not for the claustrophobic, the fort can be interesting if you have nothing else to do that day, or if you wander around on your own. Cost for entry: a modest 25¢. There's a proliferation of sidewalk salesmen who will follow you up the hill and to the door of the fort (and will be there to greet you when you come out). Buy if you want, but there are no bargains. General Gregorio Luperón, who prances on horseback in the middle of the parking area, fought to overthrow the Spanish when they were in power from 1860 to 1865. He staggered from his deathbed at age 58, pulled himself upright saying, "I refuse to meet death lying down," and promptly dropped dead.

Isabel de Torres cable car runs on an independent schedule, which will probably include a cruise ship day, but don't count on it if you've headed north on your own. (And if you have flown into Puerto Plata, you've had your spectacular view from the plane window; that offered from the top of the tower is no better.) There's a fort built under the regime of Generalissimo Trujillo near the top of the tower.

More than $36 million is earmarked for this area, with $21 million from the World Bank, $15 million from local government, and $3 million from the private sector. If you fly north on one of the small planes out of Santo Domingo's Herrera Airport, you'll land at the modern La Unión International Airport, which is ready, willing, and able to take the biggest jets. The commercial flight from Santo Domingo takes little more than an hour, with a stop at Santiago, and a bird's-eye view of the country. (Your own charter can fly you non-stop.) As you sweep in over the mountains, you may see the silver mist that caused Columbus to call the town Puerto Plata. (The excursion is heartily recommended if you have spare time.) Although completion of the project is a long way off, the Dominican Government has designated this area as zone 2 in long-range tourism development plans (the southeast coast is zone 1). Playa Dorada's facilities are flourishing, and another extensive resort is planned for Playa Grande almost 2 hours' drive along the north coast, east of Puerto Plata. Costambar, west of the town, at the foot of the station for Isabel de Torres cable car, is already under way—with the first of several hundred condominiums standing, and with the Costambar Country Club the luncheon stop for cruise ship passengers who enjoy the pool. (The "beautiful" beach was covered with gray sludge when Puerto Plata's harbor was dredged for cruise ship traffic.)

■■

TREASURES AND TRIFLES: If you're looking for something unusual head for **La Fábrica,** where Bill Everett sells handwork from his house, and the studio of **Carlos Mena,** a commercial artist from New York who transplanted to Puerto Plata. **Mildred Casacate,** who studied art in Mexico, has been bringing local artists into her shop to work when cruise ships are in port, but ask around if you want to find her—and her workshop.

   Casa Castille, next to the Hotel Castille, not far from the town square, has imaginative hand-painted rocks for about $5. (A lot for a rock? You're right, but they're clever.) The shop also has paintings (framed), plus wrought-iron mirrors, some work done by local schoolchildren, and above average handwork. The **Amber House,** also on this street, has better than average workmanship for the inevitable amber jewelry.

■■

SAMANÁ PENINSULA is one of the several special areas in this intriguing country, but it's not for those who must have everything perfect, with pampering. The spine of land that stretches off the northeast coast of the country is rugged, sand-fringed, and ideal for anyone who likes rustic settings and virtually virgin countryside. Flatlands at the midsection of the Dominican Republic rise to mountains and a terrain that looks, from the small planes you can charter to fly here, like a lumpy, green quilt, patchworked with dirt roads. Coconut groves are appliquéd along some sandy strands, many of which are accessible only by boat. Some are seldom touched at all.

   Samaná, on the south coast of the peninsula, is a cruise port for Norwegian Caribbean Line and a few other Miami-based cruises. One of Balaguer's projects, during his last term of office, was to raze the former town and "build a new one." I, for one, long for the old

small town where some of the wood houses could have been renovated to maintain a unique personality. What you see here today
are a couple of boring stucco boxes, albeit 2-story buildings, with
pockets for "freeport" shops stuffed with items for cruise passengers. (Don't count on a wide selection, but if you see what you
want in the luxury-item roster, the price will be good.) Although
the town's character is undefined, at the moment, the natural
countryside is spectacular. There are specks of offshore islands,
some of them used as beach havens for cruise passengers who don't
care about shopping (picnics are planned), and other areas that
can be seen if you hire an enterprising taxi driver and ask for a tour
of the area. Don't expect a trumped-up tourist-type spot when you
get out of town. It is rural.

■■

HOTELS AT SAMANÁ are limited to 2 to talk about. One is at the
town of Samaná, the other is on the north shore.

✤ **Hotel Cayacoa** (Samaná, D.R.: 6o rooms) is a modern bastion of
hospitality, favored by Dominicans who come here for weekends
"in the country." (The drive from Santo Domingo is rugged, and
takes a good 4 hours.) Completely modern, with motel-style rooms
in a block off the main entrance and the public rooms, the hotel has
a dining area with a view over the bay to the town of Samaná (on
the other side) and a disco that is lively when house count (or
cruise traffic) warrants. At the time of my survey, the disco music
that was piped through the halls shattered the expected silence
but, as you may know, Dominicans like their music loud—and their
air conditioning "below freezing." Best rooms for my vacation dollar are in the 5 cottages down the hill by the beach (a steep but
possible climb). This place provides a uniquely Dominican holiday,
for rates that figure to over $40 for 2, meals extra, with cabanas
renting in the $50 range.

✤ **El Portillo** (Las Terrenas, Samaná; 8 bunglows) is for beachcomber types. The place is popular with French tourists who come
in with small planes to the dirt Band Aid that lines up along the
shore near the bungalows. Oxen pull the carts that are used to collect the coconuts and carry the handful of residents for any long
distances. The beach is a gorgeous white-sand strand, with only a
handful of buildings at the shore. Bungalows are built by Maxine
and Georges Taule, who were involved with the building at Playa

Dorada. Emphasis here is on rustic, easy living. Bring bug repellent, flashlights, matches, and any other items you'd usually take on a camping trip. Although you do have the bungalows for shelter, they are simple (with plumbing, kitchen, and dining areas).

■■■

SPORTS on the Samaná Peninsula include all the Hemingway-style offerings: **deep-sea fishing, diving,** exploring, and **sailing,** but don't count on the latest equipment. This area is for self-sufficient types looking for new frontiers. A sailing group hauls boats over from Santo Domingo for regular regattas off the beach at Cayacoa. Inquire from the Dominican Tourist Information Office about dates and contacts.

Grenada

Grenada Tourist Board, Box 293, St. George's, Grenada, W.I.; 141 East 44th Street, New York, NY 10017; 3300 N.E. Expressway, Suite 4-W, Atlanta, GA 30341; Oldham Editorial Services, Box 209, Pt. Credit Postal Sation, Mississauga, Ontario, L5G 4L8, Canada.

US $1 = EC$2.60
Unless otherwise noted, $ refers to U.S. currency.

His fingers flicked at the palm fronds to make the birds dance, and as they looped in dizzy pseudo-dives, Samuel assured me he was "the best in the business." His business is weaving palm fronds into hats and hanging baskets, and business along Grand Anse beach has been slow. The few people here seem to be thinking about other things.

As he strolled off down the beach, his black chest glistened in the morning sun and the blue suspenders that stretched from his faded jeans drew vertical lines across it. The bird hats and the baskets swung jauntily from his hands. Nothing appeared important.

I stretched out again in the sun—to feel another presence by my side. The cascade of sun dresses and smocks that tumbled across the wedge of space on my lounge chair could have covered twice as many tourists as I had seen nearby. Each dress had been sewn by hand; each was for sale. "My name is Veronica. You can ask for me," I was told when I proclaimed, politely, my lack of interest in anything but her ability to sew.

Yellow birds danced with black birds in a minuet on the back of the wicker chairs. They took their intermission for the crumbs around the tables. Palm fronds whispered in the breeze and the sea sloshed near the soles of my feet. Samuel and Veronica lead an early morning parade that includes joggers, black and white, resident and tourist, all shapes, sizes, speeds, and costumes, many of them American students from the Grenada Medical School that has its headquarters on this sandy strand.

And the parade that continues through the day includes a glassy-eyed marijuana salesman, barefooted and wool-capped, who finds a buyer near the bar—in full glare of the hotel's policeman who stood and watched as I did.

So goes the life along the beach, not only here but elsewhere in the Caribbean. What makes this place different these days is a barrage of headlines. This was the day when the Cuban ship was due: December 7, 1979, and the town—perhaps the country—was throbbing with conversation, and eager with anticipation. For several years this country had been requesting assistance for an airport at Point Saline, within "shouting distance" of the capital and most of the country's hotels. Both the United States and Canada had prepared, I was told, "Feasibility studies that could stack floor to ceiling," but nothing was done.

The small Pearls Airport, in the northeastern section of this almond-shaped country, has been the island's lifeline, and it is a long and tortuous 45-minute drive from the capital. One of Cuba's first gestures of "good will," after the immediate assistance with military arms and technicians following the March '79 revolution, was to agree to build the airport at Point Saline. The fact that this point also provides superior surveillance over shipping (of oil and other items) from South American refineries to the shores of the United States, and that Cuba's magnanimous "gift" would not be forgotten should Cuba (and perhaps her sponsor) wish to use the completed airport was not lost on thoughtful souls.

But that seemed of little importance to most Grenadians I talked with at the time. They had yearned for an airport; they believed that such a prominent airport (akin to that in other new nations in the Caribbean and an acknowledged mark of "having arrived" as an important country) was essential for an increased tourism and for shipment of their crops—the two main focuses for most Grenadians' business ventures.

AUTHOR'S OBSERVATION: Grenada's situation is difficult to assess. There is no doubt that this country is not ideal for a carefree, profligate Caribbean vacation at this time in its history. Grenada is on the brink, in my opinion, and, if the country's North American tourism dries up, the scales could be tipped toward the austere "socialism" that many know as Communism. For thoughtful vacationers

who can accept the necessity to contribute to local economies while the sun and sea are sampled, Grenada can offer
an intriguing, enlightening, and interesting destination. I
have been in this country when some of the headlines
were in the making, and I experienced a warm hospitality
from the hoteliers and their staff and from all others I
met—including Maurice and Angela Bishop. For a people-
to-people experience in a developing nation of the Caribbean, Grenada should be visited.

POLITICAL PICTURE: The March 13, 1979 revolution in Grenada is now history, and anyone who is aware of Caribbean activities is also aware of the liaison between Maurice Bishop's People's
Revolutionary Government and the government of Fidel Castro's
Cuba. What is not so well known is that the "revolution" involved
about 40 people. Political oppression of any opposition had been a
prominent factor in the peculiar regime of former Prime Minister
Eric Gairy, best known to many outside Grenada for his tirades
about UFOs at the United Nations and within Grenada for implica-
tions that he had gone into political office bankrupt, owing money
to many, and within 3 years he "had enough money to buy several
buildings," including the Evening Palace Nightclub. Maurice
Bishop's father reportedly had been killed by Gairy's men. The New
Jewel Movement, precursor of the present People's Revolutionary
Party, was a thorn in Gairy's side. Although there was, apparently,
no plan for a government overthrow at a specific time, when
rumors reached Bishop and his supporters that Gairy was going to
arrest them, they decided, I was told by one member of the new
government, that "if we were going to get wiped out, we might as
well go trying." When Gairy left Grenada on a trip for the United
States, Bishop's men moved. A handful who had been watching the
sentries at the police station made their move when the sentries
crossed. They grabbed those 2 men, and then a third, entered the
police station, and talked with the police force. That was Grenada's
revolution. An announcement was made on the radio; Gairy's government capitulated—and some members of Gairy's cabinet still
live in Grenada, peacefully.

The period of "blackout" immediately following the easy and
peaceful takeover caused concern among neighboring Caribbean
countries and others who knew of the arrival in Grenada of shipments of arms and advisors from Cuba. The avowed purpose of the
known military buildup was to counteract the expected invasion by

Gairy forces, according to Bishop's government. But the new policies were immediately implemented, and the school and military programs that were put into effect in the months immediately after the revolution, are closely patterned on learning techniques applied in Communist Cuba.

The response by the United States government was to tell Grenada that it "would view with concern any move by Grenada to establish close military ties with Cuba." Grenadians still bristle when discussing the communiques that are known to have passed between a former U.S. ambassador to Barbados and the Grenada government. On April 16, Grenada and Cuba established diplomatic relations, and the relationship continues to grow stronger as Cuba assists with military training, doctors, and other technicians as well as with the equipment and advisors to build the airport at Point Saline.

▪▪

CUSTOMS OF THE COUNTRY have taken a decidedly socialist turn since the advent of the Bishop government. Vestiges of the old way prevail, but they are colored by a new look from a new nation with a new government anxious to make a strong statement of its own. Cricket, football (soccer), and tennis are national sports, but many young people are too involved with military training to participate. Common courtesies prevail. "Good morning" or an appropriate greeting precedes any conversation and you'll find the visitor reception better if you begin your transactions with the greeting even if, occasionally, it is not returned.

Official government-sponsored functions, or parties at private homes, follow a new formula that finds casual clothes, the badge of socialism, mingling with coat-and-tie vestiges from the former British tradition. Although few groups have more fun than Grenadian friends at a party, outsiders are well advised to take it slow. Guests are tested and tolerated before they're taken into the fold.

Clothes are conservative. Your peacock resort wear marks you immediately as a wealthy tourist on the prowl. For a lot of reasons, you'll probably be more comfortable if you keep your sun wear and swim suits at the beach and cover up for town. Grenadians, both men and women, are fashion-conscious, but that does not mean that clothes have to cost. If jeans are worn, they should be neat. Women will feel more comfortable in skirts. For evening dress, most men wear the tropical shirt-jac, guayabera, or whatever you call the straight-cut shirt. Leave your madras jackets at home.

AUTHOR'S OBSERVATION: Granada (Gre-*nah*-da) is in Spain. This country is Grenada (Gre-*nay*-da). The spelling is similar for good reason, but there is no reason for pronouncing it wrong once you know that: although Columbus passed by on August 15, 1492, and named the island Concepción, the Spanish conquistadors called it Granada for the far off port whose peaks they knew better. The French called the island they claimed from time to time Grenade, and the English, who ultimately took possession by the Treaty of Versailles in 1783, pronounced the French name of their new colony with its final "e" as an "a"—eventually spelling it that way. Grenada is Grenay-da.

■■

MONEY MATTERS: Eastern Caribbean currency is the local legal tender and you'll do best if you exchange at the bank where the official rate is about EC$2.60 to US$1, give or take a few cents for the current fluctuation. Hotels will happily take payment in US$, but the exchange rate will not be in your favor (which is of no concern on a small bill, but can tally up to impressive proportions if the bill is substantial). Be sure you have checked the going taxi rate before you get in a car for a tour, and do some shopping around before you commit yourself on a rental car. Rates vary, and may be quoted in either US$ or EC$.

■■

ARRIVAL by plane will be at the northeast coast's Pearls Airport probably for the duration of this edition, although Cubana planes have been flying into the airport at Point Saline, within a few minutes' drive of St. George's and most of the country's hotels. The project is not expected to be completed for commercial use, however, before late 1982. Pearls Airport, the small strip that has served as Grenada's only airport for several decades, is a 45-minute LIAT (Leeward Islands Air Transport) flight from Barbados. At the times of my visits, researching for this book, there was an obvious military feeling at the once-somnolent airport. Immigration services involve the usual checking of passport, return or onward ticket, and stamping of the immigration form you have filled out on the flight.

(Hold on to the carbon copy, which you will submit when you depart.) Once you've claimed your luggage (travel light, you won't need much in the way of elegant attire), negotiate with a taxi driver for the hour-long winding mountain drive south to St. George's where most of the hotels are located.

■■■

TOURING TIPS: The 45-minute or longer ride from Pearls Airport to the St. George's area (and the hotels) can provide your tour of the hinterland. Once one of the most beautiful Caribbean drives, in my opinion, the route is now scarred by ambitious road building and forestry projects that were inaugurated soon after the Cuban "technicians" arrived, which was not long after Maurice Bishop became Prime Minister. Grand Etang National Park, the verdant area around a spectacular crater lake that had been one of the country's major attractions, was closed to the public during one of my visits, and military personnel and police stationed in this area indicated that portions of the park have been put to something other than pleasure use. Keep your eyes open (even during the 5 a.m. or earlier departure ride from St. George's to catch the early morning LIAT flight) and you will undoubtedly notice a lot more than the impressive and awesome tropical growth.

The rate for the ride between Pearls Airport and town was about EC$50, but expect to pay more (due to rising fuel and other costs) and take a pill if you are the car-sick type. Although the route is beautiful, it also bends and weaves incessantly not only for curves, but also to avoid potholes, washouts, children, and goats.

You may opt for riding the public bus that travels the island-rimming roads on the hotel-flecked south coast, but avoid the "commuter" hours, from 7:30 to 9:30 a.m. and from about 3:30 to 6:30 at night. It is possible to take the public bus (EC50¢) from most of the south-coast hotels into St. George's, although taxis are ready and waiting at the front doorway of most hotels—and are eager for your business.

If you can find a couple of days for a visit to Carriacou, you have a choice of travel methods. Total travel time is almost (but not quite) the same. One route is to the airport (1 hour plus waiting time) for the short flight (10 minutes) from Pearls Airport to Carriacou's airstrip; the other—more adventuresome—is on the mailboat that makes regular connections out of St. George's harbor to Hillsborough on Carriacou. The crossing can be rough, but will certainly be interesting if you enjoy island traveling. Check with the Grenada Tourist Board office in St. George's for sailing times and costs.

AUTHOR'S OBSERVATION: There is a good-value travel
rate involved if you buy a LIAT triangle fare from Barbados
to Grenada to St. Vincent to Barbados. Be sure to inquire
about whether or not you are entitled to stop on any of the
Grenadine islands on that ticket. Inter-Island Air, a LIAT
affiliate, flies the Grenadine island-hopping route, and
when I last inquired, they would not accept the LIAT
triangle fare ticket for island hopping. (LIAT flies nonstop
between Grenada and St. Vincent.) If you want to fly the
small plane service through the Grenadine islands (highly
recommended), you will have to buy an Island Air ticket.

▪▪▪

HOTELS are small, and most of them are very special, with the
strong stamp of the owner/manager. Even the Holiday Inn strug-
gles to maintain its Grenadian personality. This is no place for the
sports enthusiast who must have his golf course and tennis courts
within a few steps of his room, nor is Grenada the place for people
who demand the pampered and perfect life. The inns on this island
are personality places, where self-sufficient travelers can have a
pleasant holiday quietly mingling in the day-to-day routines known
to Grenadians. Many hotels add a 10% or 15% service charge onto
your bill, and all carry the 7½% government tax.

AUTHOR'S AWARDS for places I'd like to spend a vacation
go to Twelve Degrees North (see Housekeeping) for setting and hospitality, to Spice Island Inn, where your
choice can be a beachfront room or one of the private pool
hideaways idyllic for 2, and to Ross Point Inn where the
Hopkin family continue to do what they have done for
years—make strangers into friends.

✤ **Blue Horizons** (Box 41, St. George's, Grenada, W.I.; 16 units)
beckons self-sufficient travelers who want a place of their own,
within a short walk of the beach and with one of the island's best
restaurants on the premises. When the Hopkin brothers (Royston,
Arnold, and Gerald) took over the property in late 1978, they
painted and primped the place so that foliage was trimmed,
grounds were put back into shape and all the basically sound units
were painted and spruced after a few years of neglect. There's a

pool on premises, with a gathering area that can provide sun-shelter (and cool drinks). In addition, from any of the cottage units (4 standards, 6 deluxe, and 6 superior), it's an easy walk to the pool, restaurant, or—across the road and through the "fields"—the beach. *La Belle Creole* (see restaurant coverage below) puts into practice the second generation version of the cooking made famous by their mother, Audrey Hopkin (at Ross Point). This restaurant has a grand view over the sea (and, unfortunately, also over the boxy and ugly buildings put up as "temporary" for the CARIFTA Festival almost a decade ago and now used for residences for U.S. students at the medical school and Cuban technicians), and is swept by trade winds for cooling. Rates for a twin-bedded standard room with kitchenette are $60 to $75 for 2. Two standards can connect for family use at special rates. All rooms have showers (no tubs); superiors can sleep 3 with one on the daybed/couch.

✣ **Calabash Hotel** (Box 382, St. George's, Grenada, W.I.; 22 suites) is cupped in a curve of beach at L'Anse aux Epines. The heart of the hotel is set back from the beach, partially hidden by the bower of flowers that puts you into the tropics immediately, even without glancing at the spread of sand that leads down to the sea at Prickly Bay, about 5 miles from St. George's. Guests at Charles de Gale's place settle into their own cottages, where the maid tiptoes in in the morning to fix breakfast "at home." This is a perfect relaxing place, with nothing more strenuous than a stroll on the sands and a leisurely sundown sip while you sit in one of the director's chairs that circle the tables near the bar. A casual kind of place, Calabash takes its tone from the pub pace set by Brian Thomas, an Englishman who opened it in 1964 as a gathering spot for yachting types in search of a landfall. The name comes from the gourdlike fruit that hangs from trees around the Caribbean, to be plucked off, cut in half, and used for bowl or scoop. You'll have casual comforts with your cottage, and if you want the one with the private pool, say so. One unit has this added luxury; most have only twin beds, bath, and sitting room, plus kitchenette and porch. (Units 4B and 4C share a kitchen and 11A is the pool suite.) Count on paying about $160 for 2 this winter, 2 meals daily included.

✣ **Holiday Inn** (Box 441, St. George's, Grenada, W.I.; 184 rooms plus 2 suites) happens to be on the best beach in the country. The 2-story buildings do their best to fit into the tropical planting that camouflages the walls, and considering the size of the place, they do the job quite well. The biggest hotel in the country is also the most commercial, but it is not necessarily the best. A major refurbishing in early '79 resulted in a newly painted pool and primping up of other facilities but the country's political problems have taken their toll. (It is government-owned.) A couple of signs noted on my prowls around the property indicate that directions are essential: "Shirt or robe required" for the dining room (but presumably guests know enough to wear shoes); the "Attention floor slippery" sign will save you from breaking your neck. The tiles *are* slippery when wet, and so are the stone pathways if they are covered with scum as they were when I fell! Rooms come with private patio or balcony (I opt for the second-floor room for security reasons), with a choice of view (beach or garden). A couple of shops are open on a schedule best known to the shopkeeper; restaurants are open and airy, and West Indian/Grenadian "international" fare is served. There are 2 tennis courts with night lights, entertainment a couple of evenings each week (more, if house count warrants), and a local group at the gathering bar where casual conversation prevails. There are other spots that are better for island atmosphere, in my opinion, and the beach salesmen offering pot as well as beach smocks grew tediously persistent. Your plumbing may not work, power may fail (an island problem), and service may leave something to be desired, but groups (mostly European) still use this hotel. Rates for winter hover around $80 for 2, meals extra (allow about $20 per day per person if you eat here).

✢ **Horse Shoe Bay Hotel** (Box 174, L'Anse aux Epines, Grenada, W.I.; 12 rooms) is government-owned. The surroundings are spectacular, on the hillside overlooking the cove and sea. The original plan is sound—a main building with attractive dining area that faces the sea and spills the guests out onto the lawns around the swimming pool a few feet below on the slope. Rooms are to the right as you enter the reception area, in separate buildings (2 spacious rooms per unit, connected with a laundry and utility area). Furnishings include 4-poster beds and comfortable chairs, with heavy wood Mediterranean-style chests and tables and the winter rate is about $145 for 2, breakfasts and dinners daily. Entertainment has always been minimal (a steel band some evenings). If you are part of a small group in search of a special place, try this. I suspect it might be lonely, however, as half of a twosome.

✢ **Ross Point Inn** (Box 137, St. George's, Grenada, W.I.; 12 rooms) has been my Grenadian home, and clinical objectivity is impossible for a place where personalities count as much as they do here. This is a family inn. When Audrey and Curtis Hopkin opened their small inn in 1952, they set a pace that is unmatched here and on other islands. Audrey Hopkin's flair with Grenadian cuisine keeps the menu changing (and dependably good). Many of the inn's overnighters have been repeaters for several seasons; some of them stay for several weeks. You can count on a continental mix that includes Canadians, Europeans, and a few Americans. All rooms are air-conditioned; some share the main-house spectacular view overlooking St. George's harbor. My haven has been Room #4, a separate cottage with sunset and sea viewing porch where sounds of the surf soothe. A path leads to steps to the sea (where you swim from a dock of sorts—no beach here). For beaches, rent a car or take the inn's complimentary transportation 2 miles to Grand Anse Beach. Quietly comfortable, Ross Point Inn caters to self-sufficient types who like their Caribbean pure. This is a place to call home for a peaceful relaxing holiday. No matter what else you do in Grenada, be sure to make a reservation here for a meal. Count on winter rates to rest at about $80 for 2, 2 meals daily per person.

✛ **Secret Harbour** (Box 11, St. George's, Grenada, W.I.; 20 suites) sends you into a sunburst, set in colorful tiles on the reception area floor. That's this inn's first spectacular sight. If you want to look out over an awesome Caribbean view from the minute you open your eyes in the morning to the time you close them at night, settle in here. The suites that saunter around the hillside a short walk from the main building (with the restaurant and check-in area) are huge, with tiled floors, a sitting area that sets you up to overlook your terrace and view, and 2 full-size 4-posters, some of which are genuine island antiques. All modern accoutrements punctuate your room— and when you feel like wandering, a spacious pool is just over the crest of the hill with deck chairs set up for sunning. Godfrey Ventour is the man on the spot. A sliver of sand at Hartman Bay is a steep walk down to sea level from the hillside hotel. Barbara Stevens is the other half of the team in control of your daily diversions, which can include a few swings at the pitch-and-putt course or the tennis courts as well as island touring. The opulent Mediterranean-style elegance of the dining room was far grander than the food when I dined. Count on at least a $30 tab per person for full dinners with flourishes; the elegant ambiance is most of what you're paying for and I found service surly on my visit. Room rates for 2 this winter range from $155 to $175 and are worth every cent if any place is. Breakfasts and dinners daily are included in that rate.

✣ **Spice Island Inn** (Box 6, St. George's, Grenada, W.I.; 30 rooms)
sits beachside, groomed for hospitality by Desmond and Charlotte
Campbell. Guests are sifted into 20 beachfront suites or 10 pool
suites, each in its own tropical nest, surrounded by planting that's
perfect for privacy. When this inn opened, more than a decade ago, it
was a typical tropical retreat, favored by yachting types and those
who want their sea, sand, and sun in Robinson Crusoe style. Mealtimes on the terrace, in sight of sand and sea, are special occasions.
This is a small place with a special feeling. Spice Island guests in
recent seasons have included Europeans who came in on quality
package holidays. The beach that stretches right and left from the
inn is one of Grenada's best (Holiday Inn is a pleasant stroll away),
and the beachfront units stretch along it. (Numbers 1 and 2 face the
fence that marks the "end" of the hotel's property.) The constant
parade of people that saunter along this strand may make the private
pool units preferable, but all surroundings are superb for leisure
comforts. Unless you head here as part of a charter or group plan
(from Europe, look into Kuoni and Caribbean Connection), count
on paying about $150 for 2 at the beach; $186 for a suite with a pool;
both rates include 2 meals daily per person.

■■

HOUSEKEEPING HOLIDAYS have been a way of life for visitors to
Grenada for several decades. The English started it, with the "cottages" they rented around the shores of Grand Anse Beach and
other shady coves, and wise Americans and Canadians followed the
trend in the late '50s and through the '60s. Although some of the
apartments and cottages have been swallowed up on long-term
rental by Cuban technicians and students at Grenada's Medical
School, which occupies a beachfront building next to Holiday and
Spice Island inns, there are several places to look into if you want to
spend a few weeks or more in Grenada.

As far as food shopping is concerned, you can find plenty of the
locally grown fruits and vegetables at the market in St. George's.
Some of the top stores to head for, when you're looking for produce,
are the Food Fair at the Grand Anse shopping center and in St.
George's, but don't count on finding the shelves stacked with familiar names from home—or from anywhere outside the Caribbean
community. Imports are a drain on locally strained coffers and are
kept to an essential minimum. Bring what you *must* have from
home, and that includes steaks and beef from your hometown
butcher (who can pack from his cold storage, wrapping the beef in

newspaper to keep it cold for your journey to Grenada. On arrival, put it into your own refrigerator or cold chest (if your rental unit has one) and it will last a lot longer than you think.

✤ **Cinnamon Hill** (Box 292, St. George's, Grenada, W.I.) is worth investigating if you want top luxury for surroundings (can't vouch for service because when I saw the facilities, the place was not in full swing). The spectacular series of homes-intended-as-condominiums, caught in a mire of local politics, stand ready and waiting, at special locations on a hillside with sea view. Luxury is the keynote; lavish but tasteful furnishings are in place; leisure living with class will be the tone—but check for status and there's a pool at viewful level on the hillside it you don't want to walk to the beach. Richard Gray's dream only needs the reality of management, money, and many more guests. Rates for a luxury 1-bedroom villa are $92; 2-bedroom rents for $116; no meals.

✤ **Coral Cove Cottages** (Box 187, St. George's, Grenada, W.I.; 6 cottages) capture a hillside overlooking L'Anse Aux Epines, not far from Secret Harbour Hotel. The 1 and 2-bedroom villas are modern, well-built and attractively furnished, with plenty of space, a pleasant porch-with-view, and beach and pool for cool-off times. Count on paying about $300 for a winter week for the 2-bedroom villa and $150 for a week in the 1-bedroom version.

✤ **Southwinds Cottages,** rented through Mr. Chasley David (Church St., St. George's, Grenada, W.I.; about 6 2-bedroom cottages) are within walking distance of Grand Anse—and the supermarket and a couple of small restaurants. Good value, with accommodations that give you what you are paying for, and usually in working order, the units include a mini-moke at about $300 per week for cottage and car. The 1-bedroom apartment is $150 per week. Accommodations are simple, but acceptable for a beach-and-sea holiday.

✤ **Twelve Degrees North** (Box 241, St. George's, Grenada, W.I.) is tops for quality accommodations at a curve of sand, with pool-and-gathering area near the sea. All units slope down the hillside, giving you your own view out to sea. Joe Gaylord puts hospitality at the top of the list of priorities and there's plenty of it here. There are twin beds in bedrooms, modern bathroom equipment (that usually works), and a living room-terrace area that will quickly feel like home. Kitchen facilities are compact but more than adequate. There's no air conditioning, but the trade winds more than take care of that problem, and for my vacation dollar, this place is just about perfect. Rates this winter will run about $70 per apartment per day.

Others to consider (but count on finding facilities spartan, with emphasis on being outside—and on the beach) are:

✤ **Carifta Cottages** are at Morne Rouge and some are now being used by Cuban visitors. The 3- and 4-bedroom cottages put you within a short walk of Grand Anse Beach. Rates in the winter time have been from $150 to $225 for a week at the cottages, with all your meals extra. (Carifta stands for Caribbean Free Trade Association, the organization for which Expo '69 was held.)

Other places to investigate are Blue Horizons (see hotel listing) or the **Flamboyant Cottages** (Box 214, St. George's, Grenada, W.I.), which march up the hill near Grand Anse Beach and rent for $40 to $80 per day, depending on the cottage. For general rental information, contact Grenada Property Management, Box 218, St. George's, Grenada, W.I. Two large developments, planned as condominiums, with many units filled on a year-round rental, are **Coconut Hill** and **Westerhall Fort Jeudy.**

■■■

RESTAURANTS are popular with Grenadians as well as with visitors, and although those of us from elsewhere may prefer the excellent island cooking, Grenadians go where the steak is good. (Spice Island Inn's steaks are so good that the Cuban Ambassador's American-born wife reportedly buys them by the carton for home consumption.)

AUTHOR'S AWARDS for exceptional food in Grenada go to La Belle Creole where a memorable meal was enjoyed with the view, and to Ross Point Inn, where the Hopkin sons were "tutored" in their trade and we from the outside can settle into family surroundings for traditional island cooking.

Apple Inn is a casually comfortable place that is good for West Indian food.

Ross Point, on the hill road leading from St. George's, is where Audrey Hopkin controls her kitchen and keeps the best-tested recipes coming to the tables in her dining room. There's no telling what will be on the menu, but you can count on excellent local fish, mouthwatering *lambi* (conch, pounded tender and seasoned to perfection), and an occasional breadnut soufflé. Reservations are essential for dinner time since this is one place that wisely decided to serve one group well rather than pack them in for maximum profit.

La Belle Creole, at Blue Horizons, has the Hopkin flair, as translated by the younger generation. After the winding walk up the hill from the parking lot, you are rewarded with the view—daytime or with night lights. Hope to find stuffed crab and callaloo quiche on the menu (both were delicious), and count on entrees such as ginger chicken or curried lamb (usually goat) with condiments, plus vegetables such as fried plantain, black-eyed peas, yam, and whatever else is growing at the time of year you visit. Coconut cream for dessert was mouth-watering. The meal costs about EC$40; entree alone is about EC$25.

The **Red Crab** at L'Anse aux Epines, just outside the gates of Calabash Hotel, continues to capitalize on its pub atmosphere that has made it a favorite halting spot since it first opened more than a decade ago, but do not expect much special attention from owner or staff. If they feel like it, they'll be pleasant; if they don't, they may not be—even when you're paying EC$25 for a lobster dinner. Fish and chips are EC$8.50, and the owner is Julian Pieniazek. U.S. medical students attending St. George's Med School use this place like a club. On the main road to and from the beach, the pub gives you indoor or terrace choices for dining on barbecued chicken (which I found better than the steak).

Bird's Nest, folded in behind the other stores at the Grand Anse Shopping Centre (just outside the gates of the Holiday Inn and within walking distance, also, of Spice Island Inn), specializes in Chinese food and it is *good!* Best when a group orders several different dishes (smoothed down with the local Carib beer), here are some specialties to try: lobster Cantonese (EC$15), curried lobster (EC$15), and any of several chicken dishes (all in the EC$5 range). A "Yin Wo" lunch combination, with fried rice, chicken, and chow mein, is about EC$6.50. Atmosphere is typical Chinese-restaurant-style: chairs, tables, plain walls. Focus on the good food.

The Hill serves local food in casual Caribbean surroundings. You can dine at any of 3 locales—terrace, patio, or inside air-conditioned—but the food will be reasonable and reportedly good. You'll find the Hill about a quarter mile from the Red Crab, and you may find the atmosphere far more congenial if staff and management at the Crab are not their most hospitable.

Three other spots to find for lunch are **Turtle Back, Rudolf's,** and the **Nutmeg,** this last an island classic that has survived and still gives casual, reliable food in town.

Plantation dining is possible, with advance reservations and a long drive, at Betty Mascoll's home in the north. Inquire through your hotel about how to make a reservation on a day you're touring; the experience—wonderful West Indian food served in a 70-plus-year-old plantation house—will be unforgettable.

■■

PLACES WORTH FINDING are mostly natural ones. If you miss the sites on the official list, chances are you will have found others that you prefer. There is no pressure to check off the spice plantation, or Grand Etang (off-limits as we go to press), or Sauteurs Leap, or even Fort George (renamed Fort Rupert in honor of Maurice Bishop's father, who was assassinated), but to miss the cove that is St. George's would be to miss the point of Grenada—and certainly of its capital. Since Pearls Airport is in the northeast section, at the top of the almond-shaped island, you'll have a full island tour on your way to your south-coast hotel. For some, that's enough. **Grand Etang,** the vast, calm crater lake, is at a high point, although it hardly seems so when you look north and south to Mt. Catherine and Mt. Sinai, 2 of the 3 highest peaks of Grenada.

ST. GEORGE'S, the capital, is in St. George Parish, in the southwesternmost of the country's 6 parishes. (The other parishes are St. Andrew, St. David, St. John, St. Mark, and St. Patrick.) The curve of the coast makes a huge bay, with an inner bay that is the harbor which some say is the bowl of a submerged volcano. In the harbor, the lagoon (home for charter yachts) and the Carenage (the waterfront village "square" where the boats were hauled in the old days) are prickled with yachts and service ships, carrying people and produce to and around the islands. The "newness" of town comes from rebuilding after Hurricane Janet, which swept through on a path that is far from the usual hurricane course, on September 22, 1955. The traditional look comes from the British, who took the city in 1763, the French, who took it back again, and the British who claimed it by treaty in 1784. Typical West Indian buildings, some of them tumbling against their neighbors, parade up and down the hills of town, shoved apart from time to time to make a road now used by taxis, or more often by footfall. The waterfront where the interisland boats tie up, and the central market square, are focal points for daily life. **Bay Town,** connected to St.

George's by the Sendall Tunnel, is the place where you will find the fish market on Melville Street.

Fort George, renamed Fort Rupert in honor of Bishop's father, will fascinate bulwark collectors. It was built by the French in the early 1700s, taken by the British, and is now the country's police headquarters, honeycombed with tunnels and complete with walls you used to be able to walk around.

Botanical Gardens, near Government House on the hill, are well worth some time, especially if you are interested in tropical flowers and trees.

For a **drive-yourself excursion,** dipping and weaving on Grenada's roads, with views and villages punctuating almost every curve, head up the west coast. You'll pass through a selection of fishing villages and small towns where both you and your car will be obvious outsiders, but don't let that deter you. Mt. Moritz (a white community on an island that is 98% black) is the first village north of the capital of St. George's, with Fontenoy just below. Beyond the old estate of Beausejour is **Halifax Harbour,** but it is **Gouyave** that is the goal for many visitors who want to visit the **nutmeg cooperative,** in a 3-story building at the edge of town. (Gouyave is the town's old French name, used today in spite of the fact that the British officially called this place Charlotte Town.) Beyond Gouyave, in the parish of St. John (which the French called by the name of the town), are acres of banana, cocoa, and nutmeg, and then you come to the spectacular **Black Bay** where volcanic sand makes a black line at the sea. The **Concord Waterfall,** high in the hills, tumbles down the Concord Valley as Black Bay River.

In the town of **Victoria,** there are some Indian rock carvings (just south, before you reach the town), and the country's highest mountain, **St. Catherine,** pierces the skyline in this parish of St. Mark (known to the French as Grand Pauvre). St. Patrick parish's town of **Sauteurs** is more noteworthy for history than for current sights. The scenery is spectacular, but it is the fact that this is where the Caribs leapt into the sea in 1652, rather than yield to the French, that is the story every Grenadian schoolchild knows. Beyond Sauteurs, known to the French as Bourg des Sauteurs or town of the leapers, there is **Levera Bay** with its spectacular powdery beach, and the offshore small islands officially known as Green and Sandy.

Your choice now is to return back along the west coast, after your swim at Levera Bay, in time to see the sun set at **Point Saline**—the southwestern point where the Caribbean washes over white sands and the Atlantic crashes in on black sands that fringe the peninsula you drive over to get to the point, or to continue around, through the Parish of St. Andrew (which the French knew as Grand Marquis). If you continue on around the east coast, you will follow your arrival route from Pearls Airport through the **Grand Etang Forest Reserve** to the city, but detour for **Grenville,** where schooners set sail for Carriacou and other islands, and the nearby town of **Boulogne** with its cocoa experimental station and nursery for tropical plants. (Grenville is really worth an excursion of its own, if you don't want to pack all your touring into one exhausting day.)

Other places worth finding are the offshore islands on the south. Check at the tourist office to see if visitors are welcome on the beaches of **Hog Island** or on **Calivigny.** Both small islands have been my goals on fishing boats, heading out from Woburn village, but the recent Cuban activity has changed their holiday status. **Glover Island,** off the True Blue Peninsula (the site of Expo '69, an expensive Gairy-administration exercise for Caribbean colleagues that helped put Grenada seriously in debt), is the third of the south-shore triumvirate, and its status, also, is in question as we go to press.

■■

SPORTS have settled into a Grenadian pattern of water sports, soccer, cricket, and tennis for local folk and tourists. Sailing put this place into print in yachting magazines a decade or more ago, but present politics have taken some of the wind out of the sails. The biggest of the charter firms—those with U.S. connections—have sailed north to St. Vincent, the northern mark on the course through the several Grenadine islands, but there are reputable firms from which to charter "your" yacht—as many European vacationers are realizing.

AUTHOR'S OBSERVATION: One of Grenada's most spectacular beaches, and the one most talked about, may seem to the novice to be three. The name is pronounced vaguely as "Lance-eh-peen," and will be spelled—in print—as Lance aux Epines, L'Ance aux Epines, and L'Anse aux Epines. All mean Beach of Pines, and I choose L'Anse aux Epines, the true French spelling, for the copy that follows.

Sailing these days centers on yachts registered at *Spice Island Charters,* with facilities at what used to be the Stevens Yachts' dock at L'Anse aux Epines, and at *Grenada Yacht Services* (Box 183, St. George's) with marina and other facilities at the lagoon at St. George's. Included on the listings for both firms are several yachts that cruise through the Grenadines (some of which can be reached on ship-to-shore phones; others are available only when they cruise into port), as well as some bareboat charters (no crew) that are advisable only for experienced skippers who are also experienced at makeshift maintenance that may be needed when you are mid-cruise. A careful countdown of all facilities, and a careful look at all shackles, fittings, and sails, is advisable. Experienced yachtsmen well know that, and others, in my opinion, shouldn't be taking a bareboat through the Grenadines.

Carriacou's Regatta, held on the first weekend in August (Britain's traditional August Bank Monday), is a sight to be seen if you can manage it. The island's hand-hewn work boats, with their hand-sewn sails, compete in a race series that also includes the most modern fiberglass yachts. This is a regatta that pulls boats and yachting types from the entire Caribbean.

Snorkeling is spectacular off many beaches, but the flat, sandy shores of Grand Anse are not the best areas. Some of the rocky areas are more interesting, and your hotel and fellow guests can suggest the best of the nearby spots. As far as **scuba** is concerned, Grenada Divers had the concession in control when I visited, but check on the spot for any changes. Their rates were $6 for mask, $25 for regulator, $8 for refills, and they will deliver equipment to your hotel if you have a Scuba card. Their offices are at Grenada Yacht Services as well as Spice Island. (Half-day of scuba figured at about $25, using a 19-foot dive boat to reach the sites.)

Tennis courts can be found at the *Richmond Hill Tennis Club* and at the *Tanteen Tennis Club*, on the grounds of the special site cleared and built upon for Expo '69, a Caribbean Free Trade Association festival sponsored in Grenada. You can also use the courts at the Holiday Inn, Calabash, and at Secret Harbour if you make arrangements ahead of time.

■■

TREASURES AND TRIFLES in Grenada are full of spice—literally. Known as the spice island, Grenada sells its fresh bay leaves, ginger root, ground coriander, pepper, cinnamon sticks, and other spices in neat baskets in local shops or in bulk at the market in St. George's. Considered treasures by any hometown culinary expert, fresh spices are plucked from the trees and bushes of this island. If you haven't latched onto any in the several markets and shops around the south, in and around St. George's, there are spices in baskets and glass jars for sale at the small shop at the airport.

Spice ladies proliferate on the streets of St. George's, hovering around the exit to the cruise ship dock on days when a ship is in port. $5 is the going price for a couple of small spice baskets, but be sure to bargain—and specify whether you're talking US or EC $.

For shopping on the streets of St. George's, one of the best bets for my money is the **Government Handicraft Center,** behind the public library just after you pass the Carenage (where the boats are hauled for repairs). You can find some well-made baskets and other items made from island grasses. Production in recent years seems to include a lot of colorful raffia designs that I find too "touristy." If you agree, stop here early in your visit to talk to the craftsmen before they get carried away with all that color spelling out "Grenada" and bubbling in flowers. Other places to prowl around before you make your final decisions on island straw work are **Pitts Handicraft** at the pier (where the torrents of tourists pour off the cruise ships) and the **Straw Market** at Granby Street, opposite the market square.

Yellow Poui, an art gallery upstairs off Granby Street at Market Square, has expanded, and still carries a good selection of local art.

For clothes, **Dinah's Original** is still in operation, but Bessie Wildman (Dinah's sister) has moved over to **The Island Shop** which she opened at the new Charles of Grenada center. Careful attention to details and tailoring makes her fashions some of the island's most interesting. If you have a special design you like for summer clothes, it's possible to have something made up, but bring the pattern (or a dress in that style) with you for Bessie Wildman's talents to touch.

Charles of Grenada has Liberty fabric, Pringle sweaters and a startling assortment of English imports, as does **Y. DeLima,** operating as an eastern Caribbean chain, anchored to its Port of Spain, Trinidad, base. The expected crystal, Wedgwood, china, watches, perfumes, etc. can be found here, as well as at the **Granby Stores.**

At the Holiday Inn, the **Dolphin Shop** is the boutique, having moved here from its in-town location a couple of seasons ago. The fashions are attractive and the workmanship above average on the handcrafts. (You can get suntan lotion at exorbitant prices that respond to the local taxes and the fact that it's a tourist item.)

The usual store hours are 9-12, and after lunch until closing time—worded that way because that is the way it is in Grenada. If it is important to you to get to a shop when it is open, research on location or phone the entrepreneur at home if necessary. Although you can usually count on places in downtown St. George's being open (and crowded) when a cruise ship is in port, shop hours are not dependable in spring, fall, and even summer, when the tourist season is slower. Shops frequented by Grenadians open, certainly for morning hours, and usually also in the afternoon—until about 4 p.m. or so. The island market, at Granby Street on Market Square, is at its liveliest on Saturday morning, but there is something sold there in the way of produce every day of the week.

Carriacou

Maxman leaned out the window of his car, his red cap accenting the ebony face. "Wanna ride?" I nodded, tossed my bag and myself into the back seat of his car, and slammed the door, all set to slumber. After all, it was about 6:30 a.m. and I had been traveling since a pitch-black 4 a.m. when I stumbled out of my hotel on the southwest shore of Grenada, near that island's capital of St. George's. The weaving and darting ride up and over the mountain route of Grenada to Pearls Airport was an hour-long endurance test, where only agile skirting of potholes by an experienced driver kept the car on some sort of path. There was a broken ribbon of traffic, mostly pedestrian, wandering along the way to . . . where? Maybe work? Maybe not.

The check-in at the Island Air counter at Pearls is casual at best, and capable of being overlooked at worst. Only a "You going to Carriacou?" to the man at my elbow yielded the essential information that "No. That plane's taking off." I scampered out to the runway, to gain permission to sit in the seat next to the pilot, the only seat left in the 7-passenger plane.

My arrival on Carriacou about 10 minutes after takeoff from Grenada was greeted with the sunrise. Spectacular! It seemed a shame that only a dozen or so of us were there to enjoy it, but others undoubtedly saw it from their vantage points. People get up early around these islands.

But not everyone. Two men were rocking on the terrace facing the sea when I finally figured out how to get behind the front gates and onto the patio of the Mermaid Inn. "Hi. Do you know where I can find somebody?" "No." Continued gazes at the sea. Rock, rock, rock. Pause. "But someone will turn up around seven or so."

I pulled up my rocker next to theirs, and settled into what was obviously the local system. Slow rocking. I looked off to the wedge of green mountains that sat in the sea not far away, and watched a couple of sloops sail across the view. That was Union Island—and that was the day of the "rebellion" that made a 4-inch article in *The New York Times*. No one here even knew it was happening, and I suspect that the people on Union only knew it when they watched a small plane land at neighboring Palm, on a strip that had been closed for scheduled service because the clumps of grass on the strip had grown too high. (The plane carried the police from St. Vincent, several stepping-stone islands to the north and the seat of the government of which Union is a part.) The dissenters were arrested within hours.

So much for the effect of "rebellion" on daily life in the Caribbean. The main concern this morning was when I could get breakfast and get going—to my survey of Carriacou. Soon after Agnes arrived, she delivered my requested two eggs sunny-side with a selection of fresh-baked bread, still warm from Cecilia's stone ovens down the street. Conversation began, at the table I shared with the two previously unknown fellow travelers—and none of my pressures to "do" something seemed to be important anymore.

That's life in the unusual Caribbean, in the little-known islands where tourists are almost as scarce as iguanas, the prehistoric-looking lizards that islanders love to eat. Down the beach, a while later, Mavis Brown had scooped her skirt into her belt to keep it from dragging in the sea while she washed the conch she had been pounding with a chunk of two-by-four against a rock. Conch, known locally as "lambi," is the animal that lives inside those gorgeous curved shells that sometimes see later use as horns, or bookends, or edges for garden paths. The shells are beautiful; the conch meat being pounded is not. But Mavis Brown is, in her way. She smiled, and shared her recipe for cooking (a lot of rinsing in the Caribbean, a lot of pounding, some paring away of inedible parts, and then a series of soaks and boils eventually with tomatoes, onions, and spices plucked from nearby bushes).

With that knowledge entrusted to my notebook, I wandered off along the beach that fringed the couple of streets that make up Hillsborough, the main town of Carriacou, to see the small museum of island artifacts, a labor of love by a devoted outsider who has made her home here for several years.

Windward, a spray of houses along the shore on the other side of the island, is a boat builders' village. Framed wood boats rest on the beach. No one was working on the day I looked, but the half-built boats were there. "No boats building these days?" a Windward resident was asked. "No, man, not now," was the easy answer. "How's things?" "Nothin' special." Smiles, waves, and a revving motor completed the transaction as we rolled on around the rutted and pot-holed threads that link communities on this island. On Sundays, small boys sail handmade boats at Windward, but the once-thriving boat building "industry" has fallen on hard times. "All these people care about is boat building," I was told. "If we could just get some electric hand drills, they'd be happy."

▪▪

POLITICAL PICTURE: Although Carriacou is part of the country of Grenada, with the same central government, the island has its own administrator, Lyle Bullen, whose office is next to the pier at Hillsborough.

▪▪

MONEY MATTERS: U.S. dollars are in demand (as hard currency). Hotels, cab drivers, and others will be happy to have them. If you're staying for a while, change your money into Eastern Caribbean dollars at the Barclay's Bank on the main road in town, for the best rate.

▪▪

ARRIVAL on Carriacou can be Island Air from Pearls Airport on Grenada, or by the mailboat or other inter-island craft that make regular runs out of St. George's on the south coast of Grenada and/or coming south from St. Vincent, at the northern "end" of the string of Grenadine islands. Private, chartered yachts have made Carriacou a port of call in past seasons. Depending on the political climate, and the treatment they get by the local customs officials, they still do. If you are chartering through the Grenadines, you can count on your skipper to know the "temperature of the water" at the time you are sailing these islands. Rely on his judgment as to whether or not this is an attractive port of call. In spite of the size of the island, and the planes that fly in here, be sure to follow all the most formal procedures for flight check-in. Reconfirm your onward flight soon after you arrive on Carriacou, and reconfirm more than once. If the Island Air agent tells you to be at the airport one hour ahead of time, do so. I was not allowed on "my" flight because I turned up for the 7-passenger plane (which you can see in the sky from Hillsborough, 5 minutes from the "airport") only half an hour ahead of time. Two standby passengers, friends of the agent, had already been ticketed!

■■■

HOTELS ON CARRIACOU:

✣ **The Mermaid Inn** (Hillsborough, Carriacou, Grenada, W.I.; 10 rooms) is one of those small and special inns that makes the Caribbean the kind of place you want to come back to, if you *like* real islands, with no frills, no fancy nightlife, and no fussing over the size of your room, the luxury of your bath, and whether or not the lights stay on at night. But the publicity about politics has taken its toll, and there is talk of closing at press time. Inquire about the status at the time you plan to visit. Trevor and Hazel Ann Kent left Carriacou to live in and educate their young children on Barbados. The Kent family (parents and sister) continued to maintain the homelike atmosphere of Mermaid. If they do so, you can be assured of a very special, typically West Indian, place to stay. If the property is now being run by others, it's worthwhile checking on the atmosphere before booking for an extended stay. The Mermaid Inn has a legendary past that includes the "founding" of the place by J. Linton Riggs, a yachtsman and writer who moored himself on Carriacou in his 60s in the early 1960s. A main house with a small appendage of a trio of rooms is the extent of accommodations. Meals have been served in the courtyard, or under cover next to it, as congenial candlelight events with good local food (mainly fish). Make no mistake about it—this place is an outpost, with only the 2-street-wide village of Hillsborough and miles of beach plus acres of ocean to keep you occupied. The inn is simple, in a stucco structure on the road through Hillsborough. It operates, according to the Kents, as an "old-style West Indian hotel with good food and atmosphere of friendly intimacy, typical of our island."

If you want a room with private bath, request it when you write; most rooms have shared bath, and the entire nest offers lots of genuine hospitality. Rates for winter have been about $60 for 2, with breakfasts and dinners daily. Day sailing can be easily arranged, usually with some of the local folk or those who have chosen to anchor at nearby Tyrrel Bay.

✣ **Silver Beach** (Hillsborough, Carriacou, Grenada W.I.: 4 units) sits at the shores of Beausejour Beach, which is the strand of sand that lines the shore of Hillsborough. The 4 single-story, cement-block units each have 2 simple apartments, with bedroom area, small kitchen and living area, as well as a porch that is shared with your other half. Don't count on lavish furnishings, but then, rates this winter are $35 for 2, for a room ($150 per week). There's a warped ping-pong table and a pool table for shoreside play and a beautiful beach for strolls and swims. This place is popular with local folk who know about the good food (which includes crab soup for EC$8 and lobster for EC$40) and the good conversation that thrives around the bar. For people who like their islands "pure," Silver Beach can provide an independent "home."

Guadeloupe

Office Départemental du Tourisme de de la Guadeloupe, 5 Square de la Banque, B.P. 1099, Pointe-à-Pitre, Guadeloupe, French West Indies; French West Indies Tourist Board, 610 Fifth Ave., New York, NY 10020; 9401 Wilshire Blvd., Beverly Hills, CA 90212; 1840 Ouest Rue Sherbrooke, Montreal, Quebec, Canada H3H 1E4; 372 Bay St., Suite 610, Toronto, Ontario, Canada M5H 2W9.

US $1 = 5 French francs (Confirm at travel time.)
Unless otherwise noted, U.S. equivalents are figured at the above rate.

It was almost ten years ago, at a mountainside inn above Basse-Terre, on the flanks of La Soufrière, that I first encountered French West Indian hot sauce, the pungent pepper potion that turns your mouth into a raging volcano and sends lava down your gullet.

I now suspect, considering the obeah known to the weed women of Guadeloupe (and most West Indian islands), that that established my addiction to the French West Indies—and, I might add, my respect for the perils of hot sauce and admiration of French creole cuisine.

No waterfall in Guadeloupe's 74,100-acre National Park cascades more profusely than the tears did down my cheeks on that first encounter. I am older and wiser now. I slice the pepper paper-thin, pierce it with my fork, and waft it over some gourmet delight with the care many people reserve for vermouth when it comes near gin or vodka.

The French West Indies are like that. Their effects are felt immediately, and the impact carries extra voltage. The Antilles Françaises don't *intend* to be different; they just *are*. And most who head here on holiday from the English-speaking world are totally unprepared for a completely different culture, especially when bedded down in a place that *looks* just like home.

Even the most basic primer of these French islands has to include Guadeloupe, with the satellites in its orbit (the 8 islands of Les Saintes, plus Marie Galante and Désirade) and Martinique, reached by leapfrogging south over British-affiliated Dominica (Details in Chapter 10). And now, deservedly claiming places of their own for French flavor under the sun, are also the other dependencies governed from Guadeloupe: the French part of St. Martin, 140 miles to the northwest and sharing an island with Dutch Sint Maarten (Chapter 27); and St. Barthélemy, reached in 12 minutes by small plane from Sint Maarten or 45 heading northwest from Guadeloupe (Chapter 21).

Guadeloupe's 2 islands of Basse-Terre and Grande-Terre are linked by a drawbridge and shaped like the top of a bikini—an item most women discard on the French beaches. Basse-Terre, the westernmost of the 2 islands, has verdant mountains (ideal for walks) and the awesome, moon-like volcano peak known as Soufrière. Grande-Terre, flatter than its sister island, and often parched and dusty, is home for most of the tourist hotels, and the site of the island's 18-hole golf course and best beaches.

The French West Indies are tied to mainland France by the long tether of Air France (with preferential rates for vacationing French people.) Since they operate as *départements* of France, equal to the *départements* on mainland Europe, they have the same social benefits: hospitals, modern low-income housing, vacation pay, tax benefits, educational opportunities and a staggering government payroll.

"Bonjour" is the key to unlock the French West Indies. Without it, you'll survive, but you'll have to be content to glide along on a surface slickly prepared for American visitors with no language but their own. With French in your kit-for-travel, you'll be a free agent, one able to negotiate with the market ladies, colorfully dressed in their madras layers, and sometimes offering herbs, spices, and piles of little black or white dolls on which to work your obeah.

■■

POLITICAL PICTURE: No *département* on mainland France is more firmly committed to the vagaries of French politics than the two *départements* that speckle the Caribbean. Most of the mainland political parties have representation in the islands (the communism that is practiced here seems to be a capitalist variety that makes private homes and big cars part of the traditional doctrines). Guadeloupe is the seat of the government not only for the 2 wings of the butterfly-shaped "island" of Guadeloupe, but also for the satellites of Désirade, Marie Galante, the 8 Iles des Saintes, and, some 140 miles north, of St. Barthélemy and the French part of St. Martin. The Prefect is appointed by the government in Paris; The Conseil Général is elected by the citizens of Guadeloupe. The French portion of St. Martin has a resident Sous-Prefect. Each town has its local mayor, the reigning political figure in his orbit, and the links are firm with the representatives of the Conseil Général, who are responsible for passing the legislation and putting it into practice. The ties that bind to mainland France give these Caribbean *départements* a role to fill in Europe's Common Market, but no place in the Caribbean community in the middle of which the islands sit. It is easier to trade with Italy and Austria than with Trinidad and other countries a few miles north and south!

Wage scales are set by mainland France, giving French West Indies residents one of the Caribbean's highest standards of living. You'll see little of the poverty found on some of the other, smaller islands—even when you visit the specks that sit off the shores of Guadeloupe. Medical services and education are patterned on the mainland's, with modern schools and equal opportunities for university in France. Specialists and surgeons make frequent visits to French West Indian hospitals to diagnose and to perform operations.

CUSTOMS OF THE COUNTRY are French, and if you speak French you'll enjoy life in these islands more. Not only will you be able to understand what's going on (perhaps not in a conversation between Guadeloupeans because they will speak their patois or dialect), but you will be able to read signs and menus and order in restaurants.

This is creole country, and that means a lot of magic in the air— and in the recipes for living as well as for table. Obeah (witchcraft) is practiced by many in the countryside; weed women are locally known as some of the most reliable medicine ladies; pageants and customs are colorful.

Clothes on the city streets are French. Midcalf sundresses or swirling skirts with T-shirts, and sandals are the local fashion for ladies; European-cut trousers and slick-fitting shirts for men. And on the beaches? Nothing goes. Even visiting maidens from the Country Club cloistered set doff their bikini tops after a few days under the French West Indian sun. *Very* casual attire can be seen (if not admired) in hotel lobbies and around the cluster of vacation places at Gosier and Bas du Fort. The preponderance of sloppy clothes and T-shirts on men and women in once-formal hotel dining rooms is a trend I notice (especially for off-season travelers), but do not applaud. Wintertime travelers are usually a dressier group, and some of the evening garb can be fashionable. Men seldom (never?) need jackets; open-necked shirts are acceptable everywhere. Many women choose to dress up for evening, but resort-wear pants, jump suits and other fashionable outfits are seen more often than the traditional long skirts of yesteryear. Midcalf dresses, in very lightweight materials, are popular.

AUTHOR'S OBSERVATION: If you're unfamiliar with the ways of the French West Indies, write to the Tourist Board office for a copy (free) of *Helpful Hints for Visitors to Guadeloupe and Martinique.* The 28-page booklet is filled with tips to smooth the way for strangers.

Tipping is a troublesome matter here, as it is everywhere. Most restaurant bills include a 10% or 15% item for service. Ask when in doubt. "Service compris?" (Is service included?) will bring a "Oui" (yes) or a "Non" (no) from your waitress. If service is *not* included, an additional 10% to 15% is sufficient. You need add no more if the answer is "oui." In one or two restaurants, there is a notation on the menu that says "Prix nets." This means that each item carries its own service charge; you need not leave additional money when your bill is presented. For special service, from watersports personnel, for tennis, for some exceptional service at the hotel, or from a taxi driver a small additional sum may seem appropriate. In most instances, though, the fee you are being charged is more than enough.

Expect to find dogs, cats, and sometimes chickens wandering around your dining table in some of the places that serve excellent local food. The custom doesn't bother the islanders (or most of the visitors). If you think it will bother you, you'll have to limit your dining to the major hotels' enclosed dining rooms, and you'll be missing some of the best island food.

MONEY MATTERS: French francs are the currency of record, and you'll be wise to get some before you land, or transact at the banks when you get into the airport or the city of Pointe-à-Pitre. Hotels will change U.S. dollars to French francs at a lower rate of exchange than the banks and, while that difference may not matter on small transactions, it can add up for big ones. You'll be happier with French francs for your travels around the island and to the offshore satellites, and certainly if you've rented a "cook at home" place where you are negotiating with the local bread lady and the fishermen. On the satellites for Guadeloupe (Les Saintes, Marie Galante and Désirade), most of the visitors are French and French currency and customs prevail.

Fluent French can bring prices down, perhaps not at hotels where rates are published, but certainly in local markets and when you're taking care of daily routines if you've rented a villa or another housekeeping facility. Taxi drivers here, as elsewhere are seldom intimidated by anything, but they are at least fair when you negotiate in French. The same goes for clerks in shops, personnel at hotels, and for trying to accomplish anything on the French islands.

Be sure to inquire about, and pursue when shopping, the special discounts available at some in-the-city shops when you buy with traveler's checks or some credit cards. Many of the bigger stores give some discount, and some others will when asked.

AUTHOR'S OBSERVATION: As the dollar gets stronger, its ratio to the French franc is better for U.S. currency travelers. However, since hotels print their U.S. dollar rates months in advance of the time you travel, you may do better to settle locally with francs (if the rate has risen to more than 5F to US$1). One way to avoid any cash confusion is to purchase the Fête Française vacations packaged by the French West Indies Tourist Board and cooperating hotels and airlines. Read the fine print carefully in the promotion brochure, and know that there *are* some very good values.

■■

ARRIVAL ON GUADELOUPE at Raizet Airport is usually easy and efficient. The big modern airport with its air conditioning is a refreshing change from other, smaller terminals you may have known as you fly around this area. Immigration and customs formalities are standard: Stand in line to show your passport (the easiest and most effective proof of citizenship), your filled-in immigration form, which you probably will receive on the plane but may have handed to you on arrival, and perhaps your return ticket if you look like you might not have the wherewithal to support yourself while here. Porters are scarce, but you can find luggage carts (European-airport style) around the baggage claim area.

When you leave from Guadeloupe, there's a band of small boutiques at the airport departure lounge. The ones near the airline ticket counters are *not* duty-free, but do have some locally made items for sale (if the shops are open when you are there). If you see several people rambling around the airport with the long loaf of French bread tucked in the crook of their arm, you should know that the "best bakery in town" is the restaurant up the stairs to your left as you face the terminal departure lounge. The small counter for duty-free items (mostly perfume and liquor) is "tended" by staff whose casual sales approach borders on indifference. My advice is to shop elsewhere if you like smiles with your service.

Air Guadeloupe and other small plane flights to the satellite islands leave from the left end of the terminal as you face the entrance. You can buy your ticket just before check in, but allow at least 45 minutes before boarding time—and be prepared for the shock of reentry at the end of a day spent on one of the small spots. Guadeloupe's Raizet Airport takes on all the aspects of metropolitan France, with the unexpected hustle and bustle after a leisurely day on a remote speck.

AUTHOR'S OBSERVATION: When you arrive at the Office du Tourisme or at your hotel, ask for a copy of "Bonjour Guadeloupe" in English. The fact-filled information booklet is published at regular intervals, and although it may not have all the latest hours and times, the basic information is sound. Armed with "Bonjour Guadeloupe" supplemented by inquiries at the Office du Tourisme, your hotel's activities desk, and conversations with residents you may meet, you should be able to enjoy a Guadeloupean holiday that is uniquely your own.

■■■

TOURING TIPS: *Be sure* to ask in advance at your hotel, the tourism desk at the airport, or at the taxi stand for the fare between where you are and where you want to go. Taxi drivers here, as almost everywhere, recognize a novice when they see one, and have sometimes charged what they think the traffic will bear. (For the ride from the airport to Gosier, expect to pay 40F or more, and change your money at the airport as soon as you arrive if you have not gotten French francs before you head south.) Speaking French will save you anguish and money.

Rental cars are available through the activities desks at most of the big hotels. As everywhere, gas is expensive (but the investment is "nothing" by comparison to the going rates for hiring a car-with-driver, and having the driver wait while you swim, explore, or have a leisurely meal). If you want a car at height of winter, request it when you book your hotel so that your reservation is set. Even with that "confirmation," you may find that your car is not ready when you are, but with some protesting, one will usually appear eventually. French is essential if you want to stray from the usual tourist routes (and even when traveling along some of them); your alternative is a lot of smiles, sign language, and silent prayers if you have a breakdown or otherwise need help.

What about finding your way? Good luck. Roads are not well posted but they are direct. The main routes are well paved, but watch out for the Frenchmen who drive at breakneck speed down the middle—or squarely on your side of the road. You may follow a well-paved road that dissolves into dirt. You won't be the first, and some of those dirt roads lead to the best places. Exploring types will love driving on Guadeloupe.

Other getting-around options include the public bus service, which is relatively comfortable (buses are new, usually Mercedes vans) and easy to travel from, for example, the Gosier hotels to Pointe-à-Pitre or, in the other direction, to Ste. Anne, or on to St. François. Routes are highlighted in writing on the side of the bus. All you need to know is the name of "your" town, and—with payment of a few francs—you're on your way.

For those who want commentary with their travel, tour companies that operate in Guadeloupe give efficient service, pick you up from your hotel, and deposit you back there after your carefully coddled day of exploring. The services offered by Georges Marie Gabrielle, the ground-tour operator for the Fête Française package I purchased, proved to be efficient, and representative Danielle Wilheur was a valuable source for on-the-spot information. Their offices are at 21 rue Alexandre Isaac in Pointe-à-Pitre, but representatives come to most hotels at appointed hours each day.

Guests at Gosier and Bas du Fort hotels should check about boat services that sometimes make the run from beachside to downtown Pointe-à-Pitre. For seafaring types, the motorboat ride can be fun—and faster than the traffic clogged road routes.

■■■

HOTELS ON GUADELOUPE speckle both wings (Grande-Terre and Basse-Terre) of the butterfly shape of the island. The greatest concentration of resort properties is on Grande-Terre at Gosier, a once-small fishing village now taken over by tourists, and at Bas du Fort, a hump of land between Gosier and Pointe-à-Pitre. When you bed in here, you'll be about 5 miles from downtown Pointe-à-Pitre and almost the same distance from the airport, on two branches of a Y. Meridien and Hamak (and some of the country's best restaurants) are *miles* away, along the southeast shore of Grande-Terre, beyond Gosier, at St. François. There are a couple of small spots plus Caravelle Club Med scattered along that south shore of Grande-Terre. The other Club Méditerranée, at Fort Royal, is about as far away as you can get from hub activity. At Deshaies on the west side of Basse-Terre, it's a generous hour's drive from Pointe-à-Pitre and the airport. The capital of the *département* is at the town of Basse-Terre on the island of Basse-Terre, and you'll find La Grande Soufrière in the hills behind that area. (All this is not *quite* as confusing as it sounds if you look at a map.)

Variety is the keynote. for Guadeloupe. Almost 1000 new hotel rooms were added in the season of '75–'76. After that surge, tourism officials and hotel operators recognized the need to *fill* the rooms for more than the 3 peak winter months. Activity programs, promotion with European groups, and special package tours, most notably the Fête Française, have helped, and season of '79–'80 saw more building, especially at Bas du Fort and St. François.

Francophiles who like small spots will applaud (as I do) the establishment of Chaine des Relais de la Guadeloupe, an association of small hotels around Guadeloupe and its offshore islands. For information, contact the Chaine des Relais at the Office du Tourisms, 5 Square de la Banque, B.P. 1099, 97181 Pointe-à-Pitre.

There are a few excellent inns, many of them beachside, and some good big hotels, a few of them with special personalities that help to simmer down the overwhelming mass-market mix. *All* are very French, no matter how "American" they look, and you will be far happier if you speak French and are willing to "do it their way"—which is often slowly.

Tourism troops at top spots are 65% U.S. (most of the rest are Canadian and French, many of whom come on charters as part of their government-granted annual holiday) in winter months, with many Europeans in summer.

AUTHOR'S AWARDS go to Auberge de la Vieille Tour, for providing atmosphere and hospitality in comfortable surroundings convenient to town and the action at other hotels; to Hamak for comfortably casual surroudings with a housekeeping option; to Relais de la Grande Soufrière for maintaining a traditional "private home" in the country; and to Auberge du Grand Large for specializing in the simple, uncluttered beachside life that is reminiscent of that offered by small inns on the Mediterranean shore of France.

✤ **Auberge JJ** (Gosier, Guadeloupe, F.W.I.; 12 rooms) is a special small spot where Jose Mormont and his wife are your hosts. Rooms are simply furnished in French guesthouse style. The inn is clean, and the restaurant *Le Saramaca* is more prominent than the hotel facilities when you glance up the entrance steps from the street in Gosier. For anyone who has traveled in France, and likes being within walking distance of in-town things, this inn provides clean, convenient, and modestly priced (at about $40 for 2, breakfasts and dinners included) accommodations.

✤ **Auberge du Grand Large** (Route de la Plage, Ste.-Anne, Guadeloupe, F.W.I.; 10 rooms in bungalows) is a gem, if you like French beachside places where life is casual and uncluttered. You can walk on to Ste.-Anne beach, a long stretch of sand that is shared with the village folk, the fishermen, and guests of the Club Med who come down the hill from their Caravelle. This is a simple place, with a marvelous gathering area decorated with an old sewing machine, a Gauguin copy, some small wood carvings, ice cream parlor chairs and tables, with colorful mats, topped with napkin "hats," ready and waiting for the very special creole fare that's served lunch and dinner. Josette took me to a room, on one visit, and it was like being escorted to meet the queen. The room was simple, in one of the bungalows near (but not on) the beach. Rooms 2 through 6 are closest to the beach, but they face the fence that discourages local walk-in traffic. The rooms nearest the main building (where meals are served) are more protected from beach strollers. The small staff seems to feel as at home here as you will when you settle in (especially if you speak French). Mme. Georges Damico manages the place, with her own chic and warm brand of hospitality. Speaking

French is essential if you want to fit in. Rooms rent for about $80 for 2, continental breakfast included. (Summer rates are about half.)

✤ **Auberge de la Vieille Tour** (Gosier, Guadeloupe, F.W.I.; 82 rooms) incorporates its sugar-mill tower into the complex, weaving the entire set of buildings that make up the Auberge together with lush planting. The feeling here is one of permanence, even though the inn has only been open for a decade or more. It was the precursor of Gosier development, and followed itself with Callinago and Salako, down the stretch of shore (sometimes beach) shared also with Arawak and Holiday Inn. The inn is now part of the Frantel operation, but for my vacation dollar, Auberge still reigns supreme. Not only is it the closest to Gosier (making it possible to walk into what used to be a small fishing village and still is a typical Guadeloupean town), but it is also "above it all," literally. The place perches on a knoll, so that you walk from the main check-in area to the boxy buildings on the left where most of the rooms are located (24 in one section with 12 on 12, 36 in another, and 9 in each of 2 more) and down to the curve of sand that is the beach. There's a freshwater pool, and 2 of the 3 courts are lighted for night tennis. Responding to the enthusiasm for scuba and organized water sports, there is a water-sports concession near the pool, with the snack and light meal area nearby. The dining room in the main building has a reputation as one of the best, but I have found prices high and food only fair on a couple of recent visits. It seems possible that increasing groups of tourists unable to converse in French may have taken their toll on the patience of the staff. The place still *looks* serene, with waitresses in the Guadeloupe madras creole dress. (Most of the staff have been trained on the spot, after time at the hotel school and the ceremony of service wine pouring and food preparation is noteworthy.) Rooms are nothing spectacular, unless you get one of the 3 2-bedroom villas which seem like a home. The usual nooks are small, with narrow beds and plastic-covered furniture you'd expect to find in a middle-class hotel. But this place is tops—and so are the rates, at about $130 for 2, breakfast daily per person.

✤ **Bougainvillée** (9, rue Frébault, Pointe-à-Pitre, Guadeloupe, F.W.I.; 32 rooms) bids for the business traveler, with its in-the-city location on a busy corner a short walk from the cruise ship dock. No place for those seeking sun, sea, and sand, the 7-story modern building is honeycombed with good-value rooms, ranging from a simply furnished suite with balcony to small singles with shower and w.c. down the hall. Rates are listed at about $55 for 2, meals extra, but there are rock-bottom rates for the rooms without private bath that you can learn about only by asking. (They're not listed on the official rate sheet.) Speaking French is essential for any conversation at this in-town spot. The snack bar on the 6th floor (also air-conditioned) is used by residents and returning guests who know their way around. Not for a typical Caribbean vacation, the small-but-modern hotel may be ideal if budget and being in town are top concerns.

✛ **Callinago** (Gosier, Guadeloupe, F.W.I.; 41 rooms) opened for season of '75 and now, with its related Callinago Village (see Housekeeping Holidays), is an imposing conglomerate at one end of a beach. The white stucco walls are softened by the planting in the center courtyard where you'll find a couple of shops. The restaurant and bar, down the stairs from the lobby entrance and to the left, are sparse but adequate (I prefer the open-air drinking and dining nook that opens out to the pool and beach). Liveliest action here is the Tuesday welcome cocktail, with a creole lunch—and that is very special when the folkloric group performs (otherwise you'll listen to the steel band). For scuba, check the concession at Auberge de la Vieille Tour. Other water sports available on the beach include waterskiing, windsurfing, pedal boats, and sailing in a 36' boat. A room at Callinago gives you an opportunity to visit the nearby hotels—Auberge, Salako, Arawak, and Holiday Inn—all a short stroll away. Rates this winter for 2 settle at about $90, breakfasts included.

✛ **Club Méditerranée La Caravelle** (Ste-Anne, Guadeloupe, F.W.I.; 275 rooms) cavorts according to the familiar formula: staff of GOs (*gentils organisateurs*), guests called GMs (*gentils membres*), no tipping, no money (only beads for cash which you convert as soon as possible after arrival), shared rooms which start off with same sex but have no keys or locks, and an action plan that would leave a whirling dervish breathless. I've been told you don't have to do everything, but I suspect you'll spend a lot of time explaining why if you don't. This is not a place for peace and quiet; it's an action-packed purchase that puts you shoulder to shoulder with others in search of the same. For sports, there's windsurfing, volleyball, water polo, tennis, ping-pong, yoga, calisthenics, bocce, horseback riding, sailing, snorkeling, waterskiing, and you name it. Your wish is a GO's command, but chances are they've already thought of it (including eating sea eggs on the pier).

Intertwined with the mix of activities is a mix of guests that is several parts American, some Canadian, some French, and some other Europeans on an 80% North American, 20% others tally that changes slightly in summer months (Europe's vacation season). This property opened as a private hotel, to be incorporated into the Club Med plan in 1973. All rooms have private bath, air conditioning and simple, standard Club Med furnishings—plus 2 people. (You either arrive with your own partner, or get put with one of the same sex.) Children age 5 and over are welcome guests, but there's no special action plan as there is at the Fort Royal.

Rates for a week of fun in the sun, paying a price that includes your room, meals, and most activities, will figure from $680 to $740 for each of 2 sharing a room at high season; and about $500 to $535 at lowest rate spring and fall, with airfare extra on all rates.

✤ **Club Méditerranée Fort Royal** (Deshaies, Guadeloupe, F.W.I.; 150 rooms) sits shoreside, near the westernmost point of Guadeloupe, on the island of Basse-Terre and is the best spot on Guadeloupe for sun-set watching. The route over the hills and through the National Park to Pointe-à-Pitre is one of the island's most scenic; it will take about an hour, whether you do it on your own in a rental car or as part of the half-day excursion offered by the tour desk. Sometimes referred to as the "family place," the routines at Fort Royal might be a shock for conservative folk who picture a quiet holiday playing in the sand and sea. This Club perks at the same peripatetic pace as the rest of the Club Med clan. Children from 4 to 14 are swept off with their own hourly roster of activities, *always* separate from the grown-ups, but often including the same action options (water-skiing, snorkeling, swimming, volleyball, etc.). For adults, the rites of revelry that set the pace at all Club Meds can be found here: the GOs (*gentils organisateurs*) plan the activities for the GMs (*gentils membres*), and the bikini and sun-basking atmosphere prevails with a disco with thatch roof and terrace that keeps toes tapping 'til dawn. "Un village où vous parlerez souvent l'anglais," is the comment in the French version of the Club Med catalogue, but *souvent* (often) doesn't mean always. Life will be a little easier (and certainly more interesting) if you have a working knowledge of French. The western hemisphere mix puts a house count at about 65% North Americans (Canadian and U.S.), 35% European— with many Europeans coming in summer months when they have their long vacation. Meals are served family style at tables that fill as people arrive; you sit where the next seat is vacant. Meals are plentiful (lavish buffet lunch that one guest claimed was "recycled" and family-style dinner) but there's plenty of food for all, and plenty of red or white wine to wash it all down. Young and old mix at mealtimes, but families are housed in the main hotel building, where rooms have a connecting bath-with-tub; singles and adult couples settle into the bungalows. From the Dive Center, groups head to Pigeon Island—for snorkeling and scuba with instruction. Arts and crafts courses are a recent addition to the action plan that includes all the water sports plus tennis, volleyball, Scrabble, badminton, dance lessons, party games, musical shows, and any activity anyone can think up.

From the Fort, day tours set off for St. Barthélemy (by plane), Terre de Haut, one of the Iles des Saintes (also by plane) or by car to Pointe-à-Pitre for a half day of shopping, or a full day touring the island of Basse-Terre. If you want a 2-day excursion, look into the overnight journey (plane and jeep) to Dominica, the British-affiliated island with a French patois several miles to the south.

Planned as a week-long holiday happening at an all-inclusive price, the Club Med mix appeals to gregarious types who want quantity and don't care so much about country club quality, and to voyeurs who want to be where life looks good. If you want to sample the selection for a couple of days, check to see if house count allows for a 2- or 3-night stand, at a price to be negotiated with the front desk clerk. Rates for the all-inclusive week are the same as at La Caravelle above, with special considerations for children who will tally up at a little more than half the adult tariff.

✜ **Ecotel Guadeloupe** (Gosier, Guadeloupe, F.W.I.; 44 rooms) is one of Guadeloupe's inns that operate as hotel schools offering a unique holiday option. Everyone learns: The staff learns service; you learn French. Both Ecotel, on Grande-Terre, and its Basse-Terre relative, Relais de la Grande Soufrière, are staffed by students learning the specialties of hotel service and operation after they graduate from the lycée. In addition to the financial support by the department, Ecotel is supported by the Pointe-à-Pitre Chamber of Commerce. Hotel managers are required to set aside 1% of the employee's salary for schooling, and many students use that 1% for special studies at Ecotel or Le Relais. When they complete the course, students receive *le brevier de Technician du tourisme* and special status as a hotel employee. Although very different in appearance and personality, the two schools have the same goal: training young people for the hotel business—and helping you to learn French. This modern 2-story complex of buildings is at the fringe of most of Guadeloupe's hotel activity in Gosier and is one of the island bargain spots, not only for the room rates (about $70 for 2, breakfasts daily), but also because you can learn French while the students learn the hotel business. Rooms at the Ecotel are modern, comfortable but not lavish, and many have views over pool or gardens. Although you're on the public bus route, you may feel more carefree with a rental car, especially if you want to escape to the beach.

✤ **Frantel Guadeloupe** (Bas du Fort, Guadeloupe, F.W.I.; 200 rooms) filled a plot on an area marked for development when it opened in December '75 on a man-made beach that is better than some of the God-given ones on this island. Typical of a lot of Caribbean hotel building that was "rushed" to completion for a winter season, cracks appeared in cement poured and dried too quickly, and other nicks and niches made this place look worn in spots when I inspected it. What you have here is a good hotel for middle-income travelers, at rates that are high (in my opinion) for what's offered. A daily double in winter runs about $90, meals extra, with free use of tennis during daytime (charge at night), shuffleboard, volleyball, Sunfish sailboats and pedal boats—plus the pool and beach— but you'll pay top price for any sipping and snacking at the poolside places or the fancier rooms on the main level. Green formica covers counters in the lobby area, and a gray and black brick floor sets a dreary tone that disappears the minute you glimpse the sea and pool.

Frantel gives you a place on the beach with relatively easy access (10 minutes by car) to Pointe-à-Pitre. (Your taxi to town will cost about 30F.) Planting almost covers the thermogas tanks on the "front lawn." You can notice them as you go to your room, but once inside your air-conditioned room with sea view, you won't care. This resort is reasonable, if you can get a group rate where enough extra is included to make the overnight rate worth it. As of the moment, even on European plan, I'd rate a lot of other places ahead of this one.

✤ **Holiday Inn Guadeloupe** (Gosier, Guadeloupe, F.W.I.; 156 rooms) has a look of its own, without the stereotype U.S. Holiday Inn image (except for its entrance sign). An orange tile floor leads from the lobby to the colorful pool and terrace area; management thoughtfully places a *sol glissant* sign near the tiles when it rains, and they mean it—the floor is not only slippery, it is treacherous! So treacherous, in fact, that a resurfaced "path" cuts through the middle of the tiled areas. *Ste. Anne* is the fancy, air-conditioned dining room (with OK general food, and good fish, if my sampling is typical). *St.*

Tropez, the airy snack bar is far preferable, and hopefully the mildew that has plagued the plastic cushions every time I have been here has been cleared up by the time you visit. The pool is big, plunked right in the middle of the social complex, and sometimes fringed with the same topless bathers you will find on most French beaches. Rooms are in several wings, off to the right as you face the sea. They all have narrow balcony or terrace, depending on your level, and require an excellent sense of direction and a desire to walk long distances to find the room where your key fits. There is one of the Holiday Inn handicap rooms, with special railings, etc. There's a 5F charge for "outsiders" to use the pool and beach facilities for the day, but you can sample snacks from the poolside barbecue and order a drink in the colorful and pleasant bar area, and pay only for what you eat and drink. The *Ti-Racoon Club* has a pleasant breeze-swept terrace overlooking the pool, and a dark and freezing (when the air conditioner works) disco that brightens the nightlife. For those who want to swing on the tennis courts, they are night-lighted. Tour groups keep the house count up in winter months. Count on things being quiet in spring and fall, with a puff of people in summer months. Rates are over $100 for 2, continental breakfasts included, in winter months.

✛ **Meridien Guadeloupe** (St. François, Guadeloupe, F.W.I.; 272 rooms) is coming into its own, after 7 years of "settling in." The property is a marvel of survival. Part of a pact with the local government to spread tourism out of the clutches of hotels at Gosier, and give some jobs to people in other areas, the big French chain built a huge property 25 miles east of Pointe-à-Pitre. Big plans for golf course, airport, and marina were premature for the 1974 opening, but are now in full swing and fun. Prior to opening at this then-desolate shoreside outpost, the Meridien man-on-the-spot had to establish a school as he was building the hotel, to train the people from St. François, not only in the operation of a huge modern monster like this one, but also, for the older employees, first in French and then in at least minimal English (they spoke only Creole). The wells and the water that was piped from Capesterre not only allowed the hotel to have running water in the rooms, but it also allowed the local folk to grow vegetables in their yards (the area is parched dry by the sun you tan by). When the place opened, plans were grand—for 450 rooms by 1975, with private homes all around, the marina chock full, and in effect, a whole new city. The plans are now in focus with the complete resort complex shared by guests here plus those at neighboring Hamak, Residences de Lagon, and

Les Trois Mats. As you stretch out on the beach, just imagine what running a complex like this entails—even now when the kinks are supposedly out. All rooms have spectacular sea view (and minute balconies) and overlook beach and pool. Food served at the elegant, expensive *Le Saint Charles* restaurant is acceptable restaurant fare (but several good bistros and restaurants in this area make it almost impossible for me to heap high praise on this enclosed, air-conditioned hotel dining room which, like its counterpart in Martinique, could be anywhere). There's a coffee shop of sorts where you can expect croissants and black coffee, but you should not expect fast service. The usual number of tour desks, boutiques, and even a drugstore are in the lobby area. The casino, long talked about and finally opened in late '77, is a short stroll from the front door. There's entertainment in the evenings; a lively water sports program during the day with use of all equipment free; options for interesting day excursions, offering—if house count includes charters—a flight to and frolic around Terre de Haut, one of Les Saintes islands; and tennis courts nearer to your room than the Robert Trent Jones golf course, which is not too far away. Rates this winter range around $150 for 2, breakfasts only. For eating options, you can head for the marina to Le Barokko and some of the very special places (Mme. Jerco's for one) in St. François.

✣ **Novotel Fleur d'Epée** (Bas du Fort, Guadeloupe, F.W.I.; 190 rooms) is another of a French chain reaction for middle-income travelers. Nestling next to the Frantel, on an area designated by the government for tourism development (and, therefore, eligible for good tax incentives if you build here), the 2 properties are similar in tone: lively if the usually young crowd is, used by groups from Canada and Europe, *very* casual (bathing suits go almost everywhere, and tops go off when you're by the pool or at the beach). Looking more like a giant Lego building than a hotel, the 3-story Y-shaped building stretches along the coast on a pretty good, man-made beach. The public areas are in the yawn of the Y, and filled (when the hotel is) with bathing-suited enthusiastic vacationers who wander in and out of the shops and other spots. Beach action includes volleyball and ping-pong, plus a selection of water sports and free use of pedal boats (which have been well used, from my glimpse), windsurfers, and Sunfish sailboats. The 2 tennis courts are free by day with charge for night-light. The restaurants here and next door at Frantel are open until midnight or thereabouts, depending on house count. You will find some interesting small restaurants along the road near the entrance. Budget-conscious travelers can walk down the road to the shopping center, to *Escale,* to stock up on nibbles and liquor which will be less expensive. Rates at the Novotel will stretch over $100 for 2, breakfasts included, which seems to me to be a lot of money for this hotel. Check about groups or charter plans which should bring the room rate down. (It will take you about 10 minutes by car to get into downtown Pointe-à-Pitre from here, and about the same time in the other direction to get to the Gosier hotels.)

✣ **PLM Arawak** (Box 396, Gosier, Guadeloupe, F.W.I.; 160 rooms) puts you right on the shore, between Salako and Callinago on the stretch of sand that reaches from Auberge de la Vieille Tour to the Holiday Inn (you can walk from one to the other in a leisurely, but nonstop 20 minutes). The Arawak came under the PLM wing not long after its opening in the early 1970s; it's the "skyscraper" on the shore, stretching to a 10th-floor crown of 6 suites that are *huge,* with terraces, and a choice of 3 sea-facing outlooks. Lobby facilities include a shop, a welcoming-bar area and a terrace where a piano player entertains for evening relaxation. The Laffitte dining room downstairs is like a dressed-up coffee shop, with lobster creole at 70F (about $18) and a house menu at considerably less. There's a pool near the 48-room annex (a boxy 3-story building with minimum-rate rooms) and the very active (very topless) beach. The 2 tennis courts get steady play, but those who want to head out to sea should check at the water sports pavilion on the plot of land near the Callinago side of the hotel. The *Tchapp* disco has been a drawing card for several seasons, but it is only lively when the crowd is (and has a steep cover charge all the time), and a European casino is now in full swing. I don't think the regular rooms are anything spectacular, but if you get one facing the sea, the view makes up for the mundane furnishings (all the basics are here, however). Best rates come with group travel; if you're on your own, you'll pay from $75 to $100 for 2, or $136 for a spacious top floor suite, breakfast included.

✣ **PLM Village Soleil** or **Sun Village** (Bas du Fort, Guadeloupe, F.W.I.; 105 rooms) rose from its hillock-top and opened in December 1979. The several buildings that encircle the pool and gathering area hold attractively furnished studios and suites and a couple of duplex units that are suitable for 4 people. Village Soleil is comfortable for self-sufficient, nautical types who like being able to wander down the slope to the activity and restaurants at the Port de Plaisance, the Bas du Fort marina area. Most action at Village Soleil centers on the pool, or you can go exploring in a rental car. Buildings are named for the satellite islands (Désirade, St. Barthélemy, Marie Galante, etc.), and most rooms have a view over boats and sea activity. Although the hotel is promoted in the U.S. as "Sun Village," signs on location and conversation about the hotel to residents (who speak French) refer to Village Soleil. Rates for winter range from $52 to $70 for 2, all meals extra. On-the-spot dining is in the open-to-breezes restaurant near the pool (a glass baffle protects from prevailing winds).

✣ **Relais du Moulin** (Chateaubrun, near Ste. Anne, Guadeloupe, F.W.I.; 20 rooms) rests amid grazing grounds for cattle and an occasional horse. Marked by a sugar-mill tower that is the main reception office for the cluster of small buildings that hold the rooms, the Relais provides a very special resting spot for those who want quiet, countryside surroundings. The small pool that punctuates the top of the rise on which the Relais perches can be lively with children or completely "yours," depending on the house count. Rooms are neat, comfortable, and small—with a hammock strung on some of the porch areas. A pleasant dining area called *La Marmite* is there for mealtimes near the pool. You'll want a rental car for mobility and plenty of books to read if you intend to stay "at home." Guaranteed to give you a very different look at Guadeloupe than that provided by the action-packed places, this special spot has a lot to recommend it. (You'll have a long walk, or short drive, to the shore for sea swimming.) Rate for 2 is about $60 this winter.

✣ **Relais de la Grande Soufrière** (St. Claude, Basse-Terre; 20 rooms) is in the grand old island tradition and is one of two hotel schools (Ecotel is the other). The Relais is in a residential suburb, up the hill on your way to reach the sulphur-puffing Soufrière. Rooms, named for great hotels in metropolitan France, are white-walled, high-ceilinged, airy affairs, some with duplex status (bedroom on the second level) and some with garden view. The nearest beach is Rocroy, 10 miles away, and you're about an hour's drive from Pointe-à-Pitre and the airport. Service is diligent and willing. Meals are excellent, carefully if slowly served; the place is a Guadeloupean treasure. Forget about this Relais if you need action; if there is any, it will be a private party of one of the well-to-do local families. A special place for self-sufficient types who want to be carefully cared for, and don't need a beach at the first footfall. Winter rates range around $50 for 2, no meals included (but all meals available at extra charge). Figure about 12F for breakfast and 65F for lunch and dinner.

✤ **Callinago Village** (Gosier, Guadeloupe, F.W.I.; 118 apts.) casts its guests onto the sand that stretches from the hillside units along the bay as far as the Holiday Inn. Located between Auberge de la Vieille Tour and the Callinago Hotel, guests who choose to do their own housekeeping in the studio and duplex apartments can be near the daytime and the nighttime action. You can walk to all the Gosier hotels, and to the beach concession that has windsurfers and other small sailboats, which is between the apartments and the Callinago Hotel. Be sure to ask for a room with sea view if you do prefer that to a view of the backside of a building. Although the 8 buildings are scattered around the patch of land, the lower level rooms don't have much in the way of porch-level scenery. Walls are thin, and some vacationers have complained about bugs (a Caribbean problem which management claims is controlled with sprays and intensive, periodic cleaning). If you're concerned, bring your favorite anti-bug spray and a "roach hotel" (available in many hardware stores) with you. Rates for the Callinago apartments figure at about $75 for 2 this winter, for room only.

✤ **Salako** (Gosier, Guadeloupe, F.W.I.; 120 rooms) stands at the shore, wedged between Arawak and Holiday Inn. Named for the hat worn by the fishermen of Les Saintes, Salako settled into the sands on this shore in 1975, as part of the government's tourism program that more than doubled the island's hotel room count. From the outside, the building looks like many other balconied boxes sitting seaside, but this box is honeycombed with attractive, modern, small rooms. The public facilities range over a separate area, connected by walkways and including check-in and activities desk, shops, and the very special *Le Santoise Restaurant,* the rotisserie. Other dining options include *Le Salako* (sparse, serene, air-conditioned, with huge menu) and *La Pizza,* the beachside snack spot that serves pizza (18F) and crepes (about 6F) cooked on the spot. *La Grappe Blanche* is the dark, air-conditioned bar, to the right of the restaurant off the lobby. Pool and 2 tennis courts supplement the beach for day activities. Tennis can also be your nighttime game (courts are lighted), but you may prefer the band that plays in the bar from 9:30 to 12:30 (on Saturdays, it's a steel band). Rates for your Salako stay will be over $100 per day this winter for room and breakfast for 2.

■■

HOUSEKEEPING HOLIDAYS ON GUADELOUPE allow for complete independence, with the freedom to sample the special cuisine at the many small creole and fish bistros, as well as at the haute cuisine French restaurants. Agence Molinard, with offices at Galeries Nozieres, B.P. 372, Pointe-à-Pitre, lists several seaside houses for long-term rental near the marina at Bas du Fort, as well as some houses elsewhere around Guadeloupe. There are individual homes, apartments, and villas available for week-long or longer rental through Gîtes de France (contact the Office du Tourisme in Pointe-à-Pitre) and M. R. Adolphe at Bungalows-Village, Montaubon, Gosier, Guadeloupe, F.W.I., for places near the resort hotels of Gosier. Do *not* count on flourishes and fancy fixtures, or even, in some cases, hot water. Some places listed are second homes for Guadeloupeans who use their beach villas during very casual, carefree summer holidays but are happy to rent them to visitors during the winter months. Rentals will range from about $150 for a small villa to about $400 per week for a 4-bedroom villa.

Speaking French is essential, not only for negotiating the rental, but certainly for shopping for food and making arrangements with the maid and/or cook if you hire one with your island "home."

✛ **Hamak** (at St. François, about 25 miles east of Pointe-à-Pitre; 56 rooms in 28 villas) made a name for itself as the site for the summit meetings, and the place where the Carter family was a sight. The complex opened in the season of '77–'78 with its 250 acres barely covered with greenery and its planting and flourishes still in the nursery stage, but it has now burgeoned to a full-fledged resort, next to the Meridien Hotel. Conveniently located near the 18-hole golf course and the lagoon that is slowly breaking out in a rash of lavish yachts, the complex has villas: the 2-suite version (590 square feet each suite), has private patios sparsely furnished, twin-bedded room, kitchen, bathroom and terrace—with hammock, of course. One of Guadeloupe's several airstrips is a short walk away (and you can take flying lessons while here, if your French and fear dispersal are high). The Meridien is your nearest hotel neighbor; Le Barokko at the marina is one place to dine.

Count on paying over $200 for a room for 2, with breakfast, greens fees on the golf course, and facilities for tennis, windsurfing, sailing, and other water sports—and that is daily with no dinner!

✛ **Les Trois Mats** (St. François, an hour's drive east of Pointe-à-Pitre; 36 apts.) perks at the boardwalk of the marina. All residents can cook at home, in one of the studio or duplex units, or dine at one of the restaurants (La Ciboulette is tops, see below) in the marina orbit or the special spots in the village of St. François. The 2-story buildings nestle up to the shore (not beach). Each sets you up with an "outside" kitchenette, with cooking and sink facilities on the outside wall so that you cook and dine on your patio or porch. Ideal for self-sufficient types who like open-air living (bedrooms are enclosed, as are the living rooms of the duplex units) and the chance to walk to the Meridien Hotel, the casino, the golf course and the beach (at Meridien). La Chaloupe restaurant serves snack fare, including breakfasts, if you prefer not to prepare your own. Studio rates for 2 in winter figure to about $100, duplexes can take 4 (at about $150), breakfasts included. Lowest rates are spring and fall, with summer rates slightly under the winter highs. You may want to rent a car for a couple of days, but it's not essential for day-to-day living. There's a small commissary, *Aka Denis,* in the marina complex, but for stocking up you'll need to bring things from home or head to a market in St. François.

✛ **Residences du Lagon** (St. François, Guadeloupe, F.W.I.; 20 houses) ribbon the shore, to the left of Hamak (which is to the left of Meridien Hotel) as you face the sea. The "houses" are in a string, linked by their garages which provide buffers between "your" house and "mine." All units are attractively furnished, according to the tastes of the individual owners, who rent their vacation homes when they are away. The golf course is across the road; the casino is a reasonable-to-long stroll along the road; and the sea stretches outside your front patio. All the action options (water sports, tennis, etc.) are available at Meridien, but you can come home for peace and quiet between forays for fun. For details and prices, contact M. Bourgeois, E.M.I., Immeuble Leclerc, Avenue General Leclerc, Raizet, Abymes, Guadeloupe. F.W.I. Mr. Bourgeois is conversant in English as well as in his native French.

CAMPING ON GUADELOUPE is possible by arrangement with some property owners. Check with the Office du Tourisme about specific locations and, if renting a camper appeals, contact Caraibes

Loisirs Sarl, 40, Chemin de Simonnet, Section Marie Gaillard, 97190 Gosier about the small Datsun camping cars that have kitchenette, refrigerator, toilet and sleeping space for 4. Rental can include unlimited mileage.

■■

RESTAURANTS ON GUADELOUPE have only those on Martinique for competition. While other Caribbean islands/countries have one or two places for excellent food, the Antilles Françaises are speckled with them—and many of the places provide unpretentious, simple surroundings where the food reigns supreme. There are places on the 2 major islands where French haute cuisine is served, but the spice of life, for my money, comes in the creole cooking that is the essence of the French West Indies. Time-honored French culinary methods have been adapted to Caribbean ingredients. Sauces are spicy to cope with the tropical heat. Fish, beef, and chicken were curried and otherwise spiced to keep them edible in the days of no refrigerator and the recipes have been refined to thrive today. Guadeloupe's *Fête des Cuisinières,* held annually in mid-August, begins with the blessing of the platters of food prepared by the island's culinary experts and culminates in a bacchanal that follows the exuberant parade. Although the fête honors the island's best cooks, it is not the best day to sample the foods. Wait until the cook has returned to the kitchen to enjoy the best the Caribbean islands have to offer.

Special creole foods that appear on small bistro menus include *soupe du pecheur* (fisherman's soup), *blaff* (a French West Indian bouillabaise), *lambi* (conch, pounded tender and cooked), *ouassous* (local crayfish), *colombo* (curry, often *des poissons,* which means fish), *calalou* (a hearty soup, often flavored with garlic, that bears a resemblance to spinach soup), and *langouste,* the Caribbean lobster served in a variety of ways. *Accra,* a crispy, fried, spicy "fritter," usually made with cod, is often served as an appetizer, as are other nibbles with names best known to the cook.

AUTHOR'S AWARDS for Guadeloupe go to Chez Violetta, for memorable créole food, and to La Langouste on the beach at Pointe des Châteaux for an overpriced lobster that seems worth any cost with the simple setting.

During peak winter season, reservations are advisable, especially for dinner. Summertime meals can usually be spur of the moment, especially if you're willing to wait a while if all tables are filled.

Chez Rosette, in the village of Gosier, not far from most of the hotels, has become a prime example of the sad saga of tourism, in my opinion. Mme. Rosette Limol has expanded her enterprise from the single small room I first knew several years ago, after she left Auberge de la Vieille Tour to open her own place. The present modern restaurant, with creole touches in the decor and the culinary awards prominently posted, was one of my favorite places even in the new surroundings, and I said so in copy for another major guidebook when I was its author/editor. That book, I have learned, was the guide for the White House corps when they set up shop for the summit at the St. François area (with the Hamak as hub), and the press corps partied at Chez Rosette! All that publicity, and prior press, brought too much prominence to what had been a strictly personality place. On repeat visits, including one when researching for this edition, the food was merely edible and not the special memory of ages past.

La Créole-Chez Violetta, is on the outskirts of Gosier, as you head down the hill toward Ste. Anne. This was a small and special spot until additions during summer of '80 nearly tripled the size of the place. A meal shared when the building work was still in progress proved to be better than ever before, and I hope the new size hasn't interfered with the old-style cooking. Red checked cloths cover tables, and various madras patterns parade around the room on waiters and waitresses. A meal that included a mouth-watering poisson en papillotte (fish cooked in a "paper bag" of aluminium foil), spicy accras, colombo poulet (chicken curry), and soupe du pecheur (a hearty soup with fish) proved memorable for 2 of us, and—with wine and dessert—came to about 150F.

In Gosier, in addition to Chez Rosette, La Créole-Chez Violette, and Ecotel's dining, consider **Le Baoule,** on the water side of the lower road through Gosier toward Ste. Anne. **Restaurant Vietmanien** on the opposite side of that road, near Le Baoule, or **Mahogany,** the small spot to the right of Vietnamien all have casual surroundings where camaraderie is part of the mealtime ritual. **Chez Lydie** has been recommended for good créole food in surroundings simpler than Chez Violette or Rosette but speaking French is almost essential. **Chez Jacqueline,** across the road on the right heading toward Ste. Anne, is another to consider. **Le Guillaume Tell** offers some Swiss-style food on the road between Gosier and Ste. Anne. **La Finca,** in Gosier on a one-way street heading toward Pointe-à-Pitre, and **Sud American,** on the main road between the Gosier hotel grouping and the village, have South American (beef and barbecue) specialities. **La Fourchette** is a simple place by the side of the road near the juncture of the road from the Gosier hotel group and the main Pointe-à-Pitre-to-Gosier-village road. (You can walk to La Fourchette from any of the Gosier hotels.)

In the Bas du Fort area, restaurants are growing as fast as the tropical plants. **Le Marine** (seafood), **Bois Lélé** (Créole) and **Marie-Lou** (more commerical-style restaurant and disco) are cheek-by-jowl near Frantel and Port Madras hotels. **Ti Quebec,** a small white house at water's edge, and **L'Albatross** next door is also known for good seaside food. All are also easy walks from Novotel and Frantel.

On the marina side of the stub of a peninsula that is Bas du Fort, there are **Le Boucanier,** the **Route du Rhum** (snacks and entrees at picnic-style tables at the marina) and **La Plantation,** at the marina area (Port de Plaisance) where elegant surroundings help good food and service seem even better. **Le Bistrot** at Petit Havre is open only for the winter season but well worth the forethought and telephone time it takes to make a reservation for a special dinner.

In Pointe-à-Pitre, there is **L'Oasis,** known for its grilled meat, on the corner of Nozières and Boisneuf. **Le Grenier,** an air-conditioned spot not far from Place de la Victoire (and the Office du Tourisme), serves canard à l'orange (duck) for about 35F, filet de poisson (fish) and a poisson en papillotte (which I'm told is superb and is fish baked in a foil wrap) for about the same. An omelet tallies at 16F and the hors d'oeuvre offerings are exceeded only by the desserts. Frankly, I have never found myself in the heart of hot and seething Pointe-à-Pitre at noontime with a desire to linger for a long and lavish lunch and have never found much reason to head in here for dinner. When I'm on Guadeloupe, it's the Caribbean/West Indian ambiance I'm looking for, and that can't be found in downtown Pointe-à-Pitre. There are some casual, snack/bar places around the Place de la Victoire for a respite from city strolls or marketplace meandering.

For the best in-hotel dining, head for **Auberge de la Vieille Tour,** pausing perhaps for an aperitif in the Rum Keg if you have to wait for your table. Credit cards are accepted, the food is usually good, and the service is about the best in Guadeloupe. (The other hotel dining room worth visiting is that at **Salako.**)

Auberge au Grand Large, on a side street off the beach at Ste. Anne, is a bowered open-air spot for a good creole meal. You will have to have French firmly in command to know exactly what you are ordering (and to make your wants known), but a reservation here will put you in touch with some of Guadeloupe's creole atmosphere and near enough to the sea to have a swim for dessert.

Le Galion, the restaurant at Ecotel, the hotel school on the outskirts of Gosier, offers traditional Guadeloupean cuisine, as well as the best French fare. Everything is prepared under the watchful eye of a master chef who is training those for the future and served by eager staff who are learning the arts of the profession. The surroundings are antiseptic (in a modern air-conditioned room), but the service is sincere.

Relais de la Grande Soufrière, the other hotel school, is in more spectacular surroundings. Not only is the hour-long drive along the coast of Basse-Terre an interesting way to see the island, but the location of the mansion-turned-hotel in residential St. Claude is a superb, suburban setting. The food will be exceptional, if my meals are representative. Count on about 65F for a full luncheon with all flourishes (and luncheon is recommended so that you can enjoy the tour and views).

Karacoli, north of Deshaies, near the Fort Royal Club Med on the "wing " of Basse-Terre, is an informal, bathing-suit kind of place where you can leap into the sea while you wait for the next course to come—and the favorite food will probably be poisson grillée (grilled fish). Owner Lucienne Salcede speaks English, if you're timid about trespassing where you are not on firm footing with French. (A good goal on your car rental day.)

Le Barokko, near Hamak and the Meridien Hotel at St. François, occupies the space first claimed by a restaurant serving nouvelle cuisine. The menu now is mostly creole. The marina surroundings are the best of French West Indies modern. The simplicity of the straight line furnishings and decor provides a perfect foil for some interesting cuisine.

Mme. Jerco, when she was supervising the daily scene, didn't really care whether Jackie Kennedy Onassis and ex-Queen Saroya are among those who have eaten at her St. François restaurant, as some report with awed tones and wide eyes. The surroundings certainly didn't change for them, and the full creole meal continues to be the solid, substantial 8-course meal that has sent pungent aromas from the open doors and windows of this creole house since Mme. Hortense Jerco first started cooking for guests. She has now retired, but the place lives on. During a mid-day meal, researching for this edition, we were the only 2 in Mme. Jerco's small-but-special spot. Chickens wandered around underfoot, a gentle breeze blew through the open doors, and good creole food was served on glass plates perched on the plastic that covered the red-checked cloths. Pictures of Christ punctuated spots on the blue walls, and a young waitress served our meal. During height of season, seats may be full, but you can count on plenty of space on most days at other times of the year. (Credit cards are accepted, and seem an anachronism in this simple spot.) The wine you order with your meal is best by carafe, and is customarily spelled with an ice cube as your meal dawdles on. For this feast, the going tariff is about 50F; the surroundings are priceless. If you think the service takes a long time, remember that the memory lasts forever.

La Pecherie, on the shore at St. François in a reborn, patched, and re-plastered 200-year-old stone house, serves a standard menu that will cost about 55F and will give you 3 courses and a carafe of wine. The main course will be the expected grilled fish, perhaps even local lobster if that pleases your palate. Wood tables and chairs stand in porch-like surroundings, and there is usually a nice sea breeze. This has the European atmosphere known to those who head for Mediterranean shores.

■■■

PLACES WORTH FINDING ON GUADELOUPE are natural sights, with a sprinkling of fishing villages around the shore and the satellite islands offering special sights of their own. I find Pointe-à-Pitre overwhelming, and a city that is best seen from the marketplace near Place de la Victoire. (There are other city markets elsewhere, but the sloops that tie up to sell from the waterfront give this one an added ambiance.) Check at the Office du Tourisme, in an imposing Victorian building on the left as you face the park with the sea at your back, for any special events or tours that may be planned during your visit.

Basse-Terre, the westernmost wing of 2-island Guadeloupe, is mountainous, verdant, and the site of the **Parc Naturel,** which is pinpointed by the 4813-foot peak of La Soufrière. There are more than 74,100 protected acres to the park, with the waterfalls at Carbet one of the hiking goals. If you're driving on your own, make your first stop the Maison de la Forêt where you can get full details. You'll find the park headquarters by veering off at the sign on the main *traversée* which runs more than 10 miles through the park. For those who like to see their parklands in comfort, it's possible to drive along the well-paved roads, circle around to the town of Basse-Terre, and drive to the hillside suburb of St. Claude (note the affluent suburban homes, many of them well-kept models of turn-of-the-century French West Indian architecture). Your goal, before or after the drive up the mountain to the sulphur-seething vents in La Soufrière, should be Relais de la Grande Soufrière, the hotel school inn that is a special place for meals. (Call ahead to make a reservation.)

Any serious trek to and through the Parc Naturel should be preceded by a careful reading of the "Walks & Hikes" booklet (*Promenades & Randonnées*), with diagrams, description of sites and suggested hikes with approximate times and a code for degree of difficulty. (Ask for the booklet at the Office du Tourisme.) Even those who don't hike will enjoy the 10-minute walk to the *chutes* (waterfalls) from the first parking pull-off after you head into the park from Pointe-à-Pitre, following the island-splitting, well-paved *traversée*. You can swim in the rock-lined pool at the base of the falls.

The **Parc Archéologique des Roches Gravées** (Engraved Rocks) is a wide spot off the road near the wharf at Trois Rivières, which I find more interesting for the local boat service to Terre de Haut. (The rugged boat trip can be an exceptional travel experience if you like the sea and have an adventuresome spirit.) The rock carvings that "were more than likely carried out by the Arawaks" are more of a tourist lure than I care to spend time on. If you want to take a look, head to the wharf (*embarcadère*) where the boat departs for Les Saintes. (Trois Rivières is about 30 miles from Pointe-à-Pitre).

Heading east along the south coast of relatively flat Grande Terre there are fishing villages and, eventually, the easternmost point of 2-island Guadeloupe, **Pointe des Châteaux,** where a majestic tumble of black rocks is etched on the horizon. The surf comes pounding in against the rocks, and after you have "oh-ed" and "ah-ed," there's not much more to do here—unless you want to slither off to the naturalists' beach that draws enthusiasts from the nearest hotels (Meridien and Hamak), both about 20 minutes' drive away, or settle into one of the several small-but-expensive bistros and cafes that are scattered around the area.

Offshore islands are intriguing outposts which can be seen in a hurried day, flying over and back to Terre de Haut, Marie Galante, or Désirade. (The flight to Terre de Haut on Air Guadeloupe takes about 15 minutes; Désirade and Marie Galante are about 20 minutes.) A bag with your bathing suit and a towel, plus your tongue firmly wrapped around French is all that you need for an excursion to one of the small islands. (A group tour is *not* the ideal way to visit the small islands; *you* become the sight to see, and there is no way to mingle with the local life, which is about all there is to offer on these islands.)

Many of the tour desks at big hotels arrange excursions to neighboring Dominica and to St. Lucia for a day or two. Even if you are not staying at one of the biggies, it may pay to read their activities board. If there is space on one of the tours to get you to and from another island, the tour operator is usually very happy to have an extra fare. The alternative is to check with one of the travel agencies with offices in Pointe-à-Pitre.

Dominica is definitely worth finding, when you are as near as Guadeloupe. Not only is your flight south, and the swoop into Dominica's Melville Hall Airport an excursion for the adventuresome, but the island is unique and the 1-night and 2-night packages offered through the Anchorage Hotel (Box 34, Roseau, Dominica, W.I., or telex DO 619) give you the best of the island highlights in well-planned order. With a morning arrival, you will start with your safari tour through the Carib Indian Reservation, to Castle Bruce (black sand) beach and Emerald Pool, punctuated with rum punches poured from a caldron that miraculously appears from one of the Land Rovers you've been riding in. After dinner, entertainment, and overnight at the hotel, you can visit Roseau, or boat to Portsmouth to row up the Indian River before continuing for a picnic on Picard beach before you are taken to the airport. That's just one sample, and it will cost you about $120 per person, each of 2 sharing a room. (Summer is $100, and both are worth the investment.)

■■■

SPORTS ON GUADELOUPE are resort-centered. If it's action you're after, Club Méditerranée (either Caravelle or Fort Royal) are the places to head. And if **water sports** are your French focus, all major hotels have good facilities. Meridien, at St. François, includes use of equipment in your room rate. The Gosier hotels have beachside concessions for windsurfers and small sailboats. (Windsurfing has taken top action spot on the sports roster. You'll find windsurfers at *all* major hotels.) The Fort Royal Club Med is closest to Pigeon Island where the diving is best organized. The Club Meds have tennis, volleyball, sailing excursions, and all the usual water sports.

Golfers should reserve a room at Meridien, Hamak, Trois Mats, or Residences du Lagon, all on the fringes on the St. François course which opened in early 1978. (Hamak guests have no greens fees; Meridien mavens pay $15 per day of play.) If you're staying at the Gosier hotels you will have almost an hour's drive before you can negotiate for your caddy and cart to play. Greens fees for visitors who are staying at other places figure to about $20 per day, but ask specifically about greens fees and other charges if it matters to you. The 18-hole course was designed by Robert Trent Jones's group, and the pro is English-speaking (but all the caddies are not fluent in English).

Tennis enthusiasts will find courts at Holiday Inn, Arawak, Auberge de la Vieille Tour, and Salako at Gosier and the Frantel and Novotel in Bas du Fort. Meridien and Hamak also have tennis courts, near St. François.

Yachting around Guadeloupe often involves heavy seas and stiff winds when you head out as far as Terre de Haut or some of the other satellite islands. Experienced charterers can take a good-sized skippered yacht for a few days or a week.

Guadeloupe-Chartaire with offices at Appontement du Carenage, on the Gosier side of Pointe-à-Pitre has some yachts listed, as does *Guadeloupe Yachting* at Ponton du Carenage next door. *V.E.B. Nicholson & Sons, Ltd.*, the Antiguan firm with U.S. offices at 9 Chauncy Street, Cambridge, MA 02138, and *Stevens Yachts*, reached through Box 129, Stevensville, MD 21666, carry listings of yachts that put into Pointe-à-Pitre and can take on passengers for a couple of days or more.

Port de Plaisance (Pleasure Port) was established in early '80 at the Pointe-à-Pitre side of the Bas du Fort nub of land, and the yachts tied up at the marina are an impressive fleet. Check the bulletin board at the cafe, Route du Rhum, if you're an enterprising sailor looking for a bunk to some other island. Ask as you wander the marina if you are interested in picking up a charter yourself. Several of the skippers are happy to talk business, for a day or longer sail.

Guadeloupe came into sailing headlines as the western port for *La Route du Rhum,* a race from St. Malo on mainland France to Pointe-à-Pitre in fall of '78, when yachts sailed trans-Atlantic to arrive in early December. Check for information about a repeat journey if the adventure interests you.

■■

TREASURES AND TRIFLES ON GUADELOUPE are best found in seething, steamy Pointe-à-Pitre, where most of the stores for residents are located, and along the street and lanes in Gosier, the former fishing village turned holiday hub. There are shops in the hotels for essentials, and many of those shops carry resort wear imported from France as well as a few local items. In the city, the fruits and vegetables, plus dolls on which to work your witchcraft with the "weeds" (herbs) the weed women use for theirs are sold at the local market, along with a selection of baskets that the local folk use for carrying their produce and brooms they use for their housekeeping.

Boutiques are gathered at several spots, but especially in a cluster known as **Galerie Nozières** on rue de Nozières. Schoelcher, Frébault, and Nozières are the threads for most of the shops, but do not expect displays geared for visitor consumption. These shops feature household items and furniture as well as tropical clothes that visitors can buy (and use) for resort wear. Perfume is sold at **Phoenicia Rosébleu, Champs Elysées, Albert Kattar, Au Bonheur des Dames,** to name only a few stores. Most offer a 20% discount for U.S. currency traveler's checks and on some credit cards.

Vendôme features clothes, **Au Caraïbe,** and **Champs Elysées** carry an assortment of items, and fabric by the yard can be a good buy if you want to have something made up while you are here. (Ask at your hotel for the name of someone who sews; usually they will have some names and, failing that, check with the Tourist Office at Place de la Victoire.)

Across from the string of hotels that stretch out of the point from Gosier (nearest Callinago) is **La Galerie,** an attractive boutique, in its own small house, with an interesting selection of handmade dresses and other resort wear, plus some accessories and wall hangings. The **Boutique des Arts Caraïbe** is nearby, at the corner, with, as its name suggests, island made items, many of them with a creole theme.

If you are interested in quality wall hangings (and are willing to pay for them), find **Estel** at her shop near the Ecotel. All of her work is done by hand, and although she no longer puts together all the appliqués she sells, her quality is attached to everything that is available in her small-and-special shop. In addition to the appliqués that made her island-famous, she now carries some fashions and other colorful items with good design.

The main feature with shops on Guadeloupe is *not* bargain prices, but fashion. The prêt-à-porter (ready-to-wear) carries prices akin to those in Paris, and follows those fashion lines. Count on stores being closed from about 12:00 until 2:30 or so, when they open until about 5:30. Most places are closed on Saturday afternoons.

Les Saintes

When the first smudgy-faced child looks at you, silent with saucer eyes, and then looks down at his basket of warm tartes d'amour, it is difficult to resist pulling out the franc or two it takes to buy one. I've seldom hesitated, and sorrow some at the fact that commerce is now putting the tartes d'amour on the tables, sometimes just after you check into one of the small inns, and usually with a little thought to the several hands that have patted the pastry and put in the filling before cooking and handing it to me.

A tarte d'amour is a special pastry that, for me at least, is the symbol of a special island. **TERRE DE HAUT** is a few miles off the south shore of the western wing of Guadeloupe. The choppy ride across the channel to the cove that is the island's main town, also called Terre de Haut, takes about 1½ hours. Departure port is Trois Rivières, which is more than an hour's drive from Pointe-à-Pitre, across the bridge over the Rivière Salée that divides Basse-Terre and Grande-Terre, heading southeast along the coast. (The alternative route, the one followed by the day trippers who wash over the town in winter months, is to swoop onto the airstrip like a frigate bird dipping for food, after the 15-minute flight on Air Guadeloupe from the cosmopolitan (by comparison) Raizet Airport at Pointe-à-Pitre.)

Tourists are siphoned off with the locals, the fish, and the fruit, at the pier. "When we arrived here there were only 2 cars. Now there are 20, plus 2 small buses," Jacques Bouny laments. And the naturalist beach that put the Bois Joli hotel into Vacations-in-the-Buff tours in past seasons has created some problems with the island's longtime traditional population. Naturalists on the naturalist beach over the hill? Fine. But not on the streets of town. Mme. Azincourt agrees. From a perch on the narrow balcony of her *Au Coq d'Or,* a bistro overlooking the pier in the village, you can watch (and cluck over) the sprinkling of bikinied outsiders sauntering along the fisherman's beach, and then up the dock to the main street of town. They look remarkably out of place with the fishermen—who wear the big straw hat called a salako, plus blousy shirt and pants. Only the fisherman's feet are bare.

✢ **Bois Joli** (Terre de Haut, Les Saintes, Guadeloupe, F.W.I.; 21 rooms) looks like a lump of sugar, sitting on a green hillside, about 10 minutes' drive from the small airstrip, less from the town of Terre de Haut. Although the inn is "home" for many who head by daylight to the nudist beaches, Mme. Bouny plainly says in animated French that vacationing in the buff is "pas pour tout le monde," and is certainly not for her dining room, for the hotel's own beach, or for her young children who call this inn home. Speaking French will add to your holiday, whether you stay in the modest but comfortable rooms (shared bath) in the main house or in one of the simply furnished cottages down the slope, nearer the beach. Jacques Bouny assists with fishing, scuba diving, exploring, and speedy boat trips around to the nude bathing beach if you don't want to walk up and over the hill. A rare treat, this place will appeal to Caribbeanists who like their islands casual, with French flair and natural surroundings. Winter rates for 2, breakfasts included, are about $40.

✤ **La Saintoise** (Terre de Haut, Les Saintes, Guadeloupe, F.W.I.; 10 rooms) stands at water's edge, in the village where the boat docks from Trois-Rivières on the main island of Guadeloupe. The building is boxy; rooms are on the second floor, simply furnished and had an extra charge for water which I hope will have been incorporated into your room rate by the time you visit. A very simple place that has a popular restaurant, seaside. Fresh seafood is excellent, as are surroundings at evening, or at lunch if you are there when the groups from Guadeloupe are not. Daily rate of about $40 for 2, is modest enough but double it for estimates of meals, water, taxes, and tips. (The price is high because the demand is; there aren't many rooms on this speck and the inn is popular with the French.)

✤ **Kanaoa** (Terre de Haut, Les Saintes, Guadeloupe, F.W.I.; 10 rooms) punctuates the northern "end" of the harbor cove of Terre de Haut, at the shore below the hill capping Fort Napoléon. The 2-storied small spot sifts its self-sufficient guests onto a breeze-swept terrace for sipping and supping. There's a patch of gray sand shared with the fishermen, and a village ambiance at the inn. Surroundings are simple and hospitality sincere, but there's nothing fancy about the inn that is run by Theo Giorgi from Guadeloupe's Basse-Terre and his wife, who was born on this island. Most rooms have showers, 3 have sea view, and you can count on paying about $30 for 2, all meals extra.

✤ **Jeanne d'Arc** (Terre de Haut, Les Saintes, Guadeloupe, F.W.I.; 10 rooms) is a new place opened by Monsieur Vala, who hails from another of Les Saintes. Rooms in the boxy cement building, shore-side, are simple, and convenient to the heart of town where the fishermen pull in their boats. Rates are about $55, with breakfasts and dinners for 2. Hospitality is high (if you speak French), and the terrace at "back" faces on the seashore.

■■■

HOUSEKEEPING HOLIDAYS are possible on Terre de Haut, if you are lucky enough to get one of the apartments at **La Colline,** up a perilously steep cement slab drive with a gate that is sometimes closed. There are 8 bungalows, but a couple of them are on long-term rental (wise folk), so what's left is about 6. *Allamanda* has an open kitchen unit, with orange formica counters, a living room, with a black plastic couch with cushions, bedroom and bath. There's a balcony with a spectacular view—and that view is shared by any of the cluster of cottages. If you rent one of these (for about $200 per week) you can cook at home, after you've negotiated with the local baker and fishermen (in French), or you can go to one of the restaurants a long walk down the hill and around the bay (and an even longer walk home).

For other homes to rent on Terre de Haut, contact the Office du Tourisme in Pointe-à-Pitre, Guadeloupe.

■■■

PLACES WORTH FINDING ON TERRE DE HAUT begin with the island itself. This is a gem for people who like their islands "pure." The town of Terre de Haut is the main metropolis—with its half-dozen short streets, its gray sand strand that separates sea from seawall and provides platform for the fishing boats that get pulled up when the catch is completed, and the few small bistros that speckle storefronts. Chickens share the sandy streets with the dozen or so cars—and the day trippers that come by small plane-load from the Club Meds and other Guadeloupean hotels.

Fort Napoléon (open 8:30 to 5:30 daily; 30F entrance) was built in the 18th century, when British Admiral Rodney grappled with French Admiral de Grasse for supremacy of the seas. (Rodney sent de Grasse scuttling in the Battle of Les Saintes in 1782.) There's a small museum of island history and artifacts, but it is the fort walls and the buildings inside the walls that are worth the climb to get here. Club de Vieux Manoir, a French-based organization that moves into derelict forts and buildings and puts its members to work patching and pulling weeds from buildings and grounds, has a group that sets up camp here. For a small fee, campers/workers spend part of the day working on the restoration and the rest of the time enjoying their vacation on Terre de Haut.

Haiti

Office National du Tourisme, Avenue Marie Jeanne, Port-au-Prince, Haiti. Haitian Government Tourist Office, 1270 Avenue of Americas, Suite 508, New York, NY 10020; 7100 Biscayne Blvd., Miami, FL 33138; 919 North Michigan Ave., Chicago, IL 60611; 5959 West Loop South, Suite 500, Bellaire (Houston), TX 77401; 44 Fundy, Etage F, Place Bonaventure, Montreal, Quebec H5A 1A9, Canada; 920 Yonge St., Toronto, Ontario M4W 3C7, Canada.

US$1 = 5 Haitian gourdes.
In the following text, $ refers to U.S. currency.

The pyramid of purple eggplants and uniformly scarlet tomatoes rose from a woven basket in an arrangement suitable for the centerpiece of a gala dinner party. The Haitian woman carrying this burden on her head through the pulsing, dusty downtown of Port-au-Prince seemed impervious to the commerical chaos around her. So did the man who had linked 8 chairs into a sort of hat, and his counterpart, whose headpiece was a load of intricately wrought iron. Haitian salesmen use their heads.

Sidewalk level gaps in the Victorian buildings that line the city's cross-hatch of streets ooze with colorful fabric, plastic, spices, machinery parts. and almost anything else. Ready-made clothes dance in the breezes over doorways, in a city version of the kites that thread sky-high from small settlements around the countryside.

Outside of the city, the border of the paved road is embroidered with river-washed laundry draped over cactus hedges, and small adobe houses. Haitians "from the country" weave their lifestyle onto the asphalt road. Brilliant yellow-orange mangoes loll on wood slabs, waiting for sale. The juice runs down your arm when you bite into them, and the sea that laps the shores nearby is the best wash basin.

"Give us something for our music if you're gratified; donnez nous quelque chose. . . ." The message was written in ragged letters on a board that was propped against a nearby post. The quartet that wedged itself onto a fringe of the hotel's front porch created a panoply of sounds that set smiles on the faces and sparks in the eyes of even the most somber diners. (And the couple who left without sprinkling some coins into the upturned hat by the post were greeted with a clash of cymbals.) Haitians are enterprising and good-natured about the need of money, but the average Haitian income is only about $200 per year, with a daily wage that is up to about $2.50 per day—up from the 70 cents of ten years ago.

The small boy that grew on the side of our car as soon as we slowed to stop began rubbing the headlights with a dirty cloth. A gentle cascade of "No, thank you's" had a reverse effect; the rubbing stretched onto the hood, and—after a dousing in the attending pail—the rag wrapped around the hub caps, along the doors, over the top and around to the back. His sidelong glances to the porch where we were devouring homemade *aubergine* (eggplant) with *roti* (a Haitian stew) and *poisson* (fish) seemed to get enough encouragement to continue. "No" begins to mean "yes" in Haiti, when a Haitian salesman persists. And a car wash can be accomplished for a quarter or two.

Haiti is a colorful country—sitting a few rungs up from the bottom of the list of most impoverished nations. It is full of people who use their wits (and perhaps witchcraft) to overcome substandard living conditions and whose priorities seem to be on something more immediate than material possessions. Having a big house is not a realistic goal for most Haitians, although it does seem to be top priority for some who aspire to keep pace with the President-for-Life Jean-Claude Duvalier, who maintains the Palace and several other homes. Haiti's official tourism slogan has been "Vive la différence," and nowhere in the Caribbean is "la différence" woven more tightly into the web of life than it is in this country—the first Black Republic, declared independent by its free Negro King in 1804.

Any ride through the Haitian countryside carries the impact of a Haitian painting, brilliant in its patches of primary colors. The angles and juxtapositions are all part of the scene: the maze of black people and colorful fruits; the ebony faces that crack to show a quarter moon of white shiny teeth; the iron market, so-called for its frame and lid of corrugated tin, imported from France in the 18th century and creating a chiaroscuro of hot dark people sheltered from hot brilliant sunshine in the 20th. The slant of the hillsides is just as sharp as those in Préfète DuFaut's paintings, with little ant people wearing colorful patches of clothes (when they are wearing any at all), zigzagging up and down line roads. Some say that the 5 million Haitians are scattered all over the country, hunkering in remote areas, because there they are free to do their own thing, away from the watchful eye of Haitian politics, and the toll it takes.

The sharp angles of the mountains are accentuated because there are no trees. They have been shaved off in most places—for building and by fires, sometimes for fuel. Few know (or care) that indiscriminate destruction allows the rain to wash the topsoil to the valley, or out to sea, leaving the slopes barren and incapable of bearing the fruits and food the country so desperately needs.

Haiti does not leave people untouched. It reaches into your soul with the gnatlike persistence of the swarms of its children-turned-salesmen, and tugs at your heart—and your conscience.

William Larimer Mellon, grandnephew of onetime Secretary of the U.S. Treasury Andrew Mellon, would leave the family bank and fortunes a few years after graduation from Princeton, to head into the Artibonite Valley with his wife, Gwen Grant Mellon. At this outpost, at least 3 hours' travel from Port-au-Prince, they would set up the Schweitzer clinic, now with 10 doctors, all of whom follow the devotion of their profession that led Albert Schweitzer to found the clinic in Gabon (Africa) from which this place takes its name—and ideology.

Wallace and Eleanor Turnbull came to Kenscoff in 1946, to birth and nurture their Baptist Mission, which would eventually and unobtrusively speckle the countryside with clinics, schools, and solace. Villagers would be encouraged to do handwork at home, and to bring it to Kenscoff on market day, to sell or trade for a few essentials for home.

In downtown Port-au-Prince 1700 children fold into the classrooms of Holy Trinity School where Sisters affiliated with St. Margaret's Convent in Boston, Massachusette teach and work. Some of the children will go on to the school-affiliated College of St. Pierre; others will weave their way into the Margaret Woodbury Strong (Holy Trinity) Trade School; and still others will go back to the streets or the countryside because there is no funding to do anything more. Goods in the Holy Trinity Gift Shop are parental and student efforts to help with tuition and school expenses, and all shop profits go toward scholarships.

History in Haiti is being made on the foundations of the first Black Republic which was built by four flamboyant Haitians. Toussaint L'Ouverture gained his nickname, some say, from the fact that he could make an opening (*ouverture*) in the lines of invading forces, which in the late 18th century were mostly French. He inspired Haitians to throw off the bonds of slavery. The rebellion began on August 14, 1791, with a holocaust that devoured plantations and destroyed the white privileged society, to end with the beginning of an independent Haiti. Toussaint was killed in France in 1802; Jean Jacques Dessalines declared Haiti independent in 1804—and himself Emperor Jacques I. Two years later, after he had been assassinated, Haiti would be divided north and south. The northern section, with thriving Cap François, was claimed by Henri Christophe who took a crown for himself as King Henry I and set about to build himself palaces and fortresses worthy of his kingdom. Alexandre Sabes Pétion made his capital at the coffee port at the south. Simón Bolívar, who set out from the town of Jacmel to liberate South America, would promise Pétion, in return for his protection, that he would free South America from slavery.

On these flamboyant beginnings the country of Haiti stands.

■■■

POLITICAL PICTURE: President-for-Life Jean-Claude Duvalier was 19 when he came into office on April 22, 1971, after the death of his autocratic father who became President-for-Life in 1964. "Papa Doc," as the father was known, had been elected President in 1957, after turbulent years that had included occupation of Haiti by U.S. Marines from 1915 to 1943. July 1971 marked the start of the return of U.S. aid, which had been suspended by President Kennedy in 1963 because "the money was going into pockets rather than projects and because Congress objected to propping up a dictator who was less than respectful of human life," according to Alan Riding in an article for the *Saturday Review* (5/17/75). Almost 6 months later, the Inter-American Development Bank announced a $3.2 million loan for agriculture and industrial development and $500,000 for roads and hospitals. The bank more recently has loaned $22.2 million for a road southwest to Les Cayes while the World Bank, in 1975, loaned $10 million for the road to Cap Haitien and more recently has provided funding for other agricultural and infrastructure projects. The International Development Association, a World Bank affiliate, announced a $14 million loan in May '81, and, in the past, the French government has found the money for the road to Jacmel and improvements to the airports. President Jean-Claude Duvalier raised the daily wage from 70 cents in 1971. The figure mentioned in 1980 was $2.20 *per day*. From

1971 to 1978, the national budget is reported to have risen from $51 million to $233 million, with loans and grants totalling $108 million in 1980.

Tourism in Haiti began to come into clear focus a few years ago under the able management of Haitian-born Director of the Office National du Tourisme, Jean Saurel. Saurel has been replaced by his former assistant Theo Duval, and promotion continues. Haiti's Hotel and Tourist Association is working closely with the National Tourist Office and feeder airlines to promote the country. Investment is coming into Haiti and facilities are being improved, for the estimated 5 million Haitians as well as for the expected tourists. Meanwhile, prices for tourists in many areas have just about doubled with the increase in visitors but they still are among the Caribbean's best values.

AUTHOR'S OBSERVATION: The extreme poverty that has torn at my conscience on Haitian visits in the past seemed slightly alleviated when I researched this edition. I am not inured to the poverty as much as I am impressed by the innate pride of the Haitian individual that causes him to make the most of the little he has. Cement-block houses are replacing some of the shacks in the streets and the hills around Port-au-Prince. But the cross-hatch of roads, many gutted and rock strewn, in the heart of the city are still overwhelmed by the heaviest concentration of people I have noted anywhere in the so-called modern Caribbean. Haitians seem to be happy people, but that cannot mask the poverty and the lack of economic opportunity that has sent more than 15,000 (since 1972) across treacherous seas, often in flimsy boats, in hopes of finding a better life in the United States—which many still regard as the land of opportunity. Tourism is only one crop harvested in this country, but there must be more before the Haitian economy can show signs of real stability.

CUSTOMS OF THE COUNTRY are a curious mixture of French and African. Today the recipe is distinctly Haitian, and that includes voodoo (spelled vaudou in French), which seems to pervade the air, even when you don't get to a tourist performance yourself. (It's highly unlikely that you will see anything *but* a tourist performance; the real thing is taken very seriously by the Haitians who participate. It's not a spectator sport; it is a religion.) For an interesting version of the ritual, make a reservation at Le Peristyle, south on the main road out of Port-au-Prince, where Max Beauvoir is available for "consultations sur rendez-vous" if you want some special help with a supernatural solution to a problem. He's told me about special flights—paid for by the client—to Paris and other spots to work out people's problems.

Clothes are casual, often with French flair, on the wealthy Haitians. Visitors will be comfortable in casual (not sloppy) tropical clothes, with sweater or long-sleeved shirts for evening wear and mountain journeys. Bring jeans or some sturdy trousers if you plan to ride the nags to the top of Christophe's Citadelle at Cap Haitien, or horseback ride or jungle-walk anywhere. Hiking shoes will be better than supportless sneakers if you plan to get into the hinterlands; crepe soles are better than leather for the streets in town, and for any walking you will want to do around Haiti's rutted roads. Beach resorts have French class, for the most part. Some wrap over your bikini will take care of daylight hours—and at some spots well into the evening. Keep luggage light; you can buy some things if you find yourself short.

Business suits or elegant casual clothes are worn by the upper crust—and most of those with whom the high-paying tourist will mix. The crowd in the best restaurants will be well dressed, but jacket and tie are seldom seen these days. The new equality that sets the fashion pace for other Caribbean countries is present in Haiti also. Only at the most formal special occasions will you see long skirts. Otherwise elegant, but low-key, clothes can go anywhere, and guayaberas or jacket without tie is suitable for men.

■■

MONEY MATTERS: There are two ways to travel around Haiti, and your travels may be a mix of both. The first is true tourist, paying everything in U.S. currency—which is what your hotel prices will show, and what Issa and the other art galleries will want. U.S. dollars are also what the market ladies and the omnipresent street salesmen, young and old, will want. The Haitian gourd is local currency, figured at 5 to the U.S. dollar (20¢ per gourd), but worthless outside the country although you may often receive gourds as change. If you do exchange, for small purchases on the road or in the markets, be sure to exchange only what you will use (or what you want as souvenirs). For bargaining, U.S. currency is in demand, but in a country where the annual income average is not much more than you pay a day for a hotel room, it's hard to bargain—even when you know that the local salesmen like it, think of it as a game, and price their merchandise accordingly. They seldom *expect* to get the price they ask; slightly more than half is usually more than enough.

Prices for tourist places (restaurants, most hotels) are reasonable, in my opinion, for services (and food) offered—at least according to accepted Caribbean standards.

AUTHOR'S OBSERVATION: Le Grand Value, a special April 16 through December 15 holiday inaugurated in spring of '80, is worth considering if getting the most for your dollar is crucial. It was planned to build up the slower seasons. But (as wise Caribbean travelers know) summer season is "just like winter" insofar as weather, etc. is concerned, and Haitian hotels put their best foot forward. Inquire about the 3- and 7-night holidays which you can buy with or without meals included. (My recommendation is to buy without, if you choose to base at a Port-au-Prince or Pétionville hotel. There are several excellent restaurants in and around the capital.)

ARRIVAL at the airport is much better than it used to be, now that the airport expansion is completed. If you arrive as part of a special group, you'll be whisked through, oblivious of the ritual everyone else goes through. If you come alone, speaking French will help with some of the customs questions, if any are asked. Count on "people confusion" at the luggage pick up and the departure areas. Customs will be cursory if you are an obvious tourist bent on having a good time and helping the local economy. Luggage will be lifted by handy porters, unless you get to it first. There's a tourist desk just to the left of the immigration booths; helpful staff can answer questions, advise with hotel reservations if you've arrived without any (assuming the telephone is working), and head you in the right direction for rental car or a taxi to take you where you want to go. Ask what the fare should be, if you haven't noticed the posted sign listing all hotels and their official taxi rates from the airport.

Reconfirm your flight out when you arrive and are still at the airport. Getting through by telephone may take the better part of your vacation, and if you do not reconfirm, you may be canceled—especially at height-of-season winter. Be prepared to wait (bring a book, write your postcards) at all airports, not only for the intraisland services to Cap Haitien and elsewhere, if you make those jaunts by plane, but also for your return trip away from Port-au-Prince. Haitians move at their own pace, which may not be the one you're used to.

■■■

TOURING TIPS: Taxis proliferate, but be sure before you get in one that you know what you will be paying. If you want to go touring, check with your hotel and/or the tourist office about a good guide, unless you are more interested in experimenting than in having your facts straight. Taxi rates are set for regular tourist routes: from the airport to Port-au-Prince, figure on paying about $10; to Pétionville hotels (up the hill) from the airport is about the same; and for the ride between Port-au-Prince and Jacmel, where you will be hiring a driver for the day, the rate will be about $75. The 4-hour drive to Cap Haitien is best done over a 2-day period if you want to do more than say you've been there. If this is your first time in Haiti, and you consider yourself a "timid tourist," sign on for a tour—which is usually you and your party in a car with driver/guide.

> Author's Observation: If you don't see a copy of the weekly *News of Haiti* in your hotel lobby, ask for one. Peter Hall's information-packed newspaper is invaluable for anyone wandering around Haiti with hopes of making a discovery. Air mail subscriptions are available for $25 per year, from: News of Haiti, Box E, Delmar Phipps, Port-au-Prince, Haiti.

There are flights between the Port-au-Prince airport and Cap Haitien, as well other Haitian towns, but do not expect the plane to be faster than driving. From my experience, by the time you get through waiting for the plane to depart, you could have driven.

There are rental cars, and experienced travelers may want to rent one. At height of season, plan in advance and secure a car *with* deposit. At other times, all the major firms (but by no means all the car rental firms in the capital) have a representative at the airport. Count on finding Budget, National, Hertz, and Avis. Be forewarned that many Haitians have gotten their cars in the past couple of years, and the paved roads are—for them—speedways, even when the roads curve continually. Driving is often "in the middle" of the road, and signposting is almost nonexistent. If you are staying at one of the beachside properties and want a car for mobility, write in advance to the management to make arrangements for your car at the airport. It is possible to follow those routes with a minimum of inconvenience, and, unless you want to be confined to your beach-front accommodations, you'll need a car to get into Port-au-Prince or anywhere else.

Much is said about the "tap-taps," the colorfully painted buses that the locals use. You certainly *can* use those buses yourself, but be prepared to be *very* conspicuous in this land where the average daily wage is about $2.20. You will probably represent more than the entire packed busload earns in a week! (For that reason, my recommendation is to take the taxis or even the autos that sell a seat-in-car for the regular runs between Pétionville and Port-au-Prince, where the more affluent travelers are less obvious.)

In April 1980 a fleet of air-conditioned buses arrived in the country. The buses are used for transporting groups, and, if available and not needed for group travel, some of the buses may be used on regular beach-to-the-capital routes. Check with the National Tourist Office.

■■

HOTELS in Haiti show more character (and individuality) than the crop on any other island. Some of the reason, I'm sure, is the special nature of Haiti, where all who live here seem to have magic in their souls. But another part of the reason is that there are none of the expected Caribbean assets (beaches, for example) for those staying in Port-au-Prince, or even at Pétionville, where most of the Haitian hotels are located. Only in the past few years have places begun to sprout on the beaches, and most of the beaches are an hour or so from the center city or its hillside suburb, Pétionville. Haitian inns are among the most difficult to capture in print. Each is so different from the other, and whether it's *your* kind of place or not depends on you—at the moment you are visiting this unique country. Haitian innkeeping is definitely an individual affair. In a bid for as much business as possible, some of the properties have more than one hotel representative in the U.S.; others have none. Your travel agent can track down a reservation, but know before you go that what you find when you arrive may not be what you (or he) thought you were getting. Haitians follow their own spirits. For beachside hotels, see the end of the Port-au-Prince and Petionville hotel listing.

All rooms carry a 5% government tax, and most also have a 10% gratuity which I hope reaches the staff that works for it.

AUTHOR'S AWARDS for Haitian innkeeping go to Villa Creole, a very special small hotel that offers hillside breezes and view with uniquely Haitian hospitality; to Le Plaza Holiday Inn because Fred Pierre-Louis had the vision to adapt the assets of a chain operation to a place that is Haitian to its core; and to Le Jacméliene an unusual property created by the foresight of its owner, Erick Danies, who set a precedent for modern tourism at Jacmel.

✤ **Beau Rivage** (Box W1117, Port-au-Prince, Haiti; 40 rooms) gives you a glimpse of the harbor from its place on the boulevard not far from the Yacht Club and the downtown casino (the one Miami's Mike McLaney opened about 1970). One of the buildings for the 1950 Exposition, the Beau Rivage became a hotel in 1954. Albino Mossoni has added Italian touches (and tastes) to his inn, with homemade pasta on the menu along with the creole cuisine you expect. Friday night is the creole buffet; Saturday is a barbecue by the pool with a band—and the rest of the time the downtown noises are the background "music" for your daily (and nightly) activities. There's a pool on premises, and arrangements can be made (at an additional charge) for scuba lessons, sailing, tennis, and trips to the beaches. Count on spending $60 for 2, with all meals extra this winter. One of "Haiti's 8 Hotels of Distinction," the Beau Rivage is the only inn with an Italian flair (and wine cellar) and a past that gives it the excuse for the marble and "modern 50s" architecture that has become a style of its own.

✤ **Castel Haiti** (Box 446, Port-au-Prince, Haiti; 100 rooms) is a family affair, started by father Jules Thebaud and now being managed by son Joel. The 8-story mansion is Haiti's only "high rise," perched on a hilltop on the southeastern fringe of downtown Port-au-Prince, "above" famed Oloffson, and providing the perfect landing pad for groups from Europe, Canada, and the U.S. as well as for small plane-flying clubs. The mix includes a lively vacation crowd that seems to thrive at this hive, with pool (with green plastic "grass"), recently refurbished restaurant, and a program of nightly entertainment that mingles its music with the constant noises that float up the hillside from the life in downtown Port-au-Prince. All the rooms have recently been refurbished, which means a smaller balcony for some and new Italian bathroom fixtures in most. A hotel-operated minibus service takes guests to the beach and to Port-au-Prince center on scheduled service. (Beach cost is about $4.) Although there are special rates for groups, 2 will pay between $60 and $90 for a room, with meals extra this winter. Cars can be rented through the management; taxis hover around outside for the 5-minute drive to nearby art galleries and shops.

✣ **Hotel Choucoune** (Box 693, Pétionville, Haiti; 42 rooms) has the look of a rambling private home, with each addition built according to the taste of the members of the family who were going to live in it. The hotel sits on the downhill side of the Pétionville town square, and was, in fact, a private home that became a hotel in the late 1930s. The variety of architectural styles are tied together with several coats of white paint, and wrapped in lush foliage that softens the variety of angles, curves, and straight lines that give this place its unusual personality. Cabane Choucoune, the hotel's island-famous nightclub, was officially opened in 1940. Selden Rodman refers to Haiti's "two modern architects of taste." The "more traditional of the two is the late Robert Baussan, who had already (1937) experimented with the adaptation of African materials and forms in Pétionville's conical thatched nightclub, Cabane Choucoune, when he became Haiti's first Minister of Tourism." (The Baussan family owns Ibo Lélé Hotel and the Ibo Beach Club.) All the rooms at Choucoune (which means "thatched roof") have private bath, each has its own view and personality, some are huge, and all have air conditioners (and most of them work). There's a pool at the "back" of the house, which you'll find when you stroll through the front "lobby" that has the cluttered feeling of a home built more for winters known to the north than for the sunny, tropical, hillside hotel. Saturday evening is the liveliest time, when the Cabane Choucoune Night Club thunders with one of the special Haitian shows, drums, and Haitian merengue rhythms. (The $5 entry charge paid by the general public is waived for guests over-nighting at Hotel Choucoune.) Rates for a winter night for 2 at the Choucoune run about $70, meals extra, and the hotel is reportedly popular with Dominicans who fly in from the other "half" of this two nation island.

✣ **El Rancho** (Box 71, Pétionville, Haiti; 115 rooms plus 15 suites) seems like a stage set, and when Albert Silvera's silver Rolls–Royce revs up in the porte cochere before it roars (perhaps with you in it) down the circuitous route to Port-au-Prince, you could be in another world—far, far away from the surroundings where the average income is the lowest in the Caribbean at about $200 per year, and the "salesmen" besiege you when you walk away from the carefully enclosed confines of this lavish spot. Back in 1950, Albert Silvera called this place home—and a spectacular home it was, with a view over the plains that is breathtaking when the mist is rising (and at almost anytime, as you stand beside the pool and overlook the valley). The building on the left of the entrance (now filled with luxury suites) was the original house. The string of bungalows, now the minimum-rate rooms, were the first expansion into the hotel operation—and all those rooms were completely refurbished in fall of 1977. They rim part of one of the 3 pools that cluster at the center of the property and are terraced with a glazed pebble layer that looks like a sesame candy bar. The original home has been incorporated into what is now a resort nugget, with tennis courts; palatial suites named—in French and English—the Presidential Suite, Ambassador Suite, Apollo Suite, and Haitian Suite; a disco that is lively when the guest list is, and a dining room—or series of same, indoors and out—where you can get good food, well-served at resort prices. The newest rooms—the honeymoon rooms—are *vast*, with a bed that is bigger than a lot of Caribbean hotel rooms, and a bathroom that's a showplace of marble, "gold" faucets, bidet, and the usual plumbing. The design and fixtures for the bathroom, I was told, were seen by Silvera in Paris (where he keeps one of his Lamborghinis), designed for him by Kohler in the U.S. (where he has a Rolls and a Ferrari in Florida) and installed in his best rooms here in Haiti (where he has another Rolls and another Lamborghini). You're buttoned into air conditioning with these palatial quarters, down long halls that branch off from the public rooms. The suites, in the building to the left of the entrance, overlook the pool—or at least the balconies do. The several rooms are huge, and in the Apollo Suite, the most prominent piece of furniture is a purple plastic couch. (The Haitian Suite has colorful wood accents.)

Although there are others on his staff, and some of them spend their lives around this place, there's very little that does not know (and show) the flair and fantasies of Albert Silvera; his personality pervades El Rancho; his efforts to keep up with the travel market are some of the reasons you'll have a choice of a honeymoon package (where you *should* be met at the airport in the Rolls Royce, if all the messages get to the right people so that the people get to the right place). His own folder calls the hotel "more like a sprawling estate than a hotel, the kind you might have seen in Hollywood in the 1920s" and I'd say that the folder is right on. Rates for a suite hit $150 for 2, breakfasts included (other meals extra); the rooms with marble bath are $90, and the minimum rate room for 2 is $70. Ask about special week-long package rates.

✢ **Habitation Leclerc** (Martissant, Port-au-Prince, Haiti; 44 villas and suites plus 26 rooms) takes its name, and perhaps its lifestyle, from Napoleon's sister, Pauline Bonaparte Leclerc, who was married to the general sent by Napoleon to protect his interests in Haiti. (He failed.) This palatial spot, festooned in tropical plants, punctuated with pools (to which a barman will bring you a drink at your bidding), is reached by a drive through some of the most awesome poverty of Port-au-Prince. I find the juxtaposition difficult, but if you can go into some trance that leaves you untouched by the squalor you pass to get here, the elegant estate leaves nothing out for the sybarite's life. Opened with fanfare, and a planeload of the "beautiful people" that brought the guest list to 1500 on a January Thursday in 1974 (the 3rd, if it matters), Habitation Leclerc was called "the most extraordinary, lascivious and decadent place in the world." More than $1.8 million has been pumped into bringing (and keeping) this resort alive, and one glance at the spectacular stone construction, the eye-blinking chandeliers that punctuate the elegant open-to-breezes dining room, the lush foliage, and the picture-perfect appointments tells you where some of the money went. Service may have slipped some since the first few opening weeks, but as a resort that recreates the opulent era better known in Europe, this place sets high standards. Habitation Leclerc set a pace for itself that it seems hard put to maintain in these days and times. Although package holidays were not part of the original dream, they are now part of the plan. Check with your travel agent about special honeymoon and other plans. Count on a lot of walks through almost jungle-like growth to reach some rooms. The food *is* good, if my sampling is true to form; the setting is superb. Olivier Coquelin, the talented dreamer who served as president of Habitation Leclerc (and who spirited New York's first discos to instant fame and still maintains the tempo at that city's Hippopotamus), was the creator of this special place, but he "stepped out" in early '80, and Pyramid Management (based in Louisiana) took over. They have lavished more than $500,000 and countless hours on this place. For people who want the pampered and perfect life, and can enjoy it amid poverty, this place may be ideal. The $200 per winter night for 2, includes breakfast with your room, and allows you to dally in a dream that can include a sumptuous tile-floored, open-air room with

sunken bath and no-wall bathroom, or a room (at about $150 for 2)
in the newer Résidence Pauline, where you will also have a sunken
bath (and a bathroom with walls), plus a shared pool with your air-
conditioned, balconied room. The *Hippopotamus* disco on location
draws its following from guests here and at other hotels, and the
handful of Haitians who can afford it, but the addition for the season
of '80–'81 is the sister resort at Cocoyer (see below) to which day
excursions are planned.

✝ **Ibo Lélé Hotel** (Box 1237, Pétionville, Haiti; 70 rooms plus 16
suites) comes closest to being Haiti's complete resort, although the
"annexes" that make that comment possibly involve a 45-minute
ride and short boat trip to Caique Island for the Ibo Beach water
sports and sand and a half-hour drive up to a height of 6000 feet to
the riding stables where the Baussans keep their horses, which
guests are encouraged to ride. On the Pétionville premises for the
core hotel, there's a pool, a game room (with slot machines), and the
Club Shango cabaret, which has some of the best Haitian talent for
shows. (Arrangements have been made for weekly performances by
the Bacalou Folkloric group.) The Baussan family-owned hotel has
grown from modest mansion beginnings to its present size with the
help of the late Robert Baussan, whom Selden Rodman, noted Haitian enthusiast (and art patron) called "one of Haiti's two modern
architects of taste." Robert Baussan, father of Jacques Baussan and
of Michele Chassagne who manages Ibo Beach, built the Cabane
Chouconne nightclub in 1937 when he was the country's Minister
of Tourism, and turned Ibo Lélé into a hotel in 1949. Pictures of him
with recogizable celebrities festoon the entrance walls. Son Jacques
Baussan has taken the management reins, adding his own innkeeping flair, some of which was acquired during studies in Lausanne and Madrid, and a lot acquired "on the job" here. Rooms vary,
depending on when they were built as part of the complex of several
buildings that now sprawl over the hillside above Pétionville (you
can count on a breeze at this lofty perch). Most have a spectacular
view over the valley that spreads out below, but if you want a room
near the pool, say so. Some are a long stroll from the sun-sitting area.
Jacques Baussan has been an active member of Haiti's hotel association, and a participant in the activities of the Caribbean Hotel Association; Ibo Lélé's membership in "Haiti's 8 Hotels of Distinction"
gives guests dine-around options at one or more of the other 7 (depending on how long you are staying). Count on paying between
$65 and $85, with higher rates for the new suites, for 2, breakfast
included.

✤ **Marabou** (Rue Archer, Pétionville, Haiti; 14 rooms) is one of the Caribbean's marvelous inns that mixes the special qualities of its owner/manager with a variety of guest services to come up with a unique recipe of hospitality. Mme. Odette Wiener, a dedicated dancer who sparked enthusiasm among many of Haiti's young and has "created" a talented dance company, oversees her home-turned-inn with an occasional glance that is all that most guests need. There is nothing fancy here; simplicity in rooms, furnishings, and style are the keynotes, but the hospitality is sincere. There's a small pool that can be reached from the few rooms that border one side or by the main entrance, and a dining room at the back of the house where you have to advise at breakfast if you plan to be "home" for dinner. The house is nestled on a side street just off the main park at Pétionville "behind" St. Pierre Church (and a short walk from several restaurants, including Chez Gerard and La Belle Epoque). Not for demanding travelers, Marabou may be ideal if you want to sink into an anonymous existence where you will be accepted for just what you are. This is no place for pretenses. Room rates for 2 figure at about $40, breakfast included.

✤ **Montana** (Box 523, Pétionville, Haiti; 50 rooms) makes the most of its solitary location, at a residential Cul de Sac, on a hillside half way up from Port-au-Prince and halfway down from Pétionville. This is a family operation, owned and managed by Frank Cardoza and his daughter, Nadine Riedl. Moderate rates (from $40 to $60 for 2, breakfast included in winter) make this a haven for those who appreciate a family-style hotel, with pool and picture-perfect view. The modern rooms are boxy with stucco walls that are painted white, glass-louvered window panels to open up for breeze and view, private bath, and adequate furnishings. This is a simple, modern home-turned-inn, with a growing following of value-seekers. (The public cars that make the run between Pétionville and Port-au-Prince pass not too far from the main road turnoff to the inn.) One of "Haiti's Hotels of Distinction."

✤ **Oloffson Hotel** (Box W120, Port-au-Prince, Haiti; 23 rooms) has a mystique. There's no doubt about that. I also suspect a bit of Haitian vaudou, because those of us who have stayed here *know* the place is outrageously priced for rooms I've seen with wilting wood walls, bugs that share the corners, faucets that may not work (and that spurt tepid water when they do), clothes "racks" that subsitute as closets, and a series of rooms that can charitably be said to "have personality"—and legitimately do. This is a place the late Oliver Messel, a man who was wise enough to live in comfortable (elegant) digs in Barbados, suggested for his former niece-in-law, England's fun-loving Princess Margaret. (She went elsewhere, I believe.) Among the names bandied about (and attached to special suites and rooms) are John Gielgud, James Jones (who married here), Anne Bancroft, Truman Capote, Charles Addams, and a host of lesser lights. It is turning into a place where people go to see who goes here, and usually end up looking at each other. It was a Frenchman, Roger Coster, who injected the first shot of individuality—if you want to discount the living legends about late-19th-century President S. D. Sam who built it as his Palace and the fact that the hotel did hospital duty during a tenure from 1915 when U.S. Marines added the maternity wing. The Victorian mansion, with its 3 stories, its bowered entrance stairs, its separate "cottages," some of which are air-conditioned, is a wicked wood structure that would have been the perfect dwelling for the Charles Addams spook characters if it was painted something other than its pristine white. There's a small pool, a bar percolating with wicker, wood, calico, and Haitian art, a dining area that seems more like a bowered courtyard, and a range of rooms that defies easy description. If character places are your choice, and you have a character that fits in, paying from $65 to $120 (for the Sir John Gielgud Suite) for 2 in winter, breakfast included, may seem perfect. Al Seitz bought the inn in 1960, married Suzanne here, and now is owner-in-residence, overseeing a staff of 30 who care for the guests in the 23 rooms.

✤ **Park Hotel** (25 Rue Capois, Port-au-Prince, Haiti; 40 rooms) claims a patch of street a few doors from Le Plaza Holiday Inn and facing the park near the Palace. Air-conditioned rooms in the single-story motel-style blocks surround the swimming pool. The porch facing the garden has become a popular spot for in-town meeting and greeting, since the small hotel faces the central square, only a short walk from the museums, the National Palace, several shops, and a longer walk from the confusion of the iron market. Rates for 2 are under $50. Guests have the option to head out to sea on a 40-foot trawler, the Marie Ange II owned by Eyroll Assad and Jean Grimaldi. Charge for an excursion to Grand Banc is $9.

✤ **Le Picardie** (Petionville, Haiti; 11 rooms) places high on any list for its restaurant, always a favorite for those who search out small places with very special food. Each room is different, but all are furnished Haitian-style, with artistic touches. Count on finding casual, guesthouse atmosphere with memorable mealtimes. Rates for 2, breakfasts and dinners daily, figure to about $75 this winter.

✤ **Le Plaza Holiday Inn** (Box 338, Rue Capois, Port-au-Prince, Haiti; 80 rooms) sets a new and welcomed standard for Holiday Inns in foreign countries. Thanks to the exceptional talent (and patience) of owner Fred Pierre-Louis, the Haitian element is intertwined so skillfully with the expected Holiday Inn requirements that the result is a splendidly efficient hotel—with phones in rooms, ice machines, and even television (in a country that only has TV from about 7:30 to 10 in the evening), plus the international connections that include the reservations service—that is uniquely Haitian in appearance. Furniture is the woven-reed work and carved wood that is made in Haiti; food in the restaurant (especially the Sunday-night buffet) is Haitian (be sure to try the aubergine, as eggplant is known in French). The pool is an oasis in the middle of a steamy, throbbing city, and all rooms have the HI 2 double beds, plus modern bath. As the first chain hotel to establish in Haiti, Le Plaza Holiday Inn sets high standards. Businessmen will love it, as will vacationers who want to know they will have the expected American conveniences. Rates this winter may range as high as $90 for a 2-bedroom suite, but comfortable doubles are from $53 to $65, all meals extra.

✤ **Prince Hotel** (Box 2151, Port-au-Prince, Haiti; 32 rooms) preempted one of those marvelous old mansions and put the whole thing to rights with a scrub-and-paint routine that was worked in tandem with a lot of hammering and sawing to give you a special inn. It opened in January 1975 and 11 new rooms with good views of the busy port of the city were added in early '80. Raymond Chancy is your host, and the paintings of his late wife Nanotte hang around many of the walls, along with works by other Haitian artists (Bernard Sejourne for one). A waterfall "tumbles" through the bar (intentionally), and French and creole specialties are served in the small, attractive dining room. Haitian mahogany furniture puts the struts under you as you lounge around your inn, where you'll be paying about $40 for 2. (Another of the Hotels of Distinction.)

✤ **Royal Haitian Hotel and Casino** (Martissant, Port-au-Prince, Haiti; 80 rooms) coddles the casino crowd. When Mike McLaney took over this property a couple of years ago, he poured cash into the concrete, air conditioning, and creature comforts, to open with fan-fare in 1974. In spite of its casino with overhead fans that whirl at a steadier tempo than the wheels at the tables below, the hotel has little of the high-rise Las Vegas sparkle and glamour; this is a Haitian hideaway for the gaming crowd, some of whom come in on charter group junkets. Set in 15 acres of "gardens" off the main road leading out of downtown Port-au-Prince toward Habitation Leclerc, the hotel has 2 pools, tennis courts lit for night play, and a boat to take you to Sand Cay for scuba and snorkeling. (Don't dream of a powdery beach; the shore near the hotel is rocky.) There's a thatched bohio near the pool for snacking and informal dinners, plus the air-conditioned "French-style" restaurant. In addition to the original rooms, which have been completely refurbished, there's a cluster of 2-story units with a separate pool behind the main building and two lavish suites, each with its own pool. The casino is at the front, closest to the drive and convenient for all with the gaming instinct. Rates for this winter run from $75 to $95 for 2 with breakfast included. (Check with the Miami office at 420 Lincoln Road, Miami Beach, FL 33139 for special gambling junkets.)

✤ **Sans Souci** (Box 722, Port-au-Prince, Haiti; 24 rooms) settled into its spot in the 1950s, when George Heraux and Viennese wife Gerty first opened their mansion-turned-inn in downtown Port-au-Prince. One of the character places, this 18th-century former indigo-plantation house has survived all the vagaries of Haitian politics, and seems to be doing just fine. The 3-story stucco-and-stone structure shows its past but pleases those who must have running water (not always hot *and* cold), and who require a modicum of comforts. Do not expect a high-rise Hilton ambiance, but then, no one coming to Haiti should be looking for that. The pool and gardens make a nice respite from the heat of center city; Sans Souci specializes in food service alfresco, including breakfast under the bougainvillea (or in your room, if you insist and advise the night before). The air-conditioned bar, through the lobby and on your left, has its collection of regulars, as does the creole buffet on Sundays at noon. Your room for 2 this winter figures to about $50, including breakfasts.

✤ **Splendid** (Box 1214, Avenue N, Port-au-Prince, Haiti; 52 rooms) sits in a residential area, about 7 minutes from the heart of downtown Port-au-Prince. The minute you see the white front steps that lead out of the courtyard, you will know this is special. Built at the turn of the century, the hotel was a Danish merchant's mansion before it became one of Haiti's first hostelries. *La Bougainvillée*, with its noteworthy tapestry and memorable food, is a restaurant worth finding! Although most of your meals will be served in the newer section of the main house (with view over pool and garden), there's an open-air dining area near the pool that is used for breakfasts. The pool is perfect for sunning and splashing, and a conversation with Wolfgang Wagner, German-born hotelier who has called this home for 25 years or so, can head you in the right direction for island exploring. Twelve very modern rooms were added in spring of '80. All the rooms have air conditioners, private bath, telephone, and radio, but the 7 rooms in the original old mansion give you a lot of character for your cash. All year rates range from $50 to $55 for 2, meals extra. One of "Haiti's Hotels of Distinction."

✛ **Villa Créole** (Box 126, Pétionville, Haiti; 80 rooms) continues to top my list of Haitian favorites. It climbed into my heart a decade or more ago when it was "home" by happenstance on my first visit to Haiti. Since I found the Haitian encounter a baffling convolution of appalling poverty, happy people, consummate luxury, and wretched illness, the comforting confines of the stretched out home-turned-inn that is Villa Créole suited my soul. Dr. Reindal Assad, a handsome gentleman, accomplished medical doctor, and former head of the Conseil National du Tourisme in the days of Papa Doc, actively oversees his hotel. The place when I first knew it was small (about half its present size), but the feeling today is the same. The food (now breakfast only, with your room rate) is best when served under the almond tree, poolside, but dinner—served under man-made cover on the other side of the pool—is special also. Gaze out over the view of the valley that stretches out "behind" the pool, and somehow speed becomes unimportant. As one of the hotel's leaflets claim, "With us you have time for everything because we have time for you." You will and they do. Rooms are air-conditioned, all have balconies (or small porches), some are bigger and better than others and room 400 by the pool (where you can hear the staff whisking the eggs for the breakfast omelet) is a special favorite. Rates for 2 this winter run about $70 for the deluxe room; special deluxe (bigger and better view) is $80, full breakfasts included—and dinner available at $10 to $12 per person.

Hotels on the beaches: Haitian beaches are a varied lot, and some of the strands of sand are a far cry from the white powder you may have come to expect if you've sampled the shoreline of Grand Cayman, Aruba's Palm Beach, or places in the Virgin Islands. Some

Haitian beaches are pebbly, and some of the resorts bear close resemblance to places you'll expect to find on the Mediterranean shores. Sophisticated travelers will probably enjoy these sometimes off-beat spots; those who prefer the conservative Caribbean, with white sand and country-club lifestyle will probably be happier elsewhere.

✠ **Club Meditérranée** (Montrouis, Haiti; 350 units) captures one of Haiti's best beaches, for Le Club's 4th Caribbean venture. (Other Club Med's are located in Martinique and Guadeloupe, which has two and the 5th Club Med is at Punta Cana in the Dominican Republic.) Following the ritual of one week with beads to use as on-the-spot cash, the Haitian Club Med is a great addition. The spirit of the Haitian seems to me to be closer to what Club Med is all about than any of the other CM properties I know. The facilities are spectacular—with colorful, bright (to fade to pastel, I hope) stucco units scattered at the beach, surrounding pools and public rooms, and a complete activities schedule, with a special grill restaurant (for those who want their fresh fish simply served), an area serving Haitian specialities, and the usual trays and tubs of "good old American" expecteds served family style with carafes of wine. American Airlines is the carrier from New York for the Club Med weeks, and Air Florida serves the club from Miami. Inquire about special weekend plans, an innovation for summer of '81 that may be continued if it proves successful. "Discover Club Med in a Long Weekend" was offered for $150 per person. Know before you go that the club is almost a 1½-hour drive north along the shore from Port-au-Prince airport, so an excursion to any place else in this country (expect Xaragua Hotel nearby) is an all-day, extensive-driving affair. The club is intended as a one-stop, one-price holiday, and all the action options (tennis, water sports, horseback riding, etc.) are here. Count on paying $655 to $745 for a winter week, for each of 2 sharing a room, and all "on the spot" expenses including tipping are in that fee; airfare is extra.

✠ **Cocoyer** (off Petit Goâve, Haiti) is a dream of Oliver Coquelin, the super-imaginative, talented creator of Habitation Leclerc. This place may also be your dream, if symbols of the sumptuous, tropical life Haitian (akin to Tahitian) style, set among palms on a powdery beach, are your idea of heaven. Opened "officially" in spring of 1980 but not really "in full swing" at press time, the idyllic island is reached by boat from Petit Goâve. Check at the Relais de L'Empereur when you arrive in Haiti for current information. I predict that this place will become a hideaway for discerning islomanes (as Laurence Durrell calls those of us who are addicted to islands), Le Relais de l'Empereur (Petit Goâve, Haiti; 10 suites) is a remarkable mansion that was home for a parade of Haitian royalty in the earliest years of the country's independence. More than $250,000 was lavished on the restoration, and the resulting 10 suites are palatial. Day trippers linger here only long enough for the speedboats to arrive to take you—and opulent picnic with plenty to drink—over to Cocoyer for a "day at the beach." Secure in paradise, you can splash around—or sunbathe—(dressed or undressed as you will). The atmosphere at Le Relais is cosmopolitan, jet set-style and may be comfortable for you if you fit in easily with "the beautiful people." Not a place for "just anyone," the Relais has assured its exclusivity by being difficult to contact. At press time, the best route is c/o Post Office Box 11399, Carrefour, Port-au-Prince, Haiti. Phone in Haiti is 5-0810, and this is one route for getting rates for the winter. They weren't available when this edition went to press.

✤ **Ibo Beach** (Box 1237, Caique Island, Haiti; 90 cottages) begged sand from nearby Gonave Island to make its beach, but its personality comes from its creator, Haitian architect Robert Baussan, who designed the simple cottages that accent the beach. His daughter, Michelle Chassagnes and her husband Raymond are resident managers. The place began as a quiet sandy retreat for the sea-seeking vacationers who had booked into the hilltop Pétionville Ibo Hotel (a good, hot 1½ hour's drive away). Settled into its own reef-rimmed island, the Ibo Beach scatters its guests around the grounds in simple cottages with private bath (shower) plus sunning area. Getting here is a sort of safari—with a combination of car or jitney bus, plus 20-minute boat ride with a liberal portion of waiting time, although Ibo Beach is "half an hour from downtown Port-au-Prince." The real pros bring some of their own equipment, but there are masks, fins, snorkels, belts, regulators, etc. on location—as well as compressors and Zodiac dive boats that can take 12 divers out to sea, but if scuba diving is crucial for a successful holiday, be sure to check about facilities prior to the time you travel. Marina facilities are available but limited. There are plans to have 500 feet of docking space with full equipment to service sailing and motor boats. The triple-tiered swimming pool has a waterfall at one level, a kiddie-sized pool at another, and a third for those who really want to swim is about 15 minutes' walk from the dock. The 3 tennis courts are lighted for night play, when you finish with dinner at the open-air casual, seafood-focused restaurant. Shuffleboard and minigolf round out the action options, for which 2 will pay from $65 to $75 for a shared room and 2 meals daily per person. Inquire about the special 3-night and 7-night sports package plans, and the split week with time at the hillside Ibo Hotel.

♣ **Kaloa Beach Resort** (Box 2161, Port-au-Prince, Haiti; 39 units) was a dream of Eden in the minds of its owner/builders. Unfortunately, as all have found, the Garden of Eden doesn't spring full grown into the modern world. For one thing, this place is *way* out (more than an hour from Port-au-Prince), and by the time most people have survived the unusual atmosphere of Haiti's Port-au-Prince airport, and have hired a cab for the 36-mile ride to get here (and paid the $60 fare), one's expectations can easily exceed the reality. Kaloa can be paradise, if you are relaxed enough to take things as they are: thatched bohios to sit under to keep sun off at the shore, a small pool, sandy beach, shingle-roofed center hub where dining is slow, alfresco, with the best bet the grilled local lobster (expensive, but good). Property owners have 385 acres to develop, part of it as a long-promised golf course *still* in the works (a comment correct since the '79 edition!), but at the moment you'll be housed in one of the bungalows. Each has private sitting terrace, spacious room with a sliding glass section to open to your terrace, and a sunken bath. Haitian paintings and mahogany furniture fill the gaps, but this is essentially a rest and relax kind of place where skimpy bathing suits (if you're built to wear one) are covered with see-through fabric, when they're covered at all. "Come to nature . . . it will bring you close to each other," the colorful folder says, but you have to go a long, hot route to get here. You'll be paying about $70 for 2, 2 meals (and you'll probably take the third here too), this winter. Most people will want jeans for horseback riding in the hinterland; sun-bleached Sunfish are available for sailing from the beach; snorkelers can enjoy casting off from shore; scuba folk should come fully prepared; and bring your racket if tennis is your game. My suggestion is to take a look at this place as part of a package week (time in Port-au-Prince or Pétionville, part at the beach) before you plunk all your hard-earned cash on a week here.

♣ **Kyona Beach** (Box W-47, Port-au-Prince, Haiti; 12 units) is casual living seaside, about 45 minutes' drive from the airport and Port-au-Prince, but near enough so a lot of residents-in-the-know come here for very special alfresco dining. The thatch cover that keeps the occasional quick shower, and more often the steady sun, off your head while you dine is like a great big umbrella, with tables set beachside so you can watch the sea while you sup. Meals will run about $9 to $12 for dinner, and will be what Murial Martin and her chef dream up. (There'll be fish, and good food.) Rooms are being refurbished, but don't count on anything fancy for your beach break. A twin-bedded nook this winter will cost $60, breakfasts included, with children under 12 at $10. In addition to the beach, there's horseback riding (free), but don't count on tennis or organized sports. Skin diving is possible, if you're sure of yourself, and chances are that a 50-foot sloop may be anchored offshore for day sails.

✤ **The Bay Hotel,** also known as **Ouanga Bay** (Carries, Haiti; 40 rooms) admits that it is pronounced "Wanga" and takes its name from a Haitian vaudou word meaning "to touch with affection." That sets the tone of yet another inn that opened on Haitian beach, more than an hour's drive southwest from Port-au-Prince, but worlds away in feeling. This was "the first" place to open on the beach, in a sandy pocket not far from the holiday home of the President-for-Life who shares this strand with the likes of us. The architectural style is hard to define. There are some buildings that are low single rooms (which are to be used for the scuba groups coming from Italy this winter) and there are other balconied octagons, 2 stories with wood standing on a cement first floor. A thatched beach and water sports bar is pillar-supported, at the end of a boardwalk that leads out to sea. This complex is different, but its water sports offerings are traditional: fishing, skin diving, sailing, scuba (if you know the sport and come prepared), and waterskiing, if the boat is working. Rates for 2 are $50 to $60 with breakfast included, but this far out, you're almost captive for all meals.

✤ **Taino** (Box 1253, Grand Goâve, Haiti; 44 villas) talks about its Quisqueya rum punch, and if you have enough of them, this setting can be perfect. It's a long poke from civilization, and from the airport at Port-au-Prince. The 30 miles will take you almost an hour in a car, following the good, new road and fishhooking back toward the sea on a dirt one. (You'll pay a Haitian taxi driver about $50 or more to find it for you). The place takes its name from one of the tribes of Arawak Indians, the first settlers on this and other Caribbean islands—before the Caribs ate them all—or drove them into the sea. (Puerto Rico and Cuba are 2 areas that praise the peace-loving nature of their earliest Taino settlers.) Your villa will be an intriguing combination of Haitian beachside architecture (wood, thatch, open space), and modern, functional furnishings. The thatched roofs and wooded walkways give the place a rustic feeling that is perfect for its casual atmosphere. Built as big A-frames, units have either 3 or 5 rooms-with-bath, plus balcony or porch. There's a pool not far from the long stretch of sand bordered by trees and shared with the villagers, who sometimes set out for fishing excursions in their handmade canoes, carved from tree trunks. You can rent a piroque to paddle your own canoe. Constantly casual (no dressing up necessary), Taino Beach Village is a place to come with a couple of good books, or a very good friend—or both. It is popular with the burgeoning European groups. This is another of the beach bunks included in a split-week holiday, offered on an American Airlines package in combination with a Port-au-Prince Hotel. For *my* money, the split-week plan would be the way to survey the scene to see if this is a place you want to come back to. It deserves a look before you make your commitment. Rates for 2 this winter range from $70 to $90, depending on your room and including breakfasts.

✛ **Xaragua** (Box 1734, Deluge, Haiti; 48 rooms) looks like a piece of honeycomb. Paul Latortue's hotel sits on a sandy shore almost 50 miles (and about 2 hours' drive) north of Port-au-Prince. Few bees found this hive in the first months after the 1978 opening, but some essential promotion and some 7-night and other tours helped a bit. Heralded by Haitians (and the few others that found this place that opening year) as the first real resort hotel built with all the amenities, the Xaragua gives you a h-u-g-e room with 2 queen-sized beds, a balcony big enough for tables and chairs, and a spectacular sea view from all rooms. There are 6 suites that seem to be full-sized apartments. Although the place looks like luxury hotels you may see other places, the decor (and the staff) are beguilingly Haitian. Speed is not part of the service, but smiles are. Do not expect fast service or foolproof electricity and waterpower. There was "nothing much" around here before this hotel was built, and everyone is learning the resort systems together. Being almost 2 hours' drive from Port-au-Prince, with the new Club Med your nearest neighbor, also means that only 2 hours separate you from the north coast attractions, Cap Haitian's Citadelle and the ruins at San Souci. Check for winter plans. The water sports facilities are here but be sure someone will be on premises to guide you during your visit. Sometimes there's no one.

▪▪

RESTAURANTS are personality places in Port-au-Prince and Pétionville, the seaside city and hillside suburb that are the heart of Haiti's tourist activity. Although (alas!) you can now find "standard fare" of the Kentucky Colonel or Burger King variety, the specialities that make Haiti famous are spicy creole cooking, and some spectacular French service, sometimes with spectacular prices as well. There are few bargains, especially at the "name" places, but food is good and surroundings special. When you make your reservation (essential at all the small, special restaurants of Haiti since personal service is part of what you are paying for), be prepared to part with $25 per person. Some of the meals at hotels are worth a reservation, especially the creole night and the lobster buffet at Villa Creole.

AUTHOR'S AWARDS go to La Belle Epoque, for exceptional ambiance and unusual-and-excellent offerings; to La Lanterne (once again) for the pleasure of dining by the pool even when it rains; and to 2 less orthodox choices, Pension Craft at Jacmel for simple, island food and Ibo Beach for a mouth-watering local lobster, grilled and served in a beachside setting where bathing suits were acceptable.

La Belle Epoque on 23 rue Gregoire, near the corner of rue Villate in Pétionville, is another of the former private homes-turned-restaurant. A marvel of Victorian gingerbread, La Belle Epoque devotes its main-floor rooms to the informal pub-like bar. The dining area with main room and balcony tables is upstairs. Even when the weather's "inclement," as it was during our recent visit, the surroundings are straight from a stage set. A huge tree, known locally as a Sopodillo, umbrellas the outdoor-terrace area. Diners lucky enough to get an upstairs terrace table are practically tucked into its branches. There's a 1920 Mercedes–Benz parked in the driveway, permanently from my observations, and a 1920s atmosphere that washes over all. Repeaters know that you can help yourself to the salad bar, usually set up on a corner of the upstairs balcony. Staff are costumed: the men accented with boaters and vests; the ladies in long, organdy-type dresses. Food is exceptional, with soupe de lambi (conch), delicious escargots de Kenscoff (local snails). Red snapper, crevettes panees (fried shrimp), and other interesting entrees. Count on a total tally of $20 per person if you go all out. Well worth the evening out, La Belle Epoque is open daily except Sundays.

La Bougainvillée, in the Hotel Splendid on rue N in downtown Port-au-Prince, deserves special mention not only for the setting, but also for the food. Popular with businessmen who don't want to battle traffic to get out of town at noon, the poolside-but-covered dining room is at its best by night-light. Study the intriguing rope weaving that provides the focus for the "end" wall if you are interested in art forms. A piano player adds to the atmosphere most evenings, but the food and surroundings are worth the visit without any other entertainment. Call for reservations for dinner.

Le Chalet Restaurant, 12 Route de Laboule, on the Kenscoff Road, past the Pétionville Police Station (follow rue Lamarre off rue Pan Americaine), features creole food with a menu that includes some specialities you may not recognize. The setting is special (as you will learn to expect from any Pétionville restaurant) in a home-like new building on the left-hand side of the road as you head toward Kenscoff. If you're not sure about your enthusiasm for creole cooking, stop by midafternoon to look at the menu. Make a reservation for dinner if you like what you see. Le Chalet is also open for lunch.

La Lanterne, on rue Borno, still sits near the top of my list of special places for Haitian dining. Follow the signs from the Pétionville Police Station at Place St. Pierre out, up and over the bridge. Brace yourself for a labyrinth of one-way streets that make returning to Pétionville center a challenge. Edwidge and George Kenn de Balinthazy continue to offer some of the country's best food, and the surroundings—especially if you sit poolside—are superb. Built on some property that has been in Edwidge Kenn's family for generations, the restaurant building is new, but noteworthy not only for its own structure but for the collection of Haitian paintings that George Kenn has put on the walls. Although the back-room cocktail lounge is not my favorite part of the decor (too much like New York for my taste), its function as a "waiting room" for those who arrive before their table is ready is useful. The list of offerings is awesome, and enough to make me wonder how a chef can prepare *all* those selections with equal finesse. Count on fish to be fresh, lobster to be local, and sauces to have a Swiss flair from a former Swiss chef who taught some secrets to the present Haitian one. This is a place to enjoy the ceremony of good dining in serene surroundings. Count on parting with at least $40 for 2, even without all the flourishes. Make a reservation, especially for dinner in winter season, since this nook has a devoted following among residents. Open for lunch and dinner daily, except Mondays.

Chez Gérard, off the square in Pétionville, settles its guests in an inside room, or on the alfresco "porch" where the trees dip into the dining area. Another home-turned-dining-spot, the atmosphere is that of a tropical hideaway, but the food is essentially French. Count on top quality with your top prices, and order wine to set the proper tone. No place for a rushed meal, Chez Gérard will turn your dinner hour into the evening's entertainment.

Sans Souci, a 24-room inn in a residential area of Port-au-Prince, serves dinner to outsiders by reservation. In addition to the expected creole fare, Gerty Heraux's Viennese specialties are worth investigating. Tuesday night is the traditional evening for candle-light barbecue and dinner dancing, but plan on coming here for Sunday luncheon if you want to sample the very special creole buffet.

Beau Rivage, not far from Sans Souci, on the waterfront port, and takes its culinary cue from its Italian owner. Homemade fettucine, lasagna, and delicious gnocchi as well as veal piccata are specialties, and all are best when sampled with a bottle of Italian wine from Albino Mossoni's cellar. The dining room setting, with fountains, tropical plants and a talkative parrot named Mademoiselle Cocotte, makes the evening special, even if you order the creole cooking. Count on spending at least $15 per person, and more if you're hungry (and thirsty). Friday night is the creole buffet; Saturday is the poolside barbecue here.

■■

PLACES WORTH FINDING are a captivating combination of man-made sights, each with its own powerful appeal for its own special reason. There's Henri Christophe's Citadelle and Palace of Sans Souci in the north, the Schweitzer Hospital in the Artibonite Valley, and the Baptist Mission in the hills at Kenscoff. There are the coral reefs off Sand Cay, easily reached from Port-au-Prince and the suspected wreck of Columbus's *Santa Maria* off the north coast near Cap Haitien. And then there are the intriguing, once-thriving coffee town of Jacmel, now slumbering on the southern coast, and the hinterlands that can be visited by hiking or by horseback. The sights of the city of Port-au-Prince and those seen on the package tours put together by the island's professional promoters are by no means all of the places worth finding. Haiti has been mired in its own political problems for most of the years since its independence of 1804. The country may be slowly emerging from years of neglect and poverty, but at the moment Haiti represents a unique Caribbean country where pioneers can find plenty to challenge mind and sight.

"PORT-AU-PRINCE has 30,000 to 35,000 inhabitants, but though it is the centre of nearly all the foreign trade, it is a shabby, ill-kept, foul smelling, and most unwholesome place. It was shaken to pieces by an earthquake in 1842 and has been several times nearly burned up, but it retains its flimsy construction, speedily becomes dingy after being rebuilt, and reeks with filth at most times." The comments are those of Amos Fiske, in his *The West Indies,* published in 1899. While my own writing will not be as harsh, it is only an affection for the Haitian people that softens my sentiments. The city, in spite of an investment of millions of dollars for an exposition slated by President Dumais Estime and enthused over by Papa Doc for the 1950s, is a seething caldron of humanity that I usually find overwhelming. The brilliant white **Presidential Palace** is prominent, and best viewed across the huge park with its statue of the Maron, the Haitian slave blowing the conch shell heralding the uprising for independence which began in 1791, resulting in success in 1804. The vast, and usually people-flecked park is known as **Parc des Héroes;** some claim that the Palace was designed by a Haitian architect to resemble the Petit Palais in Paris. The main street of the city is Boulevard Jean Jacques Dessalines, named for the lieutenant of Toussaint L'Ouverture who has been called "the most powerful spirit" in Haitian history. Dessalines crowned himself Emperor in 1805, after he had proclaimed Haiti independent from France. In fact, it was Dessalines who named "Hayti," which had previously been known as Sainte Domingue. (Dessalines was a tyrant, who was murdered for his trouble on October 17, 1806, at Pont Rouge, the site of Bowen Field which is the present Military airport.)

Port-au-Prince is hot dusty and people-packed at midday. If you are interested in touring the town, head into the city streets at sunup and linger until midmorning before you head to beach or the hills—or your hotel pool, to emerge after the heat of the day.

AUTHOR'S OBSERVATION: The same laissez faire that makes this country a perfect place for a holiday can make an excursion to the museums an infuriating experience. Check, and double check, on hours that public buildings and stores are open (or not open) before you head for an entrance door to find it locked. A similar casual regard for hours makes meal service slow—and reservations (to be sure the place is open more than for a specific time) essential.

Cathédrale de la Sainte Trinité, rue Pavée at rue Jean Marie Guillox, is the country's best museum of Haitian art. The paintings that cover the walls are much more than decoration for the church; they represent the first real impetus for Haitian painting. The project was undertaken in 1951, and the painters took about a month to complete their works. Bishop Voegeli agreed to the decoration of his church, and the artists began their project while he was out of the country. When he returned, according to Rodman's commentary, he looked at the paintings with their religious themes and said, "Thank God they painted Haitians." The paintings were sponsored (at about $5000) by anonymous patrons. Wilson Bigaud's *Marriage of Cana* on the south transept wall covers almost 528 square feet, and incorporates two windows in the painting. (Bigaud, who was discovered at 14 by Hector Hippolyte, started with a charcoal drawing and later covered the wall with paint.) The entire work was accomplished when he was 22, several months after the mural at the altar, which is one of the main murals in the cathedral. The 3 panels are painted with different approaches: Rigaud Benoit focused on detail in his painting of the Virgin and Child; Castera Bazile makes flat figures in his Ascent to Heaven, and Philomé Obin, in the center panel of the Crucifixion, paints Christ without his beard. Overhead, tying the panels together, Gabriel Levêque sends his angels upside down, plunging between the windows with sprays of flowers. The Last Supper, logically, shows a white Judas betraying a black Christ, with his black Apostles. Obin painted this, and Bazile painted the Baptism of Christ. The intricate carvings of the choir screen were worked in 1954 by Jasmin Joseph as a memorial for Hector Hippolyte, one of the first Haitian painters to be recognized by the American artist DeWitt Peters, and a vaudou priest who painted black magic scenes. Philomé Obin, born in Cap Haitien, was the other Haitian painter singled out by Peters.

When you are saturated with the paintings, and the people they represent, leave by the side door to walk across the street to the small shop that is operated by the Episcopal sisters. You can buy handicrafts made by parents of the children who attend the school as token payment for their tuition, but check for hours when the shop is open or knock at the door of the nearby residence to see if they can open up if you are serious about buying.

Le Centre d'Art, in an old house at 56 rue de 22 Septembre, (9-5

M–F; 9-1 Sat), was the first organization to sell Haitian paintings, in the 1940s, when DeWitt Peters, who came to Haiti during the war to teach English, was director—Selden Rodman worked with him to encourage the popular arts. The Haitian elite was not enthusiastic about encouraging the development of the naive art we know today. Having been schooled on the French masters, they seemed to feel the style was too primitive. In spite of the lack of Haitian encouragement, William Calfee of the American University in Washington was invited to come to Haiti to instruct a group of local artists in the tempura technique. According to Selden Rodman's account, in his *Haiti: The Black Republic* published in 1954, five noted Haitian artists were set up in the upstairs rooms. Those who were painting primitives were given the stairwell, and Philomé Obin was ensconced in the library. While the "professionals" fussed and dawdled, Benoit, Levêque, Bigaud, Bazile, and Obin excelled, using the clear, bright colors in fast succession to bring the unique world of Haiti alive on canvas with the touch of the brush.

The **Foyer des Artes Plastiques,** established in 1950, was a splinter group from the Centre d'Art, and today there are several schools— some of them as commercially oriented as the studios set up in the lower level of Issa Gallery.

Le Musée d'Art Haitien du College St. Pierre (check about hours which change depending on interest and available funds) is another "must" for your art tour of Haiti. Opened in May 1972, the Musée's main purpose is to house the works of art sponsored by Bishop C. Alfred Voegeli when he was at Sainte Trinité Episcopal Church and responsible for sanctioning the paintings on its walls, and encouraged by American artist DeWitt Peters, who is given the credit for focusing on the talents of Haitians and establishing the Centre d'Art in the 1940s. The modern boxy Musée seems almost too stark for the colorful paintings, but perhaps the blank walls (with their supply of fingerprints) are an acceptable foil for the work of the people. The museum opened with donations from private sponsors and Le Centre d'Art plus $10,000 from the discretionary fund of Knox when he was Ambassador from the United States, but its present status depends almost entirely on private donations. Although the Musée is owned by the Episcopal Church, the independent, self-perpetuating Conseil d'Administration is charged with the responsibility of funding and daily operation.

Musée Defly (open at midday, but check for specific times, which seem to be flexible), perches not far from the Champs de Mars and the Musée d'Art Haitien. Restored and refurnished, the gingerbread mansion gives us a chance to see surroundings suitable for turn-of-the-century life in downtown Port-au-Prince. Even if museums do not usually intrigue you, this is one to be sure to see if you're curious about the intricate artistry that is in the soul of Haitians. This is a place where the Haitian heritage could have been born.

Musée National (usually open M-F 8:30-12) holds its collection in what was once a Presidential mansion, but has been the home for the National Museum since its founding in 1944. The collection assembled in the several rooms has a naive quality that relates to the Haitian paintings. The eclectic displays cover centuries and events, in no particular order and with no apparent regard for prominence. The silver pistol with which Henri Christophe shot himself is one of the prize exhibits, as is one of the 7 anchors of Christopher Columbus's *Santa Maria,* which was wrecked on Christmas night 1492 off the shores of Cap Haitien. Henri Christophe's jawbone rests near his spurs, a few buttons, and some silverware from table service at Sans Souci, and then there are some personal effects of Toussaint L'Ouverture, the impressive fighter who drew the awe and eventual wrath of Napoleon, who ordered him to France for "special honors" which included his death. President Alexandre Pétion's help to Simón Bolívar (who set off from Jacmel to liberate South America from Spanish oppression) is noted in another display with a sword given by Bolívar to Pétion. A gold plate given by Lyndon Johnson to the late President François Duvalier is in another room, with a gold sword given to President Dumarsaid Estimé (elected 1946) by Argentina's Juan Peron. Slave bells have been assembled in one of the hallways, where special prominence has been given to the bell used to herald Haiti's independence in 1804. There are a few artifacts from the country's earliest Indian settlers, as well as a room with dolls dressed in Haitian costumes of earlier times. You can count on finding a little bit of everything in this museum. While I am not a devotee of enclosed museums in tropical climates, this one has its charm.

Up in the hills, outside of shoreside Port-au-Prince the sights are limited to views, when you can glimpse them through the trees, as your road climbs to Pétionville and beyond. This residential area of private homes now has its crop of hotels, most of them low-rise places that have grown with a residential feeling of their own.

Jane Barbancourt Castle, on the road leading to Kenscoff, is a commercial place. Taxis will take you here, tours will stop here, and your own curiosity will pull your self-drive into the parking area for a visit to what I can only call a tourist trap. The Barbancourt name came to Haiti with Louis in 1765, when he arrived in the then-

French colony of St. Domingue from his home in Bordeaux, France. The sugar plantation he started near Arcahaie was where the family rum enterprise began, and it was Jane Barbancourt's grandfather who is credited with winning the international awards for L'Abbé Barbancourt. Rudolph Linge, with the Barbancourt connection, trained in a perfume factory at Grasse on the French Riviera for the liqueurs he blends! It's difficult to find pure rum here; the claim to commercial success is cordials—in a syrupy-sweet array of apricot, mango, coffee, and other flavors that I find best over ice cream (or in conversation). The huge rum casks, the castle walls, the chains and shackles are more like a Disneyland amusement than an authentic sight to see. For a hokey spot in the hillside, this place wins a prize.

KENSCOFF is a different story, especially if you head here when the bus tours are not depositing their loads of cruise ship passengers. As you weave up the mountain road, the children that thrust the trussed-up bunches of brilliant blooms in your car window on one curve will meet you at the next (they climb hills with the agility of mountain goats while you weave roads at a slightly slower pace). If you succumb to a bouquet, they expect some coins in return, and the market ladies of Kenscoff have their price as well (Friday is the big market day.) They sell for the country folk as well as for the tourists. The array is slightly less overwhelming than the caldron at the iron market in Port-au-Prince, but the sales pitch is just as persistent.

The **Baptist Mission** near Kenscoff was started with the arrival of Eleanor and Wallace Turnbull in 1946. The projects, which now include some 60 churches and many small missions ministering to country people both spiritually and through the hospitals and schools, is supported by its headquarters in Grand Rapids, Michigan. Most visitors arrive in response to the wares sold at the handcrafts center, the outlet for work done at home by Haitians who live in the countryside. This is one of the better places to buy Haitian handcrafts, and well worth a visit. Talk with some of the staff who work here about the less obvious accomplishments of the Wallaces' mission.

MILOT, the town from which you get your start, is about 45 minutes' drive from your overnight base (Mont Joli recommended) at Cap Haitien. **Sans Souci Palace,** just outside Milot, stands in ruins, majestic even with its present coats of moss and mold. When Henri Christophe, King of the north (who was born on St. Kitts) ordered this place built in the early 1800s (completed 1813), he pictured himself regal in robes, surrounded by marble and mahogany, with chandeliers providing the physical light while he provided his country's emotional light. And that is the role he played. The closest anyone has come to recreating that grandeur, according to some who tell about the ceremony, was when Marian Anderson stood on the remains of the grand staircase on January 1, 1954, to sing a celebration of Haiti's 150th anniversary. Sans Souci was Christophe's answer to the elegance (and excesses) of palace life in Europe. Versailles was one of his models, in lifestyle if not in design, and he picked up local clues from the palaces of Napoleon's sister, Pauline, married to General Leclerc and living a sybarite's life in Haiti. Although Christophe's dream may not have equaled the style of Europe's royalty as practiced on the Continent, it was far grander than anything the average Haitian had known. Selden Rodman noted that Sans Souci Palace "is built of brick overlayed with stucco four stories high and covers twenty acres of sloping ground from the sentry boxes flanking the regal steps to the royal stables which housed the King's £700 English carriage. . . . Completed in 1813, Sans Souci in Christophe's time had floors of marble and mosaic, walls of polished mahogany, and pictures, tapestries, and drapes imported from Europe. Under its floor, conduits carried a cold mountain stream—ancestor of air conditioning—to emerge below as a fountain. Installation of numerous bathrooms was a notable feature of the time." The ruins are impressive, but travelers with romance in their souls will want to make arrangements to get here at other than cruise-ship-visitor, top tourist time. A lot of the mystique is lost when guides and tourists vie for space on the moss-covered steps and around the grounds.

The **Citadelle,** hung on its clifftop like a monstrous freighter aground on a rock, overlooks the town, plains, and Caribbean Sea from its superior peak. Many of us who have made the 4-hour muleback trek to some 3000 feet above sea level scoff at the fact that cars can now travel the rutted, bumpy road that winds through the hillsides and wraps around the ridges to a flat spot that leaves only a hefty half-hour ride on a pathetic nag to reach the haunting ruins. The fact that you still have to walk for about 20 minutes, and certainly have to walk all over the ruins, is small penance for what used to be a real pilgrimage of tourism. However, it is a *little* easier (although still an adventure) to see the Citadelle now that the road is at least cleared, and I am told (but have not yet seen) that "they are fixing up the ruins." I hope not too much, since the moss and weeds were part of what gave this place its personality, providing the punctuation marks for a period in Haitian history that saw a black man, born of free Negro parents on the island of St. Kitts, move from his job as a waiter in a small Capois hotel to become King Henry I, ruler of Haiti's north. It is claimed that he took the name Christophe from the formal name of his homeland (St. Christopher), the name Henry from his love of the English rule, and his portion of land from wars with Pétion which left the latter with control of the south of Haiti. Christophe's ties with the fledgling United States included fighting in the Battle of Savannah during the American Revolution and hiring a Quaker lady as governess for his daughters, whom he called Princess Amethyst and Princess Athenaire. Devoted to creating a culture for his people in the early years of his rule, Christophe's Citadelle was the result of his eventual paranoia about invasions from the powers of Europe. The benevolent king turned tyrant to order, cajole and whip hundreds of thousands of men into submission (and 20,000 to death) to build the Citadelle. The promontory is imposing, but it would have taken an incredible advancing force to come close enough to the monumental walls for any of the 365 cannons that were hauled to this place to have been useful. The walls are *thick.* Just how thick depends on whether you follow an official Haitian tourism office folder—"12-foot thick walls took ten years to build,"—or Selden Rodman—"20-30 feet thick" and "tens of thousands toiled for sixteen years"—or the National Geographic article of January 1976, which states that "20,000 men died and hundreds of thousands of others suffered cruel hardships during some 15 years of pulling up stone, cannon, and supplies for the fortress" with "walls up to 20 feet thick. . . ."

Both the Citadelle and the ruins of Sans Souci have been designed as National Monuments, and the long-term restoration plan is in the capable hands of Albert Mangones, with assistance offered by the U.S. National Park Service.

AUTHOR'S OBSERVATION: Plan for your trek to the Citadelle in the early hours of the morning. As is the case with many Caribbean high points, the clouds settle (and the rains may come) on the peaks at midday and later. Although the ruins are impressive on their own, it's the backdrop of sea, mountains, and miles of space that makes the entire experience unforgettable.

■■

SPORTS in Haiti are not highly specialized or finely tuned. The same *laissez faire* that makes the country appealing, and puts its personality first, applies to the sports facilities. Don't count on the best court surface for your tennis, or immaculate shipshape yachts for your sails—or even a meticulously manicured course for your golf. The best sports are those pursued by the rugged individualist who gets part of his kicks out of climbing the last mile or 2 to the Citadelle in the country's north, or bushwhacking along the south shore, in spots suggested by those who live in and around Jacmel.

There are interesting places to **hike,** and some of the hotel managers are your best sources of information about where they are. **Horseback riding** can be arranged from several spots, with one of the best places the stable the Baussan family maintain at their mountain retreat about 6000 feet high. The nags that meander up the route to the Citadelle are used only by the horse-hardy these days, now that the road weaves almost to the top of the peak. Check with Walter Bussenius at Mont Joli for information about horseback riding when you head to Cap Haitien.

Golf is available at the 9-hole Pétionville Golf Club, where clubs can be rented along with your caddy. The course isn't worth hefting your clubs all the way to the country; if you're that much of a golfer, go elsewhere.

Snorkelers based in Pétionville and Port-au-Prince set out for Sand Cay by boat from the dock near the International casino at the downtown waterfront. Check with the activities desk at your hotel about taxi and/or car arrangements to get to the boat in time for the usual 10 a.m. departure. Return is about 1 p.m., but if you want to head to the cay for a picnic lunch, you can make other arrangements for return (and bring a long-sleeved shirt and plenty of sun protection).

From the beach resorts southwest of Port-au-Prince (Taino Beach) and north of the city (Kaloa, Kyona, Ouanga Bay, Xaragua, and Club Med) all **water sports** are offered. You can snorkel from the sands, or go out with guide by boat. Club Med specializes in scuba and skin diving. *Yellowbird,* a huge catamaran, takes people sailing. Departures are from the Beau Rivage marina in Port-au-Prince.

Ibo Beach Club's *Baskin in The Sun* operation seems to be the most professional **scuba** setup for beginners (and for advanced divers who want guides and suggestions). Check with the hotel, either through the Pétionville perch (Ibo Lélé) or at the beach resort if you plan to go out for the day. If you're staying here, you can find out all the details before you book.

■■
TREASURES AND TRIFLES are related to art, either painting or sewing, both done well in this country. However, for every treasure you find, you'll find yourself plowing through piles of trifles—and there comes a point when even they look good. Haitian art features bright, lively, clear colors in imaginative scenes, some so cleverly done that they look like the countryside you travel through when you head out of the city.

Individual entrepreneurs are what make Haitian shopping special. The artistic elements and love of color in every Haitian's soul come to full flower in the plying of a craft and in the selling. Sometimes (often) the actual purchase is only worth half the price you finally pay, but the ceremony of salesmanship is worth a good price of its own! Haitians are persistent salesmen, but they smile and bid you good day when they realize, finally, that you do not intend to buy. There's no grumpiness.

Prime products this season are crocheted skirts, blouses, blankets, shawls, almost anything, and the items for sale are strung from trees, walls, and arms. One of the best reasons I know for renting a car is so you can stop at will along rue Panamericaine which becomes Avenue John Brown as it slopes into Port-au-Prince fron Pétionville. Among the items for sale, in addition to the crochet work, are goatskin rugs, carved items of every sort, baskets, and other woven mats, hats, rugs, paintings (of course), and huge-and-heavy cement planters and urns. In all cases, bargaining is the only way to buy from the roadside merchants. Start at half the price and work up as they work down. The game takes time, and I, for one, have trouble bargaining when I think about the difference in the artists' and my own "disposable income."

Prices are higher than they should be at many of the art stores. I don't doubt for a minute that Issa, Nader, and other entrepreneurs are making a healthy profit on the paintings I and countless others buy. However, Issa does have a "warehouse" filled with good work, and sets some of the artists up in the studio below the main sales floor where you can watch them paint when you buy. S. E. Bottex was working on a huge canvas during one of my visits, and others come in to work with paints and supplies provided as part of their "business benefit." In addition to the hundreds of paintings at places like **Issa's** and **Nader's,** there's a pile of amateur work for $10 and $15 per painting and, when you get them away from all the others, some of them don't look so bad. Issa's gallery has a table of the ubiquitous wood carvings, most of them not worth much in my opinion, but Issa is too good a businessman to have them if no one buys. (Some artists to look for are Obin, A. Bazile, and Dubic—there are several Dubics; Abner is one). But know ahead of time that a lot of present-day Haitian art, although it is original, is mass-produced by painters who knock out several "in the style of" canvases and boards per day.

Le Centre d'Art, at 56 rue de 22 Septembre (9-5 M–F; Sat 9-1), is worth an entire day (and is mentioned as one of the "Places Worth Finding" earlier). Not only is it a museum on the second floor (which has the Collector's Room), but the center is also a shop for better-than-average crafts. Search the lower level for works by budding artists. The main floor also has works for sale, with some of them unusual modern paintings.

Red Carpet is too touristy for my investment, but the store at the end of El Rancho's driveway near the town of Pétionville is convenient.

There was a small shop just up the road in Pétionville, where a woodcraftsman was carving furniture, spindles for chairs that would have cane seats and backs and the like. I neglected to get his name, but the shop is to the left as you face Red Carpet.

Bagatelle, 84 rue Panamericaine, is a short walk up the hill along the main route to Pétionville's town square from El Rancho and Villa Creole. Although the selection, when I looked, wasn't quite as carefully chic as that at either Bagaille (farther up the hill) or at Ambiance (down the hill in Port-au-Prince), Bagatelle has several interesting dresses, shirts, and some children's clothes not seen in the other two shops. Check here for Haitian handwork (tablecloths, wall hangings, etc.)

The **Iron Market** appalls me. In spite of the number of times I have girded up for this fray, I am still overwhelmed by it and am frank to admit that the entire caldron of humanity, most of it converging as I walk through the open arches, is too much. I am easily "intimidated" by young children, old women with no teeth, cripples of both sexes, and talkative salesmen, all urging me to buy. There is mahogany among the items to buy, but watch out for the bugs in some of the woodwork (which, if bought, should be stuffed into the nearest freezer for several days to de-bug). Be sure that you know what you are bargaining for—and in the Iron Market you *must* bargain (only fools and very rich people do not). As a swarm of life, the Iron Market is akin to the souks of the Middle East. You will find tap-taps, the colorful painted Haitian buses, parked outside a vast span that piles mangoes, pineapples, potatoes, and spices with sewing machines, shoes, plastic bags, and other items that appeal to the local folk. Tortoiseshell bracelets are a good buy, but you are not supposed to bring them back into the U.S. Customs may take them; tortoise is an endangered species.

Bagaille, 23 rue Panamericaine, in Pétionville, is pronounced "bagay" and means "everything" in Creole. The shop has comfortable ladies' clothes (well-made caftans and colorful, Haitian appliquéd skirts and tops), plus sandals, crocheted tops, stitched mats with Haitian motifs, and citrus cleansing lotion from the Haitian perfume factory. Located in a stucco house-like building on the left as you head up the hill toward the town square, Bagaille is a boutique in the best sense of the word.

Holy Trinity Gift Shop, at the Ecole de la Sainte Trinite (Holy Trinity School) near the Cathédrale, has an interesting collection of handmade items, many with detailed and sometimes colorful embroidery. Monies that come from goods sold at the shop go toward the scholarship fund for the school. Everything has been made by parents or students at the school, often as a partial contribution toward tuition expenses. You can have things made to order, but allow enough time. For information about items sold, with prices and—if the catalog is still available—some descriptions, write to Ecole de la Sainte Trinite, Box 857, Port-au-Prince. Although there's no charge, I'd suggest sending a contribution, at least to cover mailing costs. This entire venture is the province (as is the school) of members of St. Margaret's Convent in Boston, MA.

Ambiance, in a marvelous gingerbread house on property that runs between Avenue N and Avenue M in downtown Port-au-Prince, has an eclectic assortment of decorator items as well as some neatly tailored clothes. Haitian-made ceramic ashtrays and other pottery are especially interesting, as are the elegant beach and evening clothes. A high-quality shop, in interesting surroundings, Ambiance gets my vote for one-stop shopping—if you want something out of the ordinary. Be sure to ask to see the work of Les Ateliers Taggart. Their tapestries and the Haitian cotton items are original, impressive, and worth trying to find a way to carry home.

Mountain Maid Self Help Project has a link with the Baptist mission in Haiti. The shop and snack place is popular for cruise-ship passengers, but is well worth a visit on the day you go up to Kenscoff. It's on the road up into the mountains, in Fermathe, and you'll find an impressive selection of quality wrought-iron work as well as hand-carved furniture that can be shipped (reliably) to arrive—eventually—on your doorstep. All the items for sale have been made by Haitians, usually at home. In addition to the usual mats and hats, inquire about the furniture that can sometimes be made to order. The Haitian chairs with woven seats are sturdy, useful reminders of your holiday here (and small ones can be shipped home with your luggage).

For last-minute shoppers: After you have come through immigration at the airport, there are a few shops with good, representative merchandise (including full-sized chairs which can be packed for shipment on your plane). Macrame bags, a small supply of overpriced paintings if you "just have to have" one and don't much care what it looks like, and bottles of special Haitian rum—Barbancourt, of course.

■■■

CAP HAITIEN was known as Cap François when it was the "Paris of the Antilles," a title also claimed by Saint-Pierre when it was a thriving city on northern Martinique. There were 25,000 people living in the city in the 18th century, when it was a social and shipping center for activities in this part of the Caribbean at a time when the riches of Central America and Mexico led adventurers farther to the west. Burned to the ground in 1802, when Henri Christophe was waging the war of independence in the north, the town was to become his capital—and his monument (also the site of his grave)—in the first quarter of the 19th century. Even if you are making your main base elsewhere, this is the first-priority daytripper's goal.

After years of slumber, Cap Haitien awakened slowly in the late 1950s. The alarm was the jubilant celebrations of 150 years of Haitian independence, when costumed Haitians reenacted the battles and lifestyle of the celebrations of January 1, 1804, and Marian Anderson sang at Sans Souci. The Norwegian Caribbean Line, to be followed by other cruise lines, discovered the port in the early '60s. Cap Haitien proved to be not only a convenient halting spot when the fuel crisis hit, but also an interesting port for an ever-increasing cruise market. The Citadelle was the main attraction, and although not everyone made the then-rugged journey to the top, everyone did talk about it—and about Cap Haitien. In 1977, the new road from Port-au-Prince brought the journey from that city to a reasonable 4-hour drive, replacing a staggering and spine-snapping almost 12 hours.

■■

HOTELS IN CAP HAITIEN are few, and all are small with the personality of the owner/manager.

AUTHOR'S AWARD goes to the properties cared for by Walter and Marie Bussenius: Mont Joli, Roi Christophe and Cormier Plage.

✣ **Brise de Mer** (Carenage, Cap Haitien, Haiti; 18 rooms) is a guesthouse by the sea. Anyone who wants a comfortably casual kind of place where hospitality is sincere, and prices are joke-low, should search out this inn. Roger and Maggy Pinkcombe are your hosts, and $35 for 2 with 2 home-cooked meals per person per day is the going rate for this winter. Don't count on fabulous furnishings, or any lavish entertainment, but you can certainly count on getting your money's worth—and much more.

✣ **Cormier Plage** (Box 70, Cap Haitien, Haiti; 30 rooms) is a spectacular and very special spot, far removed from hectic day-to-day, even any place as "hectic" (which it is not) as downtown Cap Haitien. Claiming a marvelous mile of beach, the thatched roof villas are elegantly furnished. Wood slat roofs (from what you see inside the rooms) provide a cooling atmosphere; the tradewinds do the rest. Haitian woods, burnished to fine gleam, punctuate the white walls, and the suites are places you'll be pleased to settle. Kathy Dickemare is on the spot to help with suggestions if you ever want to leave this spot for some touring, and to set up any water sports activities if you want something more strenuous than swimming and sitting in the sun. A lovely place for the languorous life, rates this winter will be $65 for 2, breakfasts and dinners daily (and you have choices for dinner here or at Mont Joli or Roi Christophe in town).

✣ **Hotel Beck** (Box 48, Cap Haitien, Haiti; 12 rooms) perches at its mountainside peak, luxuriating in acres of gardens and the option for long walks around the grounds. There are 2 pools on premises, and beaches are about half an hour's drive or a boat ride along the coast. Kurt and Kuno Beck keep this place running with German-born efficiency, mingling enough of the natural Haitian nuances into the mood to create a special enclave out of the mainstream (which admittedly runs slowly) of the life of Cap Haitien. Guests who come here seeking solace and solitude may want to head for other hills on the days and evenings when cruise ships heave into view. Passengers are invited to this inn for a folklore and voodoo show! Rates this winter for 2, with 2 meals daily per person, are about $50.

✠ **Hostellerie du Roi Christophe** (Box 34, Cap Haitien, Haiti; 20 rooms) settles at the edge of town, resplendent with legends. Not only was this a home for Napoleon's sister, Pauline Bonaparte Leclerc, and her general-husband, whom Napoleon dispatched to Haiti to control the slave uprising, but it was also Henri Christophe's jail for insurgents who did not follow the rules of the new kingdom after war had been won and independence declared. The house was built in 1724, as home for French Governor de Chatenoy, and it still looks the part. The architecture is not the wood fretwork "gingerbread" style that you may have heard about (or seen) at Port-au-Prince. This is a sturdy stucco sanctuary that has been completely refurbished and rewired by former owners Kip (Richard C.) and Caroline du Pont. When you flick the switch, the lights go on—with a little bit of luck. Walter and Marie Bussenius, known to longtime readers for their considerable accomplishments at Mont Joli, took over Roi Christophe in early '81 and linked it with Mont Joli and Cormier Plage as a trio of "fine hotels in Cap Haitien." On the spot manager is Henri-Paul Mourral. Planting thrives—and so do guests who settle into one of the superior, moderate, or standard rooms which rent at about $50 to $65 for 2, 2 meals daily included, this winter. The superior rooms have a balcony (and air conditioners). Some of the moderate rooms face the generator, and the standard rooms with ceiling fans are the ones that are sometimes affectionately called the "dungeon" rooms.

Hanging baskets help the decor in rooms, and the bar around the pool is intended as the daytime focal point for those who don't make the trek up to the Citadelle, or to one of the north shore beaches. Count on meals to be interesting Haitian fare, with true French flourishes. Don't count on finding snap-finger service and high-rise hotel flourishes but the casual, cosmopolitan air is natural—and apparent.

✠ **Mont Joli** (Box 12, Cap Haitien, Haiti; 45 rooms) caps its own hill on the northern fringe of the town that was known as the Paris of the north, not far from the ruins of Pauline Bonaparte's palace (which shouldn't be confused with Habitation Leclerc, on the site of her estate at Port-au-Prince). The nearest beach is about 20 minutes' drive ($15 taxi fare round trip) and the inn that Walter Bussenius and his wife, Marie Christine, have created for your home provides transportation to its private beach at Cormier, leaving in the morning and returning after lunch. Most of the other escapades are longer excursions, but if you follow the advice of your hosts, you can find plenty to while away several days of picnic-and-pursuit. The map that the hotel puts into your hand (or at least your room) carefully diagrams the town and the major sights, one of which is this haven of hospitality. The 45 twin-bedded rooms, many air-conditioned and all with private bath, are in several buildings around the hilltop, with villas, each with 3 bedrooms, kitchen, 2½ baths and a dining area and porch-with-a-view. Meals are served in casual comfort (jacket and tie for dinner are not required) near the pool, either on the terrace or in the restaurant. In one of the information leaflets, Walter Bussenius has said, "All of us at Mont Joli Hotel are delighted that you chose to visit us. We hope that during your holiday here the serenity, beauty and historical uniqueness of this area will refresh you, for that is the purpose of this resort. The staff and I would like you to feel free to call on us should there be anything you need. We are here to serve you, help you enjoy and refresh yourself. Please let us know if you hear water running or if a window is jammed etc. . . . Such things may escape our notice and we love fixing them! Also remember that lights attract insects (such as mosquitos, etc.); when not in use, please turn lights off." That diplomatic message just about sums up the exceptional brand of hospitality offered at this very special inn. The most expensive double figures to about $60 this winter, meals extra (at about $3.50 for breakfast, $5.50 for lunch and $8 for dinner).

✤ **PLM Village Labadie** (Cap Haitien, Haiti; 133 rooms) is an awesomely ambitious project for a spectacular tract of land, a peninsula jutting into the Caribbean not far from the town of Cap Haitien on the north coast. Planned by pros who have had plenty of Caribbean experience (the French chain is active with several properties in Guadeloupe and Martinique, in the French West Indies), the village hopes to be open by December '81. Plans at press time are to have the first of an intended 270 rooms open for vacationers, but check through your travel agent and the Haitian National Tourist Office for latest details. There are at least a half dozen beaches that fringe the hotel's property, and although 3 restaurants are planned, I'd be surprised if they are all open for this first season. This will be a "total" resort, with sea-focus. Labadie village is about 15 minutes' drive and there's very little there except fishermen and humble dwellings.

■■

JACMEL is now a speedy 2 hours' drive from Port-au-Prince. (The south shore town used to be a tortuous excursion of 8 to 12 hours, depending on how many times your car broke down and how full the streams were that you and the car would have to ford.) Any Haitian taxi driver will take you, or you can drive yourself (if you know a lot about car maintenance and enjoy wiggling and weaving roads that oncoming Haitian drivers think they own and that cows, goats, and people don't realize are used by anything that moves faster than they do).

Selden Rodman, noted art critic credited with promotion of Haitian art, has a home in Jacmel. Rodman notes that "Albert Mangones, Haiti's leading contemporary architect, thinks that the country's Victorian Gothic, in its iron as well as wooden manifestations, owes more to New Orleans than to Paris. Much as I would prefer to see the credit go to America," he comments, "I am inclined to think the style came to Haiti from France—by way of Jacmel. The Renaissance II structure carries the date 1888. It was in that year that Alexandre Gustave Eiffel was completing the famous tower that bears his name; three years before, he had designed the skeletal structure of the Statue of Liberty. But this was engineering. The *art* of wrought iron, freed from its hitherto almost exclusive dependence on ivy and acanthus motifs, was being perfected in the workshops of such master craftsmen as the Moreau brothers, Emile Robert and Edgar Brandt. Iron was 'in.' Art Nouveau was just around the corner. And Jacmel, perhaps without being conscious of it, became a repository for some of the fanciest experimentation in forged filigree and cast columns." Rodman points out that "Jacmel's glory is its dozen or so 'coffee places' built in the 1880s and 1890s out of cast iron columns, balconies and doors shipped from France and Germany as ballast for the incoming freighters," who would return to France with cargoes of coffee and other produce.

Note especially the Jacmel marketplace (which you can't miss—it's in the center of the town and all streets lead to it), and then saunter the zigzag road down to the sandy shore, past the shops that have a few good items for sale, and Selden Rodman's house, painted white, with blue trim and a plaque that says "Renaissance II." The house has an art gallery on its first floor (9:30-11, 2-4 from Dec 1 to March 1) and is open for visitors on the second floor when he is not in residence (and sometimes, also, when he is). The beach at Jacmel is not much, by other Caribbean standards, in spite of the enthusiasm of local folk (Erick Danies among them) for building a "large hotel on the beach." Ask Erick Danies about the better beaches that are a drive along the coast. I have not seen them, but he says they are there—and spectacular.

■■

HOTELS IN JACMEL are personality inns, and there are 3 I know at the moment that are worth writing about.

✤ **Hotel Craft** (Jacmel, Haiti; 20 rooms) carries its past as an important part of the present. Even when you sit on the small terrace, roadside, sipping a cool drink, the past pervades—and parades along in front of you with the people going to the market down the street. This is another world, one not yet stamped upon by the firm foot of tourism. The small inn that Erick and Marlene Danies operate with flair may have changed since my recent visit, but I hope not. It was a perfect oasis just the way it was, with the simple wood walled rooms, not all with private bath, but #8 and #9 with balconies overlooking the street. The walk up to the rooms is on a wide mahogany staircase that was once covered with a painted Haitian flag, in honor of a visit by Papa Doc when he came to see Erick Danies's grandfather. Around the walls lining the staircase are family photographs, showing the grandfather, who had used what is now the attractive, airy dining room as his office, and the grandmother with some of her grandchildren (Erick is one). This small inn is known to Haitians who come here for weekends, but it's off the beaten path—as is the whole town of Jacmel. Especially at other than winter time peak, you'll find this a very special spot. Rooms rent for a modest $35 to $50 for 2, with breakfast daily per person. There's only one place like this one in town. (Erick Danies also rents 4 "villas" in a building with a seedy entrance off one rim of the Jacmel marketplace, a slightly smaller caldron than the one in Port-au-Prince. The villas, which I'd call apartments, have modern facilities, attractive furnishings, varying sizes, and a view out the back that is better than the entrance. Inquire if you want to do your own housekeeping, with the help of a maid.)

✤ **Hotel La Jacmélienne** (Jacmel, Haiti; 26 rooms) nestles into palm trees at the edge of a pebbly beach punctuated with fishing boats and much better known to the Haitians who live in Jacmel than to the few tourists who find this enclave. Taking its cue from the former prominence of this now-sleepy town, La Jacmélienne recalls an elegant era not known in Jacmel for many years. The pool has been pressed into cement casing at the edge of the gray-sand beach, with an attractive poolside dining and drinking area, and the arcades of the 2-story hotel as a background. On the inland side of the hotel, the small and simple homes of the Jacméliennes who live in the area have been fenced off, but anyone living in a second-floor room can look into the "residential" area (where most of the living is done outside the small shacks) as you walk along the open-to-breezes hall. Rooms are designed to take advantage of trade winds, and to give every guest a very special sea view. There's an understated elegance at Erick and Marlene's new property that suggests the resort life of the French Riviera. Don't expect a lot of action, unless you head here with a cluster of friends, but count on living in a dream world where languorous life can be enjoyed. Jacmel is definitely not (and I hope never will become) your "typical tourist town." Rates are a very reasonable $50 for 2, with 2 meals per person daily, all year, making this one of the best buys in the Caribbean!

✣ **Manoir Alexandra** (36 rue d'Orléans, Jacmel, Haiti; 6 rooms) is a marvelous mansion, peering over the far edge of the park, across the expanse from street-side Hotel Craft. The building is bigger than it looks from the park; it hangs down the hillside in a couple of balconied levels, the old wood frame held to the land with lush planting. This is the home of Mme. Alexandre Vital, and speaking French when you stay here will be helpful (essential, if you want anything special). The Vital name is one of Jacmel's most venerable. Grandfather Vital arrived from France in the 1870s, to set up a coffee business buying from the locals for less than 19¢ per pound and exporting his healthy portion of what's reported to have been 700,000 bags in 1900. The legends of Jacmel include many about the German owner of this house, who was asked to leave the country in 1910. Rooms are simple, most have view, but all do not have private bath. The rate is about $20 for 2, without meals and $44 to $48 with *all* meals for 2. Ideal for adventuresome travelers who care more about people and a place with personality than about being pampered.

■■
RESTAURANTS IN JACMEL in addition to the very special dining rooms and terrace/porch areas of the 2 small inns, include a few places in former private homes on the winding streets of town.

Choubouloute is now on the "beach," having moved from its nearby corner spot. The "new" location puts it within easy stroll from La Jacmélienne (and any place else in this small town). Seafood, especially lobster, is the specialty.

The Ruins, another enterprise of Erick and Marlene Danies, has an opened-and-closed history. It is near the beach and *in* actual ruins. Comfortable settees have been built into the remains of the stone walls; the sky is the roof over your head.

Jamaica

Jamaica Tourist Board, Box 360, 79–81 Knutsford Blvd., New Kingston, Jamaica, W.I.; 866 Second Ave., New York, NY 10017; 1320 S. Dixie Hwy., Coral Gables, FL 33146; 36 S. Wabash Ave., Chicago, IL 60603; 3440 Wilshire Blvd., Los Angeles, CA 90010; 2221 Yonge St., Suite 507, Toronto, Ontario, Canada M4S 2B4.

US $1 = approximately $J1.78.
Unless otherwise noted, $ refers to U.S. currency.

Most of the birds were blobbed with shellac. I liked the one that was one piece of wood, but it had no legs or stand. When I looked more carefully, it had only one eye. I asked what happened to the other. "A rat ate it," Almon said with a wide grin. I gasped, said I might buy it if he put in another eye, gave it inch-long legs, and set it in a block of wood. "How much?" He looked down at the sand. "Five dollars." "Five dollars Jamaican?" I said. "No, U.S." "That's too much," I said—and put down the weathered gray bird body. "I'll put the legs on it, and you come back to see if you want it," Almon said—and I shrugged, smiled, and walked away.

Several hours later, after I had slithered my way up Dunn's River Falls with some friends who hadn't been there before, I returned to the end of the beach, beyond the wire fence, where Almon and friends had laid out their handwork, and were polishing black coral with Noxon. They welcomed me like an old friend—even the three Rastafarians who lounged on the overturned wooden fishing boat, glassy-eyed. We talked some more—about the boat that was being built on the frame a few feet away. "Who's building that?" I asked. "We are," said one of the glassy-eyed Rastas, hardly able to move from his lounge position. "Not the way you're going" I noted. They laughed—and we talked about Rastas for a while.

Rastafarians have been known in Jamaica for almost 50 years. Marcus Garvey prophesied that Jamaicans should "look to Africa where a black king shall be crowned, for the day of deliverance is near," and the Jamaicans saw Ethiopia's Emperor Haile Selassie, who was known as Ras (Prince) Tafari. To many Jamaicans, he was a living god—and I have not talked to many Rastas who want to comment on his eventual fate. Some estimate that there are about 100,000 Rastas, devoted to "peace and love," and to ganja, as marijuana is called in Jamaica.

The group withdraws from society, but has made major contributions in the arts—notably to the reggae music that has washed over the Caribbean (including Cuba) and sent waves around North America and Europe. You can notice the Rastas by the locks—the long plaited hair fixed to position with wax. While the true Rastas—as they'll tell you themselves—are peace-loving and gentle, a league of copycats began to spread through the Caribbean as the area's equivalent of the world-wide hippie movement. They acquired the name "dreadlocks" or "dreads." And like the hippie movement, that seems to have run its course. A lot of the mimics were menacing, causing trouble where they live and abusing the credo of social involvement, translating it to mean no work and a lot of stealing. The three men I talked with were in their late 20s; none of them had a full-time job, but all worked at something—for a while. One had some friends who sang with one of the bands, and one of the loungers said he carved big wooden heads with Medusa locks like those I had seen in the straw market that morning—and everywhere else as the days went on. They are made by craftsmen who carve and polish. I didn't buy a head, but I bought the bird. It was worth the $5 U.S.—maybe not to you, but to me. The price was outrageous, but not for the lesson I'd learned.

And the next day, when I hoisted myself into the front seat of the 12-passenger minibus that Raphael had brought to bounce me along to Port Antonio, I heard about his family—all 7 of the children. "With the same mother?" I asked. He laughed, the loudest he laughed all day. "Not all," and then he told me how angry his wife is now—about his new baby with a woman in a nearby village, and how pretty the baby is. He loves his children—all of them. Raphael works hard.

As you bounce around the countryside, with "your" Raphael, or in a car you rent yourself, it's impossible not to notice the lush crops of bananas, sugar, pimento (allspice), coffee, and citrus fruits that cover valleys and slopes. Almost all of Jamaica's 4400 square miles are blanketed with lush growth—or could be. Almost any one of the 2.1 million people could live out of his backyard. Many do. Too many have to, in a country where unemployment hovers around 25%. Tourism is essential to the economy of Jamaica. There's not much else that gives jobs and brings hard currency; the government is working on that, and bauxite is the big booster, but for the moment, tourism helps the tallies.

It was obvious that Raphael had a lot of friends. He beeped and waved for most of the 4-hour drive along the north coast from Ocho Rios to Port Antonio, past Port Maria, where Noel Coward lived, and Boscobel, where I had dined at Moxon's restaurant a couple of nights before, past long stretches of beach and fields of cane, and over the railroad tracks for the train that goes between Kingston and Port Antonio. (It's a good ride, Raphael added, but take the diesel; the other train takes forever.) He waved and beeped so much that I wondered whether this journey, for which I was paying US$50—was for his benefit or mine. I guess, looking back on it, for both—and that's part of the purpose of tourism.

■■■
POLITICAL PICTURE: October 30, 1980, was the historic day that turned the tide of Jamaican government. Prime Minister Edward Seaga's Jamaica Labour Party soundly defeated the People's National Party, led by former Prime Minister Michael Manley. One government official noted that "what emerged out of that election was a clear message that the people of Jamaica have decided, after a long and painful experiment, that the route we will go is the route of the western democratic system and the free enterprise method of economic development."

Prime Minister Seaga lost no time in reestablishing the once firm friendship with the United States and other western nations. As the first leader of a foreign country to meet with President Reagan not long after the United States elections, Seaga set in motion a series of meetings and conferences that have resulted in a resurgence of outside investment in Jamaica. Former Chairman of the Chase Manhattan Bank, David Rockefeller, agreed to serve as Chairman of a committee to assist with investment advice for Jamaica, and the local legislature lost no time in approving JLP recommended relaxation of import restrictions and in inviting western businessmen to meet in Jamaica to look at possible investment opportunities. The Jamaica National Hotel Properties, formed when the Manley government assumed operation of several of the country's biggest hotels (when the U.S. chains and management groups that had been running the properties chose not to continue), expressed interest in leasing the hotels to foreign management companies and it seems certain that, by the time you visit this winter, most of the NHP hotels will be under new management.

Much needed hard currency was arranged under new loan agreements with the International Monetary Fund, the group with whom Manley had broken off discussions in March 1980, and more than J$900 million will be received in assistance from the IMF during this fiscal year, in addition to extended loan facilities and compensatory financing and credit.

Shortages of food have been alleviated, and the lack of raw materials that had caused a 40% decrease in factory output toward the end of the Manley years has been replenished by the relaxed import restrictions.

Tourism was elevated to Ministerial status, with a Minister of Tourism and a Minister of State for Tourism, one charged with marketing the country and the other charged with responsibility for improving the product. Much has already been done, but vacationers heading here for winter of 1981–82 will find all the elements for a good vacation.

AUTHOR'S OBSERVATION: During survey travel for this edition, the change in the course of Jamaica's history—and the related enthusiasm for the future—was evident in conversations with people in villages, restaurants, shops, and shores. There is much to be done, but the Jamaican people are determined to revitalize the country and the government is dedicated to creating a climate that is comfortable for visitors and businessmen, and to nourish new industries.

CUSTOMS OF THE COUNTRY are changing as the country readjusts to the free enterprise system, following a well-publicized experiment with "democratic socialism." Many of the "traditional English" customs have been adapted into a uniquely Jamaican lifestyle that, once again, makes times for the nice touches. You can count on teatime at the best resorts and at those with a British clientele, and you can plan for polo matches and other events that are part of the routine of this once-British country.

Clothes are casual, but the *kareeba*, the Jamaican version of the shirt-jac or the "leisure suit" with short sleeves, is giving way to the

Seaga style of coat and tie. (The egalitarian kareeba became the hallmark of the Manley administration and still marks Jamaicans as PNP supporters.) You can count on parties at private homes and any Jamaican-initiated hotel receptions to be elegant, with hospitality assured. Although casual summer clothes can go anywhere in daytime, many hotels are encouraging something special come nightfall.

> **A**UTHOR'S OBSERVATION: Tourists of past seasons seemed to take their clothes cue from the Jamaican Rastafarian look (unkempt, earthy, and "hippie" style), leading to an anything but a stylish atmosphere. Hopefully, the Jamaican change in government will lead to a change in style, with a return to attractive (but not necessarily expensive) clothes. We who visit can help by keeping the casual look under control and by covering up with something decent when we walk through towns and go touring.

MONEY MATTERS: In shops and restaurants around the country (non-tourist places), all quotes will be in Jamaican dollars. Changing money on the street or on the black market is illegal. All hotel bills *must* be paid in U.S. dollars, and you may have to insist on your change in U.S. dollars if you do not want Jamaican cash. Even banks will not give U.S. dollars in exchange for U.S. dollar travelers cheques, from my experience. Jamaican dollars are worthless outside the country.

Most restaurants quote prices in Jamaican dollars. Admission for attractions is usually quoted in Jamaican currency unless you are on an organized tour. You may get a slight advantage if you pay in U.S. currency since businesses are eager to have it (for its stability and their foreign purchases). Car rentals are transacted in U.S. currency; gas will be paid in Jamaican currency. As far as shopping is concerned, many stores quote prices in both currencies if they have Jamaicans and tourists as customers; local stores (food shops where you will want to buy coffee, Pick-a-Peppa sauce, and other Jamaican foods) will charge in Jamaican currency; in-bond shops (where you buy, obtain a receipt, and pick up at the airport—see comment below) are priced only for U.S. dollars.

Do not change more money into Jamaican currency than you expect to use; it can be time-consuming (if lines are long) and tedious to change it back to U.S. dollars. Be sure to hold onto your receipts for exchange; it is impossible to exchange Jamaican dollars to U.S. dollars without them, plus an explanation of what you purchased.

> **A**UTHOR'S OBSERVATION: *Do not* get into the "in-bond" shopping routine unless you allow a lot of time to look for your merchandise at the airport and, perhaps, call the store to have it delivered if it has not shown up at the airport as promised. Complaints about non-delivery are legion, and my own experience involved chasing around to at least five people at the airport to find the proper pickup place and anyone who knew anything about the procedure. My advice is to buy only what you can carry with you out of the store or what you see that you want at the airport after you have checked in for your flight. The anguish with "in-bond" is not worth the money saved, in my opinion.

■■
ARRIVAL: The country's two major airports are Kingston (Norman Manley International) and Montego Bay (Donald Sangster International), and it is the latter that is used by most visitors/tourists. Passenger lines are apt to be long and vacationers "confused" if they are arriving in bulk off one of the several Air Jamaica or other commercial carrier flights. The welcome is courteous and well-organized. The first line is for health clearance; just saying you're a tourist and flashing your U.S. passport is enough. The next line is immigration, with somber-faced, polite immigration inspectors who will stamp the immigration card you have filled out on the plane, and will ask you for your local address (hotel). The wait for the luggage allows time for changing currency at the bank and sipping Jamaican rum punch, proffered at the Appleton Rum booth. (If either or both are operating when you go through the airport. They have not been on my recent survey trips.)

Customs inspectors are businesslike and serious. Flip, "funny" comments do not amuse them, and don't try to bring in anything duty-free except what is for your own personal use. If you are housekeeping, you will be allowed to bring in some staples for your use, but anything that seems like an excess (and destined for Jamaican friends) will be charged with duty. (The emphasis in Jamaica is on using things Jamaican, not only to encourage local production, but also to try to control a serious balance of payments problem.)

MoBay's airport is BIG and relatively modern, but count on flights of stairs. There's a good restaurant/bar to the left, up the stairs, as you face the building from the parking areas, but it is in the public part of the terminal (you'll have to go back through immigration if you decide you want something to eat *after* you have gone through your exit formalities). Additions and extensions to the MoBay terminal have provided room for the hordes that swarm off the Air Jamaica and other charter and group flights, but be prepared for a long walk—with the first steps down the ramp from the plane door and another set to take you up to the second level where the immigration and arrival facilities are located. (Think ahead if you have heavy carry-on luggage; you'll be your own porter for that long walk.)

On departure, when you pass through immigration (forfeiting the card they stamped on entry), you will be in a huge room lined with booths to lure your last few dollars from you. Worth considering, if you're interested in Jamaica today, are some of the books at the bookstore. There are also attractive small booths selling the expected perfume, liquor, camera and watches and the **Coffee Mill** carries Jamaican coffee, special sauces, jams, and other foodstuff. The standing and waiting room at Kingston's airport, although rimmed with "duty-free" shops for watches, cameras, liquor, etc. (limited selection of items, with Jamaican liquor featured) is not air-conditioned and seating capacity is limited. There's no restaurant in the waiting room (and the bar is small), but you can get sandwiches to take out from the upstairs restaurant that caps the main check-in terminal. Allow at least ½ hour for your takeout order to be ready.

In both terminals (Montego Bay and Kingston) walks from check-in area to plane boarding are l-o-n-g, and if you have saddled yourself with the usual huge baskets, mats, hats, liquor, etc., think ahead about how you are going to carry it all that distance. (I've found that the fold-up luggage wheels are indispensable for Jamaican airport travel.)

■■■

TOURING TIPS: Ground transportation in Jamaica is handled by several firms including JUTA, the Jamaican Union of Travellers Association, formed a couple of years ago from some of the members of the previously independent taxi associations, Blue Danube, Scenic Tours, and Martins Tours.

Cars and buses vary insofar as upkeep is concerned, and my experience on one short run between Ocho Rios hotels proves that rates are negotiable although there is a posted sign stating the official rate at the departure point (usually your hotel). Always be sure to ask the rate, which, although usually posted in Jamaican currency, is readily accepted in the hard currency U.S. dollars.

At the airport, taxis are available but check first with the uniformed Courtesy Corps representative at the desk to the right, just outside the door. Ask him what the fare should be if you are not being met by a representative of your tour agent. If you are heading for Negril or Ocho Rios, ask the Visitor Services representative where the limousine is located. There is a standard fare and service for hotels at both towns. (Bargaining with local drivers can be beneficial if you have the time and inclination.)

Rental cars are available—sometimes. High duties and restrictions imposed by the Manley government have resulted in a shortage of cars and parts, and by my experience even if you have a "confirmed" car, you may find that no one but you knows about it when you arrive at the airport. Avis, Hertz, National, and Jamaica Car Rentals have booths at the airport. My experience with Jamaica Car Rentals was a series of time consuming problems resulting in a 24-hour charge of over $80 U.S.! I've been told you'll do better with weekly rentals, but my advice is to brace yourself for the worst if you want instant mobility. Roads are good (at least the main roads are), driving (on the left) is easy, and I suspect the best service comes with cars rented through your hotel when you make your reservation for rooms.

Trans Jamaican Airways connections can be haphazard. No matter what you have been told by your hometown agent, brace yourself for delays with departure of Trans Jamaican flights, if there's any flight leaving when you expected it to in the first place. The airline is safe, but very independent. If you are very lucky, the small plane may dart off to Negril, Port Antonio, or Ocho Rios (if you are going to Kingston, you can fly direct) within a reasonable time after you and your luggage have arrived, but that has yet to happen to me. In all cases when I have tried Trans Jamaican Airways, the actual flight time bore no relationship to the printed schedule, and the only satisfactory part of the small plane flight was the view. If you think of the excursion as a sightseeing venture, it's worth every penny, but don't count on it to save time.

AUTHOR'S OBSERVATION: Efforts by the new government to improve the tourism product will result in changes-for-the-better throughout the year. Jamaicans are dedicated and enthusiastic, and you are guaranteed genuine hospitality in Jamaica this year.

■■■

MONTEGO BAY has grown like a weed from its roots in town to cling to the shores—both east and west—and climb all over the reclaimed land that was to make it one of the Caribbean's most alluring ports. Frankly, this town-turned-city of 30,000 is not one of my favorites. The downtown area is a knot of commerce and, although bypass roads divert some of the traffic, it is confusing (and hot). There are some special small hotels amid the clutter, but most of the better resorts are east and west of the north coast city. Check with the Jamaica Tourist Board at Cornwall Beach for their suggestions about what to do while you are in the area. In my opinion, after you've seen Sam Sharpe Square—which isn't a square at all, but is named for one of Jamaica's Emancipation patriots—then all that's left are the barnacles of buildings that house the heart of a tourism industry: shops, hotels, restaurants—some good, some excellent, some terrible.

The Cage, built on the northwest corner of Sam Sharpe Square in 1806, and the building used to imprison runaway slaves, has become a small museum of slave memorabilia. Check on its status when you're in town. Cast a glance at St. James Church, built in the late 1700s, at the Georgian house that stands at 16 Church Street, and at Burchell Memorial Baptist Church, while you leap around, sidestepping people and traffic.

MoBay was THE resort area in Jamaica more than 25 years ago when the freezing northerners' lunge toward the sun included traveling with trunks of top-notch clothes for black-tie evenings. That way of life has gone—and so has the excellent service that the handful who could afford it enjoyed. Egalitarians will applaud the disappearance of the servant-master syndrome, but one result of the changing lifestyle has been that hotels built from the late '50s to the early '70s, before architects and investors woke up to the fact that their local climate—and visiting clientele—had changed, are struggling to move to the modern reggae tempo. Some suffer from groups that come and go; others survive by being small personality places.

■■■

HOTELS IN THE MOBAY AREA (which stretches all the way from Round Hill to Falmouth) give you more choice for your money than any similar cheek-by-jowl lot of hostelries in the Caribbean. The only place with as many (perhaps more) rooms is the San Juan strip, but the MoBay area hotels have more variety, and much better beaches than the Puerto Rico cluster. For example, you can head for the ultimate of the '6os-style vacation life (plantation style) at Round Hill, or the action-packed Seawind Beach Resort and its counterparts. You can cook for yourself in several spots, or fold into a room in one of the small inns. There are beach-side/shoreside places and places in the hills; there are even rooms for rent on the reclaimed land, where high-rise towers designed as condominiums are let for overnighting.

At MoBay hotels, as elsewhere around the country, you will find a heap of extras tallied on your bill. Those to expect are the per night per room occupancy tax, fixed at $4, $5 or $6 dollars per night in winter (slightly less in summer) depending on the category of your hotel, and 10% service charge at some hotels. Separation of "room" and "restaurant" charges is sometimes cloudy on the all-inclusive week plans, so ask in advance as to how the bookkeeping is handled so that you aren't in for a surprise when you check out.

AUTHOR'S AWARDS for overnighting in the MoBay area go to an eclectic lot. Half Moon Bay, whose General Manager received the 1981 Caribbean Hotelier of the year award, is an exceptional total resort. Round Hill and Tryall offer luxury, and small, innlike Coral Cliff can be ideal if you want an island inn.

✤ **Beach View** (Box 86, Montego Bay, Jamaica, W.I.; 54 rooms) is buttoned onto the side of the hill, on the inland side of the coast-rimming road, across from the beach (Doctor's Cave and Cornwall are easy walks). The traditional part of the hotel is West Indian wood-walled, with white paint; some new rooms with stucco walls are punctuated with furniture in Jamaican wood. All rooms have porch or balcony (and some of the older rooms have a bed on the porch for sleeping "outside"). There's a pool in the back, and the restaurant on the street-level front (where traffic noises can accompany your mealtime). Count on good value at about $50 for 2, this winter, meals extra (and readily available at several restaurants within a short walk of the front door).

✤ **Chalet Caribe Hotel** (Box 365, Montego Bay, Jamaica, W.I.; 30 rooms) concentrates on scuba diving, and its location near one of Montego Bay's most spectacular reefs assures interesting underwater sights. With rooms that range from regular hotel style to studio and 1-bedroom apartments, the hotel gives its guests sea-oriented surroundings about 10 minutes' drive west of Montego Bay city. There's entertainment some evenings when house count warrants, but the property can seem isolated if you don't have a car for mobility. Inquire about the special scuba rates with Montego Reef Divers and plan to pay about $50 for 2, meals and taxes extra, on a regular daily rate.

✤ **Coral Cliff** (Box 253, Montego Bay, Jamaica, W.I.; 32 rooms) captures a piece of land on the inland side of the road, with a view of the sea. The main house is a marvelous West Indian, open to breezes manse, well kept and painted white with chandeliers on the dining terrace and a feeling of hospitality throughout. Rooms may be in the older buildings (which I prefer because they have some character) or in the new blocks back by the hillside pool. Count on steps and walkways, a European clientele, and a casual, comfortable traditionally Jamaican atmosphere. (Coral Cliff and Beach View are both owned by the Maffessanti family, architects and builders of top resorts such as Tryall and of many elegant Jamaican homes.) Count on winter rates of $39 for 2 in the old wing, $49 in the new, plus meals and taxes.

✤ **Doctor's Cave Beach Hotel** (Box 94, Montego Bay, Jamaica, W.I.; 75 rooms) is right across the road from the beach of the famous name amidst the tourist hub of Montego Bay. There's a pool for playing on location, and all the action of MoBay a few steps away. (You can walk to the Cornwall Beach evenings, for example.) The basic structure (rooms in a few floors of an assortment of buildings within an easy stroll of the beach) is sound. The terrace restaurant in the back is pleasant; a pool is to right of the entrance, and the atmosphere is pleasant. Count on room rates from $55 to $70 for 2.

✤ **Half Moon Club** (Box 80, Montego Bay, Jamaica, W.I.; 128 rooms and 62 apts.) is in a class by itself, with Austrian-born Heinz Simonitsch and his wife, Vi, in charge. Accolades from his peers throughout the Caribbean include the Caribbean Hotelier of the Year award, bestowed in June 1981, for the unique and effective concern this couple has shown for the Jamaican community, the hotel staff, and guests. Dinner on a tropical evening, served by candlelight at the seaside terrace, is one of Jamaica's special experiences. The surroundings and service are special—and I have the same feelings about the cottages that stretch out on the left of the main building as you face the sea. Each has its own pool, and the privacy of a private home—well worth the price tag that puts rooms, with breakfasts and dinners daily at rates that range from $189 to $319 for 2. The 32 1-bedroom apartments and 30 studios added last year are elegantly furnished in Jamaican-made antique reproductions and have full maid-service. They rent, without meals, for $119 to $209 for 2. The regular rooms, in the 2-story wings on the other side and around the grounds, have sea view—and the ground level has a slight edge over the top because you can sprint to the beach for your jog and swim with the first rays of morning sun. Popular with Europeans, honeymooners, and anyone wise enough to want "the very best," Half Moon thrives as the one "complete" resort in the old MoBay image. It has had to cater to groups to fill rooms at shoulder and summer seasons, but height of season winter will find most of you paying the same high tariffs. Check with your travel agent about the package for tennis, golf, and honeymoon holidays. The full range of sports includes golf at the nearby Rose Hall-Half Moon course, tennis on the premises, squash at the 6 courts near the golf clubhouse, sport fishing from the pier at the shore, horseback riding not too far away, plus shopping trips into MoBay (½-hour drive west), when you tire of the boutiques on location. Be sure to have at least one dinner at the Golf Club (by reservation only).

✝ **Miranda Hill Hotel** (Box 262, Montego Bay, Jamaica, W.I.; 40 rooms) made a name for itself when it switched from being the elegant private home of Edward Molyneux to becoming a classy inn for luxury lovers. A few personality changes, mostly due to the era when elegance was unfashionable (during the Manley years), have taken their toll on the hillside property, but it looked to me as though the enthusiasm of Pamela and Bert Wright will put this place back in first-class shape. There's a lot to do, but the basic setting—plenty of lush foliage and a private estate atmosphere right in the "middle" of Montego Bay's resort area—is sound. The best rooms for my money are those in the several separate buildings; the 2-story block added by the previous owners seems pretty standard motel-hotel style. You can walk to downtown Montego Bay, in about 10 minutes to Doctor's Cave beach and in a few minutes to a choice of several restaurants. Count on paying $80 and up for 2, with meals and taxes extra.

✣ **Montego Bay Racquet Club** (Box 245, Montego Bay, Jamaica, W.I.; 38 rooms), in the hills and focused on its 7 Laycold courts, became part of the hotel enterprises of Robert Garth when it was linked with his neighboring Blue Harbour Hotel for the season of '76–'77. The marriage included a complete new wardrobe, with bedrooms refurbished and the main rooms spruced up. The new look makes the former private club worthwhile to consider if you want a place in the hills with a tennis emphasis. So great is the interest, you can play all night, to end your play and start your day with a lavish breakfast at 7 a.m. Winter rates for 2 can reach $120, meals extra, but inquire about the special tennis holidays that include lessons, clinics, and playing time. There's a pool on the premises, and access to the beach, about 10 minutes' drive to the coast. All rooms are air-conditioned, with private bath and comfortable surroundings. If you want more space, ask for the suites.

✣ **Montego Beach Hotel** (Box 144, Montego Bay, Jamaica, W.I.; 129 rooms) used to be a pacesetter for places near the airport (5 minutes' drive) and the center of MoBay (another 5), but that was when the hotel was owned by the Morrow family (who still own the Ocho Rios Jamaica Inn). Today groups from Europe, Canada, and the U.S. take over this multistory complex where every room has a sea view, and the place has a small beach held in place by the cement retaining wall. Taken into the government's National Hotel Properties group under the Manley administration, this hotel may be under refreshing new management by the time you visit, since Seaga's government plans to divest itself of hotel management. If you like your privacy, pay the premium for one of the rooms at **Sunset Lodge** next door. The 40-room resort, once independent, was incorporated into the week-long-tour mix when it was acquired by the government in 1977. The beach at Sunset had completely disappeared during a period in winter of '78, but there are cement slabs seaside to sit on if you don't want to stroll the several yards along the shore to the people-covered sand in front of the Beach Hotel. Water sports available; beach bar congenial. A good place for the action-oriented who aren't demanding about snap-finger service and immaculate housekeeping. Shops of all sorts, all of them for tourists, have been spread along the edge of the road from Montego

Beach and Sunset all the way into town (put cash in your pocket and you will have difficulty making it that far). Straight room winter rates are about $120 for 2, all meals extra, but ask your travel agent about package tours.

✣ **Richmond Hill** (Box 362, Montego Bay, Jamaica, W.I.; 23 rooms) perches on a hilltop, with a magnificent view over all the hubbub and confusion of the city to the sea beyond. Surroundings are special, with an elegant former home atmosphere at the main house, where terrace dining wraps around two sides of the pool (opening to the view). Rooms are in several strands, with some down the hillside "under" the pool's platform; all are neatly furnished, with air-conditioning units if the breeze doesn't blow through the louvers enough to keep you cool. A rental car will give you maximum mobility, but you can easily take a taxi into the city that stretches out below, to the beaches and to some of the other restaurants (there's good seafood served right here with romantic surroundings). Count on paying about $70 for a room for 2, meals and taxes extra, this winter.

✣ **Rose Hall Holiday Inn** (Box 480, Montego Bay, Jamaica, W.I.; 558 rooms) will hold 1080 people—and if that sounds like a lot to you, it has proved to be too much for the ownership/management here. The place survives with groups, who bed in to the 8 multistory units that stretch along the beach from the main-building hub, where the pool and restaurants are located. Patterned on the Holiday Inn-building formula, the hotel is about 20 minutes' drive east of the airport, next door to the Half Moon Club. If your group rate is low enough to please your pocketbook, then you might be happy here, but even with tennis courts, nice beach, air-conditioned rooms, and proximity to the Rose Hall Golf Course, the printed daily winter tariff of almost $80 for 2, no meals, is too much. Most meals are served cafeteria-style (you push your own tray, and take it to your table). There are some shops on the grounds, but the complete MoBay roster is a ½-hour's drive west.

✣ **Rose Hall Inter-Continental Hotel and Country Club** (Box 999, Montego Bay, Jamaica, W.I.; 487 rooms) is big, beautiful-if-you-like-convention-hotels, and operated by a staff that is part of the international Inter-Continental family. Count on comfortable rooms, plenty of bustling (if a convention group is registered), and action options on the premises. Among the amenities are 6 all-weather tennis courts (extra $ for night play), 2 restaurants, bar/lounge areas, an active poolside life, and a nightclub/disco that blares until dawn. The two towers are linked by a carpeted, spacious lobby, with shops rimming one wing. The grounds include a golf course (special golf packages in recent seasons have offered 3 day and 6 day all-inclusive holidays with greens fees, shared golf cart, and the challenge of the 18-holes—once). Rates this winter range from $96 to $111, meals and taxes extra, and can hit $550 per day if you want a palatial suite with sea view and spectacular surroundings.

✤ **Royal Caribbean Hotel** (Box 167, Montego Bay, Jamaica, W.I.; 168 rooms) gives guests the opportunity to settle into traditional surroundings, in an older hotel that keeps spruced up. The long driveway that leads to the porticoed entrance, and the beach that's cupped at Mahoe Bay is a nice patch of sand. You're about 4 miles' drive from the heart of MoBay, following the shore-rimming road past the airport for part of the route. Rooms all have private balcony, and all are a short walk from the beach that spreads out seaside. The roar of airplanes is only a temporary intrusion, and the convenience of being a few minutes' drive from MoBay's tarmac means that you can spend maximum time in sun-and-sea. Open-air terrace dining is lovely (when the weather is), screens are wrapped around all porches, and a water sports concession keeps a sport fishing boat at the dock for charter. Gathered into the Jamaica Resort Hotels clan in the season of '78, after years of private operation and a brief era as a classy relative of the Ramada chain reaction, the Royal Caribbean is a prize property, still comfortable for people who want a personalized holiday with what is now known as "casual elegance." Check through your travel agent (or major city newspapers) for the all-inclusive air-and-hotel plans that include this spot for your best value this winter. Otherwise, your room rate will be about $100 for 2, meals extra, with the usual Jamaica taxes and surcharges.

✤ **Round Hill Hotel** (Box 64, Montego Bay, Jamaica, W.I.; 111 rooms, most of them in elegant houses) nestles into a nub of land that flourishes with tropical planting and is the epitome of elegance. This awesome crop of luxury homes survived the Manley experiment and remains one of the Caribbean's most spectacular resorts, *the* pacesetter for any of the resorts that followed its opening in 1954, and well worth your weekly allowance if this is how you choose to spend it. Once you pass through the stone gates and start your drive around the hillside to the main house, you are in another world—a carefully manicured world, where anything but the best seems joltingly out of place.

Michael Kemp, as general manager, is the man who keeps this ship on course with a loyal staff who have become part of the Round Hill family. The surroundings are special: A curve of beach where vacationers bask is just below the restaurant terrace and a few steps from the beachside sipping spot where you can hop on a stool in your bathing suit to sit while the sun goes down (or at any other time of day). There's a small shop near the reception area and a big staff to take care of your every wish. Some water sports (Sunfish, for example) are available beachside, but most of the action will be elsewhere. This has traditionally been a retreat where tired souls come to revive. Rooms 101 through 117 are on the ground floor (beach level) of the 2-story unit that stretches to the right of the reception area as you face the beach; 118-133 are upstairs, and the cluster that is cottage 26 provides 4 rooms at, but above, the shore. "Cottages" 1 through 25 are an amazing variety of private homes, all of which split to separate rooms, most of which can be enjoyed as a home where your maid comes in to cook your breakfast. The evening entertainment is limited to a winter weekly roster that includes beachside barbecues, dancing some evenings, and all the action far enough away from your room so that you can go to sleep by 9 P.M. if that's why you're paying $200 or more for 2 (depending on your room) with 2 meals per person daily, and without the extra taxes, meals, drinks, tips, and everything else that gets added on. Here's an enclave that provides a pampered and perfect holiday.

✣ **Seawind Beach Resort** (Montego Freeport, Jamaica, W.I.; 340 units) has changed direction with the prevailing winds, from separate complexes (a dozen stories of what had been Heritage Beach Hotel, and some 2-story apartments that opened as Seawind) to one big action-packed resort, complete with jogging trails. This sprawling complex puts plenty of action options into your holidays in the sun (many of them at extra cost). The hotel has a unique location, in what used to be "the middle" of the bay, before the land-fill project created a hunk of land earmarked for major development as the location for the cruise ship docks. If you're going to head out to this enclave, my vote goes to the apartments at Seawind, the 2-story complex with attractively furnished units with Pullman kitchen; the high-rise tower aims to be a modern hotel, but the condominium concept just misses in my opinion, and the elevators essential for top floor viewful living are an incongruity in a country that should send its vacationers onto sand and sea. Acceptable if you get a good package tour rate, this would not be my choice otherwise (because you need a car to get anywhere, and when you're here, you're isolated from everything except the commerce of tourism). The property offers pools, beach, bars, restaurants—and plenty of Montego Freeport shops (where merchandise did not have a lot of true freeport prices when I looked), with some comfortable, casual Caribbean clothes at reasonable prices.

✣ **Toby Inn** (Box 467, Montego Bay, Jamaica, W.I.; 26 rooms) is tucked at a wide spot at a bend of the shore road, as it curves past Montego Beach and Sunset Lodge on the way to the airport (5 minutes away). The former home that doubles as front office and **Pagoda Kai** restaurant marks the entrance (and the only way to get to the rooms in several separate buildings connected by paths through the lawns in the back). Rooms are attractively furnished, with modern conveniences, but can be dark when louvers are closed to keep in the air-conditioning. One of the small inn oases amid the hubbub of commerce that is Montego Bay, Toby Inn allows guests to walk across the road to the Montego Beach/Sunset Lodge beaches or down the road to a selection of shops and other hotels, as well as to Cornwall Beach and Doctor's Cave. Count on winter rates that hover around $50 for 2, meals extra.

✣ **Trelawny Beach Club** (Box 54, Falmouth, Jamaica, W.I.; 333 rooms) tied into the government owned hotels a few years ago and focused on a week-long, all-inclusive holiday that gives you all the water-sports equipment plus use of tennis courts and volleyballs along with opportunities for horseback riding, scuba diving, crafts classes, and excercise courses. It's an around-the-clock action plan that gives you all the options amid attractive hotel surroundings that include tower rooms and 4 low buildings that stretch toward the beach. Special events every night, year around, means that you never have to wonder what to do next, and the initial enthusiasm for a sensuous *Ecstacism Experience* seems to have simmered down to just plain fun. Count on weekly all-inclusive rates to range from the $650 December 19 to mid-April high, down to about $500 during shoulder seasons (spring and fall). Rates are for each of 2 sharing a room; air fare is extra as is the departure tax.

✣ **Tryall Golf & Beach Club** (Box 1206, Montego Bay, Jamaica, W.I.; several elegant villas plus 30 rooms in the Great House) holds onto the dream of past luxuries. The U-shaped main building that clings to a hilltop overlooking some of the undulating lawns and golf course of the 3000-acre plantation and the calm Caribbean seas seems more like the country club it aspires to be than the hub of hotel it is. Hotel operation is now guided by Count Kenneth Diacre de Liancourt and plans are to restore former elegance. The villas, planted at auspicious spots close to the fairways and tennis courts or at the shore, were built in the era of ultimate luxury. Rentals range from $1400 to $2500 per week. Some (most) have private pools, several have as many as 5 bedrooms, and all come with "your own" staff, which includes maid, cook, and gardener. If you're beach-oriented, ask for a villa near the beach café and pro shop (107 & 109 are nice). Dedicated golfers will be pleased to know that attention is being paid to the 18-hole, 6880-yard course. Those who like their surroundings special (and can afford to pay the price) can rent a double superior room here for about $150 per day, meals and taxes extra. Count on an additional $15 per day, for greens fees, and another $25 for a cart or $9 per round for a caddy. The 4 tennis courts go for $8 per person per hour. Tryall is an oasis, out of the mainstream of Jamaican modern life—and about half an hour's drive (allowing for MoBay traffic) from the airport and slightly less from town. If you have any question, check with the 800 number in Virginia (800-336-4571).

■■

HOUSEKEEPNG HOLIDAYS IN MOBAY are a big thing in Jamaica. Past seasons have seen a string of villa vacations, where you live in a house, complete with maid/cook and gardener, at rates that depend on the size of your house, its location, and how long you plan to stay. Tops on the list of homes to live in are those at Round Hill or at Tryall, where grounds are spacious, appointments elegant, and prices high.

✤ **Caribbean Home Rentals** (Box 710, Palm Beach, FL 33480) lists several Jamaica properties, many of them with full maid service, pool, and luxury furnishings. Some come with rental car and prices range from relatively modest to sky high.

✤ **JAVA,** the Jamaica Association of Villas and Apartments (200 Park Avenue, New York, NY 10017) carries a listing of properties on the north coast, and can provide details and prices for several houses of varying sizes as well as apartments in clusters and high-rise buildings around Ocho Rios and Montego Bay.

✤ **Montego Bay Club Resort** (White Sands, Montego Bay, Jamaica, W.I.; 97 rooms) is a high-rise hotel on the inland side of the coast road, in the middle of the tourism center of the city. Mentioned here so that you won't confuse it with the Montego Bay Racquet Club (which has a hillside location on the airport side of the city), this place has studios and 1-bedroom apartments, many with sea view but all with the inconvenience of an elevator that I found sometimes worked (and sometimes didn't). A glassed-in walkway off one of the top floors leads onto the upper ridge road, giving guests the option to walk to some of the hotels and restaurants that are along the strand. OK, perhaps, if you're cost conscious and want housekeeping; although this place is not tops on my personal list.

✠ **Montego Gardens Apartment Hotel** (Box 220, Montego Bay, Jamaica, W.I.; 24 apts.) gives you a base for independent housekeeping within easy walk of the restaurants, shops, and shoreline of the tourism area of the city. For about $50 per day for a studio, with better rates for longer stays, you are sequestered in the hills, but can use the glassed-in walkway to get piped into the Montego Bay Club Resort and sink (in the elevator) to shoreline and the sea. Near Miranda Hill and the Racquet Club, the Gardens gives good value.

✠ **The Upper Deck** (Box 16, Montego Bay, Jamaica, W.I.; 109 units) has captured some of the aura of the old days while offering the convenience of kitchen units. You're self-sufficient at this perch, no matter whether your home is one of the studios, with terrace angled for sunset viewing and living room where the "couches" turn into twin beds (or swing together for a double), or the suites where your bedroom is at the back, terrace at the "front," and living room with couch and dining table in the midsection, or the 4 elegant duplexes, with 2 twin-bedded bedrooms upstairs and a full-floor living-dining-cooking area on the first level. Talk at press time suggested that the former restaurant, *Admiral's Inn,* might be turned into an exclusive gaming club, but the only thing that is certain at this point is that the restaurant is closed. Guests have to fend for themselves, but there are several choices nearby (*Brigadoon* is one; *Marguerite's* is another—and the best, in my opinion). Lunch can be served poolside, before or after your Jacuzzi. Winter rates hover around $90 for 2, everything but your overnighting space at additional cost.

✠ **Villa Leisure** (800-526-4244) assembles villa holidays, and offers 7-nights at prices ranging from $1785 for 4 to $2100 for a 3-bedroom house, and many other combinations this winter. A car is included in the villa package, and there are some villas with a tennis court at extra charge.

If you rent a house or apartment and will be cooking at home, be prepared to find fruits and vegetables in season, and sometimes local fish—but everything else will be at a premium in the local markets for you as it is for the residents. Local taxes geared to encouraging home production and slowing the drain of funds on imports have put the prices on the items you will find at top dollar (J$). If you are staying a couple of weeks or longer, bring staples from home (even flour and other basics), and you can try to bring in a canned ham or similar tinned meat, although Jamaican customs folk may sweep it away.

(Following relaxation of the stringent customs restrictions imposed by the Manley government, produce in markets increased and the shortages were not as severe.)

■■■

RESTAURANTS IN MONTEGO BAY are tucked into the crevices, cottages, and even condominiums, providing a baffling roster that makes a legitimate listing of "all" places to dine impossible. The erratic chart of Jamaican tourism over the past decade—with the highest, and then the lowest, visitor count—has put the test to restaurateurs who may have braced for the tidal wave of tourism that did not come, and then closed their doors when the tourist tide returned. Many are reopening, and this winter will undoubtedly yield new places to try.

Brigadoon, just off Queen's Drive where the road breaks to head to Upper Deck Hotel, is a dining depot and more. From opening hour (at 5 p.m. when you'll be virtually alone here) until late night at floor-show time, the place is popular when there are tourists around. Seafood is a speciality, but the floor show is the real drawing card.

Calabash, on Queen's Drive a few paces from the Diplomat restaurant, comes up for accolades as much for the view as for the food. Seafood and Jamaican recipes are featured, and accompanied by background music on some evenings. A bright blue awning marks the entrance; about $25 per person will permit carefree dining.

The Diplomat, in a millionaire's mansion on Queen's Drive, is hard to beat for all-time elegance insofar as surroundings are concerned. Ralph Chapman's home has been turned into a seafood and steak place, where surroundings were more elegant than the fare I sampled

Marguerite's is a must. It's the one place I would choose more than once. Wedged onto a nub of shore, tables give some diners a sea view, and everyone can enjoy the elegant surroundings. Food is well served, the evening's specialties have never failed to please, and the tab of about $25 per person seems acceptable for top-notch dining. Across from Coral Cliff Hotel and within a stroll on any of the cluster of MoBay hotels, Marguerite's is a special experience.

Pagoda Kai, at Toby's Inn across the road from the Montego Beach Hotel, serves its fare on the enclosed porch of the main house, overlooking the pool. Selection is varied, but my samplings of lobster and shrimp specialties are worth recommending. Count on about $15 to $20 for a multicourse meal with drinks.

Town House, 16 Church Street across from the Parish Church, in the heart of "old" Montego Bay, has survived the vagaries of fickle tourism. The shell was built in 1765, but the menu is strictly '70s. I've found the Jamaican stuffed (and very rich) lobster excellent, but there are steaks, spare ribs, and other familiar U.S. fare offered as well as some local fish (usually fresh). Count on paying the equivalent of $20 to $25 per person for a feast; less for entree only.

For basic in-a-basket fare, try the **Chicken Joint** (pizza, chicken) at the Overton Plaza downtown, and if you want Italian food, I've heard acceptable comments about **Casa Italiana** at the Casa Montego hotel annex (but don't count on atmosphere); this is a casual place where the pizza has been known to make its way across the road to the beach. For good Jamaican food at reasonable prices, a colleague touts the **Front Porch** at Wexford Court.

Highpoints for dining out of town, for those who have a car (or the wallet to support an expensive taxi ride) are: about ½ hour west, **Round Hill** (make a reservation, and know that you will be paying for elegant atmosphere and average food) and, about ½ hour east, the **Half Moon Club House Grill** (roast beef, steak, lobster, and fish) at the 18-hole Robert Trent Jones golf course, near Rose Hall and Half Moon Hotels.

■■

PLACES WORTH FINDING AROUND MONTEGO BAY have been found by hundreds before you. Although the magic of "discovery" may have vanished with increasing tourism that has totally changed this once small resort on the north shore, there is comfort in knowing that most of the tourist attractions are in the hands of the government's Jamaica Attractions Development Company Ltd., which is a wholly owned subsidiary of the Jamaica Tourist Board. The programmed pleasures you follow are part of the government plan to show you their country's "typical" experiences.

Governor's Coach, sometimes called the Catadupa Choo Choo, runs from the MoBay railroad station 40 miles up into the mountains, with stops at villages where it has been stopping for its couple of decades of service. The train trip is fun and does show something more than you can see from your lounge chair at beach or pool. After going through banana and sugar fields, passing small villages (Anchovy is one), and pulling into a siding at Cambridge so that the Kingston Express can sweep through on the track they share for this part of the run, the train stops at Catadupa. Sewing ladies have made a home industry of measuring, cutting, and stitching from the time you pass through town on your way up to the Appleton rum factory at Magotty until the time you return in the afternoon to pick up your home sewn dress. Don't expect Christian Dior, but do expect genuine enthusiasm and a few laughs—by all. (Don't settle for the ready-made; it's fun to see the results of the cut-and-sew routine.) Most stops are made on the way up; the late afternoon sweep back to MoBay stops only for your new clothes.

An Evening on the Great River, a JADCO activity, is available several nights a week in winter season (usually Tu-Th) and your price of about $25 includes transportation from your hotel to the river at shoreside, west of the town of MoBay. The ride includes paddling in a dugout canoe (worth a lot of laughs) upstream to the clearing where you walk through the "jungle" to reach your Jamaican feast with lively, colorful entertainment. As with the White River trip offered for guests in Ocho Rios, this trip is fun if you've gathered a group at your home-base hotel, but if you're on your own go along anyway because you will be with sunburned vacationers from other hotels and introductions are easy when you're all at sea.

Cornwall Beach, opened up a few years ago in response to the crowds that were inundating the small patch at nearby Doctor's Cave and is the hub for the **Cornwall Beach Party,** offered at 7 on Friday night, with a show, music, open rum bar, and plenty of casual beachside fun, including the party games that have taken over at the government's Negril Beach Village, a couple of hours farther west on the north shore. For this evening, you'll also pay about $20, unless the evening is included in the package tour you bought for a Jamaican week.

Maroon Country is for adventuresome travelers. The mountain cockpit country is off the beaten path around the coastline. If you drive about 2 hours into the hinterland, you will reach a separate "country" in Jamaica where the first freed slaves created their own community and kept it secure with a guerrilla war against the British. The war ended officially in 1738, but the cockpit country has been a law unto itself ever since. Perceptive readers will recognize that this tour is not for everyone, but those who want to head for the hills can check with the Jamaican Tourist Board at the Cornwall Beach office for the best ways and times to go, and the best guides to take you there.

Miss Lisa Salmon's **Bird Sanctuary** is a special pursuit for those who are intrigued by our feathered friends. Miss Salmon settled into her hillside retreat at Rocklands, about 4 miles up the coast toward Anchovy, west of MoBay, in 1952. Her original reason was to paint, but she found that the birds who were her tenants demanded more than full time. Her feeders drew grass quits, doves, and finches who told their friends about the new tourist resort for the birds. Visitors are invited to come, quietly, to observe and feed the birds—in the afternoon from 3:30 until just before sundown. If you want to make a special pilgrimage, call Miss Salmon to set a convenient time.

Great Houses in the MoBay orbit include Greenwood, Rose Hall, Good Hope, and Sign. These elegant former homes of plantation owners vary in style and furnishings, but all are fascinating for inveterate house tourers. **Greenwood** (daily 10-6) about 15 miles east of MoBay and 7 miles west of Falmouth, was the private home of Richard Barrett between 1780 and 1800, and although much is made of the possibility that relatives of Elizabeth Barrett Browning may have visited here, this doesn't make any difference in your appreciation. The place is fascinating, with authentic furnishings, a collection of 18th-century musical instruments, and the island legends that surround the property presented for the public by owners Bob and Betty Betton.

Good Hope Estate (in the hills behind Falmouth; by appointment), where the lower floor is said to have been a slaves' prison, has spectacular lawns and gardens in their natural state. The estate was started by Thomas William, Jr., in 1755, and legends are rife (and carefully told by your guide). Among the buildings on the estate are the icehouse, the estate offices, the counting house and the sugar works. Elegant Oriental rugs cover the wood floors, and mahogany furniture punctuates all rooms. The grounds are best seen on horseback, easily arranged by appointment (about $15 for 2-hour ride).

Rose Hall Great House, set inland from the resorts of Half Moon and Rose Hall Intercontinental, was restored to look better than it probably ever did. The fortunes and leisure time of former governor of Maryland John Rollins and his wife brought this place back to life—to the dismay of some Jamaican friends of mine who remember playing around the ruins, terrified by the legends of Annie Palmer's ghost. The legends are now politely recited by the well-trained guides who take you through the property, pointing out historic highlights and giving you prices for the restoration. (Read *The White Witch of Rose Hall* and *Morgan's Daughter,* both by Herbert deLisser, to set the tone for this sight, and try to carve off all the Hollywood theatrics that have been added in the name of restoration.) If this is the only Great House within your touring orbit, make a stop here—but if you can get to some of the others, they seem to me to have more "life." In addition to the Great House 2 floors to tour, there's a comfortable bar/lounge area where you can wait for your tour to start or linger when it is finished.

SPORTS: See special section at end of chapter.

■■■

TREASURES AND TRIFLES range from the straw baskets, etc. you will expect to find to island gems you may not. Between that range there's resort wear made in Jamaica, sometimes designed with flair, and often for sale at reasonable prices, as well as the freeport shops, with their cameras, perfume, watches, crystal, silver, and other luxury items.

To begin with the last-mentioned, be sure you know the "best price" you can get from your hometown store before you buy a bargain that is not. There are some good values, but the onus is on you to do your research so that you know that you have found one. **Swiss Stores** punctuate tourist towns, specializing in Tissot, Patek Philippe, Piaget, Rolex, Omega, and other watches, as well as an eye-popping assortment of other jewelry and luxury items. Peter Bangerter, the man in charge of the several shops, has an eye for merchandise that could keep you in hock for decades. The selection is superior, and some of his specials are worthy of the claims made for them. This is a place to survey on the day you arrive and shop in just before you leave—when you have had time to think carefully about what you really want. **La Henriques Ltd.** and **Harts** are 2 more Jamaican chains to wander around for your "duty-free" shopping.

T-shirt collectors will find a happy hunting ground in the shops of MoBay (and all over Jamaica). The shirts are Jamaican made, and very professional—good quality, little shrinkage (count on some—the shirts are cotton). When you see a saying you want, buy it; all shops do not have all shirts in all colors.

Resort clothes were "born" in Jamaica, not only because the Jamaican seamstresses were adept at copying the styles from the top designers, but also because the now-defunct Jamaican Fashion Guild set high standards when local designers formed it more than a decade ago. Styles have changed from the bright designs and cotton fabric that appeared in long skirts, shirts, hats, bathing suits, and everything for sunwear, and so has the Fashion Guild. A name to look for if you are in the market for the Lilly look is **Ruth Clarage** (there are several shops, but the one at the Montego Freeport has a good selection even though Ruth Clarage sold out a few years ago). Beverly Clarke's **Pineapple Shop** has well-made clothes and other interesting items that bear the imprint you'd expect to find from the name. **Caribatik,** a batik studio started by Muriel Chandler from Chicago sells its fabric by the yard and made into clothes. There's a shop near Doctor's Cave Beach, and the studio is about an hour's drive east along the north shore, on the shore at Falmouth. You can't miss it when you follow the north coast road toward Ocho Rios.

Harald's, with a store at the Montego Freeport Shopping Centre, specializes in English silver at "less than London prices" and enameled boxes, small and special, by England's Bilston & Battersea in the style of the 18th-century snuffboxes. Some prints of Jamaica (most of them interesting; some of them blatantly tourist/commercial) and the silver slave bracelets that are the fashion for all in today's West Indies are worth investigating. In fact, for one-stop quality shopping, where what you buy is worth the price even when the price is high, head for Harald's.

"Crafts" seem buried in an avalanche of items that are "tempting for tourists" but as an experienced Caribbean shopper with a lot of sales resistance, I must warn you that you will return with something, and—happily—it will look a lot better at home than the piles do when they're gathered like bees in a hive. Bargain when you buy from the "straw ladies" at beaches, roadsides, and in the craft market. They expect it, and price accordingly.

For Jamaican items, find the nearest shop for **"Things Jamaican"** and look at the ceramic figurines and other local artwork. The wood carvings are sometimes good, sometimes terrible, and you're the best judge of what's best for you. **Appleton Rum** is Jamaica's best; investigate **Rumona,** the very special Jamaican liqueur. Cigar smokers should try **Royal Jamaican.**

At the MoBay airport, there's a bookstore-magazine shop with sales counters that face into the ticket area as well as into the departure lounge (which you reach after you have gone through immigration). If you have a sincere interest in what's going on in Jamaica these days, some of the books by Prime Minister Michael Manley and other Jamaicans will be of interest. Other shops in the departure lounge include the Coffee Mill with high-quality food, coffee, and other items made in Jamaica, sold at standard prices (no bargaining); Duty Free Shop, with a limited selection of cameras and camera equipment, plus watches and the usual; and a liquor shop where the selections of imported brands is better than that of the local Jamaican products. (See also Treasures and Trifles for Ocho Rios and Negril.)

AUTHOR'S OBSERVATION: The Jamaican government's crucial balance of payments problem means that you pay for your purchases in U.S. currency or with a credit card in most tourist stores. Some stores that are frequently used by Jamaicans list prices in Jamaican and U.S. dollars, but you will be expected to pay U.S. In-bond shopping or duty-free in Jamaica means that you pay a special (lower) price for luxury imported items. You may take nonconsumable purchases with you from the store, but consumable items (liquor and cigarettes/cigars among them) must be shipped to the airport or cruise dock, for pickup with receipt when you depart—and heed my earlier warning about the in-bond airport delivery problems.

MANDEVILLE's coverage represents an exception. It's been almost 5 years since I have headed into this mountain village, and less than that since I met Diana McIntyre, who is the reason this copy exists. My comments are not based on firsthand observations—I hope to rectify this well before the next edition is printed. These observations are included because Diana is an enthusiastic Jamaican, who knows and loves her country and is willing to share her time with visitors.

✝ **Astra Hotel** (Ward Ave., Mandeville, Jamaica, W.I.; 24 rooms plus 2 suites) is the McIntyre homestead, and the entire family will do its best to make visitors welcome. An island inn in the best traditions, Astra's owners arrange for guests to meet the people and see

the countryside in ways known best to those who have detoured
from the beaten path. Do not count on any tourist-type activities.
From what Diana tells me, your time can be spent exploring areas
little known to outsiders, including the southcoast resort area that
Diana and Jamaican colleague, Desmond Henry, are planning to
develop in the Jamaican way. Next year's coverage will have a complete report, but if this sounds like your kind of place write for reservations and know that the hospitality will be sincere. Rates this
winter figure from $92 to $105, breakfasts and dinners daily, for 2,
with Jamaican meals guided by the expertise of Mrs. McIntyre,
Diana's mother.

■■

HOTELS IN NEGRIL: Long before the sun-and-sin of Negril
Beach Village burst on the scene in season of '77, the small village
of Negril had been savored as a hideaway for peace-loving vacationers, including hippies who liked the grass that grows around here.
As often happens when the Big Boys come in with trumpets blaring, the small-and-quiet places get lost in the shuffle. Happily lost in
this case, because many have survived the government-sponsored
hullabaloo about Negril Beach Village (which is headed for a reor-
ganization under Jamaica's new government policies).

The village of Negril is offbeat, barefoot, natural—and those who
want a no-frills holiday with an option for the easy life can find it
here. The peripatetic pursuits of the Negril Beach Village are in a
class by themselves; the rest of the town and the long stretches of
beach that are too far from the hub for most of NBV's guests to find
are blissfully quiet even in the height of winter season. Property
values have soared, village folk who had known little about the outside world (or even the rest of Jamaica) a couple of years ago are
rapidly learning the ways of commerce, and Negril has become a
beach-and-sun oriented resort where ganja (as marijuana is called)
is a fact of many lives.

AUTHOR'S AWARDS for Negril hotels go to Sundowner,
for having the courage to be exactly what it is—a beachside resort with a casual, comfortable atmosphere at realistic rates, and to Charela Inn, a small homelike place that
operates as though it might be your own.

✝ **Charela Inn** (Box 33, Negril, Jamaica, W.I.; 10 rooms) can be
ideal if you want a small haven where you'll feel more like a paying

houseguest than a body beloved for your dollars. What stands, beachside, about a half-hour's walk along the beach from the town of Negril (or a five-minute drive), is a Spanish-style house that is bar, restaurant, and a couple of rooms, with its ribbon of rooms trailing inland (no sea view, but well air-conditioned). Best-bet rooms are #201 and #203, over the dining room with a spectacular look out to sea. There's a honeymoon suite at the back of the house, up a spiral staircase to complete privacy. A glorious long strand of sand is a few steps from your room; water-sports arrangements and rental of a sailing yacht can be easily arranged. New owners, the Grizzles, took over from the Mucklows in December '80. A French influence has come to the cuisine which now mingles French flourishes with Jamaican produce for interesting (and enjoyable) results. Rates this winter range from $120 to $130 for 2, breakfasts and dinners daily, with the honeymoon suite at $150.

✣ **Coconut Cove** (Box 12 Negril, Jamaica, W.I.; 46 rooms) nestles at the beach, between the action-packed Negril Beach Village at the northernmost end of the strand and the small-and-special Sundowner, an inn at the beachside. This cluster is an oasis of hospitality favored by sun-loving Europeans. The clutch of rondavels set where green trees grow at the inland side of the beach holds the dining room and the bar and surrounds a small pool (for hotel guests only). Tables have sprouted around the thatch-covered beachside bar in recent seasons, in acknowledgement of the fact that many bathing-suited vacationers want to dine in the sun-and-sand. Food is acceptable, with a few good Jamaican offerings. White stucco 3-storied buildings hold the rooms, each with 1 or 2 bedrooms, full kitchen, air conditioning, and with a patio or balcony angled so that everyone has a view of the sea. Top-floor rooms have best view; ground-level rooms have easy access to the beach. Winter rates are about $90 for 2, rooms only. Meals are served in the pleasant dining room, near the pool, or you are free to walk down the beach after you've made a reservation at Sundowner or one of the beachside restaurants. All water sports are available through the hotel's concessionaire or at beach shops a few steps away. There is evening entertainment some evenings (and all of Negril Beach Village action a few barefoot steps away; you'll hear the noise most of the night). Small conventions and special rate package groups book in here even at winter season.

✣ **Negril Beach Club** (Box NBC, Negril, Jamaica, W.I.; 72 rooms) should not be confused with its pulsating Negril neighbor. The

Beach Club, almost as far away in atmosphere and distance as you can get from Negril Beach Village, spreads out at the shore just northeast of the town. You can easily walk into the straw market, the supermarket, the bicycle shops, and the handful of small restaurants. Blocks of 2-story, balconied motel-style buildings grow between the road and the sand-and-sea. Accommodations are modest, air-conditioned, newly furnished with the necessaries (nothing lavish). Built in the season of '77–'78, the place has developed its own personality with a beach-focused life. Rates depend on the tour you are on, but they dropped to a modest $45 for 2, meals extra, in summer months. Tennis courts, pool, and special rates for children turn this into a family place. All water sports easily arranged from the concessionaire. Long beach runs from the hotel northwest to other inns and resorts.

✛ **Negril Beach Village** (Box 25, Negril, Jamaica, W.I.; 250 rooms) is not one of my favorite spots, although hundreds of vacationers are lured here annually. In my opinion, this place tries too hard to be Eden and an orgy. The whole bacchanal is too carefully planned for profit to send me into ecstasy. Activities planned by the "with it" staff include bikini judging contests for men and women, contests with beer and wine around the pool midmorning, "thumper" games with obscene gestures as choices for your signal, and a constant round of evening activities that has been known to include a "dance" where a bottle held between legs is passed from one partner to the next and a sheet night where you wear only sheets—and some dispense with even that. If this is what you're looking for, then maybe this place is for you. Negril Beach Village, with its shark's-teeth takeoff on Club Med's beads-for-cash system, *looks* attractive. Rooms in the several 2-story buildings are colorful, with spartan but adequate furnishings, air conditioning, private bath, and a roommate. (You can bring your own or be assigned one of the same sex.) The main reception and activities area at the top of the slope, near the tennis courts, riding stables, shops, and pool, is airy and attractively furnished. It's just the mass-with-no-class action that overwhelmed me. For a winter week, you'll pay about $500 per person, *everything* except drinks and airfare included. Horseback riding, sailing, scuba lessons, snorkel sessions, lessons in Jamaican politics, dance lessons, and the entertainment mentioned above are all part of the action. If you're fazed at all by the sight of a man wearing only his scuba tank or a woman wearing only sandals as she climbs over coral rocks for a place in the sun, then don't walk past the gates to the nudist "beach" which is a strand and shoreline that the sea washes out regularly.

✤ **Rock House** (Box 12, Negril, Jamaica, W.I.; 12 rooms) could be Robinson Crusoe's lair, with a half-dozen thatched cottages that grow on the rocks. Ideal for folk who want to put their feet up on the railing and spend the days—and nights—watching and listening to the surf pound at the rocks at their feet, the small inn has no beach. Your next-to-the-water nest will be of wood, spruced up with colorful fabrics, lighted with kerosene lamps and with a choice of 1 or 2 bedrooms, plus a simply furnished kitchenette. Renting a bicycle is one way to get around; otherwise walk or hail a cab or pay for a seat in the car that passes the entrance and is used by the residents. For this thatched retreat, wedged on the rocks within walking distance of Negril, you'll pay about $60 for 2, meals extra in winter.

✤ **Sundowner** (Box 5, Negril, Jamaica, W.I.; 26 rooms) seems secure in the knowledge that it still offers Negril's best vacation. When the Hojans opened this place about 10 years ago, they offered the only comfortable overnighting spot in the area. As far as I'm concerned, Rita Hojan still manages the best inn at this west end of Jamaica. Today's hotel is a band of rooms in a 2-story block on the south side of the original building, which has become the indoor dining area, reception desk, and kitchen. Dining is usually alfresco, on the terrace, where you can enjoy Jamaican food. The higher room rates give you more space and a small refrigerator, but standard accommodations are more than adequate if you want a seaside vacation, air-conditioned room (I turn it off and open the doors to the sea breeze), with options for pre-breakfast swims and jogging on a long and powdery beach. This inn is for repeaters. Many of the guests have been hiding out here for a couple of winter weeks over a period of years and they arrive to find few changes (which is the way we want it). If you tire of lapping waves and spectacular sunsets, all the lascivious, lively life of Negril Beach Village pulsates a short walk down the beach. Rates have climbed to $115 to $125 for 2, breakfasts and dinners daily, winter rate. This is a casual place with a comfortable style, but leave your fancy flourishes home. A local band plays a couple of evenings a week; Wednesday buffet and Sunday barbecue are the main events and may be cancelled if house count is low. Water sports are available from *Aquasports* concession next door.

■■

HOUSEKEEPING HOLIDAYS IN NEGRIL are casual and easy. You can buy your fish from one of the local fishermen when he returns with his catch, and it won't be long before you know where to find the best lobsters. Supermarket shelves are seldom filled, and what's there is either made / grown locally or very expensive, thanks to taxes on imports. Chicken you can find, but beef will be hard to come by and you may not be successful at bringing the tinned ham or other meat through customs. If it matters, be sure to check to see if your housekeeping setup has a refrigerator; some of the small and inexpensive places in Negril are very simple, geared for communal living. There are many places that are one step away from rustic camps. Some cost as little as $5 per person per night, on the commune system. Up the ladder from that rung are the places to be found through Richard James Real Estate in the village at Negril.

✢ **T-Water Cottages** (Box 11, Sav-la-Mar, Jamaica, W.I.; 38 rooms) comes in several versions, all beachside. There are studios, 1-, 2-, and 3-bedroom units, all with private bath, minimal furnishings, and a gorgeous location at the sea. Desmond Segree, overseer/owner of the cottages, is worth finding just for himself; his local lore is some of Negril's best. Count on paying about $50 per person per day (no meals) for the best accommodations.

✢ **Villas Negril** (Box 35, Negril, Jamaica, W.I.; 46 units) roam around the hillside behind (and up from) the supermarket, not far from the water and a beach. There's no beach at the Villas, but once inside this enclave (which looks like many small condominium developments in the States, except for the view from your windows), you'll find the pool, hillside breezes, a poolside/restaurant/gathering area, and housekeeping comforts that are new enough, and modern enough to provide the best in the area. All the man-made elements are here; only the beach is missing—and your winter rate for 2 will rest around $60, all meals extra. (One plan offers meals included, but part of the fun of Negril is visiting the other spots; mealtime is the best time.)

✢ **Crystal Waters** on Negril Beach is a cluster of several cottages, all of them very simply furnished. The reasonable rates include air conditioning, except for the 2-bedroom "minimum" unit at the lowest price of about $400 per week for the house.

Other places to investigate if you want housekeeping, with maid available and at least a caretaker roaming around the premises, if there is not an on-the-spot manager, are **Caribella,** with very casual accommodations that may not have much in the way of kitchen implements and extras; **White Sands,** with a 1-bedroom cottage, a non-air-conditioned studio apartment, and a 4-bedroom house with its private pool and use of the tennis court; **Yellow Bird Sea-Tel** with 2-bedroom, 2-bath units on Negril Beach; and the 10 houses on the hillside at **Negrillo.** Each house has a sea view, houses are available with 1 or 2 bedrooms, with the 2-bedroom versions ranging from standard to deluxe depending on the size of the house and its hillside location. You'll want a car if you choose Negrillo.

Very informal living arrangements, often with a thatched roof over your head and a barefoot existence, are offered at Negril Cliffs west of the village where people are not interested in phones or electricity. **Samsara, Aweemaway Village, Home Sweet Home,** and **X-tabi** are some of the clusters to investigate, if you are the casual kind. You're on the rocks at these places, or across the road from the sea; beaches are a walk away.

■■■
RESTAURANTS IN NEGRIL: Count on places to be casual. Hotel dining rooms—most of them open to the breezes—are the dressiest of the lot, but even on location men seldom wear jacket (never tie), and women wear what they please.

Sundowner's special nights are worth searching out, especially the Sunday night buffet when Miss Hortense loads the groaning board with everything Jamaican and ends the meal with a final flourish of cakes warm from the oven and coconut candy, made only an hour before, that will melt in your mouth. Reservations are essential if you're not lucky enough to be one of the houseguests.

Other Negril nests to try for meals are **PeeWee's,** a small spot (a couple of tables under a shed) on the inland side south of the town; the **Banana Spout** (also casual); and certainly **Rick's Inn**—at least for the sunset view. Rick's draws all the visitors and some longtime residents in Negril at sunset time. Perched on an enviable westernmost promontory, splashed with the sea, Rick's Inn is open for lunch and dinner, at least at high winter season. I've found that the mealtime offerings have wavered and count on finding the view better than the food. Cash count is higher than food warrants, I think, but I suppose there's a price to be paid for perching on the westernmost point of Jamaica.

SPORTS: See special section at end of chapter.

■■

TREASURES AND TRIFLES IN NEGRIL are legion. Selection varies between well-made clever items and outright junk. You can buy both (plus ganja) from the salespeople who set up their stalls near the beaches and in the village of Negril. You'll find a surfeit of carved wood heads, bowls, plates, and platters, plus plenty of woven baskets—with and without the name of the village woven in colored raffia. Flour-sack shirts and skirts have been "the rage" of recent season, with rapidly rising prices—and local grass (*ganja*) is surreptitiously sold along the beach, in town, and almost everywhere else. You don't even have to look eager to be approached. Buying is illegal here; but a proposal a few years ago to make 2 ounces of ganja legal drew laughs from those in the know. (I suspect that ganja is the most lucrative local product offered for sale in Negril.)

Negril Beach Village shops have reggae records, better-quality (and higher priced) woodwork and baskets, plus some resort wear made in Jamaica and stacks and stacks of T-shirts, with the marijuana leaf "Weed of Wisdom" or "Ganja University" being top sellers.

The local supermarket is the place to buy Jamaica's Pick-a-Peppa sauce (which is such a popular export that it's often scarce "at home"), local jams and jellies (good gifts for the homefolks), and Appleton or another Jamaican rum, which will cost much less than the per drink price at any of the hotel bars.

■■

OCHO RIOS has developed a rash of high-rise buildings at a knot near the Reynold's bauxite depot and Ocean Village, but the north coast region has been spared the scars of overdevelopment that blight Montego Bay. One obvious reason for development being paced along the shore is that the airport at Boscobel, east of Ocho Rios, is small, served only by the flights of Trans Jamaican Airways and private planes. Most people who come to resorts at this part of the north shore have spent anywhere from 1½ to 2½ hours in a limousine, bus, taxi or rental car to get to the hotel. Low-slung properties snuggle up to the seaside coves but the too-obvious punctuation marks of high-rise hotels are few and far between— except just west of the town of Ocho Rios, at the Ocean Village area where Turtle Beach Towers, the Inter-Continental, and Mallards Beach stand tall. The Jamaica Hilton, at St. Ann's Bay, about 6 miles east of the town of Ocho Rios, is sheltered from the road by planting that has grown almost as tall as the hotel in the 20 years both have grown here.

Ocho Rios was not named, as everyone commonly supposes, for 8 rivers. There are many rivers flowing to the shore in the area of the town but not 8. *Las Chorreras,* Spanish for the waterfalls, is the earliest town, the one that Don Ysassi, the last Spanish governor, made his headquarters, just before he and his men fled from the shores at Runaway Bay (named for their hasty departure) for more secure settlements at Cuba. The town was spelled Chereiras by the English in records of 1744, and Cherreras by 1800 when a fort was built for protection from invasions on the north shore. By 1841, the almanac lists the town as Ocho Rios and comments that "It is an old harbour sheltered to windward and affords anchorage to vessels of thy burthen."

"The people here complained of want of employment. Some go sixteen miles to get work on sugar estates at St. Mary's. A few years ago it would have been described as the most advanced in the intelligence and prosperity of its population. But it has suffered perhaps more than any other from the drought and also from the diminished value of its staple pimento." That was in 1866; the problem in the 70s became countrywide: the "drought" of tourists and the "diminished value" of the Jamaican dollar, but Jamaica's renewed emphasis on free enterprise will undoubtedly revitalize the sluggish economy.

■■■

HOTELS IN OCHO RIOS get high marks in my book for having their own personalities. There are excellent, elegant inns tucked into the trees along the shore, and some places up in the hills where you can enjoy a "home" of your own. There are condominiums for rent, and commercial high-rise towers—with elevators and constant action—that have cropped up in the past few years.

AUTHOR'S AWARDS go to the Jamaica Inn, for preserving the best of traditional Jamaica in a climate that seems to appeal to the staff as well as the repeat visitors; to Couples for giving good times, good value, and good quality and to Hibiscus Lodge for preserving a small and special innlike atmosphere.

✤ **Couples** (Tower Isle Post Office, St. Mary, Jamaica, W.I.; 141 rooms) is only for couples, and operates on an adaptation of the

Club Med theme with an all-inclusive price for a week's stay for 2.
This winter figure about $1500 per week for 2 for everything, more
for ocean-view rooms. This place started its stateside promotion
with a pacesetting poster showing two tigers—coupling. Born almost 30 years ago as the sedate Tower Isle of Jamaica's Issa family
fame, the hotel added layer after layer of "modern" flourishes to
keep up with the times. The newest flourish came with the January
20, 1978, reopening with the Couples name—and theme. You're
invited to sample "exotic Caribbean delights" at the bar, complimentary, as are cigarettes, wine served in a special Couples pitcher,
tennis on 5 courts (3 night-lighted), scuba, snorkeling, volleyball,
backgammon, ping-pong, yoga, chess, bicycle riding, dancing, and
a "photograph of every Couples couple at Couples." The formula
caught on so quickly that the place often boasts 100% occupancy.
Couples noted on my swing through for this edition seemed to be
enjoying themselves, and all ages were included in the groups
gathered at tables for mealtime. (The management, incidentally,
reports that although you who come here go wild with all the free
drinks and smokes for the first couple of days, life settles down to
"normal" after that—and the new system seems to satisfy both you
and the management, who have found that their initial largess is
not abused.) The complete redecorating that came with the new
life of togetherness brought the dowager hotel up to modern standards, with colorful fabric on couches in lounge areas, plants flourishing in lobbies and lounges, comfortable furnishings in rooms
(if you settle into the 111 to 158 series of rooms, ask for a room
that faces the sea), and an overall atmosphere of fun. You're
about 20 minutes east of Ocho Rios on the north coast, but you're
not too far from Boscobel airport where Trans Jamaican Airways
flies.

✤ **Hibiscus Lodge** (Box 52, Ocho Rios, Jamaica, W.I.; 20 rooms) has
a shoreside location (its *Almond Tree* restaurant almost hangs over
the sea), in the heart of the classic Ocho Rios. Shops, etc. are
within an easy stroll and the original house, wood-walled West Indian, is a charmer. Porch sitting, sea-viewing, and reading are natu-
rals here, although all the touring options are available. Favored by
wise Europeans who like the small spots, and by others who settle
into the few bands of modern rooms that are in separate buildings
(with sea views from their balconies), Hibiscus Lodge is one of the
area's (and Jamaica's) best bets. Your winter double for 2 is $44,
with meals and taxes extra.

✣ **Inn on the Beach** (Box 342, Ocho Rios, Jamaica, W.I.; 46 rooms) is a great spot at reasonable rates, as long as you look out to sea. On the inland side, recent developments have made the surrounding terrain look like your local hometown shopping center. The area is known as Ocean Village and *is* a shopping center, with a supermarket, where you can stock on room nibbles, the local office for the Jamaica Tourist Board, and a couple of restaurants and many shops. One of the hotels for charter groups who come into Jamaica on week-long stays, Inn on the Beach has a smaller, simpler feeling than the high-rise Turtle Beach Towers next door. Both are National Hotel and Properties and available for lease agreements at press time, so check for status. Rooms have sea view, small balcony, phony wood-beamed ceilings, and white stucco walls. Furnishings are simple; rooms can be set up for triples. Two will pay about $60, all meals extra, but ask your travel agent to research special charter weeks. There are no pool, tennis court, or other extras on the grounds, but all are nearby and you border a good beach. It's a good value.

✣ **Inter-Continental Ocho Rios** (Box 100, Ocho Rios, Jamaica, W.I.; 335 rooms) is known as the Inter-Con by the regulars, and the activities schedule is geared to filling the minds, hearts, and hours of the most world-weary vacationer with a program of Jamaican fun. Even the children are not forgotten, with a small pool, a playground, and a special program geared for young visitors. Check with your travel agent about status since this member of Jamaica's National Hotel and Properties may have a new management team for winter '81–'82. The 11-story tower burst upon an already surfeited hotel-room scene in the season of '77, just in time to be folded into the Manley governments NHP group, the result of a financial arrangement that found the government of Jamaica picking up the mortgages on about 40% of Jamaica's hotel rooms. Open-air bar area and *Spanish Retreat* terrace are the main gathering areas to the left as you enter (with the food at the restaurant making up in quantity what it lacks in quality); the *Victoria Restaurant* is straight ahead (with attempts at high quality and high service and success with high prices); and the shops and other entertainment areas are scattered off coves to left and right. Rooms are modern, comfortable, and in pretty good shape considering the wear they get. Exchange privileges are all tied into an action-packed, never dull week that carries one price to cover all—except for personal purchases and drinks. The hotel is at the shore, just west of Ocho Rios and the Ocean Village Shopping Center.

✤ **Jamaica Hilton** (Box 51, Arawak Postal Agency, Ocho Rios, Jamaica, W.I.; 265 rooms) rose from the sands on the north coast in 1958 as the Arawak, with a gambling connection that had roulette wheels spinning—briefly. Since then, wheels have been spinning in other directions, to keep this place open and full. Hilton Caribbean's emphasis on sports and family action helps a lot. The hotel is a lively resort, with a family feeling that found me asking barman Erroll about the best reggae records, which he bought and brought back to me on his day off. Talk to the staff; most of them have come from the neighboring inland village of Steer Town, and many will help you to see another side of Jamaica. That's all in keeping with Hilton's person-to-person emphasis that puts Jamaican patois lessons along with bread sculpture, raffia weaving, and coconut-palm frond plaiting on the activities roster. The Aquatic Centre that opened in summer of '77 is your source for scuba, sailing, deep-sea fishing, and even snorkeling, if you want to head out in the boat to some of the reefs offshore. Tennis pro Cecil Heron is Jamaican, and reconstructed my weak backhand to a 2-handed wham in a couple of lessons. Not for the super-proficient (who can sign up to pay for play), the lessons are best for beginners and intermediates. The 5 courts (3 night-lighted) are in almost constant play (ask about tennis holidays). The "elegant" *Arawak* dining room fell short of my expectations for food, if not for service, at high à la carte prices, but the coffee shop terrace area had excellent salads and a special Sunday "salt fish and ackee" native Jamaican fare. The peacocks that parade around the ground wore more finery than most of the guests who lodge in one of two 6-story wings. All rooms have sea view; some have bigger balconies than others; all are air-conditioned and offer the Hilton expecteds. Beach, pool, choice of several restaurants, and some shows (which range from very good, to entertaining, to very bad, from my observation) round out the evening action on premises. Horseback riding and golf are available at Upton Country Club, about half an hour's drive through and into the hills beyond the town of Ocho Rios (which is a 20-minute hotel shuttle bus ride from your room). And for all this you pay a daily double winter rate about $100, no meals, unless you're smart enough to take the time to have your travel agent find the special package rate that's ideal (and less expensive) for you.

✤ **Jamaica Inn** (Box 1, Ocho Rios, Jamaica, W.I.; 50 rooms) is just about perfect, and that's largely thanks to the loyal staff who are the heart of this place. They are part of what keeps Jamaica Inn regulars returning. The steadying influence of the ownership team (Charlie Morrow and Matthew Archibald) keeps the inn on an even keel. The first 35 rooms opened on this beach in the season of '51, but constant painting and polishing keeps them at top quality. The 2-story wings that cup the section of sand house guests in colorful, neat, and pleasant rooms where your terrace is your own, for reading, snoozing, sipping, or entertaining some of your fellow guests should the spirit move. The lounge area, to the left as you walk in, passing the check-in desk, has the cozy feeling of a country home, with comfortable couches, puzzles for playing, and backgammon board at the ready if you can find a partner (or have brought one with you). The inn is marked by a pirate sign on the roadside, a polished brass plaque on a stone pillar, and you'll be slowed by the "sleeping policeman" you ride over to get to the entrance. There are facilities for tennis, Sunfish and snorkel gear at the beach and entertainment most evenings in winter (when the pre-Independence peacock wear is still worn at dinner). Dinner by candlelight on the terrace, and a rum punch, brought to you at your bidding (and compliments of the house) as you bask in the sun at the beach before you order your lunch, set the special tone that makes this place worth the investment. Jamaica Inn practices innkeeping at its best, and people continue to pay from $180 to $215 all meals (and the pre-lunch punch) included in winter.

✠ **Mallards Beach Hotel** (Box 245, Ocho Rios, Jamaica, W.I.; 394 rooms) moved onto the shore at Ocho Rios in January '77, with most of its rooms in a sky-piercing tower; 40 cabanas stretch off in a 2-story building to your left as you face the sea, with 32 of them suites with living room, and 2 deluxe with 2 living rooms. That's nothing compared to the 14th floor Presidential Suite with its living room, dining room, bedroom, study, bath, bidet and tower-top view of the Caribbean. The top of the tower is high enough to overlook all the shops and busy beach at ground level, but only an elevator drop away. Planned for convention business, the hotel contented itself with the group programs planned with the JTB's action focus when the property came into the National Hotel & Properties Ltd. fold. (This property may have new management by the time of your visit. If it matters, check.) You have the option of spending your nighttime at the *Sea Gull Restaurant* or the downstairs disco, after sipping a sunset potion (or even a Red Stripe beer) from your perch in one of the wicker chairs at *Hugo's Bar,* or heading out to nearby nightspots, some of them at other hotels. The *Pimento*

Room is the coffee shop (air-conditioned), and the *Garden Terrace* and patio are open for all meals, with breakfast by the trayful, cafeteria style. Sunday night has been barbecue night, and package tours are full of fun—and food. Swimming pool, 2 tennis courts, volleyball net set up at the beach, ping-pong tables, and a health club occupy daytime hours, unless your week-long plan includes some of the Ocho Rios day touring options. If you're a light sleeper, pack ear plugs. Disco dancing goes on until dawn, and the pong of tennis balls bouncing on the 2 courts starts at the first light of day. Both can be heard clearly from room 1305, and comments from colleagues report that ground-level noises float up to lofty floors even on the ocean side of the tower. Check for special rates with the all-inclusive weeks that include air fare, or be prepared to pay from $80 to $100 for 2, everything extra including the 10% service charge and the usual taxes. From the Mallards lobby you can stroll to the Ocean Village shopping center, to the facilities at the next-door-neighbor Inter-Con, or along the beach to the Inn on the Beach and Turtle Beach Towers; or you can take a taxi for the ride to Port Maria to visit the home of the late Noel Coward.

✤ **Plantation Inn** (Box 2, Ocho Rios, Jamaica, W.I.; 65 rooms) was planted on the shore at Ocho Rios in the season of 1955 and now is owned by the Watson family from Kingston (known locally for their race track connections). The first 46 rooms bloomed through several successful seasons, when guests who paid top dollar even then enjoyed a lifestyle akin to what you'd expect from the name. The imposing drive into the property and the elegance of tea on the terrace helped the image along and the addition of a pool and one of Jamaica's most respected hotel managers this season suggests a return to high quality. When John Young, of Bermuda's Lantana fame, bought the inn several seasons ago, there were additions and changes to support (and be supported by) the upper crust. To reach the sandy cove of beach, you have to climb down a winding and flower-festooned series of steps; and after your swim, it's an uphill climb to tea on the terrace. As you drive into the property, there are a couple of shops (one of which has been a beauty shop) on your left and a tennis court off to the right, but a complete shopping center is across the road outside the gates. Once inside the enclave, count on finding a "gone with the wind" lifestyle. Rates for the season are from $150 to $200 or more for 2, breakfast and dinners daily, plus high tea and the option of ordering—and paying extra for—lunch.

✣ **Sans Souci** (Box 103, Ocho Rios, Jamaica, W.I.; 44 apts.) began life with a statement for luxury, and when candles flicker on terrace tables on the patio and around the pool, there's an elegant ambiance. About 10 minutes' drive east of the shopping areas of Ocho Rios, Sans Souci is self-sufficient—with elegant Great-House-style surroundings so submerged in tropical foliage that it's hard to realize you are wedged in a narrow strip between road and sea. (The beach is down a series of stone steps to the left as you stand at the main building, facing the sea.)

Casanova's kitchen continues to serve some of the best meals in town, even though the original chef has gone, and they'll taste even better for the kids when you realize that the special MAP plan available for them costs "only" $15 per day. The straight tariff for fancy food is sky high, and the lengthy wine list on one night I dined here seemed to have melted—only the top-priced selection (which settled at about $30 for a bottle) was in stock. You can, of course, cook in your suite, where there are full kitchen facilities with nice "linen, cutlery, crockery and chambermaids." Housekeepers are available at about $15 per day. Room choices range from the 1-bedroom apartment for 2 to a 1-bedroom suite, 2-bedroom apartments, and the very lavish 2-bedroom and 3-bedroom penthouses at rates this winter from $150 to $220 for 2, everything extra.

✣ **Shaw Park Beach** (Box 17, Ocho Rios, Jamaica, W.I.; 118 rooms) sits on the shoreside but takes its name from an imposing hotel that used to stand inland, on the hillside in the middle of what are still Shaw Park Gardens. The Beach hotel rose on this spot of shoreline in the season of '59, with a string of 2-story units with modern furnishings and an action plan focused on the beach and sea. Fame rested for several seasons on the fact that scenes for the movie made from Ian Fleming's *Dr. No* were shot at a creek down the sand, but life now percolates to a lively mix that comes from small group tours, European visitors (Germans and others), and other international guests. Dining is alfresco on the seaside terrace near the beach. Sailing can be arranged at about $5 per hour, $10 for a lesson, through the water sports concession, windsurfers scoot along the sea surface from here, and there are tours to the White River for the boat trip and island buffet that has been organized through the Jamaica Attractions Division of the Tourist Board. Bus tours take guests along the road (15 min.) to Ocho Rios for shopping, but otherwise daytime visitors stretch out to enjoy the sand and sea. The hotel has a lively, action-packed plan during winter months when things often operate with a full house. Spring and fall, as with most spots, are quieter, and summer sets its own pace. Rates for winter are $120 to $202 for 2, full American breakfast included. All other meals and activities are extra, as are taxes. (Special holidays available from April 15 to December 15 offer good value.)

✢ **Turtle Beach Towers** (Box 73, Ocho Rios, Jamaica, W.I.; 360 rooms) stretch to touch the sky from a shore point just west of the town of Ocho Rios at the end of the sandy strollable strand that passes Inn on the Beach to stop at Mallards Beach Hyatt, just short of the Inter-Con. The high-rise towers are air-conditioned, and look like modern apartment buildings in Miami or a lot of other cities. Ocean Village Shopping Center is at your feet; you can do all your shopping at the Family Food supermarket. (Count on paying budget-breaking prices for imported foods.) Rates run from just over $60 for a studio to over $200 for the 2-bedroom units this winter, but check about special week-long plans and charter packages where the rates are much lower.

■■■

RESTAURANTS IN OCHO RIOS are better on interior decorating than on the culinary arts with the exception of Almond Tree which if good on both. You can count on the fish to be fresh (or recently frozen from the surrounding seas) and the vegetables to be locally grown. Restrictions on imports, and high taxes, from which some restaurants are supposed to be exempt, mean that the expected extras you may be used to at your hometown favorite spot may not appear on the table here. The atmosphere—when it's tropical, West Indian, and alfresco—will be superb. Even some of the air-conditioned places where, once inside, you won't know where you are, make up in food what they may lack in atmosphere. In strictly tourist places, you will pay tourist-high prices; if you eat at favorite Jamaican spots outside the vacationing arena, you'll pay Jamaican prices which are reasonable to low.

Almond Tree, near the modern Catholic church and part of Hibiscus Lodge, claims top spot among the area residents and has become a favorite for many of the rest of us. The alfresco dining on the terrace-with-sea-view, amid trees and tropical shrubs sets the tone for local fish, lobster, and other succulent specialties (many with an ambitious Continental flair) served to specifications set by owners with English and Swiss allegiances. Good local food with foreign flourishes makes the $25 to $35 price tag for dinner acceptable. Lunch is a lot less expensive.

Chez Robert, an air-conditioned boite in a part of the Coconut Grove Shopping Center on the main road running through Ocho Rios serves good food (the present owner was chef at the Mallard's Beach when it was part of the Hyatt chain). Plan on parting with $25 per person if you want a meal with all the extras and a sip or two of wine. You can dine at one of the handful of patio tables or buttoned into the air-conditioned room. (There's no sound of sea on tropical evenings.)

Jamaica Inn's terrace dining is worth a reservation, for the surroundings if not for the food. The menu is substantial hotel fare, thriving on homemade hot breads. Do not count on flambés and flourishes, but the ambiance is true plantation, traditional to its core.

Moxon's of Boscobel, almost 10 miles east of downtown Ocho Rios, gets high marks for surroundings, which are just about ideal. The food is—well, interesting, often unusual (at least by name) and sometimes extraordinarily good. As with personality places, this one too has its good days and bad days. Dinner is served from 6:30 on and you'll be told that you're dining in the bowered gardens where Henry Kissinger, George McGovern, Edward Heath, Alex Haley, and Pierre Trudeau have dined—not all at once. I wonder if they were handed the same small card that I was: Mine said, "With the compliments of Moxon's, Boscobel, Jamaica. Please note: Eating at a place like ours resembles taking the pill. You get a feeling of faith, warmth and security while being screwed. Reserve for Rip-Off 974-3234." One of the menu offerings, with the same sense of humor, is the fertility cocktail. Entrees are local fish, lobster, chicken, or beef. The back-of-the-house terrace is the treasured spot, where you'll find yourself paying somewhere in the vicinity of $25 per person for a priceless evening. (Jacket and tie are a compliment to surroundings and management.)

PLACES WORTH FINDING AROUND OCHO RIOS have been found by the tour operators and the Jamaica Attractions division of the Jamaica Tourist Board. All are well marked, well promoted, and well peopled at the tour times. Even if you are a loner, some places are still worth seeing—but on your own terms and time.

Dunn's River Falls have cascaded over their rocks and rills for centuries, and they're still spectacular. If the thought of wallowing around in a freshwater pool formed by the falls as they tumble down a 600-foot drop appeals at all, head for the area with a handful of friends and start climbing from the roadside ticket window, beach level. Your human chain snakes up the rocks, slipping and sliding all the way. Bathing suits are proper attire, although the folk who live in the village at the top of the falls make this wet climb daily in their regular clothes. Anyone who jogs and is staying within a reasonable distance could consider heading here for variety. One climb up and your legs will get their wanted workout. The beach on the other side of the road was a muddy slab when I last saw it. Remnants from the Jamaica Activities Development Corporation-sponsored "Evening at Dunn's River Falls," which was "a blast" according to some recovering tourists I talked with, littered the "beach" with paper cups from the obviously successful rum punch. I wouldn't bother coming to this "beach" to swim.

Fern Gully is a few miles inland, on the winding road to Kingston from Ocho Rios, and appeals mostly to botanists. The overhanging ferns are huge—but not a highlight for everyone.

Shaw Park Botanical Gardens, up in the hills on what used to be a famous plantation, are gorgeous if they are well tended. If you like to go where the wild group goes, try it. Otherwise, wander on your own. Guides are available, but most of the plants are tagged (and the grounds are ideal for a quiet, mountain garden picnic for 2 on a day when you're recovering from too much sun). There are 34 acres, with views, streams, ponds, and plenty of planting. (The gardens are inland, west of the town of Ocho Rios and about 25 minutes' drive from beachside Shaw Park Hotel.)

Firefly, on the coast at Port Maria, just east of Oracabessa where banana boats used to load, and about 35 minutes' drive east of Ocho Rios, is Noel Coward's home-turned-museum. Donated to the Jamaican government on his death on March 23, 1973, the home holds memorabilia of the famous playwright, actor, director, painter. The 4½ acres include his tomb—and a lot of memories of the life of the man who wrote *High Spirits* (a musical version of his play, *Blithe Spirit*), *Quadrille,* and other plays here. Sir Noel lived in Jamaica for the last 25 years of his life.

"Jamaica Night on the White River" is part of the government-sponsored action plan, where you row up the river (or are rowed if you prefer) for drinks and dinner in a side-of-the-river setting that takes on a whole new personality, helped along by those of you who come in the boats and the sound of the steel band that greets you. You can buy a ticket for this evening (usually Sundays, but check) at your hotel activities desk if it has not been included in your package tour. You will be picked up at and returned to your hotel and—even if you can't go with a group of friends from your own lodging—the evening can be a fun one if you're in the mood for it. (Slather yourself with your favorite mosquito deterrent if those pesky intruders bother you.)

Spice plantation tours should be on the activities program for any first-time Caribbean visitor. **Prospect Estate** offers a complete and enthusiastic tour, with talks about all the produce and a horticulture lesson that will not be too pedantic but will let you know something about all the trees and bushes you will look at during the rest of your stay. The usual conveyance is a truck-turned-bus-called-jitney where you bounce around in the back, sometimes sipping a rum punch (which you can certainly get at the "filling station" that is the last stop). You will see a local boy climb a coconut tree (fascinating, for the first time), and then will taste fresh-cut sugar cane in season, a favorite for all the school children you will see munching it as they walk along the roadside. Count on spending about $6 for the tour. Inquire about the possibility of pickup at your hotel, but the usual route is to take a taxi to either plantation, with arrangements for the cab to pick you up when you're finished. If you like horseback riding, that can be the ideal way to tour the plantation.

SPORTS: See special section at end of chapter.

■■■

TREASURES AND TRIFLES IN OCHO RIOS are part of the planned tourist scene, as is the case in Montego Bay. Most of the "real" bargains have long since gone, but the game of bargaining can still be played at the straw market stalls and with the beachside vendors, with a modicum of fun (and profit) for all. If you pay attention, you can avoid being taken completely. Although the shops that honeycomb Pineapple Place, on the shoreside of the main road, and Coconut Grove on the inland side and a short walk east of Pineapple Place, have luxury goods (crystal, china, Wedgwood, perfumes, etc.), the best buys these days are some of the Jamaican-made goods. For those who want T-shirts, Jamaica has them all—including a large selection in colors and size for "Weed of Wisdom" and "Ganja University" as well as several other slogans. The T-shirts of Jamaica are well made and do not shrink too much when washed (because they are cotton, count on *some* shrinkage). Going price is $3.50 for small and $5 for adult size. Buy when you see what you want. Although the shirts are "everywhere," the stock and slogans vary.

At Pineapple Place, find the shop that carries the name of **Ruth Clarage**—one of the original members of the Jamaican Fashion Guild when that organization started to claim the publicity that Jamaican designers deserve. Items for sale include well-made resort wear. Fashions are conservative; colors are not. Clear, bright Caribbean tones are used for the island designs (flowers, palms, boats, etc.) and cloth is cut to standard styles seen at posh resorts in Florida and classy-but-conservative resorts elsewhere. The **Indian Palace** had a potpourri of imports. Some looked better than others and anything I lingered over was offered—intensely. Tortoiseshell bracelets and assorted bangles filled a couple of cases (but the tortoiseshell is an "endangered species" for U.S. customs lists and may be confiscated).

When you buy liquor by the bottle, you will be paying standard rate paid by all who live here *unless* you buy "in bond," which means you make up your mind a couple of days (at least) before you plan to leave. Place your order and pay for it, receiving a slip of sale in return. Your package of liquor purchased will be available for pickup *at the airport* or the place your ship docks. (I have found that the peace of mind that comes with having whatever I thought I needed securely packed with my luggage was worth more than the $ I might have saved.)

Straw baskets, mats, hats, etc. are sold by the ladies who make them, at the **straw market** near the Ocean Village Shopping Center, not far from the Family Food supermarket. You'll find all kinds of straw work; several varieties of flour-sack shirts, skirts, hats, etc., carvings that have been toned with shoe polish, and black coral that is rubbed with Noxon. Bargain for everything: The rapid increase in prices has put some of the poorer-quality merchandise into the "rip-off" category.

A warning about the street and beach vendors: Put your sales resistance into your pocket with your wallet when you go shopping, and use them at the same time. Some of the sales folk will slide up to you as you saunter, offering you a gleaming selection of trinkets, etc. that are surreptitiously slipped from their pocket, or a covering/polishing cloth. During a flurry of whispered conversation that could not have taken more than 10 minutes, I negotiated for a selection of 6 etched "gold" bracelets. Both the salesman and I knew they were not the gold he said they were; only he knew where they came from, and only I knew how much I wanted them. The same sales process is in effect for *ganja,* Jamaica's marijuana, which is illegal but freely offered—even when you show no interest. If you consider shopping a sport, as I sometimes do, then the streets and shores of Ocho Rios have a lot to offer. If you're looking for real bargains, you'll be disappointed.

The expected resort clothes and island trinkets are sold in the air-conditioned, commercial shops at the centers such as Pineapple Place, Coconut Grove, and Ocean Village, near the Turtle Beach and Mallard's Beach complexes on the West side of town, and at big hotel boutiques. Special Jamaican items that are sold (and priced) for local consumption are Pick-a-Peppa spice sauce found in the Family Food supermarket (open daily until 5, and all night Friday) at Ocean Village and the firm and well-made market baskets and reed brooms used by Jamaicans for their own housekeeping. You can buy those on the street. The Jamaican reggae records are priced sky-high—for Jamaicans as well as for us—but there are some labels sold in the record shops in Ocho Rios that are not easily found at home.

■■

HOTELS IN RUNAWAY BAY: Nestling on the north coast, within a few minutes by bus or rental car from the shopping centers and attractions of Ocho Rios and about an hour's drive east of Montego Bay airport, the cluster of hotels at the area known as Runaway Bay offer comfortable accommodations and all the vacation options—including golf.

Club Caribbean (Box 65, Runaway Bay, Jamaica, W.I.; 116 rooms) captures a piece of shoreline and covers it with "cupcake" style rooms that give you a hub of your own. Used by some of the big tour operators from Europe, the U.S. and Canada, the hotel hums when it is full of groups but can seem lonely if the house count is low. Not far from Eaton Hall and Runaway Bay hotels (for elegant evenings out), the Club gives its guests a small commissary for food supplies, a snack shop on premises and the option to take the public bus that roams the shore road into Ocho Rios and elsewhere for shopping and sightseeing. Acceptable for cost-conscious vacationers who like independence and don't need elegant surroundings, rates are about $60 this winter for 2, but much better if you're part of a week-long-or-longer plan.

✤ **Eaton Hall Great House** (Box 112, Runaway Bay, Jamaica, W.I.; 71 rooms) has an elegant aura, with a personality that takes its spark from the staff. Hotel rebirth of the 17th-century fort cum

18th-century slave depot was in 1947, when 10 rooms were offered
at the seaside spot. Since then, a series of owners/managers has
seen this place stretch, to add—when it came under Haitian ownership—a team of rooms that ribbons the sea and beach in 2 new
wings, with additional 5 villas on the seaside and another 3 across
the road almost within putting distance of the golf course (for use
by guests, although it's the Runaway course). Bulk of the rooms
are in the main block, most have sea view and all are attractively
furnished doubles that are $85 to $105 for 2 this winter. When you
bed into this atmospheric spot, you're about an hour's drive from
the heart of downtown MoBay, and almost the same from the Ocho
Rios nooks, farther east along the coast. A rental car will make getting to the golf course easier, but you have tennis here with 2 pools,
and the option to hitch a ride on the bus to go east and west at will.

✛ **Runaway Bay Hotel & Golf Club** (Box 58, Runaway Bay, Jamaica,
W.I.; 152 rooms) rambles along the shore at the spot named for the
departure of Spaniards, and perhaps some slaves, not too far from
Discovery Bay where Columbus landed, and about 45 minutes'
drive east of the MoBay airport on the north coast. The beach that
spreads out at your feet, shoreside, is one of the best reasons to
check in here. The terrace offers dining alfresco. The shops are sufficient for last-minute purchases, and the tour options are endless if
you want to see something of Jamaica. Tennis courts and pool are at
the hub. Golfers play the 18-hole championship course or the 9-hole
executive course with equal enthusiasm (and interminable instant
replay as they relax after the game). Check about the special golf
packages especially after April 15. Recent specials have included
greens fees, balls, club and shoe cleaning, shared golf cart—and a
free golf cap.

■■

HOTELS IN PORT ANTONIO: Port Antonio is the secret salva-
tion for shattered souls, Jamaican as well as the few outsiders who
persevere long enough to get to this place. The route to reach what
was the first great resort area of Jamaica (when the banana boats
docked here at the turn of the century), is to drive from Kingston or
Montego Bay. From Kingston the ride is about 4 hours; from Montego Bay, at least 5 hours, along the north shore. Alternatives are to
fly Trans Jamaican Airlines from Montego Bay or Kingston to Ken
Jones Airfield; from there you can be taxied to your hotel, which
will be in, or on the other side of, Port Antonio, about 20 to 25 min-

utes' drive. If your departure point is Ocho Rios, it will take you about 3 hours' leisurely drive east along the north coast.

Why go? Because the area is beautiful and unspoiled, with comfortable resorts, and out of the mainstream of resort and commercial life. Except for some slogans painted on the road for a political campaign, there's not much evidence of problems here. Jamaican and off-island guests share all the facilities, some of which are exceptional, all of which are clean, neat and near some interesting natural sights (Blue Lagoon, which is deep, deep blue; Annotto Caves and the tropical gardens, and the Rio Grande with its river rafting).

✠ **Bonnie View** (Box 82, Port Antonio, Jamaica, W.I.; 30 rooms including 1 cottage with kitchenette) perches on its hilltop, overlooking the town and bays of Port Antonio, some 600 feet below. The air is just about perfect, the silence awesome, and the surroundings unpretentious. When you head straight up the narrow weaving road from an intersection in downtown Port Antonio, you'll drive into the parking lot, near a cannon posed to protect the Bonnie View. The main house has a huge porch, ideal for view-watching and sampling some of the West Indian food. (Your alternative for meals is the dining room, with simple tables, chairs, and overhead fans.) There's one tired tennis court that looked as though it hadn't seen play in a while and a pool with mountain view behind the main building and the string of motel-style rooms that stretch off the back. Noted on the doors to the rooms on a previous visit: a sign that advised "In order to protect you better, all furniture, fixtures and linen are inventoried every day. Shortage or damage are reported to our management and may result in charge back to occupants last using the room," so watch the wild parties! The inn has been operating for about 40 years, but many of the rooms are new. Jamaicans enjoy this mountain inn, and so will outsiders who want a quiet aerie. West Indian food and hospitality are dependable; but don't expect fancy surroundings. Bonnie View is simple and can be pleasant if you don't need a beach to be happy. Rates this winter are about $40 for 2, meals extra.

✠ **DeMontevin Lodge** (Box 85, Port Antonio, Jamaica, W.I.; 15 rooms) supplies homelike surroundings at modest prices, within a reasonable walk from Port Antonio's marketplace. In a residential area, up the hill at 21 Fort George Street, on the corner of Musgrave, DeMontevin Lodge (Private Hotel) is so called, said Mr. Mullings, because "we don't want afternoon visits." This is a family hotel, he explained, and you can see that when you look at the pictures on the walls. Queen Victoria is prominent near the living room, with Jamaican Premiers Bustamante and Sangster; upstairs you'll find England's royal family, in the days when Queen Elizabeth and Prince Philip thought of Charles and Anne as all. The many coats of paint have not succeeded in covering up the Victorian fretwork and carved moldings, but they do keep the rooms looking neat and clean. Not all rooms have private bath: #4 is a blue room with balcony; #14 is a good-sized double; #7, where the royal family hang, is known as the family room and could easily hold a family of 6 in the huge 3-bedded room with balcony, private bath, and view over town. Mrs. Mullings's local recipes are served on reservation in the dining room. Call ahead for a special Jamaican meal at about $J15. Overnight rates in winter top off at $50 to $60 for 2, breakfast and dinner daily.

✢ **Dragon Bay** (Box 176, Port Antonio, Jamaica, W.I.; 105 rooms) dapples the hillside with several imposing white colonial-style buildings. The main house, at the top of the hill, has the parking area, a small, air-conditioned reception room where Falstaff and other Shakespeare characters peer over your shoulder from their frames around the walls, and the entrance to the stairs leading down to the first courtyard with its dragon fountain. Rooms are glorious, and planned to divide and conquer in 1-bedroom or 2-bedroom versions. The single bedroom is usually "downstairs," which on the hillside means equal, but lower, view. The living/dining area curves to the well-equipped kitchen; furnishings are color-calculated to cohabit with what nature offers—and at this place, that is a lot. Now Jamaican-owned, Dragon Bay was opened in 1970 by Michael Rosenberg. There's a winding drive to reach the main building (blink as the car passes the corrugated-tin-roof utility building, an eyesore, on the left). The other branch of the Y leads down the hill, to the fence-surrounded beach with its volleyball net, well-tended lawns, and beach house, serving lunch and beach barbecues when the house count warrants. Food at the beachside pavilion can be inconsistent. The best bet on one visit was the Jamaican patty (a pastry tart stuffed with spicy meat); the hamburger was dry and tasteless. The canned music can be too loud at the beachside pavilion, especially when the sound of the waves is more than enough music for most of us. Tennis courts and a boutique supplement the sea for daytime diversions; at night, count on elegant dining under the stars or beach buffets. Dragon Bay is about 20 minutes' drive curving around the coast from Port Antonio (which puts it about 30 minutes from the airstrip), not far from famous Blue Lagoon and the SanSan golf course. Winter rates for a 2-bedroom villa are over $150, with no meals; the 1-bedroom unit is about $120, also with all meals extra.

✤ **Frenchman's Cove** (Box 101, Port Antonio, Jamaica, W.I.) made a name for itself as the place where "two people spent $2000 for two weeks" which was a huge sum more than ten years ago when the slogan applied. The complex has struggled, in recent seasons, not only to keep the vines from growing over the sign, but also to make a new name for itself without sacrificing the innate elegance of the Jamaican stone houses set on perfect sites around 40-plus acres. Rumor as we go to press for this edition is that a buyer has been found, and Frenchman's Cove will flourish, but check before you head south if that matters to you.

The facts are these: Canadian money started the dream resort in 1960 with the first of a few resort houses, each staffed with its own maid and butler and linked to the main hotel house by a drive-your-self golf cart. Expense was never a consideration; elegance was. The houses still stand: 10 hotel bedrooms and the formal dining room (one of the few places where dressing up is still in vogue) are in the main house nearest the imposing entrance gates, and far-thest (they claim 640 yards) from the beach. Golden Vale (2 bed-rooms) is in the hills, not far from Holland (1 bedroom) and the 200-year-old sugar mill that punctuates the property. Other houses to call home are Harmony Hall (3 bedrooms) near the bluff at the west edge of the property; Montserrat, Pinnacle, Trinity Hall, and Montpelier, each with 1 bedroom; and Silver Hill, my favorite with its living room in ruins—ancient ruins—a balcony with a beach view, and its one bedroom below the main living area. From Quar-terdeck, on the point near Keyhole Rock, you can hear the surf pound, and Bryan's Castle is right above the beach (a stiff walk up-hill).

✤ **Jamaica Hill Estates** (Box 26, Port Antonio, Jamica, W.I.; 44 rooms) opened as Goblin Hill, popular as a family place, with pool, night-lighted tennis courts, and 40 acres to roam. The 1- and 2-bed-room units, each with kitchen, are in a boxy white stucco building up the hill from the pool and main house, with a fabulous view from any room's balcony. The property has been purchased by Norwe-gian Caribbean Line and they have put it into a combination cruise-and-ashore program that will give you an all-inclusive holi-day. Lush planting percolates around the grounds, helping to tie the brilliant white buildings into the landscape. The terrace dining room to the right of the check-in desk is open and airy, pleasant for alfresco dinners. Ask at the desk about the walking tours of Port Antonio with young people from the town—arranged to start at the Town Hall. For a resort that mingles with the community, where your fellow guests may be well-to-do Jamaicans from Montego Bay and elsewhere, Jamaica Hill is a special spot. Only the beach is missing, and that is down the hill, a short drive away. Rates are $150 to $200 for 2, 2 meals daily per person, and ask about all-inclusive week-long plans that focus on a Jamaican experience, with island authorities and craftsmen holding lectures and classes at the hotel and special events geared to making you part of Jamaican life in an unusual vacation "happening." Congratulations to Norwegian Caribbean Line for, once again, personalizing the vacation experience and integrating your holiday with the home life of the people you are visiting. (They set the pace a few years ago when they started carrying guest Jamaicans on their cruises to this country.)

✤ **Trident Villas** (Box 119, Port Antonio, Jamaica, W.I.) slipped into the sea—antiques and all—during the dashing winds and lashing seas of the hurricane of August '80. The place is being rebuilt as we go to press, and I've been assured that the former elegance and aura will be recreated. Check for status; the place is sure to be special.

KINGSTON is the capital, and the biggest city in the West Indies. Not since the venerable Myrtle Bank Hotel went down in a heap more than 25 years ago, to make way for a redevelopment plan, has this town been a tourist place. Kingston is a business city, and a hive that has made headlines in recent years. The city is, in fact, as far from the north-coast tourist resorts as you probably are from your nearest metropolitan city—and even if you live in New York, Kingston is farther from Ocho Rios than Chinatown is from midtown. If you live in Chicago, the two Jamaican towns are farther apart than downtown Chicago is from the lake shore.

HOTELS IN KINGSTON are used by businessmen, and services are geared more for them than for "Joe Average Tourist." The city has the intrigue-outpost atmosphere some will associate with other

Third World cities. Here, as elsewhere in the country, hotel bills carry the daily occupancy tax, plus service charge.

✣ **Inter-Continental Kingston** (Box 986, Kingston, Jamaica, W.I.; 388 rooms) provides new rooms in the heart of a commercial complex. The first part opened at the end of '77, with additions and more facilities (restaurants to supplement pool and shops) coming at well-spaced intervals. The *Port Royal Fish House* is worth a try. Rates reach almost $90 for 2, everything extra!

✣ **Jamaica Pegasus** (Box 333, Kingston, Jamaica, W.I.; 350 rooms) provides full and modern facilities at a commercial hub a few doors down from the New Kingston Hotel (formerly the Sheraton). Between the two, standing tall in what had been another hotel, is Jamaica's Ministry of Foreign Affairs. (New Kingston and Pegasus make a good combination for convention groups since both provide plenty of rooms and full group facilities.) You can count on plenty of action for businessmen and others in Kingston for short stays. Pool, restaurants, nightclubs are all here, although the Trust Houses Forte management may not be by the time you arrive. There is talk, as we go to press, of the government running the hotel. Rates are about $90 for 2, everything extra.

✣ **Morgan's Harbour Hotel, Beach Club and Yacht Marina** (Port Royal, Kingston, Jamaica, W.I.; 25 rooms) sounds marvelous, and the folder looks good. The place should be, could be, but in my opinion is not. I'd rate it as acceptable only if you are stranded at the Kingston Airport and have no other place to go. Morgan's Harbour has plummeted from the old days when it used to be a fun spot for boating folk who wanted something more casual than city Kingston. The inn is across the harbor from the city, and my feeling is that it has everything going for it but decent management. Rooms were grim on a recent visit, and the always casual dining area even worse. The "beach" is a patch of sand, and you swim in a "pool" carved into the same sea that the anchored boats use for their refuse. It is at least a place to rest your head, but I wouldn't expect much more than that for your $60 double (no meals) rate, unless management when you arrive is brand new and eager.

✣ **New Kingston** (Box 83, Kingston, Jamaica, W.I.; 200 rooms), formerly the Sheraton scatters its rooms around the pool and in the tower, in a city neighborhood that makes taxi service necessary.

The hotel shows the wear of its decade in the city, but there is a loyal following of repeaters who wouldn't stay anywhere else. There are 2 night-lighted tennis courts, and a throbbing disco called the *Jonkanoo Lounge* for evening action. For pool, restaurants, shops, and your room, winter rate is about $90 for 2, everything extra.

✣ **Terra Nova** (17 Waterloo Road; Kingston 10, Jamaica, W.I.; 35 rooms) was an elegant Kingston private home until almost 20 years ago, when it turned inn. Wings with rooms were added, the main rooms of the home were air-conditioned for dining areas, and a pool appeared on the front lawn. If you have to be in Kingston for business, and don't mind being a little bit "out of the city center" in a residential area, this is worth considering. Winter rates, meals extra, are about $60 per person, and unless you know people in Kingston, you won't want to roam much at dinner hours. Food here carried a steep tariff on my check.

■■■

PLACES WORTH FINDING IN KINGSTON, if you happen to be here on business, are **Devon House,** on Hope Road near the Governor General's residence, and the **Botanical Gardens,** which needed a lot of work when I last saw them, but are interesting if you like tropical plants in profusion. **Devon House,** administered by the National Trust and home of Jamaica's National Gallery, is almost worth a day for itself. The total complex, with restaurants, shops and the gallery, is an 18th-century mansion, restored and fitted out for visitors interested in Jamaican history—past and in the making.

■■■

CAMPING IN JAMAICA is not recommended unless you know what you are getting into. Strawberry Fields (Robin's Bay, Jamaica, W.I.) was a great idea when it first opened almost a decade ago, but it has gone steadily downhill—to the point of closing entirely for summer of 1980. Plans are to reopen in December, for the 1981 season, but unless the place has a complete overhaul, and the ganja (marijuana) purveyors are kept under control, I'd suggest going elsewhere. Check with the campsite's New York City office at 1780 Broadway for details, or give some thought to one of the several small hotels, especially those in Mandeville, where housing is provided and hospitality is sincere.

■■■

SPORTS ON JAMAICA are spread out around the country—and the country is probably a lot bigger than you expect. It is not practi-

cal, unless you want a *long* day's excursion, to plan to go from
Montego Bay, for example, to Negril for a day of scuba diving. The
drive each way will take you at least 2 hours (for a total of 4) even
though the road is a good one, and then there's the time spent negotiating for your boat and getting out to an area where the diving
is good. The same is true for Montego Bay and some of the hotels in
the Ocho Rios area. Hotels are the hubs for special water sports
that need professional equipment, so be sure you know the distance from where you are staying to where you want to go. While
Half Moon Hotel and Rose Hall are not much of a trek from downtown MoBay, to get from Round Hill, on one side of the town, to the
Rose Hall golf course on the other side of town, will take more than
an hour, door to door.

Sailing is not a special feature for Jamaica, even though MoBay is
one port for a biennial race from Miami. Yachts are anchored at the
Montego Bay Yacht Club, now at quarters on the landfill project
that added acres to the waterfront, but the yachts for charter are
few. There are occasional yawls, ketches, and sloops that make day
sails along the northwest coast between Montego Bay and Negril,
but the schedule depends on which area offered the most business
at the time and, before you book a hotel because it's close to sailing
yachts, check to be sure there's a yacht for charter. One is usually
available off the shore at Negril. The yacht books through the Negril Beach Village and at all hotels. Your chances of going out when
you want to are better if you can put together your own group of 6
to charter the whole boat.

When I checked out the facilities from Ocho Rios to Port Antonio, sailing was limited to a couple of Sunfish or Sailfish or equivalents, for use from the resort hotels. There were no big yachts for
sunset cruising.

Scuba facilities are available at Negril Beach (through **Aquasports**
next to Sundowner Hotel and Negril Beach Village hotel), and the
Chalet Caribe on the Negril side of the city of Montego Bay (and
about 10 minutes' drive from city center) has special scuba weeks
where the **Montego Reef Divers** course has facets of interest to experts as well as beginners.

Scuba facilities at the Jamaica Hilton, west of the town of Ocho
Rios on the north coast, are the most professional ones I saw with
Mike Drakulich in charge. His courses offered through the Aquatic
Centre at the Hilton's beachside vary from instruction for begin-
ners, through the resort course which gives you the basics so that
you can go offshore to dive sites in safety, to the ultimate, a 36-hour
NASDS certification course. All the equipment is in good condition,

with flotation collars that are far less cumbersome than many I have seen. Check with the Jamaica Hilton about about special scuba holidays where your lessons are included in the tariff.

Other places with scuba programs are the Ocho Rios Inter-Continental; Couples at St. Mary; Dragon Bay at Port Antonio; Round Hill and Tryall, west of Montego Bay; Bay Roc and Seawind Resort in Montego Bay; and Half Moon, east of MoBay. For a complete listing, contact the Jamaica Tourist Board.

Fishing focuses on Port Antonio. Although there are fishing craft to take you out on deep-sea half- or full-day excursions, a fisherman friend of mine noted that the gear had not seen a lot of use on the top-notch boat aboard which we wallowed off the north coast. If you like a day on the sea, try it—but don't be disappointed if you don't come back with much. Luck is better out of Port Antonio, where record blue marlin and other big game have been hauled in by enthusiastic folk who flock to this east-end port. Check with the Jamaica Tourist Board about dates of any fishing touraments which may be planned. From March through October are best months for big fish, according to local authorities, and unless you make some other deal, the fish you catch is the boat owner's prize.

Arrangements can be made for a half-day (or full-day) of deep-sea fishing out of the Jamaica Hilton near Ocho Rios and the NHP hotels (Mallards Hyatt, Inter-Con, Inn on the Beach) at the town.

River fishing is written up in some of the promotion booklets, but when some colleagues proficient in the sport wanted to find a place to cast, none of the Jamaicans asked in the Ocho Rios area knew any place to fish (and there was some talk of the small worms that get into the river fish to make them less than ideal eating). One of the Jamaican Tourist Board information booklets talks about rivers "so chock-full of mullet one could wade into a stream and catch them with one's bare hands" but those days are gone. It's hard to even find any now.

Golf is great on Jamaica, with 9 courses spread around the country, even a 9-hole course undulating around the hills at Mandeville, in the mountains. Prize spots for top golfers are the courses at Tryall (6398 yards, par 71) and at Rose Hall (6598 yards, par 72) but that's only the beginning. The Tryall course, west of Montego Bay and therefore most convenient for guests at Tryall and Round Hill, slopes toward the sea, with the golf club near the beach. Charge for 18 holes in winter is about $15, but check to see about special weekly rates if you are going to be in the country for a while. For those at the east of MoBay's clutter, the familiar course for those who have been here before is the Half Moon course, where the golf house, set at the fringe of the course, on the inland side of the road, is almost as famous for its candlelight dinners as for the pro shop and starting times (which in season have to be signed up for in advance). Rose Hall Inter-Continental's course (6598 yards, par 72) is used by the hotel's guests, especially those on golf week holiday packages. For guests in the Ocho Rios area, the Upton Country Club is another world, far removed from the commercial life that lines the shore below. The club is in the hills, surrounded by mountain views and with the 6600 yard course starting tees a few steps away from the stables for horseback riding. This course has a small-town country club feeling that makes it a popular place to play for those who are used to getting up at the break of dawn to get on their hometown courses in the north. The pace is leisurely, and the course appeals to golfers whose enthusiasm exceeds ability. Lessons are available from a resident pro—sometimes, but you can count on pros at the other courses mentioned above.

Horseback riding in the hills of Jamaica is a never-to-be-forgotten experience. Make arrangements, if you are in Ocho Rios orbit—or can be—to ride at Upton Country Club. Rates are about $10 per hour, $15 for 2 hours of trail riding through spice and coconut plantations, around the rim of the golf course and to some special spots that your guide knows best. After the ride, a refreshing cooler at the clubhouse will set you up for the evening. An alternative is Prospect Estate (see Places Worth Finding in Ocho Rios).

Near Montego Bay, the *White Witch* stables has horses as well as *Vernon's Ranch,* the *Double A Ranch,* and *Good Hope*—which was closed when I last checked but is the best of the lot if it opens again for this season. At Negril, there are horses at the stables nestling up to Negril Beach Village, and horseback riding is included in the activities (and can be arranged at extra fee from other hotels). There was a shortage of horses due to the enthusiasm for riding, but when I checked there was talk of getting more mares for the stable so perhaps that problem is solved. Riding horseback through the scrub of Negril is a special way to see what used to be the remote west end of the country. (Late afternoon riding puts you in the spectacular sunset, but early morning light is just about as good for the shore routes.)

Tennis courts are being plastered any place there's a slab big enough to take them. More than 50 places have courts for play this season, and there are those who are playing in Caribbean sun at high noon with no ill effects (although you know what they say about "mad dogs and Englishmen"). Jamaica Hilton's Jamaican-born pro, Cecil Heron, offers tennis clinics as part of the hotel's week-long tennis package, and most other tennis hotels have special weekly rates in summer. Court use for guests of the hotels is usually free, with costs (of course) for pro time, and tips to ball boys who are omnipresent many places. Best bets I found when checking the tennis racket for players who want to be sure of a game are the Montego Bay Racquet Club and the Jamaica Hilton, where special programs keep the action constant. Check also at the Half Moon Hotel for their special tennis weeks, which read well (but I haven't tried them).

The constant action places (Negril Beach Village, Couples, Trelawny, Turtle Beach, etc.) have tennis lessons and tournaments included in their all-inclusive week-long tab, but when I scouted the NBV courts, they were empty. Everyone was gathered at the pool for the morning chug-a-lug contest.

Martinique

*O*ffice Départemental du Tourisme de la Martinique, B.P. 520, Fort-de-France, Martinique, French West Indies; French West Indies Tourist Board, 610 Fifth Ave., New York, NY 10020; 9401 Wilshire Blvd., Beverly Hills, CA 90212; 1840 Ouest Rue Sherbrooke, Montreal, Quebec, Canada H3H 1E4; 372 Bay St., Suite 610, Toronto, Ontario, Canada M5H 2W9.

US $1 = 5 French francs (Confirm at travel time.)
Unless otherwise noted, U.S. equivilents are figured at the above rate.

Almost 15 madras-wrapped, white-lace-trimmed dolls peeped out from the woven basket on the deck. Nearby, experienced fingers assembled another small person to tuck into that same nest. The dolls, dressed in traditional Martiniquais costumes, are relatives of those that smile shyly from store windows in downtown Fort-de-France and the ones that look up from baskets or hang from pegs wherever tourists are expected to cluster. But these were living on a boat.

It was 6 a.m., and the light around the harbor was as crisp as it would be that day. By 10 a.m. or so, there would be a lot of action around the boats, and some of the craft would have headed out to sea, but at dawn there were only a few of us around: The Queen of the *Roi du Balata,* sitting on the deck of her orange-hulled craft, working with her dolls as though unaware of the "For Sale" sign that hung from the rigging, was one of them.

The community at the marina creates a world of its own, a new world plastered on the traditions of Martinique. The boat people come from Nantes, Nice, or some other European port, and one, at least, was from Portland, Oregon. They have nested in the new facilities and created a village focused on the Bora Bora, the nearby commissary, which supplies that early morning baguette of French bread. The hose on the finger pier is where they all wash up.

Martinique has always been a community of the sea, but these days outsiders outnumber the fishermen on the sand of many shores. You have to head out—away from Pointe du Bout and the other tourist nests, to the far south, to Tartane on the east coast, and even to the north to Prêcheur or Grand Riviére to find the "real" Martinique, and the soul of this special place.

■■■

POLITICAL PICTURE: As a full-fledged *département* of France, Martinique joins its sister Caribbean *département* in having an enviable standard of living insofar as the rest of the West Indies are concerned. Political overlays, and a puffed up payroll of government employees, puts a large percentage of the population on financial footing provided by the mainland's coffers. Tourism brings the most hard currency into Martinique, Guadeloupe, and the satellite islands. The French presidential election which took place in spring of 1981 created a rash of political slogans on walls around the countryside of Martinique. Talks of independence are being nurtured by the very active left. A smoke screen of Castro-from-Cuba involvement in the already firmly entrenched French communist party has made headlines, and there's no doubt about the fact that Martinique's communist party is actively encouraging residents with leftist leanings. It's important to note, however, that top members of the Communist party in Martinique live with most of the so-called capitalist trimmings. Severe socialism—except insofar as housing, schools, and medical care are concerned—will be difficult to maintain in Martinique.

■■■

CUSTOMS OF THE COUNTRY are uniquely Martiniquais, taking the cue from mainland France but adding elements from a Créole Caribbean history. French is the language of the island, and speaking some is essential for transactions outside the well-traveled tourist routes. Although there will be some staff who speak English at the hotels, it is seldom the primary language. Knowledge of French is invaluable for understanding directions, reading menus, or carrying on a complicated conversation. Familiarity with the style of life on mainland France will add to holiday pleasures here, not only because many fellow vacationers will be from Europe but also because many customs are patterned on those of the mother country.

AUTHOR'S OBSERVATION: *Helpful hints for visitors to Guadeloupe and Martinique,* a 28-page booklet packed full of good information, is available through the French West Indies Tourist Board at 610 Fifth Avenue, New York, NY 10020. Write for your copy so you can have it in hand when you arrive. The tips can prove invaluable.

Service (the tip) is often included on bills presented for meals. Sometimes the sum is added as a final item, at a standard 10% or 15%; sometimes prices include the service. There is usually some notation on the menu, but do not be shy about asking "Service compris?" (Is service included?). If the answer is "Oui," you need not leave more. If it is "Non," then 10% to 15% is plenty.

Dogs, cats, and sometimes chickens may linger near your dining table or loll at you feet in some of the casual island restaurants. No one seems to think much about it. If it will bother you, limit your dining to the enclosed hotel dining room but know that you will be missing some of the best island food.

Clothes are chic and casual on the best-dressed folk. There are several small boutiques (some of them in the larger hotels) where women can buy suitable French-style sun dresses and cotton evening wear, but there's not much in the way of men's fashions. Jackets for men seem to be a thing of the past, except for the most formal occasions. Even the best restaurants do not require coat and tie. Open-neck shirts go everywhere (and plain, tired T-shirts seem to be in too many dining rooms these days). On the beach, anything—or nothing—goes. Although there are no official naturalist beaches in Martinique (where nude bathing is acceptable), most Americans will be wide-eyed over the topless bathing on some beaches and at all of the major tourist hotels. European women—and now, also, a lot of Americans—think nothing of doffing bikini tops along with their sandals when they sit on the beach.

■■

MONEY MATTERS are franc-ly French. You can change other currency at the airport as well as at branches of the main banks at the Pointe du Bout marina area and around Fort-de-France. (Chase Manhattan has a prominent air-conditioned bank on the Cathedral square in Fort-de-France.) Hotels will accept U.S. dollars, but usually give a lower rate of exchange, keeping a few points for their service.

AUTHOR'S OBSERVATION: Investigate the international money market at the time you plan your French West Indies holiday. The stronger dollar means more francs for your U.S. currency. You may do better (as I did when researching for this edition) if you buy French francs and pay your island bills with them. Dollar rates are fixed (usually months in the past) at a rate that may be less favorable than the one prevailing during your travels.

■■

ARRIVAL ON MARTINIQUE puts you into the modern, bustling Lamentin Airport, about 5 miles from downtown Fort-de-France. In keeping with the status as a *département* of mainland France, Martinique had a modern airport and terminal facility long before many of the nearby Caribbean islands. You can count on phones that work, cafes that are open, shops that have a few things (mostly liquor and perfume) worth looking at (and even buying), and a general ambiance that makes coming and going a little less of a project.

The immigration procedures are fairly standard: show your identification (passport is best), your return ticket, and your arrival card which states where you will be staying, answer the question of "how long" you will stay, and proceed to customs to collect your luggage.

When you leave from Martinique, there's a good restaurant at the airport (if your plane is delayed) but it is upstairs (*not* the cafe near the airline check-in counters), and you will have to dine *before* you pass through the departure immigration systems. The few booth-like shops *may* be open but they have a very limited selection of purchasables. (Many times when I've gone through, the shops have been closed—Sunday, late in the day, lunch hour, etc.)

■■

TOURING TIPS: Martinique is an ideal island for self-drive cars, but it is also the only place, during countless thousands of miles of travel, where I have had a tire stolen. My experience seemed to be part of a rash of tire thefts at that particular time and I trust the practice has now been stopped. Gas is always an extra charge, but the small cars do not use excessive amounts. Unlimited-mileage rentals are advisable if you want to do a lot of touring. It's easy to put 200 kilometers on your car in a day.

Taxis are ready and waiting at the airport when you arrive. If you

have arrived on a package holiday, with a coupon for transportation to your hotel, someone will probably be asking for you. If you
do not see someone after you pass through immigration or while
you are waiting for you luggage, check with the Office du Tourisme
desk that is in the airport lobby, near where you come through immigration.

Many taxi drivers speak some English. My experience with Michel, a driver for Caribtours, was helpful and pleasant. He proved
an invaluable source of accurate information and can be found by
asking for either Americanized "Michael" or, by his name in
French, pronounced *Mi-shell*.

If you know no French, be sure to ask someone who does about
the fare and the length of time it takes to drive to your hotel before
you leave the airport. Taxi drivers in Martinique can be like taxi
drivers anywhere; if they know you are a novice, they also know you
are "fair game." When you know the approximate fare in advance,
you can just present it as though of course both you and he know
what it is. (Be sure you have French francs—which you should be
able to get at the exchange booth at the airport when you arrive if
you haven't gotten some at your hometown bank before you leave.)

If you are cost-conscious, and traveling light (and you should do
the latter, even if you don't have to worry about the first), there are
several reasonable ways to reach a Pointe du Bout hotel from the
airport. Taking a taxi direct is fastest, and most expensive at about
90F (because the taxis have to drive all around the huge bay of
Fort-de-France). Alternatives are taking a taxi into Fort-de-France
(figure 35F), or better yet, the bus that makes the run from town
to the airport at regular intervals for 3F. At the pier at La Savane
(the park) wait for the boat across to Pointe du Bout, or Anse Mitan
(the neighboring beach), and walk from the dock to your hotel.
None of the hotels are far from the boat dock at Pointe du Bout; if
you disembark at Anse Mitan (for Caraïbe Auberge, Bambou, Auberge Anse Mitan, or Eden Beach), you'll be at the beach and can
stroll along it to your hotel.

Between the cluster of Pointe du Bout hotels and the city of
Fort-de-France, there is frequent boat service. The charge is 10F
round trip to Pointe du Bout, and slightly more for Anse Mitan, but
the journey is far preferable to the around-the-bay road that takes
about half an hour by car.

The major hotels have an activities board that shows day-touring
options. Although many of the tours (to neighboring island Dominica, for example) are set up for groups that book package tours, individual travelers can often get space if they inquire a day or two in

advance. The small bus tours that thread sites of Martinique are interesting, and often give commentary in English as well as French so that you can learn some of the historic background.

Public bus service, often aboard small Mercedes buses, is good, inexpensive, and can be an interesting way to travel if you are not pressed for time. Villages on the routes are written on the side of the bus. The main depot is in Fort-de-France.

AUTHOR'S OBSERVATION: Ask at your hotel for a copy of *Ici Martinique* if you don't see one around. The fact-filled booklet for visitors is essential for finding out what's where and when. Although the paper is printed on an unpredictable schedule (and the information may be slightly out of date), it's the best there is for an instant, on-the-spot source of information. Other weekly newssheets are *Choubouloute* (free) and *Caribscop* (5F).

■■

HOTELS ON MARTINIQUE range from very simple homes-turned-inns, some of them historic, to big and brassy modern hotels that look as they should have finger-snapping service, but don't. Remember, no matter how familiar the surroundings may seem, you are in France and French ways prevail.

AUTHOR'S OBSERVATION: With fluctuating currency rates and the growing strength of the U.S. dollar against the franc, you *may* do better paying your hotel bill in Franch francs. However, if you want to avoid the franc/dollar gamble, consider buying a package tour from your hometown travel agent. The Fête Française holidays packaged with a nudge from the French West Indies Tourist Board and the cooperation of some local hotels can offer excellent value. Read the small print carefully to be sure of the elements you are paying for.

For those who want to be where the action is, the several hotels at Pointe du Bout await—and so does the Club Méditerranée in the south (at Ste. Anne), which keeps unto itself. For those who seek peace and quiet, in traditional surroundings, there are two inns in the north and a few in the south that will put you into another, quieter, less cluttered world. And for those who want housekeeping, there are several options (see below).

Brace yourself for some confusion with the exchange rate if you've been quoted your room rate in dollars by your travel agent. Plan to pay a service charge, which varies from 10% to 15% depending on the property.

AUTHOR'S AWARDS for Martinique go to Bakoua for retaining some of the special Martiniquais qualities while it strives to be the island's best hotel, to Hotel PLM Marina-Pagerie for giving independent travelers a housekeeping option in the middle of a nautical hub, and to Ecole Hôtelière de la Martinique for giving outsiders a unique opportunity to learn about Martinique while Martiniquais are learning about hotel work.

✤ **Auberge de L'Anse Mitan** (Anse Mitan, Trois Ilets, Martinique, F.W.I.; 20 rooms plus 2 cottages) is an old-timer that nestles at the end of the popular Martiniquais beach of Anse Mitan across the bay from Fort-de-France. Ferries make scheduled trips. The inn has air-conditioned rooms with bath/shower in its 3-story beachside stucco main house, where the open-to-breezes dining patio is at beach level, and 2 one-bedroom cottages along the beach (often taken on long-term rental). This is a comfortably casual, friendly inn where you should ask (and pay the extra for) a room with a sea view. Rooms 15 and 16 on the top floor open to the view, and 6 and 9 are doubles on the second floor. Going winter rate is about $45, breakfasts included for 2, and French will get you further.

✤ **Bakoua** (Pointe du Bout, Martinique, F.W.I.; 99 rooms) spent a hefty sum sweeping in sand for its band of beach, and funds have also been lavished on some of the rooms and a beachfront wing that puts you a few steps from the sea. The hotel is named for the platter-shaped hat the fishing folk used to wear and is one of the island's most traditional hotels in spite of all the modern flourishes that owner Guy de la Houssaye has added since the hotel opened in 1965 with 27 rooms and 30 employees.

Bakoua's top-floor balconied rooms have spectacular views of the sea. But here—as in most Caribbean spots—air conditioners can be temperamental. In addition to being land contact for many of the yachts that cruise these seas (anchoring offshore and often willing to take people for day sails), Bakoua has become a tennis hub with the addition of its courts. The pool perches near the hilltop with the main hotel; beaches are down a path—and get constant attention, and plenty of French francs worth of pumped-in sand to replenish what the seas regularly carry out. The snack bar/light lunch pavilion is midway on the slope, convenient to both beach and pool. Helped along for action options by the fact that Meridien-with-its-casino plus all the hotels and bistros around the boat-filled marina are a few steps from the hotel's door, Bakoua has dinner dancing in winter, plus a circular bar that draws a lingering crowd, and a couple of shops near the check-in desk. Rates are close to $200 for 2 this winter with breakfasts and free use of water-sports equipment included.

✝ **Balisier** (21 rue Victor Hugo, Fort-de-France, Martinique, F.W.I.; 19 rooms) beats the high cost of living elsewhere, if you're content to be in the downtown area, a few doors from the famous Roger Albert store. The 5-story building is nondescript; rooms are simple but adequate (don't expect atmosphere), and the price is right at about $40 for 2, no meals, this winter—especially when you note that you are a short stroll or stroll-plus-boat-ride from some of the best restaurants in the Caribbean.

✝ **Bambou** (Anse Mitan, Martinique, F.W.I.; 26 rooms) basks in the sun, shoreside on the beach at Anse Mitan. The 12 2-bedroom wood units with their slanting red roofs are scattered around the grassy area, behind the main gathering spot, the open-air beach pavilion where you can get some of the best soupe de poisson (fish soup) with a glass of wine for lunch in your bathing suit. This is a very casual spot, with *very* simple accommodations, in small nests that are favorites for those who like to spend the whole holiday in bathing suit. There's *nothing* formal or fussy about this place, and speaking fluent, colloquial French will add to your sense of belonging. You can dress up and walk along the path and road to several small bistros or to all the hubbub at the marina area, where you'll find the new neighbors (Meridien, Hotel PLM Marina-Pagerie, Madinina, et al.). Rates run about $50 for 2, bread and coffee for breakfast.

✝ **PLM La Batelière** (Schoelcher, Martinique, F.W.I.; 215 rooms) bounced into the '78 season with a new look, a new sponsor and a new name, but the building is the former Hilton that rose on the rocks north of Fort-de-France almost a decade ago. PLM, the French chain that got its start with trains and evolved into the hotel business by putting overnighting spots at appropriate places around mainland France, has been picking up appropriate places in the French West Indies during the past couple of years. The collection now includes this spot, plus the Manoir de Beauregard and the PLM Marina-Pagerie also on Martinique, PLM Village Soleil and PLM Arawak on Guadeloupe, PLM Jean Bart on St. Barthélemy, PLM St. Tropez on St. Martin, and a new PLM hotel on the north coast of Haiti. All the rooms in this modern curve are air-conditioned, pleasantly furnished in bright colors, with a good sea view overlooking the cove of Fort-de-France about 8 minutes' drive from the hotel's front door. The lobby is an action-packed place with bar, entertainment (including bingo with cocktails some evenings) and shops. A huge freshwater pool was the only dunking spot in Hilton days; it's been supplemented with a very special span of dredged sand that rims the cove (and is kept there—hopefully—by a series of groins). Tennis courts (lit for night play) supplement the pedal boats, Sunfish sailboats, windsurfers, and snorkel equipment for action options, and *La Batelière II* and *Bois Normand* are available for days at sea. The car rental desk at the hotel can set you up for your day or more of island exploring; a taxi into town takes care of the boutiques that line the streets of Fort-de-France. Although the casino captures the gambling group, the Grand Ballet de Martinique performs here once a week in season, and other local groups provide entertainment when the house count warrants. The *Club 21* disco is popular with local folk, so you can count on action, especially on weekends, no matter what the house count may be. Non-linguists can be comforted by the fact that some of the staff are fluent in English. Groups get good-value rates for the facilities (which include good-sized meeting rooms according to the Hilton formula), but those heading here on their own should expect to pay up to $150 for 2 this winter, American breakfast included!

✤ **Bristol Hotel** (Rue Martin Luther King, Fort-de-France, Martinique, F.W.I.; 10 rooms) was a private home, and if you choose it as yours you should know that you will be in a wood frame house in a residential area of Fort-de-France. Your simple room will be air-conditioned, with private bath, but don't count on anything grand. No good for the beach buffs, this place is OK for those who like old island homes, want to be near town, and like the low rates (about $35 for 2, breakfasts included).

✤ **Calalou** (Anse a l'Ane, Martinique, F.W.I.; 30 rooms) cares for its guests in a way that has turned most of them into annual visitors. A sprinkling of North Americans assures some English spoken at this cluster of beachside units on a bay near the action of Pointe du

Bout. On-premise cars allow for day rentals, or an evening rental to go to a nearby restaurant with friends; otherwise the beach will provide the activity. The main building cups the alfresco dining area, and the desk where day tours (to the north, the south, and neighboring islands such as Dominica and St. Lucia) can be arranged. The block of 12 rooms (6 on 6) is nearest the beach, with the others in 2-story blocks nearby. The hotel usually closes in June for refurbishing. Winter rates will be about $80 per day, 2 meals daily included per person.

✤ **Caraïbe Auberge** (Anse Mitan, Trois Ilets, Martinique, F.W.I.; 12 rooms) began its inn life when the former owner decided she would welcome guests in her shoreside home. Mme. Guatel sold to L. Yang Ting for season of '81, and some refurbishing of the rooms results in comfortable surroudings for this winter. The modern cement building has a dozen adequately (not lavishly) furnished rooms with the best being those with sea view. You're on the beach, a short walk from the yachting action at the marina, with its boats, bistros, and big hotels and near the windsurfing concessions that now fleck this beach. (The ferry run to Fort-de-France takes about 25 minutes.) Ideal for sensitive barefoot and boating types who can pay about $40 for 2, with continental breakfast which includes piping hot coffee and fresh croissants.

✤ **Club Méditerranée Les Boucaniers/Buccaneer's Creek** (Point Marin, Ste.-Anne, Martinique, F.W.I.; 300 rooms) is a long and winding route south, about an hour from the airport. Once you're here, you won't have to budge—except to meander from one pleasure pocket to the next. Planned for the sex-with-sun seekers who are good sports, the enclave is so self-contained that some boosters make the dubiously complimentary but accurate claim that you can spend a week here without even knowing you are on Martinique. In addition to the familiar Club Med formula of GOs (staff, called *gentils organisateurs*) and GMs (guests, known as *gentils membres*), with a Chef de Village in charge of the recipe and a long list of activities often announced on loudspeakers, there's a naturalists' beach for sunbathing au naturel and the option to walk into the village of Ste.-Anne, once a small fishing village known only to a handful of residents. For those who want to improve their minds as well as their social life, there's a language lab for learning French. A boat departs from the beach for the offshore snorkel and scuba sessions, with spectacular sights to see off Diamond Rock and afternoon rum cruises that provide cocktail conversation for those who can still talk. The disco has moved from the base of the trademark tower to a thatch-and-terrace open-air spot that serves creole food until 12 when the pulsating ear-pounding rhythms start. (The afternoon *creperie* is still in the tower.) Waterskiing, volleyball, tennis, yoga, calisthenics and other team sports can keep you moving from dawn to dusk, with a few spare minutes for the shops where you can buy the *pareau* (the piece of cloth that you will learn to wrap over suit and/or self as your all-purpose garb), suntan lotion, magazines, and a selection of other tourist-tested items. There's a library for quiet times, but you won't find many people in it; most head to the sun, for socializing.

In addition to the island tours (half day into Fort-de-France, full day touring sights), there are visits to neighboring islands: Dominica by plane and the Grenadines by boat, one of several that leave from the dock to cruise through the Caribbean's most spectacular sailing area.

Your home for the week you buy at all-inclusive rates will be in a 2-bed, air-conditioned, simply furnished room that you can share with the friend you bring with you or, at first at least, with a fellow guest of the same sex. No locks, and no restrictions on visiting hours. A one-week, all-inclusive rate for each person, with 2 sharing a room, ranges from $680 to $740 at peak season, winter. The lowest rate for the all-inclusive week is $500 to $535, and that usually applies for spring and fall, the so-called "shoulder" seasons, when everything is the same as peak season except the rates. (The lower rate has been offered because those times are traditionally when fewer vacationers head into the Caribbean.) Check also for other rates for mid-summer and special events, and inquire about airfare-included fares; the rates given are only for the land portion.

✛ **Diamant-Novotel** (Diamant, Martinique, F.W.I.; 180 rooms) is now set in the Novotel chain. A history that flickers with open-and-shut status gives this unique spot more legends than most island properties. Built in the early 70s, and one of the first properties to have a sort of golf course, the Diamond Roc had been closed for a couple of years. With the burgeoning tourism for Martinique, and the protective and professional hand of Novotel, perhaps the time is right. (Novotel operators are pros with group travel and also manage Salako and Fleur d'Epée on Guadeloupe.) You can count on modern rooms with bath, some with a spectacular view of Rocher de Diamant (Diamond Rock). The Rock, according to my mentor Sydney Clark, is "a historic oddity offshore . . . rising 600 feet sheer from the sea. Here, in the year 1804, Captain (later Admiral) Samuel Hood, in command of a British fleet, landed a garrison of 120 men, together with cannons and ammunition—a most hazardous undertaking for those days—bidding them hold the Rock against the French. They held it for almost a year and a half with such unfaltering heroism that Hood commissioned it as the sloop-of-war HMS *Diamond Rock!*" This south-coast hotel, almost 2 hours' drive from Fort-de-France, has a panorama restaurant, a disco/nightclub that is lively when the houseguests are, and a winter rate of close to $120 for 2, breakfast included.

✛ **Dunette** (Ste.-Anne, Martinique, F.W.I.; 11 rooms) is a small inn nestling at the edge of the seaside village of Ste.-Anne. The 3-story stucco building, with its blue canvas awnings and sun-umbrellas, is on the fringe of the small town made busy by a few lingering Club Med types who sneak off the compound to come into town. Rooms range from 8 that overlook the sea to others that do not; all are air-conditioned, but some are small boxes with shower only (no tub). For adventuresome French-speaking travelers who like the idea of a French seaside village, Dunette will provide a comfortable home. You're an hour's drive from airport or Fort-de-France, in another world of Martinique. There's a strand of sand about 5 minutes' walk from the hotel, and fabulous French and creole food at your dinner table. Rates run about $70 for 2, 2 meals daily per person in winter. (Mme. Marie-Louise Kambona usually closes down in fall, so check if that's when you plan to arrive.) Nearby nests include Manoir de Beauregard, over and out on the other side of town.

✛ **Duparquet** (68 Ave. Duparquet, Fort-de-France, Martinique, F.W.I.; 20 rooms) demands some mention because it, like some of the other Fort-de-France small hotels, has reasonable rates. *If you're willing to accept a stucco box*, with sparse-but-adequate furnishings, in a convenient location within walking distance of shops and sumptuous food (at special high-priced restaurants), consider this. Rates this winter, for 2 with continental breakfast, will hover around $50, leaving you something to spend on water sports, which you can find across the harbor at the marina-Meridien area (ferries run on regular service and cost 10F round trip.).

✛ **École Hôtelière de la Martinique** (Anse-Gouraud, Schoelcher, Fort-de-France, F.W.I.; 14 rooms) is a special place for special people, both those who are learning the hotel business (and share their enthusiasm with you by giving wide smiles) and guests who want to learn French (which you can do while the staff practices their English). In a difficult to find cul-de-sac off the main road out of Fort-de-France toward Schoelcher, the hotel is just off the beaten paths. The white-stucco building is surrounded by lush, tropical planting, and the lobby has been decorated with bamboo-style furniture made in Martinique, and there are attractive bar and dining areas where the students practice their skills. The pleasant pool in the garden to the right as you enter is an ideal cool-off spot, but you'll need a car for mobility or island touring. Bedrooms are modern, comfortable and well-maintained, and you won't find a better buy than this spot on this or many other islands. Rates for 2 range around $60 at high season; the hotel school is closed from June 1 through November 14. If your French is good, and your interest in things French is strong, settle in. (Most of the staff will speak some English; it's part of their hotel training.)

✢ **Eden Beach** (Anse Mitan, Martinique, F.W.I.; 14 rooms) is a small, recently built hotel on the beach shared with Auberge Anse Mitan, Caraïbe Auberge, and Bambou. The 3-story building holds 8 of the rooms; the other 6 are separate bungalows on the grass behind the beachfront building. All are simple, air-conditioned (because they have to be; they're in pockets), and within a stroll of the marina activity at Pointe du Bout. Rates for winter hover around $40 for 2, breakfasts included. There's a restaurant (Caridad) to the left as you face the hotel with the beach at your back.

✢ **Frantel Martinique** (Pointe du Bout, Martinique, F.W.I.; 210 rooms) wraps the French chain around the east side of the marina at Pointe du Bout. The uninteresting strips of buildings, with brown doors and railings, have settled into flourishing planting over the years, and this place has mellowed nicely. Rooms are cozy (and small), but modern and more than adequate. (One problem is that when you close your louvered windows, you've cut out all the natural light.) Names like *Vanille, Corossol, Avocat* help you to find your buildings (these are around the pool). *Coco, Pomme, Cajou, Sapotille* and *Cannelle* overlook the marina activity. Action options include tennis, a small beach (usually windy), active water-sports concession, and all the opportunities for strolling around the boating activity at the marina, trying restaurants and shops and talking to boat people. The *Café Créole*, near the pool, is a pleasant resting spot, with swinging wicker chairs and big overstuffed furnishings under the dunce cap roof at the upstairs bar. *Le Boucaut* is the restaurant (where you should get a table with a view of Fort-de-

France). *Le Vesou* disco, with caves, caverns, and a peek-through hole to the sea, is usually lively. This is a big hotel, part of a big French chain, with all of Pointe du Bout a short stroll from your room (golf is a short ride to the course at Trois Islets). Made for the middle-income market, the place is popular with groups who get good rates. If you can sign on for one of those, do so; otherwise you're paying about $100 for 2, breakfasts included. There are several good restaurants within walking distance, or across the harbor at Fort-de-France.)

✤ **Gommier** (3 rue Berlin, Fort-de-France, Martinique, F.W.I.; 17 rooms) is a dining spot that also has rooms, but the fact that it does not appear on the official list from the Office du Tourisme could (and should) make you think twice. Don't be tempted to overnight here unless you like *very* simple surroundings (rooms do have air conditioners) and a low rate is prime concern. Two can lodge here for about $20, coffee and bread for breakfast included, but the location, at the inland side of La Savane (the park), in a busy commercial area, is far from ideal for a Caribbean vacation. Restaurant *and* rooms are very casual.

✤ **Impératrice** (Place de la Savane, Fort-de-France, Martinique, F.W.I.; 24 rooms) rises like the grande dame she is, from the west side of the Savane, right at the heart of the boutique area. The ground floor level has a sidewalk cafe that looked pretty seedy when I last saw it, but it has potential if it's been cleaned up. Although the house turned hotel in 1957, the place looks a lot older—and is not for fussy travelers. Rooms range from minute to relatively spacious; the ones on the front have all the view (and the noise) of the Savane. I recommend it only for Francophiles who are familiar with West Indian inns. Rates are for 2, close to $60, continental breakfasts included. There are several excellent restaurants within walking distance, and when you get bored with them you can take the 20-minute ferry to Pointe du Bout.

✤ **Lafayette Hotel** (Place de la Savane, 97200 Fort-de-France, F.W.I.; 24 rooms) claims a historic spot (on the site of the former Europe Hotel, facing the city's garden park) and an impressive management link (Carl de Pompignan is married to the daughter of Bakoua's Guy de la Houssaye). Rooms are modern (showers/no tub), and ones with park view are preferable—even considering the street noises that waft up to second-story level. Full hotel facilities are available, and everything the city offers is within a stroll.

Count on paying about $60 for 2, everything but the room extra, this winter.

✢ **Latitude Hotel** (Carbet, Martinique, F.W.I.; 90 rooms) lingers on the east coast, a few miles south of St. Pierre, but more than 20 miles north of Fort-de-France and the airport. When you're here, you are here—with the gray sand beach at your feet, a simple but colorful bungalow room to call home, and a main house that has all the group activities (dances, when there are any; meals and bar). Special scuba and snorkel holidays help give this hotel a single focus, and enthusiasts enjoy that. (There are 17 blocks of air-conditioned twin-bedded rooms.) Used by groups, and I suspect best when you are part of one, this hotel has action some evenings, but don't count on it. The pool lures some folks for daytime; others head to the hills for horseback riding or take to the sea (water sports concession) for scuba diving, waterskiing, boating, and fishing. Rates for 2 figures to $150, all meals included but inquire about special package rates.

✢ **Leyritz Plantation** (Basse-Pointe, Martinique; 25 rooms) gained fame with a *Gourmet* Magazine piece that touted the chef who thrived on press and left for a higher paying job elsewhere. Charles and Yveline de Lucy de Fossarieu headed for Florida in summer of '78, making frequent trips and telephone calls to coach the manager and team that work and play with the teams of tourists who come in on day trips. The place is popular for lunch on day excursions (it takes a couple of hours to wind the 40 miles north from the airport or Fort-de-France, at a taxi fare of about 125 francs one way but it is a pleasant and interesting drive in a rental car), and that detracts if you've sought out this lofty plantation perch for its spectacular isolation. Lawns slide from the main-house doors into lush tropical foliage that would completely take over if things were not carefully tended. Most guests are content to sit by the pool, wander around the gardens, read, or go off to a nearby beach with a picnic lunch and a will for leisure time. This is no place for rushing or for the disco-action-oriented. There's a tennis court and horses to ride, but arrangements have to be made with Latitude for use of their waterskiing, snorkeling, scuba and sailing equipment if you want more action than an isolated beach can provide. The 10 bedrooms in the main house are the best for my money (more charm). Around the grounds, the former slave quarters have been turned into 15 small cottages, with new ones added in the old style. Rooms are rustic. Rates for winter are about $95 for 2, breakfasts included.

✣ **Madinina** (Pointe du Bout, Martinique, F.W.I.; 15 rooms) makes its mark more for Mme. Sidonie's restaurant than for the modest, air-conditioned rooms that fill the top 2 floors of the small 3-story building angled into the action plan at busy Pointe du Bout. The price is right at about $40 for 2, meals extra, if you care more about being at wharf-front on the marina than about the size and shape of your room. And you're right in the heart of the nautical life.

✣ **Madras** (Tartane, Martinique, F.W.I.; 18 rooms) made a name for itself as a restaurant, serving excellent creole food at a beach-side setting. All that is still true, but Madame Nelcha has given those of us who lean back in our chairs, after a full meal, to say "I wish I could stay here forever" a chance to do so. New rooms were added in late 1980, and those that existed (over the patio restaurant and in a separate building at the side) have been painted and fixed up. Accommodations are sea-oriented simple, with tepid water that is sun (not oil) heated. Tartane is a fishing village on the east-coast peninsula that juts out at Trinité. Rates are about $40 for 2, with breakfast, and you'll need French for conversation.

✣ **PLM Manoir de Beauregard** (Chemin des Salines, Ste.-Anne; 30 rooms) has a lot of potential but what appears to me, after several visits, to be lackadaisical management. The Manoir is attractive, and could be more so if someone would weed, clean up, and help the place to look as though someone cared about it. There's no action here, but plenty available nearby if you want to go to the Club Med, or the shops and bistros of Ste.-Anne. If the other guests are total strangers when you arrive, chances are they will be so when you leave, unless you are fluent in French and exceptionally outgoing—and they want to be too. The core of the inn, and what has made it special, is the 18th-century main house with decorator touches that put the old world into modern times. A speck of a pool is a cool-off spot; French and creole food are served alfresco at the back of the house, but readers have written to complain about last season's fare. All rooms have antique furnishings (or good copies), most have 2 double four-poster beds and, for those who stay in the new wing, a small terrace. I prefer the more interesting rooms in the main house. Taxi fare from the airport (30 miles north) will be a staggering 130 francs, but once here, you can walk to Ste.-Anne. The nearest beach is Plage des Salines, about 3 miles south. Winter rates for 2 will tally around $70, with breakfast only. Count on paying about $15 if you stay "home" for dinner.

✛ **Meridien Martinique** (Pointe du Bout, Martinique, F.W.I.; 303 rooms) mesmerizes with an action plan that gives vacationers free water-sports equipment (including windsurfers) several dining depots, and casino-plus-disco for after dark dalliance. After a half-dozen years, and countless calamities, the hotel pulsates to its disco, casino, and the wishes of the group tours (French, Canadian, and American). Perched on Pointe du Bout, across the harbor from Fort-de-France, the hotel has become the queen of the court of tourist pleasures that surround this place. Sports facilities are on the spot (tennis courts, scuba school and shop, windsurfers, water-skiing, and arrangements for sailing). Meridien management regularly pulls the sand back onto the small stretch of beach, and tries to keep it there with a cement and stone groin that some use for sunning. The pool is picture-perfect, rimmed with yellow and white metal umbrellas that help keep the sun off (but watch your head when you get up from your chair). Dining facilities range from the French idea of a coffee shop (which looks like home, but doesn't act like it) to an elegant restaurant, *St. Louis* (Lewie, not Loois), where the menu is huge, the prices are high, and the quality ranged from average to fair. Surroundings in the restaurant are certainly not tropical; it has the aura of a New York spot. Rooms all have small balcony and sea or marina view; there are tennis courts (and some also next door at Bakoua) and the whole range of activity around the marina to enjoy. The boat to Fort-de-France makes the 20-minute run several times daily, at 8F one way; 10F round trip. Rates run about $120 per day for 2, continental breakfasts included, but ask about special charter and group tours and the Fête Française plan. Your travel agent should have details.

✛ **St. Aubin Hotel** (Petite Rivière Salée, 97220 Trinité, Martinique, F.W.I.; 15 rooms) is a gem, sitting on a hillside overlooking the seaside village of Trinité. You'll need a car for mobility; the public bus that passes along this road continues, eventually, from Trinité to Fort-de-France, but the ride involves a day's excursion. Otherwise, settle into this former private home on the hillside, or walk around the grounds (a clearing among plantation fields) to look carefully at the fanciful gingerbread fretwork that trims the eaves of this marvelous pink-beige house. The veranda is perfect for rocking in the soothing tradewinds, and you can count on Guy Foret to serve you special island recipes with his native-French flair. All rooms have private bath, but each room has its own personality, depending on the view and the furnishings. A very special spot for an unusual Martiniquais holiday, St. Aubin's rates are about $50 for 2, with breakfasts this winter. (You'll probably take most of your dinners here too, unless you like driving wiggly island roads in the dark.)

✙ **Victoria Hotel** (Rond Point du Vietnam Heroïque, Fort-de-France, Martinique, F.W.I.; 20 rooms) is a hillside home turned inn, popular with businessmen and others who want to be near center city (although you'll need a car or taxi access to get here). There's a small pool, and a simple dining room (where I've heard good food is served). The house is not historic, but the hospitality offered by M. Victoire is sincere. Rooms are simple, with the newest in a half-dozen separate units surrounding the pool, and some of the older rooms with very low rates (and no private bath). Most rooms are air-conditioned, some have small sitting area (this perch is apt to be *hot* at midday when, chances are, you won't be "at home"). Doubles are about $40, with coffee and croissant for 2.

▪▪

HOUSEKEEPING HOLIDAYS ON MARTINIQUE range from apartments at places like PLM Marina-Pagerie (see below), to the several homes, most of them second homes for Martiniquais families, rented through the Villa Rental Service of the Martinique Pavillon du Tourisme (B.P. 520, Fort-de-France, Martinique, F.W.I.). Do not expect furnishings and facilities exactly like what you have at home. Most of the homes for rent on Martinique have been built on or near the sea, many of them in the hills overlooking the sea. Beaches on Martinique are not the Caribbean's best—at least those that are near Fort-de-France or any other hub of action are not. A home of your own in Martinique is ideal if you speak French (or want to struggle along with it to learn how to speak French), like to read, and do not insist on a beach at your doorstep. Most of the homes have tepid water (sun-warmed, not heated) and adequate but not lavish furnishings, and you will need a rental car for mobility.

For stocking up, you will find good French bread, and should be able to track down a fisherman who will keep you supplied with fish and langouste (as the local lobster is called). There are no supermarkets as you know them at home, but there are good stores for provisioning. Bring the few things you cannot live without in a box packed from home.

✣ **Hotel Caritan** (Anse Caritan near Ste.-Anne, Martinique, F.W.I.; 94 rooms) is a newcomer to the south-coast overnighting nooks. The several buildings that hold the rooms are on a lovely beach, near the village that has developed a few restaurants and boutiques in response to tourism interest sparked, some say, by the nearby Club Meditérranée. This place, also, seems to take its cue from the Club Med system, with buffet lunch, extensive sports facilities (windsurfers, sailboats, scuba, boat rides, fishing, etc.) and nightly entertainment. The air-conditioned modern (small) rooms are geared to family-style beachside living, with kitchen facilities and narrow, French-style beds. A camplike program for children (with French the language for communication) is part of the activities plan. Although 1-night rates are offered (at about $100 for 2 with continental breakfast), you'll do much better with the all-inclusive weekly rate which is about $600 for 2. You'll need a rental car for mobility.

✣ **PLM Marina-Pagerie** (Pointe du Bout, Martinique, F.W.I.; 240 apts.) puts a high price on its location, which is wonderful if you like being in the middle of everything and don't demand a lot of wide-open space with your investment. Part of the barnacles of rooms that grew as soon as the marina was ready, this complex has studios, 2- and 3-room apartments that have a living area plus bedroom. All units have an ideal location for those who want a lot of action. Walls are thin in the 30 or more 3-story buildings, but you'll have air-conditioning (which you'll need with some of the pocket locations), a small efficiency kitchen with a few implements for home cooking, and a modern room with narrow twin beds that sit about 12 inches off the floor. (The first-built rooms are about 6 years old.) Shops, restaurants, cafes, and lingering spots have hatched at the ground level, so there are plenty of places to spend your time. Across the road, there's Bakoua and the Meridien, both with nightclubs, beach, and tennis courts plus the Meridien's casino. PLM Marina-Pagerie's rates, for compact accommodations in the heart of the marina activity, are some of the best values in this area. Even though $100 per night for the 2-bedroom unit (3 rooms) in winter may seem steep, you are in the heart of the high-rent district and that rate is reasonable. Studios are about $80 for 2. Check for summer Fêtes Française rates for the best deal.

✣ **Village Vacances** cluster at the shore on the east coast at l'Anse L'Etang near Tartane, and on the south coast near Sainte Luce (and there may be others that I have not seen). Built as vacation homes for Martiniquais, the bungalows are self-contained housekeeping units, some of them quite spacious and comfortable, around a central pool and at the beach. Since most residents vacation in summer months, the units are often available for rental by outsiders during the winter months. Contact the Office du Tourisme in Martinique for details. (People who speak French will be more comfortable in these surroundings than those with no knowledge of the language.)

■■
CAMPING is not organized according to U.S. National Park routines, but there are some small Toyota campers that can be rented at Pointe du Bout for driving around the island to pull off the road near a beach when you want to. The compact units, known as Sunraders, have a boat-like interior, with small kitchen equipment (including refrigerator) and toilet in addition to 4 sleeping berths that are covered as couches during the day. Rentals have been 900F for a weekend, 400F per day and 2800F per week, plus gas and your food. Ideal for families with small children or for a couple, the campers would be too crowded for 4 adults.

■■
RESTAURANTS ON MARTINIQUE share the kudos heaped on those on Guadeloupe; the unique French West Indian offerings on the menu are about the same. Here, as on Guadeloupe, the informal bistros offer some of the best eating experiences for my vacation dollar. The cluster of new restaurants at the marina of Pointe du Bout offer many options as do the simpler, older surroundings at some of the country villages and those places slightly off the beaten path. Food is expensive. Count on more than $10 for luncheon, and at least $20 and probably more for a complete dinner.

AUTHOR'S OBSERVATION: If you are addicted to your American cocktail, beware. Your "martini" may be presented as Martini & Rossi vermouth in many hotels—and will be that in small bistros not used to American travelers. Your "scotch and soda" may appear, as a colleague's did a few years ago, as Irish whiskey and orange soda, and highballs as Americans know them will be very expensive. If you *must* have your martini, bring your own small supply of dry vermouth (you will often get sweet vermouth even when you give the bartender instructions). The problem is not that the bartenders are not willing (they *are*); it is simply that American tastes are not, in fact, universal—and European customs prevail in the French West Indies. If you want to follow the "when in Rome" principal, you will content yourself with wine, rum (usually as "poonch" or a "planteur"), and an occasional *bière*.

The accepted accompaniment for main meals is wine which you can order by the carafe in the casual places and will be expected to order by the bottle, from the wine list, in the best French tradition at the more formal restaurants. For a bistro lunch, you may get by with French beer (Kronenborg from the Alsace is sold here and Lorraine is locally brewed) but water marks you as an obvious American—and in many places should be ordered with discretion. Bottled water appears on most mealtime tables, but you will have to order it (for about 4F). The French West Indies *punch* is the classic drink. Pronounced "poonch," the drink is a potent potion that is served with the ceremony of English tea in the traditional places: On the table will be set a tray with a small bucket of ice, a small carafe of what will prove to be sugar syrup, a plate with limes, and a bottle of powerful rum. Your host—or you—can mix the ingredients in the small shot-sized glass provided for the purpose. Water is not usually part of the recipe, but a generous squeeze of lime with your rum and sugar syrup on the rocks is. A *planteur,* also popular, is rum and fruit juice.

AUTHOR'S AWARDS for dining on Martinique go to La Vraie Bonne Auberge Chez François et Raymonde, not so much for the atmosphere as for the fact that the food (especially fish) is fabulous; Madras at Tartane, for its beachside atmosphere and bistro setting; to Le Foulard at Schoelcher for uniquely Martiniquais surroundings and very special food; with a special mention for L'Ecole Hoteliere, where your meal is prepared by students eager to please and learning the best preparation.

La Grand Voile, at the Yacht Club in Fort-de-France, is constantly touted as offering the best food on Martinique. I do not doubt the claim, but you will have little difficulty finding this place. Prices are very high—and going higher according to recent predictions. The haute cuisine is worth the praise heaped upon it and an evening here should be reserved for a very special occasion. There's a small, icebox of a bar (air-conditioned to sweater temperature) with nautical decor just at the top of the stairs you climb to get to the second-floor restaurant at the harbor. Try to get a table near the window for best view, and be sure to make reservations in advance.

La Bonne Auberge Chez Andre nestles between 2 small houses on a side street not far from the Pointe du Bout marina, near the beach at Anse Mitan. Your fish will be grilled, and whatever you order will be simple and good. Although the menu is written in English and French, the waitress or waiter will respond best to French or slow and precise English. Count on about $10 for a full lunch (in bathing suit with cover-up if you want) and $20 for dinner. (This was the first Bonne Auberge building, but the original owners who made it famous, are at the other.)

La Vraie Bonne Auberge Chez François et Raymonde, farther down the road (away from the beach but closer to the turn off from the Pointe du Bout road) is in a new and expanding building on a plot of land that was formerly a vacant lot. François and Raymonde are the originators of La Bonne Auberge—and their food is fresh, excellent, and well worth the reservation you will need at peak season winter. Rooms have been added and, if you want a simple inn, with what should be very reasonable rates, a few steps from the beach at Anse Mitan, consider this. As far as dining is concerned, count on good, fresh fish and the chef's special (whatever it may be) to be excellent—and the atmosphere to be favored by residents who know good food.

Bambou, popular with Martiniquais, especially on holidays and weekends, is another beachside place at Anse Mitan, with the terrace restaurant at the main building for the cluster of simple cottages that makes up the small inn. This is also a fish and/or soup spot, with the soupe de poisson especially good.

Chez Sidonie, at Mme. Sidonie's small Madinina Hotel right on the boardwalk at the Pointe du Bout marina, I think has suffered from the leap into the commerce of the marina. My meals here have been only average, although Mme. Sidonie made her reputation for a very special, simple spot where the food was exceptional. The new surroundings are at the edge of the boardwalk at the marina and appeal to nautical types.

Le Cantonnais, sets back from the boardwalk at Pointe du Bout's marina, is an air-conditioned Chinese restaurant favored by residents. The menu is extensive, the food good, and if you want a break from creole cooking, this is worth a try.

La Marine, the restaurant that grew at the feet of the ever-expanding La Marina apartments, is a "quick lunch" or informal dinner place where you can get acceptable food at reasonable prices. Pizza had become a favored item now that the ovens are installed. If you get one of the chairs in the front, near the bar, you can enjoy the waterfront panorama as entertainment while you dine.

D'Esnambuc, in Fort-de-France, up the stairs near the building on the corner to your left as you get off the ferry from Pointe du Bout, resides on venerable ground. For several years, the location was that of Le Foyal (now closed), the most famous haute cuisine restaurant in the city. D'Esnambuc has good food, but the surroundings are crowded and closed in so that you could be anywhere. There's no view, and a lot of noise if the place is full. Look it over before you make your reservation here, but count on above average French cooking and good seafood—with wine—for your meal. Prices are high.

Le Tiffany, outside Fort-de-France, is a gem, with prices in keeping with the excellence. Surroundings are almost reason enough to make a reservation for dinner here, but food preparation and service are also superb. A traditional French West Indian house has been preened to perfection. Count on planning ahead for a dinner reservation and hope that the place is open (and your wallet can cope with prices) if you are on Martinique at other than peak season winter.

Le Foulard is at Schoelcher (northwest, along the coast from Fort-de-France; named for Victor Schoelcher, a leader in the 1848 abolition of slavery in the French West Indies). The taxi fare can be staggering, and you'll have to make arrangements for the taxi to return for pick-up. If you drive yourself, be sure to get specific directions. The restaurant is unpretentious, and therefore not easy to find. The food is exceptional. Call for a reservation and inquire about the evening's special, which should be preceded (if you are hungry) by the soupe de poisson. Pastries and bread can become an addiction.

Madras, a small informal bistro at the simple inn on the beach at Tartane, is the special domain of Mme. Nelcha who set up Les Brisants. When you are driving in the country, and heading east out to Presqu'île de la Caravelle (the nature preserve being developed for recreational use for Martiniquais) and Trinité, this is a thought for a late lunch and leisurely afternoon. Our meal of poisson grillee (grilled fish) and other seaside specials was superb.

Plantation de Leyritz, the 18th-century estate in the northern quarter of Martinique, has developed its dining for groups and tourists. Food is served in a building near the pool, and reports were good when I stopped by for this edition. Satisfied diners liked their meal; I was too late for mine. I suspect the place is better for dinner (if you are staying here), than it is when it is full of day-trippers who arrive for lunch and fill the place with lively conversation.

Other places to head for when you're touring the island are **Mme. Edjam's** in Basse-Pointe (almost at the northern tip of the island, at the village near the turn off for Leyritz) and **Mme. Palladino's** in Morne des Esses, a worthy goal for creole cooking in typical home-like surroundings on the day you tour the north. Called **Le Colibri,** Mme. Palladino's place has had a shower of publicity in U.S. newspapers and magazines so calling for a reservation is essential to assure a seat. **Poi et Virginie,** a casual thatch-roofed seaside spot at Ste.-Anne, a short walk from Dunette Hotel and at a corner of the town's main square, is related to **Filets Bleu,** both good spots for a break from your Club Med routine if you're staying in the south.

■■■

PLACES WORTH FINDING ON MARTINIQUE are a marvelous mixture of small fishing villages, legitimate and interesting historic sites, and plenty of verdant tropical countryside—occasionally shored with beaches. The big tourist hotels have activities desks where you can sign on for a group tour, with daily options that vary according to the prevailing plan, but there's a lot to be said for striking out on your own—in a rental car—especially if your French is fluent. Martinique is a very special island, where the French flair is so ingrained in the lives and looks of the people that even the smallest villages have an ambiance all their own, more reminiscent of places on the French Riviera than of other Caribbean islands you may know.

Musée de la Pagerie (daily except M, 9-5:30; 6F) at Trois Ilets is on the site of the house where Napoleon's Josephine was born, but don't be misled into thinking that the present museum was her birthplace. It was the former kitchen for a plantation on the site, built after the 1860 hurricane blew the former plantation to bits. The gigantic African tulip tree may have stood on the property when she played here, but the museum and most of its collection are the result of a local doctor's interest in the famed Martiniquaise. In addition to costumed dolls in cases, and letters written by Napoleon to his wife (whom *he* called Josephine; her birth name was Marie Josèphe Rose), there are mementos and portraits of Beauharnais (Josephine's first husband), comments about Josephine's two children (one of whom married Napoleon's brother to become Queen of Holland and mother of Napoleon III), and her divorce from Napoleon in 1809.

The small museum is a short drive from the hotels at Pointe du Bout and Anse Mitan, on the road to the airport. You can allow an extra hour or more to visit the museum and to pause for a stroll around the lovely gardens with pond that you pass on the way to get to the museum. Known as the Parc des Floralies, the compact garden nestles near the golf course, and is worth a look if you are interested in tropical flowers (and the gates are open). The road off the main road at Trois Ilets is well marked. A guide is usually available—and even in French, with a few words in English, can help with highlights.

Mont Pelée, the peak that put the island into the headlines in 1902 when the volcano erupted, is often cloud covered. The northeast coast site is about an hour's drive up the coast from Fort-de-France. You can climb the mountain, but arrange for a guide and don't attempt the trek unless you're in good shape and a competent climber. The route is not difficult, but it is steep in spots and often tangled with tropical growth. For most, the **Musée Volcanologique** (daily 9-12, 3-5; 3F) tells the story in vivid enough displays. There are twisted and tortured clocks that stopped at the hour the volcano erupted (8 a.m.), as well as before and after photographs that are hard to believe when you look at the sleepy village that has taken the place of once-thriving Saint-Pierre. The pictures and remnants give another dimension to the most monumental event in Martinique's history, and you can stroll through the couple of rooms in a quick 20 minutes.

Saint-Pierre is described as "the quaintest, queerest, and prettiest withal, among West Indian cities," by Lafcadio Hearn. He comments about the town being "all stone-built and stone-flagged, with very narrow streets, wooden or zinc awnings, and peaked roofs of red tile, pierced by gabled dormers. Most of the buildings are painted in a clear yellow tone, which contrasts delightfully with the burning blue ribbon of tropical sky above; and no street is absolutely level; nearly all of them climb the hills, descend into hollows, curve, twist, describe sudden angles. There is everywhere a loud murmur of running water, pouring through the deep gutters contrived between the paved thoroughfare and the absurd little sidewalks, varying in width from one to three feet. The architecture is quite old: it is seventeenth century probably and it reminds one of a great deal of that characterizing the antiquated French quarter of New Orleans. All the tints, the forms, the vistas, would seem to have been especially selected or designed for aquarelle studies, just to please the whim of some extravagant artist. The windows are frameless openings without glass; some have iron bars; all have heavy wooden shutters with movable slats, through which light and air can enter as through Venetian blinds. These are usually painted green or bright bluish-gray." Lafcadio Hearn's description of the town in the 1880s continues; the town does not. When Mont Pelée erupted on May 8, 1902, the entire thriving metropolis of Saint-Pierre, known at that time as the "Paris of the West Indies," was extinguished by clouds of poisonous gas, horrendous heat, and a blanket of hot ash. Today Saint-Pierre is a small village, with a big history—and its interesting small museum.

In **FORT-DE-FRANCE,** **La Savane** is the town's central park. Tourism has touched the shoreside section, across the road from the place the ferries dock from Anse Mitan and Pointe du Bout. That end is cluttered with shoppers' stalls stuffed with Haitian carvings and other tourist trinkets. At the other side of the park, not far from the imposing **Schoelcher Library** with its intricate facade, leisure time is enjoyed by the islanders who linger on the benches that have been sifted around the sometimes well-trimmed gardens.

Musée Départemental de la Martinique (M-F 9-12, 3-6, Sat 9-12; 5F) will fascinate anyone interested in island archeology. Relics retrieved from the early Arawak and Carib civilizations have been organized in display cases, with some explanation (usually in French, but simple enough for anyone with rudimentary knowledge of the language to decipher). Documentary films and slide talks are sometimes sponsored by the Musée; check with the tourist office, which is along the waterfront in a special building you can easily find, if you walk along rue de Liberté to the shore. **Musee de Gauguin** (daily 10-5; 3F) is off the shore-rimming-road south of St. Pierre and is near the place where Gauguin lived and painted for 4 months in 1887. A nice interlude after a day of natural sights, the small museum holds the expected memorabilia—letters and small items relating to his life on the island—as well as some copies of his painting while here.

Parc Naturel Regional de la Martinique is the overseer of the verdant area around Mt. Pelée, in the northern section of the island (in the vicinity of Leyritz Plantation). Check with the Office du Tourisme for information about hikes and walks and other activities that are planned from time to time. Anyone interested in island flora and fauna should at least make the drive north, coming down the windward side of the island from Leyritz. Cecile Graffin, tireless French West Indies touter in the New York City tourist office, tells of a 6-hour hike along the shoreside trails in the vicinity of Grand Rivière and Prêcheur on the northwestern tip of the island. It took her half an hour to return to the starting point by boat!

In addition to the northern area, including the peaks and flanks of Mt. Pelée, the Parc Naturel includes **Presqu'île de la Caravelle,** a peninsula jutting into the sea on the east coast and an area now undergoing development for recreational facilities for the Martiniquais. Plans include a marina in addition to full water-sports facilities for scuba and waterskiing as well as tennis and other facilities, but at this writing you will find only beautiful scenery, the small fishing village of Tartane, and some dirt roads leading to remote coves.

Fishing villages are liveliest in the morning, when the fleet has returned with the catch and the stalls are set up at the shore. At their best when you go on your own, so that you can mingle with the local folk (who will look you over because you will look different), the villages are perfect places to settle into one of the small cafes that set up seaside to serve the fresh grilled fish—sometimes served with lime and usually best with a fiery shot of rum. Places like **Marin** not far from Ste.-Anne in the south, and **Vauclin** or **Le François** on the west coast are special spots to sample the Antilles Françaises. Both are about as different from the tourist tempo at Pointe du Bout as you would wish to get (and a detour for a broiled langouste at Les Brisants near Le François can put the final touch on a perfect island day).

■■

SPORTS ON MARTINIQUE stretch from north to the south, and from the calm western coast of the *département* to the rugged east. While most of the sports that need special equipment (scuba diving, which is known as *plongée,* windsurfing, and sailing) are centered on the resorts, the individual sports (horseback riding and hiking) can be found in the country, in places seldom seen by most tourists but well known to the Martiniquais. Action centers are the area of Pointe du Bout, a 20-minute ferryboat ride from the waterfront of Fort-de-France, and the Club Med in the south.

Sailing centers on the Pointe du Bout marina, where yachts can be chartered at *Dufour Antilles,* operating from their own boat moored at the marina near the Frantel waterside gate. Bareboat charters through Dufour are priced to include fuel and water, and have high quality radio and other equipment on board. Charterers are given a copy of the French Guide to cruising the Antilles; if your language is not French, there is an English guide by Wilensky that is an essential companion. *West Indies Bird,* a 39-foot sloop, is available for charter through *Caribtours,* from their office near the entrance to the Hotel PLM Marina-Pagerie, and the water-sports desks at Frantel and Meridien can also arrange for day and longer sailing on bigger boats. *Martinique Charter & Services* carries listings of about 35 yachts that are cruising through the Caribbean, some of them tied up temporarily at one of the 140 berths that are the teeth of the marina. Since the favored cruising area in this part of the Caribbean is the several specks of the Grenadine islands, the firm sometimes includes flight to St. Vincent in your charter fee so that you can board at the best sailing area, and not have to pound your way across the often rugged seas from Martinique, southeast to St. Lucia and on to the north of St. Vincent, where you sail down the coast to reach the string of Grenadines that stretch out from the south. *Tabarly Yachting* has shifted its island base a couple of times in recent years. Although Eric Tabarly talks about returning to the Pointe du Bout area, at presstime he has a sailing school at Le Marin in the south, on the 60-foot *Pen Duick III,* an ideal craft for one-week sail-and-learn programs. Tabarly's Pen Duick 600s are good for day sailing. Out of the Club Med, at the south at Ste.-Anne, there are several yachts for day or week-long charters through the Grenadines. Arrangements can be made when you book a Club Med holiday. For true yachtsmen with club credentials from home, the *Club de la Voile de Fort-de-France* is at Pointe Simon. You can look over the facilities while you sample an elegant meal on the glassed-in terrace of La Grand' Voile restaurant, or you can make a point of going over to talk with some of the local yachtsmen in your best French.

If you want to head out on plans you make yourself, stop at the front desk at Bakoua Hotel to see what yachts are anchoring offshore. It is often possible to make arrangements with the skipper; someone at the hotel can send you off in the right direction to find him (usually through the *Ship Shop* at the shore). You can usually count on finding a big boat for a cruise along the coast out of PLM La Batelière. There's a "Buccaneer Cruise" offered from some of the big hotels, where you head up the coast by yacht and return through the rain forest by bus. Check the activities boards at the large hotels in the Pointe du Bout area, especially at peak season winter when activities are running full tilt.

Scuba has surged to the forefront of water activities in the French West Indies, as you might expect from an area that can benefit from knowledge of Frenchman Jacques Cousteau who developed the underwater lung. The instructors are French, and are licensed in international scuba organizations such as the World Underwater Federation and the French Federation of Underwater Sports. Spirotechnique and scubapro regulators are used, and although the bilingual instruction is excellent, the teaching procedure varies slightly from what you may be used to in your hometown pool. Meridien Hotel was the first to get into scuba lessons for American tourists, when the property opened in the early 1970s. The 37-foot boat takes you and your group to Anses d'Arlets and the Ramier inlet where there is a wreck as well as plenty of coral. Frantel, on the other side of the marina, has started a similar program. Latitude Hotel, up the west coast, at Carbet, just south of St.-Pierre, also offers an official scuba course through its *Carib Scuba School* (guests at Leyritz usually sign on here). French instructors take experienced divers to spots off the coast at St.-Pierre (to shipwrecks like that of the *Roraima*) and farther north at Prêcheur. Club Med, on the south coast, includes basic scuba lessons in its week-long all-inclusive holiday (no extra charge), but complete novices may find that the group technique offered does not give the very special personal touch that timid beginners may need.

Snorkeling is good off most shores, but especially off the beaches at the south near Ste.-Anne, and at some of the small coves that cut into the west coast around the point below Anse Mitan at les Anses d'Arlets.

Deep-sea fishing has not been organized for tourists as it has been in places like the U.S. Virgin Islands, Puerto Rico, Barbados, Bonaire, the Caymans, Jamaica, and some of the other islands. The PLM La Batelière has a fishing boat at its pier, but otherwise, check through your hotel when you arrive on Martinique, and ask around at the Pointe du Bout marina to see if there's some news on this subject. For adventuresome tourists who speak French, it may be possible to go out with one of the local fisherman when he goes to collect his nets, but this is *hard* work (as you can see when you stand on shore and watch them return) and not a sightseeing expedition. Your space and your brawn are important.

Golfers should book at Pointe du Bout hotels if being near the 18-hole Robert Trent Jones course is important. The course finally opened for the season of '77–'78, after a couple of years in the laying and pruning and another couple trying to decide how the operation would be run. The fact was that, for a while, there were so few people on the island who knew anything about golf (an American passion, but not necessarily the only sport for the rest of the world) that finding people to staff the course, tend greens, and the like, turned into a major project. *Golf de l'Espérance* is the name of the course which undulates over several acres (6640 yards) near the village of Trois-Ilets. Greens fees depend on your hotel. Bakoua, Frantel, PLM Marina-Pagerie, and Meridien guests can play the 18 holes for $12 a day; guests from other hotels pay $15. (The Club Med may negotiate some special rate, but if you go on your own from that southern spot, you will have almost a 300F taxi fare to get to and from the course; playing golf on the day you rent a car turns out to be the most economical way to play from the south coast.)

Hiking is popular with the Martiniquais, and guided walks are arranged through the Parc Régional. Check at the Office du Tourisme on the waterfront in Fort de France for details about possible hikes, dates, and times. The day will be a lot pleasanter if you speak some French, but it is possible to survive without it. One of the popular hiking areas, with some occasionally marked trails is Presqui'île de la Caravelle Nature Preserve, on the east coast. Hikes are also planned around and up the flanks of Mont Pelée in the north.

Horseback riding is "outlawed" on beaches in France—and that applies to the French West Indies, but there are plenty of interesting trails inland. If you ride at Ranch Jack Galochat, near Anses d'Arlets which is less than half an hour's drive from the Pointe du Bout hotels, you can canter around on small and nimble creole horses. Some who have taken the ride think that a stop at the California Saloon is an essential part of the experience. (The restaurant, with a chili special some days, is operated by an island entrepreneur who spent some time in the American west. His combination of creole and "California" is intriguing.) Do not count on English Riding School technique. The Antilles Françaises consider horses a means of transportation and the method of riding is not showmanship as much as survival.

Tennis facilities are improving. The PLM La Batelière has 6 courts and the hotel's location just north of the city of Fort-de-France and across the harbor from most of the tourist activity has led to a focus on tennis. Other courts are available (and in constant play) at Bakoua, Meridien, and Frantel in the Pointe du Bout area as well as at Latitude (1), Leyritz (1), and at the Club Med (6, with 4 of them floodlit).

Windsurfing, the surfboard-and-sail sport that got its start in California in the late 1960s, has put a fringe of colorful sails at all the major tourist beaches. The sport is so popular, in fact, that the International Windsurfing Championships, held in Martinique in mid-November 1978 are planned as an every other year event. There are several small booths (or tables) for rental and instruction on Anse Mitan and Meridien, Frantel and La Batelière have windsurfers as does the Club Med.

Pilots who would like to take a Cessna or Cherokee from the Aero Clubs de Martinique or les Ailes de la Martinique will have to have a French license, which you can get on the spot from the local civil aeronautics board (but allow at least a day to track down the person and price).

■■

TREASURES AND TRIFLES ON MARTINIQUE are clustered along the side streets of Fort-de-France, running parallel to the sea from rue de la Liberté, bordering La Savane, especially along rue Victor Hugo, rue Blenac, and rue Antoine Siger. You may see booths set up on La Savane as soon as you step off the ferry from Pointe du Bout, and there may be something among the obvious tourist trinkets that will interest you. It's impossible to miss the sign for **Roger Albert's** perfume and luxury item store. The store is on rue Victor Hugo, but the sign hangs over the waterfront as you pull into the dock. Each time I write about his perfume prices, I receive a flurry of comment from interested parties that his prices *are* the best in the Caribbean. Check for yourself. Cabinets in the store hold luxury items imported from France (Lalique, crystal, china, etc.), plus watches and a selection of souvenirs. And there is an announced "20% tax refund for payment in Travelers Cheques and American Express credit card," so don't be shy about asking for it.

Cadet Daniel, at 72 rue Antoine Siger, also carries Limoges china and Lalique crystal in addition to Baccarat, and gold and silver jewelry plus some less expensive (but imaginative) creole jewels. And Cadet Daniel also advertises a "20% discount for payment in travelers cheques and credit cards."

Au Printemps, with no direct link to the name you may know from mainland France, is at 12 rue Schoelcher, by the cathedral. It is one of the few department stores in the Caribbean that I think is worth my shopping time. I have found some excellent values (often at sales) and some interesting, and reasonable, French fashions and imports from elsewhere, sold at prices that big chain reactions can afford. **Prisunic** on a main route parallel to the waterfront is another department store, with slightly lower prices than Au Printemps.

The **Caribbean Art Center,** also called Centre des Metier's d'Art, is in its own building opposite the Tourist Office on Boulevard Alfassa, which is the main waterfront road. The selection sold here is all handmade, and although there's been a change in quality (some of the naïveté has gone with the standardization of designs) as the place has gotten more commercial, there are interesting colorful wall hangings as well as a number of paintings, wood bowls, carvings, and other items that have been made on the island. For one stop shopping for island made items, this is the place to find.

Most (all?) shops close at about noon, to open again at 2:30 or so, except on Saturdays when the morning hours are all the time you'll have for shopping.

Montserrat

*M*ontserrat Tourist Board, Box 7, Plymouth, Montserrat, W.I.; Caribbean Tourism Association, 20 East 42nd St., New York, NY 10017; Montserrat Tourist Board, Box 494, Station A, Toronto, Ontario M5W 1E4, Canada, Eastern Caribbean Tourist Association, 200 Buckingham Palace Road, London SW1W 9TJ, England.

US$1 = EC$2.60
Unless otherwise noted, $ refers to U.S. currency.

Aldolphus Morson rode his donkey, Mary, to school. By that time of day he had already been to the fields to tend his family's cattle. He would have to go back to the fields when school was over, but during the day his donkey munched grass with the other schoolboys' donkeys while the children learned. That was about 10 years ago, and while boys still ride their donkeys to school, Aldolphus Morson has earned enough money driving his taxi and taking people on tours around the island to spend about EC$2000 going to London to visit his sister. He bought his 1969 car secondhand about 5 years ago from the airport supervisor. He paid about EC $3000 for it, and could sell it now, he says, even with all the extra mileage, for EC $7000. A new car would cost EC $20,000 or more—if you could get on the list to get one. Imagine what's happened to the rest of the prices on imports.

But prices aren't the only things that are changing. Morson works the airport now. He lives nearby, and goes to the small blue shed with the separate tower and the neat sign that says "Welcome to Montserrat" when the plane comes in. The airstrip is well paved, but the small planes from Antigua still touch down on the tarmac just in time. Not long ago, when the strip was dirt, small-plane pilots talked in awed tones about the drop "of about 50 feet" just after takeoff—in response to downdrafts because the "runway" dissolved with the face of the cliff. That was about 20 years ago, and most of the people who came here then sailed on an island schooner, perhaps from St. Kitts, about 60 sea miles northeast and temporary home for Montserrat's first settlers.

They were Irish. Bishop Demets, who was the Catholic prelate on this island until a couple of years ago, noted that an "old Catholic register refers to Montserrat as 'Tirey Erin of the West Indies,' " and that "colonization began with the arrival of Catholic Irish fathers in 1632. That makes the Catholic Church the oldest church on Montserrat, though now, only third in number."

One of the first services was held, Cedric Osborne tells me, in his family home on Parliament Street in Plymouth. The house is called "Treicellian House" which means "3-leaf house" or "Shamrock House," and it seems only fitting that Cedric Osborne should have been the one to design the new host table for Plymouth's Catholic Church. It's made of local wood, burnished to a gleam the mother tree never expected, but that "Felix A.K., the wood doctor" knew was there.

Why the first settlers came to the island that Columbus had officially named Santa Maria de Montserrat (for the famous monastery in Spain and in recognition both of Queen Isabella and King Ferdinand) is a matter of speculation. For freedom of worship, probably, but whether or not for the freedom from Cromwellian oppression (since the eventual architect of the Dissolution of the Monarchy only became a Member of Parliament in 1628) is a matter of conjecture.

Whatever the reason, Bishop Demets had records of 1678 that note the population of Montserrat as "761 English, 52 Scots, 992 slaves and 1,869 Irish"—and the Irish quota included a handful of Catholics who arrived in 1634 after temporary residence in the state of Virginia. Sugar was introduced to Montserrat in 1650, but you will see few fields of cane waving now. Not only did the crop dissipate after the freeing of British slaves in 1834, but the recent attempts by Chief Minister Austin Bramble to make Montserrat the vegetable market for the Caribbean has meant that a lot of acres grow some of the Caribbean's best fruits and vegetables.

Limes became the replacement crop for the sugar era. Joseph Sturge, a Quaker from Gloucestershire, passed through Montserrat in 1836, in pursuit of his project for bettering the life of the former slaves and established what would become the island's biggest land holdings for the growth of limes. His timing was perfect. Not long after his trees were bearing, the crop of lemons in Sicily failed and the British turned to Montserrat's lime juice.

In the early 1800s Olveston and Woodlands Estates would

prickle with profitable lime trees; today both west coast estates prickle with private homes and a couple of small hotels. The new crop for these lime groves has become vacationing Americans, Canadians, and Englishmen. Vue Pointe stands on Old Towne plantation grounds, and Olveston, a short weave up the hill, takes its name from the Estate. The house was the former home of one of the Sturge plantation employees.

Life on Montserrat is not one of big plantations now. Prices have risen, places have changed, but the Montserratians maintain the personal pride that makes them—and their homeland—special. Montserrat is a people place, where your invitation to visit is sincere and the hospitality as warm as the tropical climate.

■■■

POLITICAL PICTURE: The wind shifted in fall of '78, when elections ousted the Bramble family, and John Osborne—running with the People's Labour Party—was voted in as Chief Minister of the British colony. Up until now, Montserrat has opted to maintain colonial status in the realization that the island does not have the financial base to go it alone, but with the examples of Dominica, St. Lucia, and eventually St. Vincent to look at, Montserrat can hardly be expected to lag behind in the push toward national identity. The Osborne government has given some attention to the tourism industry, with incentives for existing and new hotels.

■■■

CUSTOMS OF THE COUNTRY are uniquely West Indian. On this island, untouched by the heavy foot of tourism, life has proceeded naturally to full integration. Any comments about color seem distinctly out of place. This spot has moved far beyond that problem, which only came here through outsiders.

The local population of 13,000 moves along at its own pace, gradually improving the quality of life for all. Although things may have progressed beyond the days when a Montserratian told me there could be no thievery because if someone appeared with something new, everyone would know where it came from, life is mutually supportive here.

■■

MONEY MATTERS focus on the EC$. Change your greenbacks at the bank and spend local. This is not a tourist island (although visitors are welcome), and one of the several small courtesies to your hosts is to follow their system instead of imposing yours. Exchange is fixed at about EC$2.60 to US$1, but you will find some shops giving only EC$2.50. Taxi fares have climbed as they have on all islands due to increased costs (figure about EC$17 to Plymouth; EC$30 to Vue Pointe, and about EC$80 for an island tour). Taxi drivers are helpful, even though some will swarm around you when you land on a winter flight. Their rates are fixed by the government; any abuses should be discussed.

■■

ARRIVAL at Blackburne Airport is unfettered by the presumptuous routines of busier resort areas. The 15-minute flight from Antigua sweeps into Blackburne Airport with a breathtaking pass at the north coast mountains before gliding onto the tarmac strip. Antigua-based Caribbean carrier LIAT (Leeward Islands Air Transport) makes the flight a couple of times daily, sometimes leaving ahead of schedule, so be at Antigua's airport when they tell you to be there! (LIAT also sometimes leaves late, so come prepared for lingering.) Round trip Antigua-Montserrat is about EC$80, but fitted into your U.S.-purchased fare, the difference between fare to Antigua and to Montserrat can be only a few dollars. A 17-passenger Trilander given to Montserrat by the British government has been leased to LIAT to be used as a shuttle between Antigua and Montserrat.

Blackburne Airport is at the northwest coast, near the site of one of the early Arawak settlements (as shards found on the site have proved). The tidy turquoise-painted terminal is sufficient for service these days; immigration is quick and easy (your U.S. passport gets a shamrock stamp), customs perfunctory—even when you are bringing in food for meals at the house you've rented.

Departure involves flight check-in, forfeit of immigration slip, payment of a $5 departure tax, and a wait in the breeze-swept lounge. Don't count on shops. The few items for sale will not be of interest to tourists, but a cool beer from the bar might.

■■

TOURING TIPS: First-timers should take a taxi, not only to get where you're going, southwest across the island, but also for the lore and the option to have a lot of questions answered. If you advise you hotel about your time of arrival (and manage to arrive, with the erratic plane connections, pretty close to that time), chances are they will have someone there to meet you. If not, negotiate yourself, but be sure the fare is understood (and know whether the dollars are EC or US) before you start riding. Once settled at your hotel, you can rent a car for maximum flexibility (and should have arranged for one in advance if you have rented a home to set up housekeeping). In height of winter season, write in advance for your car reservation as well as for hotel/home overnights.

■■■

HOTELS number less than a handful, and each has its own personality. Not one has more than 40 rooms, and some of the places to stay are simple, without private bath. On this tropical garden, more than half the overnight rooms are in private homes for rent in owner's absence. There is a 10% service charge and a 7% government tax added to your hotel bill.

Summer rates are about half of the winter tariff, and the weather—as is the case throughout most of the Caribbean—will be the same glorious climate that most northerners think of only when the snow starts to fall.

ＡUTHOR'S AWARD goes, again, to Vue Pointe Hotel, not only because the facilities are comfortable, but also—and probably more important—for the very special Montserratian hospitality that the Osborne family (children included) and the hotel staff have made their specialty.

✤ **Coconut Hill Hotel** (Box 65, Montserrat; 10 rooms) is one of the Osborne enterprises. The old Montserratian mansion has added personality with its years (there's a lot of both), but don't count on luxury living. This place is strictly West Indian informal, with the newest flourish a main floor bedroom-turned-bar, with soft green walls, rattan bar stools, an outdoor deck, and the swish of the sea (a distance away) as the symphony to sip by. When another old house was being sold a couple of years ago, Cedric Osborne and family swept up some of the choice antiques. Most of Coconut Hill bedrooms now have island four-posters, painstakingly scraped of their layers of paint to be refinished so the old wood shows. Some rooms have private bath; rooms 5 and 7 face front, with a shared upper deck for open air lounging. All rooms have thin walls, and budget-conscious guests are often folks in Montserrat on government grants for studies and work. Rates for 2 are US$68, 2 West Indian meals daily per person. Lunch is served in the dining room, at an eclectic collection of antique tables with nonmatching chairs. (The menu features hamburgers, hot dogs, cheese sandwiches, and other familiar fare, at EC prices.) The hotel is in Plymouth, so getting to town is no problem. You'll pay about EC$20 for your ride from the airport.

✝ **Emerald Isle** (Box 259, Richmond Hill, Montserrat; 16 rooms) takes its name from the island, but can't take first place away from Vue Pointe, in my opinion. As the only other hotel worthy of the name (Coconut Hill qualifies as an inn), the French-owned complex nests on the hillside, overlooking Plymouth with new neighbor, Shamrock Villas. There's a pool for cooling off, but any beach (black sand or otherwise) is a drive away. Your room for overnighting will be in one of 3 band-aids on the hillside to the left of the check-in area under the green-and-white striped roof of the main building. I have to admit that my longtime friendship with the Osbornes makes it impossible for me to be objective, but it doesn't seem to me that the same warm hospitality exists here. OK for people who want to be near (but not in) town, the Emerald Isle is reached by hillside climb in a car, from the turning by the technical high school. Taxi fare from Blackburne airport runs about EC$20, and you can expect to pay about US$158 for 2 for winter overnight, 2 meals daily per person.

✝ **Vue Pointe** (Box 65, Montserrat; 28 cottages plus 12 rooms) freckles a hillside by the sea with sun-bleached shingle roofs, about 15 minutes' drive from Plymouth and about 25 from the airport (EC$30 taxi fare). Vue Pointe is a hospitable, family-run inn where guests have been returning to their favorite of the 28 cottages for long enough to create a house-party feeling. The check-in desk to the right as you enter the airy lobby is always manned by a friendly Montserratian who really makes you feel that "our house is your house," as the Vue Pointe literature says. Cedric Osborne's father started the place more than 20 years ago. Cedric and Boston-born Carol keep it operating, with a brand of island hospitality that mixes and mingles guests and Montserratians. (A group of schoolchildren who come to sing some evenings got so enthusiastic about their project that the whole school started appearing; Cedric had to reissue the invitation—for the choral group only.) The hub of activity is at the top of the hill: the dining room overlooking the sea (where I've had some of my best West Indian meals), the bar/gathering area, and the pool with its spray of lounge chairs. The 6-sided cottages sprinkled around the slope below, on the way to the brown-sand beach that fringes the bay, offer twin or double-bedded rooms, with bath (shower), sitting area and private terrace. Rooms count on the natural breeze that sweeps steadily over the hill for air conditioning. The 12 rooms are in 3 stucco blocks of 4 rooms each, with the 2 middle rooms connecting (ideal for families who want to be close, but not share a room). Cottages A, B, C, or D are on the lowest level, with view and an easy walk to "The Nest," the shore-side bar area that draws the nautical types who anchor offshore, or tie up to the small government-built Vue Pointe-maintained pier that should be completed by the time you get there. Winter rates for 2 in a cottage are $140, 2 meals 'aily per person; a room for 2 in the 3 blocks is $115, children 2-10 are an extra $30 in winter. As the Osbornes point out, for entertainment, in addition to dancing to island bands some nights, there is "bingo—if enough people want it, or movies—if the film arrives." Otherwise, Cedric and Carol do their best to include whatever is the island's highlight for guest en-tertainment, either bringing the group to the hotel, or, as in the case of the Montserrat Museum, arranging transportation for guests to get to the spot. The 2 night-lighted tennis courts were completely resurfaced in summer of '78 (after they sank 19 inches at one end due to a landfill problem). There's a West Indian buffet that draws all the island's visitors and many of its residents on Wednesday nights in season, plus rental cars available for self-mo-tivated exploring and the opportunity to walk down the hill and around the tennis courts to be at one of the holes on the Belham River Valley Golf Course, when you've practiced up on the hotel's own putting green. The inn is at its most formal—shirt-jac or jacket and tie for men—on Wednesday and Saturday nights; the rest of the time, life is casually comfortable. This is one of the Caribbean's "best inns" and will give you a vacation you'll never forget.

■■■

HOUSEKEEPING HOLIDAYS in Montserrat keep 4 real estate firms in business and have led to a rash of apartment and condo-minium units in recent years, sparked by the fact that Canadians and people from the United States have built second homes here. The house-rental-in-owner's-absence business thrives. There are all kinds of houses for rent, most of them with small private pool. Three names to try for rental, all with offices in or near Plymouth, are Jac-queline Ryan, Box 425; Neville Bradshaw, Box 270; and Montserrat Estates, operated by Frank Edwards, Box 58.

When you're investigating houses, know that the places that are priced low are priced that way for a reason—and it's often that the location is inconvenient, that the rooms are small, that the view is nonexistent, or that you'll be without some of the qualities you've come to the Caribbean to find. ("When it's in the low price, it's not much of a much," according to Jackie Ryan when she was showing me around.) Most houses are *not* air-conditioned because people on this island have been smart enough to continue the tradition of building to take advantage of tradewinds. Most bedrooms have double (sometimes triple) exposure so that cross ventilation is a fact. Kitchens are modern (some places have freezers), appointments are adequate-to-luxury, and a rental car is essential if you want to get around. Count on spending from US$25 to US$35 per day for your car, depending on size and shift, with no charge for mileage and a hefty wallop for gas.

Many of the houses are in the area around Vue Pointe hotel in the hills north of Plymouth. If you rent one of those places, you can shop in the "supermarkets" of Plymouth, or at the local market where fresh produce and fish are offered by market ladies, or at the small shop in Salem. If you can't survive without your U.S. steaks and beef, bring them from home, packed by your favorite butcher from his cold storage and plunked into your own refrigerator when you arrive on island. Same goes for other special foods you can't do without, but you should be prepared to pay some duty, which will be levied by an understanding customs officer on arrival in Montserrat. Most customs officials are aware of the housekeeping needs, and are not too harsh on vacationers who are obviously bringing food for their own use.

✣ **Lime Court Apartments** (Box 250, Plymouth, Montserrat; 8 apts.) provides homes right in the center of Plymouth, across the road from the Legislative Building and a few doors down from the Tourist Board offices. Prize spot is Apt. #1, the house that started it all (but this one is often on long-term rental). If you can rent this unit for a week, you have 2 bedrooms, private baths, good kitchen with electric oven, washing machine, large living room, and a plant-filled veranda. A winter month costs US$850; a week is US$265—and you won't need a car unless you head for the hills (and a taxi can take you). Other apartments are wedged into whatever space could be made available to provide 1-bedroom and 2-bedroom units. #3, #4, and #5 face out to the back garden, on the ground level; #7 is up narrow cement stairs, but you can pick mangoes (when they're in season) from your back patio. #8 and #9 are on the third floor (2 flights up narrow, outdoor, cement stairs), with #9 known as the "penthouse"—a 2-bedroom unit, one a double, one a small single, with stereo, view over the harbor, and a winter weekly rate of $175 ($600 per month). Best bets for my vacation dollar would be #1 if you can get it, or one of the ground-level units at the back: #3 rents for $150 per winter week ($550 per month), for 2 bedrooms with narrow twin-beds and simple furnishings.

✤ **Shamrock Villas** (Box 180, Plymouth, Montserrat; 2 dozen units with more building) sells condominiums, but offers you a good place to settle if you're not up to the $60,000 purchase price some of the units were commanding in early 1981. The apartments are new, with view over Plymouth, the black beaches, and the sea. Plans for a pool and tennis courts at the base of the hill-clinging development are slow to be realized but the white cement units, furnished in the taste of the owners, are ready and waiting: 1- and 2-bedroom units, plus 2-story townhouses with bedroom and balcony on the second floor. You'll need a car for mobility (you have a shelter to park it under). Maid service is not included in the $275 to $400 winter weekly rates for 2, but maids are arranged at about EC$12 per "day" which is about 9 a.m. to 2 p.m.

During a quick survey of houses listed with Jackie Ryan, I found a nest for 3 compatible couples, with a spectacular view over the hills and the Caribbean, with the granite isle of Rhedonda plus Nevis on the horizon. The quarter-circle house, built by a young Monsterratian "who didn't have much formal schooling but made his money with his wits" and who spends most of his time off-island, is modern. The living area is in the central portion, overlooking the wedge of pool and stretching out to 2 bedrooms at the end of one wing, one at the other. Rental for a winter week is $600, with 5-day maid service. A smaller home, also in the hills above Vue Pointe, but without the expansive feeling of the first, rented for $300, with 2 bedrooms, also separated by the main living area. Both bedrooms are twin-bedded (narrow beds); the pool is a rectangular dunking area.

A third home, with a country-home feeling and small pool offers 2 bedrooms at opposite ends of the house, each with cross ventilation and very skinny twin beds, plus bath, for $400 for one couple, $450 for 2. And a fourth offers all luxuries, airy surroundings when the louvers are opened to the breeze, and a pool, with a separate efficiency unit downstairs for the visiting in-laws. The bright kitchen with yellow appointments has a dishwasher; a freezer spells the efficient refrigerator. Two of the 3 bedrooms on the main (pool) level are at one end, the other at the opposite end of the house; the efficiency bedroom with kitchenette and big closet-dressing room was down the stairs around the pool along a bowered path to its own entrance. Rental for the whole house is $800 per winter week, but the 3 bedrooms on the main level rent for $700; the efficiency for $200 when negotiated separately.

A UTHOR'S OBSERVATION: It's almost impossible to set foot on this island and not want to share in its past, present and future. Here's one way: contact the Montserrat National Trust, Plymouth, Montserrat. You can reach the museum curator by writing Box 120 in Plymouth. The National Trust has about 150 members, most of them local. The annual membership fee is EC$5. Interest and membership are welcomed from visitors.

■■

PLACES WORTH FINDING will be those that your hosts and Montserratian friends tell you about. Plans should start with rental car, easily arranged and easy to negotiate around the usually well-paved and adequately marked roads. Only when you get into the hinterlands and out-of-the-way places will you find that your road dissolves; local drivers know the routes for those jaunts.

Montserrat Museum (W & Sun p.m.; call 5334 for other times), in a sugar mill on Richmond Hill, is the place to start any touring. The museum was created with the obvious devotion (and talent) of Walter Connell, a "new" Montserratian who splits residence between this island and Connecticut. His interest in island history has brought together a fascinating, well-displayed collection of artifacts. First exhibit inside the mill is a map showing location of Montserrat, and your location on the island. From that point, you whirl around cases with shards and relics unearthed on island prowls, with pictures of Montserratian life in the 1900s and some copies of advertisements of Montserrat Lime Juice from 1885 (about the time when island production was tallied at an astounding 180,000 gallons exported to Crosse and Blackwell in England). Although limes have been the biggest business for Montserrat, the island's era as a sugar producer is recorded not only with pictures and commentary, but also with the 150-year-old donkey saddle with its rack for sugar cane, traded with an elderly Montserratian for the new saddle he wished for. Maps and comments on the migration and culture of the island's first settlers (the Arawaks) help put the move from South America through the Caribbean islands from about 500 to 1500 A.D. into perspective. The diagrams are interspersed with exhibits showing witchcraft ceremonies and items actually found at the Arawak settlement unearthed near the island's airport. This is also the place to note some relics and newspaper comment about the Pan Am jet that crashed into Chance Peak on a swoop into Guadeloupe in September 1965, and a photo of the black Lady of Montserrat at St. Patrick's Catholic Church.

The small museum is easily reached in about 5 minutes from downtown Plymouth. Manned entirely by volunteers and supported by private donations, the museum was started in October 1975. It opened in the restored mill, with special display cases designed by and built under the watchful eye of Walter Connell, and has educated more than 4000 visitors since opening day. Among the most interested viewers are the troops of schoolchildren who come through to learn about their heritage and to note the original artwork from their local stamps. (The Montserrat National Trust has tracked down an almost complete collection of stamps, many of which are kept in the bank vault when not on display.) For intrepid historians who make it up the 2 short flights of very narrow wood steps, the top-floor research library's wall displays (to pad the echo) were drawn by island schoolchildren on bags supplied by Walter Connell. If the recounting of exhibits sounds like a lot, know that you can almost touch wall to wall in the mill with arms outstretched and that the total collection is housed in a typical small mill.

The other sights to see are natural ones: the Galway Soufrière, the Great Alps Waterfalls, Plymouth (especially on market day), and perhaps the beaches at Carr's Bay and other coves you find. Most of the sand will be black and volcanic—in spite of the gleaming white beach pictured on the island's official tourism folder.

As for the **Great Alp Waterfalls,** the challenge is in getting there, in spite of what the folders say about excellent walking paths and modern roads. This is no place to attack in the afternoon "after a round of golf." It's a hike to be enjoyed, at leisure and with time to relax and enjoy the tropical surroundings. In fact, I will even go so far as to say that you can't be part of the climbing club unless you've plodded along after surefooted Mr. Greenwood from Shooters Hill Village, who used to march along the old route, a rugged "path" speckled at some parts with volcanic rock, with his bare soles providing far firmer footing than the shoe-covered ones of the timid hikers behind him. A picnic for this spot is perfect, but don't bother racing up to check off a sight just to say you've been here. Falls are falls, here as elsewhere. If you plan to climb, hiking shoes make sense for most of us.

Galway Soufrière, a phenomenon of interest to anyone who has never seen a sulphur vent, perks not far from the village of Upper Galway in the middle of the southern half of Montserrat. Its rugged volcanic rock is a sharp contrast to the small village cupped in verdant hills, and your reward at the end of the 20-minute walk to the crack in the rocks is bubbling vents, very hot water, strong-smelling sulphur fumes, and a roaring and rumbling guaranteed to send you back to more peaceful surroundings. This is another excursion that should be considered for enjoyment of nature-en-route for those who have seen other volcanoes.

■■■

SPORTS in Montserrat are usually the do-it-yourself variety, unless you get involved in some of the local tennis matches and can find space on the 2 courts at Vue Pointe Hotel. Hiking and climbing are natural pursuits on an island that has verdant hinterland, several dormant volcanoes (the best known is Galway Soufrière) and the Great Alps Waterfalls (which have become relatively touristy with walks and markers).

Golf is played on the new 9 and the old 9 (which total to 11, played in 2 versions). The Belham River Valley course stretches out at the foot of the Vue Pointe Hotel's hill and ranges over a respectable length. The clubhouse is in an old cotton gin. (Note the hand slots for pulling the machinery in the clubroom near the downstairs locker rooms.) There's a small "19th hole" bar area, and a pricing system that lets you play for EC$20 greens fee, EC$3.50 for club rental. Caddies with blue caps (the best) command EC$2.25, yellow hats are EC$2.00, and red hats are EC$1.50. Saturday is caddies' day. Otherwise, the course is used mostly by retirees who live nearby and by visitors.

Sailing, scuba, and the expected **water sports** are all highly organized as on other Caribbean islands. Charter yachts occasionally cruise over from Antigua and elsewhere, and there are Sunfish sail races on Sundays from the Yacht Club. (Don't expect formality at this Yacht Club.)

■■■

TREASURES AND TRIFLES are not going to take you long to find, unless you linger to watch some of the craftsmen at work or search out your own contact to weave one of the grass rugs that are still made by hand by some of the Montserratians. In downtown Plymouth, there's not much in the way of traditional tourist shops after you've glanced around the few imports at **John Bull** and some of the items in Mr. King's **Gifts of Quality,** with a window display of vegetables when I passed by on one trip. (Inside you'll find Waterford Crystal, fine china, watches, jewelry, and the like.) The woodworking shop Mr. King started with a Guyanese craftsman has now been taken over by his former partner. The **Richmond Hill workshop,** across from the Montserrat Museum mill, bears the sign "Quality Furniture/Felix A.K. the wood Doctor Reliable Man." Felix can make things to order, if you supply drawings and have plenty of time, and he has the inclination. Very special gold and silver jewelry is handcrafted by **Mrs. Liburd,** who operates her small "shop" at her home, up by Galway.

The Fort Barrington Weaving Studio, where craftsmen work at looms to make fabric for mats, shawls, and other items is well worth a visit, and Sea Island Cotton is made on Montserrat, where cotton fields supply the raw material.

The Government Crafts Shop on Parliament Street, the main street of town, has been operating for a couple of years as outlet for weavers' work and other locally made items. Hand towels run about EC$3.50, big runners are EC$5.95, a Montserrat T-shirt was US$7.50, macrame bags for evening are EC$35, and block print by the yard on white cotton ran EC$35.30 for 2⅓ yards. Items are priced for the U.S. and Canadian market, but workmanship deserves the price. Note the pottery; some of it is quite interesting and packable. Guava jelly is also for sale. **The Handcraft Shop,** a few doors down on the other side of a spur street, had a larger selection of pottery when I was in town and **Dutcher's Studio** at Olveston focuses on ceramic jars, bowls and other items as well as glass work.

If local history with a local outlook interests you, you can spend EC$5.25 on *History of Alliougagana—A Short History of Montserrat* by Howard Fergus, author and first Speaker of the Legislature under a government expansion in 1974. Another book edited by Fergus is *Dreams of Alliougagana,* an anthology of prose and poetry.

Nevis

St. Kitts-Nevis Tourist Board, Charlestown, Nevis, W.I.; c/o Caribbean Tourism Association, 20 East 46th St., New York, NY 10017.

US$1 = EC$2.60.
Unless otherwise noted, $ refers to U.S. currency.

Nevis has its head in the clouds, and that's what gave the island its name. Although the earliest map—the Mapus Mundi—splotches "Nieves" as a name across an area that could refer to Saba and other islands in the neighboring seas, it's Nevis that has claimed the name as its own. During his second voyage to the New World, Columbus hung the tag on the cloud-covered peak, here or elsewhere, that reminded him of the snow (nieves) of the Sierra Nevada of Spain. The first settlement—Jamestown—was swept into the sea by a 1680 tidal wave, according to island records, and although it may be interesting for scuba divers, there's nothing on land to note from that time. Charlestown's 17th-century prosperity was as the depot for flourishing slave trade in the British Leeward Islands. Records in the late 1600s count as many as 8000 slaves prepared and sold on the market at the west coast town, and notes made about life in the early 1600s show that slaves were being used in those years on British plantations here and on other islands.

But it's Alexander Hamilton that forges the American link to Nevis. He was born here and spent his early childhood on Nevis before heading off to St. Croix to work in a relative's hardware store. Much is made of Admiral Nelson wooing and winning Fanny Nisbet, daughter of a prominent merchant, but the present church at Fig Tree Hill probably wasn't standing here in 1787 when they were married across the road at Montpelier Estate.

The historical facts are only of passing interest to most visitors who search out Nevis for peace, quiet, and a go-slow pace that is contagious. Although the 20-mile "rim" road that circles the island

and goes inland for a portion of its route can be driven in less than 2 hours, there are some people that never make it. Not because they can't, but because there are too many spots to linger—and the only people who speed around the rim in the 10-mile-per-hour race are those that are heading to the airport—where they will probably wait for a while.

■■■

POLITICAL PICTURE: Official status puts Nevis as part of the Associated State of St. Kitts–Nevis, a link that had included Anguilla (and still does include Anguilla on some official documents, although not in actual practice). Anguilla left its associates, with special status granted by Britain in February 1976 and confirmed with formal separation on January 11, 1981. Nevisian politicians have been outspoken in their belief that they had not been getting a fair shake from the government based in St. Kitts but Prime Minister Kennedy Simmonds, elected to office in March 1980, formed a coalition government that has included prominent Nevisians, and the two islands seem to be cooperating for the mutual benefit of both.

There is a coterie of very active politicans on Nevis, and they are Nevisian first of all, wanting good roads, higher wages, and better facilities for their island. You may come upon political slogans, or hear talk of political events, and should know that the St. Kitts Labour Party, founded by former Premier (now deceased) Robert Bradshaw, was in power for almost 30 years, until it was ousted in the elections of early '80. Dr. Kennedy Simmonds is head of the People's Action Party; Mr. Simeon Daniel, the present Minister of Finance and Nevis Affairs, is head of the very active Nevis Reformation Movement.

■■■

CUSTOMS are those of a rural Caribbean island with a British history. Tourism has not stepped onto Nevis with a heavy foot, although the island claims some of the Caribbean's most noteworthy inns. The hotels are either restored plantations, or new structures that fit into the surrounding countryside. All are low-key, unpretentious places where hospitality is natural and warm. Forays into Charlestown, the hub for the life of the island, will find visitors in a minority among the Nevisians. "Good Morning" or some other appropriate greeting should start any transaction, and the greeting is usually part of passing on the street. The pace of life is s-l-o-w, whether you live here or visit. Do not expect split-second timing, and be prepared for candlelight dinners even if a place *usually* has electricity. Power failures are a fact of life, as is the case on many islands. The island water supply can be sporadic, but all hotels are familiar with that situation. You will always have plenty of water (and rum) to drink, but what comes out of the faucet may be a trickle, or only a drop or two, at times when there are power problems.

What you wear at your resort home is a matter between you and the management, but for exploring the island—or even a quick trip to a nearby beach, covering up the bikini is proving your awareness of the local sensibilities. Nevis is home for the 12,000 people whose families have lived here for generations. Most island families are deeply religious and not ready for (or happy about accepting) the freewheeling, carefree, unfettered life that can be acceptable on some other islands.

MONEY MATTERS will be transacted in U.S. dollars and cents at your hotel and at some of the stores in town (those expecting to deal with tourists), as well as with your taxi driver. If you are mingling with the Nevisians at some of the rum shops or other primarily local spots, have some E.C. currency on hand, and don't bring bills in big denominations. (Not only can it be ostentatious in simple, village surroundings, but, for a practical matter, the place or person probably won't have change.) Change your U.S. dollars into E.C. currency at the local bank for the best rate. Hotels usually offer a slightly lower rate to cover their service. On a small bill, it won't make much difference; on big transactions, it can.

ARRIVAL ON NEVIS at the airstrip can be aboard LIAT subsidiary 4-Island Air, from Antigua or St. Kitts, small planes on charter from Antigua, St. Kitts, and nearby islands, or on a plane from St. Croix, usually connecting with American and other flights that head south from U.S. cities. The island connection is by ferry between Basseterre and Charlestown on a "schedule" that can be checked with your hotel and/or the Tourist Board. The fare is geared for the local folk who make up most of the passengers and having E.C. currency for the crossing is advisable.

TOURING TIPS: There's only one main road on Nevis. It makes a ring around the rim of the island. Spurs stretch off to reach hotels and a few sights in the hinterlands, but don't count on much in the way of paving on the spur roads. Rental cars can be arranged through your hotel, but request your car when you make your reservation if you are vacationing at peak season. Cars can be scarce.

Taxis take you anywhere you want to go and will wait (or come back to get you) if you're planning to stay for a while. Most Nevisian inns have links with "their own" drivers. Rates are set by distance; drivers, from my experience, usually stick to the rules.

Boats are best for "touring" in my opinion, and most hotels can make arrangements to send you to sea. True island aficionados make the run between St. Kitts and Nevis on the local ferry that makes daily crossings between Charlestown, on Nevis, and Basseterre, St. Kitts. The alternative is LIAT or other small plane service between the two islands' airports, but the air schedule when I was traveling made it difficult to do that trip in one day from either starting point. Horses can be rented for rides along the shores and into the verdant midsection of Nevis.

■■■

HOTELS ON NEVIS are a half-dozen-plus of the best inns in the Caribbean. Each spot has its own personality, and most have Nevisian history intertwined, either with the buildings or the owner and sometimes both. There's nothing on the island for those who need manufactured entertainment; everyone turns in by dark—unless there's some houseparty-type entertainment at your chosen inn, or a big do that sounds interesting in Charlestown or one of the local places. An islander's island, Nevis welcomes anyone who wants to fit into the accepted pace—which is slow, relaxed, and tropical.

Most hotels include a 10% service charge, and the mandatory $1 per night government room tax, but something extra for special service by some member of the staff is always appreciated.

✤ **Cliff Dwellers** (Tamarind Bay, Nevis, W.I.; 14 units) benefited during season of '80–'81 from the expertise of an enthusiastic island aficionado, Harriet Turner, known to some of us since her residence at Nisbet Plantation a few seasons ago. With Harriet at the helm, Cliff Dwellers acquired the easy and comfortable "house party" atmosphere on which it can thrive. The property had slumbered for several years and awoke at the start of '79 to rub the sand from its rooms, wash its face, and stand tall on the slant of shore that has provided its prominent resting place for more than 10 years. Opened in the mid-60s as an exclusive resort with about

2000 feet of beachfront land and a hill-capping restaurant that perches at 150 feet (a short-but-steep climb up a narrow cement-strip "sidewalk"), the place perked happily for a few seasons and then fell into the doldrums. Since the basic structures survived their slumber, Cliff Dwellers at Tamarind Bay is once again rising to its potential.

Your room will be in one of several cottages—called Japanese-style by some—between beach and hilltop dining room. Cottage 2, at the top of the hill, is a special favorite for view and tradewind "breeze." The plan is to "close" the dining area as soon as you've had your breakfast, and hope that you will go to sea for the day. The dining area opens again after its day-long nap, to serve dinner-by-candlelight. Surroundings are some of the Caribbean's most romantic.

Your view from any angle at this perch is spectacular—out to sea and toward neighbor St. Kitts, an easy boat trip away (speak to the management) or a short flight (about 10 minutes) from the patch at Nevis to the strip at St. Kitts. Tradewinds cool (and blow incessantly). There's a pool with bar and snack area nearby, plus that strand of sand that makes this place special. Count on rates to be about $130 for 2 this winter, with 2 meals daily (and wine with your dinner). 10% service charge and your lunch and bar costs are extras.

✤ **Croney's Old Manor Estate** (Gingerland, Nevis, W.I.; 10 rooms) is an elegant oasis on which Texas interests have lavished millions in hopes that the estate will grow. Initial plans for a condominium-style development were shelved, but what stands ready and waiting for guests is a statement of spectacular recovery. Stone buildings that stood (at least partially) have been replastered and, in most cases, rebuilt to hold vast attractively furnished units with a variety of floor plans. There are 2-story units, 2-bedroom suites (which are attractive for families), and 1-bedroom setups that preserve the old feeling while providing the most modern plumbing. The estate was a sugar plantation, a stud farm for slave-breeding, and, after slavery was abolished in 1834, a sugar and sea-island cotton plantation. All the history has been cultivated, along with the grounds. The original Great House, built in 1832, cradles the alfresco dining area. The swimming pool is nearby, as are horses to ride; the couple of houses that make up the village of Gingerland are just down the driveway at the crossroads. Rates for 2 this winter will depend on your choice of rooms, but figure on parting with well over $100 for elegant room, 2 meals per person daily, laundry service, use of pool and facilities, and excellent service. To reach Croney's (which takes its name from the promise of owner King Koch to immortalize the man from whom he bought the property), you'll have a long, sometimes bumpy ride either from the airport (about an hour) or from Charlestown (about 35 minutes).

✣ **Golden Rock Estate** (Gingerland, Nevis, W.I.; 10 rooms) has captured vacation budgets since the Galeys opened their inn on this spot in 1957, when, as part of a group of investors, they purchased the 200-acre estate. Present managers are Frank and Pam Barry, whose ties to the property go back long before 1964 when they moved down here. Pam's great-great-grandfather owned this estate back in the days when it was a working plantation. Today it is a playing one, where the Barrys are working—hard. Guests cavort around the tennis courts and toss darts along with conversation in the gathering bar in the main building (restaurant) overlooking the courts. There's a pool on premises, and excursions to the beach arranged by management. Your holiday home will be half of a 2-unit cottage up the hill from the pool. Island woods and other products have been used for all furnishings with very appealing results. Good for self-sufficient types who enjoy a houseparty atmosphere helped along in winter months by steady repeaters. Count on paying about $130 for 2, 2 meals daily, in winter.

✣ **Montpelier Estate** (St. John's Parish, Box 20, Nevis, W.I.: 19 rooms) claims fame as being near the Fig Tree Church where Admiral Nelson married local belle Fanny Nisbet. According to some of the island legends, the estate was flourishing at that time and it is certainly flourishing now. About 15 minutes' drive from Charlestown, Montpelier is on a knoll, with its Great House open to the trade winds, its huge pool worth a couple of laps, and its dining room by night light a dream place. The old mill still stands, and the sugar crushing building has been roofed over as the bar/lounge. James Gaskell returned to the island following the change in government, and lavished dollars and attention on this special property. A complete refurbishing included comfortably colorful fabric to supplement the wicker furniture in the bedrooms and welcoming basket chairs in the bar area. The otherwise standard dining room is punctuated with a planter of tropical foliage, and the main lounge areas in the great house have overstuffed, chintz-covered furnishings that make relaxing easy. Rooms are in cottages with sea view (if the foliage has been pruned), and air conditioning supplements overhead fans. Showers are small in some rooms, but all rooms are comfortable. James Gaskell is rightfully proud of his vegetable and herb gardens. Ask to see them. Your $100-plus for 2 will include breakfasts and dinners daily in winter months.

✠ **Nisbet Plantation** (Newcastle, Nevis, W.I.; 20 rooms) has a modern history that matches any of its earlier legends as the place where Fanny Nisbet used to come to play. Her uncle owned the house, and more recent owners—legends in their own rights— have been Mary Pomeroy, who flew away in her own plane, ferrying her furniture after her, when the local politics got too hot, and 7th-generation Kittitian Geoffrey Boon, who died in a crash of his own small plane in late March 1978. Present managers are the Brewers who have been on Barbuda and other island spots and claim a link with New York's Southampton. The plantation atmosphere prevails, with guests enjoying a game of darts along with lively conversation at the main house and spending the days horseback riding, exploring, swimming, hiking, biking, or swinging in a hammock. Set amid 300 acres of coconut plantation, with sentinel palms around the grounds, the lodging units are several separate cottages, some new twin octagons with 2 units in each and others in old plantation buildings, spruced up for guests who like more traditional surroundings. The tennis court gets frequent use, often at early morning when the "pong" of tennis may be your wake-up call, depending on the location of your cottage. Rates for season of '81–'82 hover around $150 for 2, 2 family-style (and hearty) meals daily, served in the plantation house. The hotel's lovely strand of sand makes a pool unnecessary. Town is about half an hour away; the Nevis airstrip is a little more than walking distance.

✠ **Pinney's Beach Hotel** (Charlestown, Nevis, W.I.: 35 rooms) is parked on the south (Charlestown) end of a stretch of beach that shows the effect of periodic sea swells. (The beach is a sliver or a wide band, depending on how much sand the sea has swept out— or in.) The rooms are simply furnished, with all the basics, but nothing lavish, and air conditioning in some. The deluxe suite has plastic "coats" on furniture, T.V., refrigerator—and an air-conditioner that works overtime. Some rooms have shower only, but overnighting in any one of these nooks will give you golden opportunity for early morning swims. The public rooms, clustered where you will park (or step out of your taxi), are furnished in assorted metal and plastic. There's entertainment (band) some evenings, and the restaurant and bar are popular with Nevisians who enjoy the proximity to town, the Nevisian food at good prices, and the chance to find whatever action there is on this island. Rates for your room with bath for 2, will be about $50 this winter, with breakfasts and dinners daily.

✜ **Rest Haven Inn** (Box 209, Nevis, W.I.; 33 rooms) is for people who like their islands pure. Almon Nisbett has expanded his place on the shore with 12 new rooms that I climbed over and through before the doors were set and the flooring secure, and have seen again since they were finished. Spacious and very comfortably furnished, the view from any one of them is spectacular, out to sea. Of the original rooms, 12 have simple efficiency units for basic cooking at home. Some of the furnishings (and all of the rooms) are made on Nevis; plumbing comes from the States, and hospitality that makes the management one of the island's most sincere is strictly Nevisian. There's a small pool set into the shore not far from the main restaurant/resting area. Lowest rates are for the original rooms, in a 2-story building across the road, or in the few units that cup the pool area. Rates this winter are good value at about $50 for 2, breakfasts and dinners daily. (There's no beach in front, but the 3-plus miles of Pinney's is a short stroll north, and Charlestown is an easy but hot walk south.)

✜ **Zetlands Plantation** (Gingerland, Nevis, W.I.; 22 rooms) has become the epitome of island inn-keeping. A tireless team (that includes a fleet of children) keeps this place running, and full credit goes to Maureen and Richard Lupinacci. Their brand of hospitality seems to guarantee that guests become friends (and often return). The seven 2-unit cottages that hold most of the rooms are scattered around the manor house (recently built, not traditional/historic) and the whole complex caps a hill, a long-for-Nevis and wiggly-for-anywhere ride around the coast from the airstrip or Charlestown. The bedrooms are in "square" one-story houses (called plantation suites), the 2-bedroom, 2-bath mill tower and the 2-bedroom, 2-bath cottage with kitchen. The main building is the source for meals and meeting fellow guests. This remote haven is ideal for self-sufficient vacationers who want a "home of their own" in the hills, where the trade winds are steady and the sea is a part of the view. The nearest beaches require a car, but you'll need some transportation to get anywhere from here. You can walk up and down hills and around to the pool, but otherwise your entertainment is other guests when you find them at the heart of the plantation. Local produce appears in intriguing (and delicious) disguises at mealtime. Lemon bread and eggplant nibbles are two specialities. Rates this winter figure to about $125 for 2, 2 meals daily per person.

■■

PLACES WORTH FINDING ON NEVIS include the other hotels, most of which represent interesting modern adaptations of once impressive plantation estates (Croney's, Montpelier, Golden Rock, Nisbet); the town of Charlestown, sleepy today and hardly hinting at its 17th-century prosperity; perhaps the Morningstar Nelson Museum and the Fig Tree Church, but more probably the verdant hills and wild growth on mountainsides with an occasional spectacular view over the Caribbean sea.

CHARLESTOWN is a grid of short streets fringed with West Indian wood buildings, most of them small and filled with the commerce of a West Indian town. The place comes alive when the ferry from Basseterre, St. Kitts, chugs into port (at the end of a 2-hour ride that costs about EC$5). The ferry is the local service, used by Kittitians and Nevisians to get back and forth to market and home, since most of the jobs are on St. Kitts—and some of the fun is on Nevis. (Market collectors will want at least a whisk through the Charlestown market, to the right as you walk off the pier.) When Queen Elizabeth visited Nevis, on February 22, 1966, the entire town was dressed for the occasion—and that has been its biggest recent event. Although the action at Pier 2 is the town's liveliest, walk over to **Memorial Square** and the **Court House,** with the library on its second floor. There's a plaque on a wall that mentions a visit by the Jamestown (Virginia) settlers, who spent almost a week here before they continued on to settle in Virginia.

   Fort Charles is for ruin collectors, since you have to walk through an overgrown field (passing garbage and goats, when I walked through) to find the ruins—and nothing has been done to restore the little that is left (a cannon, a few walls, some stones, and the site). Rumors run rampant about the **Bath Hotel,** built in 1778 and the place in the West Indies to recoup and regroup in the 18th century. All the top people came to the spa at Nevis, where commerce was contracted and gossip shared. The major building you look at these days was restored/rebuilt in the 19th century and the fledgling museum inside is worth a glance. The springs are still gurgling, the basic structure is still sound, but no one has yet turned this potentially elegant hotel into the top resort it could be. (Someone tried around the 1900s, but the place didn't stay open for long.)

   Fig Tree Church is actually St. John's Church at Fig Tree Hill. The faded register has a couple of documents—namely one dated 1787 that supposedly tells that Horatio Nelson, Esq., was married to Frances Herbert Nisbet, widow, but speculation continues about the document, since the original register is so blurred and illegible that the present "statement" is mostly supposition.

The **Morningstar Nelson Museum,** in a room of the private home of a Philadelphia lawyer, Robert Abraham, contains an eclectic collection of Nelson memorabilia. Included among the pictures, tokens and Nevisian artifacts, is an invitation to Nelson's funeral. (There's no charge for the museum, if it's open when you're in the area, but donations are gratefully accepted.) It's worth venturing up the road just to look—from the outside—at the attractive home that has been molded around the turret of an old stone mill.

■■

SPORTS ON NEVIS are what you dream up yourself. Check with Nisbet Plantation about possibilities for boating, or at Croney's if you are staying there. The hoteliers have their contacts for whatever access to sea sports are available at the time you visit. **Snorkeling** and **scuba** are popular off the beaches, and around the shores if you are experienced and have brought your own equipment. Perhaps your hotel can make arrangements for the Barracuda Diving Company instructors to come over from their Ocean Terrace Inn base across the 2-mile channel and up the Kittitian coast at Basseterre.

There's no golf, but you'll find courts for **tennis** at Montpelier (check to see if the court has been fixed), at Nisbet, and Golden Rock. **Horseback riding** can be arranged for trail rides around mountains and plantations.

■■■

TREASURES AND TRIFLES ON NEVIS center on Charlestown.

The **Nevis Crafts Studio,** in a yellow house on the inland side of the road through Charlestown, has an intriguing selection of island-made items. In conversation with Michael Brooks (who carves calabash shells) and Ashley Liburd (whose bamboo wind-chimes fill the air with "music"), I learned that the 8 craftsmen who started the cooperative in November 1978 have been joined by others for a total of about 25 members. Aided by an Inter American Foundation grant and other donations, plus the profits from their sales, the group are working with other Nevisians, especially young people, to encourage high quality handcrafts and individual entrepreneurs. Any profits from purchases made here go for a good cause, and items for sale are interesting and well made. Expect to find pottery, baskets, bamboo items, shellcraft, macrame, and other items—all of which can be brought into the U.S. duty free under the customs allotment.

Caribbee Clothes is a Nevisian enterprise that claims to be the island's major employer (35 people). Started almost a decade ago by Betty Robey, the shop and workrooms are now owned by Kathy and Tip Todd who moved south from high-pressure jobs in New York to oversee (and labor at) the enterprise. The shop sells colorful continental (that's us) style clothes, made by a team of local seamstresses. Some of the workers embroider designs on the dresses and other apparel. Their names appear on a tag with the garment. The fabric is colorful cotton, the garments are styled as "respectable resort wear" for the Palm Beach, wealthy-suburbs set.

Tradewinds Ltd., the newest enterprise of Betty Robey, is another "home industry," with Nevisians schooled in needlepoint and embroidered designs making "paintings" in a simple, Grandma Moses style.

The Arcade, in Charlestown near Memorial Square, carries the colorful Caribelle fabric and fashions made on St. Kitts. The **Handcraft Shop,** up a side street and the workshop for the blind, is a hard place to leave without having bought something. Head here only if you are prepared to buy; the crafts are the only livelihood for the elderly and infirm who weave local grasses into mats, hats, etc.

Nevisian pottery, sun-baked-clay bird ash trays and other small items, makes ideal gifts for the folks at home. You'll find it in the Handcraft Shop and can go to the source if you ask directions. Mrs. Elena Jones, now in her 70s, was the originator of the Nevis pottery. Her disciples include her niece, Almena, and others who now make most of the items for sale.

Nevis Philatelic Bureau, in a modern air-conditioned building near the pier in Charlestown, has collections of Nevisian stamps that will appeal not only to stamp collectors but to anyone intrigued by this island. Artists' renderings of island scenes—including the hotels, local boats, birds, and other uniquely Nevisian subjects—appear on colorful stamps, sometimes affixed to postcards with the same picture. Inquire about special issues, well worth framing.

Puerto Rico

Puerto Rico Tourism Company, Banco de Santander, San Justo at Recinto Sur, Old San Juan, Puerto Rico 00902; 1290 Avenue of the Americas, New York, NY 10104; Suite 1007, 150 Second Ave. S.E., Miami, FL 33131; 11 East Adams St., Chicago, IL 60603; 10100 Santa Monica Blvd., Los Angeles, CA 90067; 10 King St. East, Suite 501, Toronto, Ontario M5C 1C3, Canada.

US currency is used.

When Juan Rodriquez bent over the seedlings in the plastic pots on the porch to pour in a gulp of water with a sagging paper cup, he didn't seem to notice that more water was dancing into the pots by chance after it pounded the wooden railing where it sloshed down a pleat in the tin roof. And, while I watched the old man, partially hidden under his tattered straw hat, I listened to the symphony of rain on the tin roof of the parador. The only other sound was the occasional squeak of my cane-backed rocker—when I felt like pushing it back.

Juan Rodriquez probably didn't notice the rain because he has been noticing the plants, tending them, for the past 60 years or more, since he was a young boy and grew up in the village. He knew the place when it was the home of the overseer of the coffee plantation, and he had watched it through its recent metamorphosis into an inn. He is now official gardener. His creased face followed some of its patterns when it broke into a smile on greeting, and when I shared his weathered handshake, his dark eyes darted over his smile. He truly loved this spot, and the horses that he tended when he wasn't taking care of the plants. He proved that later when we rode.

At Barranquitas, another mountain town many hours' drive from here, José Morales manufactured a truck with the same loving care that Juan Rodriquez watered his flowers. Morales's truck was made from cut-off soft-drink cans, with hub caps of bottle tops and a corned beef can for the engine box. The body was wood and José Morales is well over 40. He was showing youngsters what he used to do to make a toy when he was young, and many gathered around him—and more than 70 other craftsmen who were making toys, decorations, baskets, and other items remembered from their past.

And in San Juan Antiguo, as the old city is known in Spanish, my guide for the tour of La Fortaleza stepped around the edges of the V'Soske carpet that had been handmade in Puerto Rico and pointed out the portraits on the walls. Most of them made up in prominence what they lacked in artistic talent, in my opinion, but it was interesting to note all the wives of the governors' over the past several administrations (including the two wives of Governor Roberto Sanchez Vilella; they hang in separate rooms). The blue room was my favorite, and the favorite of my guide. We both liked the color, he because it was the blue of the palm that occupies the center of his party's flag. The Kennedy bedroom, so called because that is where John F. Kennedy slept, has a mahogany antique four-poster and a blue tone to the trimmings. The window looks out from the top of the walls of the 16th-century fortified city, over the harbor and a wide expanse of sea. The open-air veranda, with cane backs and seats in its mahogany rockers, is a Puerto Rican home at its best— which isn't surprising since La Fortaleza claims to be the oldest continuously inhabited executive mansion in the New World. The first Spanish settlers gathered inside the first small fort on this site for protection against the Caribs in 1533. By 1540, the fort had a tower and a patio enclosed by four walls. It was remodeled in 1640 for an executive mansion, and by 1896, at the order of Queen Isabella II, the 19th-century touches were added to what had become a palatial mansion. The obvious enthusiasm of my guide for his home—and his homeland—is one reason why Puerto Rico is changing. My guide was Governor Carlos Romero Barceló, and the quick tour preceded a long interview about where tourism and Puerto Rico are heading. Puerto Rico's governor says that "the service industry is very important to Puerto Rico . . . and tourism is our most important service . . . We have not yet fully explored or developed our natural resources of nickel or offshore oil. Our people are our biggest natural resource and tourism provides jobs for them.

"Most visitors know only the beaches-casino-nightlife image of Puerto Rico. They know us through our ads, but they don't know the *real* Puerto Rico," Governor Romero Barceló said. In addition to the obvious attractions of beaches and climate, the governor knows, as tourists are slowly learning, that the real Puerto Rico is the people, the country, and the culture. "We want people to come because they like Puerto Rico—what we are. Then the visitors will leave with a new image. When they read of problems in their hometowns with street gangs and war lords, they will know that our Puerto Rico is very different," the governor added.

■■■

POLITICAL PICTURE: Puerto Rico is unique. With Latin links to the Dominican Republic, Cuba, and places in Central America that go back for centuries—long before Puerto Rico "became American" after the Spanish American War in 1898, this 3500 square mile island is becoming schizophrenic.

United States links, more economical than emotional, have appeared to take precedence over the past three decades, but recent years have witnessed a ground swell of "national" feeling—without any clear definition of what this complex island/"nation" really is.

Known as the "poorhouse of the Caribbean" at one time in its not too distant past, Puerto Rico responded to the herculean efforts of its workers and U.S. industry subsidiaries to create a Puerto Rican middle class, and to shore up the local economy, raising the standard of living for Puerto Ricans and offering high level training to many people who now hold top executive positions in their own or major multinational companies.

The worldwide ground swell for independence periodically washes over Puerto Rico where a small portion of local residents, with vocal support from the Puerto Rican Communist party, feed the fires. More practical folk look toward a modified Commonwealth status, with more independence than Puerto Ricans feel they are currently enjoying under a Washington-linked system that gives them food stamps and other welfare benefits as well as many other substantial financial supports. Others, the present Governor among them, advocate statehood, with a gradual weaning away from the Commonwealth status toward full States rights.

Gubernatorial elections, held at the time of the U.S. national election (November 1980), reinstated incumbent Governor Carlos Romero Barceló. The election was so close, however, that recounting continued well into 1981, and former Governor Rafael Hernandez Colón, candidate of the Popular Democratic Party, reluctantly yielded to Romero Barceló's New Progressive Party. Governor Romero Barceló has no clear mandate to move ahead toward Statehood, and efforts during most of 1982 will undoubtedly be devoted to shoring up his lagging popularity and to finding practical (and, I hope, popular) solutions to the drastic welfare cuts outlined by the Reagan administration. (At the time the budget cuts were announced, Baltasar Corrada del Rio, Puerto Rico's resident Commissioner to Congress in Washington, made headlines with his statement that, if implemented as proposed, budget cuts would add to about $650 million and would put an estimated 30,000 Puerto Ricans out of work. One tally puts the figure for Puerto Ricans receiving food stamps at 58% of the population of 3.2 million.)

Tourism, while employing only 8% of the Puerto Rican work force and bringing in about $600 million to the Puerto Rican economy, is regarded by Governor Romero Barceló and others as being as important for its role in increasing awareness about life in Puerto Rico as for the jobs and dollars.

The Tourist Development Company, under the leadership of Pedro de Aldrey, continues to work with U.S. travel agents and with airlines and island hotels to build and support a tourism structure that gives vacationers good value. Major emphasis has been put on activities programs to share Puerto Rican culture and pleasures with visitors and on labor negotiations to attempt to control skyrocketing labor costs so that hotel rates and other ancillary charges can be kept within reasonable range.

AUTHOR'S OBSERVATION: Some of the Caribbean's best bargains are available in Puerto Rico. Competitive pricing and the introduction of service by Capitol Airlines has resulted in very low airfares (as low as $99.50 one way in mid-1981). A surfeit of hotel rooms (and a drop in demand for them) resulted in cut-rate pricing that could not bring profit for the hotels but did succeed in bringing people (who were getting a good product at a "fire sale" price) and in partially defraying the loss incurred with a full staff and an empty hotel. At press time it is difficult to see into the future, but I suspect there will be bargain periods in the year ahead. Be ready to travel "on the spur of the moment," and you may get your tan at a very low price.

■■

CUSTOMS OF THE COUNTRY in Puerto Rico, when you go to the countryside, away from the Condado/San Juan tourism veneer, are adapted from Spain. Not only is Puerto Rican-style Spanish the language of the country, but also there are local village festivals that take their cue from Saint's Days, and the evening paseo is still part of village life. Even such developed towns as the northwest coast's Quebradillas and the south coast's San Germán, to mention only two, center the social life for the community on the central plaza or park. The young people still come to the park in evenings, if not to stroll—girls in one direction, boys in the other—as was the custom of their parents, then at least to look at—and perhaps to meet—their counterparts.

To understand the customs that are still part of Puerto Rico, visit the small museums and homes in Old San Juan, where some of the traditions are explained, and then take a car to drive into the country, away from the usual tourist routes. Even the country's most sophisticated citizens continue the tradition of their childhood (and long before) of the celebration of San Juan Bautista Day, the day of the patron saint of Puerto Rico. Families and friends gather for festivities, fun—and the midnight swim, walking into the water backwards to keep evil away for the year.

Roadside stands sell traditional Puerto Rican foods, even on the busy road from the airport to the commercial caverns along the north coast, and in the mountains and fishing villages, people are being encouraged to practice, and perhaps learn again, the hand crafts of their fathers. Puerto Rican culture continues—with encouragement from the island's dynamic Instituto de Cultura Puertorriqueña, with its head office at the convent on San José Plaza in Old San Juan.

Many of the houses in small villages in the mountains are painted the pastel colors that were popular around the turn of the century. Although municipal governments have focused in recent years on a cleanup and improvement campaign that benefits visitors as well as residents, you will find small-town life still carries many of the customs of many years ago. Children are sheltered by their parents, nightlife as it is known in the sophisticated centers is nil, and the strict discipline of old Spain, almost to the point of chaperones for young women, is still practiced in many towns.

Clothes are casual, colorful, and comfortable. Blue jeans are worn, in all shapes and sizes, on Ashford Avenue, that commercial thread through Condado's hotel area. Anything that is comfortable in warm weather appears on the streets of Old San Juan. Puerto Ricans will not wear sundresses and other half-dress in their cities; sometimes tourists do—and those who do stand out. In churches and cathedrals, as in any Catholic country, covering the arms and back is the custom, and beachwear is best at the beach.

When you're touring in the country, you will find that people dress conservatively. In many of the villages, tourists are a sight, especially as they parade through town on their way back from the beach.

Evenings at the better resorts are dress-up affairs, although there are plenty of places in Old San Juan and the Condado-Isla Verde areas where you can go for dinner in casual clothes (Kentucky Fried Chicken, Burger King, hotel coffee shops, and the assortment of snack places that rim the roads around the cluster of hotels). Coat and tie are not required at many places (not even in some casinos, but check) although most men do slide into something respectable when they go to one of the top spots, or to a concert, play, or another social event where residents and visitors mix. Dress for women in the evenings ranges from a comfortable dress to elegant long skirt, with the latter usually seen only at some special hotel function, one of the gala evenings of "your" convention, or a social event. At beach and poolside, anything goes—even hair curlers (in too many places).

■■

MONEY MATTERS: U.S. currency is what you will spend, quickly, in Puerto Rico. If you travel with a lot of cash, keep it in the hotel's safe deposit boxes, or in traveler's checks. Credit cards are widely accepted, especially in the San Juan area hotels, restaurants, and shops, but do not count on using personal checks. Make arrangements with a local bank if you will need a lot of cash.

■■

ARRIVAL at the airport in San Juan is like arriving at any modern airport in cities around the U.S., except that every Puerto Rican traveler's family and friends are there to greet him/her and you will have to wallow around in people until you can find your way to the luggage claim conveyor belts. The walk is long, and if you have carry-on luggage that gets heavy, bring luggage wheels—or your own porter. Most airlines arrive at the main terminal building (for Eastern, see below). On your way to the luggage claim, stop at the attractive, efficient Puerto Rico Visitor's Bureau information office, where you can get the current copy of *Que Pasa* (a fact-filled book that will become your thumb-worn bible), and if the bar is open for service, a free Puerto Rican rum potion. Thus armed, head for the fray—the luggage tug that finds you either stamping on your best friend (or some stranger) or standing back to be the last to claim your battered suitcase.

When you and your luggage are reunited, claim a porter (if you can find one) or—if you have been smart enough to travel light—take your suitcase and yourself to the left, after you go past the sometimes-checking-checks clerk at the gate, and locate transportation to your hotel.

Eastern Airlines arrivals and departures are handled expeditiously "within the family," albeit with long walks along corridors that link the multi-pocketed terminal area. Eastern occupies the western end of the terminal (to the left as you face the main building). In addition to allowing for convenient, and relatively quick, connections between its flights down-island and to cities in the States, the Eastern complex gives you "your own" baggage claim area and a separate pickup station with all the same options for ground transportation, plus the inconvenience of a long-but-not-impossible walk to the Dorado Wings or other commuter airline check-in area if you are flying within Puerto Rico or to other islands on the small plane services.

In addition to shops, a wide range of airline ticket counters, and a selection of places to drink and dine (on average food), San Juan's airport has the International Hotel (Airport Terminal, Isla Verde, P.R. 00913; 57 rooms), a hermetically sealed honeycomb of rooms that can provide overnighting if you have a very early flight, or arrive on a late, late flight and are heading on in the a.m. Don't count on anything sumptuous or special in the way of rooms. This is, in my opinion, strictly subsistence.

Departure from San Juan is routine U.S. airport procedure. If you are flying American, and are staying in the Condado area, you have the convenience of picking up your boarding pass at the Ashford Avenue ticket office, across from the Condado Beach Hotel near El Centro (convention center). If you do that, you can leave the beach about 45 minutes before you fly, to whisk to the airport in a taxi and be there the "required" 30 minutes before flight time to go through the usual security check and sink into the seat on your plane.

■■■

TOURING TIPS: The situation for transportation from the airport is much improved, although it can lapse into the common chaos on occasion. Your choices are three: a rental car; a taxi, ready and waiting at the far end of the terminal outside of the area where the Virgin Islands and foreign travelers clear customs and outside the Eastern Airlines area (which is at the opposite end of the terminal); or the airport bus/limousine that is supposed to take a busload to the nearby Condado, Isla Verde, and San Juan hotels. The fare for the bus/limousine service is about $3 for a trip to San Juan, but it is not always easy to find the bus; a taxi costs about $7. If you are heading to Dorado, Palmas, or one of the outlying areas, reasonable transportation choices for first-timers are two: by bus/limousine (there is usually one waiting if you are expected on the flight); or by small plane. Dorado Wings flies to Dorado and to Palmas. Advance arrangements (through your travel agent, or by writing the hotel) are advisable, but not foolproof, so be patient. You should know before you assume that flying is faster that although your time in the air is about 15 minutes, the waiting time to connect with the pilot, to board, and to take off puts the total travel time about the same—between one and 2 hours, depending on traffic and "takeoff" time. Those who know the routes to Palmas and to Dorado can pick up their rental car and arrive at either place within the hour.

Rental cars are available through a variety of sources. The names you know (Hertz, Avis, Budget, National, etc.) are easy to find. From my experience, their rates are highest, and good values are available from some of the smaller operations with only a dozen or so cars. I have had very good luck with Caribbean Auto Rental, located at Condominio Ocean Tower in Isla Verde, but it is worth investigating Danty and some of the other local rental offices when you are walking around the busy Condado and Isla Verde areas.

Prinair, a Puerto Rico-based commuter airline, has flights to Mayagüez, the west-coast town that offers an entirely different kind of Puerto Rico holiday, as well as to neighboring islands and islands as far south as Guadeloupe.

Prinair is worth a book of its own. During my years of travel on assignment (and for fun) in the Caribbean, I have folded myself into the small seats of Prinair's DeHavilland Herons on countless occasions. Sometimes my ticket has been a government order; most times I have rushed up to a counter for a last minute purchase for "the next plane out." For San Juan's airport (the airline's base), that means a choice of about 100 per day, with as many as 300 at peak times for all routes. With its network extended to provide service between Haiti and Santo Domingo since giant Pan Am stopped its service almost overnight, Prinair's planes serve about a dozen island destinations. Do not count on 747 service on these 19-passenger planes. There's a hump cross the center aisle (for the wheel axle, I suspect) and one small seat on each side of that aisle. The noise of the propellers is conversation stopping during flight, but this only adds to the sense of adventure that some of us enjoy with island travels. In late 1980, Prinair added a couple of Convair 580s to the fleet and these 48-passenger planes are usually used for the most popular links. Although Prinair is expanding to provide better service, its check-in and island offices are informal, competent—and crowded.

AUTHOR'S OBSERVATION: If you are driving, or taking a taxi, to the airport on weekdays, between 4 p.m. and 6:30 p.m., allow plenty of time. Automobile traffic in and around the airport, and especially on the gnarled routes from Old San Juan to Isla Verde, can be overwhelming; cars crawl, tempers rise and the cacaphony of horns can bring city realities all too clearly into focus even though this is a lovely tropical island.

Although traffic can be "impossible" at rush hours around the San Juan area, once you get into the country, roads are good and usually well posted, and rental cars give you a chance to be independent. There are some tours into the interior (check with your hotel activities desk), if you prefer to head inland with a guide. The most popular areas are the El Yunque area for the rain forest and, for those with an interest in the island's history, to the mountain village near to the Taino Indian ballpark.

In addition to the taxis that wait outside the doors of most of the big hotels, there is frequent bus service from well-posted LeLoLai stops, running between most of the Condado and Isla Verde hotels and downtown Old San Juan. The cost for the tourist bus is 50¢.

AUTHOR'S OBSERVATION: *Walking Tours of San Juan,* a comprehensive guide to the sights, shops, restaurants, and nightspots of the San Juan area is well worth its $2.50 cost ($4.50 if ordered by airmail return). Compiled by Al Dinhofer, the 100-page magazine-size guide is issued twice a year and tells all you need to know to get the most from a San Juan visit. Copies are sold around San Juan or by mail from Caribbean World Communications, First Federal Building #301, Santurce, P.R. 00909.

■■■

HOTELS in Puerto Rico give you more choice for your money than almost any place in the Caribbean. You can choose between action-packed, 24-hour casino cavorting high-rise hotels or small spots within a few steps of discos and the beach. You can head for the hills, to some of the government-encouraged paradores, where you will think you are in Spain, or you can tap top elegance at the west coast or the southeast. You can book into a tennis clinic, or concentrate on golf, or you can see the new Puerto Rico, that is old to traditionalists, but little known to the hordes of tourists that sweep through the San Juan strip. There's no island that has more to offer than Puerto Rico, and few that have as much, but you may have to do a lot of looking on your own, and careful reading of these pages, to find the lesser-known spots.

When it comes time to pay your bill, almost all Puerto Rican hotels accept the standard U.S. credit cards, and that is certainly true of the places in the San Juan area and the major hotels out and around the island. If card pay is crucial, ask in advance; there are a few properties where cards are not accepted.

There is a 6% tax on rooms renting for more than $5 per day, which is any commercial room I've ever been able to find in Puerto Rico. In addition, you are expected to leave something for the maid if you stay more than a night or two, and to tip as you go at the coffee shop and restaurants and for other services.

Hotels around Puerto Rico are grouped for the San Juan area (pages 562 to 576) and around the island (pages 580 to 591).

■■■

HOTELS IN SAN JUAN AREA: The name San Juan is used for everything between the airport and the old city. In fact, there are several small districts, plus the big zone called Santurce, that cover that area. The addresses in the hotel comments include the districts, namely Condado, rimming the Atlantic, with Ocean Park to its east at the shore and Miramar to its southwest, on the inland side of the lagoon. All are east of the bridge (Punta dos Hermanos) that separates San Juan Antiguo (old San Juan) and modern San Juan from the Condado and Miramar sections. The area nearest the airport, east of San Juan/Santurce, is known as Isla Verde area, and is in the Municipality of Carolina. (All the others mentioned are in the Municipality of San Juan.) You can drive from the airport to the tip of Old San Juan in about 20 minutes, traffic willing (but the ride can take an hour or more at peak-traffic times).

Condado area properties rose with a leer in their eyes, and lucre and lust still seem to me to be the name of the game here. Government cleanup efforts have helped some, new buildings are replacing some of the scruff, and the Convention Center, *El Centro*, that has joined La Concha and the rejuvenated Condado Beach Hotel in what all hope will be holy matrimony, seems to have birthed a new kind of tourism here. At the moment, anything goes—from young carefree types to older reprobates, to unisex and homosex, in addition to heterosex blatant everywhere. The only reasons I can imagine paying money to stay in this area are (1) the convention you attend is held at El Centro, (2) you want to flaunt it or watch it, and (3) budget-and-being-where-the-action-is are prime concern.

If number 3 is your reason, recommending some place to stay presents a problem. I glide through and around the small hotels at regular intervals, always unexpected by management and usually without their knowledge. What I find now is that a lot of the formerly family-operated places are being sold—often to one, two, or three men. Life is turning gay around here, and you can decide if this is the place for you, depending on your persuasion or tolerance. Several small spots investigated for this edition are detailed below. There are some good deals in condominium and apartment rentals (especially along the Isla Verde shore near the airport). Efficiencies may be your best route to cut costs and stay in the hive.

A UTHOR'S AWARD for the San Juan area staying goes to Caribe Hilton, the only high-rise hotel I know where the several stories contain a total resort; around the island awards go to Palmas del Mar, for trimming hundreds of acres with a total tasteful resort—golf, tennis, yachting, shops, beaches, pool, casual and elegant restaurants and to Dorado Beach, for maintaining an aura of the elegance that marked this resort when it first opened.

✣ **Arcade Inn** (8 Taft, Ocean Park, PR 00911; 19 rooms) is small and moderately priced. Owned by Aurelio Cinque, the stucco home sits in what was once a residential area, now incorporated into the tourist sprawl. A good bet for the budget-minded who want to be within shouting distance of the Condado chaos at about $40 for 2 for an air-conditioned room near the beach. Efficiencies are available; breakfast is served "at home."

✣ **Arcos Blancos** (10 Carrion's Court, Condado, PR 00911; 19 rooms) is a couple of homes-turned-inn on a side street that taxi drivers seem to have a difficult time finding. It leads to the beach in the Condado area, but not all guests follow that path. Some stay, well-greased and minimally bikinied, by the speck of the pool that Peter Bessie maintains for his guests-cum-friends. Rooms are simple air-conditioned boxes. Rates are $50 or more for 2 in winter, meals extra.

✤ **El Canario** (1317 Ashford Ave., Condado, P.R. 00907; 44 rooms) sits at the feet of the highrises, almost "in the shadow" of the Dupont Plaza hotel. A former home-turned-inn, El Canario still has a homelike feeling (and many repeat guests that make winter rooms worth booking well in advance). Dennis de Castro is the man to see for details. About half of the rooms are in the original house, on Ashford Avenue; others are in a separate building known as El Coqui, near the small pool at the back of the house. Guests have use of the kitchen area and appear to enjoy making themselves at home. An ideal base for cost-conscious folk who want to be within walking distance of the Condado attractions (including casinos), El Canario costs about $40 for 2, continental breakfast included. Rooms with private kitchen facilities rent for about $50 for 2.

✤ **Caribe Hilton** (Box 1872, San Juan, P.R. 00903; 703 rooms) is in a class by itself, in my opinion, at the top of the list for Puerto Rican properties. The fact that a hotel the size of this one can maintain a personal, welcoming feeling of hospitality is a credit to the staff (some of whom have been affiliated with the hotel since it opened over 30 years ago) and to the General Manager, my colleague and friend, Jag Mehta, who came to this property from Jamaica in the early '80s. The Caribe Hilton opened with Hilton management of an 8-story block of rooms in December 1948, the first of the Puerto Rico government's efforts to cultivate tourism. This hotel is *the* best in the battalion of properties that stands along the coast east of Old San Juan. It is also the closest (about $4 cab fare) to Old San Juan, and a stone's throw (but another $4 cab fare if you choose not to walk) from all the hubbub across the inlet at the Condado area.

The Caribe has class, a scarce quality among the upstarts that leapt to quick fame (and notoriety) along the San Juan coast. The Caribe in its 30s is better than ever, with the garden suites in the unit added in 1963, the 18-floor tower rooms added in 1972, and the refurbished room in the main (original) building that are all now capped with a health club. Some 1400 people mill around this place when it is full (which is most of the winter months!). The Viviana Albani solarium has the town's best view of the Condado section and the sea. Men's health club active also. Tennis & Swim Club has local members, constant action on the 6 courts (from sunup to long after sundown when you pay $10 for night-lights), pro shop, and lesson options.

Action plans for sunseekers include feeding the fish along the reefs (so they will stick around for the snorkelers), merengue lessons by the pool, surfside bingo, chess, checkers, and a classical concert, a gala evening Fiesta Jíbara (buffet and music poolside), craft classes, exercise classes, guided tour of Fort San Jerónimo on the hotel's grounds, and a piragua tasting (that's a Puerto Rican snow cone). There are entertainment plans for children as well as for adults. This is a family place.

Aquacenter water-sports headquarters are by the pool. Scuba resort course with pool and one hour of diving is offered. Inquire about the all-day excursion to Culebra, an island off the east coast. Don't miss it if the tour is offered while you're in town.

When hunger hits, options are endless amid a confusion of names. On the lobby level, the air-cooled coffee shop (alias *Terrace Cafe*) looks like any modern coffee shop in the States (and operates like it, except for the Spanish accents); the open-air terrace is far preferable, in spite of the cafeteria-style push-your-own-tray at breakfast and lunch. Twilight transforms the place; tablecloths and candlelight plus good, relatively reasonable ($15 for full dinner) menu. Reservations essential, unless you eat between 6:30 and 7. The elegant *Rotisserie* up one level, near the Casino, is one of Puerto Rico's top dining spots. Reservations imperative in season. Make them very early in the a.m. or the day ahead to be sure. Figure at least $30 per person. *Club Caribe* is the floor-show spot, which comes alive after 10:30 p.m. *Juliana's* is the island's most popular (and exclusive) disco, with jacket required and a $10 cover. *Casino* is open from noon on. Shoppers stroll in lobby area for Olga's Shop (linens and embroidered items), Chantilli (jewelry), and Sabrosa (homemade snacks).

Count on a room tariff, no meals, that ranges from $113 to $165 for 2, with good value *Pleasure Chest* summer holidays. Shoulder season travel and group rates can bring it down some, but this is the best there is, and you'll have to pay for it. A spot of sand passes as a "beach"; get out with the first rays, glue your beach chair to that of a friend, and hold onto it. Space here is at a premium. Poolside lounge chairs stand at parade rest, moving only when the sun—and all the other chairs—do.

✝ **Carib-Inn** (Box 12112, Loiza Station, Santurce, PR 00914; 225 rooms) is not to be confused with the Caribe (although Spanish-speaking taxi drivers do so). The former Racquet Club has 8 courts, for tennis enthusiasts. Near the airport (10 minutes, about $3), Carib-Inn is a favorite with stews and crews and others who follow that flock. *La Tinajita* bar in the lobby (11 a.m.-3 a.m.) keeps the heart pumping, and you have to walk around the "corner" past *La Tinaja* coffee shop (the usual) for the pool (a nice oasis with bohio bar, surrounded by friendly folk), or saunter upstairs for *Cousin Ho's Chinese Restaurant* (which has takeout service if you want to eat in your room—or at the beach a 5-minute walk toward the water and El San Juan Hotel). "Beach buggy" connection from 9 to 6. Health Club to recoup and regroup. There's no room service, but ice machines on floors 3, 5, and 7 keep things cool. Rooms are usual modern boxes, due for some attention. Most of the staff are students at Escuela Hotelera de Puerto Rico (the Hotel School), whose building you will notice by the parking lot. Some of the flourishes have been sacrified to keep the price reasonable. A good buy for nonfussy types who like a lot of youthful action, at $65 to $80 for 2, meals extra.

El Centro, as the Convention Center is called, is a city unto itself. In addition to the 2 hotels, **Condado Beach** to the left as you face the convention core, and **La Concha** on the right (see below), there are shops, the weekend artisan's market, discos, a casino, and a choice of dining areas, including the Condado Plaza restaurant at street level on the plaza. Any of the hotel facilities can be used by guests in either hotel. You do, in fact, get double your money's worth and that can be a lot if you research some of the very low overnight rates that are advertised locally in Puerto Rico in the slower seasons (May, June and the fall) when the weather and sea are the same as always, but the will to head south is not quite as strong. Check also, if you're traveling with children, about the youth program for children 3–13, with a daily program of tours and activities at about $10 per day per child, including lunch. The program operates from June 15 to July 30, with special youth programs also over the Christmas holidays.

El Centro and its streetside links hold several service spots: *Delicias,* an attractive restaurant serving Puerto Rican specialties, is on the second floor (take the escalator up), *Los Cocteles* is the bar/lounge, and *El Teatro* is where the folklore group performs on one of the special evenings of the government sponsored LeLoLai Festival. Along the Ashford Avenue sidewalks, bordering La Concha, there's a branch post office, plus a few shops (barbershop, clothes). If you go into the drugstore (for newspaper, books, magazines and/or sundries) ask for my longtime colleagues Rafael and Olga Benitez Carle; this is their shop.

✤ **Condado Beach Hotel** (Ashford Ave., Condado, PR 00907; 251 rooms) has a venerable history. In 1919, the Hotel Vanderbilt was built on this site, and although most of the surroundings have changed beyond recognition, photographs that hang in the second-floor public room show life and festivities of that time. By the early 1950s, when the tourism tide was beginning to rise, entrepreneurs saw the potential for Condado. A wing was added, where the convention center now stands, and then in 1961, another wing of new rooms grew to the left as you face the building. Today, there is little that remains from the early elegant era, but if you look up at the facade as you stand across Ashford Avenue, you can note some of the early stucco work around the windows and imagine what the porte cochere looked like when Ashford Avenue was a seldom-traveled road. The fountain and plaza that were in the first of the new wings went with the reconstruction (to the dismay of the wife of former governor Muñoz Marin, who loved the original Patio del Fauna). The new *Patio del Fauna* is one of the special rooms (and a prized one) for Condado receptions.

Be sure to ask for a sea-view room with balcony, even if it is small. The lagoon rooms have "no" view in my opinion, and the sea-view rooms that are hermetically sealed (as some in the original hotel are) let you look at, but not feel, the sea breezes. I find that frustrating when I am in the Caribbean. Rates for your winter holiday for 2 can range between $92 and $132.

There's a rabbit run that connects Condado Beach to El Centro (convention center) on 2 levels, but you will feel as though you are walking through what hoteliers refer to as "the back of the house"—and you are: Beware the service push carts that share the space with you.

For hotel facilities on your "half" of this behemoth, there is a pool (shallow, smaller than that at La Concha, and much quieter, with poolside bar/snack service only when the house count warrants) where life is peaceful, even though Condado's hubbub stretches out along the street a couple of floors below. There are ice machines on most floors, and modern furnishings and bathrooms in your quarters, but you will walk miles if your room is in the newer wing of Condado and you are attending a convention where a lot of your pals are staying at La Concha. The Condado Plaza coffee shop faces the plaza on Ashford Avenue, but hides its preferred view (of the sea) inside its air-conditioned rooms. It is attractive and efficient, if you like being boxed into air conditioning; I prefer the open air coffee shop of La Concha (see below).

✟ **La Concha** (Ashford Ave., Condado, PR 00907; 224 rooms) crept onto the shore, with the big seashell-shaped roof on its restaurant giving it its name, in the season of 1956. The huge hotel that opened then was modern in every respect, including the fact that it was planned by Fomento, the industrial arm of the Puerto Rican government, to be leased when the $4.9 million, 12-story hotel was ready to open. A few seasons on its own resulted in acceptance of a Hyatt offer to take it over, with the Condado, to link the 2 for a convention center which the Hyatt group would operate. That was the first murmur of the big convention center that has been very successfully operated by Hilton International on terms negotiated with the Puerto Rican government and terminated at the end of '81.

La Concha Hotel seems livelier than the more staid Condado, with its *Mi Sitio* cocktail lounge just to the right of the front entrance, and its casino up a few steps to the right at the back of the house. Your choice of dining depots includes *El Patio*, bordering the La Concha pool, and serving breakfast, lunch, and an early supper. *La Concha* (mentioned in the restaurant listing for its Friday fish dinners) is the shell-shaped restaurant that gives the hotel its name. Although the chamber is completely air-conditioned, you can look at the sea you cannot smell or touch. *Solimar* is La Concha's nightclub. There are several elegant suites for very special overnighting; most rooms are modern, comfortable, hotel/motel style, with plumbing that works and doors that open to balconies if you request (and pay for) a room that has one. There are tennis courts on the roof, where the trade winds that keep you "cool" can make a normal tennis game impossible, and a ribbon of orange sand that runs along the wave-lapped shore. Rates this winter range from $92 to $132, no meals. Investigate special package plans, and the spring, summer, and fall special promotion rates for the best values.

✟ **Condado Holiday Inn** (Box 1270, San Juan, PR 00902; 590 rooms) is widely recognized as the most successful hotel in the Condado area (with an enviable 90%-plus occupancy). The 2-part hotel is the born-again Holiday Inn (which has had almost 9 other lives) and the former Flamboyan, linked by a covered tube several feet below the high wire that 73-year-old circus performer Carl Wallenda was attempting to cross when he plunged to his death in

March '78. The 2-building hotel is within a toss of the dice from the heart of Condado's Ashford Avenue action, but it cuddles close to the entrance to the lagoon, across which the Caribe Hilton stands in solitary splendor.

The seaside Condado Holiday Inn company invested $1 million, to be matched by $1 million from the Puerto Rico Development Bank to haul the 2 properties up to Condado-luxury status, and allow a winter rate of $115 to $160 for 2, room only. Condado Holiday Inn reportedly spent *another* $1.2 million on refurbishing the 2 properties, while the umbilical cord that connects them tallied up at about $800,000.

The best rooms are those with sea view in the original Holiday Inn, or those in the former Flamboyan, renamed the Laguna wing, with view of the now-cleaned-up-lagoon. Other choices hover over busy Ashford Avenue. All the rooms are modern, with Holiday Inn double beds, soap, matches, and plastic touches. Light and airy decorating puts new life in these old places. Check the group rates, package deals, and specials for summer, for something more reasonable than the price-list double.

✤ **La Condesa** (2071 Cacique St., Ocean Park, P.R. 00911; 10 rooms) is a special spot that will appeal to those who search out small hotels. A well-protected pocket (entered by ringing the doorbell at the locked entrance on Cacique Street), La Condesa is the province of Luis Citron who does his best to make self-sufficient (and hopefully interesting) guests comfortable. Rooms are nicely furnished and have a homey quality even when they have no window-with-view. A private home-turned-inn, La Condesa houses guests in a variety of rooms, upstairs and down, with entrances off the plant-flecked patio. Although there are full kitchens with a few of the rooms, light meals are served in the bar/dining area. Arrangements can be made for car rentals at good rates. Daily rate for 2 this winter figures to about $40, breakfasts included, with the units-with-kitchen costing about $5 additional.

✤ **DaVinci** (1151 Ashford Ave., Condado, P.R. 00907; 91 rooms) has been given short shrift in previous editions. During my wanderings for this '82 book, I took another look—and liked what I saw. Manager Jack Bryning has a comfortable, modern hotel which, although it is wedged into the commerce of Ashford Avenue, has beach access and some rooms with sea view that are well worth considering. The hotel's *Frascatti* restaurant is favored by local folk for its salads and Italian specialties, and *La Veranda Patio* is a pleasant place for that refreshing cold drink after hot touring. Rates this winter hover around $70 for 2, meals extra, and you're within a short stroll of many excellent restaurants—and the activities of El Centro (the convention center), Condado Hotel, the Holiday Inn, etc.

✤ **Don Pedro** (4 Rosa Street, Isla Verde, P.R. 00914; 22 rooms) dots a side street, just off the main road along the commercial route between Isla Verde and the Condado section, not far from Old San Juan. This is a casual place, with a speck of a pool, a group of repeat visitors (some of whom come through San Juan for business), and some rooms that are more comfortable than others. The top price room rents for about $40 this winter, but others are available in the $30 range for 2. Efficiencies rent for up to $50. The bar is a gathering spot at almost all hours of the day (or night), and those who want to feel sand under their feet can walk a few steps down Rosa Street to the beach. Acceptable for casual types who like being in the orbit of the action places, Don Pedro is not recommended for fussy travelers who want pampering and immaculate housekeeping.

✤ **Duffy's** (9 Isla Verde Road, Isla Verde, P.R. 00914; 16 rooms) was a fun and frolicking place when it opened more than 20 years ago, but it seems to have fallen on hard (or at least confused) times now. Still very convenient, within walking distance of the Isla Verde biggies (El San Juan resorts, Carib Inn, etc.) and the beach (across the road), the inn claims a very casual looking group of regulars who hover around the bar. Most rooms are air-conditioned, none have any view, all are boxy and simply furnished, with little more than bed and chair, plus plumbing in the way of "luxuries." O.K. if you are a casual, blue-jeans kind of traveler to whom price is paramount. Rates for 2 with breakfast are about $30 this winter.

✤ **Dupont Plaza San Juan** (Box 3312, San Juan, PR 00911; 450 rooms) was born as the Puerto Rico Sheraton but came into the Dupont Plaza family in '79. Even if you decide against this action-packed place for overnighting, weave your way through the always-busy lobby to the elevator for the sight from the top-floor *Steak Penthouse* (dancing and dining; make reservations and plan on $20 per person). The view is spectacular—with firefly lights giving magic to the Condado commercial caldron that the dark night covers up. You can usually get a table in the cocktail lounge.

Rooms in this tower offer views in 4 directions; seaside is best.

ACTION is the name of the game in the lobby, with music blaring from somewhere, people milling (often groups), and slot machines and the casino not far off. There are shops, piano bar, *Zanzibar*, and other bars around the reception desk, and people slung over every sitting area whenever I've walked through. Down one level (coffee shop, activities desks, etc.) it comes alive midmorning; lounge chairs fringe the deck around the pool; the sea is nearby without a decent beach. Figure a straight rate of $90–$120 for a room for 2, but ask about special package tours, especially the summer holidays with bonus features.

✤ **Dutch Inn & Towers** (Box 13637, Santurce, PR 00908) has dedicated hotelier Fred Dieterle as its (their) man in charge. He has been active in the Caribbean Hotel Association since that organization began and was involved with the Condado Beach in its 1950s expansion. The 2 properties that make up the Inn & Towers include the original inn, a multistory building on a side street off Ashford Avenue, and the Towers (one building) which was built at one side, successfully blocking any view of what might have been seen of the sea. Biggest bonus with the 2 buildings is the casual *Greenhouse Restaurant*, jutting toward the Ashford Avenue sidewalk. It provides an air-conditioned hamburger-plus place, with healthy plants hanging around your table and a bosky atmosphere over all. A room for 2 this winter will range from about $70 to $90, depending on size, equipment (kitchenette or not), and whether you add on the in-room movies offered. All meals, taxes, and tips are extra.

✤ **El Convento** (Cristo Street, Old San Juan, PR 00902; 95 rooms) is a special star on the Caribbean hotel horizon, but the star is occasionally covered with clouds of management problems. You haven't been in Puerto Rico until you've been into El Convento, in my opinion. A Carmelite convent when it was built in 1651, the potentially elegant hotel knew a brief reign as a member of Compania dei Grandi Alberghi, better known as CIGA and a familiar group to anyone who beds down at Europe's best (Gritti Palace in Venice and Le Grand in Rome). The firm came in with a management contract in 1977, but the CIGA liaison failed to bring the hoped-for success, and the property is—once again—in the hands of the Puerto Rican government, who are, reportedly, making a go of the operation.

Credit for the idea of opening El Convento for modern pilgrims goes to Fred Woolworth of *the* Woolworth family, who assembled a group which included Raphael Benitez Carle, a former director of

Puerto Rico's tourism efforts. The inn opened in 1962, to struggle valiantly against odds which included a run-down, trash-filled old city just beginning to awaken to its present prosperity, and a stream of vacationers who had been lured to Puerto Rico by promises of beach-plus-casino, none of which El Convento had (or has). The Spanish-style, elegant European concept was too avant-garde for crowds who wanted to toss their dice on the craps tables, and the place was almost empty.

Now that the restored area of the Old City has a life of its own, there's a lot to be said for staying here a few days. Old San Juan's shops, small museums, cafes, bistros, and elegant restaurants are a short cobbled stroll from the arched doorway off El Convento's pool-specked courtyard. Perfect for anyone who knows the good life of Europe and wants to share it under the sun, and for people interested in the restoration, small museums, and cultural or casual (non-casino) nightlife of the restored Old City, El Convento is one of the special places that brings Caribbean heritage to life.

Rooms are modern, furnished in Spanish style (heavy wood), air-conditioned and open to the arcaded walkways around the courtyard where you'll breakfast (or lunch) by the pool at an umbrellaed table. Buffet luncheon daily ($8 M–F, $10 Sat & Sun, tips included), flamenco show at dinnertime some nights (reservations recommended), and a European air, with good service, make El Convento well worth its $80 for 2, meals extra, winter tariff. Summer specials with American and Eastern give good value, as does the honeymoon package. Transportation is provided, free, to Condado Beach and tennis courts. (If you try El Convento, and like it, the next vacation should be at Hostal Nicolás de Ovanda in Santo Domingo, the Dominican Republic's capital.)

✤ **El San Juan Resort Center** (Box S-3445, San Juan, PR 00904, 1600 roooms in 3 hotels) got into full swing with the opening of the Americana-turned-Palace Hotel (see Palace Hotel below) in December 1978. The **El San Juan Hotel,** the **El San Juan Tower,** and the **Palace** comprise a "total" resort, with rabbit runs linking one to another, and a choice of a dozen or more dining depots. Of the three linked properties, my vote goes to the Palace because I like to see the sunshine I come south for. The dark-and-gloomy lobby of the El San Juan is Las Vegas style, overdone Victoriana—and last I looked, the dark-red plush lining the hallways to the rooms reminded me of a 19th-century bordello. The coffee shop at the beach side of the street-level area has good Reuben sandwiches, and other New

York-style delicatessen fare, as well as salads and fresh-fruit plates that offer a nice respite from the heavy meals at many restaurants. Back Street Hong Kong takes care of the culinary needs of those who seek out Chinese food.

If you want to have a little distance between you and all the action, consider setting up housekeeping in one of the efficiencies, or the 1-, 2-, or 3-bedroom apartments that fill the shoreside tower marked with a prominent ESJ. There's a mini-market on premises for basic stocks, but you'll do better at one of the nearby supermarkets (and at the fast food places that are not far away) if cutting costs is a primary concern. The Health Club has an exercise room and other facilities and the nursery usually has someone in charge to keep the kids occupied. The *Happy Apple* has a popular Sunday buffet. The furnishings look more like New York department store than like tropical living, but the minute you open the sliding doors to "your" small balcony/terrace you'll have a view of Caribbean surroundings and at least a squint of the sea. All the facilities of related El San Juan Hotel and the Palace (casinos, coffee shops, pools, entertainment, etc.) are "at your feet." Rates for your apartment at the ESJ Tower will run from about $90 for the efficiency unit to over $150 for some of the 1-bedroom units. The 2- and 3-bedroom units are negotiable, so ask if you have a big family or a lot of friends. Ask, also, about special package holidays that include a car rental. You can spot the tower from the left side of your plane as you land at Puerto Rico's airport, and it will take you about 10 minutes by cab to get here.

✤ **Excelsior Hotel** (801 Ponce de Leon Ave., Miramar, PR 00907; 140 rooms) is included in some of the package promotions. I am including it here—so you will know that this is, in my opinion, a moderate-priced commercial hotel, with a small drop of a pool to one side of the small "lobby" off a commercial street. Rooms are boxy and air-conditioned, with whatever view there is a look over modern San Juan sprawl. You'll have to cab to the beach if you miss the hotel's free transportation, but you have *Lindy's* kosher restaurant/delicatessen for all your meals and snacks. If budget is a consideration and you have to be in San Juan city, this place might be worth a try; but if I were counting on a Caribbean resort hotel I'd be sadly disappointed—in spite of the claims for tours, and the picture of a beach in the hotel's attractive folder. The rates for 2 range from $60 to $70 depending on the room, its location, and whether or not you've opted for a kitchenette to cook and keep costs down.

✣ **Howard Johnson's** (1369 Ashford Ave., Condado, PR 00907; 147 rooms) has its orange roof, but it is a sunstruck slab best seen from the top of the nearby Sheraton. Otherwise, you'll be aware of the HoJo connection at the coffee shop, facing the street, and at the 8th-floor pool level, where the words are posted on the side of a funnel-like tower. For budget-minded travelers who want to be at the fringe of the Condado fracas, this is the spot. Value is good at $80 to $90 for 2 with coffee shop and several Condado street spots for relatively inexpensive dining. Rooms are clean, neat, air-conditioned and, while not high enough to have much view, comfortable. The small check-in area curves around, past the elevators, to the dark cocktail *Nabori* lounge and the antiseptic dining room (I'd skip it, except for emergencies). Count on a $3 fare from the airport; you can walk to neighboring casinos, cabarets, beaches and shops. HoJo's does what it does well enough to keep an almost full house during winter months, even during the Puerto Rican doldrums a few years ago.

✣ **Isla Verde Holiday Inn** (Box 6888, Loiza Station, Santurce, PR 00914; 400 rooms) reopened with a 160-room west wing completely refurbished in late 1977. The rest of the place was spruced up about the same time. If you're looking for a Holiday Inn security blanket, here's one—on a good beach with guaranteed sunshine, coffee shops and average food. I see nothing special about the place but its size. It's a $2.50 fare from the airport, and another $3.50 into Old San Juan. Rates for a top-grade room for 2 are listed at $75 and up to $100 with everything extra. Slightly better rates are possible on package tours through your travel agent.

✣ **Palace Hotel** (Isla Verde, PR 00913; 450 rooms) plummeted into Puerto Rico's headlines with official opening in early December '78. The hotel opened as the Americana about 10 years earlier, and closed in April 1977 when the American Airlines hotel link, Americana Hotel Corporation, reported several millions lost over a 5-year period. Now the Palace perks along as part of the ambitious total resort concept of island entrepreneur Lou Puro. His business interests poured $2.5 million into renovations after the May 15, '78 acquisition. At the high-rise Palace, where floors begin with 14 and climb to 26, there are several styles of rooms: those facing the sea, those facing the airstrip, and those inland in the tower, plus cabanas (18 rooms with pull-out couch in the west wing), lanais (42 rooms with full bed and a sofa convertible in the east wing), and some gala suites. Action is the keynote for this hotel (and its relatives). In addition to the casino and nightlife (shows), there are several restaurants, including a seafood place and snacks offered poolside. A collection of shops curls around the pool-level lobby (one floor below the reception lobby), and whatever you can't find at this place you will certainly find at the cousin resorts. Rates for 2 are from $100 to $145, no meals. You can do much better with one of the week-long or other multi-day package plans. Focuses include tennis and other sports, plus special interests and, of course, casino. Check with your travel agent to find out the best deal you can get. This winter is certain to produce some new offerings since selling the product is prime goal for this action-oriented hotel. When you're here, you're about 10 minutes from the airport and almost 20 minutes' drive from historic Old San Juan (depending on traffic), but you're at the shore with option for sea-wallowing or pool splashing.

✣ **Pinky's Folly** (2073 Cacique, Ocean Park, P.R. 00911; 7 rooms) does not appear to welcome strangers, but you may be surprised— as I was. (The day I rang the bell next to the formidable wooden door and was let into the compound, a congenial group was gathered around the bar where Bob Cahill, your host, was the bartender. Know before you try to book here that Bob and Pinky and their friends like this small guesthouse just the way it is. If you do too, you'll be welcomed; but if you must have fancy trimmings and a lot of pampering, go elsewhere. If you like laughs, a few drinks with some of your new pals (who may include people working on construction projects hereabouts), watching or playing a quick game of darts, or wafting in a hammock strung from a courtyard tree, this may be your spot. Bob has been around Puerto Rico for 20 years or so; he and Pinky (whose real name is Rosita) bought this place and opened it for guests after returning from some time spent in Costa Rica. Rooms are very simply furnished; some share a bath. It's a family-style place, with a rate for 2 at about $35 this winter.

✣ **Ramada Inn Condado** (Condado, 00907; 98 rooms) expects to open for guests for the season of '81–'82 although the metamorphosis from Le Petit Hotel to the luxury Ramada Inn was far from completed when I looked in. Over $4 million is being poured into the 10-story structure. Predictions are for a European-style, elegant hotel with shops, penthouse suite with view, casino, and restaurants. Check with Ramada Inn's home base for details if this link in their chain sounds interesting to you.

✤ **Sea & Sun Guest House** (Park Blvd., Ocean Park; 00911; 7 rooms)
is one of the once-private homes that face the sea, on the inland
side of the shore-rimming road. Tucked amidst neighboring
houses, Sea & Sun is marked only by a sign on its entrance gate.
Wrought-iron fencing provides a decorative (and privacy) feature
for this place that is run more like a private home than a hotel. Most
comfortable when other guests create a compatible mix, Sea & Sun
can be a good vacation base if you're more interested in beach than
in being within walking distance of the casinos and cavorting that
are a few minutes drive either east or west along the north coast.
You're about a 15-minutes bus ride from Old San Juan and less
from the action-packed Condado and Isla Verde areas. Rates this
winter figure to about $50 for 2, breakfasts included.

▪▪▪
HOUSEKEEPING HOLIDAYS in Puerto Rico can be high-rise or
way out; you make the choice. There are as many options for places
to stay as there are people owning condominiums or second homes
in Puerto Rico—and that's a lot. If you don't know much about
Puerto Rico, and are not sure where you want to locate, my recommendation is to book a hotel for a few nights and do your own
groundwork for a long-term rental; second, look this year for some
place for next. There are *plenty* of places—at all prices. As far as
food is concerned, you can buy everything at supermarkets that
look like the ones at home: air-conditioned, shelves packed, familiar
name brands in addition to some goods canned in Puerto Rico. The
best fresh fruits and sometimes vegetables are bought from trucks
along the road, sometimes seen on the way out to Dorado, and often
are available on the main route between the airport and downtown
San Juan.

High-rise condominiums are legion, but before the mention of
some of those, you should know that there are condominiums
(houses and apartments) for rent at Dorado (Villas at Dorado
Beach are rented through Loews Representation. Call 800–
421–0530 for information on the 34 units.) Some of the very attractive, furnished-to-the-taste-of-the-owner apartments at Palmas
del Mar are rented through Robustelli World Travel, Stamford, CT
06901. Apartments at Rio Mar, the attractive resort on the north
coast, east of San Juan, also give you housekeeping conveniences
with complete hotel/resort facilities. In the middle of the Condado
confusion, with beach, casinos, shops, and restaurants within a
few paces, there are the apartments at the Dutch Towers,

plus the Regency, down the street, across the road on the seaside. At Isla Verde, consider the Caribbean Beach Club, the ESJ Tower (affiliated with El San Juan Hotel), and the Holiday Inn Isla Verde, all on the beach.

Mrs. Francis J. Gilroy (3405 East Drive, Douglas Manor, NY 11363) is one reliable source for apartment rentals in Puerto Rico. Not only does she have full details on a variety of apartments in the Coral Beach complex (attractive highrise group in the Isla Verde area) where she and her husband own a unit, but she also carries listings for about 40 places available by week, month, or season. Some are located at the east end (Fajardo area), others at or near Luquillo beach, and many are in the busy San Juan area.

■■

RESTAURANTS: Dining out can lead through an endless procession of specialty foods in Puerto Rico. In the San Juan-Condado area, you can find an international range of menus, with some of the best food served in the big hotel restaurants—usually in the dress-up dining room. Most big hotels have coffee shops, with the same assortment of food that you expect to find in your local city high-rise hotels. Some hotels (even the Caribe Hilton) have turned cafeteria-style for breakfast and lunch. In addition, there are cafes and fast-food shops that are easy to get to and fine for family fare.

AUTHOR'S OBSERVATION: Two sources for coaching on dining decisions when you are on the spot are the comments in *Que Pasa,* available free at your hotel or from the Tourist Information offices, and *Walking Tours of San Juan,* available locally for $2.50 or by mail ($4.50) from #301, First Federal Bldg., Santurce, P.R. 00909.

Count on metropolitan city prices for the better San Juan restaurants. The only dining bargains come from the roadside stands that sell empañadas and pastillitos, and fresh pineapples and oranges. Otherwise, you can expect to spend the usual at the Kentucky Fried, Burger King, McDonald's and other stateside standards, all of which are in the San Juan-Condado area. There are some restaurants that offer exceptional atmosphere; many that are enclosed, air-conditioned, dark, and expensive; a few that are open-air, casual, and comfortable to lounge in. All can be found in the heart of the colonial city, some also outside and around the island.

AUTHOR'S AWARDS for San Juan dining: Zaragozana, whenever you can get there, noon or night, for Spanish/Cuban specialties; La Fragua, for excellent Spanish-style fish and specialties by a man who may be the island's best chef; and to the Butterfly People for their very special creation.

A book could (and should) be written about San Juan's restaurants. Each season brings more, and many of them are exceptionally good. Special favorites on recent visits in San Juan, a city I swing through several times a year, are **Alfonso's,** a casual snack place across the road from the beach at Ocean Park, which I liked for the willingness of its staff as much as for its made-on-the-spot tacos and other Mexican food; **El Patio de Sam,** a popular snack-or-more place fronting on the Plaza de San Jose in Old San Juan, but actually at 102 San Sebastian; **Don Pepe,** with a speakeasy atmosphere and elaborate meals (sometimes too elaborate to taste as good as they should) on a side street in the Condado area; **Scotch & Sirloin,** in the old La Rada Hotel (102 Ashford) for steak which is better sometimes than others; **Chez Michel** (1126 Ashford Avenue) for French-style food in a pleasant atmosphere; **El Consulado,** across from La Concha Hotel on Ashford Avenue, more for its cafe atmosphere than for its cuisine (which is only average); and **Casa Blanca,** in the shopping "house" called Casabella, where you can get good meals in elegant surroundings with an option for window-shopping between courses.

Most of the hotels have good-to-excellent restaurants (and plenty of coffee shops). Caribe Hilton's **Rotisserie** leads my personal list of favorites, but I have enjoyed the Friday night buffet at **La Concha** (for fish), the buffet (and breakfasts) at **El Convento** in Old San Juan, and the **Steak Penthouse** at the top of the Dupont Plaza (mostly for its view).

If you want five special meals in San Juan, here's what I'd suggest:

The Butterfly People, upstairs at 152 Fortaleza is another world, far removed from the clutter of commerce that barnacles the street. Walk up the stairs of this grand house and you are in the world of the Butterfly People, namely Dakir and Attenaire Purington who have shared their special talents (and interests) with the rest of us. Almost like a salon, the several rooms are "dedicated" to colorful butterflies encased in plastic (and purchasable), and dining can be on crepes or more substantial offerings. It's the ambiance as much as the food that makes this place worth special mention.

Los Galanes is in a 16th-century Spanish setting in an attractively restored house on Calle San Francisco 65, a one-way street. (Walk down from El Convento unless your taxi has planned ahead. Forget about driving yourself; there's no place to park.) Dining in the restaurant that Manolo Galan opened in the building whose restoration he spearheaded is like eating in a museum. Each of the few rooms has a personality of its own, with tables set with huge "crystal" goblets and pistol-handled "pewter" (stainless steel) knives. When you have looked around—at the paintings, plants, wall hangings, and courtyards—look up to find santos, candelabra, and other treasures perching on shelves close to the high ceilings where there are overhead fans. The ambiance is elegant, right down to the few flowers stuck into sake carafes on your tables. The handwritten menu reads better than the food tasted during my meals here. Too much I saw and tasted seemed contrived and over-clever. In spite of that, the experience is one I'll try again. Count on paying $20 for a paella for 2, about $9 for fillet of sole, with the appetizers in the $2.75 range.

La Zaragozana (San Francisco 356), not far from the cathedral in Old San Juan, can seat as many as 100 people on the dark wood chairs that pull up to red-cloth-covered tables, nested in the darkened rooms of this air-conditioned special spot. The bar, where you will wait if you arrive for dinner on a busy evening, is on the left, curving to the back dining area. Food is flambé and with flourishes, taking its cue from the elegant restaurant that used to occupy a private home setting in pre-Castro Havana. When the tide turned, the brothers took their bourgeois habits and classic recipes to a side street in Old San Juan, where the violin trio still plays as you linger over a late-night dinner. The red snapper flambéed with sherry and a soupçon of lemon was ideal on a recent visit, and you must have the Cuban-style flan (which colleague Carlos Diago claims gets its special flavor from creole eggs and the Cuban touch). The high prices you pay seem to me to be for one of Old San Juan's best values, considering setting, service, and food.

On the main road closest to the shore, connecting Old San Juan and the Condado area, not far from the Caribe Hilton, **Cathay** (410 Ponce de Leon) serves Cantonese specialties, and **La Reina** (450

Ponce de Leon) specializes in Spanish food. Both places are in air-conditioned buildings, with little in the way of atmosphere except for modern versions of the traditional touches from both countries. La Reina is at the street level of Torre de la Reina, built as an elegant condominium complex a few years ago. You'll need wheels to reach both places and it's well worth the effort for La Reina. Started, and coaxed into special status by Herminio Castro (from Santiago in northern Spain), La Reina's specialty (in my opinion) is the Paella a la Reina ($13.95) which takes half an hour to prepare (just enough time to enjoy your Sangria), and is well worth the wait. Zarzuela de Mariscos is another specialty and the Red Snapper offerings are a worthwhile investment (at about $10.95). Take time for an after dinner drink, and move to the bar to do so. If you're lucky, you can look at the painting of Castro pouring his potions while he mixes one for you. (Creme de Cacao, Triple Sec, Brandy and coffee, with plenty of sugar, is one lethal mix.)

La Fragua, nestled next to the Hotel Capitol in a residential area just off Ponce de Leon in Miramar, came into focus on an after-the-theater late night dinner with San Juan friends. What a special place! The chef moved to San Juan from Lina's, the famous restaurant in the Dominican Republic's Santo Domingo, and he does his best with excellent food in unpretentious surroundings. The minute you step inside the air-conditioned room you are in an "inner sanctum" known, and respected, by food-wise San Juaneros. The focal points of the decor are hams hanging over a service bar, with an occasional painting punctuating the walls. The focus here is on good food, which is best enjoyed with good company. I had both, with the range of appetizers shared by all of us and the main courses more than most could eat. If you enjoy Spanish food, perfectly cooked and served in pleasant surroundings, make a reservation here—but arrange for a taxi to take you. It's not an ideal strolling area.

■■■

HOTELS AROUND THE ISLAND are difficult to arrange in any logical order. An alphabetical listing makes no sense because it puts resorts at opposite ends of the country next to each other. Remember that you can get from the far east coast (Fajardo) to San Juan in about 1½ hours, traffic willing, and from the far west (Mayagüez) in almost 3 hours, or about 25 minutes by plane. While it is practical to plan for a day in San Juan from the Dorado/Cerromar hotels (west of San Juan on the north coast), from Delicias and the Rio Mar to the east on the north coast, and from Humacao (Palmas del Mar Hotel) at the southeast, to try to "do" Old San Juan in a day from Mayagüez or from Ponce would, in my opinion, be exhausting, although it is possible if you travel by plane.

In addition to the "total resort" concept of the big properties around the shores of Puerto Rico, there are paradores (inns) that offer a very different kind of holiday, in the mountains near small villages. If you are unfamiliar with the size and shape of Puerto Rico, arm yourself with a map when you follow the listing below. Resorts are mentioned heading clockwise out of north-coast San Juan, to the east, southeast, south, west, and back to the northwest coast. Paradores are grouped alphabetically at the end of the listing, in the belief that people who want a parador would be happy at any of them.

✤ **Rio Mar** (Box P, Palmer, PR 00721; 111 rooms) cups all the best resort offerings in an expanse of shoreline east of San Juan and far enough away from the city to seem like another island. This north-coast resort community, about 45 minutes' drive east of San Juan (19 miles east of the airport), is a vast plan that got off the ground in '76—just barely. Hyatt had a hand in management and then departed; others have tried, and now, after a couple of islandwide record-breaking seasons, the place seems to have hit its stride. The potential is here: 523 acres along the shore and inland planned for a condominium resort community with a core clubhouse for wining and dining, tennis courts, golf course, a beach that comes in and out with the wind and sea, and the ingredients for an interesting isolated play-and-pay-in-the-sun community. Rooms are attractive, in a "village" with tiled streets and sidewalks bordered by white stucco, Mediterranean-style buildings with red-tiled roofs. Lofty ceilings in some rooms give an air of elegance (and the highest rate). Suites and terrace villas supplement regular rooms. Good for families who can afford it (get a unit with kitchen); nice hideaway for honeymooners, who get a special rate. Ask about sports packages and summer deals, and expect to be a guest with groups who will help to keep the place lively. It will seem isolated if you're alone. Room rates range from $99 to $112 for 2, everything extra.

✤ **Hotel Delicias** (Box 514, Playa de Fajardo, Puerto Real, P.R. 00740; 20 rooms) offers an opportunity for a very special Puerto Rican experience. Carlos Robles has a very special inn and, although he offered to let me buy it when I wandered through, I hope his enthusiasm has renewed by the time you make your booking.

The hotel is at the ferry landing for boats to Culebra and Vieques, two offshore islands, and the U.S. customs house is across the road. (The building is probably the only pink customs house in the U.S. network.) Rooms are relatively new, neat, and nicely furnished, with shower and modern plumbing. A center courtyard, with flourishing planting, gives a Spanish/Puerto Rican feeling to the inn, and a holiday here will be a far cry from the hubbub at the better known San Juan strip. Disturbingly modern from the outside, the Delicias captures the Old World hospitality of Puerto Rico—especially if you can speak Spanish. At rates of about $30 for 2, and opportunities for excellent seafood meals at extra cost, this place can be a happy haven.

✛ **El Conquistador** (Las Croabas, Fajardo, PR 00648; 386 rooms) "growed like Topsy" through the years. It was first a small hotel, then golf courses were added, then funiculars, then pools, then over-elaborate restaurants, then beachside units, and over all a span of plastic grass to cover slabs of cement around the pool, under the funicular, and anywhere else it seemed to fit. As we go to press, status for winter '81–'82 is uncertain. Check if it matters to you.

✛ **Palmas del Mar** (Box 2020, Humacao, PR 00661; Palmas Inn, 23 rooms; Candelero Hotel, 112 rooms; plus more than 100 villas with rooms and apartments) is burgeoning with improvements and expansion. It's great, and management decisions to continue striving for top quality seem to be paying off. Palmas is a picture perfect place, if you are content to wallow on the long stretch of beach or beside one of the 3 pools, or play tennis on a choice of 20 courts (4 night-lighted), or golf on the 18-hole, 6660-yard course that weaves around clusters of Mediterranean-style villas and to the special botanical garden where the plants for the property are raised. When you sail from the marina, or head out deep-sea fishing, or dine at one of the several restaurants (ranging from beachside bohio at the *Sun Fun Hut* to air-conditioned elegant *El Jumacao*), or ride horseback or stop for a cool drink at the pro shop, the tennis clubhouse, or the inn at the top of the hill—to name only 3 of the several choices—you won't have time or inclination to think about the fact that Charles Fraser's (of Sea Pines fame) dream of an exotic resort at a prime spot of Puerto Rico's southeast shore fell on hard times and has been doing financial flip-flops for the past few years. The hotel, however, has never closed its doors, and most of its guests have vacationed here unaware of the internal financial affairs. I do not pretend to be impartial about this place. From my first contact years ago, when a New York firm did preliminary research on resort potential for an unnamed company that wanted to develop "the site of a coconut plantation," I have known this shore. I stood on a hill-top when all that was here was a thatched bohio, a spectacular view, an enthusiastic staff, and a map. And I have anguished with the faithful who have stayed with their dream through Fraser's fail-ure, Marriott's move in and out, and a series of other problems.

For those who vacation here, Palmas is a total, tasteful resort, where your evening entertainment depends on which village you wander around. If you stay near the top of the hill, you'll lounge at the piano bar where Avo Uvezian plays; if you live at the tennis vil-lage, *La Fondita del Sol* (Puerto Rican food) is the place, and other small bistros and cafes can be found at the other villages. (*La Creperie* for 8 varieties of crepe at *Cafe de la Place,* for example.) You'll pay about from $120 to over $180 this winter for a room for 2, but the room you reside in will be palatial (and meals will be extra). No expense was spared in the building: elegant tiles, huge airy bed-room with terrace or balcony for sunning and sea-watching, mod-ern bath with tub area separate from the loo; overhead fans (plus air conditioning), colorful fabrics and white walls, plus the option to slide into the seldom used pool that makes El Jumacao Restau-rant seem like a private home. Other rooms are in the inn village, tennis village, marina village, or beach village, which has oceanside rooms at a premium; fairway villas with golf-course view are slightly less, but both are at the beach. **Candelero Hotel,** with a band of rooms at the beach, is new this season. Rates for 2 are $110 to $150 for room only, but children under 12 can stay free. Guests can share all the Palmas action options. For on-your-own-holidays, you can drive in one hour from San Juan airport, or fly on Dorado Wings to the small strip at the resort. (Rental car is advisable if you don't like walking and/or want to explore the rest of Puerto Rico.) The place has the potential to offer a pampered and perfect holiday, but missing links can be maddening if you depend on precision. If you can overlook some minor flaws while you look over some of the Caribbean's most spectacular resort vistas, you'll love Palmas. (If you want to know more about the place, try to track down Esteban Padilla, better known as Steve, the Puerto Rican-born architect who was in on the earliest dreams.)

PONCE, Puerto Rico's second city, is bigger than you can "do" in a day, but neither of the hotels rates top rung on the ladder. If you want to see the museum, and some of the surrounding scenery, you can fly Prinair in the morning, pick up an Avis car at the airport (plan for it ahead), drive around all day, and fly back. You can also rent a car in San Juan, but you have the city traffic to cope with, and then an hour-long drive (on a good and scenic highway) each way. The hotels are:

✤ **Hotel Continental** (Ponce, P.R. 00731; 170 rooms) has been reborn. Opened several years ago as a member of the Inter-Continental worldwide chain, the American-style luxury hotel has slept, eyes (and front desk) closed, since 1975. New life was injected into the always attractive property by the Puerto Rico Hotel Corporation, affiliating with *Let's See Puerto Rico Tours,* a Ponce-based sightseeing company that expects to play a major role in filling the place. You can expect to find a pool, several restaurants, plus horseback riding facilities at the hillside property overlooking the south-coast city of Ponce. Count on a circuitous route for reaching this hotel, if you decide to drive. Rates are not fixed as this goes to press, but inquire about special introductory package rates that should make this hotel a good value base.

✤ **Meliá** (Box 1431, Ponce, PR 00731; 80 rooms) on Ave. Cristina, just off the old city square with its much-photographed, freshly painted red-and-black-striped firehouse and the city's cathedral. The Old-World commercial hotel rises from a street-level band of shops and has an interior courtyard. Balconies overlooking Ave. Cristina have flower boxes, and noisy traffic. Air conditioning is essential, and if you're driving, this is no place to consider unless your car will fit in another room. There's NO place for it on the street. Rates for 2 will be about $50, room only.

✤ **Holiday Inn** (Km 255.2, Highway 2, Ponce, PR 00731; 120 rooms) is the businessman's base. It is a "just-like-home" Holiday Inn: pool, plastic-packaged glasses and jellies, soap wrappers, air-conditioned boxy rooms, and all. Nowhere near the center city (where the Ponce Museum and interesting square are), but there's a parking area. You'll be on a hill, overlooking El Tuque "beach," which focuses on its public pool because the shoreline is mostly rocks. Rates are around $75 for 2, meals extra.

MAYAGÜEZ, on the western shore of Puerto Rico, is well-known to businessmen who head here for appointments, but little known to vacationers who may not know about the spectacular gardens at the agricultural station or haven't taken the time to explore this interesting coast. The area is well worth a visit, if you are an adventuresome traveler not hooked on casinos and gala nightlife (which can only be found in surfeit in San Juan area).

Mayagüez is primarily an industrial city; the best sights are natural ones, and the gardens at the Federal Agricultural Station nearby. Tours to nearby areas can easily be arranged, but your best bet here is to rent a car and take off on your own. Routes into the mountains are easy and interesting to follow, even when wiggly and not well marked. The Spanish road signs can be mastered by nonlinguists who like word puzzles and have some confidence. The nearest beach is a 20-minute drive, and golf at Aguadilla is closer to 45 minutes, with the 9-hole course at Cabo Roja only half an hour.

✛ **Mayagüez Hilton** (Box 3629, Marina Station, Mayagüez, PR 00708; 150 rooms) makes a very different impression from the standard high-rise, action-packed places in the San Juan area. As you curve up the hill of route 104, turning left off Route 2, the main road from the Mayagüez airport (10-minute drive), you approach what looks like a quality country club. Opened on June 14, 1964, the hotel has a huge swimming pool, 2 tennis courts (nightlighted), and comfortable air-conditioned rooms that give you a view from one end of the modern double-bedded box. Request one of the pool-view rooms with balcony for the favored outlook; lanais are convenient to the gardens but in a hot pocket, and I didn't think the balcony view on other rooms was much. At the modern 5-story hotel, the *Rotisserie* serves island food and the expected grilled beef and lobster, but the special treat at this unique hotel is the Chef's Table, where the chef serves private dinners for up to 6 people. Special Royal Doulton china and Denby crystal are used for the fete, and you can dine on the chef's specials, with his selection of wines. Reservations for the elegant meal should be made a week in advance and the prix fixe is $50 per person. For general, everyday relaxing, the *Cacique* bar opens out to the pool terrace gallery, and a couple of shops can take care of necessities, but there's nothing in the area to compete with the boutiques of Old San Juan or that area's nightlife. Rates for 2, for a twin-bedded deluxe room figure to almost $90, no meals, plus the 6% government room tax. Although speaking Spanish is not essential, familiarity with the language will certainly come in handy.

DORADO is a small town that hasn't changed much since the advent of the Dorado Beach and Cerromar Hotel influx. Although there are a couple of local restaurants, bars, and shops that might interest adventuresome vacationers, most visitors will only drive through on their way to the elegant resorts. Located on the north shore, west of San Juan, Dorado is about 45 minutes drive from the international airport at Isla Verde.

✤ **Dorado Beach** (Dorado, PR 00646; 300 rooms) has come a long way since it was the Livingston homestead. Almost 20 years ago, Laurance Rockefeller spotted this plot, then known as Finca La Sardiniera and the grapefruit plantation of Dr. Alfred Livingston, and was encouraged to lend his class and cash to Puerto Rico's tourism plans by building a luxury resort in an "unknown," depressed area, with tax assistance and a $1.3 million loan from the Industrial Development group. Rockresorts set the pace and kept the stride for several years, but footsteps faltered in recent years. (Sister Cerromar, built for groups, was the bull in this china shop.) Dorado expanded with elegant homes scattered around the grounds and condominium plans promoted. Additional blocks of rooms appeared around the palm trees, and although the weaving roads still *looked* as though they led to isolation, tennis courts joined golf courses for sports enthusiasts. It all proved too much for Rockresorts. First, Rockefeller interests sold to Eastern Airlines, but still managed the properties; then Eastern sold to the group mentioned in the Cerromar commentary, and Rockresorts managed the property. On April 30, 1977, after a tumultuous tenure, Rockresorts resigned and Regent International, experts in doing things the BIG way, entered—to make a BIG investment of $3.5 million to refurbish and redo. In Regent's case, big was accomplished with a flare that would have made Rockresorts proud. The transformation was miraculously completed in less than a year. Dorado today looks more as it did in its first elegant years than I have seen it look in the past 10! Walls that should never have been walled in are opened up; the same rattan with copper and beige that perked up Cerromar has set a peppy tone for this place. Blocks of rooms have been added, but my favorite is still the Su Casa wing, near tennis courts and tennis shop, the golf shop, and a fringe of the golf course, abutting the elegant *Su Casa* restaurant, and a beach.

Regent International added another layer on Su Casa, the former home of Clara Livingston, whose family built the place in 1928. The property still looks as though it could be someone's home. Note the historic photos that line the walls to the top-floor cocktail lounge— and then settle in to enjoy the view of sea and tropics from the top. Premium of $8 for Su Casa dinners, but the dinner and breakfast are both worth the steep tariff. Lunchers will settle at the golf shop's snack area, or the *Terrace* at Dorado, near its beach and also spruced up with the new rattan and airy look. Food is attractive, well served, and offered at prices you'll soon get used to. Don't come here if you have to worry about $. Everything costs—a lot. The $150 and up that 2 of you pay for your winter room with 2 meals daily is only the beginning, and if you are in one of the 17 new and elegant casita rooms on a strip between pool and beach, you'll be paying $225 per day. A reprieve for those who search for good value comes with the special summer package plans, often focusing on sports. Ask about them. Two 18-hole golf courses, tennis courts, opportunities for dining at a choice of restaurants, are on these premises, and you have all of Cerromar's action (casino, supper club, disco) a shuttle bus ride away. Yellow jitneys roam the property for those who don't want to walk the necessary miles. You don't need a rental car, but may want to take one for a day of touring. Check at the tour desk for Dorado Wings' flights for a St. Thomas shopping spree or the transportation arrangements for Old San Juan and the airport. Extra charges for EVERYTHING and, of course, for tips and taxes. Pampered perfection pursuers may not find this perfect, but it's pleasant, and the best that Puerto Rico offers.

✛ **Cerromar Beach** (Dorado, PR 00646; 508 rooms) lures group of wealthy Venezuelans, who pay full rate, and others from elsewhere willing to do the same. No cut-rate place this, in spite of its behemoth size and the several years it took this spot to "find itself." Some $30 million was poured into the construction of the 8-story building, sometimes referred to as a "military barracks" or a "born loser" since its opening in 1972. It burst full blown on the season of '72, palm trees in place and master chef in the kitchen, but the travel world wasn't ready for Cerromar when Cerromar was ready for it. Rockresorts' discreet and elegant marketing of its fine properties elsewhere in the area (Dorado on the next cove east, Caneel Bay on St. John, and Little Dix on Virgin Gorda) didn't fill 508 rooms. Eastern Airlines bought the properties at a time when they were having enough trouble trying to run an airline. They sold in 1977 to Connecticut General Life Insurance Company and Teachers Insurance and Annuity Association, who own this and Dorado through the Dorado Beach Hotel Corp. A management company was needed. Enter Regent International—blare of trumpets. Regent International is the company of two former Hilton execs, Robert Burns, who lives in Hong Kong, and George Rafael, who is reportedly living in Honolulu. Miracles have been wrought at Cerro-mar, a property that had been a white elephant. The rooms have always had a pleasant view (the two Ys, joined at the foot, give everyone a seaview balcony), and the rooms at the ends of the arms are a long walk from the center hub, but that center hub now hums with activity. The beach and sea have always stretched across the arms of the Ys. Now there's also an attractive greenhouse in the airy and plant-specked lobby. It's a bubble off the *El Yunque* bar, completely redone and a lively spot from midafternoon on. The formerly sterile sunken bar area has been turned into *El Bucanero*, with a brass-domed kitchen aisle where bartenders used to wait for patrons. You'll do the waiting now; when the house is full, this informal dining room is packed—from its opening time at 11 a.m. until 2 a.m. or so. The bar is now on the adjoining terrace, overlooking the sea and swept by the breeze; it's a convenient collapsing spot at the top of the stairs from the beach-level terrace dining area (breakfast and lunch) and near the elevators that stretch up the 8 floors. For elegant, expensive dining, try the beach-level *Surf Room,* the *Supper Club Cerromar*, next door to the casino, or, best yet, take the shuttle bus to Dorado's Su Casa (reservations essential at all).

One of the former shops has new life after 9 when *El Coquí*, named for Puerto Rico's tree frog and making a name for itself as Puerto Rico's liveliest disco, gets into action. (Note the glass-etched coquís lighted in corners around the place and the sound system that permits talkers to talk while dancers dance; and get there early to claim one of the basket couches.) Casa Cavanagh's shop claims the space next door for daylight hours. Tour desk and other small shops in the side lobby area, near the checkout desk. Available for guests' use are 13 tennis courts with pro, swimming pool, bicycles ($2 per hour), casino, supper club and restaurants mentioned above, plus all the facilities of nearby Dorado—with 4 18-hole golf courses between the 2 properties. If you're bored here, that's *your* problem! (Old San Juan is about ½ hour away, on good highways; count on 45 minutes for the airport.)

Close to $3 million was invested in a complete refurbishing of this property and sister Dorado. It shows—in light-beige rattan chairs, furnishings that look as though they are sturdy enough for wear, with copper and brown accents that give the place the tropical feeling you expect. Cerromar visitors come close to getting their money's worth when they pay the steep $135 or more for 2, meals extra. Good values come with the special summer vacation plans including honeymoon plans and free children's day camp for ages 5–13 during summer and over Easter and Christmas holidays.

■■

PARADORES PUERTORRIQUEÑOS, patterned after the very successful restoration of historic lodgings in Spain, are small typical country inns, usually mountain retreats that were formerly coffee plantations or perhaps, as in the case of Baños de Coamo, turn-of-the-century resorts. Assisted and advised by tourism officials, the inns must have resident managers and subscribe to other standards set by the Tourism Development Company to qualify for tax breaks as paradores.

✤ **Parador Baños de Coamo** (Rt. 546, Km 1, Coamo, PR 00640, 46 rooms) is the oldest, and one of the newest, hotels in Puerto Rico. Known to the earliest Taino Indian settlers, and—some say—the Fountain of Youth that Puerto Rico's first governor, Juan Ponce de Leon, went to Florida to find, the Coamo Springs have lured the likes of Franklin Roosevelt, Thomas Edison, Alexander Graham Bell, and Frank Lloyd Wright. The renowned resort opened in 1857, to close 100 years later when the tourism tide receded to the beaches and casinos. Reopened in December 1977, with 2-story buildings of new rooms surrounding the astounding tree in the center courtyard, the Parador is a popular weekend goal for San Juaneros in search of peace and quiet. Thermal baths, the elegant main house restored for dining (Puerto Rican country food), horseback riding, and the appeal of a mountain retreat are pluses (and salve for the souls of weary travelers). Each of the 46 rooms has tiled bath, entrance to the courtyard, window view of verdant tropical growth, and comfortable, Puerto Rican-made furniture. During midweek and summer months, you can have the place almost to yourself. Bring books or a romantic pal to share the $40 double room rate, meals extra.

✤ **Parador Gripiñas** (Box 248, Jayuya, PR 00664; 19 rooms) looks exactly as it might have 100 years ago when the thriving coffee plantation that had started in 1858 issued its own currency for the plantation-owned-and-stocked stores. The main house has been restored, with tin roof the instrument for a symphony when it rains and waterfalls as background music the rest of the time. New rooms, added in early '80, have been built with modern conveniences and traditional decoration. Gardens have been pruned and tended to thrive around the grounds, especially near the pool and on the porch, where your rocker is waiting. An easy place to call home, if you—like a member of the Casals symphony orchestra—want to listen to classical tapes. Not the "everyday Caribbean inn," but an ideal place for reflection or writing poetry. Puerto Rican families make this a goal for the Sunday buffets; midweek is quiet. Winter rates for the simple, air-cooled rooms are about $30 for 2, meals extra (reasonable; local specialties).

✤ **Parador Guajataca** (Rt. 2, Km 103.8, Quebradillas, PR 00742; 38 rooms) was the first of the Tourism Company's Paradores Puertorriqueños when it opened in late '73. Adda and Manuel Chavez are excellent hosts, the perfect people to tell you what's going on in nearby Quebradillas if you want to participate in village events. On the shore, just above a windy beach (if you're timid, swimming is better in the pool), the hotel is the place for local wedding receptions and other important social events. Rooms are motel style, built recently and lacking the charm of the mountain paradores. You'll have access to an ice machine, entertainment some evenings, and an air-conditioned, enclosed bar instead of handmade furniture and country touches. On the north shore, almost 2 hours' drive west of San Juan, and about 45 minutes' drive northeast from the airport at Mayagüez. (Guajataca means "ocean breeze.") Figure on close to $40 for 2, room only.

✤ **Parador Hacienda Juanita** (Rt. 105, Km 23.5, Maricao, PR 00706; 24 rooms) nestles high in the mountains, about an hour's gorgeous drive north of Sabanda Grande (on Highway 2 between Mayagüez and Ponce). This is the other world of Puerto Rico, where you can hear birds singing, the coquí chirping, and the breezes rustling in the stands of bamboo and tropical growth that surround this place. Rockers await weary travelers on the porch, where you can watch a young staff member hook up a couple of hands of bananas to ripen until they're ready for plucking. Food is hearty country fare, typical of the region, filling, and probably not anything you are used to seeing (except for chicken). Rooms in the U of wood frame buildings that cups a courtyard where a fountain plays are simple, with louvered windows to open for trade-wind air cooling. A small pool awaits dunkers; horses are nearby for riding, and there are plenty of bowered lanes for walking in the mountains. The Hacienda that provides the hospitality was part of a coffee plantation, refurbished and revived by the Tourism Development Company to open in early 1978. By early '80, 10 new rooms were added. Rates are about $30 for one of the 24 double rooms, each with sitting room and bed-room, plus bath (living room can do double duty as a second bed-room).

✤ **Parador Martorell** (Box 384, Ocean Drive 6A, Luquillo, PR 00673; 7 rooms) is small, simple, boxy stucco house, on a residen-tial street at Luquillo. Its big plus is the big beach which is a short walk along the road. For a room at good value (6 have shared bath, one has private bath) near a beach worthy of the name, try this, and pay about $40 for 2, breakfast included, for the privilege. (Lu-quillo is about 45 minutes' drive from San Juan, at the northeast corner of the Commonwealth.)

✤ **Parador Montemar** (Aguadilla, PR 00603; 40 rooms) joined the network in fall of '79, and gives guests the opportunity to fish with the Puerto Rican residents from a nearby pier. The air-conditioned rooms all have a sea view, with small sit-outside balcony, and your dining choices include a simple room where local foods are served (my preference) and a special dining area for "international" cui-sine (favored by the nearby residents for their festive evenings out). There's a pool for swimming, and—with a rental car—you're in an ideal location to drive into the mountains (to the Taino Indian ball park) or along the coast to play golf at Borinquen. Rates are about $40 for 2 in winter.

■■■

CAMPING AROUND PUERTO RICO took on new dimensions with the organization of the *Centros Vacacionales,* clusters of simple cabins (no tents allowed) usually with a beach focus and always with *very* moderate prices. Bedding is provided, and kitchens have essential utensils, including a refrigerator. Four of the commu-nities were ready by the end of 1980, and all have similar regula-tions about length of stay. No reservations are accepted more than 4 months in advance, and vacationers can stay at the centers up to one week every 3 months. You'll need a rental car for mobility, but you can reach these spots by public transportation if you are re-laxed enough to allow *plenty* of time. Planned for families who live in Puerto Rico to use during their summer vacations, the Centros guests during winter seasons will include a sprinkling of local resi-dents and many Europeans and North Americans who recognize a good value when they see one. An interesting vacation can be as-sembled with a week at the mountains (Maricao) and a week along the shore (at Boqueron, Punta Santiago, or Arroya), or on Vieques

Island when that Centro opens sometime late in 1981. For reservations, write to the Director at the addresses given below. (No need for airmail from the U.S.; Puerto Rican mail goes airmail anyway.) Speaking Spanish will be helpful when you travel around the neighboring countryside since these areas are not well-known for tourists and for meeting the Puerto Rican residents who are vacationing there when you are.

✣ **Centro Vacacionale** (Arroyo, PR 00615; about 30 cabins) on the south coast, just east of the town of Guayama, has a swimming pool, with the cluster of cabins built in the same style as those of the other Centros (2-bedrooms, facilities for sleeping 6, with simple-but-adequate kitchen facilities). The coast-rimming highway makes it possible to drive west to Ponce (and its interesting museum) in about an hour, if you've rented a car. *Publicos* and regular buses ply the route, if you want to keep costs to a basic minimum. Overnight cabin rate will be about $15.

✣ **Centro Vacacionale** (Boqueron, PR 00622; 158 cabins) is the biggest of the communities, and claims a portion of one of Puerto Rico's prize beaches. Do not expect anything fancy in the way of accommodations, but you can expect to find a local commissary for food supplies, and a cabin with modern conveniences—stove, sinks, toilet, etc. One of the 2 bedrooms has bunk beds and can accommodate 4 people, the other has 2 beds. There are basketball and volleyball facilities (outdoor, of course), but for water sports you'll need your own equipment. Rates for 6 are $12 per night! Even with your food costs, and perhaps a rental car to reach this southwest coast community, the total figures to a bargain rate.

✣ **Centro Vacacionale** (Punta Santiago, near Humacao, PR 00661; 72 cabins) nestles on Playa (beach) de Humacao, not too far from the famed Palmas del Mar resort, and offers 2 tennis courts, a swimming pool, and the beach for recreation. Some units are 2 story, and all are arranged to accommodate a family of 6 in reasonable surroundings with a floor plan similar to the other Centro units (one bedroom with 4 bunk beds, one bedroom with twin beds, kitchen, and dining area). In addition to a commissary, there are some good supermarkets in the town and a few restaurants (including those at Palmas for an elegant evening), if you have included a car rental in your vacation plan. The east coast location is about an hour's drive, mostly on a good highway, from the San Juan airport, and the town of Fajardo (for ferry connections to Vieques and Culebra as well as fishing and sailing charter boats) is a short drive north. The cabin rate for 6 is $15 per night.

✤ **Centro Vacacionale** (Maricao, PR 00706; 24 cabins) is for those who want to be in the mountains. The weaving route to reach this verdant spot takes you through one of Puerto Rico's impressive National Forest areas, an ideal place for hiking and study of tropical flora. This small community is a favorite for Puerto Rican residents who live near the sea and want a real vacation with a change of venue. Somewhat more isolated than the other places, the Centro Maricao is apt to have a more congenial atmosphere since there are fewer cottages for rent. Cabins have fireplaces (and you'll need sweaters and some warmer clothes for cool mountain evenings). Stock up at one of the supermarkets you'll pass on the main road from Mayaguez; shopping facilities are limited here. There's a swimming pool and places to play volleyball or basketball, both popular with Puerto Rican families. Count on paying $12 for the cabin for 6.

■■

CULEBRA, a 7- by 4-mile cove-crimped island off Puerto Rico's east end, was settled in 1880. The first governor, appointed from Vieques, was killed in 1887, and from that point on the independent Culebrans appointed their own top official. In 1903, when the U.S. Navy came in, Culebrans were moved to new settlements, one at the east end and another in the midsection on the south coast. This second was known as Dewey, locally called Puebla and originally a swamp. Although there are 900 residents on the island, there are more Culebrans living on St. Croix, one of the United States Virgin Islands about 70 miles southeast, than on home territory. Dewey (Puebla) is not much to look at: a few small stores, a couple of boxy buildings, and the Seafarer's Inn. When you swoop through the pass in the twin hilltops to land at the small airstrip, you won't notice the town anyway. If you focus on anything except the peril of landing, you will notice the spectacular strand of Flamingo Bay and the protected hurricane harbor that is a pocket of sea, poked into the south shore at Ensenada Honda ("deep bay"). Arrival choices are limited to small planes, either Flamingo Airways in about 20 minutes from San Juan's Isla Grande Airport or a charter you arrange from your arrival at the International Airport, or to the 2-hour Port Authority boat trip over seas that can be rough and rolling between Fajardo and Culebra. Places to find include Punta Molines at the northwest and Punta del Soldado at the south in the middle.

Both are exceptional for snorkeling, but bring your own equipment. The small offshore cay called Culebrita, reached by fishing boat or a motorboat that your hotel may have at the ready for excursions, is good for lobster progging.

The biggest news on Culebra has involved no longer getting bombed, which the island was regularly—until U.S. Navy exercises were stopped by Presidential order in response to irate Culebrans in 1975. You can count on peace and quiet, and no planned activities, when you holiday here.

✢ **Punta Aloe** (Box 207, Culebra, PR 00645; 9 units) is a grove of Douglas fir houses that grew from the shoreside hill at Enseñada Honda in fall of '73. Best way to get here is by boat, from the small airstrip near Dewey (if they know you're coming, they'll send the *Boston Whaler* over the lagoon). Each house has angles, plenty of trade winds blowing through, plus adequate furnishings, beds for 6 people, a couple of hammocks, and a full-fledged kitchen for cooking up the lobsters you progged that morning. A small commissary fills basic needs, but bring the meat you want from home. Planned by a coterie of academics from midland U.S.A., Punta Aloe is a perfect place for self-sufficient types who want a quiet spot with tropical breeze, good view, and plenty of time for resting and reading. Figure about $500 for a house for a winter week.

✢ **Seafarer's Inn** (Box 216, Culebra, PR 00645; 15 rooms) sits at roadside in Dewey, serving fresh lobster (sometimes, to my taste, overgrilled). A *very* casual, barefoot spot opened in '73 by Jane and Druso Daubon, the inn has simple and inexpensive rooms. Paint perks them up occasionally, but there's not much going in the way of fancy flourishes for your $35 for 2. Easy-going barefoot and boating types will settle in easily.

■■

VIEQUES, a beach-trimmed island that is about 20 miles long and 3 or 6 miles wide, depending on where you measure, sits almost 7 miles off the east end of Puerto Rico. Before you sign on for the ferry that departs from the east end town of Fajardo, you should know that the crossing can be choppy, and even seafaring folk have found it more than they can take. (Seas are usually calmer in summer months.) Try the 15-minute flight on the small planes of Vieques Air Link or Air Mont that depart from San Juan's second airport, Isla Grande, somewhere close to when you want to go—if you're flexible. Your alternative is to charter a small plane to connect with your big plane flight from the international airport. Home for Arawak tribes, Vieques has yielded some interesting relics from the earliest settlements. Most modern visitors head here in search of peace and quiet, even though the island is now almost constantly in Puerto Rican newspaper headlines. The U.S. Navy has a Vieques base that has become a cause célèbre for the independence movement and for people who want Vieques to take its rightful place in a developing area. (Some say it should become the free-port tourist shopping haven for Puerto Rico.) Visitors will be blissfully unaware of most of the local problems, and for now at least, will have the island's beaches almost to themselves. The main town of Isabel Segunda, named for Isabella II, who was Queen of Spain from 1833 to 1868, is not nearly as attractive as the beaches you'll find for yourself. The small fishing village of Esperanza on the south coast is the nearest town to the island's only inn of note.

✤ **La Casa del Frances** (Box 458, Vieques, PR 00765; 16 rooms) was the house of a plantation owner from the French West Indies. It then became the home and sometime inn, called Sportsman's House, with Mr. Wemyss as host. September 1976 ushered in a new era, with American-born Paul Caron and his French-born wife as nonresident owners (they live in Brussels), and a manager in charge. Rosemary Tatsar is your on-the-spot hostess and she'll have all the helpful hints for how best to enjoy Vieques. Bahia del Sol is an easy stroll from the freshly painted wood plantation house, and the pool in the courtyard is a few steps from your air-cooled room. If you want to know what life was like in the "good old days" before everything got so complicated, try this—with horseback riding, beach strolling, snorkeling, scuba, and sailing as action options. Rates are $44 to $54 for 2, room with private bath; slightly less in summer. Meals extra, at about $3 for breakfast and $10 for dinner. Cash or traveler's checks for bills only; 10% service charge in lieu of gratuities.

✤ **Las Rocas** (Vieques, PR 00765; 1 cottage, plus 2 apts.) nests across the road from Casa del Frances and gives you a chance for housekeeping. The modern, ranch-style houses can be rented as one house (for 6 people, with 3 bedrooms) or as a 2-bedroom apartment. Contact Samuel Brick, Box 57, Vieques, PR 00765, for details and terms of rental.

▪▪
PLACES WORTH FINDING in Puerto Rico begin with *OLD SAN JUAN.* The restored 16th- and 17th-century buildings represent the

most authentic picture we have of the community known to the Caribbean's early Spanish settlers. Even the old city of Santo Domingo, in the Dominican Republic, settled before San Juan, does not represent a truer picture of an early Caribbean community. Most of Santo Domingo's buildings were rebuilt, albeit according to old plans and lines because the original city had been almost completely destroyed. In Old San Juan, the original buildings that were tumbling together about 25 years ago had survived that long not because of a man-made plan but because the original forts—El Morro and San Cristóbal—perched on clifftops. Their walls plunged to the shore or the sea, the town's early buildings were not destroyed, and no suburban sprawl from any century could be built on at least three sides of this peninsula. (When you see what has oozed out of the fourth side of the city, the commercial knot you twist through to get in and out, you can appreciate the wisdom of the Spanish settlement on the promontory.)

In mid-1978 a plan for correcting erosion of the walls of the forts was revealed. The proposal, issued jointly by the U.S. Army Corps of Engineers and the National Park Service, estimates an expense of $25.4 million to construct breakwaters to cut the force of the waves that have crashed against the walls for centuries. Other parts of the proposal include shoring up the walls, constructing foundation protection, and refilling and reinforcing the existing walls.

But for most of us, it is what is inside those walls that is most interesting. In addition to the many 16th- and 17th-century homes now restored and filled with boutiques, restaurants, and—in a few cases—apartments, there is Casa Blanca, on a site of the house built for Ponce de Leon. The Dominican Convent, home for the Instituto de Cultura Puertorriqueña, dates from 1523, and San Juan Cathedral, although mostly 19th-century, is on the site of the first wood church (1520). Tapia Theater, built in 1832 has been restored to its 19th-century appearance and is used for 20th-century performances, and La Fortaleza, where Puerto Rico's governor lives, has been home for the chief ruler of Puerto Rico since the first community was established here. The first tower was ordered built by Spain's Carlos I in 1540.

AUTHOR'S OBSERVATION: While the experts shore up the walls of the forts, I wish that the town fathers would unite on the solution to the hideous traffic problem in Old San Juan where the Sunday "paseo" has become an endless chain of cars crawling along Calle Norzagaray to turn at Plaza San José for the route down Calle Cristo to Calle Fortaleza and Avenida Ponce de Leon. Why can't this exceptional restoration have minibus routes *only*, with all cars parking in a lot to be cleared outside the old city, and the 5-block area turned into a pedestrian mall?

The **Dominican Convent** dates from the 15th century, and should be the start for any walking tour through the history of Old San Juan, not only because it is the home for the Instituto de Cultura Puertorriqueña, but also because there are always art exhibits under the arcades around the edge of the center courtyard. The small museum (ancient sheet music, convent study room, altarpiece) to the right as you enter is reminiscent of old Spain, and the walk is all downhill from Plaza San José, where the convent is located.

Museo Pablo Casals (101 San Sebastian; M-Sat 9-12, 1-4; Sun 1-5; free) on Plaza de San José opened in early 1978 as a memorial to the beloved cellist who spent the last 20 years of his life in his adopted country, Puerto Rico, and created the Casals Festival, held in June and highlight of the Commonwealth cultural season. Pablo Casals left his native Spain in protest over the policies of dictator Generalissimo Francisco Franco, to settle in his mother's home island in 1956, and was not to return until a couple of years before his death. In addition to photographs, musical scores, and memorabilia, the small 16th century house has a special library of tapes from the Festival Casals. Highlight for those devoted to the famed cellist's work will be his cello, which is upstairs in a glass-enclosed display. (The case is propped up in a ground-floor corner.)

Casa Blanca, perched on a bluff overlooking San Juan harbor, claims to be the oldest continuously inhabited residence in the western hemisphere, but that seems to me to be a loose claim since the place is a museum now, and was closed for a lot of its recent history while undergoing complete refurbishing and repair. Be sure to see this house if you have any interest in early history. Although Ponce de León never lived here, the house that stands on the site of a simple 24-square-foot wood and thatched structure was supposed to have been built for him. When the thatched building burned, in 1521, stone was used for the new building, started in 1523. The fortress was added later, with the prestige of being called a fort. The approach to the house, through the gardens (and past the building where concerts are sometimes held), is a world apart from commercial San Juan. The views out the windows and from the balconies of the house lure students and others to the parapets to talk and read. Inside, the furnishings are typical of what might have been in the house, but none of them are original.

La Rogativa, the statue at the end of Caleta Las Monjas, a right turn as you head from the Plaza San José, commemorates the saving of Puerto Rico when it was surrounded by the Dutch. The women lined up with candles to march behind the bishop, giving the impression that there were a lot of soldiers at the top of the fortress when, in fact, there were none.

After you've looked at the statue (and the view over the wall), wander down Calle Recinto Oeste (past the old San Juan gate, the oldest gate in the original walls), which is sometimes open for cars (which then drive around the outside of the walls at sea level).

La Fortaleza, the governor's residence and office, at the walls at the end of Calle Fortaleza, is open for guided visits at specified hours. The main halls are shown, but not the private residence of the governor, which is upstairs.

Casa del Libro (255 Calle Cristo; 11–5 M–F, 2–5 Sat & Sun) is almost as interesting for its 16th-century setting as for the collection of books and prints that fill the first-floor cases. Primarily of interest to bibliophiles, this special spot rates near the Casals Museum in perfect presentation of dedication to a single subject. One item of interest is the decree relating to Columbus's second voyage, signed by King Ferdinand and Queen Isabella, but there are also pages from a Gutenberg Bible and an impressive collection of 15th-century Spanish books in special rooms upstairs.

La Casa de los Dos Zaguanes (House of Two Entrances) at the corner of Luna and San Jose (Tu, Th, F, Sat, Sun 9–12, 1–4:30) opened in August '78 as the first part of a planned museum of Puerto Rican heritage. The 3 floors will eventually house folk art, early Indian artifacts (some on loan from a Taino Indian collection that had been held at the Smithsonian) and perhaps a traveling collection from the Ponce Museum. On opening day, most of the Taino artifacts from the collection of George Latimer, U.S. Consul in Puerto Rico in 1836, held at the Smithsonian, were in place in the museum, as well as a duho (Taino ceremonial stool), which was repurchased from a collector in the Dominican Republic, and a grinding stone found by Ricardo Alegria, first director of the Instituto, during digs at Cueva Maria de la Cruz in Loiza. Be sure to look at the 18th-century buildings that house the collection; they're prize examples of life in this residential area in the 18th century. (A $25,000 Citibank donation helped bring the museum to birth.)

AUTHOR'S OBSERVATION: If seeing a particular museum is important, *be sure* to check opening hours in advance. In spite of the times and days listed in *Que Pasa*, and with information given to me by the very efficient staff of the Puerto Rico Tourist Offices, I have come to places to find them closed. You can count on all museums closing *exactly* at closing hour, so don't plan to make a last-minute sprint through some hallowed premises.

MAYAGÜEZ, midway on the west coast, is Puerto Rico's third city (after San Juan and Ponce). As the port for an agricultural region, the city has become industrial. Its traditional Spanish-style square, Plaza Colón, hides in a baffling maze of one-way streets and horn-honking traffic, but is worth finding if you have the stamina. The 16 bronze statues, including Greek maidens with hand held high, supporting a now-electrified street lamp, were cast in Barcelona, Spain, to stand tall here in the 1890s. Columbus (Colón) stands in the middle of the square and the whole sight is best to see—if you can plan it—in May or June when the jacaranda trees, known to Puerto Ricans as la reina de las flores (queen of the flowers), are in bloom.

A Taino Indian town stood at this shore (and one information source claims that the town takes its name from a Taino cacique, or chieftain, Mayagoex), but was conquered by the Spaniards, who claimed the port area as their own. At one end of the square is the refurbished city hall, at the other, the **Cathedral of la Virgen de la Candelaria.**

Outside the city, the **Mayagüez Institute of Tropical Agriculture** (7:30–12, 1–4:30 M–F) labels the hundreds of experimental plants growing on its grounds. Be sure to ask about the orchid greenhouse if you are interested in plants and have found the Institute.

Halting spots from Mayagüez, south on the west coast, curving east on the south coast, include those villages and beaches along the shore road, which is not well marked but is sometimes marvelously scenic and always interesting. The alternative is Route 2, which is straight, fast, and boring.

SAN GERMÁN, in Puerto Rico's southwest quarter, is about 3 hours' drive from San Juan, via Ponce, and an easy hour southeast from Mayagüez (perhaps a midmorning halt on the way to lunch in the mountains at Hacienda Juanita). The town was settled on orders of King Ferdinand, and named (some claim) for his second wife, a French woman named Germaine de Foix, whom he married in 1505 after the death of Isabella. The first San Germán was settled on shore, but the town moved inland in 1570 to safer surroundings after ravages by French privateers and attacks by the resident Indians. The ancient **Porta Coeli church** claims to be the second oldest church in the New World (Santo Domingo's cathedral in the Dominican Republic is the first). Today San Germán is blissfully removed from the commerce of the cities. The Inter-American University is the main focus of modern activity, but this is a town about which Evalyn Marvel could write, in her 1960 *Guide to Puerto Rico and the Virgin Islands,* "along the tree-lined esplanade of the central plaza of San Germán, especially on a Sunday evening, the young people gather to promenade—the girls, arm-in-arm, circling clockwise and the boys counterclockwise, primly flirting as they pass. On the stone benches sit the chaperones, watching with viligant but tolerant eyes—for it was the same when they were young, and their mothers and grandmothers before them." The Sunday paseo is still a ritual not only in this town, but in many other smaller towns and villages in rural Puerto Rico. Small-town life exists, and there are those who are eager to preserve it.

Museo de Arte Religioso, in the old Porta Coeli church (Tu–Su 9–12, 2–4; free) is well worth the wander up the 2 dozen old brick steps at the end of the esplanade. Built as an all-inclusive fortress, church, and monastery, following the 16th-century custom, the building was restored through the efforts of the Instituto de Cultura Puertorriqueña. Little is left of the monastery, built in 1609, to the left of the church, but you can see the arched wall and the gate. The ancient church, which some date to 1583, has been plucked and painted so that it is almost too perfect, but the restoration has been authentic, under the watchful eye of the Institute. The altar is particularly worth noting, and the collection of ancient *santos*, the carved saints and holy figures that decorated the churches (and homes) in the old times, is one of Puerto Rico's most extensive. There's an exhibit area showing paintings and prints of churches from the 16th through 19th centuries.

■■

SPORTS around this big island have the variety you'd expect in a place that is home for 3.2 million people and is prepared to welcome more than 2 million tourists a season. For the planned seaside sports, the best spots are at the resort hotels, either those of the Condado area, where facilities are offered at a couple of easily accessible hubs (you can count on El Centro, the convention center, to be one), and at the Dorado Hotels—Dorado Beach and Cerromar—as well as at Mayagüez for the west-coast area, La Parguera for the southwest coast, Palmas del Mar at the southeast, the town of Fajardo at the east, and Rio Mar on the northeast coast.

There are a dozen **public beaches** with lockers, showers, and facilities for your use as well as, of course, for the people who live here. Facilities at the public beaches are closed Mondays (or Tuesday, if Monday is a holiday), but are open 9–5 in winter and 9–6 in summer. Isla Verde and Luquillo beaches are easily accessible from San Juan; Isla Verde is a taxi ride from Condado hotels, and Luquillo can be a goal on the day you rent a car. Humacao Beach, not far from the Palmas area on the southeast, and Punta Guilarte Beach on the south coast near Arroyo have fewer facilities than the north coast beaches, but if you're touring out this way, they are good cooling-off spots. El Tuque Beach, about 4 miles west of Ponce is talked about, but frankly, when I looked at it, it was an uninviting stretch of pebbly shore. Cana Gorda, near Guánica was more interesting although not quite as easy to find. Boquerón Beach on the west coast at Boquerón Bay is not too far from Punta Higüero, between Aguadilla and Rincón, and one of the few good surfing beaches in Puerto Rico. Cerro Gordo Beach, west of the Dorado-Cerromar hotels, is a popular spot for vacationing Puerto Ricans; most visitors who book into either Dorado Beach or Cerromar will find those strands satisfactory, even though they are small. Sardinera Beach, on Route 698, is also near Dorado, and Punta Salinas is the beach that stretches between the Dorado area and Cataño, on the coast. (If you drive out here, you'll see a sprinkling of the trucks that sell chicharrones and other Puerto Rican favorites for snacks at the beach.) The best beaches by far are those on Vieques, Culebra, Icacos, and the other islands off the east coast of Puerto Rico. The first two are small plane trips, if you want to make a day trip of it, and Icacos is a nice day sail/picnic lunch spot from Fajardo.

For **snorkeling** and **scuba,** the most central spot is the *Caribbean School of Aquatics* at La Concha, with its headquarters on the promenade just past the coffee shop and pool as you walk through the lobby and out the "back" door. These people are pros! They've been operating scuba courses for 16 years and have a basic course that any average swimmer can easily conquer. For 46 hours of scuba, equipment included, you'll pay about $125—with 20 hours of lecture, 20 hours of pool time, 6 hours for diving, one beach dive, and 2 trips on the dive boat *Innovation.* Advanced courses are offered, and there is also the option for nonscuba folk to go along on

the dive boat if there's space. Snorkel equipment can be rented, if
you haven't packed your own; a complete set figures at about $25
per day. For those who want a day at sea that is relaxing, there's an
"All Day Snorkel and Scuba Safari" that departs from La Concha at
8:30, driving for more than an hour east to Innovation's marina at
Fajardo. Lunch, guides, boat ride, transportation to and from are all
included for the $35, and you're back by 5, or so.

The Caribe Hilton in San Juan has its own Aquacenter with
scuba and snorkel guides and instruction. Most of the scuba is at
the reefs off the shore near the hotel, with beginners starting their
session with pool time and lectures. From the Mayagüez Hilton, on
the west coast, there are scuba tours to nearby sites, and some
training in the pool when there's a group that warrants it. Scuba
here will be more interesting for experts, and is best when the sea is
not rough. At the Dupont Plaza Hotel, back on the Condado coast
near San Juan, and at El San Juan, where *Wonderful World of Watersports* plans excursions to waters off east end's Fajardo.
(Frankly, all the building and bodies on the north coast near San
Juan fuzz up this water; there are other areas that are less peopled,
and therefore clearer for good scuba.)

For **sailing,** check at the *Villa Marina Yacht Harbor* at Fajardo.
Captain Jack Becker has a day picnic to Icacos on his 40-foot catamaran *Spread Eagle,* and includes transportation for the hour-plus
ride from your San Juan area hotel, if you want to do the trip from
there. ($30) *El Cofresi,* a sailboat skippered by Captain Osvaldo de
Jesus, has been sailing across to Icacos for half-day outings, out of
Las Croabas. Check to see if he's around if you want an interesting
sail.

La Parguera on the south coast talks about its "U-Drive-It-
Boats," but don't count on all the equipment to be in next-to-new
shape. While they're a lot of fun, the 16-foot aluminum boats with
their 6 hp outboards have had hard use. Sailors setting out from La
Parguera will probably be on the 30-foot *Pearson,* which comes with
captain for about $100 per day. The classiest sailing is offered at
Palmas del Mar, where some of the boats that come into the new
marina will take day charters, and there is a small fleet of "sail-
yourself" boats for use (rental) by experienced sailors. The scene
changes, but the excellent facilities are ready and waiting. Some
big yachts call this place home this season.

For **deep-sea-fishing,** Fajardo and the Palmas marina are the
places to start. Captain Mike Benitez, Puerto Rico's best-known
deep-sea captain, keeps a boat at Palmas. At the San Juan Marina

Fishing Center, next to the Club Náutico by the traffic circle at the west end of the Condado area, facilities have been spruced up. There are several boats listed for deep-sea fishing charters for about $300 for 6 for a day, with captain, mate, rods, bait, and ice. (You bring lunch and drinks.) Stop by the day before to finalize the arrangements.

Golf courses are plastered over rolling terrain at the east and west. The Dorado courses, 4 of them that were laid out with every effort on course challenge, not on cost, are the biggest cluster—and all can be played on golfing holidays at either Cerromar or Dorado. The pro shops at both resorts have full facilities—and a list for sign-up times, which are essential in winter months and when golfing specials fill the house at special rates from April 16 through December 15. At the far west, the former U.S. military course, on what was Ramey Air Force base and is now Punta Borinquen resort, is available for all. The pro shop is at the crest of the hill, with restaurant and all facilities—for use by those who rent the former officers' houses at Punta Borinquen that now are a housekeeping cluster sometimes used by Canadians on charters. Hotel Rio Mar has its course along the shore on the northeast coast, about 45 minutes' drive from San Juan, but the most peaceful place of all of them, in my opinion, is the 18-hole course at Palmas del Mar, spread out between the beach units and the golf and tennis units that make up part of that resort. The pro shop has a snack area as well as the expected rental equipment, lockers, caddies, and shop. Check on the status of the 18-hole course that wraps around three sides of El Conquistador Hotel near Fajardo on the east end. (At the 11th hole, golfers can stare El Yunque in the eye and blink at the Caribbean to the left.) The other courses pale by comparison to this group, but if you are going to be at Mayagüez, you can plan on the 9-hole country club course, and there's a 9-hole course at Caguas.

Tennis players who want the best facilities, and plenty of them, should check the excellent courts (and package tennis tour status) at Dorado Beach, Cerromar, Palmas del Mar, and Rio Mar, all of which are suitable for tournament play. You'll find well-maintained courts at Carib-Inn near the airport in the Isla Verde area.

In the San Juan-Condado-Isla Verde area, there are courts at several hotels. The Caribe Hilton has its tennis club, which has a lot of local members (and puts a high cost on court use), and there are courts atop the roof at La Concha, as well as at the Dupont Plaza, El San Juan, and elsewhere. If having easy access to a tennis court is at the top of your list of activities for a happy holiday, be sure to find out if there is a court—and how many of them are available *on the premises*. There are high costs for all, and the fee is sometimes more reasonable if you are overnighting at the court site.

For **horseback riding,** the guide/teacher at Palmas del Mar takes you along the shore and into the country on good trails; the paradores in the mountains have access to horses (which will be enjoyed if you have ridden before, but may not be well-trained enough if you are a timid rider), and riding is possible from Mayagüez. Rancho Borinquen at Carolina will pick you up in San Juan for the hour long ride west to their stables.

At Guayama, on the south coast, the Paso Fino Horse Show takes place in late February–early March. Those interested in watching (and riding) the remarkable smooth-gaited horses should plan a visit to Guayama. The Puerto Rico Tourism office can provide names of stables.

If your interest is **horse racing** instead of horse riding, head for El Comandante at Canovanas, about 45 minutes' ride east of San Juan, for races on Wednesday, Friday, Sunday, and holidays. (Clubhouse admission $3; grandstand $1.

■■
TREASURES AND TRIFLES are hidden in the cobbled streets of San Juan and at surprising places in the countryside, as well as at some of the hotel boutiques and the artisan markets. Although there's nothing "duty-free" in the Commonwealth of Puerto Rico, shops, markets, and special fairs yield some interesting handcrafts and a selection of worthy prints and paintings by Puerto Rican artists. Be sure to get a copy of the artists'-workshop map, available free from the tourism offices. Clearly marked are the studios (around the island) of artists who welcome visits. Al Dinhofer's *Walking Tours of San Juan,* on sale for $2.50, also has valuable information.

In Old San Juan, the Cristo Street shops give the best selection in the shortest space, in my opinion. Start at the top of the hill at Plaza de San José, by the Dominican Convent, where you can saunter through the museum, look at the exhibition around the walls under the arcades, and start down Cristo Street (at El Mesón Vasco). **Rugs and Wood,** on your left, is one of the first shops (with Guatemala-woven work and Puerto Rican pottery). Farther down the hill, on your left past the cathedral, **La Casa de las Canastas** and **Galeria Palomas** both have baskets in all shapes, sizes, and prices. The selection is bigger and better in all the small rooms at La Casa de las Canastas; take time to find the papier-mâché Puerto Rican fruits and vegetables. **The Gentle Swing,** on the right side of the street, after the San Juan Cathedral Plaza and El Convento Hotel, has hammocks strung on walls and across arches, with a recent innovation (and best seller) the "hamok" chair for your porch at home. Perfect for packing, the hammocks, that have won design awards for creator Etienne Dusart, come in several sizes, colors, and materials. Other items are also handmade, and interesting; weave your way back to the courtyard and look at leisure.

Earth (209 Cristo) is *the* store you want for one-stop shopping. Everything is high quality, well displayed, and, although I've never been a great enthusiast of shell mirrors, I saw some here that looked good. Willie Ruessner's unusual paintings and sculpture were on display during one of my visits; if his work is not on show, someone else's will be—and probably it will be as colorful and clever as Kansas-born Ruessner's art, which shows influences from his time in Mexico. Unusual clothes and accessories are part of the standard eclectic stock. There are comfortable, colorful warm-weather fashions (for men and women) as well as pottery and other above-average handcrafts. Chuck Kirtley has a good eye for unusual and interesting stock, and charges fair prices for very special arts and artifacts you won't see elsewhere.

Recent seasons have seen an invasion of cut-rate stores on Calle Cristo. Although residents (and some of us) are drawn to the Hathaway Outlet (203 Cristo) for discount shirts and sports clothes, the shop at the Don Q Rum building lures others.

Gallery Botello is worth a lingering look, if you like Puerto Rican prints and paintings and want to see some on display. For fashions with flair, investigate the selection at **Primitivo,** also on Calle Cristo, upstairs, with very high-quality (and necessarily high-priced) clothes for women.

Turn right at the corner of Calle Fortaleza, and keep your eyes open for the handcraft shop, with a skirt or shirt flapping overhead when the store is open, announcing the selection inside the small workshop by being its own banner. For shirts, skirts, or just plain yard goods printed in tropical designs on colorful fabric, the fabric here rates near the top of my list.

Butterfly People, at 152 Calle Fortaleza, was lauded when restaurants were mentioned, but the unique place is also worth a visit for a memorable purchase for friends at home (or yourself). The brightly colored butterflies encased in clear plastic make elegant punctuation marks for walls, and prices start at about $25.

The Art Store, the art gallery at Caleta de San Juan 70, diagonally across from the entrance to El Convento (M–F 10–6, Sun 2–6), has interesting displays of Puerto Rican art and handcrafts. Most of the items are for sale, and some are very interesting. Several small rooms are covered—walls, floor, and sometimes ceiling—with paintings, prints, ceramics, papier-mâché work, and other items.

Look carefully as you wander along Calle San Francisco and Calle Fortaleza, parallel streets that T off from Calle Cristo. There are some interesting stores (**Crazy Alice,** for clothes and the court-yard) mixed in with some "regular" department stores that are more useful for residents. **The New York Department Store,** with entrances on Calle Fortaleza and Plaza de Armas, carried the expected selection of department store items. If you run out of something or have forgotten a basic, head here. There's nothing touristy about this place; it's strictly functional.

AUTHOR'S OBSERVATION: Getting a taxi in Old San Juan can be a problem if you wait to find one cruising. The in-town taxi stand is at Plaza de Armas, where you can usually find one or more waiting and willing to take you where you want to go.

Patio de las Artesanias, in the First Federal Savings Bank branch at the corner of Norzagaray Street and Calle San Francisco in Old San Juan (on the hill as you follow the one-way signs to reach the Dominican Convent), displays work of local artisans (9–5, Sat, Sun, Tu), but check with the bank that sponsors the exhibit to be sure the days are the same. The booths are set up in a courtyard.

The **Puerto Rican Craft Center,** near the cruise-ship piers at the Customs House in Old San Juan, is a hive of handcrafts. A lot of the work is high quality, and the area is certainly worth browsing around.

Shops in the Condado area are overwhelming. The mixture of outright junk and *very* high-quality merchandise can be confusing, especially when some stores carry both. For handcrafts, the **Artisans Fair,** established in late 1977 at the patio on El Centro, the Condado Convention Center, takes place weekends, from about 12 to 5. Work varies, depending on which artisans have set up shop the week you are there, and if you see something on Saturday, don't wait until Sunday to buy it. There's a chance that both artisan and item may not be there. Some of the papier-mâché tropical fruits, birds, etc. affixed to a piece of old wood to hang on a wall were color-ful and worth looking at on a recent stroll, but there may be other things that will appeal more to you.

For very high-quality merchandise in pleasant air-conditioned surroundings, stop at **Ambiance,** a few doors west from the Condado Beach Hotel. Elegant imported European household items, as well as special goblets and glass sculpture, and Famous Amos chocolate chip cookies make up some of the unusual offerings here. "Million dollar" jewelry is in a side (and secure) room, with clever key chains hanging by the "check-out" counter. Prices are high, but quality is worth it—and the elegance of the place is punctuated by the unfortunate fact that a guard has to come to unlock the door when he sees you trying to get in.

Fernando Pena reigns supreme with elegant clothes sold in spacious quarters in the middle of the Condado chaos. His prices are sky high, but fashion sets its own pace and people are willing to pay for it.

With the artisans' map in hand, you can drive around the countryside visiting more than 100 craftsmen at their workshops. Some studios are devoted to wood carving (be sure to find Elipidio Collazo, in Jayuya, for a look at the carved birds), others to ceramic, santos, jewelry, furniture, and hammocks (which are made in Yabucoa and San Sebastian).

Saba

*S*aba Tourist Office, Windwardside, Saba, N.A.;
*Netherlands Antilles Windward Islands Representative, 445 Park
Ave., New York, NY 10022.*

US $1 = NAf 1.77
Unless otherwise noted, all prices are in U.S. dollars.

When the *Blue Peter* made its official, but sporadic, stop at Saba,
you hung over the side to lunge into a rocking small boat for the
plunge to the shore, such as it was. About the only thing you could
be sure of was that the Saban seamen were competent—and that
you would get wet. These days, as a handful of people wedged into a
Winair plane swirl to the airstrip on the minute meadow on a hillside, there's the same "moment of truth." I noticed the stolid face
of the Saban octogenarian who sat next to me on a recent flight.
The typical Saban straw hat with its stovepipe shape couldn't hide
the permanent crinkles in his suntanned face, and his blue eyes
darted around the brim in a look that could only be classified as
controlled panic. This was his first flight. When he had left Saba a
few months earlier, for a bout in the hospital at Philipsburg, he had
gone by boat. No such luck for him coming home, but at least he
was coming home.

The final swoop—after the wide spiral down to take stock of the
strip—is awesome. But so is this island. It's the top of a volcano and
like nowhere else.

■■

POLITICAL PICTURE is pegged to that of Sint Maarten, where
most of the commercial ventures cavort. As noted under Statia and
Sint Maarten, the 3 S islands share one delegate to the 22-member
Netherlands Antilles Staten that meets in Curaçao. As expected,
Saba's share of the coffers is small—but then so is its population,

recently numbered at 1097. The island does have its own Island Council, the government body in charge of local problems and development.

■■■

CUSTOMS survive, here, behind the shuttered windows of the small houses that speckle the communities. Visitors will see very little of the innermost heart of the Sabans, a very special people who keep pretty much to themselves, as those who have remained "at home" have for centuries. The most adventuresome souls headed out, from the island's earliest history, to become some of the world's most remarkable seamen, and to send money back home so that the family homestead could be built and maintained. Take time to talk with your taxi driver, and any talkative old folk you meet, and you will be richly rewarded—especially if you have been wise enough to bend in here for a couple of days so that you are not classed as "one of the day trippers."

■■■

MONEY MATTERS are conducted mostly in U.S. currency, with a sprinkling of guilders (Netherlands Antilles type, which have a different value from the Netherlands currency). For visitors, especially day trippers, dollars will do fine everywhere.

■■■

ARRIVAL ON SABA is one of the few adventures left in the civilized Caribbean. The name of the airport—Juancho Yrausquin Airport—is almost longer than the strip, which is served several times daily by the gnat-sized planes of Windward Islands Air Service, locally known as Winair. The STOL (Short Take-Off and Landing) flights dip in and out with tourists and a handful of residents at regular intervals, but make your reservations in advance at the ticket counter in Sint Maarten if you have not booked through your travel agent. The time you wait after check-in and before the plane takes off is longer than the 15-minute flight, but be there when they tell you to or you may be bumped. There are days when the flights are very full—and on those days, if you're flying one of the bigger Winair flights (about 19 passengers), the flight stops first at Statia, since the Saba airstrip does not encourage full-plane landings. The small strip, hacked from the only "flat" land on the island, is plastered like a band-aid on the mountainside. If all this makes you think you'd rather go by boat, you should know that that's not easy

either. The seas are often rough across the 25-mile span that separates this place from Philipsburg, Sint Maarten, the nearest port.
The crossing to Saba's Fort Bay is not in any way reminiscent of a
trip on the old Queen Mary.

■■

TOURING TIPS: Take a taxi, not only because the serpentine roads
bend and weave with perilous regularity, but also because the local
lore you can pick up from a good driver is one of the best reasons for
coming to Saba. There are a few rental cars, easily arranged
through your hotel.

■■

HOTELS ON SABA are small and special. Each has its own personality, and all are ideal for a real getaway vacation, if you do not insist
on beaches. (This island has none.) An Author's Award seems superfluous here; your personality and that of the owner/manager of
"your" inn make the magic combination.

✤ **Captain's Quarters** (Windwardside, Saba, N.A.; 10 rooms) claims
a notch on one of the side streets in the "main" village, about 1000
feet above sea level. The atmosphere is Caribbean inn at its best,
with the wood frame houses that hold the inn tied together by
blooming bougainvillea and other colorful plants, plus the careful
touches of the management. Steve Hassell is your host. Antiques
punctuate the rooms, with four-posters and a couple of 18th-cen-
tury wig stands adding to the Old World feeling that pervades this
entire island. The only drawback, if you've come here to get away
from everything, is the day-trippers who come from Sint Maarten
and stay for lunch (if they've been smart enough to make a reservation in advance). On those days, if you've come here for retreat, you
can head for the hills. Otherwise, there are comfortable common
rooms, attractive breeze-swept terraces, and a speck of a pool. Rates
this winter will top off at about $60 for 2, meals extra. Breakfast is
$5 and dinner $15 to $20. (If you want lunch, you'll probably eat
here since there aren't a lot of choices on Saba.) An innovation for
summer '81 (through the fall if interest warrants) was group rates
for 10 to 22 people traveling together and special packages with
Saba Deep, the diving operation located at the hotel. Inquire about
status for summer '82 if you can assemble a group (or have a large
family).

✛ **Scout's Place** (Windwardside, Saba, N.A.; 4 rooms) settled into another old house in town when Scout Thirkield decided to paint and put together a place that knew an earlier life as the Windwardside Guest House, but double-check before you book. Rumors that Scout was moving on proved unfounded. Ownership changed, but Scout is still the key to this spot as we go to press. Hot water is not one of the luxuries (Caribbean spots like this one know the advantages of solar heating—the sun warms the tanks), but hospitality is. This is a casual, comfortable place for people who like their islands pure. Scout Thirkield took this place over in '73, and "advertised" it with his day-glow acid yellow card that says "Scout's Place. Bed'n'Board. Cheap'n'Cheerful." Although the inn is among the "cheapest" of the few places to stay on Saba, Scout's rates respond to demand, and he can demand $45 for 2 this winter, breakfast and dinner included (and most rooms have shared bath).

✛ **Cranston's Antique Inn** (The Bottom, Saba, N.A.; 6 rooms) began its guesthouse life as the simple Bottom Guesthouse, but underwent a name change and a general sprucing up for the season of '78–'79. Rates will be about $50 for 2, all meals included.

✛ **Caribe Guesthouse** (The Bottom, Saba, N.A.; 5 rooms) is around the corner in this small town, and charges $40 for 2 this winter, all meals included.

■■
PLACES WORTH FINDING ON SABA start with the island itself. Any time spent here will be special—and you'll be one of less than 10,000 who find this peak this year. **Mount Scenery** is the highest point, at 3000 feet, and one serpentine road connects the pier, the airport, and the 4 villages. A **Sea Captain's House** was turned into a museum in early '78, with antiques furnishing the rooms in a style that might have been known in the 1890's.

■■
SPORTS ON SABA in the conventional sense have been nonexistent until this season. Although there are always hills to hike and paths to wander, scuba enthusiasts can now sign on with Jim Halpern and Rob Hassell to dive off the beachless shores. They operate **Saba Deep** out of Captain's Quarters. Special scuba holidays are offered for groups, using the hotel as base.

■■

TREASURES AND TRIFLES ON SABA are limited to the drawn
work that some have mistakenly called lace and that is getting difficult to find, and to the work of the Saba Artisans Foundation, a
screen-print workshop that keeps about 40 local women in work.
There's a shop at The Bottom, and another on Sint Maarten, at
Philipsburg.

St. Barthélemy

Office Départemental du Tourisme de la Guadeloupe, 5 Square de la Banque, B.P. 1099, Pointe-à-Pitre, Guadeloupe, French West Indies; French West Indies Tourist Board, 610 Fifth Ave., New York, NY 10020; 9401 Wilshire Blvd., Beverly Hills, CA 90212; 1840 Ouest Rue Sherbrooke, Montreal, Quebec, Canada H3H 1E4; 372 Bay St., Suite 610, Toronto, Ontario, Canada M5H 2 W9.

US $1 = 5 French francs (Confirm at travel time.)
Unless otherwise noted, U.S. equivalents are figured at the above amount.

"The little inhabitants find many sweet things in these islands. The air is wonderfully good there, serious diseases are unknown. They live a long life in good health. They derive their own food from their cattle and fowl, they plant and grow all kinds of things, and no crop ever fails. Several of them were producing indigo which sold quite well before the war. Most families have several children, which means that when the islands are well enough inhabited, we will be able to obtain from them quite a lot of cattle, fowl, and staples." So said François Roger Robert, administrator of the Isles d'Amerique, as the small French-claimed islands were known in the 1700s. The quotation comes from *Histoire de St. Barthélemy* by Georges Bourdin, published by Porter Henry. The picture recalled from the island's early history can be verified today, even though a few of the facts have changed.

When Evelyn walks the beach in the early afternoon, the shells she looks for are different from those most visitors find. She's hunting *escargots*. If you chat with her at the beach, she may thrust out a handful of the docile snails that will be steamed and served with delicate garlic butter later in the day.

The man who used to grow lettuce, with a sun-blocking palm frond roof over his several flats of crisp green leaves, has given up.

Most of the lettuce and other fresh vegetables and fruits are imported now. The *Libre Service,* as the supermarket down in Gustavia is called, carries an imposing selection of produce and special items (notably cheese) from France.

Tourists are the new crop here, and although a moratorium on new buildings will allow the recent flurry of activity to settle, St. Barthélemy is changing—perhaps more drastically than at any other time in its history.

The fishermen still tie up at the Gustavia waterfront in the early hours of the morning, and if you can get there before those who buy for the shops and restaurants arrive and are good at negotiating in St. Barth's French, you may be able to negotiate a dinner that you can grill "at home" in the cottage you've rented.

The lady on the Lorient road has a following that makes an almost daily pilgrimage to the corrugated tin house set back from the road. Once inside, the "perfume" in the air is overwhelming. The fresh-baked bread may just be emerging from her ovens, which she tends in her cotton frock reminiscent of those known in her ancestral home of Brittany. A wide-brimmed straw hat, the mark of the older women of St. Barths, serves as her baker's cloche. The modern kneading and baking equipment is her only nod to the 20th century; her bread and her bearing are traditional.

The Gustavia bakery near the Post Office is bigger and, although father may tend the ovens wearing his bathing suit and mother is more comfortable speaking French, the two teenage sons are taking over at the counter and their English can be better than many visitors' fragile French. No matter how you negotiate, the purchase is what is important—and for most who visit here in a parenthesis around church on Sunday morning, the special sweet breads, perhaps warm and crispy palmiers, are the prize.

Although small hotels and cottage communities that used to drape the laundry over nearby bushes or on lines strung between the palms are now tossing the clothes in the drier and although the bistrolike restaurants buy much of their produce from U.S. and other wholesalers, the atmosphere in St. Barthélemy is still in shades of the past. Time has not stood still, but it has certainly slowed to a reasonable pace.

AUTHOR'S OBSERVATION: The discrepancy between the spelling of the nickname of St. Barthélemy—St. Barths or St. Barts—puzzles travel professionals as well as first-time travelers. Since French is the language of this island,

and in French pronunciation the "th" has the sound of a single "t" in the word St. Barthélemy, I have used the French nickname—St. Barths, pronounced Saint Bar*t*s.

■■

POLITICAL PICTURE: Being at the far end of the political chain has its advantages for St. Barthélemy, where life among the descendents of early settlers from Brittany, Normandy and Sweden carries on in its own world. Officially linked with Guadeloupe as a district governed through the Sous-Prefecture on St. Martin some 15 minutes' flight from here, St. Barthélemy leaves day-to-day political maneuvering to others. Local needs revolve around roads, hospitals, and the like, and seem to be satisfied with a minimum of publicity. Most visitors will be totally unaware of any local politics.

■■

CUSTOMS OF THE COUNTRY life on St. Barths includes some homage, still, to the Swedish, Normandy, and Brittany past, but those vestiges are fast disappearing—except insofar as holidays are concerned. You will see an occasional older woman dressed in the traditional white bonnet and black dress, and you cannot help but notice the lean (almost gaunt), weather-worn faces of the venerable past that mingled the earliest French (from Normandy and Brittany) with the Swedes who settled here. The recent wave of tourism, building up to cresting point in the past 5 years, finds many ex-Palm Beach and other elegant resort area types from the U.S. in addition to wise Europeans and others who do *not* want a high-pressure, action-packed place. St. Barths is special, and hopefully the new tourism will not destroy what had made many of us return as often as possible over the past couple of decades.

Unlike most Caribbean islands, the population of St. Barths is mostly white (as you'd suspect with settlers from Brittany, Normandy, and Sweden). The native families stay pretty much to themselves, linking to the tourism community through their stores, car rental firms, and cottages or apartments for rent.

Reservations are "essential" for the dinner hour, which is late (9 p.m. or so). During height of season (February, March), you'll need a reservation to get a table; at other times to be sure there's food.

■■

MONEY MATTERS are transacted in French francs, if you want to do as the locals do. Although tourism has become big business, it still fits into the community on local terms, and the French franc is the official currency. Hotels will quote their rates in U.S. dollars, and will take dollars for payment, as will many restaurants, but your bill will probably be presented in French francs with a nearby calculator (if you haven't brought your own) to find the U.S. dollar equivalent. In the small shops (for those of you who do your own housekeeping), French francs are the currency.

Since the French franc fluctuates against the U.S. dollar, inquire about the dollar equivalent before you convert your money. Rates at banks, restaurants, shops, and hotels may vary by a few points and, although it may not matter for small transactions, the total in francs and dollars may not be exactly the same. To avoid currency conversion confusion, buy French franc travelers cheques from your hometown bank before you head south, and live franc-ly.

Prices have skyrocketed on St. Barths in the past couple of years, and the place is "full" in peak season, all of which seems to prove that people will still pay for "the best."

ARRIVAL this season may be to the new air terminal, being built through 1981 on the south side (the "other" side) of the runway. The concrete had been poured by April '81, and the runway-rimming road has been rerouted through what had been the football (soccer) field. Whether the new terminal is ready for your arrival or not, you can be sure that your flight into St. Barthélemy will be a small plane swoop from Sint Maarten or another airport. Winair flies from Sint Maarten several times daily; Air Guadeloupe comes up from its namesake, which is a much longer distance than that from Sint Maarten or from Esperance Airport, a small strip in French St. Martin. Small charter planes come in, as do regular flights from St. Thomas (about one hour's flight away). Some of the smaller (but still too big, in my opinion) cruise ships make St. Barthélemy a port of call. If you're on island at that time, head for the hills. Gustavia becomes a circus of sorts. There are day trips by motor and sail boats from Sint Maarten (or from St. Barths to Philipsburg, if you are staying on island), but count on crossings to be lively. The sea that separates can get rough; good seaworthy souls will love it. The *Natalie* makes the run between St. Barths and St. Martin, on the far side of the Dutch-shared island, three times weekly, and was charging about 110F round trip. Check when you're on St. Barths if that crossing sounds interesting. During recent seasons, the *Ovation* has been making the journey from Sint Maarten to St. Barths on Tuesdays and Fridays, for $17.50 one way and $30 round trip. It might be worth checking to see if you could go over to Sint Maarten on the return trip, to overnight there and return by plane in the morning, if an off-island excursion appeals.

▪▪

TOURING TIPS: Rental cars are usually minimokes or other small vehicles that rent for about $25 per day. Unlike the equipment on some islands, cars on St. Barths are usually in pretty good shape. (The "old" cars are shipped to Tortola, I was told.) Take charge of a rental car if you want to be mobile. The rates are sure to rise (there are only so many cars to rent, and demand increases with each season), but wheels are still the best for prowling around to find the best beaches. Taxis do meet the planes when they land, but they don't linger around the airport too long. You may find that all the taxis have gone by the time you're ready to leave, and finding one may take a while. This is a small and friendly island, where someone going your way will be happy to give you a lift. Hopefully, that system can continue, even with the bulging hotels of winter season.

AUTHOR'S OBSERVATION: Typical of the special allegiance that St. Barthélemy seems to nurture in its visitors, the *History of St. Barth* was translated into English and is available from shops on the island. The book is about 500 pages, and sells for about $12.50, with proceeds, after expenses are covered, to go to the Preformation School in Colombier.

▪▪

HOTELS ON ST. BARTHS are personality places, even when they are cottages by the sea. Accent on this special island is on being independent. Usually the managers are, and it helps when you are also. Places are small, with the largest being the 50-room PLM Jean Bart and the 2 runners-up, the 24-room Baie des Flamands and 36-room St. Barths Beach Hotel. For spectacular surroundings and a sophisticated ambiance, book Castelets; for cottages with a hillside view (and a walk down hill to the beach) with modern equipment that usually works, make your reservation at Village St. Jean.

✣ **L'Auberge Normandie** (Lorient, 97133 St. Barthélemy, F.W.I.; 6 rooms) is a tiny French inn, within a short walk of a lovely beach (at Lorient) with rates that make the simple surroundings a special find. Not for fussy travelers, this place can have the aura of a "hippie haven" if that's the proclivity of fellow guests during your visit. For this winter, guests will be paying about $25 for 2, with breakfast figured at another $2.50 or so, per person, for coffee and croissant. There's a small pool, and a large portion of island hospitality for anyone who puts good value ahead of a well-known name. Other meals are also available "at home," with dinner priced at 40F or about $10, but meals have gotten less than rave notices from some who know and like good food.

✤ **Autour de Rocher** (Lorient Bay, 97133 St. Barthélemy, F.W.I.; 8 rooms) perches on a hummock rising from seaside. Its open-and-shut past has allowed for a period of complete refurbishing and a couple of changes in management, with Jimmy Buffit in control at the time of research for this edition. The selection of steaks and beef that made dining here a special experience under previous management have survived the changes and are still an element for an elegant evening meal. The beach over which this inn casts its eye is a lovely one, about 15 minutes' drive from the airport and a little longer from Gustavia. Rooms offer a lot of variety, but the constant you can count on is a spectacular view. Count on paying from $85 to $120 for 2, with breakfast. Tips, taxes, and other meals are extra here as elsewhere.

✤ **Baie des Flamands** (Anse des Flamands, 97133 St. Barthélemy, F.W.I.; 24 rooms) rests at the end of a snakelike road that weaves down from the hilltop near the airstrip and about 3 miles up and down from Gustavia. Wind sweeps across the beach so that the louvers are often closed for the spray-clouded windows in the upstairs dining area. Pool sitters bask in the sun, protected on the inland side of the 2-story railroad car building. The modern French architecture is uninspiring, but the promotion of the place by a U.S. firm assures that you will be grouped with fellow Americans—if that's what you want on this delightfully French island. Families encouraged with special rates for children. Adults pay about $85 for 2 in winter for breakfasts and dinners daily, plus air-conditioned room with shower and balcony. Best bargains with summer package plans.

✤ **Castelets** (Mont Lurin, 97133 St. Barthélemy, F.W.I.; 10 rooms) preens itself, high in the hills, almost straight up from the town of Gustavia. A serpentine road makes the arrival somewhat less harrowing, but the view is still spectacular. You will be spellbound by scenery, decorating, and prices. Castelets is a gem for people with money, ably managed by Mme. Geneviève Jouany, who leaves you pretty much to yourself, unless you have a problem. This can be the sybarite's dream, if the sybarite does not need a beach and the sea at his doorstep to enjoy the Caribbean (and I do). Castelets is not for everyone, and is not for anyone who isn't prepared to be chic, attractive, and up to date on the latest international conversation, preferably in French. There's a pool, but it is *petit* and discreet. The meals (reservation only) are elegant, gourmet affairs by candlelight and after 9. (Price should be no concern, but figure on at least 120F for dinner.) Most units have kitchens; some are 2-bedroom duplex units with living room, balcony, and private (elegant) bath; others are one air-conditioned bedroom with kitchenette and living room with terrace, and then there are 2 small rooms in the main building. Each room has a tape deck. You'll need about $150 for 2 per day to wrap up just the room and breakfast. Car's essential if you want to leave this aerie.

✛ **Eden Rock** (Baie de St. Jean, 97133 St. Barthélemy, F.W.I.; 6 rooms) is an island tradition. It sits on the rocks in the middle of the shoreline at Baie de St. Jean. Chances are you'll be paying "too much" for your room (at rising St. Barth's hotel rates), but you won't begrudge a franc of it if you like seaside ports to call home. The house is historic as the home of Remy deHaenen, an island legend himself. His inn was the island's first, and in the early days he would meet you in Sint Maarten to fly you over in his own plane. Island antiques fill the main house, and less valuable, more functional four-posters and other furnishings make the several small rooms livable. One of the separate bungalows, just below the main house on the rocks as they slant to the sea, is an ideal hideaway, if you don't demand ultramodern plumbing and fancy furnishings. A do-what-you-want-to kind of place, where you'll pay $50 single, or $60 for 2, for a winter room with continental breakfast served when you sit at table. (Dinners are served on the terrace by reservation, at 9 P.M. or later.)

✛ **Filao Beach Hotel** (Baie de St. Jean, 97133 St. Barthélemy, F.W.I.; 30 rooms) sifted onto the sands between Emeraude Plage apartments and Eden Rock Hotel during '81, with opening date planned for the '81-'82 season. Owned by the Mayor who plans to have guests dine at nearby Le Pelican (which he also owns), the rooms do not have kitchens. Guests will have use of a small pool when the place is finished. Rates are expected to hover around

$112 for 2 including continental breakfast for the opening winter season, with summer of '82 at half that tally.

✤ **Grand Cul de Sac Beach Hotel** (Grand Cul de Sac, 97133 St. Barthélemy, F.W.I.; 16 rooms) claims a family link with Baie des Flamands and St. Barths Beach Hotel that gives guests exchange dining privileges as well as 3 hotels' action options for daylight and evening hours. Modern facilities assure the basic creature comforts (twin-bedded rooms, tiled baths, etc.), but I find more atmosphere at some of the other spots. Inquire about special summer programs that include some extras with a basic room-and-breakfast rate for 7-night stays, and count on paying about $85 for 2 this winter, breakfasts included. All rooms have kitchenettes, but meals are included for some daily rates, and count on your walking over to sister-neighbor, St. Barths Beach.

✤ **L'Hibiscus** (B.P. 86, Gustavia, 97133 St. Barthélemy, F.W.I.; 9 rooms plus 1 duplex) grew at the corner of rue Thiers and rue Courbet, a block inland from Gustavia's port, for the season of '80-'81. It's the punctuation mark at the foot of the town's historic Swedish clock tower. Quickly claiming a devoted following among those who want to be within a walk of all the Gustavia options, the inn offers its guests a spectacular harbor view from the balcony of the second floor rooms. Modern architecture blends with Gustavia's traditions. The air-conditioned rooms offer the choice of fan-swirled balmy breezes and are punctuated with patterns designed by island-famous silk-screen artist Jean-Yves Froment. Count on classy ambiance, cultivated French atmosphere capably administered by Laurence (that's Mme.) and Henri Thellin-Mourier, and the convenience of kitchen equipment in your room if you prefer cooking at home to dining at the inn's noteworthy *Restaurant du Vieux Clocher* or another one of the many interesting dining depots. Winter rates are expected to hover around $90 for 2, but discounted rates are sometimes offered for long stays.

✤ **PLM Jean Bart** (overlooking Baie de St. Jean, 97133 St. Barthélemy, F.W.I.; 50 rooms) is flourishing, having settled into the hillside since its creation a few years ago. By the time the place opened in season of '78, the beach had already acquired a coterie of enthusiasts. Jean Bart's premises on the inland side of the road, within walking distance of but not on the beach, have a pool, several units planted around the grounds, with subtle shingle roofs that make the potential big hotel seem more inconspicuous than its guests will be when they flock to the island. *Le Fregate* disco is lively when its habitués are, and loud whenever the music plays. Rates for this winter season are $110 for a studio for 2, with *no* meals (and an American-style breakfast will cost you $6 per person). This is a French chain reaction which, while it shows more individuality than many places, has been packaged to show profit. U.S. marketing assures a lot of English-speaking guests.

✤ **Presqu'île** (Gustavia, 97133 St. Barthélemy, F.W.I.; 13 rooms) parks at the waterfront, on the far side of the harbor as you head down the hill. It's a navy-type place that leads a hard life. More than a casual barefoot and boating spot, the small hotel which starts on the second floor (climb the narrow stairway at the left of the building) reminds me of the waterfront at Marseille—with West Indies character. An on-premise branch of St. Martin's *Caraibe Marine Service* assures scuba and boating facilities. Bargain rates (by comparison to others on this island) make it interesting for French-speaking casual, sea-oriented folk who will pay a meager $25 for 2, meals extra (you're within walking distance of several nice, small French restaurants). The rooms are basic: walls, floor, window, and bed.

✤ **St. Barths Beach Hotel and Tennis Club** (Grand Cul de Sac, 97133 St. Barthélemy, F.W.I.; 26 rooms) is big for St. Barths, and stretches like 2 shoe boxes at beach edge, a good drive from anyplace else. Owned by Guy Turbé who also owns Baie des Flamands, St. Barths Beach has become its own action center, with windsurfers enjoying the steady breezes, snorkelers and scuba enthusiasts starting out from beachside, and tennis enthusiasts leaping around on the hot asphalt courts. Not my favorite place, but perhaps yours if you get a good deal on a package plan. The 36 rooms usually go for about $100 for 2, breakfasts and dinners daily, and for that you get a private bath and balcony with the usual spartan-modern French design. You're about 4 wiggly, shore-rimming miles from Gustavia and a little less from the airport.

✤ **Sereno Beach** (B.P. 19, Grand Cul de Sac, 97133 St. Barthélemy, F.W.I.; 20 rooms) saturated its small space on the shoreline with a cluster of neat-and-new units. The place opened in summer of '80 and offers its guests a choice of two-stroke pool or beach. Not designed in traditional style, the pool has an island in the middle and skull-cracking depth. Although elegance is indicated by the rates and the hotel does have its coterie of repeaters, the place is a bit too compact for my taste. Rooms crowd around a small court, punctuated with pool, dining depots, and a beach-oriented bar. Hotel guests are joined by outsiders during daytime hours when windsurfing provides a colorful (and active) panorama. (Club Lafayette, a source for windsurfers, is next door.) Count on rates of about $180 for 2, breakfast only, this winter, and plan to have a rental car if you want mobility.

✝ **Tropical Hotel** (overlooking Baie de St. Jean, 97133 St. Barthélemy, F.W.I.; 20 rooms) nests in the lush foliage on the first rise of the hill road that leads up to a cluster of units that is Village St. Jean. A newcomer to the '81 roster, Tropical folds its guests into small-but-adequate rooms and offers full American breakfast at about $5. Beaded curtains make the break for your closet; there's not enough room for a door, but most vacationers will probably head downhill to the Baie de St. Jean where there's plenty of beachside activity including some good restaurants. There's a small pool (dunking size), and a center court that offers a verdant heart for the hotel. M. and Mme. Vial are the inn-keepers, and they've cultivated a French riviera atmosphere along with the tropics. Well worth considering, even at the $100 for 2 room only, winter tariff, and a real "bargain" during spring and fall when the double goes for about half price. (July and August rates are slightly more than half the winter.)

■■

HOUSEKEEPING HOLIDAYS ON ST. BARTHS are the experts' way to vacation. The specialty of this island is the fact that most visitors "fit in." Sibarth (Box 55, Gustavia, 97133 St. Barthélemy, F.W.I.) specializes in rentals. Among the 50 or more properties listed with code names (initials) are a U-shaped villa with 2 air-conditioned bedrooms with private bath in one wing, a master air-conditioned bedroom with bath in another, and a connecting elegant living/dining room that looks out through sliding glass doors (always opened) to the sea. Weekly rental with maid service comes to about $500. A beach villa in a palm and coconut grove, convenient on Lorient Beach, offers 2 bedrooms with one bath plus spacious living quarters for about the same tariff. My suggestion is to spell out your interests, be specific about your requirements, and contact Brook and Roger Lacour to see what they have available. Demand is great. Booking a year in advance for February and March is not too early.

One of the joys of housekeeping on St. Barths is that the fresh French bread is only as far as Gustavia or the village of Lorient, both with bakeries that bake daily. Good produce can be bought from names you will quickly learn; fresh fish can be negotiated from the fishermen *early* in the morning at the Gustavia waterfront. Only the beef is a problem, and if you insist on that, bring what you need from home.

AUTHOR'S OBSERVATION: **La Rôtisserie** in Gustavia can take care of your cooking for you. Casseroles "to go" include boeuf bourguignon, langouste créole, filet de boeuf, coq au vin and canard—and all you need to do is stop by to pick up your order when you head into town in the morning.

✢ **Auberge de la Petite Anse** (Box 117, Anse des Flamands, 97133 St. Barthélemy, F.W.I.; 20 villas) nests on the shore not far from Gustavia, but on an up-and-over-the-hill route ending at the road to Flamands. The project perked with the first 4 villas in spring of '79, and others followed along as time and money permitted. Decor is reminiscent of J. C. Penney, with gold rayon curtains and dark furniture. Porches on second floor apartments are perfect for twilight sea-watching. A neighborhood *épicerie* is a long-but-possible walk from homebase, if you want to stock up on a few staples. Florville Greaux (owner also of Presqu'île in Gustavia) is the one to find for further facts. Rates are about $70 per day for the 1-bedroom units with kitchen for 2 this winter. A rental car is recommended for mobility.

✢ **Emeraude Plage** (Baie de St. Jean, 97133 St. Barthélemy, F.W.I.; 14 rooms) stretches inland from the sand, on the western half of Baie de St. Jean, at the foot of the Eden Rock. The 7 buildings, each with 2 efficiency units, are boxy, functional places that repeaters love to call home. Well maintained and on a nice beach, the units are owned by M. Nouy from Guadeloupe and ably managed by Mme. Gil Synnaeve. It's "impossible" to get into the beach-end rooms in March, but you may get space in the units nearer the road—and that's only a short walk to the sea. Appurtenances are beachside casual, but for those who want to stroll the strand by morning light or take a midnight swim, this place is ideal. You can dress up and drive off on the evenings when you choose to, and your room-with-kitchen, porch, and lounge chairs will cost about $80 for 2, meals extra, in winter.

✣ **Le P'tit Morne** (in the hills outside of Gustavia; 97133 St. Barthélemy, F.W.I.; 8 apts.) is for self-sufficient folk who can settle in easily to island life, French style. Joe Felix's place seems like a long way from anywhere, but it's not. The drive is wiggly and around the mountain roads but the view when you get here is spectacular, the price for the simple, but comfortable rooms is right (at $45 for 2, with kitchenettes), and the holiday will be a restful one if you bring a lot of books or like to write poetry. A car is essential for mobility and for getting to the beach. (Joe Felix, for those who like to tie the island legends together, came from his native St. Barths to work at St. Thomas's Mountain Top in its early days when it was a small hotel; he wisely returned home a decade or so ago.)

✣ **Village St. Jean** (overlooking Baie de St. Jean, 97133 St. Barthélemy, F.W.I.; 42 rooms) clusters on the hillside, up a short but steep cement drive from the road, on the other side of which is the Baie and its long white sandy strand. Built in the 1970s, and adding as business and finances warrant, the Village is several separate redwood units, some (*Terrasse* or *Jardin*) with kitchen, air-conditioned double bedroom, and breeze-swept deck; others (hotel rooms) with twin beds, air-conditioned room, and refrigerator, with balcony. Equipment is new, functioning, and attractive; furnishings are simple but colorful and all you will need. There's a commissary on the hilltop, but you'll do most of your bread buying in town. *Le Patio* restaurant has been added to the facilities, and entertainment focuses on congenial guests who you may meet at the manager's cocktail party. Car is essential for mobility; otherwise stay at home or walk down to (and very slowly up from) the beach. Planting puts you in seemingly very private quarters; views are magnificent; rates for 2 in winter are from $60 to $85 depending on your view; no meals. Special rates for stays of a week or longer; children $15 per day.

■■

RESTAURANTS ON ST. BARTHS are small, and very special, with high prices and quality. Good food and elegant ambiance reign supreme at some places, good food and bistro surroundings in others. As the trickle of tourists swells into a flood, some of the places we oldtimers knew and loved are packed to the brim in midwinter.

AUTHOR'S OBSERVATION: Check for new names when you arrive on the island. Each season brings a few special spots. Reservations are recommended at all times for dinners on St. Barths. During peak season winter, places are "full" and at other times an advance reservation assures that there will be food and the place will be open.

Castelets captures top spot for location and looks. Food service at Castelets is elegant (and you'll be more comfortable if you are too). The once perilous drive to this perch has been repatterned to weave back and forth in a series of switchbacks up a precipitous slant that in previous seasons made some taxi drivers turn down a trip up. This dress-up spot at the top of the world has a perfect view, pristine table settings, and priceless food.

In Gustavia, the handful of small places to try for special dinners are **Au Port,** upstairs on rue Sadi Carnot, near the corner of the base of the U-shaped harbor, and **L'Entrepont,** also at the harbor on rue Jeanne d-Arc. **L'Ananas,** at the end of the harbor up the hill toward the clock tower, has a spectacular view that more than makes up for any failings (and there are some) with the food. I suspect that **Auberge du Fort Oscar,** a gem of a place when it opened with Madame Jacqua's creole cooking served in a small room of her house, may have changed a lot—with praise in press (*Gourmet* of January 1979). No matter what, you have to make a reservation a day ahead, and if she's kept to her cooking and not become commercial, you're in for a treat.

Le Sapotillier is a favorite for long-time island aficionados. A table "dans le jardin" is what the regulars want, since it puts you under the leaves of the Sapotillier tree that gives this place its name, but you can also dine in the house. Consistently good and more moderately priced than many spots, Sapotillier gets high marks.

Restaurant du Vieux Clocher at L'Hibiscus hotel, under the Swedish clock tower that is a famous Gustavia landmark, has a set menu at *prix fixe avec vin* for about 100F.

La Case de Clementine sur Port, and its relative **La Case de Clementine** tucked amidst the shops at the PLM St. Barths Hotel, offer light lunch and prix fixe dinners, with dinners tallying to $10 or so.

St. Jean Beach Club, on the Baie de St. Jean near the foot of the road from Village St. Jean and Tropical Hotel, serves in casual beachside surroundings. Food has always been good and may be even better now that British Hilary and her French husband

Claude Janin share the culinary skills they have put into practice at their in-town Au Port.

Le Pelican, owned by the Mayor and frequented by island residents, perches beachside at Baie de St. Jean. The bathing suit following that lounges around during lunch hour spruces up (slightly) for the more elegant dinner service. At press time plans are to bring a skilled chef from a well-known Relais in Brittany to put into practice his culinary *coups de maitre* on St. Barths. Count on good food—and high prices.

La Crémaillère is the place to settle in for the local lobster bisque and for other, more elaborate fare, if you've made a reservation. You'll find the spot near Gustavia's harbor, not far from Jean-Yves Froment's workshop.

Taiwana, an open air bistro on the beach at Baie des Flamands, puts you near a pool, amid flourishing plants. Poisson grille (grilled fish) is a favorite.

The **Pizza Parlour,** on a side street in downtown Gustavia not far from the waterfront, gets rave notices among repeat visitors for its selection of the familiar Italian pie at prices that put a meal into reasonable range. Other snack spots are **Chez Joe** (next to Sibarth Real Estate office in Gustavia) and **La Tringuette,** a sidewalk cafe equivalent that puts you at harborside in Gustavia.

Chez Francine, a one-time favorite on Baie de St. Jean, has become a haven for tour bus lunches. It's a better bet as a beachside bistro when the buses are elsewhere.

Chez Francois, often mistaken for its beachside competitor, is folded into foliage inland from the Baie de St. Jean. Occasional interludes as an entertainment spot make it worth checking on current status if you're planning on a rustic and quiet romantic meal for two.

AUTHOR'S OBSERVATION: Things slow down (and sometimes stop completely) on St. Barths in the fall. Several of the inns are closed (Castelets for one), and restaurants open when they feel like it and/or when business warrants. There will be some place to eat, but only one may be open. In spite of the "silence," the fall has been my favorite time for recollecting on St. Barths.

PLACES WORTH FINDING ON ST. BARTHS are the ones you discover yourself, as you prowl around the island. There are small villages (Corossol, where the ladies who weave the baskets and mats swarm around your car) and special beach-lined coves, but the enchantment of St. Barths is that it is a solitary place to share with someone special. This is no place for tour groups and hordes of tourists.

■■■

SPORTS ON ST. BARTHS succumb to the sea, either in it, on it or under it. **Windsurfing** has taken over here, as on many Caribbean islands. Flocks of sails flock the sea at Baie de St. Jean, starting at the beach near the road that curls up to Eden Rock and others head to the St. Barth's Beach Hotel. (Windsurfers have been known to try their boards and sails at almost any shore.) The concession at St. Jean is St. Barths Water Sports, a branch of the in-town firm near the bakery. Windsurfing is in the hands of WINDS, out of Eden Rock hotel and also at Cul de Sac.

Yachting is not organized on St. Barths (in fact, there's not much that *is* highly organized), but if you hang around the harbor, chances are you may pick up the opportunity to sail—perhaps on down the islands. The cruise that makes a day excursion to this island from nearby Sint Maarten is aboard a power boat.

The annual St. Barth's Sailing regatta, in late February, draws an ever-increasing fleet of enthusiasts from other islands as well as those on the spot, and there may be a few other events that will be organized according to yachtsmen's wishes, but don't count on there being a lot of activity for "outsiders" except on the fringe of the fun.

Tennis is only available at St. Barth's Beach Hotel and at Club Taiwana.

■■■

TREASURES AND TRIFLES ON ST. BARTHS are tucked into several small shops of Gustavia, and sold from even smaller places in some of the villages around the island. In Gustavia, check to see what's being sold at **A la Caleche,** where Brook and Roger Lacour have their home and apartment rental office. The usual selection includes clothing as well as some specialty items and island designed fabrics worked into summer fashions from St. Kitts and Nevis.

ALMA Optiques, near the waterfront, takes care of the "usual" perfume, camera (including Kodak), watches, and crystal routines. If you're in the market for any of those luxury items, visit the shop to check the prices (which are usually a shade or 2 below the better-known shopping havens in the U.S. Virgins and Curaçao). St. Barths's reputation as a smugglers' port since the time of the buccaneers is worth remembering when you shop for imported items.

Stop at the studio of **Jean-Yves Froment,** near the post office in Gustavia, for handblocked island prints, painted and printed T-shirts, and other island-made designs. The fabric can be purchased by the yard, or made up in shirts, skirts and other clothes.

The delicately woven reed work is unique to St. Barths. Although a lot of the work is whipped together by sewing machine these days, it is still possible to find some of the handsewn items that I find far preferable. Hats, mats, baskets are the usual items for sale, and bargaining when you buy from the women at Corossol is part of the process for purchase.

La Cave de Saint Barthélemy is a find for anyone who wants to buy good wine. In an enormous cement-block building that looks more like an airport hangar than a wine cellar, you can find some of France's best vintages, at very reasonable prices. Worth toting home to the states (considering the relatively low tally that customs adds to wines), the vintages are certainly ideal for "at home" consumption while you are in residence here. Located between Lorient and Grand Cul de Sac, La Cave is worth a visit if you are serious about wine.

Postcards made from the painting/collages of **Margot Ferra Doniger** are worth buying, if you can't track down (or afford) one of the exceptional works of art in the original. Available in most shops where postcards are sold, the special scenes of St. Barths help recall this island's unique quality long after you've left its shores.

St. Croix

Division of Tourism, Christiansted, St. Croix, VI 00820; Frederiksted, Customs House Bldg., Strand St., St. Croix, VI 00840; Virgin Islands Government Tourist Office, 1270 Avenue of Americas, New York, NY 10020; 343 S. Dearborn St., Suite 1108, Chicago, IL 60604; 3450 Wilshire Blvd., Los Angeles, CA 90010; 100 N. Biscayne Blvd., Suite 904, Miami, FL 33132; 1050 17th Street, N.W., Washington, DC 20036.

U.S. currency used.

The sun scattered diamonds of light on the sea. At the horizon end of that glittering path, a parade of yachts—all shapes and sizes— moved across my view. It is a Sunday in May, and I am almost sleeping—supported by the salty sea, glimpsing the sailboats over my toes as I float. Is there any better way to start a day?

Most people in St. Croix are horizontal at this hour. It is early, and they are either sleeping, in bed or on the deck of one of those yachts, or floating in the sea as I am. Those people who are bent are probably curling around a cup of coffee, perhaps at the curved counter at one of the Christiansted hotels, where your juice, eggs, and bacon may come with yachting conversations shared with strangers who turn into friends after a few converging breakfasts.

The flutters of commercial life in the north, and elsewhere in the industrialized world, can be felt here in St. Croix, but just barely. And, after a few days at sea—or in it—the pressure seeps out. What surrounds you while you're here are all the trappings of the modern life, punctuated with two stage-set towns—one historically Danish and the other replete with Victorian fretwork—and acres of tropical foliage, sometimes pruned and tended as at the Botanic Garden and at other times growing wild, with vines hanging down over damp roads as in the rain forest in the northwest quarter.

St. Croix can be a somnolent spot. Not far from where I float, the

629

sea laps at the shores of Christiansted, the town that was planned by the Danes, in an area known before that as Ay Ay by the Indians who were here and then by a handful of settlers—French who gave it its name, and English in 1645.

Even after the Danish claim, English, Scottish, and Irish outnumbered the Danes about 5 to one. English was the language of the street. It is today, even though what's spoken between Virgin Islanders bears little resemblance to the American heard at home.

The best-looking buildings in town are forced to stay that way. They're part of a National Historic Site, overseen by the U.S. National Park Service. The Danes made the plan, adapting the buildings they knew at home to the Caribbean breezes and sun—and to the ballast brick that became the building material. The arcades are from the 18th century; the people who walk under them are definitely 20th.

And it's the people who have pulled St. Croix together, not only during the early days, but in the troubled years after Peter von Scholten's decree giving freedom to the slaves, on July 3, 1848, about 14 years before Lincoln's Emancipation Proclamation in the United States. Even in modern times, when what might have been a plot for a TV horror story happened in fact on St. Croix on September 6, 1972, when there was a shooting at the Fountain Valley Golf Course.

Cruzans were outraged by lawlessness. People pulled together to create Project St. Croix, the pacesetter for the rest of the Caribbean with its programs in the community—and its involvement with the schools. Tourism is big business on this island.

The clutch of children who arrived for check-in at the hotel had paper bags with their clothes. Some of them shifted from foot to foot, cast wary eyes around the hotel lobby they were seeing for the first time, and giggled. Others chattered like magpies, and bounced from the ice machine to the pool, touching everything. A few stood silently—watching. All were part of a 6th-grade school class, making their first visit to an island hotel, where the tourists that are the backbone of the island's economy stay at regular intervals.

The school class that spent the weekend at an island hotel had participated in a school program called "Tourism is You." They had taken turns playing the role of tour bus driver (and were relegated to the back of the bus when "a tourist" asked a question that "the driver" could not answer). They had participated in word games, quizzes, and history lessons that helped paint new pictures of the places they call "home."

Now, for the first time, as a reward for several months of

study—and projects that included painting the school room and picking up litter—the class experienced a weekend at a real hotel. Encouraged to ask questions of the hotel and restaurant staff that served them, the young Cruzans could see what it's like to be a tourist, what it's like not to know the answers, and what it is like to need help from someone who does.

The "Tourism is You" program that started with one class at one school has grown to include links with several hotels and many school classes. Young Cruzans are becoming involved—perhaps for the first time—in the hospitality industry, an industry that provides more than 15,350 jobs in the U.S. Virgin Islands, and that brought in a reported $340 million to island coffers last year.

■■■

POLITICAL PICTURE: Governor Juan Luis, reelected to his office for a 4-year term in November 1978, is the head of the government for the United States Virgin Islands (which means the large islands of St. Croix, St. John, and St. Thomas, as well as the several small islets and cays included in the territory). Christiansted, St. Croix, was the seat of the government during the Danish days, from the 17th century until 1917, when the United States government bought the islands from Denmark for $25 million. The government buildings that are now part of the national Historic Site are still used—and impressive to look at. The Governor comes to St. Croix on regular visits; in his absence an Administrator for St. Croix takes care of day-to-day problems.

Virgin Island politics are a unique blend of maneuverings familiar to most West Indian islands and procedures prescribed by the U.S. federal government in Washington. As a territory of the United States (since the islands were purchased from Denmark in 1917), the Virgin Islands have a pipeline to the U.S. Department of Interior. Federal grants are crucial for the islands' economy, and many local folk are nervous about the effect of President Reagan's budget cuts.

Preferential tax and tariff regulations resulted in Hess Oil, Martin Marietta, and others establishing imposing divisions on the south coast of St. Croix, but the local reception to multinational companies has not always been enthusiastic. Protracted negotiations between the Governor and Hess Oil on a new tax agreement resulted in an ultimatum being issued by Leon Hess in March 1981 whereby, if a new tax agreement was not completed by May 8, Hess Oil Virgin Islands Corporation (HOVIC) would be instructed to suspend St. Croix operations by September 1, 1981. (The agreement was pushed through the Virgin Islands legislature on May 7 and was regarded by both Governor Juan Luis and by Leon Hess as "satisfactory.")

Tourism has followed a roller coaster path on this island, with doldrums perpetrated by adverse publicity about crime and the area's dependence on American tourism which local authorities claim is affected by high airfares and "recession." Last winter's business was not as good as local hoteliers and shopkeepers hoped it would be, and summer business was slow. Facilities are good to excellent, however, and in my opinion, this should be one of the Caribbean's best vacation spots, especially for watersports enthusiasts who bed-in at one of the many small hotels.

AUTHOR'S OBSERVATION: Headlines about crime have marked this area more than most places although the crime (robbery and muggings) is no different here than in many mainland communities. St. Croix has become the sunny suburbs, with all the attendant problems including traffic jams, rising prices, and rising crime. The Virgin Islands government and community action groups have acknowledged the problem and are working to resolve it. In the meantime, any visitor exercising reasonable precautions should have a happy and trouble-free vacation. My advice is to leave expensive jewelry at home, lock rental cars when parking, avoid dark-and-secluded streets, and visit beaches that have attendants or hotels nearby.

CUSTOMS OF THE COUNTRY are strictly American, after more than 60 years of U.S. affiliation since the pre-1917 Danish days. Life is island-casual. Although residents applaud the convenience of Grand Union, Barkers, Woolworth, Kentucky Fried, and the rest of the chain reactions known to every town in the U.S.A., the Americanization of these islands has wiped out all of the foreign flavor and has contributed to a sophisticated life style with problems (crime and pollution) familiar to many U.S. cities. Attempts were made to revive interest in things Danish a few years ago, but the prevailing atmosphere is distinctly American tourist, especially in downtown Christiansted. There are a couple of Danish restaurants, some street names, and—of course—the names of Charlotte Amalie (the capital, on St. Thomas) and the towns of Christiansted and Frederiksted.

Clothes are casual, with the ultra-elegant resort wear of *Vogue* (and yesteryear) seen on occasion (usually at private parties). Downtown, small restaurant and lively disco wear is neatly informal. Most men disdain the coat and tie, favoring an open-necked shirt; anything goes for women—who often dress up. Pant-suits are hot, and have never been ideal for tropical travel. Most women wear casual skirt & blouse or T-shirt combinations. Blue jeans and shorts are popular for boats and beach. As with all island areas, it's pleasanter for everyone if bare chests and bare feet are limited to pool or beach (and the bare chests are usually on men only, except at a beach or pool of your own, in the U.S. Virgin Islands).

MONEY MATTERS: The main concern for many is how fast money disappears. The dollars that go down the drain are U.S. variety, and everyone is overly eager to have them. Some places take credit cards, but don't count on their acceptance everywhere. Many small spots are accepting only cold, hard cash. Travelers cheques are a convenient (safe) way to carry "cash."

ARRIVAL ON ST. CROIX is by air, for most, landing at the airport that is midway between Christiansted and Frederiksted, on the south shore of the island.

The Cruzan airport is open to the tropical breezes, except for the air-conditioned enclosed upstairs restaurant. There are a few shops, including a counter where you can order your 1-gallon quota of liquor if you haven't gotten around to it in town. (The newsstand marks the place, and you'll order from a printed list; your purchase is packed and shoved out a side door for your pickup.) Taxi fares are printed on the wall near the luggage pick up, and the charge is for seat-in-car. You'll sit there until the car is full before takeoff for town. Ask, before you get in the cab, about current fares since charges are rising to keep pace with fuel and other costs. Christiansted is about 20 minutes' drive east; Frederiksted is about 15 minutes' drive west.

On departure, you will clear customs in St. Croix if you are flying straight back to the U.S. (You'll clear in Puerto Rico if you are passing through there.) Allow plenty of time for long lines at check-in counters and count on customs and security checks to be thorough. Once you check in and clear your luggage through customs, waiting rooms are comfortable, but there are no shops, only telephones and a small bar.

Islanders and knowing visitors flit between St. Thomas and St.

Croix on the amphibian planes of Antilles Air Boats. The airline is up for sale as this edition goes to press so check for status.

Prinair, the Puerto-Rico based airline that has expanded its fleet of DeHavilland Herons to include Convair 540s, links St. Croix to St. Thomas, Puerto Rico, and to several islands east and south of St. Croix. Coral Air also links St. Thomas and St. Croix as well as St. Croix with San Juan, St. Kitts, and Nevis.

■■
TOURING TIPS: Unless you're a downright novice, avoid the island tour. You can drive around on your own with a rental car for a day, heading to the opposite "end" of the island for midday (to Frederiksted if you're in the Christiansted orbit, and to Christiansted if you are staying in the peaceful, less-touristed Frederiksted area) and see all there is to see. Most of the touring options have to do with the sea, with trips to Buck Island, a day sail, scuba and snorkel excursions and perhaps a day trip to St. Thomas, soaring out of the Christiansted harbor in the belly of an Antilles Air Boat plane.

Taxis have regulated rates, but ask before you get in as to what they are. As gas prices rise and maintenance costs increase, so does the fare you pay.

Rental cars can be a good bet. During all but the busiest season (Christmas and February), shopping around can yield varying prices and conditions for car rentals. The best rates (and cars in good, if not "perfect" condition) come from the small, island-based firms with names that may not be household words. (Mid-West Car Rentals is one.) The names you know (Hertz, Avis, National, and Budget) have booths at the airport, and the highest rates. Inquire about discounts, available—sometimes—for airline employees, some businesses, and, it sometimes seems to me, for the color of your eyes! Many small hotels have their own routes for car rental, and if you're booking there, let them make arrangements. For peak season, best bet is to arrange rental in advance to be sure you have a car. It's not always possible to rent one on the spot, especially if you're on the island at a busy time. Your U.S. driving license is sufficient documentation for V.I. car rental.

Driving is on the *left,* a surprise for many in a U.S. area, but a relic from the early days when, presumably, carts and cattle followed the European system.

■■
HOTELS ON ST. CROIX are personality places. There are no big chain reactions. There's the knot of nests in downtown Chris-

tiansted in 12 small inns, plus one big hotel on its own island in the harbor. When you head for the hills you can choose from a long menu that includes plantations-turned-hotel, barnacles of condominium units covering hillsides and offering sea view, or way-out resorts that have to be self-contained because they're half an hour out of the mainstream. The north shore has its small and special inns with the personalities of the owners or manager; and then there's unique Victorian Frederiksted, the gathering spot for those who choose one of the small shoreside havens along the coast or a room in one of the 2 in-town hotels.

Considering what you get in the way of accommodations and facilities, rates seem high, but they may be understandable when you consider that most places are paying high prices for water, fuel, and imported food (which is *their* problem that hits *your* wallet). If you can arrange to vacation after April 15 or before December 16 you can save 20% or more on your room rates—for exactly the same room that hops up in price on that otherwise insignificant day. (Food prices remain about the same all year.) Investigate the summer "American Paradise" package holidays, where some extras are included with your room rate. Many hotels offer package holidays for scuba, tennis, golf, families, and honeymooners; it's always worthwhile to ask. *Be sure* to read the small print carefully, however; what is ballyhooed may not be a big bargain—especially if no meals are included.

If you're facing a pocketbook pinch, you have a choice of a simple, not sensational, small room in a Christiansted inn (where you can walk to restaurants and action hubs), or an apartment/condominium unit where you can cook to keep down the costs. Nothing is rock bottom in price on this island.

AUTHOR'S AWARDS for St. Croix go to the Buccaneer Resort for being beautiful and the best of the lot (but *not* for its food), to the King Frederik for being a good-value beachside bastion for self-sufficient folk, and to King Christian, on the waterfront in Christiansted for the view from its rooms and its special brand of hospitality.

✤ **Anchor Inn** (58 King St., Christiansted, St. Croix, USVI 00820; 30 rooms) nests in the middle of Christiansted's activities, with shops, restaurants, watersport headquarters, and gorgeous harbor views surrounding. The heart of this small gem is a plant-filled courtyard and a lively second-floor restaurant that gives you some activity at homebase if you don't want to walk the few paces that are required to reach all the other in-town spots. (Donn's Anchor Inn is mentioned under "restaurants" below.) Rooms vary. Some have view (210, 211, and 310, for example); others do not. Air-conditioning is available (and essential for some sequestered spots). There's "no" lobby, but you'll find it much pleasanter to linger at one of the viewful cafes anyway. Opened in 1968 as the Old Quarter, the place was taken in tow by Lon Southerland in 1974 when it became the Anchor Inn. Note the 200-year-old walls of a former French magistrate's house; you'll nose up to them when you park in the courtyard. Haitian-born manager Jean Perigord is your on-the-spot host. He's enthusiastically available. Room rates at Anchor Inn for this winter will range around $80 for 2, meals extra. If you're a diver, or want to become one, investigate the scuba package with Pressure Ltd. and Anchor Inn.

✤ **Buccaneer Hotel and Beach Club** (Box 218, Christiansted, St. Croix, USVI 00820; 157 rooms) is this island's best resort. It's an island tradition that is a pacesetter, offering golf, tennis, beaches, dining depots, shops—and spectacular views. The property has been an estate since 1653 when Charles Martel, a Knight of Malta, built a hospice here. Then it served a stint as a French Great House. The practical Danes made their mark in 1733 when Governor von Prock turned the Great House into a sugar factory and added the mill that still stands. Shoy bought the property from von Prock as a cotton plantation, and subsequent owners raised cattle here. In 1948, the Armstrong family built the Buccaneer Hotel and opened 11 rooms for guests on what they had operated since 1922 as a cattle ranch. My first travels to St. Croix were made memorable by joining the family at the far end of the main-house porch (near what is now the entrance to the Martel room) to hear the late Douglas Armstrong, raconteur par excellence, tell tales about life in the "old times" on St. Croix. Robert Armstrong, the present owner and the son, is the 8th generation to live here, and his young sons are the 9th.

History pervades this place, in spite of what is done to modernize it. The core of the hilltop Great House is still standing; its terrace is where you'll have your sunset drink. Rooms known in the family as the Strongbox, Lucky Farthing, Pretty Penny, and Widows Mite are along the ridge, with the newest rooms built in the old style so that it is hard to tell them from the originals. For my money, these are *still* the best rooms; the top-of-the-house modern, air-conditioned nooks are too antiseptically hotel for my taste. Rooms 64 to 71, in the Pieces of Eight—4 cottages that step down the hill to the beach

(2 units per cottage, each with 2 rooms and terrace)—are next best. The most consistently good group are the beach rooms in the curve to Beauregard Beach (try for 22, 23, 24, or 25 if you want sunset seating and best beach access); all have blue and white tiled floors, airy feeling, white walls, ultramodern bathroom, terrace, and a head-of-the bed control panel with all switches (radio, lights, music, etc.). Doubloons are beachside, near the Mermaid Restaurant.

You'll arrive through the guard-controlled entrance gate (with the golf course on both sides of the road). If fencing around the property bothers you, remember that the suitcase that sits in your room holds more clothes than the average Virgin Islander has in his closet and that the golf carts that roll over the course represent affluence with a capital A.

For your holiday pleasure, Buccaneer offers the air-conditioned *Martel Room*; the terrace for dining and sunset, open to the breezes and the best view of Christiansted; evening entertainment of steel bands and buffets; the beachside *Mermaid Restaurant* where alfresco ambiance is better than the food (hamburger, salad, and sandwich lunches are offered); plus a choice of shops, a pool at the top of the hill, tennis courts at the bottom, and 2 good beaches. Beauregard Beach is longest and seldom slathered with the turquoise dashes of lounge chairs covered with pink-to-tan bodies that obliterate the other beach in season. At Beauregard you can walk up the steps to the *Grotto* hamburger and hot dog grill as soon as you smell the first hamburger being grilled—and that is about 11:30 a.m. (Summer visitors may find the Grotto closed if the house count is low.) The beach shack at the conventional cove sells suntan oil and can book your scuba, snorkeling, and Buck Island excursions at the same price they charge from their shop in town. The hotel operates shuttle bus service, a few times daily, for the 7-minute ride into Christiansted. General Manager Kim Vohs runs a nice hotel; the big resort has small inn hospitality. Figure around $200 for 2 this winter, room only. Ask about seasonal rates and special golf or tennis holidays that give better value.

✦ **Cane Bay Plantation** (Box G, Kings Hill, St. Croix, USVI 00850; 20 rooms) claims a north coast hillside and a longtime reputation as a special small hotel. Changes in ownership over a couple of decades have modified the personality of this place, but the original West Indian house still stands (and is the heart of the activity and hospitality as well as the dining room). Appendages (of pool, sundeck, bar area, and dining terrace) have been added through the years, and an island-wide reputation for Sunday brunch continues, even though its innovators (Charles and Sally Goit) have left. Other evening meals have a theme; it's best to call in advance to check for offerings the evening you plan to come out for dinner (if you are staying somewhere else). The inn is on the hill, a short walk from the beach and about 25 minutes drive from Christiansted. The golf course is a short drive (in a car) away. Most rooms are in the newer block where B-level is the second story and 1A and B have a wraparound terrace at the west end. All rooms have balcony and good sea view. Long House and Fruit House are 2 of the old slave quarters-turned-into-cottages, at the back of the 18th-century main house (preferred by some although equipment is older). Rates this winter, for 2 with breakfasts and dinners, range from $140 to $170.

✤ **Charte House** (2 Company St., Christiansted, St. Croix, USVI 00820; 26 rooms) is another of the alcove allotment of small hotels in Christiansted. The rooms vary in shape and size, and price has risen to top limits, at about $50 for 2, no meals, this winter. If you are young in fact or at heart, and not demanding, check in. The small pool in the center courtyard gives you a place to dunk after you've dumped your clothes in your room. This is no place for light sleepers. Company Street looks across to interesting shops and eateries.

✤ **Club Comanche** (1 Strand St., Christiansted, St. Croix, USVI 00820; 38 rooms) claims to have been a doctor's house in the mid-1700s, but today it is the classic Cruzan caravansary. Ted Dale doesn't much care what you think about his place; he likes it—and has called it home for more than 25 years, charging someone else with the daily management. For the season of '79, Dick Boehm (of restaurant fame) was included in the ownership, with few visible changes in the successful holiday formula. Time was when Club Comanche was the only small spot to stay in town, if not in fact then certainly in practice. Ted Dale and Guy Reynolds opened the inn with 7 rooms in 1948, and the place is still the hub of the matter—for the old-timers and those who sense the true tempo of Christiansted. (You have only to slide up to the curved tables at *The Front Porch* for a hearty breakfast for proof.) Rooms are an eclectic lot. The 14 in the main building vary, but you can count on finding four-posters in most rooms, a view in a couple; if you luck into #5 you'll have the oldest mahogany four-poster in the house. Rooms 12 and 14–17 are on the top floor of the original house; 3–7 are on the first floor. All guests can settle into the small *Back Porch,* a 4-stool bar for in-house guests. A band of rooms stretches out to sea, with a not too auspicious outlook along Dick Boehm's *Comanche Restaurant.* The trademark windmill tower, traditional honeymooners' nest, burned in spring '81. Decision on restoration had not been made at press time. Ask, if you want the mill tower room. Bargain-rate rooms are a 4-room group with shared bath in a separate seaside building next to the mill. Comanche guests have the use of the pool, by the mill near the waterfront. Rates for a room for 2 this winter range from $45 to $60, all meals extra.

✟ **Frederiksted Hotel** (20 Strand St., Frederiksted, St. Croix, USVI; 40 rooms) focuses on giving good value. The 3-story modern building sits at the east end of Frederiksted's waterfront street. Although the best of the modern, motel-style rooms has a sea view, the nearest beach is a hot walk to the other end of town. Rooms are air-conditioned, with 2 double beds and a kitchen area that has refrigerator and sink but no cooking unit. On-premises facilities include a speck of a pool, a cement slab for sunning on comfortable lounge chairs, and a poolside bar where breakfast is sometimes served depending on house count. For other meals you can walk down the street to the Swashbuckler, or in the other direction to Piazza, or down to the deli for one of the special sandwiches. This is a good bet for independent travelers who don't have to be on a beach and like reasonable rates. This winter's tally is around $60 for 2; summer is about $45 for 2, no meals.

✟ **Gentle Winds** (Box 3721, Christiansted, St. Croix, USVI 00820; 135 rooms) is a condominium project, shoreside on the north coast near Salt River where Columbus landed. The units are in 9 buildings a safe-and-convenient distance around the beachside pool, snack shack, and open-air dining pavilion with reception area and small shop.

Units come in 2- and 3-bedroom versions that divide into separate rooms, each with its own door to the outside and plenty of privacy. Some of the buildings bear banners like Antigua Haus, Bimini Haus, St. Croix, St. John, and St. Kitts.

Tennis courts are a good distance from the shoreside buildings (originally another cluster of condominiums was planned for the tennis area) and there is some poolside entertainment when the house count warrants. Featured winter season entertainment is the Sunday buffet that clogs the parking lot and clutters the beach, making the usually lovely vista reminiscent of your central-city train station at rush hour. Other mealtime specials are offered by the group that operate the Sand Castle restaurant. Ask in advance for the events when you are on the island.

The pool provides the popular swimming area, since the constant wind sweeps the sand at the "beach" out with the sea. Reefs are good for snorkeling when the surf settles enough to keep the sea clear.

Tennis enthusiasts should inquire about any special tennis packages that make use of the 4 Aquacushion courts. Inquire also about hotel transportation into town. If the bus service is *not* running, you are tied to the temperament of the local taxi drivers unless you invest in the rental car or want to stay close to home. The 2-bedroom villas are $220 and up, depending on villa, and 3-bedroom deluxe is $300 per day, meals extra.

✣ **Grapetree Beach Hotel** (Box Z, Christiansted, St. Croix, USVI 00820; 150 rooms) is actually 2 hotels, with a tumultuous history. Grapetree Bay Hotel opened in the late 1950s, with houses intended to follow the precedent set by Antigua's elegant Mill Reef Club. The Beach Hotel was opened in the early 1960s by the Morrow family, who had (and have) property in Jamaica (most notably the elegant Jamaica Inn on the north shore at Ocho Rios).

Since the mid-70s, both hotels have been operated as one property, with guests having a choice for dining and activities. During summer of '81, Grapetree Bay closed down, and owners operated only the Beach Hotel. Plans for the season of '81-'82 are uncertain as this book goes to press. Look for some good value holidays, if the place is open for this winter since innovative sales policies will be the only way to fill these east end properties: Grapetree Bay has 67 rooms, some of them in houses that are privately owned; some are beachfront rooms made for romance and sea view. They're near the pool, in a "new" block, and are called the Beachfront Alamandas. The pool is at beach level, downstairs from the main lobby, dining room, and the Far East lounge. Poolside tables for dining have been the best bet for easy fare and a curved counter, coffee shop style, appeared in the season of '79. Tennis courts are plastered on a patch just inland from the rooms, and 2 more are at the Beach Hotel.

A short ride west (shuttle bus makes a regular run), along the south shore, is Grapetree Beach, the former Beach Hotel. Louvered glass baffles that surround the pool hint at the wind that can come from the sea. A clutch of shops are in the pool-level lobby, along with Margie's Hair Salon with her telephone number obvious if she's not.

At the arrival lobby, behind the check-in desk, there's a dunce cap roof over the dining room (don't count on dazzling food. There will be plenty, but I didn't find it perfect). Insofar as rooms are concerned, the newer units are those on the left as you face the sea. If you want sun on your terrace, request a room that has some. Since the hotel is built to the curve of the beach, not all rooms do.

✢ **Holger Danske** (1 King Cross St., Christiansted, St. Croix, USVI 00820; 44 rooms) is at the back-from-the-harbor border of the in-town action. It's aloof from the hubbub, but near enough to get to the heart of the matter when you want to. The pool perches on the roof of the restaurant (which was closed when I looked) and both have a water view. Best Western claims this island hotel as part of its chain reaction. Each room has an efficiency unit with modern equipment. It's located on your balcony (with view) or terrace (with no view). Rooms are modern, motel-style and rent for just over $80 for 2 this winter. Good for independent types who don't need lobby action. (There is "no" lobby.) Holger Danske is favored by business and long-stay travelers.

✢ **Hotel on the Cay** (Box 4020, Christiansted, St. Croix, USVI 00820; 53 rooms) has bolted along in fits and starts since its birth on Protestant Cay in the early 1970s. John Randal McDonald, architect also of homes for Victor Borge, Charles and Maureen O'Hara Blair, and the Watergate Villas on St. Thomas, built a white-walled, multiarched castle on the small cay that had to be enlarged to handle it. The buildings have been wrapped in tropical plants, with ribbons of paths and waterfalls. Jockey Club owners spent a fortune to pump sand to make a beach during their era of ownership, so there is a patch of sand (if you don't mind swimming in the harbor). Now that a harbor cleanup program dumps town sewage elsewhere, the thought of a swim is slightly more appealing. Colorful sailfish sprout from the sands, and action emanates from the beachside restaurant where the daytime sun worshipers gather. Tennis courts are to the left as you step off the boat (to the right as you come from your room). Overhead (literally) is the pool, bordered with plastic "grass" which you can ignore when you look across the harbor to the view of Christiansted. Main dining room and bar are up the hill, on the site of the historic small inn that Paul and Nora Gilles operated from the 1940s through 60s.

Bedrooms are airy, with good views and modern furnishings, but the hotel is no place for anyone who has to count steps, or wants to hoot and holler after 1:00 a.m. The last boat trip across the harbor (5-minute float) is at 1 a.m. Room rates range from $125 to $135 for 2 (room only), but ask about package tours, group rates, and special bargains. Management offers several in season and in summer.

✤ **King's Alley** (in King's Alley, Christiansted, St. Croix, USVI 00820; 22 rooms) is kept in shape by attentive manager Phyllis Simmons. The place has proved to be the best bet for many when reserving a resting spot in downtown Christiansted. The wedge of rooms that pokes from King's Alley (a shopping arcade) toward the waterfront walk keeps up appearances, and the clean-up project improves the looks of the entrance area, down an "alley" off King Street. All rooms have balconies, except those on the first floor, where you can walk out to the sidewalk or look out to the pool. *Marina Bar,* a small but popular spot inside the fence at the shoreline, draws a lingering crowd from about 10:30 a.m. on, and the pool is 2–stroke size, which is bigger than the dunking dots at most in-town hotels. Rooms 101–104 parade back from the shore at ground level but don't have much view. The open-air lobby is just off the turnaround by *Cafe de Paris* (where you may go for breakfast and other meals). Alexander Hamilton Alley, near the entrance of the hotel, leads to King Street, the main drag. Rates for 2 range from $50 to $70 this winter.

✤ **King Christian** (59 King's Wharf, Christiansted, St. Croix, USVI 00820; 38 rooms) is a unique haven, with an intriguing past and a present created from the genuine hospitality offered by owners and staff. Part of the waterfront during the Danish era, the building was bought more than 20 years ago to be revamped as a place to stay. Several metamorphoses later, the inn operated by Betty and Irwin Sperber gives guests the option of activity (you're within paces of several restaurants, shops, watersport headquarters, and historic buildings), with a small hotel base. The front desk, horseshoe-shaped with a helpful employee captive in the middle, occupies most of the entryway which is under the arches off the waterfront promenade. The 3-story building gives top-floor guests an intriguing, ever-changing panorama of Christiansted harbor life (a melange of pleasure craft and people coming and going). All guests have a choice of air-conditioned harbor view rooms with 2 queen-sized beds and modern comforts or "no-frills" low-cost rooms with

basics (and a lower bill). Count on the front desk to be able to arrange car rentals and offer suggestions for filling your vacation
days. A speck-sized elevator makes the climb to the third floor if you
can't, and ice machine and pool are placed near each other on or
about the second-floor level. The pool is better for cooling off than
for view, but deck chairs allow for sunning; the tables and chairs on
surrounding patios, although a rag-tag lot when I looked in, could
become congenial gathering spots with a little effort. Count on
being at the heart of everything if you bunk in here, and be sure to
search out owner Betty Sperber if there's anything you need to
know about what's going on in St. Croix. Inquire about combination sailing and/or scuba holidays, using the hotel as landbase for
part or all of your holiday. Rates this winter for a room for 2 are
about $80 and up, with the "no frills" rooms at $45 for 2, when
available.

✤ **Queen's Quarter** (Box 770, Christiansted, St. Croix, USVI 00820;
35 rooms) captures a hilltop location, midisland, and punctuates it
with a pool. Not a hotel in the usual sense of building-with-lobby,
Queen's Quarter is an oasis of hospitality far from a beach (but
with a shuttle bus 20-minute ride a couple of times daily for
guests). Taking their cue from the names of old Cruzan plantations, the separate buildings (where your room will be) are known
as Prosperity, Strawberry Shack, Solitude, Fanny's Fancy, Catherine's Rest, and the like. One of my favorites—Work and Rest—is
a few paces from the central core. The "eye of the needle" that is
the pool, Queen's Court restaurant, and check-in desk, is surrounded by a road that weaves up to this perch from the main east-
west road. (Restaurant specialities are vegetarian and protein
oriented, with sautes and teriyaki items popular with those who
know.) Management makes arrangements for a rental car (which
you'll need if you want mobility). Count on elegant-looking surroundings and being close to the Island Center, cultural hub of St.
Croix. Rates this winter are expected to hold at just under $100, for
2, with all meals extra.

✤ **St. Croix-by-the-Sea** (Box 248, Christiansted, St. Croix, USVI;
135 rooms) is an island legend that now faces a major turning point
in its life. The hotel opened as a small place in the late 1940s, with
Fritz Lawaetz, a member of one of the old island families, seeing
the advantages of a hostelry for off-islanders.

For more than a decade, St. Croix-by-the-Sea expanded and modernized with the hand of Herman Breidemeier at the helm. In late

1977 he left the island. The hotel was purchased by Prinair Corp., an arm of the Heron-happy carrier that claims 26 planes and routes to 10 islands, and whose first hotel venture was the Carib-Inn in Puerto Rico. Financial convolutions in spring of '79 resulted in termination of the Prinair link, and the hotel is back in the hands of the Lawaetz family. The original hotel-plus-appendages sits seaside, with the full blast of the sea air taking its toll on the spray-stained windows that face northeast. A series of expansions have made way for a bigger dining room, cooled by the sea breezes (and dark because it is set back under a low roof), plus a pool at the shoreline and a patch of sand that stays put when the seas allow. Hotel rooms and public places needed a good scrubbing (and paint) when I looked, and debris from the sea had settled into the rocks near the pool deck. Often an active nightspot (when there's entertainment here), the hotel might be worth considering if you get a good rate on some package plan. (The condominium units that fill several buildings adjacent to St. Croix by the Sea are marked by a "St. C" logo on a road-facing wall and are operated, according to my latest information, on a separate basis with homeowners in control. See "Housekeeping Holidays" below.) Rates at the hotel are expected to be $100 and up for 2, but check on current status of the hotel if you're thinking about staying here. It's hard to predict for winter of '82 at presstime.

✣ **The Lodge** (43A Queen St., Christiansted, St. Croix, USVI 00820; 17 rooms) is kept in shape by manager Romi Truninger, who uses her Swiss heritage to your advantage. There's refrigerator and TV in all rooms but don't count on much atmosphere. Small rooms (no real windows) that open onto the balcony overlooking the courtyard. Several good restaurants, not more than 12 paces from your room, are *Frank's Place* (across the street), *Eccentric Egret* (near the arch with buttercup-colored canopy that is the entrance to The Lodge and *Tivoli*, around the corner near Frank's). The residents' bar and breakfast area are up the stairs inside the courtyard; the *Moonraker* is the front-porch restaurant that opens for lunch and dinner. Rates are about $60 for 2, with continental breakfast.

✣ **Royal Roost** (48 King St., Christiansted, St. Croix, USVI 00820; 12 rooms) on a side street near shops and restaurants, had been the Phoenicia in a former life. It's dismal, in my opinion, with soggy, worn, plastic "grass" carpeting the stairs up to the rooms, all of which open off a narrow hall. Mentioned here only because it exists, the Royal Roost needs a major overhaul before I can recommend it.

✣ **The Inn** (Box 1307, Kingshill, St. Croix, USVI 00850; 25 rooms) is about 5 minutes' walk from the airport, which is in the middle of the island, slightly toward the south shore, in the direction of the Hess refinery and the heavy industrial area. Used by businessmen and others who want to be near the airport, the Inn's biggest claim to fame is an active nightclub. There's a pool for quick dips, but otherwise this place is motel-style. Rates for 2 are about $50, meals extra.

✣ **Sprat Hall** (Box 695, Frederiksted, St. Croix, USVI 00840; 25 rooms) is a special kind of place. Joyce Hurd is your hostess, and she's part of one of the island's "big five" families, the Merwin clan. Jim Hurd came to St. Croix more than 25 years ago, married Joyce, and set about settling in. Room #5 is huge, airy, typically West Indian, with a huge four-poster bed and minimal furnishings. Everything you need is here, but not in abundance. Main rooms at Sprat Hall reek with antiquity, with mahogany tables and chairs in the dining room undergoing regular bouts with lemon oil. This is a home-turned-inn, and you're welcome to enjoy it if you can fit in. Otherwise, go elsewhere, with the Hurds' blessings, in a taxi they'll summon to take you there. Rates this winter figure to from $75 to $85 for 2, meals extra.

Arawak Cottages (see below) on the grounds offer newer accommodations, the independence of efficiency units and the access to the riding stables operated by daughter Jill, one of 4 daughters who visit often if they are not in full-time residence. (Judy was working at the beach house, serving and overseeing lunches on my visit.)

■■■

HOUSEKEEPING HOLIDAYS ON ST. CROIX are easy to arrange, with a cottage, house, or apartment base. Many homes are offered complete with maid and gardener; The condominium units come with maid service, grounds keepers, and on-the-spot managers in most cases. A few apartments are family-owned and operated, with fewer than a dozen units. The result, for those who want to cook their own meals, is a long list of possibilities.

Housekeeping in the U.S. Virgin Islands has the advantage of excellent supermarkets for shopping in a system similar to home. You may pay more for what you buy, but at least you can find plenty of food. It is not as easy, however, to find good local produce. The Cruzan market ladies still set up their stalls at the marketplace off Company Street in Christiansted, where you can buy spices and homegrown fruits and vegetables. Otherwise, word of mouth will lead you to local sources for special items; the staples you can buy in the supermarkets at several modern shopping centers around the island.

You'll want to rent a car for mobility at most places. Gentle Winds and St. Croix-by-the-Sea offer housekeeping units as well as hotel rooms; they have been mentioned in the preceding hotel roster. Other housekeeping arrangements to consider are:

✤ **Arawak Cottages** (Box 695, Frederiksted, St. Croix, USVI 00840) are the self-sufficient nooks next to the great old house that is Sprat Hall. If you want more privacy (and more modern accommodations), rent one of these units. Guests here have all the options including making a dinner reservation at the big house enjoyed by Sprat Hall guests. The puffed-up winter rate is based on demand. The $95 for 2, meals extra, splits in half for 2 for summer, all meals extra. The 1-bedroom cottage is $120; 2-bedroom is $130 to $150 depending on whether 3 or 4 people use it.

✤ **Barrier Reefe Beach Club** (221A, Golden Rock, Christiansted, St. Croix, USVI 00820; 25 units) nestles on the shore next to Mill Harbour (with which it shares a high wire fence and proximity to the play yard of the nearby housing development). A mere 10 minutes' drive from downtown Christiansted, Barrier Reefe's 2 bedroom, 2 bathroom units have complete housekeeping facilities (dishwasher, washer, and dryer with kitchen) and a winter rate that makes a family holiday at about $100 for 2, no meals. Shaped like a question mark, with the pool at the scoop, the units have balconies with sea view and—although basic construction is typical Cruzan '70s—the elements are here for good value, self-sufficient holidays. Only the neighborhood (residential, with moderate income multi-story buildings) leaves a little to be desired, but then you can look out at the sea and forget about what's behind you.

✤ **Cane Bay Reef Club** (Box 1407, Kingshill, St. Croix, USVI 00850; 9 units) is on the north coast rocks, about 2/10 of a mile from Cane Bay Plantation, where those who don't want to cook at home go for most of their meals (by reservation). You can bed into Flamboyant, Orchid, Poinsettia, Coconut, or 5 other flower names; all are basic (and dark, in spite of the white wall in the bedroom). The view,

best seen from your seaside balcony, is the sea, and spectacular.
The bedroom is on the road side, the sitting room and terrace face
out to sea. During a winter visit, when I asked about house count,
Dulcy Seiffer said it was capacity. "Isn't that the way you like it?" I
asked. "Yes, but not for the whole year. I couldn't take it. My husband could, but I couldn't. He likes to count the money." There's a
pool, with the sea crashing on nearby rocks, but for the beach you'll
have to walk a few minutes along the road to share with the Cane
Bay Plantation guests. The 2 room suites (the best in the house)
are a good value at about $350 for a winter week. A package of
breakfast basics costs about $10 and will be ready for your arrival. A
West Indian buffet (Tu, reservations needed, about $15) is a
weekly feature for winter, but for most meals you'll have to (or perhaps want to) cook on an outdoor grill or go out. A car is recommended for mobility (and the Seiffers can arrange it). You're about
25 minutes' drive from Christiansted, and can ride in with hotel
staff for a small fee if you're carless.

✣ **Caribbean View** (La Grande, Christiansted, St. Croix, USVI
00820; 20 units) captures a spot near the coast, and rooms (with
kitchen facilities) cluster around the pool. Count on congenial atmosphere with the Haspels as your hosts. Rates have figured to
about $50 for 2, for one of the compact efficiency units in the 2-
story buildings. (Upstairs units give the chance for a better view.)

✣ **Coakley Bay** (Star Route, Christiansted, St. Croix, USVI 00820;
100 units) is about 15 minutes' drive east of Christiansted, along
the north coast. The best part about the unattractive, boxy units on
the inland hillside is the view from their terraces toward Buck Island. Buildings carry alphabetical identity, with F and G at the top
of the hill with the best view (and the longest hike from the pool,
restaurant, and open-air snack area). The newest units have about
12 apartments per building. There's nothing pretty about the architecture, but if you find the price right (at about $100 for 2, this win-
ter), the place is convenient if you rent a car. No beach right here.

✣ **King Frederik** (Box 1908, Frederiksted, St. Croix, USVI 00840; 10
apts.), like most royalty, sets its own pace. There's no big sign to
mark the road, which meanders off the east end of Frederiksted's
waterfront drive (turn left at the big tree if you are coming into
town from the airport or from Christiansted). Since the road is the
only one you can take, the house-scattered area is the only confusing part. Stick close to the sea, along a route you can saunter in an

easy (and hot) 10 minutes to Frederiksted shops. Built almost 10 years ago, the cluster of efficiencies and 1-bedroom apartments stands in a couple of buildings, artfully arranged so that every balcony has privacy and sea view (if not soundproofing).

Bill Owens took over in the summer of '79, with a determination to keep things in top-notch working order, maintaining the congenial atmophere that has contributed to guests returning for "next year." Your welcome gift (rum and fresh flowers) is geared to getting you started with "at home" living; the rest of the stocking-up is up to you. (If you use Frederiksted's People's Market for supplies, a "courtesy card" available at the hotel's front desk will get you a free ride home with your parcels.) There's a long stretch of sand that can wash out with the sea, but looked good when I stopped by for this edition. Acknowledging that repeat business is the best business, this place gives good value for winter rates of $38–$64 for 2.

✙ **Granada Del Mar** (La Grande Princesse, Christiansted, St. Croix, USVI 00820; 20 units) gives good value for vacationers who want a home base, with kitchen, within a few miles of downtown Christiansted. A family of 4 can slide comfortably into the 2 bedroom units (at about $800 per week or $120 per day this winter). Check with Betty and Jack Green about latest news of places to eat when you're tired of cooking at home. (A car is advisable for mobility but not essential since pool and tennis court can provide daytime activity.)

✙ **Mill Harbour** (Estate Golden Rock, Christiansted, St. Croix, USVI 00820; 86 units) meanders back from a wedge of shorefront, with white stucco walls capped with brick-colored tile roofs cupping the rooms. This enclave is elegant—all 3 tiers of each of the units. Your balcony will have a sea view, up and over whatever confusion may be at ground level; there's a moat in front of the buildings, and the precise grounds are well tended. Your choice of accommodations—both 2 and 3-bedroom versions (bedrooms air-conditioned)—have attractively furnished living rooms and complete kitchens, at rates that reach close to $200 per day for a winter 3-bedroom unit; 2-bedroom units level off at about $165. The pool is surrounded by brick-colored "tiles"; the beach, although small, is a presentable patch at seaside; and if you keep your sights low, you can ignore the high fence that owners felt was necessary for defining the area of control. You'll want a car for mobility (and for eating out). If you pick it up at the airport, you can save the $4 cab fare for the 20-minute drive, and can speed from Mill Harbour into Christiansted for groceries in less than 10 minutes. Mill Harbour has a discreet and pleasant bar/restaurant. If you sneak around the side of it, you may be able to slip through the unofficial break in the fence-barrier between MH and Barrier Reefe's apartments next door. It will save you a lot of walking if you decide to dine or drink at your neighbors.

✤ **Pink Fancy,** a collection of self-catering apartments around a small pool, has been an island legend with a history that started decades ago. A time in the doldrums is now part of its past with re-opening this season for guests. Check with Sam Dillon, at the apartments, 27 Prince Street, Christiansted, for details.

✤ **Queste Verde** (Box 278, Christiansted, St. Croix, USVI 00820; 25 units) looks like a white comb in the hillside of Mount Royale, about 15 minutes' drive overlooking Christiansted. Don't let the small number of units confuse you; the complex is gigantic, but most of the units are owned and lived in, which gives you a feeling of permanence if you stay here. Queste Verde was built about 10 years ago; apartments are owned (or for sale) as condominiums. Your 1-, 2- or 3-bedroom nook will be furnished to the owner's taste and will rent from about $600 to $1000 per week in winter. A pool and central gathering area are a few steps from your door, and the Caribbean Tennis Club is on the premises.

✤ **The Reef** (Star Route, Christiansted, St. Croix, USVI 00820; 100 units) is about 20 minutes east of Christiansted on the north coast and looks like a house of white cards on the hillside. A small pool perches at the top of the hill. Weaving roads (with young planting that's catching on) link the several condominium units. The beach, across the road at the bottom of the hill, has a casual, seaside restaurant and a pleasant stretch of powdery sand (plus a daily wind that blows in from the northeast, over offshore Buck Island). The 9-hole golf course (carts and pro shop) rambles up the hill from the road to and around some of the units. Most of the units are filled on a long-term basis, but you may find one to rent.

✤ **St. C Condominium** (Christiansted, St. Croix, USVI 00820) has an assortment of privately owned apartments for rent in owners' absence. Facilities for the most part are well-kept, and apartments have a sea view from a hillside locale. Guests can walk down to the St. Croix by the Sea pool-and-small-beach and to the tennis courts along the entry road, and one of the island's most popular dining depots (the Top of St. C) commands a good viewing spot and offers air-conditioned, stateside-style steakhouse dining. Condominiums 127-144, 227-244, and 327-344 are at the top of the hill (and the top of the price list).

✤ **Sugar Beach** (Estate Golden Rock, Christiansted, St. Croix, USVI 00820; 25 apts.) is wedged into the shore northwest of Christiansted, about 10 minutes' drive along the main road, with a turn-off through a housing development. Once you're on the shore, the complex has possibilities. It's in the neighborhood of Mill Harbour and Barrier Reefe, but there are a lot of places I would try before this one. Studios and 1- and 2-bedroom units have thin walls, but most have good view. Rental is almost $1000 for a 2-bedroom unit for a week.

✤ **Sunset Beach Cottages** (Box 1395, Frederiksted, St. Croix, USVI 00840; 10 units) are an avocado bunch of 2 story units on the beach. Of the 10 apartments, 4 have one bedroom, on the road side of the unit, with the living-sitting area facing the sea (and sunset) and the small efficiency kitchen on one side; 6 units have 2 bedrooms. Built by the Flemming family and managed for a while by daughter Jan and her husband John Peterson, the cottages are for self-sufficient types who don't need a congregating nook. Count on $60 per day for 2 bedrooms in winter; half that in summer months.

✤ **Turquoise Bay** (Star Route, Christiansted, St. Croix, USVI 00820; 8 units) is just northwest of Christiansted, too far to walk but about a 5-minute drive. Mrs. Ward, an island resident since the mid-50s, is a compassionate hostess for self-sufficient guests who want the independence of a cottage at the shore (4 of them) or an airy, well-appointed studio apartment a few paces from pool and small beach. (The property, reached by driving on a gray-rock "path," abuts the Mill Harbour complex.) The cottage rate of $575 per week in winter is excellent value with freshwater pool, small beach, and an independent atmosphere. Daily rate for a cottage is $90 for 2 with duplex apts at $475 per week or $80 daily for 2 this winter.

✤ **The Waves** (Box 3721, Christiansted, St. Croix, USVI 00820; 10 units) shares a shoreline with Cane Bay Reef. The two 2-story blocks of rooms offer housekeeping facilities and the option to be completely independent (if you arrange for a rental car). Convenient to (but not on) the beach, the Waves' guests can make reservations for dinner at Cane Bay Plantation when cooking "at home" pales. Figure $60 to $70 for 2 this winter, room only.

✤ **Villas of Mary's Fancy** (Box 770, Christiansted, St. Croix, USVI) are speckled around Peppertree Hill near Queen's Quarter Hotel. The privately owned homes are available for rent in owner's absence and vary in size, shape, and facilities (some with their own pool), depending on the taste of the owner. When you perch here, you are within a walk (short or long, depending on the location of your cottage) from the Island Center, the cultural complex where plays and concerts are held. A car is essential.

■■

RESTAURANTS ON ST. CROIX: *CHRISTIANSTED* has a selection of spots that varies with each season. Ask on arrival for new nooks, but count on the following (and on parting with between $15 and $20 for a full meal at one of the better spots).

A word to the wise before pulling up a chair to table: Look and learn before you leap through the door. Ask to see the menu and look at what others are eating to see if the offering is what you want for *your* dinner. Reservations are essential if you want to eat at 8 or after on Saturday nights, and at the other hours if there is a special place where you *know* you want to eat. Without reservations, you will find a table at one of the eateries at some time during the evening, but it may be very early or very late.

Bailey's Beach, in an old building on Company Street (stand back to take a look at it), had a kitchen fire in spring of '81 and will probably serve only snacks with drinks for this season. Decor is established with overhead fans whirling around to keep the tradewinds circulating, director's chairs that pull up to wooden tables, and interesting old prints on the wall.

Chart House, entrepreneurial U.S. restaurant chain, picked up the lease for King Christian's restaurant space, along the waterfront with a captain's view of the charter-boat fleet that moors offshore. A complete overhaul of the premises means only that there are still tables (albeit new ones) at the edge of the shore-rimming boardwalk, but all are in an enclosed area that has sea-breeze air-cooling (through windows). Food ranges from steak to lobster and around in that orbit, with a hearty salad bar that lures a lot of the local folk. Well worth a visit if you like viewful, nautical surroundings.

Dick Boehm's Comanche Restaurant (upstairs across the Strand from Club Comanche's original hotel) still draws the crowds and

Dick Boehm still stands at the cash register at the end of the evening, doling out the tips to the staff and counting the considerable cash. People pay dearly for the steak, chicken, and lobster menu that continues to offer quality that is almost as high as the prices. Reservations are essential in winter season. Plan on parting with $20 per person, at least. The atmosphere is casually elegant: no jacket or tie, tradewinds wafting around the open-but-covered deck, and a bar to ring around while you wait for your table. Count on being cozy with your neighbor; tables are tightly knit with weaving waiters.

Eccentric Egret (Queen's Cross, between King St. and the Strand) makes up in decor what it may lack in professional food service. It is enchanting, from the ballast brick steps that lead upstairs next to Cavanagh's to the plants that punctuate the several small dining rooms, with the louvered open windows, overhead fans, and an eclectic collection of art on the walls. (Note especially the lady with the rose in her left hand, with a casually held fan in her right. She hung at the door of a shop until she was swept upstairs to this front room wall.) Warm bread comes to the table as soon as you order from the menu that includes Italian sausage and noodles, chicken in curry, and shrimps in garlic butter (all about $6.50), plus appetizers in the $1.50 to $4 range, and desserts, etc. at extra charges. House wine is acceptable, by carafe, with your meal.

Tivoli moved to a new and airy location, upstairs at the Pan Am Pavilion, in April of '79. Ferns and other foliage grow where patrons, tables and chairs do not. Plan in advance for the essential reservation for delicious dinners which can include scampi, lobster, and—strange though it seems—Hungarian goulash. Count on from $15 to $20 for the lobster; all main courses hover in that range.

Across the street, **Frank's Place** serves rooms and courtyards full of people, many of whom linger to play backgammon. The menu is Italian—and one of the reasons that this is one of Christiansted's most profitable spots is that he charges $5, $6, and up for a plate full of spaghetti, fettucine, and other pastas. People happily pay. Daily homemade soups are a feature, and appetizers add another couple of dollars to your tab. You'll be lucky to escape for under $15 if you have a full meal. (Old-timers will remember that this was once The Stone Balloon, where you dropped in to see anyone who was "at home" on the island in the old days.)

Top Hat (Company St., near the Christiansted market) is Danish inspired. In 1966 Bent Rasmussen was one of 2 Danish chefs to participate in a cultural exchange with the once-Danish island of St. Croix. He stayed, and eventually opened Top Hat on the second floor of a traditional Cruzan house (stairs up the left side of the building). The place was expanded to include several rooms, with Bent *still* working over the hot stove and wife Hanne elegant as the overseer of the dining room. Ask her for the suggestion for the evening—it will be superb; and order wine to accompany whatever you've chosen. Figure on $20 per person, and relax secure in the knowledge that you're in the best restaurant on the island. (This is as dressy as anyplace at dinner time, although jackets are not required for men.)

Captain Week's Ten Grand, across from the Fort in Christiansted, is a *very* casual, island-oriented place started a few years ago because Captain Weeks knew to find (and pull in) the best local lobsters. Still a favorite among some islanders for local food in hutlike surroundings, the menu has expanded some but the native recipes for fish and lobster are still my starred items. If you're adventuresome, try this place—but don't dress up for your evening here.

1742 Great House, on a courtyard with entrance off Company Street, is worth finding—if it's open. The impressive West Indian house has had an open-and-shut history as a restaurant, and when I checked for this edition it was open. Can't vouch for the food, although the menu and surroundings are impressive. Probably worth the mealtime tariff for scenery alone. You'll be sitting in one of the inside rooms or on the small terrace upstairs, amid the leaves of the venerable trees that fill the courtyard. (There are a few shops in this courtyard also, and they provide diversion if you have to wait for your reservation.)

Donn's Anchor Inn, upstairs in the courtyard of the Christiansted hotel, has become a Cruzan legend in the few years since it's opening. Meals are served on the viewful terrace, where you overlook the Anchor Inn's speck of a pool and a wide expanse of Christiansted harbor (with plenty of boats to watch), or in the wood-walled, nautically inspired room where the folk-gathering bar is located. Count on an eclectic menu, with touches familiar to the San Francisco crowd, and button onto a terrace table for breakfast if you want a special view with your choice of 14-or-more omlettes. (Other breakfast offerings include french toast ladened with fruit and a huge dollop of whipped cream and less adventuresome portions of eggs and the usual.) Coffee comes fast here, even when service is slow—and sipping on the terrace is a pleasurable pasttime.

Other breakfast boites in Christiansted, where most small inns operate on the "no meals" plan leaving you free to sample other spots, are the Club Comanche's **Front Porch** (enter through the main entrance of the inn and turn right to go up the stairs) and the **Deli** on the Strand (the small street that parallels the main street of town), where you can munch a selection of croissant, brioche, and other delicious French-style pastries while sitting at one of the half-dozen tables or at the short counter. The Strand Deli is also your spot for packing a picnic, if you want a delicious sandwich for a beach or boat day.

On the northshore, **Cane Bay Plantation** serves a crowd-gathering Sunday brunch, and offers specialities on other nights. You'll need a rental car (or patient taxi) to reach this spot, unless you're staying at one of the north coast nests. (Call in advance, not only for reservations but to be sure that the evening special is something you'll enjoy.)

FREDERIKSTED's dining depots are a varied lot that range from sandwich places (including vegetarian specials at La Croisée) to candlelit cozy tables at the seashore and personality places with a pace set by Barbara McConnell's New Guest House in an old building. Some have changed names and some have changed places since last season.

Barbara McConnell's place is still up the stairs, in the living quarters of a memorable mansion, but the location at 45 Queen's Street is around the corner from her former spot. The two houses that are mixed and matched to provide gardens and rooms for dining have served as an Anglican vicarage. You haven't been to Frederiksted until you've been to Barbara McConnell's. Although you'll have to have a reservation for your meal, don't have any reservations about having fun. The place has a special personality: Barbara McConnell. Food fixings, which will be fashioned by Barb, may be described as "two crab patties (deviled) who have decided to go together in a cerimony [sic] of salads and garlic toast. They return your wishes" at $4.95, or "two cheese puffs in the same performance. Bubbly cheddar broiled" also for $4.95. More lavish offerings are available, and appropriately (amusingly) described. Skit will fix your drinks; Henry will serve the meal which has been helped in the kitchen by Elsie and, as you are assured by the menu, "We put an extra fifteen per cent gratuity on the bill for mutual convenience. Hope you take home a nice memory!"—and I have, often. If you come in here looking for problems, you can probably find some, but if you come in the spirit of relaxed island life that has kept Barbara McConnell in business for the past 20 years, you'll enjoy her concoctions and conversation.

Although McConnell's is the place to go when you're having only one meal in Frederiksted, other places to try with a more leisurely schedule are **Swashbuckler** (at the shore end of Prince Phillips Passage, a shopping mall at the east end of town). Menu is hamburgers, salads, and sandwiches at the walk-in level, but if you go upstairs to the al fresco dining terrace with a shoreside view you can have steak, potato, and salad, as well as grilled fish, etc. in attractive surroundings.

Piazza, next door to the Frederiksted Hotel on the waterfront street (the Strand), took over the space previously occupied by the Persian Virgin. Smells of a piquant spaghetti sauce about 11:30 one morning drew me back for lunch, to find that listings are reasonable and selections, while not supreme, are certainly substantial. A Piazza Burger starts at about $3, with the special doused in blue cheese, chili, and sour cream at close to $4. Prices may change, but hopefully the place won't—much. I liked the lunchtime atmosphere that allowed me to pick up a paper at Rosie's, across the way at the Harbour Yard, as this complex is called, and read it while munching and marveling at the view of the sea and ship at the pier.

Belardos (up the blue stairs or at the corner of Bjerg-Gade and King St., leading to the waterfront), serves good native food, but is no place for your Lilly or your Yacht Club tie. The place is loved by locals, and very informal. If you like souse, calaloo, fungi, and other island food, plus some interesting island fish potions, give this a try.

If you're planning a picnic for the beach, or have put your belongings into one of the apartment or cottage setups in the Frederiksted area, find **La Croisée,** just off King Street not far from the Custom House Road. This small place, with a couple of counters where you can munch on the spot, serves special sandwiches, with the superior selection (in my opinion) the sandwiches on black bread that tasted like it had been basted with honey. Unbelievable combinations emerge as fillers, with my Vegetarian II selection including an option for bananas instead of avocados with cheddar, Swiss, cream, and American cheese plus lettuce, tomato, sweet pepper, hot pepper, and cucumber. Total cost for a "small" sandwich, which is a full meal, was $1.75, but prices were rising while I lingered.

The **Strand's** courtyard, at the corner of Hill Street (officially called Bjerg Gade), is a traditional gathering spot, but those in the know head upstairs for the Szechuan specials at the Chinese restaurant.

Heading west from town, **Sprat Hall's Beach Club** offers the chance for a swim, a good beach, and filling but certainly not gourmet food at lunchtime. Specialties were grilled fish (a hearty hunk of some big catch), salads, and a watery conch chowder on a recent visit. Bathing suit with cover-up is acceptable lunchtime dress.

■■

PLACES WORTH FINDING: If you have an interest in the Danish history of the Virgin Islands, track down a copy of *Three Towns,* subtitled *Conservation and Renewal of Charlotte Amalie, Christiansted, and Frederiksted of the U.S. Virgin Islands.* During the early 1960s a team from the Royal Danish Academy of Fine Arts in Copenhagen came to the Virgin Islands, following a visit by 2 of its members, to document the early history and town plans in hopes that present development would be carried out with some thought and concern for the original intentions of the Danish architects. The Rockefeller Foundation made a sizable contribution to the study, as did a number of Danish and other American interests. The National Park Service has copies of the study on file if you are unable to find one to purchase. Most of the on-the-spot research was conducted by a team of 25 teachers and promising young Danish architects who spent 2 months in the islands, beginning in May 1961. Subsequent shorter visits completed the survey, which was published in 1964.

CHRISTIANSTED was established "on November 16, 1733 [when] the Directors of the Danish West India and Guinea Company sent instructions for the colonization of the newly purchased island of St. Croix [from the French] to Frederick Moth, who was to be the island's first governor. Moth was ordered to choose a suitable location for a fort and a town, which was to be called Christiansted [in honor of King Christian VI]. The town site was to be subdivided into regular building lots and the lots were to be sold with the stipulation that buyers were to build on their lots within five years from the date of purchase.

"Moth explored the island between June 20–24, 1734, and chose the site of a former French village on the north-central shore of St. Croix as the site for Christiansted. Moth described the area as large enough to contain a town the size of Copenhagen and promised that Christiansted would be well laid out with streets as straight as those in Christiania, now Oslo, Norway. He also proposed that the best buildings should be built in the immediate vicinity of the fort, while the poorer class of buildings was to be located on the outskirts of town." It's easy to see that plan today, as you wander from the fort area, west on King Street to St. John's Episcopal Church. The report goes on to comment that the town had only 20 residents by 1742, probably "due to the fact that prices for building lots in town were considered relatively high in comparison with prices for plantations." By 1800 the town had 5284 inhabitants, which was close to its high point of 5806 in 1835, after which time the population declined, to rise again to the 5000 figure in the resurgence of the 1960s. Today there must be close to 6000 people packed into Christiansted, and many more when the tourism tide is running full. Spared the 19th-century fires that leveled Charlotte Amalie on St. Thomas, and Frederiksted on the northwest shore of St. Croix, Christiansted stands today almost as it looked in the late 1700s. The core of buildings around the fort are part of a National Park Service tract.

A̲UTHOR'S OBSERVATION: The National Park Service map folder does tell you that "the historic area has uneven walkways and stairs. Use caution." But it does not alert you to the fact that the ballast brick walks that you follow, under arcades and in open areas, are littered with cigarette butts and flip-top rings. It would seem to me that a good school project would be to pick up the litter on one of the rambles around the national park site.

On the waterfront in Christiansted, at the **Scalehouse,** is the local office for the Virgin Islands Department of Tourism. Staff ranges from helpful to lounging while they talk with friends, but even if no one says a word, there's a lot of printed information to pick up. If you persevere, the staff on duty can usually provide details. When in doubt, ask for "Walking Tour Guide," a blue and white folder that tells you most of what you need to know; *This Week in St. Croix,* the green sheet which is nowhere near as complete and fact-filled (or topical and accurate) as the St. Thomas yellow sheet, but is better than nothing (and free); plus whatever other information leaflets you can find. With these, you can find most of the worthwhile sights in Christiansted on your own. (The Scalehouse, by the way, was the Customs House. The present building was constructed between 1855 and 1856 on the site of a former wooden house. It was completely restored (on the outside) and refurbished (on the inside) in early 1978. The scales on which imports were weighed for taxes still stand in the entryway.)

Fort Christiansvaern (National Park Service headquarters, M-Sat 8–4:30; guided tours start here at regular intervals), big, brick-red, and basking in the Caribbean sun, is impossible to miss. It was built of ballast bricks in the 18th century, with some additions (and the first of its countless coats of red paint) in the 19th. There's not much inside in the way of furnishings, but there are tales to be told about the battles waged from its parapets, where you can now stand to look out over the hotel on the Cay and the boats as they set sail for Buck Island or return at sunset.

The Danish Customs House, most elegantly Danish building on the waterfront, was the public library until books, use, and U.S. government funds made the new Florence Williams Public Library on King Street possible. Part of the first floor dates from 1751, but the rest of the building dates from the early 19th-century prosperity. Photographic displays join art for decor in upstairs rooms; the Park Service doles out information at the street-level entrance.

The Steeple building (museum open M–F 9–4, Sat 9–12; free) got a complete going-over in the mid-1960s. It stands as tall now as it did when it was erected as the first Lutheran Church in 1753— well, not quite as tall. The steeple that gives it its present name was added, for the first time, in 1794. The building began falling into disrepair when the town (and island) financial base dissolved with the liberation of the slaves—and the problem with working the sugar plantations—in the 1840s. After years as a bakery, a storage area, and a building to be used for whatever need was next, the former church was a shambles. Providing the launching pad for your historical appreciation of St. Croix and the U.S. Virgin Islands became its purpose after complete renovation in 1964 (Fred Gjessing, architect; Herbert Olsen, historian). You can breeze through 3 centuries in less than 20 minutes, so simplistic are the billboards on which the National Park Service chooses to tell the tales. Pictures, costumed mannequins, and wall cabinets with a few relics make up the entire exhibition. Note the polished ballast brick underfoot— and if you come in after a rain, walk *carefully;* the footing can be perilous. Among the exhibits: Indians of St. Croix 1000 years ago; the King's Life Guard, testimony to 184 years of rule by Denmark, which you can see on the map, is 3500 miles away. The Danish West India and Guinea Company was granted the Royal Charter in 1671, at the time when there was a united Denmark and Norway. In one cabinet, I noted that "an 1853 customs record at Elsinore Castle shows that there was trade with the West Indies." Elsewhere you can note that "about 100 people from Denmark and Norway went to St. Thomas in 1672." In 1733, the Danes purchased St. Croix from France and the first colonists arrived on September 1, 1734. The Danish West Indies government divided St. Croix into 150-acre plantations and sold them, mostly to English settlers who came here from nearby islands. A map of 1754 shows the island with what looks like a piece of graph paper superimposed; that's how straight the early boundaries were between plantations that still carry names like Anna's Hope, Hannah's Rest, Wheel of Fortune, Two Williams, Judith's Fancy, Betsey's Jewel.

Government House (government offices; reception hall) is 2 private homes joined together sometime in the early 1830s. The most impressive part of the present Government House, the building facing King Street, is also the oldest. John William Schopen's home, built in 1747, was purchased by the Danish government in 1771 as a suitable Governor's residence. By the end of that century, the island's prosperity and the demands of the government required more space. Planter-merchant Adam Søbøtker's dwelling at the corner of King Street and Queen's Cross Street was acquired in 1828 by Governor-General Peter von Scholten, the man who freed the slaves. The connecting link was built a few years later, as is obvious when you stand in the ill-kept garden area in the center of the U-shape of the present Government House complex. The most interesting (and most photographed) part of Government House is the welcoming staircase that leads up to the reception hall after you walk through the iron gates at King Street. The hall is used regularly for government functions, but visitors are allowed in at other times to look at the mirrors and chandeliers given in 1966 by the Danish government to replace the originals—which were returned to Denmark at the time of the transfer (1917). Although the jigs and quadrilles popular in the Danish days no longer provide the focus for a gala evening, there's plenty to recommend peeking in the windows if you are not invited to some government function. This room is spectacular when the lights are lit and reflected in the mirrors, with the festive folk attending.

AUTHOR'S OBSERVATION: Alexander Hamilton, who clerked in a Christiansted hardware store when he came up from his birthplace, Nevis, is claimed as a local boy made good. The fact is that Hamilton's hardware store is only a name and a plot of ground. The new and commercial building that stands on the site was rebuilt after a fire in the early 1960s and bears no resemblance to the store that Hamilton knew. Noting his presence here in boyhood years is about as much as any local historian can claim.

Florence Williams Library is big, boxy, modern, air-conditioned, and to my eye, very out of place in Colonial Christiansted. References made to the "Old Danish School" refer to a building that had stood since the 1800s, the home of a merchant who fell on hard times. The house was sold at auction on July 3, 1846, to the Royal Danish Treasury for Funds and Education. Modern "progress" tore the old and interesting building down in 1972 so the bigger-and-better library could be built. I mention today's building only for the historic volumes it holds (which you have to make special inquiry to find), and certainly not for the way it looks. The only old part of this building is the ballast bricks from the former structure; they were reused for the present library.

Buck Island Reef is a National Monument, "administered by the National Park Service, U.S. Department of the Interior," as one of their "hard duty" positions, I suppose. For most of us, the reef is a spectacular day excursion out of Christiansted, or Buccaneer Hotel or Grapetree Hotels if you are staying there. A fleet of boats sets out from Christiansted daily for Buck Island. The *Reef Queen,* a glass-bottom excursion boat that makes ½ day journeys, is the only boat that makes a pass over the Scotch bank, a coral forest. There are a couple of catamarans, big enough to sail flat enough so that you hardly know you're sailing, and several small and lively boats that give you a good sail on the day-long excursions. (To provision for the full-day tours, make a stop at the Strand Delicatessen, near Club Comanche, to pick up your deli sandwich lunch; beverages are usually sold by the boat skipper.)

Buck Island is for neophytes and for underwater experts. Your personal prowess will make the decision about whether you tag along on a guided tour, flipper-to-flipper throughout the marked trail, or whether you and a pal head to the deep areas away from the commercial, relatively shallow marked trail. In all cases, strict National Park Service preservation rules apply: no plucking, picking, or pinching of fish, coral, or anything else you find.

West Indies Laboratory, a branch of New Jersey's Fairleigh Dickinson University, has made great strides since it was established on a wedge of land at Teague Bay on the north shore, east of Christiansted, in 1971. Dedicated to the study of marine life, flora, fauna, and ecology of the Virgin Islands in particular, and the West Indies in general, the laboratory is justifiably proud of its Hydrolab. The habitat is at Salt River, not far from where Columbus is said to have landed on his second voyage to the West Indies in 1493, when he sighted and named the Virgin Islands for St. Ursula and her 11,000 martyred Virgins. Scientists can live on the sea floor for up to 7 days, studying the underwater life. The 12 buildings on the 8-acre campus at Teague Bay include laboratories, a compact library for student research, dormitories, cafeteria, and a small pool.

The floating dock at Teague Bay Reef is one of WIL's schoolrooms and is one of the reasons the catalog suggests that you matriculate with some scuba experience. (If you don't, they will arrange for courses at an additional fee.) In addition to formal courses for credit, offered in spring, summer, fall, and January sessions, there are seminars and field trips to which outsiders are invited, depending on space available. If you are interested in knowing more about your surroundings from the professionals, write in advance to West Indies Laboratory (P.O. Annex Box 4010, Christiansted, St. Croix, VI 00820). If you want to check for last-minute lectures, etc., when you arrive on the island, call 773-3339, or drive out to Teague Bay, about 10 minutes east of Christiansted.

St. Croix Marine Station, at Estate Rust Op Twist on the north coast, is an island base for the University of Texas Marine Science Institute. The station operates in conjunction with the Port Arkansas Marine Laboratory. If you're interested in courses and projects underway at this lab, write to the St. Croix Marine Station.

Whim Greathouse (on Centerline Road, 2 miles E of Frederiksted; winter daily 10–5; summer Tu–Sat 10–5, Sun 2–5; $1.50 adult, children under 12 free; small shop on premises). A marvel, if you know what this place looked like when a group of concerned citizens took an interest in it in the early 1960s. Under the aegis of Walter and Florence Lewisohn, part-time Cruzan residents with a full-time interest in preservation of the island's history, the St. Croix Landmarks Society got more than itself off the ground. Whim Greathouse restoration was the prime focus for the first years of the society, and all fund-raising, including that from sale of Florence Lewisohn's books and booklets (*The Romantic History of St. Croix* is one) and from the annual House Tours, was dedicated to furnishing the Greathouse and reviving the plantation buildings. You step into another century when you step out of your car for a tour of the house, small museum, working sugar mill, and grounds. The sketchy history of the man named Christopher MacEvoy gets embellished with each recounting. The presumed facts are these: MacEvoy built the house about 1794; the man was wealthy enough to move to England in 1811, to buy a refinery and castle in Denmark, and to return occasionally to St. Croix where legends about him and his assumed bachelorhood are prevalent. The 18th-century house is furnished with antiques from the period, many of them from Cruzan homes—some made on the island, copied from popular European styles of the era, and others imported to St. Croix from European centers. The building, with its 3-foot-thick walls, might have been intended as the core of a bigger estate house, but the fact is that MacEvoy lived in what we can see—complete with a moat around its perimeter. Delores was my guide for one tour of the property. She is a Cruzan teenager, one of 3 daughters of a family who lives on the estate. Although she goes to school in Frederiksted she was my teacher for some of the lore: about the Exportware that fills cabinets in the first room (it came on the trading ships), about the 1830s sugarcane prints (they are from Antigua, where the process was different from that of St. Croix, but are interesting nevertheless), about the table setting in the dining room (Bing & Grøndahl from Denmark), the rum in St. Croix today (molasses comes from Puerto Rico because cane is no longer cultivated on St. Croix), about the bedroom, with its mirrors, mahogany bed, wood floors and open windows (the bed was Mrs. Limpricht's and she was the wife of a Danish Governor; the planter's chair is a modern reproduction; and the room reminded me of Room 5 at Sprat Hall up the coast past Frederiksted), and about the items in one of the corner cabinets—especially the Queen Margarethe cup. Margarethe (1347–1412) was Queen of the united Norway, Sweden, and Denmark. The cup has 8 sides, one for each of the queen's ladies and one for herself. There's a print of Danish Prince Valdemar's arrival on St. Croix in the late 1800s, and a print of Bernstorf, an estate in Denmark that looks like Whim. The museum's few open and airy rooms are filled with treasures and with memories of plantation life now gone.

Because there was no working mill in the U.S. islands, Walter Lewisohn and others involved in the Landmarks Society at the time trekked through the Caribbean in search of a representative one. A mill with sails was found in Nevis, transported block by numbered block to Whim Estate, and reconstructed on the grounds to show what the 115-plus mills that were on St. Croix in the sugar king days looked like.

The plantation museum shows the step-by-step process for sugar cane to rum, with appropriate caldrons, wheels, and a pot-still punctuating the illustrations that make the whole process very clear.

For an interesting island entertainment, check to see when art shows, concerts, and receptions will be held here. All are welcome to attend. Open House Tours are held in February and March, providing an opportunity to see several exceptional island homes, some restored mills and plantation houses, others new and built to make the most of spectacular views and plantings. Tickets cost close to $10 per person ($8 in 1978), with transportation included. If you want to drive your rental car and take 3 passengers, you can tour free. Starting point is either Whim Greathouse or the Island Center. If you're driving, you have to be at the starting point to get your "sticker of the day and the essential directions." The St. Croix Landmarks Society has open membership (regular $15, contributing $25, sustaining $100 and up). For details, contact the Society by mail (Box 242, Christiansted, St. Croix, VI 00820).

St. George Village Botanical Garden (Box 338, Frederiksted; on St. George Estate; open 7:30 to 3:30, free admission; memberships available for individuals $10, associate $25, junior—under 18—$2; inquire about others). On the day when you rent a car, head for these gardens. The minute you turn right off Centerline Road, about 11 miles from Christiansted (or left about 4 miles from Frederiksted) and head through the stone gates, down a channel marked by royal palms, you have a glimpse of just how rich the flora of this island can be. The surroundings are the perfect setting for occasional Sunday concerts (inquire about dates when you arrive on the island, or write ahead if it makes that much difference to you). Given to the Botanical Garden, Inc., in 1972, the estate is complete with meandering stream, great-house ruins, and a historic garden that includes cassava, corn, and sweet potatoes known to the earliest Arawak settlers as well as representative contributions made by later English, Dutch, French, Spanish, and Danish settlers. Bicentennial Memorial Trees are some of the newest plantings, but there's always room for more on this estate, tended mostly by volunteers. I guarantee that a few hours here will give you an entirely different impression of this rural island where approach to the town of Christiansted was through an avenue of stately royal palms as recently as 15 years ago. (In 1977 a furor was created when road-widening activities mowed down too many of the few remaining royal palms. Some survived, but today's emphasis seems to be more on speed than on saving.)

FREDERIKSTED, according to the Danish survey *Three Towns*, follows a plan submitted by Surveyor Jens M. Beck, who had also been involved in the Christiansted plans. His plans for this west-end town, which the Danish West India and Guinea Company ordered established on October 19, 1751, to be named in honor of

Danish King Frederik V, had "two symmetrical parts separated by a lagoon and a proposed fort." Although customs duties were remitted to builders who established in Frederiksted, and work was started on the fort and warehouse that were supposed to make the location more appealing, there were only 2 houses in Frederiksted by 1755. Many of the buildings that had been built by the 1860s (when the population numbered about 3000) were washed away in the tidal wave of 1867 or wiped out by flames on October 1 and 2, 1878, when labor riots resulted in conflagrations that completely consumed many of the wood buildings. Frederiksted has never been the thriving commercial center that its sister-town to the northeast has been, although this town holds the favored harbor. Even today, when the deepwater pier juts into the sea off Frederiksted's waterfront, most of the cruise passengers that do land here head to Christiansted, in buses supplied by the local tour companies. There's almost a conspiracy to keep Frederiksted for the purists and send tourists "away."

Victorian Frederiksted was built after the labor riots, and unless someone gets some local zoning into firm effect fast, many of the enchanting wood-fretwork buildings will be demolished or "refurbished" beyond recognition by an unimaginative Public Works department. That government department has already done its architectural damage to the fort area, where a prominent, modern, and—to my eye—ugly resting pavilion has been erected. Presumably, it is for cruise ship passengers, who have plodded along a hot cement pier to reach the town park. The only redeeming factor is that when you sit at this "pavilion," you can't see it.

Fort Frederik is to look at from the outside. Construction was started in 1752, but enthusiastic if unskilled restorations have all but covered the original attributes—except for the shape. The most recent sprucing up was bicentennial inspired, in 1976. Because this port was Danish in 1776, claims are made (but not supported as strongly as those of Sint Eustatius) that the first foreign salute to a fledgling U.S. flag was made here on St. Croix. The story is that an American brigantine was in this port for supplies at the time independence was declared. A hastily hand-sewn flag was hoisted when the British flag was hauled down, and the local population responded with cheers. This fort claims to be the location at which Governor-General Peter von Scholten read his "freedom for the slaves" proclamation on July 3, 1848.

Victoria House is far more interesting to look at than the fort. It is on Strand Street between Market and King streets, is privately owned, and is a remarkable example of just how elaborate Victorian fretwork could become. Some of the original house dates from 1803, but most was burned in the riots of 1878, so that what you see is "pure" Cruzan Victoriana.

Walking the streets of Frederiksted is the best way to see the town, pausing to note some of the remarkable wood buildings and blinking to overlook too many modern, commercial boxes that threaten to destroy the one thing this town has going for it. One of the worst examples of modern trends, in my opinion, is the Kentucky Fried depot that has painted an old arcaded walkway with the ubiquitous red and white stripes. Fortunately, it is on King Street, so it's not the first sight you see.

OFF-ISLAND OPTIONS for places worth finding include St. Thomas, an easy day excursion on Antilles Air Boats, lifting out of Christiansted harbor on a morning flight, and rumbling up the ramp from the seas in Charlotte Amalie harbor about 25 minutes later, or an AAB day excursion to Tortola, to take off for a land tour or a quick zip by boat to one of the other, smaller British Virgins. The list is endless, and if you're timid about putting the pieces together yourself, search out *Southerland Tours* near Cafe de Paris, or *V.I.P. Tours* at the Pan Am Pavilion (still so called although Pan Am doesn't fly here anymore), off the Strand. Both are near Club Comanche.

■■

SPORTS ON ST. CROIX: The surrounding seas provide the playground for most of the Cruzan sports. A stroll along the boardwalk of Christiansted yields a dozen or more alternatives for heading out on and under the Caribbean. **Sailing** is usually by the day, with Buck Island the goal. Boats are skippered and varied; whatever sails into port usually goes out on charter. The choices include a 40-foot catamaran (Check at King Christian hotel.), a 32-foot West Indian sloop named *North Star,* a 35-foot Sparkman & Stevens fiberglass sloop called *Titania,* all towing glass-bottom skiffs so nonswimmers can bob over the reefs; *Capt. Teddy Clarke's Charters* aboard the 31-foot Seafarer's sloop *Juliet* or the 36-foot trimaran *Viti Viti.* (Check the office in Pan Am Pavilion.) Jim Butterworth is local man for the branch of *Annapolis Sailing School* that operates in Christiansted. Contact him c/o Annapolis Sailing School, Pan Am Pavilion, Christiansted, St. Croix, USVI 00820, if you want information in advance. Week-long programs are offered at winter and summer rates; lessons are aboard Rhodes 19s.

Caribbean Sea Adventures has survived the vagaries of several seasons and is a one-stop source for most watersports. The firm has concessions at Buccaneer and at Grapetree as well as its waterfront office. Half-day sailing to Buck Island ranges from $20 to $30 depending on the boat and which half of the day you choose. They also arrange sport fishing, scuba lessons, and windsurfing.

Sport Fishing days ($350 full and $225 half) are a feature of *Caribbean Sea Adventures,* but also look into the sport fishing offered through boats that moor at the waterfront.

> **A**UTHOR'S OBSERVATIONS: Names and numbers change. Although the firms I've mentioned have been in business for long enough to earn a solid reputation (and to print folders that have held up for a season or 2), you'll find out about other offerings on the spot. Allow a day for researching to find the deal that's best for you. Wander along the wharf and talk to the boating people. There's a great variety in boats and skippers; prices are controlled by the National Park Service so should be standard.

Scuba got a slow start on St. Croix, considering the wealth to be found in some of the underwater areas and the fact that Buck Island has been touted as a snorkel spot for several years, but it's in full swing now. Full equipment—and plenty of it—is available in Christiansted. Shops on Strand Street and along the Christiansted waterfront sell and rent equipment and have full facilities for servicing tanks. *Caribbean Sea Adventures* works with Buccaneer and Grapetree, week-long scuba holidays (and some for 4 nights). *Pressure Ltd.* works with Anchor Inn (with a 3 hour Resort Diving course with pool beginning and dive ending, for $35 per person). In Frederiksted, *Above and Below,* on the waterfront, handles scuba. If you're proficient, ask any one of the firms for a guide for the Cane Bay or Salt River drop-offs. Other favorite spots for local scuba enthusiasts are out of Davis Bay, near the golf course, and at Hamm's Bluff on the north shore.

Several hotels have special scuba package holidays, usually in summer. Among those to investigate are Cane Bay Reef Club, Buccaneer Hotel, St. Croix-by-the-Sea, Hotel on the Cay, King Christian, Anchor Inn, and Grapetree Beach in the Christiansted area, and Sprat Hall, for anything to do with water sports out of Frederiksted.

Golf gets gold stars on St. Croix, where *Fountain Valley* offers

one of the best courses in the Caribbean. The course was laid out by
Robert Trent Jones almost 10 years ago, to be part of what was then
planned to be an extensive Rockefeller resort, part of the Caneel
Bay, Little Dix, and at that time also Dorado Beach Rockresort family. The Good Hope venture never materialized, but the course
did—and it's a favorite drawing card for anyone with a golfing interest and some ability. The course is in good shape. Pro and pro shop
are on premises, with golf carts and full equipment for rent (expensive). Cane Bay Plantation is the closest hotel to the course.
Check for special golf packages.

Host hotels can make arrangements for play at Fountain Valley,
but duffers and those who like to stroll around for a leisurely swing
or two will be content with the 18 holes at Buccaneer Hotel (pro
and shop, plus carts; lessons offered). The Reefs also has a few
holes for resident guests, but there's nothing spectacular about this
course.

Tennis is taking over. Every patch that's big enough for a court or
2 is being plastered with one. The best bases for tennis enthusiasts
(and places worth inquiring about special tennis weeks, especially
in spring, summer, and fall) are the Buccaneer Beach Hotel, where
courts are lighted for night play; St. Croix-by-the-Sea, Gentle
Winds, Grapetree Beach Hotels (each of the 2 "wings" has a couple of courts) and Hotel on the Cay, with the course nearest to
Christiansted. Guests in downtown hotels can take the 5-minute
boat ride for $1 dollar round trip and pay extra for court time.

The *Caribbean Tennis Club* is a place to pick up a game with
some of the island players. There are clinics, tournaments, and
special lessons. Check with the pro shop, usually open 8:30–12,
4–8:30 during winter months, and approximately those hours in
slightly slower summer. Guests are invited to participate. Reservations must be made at the pro shop for play. Courts are night-
lighted until 8:30. If you want some information in advance, write
to the Caribbean Tennis Club (Box 3844, Christiansted, St. Croix,
VI 00820). The Club is located in the hills, near Queste Verde, just
outside Christiansted (the Breeze Inn can be a congenial place for
a Saturday night drink, with backgammon, chess, cards, and perhaps a band).

Horseback riding happens to be the love (and living) of Jill Hurd,
who grew up at Frederiksted in the homestead (Sprat Hall) near
the corral. She knows her trails and her horses well. An afternoon
riding from *Jill's Equestrian Stable,* on the grounds of the family
estate and in the neighboring countryside will be time well spent. A

punch ride will run about $20 per person, through the rain forest and around old sugar mill ruins; Mt. Victory is a little longer (and a little more than $20) when you include Rose Hill, but if you just want to go as far as Mt. Victory and back, it is $20. Beginners should check on the lessons before heading out on the trails; jumpers can also take lessons. Check with Jill when you arrive on St. Croix (phone 772-2880) to find a good time for your riding and to learn about any price changes or write in advance to Box 695, Frederiksted, St. Croix, USVI 00840.

■■

TREASURES AND TRIFLES ON ST. CROIX: Shopping is centered on small shops. Offerings are original, handcrafted in many cases, and usually worth the reasonable price tags. The only problem with writing about small shops now operating is that I'm not sure how many of the craftsmen will be around for more than a season or 2. Many of the people working in and supplying the boutiques that fill the nooks and crannies of downtown Christiansted are the college-age kids of the '60s who have flown south to set up shop. The town is turning into a modern Nantucket.

AUTHOR'S OBSERVATION: Remember: in the United States Virgin Islands you can purchase up to $600 duty free, plus one gallon of liquor per person. Items made in the Virgin Islands can be brought back to the states in any amount; they are not dutiable.

When you walk along King Street, the main (and one-way) road through town, be sure to look in "every" open doorway; some of them lead into alleys-turned-shopping arcade where you'll find several boutiques, each with its own speciality. Before diverting off the main road, however, search out these special spots: **Heritage House** where you'll find top quality jewelry, pewter, and other well-chosen items, neighboring **El Gaucho,** with an intriguing selection of South American handwork including sweaters from Uruguay that look hot in this climate but will set fashion pace for cold northern winters, colorful butterfly pictures nicely framed, and small handcrafts that are noteworthy (and easy to pack), and Barbara Kiendl's **Needlecraft,** with island themes painted on canvas and sold as kits with colorful threads. (Barbara lives on St. Thomas, where her shop is in the Royal Dane Mall.) Look for Lisa's leathercraft, at the back of El Gaucho's shop. She makes sandals, some that don't require several fittings, and an interesting writing packet that sells for $35 and up.

Around the corner, on King's Cross Street (Kongens Tvergade in Danish), **Jelthrup's** bookstore has a complete selection of bestsellers, and an interesting collection of books about the West Indies, including some cookbooks. Across the road from Jelthrup's, the **Linen Cupboard** is geared for island residents, but the elegant embroidered linens from Portugal's Madeira island are well worth considering for someone special at home. (Placemats pack flat and the selection is spectacular.)

Nancee's Leather Awl, on Company Street has readymade canvas bags (all sizes) and a lot of excellent leatherwork—sandals made to order if you will come back for several fittings, belts, bags, and vests at good prices. (There's another **Sandal Shop,** across from the Eccentric Egret, next to Franks, through the doors of Island Optique and up the stairs.)

The **Jeans Shop** also on Company Street, sells jeans (of course) and denim everything, plus some shirts at good prices, and **Classic Imports** holds a cache of elegant jewelry and Italian leather bags.

Clothes come in all shapes, sizes, colors, and prices. For consistently good quality, variety, and a staff that is willing to please and has fabric by the yard to make something of it, head straight for **Nini's of Scandinavia** (across from the downtown Post Office on Church St., at the corner of Company). This place carries Scandinavian fabrics (Marimekko by the yard) and jewelry, at high but not unreasonable prices. If you catch one of the sales (which I have found in June and January) you can pick up some REAL bargains.

Cavanagh's Butik and the **Compass Rose** are the old standbys that have been bypassed with the modern trends. You may find some old standards (sweaters, Thai silks, bright-colored straitlaced dresses), but not much that's new and swinging.

Patelli Imports (in King's Alley) has colorful, comfortable Mexican imports, sometimes on sale at good value but never *that* expensive. For batik sarongs you'll see most of Christiansted wearing, when they work in restaurants or head to the sea, try **Java Wraps** (on Queen Cross St., next to Franks).

For the children, head straight for **Land of Oz** (in King's Alley Arcade), where you'll find a floor-to-ceiling selection of games, wari boards (for that originally African bead game played in the West Indies), cars, boats, and something to please any child.

Pan Am Pavilion, one of those shop-fringed courtyards, runs between the Strand and the sea. It would be easy to spend a day here, darting from side to side. **Spanish Main,** one of the first stores in St. Thomas years ago, has a small shop with special island-printed fabric made up in summer clothes and for sale by the yard; **Cruzan Carib** next door also has summer fashions (sunback dresses and shirts) made in the Virgins; **Island Style** has belts, shirts, Bain de Soleil tanning creams, and "stubby shorts" that are the fashion here. **Happiness Is**—a little bit of everything, most of it interesting and island-oriented if not island made. Cactus, conch shells, canvas bags, Bay Rum, steel drums—you name it, and Happiness Is has it. **Many Hands** has Cruzanmade items, including seashell wind chimes, clever painted stone faces as a "family tree," stuffed dolls and toys, paintings, food (including rum balls), and other products that are locally made (and therefore not dutiable). **Steele's Smokes & Sweets** sells pipes and tobacco but has a sign in its doorway that says "chocolates are sensitive to smoke." Please do not smoke in deference to its selection of Godiva, Krums, and Blums chocolates. **Pemberton Shoes** is the place to replace your sandals or to pick up another pair of shoes, and **Rosa's Fancy** sells needlepoint kits (but not the quality of the Needlecraft kits at El Gaucho). **Pig's Ear** is a place to sip something, cook, or have a snack, and a plethora of boat services—**Teddy's Charter Service, Annapolis Sailing School, Buck Island Tours, V.I.P. Tours**—plus **Nancy's Cycle Shop** (for moped and bicycle rental) offer the link to sea or sightseeing.

Heading out from town, Antiguan **Conrad** has his shop just after you turn off the old road to Frederiksted (the road you take to weave to north shore inns). Ceramics is the specialty; courses are offered if you have the time to take one; and it seems to me that quality of items has suffered some from standardization. If you didn't know the original products, some of what's available today may seem worth the price.

Whim Greathouse Gift Shop (at the Estate off Centerline Rd. near Frederiksted) has note cards, tote bags, door knockers, bags of raw sugar (locally known as Muscouada), pineapple-patterned porcelain, steel band records, and a fascinating collection of books and pamphlets about St. Croix and other islands. Ideal for one-stop quality shopping for a cause.

Frederiksted shops are scattered around several alleys. It's best to call ahead to be sure when places are open if you are going to make the 16-mile half-hour drive from Christiansted for something special. Prince Phillips Passage, at the east end of town, is where you'll find **Island Stuff.** The small shop has some of the most colorful, quality, original fashions I've seen on St. Croix. If you're clothes shopping and like bright colors craftily worked, this shop is almost enough reason to drive to Frederiksted. Resort wear (mostly skirts and long dresses for women) has handpainted island designs and can be done to order if you allow enough time.

Sint Eustatius

*S*int Eustatius Tourist Office, Oranjestad, Sint Eustatius, N.A.; Netherlands Antilles Windward Island Representative, 445 Park Ave., New York, NY 10022.

US $1 = NAf 1.77
Unless otherwise noted, all prices are in U.S. dollars.

"Good morning, Mistress," a young girl said. "Why you walking all by yourself?" I explained that I enjoyed it. "You like Statia?" "Yes, very much," was my enthusiastic reply, and after her "It's friendly," she continued her chatter with stories—encouraged by an occasional query on my part—about going to Nevis by boat and St. Kitts by plane, her sole excursions from Statia, but remarkable by comparison to many others who have never been off the "Golden Rock." The glorious and lavish era of the 1700s is hard to imagine as you wander the paths of Statia today.

The Dutch had built a dike, behind which the good life thrived. Admiral Rodney punched a hole in it, and after he plundered what he could, the French followed, intermittently with the Spanish, the Dutch, the English—and so on for 22 changes in rule, which returned eventually to the Dutch.

Although there was some rebuilding after the Rodney episode, commerce and its contributors moved elsewhere. From the 1830s on, when freedom of slaves made plantation life impractical and the importance as a transshipment port for a rebel nation had passed, so also passed Statia's golden era. The once bustling Oranjestad harbor at water's edge began its final decline. Even in the 1900s, the pillaging continued. Stones from former mansions were sold to neighboring Saba in the 1940s, when that island began building its miraculous serpentine roads. Further sales of whatever had a market elsewhere helped the continued destruction of the Lower Town.

As I sat in the sun on the low stone wall that casually and occasionally borders the main street into Oranjestad, local people passed by, all nodding and echoing my "Good Morning," in the best West Indian tradition. A teenage boy circled me, looking unabashedly as I scribbled in my notebook. Finally he sauntered up, perched on the wall next to me with a "You take stories?" "Yes," I replied, and we talked for a while. The blue beads hanging around his neck set him apart from others I had noted. Clearly he was a member of the new generation. No, he didn't have a regular job. He played with a local band some nights. "Not a big band, but big for here."

The catcalls from his pals in the small building in the field behind me put them into the conversation. "Is that a school?" I asked naively. "No." He smiled. "It's a sort of bar. It's where we sit when we have nothing to do." A fact that bothers his 80-year-old grandfather no end, he added.

And when we changed the subject to his grandfather, Mr. William Roosberg, my young friend said, "He tells stories. Would you like to talk to him?"

He pointed with obvious pride to the neat West Indian house across the street and left saying he would find out if it was convenient. In a few minutes he returned. Mr. William Roosberg it turned out, was at home.

I came from the brilliant Caribbean sunlight into the shuttered, cool West Indian cottage. Mr. Roosberg's love of flowers was immediately evident, not only in his garden, but also in his house. The wallpaper draped from the walls like the bougainvillea that brightened the fence outside. "It's been on for twenty years or so," he offered, when I noted how pretty it was. Mr. Roosberg is a gardener, by inclination and for pay. Although in his 80s, he still tends the property of a wealthy Canadian, in residence only a few months of the year.

Life has not been easy. He has worked long and hard, in the soil and the sea, to make a living for his family. His own home, with its memory-filled main room and corrugated tin-roofed kitchen where a teapot whistled, is warm and hospitable. And so is he.

Most of his legends, painstakingly handwritten, had been taken away sometime previous, to be recorded in the archives in Curaçao, he's been told. Six of his children live there. Three more live on Statia, with their children.

When I asked about his schooling, remarkable among the older generation on many West Indian islands, he told me that "my mother and father were poor, but I studied a little at night, a little here, a little there." He had learned a lot, but is not so sure about his grandson, who has "got more learning, but he just study to get in a motor car."

Pride in Statia is part of the island's spirit, even though the island seems the last on the list for economic favors doled out by the central government of the Netherlands Antilles based in Curaçao. About 2/3 of the 1600 Statians now living on the island are without regular employment. The school, reportedly, has no funds for notebooks—or regular books. And the local doctor takes barter for his services. Cash is in short supply, but friendly West Indian hospitality is not.

POLITICAL PICTURE is a dim one on this island. Although the local politics are very important to the residents, the fact that Statia, Saba, and Sint Maarten share just one delegate for the 22 member Staten that meets in Curaçao for the government of the Netherlands Antilles, means that Statians are usually last on the line for any financial attention. Special pleas have made some impression in recent years, but you'll still find the roads, electricity, and other infrastructure a little more rustic than on other islands—and a lot different from what you find on Sint Maarten, only 15 minutes' flight away.

CUSTOMS of Statia are those of the old-time Netherlands Antilles, for the few Statian families who have stayed "at home." (Most Statians have moved elsewhere in their wage-earning years to find jobs and send money home.) The handful of visitors who come here haven't made a big dent in the lifestyle, although on the days when the windjammer that anchors in the bay sends its folks ashore the streets of the small town that is Statia's capital are full of barefoot-and-boating types. A couple of stops per season are made by the smaller ships of the major cruise lines, and those are days to go climb the Quill, in my opinion.

MONEY MATTERS used to be conducted in blue beads in the earliest history. Now U.S. curency is the key. Any store, and certainly the handful of hotels, will happily accept your dollars, as many of them as they can legitimately pry from your wallet. The official currency is the Netherlands Antilles guilder or florin, noted as NAf and worth 1.77 to US$1.

■■■

ARRIVAL AT SINT EUSTATIUS's airport usually involves a Windward Islands Airways flight from Sint Maarten, unless you float onto the runway in a charter plane. This airstrip, unlike some of the neighboring ones, is on flat land, with plenty of space to stretch—when that seems worthwhile. At the moment, the small box of the airport, often filled with friends and relatives of Statians returning home, is more than adequate. Perfunctory immigration (since you are presumably coming from Sint Maarten where you've gone through the official clearance) includes a request to know when you are planning to leave. That's not an inhospitable gesture; often it's so that officials are sure there's a plane to carry you out when you think you have to leave. Check-in for your return flight is much more casual than on bigger islands, but you should be sure that a plane is scheduled when you think you are leaving. It's wise to look at the sky around plane arrival time. Sometimes flights arrive—and leave—early; you can still make the flight if you are in the town as long as you start for the airport when you spot your plane in the sky.

■■■

TOURING TIPS: The 10-minute taxi ride into town will deposit you at the heart of the matter, if you want to wander around on a day trip (or even if you're staying overnight). When you leave for the airport on return, allow an hour or so for a grand circle tour, and you'll have seen the highlights. By foot is the best way to get around, not only from Oranjestad down to shoreside (Mooshay Bay and Old Gin House), but also to climb "The Quill." If you're planning on being on the island for a while, renting a car for a day can prove interesting.

■■■

HOTELS ON STATIA are a trio of inns with prospect for more in the near future. All are small. The one that is the most "hotel-like," and that's a relative term, is on the windy coast. In addition to the 3 hotels, there are a few rooms in private homes and a couple of homes to rent in owner's absence, but do not count on anything fancy here. A room in a private home will probably not have private bath, and the bath that does exist may have sun-warmed water only. If you're heading to Statia for the first time, check into one of the inns, and look around to make your choice for next year.

✛ **Antillian View Hotel** (Oranjestad, Sint Eustatius, N.A.; 40 rooms) was scheduled to reopen when I passed by in April of 1981. Built a

few years ago, and discreetly closed, the white stucco building sits
on a slope on the outskirts of town. Always popular with the residents when it was open in its previous place, the hotel offers simply
furnished, motel-like rooms with modern conveniences that include balconies on some rooms. Coffee should be free (according to
my advance information) and breakfast is served at a sum in addition to your up-to-$40 for 2 rate; dinners here are expected to tally
to about $10. Check for status if you're considering a room here.

✤ **Golden Rock** (Box 157, Sint Eustatius, N.A.; 10 rooms) has a
name I find more imposing than its facilities. The several units that
line up on the slope of an east-coast hillside are open for sea breezes
that keep the rooms cool. But these breezes also cloud the louvered
windows with salt spray and otherwise show their effects. Purchased in 1976 by Don Lewis from New York, the Golden Rock was
lavished with a lot of money, but I regret to report that the atmosphere around the place when I stopped by bordered on "I don't
care." This place seems to need a soul, in my opinion, and perhaps
a congenial manager will be around when you visit. Those same
cooling trade winds make growing anything tall impossible on this
shore and, although you have a long stretch of gray-sand beach
within a short walk of the hotel you can also have splintering sand
when the winds pick up the surf. There's a pool (which needed
paint and cleaning when I looked), and food reports from guests
were depressing. Some of the day tourers who come over from Sint
Maarten swing by here on the way to the plane. (It is the closest
hotel to the airport and about 20 minutes' drive from town.) Bring
books (and bug repellent for nights when the wind drops), and
plan to rent a car or hire a taxi for at least one day of island exploring. Golden Rock rates are about $80 for 2 this winter, with 2 meals
daily included.

✤ **Mooshay Bay Publick House** (Lower Town, Sint Eustatius, N.A.;
14 rooms) makes its mark across the road from the seaside Old Gin
House. The stone walls of the old cotton gin hold the inn that
opened in late 1976. Old was preserved where it could be, patched
to permanence where it had to be, and copied where it seemed to
help the atmosphere. The result is museumlike, with a modern interior in the old style, except for baths, etc., which are (obviously)
modern in the new style. Delft and pewter recall the 18th-century
days (and Holland) and the appointments in the dining area are a
pleasure to look at while you wait for your meal to be served. Menu
here, as at the Old Gin House, is a marvel of creative ingenuity on

the part of the owners. Almost everything (except fish, langouste, and a few vegetables) has to be imported; you can count on finding your steak, but I prefer the fish. There's a small pool in what was the cistern, and all the facilities at the Old Gin House across the road at seaside. Although some guests prefer to be "separate but equal," most mingle with the visitors at the sister resort, which makes for a slightly larger, comfortable house-party atmosphere. No matter which place you call home, unless you are an owl by nature, or get hooked into a percolating backgammon game, bedtimes and wake-up times will be early. The choice is yours. You'll pay about $80 for a room for 2, meals extra (but you can figure about $7 for breakfast, from $3 to $12 depending on what you choose for lunch, and $22 for dinner).

✢ **The Old Gin House** (Lower Town, Sint Eustatius, N.A.; 8 rooms) stands at the shore, near the ruins of the old cotton gin which metamorphized into the neighbor hotel, Mooshay Bay. When John May and Marty Scofield decided that Statia had more to offer than the cold winters they had known in the northeastern U.S., they opened a small restaurant on the island. The few rooms came later, in response to guests who flew over from Sint Maarten for the day and wanted to stay. At this point, you have to make winter reservations as far in advance as you can make up your mind; the special spot they've perked into prominence at the shore where the old town of Oranjestad tumbled into the sea is very much in demand by their friends and a handful of others. Although the primary emphasis is on relaxing, there are a few things to do—things as strenuous as jogging along the silver beach that follows the shoreline a few steps off the terrace, or climbing the slope to Upper Town. Nightlife is as lively as the guests; dinner will be by candlelight, and your dinner music will be conversation to the accompaniment of the swish of the waves. Furnishings in the 8 rooms in the 2-story unit that faces the sea are exceptionally attractive, with island and stateside antiques, flowered fabrics, and mosquito netting to pull over you at night. Rates this winter will be in the $90s for 2, meals extra (at the same rates, with interchange privilege with the sister inn).

■■

HOUSEKEEPING HOLIDAYS are possible at **Fairplay Villas,** a cluster of modern stucco boxes with modern kitchen equipment and adequate, if simple, furnishings. There are plans (not yet realized) for a tennis court and swimming pool, but when I looked in there were only about a dozen units, each with separate apartments connected by a covered patio. Check with *N. C. Wathey, Bicen Development Corp., Box 18, Philipsburg, St. Maarten,* for details—and count on simple dining or stocking up at shops in Sint Maarten before you fly to Statia. There's not much in the local shops, although fish and lobster are usually in good supply.

■■■

PLACES WORTH FINDING ON STATIA: "The town consists of one street, a mile long, but very narrow and disagreeable, as everyone smokes tobacco and the whiffs are constantly blown in your face.

"But never did I meet with such variety; here was a merchant vending his goods in Dutch, another in French, a third in Spanish, etc., etc. They all wear the habit of their country and the diversity is really amusing . . . From one end of the town to the other is a continuous mart, where goods of the most different uses and qualities are displayed before the shop doors.

"Here hang rich embroideries, painted silks, flowered muslins, with all the manufacturers of the Indies. Next stall contains the most exquisite silver plate, the most beautiful indeed I ever saw. . . ."

Statia's Oranjestad? Yes. Today? Definitely not! The notes are those of an English lady of the 1700s, from her *Journal of a Lady of Quality.* You can find the journal in the small library in Oranjestad's Upper Town, if you can find the library when it's open, that is.

Today, the fort, churches, and a few shops are in Upper Town (also known as Oranjestad), some 300 feet (90 meters) up a sheer face from the sea, safely over the hill from boat-based marauders. Even with the utmost effort, your sightseeing will be limited to a saunter around Fort Oranje—now the seat of the local government and the heart of town gossip at mail time, which is midmorning at the Post Office, and a visit to the small museum that opened during U.S. Bicentennial celebrations.

The **Museum,** spurred into reality by tireless efforts of a Dutchman teaching in Statia, Jan Smid, and Statian-born tourism official Jim Maduro contains mostly Victoriana—an old sewing machine, broken eyeglasses, and bits of memorabilia from homes in Statia. Around the walls are impressive photos of Statian historic ruins, taken by Smid and worthy of greater exposure.

If you are interested in archaeology and early Caribbean history check with the local Tourist Office about any interesting digs that may be underway during the time of your visit. Some relics dated to A.D. 300 have been unearthed in the midsection of the island, and, although too much material was tragically bulldozed into the sea to make way for the pier, there are probably many more early items to be unearthed. The rich history of this island, where society thrived in the 18th century, may lie under its surface.

■■■

SPORTS ON STATIA are limited, but you can look for some changes that will be as dramatic as the *Happy Hooker Watersport* Center, operated by Tony Durby, formerly with Aquaventure in Bonaire, and a resident here since early '78. He has **diving tours** with full gear and also rents Sunfish **sailboats** and makes arrangements for **deep-sea fishing** from his quarters near the Old Gin House.

You can **snorkel** among the ruins of the Lower Town; the parts that have slid into the sea can be clearly noted from the fort ramparts on a day when the sea is calm. Then there's the experience of **climbing** Mount Mazinga and of going down into "The Quill," which is the core of the dormant volcano. This is the high point of the island, rich with verdant growth and an impressive herd of land crabs that are hunted at night by flashlight and end up on table, in stews and other local dishes.

Beaches can give you Atlantic surf, or Caribbean calm—and plenty of silver-gray, "black" sand where yours will be the the only footprints. You'll share the roads with Statians and their donkeys, the local transportation for most people.

Don't count on golf, but tennis courts may be part of the plan for this season.

■■■

TREASURES AND TRIFLES ON STATIA are limited. The blue beads discovered a few years ago are hard to find today, but if you take the time to find Jan Smid or some of the local folk interested in historic digs, you may share with them the glee of finding *real* treasure. The rubble of the town blasted into the sea has still not been sifted as it should be, and someone on the spot might be able to send you to some areas where other settlements are known to have existed.

There is a handful of small shops in Oranjestad but not much for visitors to buy. The friendly Statians are natural salesmen—smiling, pleasant, talkative, and neat. But even without all those qualities, **Mazinga's** small shop would probably be sold out of Bicentennial shirts by the time you get here. They were printed for 1976, and ought to be printed again. For other souvenirs, consider some Statia sand, or pieces of rock, or some blue beads—uncovered a couple of years ago in a seaside cache and reported to be, perhaps, the kind of beads used to buy Manhattan from the Indians. You can join the Historic Foundation, a continuing organization, for $60 as a Life Member, $7 for a one-year membership.

St. John

St. John Visitor's Bureau Information Center, Box 200, St. John, VI 00830; Virgin Islands Government Tourist Office, 1270 Avenue of the Americas, New York, NY 10020; 343 S. Dearborn St., Suite 1108, Chicago, IL 60604; 3450 Wilshire Blvd., Los Angeles, CA 90010; Suite 904, 100 N. Biscayne Blvd., Miami, FL 33132; 1050 17th Street, N.W., Washington, DC 20036.

US currency used.

Sea splashes from the bow of the boat that cuts the channel to St. John, but the shower, if you choose to stand in it, lasts less than half an hour. It sets the stage for the special experiences of this unique island, set in the middle of commercial options, but content to carry on along a clear path that has known changes of faces but not drastic change to terrain. When you step off the Cruz Bay ferry, wet from the spray, you can amble along the few roads of town, past the small shops and handcraft places.

The car that carries you to your island home will curve around coves edged with whitest sands and plunge down from hilltop to gully, following the cane-cart paths that made the first roads on this island. The minute you see the manicured lawns and the perfectly placed planting, you're passing the grounds of Caneel Bay, the Rockefeller-funded resort. The road runs on, and you may too, to rise again and fall into Trunk Bay, where a spectacular ribbon of sand breaks blue sea from green hill.

At the end of that line, down a path from the place the car is stopped, is a beautiful beach of talcum sand. This is a peaceful place—a playground for the world weary. A couple of windsurfers had found this spot the same day I did, and their taut sails added a new dimension—as well as color and entertainment —to the otherwise somnolent scene.

St. John had about 400 residents in the early 1950s when the island caught the eye (plus heart and wallet) of Laurance Rockefeller. Caneel Bay had a fishing camp, enjoyed by a handful of St. Thomians and some off-islanders who sold their property—held as the Rhode Island Charity Preserve—to Rockefeller in 1952. The late George Simmons, Administrator of St. John for the better part of 20 years, told about an excursion of his boy days from St. Thomas to St. John. It took 24 hours and depended on the winds. Most people never made the trip. If you were born here, you stayed here. The island had no electricity until Rockefeller guaranteed that Caneel would use enough to make an underwater cable worth the investment. And even then, in the early days, lights only went on for a few hours at night.

Life is not much different now—and the people who live here like it that way. St. John is still a perfect place to step off the treadmill of "civilized" life.

POLITICAL PICTURE:　St. John is governed as part of the United States Virgin Islands (see coverge of St. Thomas), with the Governor elected every 4 years, 2 years after the U.S. Presidential elections. Governor Juan Luis will be in office at least until elections are held in November 1982. He administers from Government House on St. Thomas, leaving the daily affairs of St. John to the duly elected representatives. The Administrator for St. John lives at Cruz Bay, but—except for improvements for roads, water supply, electricity, schools, and hospitals, life seems to go on "without" much government on this island. You will not be aware of local politics here.

CUSTOMS of St. John have modified some in recent years, although village picnics and the July 4th celebrations are still festive occasions that call forth traditional entertainment such as the greasy pig contest. Check with the Tourist Office about any special events that may take place when you plan your vacation, and be sure to hear the steel band wherever you can find it playing.

MONEY MATTERS are conducted in U.S. currency. Prices have gone up here, as everywhere, and those services that are geared for visitors charge accordingly. There are a few places to get reasonable meals, but you can count on medium to high prices most places. Don't count on using your credit card, except at places such as

Caneel Bay and a couple of the shops that are used to dealing with visitors.

■■■

ARRIVAL ON ST. JOHN is usually by boat from Red Hook landing. The sea crossing from the east end of St. Thomas (Red Hook) takes about half an hour, and there are several trips daily, with the first crossing from Red Hook at about 7:30 a.m. weekdays (slightly later on weekends) and from Cruz Bay (to get to St. Thomas) at about 7 a.m. The last crossing from St. John is at about 6 p.m. The public ferry goes to the village of Cruz Bay, the island's main town. The Caneel Bay ferry goes, obviously, to Caneel Bay and is more luxurious (and more expensive at about $7 each way). If you're a nautical type, the best way to arrive at this island is under sail, easily arranged on a day excursion out of St. Thomas (several charter firms have day sails, with lunch provided at about $30 per person charge).

■■■

TOURING TIPS for St. John center on taxi or rental car, plus a taxi-bus (used mostly by the camping folks who head to Cinnamon Bay and other sites), but don't forget the walking option. The National Park Service has posted trails that are the best way to explore this island (since the reason you came over is, presumably, to get away from blatant commerce). Check with the National Park Service center, at the fringe of Cruz Bay on the Caneel Bay side of town, or the Tourist Information Center in the park behind the Morris F. DeCastro Medical Clinic. They can tell you the days and times for guided walking tours, or—if you know all about local lore, flora, and fauna—strike out on your own with a copy of "St. John on Foot and by Car" in hand. (The small booklet is available for about $2.50 at the Gift Shop at Caneel Bay and elsewhere where books are sold.)

Car rentals are available at the Dock Shop on your right as you walk off the pier (from the boat). Although rental cars may not be "straight from the showroom," consider the hazards of getting any car from St. Thomas to St. John and be glad to have one that runs relatively smoothly.

■■■

HOTELS ON ST. JOHN: There is one exceptional resort; one National Park Service campsite; one unique camp-cottage set-up; a handful of small guesthouse/inns; and a liberal portion of private homes, available for rent in owner's absence. Rates fall from sky-high Caneel Bay (which is one resort in the world that can demand what it does because what it gives is worth it, if anything is) to campsites where you pay 1/20 of CB's daily winter rate. St. John, with the exception of Caneel, offers cultivated camping, whether you're on a site or settled into a small guesthouse.

AUTHOR'S AWARDS go to Caneel Bay, for being in a class by itself on this or any other island, and to Stanley Selengut and his colleagues for having the sense and perseverance to create Maho Bay Camps.

✢ **Caneel Bay** (Box 120, St. John, USVI 00830; 148 rooms) is Eden to those who know and go and to those who hear it spoken of in reverent whispers. This resort sets the standards that the best resorts in the rest of the Caribbean aim to reach. The place may have some flaws, but most people get hung up in a hammock or sink into the sea before they can get too excited about them. Only golfers will be disappointed; there is no course, but there are 7 tennis courts, several powdery beaches lapped with sea, and the option to take the ferry to St. Thomas to play golf at Mahogany Run.

In December 1956 Caneel Bay Plantation opened for its first guests, who stayed in what have been updated to be the beachside rooms nearest the check-in area. Rockefeller interests' gradual purchase of almost 5000 acres, eventually presented to the U.S. Government to be the 29th national park, raised storms of protest on quiet St. John. Life in those times was unfettered and free from the problems of the "outside world." Few wanted the interlopers, and all (except those who saw the value of cash) feared what progress would bring. Families split over whether to sell or not to sell. There are still some hold-out homes in the middle of the 5000 acre National Park. Few understood that the profits from Caneel would be plowed back into the property or into the conservation interests of Jackson Hole Preserve, Inc., which also operates the Grand Teton National Park accommodations in Wyoming.

In spite of all the turmoil, Caneel Bay Plantation progressed, adding rooms along the beach (discreetly hidden behind sea grape trees) and ultimately acquiring the Oppenheimer estate that would become the elegant Turtle Bay section of today's hotel. Operating more like a residential community than a resort hotel, Caneel Bay sprinkles its guests around the fringes, near the beaches. The 2 double rooms in Turtle Bay Estate House are prize possessions; there are also 4 rooms in a nearby building, and a block of 12 facing Turtle Bay Beach, over the hill-hump from the boat dock and main center. There are 20 rooms at Scott Beach, and 24 rooms in 3 buildings along Hawksnest Beach, farthest from the main hub (if one can call it that), nearest the Cinnamon Bay Beach National Park campsite and my favorite haven because you *feel* as though you are miles away but can easily walk to find your friends. All rooms have overhead fans, no phones, modern-and-working facilities, elegant decor, and everything you'd expect to find when you and another are paying up to $310 per day in winter for 2 meals daily per person and a roof over your head. Rates drop some from April 16 to December 15, but this is no place for those who have to worry about money. This is paradise, and the price is high. The excursion to Caneel is accomplished frequently by Kissingers, Mondales, McGoverns, international luminaries, diplomatic dignitaries, and an assortment of other names you may not know, but whose products you do. Arriving involves a reservation (difficult, but not impossible at height of winter season) and then, for most, flying to St. Thomas, then by taxi to Red Hook landing for the boat to Caneel Bay's dock.

✣ **Cinnamon Bay Campgrounds** (Box 120, St. John, USVI 00830; 40 cottages, 56 tents and 10 bare sites) put you in an almost idyllic situation, if you plan far enough ahead to assure a spot. On national park protected grounds abutting the luxurious Caneel Bay, campers have the use of an efficient subsistence snack area plus sailfish, windsurfers, snorkel and scuba equipment (rented at the beachside water-sports center), and plenty of trails. Beds are canvas and steel (bring your own sleeping bag if you are fussy); cottages come with foam mattress, folding canvas chairs, and electric lights—plus sand flies at twilight. (Travel with your favorite bug repellent and a flashlight.) Picnic tables are near the tented sites where gas lanterns, stars, and moon provide night light. Park rangers conduct walks and talks. Stays are limited to 2 weeks; count on spending $30 per day for a cottage, $15 per day for a tented site, and a mere $3 for a bare site. Your taxi from Cruz Bay will cost $7 for the first person, plus $1 additional, but the taxi-bus that runs on regular schedule brings the price to $2 per person. (The foray from the airport in St. Thomas to Red Hook Landing for the ferry to St. John will involve $7 for the first person, $1 each additional, plus $1.50 adults, 75¢ children on the ferry. Include a stop at Grand Union, just after you go through Charlotte Amalie, if you want to stock up on food at the best island prices.) If you're a camper, the situation at the 29th national park is almost ideal—with stretches of white, powdery sand and excellent places to scuba and snorkel, plus sugar-mill ruins to prowl around on land.

✣ **Maho Bay Camp** (Cruz Bay, St. John, USVI 00830; 96 units) made a name for itself in its very first season of '77 for good value in surroundings that proved to be just what they said they were: tent-cottages with canvas flaps on a 14-acre preserve that "is dedicated to an artful grooming of nature, not its alteration." That includes an extensive system of boardwalks, elevated above the growing things so that you won't step on them as you hike down to the beach. Ideal for self-sufficient outdoor types, the tent-cottages are hidden in the foliage so that only the occasional noise makes you aware of your neighbors. Furnishings are functional and sparse, and include the planked deck that hangs out toward your own special view. The sleeping area can be supplemented with the couches-turned-beds in the living room, with a screened area for dining. (Also included are a 2-burner propane stove, 4-cubic-foot icebox, 6 chairs around your dining table, bed linens, blankets, towels, pots, pans, and dishes.) A community bathhouse (showers, toilets, sinks) is a short walk from your cottage. Hurrah for Stanley Selengut and his colleagues for their perseverance (which included carrying supplies and building materials along carefully tended walkways) so that those who seek it can have a very natural place to stay, at very realistic prices that have risen to a still-reasonable $45 per day for 2 at peak demand winter months. Brace yourself for the hike back up from the beach to your cottage; bring food from home if you're fussy. For the rest of us, there's plenty of simple food available.

So successful is the Selengut plan for holidays that I've heard he has taken an option on about 60 acres at another part of the island to set up a similar project. Check with the Maho Bay Campgrounds for details as plans progress.

●●●

HOUSEKEEPING HOLIDAYS don't have to be any hard-up affair on St. John. For those who want it, there are very simple setups such as those at Maho Bay Camps and at the National Park Service cottages at Cinnamon Bay, but there are also 8 **Holiday Homes** (Box 40 Cruz Bay, St. John, USVI 00830) managed by Sis Frank, who was the pioneer with the Holiday Homes arrangement, when she started listing homes available for rent in owner's absence. For culinary successes, don't count on a lot of local food. You'll probably

want to bring some items from your favorite meat man at home),
and for suggestions on places to find when you are an island resident check at the Tourist Office.

For those who can plan ahead, it's worthwhile stocking up on
staples when you pass the Grand Union or other supermarkets on
the ride from the St. Thomas airport ot Red Hook landing for the
boat to St. John.

Other homes for rent are the 6 managed by Mary-Phyllis No-
gueira (Mamey Peak, St. John, USVI 00830) and the 5 managed by
Ruth Wilford (Box 39, Cruz Bay, St. John, USVI 00830). Check for
specifics about exactly what is included with your rental. Maid service is usually part of the deal, but beach gear is sometimes included, and 2 of Ruth Wilford's homes come with a rental car.

✤ **Gallows Point** (Box 58, Cruz Bay, St. John, USVI 00830; 7 cottages) is an island legend nurtured by the Ellington's, who owned
the place for about 30 years. Reports of sale to a Redbank, NJ resident hint of a change, and some change is desperately needed. Although the very rustic, haphazardly furnished cottages had been
ideal for a very carefree holiday, several basics for comfortable living had been neglected in recent years. I hope new ownership
means a refurbishing; check if you're interested.

✤ **Serendip Apartments** (Box 273, Cruz Bay, St. John, USVI 00830;
10 units) are about $350 for a week, and that's how long it will take
you to unwind and settle in to enjoy this quiet spot, so forget about
the daily rate even though there is one. About midway through
your holiday, rent a jeep for bouncing and weaving around island
roads. (It may take you the next couple of days to recover from
that!)

▪▪▪

RESTAURANTS ON ST. JOHN are an interesting lot, better
known—in most cases—for their special character than for the
gourmet quality of the cooking. Prices are HIGH at Caneel and as
high as the traffic will bear at the other places. It seems to me that
restaurant prices bear little relationship to the actual cost of obtaining the food, unless the local restaurateurs are price averaging.
Even then, I think there's a strong relationship between demand
and price. If one is high, so is the other—in hopes, I suppose, of
early retirement.

Everyone knows about **Caneel Bay's** beachside buffets and expects them to be exceptional; they usually are, but frankly, for me

they are overwhelming. Try the *Sugar Mill,* where you get a hilltop view with your meal, which is lunch or snacks and sometimes special dinners. Caneel's restaurant at *Turtle Bay* has a slight edge for my money, again because of the view—which you miss when you settle into the shoreside dining room in the main building.

Miss Meada has a long tradition of serving good island food, at her home. She's spruced up the surroundings, off to the left through the small park by the travel office, as you walk up the Cruz Bay dock and surrounded by a cluster of small shops. It's worth making a reservation for dinner if you want to be sure to be served, but at least linger for lunch. **The Back Yard** is next door with grill-cooked items and health food featured in a picniclike atmosphere. **Joe's Diner,** up the main road from the dock, has switched from Chinese to Southern fried, with cheese-filled johnnycakes and other surprises. **Oscar's Luncheonette,** across the road next to the apothecary, is a glorified diner with formica tables, plastic and chrome chairs, and some of the best sandwiches around. (A lot of the local folk like it for breakfast and ice cream.) You have to head for the **Lobster Hut** if you want a local lobster roll or better yet, a conch fritter, and to **Fred's Patio,** behind the Lutheran church on one of the side streets, for some good island food (but don't count on knowing what it is unless you know island cooking). For a real island evening, find **Bamboo Inn,** not far from Enighed Pond, but very far from the Caneel Bay aura. Everything really leaps and cavorts when there's live music, but it's difficult to say when that will be. Check when you get on the island. All of these places are casual, ideal if you want to become an instant islander and favored by the boating clan. There's no room for pretensions at any of the small places.

Try **The Out,** open-air and casual, next to Islandia, across from the national park headquarters—a couple of jogs to the left and about a 10-minute walk from the Cruz Bay dock. There's supposed to be music on Wednesday and Sunday nights, and that will probably be the case if you're here at height of winter season. Always inquire. If the band doesn't feel like playing, it doesn't. Find a ride to the **Upper Deck** (or take your jeep up the tracks that lead here) for a spectacular view and romantic setting, ideal at twilight and then for dinner. Closed on Monday and Tuesday. Dinner is by candlelight, when everything seems delicious and, if you don't like waiting, dine early or close to the 9 p.m. closing. No reservations taken.

The Ship Lantern at the Boulon Shopping Center has a luncheon menu with omelettes and quiche, and gets fancy for dinner with escargots, scampi—and even caviar. There's entertainment on Friday and Saturday, and a steel band on Wednesday nights in season;

check for the sometimes slower spring and fall seasons. **The Ice Cream Store** at the Boulon Shopping Center is the place to find when you crave a cone.

Trunk Bay's never been the same since Erva Boulon left, and if any readers remember her, I'd like to hear from them. This place in those days (20 or so years ago) was unique, and its view still is. It was an island inn, pervaded by the personality of wiry and witty Erva Boulon. She brewed and stewed almost any vegetable, fruit, chicken, or fish that thrived in these surroundings, and her meals are an island memory to be cherished. The hot dogs and hamburgers that are served in the new place the National Park Service built are pale and boring by comparison, but if that kind of food appeals, it's here (and pricey). And then, if you are *really* hungry, there's always the cafeteria at Cinnamon Bay.

■■

PLACES WORTH FINDING ON ST. JOHN are natural. There's not much in the way of thriving restoration. Even the Annaberg ruins, gradually coming back to life under the aegis of the National Park Service, are still ruins. The views are as interesting as the coral stone buildings. Before you set out on any prowls, it's worthwhile finding a copy of Randall Koladis's *St. John on Foot and By Car*. In addition, ask at the Virgin Islands' Government Tourism Office at Cruz Bay for the map folder about St. John. (Try writing to one of the U.S. offices if you want the map in advance.)

The St. John Visitor's Bureau Information Center (with a name that's almost bigger than its office) is near the DeCastro Clinic and is the source for any special events that may be taking place (but not well posted) while you are on the island. Bring your questions here for answers, and pick up leaflets that will help you get your bearings.

The National Park Service Visitors' Bureau, to the left as you get off the boat at Cruz Bay, sets the stage for what you can see. In typical "basic information" displays, the history of St. John stretches around an airy room, with special exhibits on flora and fauna. Ask about the guided tours, operated by park rangers when there is enough interest. (Check also at the Cinnamon Bay Campgrounds, if you are staying there.)

Coral Bay was the site of the original settlement, some say by the Arawaks in 200 A.D. This was the main town for the European settlers who had their plantations on St. John, under grant from the Danish government. You'll need a 4-wheel-drive jeep to find Coral Bay Overlook, and the rest of the sights worth seeing—including

Reef Bay Estate, a hiking goal, where the remains of one of the island's steam-operated sugar mills is almost buried in tropical growth. The Estate House, built around the 1830s, is closed, but the grounds are open for visitors who want to poke through an unattended area.

The most spectacular sights for St. John are underwater, for those who want to don snorkel gear to follow the underwater tags that mark the trail.

■■

SPORTS ON ST. JOHN: For **sailing,** there are Sunfish for rent at the Campgrounds, where windsurfing has become popular in recent years. *Trade Wind Charters* has a couple of small sailboats for day sailing. Occasionally big boats that come into Caneel Bay will take day charters, or a day charter can be arranged if there are enough of you who are interested.

Scuba is professional, at Caneel Bay's water-sports center and at Cinnamon Bay, where the concessionaire has scuba courses for beginners as well as a range of escapades for experienced divers. In the neighboring British Virgins, you can find some of the Caribbean's most exciting diving areas—especially off Anegada, which is a possible day trip if you have a fast dive-boat and start early. Two water-sports operators have responded to the increased interest. Contact either the **St. John Dock Shop,** or **The Dive Shop,** for prices and details about services offered.

Deep-sea fishing can be arranged through Caneel Bay. In fact, look to Caneel to take care of everything. If what you want to do is possible, they can arrange it—at a price. Otherwise, do not count on things to click along as they might on neighboring St. Thomas, where several professional firms operate flourishing businesses. Many of the boats you use out of St. John will have been brought over from St. Thomas or Tortola.

■■

TREASURES AND TRIFLES ON ST. JOHN: Shopping is casual and craft-oriented, but 2 books to buy (at opposite ends of the price range) are Randall Koladis's *St. John by Foot and Car* (about $2.50) and West German industrialist Peter Ernst's *Impressions of a Happy Island*, written under his pseudonym Peter Buruba (the name of his estate) at about $40. The photographs he has included are priceless. If you don't see these books around, ask for them at **Islandia** or the **Caneel Bay Gift Shop.** If all else fails, find Sis Frank at

Holiday Homes. She'll track down copies for you, and can also sell you the island's best steel band records, those of Steel Unlimited, a group of schoolchildren trained by Trinidadian Rudolph Wells. The group has been practicing and playing since 1972, promoted for off-island performances by the enthusiasm and contacts of Sis.

For sandals, find **Nereide Ellis** at her leather shop next to Fred's Bar. **Kit and Caboodle** is the bastion of Bish Denham, who makes a lot of the craft items sold herein. **Bob Couse** makes buckles and other brass fittings, and **The Art Product** has local painters' and sculptors' works. Look at the handmade jewelry at **Barsel Jewelry** and the colorful Batik Caribe fabric (and resortwear), imported from St. Vincent. **Islandia,** the first "real" shop at Cruz Bay when it opened a few years ago, still specializes in the Marimekko fabric and sunwear (you can have what you want made to order if you don't see it on the rack), as well as silk-screen island designs on fabric, Topsiders, and books about the island, plus coral and island products (including St. John bay rum).

Batik Caribe fabrics made in St. Vincent are sold at a corner location across from the social welfare building, and **The Side Door** is packed with T-shirts, Indian cotton dresses, and an assortment of shorts and shirts. (It's wedged between the social welfare building and The Back Door restaurant.)

The Lemon Tree, to your right at Chase Manhattan's St. John branch office, is a small collection of shops, with **Virgin Canvas** selling bags and other items (and making things to order if you give Lina enough time) and **Sailor's Delight** where someone was working on handmade jewelry and another person turned out to be the one who paints the island scenes on T-shirts for sale.

Caneel Bay's boutique will be found by day visitors who land at the hotel's dock; its clothes are chic—and mostly from the States, Mexico, and elsewhere in the Caribbean. Elegant resort wear is here in limited but colorful quantity and high prices, befitting the budgets of Caneel Bay's guests. My preference for one-stop shopping is **Mongoose Junction,** a marvelous madhouse of small shops with some very exceptional artisans making and selling wares. It's off to your right (with the sea at your back) past the National Park Service station and Islandia. Be sure to search out **Rudy and Irene Patton.** They design and work silver and gold jewelry; expensive but worth it. **Donald Schnell** makes pottery while you watch, and will make a special bowl or planter if you state your interests and give him plenty of time. **Charles Benbow** makes mobiles, some of them with sailing ships and all with tropical motifs. **Linda Smith** adds flourishes to children's and adult wear. **Virgin Canvas** set up a shop to sell Cheri Butt's standard bags or to make the size and shape you need to carry your purchases home. And when you tire of looking, try eating a sandwich or nibbling at a cheese plate from **The Moveable Feast** or pluck a pastry from **Marcellino's Bakery.**

St. Kitts

S*t. Kitts-Nevis Tourist Board, Box 132, Basseterre,
St. Kitts, W.I.; Eastern Caribbean Tourism Association, 220 East
42nd St., New York, NY 10017.*

US$1 = EC$2.60.
Unless otherwise noted, $ refers to U.S. currency.

When the bread was bought at the bakery not far from the Circus
one morning, it was warm. Now the sun was, and the bread was
being broken on the ramparts of Brimstone Hill, the fortress that
was started in 1690 by the British, "finished" more than 100 years
later by the French, and not often used for battles. Some say that
more men were lost from plagues than from wars at this fortress,
but none of that seems important as I face toward the sun, to
stretch out on the wall after looking through a crenel that framed
the island of Statia, several miles northwest.

The turning to get here is at Half-Way Tree, and the road that
winds up is treacherous—unless you're used to cars and goats that
weave and meander, not always synchronized with the turnings of
the road. Not too many people come up here, because—in the tourist scheme of things—not too many people come to St. Kitts. That's
their loss. I first found this perch more than a decade ago, and have
been waiting patiently to bring a book and a quiet friend or two up
here for some thoughtful sunning, spliced with a spontaneous picnic. Today's the day—and getting here took some perseverance,
not only because the pace has slowed so much that following any
plan seems like too much of a project, but also because when Grenville stood by to fill my coffee cup this morning on the terrace at the
inn, he announced he was going home to Nevis and asked if I'd like
to take the boat across. When I bought the bread in Basseterre
(which is where the Circus surrounds Berkeley Memorial, named
for a former president of the Kittitian legislature) I watched him go

with the what seemed like hundreds of others to make the crossing to Charlestown.

There's been a lot of crossing between St. Kitts and Nevis through the several centuries that they've been linked. Nevisian settlers came from St. Kitts, but the Kittitian settlement came first. In 1623, Sir Thomas Warner stepped ashore with a small group that included his wife and a son who would later go to a new settlement in Antigua. They established Old Road, where a marker can sometimes be seen amid a tangle of brush and where the sea pounds against what's left of an old fort's walls. The island had been known to Spaniards, and then to the French, British, and Dutch, but no one had settled until the Warner group arrived. Not long afterward, when Sieur d'Esnambuc brought his crippled ships ashore to career and repair, the Frenchman and his sailors stayed, and others from nearby French settlements followed. The split personality still known on Sint Maarten/St. Martin to the north was known also on St. Kitts. The British held the middle; the French claimed both ends—and named Basseterre (the low land).

Even today, this West Indian town turns to its own tune; there's nothing touristy about it. Since it became the British capital in 1727, the town has known the floods and fires familiar to many 18th- and 19th-century West Indian towns. A few buildings—and the street plan—date to the rebuilding after the fire of 1867, and some of the newer changes at the shore came after the earthquake and floods of 1974. Basseterre has been too busy rebuilding to think much about building up.

Only the development plans for Frigate Bay attest to the country's tap dance with tourism—and although sugar and peanuts have replaced the first crops of logwood and salt, it seems safe to say that it will be a while before tourism overwhelms this primarily agricultural island.

■■■

POLITICAL PICTURE: Elections held in March 1980 tossed the St. Kitts Labour Party out of the Premier's office and changed almost 30 years of party tradition. St. Kitts-Nevis-Anguilla had become an Associated State of Britain in 1967, when Robert Bradshaw, head of the St. Kitts Labour Party, was named premier. Anguilla, disenchanted with its share of the funds and attention from government based in Basseterre, St. Kitts, petitioned for, and was granted, special status in February 1976. Although Nevisians also, used to talk of secession to "go to alone," the leading political party of Nevis is now woven into the present government of St.

Kitts-Nevis. Dr. Kennedy Simmonds, head of the People's Action Movement, is premier, and his alliance with Mr. Simeon Daniel, his Minister of Finance and (perhaps more significantly) head of the Nevis Reformation Movement, are what created the necessary majority to oust the incumbent Lee Moore who is still active politically and otherwise as head of the St. Kitts Trade and Labour Union.

Talks of independence have been merely whispers in this two-island Associated State (of St. Kitts–Nevis). The present government has long held the opinion that indications of a sound financial base must precede the "go it alone" move, and Britain now seems more disposed to offering support for its former colonies through the earliest years of self-government. (Lessons have finally been learned, it seems, by the troubled times of Grenada and Jamaica, where independence was granted to people who were novices at self-government in today's complicated world.) The islands of St. Kitts and Nevis are primarily agricultural, and since they have been out of the mainstream of tourism until the past two years, they are only now beginning to take their rightful place as a pleasant and comfortable Caribbean vacation destination. The appointment of Michael Powell as Minister for Tourism bodes well for this area. Powell's involvement with a car-rental business has put him in touch with visitors, and his interest in the gradual and sound development of his country, with a tourism that is compatible with the needs of his people, is an obvious concern.

■■

CUSTOMS OF THE COUNTRY are basically British, although there is a Kittitian modus operandi that comes with the confidence of knowing that this island was the first English settlement in the islands—Sir Thomas Warner established his small community in 1623. More than 20 years ago, when the late Premier Robert Bradshaw became the spokesman for the workers on the sugar plantations and set up new systems in the country, St. Kitts established a "new" lifestyle. More obvious on St. Kitts than on rural nearby Nevis, the local customs that will appear for the sensitive traveler include the familiar greeting, either a "good morning" or a "good afternoon," to anyone you pass, and certainly before starting any business transaction in a hotel, restaurant or shop.

There is tremendous pride among Kittitians and Nevisians about their accomplishments over the past decade and more. Although the first-time visitor may not appreciate the good roads, clean streets, tidy homes, and impressive infrastructure that awaits full tourist development at Frigate Bay, most island residents are aware and proud. The market day ritual that you can note in downtown Basseterre is just as much a fact of life for island residents as the hauling of the fishing catch, and camera-swinging tourists are distinctly out of place, although welcomed to wander around and look. The situation, however, is like having a total stranger come into your office or home to peer at you, and although you may welcome the intrusion, you may be too busy to talk.

Tourists are still in the minority on both these islands, and emphasis seem to be more on fitting into the system that is working here than on parading through town, either Basseterre or the Nevisian town of Charlestown, in peacock finery or beach clothes.

Clothes are comfortably casual tropical wear. Most local businessmen have yielded to the shirt-jac, or whatever you call the straight, sometimes pastel-colored shirt that is both comfortable, and a statement of equality in today's Caribbean. Coat and tie may be worn by some businessmen, and at some formal evening occasions, but the more common attire is a neatly comfortable open-neck shirt for men and skirts or dresses for social events for women. Touring togs are, of course, whatever is comfortable—with top resort finery appearing for an occasional dinner at the Golden Lemon or a special elegant evening at Rawlins Plantation.

■■

MONEY MATTERS on St. Kitts revolve around Eastern Caribbean currency. You would do better to change US or other foreign currency into EC at the bank, at the rate of about EC$2.60 to US$1. Although there may be slight variations, due to the nibble for exchange services at the hotels, stores, and banks, the rate is "pegged" to the US$ and therefore fairly steady. Do not count on using credit cards, although some hotels will take them, and if you want to cash a personal check, be sure to ask the hotel's owner/manager in advance. Some owners will accept personal checks, but most will not—for obvious reasons. When you are dealing with taxi drivers, ask *in advance* to be sure whose dollars you both are talking about. Kittitian cab drivers, from my experience, are not above taking US$ when the price is actually EC$, thereby making a quick 100%-plus profit for themselves.

■■

ARRIVAL ON ST. KITTS is relatively easy, now that the new terminal is finished. The 8500-foot airstrip that can easily take a fully loaded 747 was completed in 1976, but the expansion of terminal facilities was a slow-going project that made the airport a mess for all of the '79–'80 season. When you get off your plane, you will be directed to immigration (a slow process, especially if you arrive on one of the small Prinair planes with the relatives and friends of the immigration officials), and then to the ramps for customs clearance. Brace yourself for the onslaught of taxi drivers when you push open the doors to step outside. Unless repeated comments have been taken to heart, you will be beseiged by a flurry of young and eager taxi drivers, each of whom will be willing to take you where you want to go—at a price. Ask about the fare when you are in the customs area (if you haven't been advised by your hotel when you made your reservations), and always start asking whether the price you are being quoted is in EC$ or US$. Most price quotations—except at strictly tourist traps—are in EC dollars because this is still an islander's island.

■■

TOURING TIPS: Kittitian taxi drivers have been known to swarm around the exit from the air terminal and latch onto you as soon as you walk out the door, but I have been assured that a local effort will eliminate that problem. Even so, my advice is (1) find out, in advance, the name of the driver your hotel uses, and ask for him by name, and/or (2) ask inside the door at customs before you go outside what the rate should be between where you are and where you want to go. Rates have been changing so rapidly (upwards) that chances of seeing a prominent list of current rates are slim. Pay the specified amount only. Tipping is not necessary unless some special service is involved. Kittitian drivers own their own cars, and except for what they pay for maintenance, license, running costs, and union dues, the fare is theirs.

First-timers will learn lore from local drivers, but there are an eclectic group of rental cars for those who want to be independent. My mini-moke rented from J. Irving Howell, manager of *Holiday Transport Ltd.*, on one journey became my alter ego, not only because the metal pipes at the back of the seat were welded to my spine after the first few potholes, but also because we got used to each other. My ability to shift gears (resurrected from my learning-to-drive days) seemed to synchronize with the gears of my moke. The small car rented through *Michael Powell's* firm on a subsequent journey proved to be dependable and good on gas, which is an astounding EC$5 per gallon, and expected to rise higher. Be sure you know the exact charge when you sign for your car. (Mine, with extras, was much more than I had expected.) Driver's license, available from the police station in Basseterre, costs EC$4 after the form filling and proof that you are eligible to drive in your own hometown. There are cars (at higher prices) available through the local *Avis* representative, and through some other small time entrepreneurs. Your hotel can arrange a rental.

Local bus services will not appeal to most tourists, especially those pressed for time. Waits are long and rides are stop-and-start affairs. Hitchhiking is prevalent.

Mopeds are popular; helmets are not, but should be. Roads are potholed and moped riders looked hot (and scorched) when I saw them. Your hotel can make arrangements for a moped rental; Royal St. Kitts hotel has a fleet.

For inter-island transportation (between St. Kitts and Nevis) pros travel on the official ferry service between Basseterre and Charlestown; others take small planes, usually private if you want to go over and back in one day, unless the LIAT schedule has been modified since my visit. Although the flight is only 10 minutes, LIAT's links with the rest of their route make a day excursion to either island "impossible." I hope this will have changed by the time of your visit (or perhaps there are enough of you to arrange a small plane charter).

■■

HOTELS ON ST. KITTS are personality places. The half-dozen havens include some of the prize small properties in the Caribbean. Until a couple of years ago, there wasn't a big hotel worthy of the name. Even the Fort Thomas, which skipped through its early life as a Holiday Inn, and then was called Liamuiga (an early Indian name for the island), is a big place with a small-hotel feeling, and the Royal St. Kitts is just now coming into its own, at the golf course, with tennis courts and full resort facilities that include gambling. There are ambitious plans for several hotels to add 786 rooms in the Frigate Bay area, and some rooms *may* be open in early '82.

In addition to your hotel bill, you'll be paying a service charge, usually figured at 10% but sometimes 15%, and US$1.50 per room per night government tax.

AUTHOR'S AWARDS go to the Golden Lemon, for picture-perfect surroundings and a unique nugget of hospitality, and to the Ocean Terrace Inn for offering traditional Kittitian hospitality and cuisine, as well as activities' options in a special small hotel.

✤ **Banana Bay Beach** (Box 188, St. George Parish, St. Kitts, W.I.; 10 rooms) is a speck on the south coast reached only by boat (45 minutes' ride) from Basseterre. (The Cockleshell is "next door," over the hill). The hotel's guiding spirit eventually sold the place last season (after a couple of false starts) and you can count on new owner Carl Fuchs, friend of Golden Lemon's Arthur Leaman, to turn this outpost into a gem. There is no road from Basseterre, and no immediate prospect of one for this season. If you want a Robinson Crusoe hideaway, with privacy assured and the beach, sea, and conversation with other guests (if there are any) as your only activity, then paying the winter rate of about $100 for 2, two meals daily included, might seem acceptable.

✤ **The Cockleshell** (Box 284, St. George Parish, St. Kitts, W.I.; 10 rooms) is on a beach, about 45 minutes' bouncing boat ride from Basseterre or anywhere else where there's a telephone. Bill and Georgie Bowers sold their south-coast haven in spring of '80; so there's a new feeling at this nest now that Laddie Hamilton is running it. The main house is the hub; your room will be one of a string that reaches toward the beach and sea, overlooking both from a small terrace. There's a tennis court with house-owned rackets, plus ideal snorkeling and scuba area. (No place to replenish equipment; bring your own.) This is not an inn for peripatetic types who must be near a phone or might need to make a quick exit. You are isolated—blissfully and completely. All the comforts are here (you can marvel at how), as are several repeat guests from upper crust communities. Winter rates are $130 for 2, 2 good meals.

✤ **Fairview Inn** (Box 212, Basseterre, St. Kitts, W.I.; 30 rooms) is more like a home than a hotel for those of us who have been traveling this area for many years. It's impossible for me to be totally objective about this special inn. The owners and I have "solved," mourned over, and laughed about so many Caribbean events through several years of friendship that it is impossible to separate them, and their personal and inn family, from the surroundings. When Freddy and Betty Lam took over their 18th-century Great House more than 10 years ago, they were among the first on this island to tackle the operation of a small inn for today's tourists. Betty Lam's Kittitian traditions and recipes give the inn its special atmosphere, and Freddy's Trinidadian enthusiasm and drive have kept this place up with the times and active in promotions. Although the original Great House is the heart of the inn, there are modern features (pool, easy car rental, and evening enterainment that often includes top performers from other islands, lured to St. Kitts en route to other places). Most rooms are 2 per cottage in buildings at the back of the main house, up the path beyond the conflagration of bougainvillea blossoms. The "best room in the house" is in one of the buildings to the left of the main house: Room 107, the Maureen O'Hara suite, perfumed by the jasmine bush that grows outside the door. Furnishings throughout the inn are comfortable, not lavish, and hospitality is sincere. It is the combination of real West Indian tradition and modern comforts that makes this place worth its $50 for 2, meals extra. Inquire about special rates for long term visits and know that you will have to walk from an inland location or drive to a reasonable beach. Basseterre and the airport are about 15 minutes' drive south.

✛ **Fort Thomas Hotel** (Box 407, Basseterre, St. Kitts, W.I.; 64 rooms) is comfortably modern and favored by package tour operators because rooms are standard hotel style and because the hotel is convenient to Basseterre. Taxis are available to take you to other spots if you choose not to rent a car. The hotel appeared on the drawing boards almost 10 years ago. Past history called it Liamuiga (the original name for this island) and funneled it through the Holiday Inn routines. Today it belongs solely to the Kittitian government, to stand at the site of Fort Thomas, giving poolside visitors a nice outlook over the sea. Built for big-time tourism before there was any to this island, Fort Thomas languished at the fringe of Basseterre until touring groups—those planned by Chicago-based, London-birthed Thomson Vacations and other firms—began to use it for their home base. Tied into promotions with the island's other biggie (Royal St. Kitts with its casino), this hotel is coming into its own. You can count on the standard Holiday Inn-style rooms, without the processed maintenance that the Memphis firm demands. When the package tour operation is running full tilt, there's life at the hotel. Otherwise, the staffing and other guests may be sparse. You'll be overlooking Basseterre (and can drive into downtown in 5 minutes) and can count on paying $75 this winter for 2, meals extra. (The package vacations are well worth considering. See your travel agent.)

✛ **Golden Lemon** (Dieppe Bay, St. Kitts, W.I.; 12 rooms) is elegant, small, and very special. Arthur Leaman's dream, painstakingly turned to reality with his decorator touches, is at the north coast village of Dieppe Bay, named by early French settlers for a better known bay across the Atlantic. The inn is an oasis—with small pool in the entry courtyard, a gray sand beach shared with the fishermen, and a grove of palms outside the gates. If the antiques that furnish this 17th-century house don't impress you, the color and placement of the fruit and flower arrangements will. Each room has its own personality, plus patio or gallery, private bath, and overhead fan to keep the trade winds whisking through the open windows. Not for everyone, the Golden Lemon is certainly for sybarites who know and like the good life. Golden Lemon is a quiet place on a quiet island. Leaman says it "takes a week and a half to get used to slowing down," so minimum stay is 4 days, maximum 2 weeks. Children are not invited. Breakfasts and dinners are included in your $160 to $195 daily double winter tariff. The Golden Lemon thrives about 15 miles north of the airport and the town of Basseterre. A taxi can guide you up the coast in about 45 minutes.

✛ **Ocean Terrace Inn** (Box 65, Basseterre, St. Kitts, W.I.; 30 rooms) continues to be one of my favorite inns, partly because of the tireless attention the owners pay to their place and partly because the location, on the outskirts of Basseterre, makes in-town visits easy (allowing for escape to cool in the OTI pool when time permits). OTI hangs on the hillside, overlooking Basseterre. Colin and Leslie Pereira opened an inn with 2 rooms in the family homestead almost 12 years ago; today, with additions and modifications, the small hotel gives full vacation facilities plus warm hospitality. The food served at the inside dining room, or poolside on occasion, is some of the best Kittitian cuisine on the island. Your taxi fare to town or airport won't be more than EC$10, and you'll be at the site of whatever there is in the way of evening action on St. Kitts. The island's disco, *Bitter End,* is here near the pool, on week-ends and at other times when house count and/or local interest warrants, but don't count on the disco being an "every night" activity. Rooms are modern, comfortable, and air-conditioned. Some have views over the town, and all give you glimpses of the sea. Ambitious plans for a related unit of condominiums, planned for rental in owners' absence, are underway down the hill (nearer the water's edge but with no beach), but guests at the hilltop hotel will find hospitality unhindered by the contingent plans. Colin Pereira acquired a 33-foot fiberglass cabin cruiser when he built the 12 new rooms in 1977, and he has built up a substantial water sports business with deep-sea fishing for a minimum of 6 at $15 per person for a half-day, a Nevis all-day excursion with lunch included for $30, and a beach picnic, usually at the Salt Pond Bay area south of the inn, and other boat outings as requested. Rooms this winter will range from $64 to $80 for 2, meals extra. Figure on about $5 for a full breakfast and about $15 for a dinner with Kittitian specialities (and top grade steaks on barbecue night).

✤ **Rawlins Plantation** (Mount Pleasant, St. Kitts, W.I., Box 340; 8 rooms) puts you in a stage set. The Walwyns turned their home into an inn when government pressures put them out of the plantation business, and the exciting addition, through purchase, of the original main house has turned this property into a spectacular gem. The 260 acres still grow, mostly in cane, and you can scan them from the main-house porch or poolside as you stretch out in the sun. At the northern tip, inland from Dieppe Bay (where the Golden Lemon grows), Rawlins is just about perfect if you want a plantation. Innkeepers only since 1973, the Walwyns prove that 300 years of tradition (theirs) on St. Kitts create excellent (and delightful) hosts. The senior Walwyns have turned over daily management to son Philip and his wife Frances. Both are able hosts, experienced in the art of hospitality and knowledgeable in the ways of the island that can put you on horseback or out at sea on their 34-foot catamaran for a $30-day of sailing, sunning, and sipping rum punches. Choices for rooms are the duplex in the sugar-mill tower (if you're lucky enough to get it), 2 rooms in the original main house, or a room in one of the other cottages on the property—all private, some with kitchen facilities for complete independence. Meals are served, family style, in comfortable antique-furnished, homey surroundings in a recently built stone house incorporating the ruins of one of the original plantation buildings. The rates of $160 for 2, 2 meals and tea daily, are worth every penny. (The minimum 3-day stay in winter is far too short a visit.) Plan far ahead to book here at height of season.

✤ **Royal St. Kitts Golf and Racquet Club** (Frigate Bay, St. Kitts, W.I.; 100 rooms) has known a couple of seasons as "home" for groups who fly south on charters for a week of fun in the sun, spending evening hours (and U.S. cash) at the hotel's casino and daytime on the golf course, tennis courts, beaches, pool deck, or touring the island by moped or rental car. For its first 3 years, Royal St. Kitts was used mainly to impress government guests, who came in groups and with retinue from neighboring Caribbean spots. Rooms vary in size and shape, but all are modern, attractively furnished, and have white stucco walls with colorful fabric punctuation. The Mediterranean-style units are around the pool and near the tennis courts.

Beware of the perilous spiral stairway that leads up to the bedroom of the duplex units. It must be the bane of maids and bellhops, not to mention the trauma of guests. In addition to rum punch parties and golf and tennis privileges, you get 7 full breakfasts and the option of eating here (there are better places, in my opinion) or driving elsewhere for dinners. (Ask your travel agent to check Thomson Vacations week-long holidays for an all-inclusive week.) You're 20 minutes from Basseterre and the airport.

■■

RESTAURANTS on St. Kitts are some of the Caribbean's most authentic, in restored surroundings serving local food. You can count on some truly special food at a handful of places, but reservations in advance are essential at peak season in winter (and advisable at other times since some of the smallest places don't serve every night).

Anchorage, on the beach at Frigate Bay, serves mouth-watering local lobster at a beachside setting that allows for a dip in the sea to wash up after grappling with the spiny speciality. When I last sampled, the cost was EC$28, but that included the whole broiled lobster, with coleslaw, french fries, and a leisurely meal. A favorite spot for a local-fish lunch, Anchorage also serves sandwiches and a regular snack-bar menu. Count on very simple, open-air surroundings.

Georgian House, on Pall Mall Square in one of the town's true architectural gems, is worth the visit as much for the ambiance as for the food and hospitality. This is the Bowers' place, and it's just about perfect. Dining in the garden, where flourishing trees and shrubs have been pruned and cared for, is pleasant at any time, and the inside rooms (where furnishings are elegant reproductions of Queen Anne style) is romantic by candlelight. Check with Georgie and Bill Bowers about reservations and the house specials, and count on a memorable—and pleasant—interlude.

The Palms, on the Circus (as Berkeley Square is called) in Basseterre, is Carl Fuch's place, and he has put his considerable decorating talents to use designing a delightful dining area, amid the courtyard and rooms of one of the venerable Kittitian buildings. The food is excellent, with unusual combinations of spices and local produce as well as more standard fare. Open for luncheon and dinner, the place has been popular since the day it officially opened in November '79.

Ocean Terrace Inn, overlooking the town of Basseterre, has made a name for itself with a very special cuisine using local vegetables and fish. Each of the many meals I've eaten here has been better than the last, but the special buffet evenings have gained staunch support from Kittitians as well as from island visitors who know about them. Be sure to call for a reservation.

Reservations are accepted at Fairview Inn, Golden Lemon, and sometimes, also, at Rawlins Plantation, but a telephone call in advance to each of these places is essential. For the protection of hotel guests, and in an admirable attempt to maintain the atmosphere that made these inns unique in the first place, the number of outsiders accepted for meals is limited.

■■

PLACES WORTH FINDING ON ST. KITTS are going to be those you find for yourself—perhaps the fishing village at Dieppe Bay in the north, some of the small towns you pass through as you drive around the rim road from Basseterre north on the west coast and south on the rugged and windy east coast, and coves and beaches you can reach only by boat at the midsouth section and along the south shore, facing Nevis, which lies across the 2-mile channel. Many of the villages were the original settlements of this island that proudly calls itself the Mother of the Caribbean (because many early settlers on other islands came from the original Sir Thomas Warner 1623 settlement on St. Kitts). Today the villages are quiet settlements, where some people make their living from tapping rock into pebbles for paving the roads. The inland villages, encouraged to move to the rim road for better transportation to school and commerce, are again surviving; many of the people who moved obediently to the shore at the strong urging of the Bradshaw government returned to their more familiar, if less modern, communities in the hillsides, near the heart of the old plantation where they recognized their favorite trees, streams, and way of life.

BASSETERRE, the capital of St. Kitts-Nevis, was in the French portion of the island when the north and south sections were held by that country and the midsection was English. Extensive restoration is underway on some of the most interesting buildings, especially those around **Pall Mall Square** where the lines of sectioning in the park still follow the 18th-century tradition of special areas for slaves and freemen. Some of the renovations in the unique houses that rim the square (notably Georgian House) have made the space available for artists and small shops, as well as for private homes and a couple of restaurants. The **Court House** is imposing, and has been partially refurbished. The library at the Court House has some old West Indian books, but the archives room in the Government Headquarters is more complete if you are interested in documents relating to the island's early history. (Call for an appointment to be sure the archives are open and there's someone on duty.)

St. George's Anglican Church, on Cayon Street, which runs parallel to the waterfront, reached easily by walking up Church Street, was built as it now stands in 1867, on the site of a church which was first built in 1670. When you wander around the grounds and look at the old wood pews and decoration, modern commerce seems to be in another world. Note the gravestones in the unkempt cemetery—with Woodley (1795), Cunningham (1847), Pilington (1748), and others reminiscent of the previous planter-dominated world of St. Kitts-Nevis.

For ruins around the island, check for permission to prowl around **Fort Smith** on the St. Kitts Sugar Factory grounds. There used to be rusted cannons here, as well as some old stairs and walls, with some bits that might be from some 18th-century pottery, but it was a couple of years ago that I climbed around this site, so things may have changed. Check at the Tourist Board office, or ask at your hotel, if poking around old sugar mill ruins seems like an intriguing pastime for your holiday.

AUTHOR'S OBSERVATION: If you want to prowl around the ruins and restoration, wear rubber-soled shoes (something firmer than sneakers) for the cobbled walkways, and bring some mosquito repellent if you come after a rain or on a humid day.

Brimstone Hill, a fortress built on the top of a cliff on the western coast of St. Kitts, continues to claim its spectacular outlook with imposing silence. It will celebrate its 200th anniversary of a French defeat in 1983. Walking around the fortification, the parts that have been restored and the parts still left in weeds and disrepair, recalls the past when English and French jockeyed for control of this fort. The English built the first battery on the hill starting in 1689, after they'd tossed the French out of this part of the island. By 1736 there were 49 cannons on the hill and, during the French seige of the fort in 1782, some 600 troops of the Royal Scots and the East Yorkshire brigades plus 350 militia lived in and fought from here. Even with all that might the English surrendered—with dignity, however. In keeping with war maneuvers of the time, the French reportedly stood by while the English forces—all of them—

marched valiantly out of their fort and down the hill, a ceremony that was to be repeated in 1783, when the French were defeated by the British and *they* marched safely to French enclaves elsewhere on the island. The fort was damaged by the hurricane of 1834 and abandoned in 1852, to come back into Kittitian and Caribbean prominence when the Island Resources Foundation, based in St. Thomas, focused on the prominence of the remains and helped raise funds for a partial restoration of the Prince of Wales Bastion in the early 1970s.

Romney Manor, along the west coast about 20 minutes north of Basseterre, is a sight worth seeing even if you do not go inside the batik workshop (but you should if you haven't on a previous visit). Grounds and building are classic and well maintained, making both a special experience. The turn-off (to the right coming from Basseterre) from the shore-rimming road is marked.

■■■

SPORTS ON ST. KITTS: The picture is changing rapidly as the Frigate Bay tourism center comes clearly into focus. You can count on finding more sports facilities as business warrants, and this season is expected to be the most active for Kittitian tourism. Frigate Bay, the ambitious project for developing a resort hotel/private home community at the handle of the cricket-bat shape of St. Kitts, sat for several seasons, serene with its infrastructure intact, waiting for the investors to build hotels and other tourism facilities. With the advent of the quality operation of Thomson Vacations, a Chicago-based tour operator, life took hold at this resort area. The God-given beaches have been supplemented by "mile-high" aluminum lightposts—which I hope will someday be changed—as well as a web of well-paved roads and an undulating golf course.

Golf is the prime possibility, with a Trent Jones designed course, the clubhouse at Royal St. Kitts, plus caddies. Don't count on all the accoutrements you find at your local country club, but count on being one of the few on what has the potential to be an exceptional course.

Tennis courts have been built at Royal St. Kitts hotel, and there is a hot, asphalt court at Cockleshell for use by guests who may also use the house rackets since the court isn't worth carrying your own racket this far, especially when you see how one reaches this outpost.

Scuba and **deep-sea fishing** are firmly in the hands of Colin Pereira operating out of Ocean Terrace Inn. Qualified guides operate the dive station, offering beginners' and experienced divers' sessions.

Equipment for 20 divers includes wet suits, masks, snorkels and fins, compressors, regulators—and underwater cameras. The dive boat, a 33-foot fiberglass twin diesel, is also used for deep-sea fishing. (It has a flying bridge.) When there are no scuba groups scheduled, the boat is available for excursions to nearby islands—Nevis, Statia, Saba—for beach parties and picnics. If you want details about special equipment in advance, contact Barracuda at Box 65, Fortlands, St. Kitts, W.I.

Sailors can check with Philip Walwyn at Rawlins Plantation to see if he's planning to sail his catamaran offshore ($30 for a full day with drinks and lunch). Otherwise, talk to Hillary Wattley at the Tourist Office to see what she has for suggestions or go to the waterfront at Basseterre and negotiate with one of the Kittitian fishermen. If you're experienced with Sunfish sailing and the vagaries of Caribbean offshore breezes, there are Sunfish for rent at Frigate Bay.

■■■

TREASURES AND TRIFLES ON ST. KITTS range from the exceptional wall hangings and printed fabric for clothes and other uses designed at **Caribelle Batik,** with studios at 17th-century Romney Manor, to the simple handcrafts that make up in earnest attempt what they may lack in finesse. Caribelle's studio at Romney Manor is worth an excursion, with a stop at the Carib petroglyphs carved on the stones, up the road to your right as you pass through Old Road Town heading northwest on the west coast. The batik and tie-dying (wax painting on fabric which is then dipped in color vats) is fascinating to watch, and the designs are worked on West Indian Sea island cotton which used to be made in the islands—and is now made elsewhere occasionally from cotton grown here. Prices for T-shirts hover around $10; sundresses can be $35 or more; wall hangings range from $15 to $30 and up.

Cameron and Spencer, with a sign over the front porch of one of the buildings that fronts on Pall Mall Square, is an artists' studio, and the artists are 2—Kate Spencer and Rose Cameron Smith—who came from England to settle in St. Kitts, at least for part of the year, a couple of seasons ago. With a flair for capturing the special character of West Indian scenes, buildings, and people, Kate and Rose parlayed their expertise with watercolors into a commercial venture that gives vacationers something of quality to buy. Visit the studio (or look around your room if you're staying at the Royal St. Kitts where their pictures hang on the walls).

In Basseterre the **Cellar Shop,** where Lesley Pencheon selects the merchandise for sale, has Jean Yves Froment fabric designs by the length or made up in shirts and skirts plus handwoven (in Montserrat) Sea Island cotton mats for EC$8 each in packets of 4, or EC$9 apiece. T-shirt collectors will not want to leave the shop without the "Mind Your Head 'n Watch Your Step" shirt that is the store's motto. You have to stoop to enter through the low cellar arch. (Other items to look for are Mrs. Jones pottery from Nevis, dolls made on Antigua, and basketwork from St. Lucia.) The **Corner Shop** has a selection of "free-port" merchandise, displayed on shelves with Lalique, Lladro, and other name-brand figurines prominent and china in the next-best spot. Search out the **Lotus** where you may find some local crafts (but I did not find much of interest when I last looked). Check with Hillary Wattley at the Tourist Board office near the boat landing for the Nevis ferry to see what places she suggests for island-made items when you are vacationing. The Tourist Board office occasionally has a few things for sale.

Ram's also has a duty-free shop near the Tourist Board office—for the winning gamblers to spend their money on crystal, perfume, china, and other luxury items that have not been readily available heretofore, but I suspect the best buys will continue to be the Mt. Gay rum and other liquor that can be bought from the limited selection at **Kassab's** airport nook (which is not always open, and is big enough to hold about 2 shoppers at a time when it is).

A Slice of Lemon is a very special shop which will be no surprise to any readers who already know just how unique the Golden Lemon Inn at Dieppe Bay has become. Martin Kreiner's considerable talent sets the tone for the 2 shops (at Golden Lemon and in town). Elegant jewelry with interesting design is a specialty.

Palmcrafts, at "the Circus" in downtown Basseterre, has enough interesting items to offer one-stop shopping for purchases for all your friends at home. Culling the best from this and other islands' handcrafts, the small store is packed with "the best" available from Haiti, St. Vincent, and other spots. Although prices reach the highest ranges, there are shell bracelets and other items at reasonable cost. Carl Fuchs has a noteworthy sense of design and commerce.

Wall's Bookstore, with an around-the-corner entrance marked as Deluxe Records, is a Kittitian tradition, and your source for reading matter including an interesting selection of paperbacks. Investigate the records by West Indian artists and ask to see Betty Lam (who with husband Freddy is responsible for Fairview Inn). This is her family store.

St. Lucia

St. Lucia Tourist Board, Box 221, Castries, St. Lucia, W.I.; 41 East 42nd St., New York, NY 10017; 151 Bloor Street, W, Suite 425, Toronto, Ontario M5S 1S2, Canada.

US$1 = EC$2.60
Unless otherwise noted, $ refers to U.S. currency.

The boat bobbed on the waves, as did the English and French flotillas when they cruised these shores in the 18th century. We had boarded in Castries to sail down the Caribbean side of St. Lucia, aiming for the twin peaks, the famous Pitons, that are navigation marks for the area's sailors. We would eventually anchor in their shadows, but not until we had tacked into Marigot Bay, to swirl around with some other yachts and to reminisce about what the place might have looked like in 1778 when Samuel Barrington, British admiral, tied palm fronds to the masts of his ships and convinced the French that there was nothing but a palm grove here. When you sail in, you can see how Count d'Estaing could have been fooled—not often, and not for long.

The peaceful place that proves a haven for vacationers, some of whom turn into residents, in search of sun had a tumultuous history that saw the island tossed back and forth between French and British for most of its early history. The town of Soufrière, for example, was home for a band of French republicans sent to the colonies in the French Revolution to retrain the settlers in the ways of the new government. The slaves who were freed turned to the British rather than submit to the rule of the French and were sent on military maneuvers in the British colonies in Africa.

Fishnets hang from posts along the shore at most villages, certainly at Anse la Raye, where they blur the scene of the sea and are punctuated with bright bougainvillea and other blooms that spill from nearby bushes. The history braided with French and British strands is obvious not only in the costumes and customs but also in the place names: Moule-à-Chique, Anse la Raye, Choiseul, Vieux Fort, and even Troumassee, an archaeological site worked first in 1955—and an area now marked for a big hotel.

When the British took the fortress that capped the mountain known as Morne Fortuné, above St. Lucia's capital of Castries, Admiral George Rodney set the place up as his headquarters. He would watch his fleet from vantage points here and could set sail— soon after the acknowledgment of America's united colonies—to pillage Statia in reprisal for the Dutch island's recognition of the sovereignty of the fledgling United States.

It's not only the naval battles that mark the shores and hillsides of this island. On the Cas-en-Bas estate, near Lavoutte Bay at Gros Islet, there's an intriguing 3-level sugar mill. They say that animals turned the mill by walking around the top level (most St. Lucian mills weren't powered by wind). The middle level held the hearth, the boilers and the rest of the heavy equipment and the lower level is lined with vats and canals—for the molasses that was crushed and boiled, leaving the bagasse that was rich in nutrients and used for fodder. Today the place is in ruins, and few know it is here. Sugar was finally abandoned as a St. Lucian crop in 1960, almost 200 years after it was first planted.

It's banana plantations and some copra plantations prickling with the coconut trees that provide the source for the copra that make the quilt in shades of green that lies over St. Lucia. Those have been the crops for the past few years, but the newest crop is tourists, well fried in coconut oil, which is sold with lessons about the application by wily young St. Lucian salesmen who saunter along the beaches.

■■■

POLITICAL PICTURE: St. Lucia's political situation is unclear at press time, but it will have been resolved by the time you visit. Readers planning to vacation in St. Lucia are invited to contact me, c/o William Morrow Co. 105 Madison Avenue, New York, NY 10016, for comment on status during the vacation period covered with this 1982 edition. In May 1981, after Prime Minister Alan Louisy had been encouraged to step down and his former Attorney General, Winston Cenec, had taken the post as Prime Minister, George Odlum, former Minister for Trade, Tourism, and Foreign Affairs and Deputy Prime Minister under a fragile liaison with Louisy, split from the ruling Labour Party and formed the Progressive Labour Party. The PLP's symbol is a heart, and at the party's launching on May 17, 1981, Odlum made clear what many had known from the time he first emerged as a political figure: George Odlum believes he is the best man to lead his fledgling nation for the foreseeable future. Elections may have been called, following the British system, by the time you visit. Whether or not former Prime Minister John Compton, the man at the helm of his country's ship of state at the time of independence, will lead his party to victory remains to be seen. St. Lucia became an independent country on February 22, 1979. Although the order to end the Associated Statehood status was passed on December 15, the St. Lucia Labour Party (SLP) fought the independence move promoted by the government, with John Compton as Premier, because they claimed, through SLP leader Alan Louisy, that independence "was not the will of the people." Louisy's sentiments were overruled and Compton became Prime Minister of the new country of St. Lucia, but not for long. Elections on July 2 resulted in a landslide victory for the SLP. Prime Minister Louisy assembled his new cabinet, appointing George Odlum as Deputy Prime Minister and Minister of Foreign Affairs. Politics within the SLP party resulted in a seesaw of power plays during the end of '79 through '80 and well into '81. Odlum was acting as spokesman for St. Lucian policies in his travels in the U.S. and elsewhere, and his close friendship with Grenada's Bernard Coard and others active in the new socialism in the Caribbean were under careful scrutiny. St. Lucia has traditionally held regular elections for the 17 members of the House of Assembly who govern with the 3 nominated members and the Attorney General, who is appointed. The Cabinet of St. Lucia consists of the Prime Minister and 7 Ministers in charge of the various departments of the government. The Governor is appointed by the Queen on recommendation of the Prime Minister.

AUTHOR'S OBSERVATION: St. Lucians speak English, but you may not be able to understand it. The dialect is their own, as is the case for each island of the English-speaking Caribbean, but the colloquialisms link French and African words and sayings with perhaps-familiar English words. When you're trying to make your wants known to staff at your hotel, and to people you may talk with elsewhere, speaking slowly—and without too many Americanisms—will be the easiest route for clear communication.

■■■

CUSTOMS OF THE COUNTRY of St. Lucia are a marvelous mixture of French Creole, a token from the days of French rule and the present proximity to French neighbor Martinique, and English tradition. Over the basic French and English, there is a liberal layer of modern independence. Government efforts for a domestic education plan about the benefits (and liabilities) of tourism will, many hope, counteract the advance of a kind of diffidence I noticed on a recent visit. Tourism has taken firm foot on some areas of St. Lucia in recent years, and some local resentment was obvious among young people who cluster around some of the Castries stores and who saunter the tourist beaches attempting to sell baskets, sundresses, and suntan oils.

Tourism was late in arriving on St. Lucia, by comparison to some other Caribbean destinations. Hotel rooms came into flower in the early '70s, long before many people had really heard about St. Lucia and not long after British entrepreneur John Young made this one of the terminals for his charters full of tourists from England, moving along a formula he had found financially successful (for someone) during his empire-building that included Court Line acquisitions of airlines and hotels and a building boom that put a bumper crop of boxy rooms on the beach at the south of this island. The problem was that John Young/Court Line went bankrupt, leaving a lot of St. Lucian operations gasping for breath. The southern tip of this island, where most of the foreigners who had intruded in the early '40s had been the U.S. military stationed at Beane Field during World War II, responded to the huge hotel that grew on the beach at its southeast shore—and became the major employer. But the fact remains that many of the people of the village of Vieux Fort had never seen anything like the modern Halcyon Days hotel in their lives—and most had never been out of Vieux Fort. There's bound to be a culture shock for local villagers whose quiet country traditions are suddenly trampled upon by a lot of bare-breasted tourists, burned from tropical sun, gaily garbed in a variety of resort wear the likes of which had never been seen here before. Vieux Fort has changed, but it still survives. The same is true of Soufrière, always a place for visitors to come to see the sulphur vents, but only recently "filled" with cruise ship passengers and the handful of guests who can fit in the few small hotels in this area. When you head into the hinterlands, however, you will be an obvious outsider—welcomed, but looked at askance. Only Castries caters to commerce, but it does so keeping its own West Indian character intact.

Clothes are comfortably casual. Business dress in downtown Castries is more casual than it used to be, but you will still find men in business suits and women in "proper" dresses. Unlike Willemstad, Curaçao, and Charlotte Amalie, St. Thomas, the streets of downtown Castries do not throb to the tourist beat. St. Lucians outnumber the visitors, and St. Lucians put on their best for the excursion to town—especially if it is market day. Colorful resort wear and shorts are conspicuous, marking you immediately as an outsider. At the luxury hotels (La Toc, Cariblue, and others), most of your fellow vacationers will be North Americans and Europeans who dress up for the tropics. Evenings can be elegant, especially if you are with a group who likes to be more formal in the evenings. About the dressiest anyone gets is jacket and tie for men, and the loose-fitting white or pastel shirt is more popular with many St. Lucians than the northerner's jacket and tie.

■■

MONEY MATTERS: St. Lucia uses Eastern Caribbean currency, exchanged at the official rate of EC$2.60 to US$1. Since most of the stores, restaurants, and other services are for residents first—and tourists also—$ and ¢ refers to EC currency. Some places will also print U.S. prices, but most leave you to figure equivalents for yourself. Although you can pay your hotel and services in U.S. dollars at the end of your stay, it's wise to change some money at the bank or your hotel cashier to have the currency of the country for purchases when you are touring. (Bagshaw's marks its prices in U.S. dollars, which should give you some indication about who does most of the purchasing there. See Treasures and Trifles below.)

■■

ARRIVAL at St. Lucia's airports offers you options, depending on your starting point. For most hotels, the small airstrip at Castries, about 5 minutes' drive from downtown and no more than 20 from most hotels, is by far the most convenient. However, the big jets from major international destinations do not land here. They fly into Hewanorra (Hugh-an-*no*ra) Airport at the south. It was a former U.S. military base, Beane Field, and is almost an hour's drive from Castries. The time varies according to your advisor. My St. Lucian friends say 45 minutes, but I find it difficult to cover that distance—when I don't know what's around the next curve—in less than an hour; the drive is especially difficult since most first-timers don't know where they're arriving in Castries as they curve down the hill into town. (Signposting is sparse, if it is present at all.)

■■■

TOURING TIPS: As on other islands, your options for getting around include taxi or rental car (and you'll drive on the left). Main roads are good, and taxi fares between the southern airport, where most of the big planes land (at Hewanorra), and Castries are about $30 per car (for 1 to 4 people). Although the big-name car-rental firms do have representatives on the island (and offices at hotels such as La Toc and Cariblue), you'll usually get better rates from the local entrepreneurs who may have a couple of cars for rent. If you're a stickler for maintenance, stay with the big firms and pay the price; otherwise gamble with the smaller firms (Rufus Branford for mini-mokes or Fletcher's, Fredie's Garage, and, in Vieux Fort, Boriel for regular cars). They will usually have a relative or friend handy if you have any mechanical problems.

Roads are not well signposted, but the main road that is the backbone of the island is easy enough to follow (just stay on the paved part); the side roads often dissolve into rutted routes of dry and dusty dirt, but the rewards at the end may be a remote fishing village or a sandy cove. (Avoid swimming on the surf-pounded east coast, unless you're with an island resident who knows the area. The surf may be tempting, but the undertow can be treacherous.)

For quick trips between airports, inquire about chartering a small plane, or taking the sometimes scheduled service St. Lucia Airways makes the air link with small planes (and *very* casual service).

Taxi drivers take visitors on tours and are willing to wait while you prowl at some spot that interests you. Often their conversation adds a lot to the experience. For those who like the water and want a quick glimpse of the highlights, the trip from Castries on one of the sightseeing boats captures the top of the list. (The boat trip, plus a taxi drive overlooking the east coast from Hewanorra Airport to a northwest coast hotel, will give you an idea of the island, but there's nothing to compare with prowling around on your own.)

AUTHOR'S OBSERVATION: St. Lucia's largest hotels cooperate with tour operators to provide an all-inclusive week (or longer) at one price with options. Ask your local

travel agent for information on good-value week-long
stays, but read the fine print carefully so that you know
what the extras (usually all meals) will be.

■■■

HOTELS on St. Lucia run the whole range, from luxury resorts to
small and very special guesthouses tucked on their own coves at
the sea end of rutted, winding roads from airports, villages, or Castries. There are interesting housekeeping facilities where you are at
the heart of St. Lucian activity, with the convenience (and cash
saving) of cooking for yourself, sometimes with the help of a St.
Lucian cook.

During the several years since the burst of early 70's building,
hoteliers and others have concentrated on filling the rooms and establishing a viable tourism. Rhetoric of local politicians and turbu-
lence within the various political parties has meant, unfortunately,
that government officials have been too occupied with domestic
problems to concentrate on the much needed support systems for
sound tourism development. Although private industry has continued to operate the existing hotels, there has not been much government support in the way of tourism promotion, and the island's hospitality industry has suffered. Ambitious plans are on drawing
boards, but I suspect they will stay there until the political situation
is resolved and the government ship of state is sailing again. There
has been talk of two large European developments and a Midwest
U.S. venture. Smuggler's Cove at Cap Estate in the north of St.
Lucia is programmed for 500 holiday homes (none open, few
started as we go to press) and the Rodney Bay area is expected to
have 300 holiday units within a couple of years.

On-the-spot training for St. Lucians interested in hotel work has
been implemented. Instructors affiliated with L'Ecole Hoteliere of
Lausanne, Switzerland, were the teachers, all of whom were
backed by the enthusiastic support offered by Bill Stewart (Caribbean Hotel Management Service), an active member of the Caribbean Hotel Association, which inaugurated the Swiss program.

AUTHOR'S AWARDS go to La Toc, the Cunard Trafalgar
hotel and to East Winds for casual surroundings seaside.

✜ **Allain's Guest House** (Soufrière, St. Lucia, W.I.; 3 rooms) is a
small spot in downtown Soufrière, a seaside village almost untouched by the swish of the '70s. Mr. Charles Allain's rooms take 2,

in simple surroundings that are OK for self-sufficient travelers and for those not seeking resort facilities. His rates are about $50 for 2, 2 meals daily served family style, with the option for some good St. Lucian food.

✤ **Anse Chastanet** (Box 216, Soufrière, St. Lucia, W.I.; 20 doubles plus suites) arranges itself on a hillside, rising from a curve of beach that is best reached by boat. That's the way I first saw this place more than a decade ago, and that is still the best way—if it is *my* vacation—to arrive. The rutted, bend-and-weave road that snakes here from Vieux Fort's Hewanorra Airport is enough to make *any* hotel seem like an oasis. Each room has its own personality, none is lavishly furnished, and the best ones for me are those that put you at eye level with the 2 peaks of the picture-perfect Pitons. This is no hotel for cardiac cases; the hike from the beach up to your room is 100-plus steps, with a couple of bird-feeding stations placed at appropriate pausing spots so you can claim you're stopping for them. The beachside bar and restaurant have flourished with recent seasons; together they offer a self-contained unit that can keep you in and near the sea all day. At the top of your climb, you'll find the modernized, open-air original house that the Cummingses built and ran as an inn when they opened in the late 1960s. When Nick Troobitscoff and Wayne Brown bought the inn in 1975, they added and padded facilities, so that the small resort has something for anyone who likes peace and quiet in comfortable tropical surroundings. Manager John Barker takes care of the day-to-day operation, and any special requests you may have while here. Count on paying about $160 for 2, 2 meals daily per person this winter, unless you want one of the suites where you'll be paying more.

✤ **Cariblue** (Box 437, Cap Estate, St. Lucia, W.I.; 102 rooms) captures a west coast cove, in the north of the country. (You can make the 9-mile run into Castries in an easy 20 minutes on good roads.) Advertising includes prominent mention of Steigenberger, a name well known to Europeans who are familiar with the other properties of this German chain, but unknown to most North American travelers who may be surprised by the quantities of European guests that the Steigenberger link helps explain. Most of the modern air-conditioned rooms are in a couple of 4-story buildings, a short walk from the main dining, dancing, drinking hub and the patch of beach. Full resort facilities (shops, water-sports concession, etc.) are available here, and the foreign accents of many of the guests give the resort a cosmopolitan aspect that adds a special aura to an English-speaking island. There are horses for riding around the estate ($10 per hour or $12 per hour with instructor), and the 9-hole Cap Estate golf course is a 10-minute walk from the hotel gates, with tennis courts on the premises free for guests who don't want instruction (and a charge of $10 per ½ hour in winter if you do). The Sunday morning concert that is part of the usual action plan is a European innovation welcomed by those who haven't expected it; it's followed by the buffet that draws visitors from other hotels as well as island residents to this northern point. The food that is called "international" is heavy enough on steak and roast beef to please most American palates. You can expect to find the menus written in German as well as English, and the staff will speak most fluently in their own island patois. Your English is not theirs. A hotel bus makes the run into Castries Friday afternoons for a 2-hour shopping excursion (at a $5 transportation fee). Rates for your winter holiday for 2 can range from $200 to $250, with 2 meals daily per person; one of the 2 suites reaches close to $300 for 2. The Christmas holiday surcharge of $10 per person (December 23–January 2) may be a Christmas present for the hotel, but certainly not for you.

✣ **Cloud's Nest Hotel** (Vieux Fort, St. Lucia, W.I.; 14 rooms) gives you simple surroundings in downtown Vieux Fort and an option to see more of the St. Lucian daily life in this south-coast town than the high-rise Halcyon Hotel does. This hotel is not for the timid tourist or the demanding visitor; Ms. Gildette Williams's hospitality at Cloud's Nest has appealed to barefoot and boating types who are Caribbean converts. The location is convenient for town, and a short distance from the beach. Rates of $60 for 2 seem high to me, even when 2 good meals daily are included, since most people who stay here will want the opportunity to eat at some of the other local spots.

✣ **East Winds Inn** (Box 193, Castries, St. Lucia, W.I.; 10 rooms) is buttoned to its beach, providing a self-contained vacation unit that is a haven for the world-weary who pay $60 for 2, meals extra, for seclusion on the sea. Marguerite Egerer is one reason why this place is so successful. While you bask on the beach or curl in one of the corners of the thatched-roof reading, sipping, dining area for an afternoon on your own, she is working to be sure that everything is at the ready for whatever you want when you want it—and that includes the food in the kitchen, which has become island-famous.

The Sunday beachside buffet draws knowing folk from town and other resorts. The rest of the time, those who have rented one of the rondavels within earshot of the sea and the birds have the place pretty much to themselves. There are Sunfish for guests' sailing, and the option to follow the dirt road away from the sea to the asphalt strand that stretches into Castries, about a 15-minute drive but a world away in atmosphere. This is a place for people who like their comforts casual and who don't care if the stove in the housekeeping unit doesn't cook on all burners and there are lumps in the bed.

✣ **Green Parrot Inn** (Castries, St. Lucia, W.I.; 30 rooms) gives you a bird's eye view of the town and the sea from a mountainside perch on the Morne, that historic hill that rises "behind" the town of Castries. The rooms are comfortably furnished, and guests have easy access to what has been one of the best restaurants in town (a place that's been recommended in the restaurant listing since it opened a few years ago). You'll need a car, or willingness to thumb a ride, if you want any mobility here. The mile or more from downtown Castries is up a wiggly route, and getting to any beach from here will take a good 20 minutes but there's a pool on premises. OK for island aficionados who want a hillside setting, but no good for beach-baskers. Rates are about $90 for 2, breakfasts included and other meals a la carte.

✣ **Halcyon Beach Club** (Choc Bay, St. Lucia, W.I.; 98 rooms) is under the wing of Caribbean Hotel Management Service, a St. Lucia-based firm that manages this and three other St. Lucian properties. Your fellow guests will include many British and Swiss and other Europeans, as well as Canadians. The facilities include 2-story units in the gardens at the beach, a main building with shops, restaurant and convening nooks, and a *Fisherman's Wharf* that sits on stilts in the sea. The pool punctuates a place near the sand, the tennis courts are ready for play, and there's plenty to keep people busy here—even without heading out for a sail on a yacht, or to water-ski, or scuba dive, or to take a ride into Castries, about 5 miles south and the source for downtown shopping. All water sports are included in your room rate, and you'll settle into one of the several buildings around the property. Rooms without a sea view often have a patio and semi-private sunning area; rooms with a sea view are preferable (in my opinion) and carry the highest tally. Count on paying over $150 for 2 if you take 2 meals daily per person here this winter, and know that you have a dine-around option at other

CHMS properties (Halcyon Sands, and St. Lucian). Anyone who books in on a group rate will be paying a lot less for more. Ask your travel agent about how you can too.

✢ **Halcyon Days** (Vieux Fort, St. Lucia, W.I.; 256 rooms) is *huge*, far bigger than its 256 rooms make it sound. The 4-story units rose on this windswept southeast-coast beach in the season of '71, with plans for filling the small pockets that face the sea with vast numbers of sunseekers who would pour onto charter flights to be funneled into the vacation plan at Halcyon. The hotel is built for moderate-income travel: Rooms are small (by American standards), as are the narrow twin beds; furnishings are colorful but sparse; meals are served in quantity—in big rooms with small tables. When the house is full there's an aura of camaraderie even if you have not come with part of a group. There's a pool, plus l-o-n-g strand of sand. (Someone said 5 miles, but all I know is it was as long as I wanted to walk turning left and turning right from the hotel.) There are tennis courts, volleyball, and arrangements can be made for water sports (usually on the other, more protected, side of the point when the wind is strong, which is almost always) and for horseback riding. There are a couple of shops in the lobby at the hotel and an activities board that posts island tours as well as flights to nearby islands (Martinique, St. Vincent, etc.) for day excursions. Sailing can be planned for sunset cruising or longer, and while your surroundings here may not be the island's most luxurious, there's a good chance they may be the island's most active. There's disco dancing some evenings, and a lively cocktail bar/lounge that starts with some music just before sunset. Rates on the regular plan are about $135 for 2, 2 meals daily, or just over $100 with meals extra. If you are a light eater and/or like island food so that you'll be happy trying the half-dozen St. Lucian dining depots at this end of the island, you might consider the no-meal plan.

✢ **El Leon Rojo** (Vigie Beach, Castries, St. Lucia, W.I.; 57 rooms) has aged well, with a name change that came with each marriage with a new owner. With each new name came new layers of "improvements." In the late '60s, the hotel was known as Blue Waters Beach, and then in the early '70s it became Vigie Beach, a name it held onto through about 5 seasons. The Halcyon group took it over, changing the name to Halcyon Sands, adding new rooms, opening up some of the public facilities, and filling the place with groups. The newest owners, who arrived in mid-1981, have changed the name again and are adding "Inn on the Beach" for the non-Spanish-speaking group. Through all the changes, the property at the south end of Vigie Beach (Malabar is at the northern end of the cove) has held onto the personality of a small resort, dedicated to the beach, sun and fun life. Rooms are in 2-story units that sprawl along the shore; the public rooms are open to the breezes, with the dining area out near the beach bar at the shore. Informality has been a key, not only because the groups that flock here enjoy the sun and sea, but also because the beach is shared with St. Lucians who arrive in invasion force on weekends. There are all shapes and sizes of rooms, some of the simplest at good rates. Count on paying close to $100 for a room for 2 with no meals this winter. You can just about name your price if you check with your travel agent about special tour rates and know that whatever you pay, you're near the town, on the beach, and at an action hub.

✤ **Hotel La Toc** (Castries, St. Lucia, W.I.; 164 doubles) is so closely linked with La Toc Village that it is difficult not to talk about the two together. However, they are separate but equal, the village being villas and apartments with kitchens where guests are free to cook at home and to use the hotel facilities, especially the pool and beach nearest the village, and removed from the bigger beach and livelier facilities of the hotel. Both were part of a grand plan that opened in April '73 on the shores above a sandy beach in a residential area about 3 miles south of Castries. Guests at the main hotel, with the central building shaped like an angular question mark cupping the sand and the hotel pool in its bowl, have air-conditioned rooms in several tiers, most with view of the sea and all with modern facilities. The Cunard-Trafalgar hotel links some vacation plans with a week aboard a Cunard cruise ship and a week here; other vacationers bed in here to stay the full time. But beware the day the cruise ship lands if you came here seeking peace and quiet. Coffee shop, poolside, is casual; evenings at the main hotel can be resort-dressy, when the complement of guests who spend their days on the golf course, the tennis courts, the beach or sailing and scuba diving want to dance until dawn. If you are a hamburger, sandwich, salad and seafood soul, you'll find the surroundings and food acceptable; more demanding types would do better, I suggest, by renting a villa and dining around. At the driveway entrance shops and a car rental desk speckle the main lobby, one floor above the beach and pool. Rates for 2 this winter will range from about $150 to over $200, meals extra but investigate special week-long and other package plans for good value rates. Inquire about the Cunard cruise plan, and special golf and tennis weeks as well as honeymoon holidays. (See La Toc Village under Housekeeping Holidays, below.)

✢ **Hurricane Hole Hotel** (Box 568, Castries, St. Lucia, W.I.; 12 rooms) is not at Castries, as the address suggests, but about 40 minutes' drive down the west coast, at Marigot Bay, a favored port for yachtsmen and a prized bay in the countless wars between the British and French during the tumultuous island history. Accommodations here are simple, and sea-oriented. This is no place for the fussy traveler, but surroundings are ideal for barefoot and boating types who are willing to put on shoes—occasionally. The cottages that cup the rooms are set around the grounds, not very far from each other, but with enough distance to give some privacy. The main hub is the "yacht club" area that is favored by sailors who anchor offshore and the bay is good for waterskiing (arranged through Nick Bowden). Meals include full breakfast and a 3-course dinner, often fish and always filling, at winter rates that figure at just over $800 per person for 2 weeks, when you're part of a group of 8 on the week-on/week-off plan. Write to Nick Bowden at the hotel for information on rates by the day or more. (Bar bill is extra, and there's a slight charge for waterskiing, but the room and board, on land or sea, has been paid for with the 2-week tariff.)

✢ **Malabar Beach Hotel** (Vigie Beach, Castries, St. Lucia, W.I.; 86 rooms, some cottages) makes its mark at the north end of Vigie Beach, just off the airstrip on this island's small, near-town airport of Vigie. The main part of Malabar began life as a private home at the beach, and the Barnards have expanded to make a comfortable hotel. Do not count on a modern, American-motel-style place; but you will find personality and more character than some of the newer places can claim. The beach at Vigie is not the island's best, but the part that stretches north from the main part of Malabar is pleasant to stroll along—when the sea hasn't swiped out the sand. (When that happens, chances are it will soon swoosh it in again, but maybe not during your vacation.) The 2-story block of rooms that is back from the beach is near the pool and the casual restaurant/bar with plastic-wrapped aluminum chairs that is a gathering spot for St. Lucians during their lunch break from business in town. Malabar's cottages are nothing fancy, but they are within the sound of the sea, and quiet, comfortable nests for a relaxing vacation, except on the nights when there's entertainment at the hotel. On those nights you'd better opt for dancing and drinking instead of sleeping. Rates this winter for a room for 2 are about $110 with meals extra; the cottages claim from $100 to $125 for 2, depending on which cottage you have.

✤ **St. Lucian Hotel** (Reduit Beach, Gros Islet, St. Lucia, W.I.; 185 rooms) hove into view on this shore in the season of '70 as a Holiday Inn with careful attention to fitting in the landscape as much as possible. The hotel, which incorporates the former St. Lucia Beach Hotel, tries—and succeeds, I think—to have a personality of its own, even though you have wings of standard air-conditioned rooms, modern furnishings, ocean view from terrace or balcony (depending on your floor), and the usual public rooms and poolside terraces. Caribbean Hotel Management Service runs this place in consort with other properties around St. Lucia. Inquire about the dine-around plan with the other CHMS hotels, and know that you are within walking distance of popular *Pat's Pub,* plus the *Islander* (known for lobster) and *Mortar & Pestle* (featuring Chinese and Indian food). The marina (used by *Stevens Yachts* for charters) is across the road from the hotel, and the beach and pools on the premises offer plenty of space for sun-worshiping. For casually comfortable Caribbean pursuit, it's hard to find a hotel with more to offer on-the-spot than this one. Groups book here summer and winter, which means that even the lone ranger can find other people here—even during the slowest travel times. Count on a friendly, informal atmosphere. *Lucifers* disco opened with top decibel gaiety in June of '80 and will pulsate through the season and after that as outside enthusiasm warrants.

There are some shops on premises, plus 3 tennis courts with night lights (extra fee), and arrangements for scuba, waterskiing, deep-sea fishing, and all the Caribbean vacation expecteds offered right offshore. The beach is once again, the country's best. Your room for 2 this winter will cost $125 and more, meals extra if you book on your own, but ask your travel agent to investigate package tours. You will be about 7 miles north of Castries, so town is a taxi ride or shuttle-bus trip away. (Cap Estate's 9-hole golf course is about 5 miles north.)

✤ **Villa Hotel** (Box 129, Castries, St. Lucia, W.I.; 20 rooms) perches on a patch on the flanks of the Morne, and gives you mountain breezes and a spectacular view of town and the Caribbean, up and over the heat of downtown Castries. This is one of St. Lucia's traditions, run by an island family in true West Indian fashion. There's a pleasant dining area, and linoleum covers the floor of the bar. Aluminum-pipe chairs are backed and seated with plastic-wrapped cushions, and all pull up to round formica-covered tables. The atmosphere is casual, comfortable, and very much West Indian inn. Rooms are tucked into a 2-story building that stretches out in back (so you probably won't have the spectacular view all can enjoy from the front of the house). You can count on good West Indian food and hospitality, and a complement of guests who enjoy being self-sufficient. Not for people who demand beachside lodgings and all modern resort facilities, Villa is ideal for anyone who wants to know St. Lucia better. Hamilton Gidharry manages this and the Villa Beach cottages, is a good host. (See Housekeeping Holidays for mention of the beach cottages, reached through Castries and north up the west coast, about 15 minutes' drive from here.) There's a write-up about the hotel that talks about its being a short walk from town; if you read that, you should know that the walk is straight up—or straight down—on a weaving asphalt road hardly wide enough for 2 cars to pass, and the passing is often 2 trucks. A rental car is recommended if you plan to stay here and want to be mobile, but there's plenty of traffic that passes by the driveway, so you can probably hitch a ride down if you want to. Rates for 2 this winter will be about $80 for room, breakfasts and dinners daily.

■■■

HOUSEKEEPING HOLIDAYS on St. Lucia have led a lot of people into buying or building their own house here. Life is easy and pleasant, and there are adequate to luxury places to rent. For stocking up, the markets in town have fresh vegetables, there is a good bakery on a back street in Castries for marvelous crusty St. Lucian bread (which shows its French influence), and fish and chicken are relatively easy to come by.

Houses for rent range from luxury accommodations (some of them condominiums rented in owner's absence at La Toc Village) to the simple small apartments and cottages away from the tourist hubs, in villages such as Soufrière, Gros Islets, and other towns. Rent-a-Home, Box 337, Castries, St. Lucia, W.I. and Caribbean Home Rentals, Box 710, Palm Beach, FL 33480, list several special properties.

✛ **Bois d'Orange Holiday Villas** (P.O. Box 98, Castries, St. Lucia, W.I.; 11 units) are inland, a hot (and long) walk from any beach. Surroundings are very simple, but you'll find the basics in a 1- or 2-bedroom villa, at about $300 per week tops. The summer low rate of $35 per day for a 2-bedroom villa makes this an ideal family place, but even in winter, when the rate goes up to about $50, it's an OK spot to have a very casual holiday. Facilities are new, adequately (but not lavishly) furnished, and geared to a carefree holiday.

✣ **Dasheen** (Soufrière, St. Lucia, W.I.; several villas) is picture-perfect in my opinion, but part of my enthusiasm is due to the God-given view of the Pitons, and the relief of finding this spectacular spot after bumping and weaving for almost an hour from Hewanorra Airport in the south. The villas that are Dasheen are privately owned, furnished according to the tastes of the individual owners, with maximum use of the breathtaking view and the mountain air that wafts around. You'll have to drive to the beach; management sometimes provides transportation to the strand at Anse Chastanet. At this hilltop perch, there's a speck of a pool, a small gathering spot where meals are sometimes served (when house count is high enough and staff is willing), and wood-frame houses that stand tall at several angular levels, each with its own special outlook. There are 1-, 2- and 3-bedroom homes, all with decks for sunset and Piton viewing, modern kitchens, and several steps to climb to get from one living unit to the next. An ideal hideaway for people who like their places simply perfect. Contact Francis James for details and plan to pay from $50 to $85 daily for 2, depending on the size of the unit you rent this winter.

✣ **Edgewater Apartments** (Vide Bouteille, St. Lucia, W.I.; 6 apts plus 1 cottage) are about a mile from Castries, to the south. The apartments are air-conditioned, but don't count on anything grand. The price is what makes these appealing for people who are watching the budget. Mr. Thompson charges about $30 per night for 2 to share an apartment, and the 2-bedroom cottage goes for about $50.

✣ **Estate Cas-en-Bas** (Lavoutte Bay, St. Lucia, W.I.; 10 cabins) gives you a wood-frame unit in very special surroundings, at a level plot not far from a sandy beach. Furnishings are shoreside simple, with new wrought-iron furniture, colorful fabrics, and an efficiency unit at one end of your living/dining room that is sufficient for cooking. Emphasis is on the uncluttered life in these recently built units with louvered windows (that get cloudy when closed). There's a door that opens onto your own sundeck, but nothing here yet in the way of regular "hotel" services. Self-sufficient types who want a place in the sun should contact Estate Cas-en-Bas, 645 South St., Roosevelt Field, Garden City, NY 11530.

✣ **La Toc Village** (Castries, St. Lucia, W.I.; 50 units) offers 1- and 2-bedroom villas that climb the hill up from the beach, across the La Toc road from the sea. All villas are air-conditioned, with private patio, attractive furnishings, and a higher price than most villas on St. Lucia. Daily winter rates for a 2-bedroom villa start at about $200 and reach close to $300, for 4. You can have a maid/cook included, and will have access to the separate pool (there's another down the beach at La Toc Hotel) and restaurant under the dunce-cap roof in front of the villas. In view of the busyness at the hotel complex, especially when the cruise ship is in port, the peace and quiet you can find just a few steps down the road at these villas is surprising.

✣ **Marigot des Roseaux** (Box 262, Castries, St. Lucia, W.I.) occupies 7½ acres at Marigot Bay and freckles it with glorious open-to-breezes hillside homes that are attractively furnished. An ideal oasis with a nautical atmosphere, the homes have access to *The Moorings Yacht Charter* and *Dolittles* restaurant.

✣ **Morne Fortuné Apartments** (Morne Fortuné, Castries, St. Lucia, W.I.; 12 apts.) are up the hill, just outside the town of Castries. Most of the apartments give you a good hillside breeze and view, but some are pockets, so inquire about what's available for you. The 1-bedroom unit suitable for 2 is about $50 per day; a 2-bedroom unit, ideal for families, is over $50, and Mr. Leonard Headley is the man to see when you have questions. Count on facilities to be simply furnished, and hospitality to be sincere.

✣ **Villa Beach Cottages** (Choc Bay, St. Lucia, W.I.; 5 apts.) are right on the shore, about 3 miles north of Castries on the west coast. They provide a peaceful, shoreside place for independent folk in search of an uncluttered life. There's nothing fancy about these places, but the basics are here and if you want a reasonable holiday on the beach in the sun, this is one place that offers it. Count on about $50 per night for an apartment for 2; contact Mrs. Laura Hunte for details.

■■■■■■■■■■■■■■■■■■■■■■■■■■■■■□■■■■■■■■■■■■■■■■■■■■■■■■■■■■■■■■■

RESTAURANTS in and around Castries are personality places that count as much on their atmosphere as on their food. **Coal Pot** (take the road that runs along the Castries side of the runway, and turn left after the marina) sits at the shore in what might be humble surroundings if extra effort hadn't been put on hurricane globes for table lamps, fishnet, etc. over the bar, and a lot of nautical touches that make a very simple building something special. The food is better than average, but the quality is not as high as the prices. This boite has a following of nautical types and a reservations roster that makes advance planning imperative. The menu is interesting (featuring fish, beef and chicken in St. Lucian and French versions). Count on at least $25 per person, probably more.

Le Boucan, in downtown Castries, near the library at Columbus Square, takes its name from the roasted boar that was the staple in the diet of the early seafarers, otherwise known as "boucaniers." Surroundings are comfortably casual, and food includes roasts as well as some St. Lucian specialities and fish.

Green Parrot Restaurant, up the winding road to the Morne, about 15 minutes' drive out of and above Castries, is in an unusual setting next to the St. Lucia perfume factory. The restaurant, to the left as you walk up the steps after you've parked your car, is set up for the elegant service it offers, and food focuses on local specialties, well prepared and presented. (There are also offerings to placate tender palates.) Ask the maitre d' for some suggestions from the chef, and leave yourself in his hands. You won't be sorry. Prices run about $15 for an entree, but with full meals will be much higher (and are quoted in E.C. currency).

Rain, on the square near the Catholic church inland at downtown Castries, is a St. Lucian institution. Pinpointing a special small, wood frame building almost a decade ago, the restaurant is casual, with a very special Somerset Maugham aura all its own. The 2nd-floor balcony is the prize spot—not only to read from the blackboard to learn the day's offerings, but also to watch the view over town. Count on everything from hamburgers to interesting specials—including ice cream, delicious desserts, and a panoply of rum and other concoctions. White walls, wicker, and pinpoints of color, plus interesting pictures, posters, and notices make this place a "must" stop on any St. Lucian visit. Fortunately, Rain is open from about 10 a.m. until late evening, when the atmosphere changes with the light.

Pat's Pub, at Rodney Bay's new development, within walking distance of the St. Lucian Hotel, draws those who like a nautical setting (Stevens yachts are moored nearby when not out on charter). Seafood and steak are staples, but it's the hospitality as well as the food that makes this spot so special. With a publike place that perches over the harbor area (and often has some yacht tied up within arm's reach), Pat's place draws St. Lucian residents for friendly, fun-filled evenings. Reservations are recommended, and plan on parting with about $25 per person if you want to go all out (with wine). Pub meals cost less.

At Soufriere on the southwest coast, **The Hummingbird** has made a name for itself as an unusual and comfortable dining depot. Paul and Joyce run their shoreside place with easy hospitality, taking their cue from the boats that anchor offshore. Try some of the Creole specialities (and be sure to ask for local hot sauce if you like lively spices). A good place to park for lunch on a day of touring or to go if you're lodging at Anse Chastanet or Dasheen, The Hummingbird also has French wines and a pleasant bar.

The Still, on a side street in Soufrière, is a long way to go from Castries for dinner, but there are those so enthusiastic about the opportunity to dine in refurbished ruins of a plantation house that they make the effort. For most visitors, this is a luncheon stop (but be sure to check about opening hours) on a day of touring. Guests at Dasheen, Anse Chastanet and a few nearby homes for rent plan special dinners here, where the verdant growth disguises the remains of the 1900s rum distillery.

Dolittles, at Marigot Bay, takes its name from the fact that the film of *Dr. Dolittle* (starring Rex Harrison) was filmed here a decade or so ago, but the seaside bistro's fame comes from a casual, nautical atmosphere that would make almost any meal taste good. Desmond and Jenny Bascomb are in charge. Favored by sailing types who have anchored offshore, the place features homemade soups (pumpkin, calalloo, groundnut) all served with homemade banana bread. Sound good? It is, and well worth the drive down for lunch if you are staying in the Castries orbit. A Sunday luncheon special last season was curry chicken with a full complement of condiments for EC$20. The lobster dinner by candlelight casts some kind of a spell; it's marvelous!

■■

PLACES WORTH FINDING around St. Lucia are natural, unless you count ruins among your interests. The best view over Castries is from the top of the Morne Fortuné (the mountain that rises behind the town), but the Morne itself is not much to look at, having been subdivided into building lots in the last half of the '60s. There's part of Fort Charlotte, started in 1794 and named for the mother (Queen Charlotte) of Edward, Duke of Kent, that is worth a wander, but otherwise look into the studio of Design St. Lucia, watch a cricket match or a football/soccer game played by some of the young people who attend the school and university in some of the refurbished buildings, note the hospital (which has been used for a St. Lucian government-Rockefeller Foundation study of schistosomiasis) and head for a beach. The hospital is in what was a barracks building; the Batmen's Quarters, shown on a map of 1846, are the museum for the **St. Lucia Archeological and Historical Society;** the Canteen (on maps of 1846) is a lecture hall for the university, and the Combermere Barracks is a technical school. Although most of the authentic historical feeling has been lost with the new building uses, the site *is* worth visiting, mainly for the views on the way up and from the top. (Typical of new uses for old buildings, the Top of the Morne apartments are in what was the headquarters building, erected in 1891 but unrecognizable for its venerable past now.)

Pigeon Point used to be an island until the 1970–71 landfill project that was intended to drain the swamp (and take care of the plague of sand flies that pestered Choc Bay resorts) created a causeway. Conservationists shrieked, to no avail, as almost one third of a spectacular reef was covered over (and the rest changed irrevocably). Plans for Pigeon Point to become a recreation area have moved along slowly; but those who take the time can still find some of the military graves in the cemetery on the south shore that dates from Admiral Rodney's day, when he had a base on Pigeon Point in the early 1780s.

CASTRIES has been burned and rebuilt so many times in its history that there's not much of historic interest, as far as buildings are concerned. The town thrives as a West Indian port, with the fishing boats lining up in the morning on the north side of the harbor (easily seen as you drive out of town to the hotels on the northwest shore). Find the town square, a couple of streets back from the waterfront, for the most interesting buildings. One is **Cathedral of the Immaculate Conception,** built in 1894 on the site of previous churches and completed in 1897. The wood inside is worth noting, if you like imposing buildings. Otherwise, look from the outside (you can't miss it) and head for the upper porch at Rain restaurant to watch the meandering activity around the square. The **Market,** at the north end of town, is the only other sight of note. The market building was formally dedicated in 1894 by Sir Charles Bruce, but it will be difficult to imagine an imposing proper Englishman in the middle of the fray you'll witness on market day. Take time, when you wander around here, and be sure to look at the buses as they get stuffed to the splitting point before they head out of town back to the villages.

AUTHOR'S OBSERVATION; Invest $3 in *St. Lucia Historic Sites* (1975) by Robert Devaux, published on behalf of the Saint Lucia National Trust. The ponderous book lists sites, monuments, buildings in a strictly functional fashion, but the background information will be interesting if you want to explore on your own. Copies have been available through Shipwreck Shop at Halcyon Days and shops in Castries. Inquire at the Tourist Board if you have trouble tracking down a copy.

Moule-à-Chique, the southernmost point, near Vieux Fort, is an interesting ride for the view, but the lighthouse perched at the point, and the stone buildings you can note around it, were built in 1911, so there's no point in heading here for history. The view, along the shores where Halcyon Days reigns supreme, and out to sea is spectacular.

For a more interesting route, in my opinion, drive through **Vieux Fort,** a village with small buildings, cluttered with people, chickens and sometimes pigs on dirt roads, with shops tucked into the wood West Indian buildings (Agatha's Art & Boutique; Kitch Tailoring Boutique, Charles Supermarket, all small and surviving on local business). **Laborie,** another village, about 25 minutes' drive west, has an imposing Catholic church at the turn in the road as you snake around the coast. Follow the road up, down and around the shore toward **Choiseul,** a town which rumor claims is destined for a big hotel. The waterfront street in Choiseul spills into the sea, there's a handcraft center on the hill as you head into town, and then you'll wind past the graveyard, the Catholic Church, and the fishing boats, nets and traps at the shore. (About 1½ hours along this route, you'll come to the turnoff for Dasheen apartments—see Housekeeping Holidays.) **Soufrière,** half-burned in the 1900s, is a clutter of pastel houses set on the shore. The town was the earliest French community, and is a goal these days for the sulphur vents at the volcano in the hills where your guide will either talk about—or actually perform—cooking an egg in the steam. At **Diamond Estate** (a banana plantation) there are mineral baths that periodically come into conversations as "about to be developed." At the moment, you can wallow if you want, but there's nothing fancy or even very organized about the facilities. (The claim is that Louis XVI used the baths during a French reign over St. Lucia, in the years of English-French squabbling over possession of the island.)

■■

SPORTS simmer down to a complete list, with a little of everything, if not the best for some. Facilities for visitors are centered on the hotels, at Rodney Bay, home port for the island operation for *Stevens Yachts,* and at Marigot where The Moorings Yacht charters are based. Stevens has its land base near Annapolis, Maryland (and a mail drop at Box 129, Stevensville, MD 21666). Bill Stevens was the pioneer for bare-boat and small crewed boat chartering when he started his operation in Grenada almost 2 decades ago. The only other island network at that time was the Nicholson operation, and they sent yachts out from their home port of Antigua. But it was Bill Stevens who originally set up the Grenadines for many who have cruised these islands. The Custom 50 ketches and sloops listed with Stevens charter with crew for a week, between $2500 and $3000, depending on whether you have 2 or 6 aboard, and include everything except gratuities. You can pick up your boat and/or jump ship at any port between Antigua and Grenada, giving you the best cruising grounds to call your own during your week or more aboard. Check with the Stevensville office for details on other sailing opportunities, including sail-and-learn programs, available for Grenadine and other cruising. Anyone planning to charter in this area (the Windward Islands) should not consider leaving home port without *Steven's Cruising Guide to the Windward Islands,* available through the Stevensville office.

The Moorings operation is linked with Charlie and Ginny Cary's very successful British Virgin Islands' charter firm, the leader of the Tortola-based fleets. St. Lucia's venture started last season, with Custom '50s available at Marigot Bay, and a land base, at the former Marigot des Roseaux Club which has been home for Desmond and Jenny Bascomb's Dolittle restaurant. Details on The Moorings Marigot are available from the U.S. headquarters: Box 50059, New Orleans, LA 70150.

Yacht Cariad combines with Hurricane Hole Hotel at Marigot Bay for a week-on, week-off cruise/land setup that puts you aboard a 115-foot ketch with a full crew for your 7 days of sailing. Ideal for those who like the water but don't really want salt spray, the *Cariad* anchors at Marigot where she becomes part of your breakfast view during your week ashore. For details, contact Nick Bowden at Box 568, Hurricane Hole Hotel, Castries, St. Lucia, W.I.

Other **boat trips,** fun for nonsailors as well as those who love the sea in social settings, are the *Buccaneer Day Cruise* and the *Unicorn*, both of which set sail from Castries to cruise south down the west coast to Marigot Bay and Soufrière (the character ship offers an open bar and a lot of fun for its lively day; a good investment of $25), and *Ann-A*, a motor cruiser, makes pretty much the same run—with no sail but with a steel band. The price is the same, and although the character of the craft isn't as impressive, the day can be a good one if you've gathered with friends.

Golfers have a choice, of the 9 holes at La Toc, just south of Castries, or the 9 holes at Cap Estate on the island's northern tip near Cariblue Hotel. Greens fees at Cap Estate depend on whether you come from an obviously American hotel or whether you live locally. Going rates have been the E.C. equivalent of the $6 per person per day, with a $24 weekly charge, and a $40 2-week charge (Cariblue guests get a 10% discount on the US$ price). Both courses have clubhouses, the Cap Estate arrangement being more independent of the hotels than the setup at La Toc, which is obviously part of one.

Horseback riding can be arranged at the Cap Estate Trekking Center, on the grounds of the north point development.

Tennis courts are at Cariblue, La Toc, Halcyon Beach, Halcyon Sands, the St. Lucian, and Malabar in the Castries area, and at Halcyon Days on the south coast, near Vieux Fort and Anse Chastanet, on the southwest coast, at Soufriere.

Scuba diving is organized through your hotel, probably with *Dive St. Lucia*. If you want details in advance, write them at Box 412, Vigie, Castries, St. Lucia, W.I. The resort course (to give beginners confidence to make at least one dive) is about $35, with dive tours on the west coast figuring about $25 with the price variation depending on the location and your expertise. Dive packages of about 6 dives cost almost $100, but check for details when you arrive and write in advance to be sure of equipment available.

■■■

TREASURES AND TRIFLES start with **The Bagshaws** silk-screen designs, better than ever when checked for this edition. Almost 20 years ago, when the Bagshaws "retired" to St. Lucia from U.S. pressures, they put their considerable talents to work incorporating island themes into colorful designs, screening the patterns on plain fabric, and selling placemats, wall hangings, and eventually shirts, skirts, and yard goods. Today the shop and studio that sit on the shore on a hill outside Castries (you can walk along the beach from La Toc if you plan ahead and bring your money and a cover-up for shopping) burst at the seams with tourists when the cruise ships are in port. At other times, you can wander around on your own to pick through the piles of merchandise, priced in US$. There's a room to the right as you enter the shop that has had some sale items worth looking at; otherwise, I've found the consistently good and interesting designs to be the birds and flowers that were some of the Bagshaws' first. If you're a nonshopper, you can swing in the wicker chairs on the porch or peek at the studio operation if it's open and running when you're here.

La Toc Hotel has a couple of shops in its lobby area, but the one with the most items of interest for vacationers is the branch of the in-town based Noah Arcade, with books, island-made items, and St. Lucian pottery. Most resort hotels have lobby boutiques that sell books about St. Lucia and other locally focused items.

Ruth Clarage, on Brazil Street in downtown Castries, carries the well-made, colorful Caribbean fashions well-known to those who knew Jamaica in the old days. Clothes include men's jackets, children's clothes and fashions for the ladies. (You can stop in on your way to or from Rain, the restaurant a few doors away.)

Downtown Castries is a mixture of shops for residents and shops where tourists can find something to buy, but commerce is mostly geared for residents. **Noah's Arcade** has some interesting West Indian books (and a complete Penguin paperback collection), plus flour-sack shirts, plenty of carved wood figures, St. Lucian pottery of good quality and an unusual selection of bowls, mats, and hats.

Shipwreck Shops have taken hold on this island also, with the stock you will expect if you have seen other Shipwrecks on other islands: plenty of wood bowls, salad servers, carved figures, woven straw items, and bags, books, and "unusual gifts," they say. (Tourist trash, I say, although you will find some average-to-good items buried in all the mass-produced bowls, etc.). The selection of West Indian books is usually good. Check the Castries shop at Brazil and Mongiraud Streets, or—in the south—at Halcyon Days Hotel, in the lobby.

The **Castries Market** is well worth a wander, but not slung with cameras and in your colorful tourist togs. You'll look different enough as it is, even if you are dressed conservatively and try to look inconspicuous as you poke around the piles of fruits, vegetables, fish, and handwork, made by people who trek weekly to Castries in hopes of selling and/or bartering for their weekly needs. On one visit through the market, I found some sturdy wood and reed chairs which, although bulky to bring home, have withstood the ravages of time. They are handmade and solid.

The **Sea Island Cotton Shop,** on Bridge Street, has a good selection of silk-screened and other fabrics, some of which can be made to order to the pattern of your choice (often by copying a dress you brought with you) while you're here.

Y. De Lima, on William Peter Blvd., the block-long esplanade in the center of town off Bridge Street, has the expected crystal, china, watches, etc. for tourist purchase. Check on prices, and don't count on a complete selection of all patterns. If you want a specific pattern or item write to the store in advance of arrival to find out if it's in their stock. Cox and Company is a department store to prowl if you are interested in household sundries.

The **government handicraft center for strawwork**—including woven grass rugs rolled up to carry out—is a marvelous place to poke around, for baskets and other items, at prices you can bargain about. The small shop is at the waterfront, toward the main Castries market from the Tourist Board.

St. Martin/Sint Maarten

Sint Maarten, De Ruyterplein, Philipsburg, Sint Maarten, N.A.; Sint Maarten Tourism Representative, 445 Park Ave., New York, NY 10022; 243 Ellerslie Ave., Willowdale, Toronto, Ontario, Canada; St. Martin, French West Indies, Information, 610 Fifth Ave., New York, NY 10020.

US $1 = NAf 1.77
Unless otherwise noted, all references are to US dollars.

The view from the second floor balcony would make a marvelous painting. Luxury sailboats bob at anchor, with hand-built island freight boats as a counterpoint. Baskets of vegetables are piling up at the waterfront, with the help of an assortment of men and boys who lift the cargo when conversation permits.

Although the scene played out almost at our feet, we took an "intermission" to savor crisp salad and fresh fish grilled to perfection and served with island limes. We could sip the wine while we watched the activity below. The price for the meal would seem obscene in lesser surroundings; for this cafe, the price included the spontaneous entertainment and somehow the total, although higher than it might have been, was acceptable.

This island is like that. There are moments that are priceless— and usually there's no charge for them. Other encounters, often involving taxis and hotel rooms, come at high cost, but there are ways to skirt those costs if your pocketbook can't stand it.

Sint Maarten/St. Martin has grown with awesome statistics and steady development. Familiar to many of us who knew this island 20 or more years ago as a relatively unknown island outpost where French and Dutch cultures sometimes braided in amusing ways (and other times stand impressively separate, even when sharing nearby plots of land), this island now has an overwash of American commerce that is impossible to ignore.

In the 17th century, after the Dutch had laid claim to the south

734

part and French from settlements in Guadeloupe claimed the north, people used to walk back and forth between French Marigot and Dutch Philipsburg. Probably not every day, but often enough to bring news—and to make it.

Scottish John Philips, for whom Philipsburg is named, always claimed that the island should be under one flag, but the 1648 division treaty held—at least for most of the island's history. When Salomon Gibbes, a Swede, was commander of the colony at Sint Maarten he saw to it that Barthélemy Curet, a Frenchman with debts on the Dutch side, was locked in the Philipsburg jail. A covey of Curet's cronies marched from Marigot to plead his case, and while the council debated, they strolled past the jail and stole the jubilant sinner, parading him and another prisoner on a flag-waving march back to Marigot.

Not long after 1793, after the Dutch had secured their possession from the Spanish but were still squabbling with the English, Commander Rink ordered a march on Marigot by his Orange Company guard. His purpose was to protect the entire island from English invasion (and his Dutch colony from problems with the French), but his immediate project was to march with his men, dragging a cannon to French Fort Louis, which the Dutch would name Fort Willem Frederik. For a few years, St. Martin was governed by the Dutch, with an administrative council of Frenchmen who reported to the Philipsburg-based island council.

The roles reversed with the political waves of Europe. When the power of France welled over the Netherlands at the end of the 18th century, Guadeloupe ordered the Dutch to give up their claim to French St. Martin and to become the occupied part themselves. A garrison of Frenchmen lived in Sint Maarten and built themselves a fort. That period lasted until 1801, when the English invaded—to clear the air during their occupation of less than a year.

By 1802, sides would be separated again, according to the treaty of 1648. The Frenchmen of St. Martin would continue with their own language, coins, and customs; the Dutchmen on Sint Maarten would do the same with theirs, and the trade, then transports, then tourists would continue to cross borders without noticing more than the view.

AUTHOR'S OBSERVATION: Comment about the spelling of Sint Maarten (Dutch) and St. Martin (French) is constant and confusing. In this chapter, when a place is on the Dutch side, the island will be referred to as Sint

Maarten; when it is on the French side, St. Martin will be the spelling, but all who have not been here to see for themselves should realize that you can drive from Marigot, St. Martin, to Philipsburg, Sint Maarten, in about half an hour on weaving roads and not even know when you've crossed the border. Whichever spelling is used, the other "country" is a stone's throw away, perhaps not politically, but practically.

■■■

POLITICAL PICTURE: Sint Maarten is the leader of the northern triumvirate of the Netherlands Antilles. The three "S islands" (Sint Maarten, Saba, and Statia) are grouped as the Windward Islands. The Dutch Windwards, that is. (They, in fact, mingle in the Caribbean Sea with what the British refer to as the Leewards). The three share one vote at the 22 member Staten that convenes in Curaçao and, for obvious reasons, have long felt that they are given short shrift by the Netherlands government. Their allegiance to North American commercial interest is stronger, with firm links forged with U.S. entrepreneurs, through the big hotels and certainly with the casinos. Commercial interests with other parts of the world include a longtime liaison with a Japanese group for a shrimp operation based just out of Philipsburg, and ventures with European, Arab, and other countries.

Politics plays an important role in Sint Maarten today. At least one local politician (Claude Wathey) had a firm hold on the tourism strategy for the several years when the arrivals leapt from insignificant to 7th place in Caribbean statistics. Only the big islands of Puerto Rico, the United States Virgin Islands (both near neighbors), the Dominican Republic, Barbados, and Jamaica, in its good years, count more tourists than Sint Maarten.

The French side of the island is governed by a prefect who eventually reports to Guadeloupe. Substantial changes, some of them improvements, in the past few years have brought an interesting tourism to St. Martin (with bistros, small hotels, and a casual, seaside focus akin to that of the French Riviera). You will note the difference in road surface (especially in the vicinity of Mullett Bay and La Samanna, on the Dutch and French "sides" of the island respectively), and in island services (such as power and water). The French side is still very much a Caribbean area with a very special French flavor. Sint Maarten (Dutch) tends to yield to an avalanche of Americanisms which includes Kentucky Fried, hot dogs, and the tempo you can except with Las Vegas or Atlantic City casinos (without the lavish floor shows).

The Dutch claimed Sint Maarten in 1631, and used it as a way station between their community of New Holland in Brazil and New Netherlands (New York) on the east coast of North America. Dutchmen came over from their colony at Christiansted, St. Croix to settle Sint Eustatius in the late 1630s, and they claimed Statia in 1640.

Saba and Sint Eustatius—commonly called Statia—slumber in the sun, while action-packed tourism rolls around and over Sint Maarten, where hotels and casinos are big business.

■■■

CUSTOMS OF THE COUNTRY are so Americanized on the Dutch side of Sint Maarten, and so French on the French side, called St. Martin, that it will be surprising to realize that there is, in fact, no *real* border between the two countries that occupy this island. Speaking French can be fun (but is not essential) on the French side of the island. Speaking English is common practice on the Dutch side, where you will only hear an occasional word of Dutch.

Ties with Holland are most obvious with place names (Queen Juliana Airport, for example), food, and holidays. Most of the Netherlands' official holidays are celebrated in Sint Maarten (but not necessarily on the French side of the island). An impressive list of strictly local holidays, some geared to political rallies and other occasions, also appear on the calendar. Stores will carry extravagant displays of Dutch cheeses (check the supermarkets), Bols gins, Heineken and Amstel beer, the best you can buy. Dutch devotion to the dollar or guilder, or whatever the going currency happens to be, is typical of the homeland and reflects its commercial history. St. Maarten is small in size but big in impact in the vacation world. People pay a lot for everything, and tourists are tapped the most. Be prepared for few bargains but acceptable quality.

Clothes for Sint Maarten/St. Martin are Caribbean casual, but usually not sloppy. Jackets are seldom seen these days, especially during summer season, but some men wear them for some of the official government functions, or special resort evenings during the winter season. The loose-fitting guayabera, or shirt-jac, popular among most West Indians, is also worn here. Men seldom wear ties. Women can enjoy dressing up in resort clothes in the evenings. Long skirts are still worn some places, usually by tourists or for parties at a private home, but calf-length summer dresses, or evening pants with a fashionable top are more common these days. Daytime wear is comfortably casual, but please—for the sake of residents if not for other tourists—no bathing suits in shopping centers or on the streets of town. Keep the bare-look for the beach and cover up when you go to town or island touring.

■■

MONEY MATTERS: Although the Netherlands Antilles guilder or florin, noted as NAf on price tags for merchandise (and in the supermarket), is the official unit of currency for the Dutch side, and the French franc is the official currency for the French side, the U.S. dollar bridges the gap and is accepted everywhere. You may get change in the local currency (especially on the French side) when you buy gas, or bread from one of the country bakeries, but you can use dollars to pay bills in any store, restaurant, hotel, or entertainment (boat trip, etc.).

■■

ARRIVAL at Queen Juliana Airport on Sint Maarten, whether you are housed on the Dutch side or the French side, is usually quick, easy, and efficient, once you have stepped from the plane to be wrapped in that "blanket" of hot, moist air blown around you by the trade winds as you walk across the tarmac to the terminal. As recently as mid '77 the first full DC-10 landed on the 7000-foot runway at Sint Maarten. When deregulation of air fares resulted in a price war of sorts, American and Eastern were joined by other airlines' flights full of sun-seekers. The small STOL and other planes of Winair (Windward Islands Airways), Prinair (Puerto Rican International Airlines), and private owners fly in and out at regular intervals several times daily.

Immigration officials are stone-faced, strictly business types who look at you—and the immigration card you have filled out on the plane (keep the copy for departure), your proof of citizenship (passport is best; voter's registration or a copy of your birth certificate will do; driver's license is *not* sufficient since it does not prove citizenship)—and then take up the next in line. Luggage claim takes a while since the carts to get the luggage from the plane are not sufficient to bring a fully loaded cargo to the terminal with anything resembling speed. This is your cue to start slowing down. The Sint Maarten Tourist Bureau information booth, open from 7:30 a.m. to 9 p.m. has leaflets and staff to answer questions about hotels, rates, and facilities. Check there or with one of the tourism aides about cab fares before you get in a car.

Departure, even for a day trip to Saba or another island, involves check-in at least 45 minutes before flight time, and a long wait in an uninteresting airport. There are chairs, tables, bar service, and a few shops in the main trade-wind-cooled rectangular room that holds all the airline ticket counters and a branch of Spritzer & Fuhrmann that is usually open at regular shop hours. Once you go through immigration, which you must do even for the Statia and Saba flights, you can sit upstairs in the restaurant—which is air-conditioned, or find bench space in the departure lounge where there are a few shops that hint that they are "duty-free" but which I found to be the usual price on a limited selection of merchandise.

AUTHOR'S OBSERVATION: If you are going to British-affiliated Anguilla or French St. Barths, or "out of the country" for the day, you will have to pay the $3 departure tax, and fill out all forms, and go through immigration *again* when you reenter Sint Maarten that evening. If you leave to come home the following day (or whenever you leave), you will be hit with *another* $3 departure tax. I find that system annoying, although I'll grant that it is good for Sint Maarten's coffers. (Since Saba and Statia are both Dutch, there is no $3 to pay for those day excursions.)

▪▪

TOURING TIPS: Plan to rent a car if you want mobility. Taxis are expensive and in my opinion seem to be a "law unto themselves." If you are going to one of the hotels near the airport, you may have some trouble finding a driver willing to take you from the airport. I cajoled one driver into dropping me at Mary's Boon by letting him fill the car with a group going into a Philipsburg hotel.

If you are planning to tour by taxi or to go to one of the several good restaurants around the island for dinner, negotiate the fare in advance, and be sure you both clearly understand how much waiting time is involved and exactly what the fare will be.

As far as rental cars are concerned, there's a lineup of booths at the airport where you can make arrangements or fill out your contract and get your keys if you have made your car reservation in advance. During peak winter months (February and March), when cars are at a premium, you may find your car "gone" even though you have reserved in advance. In my experience, if you wave your coupon and insist, a car will be produced—probably from the stock for the people arriving on the next flight. In addition to Hertz, Avis,

Budget, and National, there are local car rental companies. I have used Risdon Rentals on more than one occasion, and have also found the women who operate the Mullet Bay hotel car rental firm to be very helpful.

Gas prices are leaping here as everywhere. When you rent be sure that you inquire about gas and start with a full tank no matter what the cost.

The wounds on a tourist stretched out in the sun at Mullet Bay Beach are testimony to the fact that there are Hondas and other cycles for rent. Some love them; I do not. Rates are reasonable, and rental can easily be arranged through some of the car rental companies as well as through your hotel's front desk. Wear a helmet.

Be forewarned that although main roads around the Dutch side are in good condition, some of the French-side roads are potholed and rutted, and the backcountry or remote beach roads on both sides are often little more than dirt lanes with perilous potholes. Signposting is not ideal, but it's hard to get too lost on an island this size.

AUTHOR'S OBSERVATION: The condition of downtown Philipsburg deserves some comment. The seedy "city" is no longer a quaint West Indian town. With the landfill (from the salt flats) that added a back-of-the-town "highway," the former Front Street has been turned into the back street—even though it edges the sea. Massive (or seemingly so) buildings with apartments and shops have risen along Front Street, closing in a street that is plugged with shoppers in daylight weekday hours. Anyone who knew the Dutch side before it seethed with so many tourists will be stunned by the change in pace and profferings.

▪▪▪

HOTELS ON SINT MAARTEN/ST. MARTIN provide a curious variety in accommodations. The spelling of the two parts of this island differ and so do the customs and currency at the unobtrusive border. (During one of my island forays, I asked directions of a cluster of young boys at a turning in the road not far from Grand Case. I asked in French, the boy answered me in French, turned to his friend who answered in Dutch, and the middle fellow gave me my reply in English.) The atmosphere emanating from Marigot and Grand Case, on the French side, is *very* different from that of Philipsburg, the Dutch town. Hotels on the Dutch side are geared to, and cater to, Americans—in food, package tours, pricing, and what is purveyed. The French side is still French—with the "come if you want to, but do it my way" atmosphere that makes a vacation on the French side like being on the Continent.

Sint Maarten and St. Martin have guest houses and small inns that are often not on the beach but are personality places worthy of notice. Although prices everywhere are geared for tourists, and the top tally is taken during prime season winter months, your best value comes at the guest houses—or the housekeeping apartments. At the big places, count on big tariffs—and extra charges for everything.

AUTHOR'S AWARDS go to the French side's La Samanna, the only high-quality haven on the entire island, in my opinion, for designing rooms and a hotel that are a compliment to the natural setting, and to the Horny Toad, a small and very special place with the personality of its owners.

✛ **Beau Séjour** (B.P. 36, Marigot, St. Martin, F.W.I.; 10 rooms) beds you down in simple rooms, some opening right off the main dining room, which is up a flight of stairs off the street level in the town of Marigot. If you have been in France, and know and like small bistros-with-rooms in the southern parts of that country, here's one with a West Indian flair to try. The rate of about $50 for 2 includes continental breakfast (coffee and croissant), but the surroundings are not suggested for first-time Caribbean travelers or timid tourists. French is essential for fitting in, and if this sounds like your kind of Caribbean hideaway, plan to adapt to the custom. You're within a short walk of the water, but will need a car or the patience to wait for the local bus that makes the loop from Marigot to Philipsburg and back. You *can* walk to the sand (if there is some while you're here) at the patch in front of Le Pirate, but it will take about 20 minutes for the hot stroll through town.

✛ **Belair** (Little Bay Beach, Philipsburg, Sint Maarten, N.A.; 72 suites) bounced onto the beach in the season of '81, with official opening at special "advance booking" rates in effect until December 18. The lavishly furnished deluxe suites have 2 bedrooms and TV, an island luxury. Planted 18 suites per floor, the 4-story buildings have a castlelike appearance, with crenellated roofline. Part of an expansive project planned to move inland and up the hillside, Belair is the first of what is intended to be a b-i-g hotel. If all goes as planned, the second phase of 184 units will be built in the summer of '82. Count on all vacation amenities (watersports, dining choices, good beach, pools) and very competent management. Jan Welage, overseer also of Little Bay Beach Hotel next door, has run the gamut of island hotels with time at St. Croix-by-the-Sea in the Virgin Islands and Pasanggrahan here prior to assuming the leadership of these properties. Count on rates to climb to $100 or more for 2.

✣ **Caravanserai** (Box 113, Philipsburg, Sint Maarten, N.A.; 60 rooms) means "inn," and is the name for the way stations on the old roads of Turkey where people bedded down at the times of the crusades. The small inn that opened on the rocks at the shore of Maho Bay with 17 rooms in 1965 was an elegant spot, the dream of a New York advertising man who headed south for a new life. Caravanserai's original big rooms had ceiling fans, double exposure so that the breezes swept through, and the elegance of the owner's "cottage," a spectacular house on the rocks that a few of the special guests were invited to see—and perhaps sit in. Things change. The airstrip that was near Caravanserai is now a full-fledged runway, with planes making a dip at the inn's end of the runway when they sweep in to greet Queen Juliana's airport with a whoosh and a deafening roar. (You can watch people on the beach holding their ears as they look up to the belly of the plane.) Rooms have been added, in 2-story units around the grounds, and around the pools—and near the tennis courts. The main gathering building has been extended to give diners a choice of a seaside dining pavilion or a poolside setting that is one of the island's best, especially on moonlit nights, and nights when there's entertainment. The bar area, restaurant, and pool built out over a tumble of rocks, provide an elegant perch for cocktail hour. The overall atmosphere is impressive; the surroundings look serene and the umbrella ownership by Island Gem Enterprises that puts Caravanserai and Mullet Bay in the same "house" means that guests here have a close link with the links, beach, and tennis courts of the big resort on the other side of the runway. Peak season rates this winter range from $40 for a twin-bedded standard room to almost $150 for 2, meals extra for an elegant air-conditioned apartment.

✣ **Castle Cove** (Box 133, Philipsburg, Sint Maarten, N.A.; 18 rooms) clutches a hilltop at Pointe Blanche, just east of Philipsburg past the unsightly commercial area. In a complex that knew another life when it was Hunter House, Castle Cove guests have sea view from their rooms, the Panoramique Restaurant "next door," and a pleasant management team that will do their utmost to help them see the island and enjoy their stay. Rates this winter hover around $50 for 2, with breakfast, for a modern room and congenial atmosphere spurred along by Manager Terry Kingdon. There's a pool at the heart of the inn if getting to a nearby beach seems like too much of a project.

✤ **Coralita Beach** (Baie Lucas, St. Martin, F.W.I.; 40 rooms) is closer to Philipsburg (about 5 miles) and Queen Juliana airport than it is to Marigot (almost 10 miles), "its" main town, since it is French. The rooms are big, modern, and air-conditioned; whether on first or second floor, all have sea view and either small balcony or small patio—and big sea breeze. Facing the prevailing winds, the rooms are slightly protected by having the pool area and the slope of sand in front of them, but count on plenty of breezes. There's one tennis court, buffets and barbecues with music some evenings; and gathering areas that are seldom peopled (from my experience) but comfortably furnished. The reserved atmosphere I sense here may come from the "way out" location, or from the French ambiance with a modern hotel that verges on seeming antiseptic. If you are part of a group—so that you have your action assured, or want a quiet retreat in modern, French surroundings, consider this place. Part of the property has been used by the health clinic, which I understand concentrates on cell therapy guaranteed to keep (or make) you young. Rates for a regular vacation range from around $100 for 2, which is too much I think, even with 2 meals daily—unless, of course, you like, want, and will pay for an isolated location, to read, rest, and do what you want to.

✤ **Cupecoy Beach Club** (Box 302, Philipsburg, Sint Maarten, N.A.; 165 units) speckles the sands at a cove near Mullet Bay's beach and La Samanna. Just outside the gates of Mullet Bay resort, (and therefore close enough for guests here to enjoy the golf, restaurants, and other facilities), Cupecoy has its own activities center with restaurant, pool, and beach. Rooms with beach view are the best and carry the highest price tag, which will range from $186 to $216 for 2 this winter, everything extra. Garden view rooms range from $156 to $196, and all suites have kitchenettes. Standard rooms do not.

✤ **Galion Beach** (Baie de l'Embouchure, St. Martin, F.W.I.; 46 rooms) supplies *huge* rooms, rambling around a central area that houses the restaurant, terrace for sunning while dining, and gives you one tennis court and several l-o-n-g strands of sand, one reserved for bathing in the buff. The hotel is on a cove, about 10 miles from the airport and about 7 weaving miles from both Philipsburg and Marigot. The nationality—and local language—are French, although a sprinkling of North Americans have been known to nest here. The beaches are spectacular, the hotel's own atmosphere quiet, and too spread out to be cozy. This is a place for self-sufficient types or small groups who will enjoy the big rooms with French-modern (sparse) furnishings, and will be content to bask on the beach, snorkel and sail at will, and rent a car for around-the-island touring. Rates this winter are high, in my opinion, at almost $140 for 2, even when 2 meals daily per person are included. Investigate a package tour or group rate to put a holiday here into more reasonable realms.

✦ **Grand St. Martin Beach** (Marigot, St. Martin, F.W.I.; 60 rooms) is an old-timer that keeps trying to catch up with today's market, and is still, in my opinion, short of the mark. A curve of sandy beach stretches out a short walk from the rooms, which used to be furnished with a few old four-posters (but I have heard rumors that they have been sold in a cash crunch). Check this place thoroughly before you book. To my mind, rates of almost $100 for 2 are much too high for the offerings, and the big dining room can be grim if you are one of a few French-speaking guests, and even grimmer if you don't speak French.

✦ **Great Bay Beach Resort** (Box 310, Philipsburg, Sint Maarten, N.A.; 225 rooms) is at the southwest end of Great Bay beach. If the sun doesn't fry you in the process, you can walk along the beach to Philipsburg in a leisurely half hour. The hotel looms large, and seems to be lively during the height of season and summer months with groups who sweep through on week-long gambling junkets and other gimmick trips. Depending on the house count while you're around, daytime/nighttime action can be nonstop—with water sports, boating trips to nearby islands, and chip flipping in the casinos until the light of dawn. The wood deck around the pool packs with people in winter months; the beach is better. Coffee shop and fancier dining room fill the frames of hotel guests (I don't think the restaurants are worth booking if you are staying somewhere else). Many of the tiers of rooms have a sea view (highest price); others overlook the tennis court and usually parched countryside. Game gambling types like this place and seem willing to pay one of the special package tour rates to be here. The winter rate for 2, is $85 to $128—and you can add half again as much with lavish meals, drinks, sun oil, tips, and taxes.

✦ **Little Bay Beach Hotel** (Box 61, Philipsburg, Sint Maarten, N.A.; 120 rooms) began life in 1955 as a government-built inn, planned in the best mainland Dutch tradition. Sometime in 1956, there was the "new" building along the beach (which still holds the best rooms for my vacation dollar); then 10 years later more rooms along the beach, to be followed by cottages around an upper pool. Today, the more than 100 different rooms have just about as many different personalities and the benefit of a more than $1.2 million facelift this season. When casinos were fashionable, Little Bay added one; when shops seemed to be a good idea, the boutiques appeared across the driveway from the entrance; when tennis courts became popular they were added; and the same goes for watersports at the beach, a lunch service area for terrace dining in bathing suits, and a beachside bar with walls and windows so that you can sit here even during the quick and welcomed showers. This is an ideal family place, if you can afford it, at about $200 daily for 4 to share a family cottage, meals extra. Garden cottages (around and overlooking the pool) carry the minimum rate, which is just over $100 for 2, 2 meals daily per person this winter; beachfront figures to almost $150 for 2, room only. Little Bay is on the beach shared now with Belair, about 5 minutes' drive or a 20-minute leisurely walk (which is hot for the part along the pavement, but pleasant when you get to Great Bay beach) from Philipsburg.

✦ **Maho Reef and Beach Club Resort** (Box 306, Philipsburg, Sint Maarten, N.A.; 141 rooms) was built big (under the Concord Hotel name) and is a group-oriented hotel. The buildings sit like a fortress at the end of the runway for Queen Juliana's airport. Flags wave in the breeze, the first greeting you'll get as your plane slants to touch the tarmac. Built as a big, air-conditioned bastion in the best Pocono Mountain tradition for visitors in the early 70s, the hotel hopes that its casino, air-conditioned public rooms, dining room, and bedrooms provide cool and comfortable confines, but—frankly—I like more fresh air when I'm frolicking around the Caribbean. The cement slabs around the pool are decorated with lounge chairs, tables with umbrellas, and people when the house count is high. The casino and evening action are there for those who want it, and that includes groups who come in on special package plans. Not much on old-time Caribbean atmosphere, the big-time hotel provides familiar comforts for those who know—and demand—stateside-style surroundings. Rates this season will figure around $140, meals extra. There's a special rate for villas, and about $28 per person charge if you want 2 meals daily here, but your best bet, if you want to stay here, is to sign on for one of the week-long all-inclusive vacation plans.

✤ **Mary's Boon** (Box 278, Philipsburg, Sint Maarten, N.A.; 10 rooms) no longer has Mary, and the airplanes that land all day and well into the night do so with a deafening roar that rages through your room, which is open to catch the trade winds. The fact that Mary's Boon backs up to the airport can be forgotten between planes, when you look out (or stretch out) along the beach that rims the wide open ocean. Mary's Boon used to be filled with the personality and antiques of the creative owner, Mary Pomeroy, but in season of '78 she left for the hills, turning the property over to former Pasanggrahan manager Rush Little, who runs this inn. The structure is the same, and most of Mary's staff has stayed, but the atmosphere has changed. If you get along with Rush, you'll enjoy the casual West Indian guesthouse atmosphere here; if you want to look first and reserve for next vacation, make a reservation for dinner. The food is served when you sit in the small seaside air-cooled dining room, and the bar is at the other seaside of the main house—and on the honor system. This special inn charges $80 for 2, meals extra, which may be worth it if you put a price on personality (and aren't turmoiled by the roar of planes). Philipsburg is a 15-minute weaving, mostly shoreline drive to the east.

✤ **Mullet Bay Beach Hotel** (Box 309, Philipsburg, Sint Maarten, N.A.; 622 rooms) is a city. Although the property is closed at press time, a resort the size of this one will undoubtedly be taken into the fold of some promoter before long. Mullet Bay sprawls over some 170 acres and I suspect that you could be here for at least a week and not get to each of the bars, restaurants, pools, and beaches even once. The golf course roaming through the middle of the property assures some wide open space, and the pond in its middle puts you within sight of water no matter where you stand. The panoply of pleasures includes a powdery stretch of sand with a beach bar and restaurant on its inland side, a full range of water sports available from the shop at the beach, a casino and cache of shops on the rocky promontory that marks the eastern edge of the property, a selection of restaurants, from deli-style hot dogs and an ice cream shop to attempts at gourmet food, an 18-hole golf course and all that goes with it (pro shop, snack area), a small commissary, and a medical center with doctor, plus car rental offices. But to me potential problems are the fact that the beach is not big enough for all the guests in the 622 rooms when the place is full, and neither is anything else; reservations are essential, sometimes the day ahead, for the best restaurants on the hotel's ground; jitney service to get you around the property if you don't have a rental car can be sporadic and it can be a 20-minute ride to get to the beach if your room is near the hillside hub.

And as far as room possibilities are concerned, the list is almost endless. The original condominium units, for rent in owner's absence, crack up as 1- and 2-bedroom suites, some with efficiency kitchens, plus standard, superior, and deluxe rooms. The suites come as oceanfront or deluxe (which can be near beach, golf course, or rubbish bin, depending on which one you get). And the room tallies can range from those for standard rooms to top dollar for the ocean-front suites, but all that will be decided by whoever steps in to manage and run this vast complex when it opens again. Check with your travel agent for status.

✣ **Pasanggrahan** (Box 151, Front Street, Philipsburg, Sint Maarten, N.A.; 21 rooms) focuses on basic West Indian qualities, from its wood frame house with simple but effectively furnished rooms to its back-porch dining, seaside by candlelight with complimentary house wine and the casual beachside atmosphere beloved by repeaters, many from New England and the Midwest. I wonder how long this small spot can hold out. It is being squeezed out by the blatant, boisterous commercialism of downtown Philipsburg. Peter De Zele manages to maintain an inn atmosphere amid the surfeit of shops and other buildings. The Garden Cafe, where you can get omelets and hamburgers in addition to a cool drink amid a hot shopping session, is one redeeming factor, but even the once pleasant beach is overrun with tourists when a ship comes in—and the offshore view is cluttered with an assortment of tourist-type boats for hire. Rooms are simple, with ceiling fans. If you insist on air conditioning, it will cost you an extra $4 per day. Otherwise, figure about $100 for beachfront for 2, breakfast and hearty dinners daily; rooms at the back are less, and the efficiencies bring the rate lower with no meals.

✣ **Oyster Pond Hotel** (Box 239, Philipsburg, Sint Maarten, N.A.; 20 rooms) is a leisurely inn—with class and the possibility to drive into

Philipsburg or Marigot in your rental car. It is scheduled for extensive expansion, as part of the Rolag N.V. group that includes nearby Dawn Beach and Almond Grove, with Walter Kieser as Director of Operations. For this season, however, facilities are expected to remain as they are. You can settle into the Club that greets its guests with an antique-punctuated, open-to-the-breezes "lobby" with yachting burgees hanging around the top of the walls. Oyster Pond is picture-perfect, with the cluster of white stucco buildings with their brick-tile roofs set on a knoll at the edge of the sea. Yachts are beginning to moor at the lagoon, where you'll find water sports facilities and some yachting activity. Around the courtyard in the main building, with a ceiling of the sky, there are the stairways to the second-floor rooms (each with its own personality, all with a view of the sea). The dining room and lounge area both face the sea. Food is not as noteworthy as the elegant atmosphere at dinner hour. There's a beach a short walk along a weaving path, and an outdoor area for alfresco dining, popular for the barbecue evenings. Water sports can be arranged, but usually set out from somewhere else. Winter rates for 2 are planned to hover between $125 and $170, meals extra.

✣ **PLM St. Tropez** (B.P. 50, Marigot, St. Martin, F.W.I.; 130 rooms) was adopted (and refinanced) by the French PLM chain at the end of '77. Flurries of francs were lavished on the premises, so that the hastily built third floor, which threatened to wash away with more rains, was repaired and rebuilt to stand tall and sturdy. St. Tropez began life a decade or more ago as a small seaside bistro with rooms. The original property has been incorporated into the new complex, with a metamorphosis that is beyond belief. It's difficult to recall the old and casual bar as you glide over (*slide* over, if it's been raining) the orange-tiled floors. Most of the modern, attractive (white stucco walls, primary colors for accents on furniture) rooms are in the 3-story new unit, with 16 rooms stretching along the beach. Ask for one of the 70 rooms that face the sea for the best view. There's a swimming pool, a nice beach (that changes with the surge of the seas), plus the option for water sports—or a day sail to Anguilla, the British-affiliated island you can see off the north shore. Marigot is nearby for shops and bistros; there is a boutique here, plus good although group-served food in the restaurants. This season rates will range from $72 to $117 for 2, breakfasts included,—and count on 15% service charge plus local French taxes on your franc rate at this hotel.

✣ **Le Pirate** (Marigot, St. Martin, F.W.I.; 10 rooms) has had a complete face-lift with new owners, Stephan Helfer and Edgar Ott. The
inn has held onto its patch of sand for a couple of decades, watching
the seas sweep out hefty portions regularly—and sometimes portions of the small hotel as well. Both, however, return eventually,
the latter often at the expense of the owners. The rooms are attractive, with basic furnishings and sea view. The atmosphere is distinctly French Mediterranean shore casual-with-class. In my opinion, this is not a place for those lacking fluent French, unless you
enjoy being on the "outside looking in." Rates for the room this
winter is $110 for 2, breakfast only. Daytime wear will be bathing
suit with cover-up, but you will be expected to pull yourself together and wrap up for evening. Just west of Marigot, a short walk
from the PLM place, on the north (French) shore, the inn puts you
in France—with francs your unit of currency.

✣ **La Samanna** (Baie Longue, St. Martin, F.W.I.; 88 rooms)
stretches along what I have always thought was St. Martin's most
spectacular beach. The hotel is obscenely expensive; some complain that the rates are *too* high, but while I don't think $250 for 2 is
any bargain, especially with meals extra, I know other places that
charge as much and aren't nearly as spectacular. (Even the $10
croissant, coffee, and fresh orange juice breakfast I enjoyed on one
visit seemed worth the price as a reward for battling downtown
Philipsburg.) The main check-in area commands the highest hill,
with its white stucco, Mediterranean (almost Greek) style building
sectioned off to give you a sea-viewing dining terrace, effectively
furnished with sturdy, I suspect Haitian chairs and sea-blue cloths
on tables with punctuation of colors cued by the flowers that patch
the walls and open spaces. There's a lounge-bar area that looks out
on the pool; you can sink into puffy cushions or slouch down to see
the view while you sip. The sand of Baie Longue stretches for what
seems like several powdery miles, and is long enough for most of us.
There are dunes to slide down when the seas have carved them to
the right slope. As for the rooms, they're spectacular. Colors make
the white walls vibrant; furnishings are sturdy enough to survive
several people's vacations and still be fresh enough for yours. Rate
range revolves around your room choice: one of the 14 rooms in the
3-story building closest to the main hub; or in the 14 2-story units
that sprawl near the sands, or a 1-bedroom suite (24), 2-bedroom
apartment (16), or a 3-bedroom villa (6) for you and your well-

heeled friends. Any one of the rooms gives you an option for tennis and water sports; you'll need a rental car for touring since you're down a sea-terminating road, off the back road that leads through the Mullet Bay Golf Course, about 20 minutes from Marigot and close to 45 if you don't know how to get to Philipsburg.

■■

HOUSEKEEPING HOLIDAYS ON SINT MAARTEN/ST. MARTIN are an excellent way to beat (or at least cope with) the high cost of vacationing on Sint Maarten. Apartment and efficiency setups give you freedom at reasonable cost. With the selection at the Food Center near the Avis car rental depot on the western outskirts of Philipsburg, and another market at Cole Bay and at Marigot's *Gourmet Supermarché* far above the Caribbean average (except for supermarkets in Puerto Rico, St. Thomas, and St. Croix), you don't have to worry about bringing a lot from home. For bread, you can find your own French baker, or try the Boulangerie in Marigot.

In addition to the apartments that have full facilities at Cupecoy Beach and Mullet Bay (where there is also a commissary called *Tiffany's* that is expensive, but convenient), there are many homes to rent in owners' absence. Two reliable routes for renting are through Louis Peters' Karnel Rental and Management, Box 372, Philipsburg, Sint Maarten (phone 011-599-5-3590) and through Judith Shepherd, St. Martin Rentals, N.V., Pelican House, Beacon Hill, Sint Maarten (phone 011-599-5-4330). Among the listings carried by Lou Peters are Jones House at Simpson Bay, with 3-bedrooms, 2-baths, and maid service; Francis Carty Apartments at Mary's Fancy with 1-bedroom apartments at good value, inland (you'll need a car for mobility); and the Tradewinds Beach House with 10 apartments on Simpson Bay and on-premise management plus maid service. Judy Shepherd's elegant listings include 3- and 4-bedroom homes with pools (with the 4-bedroom at about $1800 for a mid-winter week), as well as some 2-bedroom houses at about $900 for a mid-winter week.

✤ **Aambeeld Guesthouse** (Box 256, Simpson Bay Beach, Sint Maarten, N.A.; 6 apts) claims a curve of that stretch of sand you fly over as your plane lands on Sint Maarten. All apartments, whether you opt for (and can get) the 1-bedroom or 2-bedroom variety, have comfortable, beach-oriented furnishings, adequate cooking equipment, and maid service. One of your 2-bedrooms in the bigger version has a wake-up view of the sea (the other bedroom is in the back), and host Walton Westlake is around enough to be helpful with touring tips. Ideal for self-sufficient folk, next door to Mary's Boon and not too far from Philipsburg or Marigot for dinners out, the Aambeeld is one of the island's best values at $65 for the 1-bedroom, $93 for the 2, with extra people paying $12 per day.

✢ **Almond Grove** (Cole Bay, Sint Maarten, N.A.; 16 houses) may be your ideal haven, if you're not one of those folks who demands sand outside your door. Each house has a full kitchen (with washing machine nearby), and living area which includes either 1, 2, 3, or 4 bedrooms. Located midisland, about 3 miles from the airport and less than that from the French side's capital of Marigot, Almond Grove guests will need a car. The Bali Hai restaurant is worked into the walls of a former Great House to provide an elegant on-location meal. The pool is a gathering spot. Rates for winter are $75 for the 1-bedroom, $100 for 2-bedroom; $140 for the 3-bedroom, and $175 for 4-bedroom (which is a good-sized unit suitable for 8 people). Daily rates do not include any meals.

✢ **Dawn Beach** (Box 239, Philipsburg, Sint Maarten, N.A.; 95 apts.) was new with the '80–'81 season, and freckled the beach near Oyster Pond with cottages, a restaurant, and water sports. All the beachside units have modern facilities, including a kitchenette. There's a pool, and tennis courts, plus TV in your room for entertainment. Count on $130 or more for 2 for the winter season. This place is part of the Rolag N.V. enterprises, with Walter Kieser, who had been with another Sint Maarten Hotel a few years back, in charge.

✢ **Holland House** (Box 393, Philipsburg, Sint Maarten, N.A.; 42 apts.) opened in early '80 on the main street of town, with some rooms overlooking the beach. You can walk to a choice of restaurants and shops, plus loll by the pool or beach. No car needed. Rates are about $135 for 2, meals extra, this winter.

At the other end of that price range there are several clusters of efficiencies and apartments at the west end of Great Bay, where you can walk to Philipsburg along the beach.

✢ **Naked Boy Apartments** (Box 252, Philipsburg, Sint Maarten, N.A.) has 7 units on the beach. Although a daily rate is offered ($75 to $82 for 2), you'll do better with the weekly or monthly rentals if you want a self-sufficient base.

✣ **Oyster Pond Hotel** has luxury homes for rent. The selection includes the Tower House, furnished with antiques, and costing $1000 or more per week for a place that 6 can call home—comfortably.

✣ **Town House Apartments** (Box 347, Philipsburg, Sint Maarten, N.A.) nest on the beach (you can scuff through sand to shop in Philipsburg). The 2-bedroom apartments are condominiums, for rent in owners' absence, and all are comfortable and adequately furnished, Bob Bailey is manager, and the mix of owners and regular renters gives this place a congenial atmosphere. Count on $185 for 2, everything extra.

✣ **Friendly Island Beach Homes** (Box 346, Philipsburg, Sint Maarten, N.A.) are simple beachfront units with living room and patio, full kitchen, and twin-bedded rooms on Simpson Bay Beach. Maids do the daily cleanup, and action options include a catamaran cruise aboard *El Tigre*. Rates until Dec. 15 are $200 and winter months figure around $350 per week for 2.

✣ **Beachcomber Villas,** on the south shore not far from Caravanserai (whose road you follow to get there), offer an oasis, beachside. Lynne Conner returned to the property to put the units back in shape in season of '79 so that the painting and primping assure clean, open-air surroundings—with all the comforts of home (and the right to cook to keep costs down). Also along this stretch, **White Sands Villas** are a good bet, at $400 per week for a 2-bedroom unit.

✣ **The Horny Toad** (Box 397, Philipsburg, Sint Maarten, N.A.) has apartments for $89 in winter. It slides along a side road on the beach side of the runway not far from Mary's Boon. A special place with a personality of its own, this small inn/group of efficiencies offers one of the best bets on the island—if you like casual surroundings and a congenial atmosphere. The units are fully furnished, complete with kitchen equipment, and the difference in your suite or double depends on whether you sleep on the couches-turned-bed in your living room or have a separate bedroom. The Horny Toad is a few steps from the beach, about 10 minutes' drive looping around the end of the runway from the airport, and almost 20 minutes' drive from Philipsburg. The public bus runs along the end of a nearby road so you won't need a car for mobility, but might find one convenient for touring for at least a day or two.

There are many houses for rent at the Pointe Blanche area, to the

east of Philipsburg, past the Japanese shrimp factory and an industrial area that has a lot of (I think ugly) heavy equipment around
the port and small factories. The price is less for places here, as it
should be, even considering the spectacular hillside views that
open up to the Caribbean sea when you get above the mess. You
will need a car if you want mobility. Among places to consider are
Devil Cupper Cottages (c/o D. Booy, Sint Maarten, N.A.) and **Blue
Waves Apartments** (8 apts., Canary Road, Pointe Blanche, Sint
Maarten, N.A.), the latter in a hot pocket below Castle Cove and
Panoramique restaurant.

✣ **Goetz Guest House** (Grand Case 97150, St. Martin, F.W.I.; 3
apts.), on the French side, provides very casual beachside surroundings to use as a base for a *very* casual island holiday. Grand
Case, a one-street-wide village that has been painted and plucked to
rejuvenated status, has boutiques and bistros tucked inside most of
the small wood West Indian houses that border the street at the
seaside. Count on nothing fancy in your studio with "garden" (2),
or the 2-bedroom apartment with living room, but the rooms will be
air-conditioned (the pockets are *hot* otherwise), and the kitchenettes will be adequate for simple suppers. This one is owned by
American William Forbes. Speaking French is not essential now
that this area has drawn a few Americans, but you'll feel more
comfortable if you parlez français. The place has been locking up in
the fall, so check if that's when you plan to head south. French
francs are the unit of currency for Grand Case.

✣ **Grand Case Beach Club** (Grand Case 97150, St. Martin, F.W.I.; 49
units) about 3 miles northeast of Marigot, sits at a lovely beach,
east of the Grand Case village. There are studios and one-bedroom
apartments, each with a small kitchenette and a balcony. The two
3-story and one 2-story buildings are new, and the surroundings
simple, but the facilities are more than adequate if you want a no-
nonsense beachside holiday where you can be in your bathing suit
most of the time. Winter rates for 2 range from $85 to $190, room
only.

■■

RESTAURANTS ON SINT MAARTEN/ST. MARTIN are beyond
count, with almost 60 dining options. Many menus show French
flair (especially, but not exclusively, on the French side), but you
can also find Chinese, Italian, recognizable American hamburgers
and hot dogs, as well as Kentucky Fried. There's even an ice-cream

station within the confines of Mullet Bay. Count on spending substantial sums, however, even for simple fare. Restaurants price as though they had to make whatever profit they can in the 3-month height of season (Jan, Feb, Mar), even though they have good summer business too. If you figure $20 per person as an average, you will occasionally be able to eat for less, and will often pay more for dinners. You can taxi to Philipsburg, to wander to one of several restaurants, but for all other dining depots, a rental car or taxi is essential. Spectacular settings for hotel dining are the restaurant at La Samanna and the poolside dining at Caravanserai, with Mary's Boon offering a pleasant seaside setting of a small inn with personality on the south coast, and Le Pirate for a French bistro on the opposite (north) shore.

AUTHOR'S AWARDS for restaurants go to Nadaillac at Marigot for the exceptional Perigord cuisine and to La Nacelle, the renovated police station—a gem set in a gendarmerie.

Antoine, next to the pier in Philipsburg, facing on Front Street and housed in one of the old wood West Indian buildings, makes up in atmosphere what it may lack in gourmet cuisine. The menu reads well, but the actual presentation wasn't up to my expectations. The lunch with salads and sandwiches is a safe bet.

L'Aventure, on Marigot harbor and marked by a black and white striped awning, offers informal dining at a hillside, seaside perch. Best spot is on the porch, with sea-breeze cooling. Count on simple food, with grilled fish dependably good at about $10 per serving.

Bali Hai, at Almond Grove Estates, is the place to go for the multicourse Indonesian rijsttafel, the "rice table" that punctuates your plate with more than 25 different taste thrills and mediates them with rice (and cold beer). Ambiance in the 150-year-old plantation house is conducive to comfortable dining. Plan to pay close to $20 per person for the rijsttafel, and be sure to call for reservations. The 70-person limit is often filled on winter evenings.

Bilboquet, in a former home on a hillside at Pointe Blanche, southeast of Philipsburg, surrounds you with memorabilia of the owners (Bob Donn and Bill Ahlstrom from Minnesota and New York) arranged on walls and halls, with big open spaces so you can see the view—of St. Barths. The place has atmosphere, even though it opened in these quarters only in June '77. The menu and surroundings are attractive, but the food seemed almost too flourished and "exotic" on a couple of my evenings here. Closed Mondays, and you'll have to drive up to make a reservation—partly so they can see if you are what they want for dinner.

La Bouillabaisse, on the seaside of Front Street in Philipsburg, in a West Indian house with lots of atmosphere, serves a hearty meal for lunch and dinner. The terrace view is spectacular, and so were the fresh fish, and the bouillabaisse when I tried them. Do not count on a lot of fussing and doing by the staff; the meal will be good, the service slow, and the staff automatic, if your experience is like mine. Count on paying about $7 for a full lunch, and between $15 and $20 for dinner with some extras added to your entree.

La Calanque, on the shore road at Marigot, a few doors away from L'Aventure and La Vie en Rose, was the first of this trio to offer outstanding food in special surroundings. The service can be slow, but the food lived up to expectations when I dined here. If you're planning for dinner, stop by early to make your reservation; height of season space is scarce. (And plan on parting with the equivalent of $20 per person for a memorable meal.)

Chesterfield's, on the road to Pointe Blanche, near the marina on the east curve of Great Bay, serves down-to-earth seafood and sandwiches from 11 a.m. until well after midnight. Popular when it was the "new place in town"; check here for publike activity.

Ma Chance has been a St. Martin legend for many years. The stories began when the owner started serving good creole meals in her Grand Case home, by reservation. She then opened a more "formal" restaurant, on the sea-following road through Grand Case. When her 2 top staff left to open their own places, she turned again to home cooking, by reservation only. When you pass through town on the day you're touring, ask (in French) about the possibility of a special dinner for you and your friends. Set the date and time and leave the menu to her. You'll never forget the experience, if you can make the arrangements.

Chez Christophine, on the French side, at Grand Case, is a few doors west of La Nacelle and next to Madame Chance. Christophine Knight makes up in earnest desire to please what her place may lack in picture-perfect atmosphere. The surroundings are sincere, colorful with some plastic touches, and warm (on the inland side of the road) when the day is. The food is good, spicy creole country cooking. Select some fish, and count on paying a fair price for what you eat—with some wine to cool the creole spices. The setting is West Indian sunshine-simple.

Chez Lolotte is a relative newcomer to the creole cooking craze at Grand Case. Count on being served in the outside garden.

L'Escargot is on the inland side of the west end of Front Street, Philipsburg, in a wooden West Indian building wrapped with a band of red, white, and blue for the tricolor and/or the Dutch flag. The wall coverings around and over the bar where you will wait for the table you reserved (or linger after your meal) are worth noting, but it's the food you are served that is the specialty here. Try the duck, however they're serving it. One of the first places to serve good food in this town, L'Escargot maintains its reputation while its prices rise. The place is in demand, reservations in winter months are essential, and there's an atmosphere that makes the restaurant a rendezvous spot for people who live here. Count on spending $15 per person for dinner, and if you get out with less, consider yourself lucky. You're expected to order wine, but a carafe of the house potion will keep the waiter happy if it pleases you.

Le Fish Pot hangs over the beach at Grand Case (French side). The balcony tables are the prized perches, while you dine on creole cooking that is best known in the southern French West Indies (Martinique and Guadeloupe). The fish is fresh from the sea, best just grilled with fresh lime (in my opinion) and spelled with chicken and sometimes beef if you're not a fish eater. This is a casual bistro at its best, with a late lunch that lingers well into the afternoon and a swim as the after-dining liqueur. Rates range depending on what you order, with the daily fish special the most desirable.

La Grenouille, up the stairs in the building next to Pasanggrahan Hotel at the east end of Front Street, in Philipsburg, has an uninteresting entrance. The view at the top (3rd) floor of the modern, stucco building makes the climb up the narrow, twisting stairwell worth it—especially for lunch when you can see out to sea. Sandwiches and soups are featured for lunch, but dinner (too dark to view) lights up the room with the steak au poivre flambé. One of the first places to bring good cooking to the Dutch side, La Grenouille took its cue from its French chef. The food is good to excellent.

Le Mini Club, seaside, west of Marigot (French), has been my longtime favorite since I first wandered down the inauspicious "alley" to the sea, off the main road out of Marigot. The place is "fancier" than it was at its start, with a wood-plank dining deck that puts you over the sea, the grilled fish with plenty of lime was still supreme, especially with chilled white wine, the fresh French bread, and plenty of time. The first years of the Mini Club (terrible name, but one which sticks) hung their reputation for good food on what was served in a couple of small rooms, in a house on the shore that was practically washed with the sea. Setting was simple, and so was the cooking, but both were sincere. Le Mini Club has survived through several owner/management teams, and now seems secure with Claudine and Pierre. The special evening buffets (check for Wednesday and Saturday) give you 35 dishes to dine on, with beef, lamb, and pork included, for $15 per person. The regular menu lists entrees from a $3 soupe de poisson (fish soup) to a $15 lobster soufflé, with my favorite poisson grillé (grilled fish) at about $8. French cheeses and crepes flambées complete the courses.

La Nacelle, nestled on the island side of the road from the sea at Grand Case, marries exceptional surroundings (now that they have been restored) with some of the island's best cuisine. A meal here will be memorable, not only for the experience but also for the price, which is as high as you can get on this island. Charles Chevillot, known to New Yorkers as the man who created a gem (La Petite Ferme) in lower Manhattan, is also known to many of us as the man who created the only place worth dining at in La Romana, on the southwest coast of the Dominican Republic (Canaris). His move here is a boon for St. Martin. Make an evening of a visit here (and don't plan on visiting in summer; they close from mid-April until the winter season).

La Nadaillac, at waterside in Marigot, is the best of the French bistros, with tables on the terrace and Chef Malard, who brings his native Périgord cuisine to Caribbean-island surroundings. The results are spectacular. This is a place for a celebration—of French cuisine. Not open for luncheon, La Nadaillac makes a ceremony of dinner and is open until the latest hours. Plan ahead, make a reservation, and don't count on rushing off to do anything else in the way of entertainment that evening. (You may not be able to afford it, and you certainly won't have the time.)

Le Radeau, moored at the edge of the Lagoon near Le Pirate hotel, flickers with its restaurant personality and an open-and-closed manner that makes checking the status crucial. Surroundings are houseboat style, with thatched roof and simple seafood specialities served to casually clothed guests. A good spot for diversion when you're touring around, or if you live at one of the Marigot hotels nearby.

Le Santal, on a dirt road off the main road at Pont Leyant (a narrow bridge over the lagoon-sea link on the French side west of Marigot), puts you in spectacular surroundings (and charges a spectacular price for the privilege). The former home has been painted and punctuated with plants, wicker, and decorator touches to provide special surroundings seaside. Terrace tables give you the option of looking over the sea, or down to coral. Bisque de Langouste and cassoulet proved excellent on one visit, with good wine, good company, and the swish of the sea as background music. Well worth paying the outstanding prices.

La Vie en Rose, on a corner at Marigot, near the open-air market, L'Aventure, and Vendome shop, offers pleasant surroundings and special meals, featuring the fish that is this island's main offering. The place is small, and reservations are essential if getting a table on the balcony is important (and even with a reservation, on a winter evening you'll have to wait, from my experience). Count on $50 for 2, if you want to dine well. Careful control over entrees can bring a check for less.

The restaurant list is legion, and the best spots on this island are going to be the ones you find yourself. The above list includes some —but by no means all—of the places worth trying. For casual, comfortable yachting informality (and subsistence food) check the **Rusty Pelican** down Kanalstraat on the beach, east of Pasanggrahan and west of Bobby's yacht marina at Philipsburg; **Sam's Place** on the shoreside of Front Street, has new owners but you'll still find hamburgers, etc. in very informal surroundings; and the **West Indian Tavern,** across Front Street, serving onion soup and lobster salad, etc. in a congenial publike setting in a balcony, house, and garden (backgammon and darts for entertainment). (This place boasts in its flyers scattered "all over" the island that you are dining on the grounds of the Caribbean's oldest synagogue; a tasteless touting, I believe.) For Chinese food in Philipsburg, try Steven Suen's **The Majesty,** in air-conditioned, boxy surroundings at the west end of Front Street, where the menu includes some Javanese and Spanish specialties mixed in with the expected Chinese. In Philipsburg, there are several small hamburger and snack places seaside, tucked into halls and houses. On the French side, both at hotels and at the small bistros, the French food is supreme.

■■

PLACES WORTH FINDING ON SINT MAARTEN/ST. MARTIN
are the beaches, for my vacation dollar, and they are powder ribbons at the shore end of dirt roads and overgrown paths on both the Dutch and French sides of the island. Fishing villages posted at the ends of some of the roads on the French side give those coves atmosphere, and sometimes give you the option to negotiate with a resi-

dent to head out to one of the small and palm-dotted islands off the northeast shore.

Except for minimal ruins of a couple of forts, there's not much in the way of buildings to prowl around. La Belle Creole, the ghost town dreamed up by Claude Philippe that was to be the multimillion dollar resort can be seen from a distance as you drive from Marigot toward Mullet Bay. Rumors persist that buildings may some day be taken over by Club Med, but as of now the pieces of Mediterranean-style village stand as weathered shells.

The Courthouse/Post Office in Philipsburg marks where Sint Maarten's first courthouse was built in 1793. As Commander Willem Hendrik Rink wrote when he requested funds from the government of the Republic of the United Netherlands, it was unseemly for the Island Council to continue to meet in the home of its commander, especially since *his* home, near the present inn at Mary's Fancy, was too far from town to expect the council members to walk. Rink countered the Netherlands' chastisement that the colony was lax with its taxes with the fact that, since the weights and scales had no housing, the salt air and strong sun had ruined them. People had taken to weighing and doing business in their homes, and it was obviously impossible for the weighmaster to chase all over town to be present at the weighing. The new courthouse Rink requested could hold the weights and scales and keep taxation under control. The third reason Rink gave for his need for a courthouse was that the garrison was too small to guard the jails in Philipsburg *and* at Fort Amsterdam, and prisoners were escaping. The jail could also be in the new courthouse. Rink won his case—and the money to build the courthouse—by 1793. A hurricane lifted the lid in 1819 and funding in those less prosperous years took until 1826, when restoration was supervised by Samuel Fahlberg, well known to islanders from this area as a cartographer, artist, civil engineer, and physicist. The Fahlberg restoration tore down the former (and partially ruined) second story and built a wood-beam version with a small balcony in front and the bell tower which Dr. Jan Hartog points out, in his *The Courthouse of St. Maarten,* was requested by the Council who wanted to follow the "modern" fashion in the 19th century—by making their announcements after a peal of bells instead of a roll of drums. Changes for 130 years were relatively minor, but the restoration in 1969 changed the lines of the building. Workmen got carried away with piling cement block on top of cement block and added 3 extra layers to the wood-flashed core they were recreating on the second floor. The building you look at from De Ruyter Square has an "imposing" second story that is the result of misreading the plans. The air conditioning is obviously new, but the stamp windows are where the weighing room used to be and packages fill the area where the jail cells used to be.

Other islands are the best places worth finding if you have time and inclination for an excursion from your Sint Maarten/St. Martin base. Winair has day trips to Saba and Sint Eustatius, with air travel, sightseeing, and lunch included in the price. You cannot do it yourself for less, although you will have a little more freedom if you want to put your own pieces together and pay as you go. Flights in all cases are well under 20 minutes, as is the case also with French St. Barths and half of the 2-island British Associated State, St. Kitts. Anguilla can easily be reached by plane flying north in about 7 minutes (all the other islands are south and a little east.)

Boat services to 6 islands—Saba, Sint Eustatius, St. Barths, St. Kitts, Nevis, and Anguilla—operate on specified days out of Philipsburg. Count on the schedule to be *very* flexible in all but peak season winter months; if you want to go to one of the 6 islands by boat, your best bet is to check the day you arrive to see what day the boat goes to your chosen island and plan the rest of your excursions around that. Writing ahead is no assurance; plans change at the last minute. Fare figures to about $35 round trip for the farthest distance—Nevis; all others are less with Saba and Statia at $30.

■■
SPORTS ON SINT MAARTEN/ST. MARTIN set off from one of the Caribbean's best collection of beaches. Although there's no strand that stretches as far as the Caymans' Seven Mile Beach, there are not many coves on Sint Maarten/St. Martin that don't have at least a small patch of talcum sand, and all are open to everyone, no matter whose property you walk through to get there. Pack a picnic for some of the beach days; unless you've beached by a hotel, there are no food concessions and bringing something from home port makes the day trip possible.

Scuba and **snorkeling** thread out from water-sports concessions at the hotels. Mullet Bay's beach concession *Maho Watersports,* offers on-the-spot options for guests. Novices can sign on for the 3-hour Resort Course, given in Mullet Bay when the sea is calm, or at the pool otherwise. Your offshore dive is a second part of the experience, arranged the next day with one of the instructors. Divers depart from the Mullet marina by boat for dive sites offshore. Among the special spots for experienced divers are the wreck of HMS *Proselyte*, which sank in the early 1800s and has coral-encrusted cannons and anchors that are favorite havens for colorful fish. The Alleys, underwater cliffs, and ledges are another spot, and Hens and Chickens, on the windward side, are surrounded with elkhorn coral.

If you are interested in going farther afield, it is possible to make arrangements to go to St. Barths, Anguilla, and Flat Island, in addition to the areas around Dog Island, Prickly Pear, Scrub, Sandy Island, Five Island, Barrel-Beef, and others.

Snorkeling is best at the coral reefs, but is not its most spectacular off the resorts where the powdery sand slopes into the sea and the waves often churn the waters. There are regular snorkel trips arranged by both firms mentioned above, or you can head out on your own from some of the uncluttered coves you find yourself.

Glass-bottom boat rides are offered on lagoon and sea. Departure port is the Mullet Bay marina, behind building 66. The water sports facility at Mullet Bay has the most complete facilities, with waterskiing, jet skiing, sunset sailing, scuba, and snorkeling easily arranged. Only a rolling surf curbs the man-made activity at Mullet's beach.

Sailing: for latest information on the fleet that sets sail or heads out under power from Sint Maarten/St. Martin shores, check first at the Sint Maarten Tourist Bureau on the waterfront, not far from the Courthouse/Post Office in the middle of Philipsburg's Front Street, and then, if you want to make a thorough survey, head over to the French side to check with the hotels near Marigot for information on yachts setting sail from this north side, usually to Anguilla. Look for *Sea Wolf*, one of my favorites because the 48-foot ketch takes only 8 people. Captain Don Borer will head off to Anguilla for the day or will go wherever you want to, seas permitting, for a day sail, sunset sail, or half-day sail. You can find out about *Sea Wolf* at the Charter Boat Center on the pier at Philipsburg. Others to look for are the 57-foot motor cruiser *Maison Maru*, which covers the coast between Philipsburg, Marigot, and Grand Case, anchoring off a beach for a swim. Check for the planned departure days, which are on a schedule in winter but depend on the quantity of passengers available on the slower season days. *Yacht Maison Maru* picks up at the Town Pier and sometimes from the hotels if there is a big enough group to make a special boarding stop worthwhile. The Tourist Board can give you on the spot details, as well as information about *La Esperanza*, a marvelous wood-hulled character craft that was built by Jaap and Nanda in Portugal in 1973, and sailed to Barbados in 1975 to arrive here for charters a few seasons later. It has more character than anything except the *Sea Wolf,* and will give you a lot for your money if you like sailing to St. Barths or some nearby island—if it is in port.

El Tigre, a catamaran launched in October '78, takes up to 9 for cruises, bedding them down in 4 double cabins and one triple. Weekly winter charter is about $4100 for 8 down to $2000 for 2. Summer rates are lower. Check with Courtwell, N.V., Box 346, Philipsburg, or at Friendly Homes on Simson Bay for details.

Bahamas Yachting Services opened a base next to Bobby's Marina in Philipsburg last winter. The fleet of CSY 44s (cutters) and Morgan 46s (ketches) can take 6 easily, and are available either bareboat or with skipper. If you want a 23′6″ Rhodes Tempest with a 7 hp outboard for some day sailing on your own, check at Bobby's Marina (or with management at Town House Apartments) about how to find *Cy Collins' boat.* It's available (when he's not out sailing himself). *Lagoon Cruises and Watersports* offers "Sail in St. Maarten" specials, with boat rental and a sailing school operating on the lagoon. Contact the Sailing Master at Mullet Bay or ask at your hotel's activities desk. The usual complement of Sunfish and other small sailboats are available at Mullet Bay, Simson Bay Beach Hotel, and Little Bay Beach on the Dutch side, and at Le Galion on the French side.

Golfers gather on the 18-hole course at Mullet Bay. During peak-season winter the sign up for starting times is as crucial as at your hometown course on Memorial Day or Labor Day weekends. The entire operation was planned and programmed for real pros, so that all facilities are in perfect (sometimes sun-parched) U.S.-style working order. The pro shop is complete; the pros are available for lessons as well as for helping you find players if you come on your own. Locker facilities, carts, caddies, and the 19th hole are ready and waiting. The course undulates at the heart of the vast Mullet Bay complex, and is said by some to be the heart of the resort. Count on costs to be high. (If you want to be sure of a starting time, be a guest at Mullet. While guests from other hotels are welcome to play, their starting times depend on what's available after the house residents take their choice.)

Tennis courts speckle the resorts, but Mullet Bay takes top prize for quantity, quality, and tennis shop. There are 18 courts at 2 tennis areas, and most see regular play both during winter months and when the tennis-week specials are offered, from April 16 through December 15. (Check for rates which include room, board, court use and clinics.) Other hotels with courts are Little Bay, La Samanna, Great Bay, Caravanserai, Oyster Pond, Dawn Beach and Maho Reef.

■■■

TREASURES AND TRIFLES ON SINT MAARTEN/ST. MARTIN on the Dutch side are neatly organized, and although the lark of discovering something "no one" else has found may no longer be the prime pursuit on the streets of Philipsburg, shops offer some of the Caribbean's most unusual good-quality items. The several shops are within a short walk of each other: most are air-conditioned and—if you avoid the days when the cruise ships are in port—there is plenty of space to wander.

> **A**UTHOR'S OBSERVATION: To make your shopping time count, spend some time perusing the orange newssheet *St. Maarten Holiday,* published regularly, available free, and full of suggestions for shops (and restaurants) with special items highlighted.

Shopping on the French side is very different from the calculated commerce of the Dutch. First, although the most tourist-oriented stores will welcome credit cards and traveler's checks, the common currency is the French franc. Shops sprawl around the town; those that cater to residents are mixed with the ones that focus on visitor interest. Only Grand Case, the wide spot in the road that is a separate village, has burgeoned with special shops in a cluster. One focal point of tourist shops in Marigot is the plaza near the Palais de Justice a couple of streets inland from the main waterfront drive. Count on hours to be flexible on the French side. From my experience, places seldom open at 8 as posted, and often shutter completely for lingering lunch between 12 and 2. Purveying products to outsiders is not the prime concern of Marigot's shopkeepers; if you find a treasure, it will be because you have really hunted for it.

PHILIPSBURG, Sint Maarten, is the heart of the duty-free shopping as you have heard it touted on the other Dutch islands (Curaçao and Aruba especially). There *are* real bargains to be found, but here—as everywhere—wise shoppers should do research at home, with their local discount store, to be sure that the price they are paying in Philipsburg *is,* in fact, lower than that offered at home (where repairs, if needed, will certainly be easier to negotiate). Separate stations for **Spritzer & Fuhrmann** (watches, jewelry, and all luxury items), the **Yellow House** (cameras, watches, etc.), **Kan** jewelry, and other names you may know from the southern ABC's, where the stores got their start, stand on Front Street. Their air-conditioned confines have case after case of tempters, with some "come-ons" mixed with the true luxury items. Be aware that these stores *specialize* in merchandising. (Spritzer & Fuhrmann also has branches at Mullet Bay, Little Bay, and Great Bay. On days when the streets are filled with cruise ship passengers, these shops represent a peaceful shopping oasis with the pick of the crop.)

Check at the **Royal Palm Arcade,** near the Methodist Church, for Java Wraps (batik bathing suits and beach or patio wear) and look into the **Italian Patio** for several boutiques and small speciality shops. **Gluck Galleries** has filled a building on the road near Philipsburg (from the airport) with a lot of trinkets and what I refer to as "tourist trash." It joins the **Shipwreck Shop** in filling its shelves with a combination of interesting items and outright junk that leave the final decision of which is which to you, the buyer. I find the selection at the **Sea Urchin,** on the water side of Front Street in the area near L'Escargot Restaurant at the west end of town, much more interesting, with some really creative trinkets, jewelry, and silk-screen work when I last looked. The scarves from Jean Yves Fromment's workshop on St. Barths are colorful, easy to pack, and priced right, no matter what size you choose.

The Arcade Shopping Terrace, not far from Pasanggrahan and Holland House in Philipsburg, was in a state of flux when I visited. It has had a good shop for island made items called *Around The Bend.* Inquire, or walk around to see what you can find.

Thimbles and Things has needlepoint designs and a good selection of threads. The Caribbean themes, some peculiar to Sint Maarten, are well worth the purchase. If you are not handy yourself, it is sometimes possible to order something worked especially for you. While in here, take a look at the Batik Caribe fabrics, hand-painted from original designs created at Caribee Studio on St. Vincent, and the work of **Saban Artisans,** the fabric design that's accomplished on the cone that is Saba and sold here (as well as there) by the yard and worked into floating and fun patio clothes.

I sometimes find Front Street overwhelming—with its proliferation of Indian shops *full* from floor to ceiling and back into the dark corners with possible "buys," and the several shops that sell Dutch "Delftware" that is usually not authentic from Delft but copies that are priced too high mixed with a selection of Dutch-theme tourist trinkets. Included in this shopping stew are some fashion shops that *do* carry trendy clothes at good prices. Check **St. Tropez,** which I found a cut above some of the others on a recent run through. It specializes in French Riviera styles, but the mix also includes blue jeans and casual wear.

Shops on the Dutch side are open 8–12, 2–6 daily except Sundays, and Saturdays when many shops close at 12. Shops at the hotels are sometimes open evenings, so check if it is important. Do not count on the airport shops to be open when you depart. Although most are open when there's airport activity, all have small staff and when they are sick (or late) the store's not open. When a cruise ship is in port, most tourist shops are open, even on Sundays, on the Dutch side—but don't count on the French.

At **GRAND CASE,** on the French side, wander around **Pierre Lapin,** a shop *full* of imaginative and colorful clothes, accessories and some stuffed toys for children. At **MARIGOT,** aim right for **Galerie Pergourdine,** across from the Palais de Justice, and wander around the boutiques that cluster at this new shopping courtyard. Although a lot of print has been spent talking about the French imports that you can scoop up by the armloads, frankly I haven't found much. There are some imports—the famous names of Courréges, Yves St. Laurent, Cacharel, and others including Lacoste, which is so familiar in the States that many people think of it as a U.S. firm—but they are sprinkled with the "imports" from the States, and you have to know what you are looking for. Perfumes can be a bargain. Wander along the waterfront drive to stop in the small shops that specialize in them. There is a good boutique at the alley that leads down to the Mini Club, and for some interesting French resort wear, stop at **Vanessa,** either the shop at Marigot or the branch at Le Pirate.

L'Atelier/Galerie, on the second floor not far from the Texaco Station on the main road through Marigot, has high quality crafts, displayed in a restored West Indian house. Expect to find jewelry, sculpture, paintings, and other artisan items.

Two books to buy, if you're interested in island history, are *History of Saba* ($2.50) and *History of Sint Eustatius* ($2.50), both by Dr. J. Hartog and available at shops in Sint Maarten.

St. Thomas

Division of Tourism, Box 1692, Charlotte Amalie, St. Thomas, VI 00801; Virgin Islands Government Tourist Office, 1270 Avenue of the Americas, New York, NY 10020; 343 S. Dearborn St., Suite 1108; Chicago, IL 60604; 3450 Wilshire Blvd., Los Angeles, CA 90010, 100 N. Biscayne Blvd., Suite 904, Miami, FL 33132; 1050 17th Street, NW, Washington, DC 20036.

U.S. currency used.

The picnic spread out over the slab of wood that did duty as the table was an island affair. The tub of a concoction known as *souse* was a joy for my St. Thomian friends and, after I had timidly tasted a peculiar looking part of pig (at the insistance of my hosts), not completely poison for me. There are other specialties I learned to like better: calaloo, fungi, land crabs, and even the local lobster—langouste—that 7-year-old Johnny pried from the sea-covered rocks off shore. That was his contribution to our feast.

The road we had followed to reach this Sunday beach was rutted and rock strewn. Sun-dried dirt dusted us as we traveled. At the end of the drive was a wooden gate that 12-year-old Linda leapt out to swing open for the car to pass. The day at the beach was an outing—St. Thomian style—and it took place more than 20 years ago.

Today this island's pleasures have adjusted to the stateside tempo. The road to the beach is paved. And there's a hotel, plus condominiums around the shores—here, and almost everywhere else on this island. Even the shores have changed; the sand drifts out at regular intervals, as if recoiling from the surge of people that now play at this place. As for souse, calaloo and fungi? Few people make it any more in St. Thomas. Hamburgers, hot dogs, and Kentucky Fried Chicken have taken over. And the day of the "do-it-yourself" beach picnic has almost gone. There are places to buy your food on most beaches these days, and most people do that.

The simple life of the past has vanished from the U.S. Virgins—and so has most of the extreme poverty of those days. Natural pleasures have been packaged for sale. The commerce may have crowded beaches, but it has also created jobs.

Downtown Charlotte Amalie, capital of the United States Virgin Islands and the commercial heart of St. Thomas, has always been a pirates' place. When the planters settled rural St. Croix, almost 40 miles to the south, the pirates were carousing around the free port of Charlotte Amalie, declared free for all by the Danes. Commerce was always the core of St. Thomian life; it still is. Downtown Charlotte Amalie's former warehouses are appliqued with boutiques and bistros, and the once-private houses that lined the inland side of Dronningen's Gade (known these days as Main Street) are now shops as well.

You have to head out of town—way out—to find the leisurely life that Caribbean converts come south to find. And you'll find comfortable, small hotels on most of those sandy strips these days.

■■

POLITICAL PICTURE: When Governor Juan Luis, running on the Independent Citizens' Movement (ICM) ticket, defeated the Virgin Islands Democratic Party's candidate Ron deLugo in the elections of November 1978 to win a 4-year term of office the Governor began grappling with a number of serious economic realities in the U.S. Virgin Islands. Tourism is an important employer and wage earner, and rum subsidies and other benefits that accrue to a U.S. territory are major contributors to the island finances. (Estimates of federal aid to the USVI in fiscal 1981 reach $100 million, for a population of about 110,000.)

The U.S. Virgin Islands, purchased from Denmark in 1917, are an unincorporated territory of the United States Government, governed—as we go to press—under the Revised Organic Act of 1954. Three attempts at drafting their own constitution have been defeated by the Virgin Islands populace, with the most recent constitutional referendum held in March 1978. A fourth attempt, well underway by May '81, may be passed, giving the territory more self-government.

A series of articles in the *Virgin Islands Daily News* in spring of '81 focused on "mismanagement and corruption" in the local government. FBI investigations followed the revelation of fiscal abuses and gross mismanagement at the highest government levels, and although some Virgin Islanders regretted that the "Problems in Paradise" series appeared at the time that President Reagan was calling for reduction in government spending, most agreed that public knowledge of the corruption within the local government might do something to correct it. Virgin Islanders will be voting for their governor (for a 4-year term) in November 1982.

Tourism is a major source for employment, and cash, for the Virgin Islands economy. Efforts by the government as well as by the very active Hotel Association, Retailers' Association, and Chamber of Commerce are geared to providing what the vacationers expect to find in "paradise." Recent realities—a rising crime rate, both for petty crimes (robbery, for example) and for violent crimes—have prompted the government to beef up the police protection. Highly trained police dogs, agile at tracking down criminals, are operating in St. Thomas; demonstrations of the dogs effectiveness have inspired awe among schoolchildren and others invited to watch the dogs perform at community events. The problem of security has been recognized, defined, and addressed. All hope that will result in reduced crime for coming months. Vacationers and others taking natural precautions (not leaving valuables in hotel rooms or rental cars, following well-traveled tourist routes, avoiding desolate, poorly lighted areas in town and in the countryside at night, etc.) have had no problems.

■■■

CUSTOMS OF THE COUNTRY are American suburban. St. Thomas is like any small town in sunny climates, U.S.A. You will find Kentucky Fried Chicken, plus the usual hot dogs and hamburgers for fast food. Supermarkets akin to those you know at home can be found on the outskirts on Charlotte Amalie, as well as "in the country" at Estate Tutu and in other areas around the island.

The warm and sunny weather means that casual clothes are the daily "uniform," with bathing suits best on beaches (*not* in town). Although dinner hours at the big hotels (Bluebeard's, Virgin Isle, Frenchman's Reef) and at private homes may be elegant, dress-up affairs, "fashion" elsewhere is in the eye of the beholder, and almost anything goes.

The main word of advice is to travel light. Leave all the gaudy jewelry, etc. at home, and bring as little as possible in the way of baggage on your island vacation.

■■

MONEY MATTERS a lot, and you will need plenty if you want to be carefree about dining out and renting cars, sailboats, snorkel gear, etc. Credit cards are accepted at many (but not all) restaurants and at the better stores, but cash is the essential commodity. If you have a lot of cash, keep it undercover, and consider leaving some at the front desk of your hotel. Traveler's checks are advisable since they're only negotiable with your signature.

■■

ARRIVAL ON ST. THOMAS will be on some plane that is approved for landing at the airstrip where work is going on to bring the tarmac to specifications for all but 747s. If you fly American Airlines, the convenient connecting flight on their shuttle between St. Croix (where the biggest planes land) and St. Thomas is easy, fast, and comfortable. The St. Thomas air terminal as of this writing is still the ancient military hangar that has been around so long there are those of us who love it, but no one thinks it is beautiful (or efficient). In fact, the "system" for luggage pickup can only be classified as organized chaos. The terminal has acquired barnacles of shops, car rental booths, small-airline ticket counters, and *long* covered walkways occasionally used to get you from or to your plane. Prinair Herons, Oceanair Rolls Royce-propelled planes, and the small planes of other airlines dart in and out of here like birds picking up worms; Prinair alone has about 30 daily flights, most of them to San Juan, some of them to St. Croix, and down-island runs to Beef Island for the British Virgins, Sint Maarten, and points south to Guadeloupe, and including Antigua. Neither restaurants nor shops are worth talking about at this airport now, but you can walk across a road to Lindbergh Beach for a swim after you check in—if you're smart enough to have packed your bathing suit in your pocket with a plastic bag.

■■

TOURING TIPS: First-timers would be wise to sign on for a half-day tour to get their bearings and find out what's where. From that point on, if you want to be mobile, rent a car. All the big names have spots at the airport (Hertz, National, Avis, Budget), and I have found rates to be high and staff to be haughty and not too helpful. I did much better with Sun Island Rentals, and I suggest you look into their rates and cars or those of Dotson Car Rental, Atlantic Car Rental, or All Island Rent-A-Car. Some hotels have special arrangements for rental cars for their guests. Island Beachcomber can provide a car if you request in advance (otherwise you take your chances on availability). The same is true of Point Pleasant, Bolongo Bay, and some of the other small places.

Taxi fares are posted at the airport. If you can't find the sheet, be sure to ask the dispatcher. Years of being in the tourism business seems to have resulted in "fair practices" by St. Thomian taxi drivers, at least from my experience. You'll seldom find a driver willing to share the local lore as is the case on less touristed islands, but you'll also be charged standard rates, unless you ask for something special. If you want a driver for half a day or for an island tour, be sure to negotiate the fee in advance. There is a set fee for so many hours, but if you and your driver get along, there's sometimes room for special treatment (with an expected special reward for the driver).

St. Thomas has become a commercial depot and as such has become a haven for seedy types. I do not recommend wandering around alone, on foot, along the waterfront outside of the well-traveled routes, especially at less busy hours. The same petty crimes that plague cities in the States are prevalent in these islands. There have been instances of robbery and worse crimes along the waterfront between town and the St. Thomas marina, especially in the area around the low-cost housing development. If you're timid about heading for the hills, to some of the island's top restaurants, after dark, hire a cab and ask him to return for pickup at an appointed time.

Know in advance that the mountains that give St. Thomas its spectacular vistas (the views *are* awesome, even to those of us who have been coming here for a couple of decades or more), make driving a "Grand Prix" event. Roads are winding, can be "straight" up and down, are usually potholed and seldom properly banked. In addition, island drivers are apt to stop dead in the middle of the road to chat with a friend or drive on your side of the narrow route. Driving is on the left; your hometown license is enough for legal driving here.

AUTHOR'S OBSERVATION: Make careful reading of the yellow sheet *St. Thomas This Week* your first priority on arrival. Available free through your hotel, and usually at the airport, the fact-filled weekly guide has all the necessary tidbits about restaurants, activities, and shops. It's invaluable.

■■■

HOTELS ON ST. THOMAS are personality places. Frenchman's Reef Holiday Inn is the only big chain reaction. Most of the inns on this island are small. Many have grown from being someone's private residence; some still are. In spite of modern conve-

niences (every place will have them), things may not work exactly
as you expect them to. There is a very real water problem on an island where it seldom rains, and where growth has been so rapid
that saltwater conversion plants prove to be too small by the time
they are finished. There's plenty of fresh water to drink and to use,
but there is not an endless supply—and some hotels will have a notice telling you that.

Air conditioners are modern acquisitions—essential in rooms
that have been built with no regard for tradewinds, the natural air
conditioning. With skyrocketing oil prices, some hotels add energy
surcharge and others raise the basic room rate. A few very special
places have featured the old style building, with overhead fans to
swirl a breeze; There are some very comfortable beachside hotels
on an island that had *no* hotel on the beach in the mid-1950s. Island
Beachcomber was the first, unless someone wants to count the few
rooms out at Brewer's Bay, which the guests at Bluebeard's Castle
then used.

There is no gambling in the U.S. Virgin Islands. Nightlife is in-
formal-spontaneous. You'll seldom find big-time nightclub entertainment; if you find it at all, it will be at Frenchman's Reef, or
perhaps the Pirate's Parlour at Bluebeard's Castle or the Virgin Isle.
Otherwise, hotel entertainment—when there is any—is a steel
band or some other local music for dancing a couple of evenings,
and maybe a limbo or 2. The Carib Beach Hotel has the best St.
Thomian show, in my opinion.

There are few hotel bargains, but some good values. The small
places or an apartment rental are your best bet if budget is a consideration. When you rent a cottage, or set up housekeeping, you can
keep costs down—and the supermarkets for supplies are good.
Many hotels have special package holidays, for tennis, scuba, hon-
eymoons, family vacations, and golf (at Mahogany Run), with the
best rates in spring, summer, and fall. In addition, a summer
"American Paradise" promotion has been part of the sales pitch for
all 3 U.S. Virgins for recent April 16 through December 15 seasons.
Read the "extras" carefully before you leap at the opportunity; it
may be that what you are buying really isn't much of a bargain. The
free boat rides, sightseeing tours, and occasional transportation
may be an interesting "come-on," but your room rate may not be
much lower than what you'd pay anyway. Sit down with your pencil
and paper, if you care about specifics. It *is* a good advertising gimmick, but may not be good for you. For a special scuba holiday, investigate the program offered at the St. Thomas Diving Club at Villa
Olga.

AUTHOR'S AWARDS for St. Thomas go to Bluebeard's Castle's Milan Glumidge, for giving a big hotel a coveted small hotel feeling (however, know before you go that this in-town spot has convenient shopping but is a ride to the beach); to Bolongo Bay for a beachside nest with good value and exceptional hospitality.

✤ **Bluebeard's Castle** (Box 7480, Charlotte Amalie, St. Thomas, USVI; 100 rooms) is a personal favorite that looks better than ever for this season. The hotel bubbled from this hilltop 300 years ago and it's been percolating ever since. Danish explorer Erik Smidt built a fortress on Smith's Hill, overlooking the fledgling settlement at Charlotte Amalie. The main tower, some of the walls, and a couple of cannon are left from those days. That's about all. What brews on this hillside, now incorporated into undulating Charlotte Amalie, is the result of a recipe that includes the chemical fortunes of owner Henry Reichold and the ingenuity and able management of Milan Glumidge.

Bluebeard's Castle is shown as a "dwelling house" in *The Virgin Islands of the United States of America,* by Luther K. Zabriskie, published in 1918, the year after the Danish transfer. The federal government made the home into a hotel with the addition of the first of several rooms in the 1920s. The *Virgin Islands Picture Book,* by J. Antonio Jarvis and Rufus Martin, published in 1949, says that "the Castle has many legends. It was there that Consul Henriques-Moron received 'Queen Coziah' and her black rioters who went 'to protect him,' . . . Before the present manager, E. Leonard Brewer took over, this hotel was undistinguished. Now it has an inimitable air of Old World courtesy and American efficiency." I'll say the same of 1980s management, Milan Glumidge and his team, who help give this rambling hotel a friendly, truly St. Thomian personality, no matter how many camera-slung tourists range over its grounds when a cruise ship is in port.

Bluebeard's has been my fortress countless times during a couple of decades of island travels. While I'm the first to admit that no place is perfect for everyone, this place has been perfect for me on many occasions. For one thing, it's convenient ($2 taxi ride down the hill to town; you can walk if you feel like it); for another, the view from the dining terrace is just about ideal, as countless photographs attest, with the pastel roofs of Charlotte Amalie cupped in the palm of the harbor. The dining terrace, the piano terrace, or poolside are perfect places to watch the sunset, if you don't have one of the rooms in the rectangular 3-story box that give you a view over town. You can watch Antilles Air Boats' small amphibian planes dart in and out of the harbor as you stretch out at the pool. The cruise ships tie up at the pier across the harbor. When you've had enough sun, you can go into one of the air-conditioned shops. Rooms vary—a lot! Most are modern, air-conditioned, with view. A few are the result of using every inch of limited hilltop; no view, no breeze, no high price.

Complete, almost constant, and very thorough million-dollar-or-more renovations added tennis courts, rerouted the road that used to curl around the terrace you dined on, paved and propped up the poolside area, and provided a new look from the surrounding hills by painting the hotel roofs red (they used to be blue). Transportation to Magens Bay, over the mountain on the north shore, is provided daily; day-tour options can be arranged from the lobby tour desk. The nightclub here has entertainment after dinner nightly. Room rates range from about $100 to over $125 for 2, meals extra, in winter months, but ask about the plans for honeymooners, tennis holidays, and other week-long specials that give you better value.

✛ **Bolongo Bay Beach Club** (Box 7337, St. Thomas, USVI 00801; 36 rooms) is an enclave of hospitality, cupping a white-sand beach on a cove within reasonable distance (about 15 minutes' drive) from shops and social centers in downtown Charlotte Amalie, and with sailing, scuba, snorkeling, and the sea at the tips of your toes when you wake in the morning. Dick and Joyce Doumeng have organized everything (including their capable staff) so that you won't feel organized at all. Everything seems to run smoothly—as the repeat guests have recognized. Although rooms have small kitchenettes the alfresco restaurant lures most vacationers for mealtime, and the terrace around the pool is a perfect place for a midday rum punch or a twilight potion. Tennis courts are in good shape (and in constant play when the winter regulars are in the house); water sports are included in your daily rate. This is a special small spot with private-club potential. Guests have a fun-filled sail on the *Ho Tei* included in the price of a week's stay, which comes at package-tour levels with summer, winter, and honeymoon prices, with a welcoming drink, flowers and champagne, continental breakfast, 3 dinners (with a bottle of wine included for one of them), and unlimited use of snorkel gear, Sunfish sailboats, tennis courts and rackets, a scuba lesson, and the day sail to St. John. The room rate hovers around $120 per night for 2, all the activities (but no meals) included.

When booking a room, know that numbers 7 to 12 stretch off to the left as you face the sea, and are preferable for my vacation dollars because they are at the opposite side of the main gathering spots for the beachside action. Some folks gather with friends to cook out at the area set aside for that down by the beach.

✤ **Domini Hus** (Box 2205, Charlotte Amalie, St. Thomas, USVI 00801; 7 rooms) is the island's best bet for very inexpensive accommodations in historic (not fancy) surroundings. A couple of decades haven't changed this inn, but then why should they? This venerable house is part of the island's Danish heritage. With a hillside view from a busy part of the capital, Domini Hus has a devoted following who care more about price and people than pristine surroundings. Count on paying about $35 for 2, with simple breakfast included in the rate (and the opportunity to use the charcoal grill if you want to cook your dinner "at home").

✤ **Embers Guesthouse** (Box 4434, 81 Estate Contant, St. Thomas, USVI 00801; 10 rooms) eases you into the island life with overhead fans in your room for cooling off and with a casually comfortable atmosphere. Located in a residential area on the outskirts of town, the inn is up in the hills overlooking the Caribbean—and the airport. You'll need a car (or the urge to be a hermit) to be happy here, but for anyone seeking an island hillside hideaway at very reasonable cost, this place is worth considering. Count on paying under $40 for 2 this winter (and look into the efficiency unit that rents for about $50 if you like cooking).

✤ **Frenchman's Reef Beach Resort** (Box 7100, St. Thomas, USVI 00801; 410 rooms) sits at the southeastern point of Charlotte Amalie Harbor. The lighthouse incorporated into its swimming pool area hardly seems a necessity; the hotel itself is far more obvious. This resort "city" is a far cry from the former Flamboyant Hotel which stood on this site, with some of its rooms built on gun emplacement slabs from the days when the hilltop was a World War II naval installation. All that is part of the dim, dark past and hard to imagine these days. On the present property's plus side: a lively lobby with activity circulating around the center-of-the-room planter, plenty of action at all hours with discos, dining room, pinball machines in the hall, a game room, birds in cages around the lower lobby, shops along every available space, modern air-conditioned rooms with the usual amenities, plus, for most rooms, spectacular views; and an activities desk that can put you on, in, or under the sea, a beach down from the hotel-on-the-hill, tennis courts, and a gigantic solar-powered air-conditioning system with collectors installed on 2 roof surfaces. The system, financed by the hotel owners (American Motor Inns, Inc. of Roanoke, Va.) and the U.S. Department of Energy as one of 32 projects selected from 308 applicants, made headlines when it was installed in March 1977 (and cost more millions when it had to be refined less than a year later).

On the minus side: The entire hotel could be on any island—or in any sunny climate. It is big, brassy modern, and a fortress built to create a commercial holiday atmosphere. There's nothing small and folksy, or even strictly St. Thomian about the place. Convention-eering crowds seem to like it, as do folks who prefer a hotel that looks like one back home. Frenchman's Reef is not only the first sight you see when you arrive by cruise ship, but it's also one of the places cruise ship passengers perch for a day in the St. Thomian sun. Travel agents love to book the place (dependable, commissionable, a good package tour hotel), and if you like the security of a Miami- or San Juan-style hotel, this may be your spot. There's no place like it on this island. You'll pay $138 to $188 for a room for 2 this winter, with all meals extra, so it's worthwhile investigating package plans.

✤ **Harbor View** (Box 1975, Charlotte Amalie, St. Thomas, USVI; 10 rooms) was a private home of the A. H. Lockhart family before it became an inn in the late 1930s. J. Antonio Jarvis, in his 1949 book, described Frenchman's Hill as a "residential district of fine stone houses and splendid views," and goes on to point out that "several streets of stairs as well as regular roads serve this section of the city." The "splendid views" are still here, once you are inside the "famous old mansion first built by the Huguenots," but the streets of stairs—now paved and about one car wide—are sided by dozens of people in dozens of humble homes. A taxi or rental car can take you up to Harbor View from the downtown marketplace in about 5 minutes, but it's no place to walk. Mealtime, especially dinner, is very special, with good food pleasantly served on fine china, with the wine you are expected to order served in elegant goblets. Atmosphere is A-1, and the lounges on the terrace make the long waits I've often experienced for dinner (reservations essential) seem not so bad; for after-dinner coffee, the place is superb. Bedrooms vary in size; some of the air conditioners (essential because of the pocket-size rooms, some with no view) dripped when I was there, but the ambiance makes it possible to overlook a lot if you like to travel "the inn way." Furnishings are mostly wicker, with colorful fabrics, and for that you pay about $80 for 2 in winter, light breakfast included.

✚ **Hotel 1829** (Box 1579, Charlotte Amalie, St. Thomas, USVI 00801; 22 rooms) continues an island tradition, in some of this island's most traditional surroundings. (Old stone steps, front porch, ballast-brick walls in the bar and other main-floor rooms.) The bowered courtyard is worth looking at when you have to pause for breath at the top of your climb up the front steps, and you can take a quick pace or 2 to the left or right to sit on the porch, where former inn owner Mrs. Maguire used to serve free drinks for anyone in a chair at 6:29 (18:29 by European clocks). Some of the old customs have gone, along with Mrs. Maguire's tales of old St. Thomas, but the memories linger on as you sit in the inside dining room, on the terrace, or at the backgammon boards or the bar. Bedrooms are a varied lot, all carved a little smaller with the addition of private bath and all spruced up with a recent overhaul. Air conditioners hum to keep it cool in some of the tiniest boxes; 2 rooms overhang the entry steps and make up in view what they lack in quiet. Baron Vernon Ball, 1977 world champion at backgammon, owns this place, and you can count on paying a winter tariff of $55 to $95 for 2 for a room you'll have to climb to. A small pool cools houseguests between trips by car to nearby beaches. You can walk down Government Hill to the shops and boites in town.

✚ **Inn at Mandahl** (Box 2483, St. Thomas, USVI 00801; 8 rooms plus rooms in separate buildings) has gotten into the time-sharing business and has sacrificed its "inn" status, if what you're looking for is a small spot at the top of the world. With an awe-inspiring view of Caribbean Sea and several islands from its hillside, north-shore perch, the Inn is an ideal luncheon spot if you tire of beachside sun (and care more about view than food; my cheeseburger was almost inedible). Reached by a winding, mountainous road, this inn is within the realm of the expansive (and expensive) Mahogany Run golf resort. It's not related, but it is convenient to the golf course and not too far (if you don't mind mountain roads) from Magen's Bay where you'll find the island's best beach. Inquire about use of the time-sharing units, recently built in rectangular blocks with a commanding view of the bay and the islands beyond. A special brand of hospitality and a flair for island-style decor make the Inn at Mandahl worth a visit. There's a pool on premises; backgammon boards set up in the breeze-filled "lobby" that is more like a comfortable living room, and that spectacular view from the dining room where one "wall" is glass. Sunday brunch, with special banana pancakes, has become a St. Thomian tradition, but if you're nervous about driving those wiggly roads (or want to enjoy the rum concoctions) make arrangements with a taxi driver to bring you here. Rates this winter are expected to be about $80 for 2.

✤ **Island Beachcomber** (Box 1689, St. Thomas, USVI 00801; 48 rooms) is a special vacation home that makes guests feel like family with thoughtful gifts in your room—and candies by your pillow at night. This comfortably casual inn is an owner-instigated tradition. It hides behind a fence, wrapped in tropical planting, at Lindbergh Bay Beach. Michael and Lorette Resch have lavished endless hours of work and plenty of enthusiasm in this place. The first units appeared in 1957, to be followed by a second story and eventually to incorporate what used to be Surfside, a few paces east on the beach. A very special spot on a sandy strip that parallels the road from airport into Charlotte Amalie (and the runway), Island Beachcomber has devoted followers who enjoy settling into a chair at the thatched beachside bar around sunset (sometimes earlier), This place has personality—plenty of it, even when the owners are off the island. *Surfside* restaurant (in recognition of the property's original name) borders the beach. All indications are that you will find the traditional warm welcome at this special spot, beloved by its repeat vacationers and by the congenial business folk who make this home base while in St. Thomas. Rates range to the $80s for 2, all meals extra. Rooms have refrigerators; grills are available, and the hotel's alfresco dining area offers candlelight dinners within sound of the surf.

✤ **Limetree Beach Hotel** (Box 7307, St. Thomas, USVI 00801; 84 rooms) started life as a private home, and the central building (where you'll have your evening meals) was what the Jacksons knew as their viewful villa. Things are in a state of flux as we go to press, so check about possible change in ownership and ask about present plans prior to booking this winter. The hotel's location, on a white sandy beach about 20 minutes' drive from the airport and about 15 minutes from town, on the south coast, is ideal. The overnight offerings, in a series of 7 buildings (12 rooms per unit) behind the pool, which is behind the beach, are modern and comfortable. Standard rooms are on the first and second floors; superior are top floors with view for your climb. Tennis courts (2) are lighted and an Undersea Center sells clothes, perfume, cigarettes, and liquor, as well as offering scuba, snorkeling, sailing, and tennis instruction, plus arranging for car rental if you haven't picked up something at the airport. Rates are expected to be $105 (standard) and $120 (superior) for 2, this winter.

✢ **Mafolie** (Box 1528, Charlotte Amalie, St. Thomas, USVI 00801; 23 rooms) makes the most of a mountainside location, with one of the most popular St. Thomian eateries (*The Frigate*) and a small inn, with pool. The walk down to town is possible, and some have walked up the winding, narrow road, but most vacationers rent a car for a couple of days if they've chosen to call this home. The several rooms come in all shapes and sizes, wedged into any spare inch of overhang. Air conditioning is essential for most of the pockets, a very few of which have any decent view. For casual, bargain-rate accommodations, the rooms at Mafolie might fill the bill. Winter rate for 2 hovers around $50, meals extra. Non-air-conditioned rooms are less, if you can stand it.

✢ **Magens Point Hotel** (Magens Bay Road, St. Thomas, USVI 00801; 32 rooms plus 22 time-sharing) hangs over the far side of the mountain, with a view of the British Virgins and, if you could see through the trees, over that ribbon of white sand that is Magens Bay Beach, a possible (but hot) walk down the hill. Opened as Indies House with plans for a zoo, the inn flopped—into the hands of the bank, from whom Lon Southerland and a team picked it up in late 1976. Enter the new name, new money, new furniture, new management, and extensive refurbishing. After a pause, the building began again, with 22 time-sharing units over the crest of the hill, below the pool (and with a perfect sea-and-islands view). Tennis courts, in top shape, are used for clinics and tournaments arranged by Haitian pro, Guy Larreur. The island-famous poolside *Lobster Pot Restaurant* continues to lure patrons from over the hill. Your room will be someone's condominium unit, in one of 2 blocks, with a balcony so you can look at the spectacular view. Appointments are colorful; beds are 2 huge doubles; bathrooms modern. Rates for all this hover around $110 for 2, meals and everything else extra. Hotel provides transportation to Charlotte Amalie for shopping and to Magens for sun by the sea and has an enviable location not far from the golf course at Mahogany Run.

✢ **Mahogany Run** (Box 1224, St. Thomas, USVI 00801; close to 200 units) sets new standards for St. Thomas. From the moment the golf course was ready, people planned vacations at this resort—

and that was long before most of the other facilities were finished. On the north side of St. Thomas, where there had been little development heretofor, Mahogany Run's plans include tennis courts (which may not be ready for this season), golf (on the course which is already in play), and some activities for condominium guests (whether they are owners or renters-in-owners'-absence). A rental car is essential for spontaneous mobility, but the hotel's shuttle bus will bring you from your self-sufficient apartment to the golf club that serves as restaurant and activities center, if you choose not to cook at home. Expect elegant surroundings, but don't count on a lot of group activities (unless you arrive as part of a group). What you'll stay in this season, paying rates that are expected to top off at close to $200 for 2, meals extra, will be the sound-and-sumptuous kernel of a pacesetting resort. The plan over several years is to make this place perfect, and already it has set a new tone for St. Thomas. Nearby hotels—The Inn at Mandahl and Magens Point—offer dining diversions, and Magens Bay beach is a reasonable distance toward the sea, with the hotel's shuttle bus making a regular connection. You're in the hills when you are here, with spectacular views—but no beach within easy footfall. It takes about 15 minutes to cross the spine of this mountainous island to reach the capital of Charlotte Amalie.

✣ **Midtown Guest House** (Box 521, Charlotte Amalie, St. Thomas, USVI 00801; 28 rooms) means a lot to a staunch band of repeat visitors, many of them professional folk who know and like island inns with personality of the owner. Omar Brown is a former government employee, in the days before St. Thomas burgeoned, and his local lore about the old days is well worth listening to. The rooms are simply furnished, the location puts you in the heart of downtown Charlotte Amalie (at 1B Commandant Gade), within easy walk of post office and other services and a short ride from the nearest beach (a toss-up between Lindbergh or Morning Star). Not recommended for fussy tourists who need every modern convenience at a snap of the fingers, Midtown Guest House does exactly what it has done for about 30 years: makes visitors feel at home. Count on a winter rate of $30 to $55, meals extra (and plenty of dining depots a few paces away.

✣ **Morning Star** (Box 8328, St. Thomas, USVI 00801; 24 rooms) meanders along what used to be an excellent beach, but it now seems cluttered. Simply furnished rooms parallel the sea in single-story units that were getting a much-needed coat of paint on a recent visit. One of the old-timers, this small spot has its following, but I'm not part of it. The beachside restaurant is a glorified hamburger place that has added tacos and Mexican flourishes. A couple of shops are at the beach, but bring your own effective bug spray from home—for the twilight sand flies. Rates of $70 to $80 for 2 in winter, with all meals, etc. extra, are obviously acceptable to many. I was told that "we're all filled up for winter with repeat visitors."

✤ **Pavilions and Pools** (Star Route, St. Thomas, USVI 00801; 25 rooms) turns a dark and vine-covered wall to the road but hides an Eden within. Not only is the east-end location sufficiently removed from most of the crass commercialism that has taken over parts of downtown Charlotte Amalie, but once you pass through the archway that leads to the check-in desk and get to the waterfalls and the first of several pools, you are in a romantic world. Each room is a gem, planted and screened so that you can be completely unaware of anyone else except for an occasional noise or two. There are 2 floor plans: Type A with 1200 square feet, and a 16′ x 18′ pool of your own, at about $130 for 2; or Type B, known as the International Pavilion, with 1400 square feet of space, with a 20′ x 14′ pool at $20 more. Special winter package rates give you a bottle of liquor if you stay 3 nights, and a gallon if you linger for 7. The pavilion part of your pavilion-and-pool has an airy living-dining room, a kitchen with good equipment, and bedroom, with both bath and dressing room. All units have one glass wall that looks out on your patio and pool.

✤ **Pelican Beach Club** (Box 8387, East End, St. Thomas, USVI 00801; 22 rooms) has its word-of-mouth following who know that they have to turn at the cement pelican on the post near the entrance to Pavilions and Pools (there's no printed sign). When Bob and Kay Cummings opened this unique beachside inn more than a decade ago, they ran it almost like a guest cottage for their friends—or guests turned friends. Careful coddling saved the palm tree that still grows through the ceiling of the dining room, and cultivated a crop of vacationers who make this place an annual winter event (Pelican closes in summer and fall). Air cooling whisks the tradewinds through all rooms, both those that are simply bedroom/living room with terrace where your breakfast is served or the larger 1-bedroom and 2-bedroom cottages. This is a low profile place that hides under the palms, down the beach, and in another world from burgeoning Sapphire Beach Resort. Rates of $105 to

$145 and more per day for 2, meals extra, seem to keep the house count controlled. Not for swingers or barefoot beachcombers.

✣ **Pineapple Beach** (Box 2516, St. Thomas, USVI; 164 rooms) has come a long way since the first cement igloo appeared on the beach, way back when Herb Baltic provided inspiration for Herman Wouk's *Don't Stop the Carnival,* the classic novel about building and operating a hotel in the Caribbean. The overturned cups are still standing, fortunately covered with planting and almost hidden from view (and they seem to suggest the more recently built dome of Coral World, down the road). Subsequent additions include a conglomeration of motel-style units surrounding a pool and beach-side dining place, with condominiums off to the right as you face the sea. The condominiums surround their own pool and nearby tennis courts and some can be rented in owners' absence. Many are full-time residences, giving a sense of permanence to the place.)

The variety in rooms is endless. The handful of condominium havens could be nice nests for the night (at a straight winter tariff of about $130 for 2), but it's almost impossible to tell what room you'll get until you arrive. Groups occupy portions of the hotel when they can be talked into coming here; package tours with special rates give several options (sports, honeymoon, shopping, etc.), but read the fine print to be sure of what you are getting. Pineapple is on its own beach, and across from once-spectacular Coki Point, a favorite in former times and now site for Coral World's aquarium. Count on a full range of watersports, including scuba lessons.

✣ **Point Pleasant** (Smith Bay, East End, St. Thomas, USVI; 94 rooms and growing) has perked along the way it was planned to right from the time it opened on March 1, 1974. Gradually expanding from modest beginnings, Point Pleasant is now a big community of apartments-for-rent-in-owners'-absence. From the hillside perches, you have the prize island view—and a huff-and-puff walk up from the beach to your room. It's pretty going down past the pool, along the path that has been tended to make it a botanical walk. These 15 acres of property are being developed according to a well-ordered plan. The sloping hills stretch to include Water Bay's shore from Sugar Beach to Pineapple Beach. (There's a second pool in the beach area.) Villas and studios have all the necessities (new and colorful) plus the priceless view. The main building (which isn't where the reception desk is located) holds 12 1-bedroom, 1-living room, 2-bath villas and 6 studios; all have complete kitchen.

Newer units, in small groups sifted around the grounds, are similar; all are privately owned. Maid service is part of your daily winter rate of about $100 to close to $200 for 2. Guests can sign up for 4 hour stints with the complimentary cars, and for snorkel and sailing equipment that is paid for with your rate. The restaurant has a panel of rock garden and, on the other "wall," a dramatic view over bay and islands; It has become one of the favorite St. Thomian rendez-vous for those in the know. Lunch and dinner daily package is $25 per person. A couple of tennis courts are ready and waiting at the start of the Point Pleasant drive when you turn off the main east end road; you'll need a ride or a lot of stamina to get to the courts with energy enough to play.

✝ **Sapphire Beach Resort** (Box 8088, St. Thomas, USVI 00801; 125 rooms) is a conglomerate, in more ways than one. It was almost 20 years ago when Dave and Nudi Mass put together a small spot with beach emphasis on one of the most gorgeous strands of sand on any of the islands. (The beach accolades come from the fact that the sand is soft underfoot, but also because the view is unparalleled—to St. John with some of the British Virgins on the horizon. Don't look back—actually or figuratively.)

The beach can seem buried, if not by sweeping seas and spots of trash, then by beach chairs on which slathered souls lie to toast. Behind—on what used to be a sweep of hill up to the main road around the east end—is a platoon of white-stucco, uninteresting but functional buildings. They are the condominiums. At the moment, many of the rooms are straight hotel rooms, which John Flynn from Fairfield County, Connecticut (who bought the place in 1976), is trying to turn into a profit.

If you squint as you stand on the beach, you can blur the buildings and make the place look like it was in the "good old days," when beach fun was spontaneous and sun-streaking natural. If you look at this place wide-eyed, it is a jumble of sometimes air-conditioned, sometimes breeze-swept buildings, with no theme that I can distinguish other than crass cold cash: If a store would bring money, it was built; if a cocktail lounge would, it appeared; if air-conditioned dining was what "the people want," it was built. I still like the sea-and-sand al fresco touches. Action options include a full range of water sports, 4 tennis courts, 2 swimming pools, and a marina in a man-made lagoon that is full of man-made luxury yachts.

Rooms for rent are 41 beachfront units (high rate, for the preferred location), village studio units with kitchenette and patio view, village suites with separate bedroom and fully equipped kitchen, and villas for 4 to 6 people. All the 60 or so village units (in the condominium setups) are a good walk from the beach. Rates range from the beachfront standard room only at about $105 for 2 to the villa for 6 at over $200. All meals, etc. are extra charges. Unless you can get a package deal or take the villa with a big family, the rates seem to me to be higher than quality warrants.

✢ **St. Thomas Diving Club at Villa Olga** (Box 4976, St. Thomas, USVI 00801; 12 rooms) takes the cue from a historic past and is setting precedents for the present. This is the perfect place for scuba people or for anyone who wants to enjoy a casual, shoreside atmosphere with a sea focus. Thanks to the imagination and hard work of Joyce and Dick Doumeng, and their team of family and friends, this parcel of peninsula has a new personality. Located on the waterside of the maze of Frenchtown (which is a community on the outskirts of the capital, Charlotte Amalie), the Diving Club is about 10 minutes' walk from town. Although the old Villa Olga that is next door burned down a few seasons ago (and has been rebuilt in the old style as the Chart House restaurant), the special atmosphere remains—pruned to perfection by the Doumeng team. From a hillside bed-base (a 2-story block of air-conditioned rooms, completely modern with 2 queen-sized beds) guests can sprint down the hill past the special classroom building (where the land portions of the scuba sessions are held) and the pool to the sea-level West Indian house that is the nerve center of the Club. While some guests linger on the porch swapping sea stories and sipping beers, others are gearing up for an outing or peeling off after one. Scuba gear for rental and sale nestles next to the check-in desk (so you can look while you wait to register, if no one is ready at the desk). The underwater photography center is fully equipped, and courses are offered. Special boat-and-beach holidays combine time at the Diving Club base with 3-nights aboard the 68-foot fully equipped diving boat, *Mohawk II,* for the ultimate diving vacation. For divers, this place is the *sine qua non.* Inquire about the land/sea week rates (which were $650 for each of 2 sharing a room/cabin until mid-December '81), and expect to pay about $68 per winter season night for 2 at the Club, room only.

✢ **St. Thomas Hotel & Marina** (Box 7970, Charlotte Amalie, St. Thomas, USVI 00801; 223 rooms) is big, not-too-beautiful, and acceptable (perhaps) for businessmen if they want the double advantage of proximity to downtown and yachting surroundings.

Here's the history: Colonel and Mrs. Byers from the States bought the land and opened the small Yacht Haven in the late 1950s; her son, Bud, ran it for a while, and then the place was sold; and then it was sold again, and then again, and then again. Each buyer added new rooms, extra amusements, and a few ruffles and flourishes. Sheraton was involved for a while, but not now. The lobby is small; the *Long John Restaurant* is air-conditioned and *very* dark so that what magic it has is by night light. I prefer to head straight out to the *Harbour Terrace,* an open-air patio with boat view. The adult pool is separated from the kiddie cavorting area, and if you opt to dunk from the patch of sand, keep your head up; you are swimming in Charlotte Amalie harbor. The thatched-roof snack bar and the sea and air around you are the only tropical parts of the entire air-conditioned mass. There are convention facilities, plus evening action at the *Pieces of 8,* usually one of the livelier St. Thomian boites. For this, 2 pay $80 to $120 in season, no meals. Be sure to ask about special packages. Only with some "good deal" rate is this place worth your money, in my opinion.

✠ **Secret Harbour** (Box 7576, St. Thomas, USVI 00801; 48 suites) is an oasis on a sandy niche on the south coast, not far from Red Hook, about 20 minutes' drive from downtown, where you can enjoy your own apartment, with balcony or patio on the beach, living area attractively furnished just inside your glass doors, and an air-conditioned bedroom at the back of the house where you have no view. The restaurant has a superb setting on an elevated stone terrace beachside. The sea is spectacular, perfect for pre-breakfast swims (or swims at any time), and the surroundings are worth the $85 to $140 for 2, accommodations only, winter tariff. Part of an elaborate condominium development plan that is now in phase 3, units are owned on either a club plan, where owners have a certain number of days at a low daily fee (and the unit is in the "hotel" group for the rest of the time) or on a maintenance plan where you pay extra for use of the tennis courts, pool, etc. As a hotel guest (and not an owner) you won't have to worry about all those things. If you have the car you'll need for getting around, you can drive about 10 minutes to the east to the nearby marinas for good seafood dinners and to arrange for scuba, snorkel, or sailing expeditions on the surrounding seas. A good place for self-sufficient types with healthy bank accounts.

✠ **Shibui** (Box 5017, St. Thomas, USVI 00801; 25 units) sits in its own world, a Japanese world created (but eventually sold) by Michael and Lorette Resch, pioneering couple with astounding brains, taste, and energy. After a journey in Japan where Michael had his first boat built, they returned to St. Thomas to create a Japanese-style village—with shoji wall panels that slide for privacy, sunken bathtubs with plants growing around the edges, and open-to-the-breezes rooms with terrazzo floors (on which you will break your neck if you enter wet-footed). Ecologists could make notes from this spot, which blends into its location so perfectly that it's hard to spot from the airplane windows as you look *up* to it on the hillside when you depart. From Shibui's pool and teahouse you have one of the most breathtaking St. Thomian views. The executive cottage, with one HUGE bedroom and "one exotic Japanese bath with sunken tub," carries a winter tariff of $105 to $195 for one or 2. On-location dining choices include the *Outrigger Restaurant* and *La Veranda* terrace with a salad bar in a Haitian dugout. *The Emperor's Dockyard,* a small nightclub, has its following.

✤ **Sugar Bird Beach and Tennis Club** (Box 570, St. Thomas, USVI; 66 rooms), née Water Island Hotel and on the site of one of the early island inns, is a white-stucco, stage-prop arched hub with a scattering of small buildings, some of them individual cottages and others efficiency units in blocks. The heart of it all is a swimming pool, at least insofar as the hilltop perch is concerned, but the honeymoon beach that made Water Isle a place to come to in the old days is still the main reason to take the free ferry for the 7-minute trip across the harbor. The beach is at the north side of the ferry dock, from which you and luggage will be trucked up and over to the modern mecca that sprouted from this spot as the Water Isle Colony Club in 1970. It was reborn in the season of '77 as Sugar Bird, sometimes spelled Sugarbird, and aims to be big and beautiful—and it is big. Group tours and conventions keep it alive; the individual winter room rate tops off at $90 to $145 for 2, meals extra.

✤ **Virgin Isle Hotel** (Box 3188, St. Thomas, USVI 00801; 210 rooms) did a Rip Van Winkle act, but seems to have awakened from its slumber willing to catch up with the times. The hotel opened a couple of decades ago, as the *first* new hotel in St. Thomas, and it's still the only hotel on this island that is anything close to the usual "high-rise" variety. Its hillside location, overlooking the fringe of Charlotte Amalie and the seas off the south coast, puts it about 10 minutes' drive from downtown. The property knew a tenure under the Hilton name (and the hotel was always a problem for the standard hotel operation, since its initiators and builders knew more about design than they did about building for an efficient day-to-day operation). What the VI offers now is facilities for groups or for package vacationers, and both come in at regular intervals. A rum tasting, a slide showing (of underwater sights), a sunset cocktail party at the poolside terrace, and other activities are part of the usual plan for guests. If you want a Hilton-style place, without the name and quality management but with the ambiance, investigate this property, but don't expect to find top-notch housekeeping (there was debris around when I looked, and the place needed paint.) Rates will be about $100 and up for 2 this winter but ask about special package holidays with some extras included.

✤ **Windward Passage** (Box 639, Charlotte Amalie, St. Thomas, USVI 00801; 110 rooms) is a big-and-boxy pink "fortress" with flags flying, on the waterfront of Charlotte Amalie. Convenience is its greatest feature, and if you have one of the waterfront rooms, the sea view can be interesting. Rooms are standard modern hotel-style, with carpets (that give rooms what I consider a musty smell) and pock-marked chrome on plumbing taps. The wall of rooms around the center courtyard gives guests the opportunity to shop at some of the tacky shops around the ground level, or to walk along the nearby streets through the plethora of shops, restaurants, and bars that make up Charlotte Amalie. Rates this winter will be up from $80 to just over $100, and I recommend this place only if you get some special vacation plan or can't find a room elsewhere.

▪▪

HOUSEKEEPING HOLIDAYS make a lot of sense in St. Thomas where food is easy to find (even when it is expensive) at local supermarkets with the names you may know from home—Grand Union, for one—and a large selection of familiar name brands. It's no surprise that the fodder-filled shelves go hand in hand with a long list of comfortable condominium units that can be yours for a week or 2 (or longer, permanently, if you want to buy). A rental car is advisable for mobility, but it is not essential at most places.

Some housekeeping places have been included under the hotel coverage, when management and additional facilities give you leadership at the resort. Investigate Bolongo Bay, Mahogany Run, Point Pleasant, Pavilions and Pools, Pineapple Beach, Sapphire Beach Resort, St. Thomas Hotel, Secret Harbour, and Sugar Bird.

✤ **Cowpet Bay** (Box 7699, East End, St. Thomas, USVI 00801; 100-plus units) captured an entire cove when it was built a few years ago. The 1-, 2-, and 3-bedroom villas are privately owned, and most of them are occupied (or rented directly) by the owners. However, if you want to be part of a self-sufficient residential community at the east end of St. Thomas about 25 minutes' drive from downtown Charlotte Amalie, investigate this place. All apartments have views, terraces, and very attractive homelike furnishings. In addition, you have the use of the tennis courts, beach, restaurants, and shops on the premises. Ideal for families because there is something for everyone to do (and someone for everyone to play with). First contact for rental should be the head office. If that fails, try some of the local real estate agents.

✢ **Crown Colony** (Box 3357, St. Thomas, USVI 00801; 17 units) caps a hilltop, providing perchers with a view that has to be seen to be believed. You also have to love narrow mountain roads with switchbacks, since that's the route to or from the stoplight that marks the sub-base road, off the main road between the airport and Charlotte Amalie. The route is not for the delicate driver. Your housekeeping aerie will have modern equipment, and can come in a variety of sizes, depending on your group and/or budget. Terraces are ideal for alfresco dining—and you're the cook, from whatever you've stocked at the local supermarkets in town. Count on a 1-bedroom unit costing about $60 for 2 per day, this winter, with studios costing less. A maid will come in a few times weekly (not daily) to sweep and dust, but dishes and picking up are your own problem. If you like your Caribbean comforts with a breathtaking view from a mountain "top," consider Crown Colony—but be sure to negotiate for a rental car.

✢ **Red Hook Mountain Apartment & Spa** (Box 8016, East End, St. Thomas, USVI 00801; 6 apts.) gives you a spa with a view. While the place is no match for Maine Chance and other leading spas, Dick and Barb Fulton are the first on this island to focus on the need for many of us to pull ourselves together (with help) on our holiday. There's a resident masseuse (sign up for appointments) and a redwood whirlpool under the sun, but the rest of your rejuvenation is thanks to God-given sun and sea. Sand is a drive from your hillside perch, but you can easily walk to the ferry for St. John if you want to head to another island. Located at the end of St. Thomas, away from the hubbub of Charlotte Amalie and with an awe-inspiring view spread out before you, the facilities are modern (2 queen-size beds per unit) and have studio or 2-bedroom set-ups. The efficiencies rent for $65 for 2 this winter; 2-bedroom apartments are over $100 per day, and an extra person above the allowed 2 or 4 warrants a $10 per person additional charge. For a room with a view to renew, try this spot.

✤ **Villa Santana** (Denmark Hill, Charlotte Amalie, St. Thomas, USVI; 9 units) is a historic former home where Dimitri, a legendary Russian, presided a decade or more ago. Today things are different, but the view from the hillside is still spectacular. You can walk down to town, and—if your heart's willing—hike straight back up. Units are *very* simple efficiencies, with only the basic furnishings—and not any excess of those. Rates are low (about $50 for 2), and the location above the heart of Charlotte Amalie is the main reason for mention. Only for casual, budget-conscious souls.

✤ **Watergate Villas,** on the south coast, sharing the shore with Bolongo Bay, are about 15 miles minutes' drive along the winding road east of Charlotte Amalie. These clifftop villas were started before the name became so infamous. Sam Schattner, owner of the Watergate Restaurant in D.C., is the man behind this project. John Randal McDonald, architect for Christiansted's Hotel on the Cay and many homes on St. Croix, designed the complex of several 2- and 3-story clusters to weave over and around what nature put here. The view south is spectacular. The decor of each apartment is the owner's choice, so where you stay will be distinctly your "own." Rental costs vary according to size, shape, and length of stay (studios about $95, 1-bedroom in the $100 range and 2-bedroom almost $175). All renters have the use of the tennis courts and freshwater pool. Luxury on the rocks.

■■

RESTAURANTS ON ST. THOMAS are some of the best, most atmospheric restaurants in the Caribbean, and while I deplore those that think they have to button me into an air-conditioned dark room when I want to be in the warm tropical open air, I recognize that island residents like (and support) those small dark spots. There's a place for both, but my preference goes to terrace and open-air dining, where you may sacrifice something in gourmet food, but you gain a lot in total ambiance.

You need a car to get to many St. Thomas restaurants, but there are several good places within easy walk of each other in town.

Among the special spots worth sliding into for a cool drink, a snack, or a full-fledged sumptuous meal in casually comfortable surroundings are *Sparky's Saloon, Sebastians,* and the *Greenhouse,* all on the waterfront, or *Rosie O'Grady's*, *Sinbads*, and *Yesterday* on Back Street, otherwise known as Vimmelskaft Gade.

The collection of places at Compass Point, out toward the east end Red Hook dock (and just beyond Antilles Yachting boatyard), is worth noting. The hutlike, Robinson Crusoe atmosphere of the places, most of them appearing to have been built from trees and palm fronds, sets the easy tone for the *Drunken Shrimp* (a Polynesian-style place), *Papa Leone's* (Italian food and red-checked table cloths), and *Fisherman's Wharf* (see below). Also here is *Dottie's Front Porch*, for snacks that include homemade bread and lethal desserts. Down the dirt road that spurs off to the sea at another cove, *The Dove* has a thatch wall-barricade on its car park side and the sea to look at when you sit at a table. There's a nice island atmosphere at this clutch of places, all of them open to sea breezes and frequented by the boating set.

Au Bon Vivant, next door to Hotel 1829 and on the hill that leads to Government House (overlooking some of the town activity), has quickly stepped to top spot on my list of places to spend a pleasant evening. Located on the site of Galleon House, a time-honored inn that burned down a couple of years ago, Au Bon Vivant recreates the outlook that was a favorite for those of us who knew this terrace when it had the Galleon House tradition. Lights twinkling in town make an exceptional backdrop for candelit tables, and good food and wine. Although the service was a bit shaky when I stopped here a few days after the official opening, the performance with Ceasar's salad seemed to intrigue most diners, and my oversauced coquille au poulet was helped along by a chilled bottle of good white wine. Ideal for a romantic evening (but no good for the faint of heart who may gasp at climbing the two dozen or more steps), Au Bon Vivant is worth a reservation to secure a table. Figure $25 per person.

Bartolino's, in Frenchtown (a community that buttons to the western harbor edge of Charlotte Amalie), is the best bet for northern Italian cuisine (which is lighter than the southern Italian fare). *Portofino* is almost next door, but my vote goes to the first mentioned. Other Frenchtown restaurants are the awesomely expensive *Cafe Normandie,* upstairs over the ragtag Normandie bar, once a rough sailors hangout and now filled with a mixed bag of patrons, and the new *Chart House* at Villa Olga, opened in summer of '81 with the U.S. mainland "standards" of steak, lobster tails (not local), shrimp, with baked potato and a lavish salad bar.

Daddy's was an east end small spot when I first knew it. Then fame came, and $150,000 later, Isaiah "Daddy" Venzen was immortalized in a restaurant that is a far cry from the place that made him famous. The location's the same, across the road from a fishing fleet dock, about 15 minutes' drive east from Charlotte Amalie toward Red Hook. Fresh fish is still the best fare; steaks and chops are popular with some, but to my mind there's nothing to compare with the offerings when Daddy used to leave his domino game to bring you what had been brewing in the kitchen. Rae Venzen Brunn is the owner of the place that bears her "Daddy's" nickname. This restaurant, which opened in 1974, is still a family place even though it's gotten "fancy." Count on casual, boat-style surroundings where work by Virgin Islands artists hangs on the walls; those in the know dine after 8. Figure the best part of $15 for a good, hearty meal.

Driftwood Inn gives you Italian food at low prices, if you want to drive up into the mountains to get it. Ideal if you are part of a congenial, informal group who want to gape at a spectacular view, but loners will probably feel left out. Arrive when the cocktail area opens (about 5:30) and look it over.

Fisherman's Wharf (on a barge at Compass Point, almost at East End) focuses on casual, nautical life. When the restaurant first opened (as the Fish Market), the ideal way to arrive was by rowboat from your charter yacht anchored in the lagoon. Now the road is paved (and potholed), and the place has spruced up some (not too much). Great if you like seafood and sailors' stories with a $5 fish and chips or something grander.

The Frigate is the name for two places: the original, at Mafolie Hotel, 800 feet in the hills, overlooking Charlotte Amalie, and the younger sister, The Frigate East, at east end, across from the entrance to the St. John ferry dock at Red Hook. Both restaurants feature steaks (some say the best on the island), plus lobster tail, teriyaki chicken, salad bar, and a baked potato. Count on a cost ranging from just over $7 for the chicken to close to $15 for the best steak. Favorites for the residents, and for a lot of the rest of us who need to punctuate our memories with a glimpse of the Mafolie view.

Harbor View, up a wiggly, narrow road weaving from the marketplace, is a longtime favorite. For one thing, I like the view—especially at cocktail time, when you can lounge on one of the settees and watch the lights go on downtown. Arlene Lockwood and Leonore Wolfe have maintained an enviable enthusiasm; they've been in business in the islands long enough to have wilted from the waffling. Mediterranean fare is featured, and even if you find the chef on a weak night, the goblets, tableware, and china will be enough to inspire raptures—if you are affected by that kind of thing. It's only fitting to order wine—and to make a reservation to be sure you'll get a table at one of the 2 sittings. This is #1; expense be hanged (closed Tuesdays).

Hotel 1829 has been here since before 1829. The terrace tables are surrounded by the first to arrive for dinner; if you want one, arrive early for your reservation (and ask for a terrace table when you call); the inside room, with its stone walls and overhead fans, has atmosphere, but it can be hot if the breeze isn't steady. Atmosphere is enough reason to walk up the steps from Emancipation Park, or wind up the road toward Government House. (Don't plan to park in front; space is limited.) Food ranges from roast beef to chef's specials (closed Sunday).

Jelly's Seafood House has a sense of humor and you should bring yours. The place has a style of its own. I like sitting in the light and airy surroundings, with the lime green-lemon yellow punctuation, at Pier II near what we used to call the sub base area. Jelly's claims to be "world famous since 1976 A.D. (after dinner)." You can sit seaside and munch a selection of standard American offerings that aren't as inspirational as the surroundings, but are more than enough to fill the pit. I like a management attitude that plainly states on the printed menu: "It is almost impossible to completely satisfy everyone's individual taste, and if something really goes wrong, don't wait until you've finished your meal and say it was absolutely terrible. Please bring this to our attention immediately. We will then, of course, rectify any valid complaints, while you still dine with us. This will help you and us to be happier for the time we are spending together this evening." Bravo, Jelly's—and good luck. You can dine on dolphin for about $7, but prime ribs or a New York strip steak will set you back close to $15.

L'Escargot, hanging over the sea near what's locally known as the sub base west of Charlotte Amalie, has its following, and the view on the harbor and the souffles may warrant it. Try lunch, but look out for long lines even with reservations at dinner. Responding to enthusiasm from local folk, L'Escargot opened a second lunch-and-dinner place in Creque's Alley, about midway along the Waterfront Highway at the heart of the old part of Charlotte Amalie. (The Alley runs through to Main Street.) If you're in a hurry, pick up a take-out lunch from the Waterfront entrance.

■■■

PLACES WORTH FINDING ON ST. THOMAS: The handful of historic sites are huddled in downtown Charlotte Amalie, and can be checked off in a couple of hours. The rest of the sights are of the "oh" and "ah" version: mostly scenic. Before you head out for your

sightseeing, stop at the Visitors' Bureau, facing Emancipation Park
(where von Scholten's proclamation of July 3, 1848, was read) in
what is still called the Grand Hotel building. (The Grand Hotel has
yielded to the more lucrative lure of the shops that now rim its
foundations.) Invest the $2.50 or less in *St. Thomas on Foot and by
Car,* by Randall Koladis. The compact, attractive book is not only
fact-filled, but it is small enough to be a reasonable traveling companion. The Visitors' Bureau is staffed by volunteers. It was the citizens' response to some complaints about hospitality a couple of
years ago. You can head here for information, to check packages,
to buy a beverage while you sit to collect your thoughts, and to
use the plumbing facilities. Walking around with Randall Koladis's
guidebook in hand is the best way to tour Charlotte Amalie; in
my opinion, none of the planned tours for town are worth being
packed into an uncomfortable jitney or "bus" to be portaged from
one spot to the next. You can do just as well (or better) on your
own.

Government House (open daily during working hours) is more
impressive from the outside, where you can clearly note the intricate wrought-iron railings that border the balconies. The best place
to stand to look is the small park across the road. The street on
which Government House faces is narrow from the old days, and
constantly clogged with the governor's car (when he's at Government House) and the cars of those who hover around him. Built in
1867, the 3-story house is impressive when viewed from Bluebeard's Castle (where you can pick it out from the others by its red
roof, and U.S. and Virgin Islands flags flying). In the main foyer,
when you climb the entrance stairs, are several panels of local
woods, listing the Danish governors since 1672 on one panel, with a
gap for 1807 to 1815 when the British ruled these islands. On another, from April 9, 1917, the United States chain of command is
listed, beginning with Rear Admiral James Harrison Oliver of the
U.S. Navy and carrying through Captain Waldo Evans until March
18, 1931, when government of the U.S. Virgin Islands was handed
over to the Department of the Interior, and a civil administrator,
Paul Pearson, took over. Cramer, Harwood, Hastie, Morris de Castro, Alexander, and Governor Walter Gordon (a black Californian
appointed to the position by President Eisenhower, in appreciation
for Gordon's political help to fellow Californian Earl Warren) followed. On October 7, 1955, Republican John David Merwin, born
on St. Croix, was the first native-born governor appointed to the
Virgin Islands. He was followed by Ralph Paiewonsky, a native-born

St. Thomian (a Democrat), appointed after Kennedy became president.

Another plaque starts with Melvin Evans, a St. Croix doctor, who was the first governor elected by the populace of the Virgin Islands, in November 1970. He took office on January 4, 1971. (Evans had been appointed by Richard Nixon, and then ran for the island's first election against Cyril E. King.) King was elected governor in the Virgin Islands' second election of November 1974, but died in January 1978, before he completed his term. (He assumed office on Three Kings Day, which local wags and others called Four Kings Day, January 6, 1975.)

A glimpse at all the above will take you about 5 minutes. Then walk up the stairs at the back of the foyer, to the reception room (M-F 8-12, 1-5) on the first floor. In frames around the wall of the lovely hall you can note signatures of Danish governors from 1733. (During one of my visits, a 20th-century Dane was checking out the signature of one of his ancestors who had been governor of the then-Danish West Indies in the early 1900s.) J. Antonio Jarvis's paintings of the Virgin Islands, plus paintings by island residents Ira Smith, Donaldson, and Camille Pissarro are on the walls, but the best picture is the harbor, seen through the open windows. The reception room was redecorated in 1969, when chandeliers were electrified and the walls were painted mustard color (woodwork is white). The chandeliers were last cleaned for the visit of the Queen of Denmark. The new frames around the pictures are the result, I was told by one custodian, of the fact that the old frames "were held together by termites holding hands." Flowers, gleaming silver, and other homey touches make the halls seem less awesome than they otherwise might.

As I left after one visit, the custodian said that I was "very kind to come up and see the rooms." The pleasure was all mine, as it always is when I climb the steps to these rooms. (There's an elevator, installed during the Paiewonsky regime, as the gift of "a lady who came to have tea with the Paiewonskys and didn't like the climb" to the third floor governor's residence.)

As you leave, sign the register—along with others who have said "Beautiful Spot. I love it"; "After a 10-year absence, it is good to come back to V.I."; "Gorgeous"; "Happy to be here"; and—as noted by Mr. Honnig from Copenhagen—"Most interesting and beautiful."

Virgin Islands Museum (M-F 9-12, 1-5; free) is worth seeing more for the historic fort it sits in than for the artifacts it displays.

There's no priceless collection of pirate treasure, but there are a few prints, bits and pieces of Indian and Danish eras, and a display that explains the history of the islands. The entire museum fits in a couple of small cells. Fort Christian itself stands sentinel at the waterfront, near the firehouse and just below Government House on its hill. The fort was completed by the Danes in 1672 (they had started construction in 1666), but the fort you see is the result of a scrub-and-polish routine in 1874 that dismantled a tower and reconstructed the ground plan to include several courtyards. From the 1670s, the fort was the hub of life in Charlotte Amalie. Anyone who *was* anyone was here: the governor and his fellow rulers, the blacksmith, other craftsmen, and most of the town's wealthy. The entire population gathered inside the 22-to-33-inch-thick walls when there were hurricanes, fires, pirates roaring through town, or some other holocaust that threatened peaceful days. Governors lived here; prisoners were jailed here. (The governor now lives in Government House; the Department of Public Safety maintains the small jail.) A spin through the fort won't take more than an hour.

Crown House is an up-the-steps hike from Government House, either up the "99 steps" (which are no longer 99, but still plenty to climb up if you're out of shape) or the Government House steps (also straight up). The 200-year-old house was refurbished and opened to the public a couple of years ago, as an example of the life of the luxury class in the 18th century. It was closed for public viewing when sold to new owners in late '78, but it's worth checking while you're on the island to see if the house may be open for some special reason.

Noteworthy as the home of Peter Carl Frederick von Scholten, who freed the slaves of the Danish West Indies in 1848, some of the furniture is from the period when he was resident harbourmaster and vice-governor in St. Thomas (before he moved to the main government headquarters, which were in Christiansted, St. Croix, during the Danish years).

The 2-story house is mostly stone, with a Dutch gambrel hipped roof. The inside is embellished with carved woodwork and a handsome tray ceiling. The dormer windows were typical of the 18th-century island buildings. The antiques in the main floor rooms are island versions of what was popular in England, and there are also some antiques imported (as was the custom in those days, for those who could afford it) from England and the United States, where fine craftsmen were working in New England. In the reception room, which has mirrors similar to those in Government House on St. Croix, the sparkling chandelier is from Versailles. There's 18th-century Chinese wallpaper dressing up the dining room. Crown House is the St. Thomian equivalent of Whim Greathouse on St. Croix. When you have seen them both, you can have a good picture of city life in cosmopolitan Charlotte Amalie and the plantation life of sister-island St. Croix.

Coral World (daily 9–5, Tu, F, Sat 9–midnight; $5 adults, $2.50 children; restaurants 9 A.M. to midnight) is a man-made marvel well worth paying the high fee to see, especially if you're not one of those who will don snorkel mask or scuba tank to go underwater to see freely. The cement and glass tube that was poured into the reefs just off Coki Point was a blasphemy to many of us who had headed out to this once remote east end spot for an idyllic snorkel-for-two. However, credit has to go to the builders, who splashed a minimum of reef-wrecking cement on the natural habitat of the fish this commercial venture was created to exploit. These days, as you wind your way down the staircase to the sea floor, the view out the windows is an absolute marvel. You are *inside* an aquarium— and the only place like this one is the owners' similar structure in Israel's Bay of Eilat. As you walk out to the dome, you have a spectacular view of St. John and the neighboring British Virgin Islands, and before you get to either of these places (since I have dealt with the best part first), there are the 21 aquariums in the Marine Garden area, all filled with corals, sponges, sea urchins, and fish plucked from the sea to survive here where they can be seen without scuba apparatus. The expected commercial ventures (shops and restaurants) flourish on your extra cash. The entire excursion can be a very expensive one if you've paid the full fee at the gate. Ask at your hotel, and check package tours including other things you might want to do to get a better rate.

Special considerations around and away from the island of St. Thomas include a day in Old San Juan, Puerto Rico, which is offered on special day tours conveniently arranged through the local travel agents. If you are a do-it-yourselfer, you can buy a round-trip air ticket, and arrive at the San Juan airport.

Other open-air excursions to places worth finding are by boat, to St. John for the day. Choices range from an organized tour (purchased with the assistance of your hotel, or directly from one of the downtown travel agents) with pickup at and delivery to your hotel; to a day sail you put together with some friends; to a ferry ride from east end's Red Hook (either the boat to Cruz Bay, or to Caneel Bay for the buffet)—and walk, taxi, or rental jeep ride around St. John. You'll need the wheels for longer excursions, but be sure to allow an hour or 2 for a leisurely stroll around the streets of Cruz Bay.

The town still represents an islander's island village. A day on Tortola can be via boat or Antilles Air Boats, with taxi for touring; and then there's AAB for shuttle service to St. Croix's Christiansted and taxi or rental car to tour that 21-mile-long island; plus an endless list of other options that you can dream up as you sit on the beach.

■■

SPORTS ON ST. THOMAS started to get organized about the same time the first record blue marlin was hauled in, in the early '60s. Since then, the Virgin Islands Department of Commerce has set up a separate Division of Watersports which, while responsible for all 3 islands, has its base at the Dept. of Commerce offices at the end of Main Street, near the old market place.

Sailing spokes out from the expensive slips at the St. Thomas Marina, the casual moorings at the Avery Boat Yard across the harbor of Charlotte Amalie on the fringe of Frenchtown, and out at the East End, where only Sir Francis Drake Channel separates you from St. John, and trade winds send you tacking to reach some of the British Virgins. The main marinas for day or longer charters are *Avery's Boathouse* near Frenchtown, the *St. Thomas Marina* where *Spur of the Moment Charters* and *Caribbean Discovery Charters* list boats, the *Undersea Centre* at Frenchman's Reef Hotel (boats leave from its pier), *V.I. Charter Boat League* (listing several yachts that are available for charter), *Caribbean Yacht Charters* at Compass Point on the east end where you can charter Morgan Out Island 41s and other boats for bare-boat sailing or with skipper, *Ocean Enterprises* at Home Port, near the St. Thomas marina, and *Sailor's World* at Harms Marina at the East End. If you're a true yachting type, check in for activities at the *St. Thomas Yacht Club*.

For day sailing, the catamaran *Ho Tei* has set sail daily for picnic trips toward St. John for enough years to have become an island fixture. Look for the craft near the Coast Guard dock on the waterfront, not far from Emancipation Park and ask for Richard Doumeng, the boat's captain—and son of Dick Doumeng of Bolongo and St. Thomas Diving Club fame. *True Love* is another regular, as is Neil Lewis' sloop the *Red Hooker* which is moored at the St. John ferry dock at Red Hook. *Allyn, Nightwind,* and *Le Junk* are others to look for.

The Virgin Islands Charter Boat League has a membership of about 200 craft, ranging in size from 40 to 100 feet, and most of them dock regularly in St. Thomas. If you're roaming around the island in November, it's worthwhile checking for dates of the Annual Charterboat Show, at the St. Thomas marina.

Fishing is easy to arrange. *Johnny Harms's Lagoon Marina* is one home for his deep-sea fishing boats. The *St. Thomas Lagoon Fishing Center,* a few mango groves away, is another spot to try. Know before you go that a 1282-pound Atlantic blue marlin was taken 20 miles off St. Thomas in the Puerto Rico channel by Larry Martin of Pompano Beach, Florida, on August 6, 1977. The catch was the ninth world record blue marlin to be caught off St. Thomas since John Battles took his 814 pound fish in the early '60s.

Scuba got its start in St. Thomas, when the Navy's Underwater Demolition Teams trained in the clear seas offshore. That was years ago, but many of those who trained stayed, and some of them took the first of the leisure scuba groups out to explore not only reefs but wrecks. Proof of the enthusiasm was the cooperation (too often unknown among island entrepreneurs) shown with the opening of the *St. Thomas Diving Club* at Villa Olga, around the bend and bumpy roads of Frenchtown on the outskirts of St. Thomas (see hotel listing). Most of the top instructors come to Villa Olga for their day "on," or for lingering hours, so head here first if you want to talk about the sport. Special scuba weeks, using the 68-foot *Mohawk II* as home for a few days and the hotel for the rest of the week, are popular. Bolongo Bay also has instruction and good facilities. Other spots in and around town to sign on for special scuba sessions are at *Joe Vogel*'s shop in the center of town, *Watersports Centers* at Frenchman's Reef and out at Sapphire Bay, and the *Virgin Islands Diving Schools* operation across the road from the St. Thomas hotel. Some of the best scuba areas in the Caribbean lie off the shores of St. Thomas and around the neighboring British Virgins.

Tennis has taken over. Almost every place that has a patch has a court, but you can count on good courts at Bluebeard's Castle, the Virgin Isle, at Pineapple Beach, Bolongo Bay, the Cowpet Bay Tennis Club, Frenchman's Reef, Lime Tree, Sapphire, Secret Harbour, and at the Yacht Club at the East End. The public courts on the shore between the St. Thomas marina and town are available for play. Check for special tennis weeks at the hotels with courts; most of them have good values—with some instruction and other bonuses.

For **golf,** this season is the second for Mahogany Run on the north shore abutting Magen's Point Hotel. The first 9 holes were "ready" in mid-80, with the back 9 ready in early '81.

■■■

TREASURES AND TRIFLES ON ST. THOMAS: "Know Before You Go" is the title of a U.S. Customs Service pamphlet giving all the small details and some typical duties for bringing items purchased overseas back into the United States. Although they are part of the United States, the U.S. Virgin Islands have a special customs regulation that is a remnant from the agreement of transfer from the Danes in 1917. The "free port" status was to continue. That means that goods come into Virgin Islands ports at very low (6%) duty. When the goods are sold in shops, theoretically they come to you without extra charges, but the profit added by Virgin Islands' shopkeepers in recent years has gradually edged the price up so that some of those "bargains" are not. Know your hometown "best price" for a camera, watch, or whatever before you make your island purchase; you may find the cost about the same as your local discount house. On the other hand, the selection of items for sale in the former pirate warehouses of Charlotte Amalie (and even at Christiansted and Frederiksted on St. Croix) is astounding! The crowd of shops downtown is exceeded only by the crowd of shoppers on cruise ship days, all of them carrying the bulging shopping bags like so many children after a successful Halloween "trick or treat." When you have been in the U.S. Virgin Islands, you may bring home duty free $600 worth of merchandise and one gallon of liquor. In addition, items made in the U.S. Virgin Islands can be brought back in any amount. They are not subject to duty.

I confess to being overwhelmed by the surfeit of shops in Charlotte Amalie. During three separate forays for this edition, I succeeded only in being completely confused. Many of the small shops open and close or leapfrog from one location to another. Good craftsmen work here for a while, and then seem to wander on. And, sad to say, there is an increasing amount of what I have to call junk, which succeeds only, in my opinion, in camouflaging the good items, making them harder to ferret out. Think of this place as a Middle East souk, and you'll be braced for what is here.

AUTHOR'S OBSERVATION: Two indispensable aids for St. Thomas shopping are a copy of *St. Thomas This Week,* the fact-packed yellow guide published by Margot Bachman and tirelessly researched by her team. Copies are sometimes available from the Virgin Island Tourist Offices in the U.S., or by writing to St. Thomas This Week, Box

1627, St. Thomas, VI 00801. (Enclose $1.50 to cover air-mail postage.) Another invaluable contact, if you have a specific purchase in mind, is the Retailers' Association, Box 1287, St. Thomas, VI 00801 whose motto is "shop with confidence." Member stores are the highest caliber, and all have exemplary ethics.

Liquor is still one of the true bargains, although not the bargain it once was. Best buys are in the supermarkets, where the local folk buy theirs, but you have to have space in a spare suitcase, or bring your own box, string, etc., which may be more trouble than the price-saving is worth. Next best bet is **Al Cohen's,** across from the cruise ship docking area (wise man). Check whatever he has on special. Even his regular prices are a few cents (and sometimes only that) below what you will pay at the long-established shops on and around Dronningens Gade (Main Street) in Charlotte Amalie.

A. H. Riise downtown is by far the pleasantest place to shop, if you want to pay a little extra for atmosphere. Isidor Paiewonsky is one of the special St. Thomians. He and his wife Charlotte have done more for the area, in their way, than most people I have known in the Caribbean for more than 20 years. As a pair, they have started and driven to stardom their A. H. Riise stores: hers is the gift, perfume, china, and crystal store, and his carries liquor, cigarettes, and now also perfume (on the waterfront side). Both sandblasted old pirate warehouse walls to their original ballast brick, making the combination of arches, brick, and modern commerce unique. For restoration, they've done by far the best—and I'm sure the effort (and their considerable aptitude for merchandising) shows in their profits. The Gift Shop is the first of the A. H. Riise stores that you pass as you walk down Dronningens Gade. It's worth a look even if you aren't interested in Zolotas Greek jewelry, leather pocketbooks, scarves, sweaters, china, crystal, and the other traditional "free port" buys. Go back to the art gallery, up the stairs in what was the old kitchen in the warehouse, with its living quarters in the back.

Continental, facing Emancipation Park, has consistently kept the standards up since the 1940s when the shop opened. The 2-story emporium has attractive small items (silver-backed combs and mirrors, ties, gloves) for the folks back home, as well as an entire wardrobe of imported (England, France, Scandinavia) sportswear. The men's shop has the traditional Pringle sweaters and other English and Scottish menswear.

Cavanagh's has yielded to the cruise passenger pressure to have a lot of small items for quick sale. You have to wade through counters piled high with colorful "junk," to get to the worthy items in the back of the store. The men's boutique has jackets, Daks slacks and some worthy items if you like colorful clothes; the women's shop features the lively Thai silks and other resort wear that has its en-claves at the better hotels. Step across the alley to look at the furni-ture selection. Some of the imports from the East and India would make interesting additions to the patio at home (and staff claims they can cope with shipping even the biggest items).

Alleys are a part of St. Thomian shopping. You can spend hours weaving between the waterfront and Dronningens Gade (Queen's Street) as Main Street is officially called and through to Vimmels-kaft Gada, the official name for Back Street. During the earliest days of St. Thomas the port was a haven for pirates and others who had merchandise to store and ship. The buildings that lined the waterfront in those days stretched back to what is now Main Street. Their walls bulged with commercial loot from Europe, sometimes shipped direct, but more often commandeered on the high seas, and brought in here to be shelved for sale. The same is true today, although the commandeering on high seas is minimal.

From Emancipation Park and the Visitors' Bureau, walking vaguely west, you can pass (or prowl along) Cavanagh's Alley, Raadets Gade (which is a legitimate street), Drake's Alley, Trom-peter Gade, Creque's Alley, Royal Dane Mall, Palm Passage (where you can find books about the islands, as well as a hearty selection of novels, etc. in the **Paperbook Gallery,** and **Courrèges's** colorful shop of French fashions at the waterfront end of the mall), International Plaza, and on to the traditional St. Thomian marketplace, once a slave market and now used by the vegetable ladies for sale of their fresh produce, most of it grown on the north side of the island.

Choose your mall and weave around it for hours. In the Royal Dane Mall, one shop to find is **Needle Craft,** where owner Barbara Kiendl has an intriguing collection of needlepoint designs using is-land flowers, shells, scenes, and anything you could want. Pack-aged with canvas and yarn, the kits are "made in the Virgin Is-lands" and therefore not dutiable.

Trompeter Gade gets top awards for community spirit. The entire alley, once an ugly run-down street, was malled into shape with more than 2 years of effort led by John Bensen, a founding member of the St. Thomas Historical Trust. Formal opening was July 2, 1977, and involved a Bicentennial grant of $21,375 to be matched by private contributions. When it was, another $10,000 came along the same way. Several boutiques and stores fill the niches (**Gold Mine** is one to look for if you want jewelry.)

In business since 1962, **Zora** is the expert sandal maker. Her move to Narre Gade, at the Bluebeard's Castle end of town, puts the shop out of the commercial crush, but for leather and canvas, Zora is in a class by herself. A truly fine pair of sandals takes several fittings, but there are several styles that can be finished quickly for instant purchase. Look also at the belts, pocketbooks, jackets, and vests.

Find the **Sheltered Workshop** for handmade items for sale to benefit the needy (there's a branch of the shop at Frenchman's Reef). For jewelry, my source has been **Irmela's Jewel Studio** at the open-air section of Drake's Passage, not far from the steps to the Virgin Islands film showing. Irmela Neumann set the pace that others now follow, to design imaginative pins, rings, and clips in gold and silver. (If you have some stones to set, discuss it here; if you don't have your own gems, you can buy them from the studio.) Relative newcomers, with less expensive and more trendy silver work, are Sue Frett at the **Shipwreck Shop** (where there is some good merchandise amid a lot of Haitian and other wood "junk"), and Roberta Newman at **Octopus Garden,** a variety shop of handicrafts where you can buy a sarong as well as the silver jewelry.

Jim Tillett's silk screen workshop at **Estate Tutu** has grown far beyond his original vat or 2. The complex that you can pass as you drive out to the east end is now a craftsman's haven, with the colorful screen work still the main feature, but other items are for sale—all of them made in the islands.

Compass Point, out at the east end amid the marinas and frequented (and created) by the boating set, offers interesting shops on a day when you're driving around. Look into the skirts, shirts, and shorts made at and sold from Crew Fashions, where women are stitching while you are buying/looking. Other shops are **Sugar & Spice** (handmade items) and **Elephant Fingers** (an eclectic collection of handmade and other items).

St. Vincent and Its Grenadines

S*t. Vincent Tourist Board, Box 834, Kingstown, St. Vincent, W.I.; Caribbean Tourist Association, 20 East 46th St., New York, NY 10017.*

US$1 = EC$2.60
Unless otherwise noted, $ refers to U.S. currency.

"Pssst, lady. Want a head of lettuce? Tomatoes? Nice ripe mango?" Once you've established that you are a looker, not a buyer, the market ladies at the far end of Kingstown's main street take real pleasure in showing you what's what.

The heaps of fruits, vegetables, and spices, clustered by kind, have probably grown in the fertile Mesopotamia Valley that is the backdrop for this West Indian town. And the women have carried them to market, walking or riding the wood-slatted bus, gaily painted, perhaps with "Patience and God" on its forehead, and certainly open to the trade winds—and to all passersby.

The pros will tell you that Saturday is the only day to go to market in Kingstown, St. Vincent's south-coast capital. But for most of us, any day will do. In fact, the piles of ruby-red tomatoes and coral carrots, and the bubbles of cabbage that nestle against dasheen, breadfruit, mangoes, and papaya are almost overwhelming when the Saturday crowd comes in to buy. It's much more fun on other days, when the market women have time to talk, which they will do, easily and animatedly, even when they know you are not going to buy.

And outside, close to the wharf, there's the fish market—and the charcoal ladies, hands, face, and clothes blackened with their product, which is sold for cooking fuel for braziers used in most Vincentian homes.

At the other end of Kingstown, the first part of town you pass when you drive in from most of the small hotels, there are the boat docks. Once touched only by island schooners, they now have some motorized craft that, although faster than the others, still travel on erratic schedules and still fit you in between cases of Heineken beer, sacks of potatoes, and tanks of bottled gas—all destined for the satellite islands, the chain of the Grenadines.

Boat schedules are "trade secrets." If you want to go down-is-land, persevere. No one "knows" when the boats are going, but if you head down to the wharf at early dawn, you can usually find a craft heading out for Bequia—and willing to take you there with the freight, when it is loaded. The cost is negligible; depending on how desperate you are to go at a specific time, fare can range from a dollar or two to as much as EC$10.

■■■

POLITICAL PICTURE: St. Vincent and its Grenadine Islands comprise one independent country. Milton Cato has been Prime Minister for most of the years since 1967 except for a short term when James "Son" Mitchell wrested political power from the island pros and became premier. Elections were called for December 7, 1979, less than 2 months after the island conglomerate was granted independence (October 27). Duly elected Prime Minister Milton Cato dealt with his new country's first crisis, the rebellion of a handful of insurgents on Union Island on December 7th, and de-clared a "state of emergency" to assure and maintain law and order in the new nation. Life remained calm. In the early months of 1979, the north tip's volcano spewed ash in the air and sent those who had lived on its slopes to the south, 30 miles away, and the Kings-town area. After a couple of weeks of activity, but no real eruption, things settled down and folks went back home—but the aftermath took a long time to overcome. The crops that are St. Vincent's major source of foreign exchange were damaged by the ash, fortunately, flourished in the following months when tropical rains washed the ash into the soil.

Vacationers have always been in the minority on this island, and that situation will not change in the near future, since there are no big hotels—and no plans for any that can possibly materialize this season or next. Some talk over past years has focused on turning the Grenadines (with the exception of Carriacou and Petit Marti-nique, which are part of the independent country of Grenada at the south of the arc of islands) into the tourism resort areas, a logical move since the Grenadines are lined with white sand beaches and crimped with protected coves while the main island of St. Vincent has black volcanic sand on any of its shores where you find beaches, except for a patch or two of gold sand on the south coast.

■■■

CUSTOMS OF THE COUNTRY on St. Vincent are modified from the centuries of British heritage to the trends of newly independent Caribbean countries. Vincentians, and the sprinkling of people on the several Grenadines that are governed from St. Vincent's Kingstown, are adapting some of the traditional British rituals to a lifestyle that is Vincentian. You can count on cricket and football/soccer to be popular local sports, but you can also walk down to the far end of Kingstown, the opposite end of town from the banana-loading docks, and perhaps hear the young children practicing hymns at one of the trio of churches (Methodist, Anglican, and Catholic). School children are uniformed, neat, and smiling, although curious about those of us who wander in their midst—intruders from another country.

St. Vincent is a verdant island where almost anything grows. When you drive into the country, you will see lush plantations and a simple lifestyle that finds Vincentians living off the land they till.

For those interested in the island's history and past traditions, St. Vincent and Bequia have two of the few remaining Caribbean communities where men go out after whales, bringing them back to shore as the Portuguese fishermen did in the old days out of New Bedford, Mass., and their own Azores in the Atlantic. When a whale is sighted, life among the old generation reaches a feverish pitch— with capture and cutting part of a time-honored ritual where danger mixes with daily activity.

The Carib community that has lived for generations on the slopes of St. Vincent's volcano in the north of the island was moved south in April 1979 when ominous rumbles resulted in a gigantic plume of ash in the air. Some of the younger Caribs did not return; the older generation who live on the flanks of the volcano have been integrated into modern Vincentian life more than their related community of Caribs on the reservation in northeastern Dominica.

AUTHOR'S OBSERVATION: If you are interested in some of the thoughts that are vital for Vincentians today, read any of the writings of Orde Coombs, a Vincentian whose experiences may not be typical of his countrymen (education at Yale and Cambridge, and life in New York), but a man who speaks and writes eloquently about life he knew as a boy and knows today. One of his books to find is *Do You See My Love for You Growing?*, published by Dodd, Mead & Co., New York, 1972.

Clothes are casual. St. Vincent is not an island for peacock finery. Most of the small hotels and resorts are sea oriented (often sailing, certainly swimming), and only Young Island aspires to be a resort-style property. What you dress up in there for dinner is up to you, but the rule used to be—and still is for some—that barefoot elegance sets the pace. Some of the Grenadine resorts (notably Cotton House on Mustique and Petit St. Vincent on its island of the same name) are enclaves of the good life. You will be comfortable in your favorite resort wear. When you venture into Kingstown, or any of the small villages around the country, conservative daytime wear is most appropriate. These are kind and welcoming people, many of whom have an annual income that may be less than the total value of the clothes in your suitcase.

■■■

MONEY MATTERS: The currency for St. Vincent and its Grenadine islands is Eastern Caribbean dollars and cents, at about EC $2.60 to US$1. When you are staying at Young Island, Petit St. Vincent, and a few of the other resorts, you can use your familiar greenbacks, but if you venture out of those compounds, you will find that EC currency is legal tender—in the market, shops, restaurants, and anywhere in the country. Using the currency of the country is regarded as a common courtesy by the people of recently independent countries. Flashing U.S. dollars around represents a lifestyle some West Indians resent, although you will find no resentment to you as an individual.

■■■

ARRIVAL at Arnos Vale Airfield is your first clue that this place is different. If you fly here from Barbados, chances are you will have had delays, and more lingering time at Grantley Adams Airport (Barbados) than you really needed. However, anyone destined for St. Vincent should relax on the plane flying south. Be prepared for anything and take it in stride when you make the last leap to St. Vincent. One choice from Barbados to St. Vincent is LIAT, Leeward Islands Air Transport, the Antigua-based airline that comes in for more than its share of raps. It has become "fashionable" to share jokes about LIAT, and while I have had my problems with delayed flights, indifferent staff, and the whole list of complaints, I find LIAT flights part of what the Caribbean is all about today. Most people are *trying* but in many instances, no one really knows what to do next, so *you* must. Have an alternate plan—which for the first-time traveler to St. Vincent should probably include overnight arrangements in Barbados, especially if getting to Barbados is more than a nonstop hop for you. Even with the best of the airline's intentions, smooth connections between Barbados and St. Vincent are the exception rather than the rule. The new Barbados airport has a comfortable lounge area, plus shops, but the Marriott hotel is nearby and if you have a long delay, life is pleasanter there or at the Arawak or Crane Hotel than at the airport.

Tropicair is a Barbados-based charter line that often has advance arrangements to sweep you from your international flight across the tarmac to their waiting plane. (Young Island and Petit St. Vincent are 2 resorts that group their clients, if you are one or 2, to fill a charter so that your travel is as expeditious as possible.) Air Anchorage flies from Martinique to Union Island for boat links to PSV and Palm resorts. There are other small charter airlines that are available, but you will pay a premium, usually, for your personal flight. Your alternative for the Grenadine island destinations is Inter-Island Air Service (IAS, and a LIAT subsidiary) island-hopping flight between St. Vincent and Grenada.

St. Vincent's Arnos Vale arrivals building was expanded to open, officially, on Independence Day, October 27, 1979, but it is still small by comparison to, for example, the major international airport in Barbados. Customs inspectors take their work seriously—even when there are only a handful of you to clear. The system is methodical. On a couple of occasions, the inspector would not look at the first piece of luggage until everything from the plane had been put at the luggage claim area and taken to his counter. This may have changed, but if not—relax. You'll get where you're going sometime.

The St. Vincent Tourist Board information desk is usually manned for flight arrivals (but not always if you have chartered a plane). Leaflets and information are available; ask about taxi fares. The departure lounge is comfortable, with bar, post office and a branch of St. Vincent Craftsmen's shop (which is not always staffed).

■■■

TOURING TIPS: When you step outside the airport door, taxis will be waiting. If your hotel expects you on a certain flight, they may have made arrangements for a driver to ask for you. Check with the Tourist Board desk before you wade into the sea of drivers outside. Cab fares to all hotels are reasonable; there's no place that's more than about 15 minutes' drive from the door.

Bequia and the offshore Grenadine Islands are another excursion. If you're headed there, be sure to travel light, unless you *like* to lug suitcases, crates, etc. through the several stages involved in getting from Barbados to St. Vincent airport to the docks for the boat service to some of the islands with no airfields. Boats at the Kingstown dock range from the motorized M.V. *Siemstrand*, which makes regular island runs, to island-built schooners that will take you along with the freight. None of the escapades are geared for resort wear; dress for rugged travel in warm countries (jeans, shirt, and not much luggage).

For touring around the "big" island of St. Vincent, take a taxi if you are a first-timer, and check with your hotel to find the name of a tried and true driver whose lore will add to your experience. Once you know the roads (signposting is limited or nonexistent), you can rent a car, but be prepared for a car that may show signs of wear, roads that weave and are potholed and expensive gas (with small cars you won't use much). The Vincentian bus service runs along the road past the driveway for most hotels (Young Island's dock included), and you can pay the few EC cents for the 20-minute ride into Kingstown.

On Bequia, taxis will take you touring, and you can walk (or hitchhike—cars are limited) around near Admiralty Bay.

HOTELS on St. Vincent and its Grenadine Islands are an astounding collection of super luxury—the kind that makes you marvel at how anyone *dared* to attempt to bring freezers, fresh running water, and electricity to island outposts—and small and simple surroundings, suited to the inevitable power failures, sudden tropical downpours, and dearth of fresh water that are facts of life in island communities where modernization comes at a high price—emotionally as well as financially. You will find hospitality the highlight in these islands. For years, I have fled to hideaways on St. Vincent and its islands—to luxuriate in the sure knowledge that nothing elsewhere would be/could be important enough for anyone to succeed in finding me.

Most of St. Vincent's hotels, cottages, and inns are on the south coast, within a few minutes' ride from downtown Kingstown if they are not actually in the town. There are a couple of places outside the town—one at the golf course (which is not open as we go to press), and another on a black-sand windward cove, but otherwise most vacationers will find themselves in the cluster of small places that look toward the Grenadines.

On the Grenadine islands, there are a few places to stay—some simple and some simply perfect luxury.

AUTHOR'S AWARDS go to Petit St. Vincent for being one of the few true Edens in an often complicated world; to Young Island, for an island outpost that is relatively easy to reach; and—once again—to the Heron Hotel for managing to maintain the basic West Indian values that make the small inn so special.

✤ **CSY Marina** (Blue Lagoon, St. Vincent, W.I.; 18 rooms) is the home port for Caribbean Sailing Yachts, the operation that is mainland headquartered in Tenafly, New Jersey (see Sports). The overnight facilities were built with yachtsmen in mind, for providing a place to overnight before you head to sea (or when you return from your sailing). The rooms were built in the late 70s and a scrub-up in one of the billets is welcomed after a week or two of sailing. Rooms are upstairs, over the yacht service area, not far from the convening area where sailors swap sea stories. Rates are about $50 for 2, with light breakfast included.

✤ **Cobblestone Inn** (Kingstown, St. Vincent, W.I.; 20 rooms) has had its ups and downs since it was sandblasted back to the pirate-era ballast-brick walls. The bar/restaurant on the main waterfront street is a gathering place for local folk who can afford it; bedrooms are up the courtyard stairs on the second level. Rooms have potential; at one time all the air conditioners worked and even the small-and-boxy singles were adequate. When I last visited, the place looked in pretty good shape, with #3 (twin-bedded, on the front of the building with street noises and waterfront view) and #4 (on the back with less noise and no view) ready for guests. The coralstone walls in many rooms add a nice decorator's touch. Popular with barefoot and boating types who take off for sea from the waterfront piers. $56 for 2, breakfasts and dinners daily, is the winter price tag.

✤ **Coconut Beach Hotel** (Box 355, Kingstown, St. Vincent, W.I.; 10 rooms) captures a sandy shore not far from Kingstown or the airstrip and at a perfect place for you to overlook yachts anchored in the protected passage that separates this shore from Young Island. Turn off the main road at the Coconut Beach sign and weave down for about 3 minutes toward the shore to find the place that the Gelos bought in 1970 when they moved south from the States. Helene Gelo is the moving force with this property, and with the St. Vincent Hotel Association, where she has been a vital catalyst for several years. When she's on the premises, there's a congenial, informal atmosphere for those lucky enough to get one of the 10 rooms this winter. Ask for one of those closest to the sea. Tucked under and around palm trees and other tropical planting at the shore, the rooms can seem boxy if you get one in the back, but bright colors liven up the inside, and chances are you'll spend most of your time on the seaside deck or the sands. For a winter overnight, count on paying about $60 for 2, 2 meals daily included— and the meals will be good and hearty island food, with some American flourishes but with island vegetables and fruits the best.

✛ **Grand View Beach Hotel** (Box 173, Kingstown, St. Vincent, W.I.; 12 rooms) gathers its guests at the top of the hill, with a view south over the Grenadine Islands from the porch of a house once used for drying cotton. For many years, Grand View operated as a family-run inn, popular with island residents who knew—and liked—good island food. On my first visit to St. Vincent, I dined in style on Mrs. Banfield's Vincentian recipes—and developed a lifelong affection for the food. Rooms with the view over the islands are the best for my money, and those were #3 and #4 when I last looked. Located between the airport and town, about 10 minutes from the docks of Kingstown, the main house (former home) sits on the hill, sending its guests down to the shore for a swim. The hike back up can be hard if you're not a hill climber, but the location is ideal for sea breezes and simple living. Not for those who must have a luxury resort, Grand View is ideal for people seeking good value in comfortable, congenial West Indian surroundings. Rates are about $45 for 2, 2 meals daily this winter, with special rates for children under 12, and children under 2 are free.

✛ **Heron Hotel** (Box 226, Kingstown, St. Vincent, W.I.; 15 rooms) is a hideaway for people who like their islands pure. The entrance is across from the banana boat loading docks on Upper Bay Street, through the doorway and up the stairs. The world you step into is strictly old-time West Indian, even though all the wood-walled rooms have been air-conditioned, and all have hot/cold showers, with a special electronic mosquito killer that takes care of the pesky intruders that used to be kept from their nighttime nibbles by the mosquito netting that draped around you while you slept. The inn that Doreen McKenzie runs at the top of these stairs has rockers in its center (the open-air "parlor") and on its porches where you can look over the action in town. This is not a quaint, trumped-up place. It is exactly what it appears to be: a traditional West Indian inn that has the confidence to continue operating much as it has been for the past several decades, or perhaps centuries. Heron Hotel is one of the few constants in a rapidly changing world, and I, for one, count on it to stay that way. Your rate for 2 is almost $50, 2 meals daily per person—but you're not on a beach, and there are no planned activities or bands at night. This is a place for self-sufficient travelers to see what this island is like. I wish I had more places like Heron Hotel to write about.

✣ **Kingston Park Guest House** (Box 41, Kingstown, St. Vincent, W.I.; 20 rooms) is included here because its owner, Miss Nesta Paynter, is well worth meeting if you want to learn some local lore. A traditional Vincentian home has been opened up for guests, with about a dozen rooms (varying shapes, sizes, and decorating styles) in the main house and others in some self-catering apartments on the property. Count on basic-but-adequate facilities and some memorable island hospitality and food at this in-town place. Rates this winter are a modest $30 for 2, 2 meals daily per person.

✣ **Mariner's Inn** (Box 868, Kingstown, St. Vincent, W.I.; 12 rooms) has Shirley Layne in charge, and her enthusiasm and hospitality help to hold the place together. The bar-side atmosphere, always salty, can be *very* island casual depending on who is "hanging around." The inn began to make its mark when Bill and Sandra Miller opened this overnighting nook on the south shore of St. Vincent in the 60s. The inn has always appealed to yachting types. Several changes of management have moved some of the furniture around, but haven't yet moved the antique four-posters in some of the bedrooms out. Vincentian-owned, this inn offers casual, sea-oriented surroundings, and dancing, music, and perhaps a shore-side barbecue some evenings. The indoor dining area is open to the breezes and features island food. There's a small patch of sand where you can slide into the sea, but don't count on a long stretch of powder here. You'll have to go to the Grenadines to find that, but you are within a 15-minute drive of Kingstown and can take the public bus that passes along the main road outside the entrance if you don't want to rent a car or taxi. Rates for 2 this winter will be

$70, with 2 meals daily per person. Children under 2 are free and there are special rates up to age 12.

✢ **Sugar Mill Inn** (Rotho Mill, St. Vincent, W.I.; 25 rooms) is an island tradition that has had its ups and downs since it was first conceived by a trio that included noted photographer Bradley Smith and a few other expatriates who had come to these islands back in the 50s. Today the inn has a sailing focus (even though it sits on a hillside with a noteworthy tree punctuating its open-air "dance floor") and an international atmosphere that came with the partnership formed with a German colleague. Les and Brenda Hazell are your hosts at this comfortably casual hillside haven with a nautical tone, and Brenda can be your source for tips on touring and for the recipes for some of the Vincentian specialities served at mealtime. Count on paying up to $75 for 2, 2 meals per person daily.

✢ **Sunset Shores** (Box 839, Kingstown, St. Vincent; W.I.; 19 rooms) sat firmly on a yellow sand beach on St. Vincent's southern shore in the season of '73. This property is family-managed as well as family-owned, and Compton King is the man to find if you have questions while you are claiming one of the garden-level rooms that U-shape around the pool. Accommodations are motel style, air-conditioned and comfortable but not luxurious. There will probably be entertainment some evenings, especially in winter, but most of the activity here—as at other hotels—is what you stir up yourself. From the shore you overlook Young Island and the seas to the south. Kingstown is about 10 minutes' ride, either by taxi, rental car, or the bus that runs on its own schedule past the end of the drive. Count on paying about $80 this winter for 2 with 2 meals daily per person or almost $60 without meals. (Rates are slightly higher for the bigger rooms nearest the beach.)

✢ **Villa Lodge** (Box 222, Kingstown, St. Vincent, W.I.; 10 rooms) is a home-turned-inn, with rooms in various shapes and sizes, all neat, and some with a view of the water. (Number 7 has a lovely view of Fort Duvernette, the rock hump near Young Island.) The 3 rooms off one side of the original house have doors leading out to the pool path; #1 is a big double room that can easily take 3 people. Count on sincere West Indian hospitality from the Brisbane's inn, and you can walk down the hill to the shore for swimming if you prefer that to the pool. The bus into Kingstown runs past the end of the driveway. Surroundings right here are conducive to quiet evenings "at home," either joining the other guests (and the Vincentians) who settle around the bar, or enjoying your own company after a good West Indian meal. Rates this winter will be about $80 for 2, 2 meals daily per person included. Rate for 2, without meals, is $50.

✤ **Young Island** (200 yards off the south shore of St. Vincent; 25 cottages) is about as close as I can find to Robinson Crusoe's dream, with additions of modern plumbing, good drinking water, and maid service. Each of the cottages scattered around the rocks and rills has louvered windows to let in tropical breezes plus overhead fans, modern dressing room, and toilet area, with a shower fenced in bamboo with stars or sunlight overhead. This very special place was the dream of a high-powered tourism exec, John Houser, and his wife Polly. After suffering the birth pains for 25 cottages (now wrapped in a Houser-inspired quilt of tropical plants) John and Polly Houser sold the resort to Charles McCulloch from Nova Scotia. Improvements have been made, but the atmosphere remains the same. His death in 1979 allowed for the purchase (his expressed desire) by Vincentians. In early '80 the hotel's manager, Vidal Browne, and the country's leading surgeon, Fred Balantyne, negotiated ownership of the property.

Cottages 1 through 10 curl around the eastern shore, near the small but good beach. Cottage #24 has the perfect perch for sunset viewing, and a small second room; #17, with a parrot's eye view of St. Vincent's sawtooth skyline, is close to 90 steps up the hill, with a private terrace favored by sunbathers and romantics (the climb makes it off limits for the faint of heart or families with flocks of children. #13 is almost as bad, with about 40 steps.) There's a pool tucked into the tropical plants, a tennis court over the brow of the hill, grounds to meander around, a small and constant ferry service to the main island, and the 50-foot yacht *Patricia of Camelot* anchored in the cove when it's not cruising with guests down the Grenadines.

Vincentian-born general manager and part owner, Vidal Browne began his hotel career as one of Houser's first employees, learning on the job and—with a few years away by mutual agreement—with exceptional opportunites offered to him both by Houser and McCulloch. Although most of the small hotel operation seems to run smoothly, mealtime offerings vary in quality, but service is pleasant. The atmosphere in the dining area and around the beachside bar is just what a Robinson Crusoe retreat should be. Breakfasts are cooked before your eyes (opened with the aid of immediately poured coffee) at the casual curved counter under one of the pavilions. The omelet that has become the house specialty (at least for me) makes a bold attempt at filling you until dinner hour. Atmosphere around this place is "no tie, no shoes" for guests—and often for Vidal Browne.

Plan on paying about $225 for 2 this winter, 2 meals daily per person, and brace yourself for the multihop route to get here. More for well-heeled barefoot and boating types than for the pampered and perfect set, but both will enjoy it if they're tolerant. This is an islanders' island—with flourishes. (Inquire about the special summer, spring, and fall promotions that include "everything but drinks and postage stamps.")

▪▪

HOUSEKEEPING HOLIDAYS have been popular ever since there has been tourism to St. Vincent. Surroundings are usually simple and sea-oriented, even when the beaches are just a patch of sand. You'll buy food at the Kingstown market, from a fisherman you meet and from people suggested to you by the manager of the place you rent. If you have favorite foods you cannot live without, bring them with you—but know that you can get a good supply of island vegetables and spices at the market, depending on the season.

✣ **Indian Bay Beach Hotel** (Box 538, Kingstown, St. Vincent, W.I.; 12 rooms) has 1- and 2-bedroom units, right on the beach at Indian Bay, not far from Yvonette Apartments. There's nothing fancy about the surroundings, down a road that slopes to the sea, off the main route between airport and town, in sleeping surroundings that allow vacationers to relax as the Vincentians who spend leisure time here do. Don't expect a U.S. modern apartment with the 2-bedroom unit that 4 can use, but you will be paying about $50 per day this winter. If you want hotel plan, with meals at the restaurant nearby, you can pay $63 for 2, breakfasts and dinners daily.

✣ **Tropic Breeze Hotel** (Box 761, Kingstown, St. Vincent, W.I.; 12 apts.) takes the prize hillside view overlooking the Grenadines to the south, and puts you in your own apartment with kitchenette, with the option to eat all your meals at the hotel's restaurant. There's a pool at this perch, and although the rooms are motel style, the furnishings are comfortable and the view from the balcony spectacular. If you don't insist on being on a beach, this place has its merits. Your room for 2 with no meals will cost about $50 this winter, with a 2-bedroom apartment, suitable for 4, renting at about $300 per week. There are 1-bedroom apartments and a unit that makes up for 3 bedrooms to take care of 3 couples or a family who want to be in an apartment-style complex. You'll need a car if you want to be mobile. Kingstown is about 15 minutes' drive down the hill, curling around the airport to town. Inquire about the special scuba package.

✤ **Yvonette Apartments** (Box 71, Kingstown, St. Vincent, W.I.; 12 rooms) clutch a piece of shoreline at Indian Bay Beach. The units are a cheek-by-jowl group that climb over a small slope, offering the option for 1, 2, or 3 bedrooms. All apartments have "balconies," a kitchen with adequate equipment (and a propane stove), and enough furniture to give you a comfortable, casual place to enjoy but not worry about. Roger St. Maurice is your manager on location and you'll need a car or access to a taxi, to get into Kingstown and around the island. The road that leads to the shore and Yvonette is a winding route from the main road between airport and town. Figure about $60 daily for 2.

■■

RESTAURANTS on St. Vincent feature West Indian food. Some of the most comfortable places for outsiders are the hotel dining rooms. If you are unfamiliar with the ways of West Indian islands, you'll find the dining room at Young Island the most typical of what you expect of Caribbean resorts. However, the food will be better— if you want to sample local recipes—at places such as **Sugar Mill, Grand View, Villa Lodge** and at **Coconut Beach.** Stop by a day before, or certainly in the morning, to see if you can have a West Indian meal that night.

Harbour Lights, at the shore near the Young Island dock, has a pub atmosphere popular with those who like casual camaraderie. Fish and chips are featured, along with sandwiches and full meals. Beer and other beverages are offered anytime after mid-morning until the last person leaves.

Umbrella Restaurant, also near the Young Island dock, is an easy place to have a snack or more in shoreside surroundings. **Ikhaya** in Kingstown has been suggested by a trusted scout, but I have not tried it myself. Check with the Tourist Office about any other small spots that may have opened up recently. They may have some suggestions.

Check on the status of the **Aquaduct Golf Course** dining facilities. The valley location can be lovely for lunch, if you want to see some island scenery (or to play golf), but I can't vouch for the food since plans are changing as I write.

In Kingstown, **Cobblestone** serves meals, and check with Doreen

McKenzie at the **Heron** about the possibility of a simple, family-style meal with her overnight guests if you have not booked here. She may be able to take an extra reservation. The sandwich-and-soup lunches are a noontime favorite for many who find themselves in Kingstown then.

■■

PLACES WORTH FINDING on St. Vincent and its Grenadines are natural sites. Unless you like tropical flora and fauna, there's no point in moving from your beach chair. Although you can wander around Kingstown happily on your own, looking and lingering at whim, for your first foray into the countryside stop at the Tourist Board and ask them to suggest a driver if you have not already made arrangements through your hotel. Having a Vincentian take you around, to give some local commentary, will make all the difference in the first run. From that time on, you can rent a car and get around easily on your own.

AUTHOR'S OBSERVATION: Do not take "just any" taxi driver; some are better versed in island lore than others, and it is worthwhile, if you are taking time from your vacation to ride around in a car, to take some time to do some research in advance.

KINGSTOWN is several villages, at least as I see it. First is the port area, around and down the road from the banana boat loading docks. The most fascinating part is the schooner dock, where you should be at 8 a.m. or earlier—whether you want to sign on to go down island, or just look around. Everything gets loaded—early; and you can sign on on the spur of the moment if you like spontaneous travel.

Carnegie Library, in a wood frame building where trade winds blow through the second floor while you check up on West Indian history or other subjects, is one of several Carnegie libraries dotted around the formerly British West Indies as part of a behest from the Andrew Carnegie fortune.

The cluster of churches at the west end of town, the "other" end from the docks, set an entirely different tone. Most of the churches also have schools (you will see neatly uniformed children in play yards and around the area on weekdays, morning, noon, and mid-afternoon. **St. George's Cathedral,** the Anglican church, has interesting plaques on its walls and stones in its graveyard from earlier

English/Scottish days. The view from the graveyard of **St. Mary's Roman Catholic Church,** built in an intriguing combination of several styles, is interesting. The Catholic church was the dream of Belgian monk, Dom Carlos Verbeke, who obviously carried with him European visions of the house of God. The **Methodist Church,** on the third "side" of this area, is simple, of wood construction, and usually open to the breezes.

Fort Charlotte, up and out from Kingstown, is the standard tourist stop for anyone who takes a cab (or a cruise ship tour). It's the view that is awe-inspiring. There's not much but walls to the Fort, unless you count the part where prisoners are kept (and where they bake bread for the government hospitals and schools). The drive to get here is matched (or exceeded) by the curling route you will follow around what's known as Mesopotamia Valley, a lush plant-filled "bowl" where Vincentians farm on the slant and reap some of the healthy crops you can witness at the local market.

St. Vincent Museum, planted in an interesting West Indian house in the middle of the **Botanic Garden** where the Caribbean's first breadfruit tree grows (the nut was left by Captain Bligh, legend claims), is worth a visit. Be sure to make an appointment to meet the museum's enthusiastic director, Earle Kirby, if you want more legends and lore than appear on the meager identification tags. Among the treasures in the small museum are early Arawak Indian artifacts, and items from the culture of some of the tribes (Tainos and Ciboneys). All items have been unearthed around St. Vincent and its Grenadines, and the $1 donation seems too small a price to pay for this opportunity. Allow some time to saunter around the Botanic Garden, well worth a walk in their own right.

Falls of Baleine are well worth the day's outing. Inquire about making the excursion by boat as soon as you arrive on St. Vincent. (It may take a couple of days to get things organized). The 3-hour boat trip from Kingstown area along the west coast is almost enough reason to make the journey. Views are spectacular. But the falls are a bit of magic. This is a bathing suit-and-sneakers excursion where diving into the sea swells that make a landing a challenge are part of your experience. Following the riverbed to the base of the falls is a short (10 minute) rewarding walk, with an opportunity to wallow in the pools at the base of the falls when you reach the "end." This is a special experience, well worth whatever the going rate happens to be.

The **volcano** in the north (see Sports) is a real excursion and not a place for passive sightseeing. The area was restricted, except for rescue missions and volcanologists during the April '79 activity, but check to see if things are back to normal enough to arrange a climb. Hire a small plane at the airport and fly over the area; driving up and back is a back-breaking ride, not worth the excursion unless you are intrepid.

Whaling villages on the leeward (west) side of the island are not the typical tourist traps. If you head here, take humility with you. Not many outsiders come to these villages, and you will be obvious whether you mean to be or not.

Liberty Lodge is not your typical sightseeing goal, but it is definitely a place worth finding, or at least finding out about. Located in the hills behind Kingstown, the Lodge is a self-help project for Vincentian adolescents who had been spending their childhood getting into trouble around the docks. Sparked by the enthusiasm of some local citizens and a few interested island visitors, Liberty Lodge became a residence for delinquents, who learned animal husbandry, agriculture, and carpentry, plus other useful crafts at their own community in the hills. To quote from the mimeographed folder given to me by Colonel Anderson, retired chief of the Vincentian police and a prime mover in the project, "In November 1969, a group of ten juveniles ranging from 10–16 years, who had all been known to the police, were called together to discuss their participation in a scheme which was to provide training for them in a different environment." The environment was the Lago Heights Police Post, no longer used for training officers and available as a mountainside residence for the boys. The youths have worked toward building their community and raise food for sale to hotels and stores in Kingstown so that the project is partially self-supporting. If you have the opportunity and the interest, inquire about the Liberty Lodge project, either through your hotel manager or directly from Andy Anderson, if you can find him while you're on the island. (Check at the offices of Argyle Associates on James Street, or write to Box 530, St. Vincent, W.I.)

■■

SPORTS are sea-oriented. They focus on sailing—not only out of St. Vincent, but certainly around the Grenadines. Bequia is a favorite anchorage for many yachts, in spite of the feeling on the part of a few captains I have talked with that the reception among yachtsmen is not as warm as it used to be. (There seems to be competition among anchoring yachtsmen for the charter business.)

Sailing from St. Vincent is at *Heritage Yacht Charters*, owned by Les Hazell with a German partner and operating from the cove near Sugar Mill Beach, or *Caribbean Sailing Yachts*,—a one-stop source for professional advice and well-kept yachts. Heritage has Gulf Star 50s and Pierson's in their fleet. CSY sends you out with capable skipper in one of the 35 special CSY 44s, designed for these waters with information supplied by CSY owner Van Ost and his crew. The firm got its start in a dentist's office in Tenafly, New Jersey, and CSY tried the idea of full-service chartering in Essex, Connecticut, in 1967. From there, the senior Van Ost went to St. Thomas, pulling up anchor from there to head to Road Town, Tortola, in the British Virgins, in 1969. At that time, services stretched south to the port at St. Vincent and the fleet was expanded to include the Carib 41s that the firm had pioneered in the island cruising-for-comfort market. Full details on the varieties of sailing programs, including bare boat, boat with skipper and sail-and-learn programs can be obtained from the CSY mail drop at Box 491, Tenafly, NJ 07670, or at Blue Lagoon, St. Vincent, W.I.

Young Island's yacht, the *Patricia of Camelot,* a custom Gulf Star 50, is available for Young Island guests for day sails and longer, and for outsiders if the houseguests haven't filled up the bunks. Daily cruising runs about $35 per person.

Pleasure cruising was available on *Quando Quando,* a 39-foot British-built boat with twin-diesel engines, during one Vincentian visit, and it's worth checking to see if the interesting offerings are still available. Tobago Cays, cruising to the Falls of Baleine, Mustique, deep-sea fishing, and Bequia were all offered on special days at fees that range from about $25 per person up to $50 (for the longer excursions to, for example, the Tobago Cays). Phone 84879 for details or inquire at the tourist office or your hotel on arrival.

Scuba diving facilities are no match for those on Bonaire, the Caymans, and St. Thomas, although the waters in the Grenadines and even off the coasts of St. Vincent offer spectacular sites. In the past couple of years, some pros have settled here and the start for what can become a flourishing scuba center is solid. Contact Terry Lampert at Mariner's *Aquatic Sports* near the Young Island dock at Villa, or *Dive St. Vincent* at their base at Calliaqua.

Golf is played at the course at Aquaduct, about 45 minutes' drive from Kingstown and most of the hotels. The location is gorgeous, in the valley surrounded by mountains, but be sure to check on the status of the course before you lug clubs this far. Financial problems have plagued this operation from its start and condition of the course reflects the problem. Golf is not the main reason to come to St. Vincent, but if you are a golfer, a trip here to rent some clubs and play a few rounds can make a pleasant day *if* the course is in condition for play.

The **tennis** court over the hill on Young Island is used by YI hotel guests even when its surface is "variable," but otherwise it bakes in the sun. There are public courts (asphalt) on the way into Kingstown, and there are courts at the Aquaduct area, but St. Vincent is not a tennis island—yet. Grand View Hotel's addition of tennis (and squash) facilities reflects a new interest.

Hiking on this island yields special rewards for anyone who has arrived armed with long pants, long-sleeved shirt, sturdy climbing shoes—and bug spray or repellent of some kind. The slopes of the north coast's volcano have become a sort of pilgrimage goal; only those who have conquered the paths and seen the lake at the top can really claim to have seen St. Vincent.

■■

TREASURES AND TRIFLES: St. Vincent Craftsmen, a handcraft cooperative, inspires some of the best-quality handcrafts in the Caribbean. When the St. Vincent government focused on local handcrafts in the late 60s, they recognized the need for retraining in some of the skills that had been part of the earliest traditions of the people of these islands. Responding to cooperation from the United Nations agency charged with teaching skills and defining products, St. Vincent's craftsmen relearned some of the earliest skills. Mr. Malcolm Benjamin, from the U.S., was the first director of the Vincentian operation, and with the assistance of Lennox "Scully" Hunte and 2 Peace Corps workers, the fledgling industry was born. Handmade items of highest quality are sold from the shop on the grounds of the Old Cotton Ginnery, inland along the road leading from the banana-boat docks in Kingstown, and from the second shop at the airport. It is possible to head out into the country to visit some of the home industries, and that can be the most rewarding way to visit the "real" St. Vincent.

Casuals Ltd., a home industry for fashion and made-to-order clothes, was started by Norma Grant who had operated a very successful Kingstown boutique a few years ago. When small children made staying near home important, Norma began to organize some Vincentian seamstresses to work in their homes assembling patterns that she had designed. Norma designs some of the Batik Caribe fashions, and can be reached through the shop if you have difficulty locating Casuals Ltd.

Batik Caribe, on the main street of town, is the shop of Gerry and Jan Palmer. They've put their eye for good workmanship and the considerable talent of the Stevensons together to provide the shop and sales force for some excellent batik designs on fabric. You can buy clothes ready-made or by the yard, and ask Jan for the name of the current recommended seamstress if you want to have something made while you are here.

Noah's Arkade, next door to Batik Caribe, has high quality handicrafts from St. Vincent and other Caribbean countries, as well as an interesting selection of books about the country and the West Indies. This can be your one-stop place for shopping. Variety in price and consistency for quality are hallmarks of this shop.

In the Cobblestone courtyard, there's a **Stecher's** store (you'll find them on St. Lucia, Trinidad, and other Eastern Caribbean isles as well). That's your best source, in my opinion, for the traditional luxury items: crystal, china, etc. Prices are fair, and probably less than you'll pay at your hometown store, but the real reason for looking here is that the selection is interesting, and *that* you probably won't find in your hometown village.

Two sources for interesting, typically Vincentian gifts are the **local markets,** where you buy domestic peanuts, sun-dried and bottled, as well as West Indian hot sauce. Ask about other local products bottled or canned for easy carrying home. The second source is the **Post Office,** where Vincentian stamps showing local scenes are interesting, pretty, and easy to carry home.

The Grenadines

In the books and articles I have written about the Caribbean I face the perplexing situation of trying to make St. Vincent and its Grenadines clear to those who have not been here but would like to visit. There is no easy way to explain the chain of islands and the "mother" St. Vincent (you'll have to cruise them). Some islands *are* resorts, others have resorts, and still others have several small places to stay. I have chosen here to talk about Bequia as an island, with its inns, etc. commented upon alphabetically; Canouan is next, and also an island—with some cottages for rent; Cotton House, which occupies most of the island of Mustique, follows, to be followed in turn by Palm Island (resort on an island that is officially Prune) and Petit St. Vincent (resort and island). Union Island follows, with its few small places, but look also at the chapter on Grenada if you want to know about places on *its* Grenadine islands of Carriacou and Petit Martinique.

Having said that, you should know what every Vincentian schoolchild knows: the order of the islands that string south, as you can see them or sail them from St. Vincent, are Bequia, Petit Nevis,

Quatre Island, Battowia, Baliceau, Savan, Petit Canouan, Canouan, the Tobago Cays and Sail Rock, Mayreau, Union Island, with Palm Island and Petit St. Vincent nearby. (South of PSV is Petit Martinique, the "first" of Grenada's Grenadines as you head south, soon to be followed by Carriacou, Saline, Frigate, Large, Diamond, Ronde, Caille, and Les Tantes, before you hit the southern "mark," Grenada.) Only a handful of these islands have housing of any kind for visitors, but most have spectacular powdery sand beaches, most of them unpeopled most of the time. Snorkeling and scuba are almost as exceptional as the sailing around here.

Bequia

Old-timers know that you have to jump into the water quickly to bind the mouth of the whale to keep it from sinking and to make it easier to tow. And they know that once the whale is beached on Petit Nevis, carving quickly is crucial. A clutch of sharks can devour at least half of a beached whale in one Caribbean evening. That may not matter in your daily life, but it does in the life of the Bequia whalers. This is an island of the sea. Tradition puts the folk into boats at an early age to pluck up lobsters, fish, and even whales that head south on their annual migrations. Your landing at Port Elizabeth after the crossing from Kingstown on St. Vincent will be casual. You may find one of the 30-plus taxis that formed into an association a few years ago—or you may not. It really doesn't matter because you can take off your shoes and walk in the water to the nearest small inns and you shouldn't have brought much in the way of luggage anyway.

There's a tourism booth near the shore and a few shops in the village that is Port Elizabeth, but mostly this town is a quiet, casual place, lingered over by yachtsmen who make this their first landfall after a trans-Atlantic crossing, and by some who call this harbor home port for chartering around the Grenadines.

The best of Bequia is lolling in the sun, watching, listening and learning how it's done. If you care, you can learn how to cook breadfruit or how to catch a local lobster; you can listen to whaling tales and you can learn how to build a boat—from trees cut to planking size and framed up on the beach. If you're lucky, you may even be around for a boat christening, when all the neighborhood comes to the shore to break down the scaffolding to drag the boat to the sea and to celebrate with more revelry and joy than most people show for a child.

■■

ARRIVAL on Bequia is by boat, either on one of the motor launches that brings you, freight, and the mail across the Bequia Channel from Kingstown, St. Vincent, or on an island schooner. Some boats are sturdy, hand-hewn versions perhaps with a tree-trunk mast, and others are sleek, modern fiberglass yachts for charter. There is no airstrip, and no prospect of one in the near future.

■■

HOTELS ON BEQUIA are a special group of personality places. There's amazing luxury at a couple of cottage/house "resorts," and simple, comfortable shoreside lodgings at a trio of inns. You can count on reasonable rates, casual life, and plenty of time to relax with no pressure to do anything. Author's awards on an island this special seem superfluous, but mention must be made of Frangipani, a favorite for yachtsmen—and for me. I like the Mitchells' brand of hospitality. If you demand picture-perfect surroundings and don't care about being at Bequia's heart, consider Spring Estates.

✤ **Frangipani** (Port Elizabeth, Bequia, St. Vincent, W.I.; 10 rooms) is one of my favorite inns because it has the courage to be exactly what it is and doesn't fuss a lot to become something others may think it should be. What it is is the childhood home of James "Son" Mitchell, Premier of St. Vincent a few years ago and still active in political and public life. He, his Canadian wife Pat, and her friend Marie Kingston are the trio who own/run this inn. The rooms in the main shoreside building are simple, with bath down the hall from the 6 rooms in the main house. Behind the open-to-breezes gathering spot there are a couple of cement-block cottages with rooms-with-bath and modern conveniences for fussier travelers who want more privacy than a room in the house affords. When you sit by the sea, sipping a cool rum punch dusted with fresh grated nutmeg and waiting for your lobster salad, all will seem right with the world. Frangipani has been a yachtsmen's haven for a decade or more, a place for barefoot and boating types that has become one of the world's few constants. Rates this winter for 2 with 2 meals daily per person will range from about $50 to $70, a fee the Mitchells can list because the place has its following.

✤ **Friendship Bay** (Bequia, St. Vincent, W.I.; 30 rooms), on a cove it calls its own, is a place where time stands still, but owner Captain

Niels Peter Thomsen, USCG Retired, certainly does not. He is the personality for this special place, with its Maine woods camp style and simple rooms, each with a private porch and spectacular view. Favored by doctors and other professional types who want (require) peace and quiet and no telephone/telex intrusions, Friend ship Bay has a long list of repeaters and a sign that was posted near the door admitted: "All our visitors bring us happiness. Some by coming, some by going." Captain Thomsen's yacht rides at anchor offshore, and there's one tennis court (not the greatest) if you think you have to play. Rates for 2 this winter are $120 and more for all meals and island isolation. For these simple surroundings, the price seems high to me.

✢ **Sunny Caribbee** (Bequia, St. Vincent, W.I.; 17 cabanas, plus 8 rooms in main house) was purchased by British-based Arawak Resorts Ltd. toward the end of '78. Paint and scrub brushes have been put to use, and the place looked better than ever when I sailed in. The small enclave stretches along the shore at Port Elizabeth so that you can walk along the water's edge, depending on what the sea has done, to get to the main dock. Started as a hotel by Gerry and Jan Palmer who used this place for a while as their escape hatch from "cosmopolitan" St. Vincent, Sunny Caribee has had its ups and downs since then. This is a casual, comfortable place for sea-oriented folk who want to spend their time stretched out at the shore, perched on stool at the seaside pavilion, or snorkeling and sailing somewhere else. The cottages that parallel the shore are simply furnished, with sea-breeze cooling and private bath. In the main house, the few rooms each have their own personality, perked to perfection by the tone and homey touches of the main-floor rooms. A nice place for a quiet, sea-oriented holiday, Sunny Caribbee charges $50 to $100 for 2, 2 meals daily per person this winter. Some entertainment is planned for a few evenings at height of winter season, but don't head here expecting a lot of action. This place is ideal for self-sufficient types who want creature comforts in a Caribbean setting, with someone else worrying about what's being served for dinner.

■■■
HOUSEKEEPING HOLIDAYS ON BEQUIA can (and do) involve house owning for a handful of people who have found this island and love it. There are several small places to rent; some should be surveyed when you spend your first vacation on Bequia from a base

at one of the hotels. For those who know and like island life, where entertainment options are natural, here's a pair of places to investigate for a holiday home of your own:

✠ **Spring Estates** (Bequia, St. Vincent, W.I.; 12 rooms in several cottages) stepped back onto the top of my "beds on Bequia" list when it reopened with new owners in early '79. Started as a self-sufficient resort estate in 1968, the place once again thrives as a 28-acre plantation, where homegrown fruits and vegetables will appear at the dinner table, along with fresh lobster plucked from Bequia's shores or some other fish that have been brought in by a guest or a Bequian. Meals are served in typical tropical style, in an open-to-breezes-and-view dining room. The houses vary in shape, size, and location, but most cluster like chicks around the mother hen (main house). A half-dozen people can overnight in comfort at the Great House; others bed down in the Hawk's Nest, the Fortress, the Little Fort, and Sea Gull, all within a short walk of the main building, and each one a quiet, peaceful, stone-built home of your own. All houses are comfortably furnished; each has a terrace/patio and large hammock, and most can be used as separate rooms if you and your friends don't fill—or want—the small house. For self-sufficient types who enjoy the semblance of luxury, Spring is a place to settle in, but know before you go that your "hot" water shower is sun-warmed and evening light is sometimes (when power fails) only by kerosene lamp. Rates this winter will be $100 to $150 for 2, 2 meals daily per person included, and no one who has made the excursion to get to Bequia should be fazed by the 20-minute ride on a rutted and winding road to get to this north-end estate. The cement slab that poses as a tennis court is used by some hardy souls whose thermostat can stand the steady sun. Plans for a pool were progressing when I visited, and it will provide a cool-off point closer to your room than the shoreside sand.

Private Homes available for rent in owner's absence, can give you an independent base. Caribbean Home Rentals (Box 710, Palm Beach, FL 33480) lists a couple of properties near Friendship Bay in their roster of homes for rent. One property with 3 sections is ideal if you want privacy while you are part of a group. The master bedroom and bath are in a separate building, as are the other 2 bedrooms, each with bath, and all the conversation and cavorting can take place in the main house, with living room that looks out over the sundeck and spectacular view. Known as "B" on Bequia on the CHR listings, the property for 3 couples rents for about $500 per week; if you're a family with children, cost is only $350 per week, year round.

■■■

SPORTS ON BEQUIA will be sea-centered. There may be professional scuba firms by the time you arrive, but if it's crucial to your holiday fun, be sure to contact the hotel of your choice with specific questions about exactly what facilities are available, certification of the instructors, and quality of equipment. **Snorkeling** is spectacular off almost every cove. There are several places best reached by boat, and anyone at Frangipani or the other hotels can put you aboard something to get around to the best reefs.

Yachts bob at anchor in the harbor. Although the fleet changes, you can assume there will be something in port, and that arrangements can be made for at least a day sail, if not for longer. If you want to be sure of a charter, contact the CSY marina or Heritage Yachts at St. Vincent to have a specific contract for your time.

Do not count on golf, tennis (although there is one court at Friendship Bay), or organized sports. This is not an "organized" island—and there are those of us who love it because of that fact.

■■

TREASURES AND TRIFLES ON BEQUIA are led by **Crab Hole,** started by Linda Lewis and purchased in late '79 by Carolyn and George Porter, who have hired Barbara Station as manager. The shop continues to produce, with the help of the Bequians, marvelous, colorful appliqué designs as well as silk-screen work and other high-quality crafts, and the expanded selection makes a visit even more interesting than before. There isn't anything in this small seaside shop (which you can reach by walking to the shore between Caribbee and Frangipani) that I wouldn't like to own—and it is worth dropping anchor in port just to see what is for sale.

Canouan

Arrival on Canouan is best by boat. That route gives you plenty of time to slow down so that you can move at the local pace. The M.V. *Siemstrand* chugs through the Grenadines with freight and passengers twice weekly. Arrival is scheduled (as I write, but that may change) for Monday and Thursday in Canouan, with departures north for St. Vincent on Tuesdays and Fridays. Alternative route is to fly to Barbados, to charter to fly to the airstrip on Canouan, or to fly to St. Vincent from Barbados and then arrange for a small plane flight.

✝ **Crystal Sands Beach Hotel** (c/o Canouan Post Office, Canouan, St. Vincent, W.I.; 10 rooms) opened in December 1977 as the first place with overnight accommodations for visitors. Mr. and Mrs. Phileus de Roche, natives of Canouan, know why *they* like their island, and do what they can to help you see things the same way. The main building has the small reception area, with the dining room and the place for whatever the evening entertainment happens to be (often it's just the other guests). Plans for the tennis court and mini-golf had not materialized when I visited, but they may be there when you are. If it's important, check first. Daytime entertainment focuses on swimming, sailing, snorkeling, and scuba if you've brought your own equipment and are proficient (no facilities/teaching for beginners). There are 10 rooms in 5 villas; each room mirrors the next, with twin beds, private entrance, private bath and comfortable—not lavish—beach-oriented surroundings. Rates this winter are $65 for 2, breakfasts and dinners included. The place may not be your idea of chic, but it is certainly comfortable.

Mustique

Arrival on Mustique is accomplished in a small plane or a seaworthy boat. People are flown in direct from Martinique or via St. Vincent and/or Barbados, depending on what's convenient for you and the size of your group. A round-trip Air Martinique flight from that French West Indian isle has been about 500 French francs.

✝ **Cotton House** (Mustique, Grenadines, St. Vincent, W.I.; 19 rooms) captures the prize spot on the 3-by-1½-mile island it occupies. The island was pushed to prestigious planes by Hon. Colin Tennant, who opened the main house as a private club in 1968. He held the helm through the early days of development, when the late Oliver Messel's considerable decorating talents were lavished on the verandas and public rooms of the 18th-century farm buildings he transformed. The public was invited to stay here beginning in 1972, in one of the several 18th-century houses or new ones built to look like them around the main building. They hold most of the twin-bedded, air-conditioned guest rooms. (You won't need the air conditioning; the overhead fans are enough.) About ¼ mile from the main house, at Ansecoy Bay, there's a beach cottage nestled in the palms—and it is its own resort, for rent with a maid and an assurance of privacy. The swimming pool supplements the sandy coves, and the special atmosphere here now has a layer of French, gleaned from Guy de la Houssaye, owner of Martinique's Bakoua Hotel and, since 1977, the lessee of this island resort. You can count on a houseparty atmosphere, with French flair, on this island and the same kind of carefree holiday that lured Princess Margaret here for more than one headline-making assignation. Manager Simone Boye sees to that. Rates for this winter are about $250 for 2, 2 meals per person included, in keeping with the exorbitant charges in the French West Indies. You can count on daytime activities to be beach- and sun-oriented, with options for sailing.

■■

HOUSEKEEPING HOLIDAYS ON MUSTIQUE are a special brand. If you want to live in the style of royalty, rent Princess Margaret's house, Le Jolies Eaux, between Geliceaux beach and Deep Bay; it has 3 large bedrooms, plus one smaller one, all opening out onto the center courtyard, which leads to a terrace. The living room, at the "back" of the terrace, has a dining terrace of its own (with table that can seat 12) as well as sundeck and balcony surrounding the room for maximum sightseeing. The view is spectacular, and the beach that stretches out at your feet is "the island's best beach" according to some. You can walk to any one of a selection of sandy coves, or use the car that comes with your week's renting. Cost for height of season is about $1500, with staff; after April 15, rates drop to $1050, which isn't a lot when you consider that you can live like a princess.

Les Jolies Eaux and a couple of other elegant houses, all built with island stone, wood, and view, are available through Caribbean Home Rentals, Box 710, Palm Beach, FL 33480.

Palm Island

Arrival on Palm Island is best by sailboat, but if you're heading here from home, you'll probably travel the full-day route via Barbados with a flight charter on Tropicair Service (arranged by the hotel if they know when you are coming) to fly to Union Island, where you cross the one-mile span of sea in about 5 minutes by motorboat. The cost for the Tropicair flight on a "share charter" basis is about $90 per person each way.

✣ **Palm Island Beach Club** (Palm Island, Grenadines, St. Vincent, W.I.; 20 rooms plus villas) is testimony to the dream—and hard work—of John and Mary Caldwell. (Try to track down a copy of *Desperate Voyage,* John Caldwell's book about sailing for 106 days over 8500 miles in a small boat with 2 kittens for company, from Panama to Australia to pick up Mary as his wife.) This 110-acre island was known (and still is known on many charts) as Prune Island, but its rebirth as Palm Island Resort was in 1968 when the first rooms were built and the small inn began accepting overnighters who came ashore from yachts. An airstrip, no longer used, was built in the early stages, and the tennis court plus the provisioning shop if you want to cook at home in one of the separate villas were added as time permitted. What's here now is a place that appeals to fresh-air types who like "roughing it" with creature comforts. While Palm Island may lack some of the luxury of nearby Petit St. Vincent, the casual, comfortable Caldwell atmosphere offers its own special brand of hospitality. Bring some books, your snorkel mask and fins (if your own are your favorites), and languish seaside for a relaxing vacation. The evening entertainment is as lively as the guests, and there's an occasional barbecue, perhaps with a band if one happens to sail by. A special sailing package holiday gives you a beach villa and a sailboat to sail on your own or with a crew (your pleasure). An innovative summer package for 1981 carried a tally of $450 per day for 4 people on a boat and $310.50 for 4 on land. Check for winter versions if it sounds interesting. A villa with no hotel services for your land stay lowers the cost. If you want to stay on land, your choices are the Beach Club building that runs like a beachside hotel or one of the several housekeeping villas with maid/cook. Among the villas for rent are Rum Corner or Tropical Villa (2 bedrooms near the beach), Palm Villa or Sea Villa (2 bedrooms on the beach), and Sun Villa (4 bedrooms on the beach). Contact the Caldwells for details, and count on a nautical nook.

Petit St. Vincent

Arrival on Petit St. Vincent is the end of an excursion. By the time you settle into your cottage, you will have packed and parted from your hometown, flown to Barbados to connect, hopefully expediently, with a charter on Tropicair for the 45-minute flight to Union Island where the PSV boat meets you for the 20-minute ride (included in your tariff) to the shore where you can climb (or ride the jeep) to your cottage. And after that, you deserve the pampered and perfect vacation you will get.

✣ **Petit St. Vincent Resort** (Petit St. Vincent, Grenadines, St. Vincent, W.I.; 22 cottages) is just about perfect. It's picked as one of the "ten to try for top luxury" for good reason: Hazen and Jennifer Richardson's ability to create a climate for warm and welcoming hospitality, and Willis Nichols's willingness to do what's necessary to keep this isolated idyll as faultless as possible. The 113-acre luxury platter is fluted with white-gold powdery beaches (a Grenadine trademark); the stone cottages have been built for privacy and view and are punctuated with colors that accent the sea that surrounds. Your cottage of blue-bitch stone with huge room and nice patio was designed by Swede Arne Hasselquist; the view was designed by God. Mr. Nichols proudly reports that 95.7% of his vacationers "said that as a vacation spot PSV met or far exceeded their expectations" and "95.6% said the staff was friendly, well- trained, and helpful." (Of the 175 questionnaires sent out to survey the guests, 113 were returned, which impressed the ownership—and impresses me too, even if we both assume that the questionnaires were sent to people who were known to have enjoyed themselves at PSV.) This is a special place for the world's weary-and-wealthy to revive flagging spirits, with a camaraderie that is helped along by the excursion to reach the place. There's a sense of "Outward Bound" that unites the guests.

There are no phones to bother you, a red flag on your mailbox brings a member of the staff who will then bring whatever it is you've flagged for, and tennis, badminton, snorkeling, Sunfish (6 of them), a 16-foot sailboat, glass-bottom boats with outboards, and ping-pong, horseshoes, darts, volleyball, and a choice of even more remote islands to sail to and stretch out on are part of your holiday package. What more could you ask for? Rates listed for room and 3 meals daily include use of all the resort's equipment, but you'll have to put on your glasses and take some time to figure out the exact charge, which changes almost monthly. The resort stayed open through August for the first time in 1980 and continues to do so, when the lowest rates ($166 per couple, all-inclusive) prevail, and many perceptive Europeans seem to have found this Eden. Other good value periods are November 1 through December 18 and April 22 through August 31, when you'll pay $166 per couple. Peak seasons are December 19 through January 7 and February 1 through March 15, when the going rate is $276 for 2; January 8–31 and March 16 through April 21 is $244 for 2, full American plan (all meals). Check with the office in Cincinnati, Ohio (Box 12506) for details, but you can count on getting what you pay for here. (10% is added for tips, 5% is tallied for the Vincentian government hotel tax, and personal checks are accepted.

Union Island

Arrival on Union island can be by plane, yacht, or by the interisland mail boat that starts (or ends) its run at St. Vincent. Clifton Harbour is the island's main town, but it's a speck by comparison to other places you've seen in these islands. The only other "village" of note is Ashton, on the south shore, but it's the beaches (and the airstrip) that draw some folk here. In addition to being the jumping-off point for vacationers heading to Petit St. Vincent and Palm Island, Union has a couple of overnighting spots of its own.

This small island's claim to fame is its December '79 "rebellion," which I "witnessed" from nearby Carriacou. I sat on the terrace at Mermaid Inn, enchanted by the sight of Union, peaceful and majestic, set in the Caribbean sea an easy sailing distance away. Two days later, when I returned to Grenada, the pilot of my plane told of his flight into the grass strip on Palm Island, usually "off limits" for planes since the surface is not well kept. He had followed a Tropicair pilot onto the "strip," and his passenger list included police from St. Vincent, who had to cross to Union to quell the "rebellion" of a handful of renegades. Jokes on Carriacou about the "marijuana marines" brought laughter to all who know the islands well, and no one locally seemed to waste much time worrying about a serious "revolution." Prime Minister Milton Cato declared a "state of emergency" for St. Vincent and its Grenadines, as much to curb any over-enthusiastic malcontents (displeased with the elections that returned Cato to office with a landslide vote) as for any other reason.

■■

HOTELS ON UNION are small and special places, geared to the sea and a casual, nautical life. All are at beaches, and not one has more than a dozen rooms. Count on simple surroundings, and a do-what-you-want-to, Robinson Crusoe kind of life.

✛ **Anchorage Hotel** (Clifton Harbour, Union Island, St. Vincent Grenadines, W.I.; 10 rooms) answers the needs of the nautical types. Nesting at the northern rim of the harbor, the land-based Anchorage provides a haven for yachtsmen who replenish some stocks at the pier facilities. (A recent sightseeing attraction of dubious value has been the pools where sharks play!) You may want to test the water for swimming elsewhere. Count on rates of about $135 for 2, with 2 meals daily per person.

✢ **Clifton Beach Hotel** (on the beach, Union Island, St. Vincent Grenadines, W.I.; 10 rooms) sets you at the sands, in boxy stucco rooms, with simple furnishings. Rates are reasonable, and life is casual. Count on about $50 for 2, with 2 meals daily per person.

✢ **Sunny Grenadines** (on the beach, Union Island, St. Vincent, Grenadines, W.I.; 8 rooms) settles at the shore, parallel to Union Island's small airstrip. This is the place that Frenchman Andre Beaufrand carved out of virgin sands about the same time he sponsored the first airstrip for the island. Rates this winter will be about $50 for 2, with 2 meals daily included.

Trinidad

Trinidad & Tobago Tourist Board, 56 Frederick St., Port of Spain, Trinidad, W.I.; 400 Madison Ave., New York, NY 10017; Suite 702, 200 S.E. First St., Miami, FL 33131; York Centre, 145 King St. West & University Ave., Toronto, Ontario M5H 1J8, Canada; 20 Lower Regent St., London SW1Y 4PH.

US$1 = TT$2.40
Unless otherwise noted, $ refers to U.S. currency.

Humphrey Bogart could have sauntered with confidence down Frederick Street to Independence Square in Port of Spain, brushing shoulders with East Indians, West Indians, Chinese, Africans, South Americans, French, British, Portuguese, Lebanese, Syrians and a handful of mid-Europeans, the melange that makes this city so special. He could have dallied, as we all do, at some downtown roti stand, where one "chef," sometimes serving through a chicken-wire "screen," hands you the crepe-thin pancake that is folded around spicy, curried shrimp, chicken, beef, or some other stuffing. Some of the roti stands are small buses or trucks that have been turned into possibly mobile snack stops, that don't seem to move from their place at Independence Square.

Roti stands nest amid department stores, yard goods outlets, and luxury shops that sell crystal, china, and other European imports along with gold that is fashioned into jewelry in the workshops upstairs. And the roti stands are sometimes patched on the side of well-known restaurants, where the take-out counter caters to those who want just snack food; they are never far from even the most luxurious Port of Spain restaurants, those places that are in trimmed up traditional houses, where hanging plants, historic pictures, and an elegant aura vie with the cuisine for your attention. (And where the cost for a dinner is almost 200 times the cost of a roti which can make a reasonable supper.)

The best way to respond to Trinidad's special tempo, which is overwhelming to the uninitiated, is slowly. A first look is best from afar: the hillside Hilton's terrace or the top of the downtown Holiday Inn, overlooking Queen's Park Savannah and the seething city with huge ships at anchor in its port. This is a country of contrasts. Rugged, jutting mountains plunge to the seaside. There's the Asa Wright Nature Center (walks, talks, and simple accommodations), the Caroni Swamp Bird Sanctuary (boats coast through to spot the scarlet ibis), and one of the West Indies' most cosmopolitan capitals at bubbling Port of Spain.

Elsie Lee Heung tossed her head back, almost closed her eyes, and summoned stillness to set the stage for the vivid images swirling through her mind. "Oh," she began, "Carnival is people. Carnival is a means of escape. Carnival is something I look forward to." Her dark eyes flashed; the pace of her conversation increased, like the Carnival festivities would from fall through the weeks before the big event, the two days before Ash Wednesday. Even Elsie Lee Heung's gold hoop earrings hinted of Carnival costumes as they glittered in the sunlight that crept into her small office, cluttered with costumes—the heart of a "mas" (masquerade) camp. On a side street in a residential section of Port of Spain, Elsie Lee Heung's office is the womb for one of the most astounding of Trinidad's famous Carnival bands.

"Nobody in his right mind should try to analyze [carnival]. It is all movement. It is the sun, wind, music pulsating, smell, vibration, colour, costume, sparkle, sweat, impact, confusion and bodies which saturate the senses," claims J. Newel Lewis in his booklet, which I bought at the airport. Carnival is a kind of exorcism. Weeks, months of preparation, tireless work on intricate costumes, much of the labor volunteer, go into the two days of Carnival. And by Ash Wednesday morning, all is in a heap. Costumes lie crumpled, perhaps broken, in the street. Portions have been given (or plucked) away during the festivities. Seldom does anything but the memory remain. There's no place to store bulky costumes; the remnants are last year's project—and that seems to be the way Trinidadians feel about their country's history. The British past is last year's project; Trinidadians are working on "next year's" plans—and those include a dominant role in the Caribbean Third World countries.

■■

POLITICAL PICTURE: On March 29, 1981, Prime Minister, Sir Eric E. I. Williams, leader of his country for 25 years, died. The Prime Minister had ruled his country apparently "single handedly," leaving no obvious successor. His People's National Movement (PNM) was elected to power in 1956, and he led his people through the ill-fated West Indies Federation to independence, as the nation of Trinidad & Tobago, in August 1962. Under terms of the constitution of the Republic of Trinidad & Tobago, President Ellis Clarke, the country's highest public official, appointed Dr. Williams' successor: George M. Chambers, former Minister of Trade, Industry, Agriculture, and Tourism. Elections will have been called, according to the British system, by the time this edition is published, but it is impossible at press time to do more than define some facts and mention key candidates.

Prime Minister Chambers set about immediately to address some of the problems of the 2-island country. Obvious problems involve the country's infrastructure (telephones, roadways, public transportation, housing, etc.), but most Trinidadians seem to acknowledge that the country desperately needs more efficiency with the highly paid labor force, delegation of authority (a situation relatively unknown under Dr. Williams' years of leadership), accountability for work, and decentralization of responsibility. In addition, it is felt in some quarters that the TT dollar is grossly overvalued, making international commerce difficult. The country's wealth from oil, asphalt, and the new steel mill has led to affluence unknown in other Caribbean countries, but a "distaste" for hard work leaves gaps in Trinidad & Tobago's development.

In addition to Prime Minister George Chambers, as leader of the PNM, the list of candidates for the top office includes Karl Hudson-Phillips, as leader of the relatively new Organization for National Reconstruction (ONR), and the leaders of three fragmented parties Tapia, ULF, and DAC, that have linked as the Treaty of Three and seem to have a following among segments of the population.

According to figures given in the New York Times, the 1.2 million people of Trinidad & Tobago are comprised of 43% black, 40% East Indian, and 17% "all other" (whites, Chinese, and Syrians).

AUTHOR'S OBSERVATION: Trinidad & Tobago has two good newspapers, if you want to be informed about local and Caribbean news. The *Trinidad Guardian* follows a conservative pattern, and the *Express*, has a more sensational style. A daily purchase of either (or both) will supply facts for putting this country (and its neighbors) in perspective.

■■

CUSTOMS OF TRINIDAD vary depending on the area of the country. Cosmopolitan Port of Spain, the capital, is the most fascinating city in the Caribbean. It is a port city, with the large strands of commerce woven into the tapestry of customs that keeps Indians, Asians, Africans, Europeans, North Americans, and others mixing and mingling on the streets and in shops and restaurants. Many cultures follow the traditions of their homelands, sometimes adapting Oriental fishing festivals, for example, to the Trinidadian countryside, or the Hindu marriage rites to the dirt roads of small villages. Port of Spain is a "formal" city, not necessarily in the coat-and-tie sense (although that, too, was the case until the ubiquitous shirt-jac became the style a few years ago), but certainly in the sense of formal business procedures. It is customary to make appointments, even though they often run on Caribbean time—late.

Trinidad is not the typical tourist island. Trinidadians know prosperity from oil, natural gas, a steel plant, many small businesses, and big plans for petrochemical industries. And yet, public services (transportation, telephone, water, electricity) are in such disarray as to be archaic at best and amazingly inefficient at worst. Too much has come too fast. The nation takes itself seriously in many ways, although few Trinidadians appear to respect the value of "a hard day's work," there is, however, a sense of humor that is uniquely Trinidadian. No one knows how to have a good time better than West Indians, and the pre-Lenten carnival in Trinidad sets a pace unmatched in the Caribbean. Some say that the exuberance of Trinidad's Carnival is close to that of Rio, with equally elaborate costumes and lively street marches.

AUTHOR'S OBSERVATION: If you want to know about Trinidad's Carnival before you attend one, be sure to track down a copy of Erroll Hill's excellent and informative *Trinidad Carnival: A Mandate for National Theatre*, published by the University of Texas Press, Austin, Texas. Also interesting is the annual Carnival guide. Copies of the previous year's guide are sometimes available through the Tourist Board offices.

Clothes are warm-weather conservative, with "proper" attire on the streets of Port of Spain and around the countryside. This is not a city for shorts and resort wear; it is a place where suits, shirt-jacs, and sometimes short-sleeved shirts are the businessman's "uniform," and skirts and blouses, or conservative dresses are the daily wear for women. For evenings at most restaurants in Port of Spain, clothes are dark colors, but not formal. Pantsuits are not popular. Polyester is hot in the tropics, and while evening pants appear at some after-dark affairs, they are usually partially covered with elegant, fashionable tops. Long skirts are still worn at some places (and certainly at formal business or government receptions). As a general rule, conservative can't go wrong.

■■■

MONEY MATTERS: The local currency is Trinidad & Tobago dollars and cents, pegged to the U.S. dollar at TT$2.40 to US$1. After arrival at the airport make your first stop the National Commercial Bank, conveniently located just after you pass through customs. (There's a TT$2 charge per transaction at the bank.) Traveler's checks get a slightly higher rate than bills. You can change money at the hotel, at banks, or, when you are in Port of Spain, at the bank near the Tourist Board offices, on Frederick Street. Do not expect Trinidadians to transact business in U.S. currency. For an occasional purchase, U.S. dollars will be accepted, but in the shops in this country, $ and ¢ refers to TT.

On hotel and restaurant bills, 10% is usually added for service, although the section for "service charge" is deceivingly blank. Ask, if you're unsure about whether or not service had been included in the total, or risk overtipping by more than twice the expected/accepted amount.

■■■

ARRIVAL at Trinidad's Piarco International Airport is orderly, and more efficient than it used to be now that Piarco has been cloned. (Although there are slow lines for immigration formalities here, as there are at most Caribbean and U.S. airports.) In summer of '79, the terminal was doubled in size. The original part, completed in the late '50s, was spruced up, and the new wing helps take care of the increased traffic pouring through this terminal. Beautiful? It is not. Functional and more than adequate? It is, and the procedures are the usual ones.

Immigration officials are businesslike when you hand them your immigration card with your proof of citizenship and passport. You may be asked to show your return ticket (to prove you will not be a drain on the economy), and to advise your local address. When you've claimed your luggage, head for the taxi dispatcher, and ask the fare for reaching your destination. (The taxi drivers that I've encountered that sidle up to you offering their services are not above overcharging outrageously.) Make a quick stop at the Trinidad & Tobago Tourist Board airport office for a map, another discussion of taxi fares, and some advice about anything special that is taking place while you will be in the country.

Your taxi fare into Port of Spain will be about TT$35, for a 45-minute ride. Count on traffic jams (a fact to remember when you are catching your plane for departure). The road between the airport and downtown is a knotted route that has been a driving hazard for 20-plus years that I have known it, and there's no improvement in sight. The eventual solution will be a 6-lane road that can take the considerable industrial traffic (big trucks) plus the people trying to go home or get to work—and *that* "dance" takes place 4 times daily since most people still go home for lunch in this country. Be forewarned if you have to catch a plane in early morning, midday, or after 4:30. Allow plenty of time—at least an hour from downtown.

Departure from Piarco takes stamina. Reconfirm your flight when you *arrive* in Port of Spain, and again by telephone (if you can get through) or at the downtown or hotel ticket office, and be sure to check in early. Planes from Port of Spain are often crowded, especially at peak travel times, and the cluster that convenes around the ticket counters can include a lot of people who have been waiting "for days" as well as you with your valid ticket.

In addition to the expected liquor and perfume shops, just before you have cleared immigration, there are flowers for sale (packaged to comply with U.S. Dept. of Agriculture restrictions) and a place where you can get a haircut or shampoo and set if you've allowed enough time—or your plane is late. But be forewarned: You will have to carry your hand luggage plus purchases up 3 banks of narrow stairs to the vast room that serves as departure lounge—and then down another stairway to ground level, before climbing up again to board your plane!

■■■

TOURING TIPS: Trinidad is "huge" and varied. First-time travelers will do best to link up with a good taxi driver, to learn lore as well as sightseeing lanes. It's difficult for the novice to find what's where, and you may be so independent that you miss all the highlights. Parking in downtown Port of Spain is "impossible." Even walking has its hazards, with all the building and bustle that goes on in this fascinating city. (There is a TT$40 fine for parking illegally in Port of Spain, and almost no place to park legally!)

When you step away from customs (and have changed your money to TT$), you've arrived. Taxi drivers stand at the ramp from Piarco's air terminal and proffer services. Be sure you know the going rate for your route. The 45-minute ride from Piarco to the Port of Spain and/or the Hilton is about TT$35 at press time, but ask at the Tourist Office.

For top service in a comfortable car (Buick with all the trimmings, including comfortable gray-blue upholstery) make arrangements for Samuel Tagallie. His car number is HAA 44; he can be found at the Hilton; and if you want to be sure of his services in advance, a letter to him c/o Hilton Hotel will reach him.

If you've signed on for one of the special promotion packages, chances are at least a half-day of touring is included. Take it. In this 2-island country, there *are* many sights to see, and to learn about. Hub Travel Ltd., with a desk at the Hilton and offices elsewhere, gives "standard" tours, usually by taxi unless you're part of a big group, so that you are relatively inconspicuous when you travel from here to there. (Cars are a fact of life in Trinidad, where many people are making good money—and gas costs a paltry TT$.1 for an imperial gallon, which figures—hold your breath—to about 40¢ US.)

If you want to rent a car, you can do so on your credit card, at rates geared to large profit for the rental company. You'll pay TT$90 per day, plus TT$10 for a minimum 2-day insurance coverage, plus your gas costs. In addition, you'll be expected to post a TT$300 deposit against any car damage. Although you'll get the deposit back when you return the car in good condition, you will then have an "extra" TT$300 to squander before you leave the country unless you've posted your bond on your credit card.

▪▪▪

HOTELS ON TRINIDAD are not the standard Caribbean resort style. For one thing, there's no beach at Port of Spain; you have to speed by boat to the islands off the northwest coast or by car to Maracas Bay, zigzagging up and over the spine of mountains that runs out the finger of land that is the northern peninsula of Trinidad. For another, fellow guests are often businessmen, frequent visitors from Caracas and other Caribbean countries as well as from North America and Europe. Trinidad has plans for opening new, small hotels, the first for several seasons. The country had concentrated on filling the hotels already built, and accommodating some essential needs of the local population, rather than jumping on the build-up-big bandwagon that has roared through most of the rest of the Caribbean over the past several years. Be sure to inquire (from your travel agent or the Tourist Board) about the special package tours that are available year around. Combination holidays (time on each island) are available at good value. "Just the Two of Us" packages, inspired and promoted by the Trinidad & Tobago Tourist Board, give extras such as tours, parties, and some meals along with a package hotel rate.

Trinidad's hotels are unique in the Caribbean, for offering as many styles of hospitality as there are strands in the country's multiracial, multiculture heritage. No two are alike. Many places on Trinidad are geared to business traffic, while the properties on Tobago specialize in the beach, golf, scuba diving, snorkeling, and tennis life. Hotel bills carry a 10% service charge and a 3% government tax.

AUTHOR'S AWARDS for Trinidad go to the Hilton for offering an imposing, hospitable hotel and staff at a unique hillside site, with the best view of Port of Spain, and to Chaconia, where Ken Duval has created a very special small hotel with the best advantages of a country inn.

✣ **Balandra Bay** (17 New Yalta, Diego Martin, Trinidad, W.I.; 44 units) boasts of big plans and counts on continued prosperity for the Trinidadian economy to realize them. The ambitious 572-acre project is to be a total resort, a dream that probably will not be a reality for about 20 years, according to my prediction. What was underway when I surveyed for this edition was the first part of a challenging golf course and the basic structures—4 blocks with 12 units in each of 2, and 10 units in each of 2 others—for condominiums that will be rented to outsiders in owners' absence. (The first 44 units had all been sold at time of building.) Restricted to ownership by Trinidadian nationals, the units have 2 bedrooms, 2½ bathrooms, kitchen, living room, and view of the sea. The first units also have a view over the 14th and 17th greens. A central clubhouse is available for convening and has minimal restaurant facilities. The natural honey-colored beach, a distance from the first units, is planned for "improvement," but was rough with rugged surf when I saw it. (A tennis complex is planned for future development near the beach.) Rates had not been set, and units looked as though they might not be ready for occupancy before early '82. Balandra

Bay is on the east coast, about 2 hours' drive from Port of Spain (or 1½ hours from Piarco Airport) on good roads. A rental car is essential to avoid complete isolation.

✦ **Bel Air International Hotel** (Piarco Airport, Trinidad, W.I.; 57 rooms) is one of those rare oases that travelers experienced with outpost areas know well. No timid travelers or top luxury aficionados should darken these doors unless they're prepared for a unique experience. The hotel is alongside the runway. Probably because the air conditioner in my room made such a racket (but its presence was essential since that was the only way to get air without leaving the door open), the airplane noises do not seem overwhelming. The hotel has been here "forever," or at least since the earliest regular air services. Paint covers the scars of ages; shower heads may be missing (but the compensation is that the water spurts out of the shower spigot in more or less one direction). The stopper in my sink was missing, as were miscellaneous items in the rooms of others I spoke with, but the group that convenes here, usually by virtue of travel plans, is made up of people "on the move." A courtesy car will shuttle you from the airport terminal to the Bel Air (ask the Tourist Office for someone to call for the car if you don't see it coming when you stand at the curb). Overnight rates range from $40 to $50 for 2, meals extra, and all kinds of airline personnel and others get special rates. Singh's office in the small lobby, around the corner from check-in, can arrange rental cars. The pool, through doors to the right of the check-in desk, takes on added appeal in the midst of a day of touring, and rooms around its edges are the top rate (and equipped with tv). Rooms 42 through 48 also have tv and television is available for other rooms at a TT$3 charge. The big surprise here is the restaurant, recently redecorated with an enthusiasm that put the previous owner in bankruptcy, I was told. The candlelight at night and the glow from Tiffany-style lamps over the booths that line the front of the restaurant set a nice tone, and the food was certainly acceptable. The lounge next to the restaurant has U-shaped, white-plastic-covered banquettes for gathering with your group, and an outside terrace area, with tables and chairs set to watch the plane action, is a much more comfortable lingering spot than the nearby airport, if you have a delayed flight.

✦ **Chaconia Inn** (106 Saddle Road, Maraval, Port of Spain, Trinidad, W.I.; 48 rooms) backs up to the mountains in the suburb of Maraval and gives you a small, modern hotel to call home. The complex of stucco buildings is partially hidden behind the front entrance wall with Chaconia Inn "written" in the special logo of the hotel. When you've parked your car (or the taxi driver has parked his), you'll walk past the reception desk into the pool area, an oasis at heat-of-the-day in suburban Port of Spain. Furnishings are modern, with TV available for most rooms, and kitchenettes in 16. All rooms are air-conditioned, some have better views (over the pool with a peek at the mountains) than others, and there are 10 2-bedroom suites if you're a family of 4 or more. A ribbon of rooms rims the road on the opposite side from the main complex. The restaurant serves Trinidadian and international (steaks, chicken) food. *The Baron* pub is dark, and a drawing card for Trinidadians who know and like this spot; the roof patio is used for special barbecues and open-air dining at modern plastic tables with gently curving chairs—perched like chessmen on a black and white checkerboard floor. The inn is managed by genial Ken Duval, a leader in the Trinidad & Tobago Hotel Association and staunch supporter of the Caribbean Hotel Association. Find him for some suggestions of special Trinidadian places to go when you're ready to move from the pool. Rates this winter are $65 for 2.

✤ **Farrell House** (Point Lisas, southwest, Trinidad, W.I.; 57 rooms with more planned) will be renovated and ready for the businessmen who come to this area sometime in the "near future." Part of a comprehensive rebuilding plan, the hotel has "always" been a haven for oil men, here for meetings. Check about its status.

✤ **Gasparee Grande** (Gasparee Island, Trinidad, W.I.; 80 units) offers a special experience removed from the life of Port of Spain. Located on an island that has been favored by Trinidadians for their own getaway vacations for decades, the Gasparee Grande project includes independent villas, privately owned but for rent in owners' absence. There's a central building for food and social times, and a boat service link (from the jetty near the salt mills), but there's no "regular" scheduled boat service so be sure to advise "your" boatman about your plans to return to the mainland. The Island Home Owner's service at the jetty is the best place to check for details.

✤ **Holiday Inn** (Box 1017, Wrightson Road, Port of Spain, Trinidad, W.I.; 249 rooms) punctuates a part of portside Port of Spain that has been marked for redevelopment. The hotel was the first stage; the rest is slowly following. Modern and impressive, with its 14th-floor *La Ronde* restaurant sometimes revolving as it was built to do, the Holiday Inn gives one of the best overviews of the port activity—and the bonus of a view of the Venezuelan coast on clear days. The *Calypso Lounge* on the 12th floor, with carnival costumes as part of the decoration, is dark, air-conditioned, and except for the sunlit terrace, depressing, I thought, at midday. By night, with the city lights, the atmosphere is completely changed, but this hotel is best if you are part of a vacationing group or a businessman who knows his way around town. The reception area seems clinical to me, and the rooms follow the standard HI format, for size and facilities (including TV) with the 9 suites the most luxurious air-conditioned havens to call home. Fully booked at carnival times, when "mas" bands parade past the lobby doors and the parking lot is sometimes turned into a party scene. The pool provides the cooling-off place, popular at lunchtime for people who have to be in town. Other action options are limited to shuffleboard and dancing evenings when the band plays in the nightclub on the top floor. Rates this season settle at about $95 for 2, meals extra.

✤ **Kapok Hotel** (16–18 Cotton Hill, St. Clair, Port of Spain, Trinidad, W.I.; 65 rooms) stands about 8 stories tall on a side street just off Queen's Park Savannah, and a short walk from the zoo and the Botanic Gardens. The arcade of shops on the street level almost hide the lobby entrance, but the *Tiki Village* restaurant on the 8th floor (Polynesian style) makes it worthwhile going through the small lobby and up in the elevator even if you are not overnighting here. For those who check in, there's a small pool fringed with a cement sunning area at the back of the house, and 6 suites among the air-conditioned rooms that open off the carpeted halls. The first half of the hotel was completed in 1970, to be followed by a group of newer rooms, and some refurbishing in 1973 and replacing of carpets, plus painting and a general overhaul where needed for the season of '76. This is not a typical tourist hotel, nor is it a fancy spot, but the surroundings are suitable for businessmen and others who want the experience of Trinidad and easy access to downtown Port of Spain, plus good food at Tiki Village. Rates this season will be about $60 for 2, breakfasts and dinners daily.

✤ **Monique's** (114 Saddle Road, Maravel, Port of Spain, Trinidad, W.I.; 5 rooms) is a West Indian white house, a couple of doors down from Chaconia. It's a home that has stretched its walls and hospitality wide enough to make room for you and a handful of others who want to see the "real" Trinidad with some Trinidadians who are their country's perfect salesmen. The big time at the home of Michael and Monica Charbonne is the Carnival week, when rooms with breakfast for a week for 2 cost about $400 (and if the rooms at Monique's are gone, Michael Charbonne will send your name to others who may have space for you). The Charbonnes talk about adding more rooms, but at the moment a few of the simply furnished rooms are air-conditioned ($14 for 2) and others aren't ($12 for 2). You can get into downtown Port of Spain from residential Maravel on a "Pirate Taxi" for TT50¢ for the 10-minute ride, and the Charbonnes will show you how. (A Pirate Taxi is a car that travels a regular route, making stops for passengers along the way; it's the usual "bus" service for people who live in the country.) What you may miss in familiar hotel comforts (pool, etc.) you'll more than make up for with Trinidadian hospitality. (Arrangements can be made for you to use a nearby pool, which will probably be Chaconia's.)

✣ **Mount St. Benedict Guest House** (Tunapuna, Trinidad, W.I.; 11 rooms) never fails to enchant me, partly because of its location, nested in the mountains overlooking the plains, and partly because of people like Mona, who baked the cakes I had with my tea and "sandwiches." The inn is also known as the PAX Guest House and is a retreat, but a place that is not so heavy on its religious overtones that it need turn away the profligates. The first hut built on this hillside perch, way above the hubbub of Port of Spain—or even Tunapuna, was a 15-by-9-foot thatch-roofed structure built by monks who had fled oppression in Brazil in the early 1900s. When the Abbey of Mount St. Benedict celebrated its Diamond Jubilee in 1972, people came from cosmopolitan centers around this country and from faraway ports. The church, monastery, and school that cap this hill are a few steps above the guesthouse which is now operated by the Christian Council of Churches. Although all the rooms have sink, few have private bath. Furnishings are simple, but you can expect a neat and hospitable guesthouse in the best inn tradition. Meals are served family style from whatever is bought in town that day, in an open-to-the-breezes dining area overlooking a small courtyard garden and the view beyond, or in an enclosed room at the back of the house. Best rooms for view are 1 and 7, looking out over the valley and hills. A veranda runs along the front of the house, on the 2nd floor where you'll find the rooms. Anyone who finds himself at Piarco airport with a 2-hour or more delay between planes can find a real respite from downtown commerce by taking a cab for the 45-minute ride up to this hilltop spot. (Ask the cab to wait to take you back down, after you've walked around gardens and woods for a while.) Rates are $20 per person for room and 3 meals.

✢ **Oceanus Hotel** (Maracas Bay, Trinidad, W.I.; 40 rooms) has suffered the problems of Caribbean building schedules. The shell that stood when I surveyed for this edition, *might* be ready for occupancy in winter of '81–'82, but only if things start to move faster than they did when I looked in. The location, just inland from the beach at Maracas, and next to the small church, gives each room a sea view. Although the basic structure is 2-story motel-style (and not too imaginative), the balconies should offer pleasant book-reading space—and rooms will be furnished with the usual. Except for the restaurant down the beach at the main entrance for Maracas Bay, there are no choices for dining depots. You'll need a car for mobility, and check with the Tourist Office for cost and status.

✢ **Palmiste Hotel** (San Fernando, southwest Trinidad, W.I.) is still "hardly off the planning boards as we go to press," (a comment I made in last years edition) but it is expected to focus on the needs of the businessmen who come to this burgeoning oil and industry area. If you want to look into the non-tourist areas of this country, consider staying here—and contact the Tourist Board for an update on status, and information on rates.

✢ **Pelican Inn** (2 & 4 Coblentz Ave., Cascade, Trinidad, W.I.; 17 rooms) puts personality ahead of pristine surroundings. The two Victorian-style houses that hold the rooms turn over their ground floors to the *Pelican Pub* (with darts and draught beer among offerings), the *Peppermill* restaurant, and other public rooms. Bedrooms vary, from small and very simple to airy and comfortable for 2 people who don't demand luxury. The place has a lot of potential, but no one seems to focus on housekeeping. The surroundings you sit in have an "old shoe" atmosphere, and there are many repeat visitors who like that—and the modest $40 for 2 room rate. The place had reportedly been sold when I visited, but the atmosphere was akin to what it has always been; only the clientele had changed.

✢ **Queen's Park Hotel** (Queen's Park Savannah, Port of Spain, Trinidad, W.I.; 100 rooms) hasn't changed much in the past 85 years, and therefore didn't change much since my last year's comment. The hotel has been a Trinidadian tradition since 1895 when the original hotel was built. The Fernandez family, who have a lot of other interests (rum, for one), keep the hotel off the regular Trinidad & Tobago Tourist Board listing. Prices are geared to the many West Indians and Europeans who have been coming here for years, some for decades, and who will continue to return—as long as things don't change too much. The refurbishing in the mid-1950s added a bar/lounge (that has plastic-covered chairs and an other-world atmosphere), a few shops and tour desks in the lobby; not long after, a few (but not all) rooms were air-conditioned. And those have been the most recent changes here. As you enter the lobby, turn to the right for the open-air sitting area with a good view of the Savannah and a boys' soccer/football game if no more formal activity (perhaps a horse race) is scheduled in Queen's Park. This traditional hotel is a turn-of-the-century place, with high ceilings and minimal furnishings in the public rooms. Rooms are spartan; a hotel folder referred to the style as "Trinidad Moderne," with private, old-fashioned bath; most have air conditioning, but try for a room that also has a private porch. A pool punctuates the back garden, with pavilion and patio nearby, but do not expect the typical, American-style tourist trappings here. Queen's Park has not changed drastically in the past several decades, and it is not likely to do so this season. For room rates, write to Mr. Fernandez at the hotel.

✣ **Trinidad Hilton** (Box 442, Port of Spain, Trinidad, W.I.; 442 rooms) is tops among Caribbean hotels for those who want a place with a personality of its own, distinct from the overlay of expected sun-holiday features. The property captured the top of a hill and slants its rooms down the flank, making the hotel unique. The view over Queen's Park and Port of Spain is spectacular, especially at about 6 p.m. when the sun is setting. The "upside down" Hilton, where you go *down* to the 10th floor, and *up* from there to the first, moved into the season of 1961, giving Trinidad something to talk about in addition to its anticipated independence. From the opening of the first cluster of rooms that catered to visitors on this site, the Hilton has had its following. There are many who lounge by its pool or play on its tennis courts and claim they've seen Trinidad; that's not as strange as it sounds because most of affluent Trinidad comes to the Hilton Hotel, if not to drink, dine, and dance, then to do business with some of the salesmen and others who pass through these portals on regular forays to the independent 2-island nation. Although you'll find full resort facilities (tennis courts, pool, tour desk, shops, disco for dancing, coffee shop, potentially elegant *Le Boucan* dining room where food and service now fails to live up to the high praise I once gave this place, and a full complement of air-conditioned rooms with view), the atmosphere is far more substantial than the frivolous just-for-fun veneer that is plastered over a lot of the hotels that bask in the Caribbean sun. There's no beach (Maracas is a good picnic lunch excursion over the northern mountain range), but you are overlooking Queen's Park Savannah where, with binoculars, you can follow the cricket matches and the horse races. Most of the rooms are twin-bedded, but there are singles, studios and double-bedded rooms if you request them, plus a 4-bedroom combination and some 1-bedroom and 2-bedroom suites that give you a dining room. Most rooms have self-service bar/refrigerator, and TV is available at an extra charge. If you're heading from here to the airport, allow plenty of time for traffic jams, which local drivers know better than we outsiders do. The drive *should* take under 45 minutes. Rates this winter figure at about $85 for a twin-bedded room, with meals extra and available at Le Boucan or the poolside, air-conditioned coffee shop. Check for special Hilton Pleasure Chest package weeks, and for the Trinidad & Tobago Tourist Board's "Just the Two of Us" promotions; both offer good value for spring, summer, and fall holidays here, and a good winter package at slightly higher price (but lower than the regular rate when you add up the cost of the extras).

✤ **Villa Maria Inn** (Perseverance Road, Port of Spain, Trinidad, W.I.; 9 rooms) was not open for full-time guests when I visited, but Randy Babooram walked me around the home-turned-inn with explanations of what you can expect. The pool is lovely and punctuates the backyard. It's fringe of bar and pooltable area bodes well for enthusiastic Trinidadian participation as a party place. Rooms vary in size and shape, with some of them small air-conditioned "boxes" that will increase your interest in sitting by the pool. Count on paying about $40, meals extra for 2 this winter. You'll want a car for mobility, but you can walk to the Moka golf course, a reasonable distance down the road.

■■
CAMPGROUNDS do not exist as special areas, but this island has some places that are ideal for nature study and offer very simple accommodations.

✤ **Asa Wright Nature Centre** (Spring Hill Estate, Arima, Trinidad, W.I.; 20 rooms) is a special preserve, 1200 feet up in Trinidad's mountains, 7 miles north of Arima and about 40 minutes' drive from Piarco airport, but about 2 hours from Port of Spain. The property was part of a private plantation purchased from Mrs. Wright to become a nature preserve for birding and flora. Administered by the Royal Bank Trust Company as a recreation and study area, the Nature Centre is a unique Caribbean spot. Accommodations are simple, dress is informal, as you'd expect at a place that concentrates on the woods and virgin terrain that covers the slopes of this mountain area. In addition to nature lovers who find this place on their own, Questers Tours and Travel, Inc. (257 Park Avenue South, New York NY 10010) operates two nature tours spending 5 nights at the center before continuing to Tobago and the Arnos Vale Hotel. Overnight accommodations at the center on your own are very reasonable, priced for Trinidadians and others who come here in study groups. Write to the Manager, Asa Wright Nature Centre, GPO Bag 10, Port of Spain, Trinidad, W.I., to make your own reservations.

■■

RESTAURANTS ON TRINIDAD range from some special spots to La Boucan at the Hilton, and the revolving restaurant (that sometimes doesn't) at the top of the Holiday Inn (both of which sound like they should be more elegant than they are, in my opinion), to the roti stands that proliferate along the streets of Port of Spain, and the ears of cooked corn sold from carts at the edges of Queen's Park. (You can recognize the corn carts by the strings of children lined up to buy their favorite after-school treat.) Any country that comprises West Indian, East Indian, Chinese, African, European, Syrian, Venezuelan, and an assortment of other nationalities is bound to have a varied food menu also—and Trinidad does. A visit to the local markets—the Indian market on Saturdays at Chaguanas, the Beetham Street market at the fringe of the commerce of Port of Spain, and an assortment of other markets—gives you the best preparation for what may appear on your table. If you are adventuresome, and interested, take some time to travel around to see the raw materials before you make your dining choices—and be prepared to find lavish use of mangoes (julie mangoes are special in Trinidad), coconuts, avocados, plaintains, fig bananas, and all the fresh fruits and vegetables that grow in the Trinidad countryside and on Tobago. Roti is a crepelike "pancake" filled with chicken (with bones), goat (which is sometimes proffered as lamb), shrimp, beef, chickpeas, liver, potato, and an assortment of other mixtures, usually heavy with curry. The filled roti is folded, so that nothing oozes out the sides until your first bite, which, if you're trained, is an inhaling nibble.

AUTHOR'S OBSERVATION: Prices at Trinidad's best restaurants seemed very high when I visited. I suspect meals are priced for what the traffic will bear (if you want the best, you'll pay for the best—and at New York City prices).

Long Circular Mall (yes, that's what it's called), near the American Embassy on the fringe of Port of Spain, is an air-conditioned shopping center that is peppered with interesting, and relatively inexpensive, dining and drinking spots. A fringe of snack stands— **Bubblicious** (ice cream), **Chinatown Express, Chicken Unlimited, Take Five,** and **Mario's Pizza**—surrounds a "sea" of orange plastic tables and chairs on the lower level "Food Fair" area; **Ships Tavern** is pub-like and pleasant, and the **Swiss Chalet,** on level 3, is open from 10 a.m. to midnight, serving on red checked tablecloths with an atmosphere true to its name.

The flock of fried-chicken stands expands with every season. Not only can you find **Kentucky Fried** and **Chicken Unlimited** in downtown Port of Spain, but on the major country roads (and at any cluster that calls itself a village) there are places like **Chicken Unlimited, Broasted Chicken,** and others. As one of my Trinidadian informers observed, "all the different chickens taste the same" except for Kentucky Fried.

For Trinidadian creole cooking in very casual surroundings (no place for camera and colorful tourist trappings), search out the **St. Clair Snackette,** on the corner of Marli and Picton Streets, where "we serve beef, chicken, shrimps, liver, potatoe roti" is painted on the streetside wall. Samuel Daniel led me here the first time, and I've come back for more, and not been disappointed yet. Also in downtown Port of Spain is **Cuisine Creole** in a "sealed" air-conditioned room at 31 Abercromby Street. This is a lunchtime spot with buffets of local food including callaloo (the West Indian spinach-style soup that varies from island to island), and mauby and sea-moss beverages. Surroundings at any of the strictly local spots are downtown West Indian style, with emphasis more on good local cooking than on interior decoration.

Mama Mia is the name presently on the front of what used to be Rosemary's, in one of the Victorian houses at 2 Queen's Park West, not far from the National Museum. The menu is Italian, but the surroundings are more interesting than in many of the local spots.

Peking, upstairs at Henry Street and Duke, serves Chinese specialties by the ¼ portion as well as a full plate so you can mix and match. Full portions range from TT$15 to TT$25, for a full roster of specialties. Surroundings are enclosed and air-conditioned, and your entrance may take you past stacks of Coke and soft drink cases that sometimes block the head of the stairs.

Chaconia Inn, in the residential Maravel section about 15 minutes from downtown Port of Spain (106 Saddle Road) has special Trinidadian menus, but call Ken Duval in advance to be sure that what's on when you plan to be there is something you want to try.

Jay Bee's, at Valsayn in the Valpark Shopping Plaza, is about 20 minutes' drive toward the airport from the Hilton and Port of Spain. Visitors find it because knowing locals tell them to; the local folk know this place well, not only for its upstairs hideaway (with bar to the right and dining room to the left) but also for the disco, a couple of doors away at parking lot level. Count on good food, attentive and helpful staff, and surroundings that are cosmopolitan, cool, and cozy. Wood tables laquered to shiny slate are offset by dried flower arrangements, cushions on sparkling steel frame chairs, and plenty of orange and browns punctuated with occasional soft lights. Seafood specialties (stuffed flounder among them) are good, as are steaks.

Kowloon, near Park Street at 109 St. Vincent Street, is a place for your Chinese evening out, if atmosphere is part of what you want to pay for. The several rooms have Chinese character, but to learn the specialty of the evening, or the best of the long list to try, sample several.

Le Cocrico, on Henry Street, is well worth finding, but bring plenty of cash. A reasonable, but not lavish, dinner for two cost TT$163.20 plus taxi fare. Assembled and opened by Simon Parkinson (Norman Parkinson's son, for those who know something about Trinidad), the restaurant features French cooking and has built up an enthusiastic (and affluent or expense account) local following. The West Indian house that holds this restaurant (named for the national bird) had been spruced up with paint, hanging plants and decorator touches that make surroundings special. Although prices are high, food is excellent—and even an undercooked Grand Marnier souffle, my desert on one visit, was delicious. The wine list is worth perusing, but expect to pay for the privilege of sipping.

Luciano's, in a hillside suburban, elegant setting, is the place for a romantic evening, the dressiest you'll find in Port of Spain (but still not dressy by resort island standards). Fountains splash in the center courtyard—and service was slow when I dined here. Somehow it did not matter, when the food was finally served. An "international menu" is offered, with recognizable steak, chicken, and fish, plus a few of the Italian favorites that made the name for Luciano's when the first restaurant started in a downtown spot several years ago. Count on this evening out to be your most expensive and elaborate.

Luciano's on Prince Street in Port of Spain, is a relative of the hillside spot. The mid-city place is popular with businessmen for weekday luncheons, but it offers dinners as well.

Mangal's makes an impression even before you know it's a restaurant. The imposing Victorian mansion at 13 Queen's Park East is almost interesting enough to warrant a visit, no matter *what* the restaurant serves. But if you like spicy, hot Indian food, this is the place to dine. The Indian food comes with a Trinidadian accent. Count on a lot of curry, ginger, and hot sauce, all favorites for local palates and tasty, although explosive when unexpected. Dining at Mangal's is best if you've done some homework on Trinidadian food, and that is as easy as talking with some of the residents. Count on roti, which will be served with more flourishes (but not as much local flavor) in this white-tableclothed restaurant.

Outhouse is the name for the small, vegetarian restaurant where guests can dine on the porch or in the small interior of a traditional West Indian House. Located on Woodford Street, in downtown Port of Spain, the place is expectedly popular for lunch, but is worth checking out at dinnertime as well. It's a few paces inland from Rinaldo's Bistro.

Rinaldo's Bistro, claiming a corner on Woodford Street, looks impressive with its new wood exterior, but the bistro atmosphere is secure inside. Fans flutter the breezes (and the hanging plants), and the offerings include steaks and salad bar as well as more adventuresome fare.

Peppermill, at the back of the Pelican Inn, just below the Hilton (but a taxi or car drive down the hill and around the curve), is a good bet for steak, broiled fish, and pleasant surroundings. Innovative decorating hangs the tables from the ceiling by "legs" and puts the several clusters of diners in nooks cleaned and whitewashed out of what was a storage area at the ground-floor level. Count on entrees from TT$20 to TT$50, and ask for hot sauce if you want any indication of West Indian flavor. There's a salad bar where you serve yourself, and a wine list with California and New York names as well as Blue Nun, but nothing to put sparkle in the eye of a connoisseur.

Shay Shay Tien, at 81 Cipriani Boulevard, is a good source for Chinese food, but the food will not be what you are used to swallowing at your corner, Americanized Chinese restaurant. The menu here has Trinidadian soul (and spices); you'll have the best luck if you know your way around, or have a Trinidadian friend who does. If you're well versed (but not a purist) about Chinese food, this dinner can be a triumph. Some discussion at noon, when you plan to dine at night, can result in a bonus menu; count on simple surroundings and a check that multiplies as you order a taste of this and a taste of that, which is the only way to dine at Shay Shay Tien. (If you are on your own, have an aperitif and look at what others order before either pointing or asking about something you see that looks good.)

Tiki Village, on the 8th floor of the Kapok Hotel, not far from Queen's Park Savannah, serves Polynesian-style food. It's the atmosphere here that is as interesting as the food. The place is dim, by night light, which helps to add to the romance/intrigue and view out the 8th-floor windows. The menu varies to include a selection that is grilled on your own flaming brazier set at the center of your table. Tiki Village attire is casual, comfortable but not dressy. Count on paying about TT$35 or more per person, for as much food as you can eat, with a Trinidadian beer or two.

■■

PLACES WORTH FINDING ON TRINIDAD are an endless list, shortened only by your own enthusiasm for things like Victorian buildings and bustling ports, outpost villages in back country where signposting and conversation are limited, rugged surf pounding hard sand shores that are sometimes the road you drive along, and an abundance of natural sights (bird sanctuaries, caves, mountain foliage, plummeting waterfalls, and pitch lakes) that can keep adventuresome travelers occupied for weeks. Most visitors miss the most interesting sights, not only because they are not packaged in Hub and other travel service tours, but also because it takes time to relax into the hinterlands of this big and complex country.

PORT OF SPAIN is the starting point for most visitors. To understand some of the country, it is necessary, I suppose, to put your hand to its heart—even though it is overwhelming. The port is best viewed with binoculars from the Hilton pool, or from the top of the Holiday Inn. **Beetham Street Central Market,** at the south end of the city, was moved to new quarters a few years ago, and although a short ride from where you are apt to be, it still seethes when there

are products for sale (and that is almost every morning). You ca
view piles of spices, fruits, and—when the season is right—sorre
that a local housewife will be able to tell you how to make into th
popular West Indian party drink.

Frederick Street is the heart of downtown activity for most outsid
ers, not only because it is trimmed with most of the top shops, bu
also because upstairs at #56 the Tourist Board has its main office
Don't go up here expecting people to do handstands because you'v
arrived. This is an office, not a reception area, and you'll have t
wait your turn for whatever information you seek—and the perso
who has the answer may be on the phone—interminably.

A trio of squares (some of which aren't squares at all) are foca
points for downtown Port of Spain: Woodford Square, bordered o
one side by a part of Frederick Street (across from the Touris
Board office), and the Houses of Parliament, plus Holy Trinit
Cathedral (Anglican) and Red House, prominent, impressive, an
the seat of the government. The building dates from 1906. Th
other 2 squares are Independence, which is mostly a parking lo
and stall market (with food—including roti—for sale), and Co
lumbus Square, behind the Catholic cathedral (started in 1832)
with its expected statue of Columbus.

National Museum & Art Gallery, on Frederick Street between Go
don and Keate Streets, in what used to be known as the Royal Vic
toria Institute, is worth a quick visit to look at the carnival costume
if you aren't around to see the real things prancing and dancin
through the streets at the pre-Lenten festivities. Carnival is the sou
of Trinidad; the more you understand about it, the closer you ar
getting to finding the key to Trinidadian outlook on life. Since par
of the costume is the action of the wearer, these exhibits are steril
by comparison to the real thing, but better than nothing. The rest c
the displays (some ancient relics from early settlers, maps of th
area at the time of discovery, and occasional special exhibits of mod
ern Trinidadian art) won't demand much time.

The assortment of **Victorian houses** that have been stitche
around the edges of Queen's Park have suffered from moderniza
tion and from government plans that, in a burst of activity at th
time of independence, tore down venerable buildings in the mis
taken notion that new would be better. In my opinion it is not: th
new buildings are boring, cement boxes. The Victorian mansion
left standing, and now adapted to new causes (museums, restau
rants, etc.), are fascinating to view from the outside even when yo
cannot enter. (But you can enter the National Museum in th
Royal Victoria Institute and the restaurants of Mangal and Mam

Mia, both in Victorian mansions at the park's edge.) You'll have to be content to look from the outside (unless you can get special permission to enter) at Roodal Residence, a gingerbread-fretwork house, and some of the other mansions.

Royal Botanic Gardens, across the north road around Queen's Park Savannah, stand where Paradise Estate once stood. The government purchased the land in 1816 and, when Sir Ralph Woodford (for whom Woodford Square is named) was governor, he established the 70-acre garden. A few of the original buildings remain, refurbished and put to new uses, but in the early 1800s, when the governors lived in the estate house, the garden surrounded their domain. The propagating and experimental stations have been moved to the University of the West Indies at St. Augustine, not far from Tunapuna in the direction of the airport, so what stands here is an extensive selection of trees, plants, and shrubs. (Charles Kingsley, who spent time in Trinidad in 1869–70 while he was working on his novel *At Last,* makes reference to the Botanic Gardens.) There are guides to take you around, and their services are essential if you want to learn about the plants, even though the patter may get tiresome toward the end of the grand tour. Note especially the flower beds around the bandstand (and check to see if there is any event at the bandstand while you are in Trinidad). All the park gardens could have used a good plucking and pruning when I looked, but they are in far better shape than their counterparts in, for example, Kingston, Jamaica.

Emperor Valley Zoo occupies a small section of the gardens, near the west entrance, at the opposite "end" of the south rim of the park from the Governor General's House. Its claim to fame is the collection of indigenous animals, which is more interesting than could have been assembled on many islands because it is commonly accepted that Trinidad was once part of South America. The reptile collection gets a lot of attention, but I am not an enthusiast of caged animals and have not spent much time here.

AUTHOR'S OBSERVATION: Binoculars and insect repellent are 2 invaluable items for travel in Trinidad & Tobago. No slur intended on hotel housekeeping; the reference to both is for those who want to head into the hinterlands, to the Asa Wright Sanctuary in the mountains, to the Caroni Swamp Bird Sanctuary, or on birding walks, perhaps along the old road between Hillsboro Dam and Castara on Tobago. You'll want long trousers, sturdy shoes, and a long-sleeved shirt (plus rain gear for Asa Wright) if you give any thought to reasonable comfort.

Asa Wright Nature Centre, at Spring Hill Estate, 7 miles north of Arima and a good hour's drive from Port of Spain, in the northern range of Trinidad mountains, has marked mountain walks and guides to take you on special excursions. Telephone ahead of time if you are planning to go on your own or with your own small group to be sure that there's someone available when you want to visit. The "dry" season, when flowers are at their best and weather is more dependable, is from January until May, and perhaps in mid-fall (October-November), but be sure to have lightweight rain gear, long trousers, long-sleeved shirts, and sturdy shoes for your mountain hiking. There is a supply of plastic raincoats at the Centre for those who forget to bring their own, but if you are serious about birding and the flora, come prepared. Count on humidity—lots of it—and very simple man-made surroundings amid spectacular natural ones. Some Audubon and other groups make arrangements for time here, but anyone is welcome to come up to wander—and many Trinidadians do. You can sit on the veranda and notice squirrel cuckoos, toucans, and other birds, but you will have to wander around with your binoculars and patience to find some other kinds.

Caroni Bird Sanctuary, where you can see the scarlet ibis, the heronries of the white and blue heron, as well as streaked herons and hundreds of other birds who live in this 437 acre swampland, is less than 10 miles south of Port of Spain. I made my first trip here in one of the small boats of David Ramsahai & Sons, moved to wake up in time for the 4:30 a.m. departure party by the Ramsahai folder which said "You are planning a vacation away from the maddening crowds. Come visit with us; enjoy the cultures of the world in a nutshell Trinidad. . . . First stop on this spectacular journey is at the feeding grounds, a stretch of shallow water in which small fish, crabs and shrimps abound: hundreds of Ibis pecking at their unsuspecting prey, is a sight to behold. Southwards, flying in unionism [sic] against the blue skies, the Scarlet Ibis appear on the horizon. The Ibis at home. The sun sets. Enveloping us in a beautiful cloak of peace. Other species of birds are Egrets, Herons, Spoonbills, Jacamas, Kingfishes and more and more in the deeper waters of the river; Tarpon, Salmon, Mollet, Snookers and others make good fishing. Our boats depart 4:30 a.m. and 4 p.m. each day of the year. Come, be our guest, we are anxious to share our good fortune with you." The only problem with all of this is that the David Ramsahai heartfelt enthusiasm is hard to come by these days. Tours to the Caroni Swamp by Hub have turned into routine affairs—a job for the driver/guide and sometimes a bore for you. If you are lucky enough to get a good guide, know your birds, or can go with someone who does, the experience can be fascinating. Tours operate on regular "schedules" and you'll have to plan in advance.

AUTHOR'S OBSERVATION: There are several companies that have tours: 4 hours departing at 3 p.m. daily for the Caroni Swamp, 4 hours for the "Down the Islands" boat cruise, a golfer's package, a day on Tobago, etc. I have found Hub Travel to be dependable, but be sure you get a good driver/guide. Contact the office at 44 New Street, Port of Spain, Trinidad, W.I., in advance of your touring and, if you have special interests, say so.

Touring the four corners of Trinidad can be one of the Caribbean's most fascinating excursions if you're good on car maintenance and very self-sufficient. Arm yourself with a Texaco map and a good sense of direction (a compass can come in handy). Directions you will get from local folk are as detailed as turning "at the third row of palms," "the second bay," "when you pass Burney's parlour" and similar verbal help-alongs, and that's assuming you can understand the dialect of the countryside.

Blue Basin, about 45 minutes' drive into the Diego Martin Valley, is a fresh water pool reached by a half-mile hike from the parking area. The road through the estate that leads to the parking area for the hike is bordered by hibiscus hedges, and the entire excursion (which can take about 3 hours) will provide a glimpse of "another" Trinidad. Take the Western Main Road through Four Roads and get directions from there, if you haven't mapped out your route with the experts beforehand.

Lupinot (pronounced loo-PEEN-oh) offers a special glimpse of life in Trinidad. The area, made up of villages of Siree, La Pastora, and Lupinot, is about 16 kilometers from Port of Spain and about 8 miles from Piarco Airport. It offers a *Brigadoon* setting in a valley in the mountains of the Northern Range. Many of the less-than-1000 people who live here are descendants of the slaves brought into this valley by a French settler in the 1800s. The Compte de Lupinot Charles Joseph took his band of slaves along a river path, into lush country where he started his plantation. Today the area is a natural botanic garden, with brilliant *immortelle* vivid in March and April, and coffee, cocoa, cashews, and other crops growing most of the year. Birds, butterflies, and other fauna live in their natural state, untroubled by modern commerce. The church originally stood on another site, in another mountain village. In 1948, when government plans for a dam threatened to blow up the church, the local priest put a curse on the project—and the village people moved themselves and their church to Lupinot. (The dam, incidentally, was never finished.) The caves here are a special site, toured by donning helmets with miners-light (and wearing sturdy shoes) to follow your guide through the dark halls. Because it is not too far from the airport, Lupinot is a reasonable goal if you find yourself at Piarco with a long wait between planes (perhaps from Tobago to elsewhere).

Caura Valley and the North Coast Road are 2 other driving routes to follow for a look at rural Trinidad. Both trips can be made in a morning or an afternoon (allow about 3 hours for each).

Pitch Lake is downright ugly. Unless you're heading out this direction (in the southwest, at the north shore of the southern peninsula) for another reason, there's no need to come here to see this. It is interesting (to me) to note that the pitch from the lake used to be carved out in huge hunks (sometimes 6 feet by 6 feet), put into mining cars that ran on tracks across the "lake," and then put on trucks to be taken to ships at Port of Spain. Water fills in the gaping holes, and eventually the pitch seeps back up, displacing the water and making it impossible to tell just where the cut was made. Intriguing? Maybe, but nothing to spend your vacation time looking at. (The Pitch Lake was known in Sir Walter Raleigh's time, and used to caulk his ships and those of others, as well as for paving streets of many cities in the U.S. in more recent history.)

■■

SPORTS ON TRINIDAD are limited to land sports, unless you sign on for the motorboat ride (check at the Tourist Board) to the islands that string out toward Venezuela from the northwest peninsula. There are some boats (and huge ships) at the marina and boatyards on the Chagaramus former U.S. Naval base turned recreation and shipbuilding area for Port of Spain. It is not easy, however, for you, the average tourist, to get a line on a boat for charter, unless you find something offered at your hotel's activities desk.

Cricket is played (fanatically) at the Oval Cricket Ground on St. Clair Avenue, and elsewhere around the island in more casual surroundings. If you want to watch a match (or part of one) ask at the Tourist Board for dates, places, and times.

Golf is played at the Moka course, about 10 minutes' drive from the Trinidad Hilton, and even less from the Maraval hotels, since the golf course is in that suburb. Popular with Trinidadians, the course is in demand on weekends, when starting times can be a problem. Play here is a good way to meet some residents, especially if you're in Trinidad on business and have a local contact who can set up the game. Otherwise, you'll find the course good, but the others around the club slightly standoffish, especially if you arrive with your own foursome and seem to be having your own fun.

Horseracing takes place regularly on the Race Course in Queen's Park Savannah and elsewhere around the country. You can view the Queen's Park events with binoculars from your room at the Hilton, but half the fun of the Trinidadian experience is lining up at the gate as almost everyone else in town does.

Tennis is available at the Hilton's courts (nightlighted and in almost constant play), as well as at some of the private clubs (on invitation only). Check for special tennis holidays at the Hilton if you play a lot and are interested in a break on rates for a combined Trinidad & Tobago holiday.

Swimming at beaches in Trinidad is an excursion, no matter where you're staying. There's a long stretch of sand at Maracas Bay (where there is also talk of a hotel that has yet to rise on these shores), but you will have the place pretty much to yourself, except on summer weekends when it's popular with Trinidadians. Bring a picnic from your hotel, and hire a taxi to take you over the northern mountains, on the wiggly route to the north-shore sands. There are other beaches along the leeward coast, along the peninsula that starts with Chagaramus, and at the small islands at the northwest tip, but the sand is not the powder-smooth strip that you find on Tobago. (Even Trinidadians head to Tobago for weekends.) Along the northeast shore, there are unpeopled beaches around Balandra and Toco, and at the coast around Manzanilla and Mayaro, but swimming is suggested only for strong swimmers and competent self-sufficient sportsmen who like challenges. There's nothing set up for tourists, even in the way of food and facilities, and certainly no "lifeguards."

■■

TREASURES AND TRIFLES ON TRINIDAD   Shopping here is not the usual trick-or-treat game played on many of the islands known as "freeport" or "duty-free" shopping centers. This is a place to find unique gold work ((**Y DeLima's** 3rd-floor workroom on Frederick Street makes what you want to order), useful and hardy handwoven Caribbean grass items (baskets, mats, hats and rugs) at the **Blind Welfare Association Shop** on Duke Street, and art from the art school which represents no commercial threat to Haiti, but where works are considerably more ingenuous and provocative than can be found in most places.

Long Circular Mall, near the American Embassy on the fringe of Port of Spain, is a comfortable place for one-stop shopping in air-conditioned comfort. Before you gasp at the idea of a "hometown-style shopping mall" for exotic Trinidad shopping, let me assure you that the best shops (**Stecher's** and others) have branches here, that the several restaurants make pleasant halting spots, that there's a lot to be said for air-conditioning after a few minutes in the downtown heat, and that the **Tru Valu Supermarket** that is an appendage on one side has some of Trinidad's most interesting "take home" items: Angostura bitters, local hot sauce (which is fiery hot), Old Oak rum plus Carypton (a liquer made from oranges), bottled rum punch and Trinidad-made wines, some special canned vegetables not known to your local market, spices, and other domestic items.

The imagination and ingenuity that is channeled into the elaborate carnival costumes every year contribute to some of the Caribbean's most interesting fashions. If you have the time and inclination, it is possible to talk with some of those who work on carnival costumes about some interesting patio wear that will certainly *not* be just like what you see in your hometown. You can have clothes tailored in the shops of **Sydney Shim** (101 Queen's Street), who has fitted Geoffrey Holder's imposing frame before Holder branched out into the big time with costume design and fashion of such top broadway shows as *Timbuktu* and *The Wiz*. Fly Tailoring (7 Henry Street) and **Samaroo's** (46 Independence Square) are 2 others to find.

A. George & Sons, at 15 Henry Street, has bolt upon bolt of top quality flannel, gabardine, and other winter weight fabrics and can recommend tailors to sew up a 3 piece suit for about TT$30, including fabric. For women's clothes, **A Boutique** at 54 Queen Street, and its "other half" called **Cheapside** offer colorful fabrics, some of them color-coordinated for 2 or 3 different patterns (English imports). Seamstresses can be recommended, but management is also very willing to give you all the information to sew your clothes yourself, presumably when you return home to your own sewing machine.

Althea Bastien's batik and tie-dyed fabrics are exceptional, and well worth tracking down. Check first by telephone (62-43274) before going to her workshop at 43 Sydenham Avenue in the St. Ann's section. If you find Althea at home and at work, you aie in for a treat.

Jean Downer also does exceptional batik work and can be reached at her home if you want to make an appointment for a special order.

Wayne Berkeley, one of Trinidad's top band leaders, and the winner of the 1980 Carnival costume competition with his theme of Genesis, is also talented with crafts that can come home with you (which his Carnival costumes cannot). Inquire about his colorful and interesting West Indian heads, worked on boards for wall hangings and trimmed with Carnival-style headdresses. Phone him at his home on Maraval Road to set up an appointment to see his work if you cannot find some examples in the craft shops.

Laurayn Serrao (95 Benjamin Street) works with copper, backed with wood, suitable for impressive wall decoration. The themes are often nature, birds, and landscapes, with the copper hammered to highlight the main focus of the work. Some works are "framed" in rope, and some can be designed to fill a specific space if you have a particular wall in mind.

For the traditional luxury "duty-free" items, check at **de Lima** shops and at **Stecher's,** now stretching through the Eastern Caribbean with samples of the wares that sell at Frederick Street locations as well as at the Hilton and other places. You can count on a good selection of watches, jewelry, crystal, china, and all the elegant trappings of the luxury life. As for the prices, be sure you know what comparable merchandise would cost at home. The prices will be better here—but just how much depends on your best deal in your hometown.

Expect the shops in Port of Spain to be open M–F, 8–4. Some are open until 5. Do not plan to buy liquor or food on Thursday afternoon (those stores close at 12), but you can buy liquor and food Saturday afternoon, when all the other stores close (at noon). Check if you're searching for some special item, and you can count on the shops in the Hilton arcade to be open at hours that appeal to the hotel guests; there's some variety, but inquire in advance if you're counting on a last-minute purchase on, for example, a Sunday.

Tobago

Trinidad & Tobago Tourist Board, 56 Frederick Street, Port of Spain, Trinidad, W.I.; Tobago Tourism Information, Scarborough, Tobago, W.I.; 400 Madison Ave., New York, NY 10017; Suite 702, 200 S.E. First St., Miami, FL 33131; York Centre, 145 King St., West & University Ave., Toronto, Ontario M5H 1J8, Canada; 20 Lower Regent St., London SW1Y 4PH.

US$1 = TT$2.40
Unless otherwise noted, $ refers to U.S. currency.

Emil Robinson eased his truck from Trinidad's St. Vincent Street pier onto the ferry boat. It was dark, and his day in Port of Spain had been spent driving from place to place. The gasoline was relatively inexpensive, but the cost of the cement, lumber, pipes, and other elements for his house cost a lot. Traffic clogged most roads, so wedging into a confined space on the Tobago ferry was a welcomed relief. The ferry would leave about midnight, and 6 hours later, just after dawn, he could drive to his homesite and unload the pieces for his new house.

"Driving" from Tobago to Trinidad to pick up building materials and other items has proved to be the fastest way to get them. Shipping between the two islands that make up the one nation of Trinidad & Tobago has always been slow, and now that demand for consumer goods is high in both places, unless you "go fetch" yourself, you can wait weeks for delivery.

Although joined to Trinidad by constitution, Tobago has a personality distinctly its own. Popular as a weekend retreat for cosmopolitan Trinidadians, it wasn't until sugar crop failures at the end of the 19th century that Tobago chose annexation to Trinidad over its own independence. When David Codrington revs up the "twin" engines (an Evinrude 25 and a Yamaha) on his Tobago-built glass-bottom boat, his "Johnson's Sea Tours" long-sleeved T-shirt flutters in the breeze. His wide smile and flashing dark eyes are shaded with a plastic leopard cap, but there's nothing else fake about this 2½-hour trip to the coral gardens of Buccoo Reef. The boat leaves Buccoo Village with an assortment of visitors from the nearby hotels and the trip is one of the few planned activities for visitors on Tobago. This is a place where you can do as you please.

Perching over Scarborough, at the end of a road that curls up and around, is Fort George, built by the British and imposing even in ruins. Children festooned the branches of the flamboyant tree that stood by the parking area, and their saucer eyes hovered over huge smiles as we said "good morning" and wandered on our way. Their laughter, oblivious of our pursuit, provided the melody for the constant rustle of the palm fronds in the trade winds. And, later in the day, as the sun started to go down, we watched the fishing fleet return at Turtle Beach. We sipped a potent rum punch, with a sprinkling of island-fresh grated nutmeg, while we watched the fishermen hauling in their catch. We lingered until dark, staying as long as Redman Deman did. He was sewing the fishing nets after the catch was in, as he had been doing "plenty years," and certainly long before the hotel was built on this shore.

■■■

POLITICAL PICTURE: Trinidad & Tobago became one independent country in August 1962. Separated by several miles of sea and linked politically only since 1803, the island of Tobago has an independent streak. From time to time, in recent years, there have been rumbles about "going it alone," forming a unit separate from Trinidad, Tobago's sometimes overwhelming sister island. When Prime Minister George Chambers assumed office, upon the death of former Prime Minister, Sir Eric Williams in March 1981, he noted in his acceptance speech that "with regard to Tobago, while we adhere unswervingly to the concept of a unitary state. . . . we shall seek in a spirit of equality to overcome the apparent obstacles to improvement of the administration and development of the sister isle. To this end, steps will be taken to initiate appropriate dialogue."

Energy Minister Errol Mahabir, sometimes called "Government's number one trouble shooter," and Senator John Donaldson, a Tobago-born delegate, were appointed Ministers for Tobago, and both went to Tobago (a precedent-setting gesture) in mid-May 1981 for meetings with a group of representatives from the Tobago House of Assembly. What will come from these innovations remains to be seen, but in the climate of the Caribbean today, it seems unrealistic for Tobago to contemplate becoming indepen-

dent (with no viable funding). A more equitable arrangement as a
sister island with oil-rich Trinidad would seem to offer a reasonable
future.

Unlike Trinidad, where an impressive percentage of the population is of East Indian descent, most of Tobago's populace is of African descent, a fact that will be obvious to even the most cursory visitor.

■■■

CUSTOMS OF TOBAGO reflect the African heritage of most of the
people. Tourism is the island's major industry, albeit tourism from
nearby Trinidad. Hotel facilities look like those found on other
Caribbean islands, and the beaches, tennis, golf, and scuba are the
main interests for most vacationers. The pace of life on Tobago is
distinctly island-Caribbean: slow.

AUTHOR'S OBSERVATION: During research visits for
this edition, I was disappointed to sense a lack of caring on
the part of Tobagonians in hotels and restaurants. Although the "lack of caring" for a visitor is one factor, the
seeming lack of interest in doing a good job—whether it be
waiting on a table, working in a shop, tending rooms, or
taking care of a front desk—is an unfortunate situation for
an island dependent on tourism. I noted little initiative, by
comparison to my encounters in many other Caribbean
destinations. Hopefully, attention to this ennui will improve the "enthusiasm" with which Tobago's tourism industry operates—for the sake of those who work in it, as
much as for those of us who spend our money on the hope
that we can enjoy it.

■■■

MONEY MATTERS: Trinidad & Tobago dollars are common currency here, although most hotels will take payment (at least at the
front desk) in U.S. dollars. It's best, for local courtesy as much as
for cash-on-hand, to change to TT dollars, however, and that can
easily be accomplished at the airport, before you fly to Tobago, or in
Port of Spain if you are adventuresome enough to take the 6-hour
ferry ride. Banks have a TT$2 per transaction charge. (The airport
bank is next to the Tourist Office, in the main building, which is a
short walk from the Tobago departure/arrival rooms.)

■■■

ARRIVAL on Tobago from Trinidad can be by boat, on the ferry that departs from the St. Vincent Street pier in Port of Spain and makes the crossing to Tobago's Scarborough in about 6 hours, or by plane from Trinidad's Piarco International Airport. Arrival at Tobago's Crown Point airport is easy, with the aura of the holiday place this island has come to be—for Trinidadians as well as for us from the outside. The airport is boxy, easy to negotiate, and your luggage will appear in the air terminal soon after you do. (You can walk out of the arrival building and across the parking lot to the small cafe/shop for a cool drink while you wait.) Make arrangements in advance for a rental car for pickup at the airport if you want instant mobility; otherwise—and especially on your first visit—take a taxi to your hotel and make arrangements on another day for your rental car. You won't have any trouble finding a taxi; drivers will all but tug on your arm when you walk from the luggage area.

When you are traveling to Tobago, if you do not fly direct on a charter or one of the nonstop services, check in early for the flight, which will take half an hour or less, depending on the size and speed of the airplane. With one of the long-time reorganizations of BWIA, the former Trinidad & Tobago Air Services was merged into Trinidad & Tobago's International Airline. A result has been improved Trinidad-Tobago air service, with several-times-daily shuttle service referred to as "Air-bridge" service, leaving at least every hour (and at peak times more often). Advance reservations are not essential (although they are advisble if you are unfamiliar with island airlines); you can go to the airport and go "on the next flight." If you make your reservation *in your hometown* to include the trip to Tobago, on your Trinidad ticket, you will not have to pay extra. Otherwise, your round trip Trinidad to Tobago return will cost about TT$26.

■■■

TOURING TIPS: Tobago is a beach and sand island. Except for a slither through Scarborough and a sprint down to the Charlottesville (east) end for a look at, and perhaps the boat trip across to, Bird of Paradise Island, there's not a lot else that requires a look.

AUTHOR'S OBSERVATION: It pays to do your homework on taxi fares. Ask at the Tourist Office desk and a couple of other places before you get into "your" taxicab.

On one journey, I had been told to expect to pay about TT$90 for what I wanted to do on a drive around the island. The driver who finally won out (mainly for his perseverance) said the fare was TT$140. When I all-but-fainted, we settled on TT$90—for an excursion that I noted later was similar to one posted for TT$40!

Rental cars are available, at TT$90 per day, plus TT$20 for a minimum 2-day insurance, plus your gas (you're expected to leave the gas gauge at the same spot you found it), plus a TT$100 deposit. As in Trinidad, you can sometimes use your credit card for reference in lieu of cash, but that seems to depend on the cash flow of the person you rent from, in my experience. (My card worked, but she counted the cash in her drawer before she approved the card for credit.)

Otherwise, you'll tour by boat. Out of Pigeon Point, there are several boats that make the run to Buccoo Village for the trip. Going rate is about TT$25.

■■■

HOTELS ON TOBAGO offer variety, from the looks of luxury to small, casual Tobagonian style, with a cosmopolitan climate created by an influx of vacationers from Europe who head here on charters and special tours. You'll find the expected resort facilities, including beaches, tennis, and golf at Mt. Irvine, but the island has its own style, that bordered lax when I visited. Housekeeping and service left a lot to be desired at most places.

As is the case with hotels on Trinidad, all bills are subject to a 3% government room tax, and most charge 10% or 15% service as well. Inquire when you check in to avoid a surprise when you check out.

AUTHOR'S AWARDS go to Arnos Vale, because it looks the way an island hideaway should (and comes closest to offering the expected vacation services), with an honorable mention to Sandy Point for giving the best value for its vacation virtues. Kariwak Village shows promise but was not operating when I investigated.

✤ **Arnos Vale** (Box 208, Scarborough, Tobago, W.I.; 25 rooms plus 3 suites) has all the elements for an idyllic resort, Arnos Vale is a comfortable casual, island inn that ranges from hilltop to beach, with a knee-bending walk or a short, hotel-supplied ride between the two. Don't arrive expecting white-glove treatment and French cuisine. Neither of those things are here, but what makes the place a good Tobagonian base for the bird-watching and flora/fauna tours operated by Questers Tours & Travel, a New York-based firm, and Wonder Bird Tours is the bosky setting and the peaceful perch from which to head out birding. Tropical growth spills over and around the buildings, softening the newest 2-story cement rectangle that sits near the pool at the beach.

The main house at the top of the hill is where you will find the reception rooms and the chintz-covered chairs and couches that lend a comfortable air to the place. There's an open-air patio, a much talked-about Murano (Italy) glass chandelier, and a grand piano that is supposed to have been played at the Paris Exposition of 1851 (both intriguingly out of place in the present atmosphere, in my opinion). The dining room features island food in hearty fashion. The Sunday creole buffet, served between pool and beach, draws guests from other hotels as well as island residents, but the standard lunches are sandwich/salad standard-style with a wine list. The nooks and crannies pounded into the black rocks at the east end of the beach are good for wallowing in the sea wash, and the beach sinks into deeper sea when the sands haven't been swirled by wave action. There's a tennis court, and the opportunity to horseback ride for your more than $100 for 2, this winter, with breakfasts and dinners daily. Coral, Crow's Nest and Dolphin cottages have hilltop view. A series of rooms have a beachside setting, with sea-washed coral rocks for swimming area, or you can choose one of the rooms in the main house. The small Jacamar gift shop has a few sun-covers and lotions as well as a sample of handmade items for sale near the shoreside restaurant.

✝ **Cocrico Inn** (Plymouth, Tobago, W.I.; 16 rooms) confuses some visitors by showing a beautiful beach on its promotion pieces. This boxy stucco building is *not* on the beach, although you can walk to a patch of sand down the road and Ida Boyke pointed out where the swimming pool will be when I surveyed for this edition. (The fact that it was not started when I saw the place does not bode well for it's being completed by the time you visit, if your travel plans are early in '82 or before.) Located on a side street in the small town of Plymouth, the new building has a restaurant on its first floor and several rooms, all simply furnished with modern eqiupment but not all air-conditioned, in an L-shaped arrangement on the second floor. You'll need a car for mobility, and I'm not suggesting this place for the first-time island visitor. Count on $70 to $76, breakfasts and dinners daily, for 2 for these simple surroundings.

✣ **Della Mira Guest House** (Winward Road, Scarborough, Tobago, W.I.; 14 rooms) is Neville Miranda's West Indian house, a 2-story stucco, recently built inn that is big enough for a handful of independent guests who want to be near Scarborough and like access to the island's "cosmopolitan club," the *Club La Tropicale*, and the Della Mira Beauty and Barber Salon, both in separate buildings. The beauty shop is the province of Angela Miranda and Pearl Fernando, both of whom studied hairdressing in the U.S. An ideal place to learn about the Tobagonian's island from two who know it well, with a staff that help you to see a side of island life you might otherwise never know, Della Mira is not for timid tourists who need lush surroundings or fancy service. Rooms are simply furnished, and some have balconies with view over the grounds (hillside or pool and sea). All rooms have private bathroom with shower stall. There's a pool that's popular with friends and family, and the windswept shore (and sometimes beach) a short walk away. As Neville Miranda says, "The accent is on comfort, rest, good food, a pleasant home-away-from-home atmosphere . . . geared to the needs of the average income traveler." Rates this winter run no more than $50 for 2, with breakfasts and dinners daily, or $20 and under if 2 want breakfast only. Hillside view rooms are less expensive, but if you can swing it, pay the premium for pool and sea.

✣ **Crown Reef** (Store Bay, Tobago, W.I.; 120 rooms and suites) captures a piece of shoreline, a few minutes' drive from the island's Crown Point airport. Although the hotel knew a brief era as part of the U.S. Radisson chain, it is now government owned and managed. Groups keep the place active (and the pool and other on-the-spot facilities in use) when they are in residence; Trinidadians flock here for weekends. If you're half of two or part of a small group, count on making your own fun. Innovation with summer of '81 is a 7-night scuba program, with 5- and 12-dive versions (and discounts for nondiving participants). Check for details, and count on finding a beach, surf sounds to sooth your sleeping (if you turn off the air-conditioner and open your door), and the indifferent housekeeping that I find to be part of Tobago's style. Food in the sea-view dining rotunda was mediocre when I dined, and the windows were so clouded with salt air that vision of view was blurred. An enthusiastic welcome by David, who stood at the door of "his" Shipwreck Bar when I looked in, was the most inviting part of my visit. Probably the liveliest hotel on Tobago, this place is o.k. if you're flexible, and can make your own fun. Rooms are "the usual," doubles with modern plumbing that *should* work. Some rooms have a sort-of-terrace; others are in the main building; some rooms are around the pool (which is to the right as you face the sea at the main entrance). Count on paying about $135 for 2, meals extra, this winter, but inquire about special multiday package plans that average to lower daily rates and include some extras.

✛ **Kariwak Village** (Box 155, Scarborough, Tobago, W.I.; 18 rooms) is a clever concept, with bedrooms in 9 octagonal buildings arranged like cupcakes on a piece of Store Bay. (The "chocolate frosting" is a shake-shingle roof.) Originally scheduled for opening in 1980, the cluster of cottages may make it for this season—but check to be sure. (Official opening was scheduled for August '81 when I surveyed for this edition.) The social center for guests in the cottages is an attractive main building with restaurant and bar, plus facilities for entertainment when it's scheduled (and that will be when house count warrants). Count on this to be a favorite for Trinidadians who weekend here, and ask manager Allan Clovis about the vacation village. He designed it. Count on paying $60 for 2, this winter, room only.

✛ **Mount Irvine Bay Hotel** (Box 222, Scarborough, Tobago, W.I.; 110 rooms) has most of the elements to be a top-flight resort, but housekeeping and service left a lot to be desired when I checked for this edition. Two cats with cuts and bruises hovered around my luncheon table (and tiny sugar ants provided entertainment while I waited—after asking four times—for an iced tea). On my visit, rain-soaked paper napkins and old cigarette butts had settled into the base of the lush, tropical planting around the grounds, and mildew was on the backs of poolside chairs. If all that has been spruced up, this place can be (and should be) gorgeous. The resort meanders over a prize piece of property, on the north shore of Tobago, about 15 minutes' taxi ride from the Crown Point Airport, and abutting the Tobago Golf Course, commonly referred to as Mount Irvine Golf Course. This resort puts you near the shore (you can walk to a choice of beaches), amid a cosmopolitan atmosphere helped along by the fact that many of your fellow guests, especially in winter months, will be Europeans. Rooms are in any of several units scattered around the grounds. There are houses for rent in the hills (see Housekeeping Holidays) that give you access to the hotel facilities. The terrace around the mill-with-roof is your dining area, with changes in personality between dawn (breakfast) and dusk (dinner). The pool nearby is the setting for some of the evening entertainment, all of it local, natural, and informal. A couple of shops in the lobby and a bar to the left of the reception desk are the activity in the main building (except for the addition of a tour desk). The *Shamrock and Palm* down one of the lanes, toward the rooms and the "back" of the house, comes alive as a disco some evenings, when house count warrants. There's a lot of walking involved to get from here to there, and especially to the beaches, with the best—a long quiet strand you can have to yourself—a stroll down the road, cutting to the shore to go over the hill at the public beach area. Count on paying $160 to $194 for 2, breakfasts and dinners daily, and bring your dress-up clothes if you like the resort life. This is one place where winter season vacationers wear them.

✛ **Sandy Point Beach Club** (Crown Point, Tobago, W.I.; 42 rooms) perches at the end of the Crown Point airport runway. As long as the flights are limited to daylight hours, the noise is not deafening—but beware when traffic warrants more flights and bigger planes. From the outside, the new complex (built in season of '78) looks like a cloister; white walls, tiny odd-shaped windows, and red tile roofs. Units are stacked and nestled against each other to take up minimum ground area for maximum housing density. The 20 suites give duplex living, with the bedroom up a narrow staircase. The 22 studio apartments are attractively, if simply, furnished in Scandinavian-modern style. All rooms are air-conditioned (a necessity since the angles shut out a lot of the breeze) and the bigger units have television. Modern kitchen equipment makes housekeeping relatively simple (but getting foodstuffs involves an excursion). The open-air, terrace dining at the shoreside *Steak Hut* restaurant is pleasant on warm evenings—and at lunchtime. The pool's next to the Steak Hut, and a small beach settles below the pool (unless waves have temporarily washed it out). Maxitaxi runs regularly to Scarborough, at rates that are less than taxi fares. Count on $40 for 2 in a studio and $50 for 2 in a suite this winter, and know that you have one of the best bargains on Tobago. (Breakfast and dinner can be paid in advance, for $15 per person daily.)

✛ **Tropikist** (Crown Point, Tobago, W.I.; 33 rooms) touches the shore (but not a good beach) at the side of the Crown Point airport runway. Motel-modern-style rooms are in 2-story blocks, with sea view. Popular with Trinidadian families and with value-conscious travelers, the hotel is geared for casual travelers who do not demand luxury. Count on paying $75 for 2 this winter, breakfasts and dinners daily, and know that you *can* walk to the airport, and to Crown Point and Crown Reef hotels for diversion.

✣ **Turtle Beach** (Box 201, Scarborough, Tobago, W.I.; 52 rooms) claims one of the island's prize hotel locations, at one end of a long stretch of sand at Courland Bay, with view to the Fort James at Plymouth. New ownership was resulting in a lot of scurrying when I stopped by, and perhaps there will be some changes by the time you visit. Trinidadian Michael Charbonne, whose small-and-homelike Monique Guest House makes a name for hospitality, has bought this hotel. Favorite activity for vacationing guests is viewing the afternoon arrival of the fishing fleet and watching the exhausting work of hauling the fish-filled nets to shore, to sell the catch to those who cluster around the boats. Wise vacationers claim their niche at the seaside bar, and have the bartender mix up one of his elaborate rum punches, complete with the fresh grated nutmeg on top. Your room here is in a 2-story balconied or terraced unit, with modern motel-style furnishings and sea view. Public rooms are comfortable, furnished for beachside living with scarlet fabric accenting white chairs, couches, and tables. There's a pool, in addition to the beach, for swimmers and I hope the housekeeping lapses I noticed are a temporary problem. The hotel is often filled with Canadians and other folk who have found this spot either through a European or other charter or on their own through an informed travel agent. Life is casual, comfortable and what a Caribbean holiday should be, if you don't want fuss-and-feathers and are content for informal life. The room rate for 2 with 2 meals daily should figure about $140 this season.

▪▪▪

HOUSEKEEPING HOLIDAYS ON TOBAGO can be in a luxury home, where someone else is on tap to help with the daily routine, or in an apartment, where you cook your meals yourself. There are some spectacular homes built as part of the development of Mount Irvine that provide sweeping views of Caribbean seas and sunsets as well as the option to head to the main hotel for meals if you tire of what your maid/cook fixes. And there are homes on isolated coves, away from any connection with community activities, where you can have a housekeeper and someone to tend the grounds or do what's necessary yourself. Other options include efficiency apartments, part of the development at Crown Point.

There's no supermarket in the U.S. sense of the word, but the Friday market in Scarborough proffers more than enough for adventuresome chefs. Your fresh produce may come from someone you meet in a nearby village or the market lady you find serves you best at Scarborough. Strange though it seems, you may have difficulty tracking down a good source for fresh fish. The best beef may be what you bring from your butcher at home, and a canned ham and any other special foods you think you can't live without can come in with your luggage.

Tobago Estates Agency Ltd. (Box 160, Scarborough, Tobago, W.I.; cable TEAL, Tobago, W.I.) has an extensive listing of houses and apartments available for rent near the Mt. Irvine Hotel. Several of the properties are fully furnished (and staffed) within a stroll from the golf course and the resort facilities.

✣ **Horizons** is one of the houses for rent at Mt. Irvine. The 3 air-conditioned bedrooms are perfect for 2 couples or a large family, and the modern kitchen has a bar area opening to the living/dining room and view. The maid comes in for breakfast and stays through lunch, but she can help with fixing the dinner you serve yourselves (unless you go to the hotel or another spot to dine). Figure about $130 per night Dec. 16–Apr. 15; $100 at other times. **Sunset Lodge** is another Mount Irvine house (3 bedrooms—2 share a bath and the bedrooms have air conditioners). Costs for this one are $100 winter, $70 summer. Both Horizons and Sunset are listed with Mrs. Martin, Box 160, Scarborough, Tobago, W.I.

✣ **Man-O-War Bay Cottages** are among the listings of homes for rent. The 3 2-bedroom cottages and one 4-bedroom cottage are near a good beach, not far from the village of Charlotteville about 1½ hours' banding, weaving, and often bumpy—but scenic—drive from the airport. You'll want a car if you care about mobility, but if you want the real island life, take a taxi (about TT $30) and concentrate on your beach and the people of Charlotteville.

✣ **Carefree Cottage** at Speyside is across the road from the beach. The 2-bedroom cottage is simple, but adequately furnished, with maid service available. Write to Captain and Mrs. James Davies, Speyside, Tobago, for details about this cottage about ½ mile from town.

✣ **Arcadia,** on Orange Hill Road in Scarborough, Tobago's main town, has a swimming pool and 5 double bedrooms with 4 full baths. Ten people can settle in comfortably, to be assisted with the housekeeping by a maid who knows where to buy what in town. Information about the estate (including the gatekeeper's cottage) is available through Mrs. Eamon O'Connor, Northside and Valder Hall Roads, Scarborough, Tobago, W.I.

✢ **Samaan and Flamboyant Cottages** are on a coconut estate called Prospect, about 8 miles from the airport and a little more than 3 from Scarborough. Each cottage has 2 double air-conditioned bedrooms and 2 baths, but you'll need a rental car for transportation to the beach and to Mount Irvine (even though the golf course is next door. Contact Otto Weeks, Box 219, Scarborough, Tobago, W.I.)

✢ **Crown Point Condominiums** (Crown Point, Tobago, W.I.; 70 apts.) claim the spot of a former small hotel, near the end of the runway and right on the beach. Completely revamped a few years ago, the housekeeping units are simple but adequate, in a variety of shapes and sizes, at rates that range from about $50 to $100, depending on size and always with no meals. You'll either cook for yourself, wander down the beach to Crown Reef to dine at the hotel, or get in a car you've rented to go to one of the other hotels. The Trinidadian-owned complex sold many units to local people who use this setup as a weekend retreat, renting it out to off-islanders at some times during the year. A good bet if you want apartment-style surroundings on the shore.

For efficiency apartments with some hotel amenities, investigate Sandy Point near the airport and Treasure Isle, on the fringe of Scarborough and popular with West Indians who know and like good value and don't care about being on the beach. Ida Boyke, owner of Cocrico Hotel, has a couple of cottages for rent at modest rate for modest accommodations near Plymouth.

■■■

RESTAURANTS ON TOBAGO are going to be hotel dining rooms for most vacationers, especially if you have your room on the MAP, which gives you breakfasts and dinners daily. However, when you are driving around the island, plan to have an island lunch at Speyside at the **Bird of Paradise Inn,** a place that has a personality of its own and meals served—sometimes. Call in advance to be sure about a reservation and ask about the mealtime menu if you are a fussy eater.

At **Buccoo Village,** there's a small snack shop/boutique that posts a sign that said, when I looked, "People are people and should be treated like people 'cause we all are the same people, as I was saying . . ." The place is **Hendricks,** the roti and bakes (crusty pastries with filling) are usually good, and management gives no credit—everyone pays cash. If you don't like *very* informal island surroundings, forget about this place.

Arnos Vale is one special setting for dinner and food improved when the chef from Robinson Crusoe moved here after RC closed. Fish and other specials worth ordering—and if you demand gourmet food, you'll have a hard time finding any place that's up to haute cuisine standards on Tobago. Varieties of Tobagonian cooking are what's best on this island.

For *very* casual dining in local surroundings, visit **Voodoo** or **Fairymaid,** both in Scarborough, up on the hill heading out of town toward the hospital. Fairymaid's chef made a name for himself (and his cuisine) when he was chef at a now closed hotel which was known as Blue Haven. The **Kountry Kottage** on Bernard Street is a "fast food" style place down a short alley on the hill. Local folk seem to like it, as they do the **Food Lab** with its adjacent **Atomic Lounge,** both behind closed doors on the edge of Scarborough.

Two interesting looking places with an opened-and-closed history that I suspect responds to the number or European and North American tourists on this island are **Kihlman "Gourmet Restaurant** at Black Rock and the **Old Donkey Cart** on Bacolet Street in Scarborough. Check at Mt. Irvine for status of these two and know that you can get a good sandwich at the **Tobago Golf Club,** at the entrance to the Mt. Irvine Hotel drive, at about half the price (and twice the service) of those served at Mt. Irvine. **John Grant's** place, across the road from the Crown Reef Hotel, had a patio full of diners when I looked in and their food looked good.

■■■

PLACES WORTH FINDING ON TOBAGO are led by one that is off the northwest shore. **Buccoo Reef** "ain't what it used to be," but if you are not a reef expert, it can be fascinating. Although conservation "laws" have now been instituted, they came too late for parts of this reef, and some of the interesting coral had already been plucked to be taken home, or at least to shore, for sale. Some of the fish, too familiar with bigger fish in funny-looking snorkel masks, have fled. If you have never glimpsed the underwater world, the shallow reefs at Buccoo are interesting; if you've been diving elsewhere, you'll find this pretty tame by comparison. A number of local entrepreneurs make the trip at low tide on boats out of Buccoo

Village—including the Johnson brothers, who are brothers in spirit if not in fact. You can drive to the village or take a taxi from your hotel to pick up one of the boats. No matter who your skipper and mate are, the craft will probably be locally built, with a hefty engine (and a hotshot driver). Snorkelers tumble over the side into waist-high water armed with a pair of tattered sneakers so that they don't step on spiky sea urchins, and fins and mask that have been shared with countless others. Some folks choose to bring their own equipment. The tour almost always includes a stop on the return at Nylon Pool, so called because its water is clear—a fact which I've never understood being touted here since the water is superb at most places along this leeward shore.

Fort James, perched on a point at Plymouth, on the northwest coast, is mostly ruins, but the view from here is interesting. The original fort was built by the British in 1768, occupied by the French, and is well signposted by the Trinidad and Tobago Tourist Board. The visit will take about 10 minutes, tops, but is worth a stop for the view across the bay toward Turtle Beach.

Fort King George, built by the British in 1777 above the town of Scarborough, is far more interesting, although also in ruins. Follow the winding road up past the hospital and on up to the top of the hill, where the parking area is clearly marked. The fort was captured by the French, who occupied it from 1781 until 1793, and called it Fort Castries. The British recaptured it in 1793, the French in 1802–3, the British again controlled it from 1803 to 1854—and so goes the history of Tobago. Buildings and ruins have markers so you know when you are looking at the Officer's Mess, the Lighthouse, the Bell Tower. The gardens, the chirping of birds, the giggles of children who live at this hilltop, and the spectacular views along the shore and out to the Atlantic need no signposts.

Exploring is interesting on Tobago. Your choices are poking and prowling from your rented car along shoreside points, namely **Rocky Point, Bacolet** with its beach, and **Englishman's Bay,** a small bay on the northside, with large rocks and deep white sand, all about 7½ winding miles from Mount Irvine Bay Hotel. When you head up to Arnos Vale, don't turn at the entrance, but head on another mile or so following a narrow track over a stone bridge for about 15 yards to the **old sugar mill ruins,** where you can note a plate that claims that the equipment was made in Glasgow in 1851. The boiler had a canopy over it, supported by 6 metal Doric columns.

At **Grafton,** up a very rough track, Mrs. Alefounder, an Englishwoman, sometimes welcomes outsiders when she feeds her birds. Check through your hotel if you are interested in making an appointment for a visit, and be prepared to step into another world. Upended rum bottles are strung to tree limbs and other props for suitable water bottles, and birds swoop through and around the open kitchen walls and through the house. There's a huge tree in the front (near where you'll park) that is a bird "hotel," with several varieties pecking and nesting among the foliage, sharing space with iguanas and other Caribbean animals. An experience not to be missed, if you have any interest in Caribbean birds.

At *CHARLOTTEVILLE,* about 2 hours from most of the hotels, along a hardtop road on the southeast coast, there's the **Bird of Paradise Inn** and the **Government Rest House,** very clean and right at the beach, for snacking and drinking. If you can raise the boatman and have enough time, ask him to take you around to **Lovers Beach,** which you can only reach by boat (but be sure to make arrangements for him to come back to get you!).

Speyside, on the southeast coast, is the departure point for the boats to **Bird of Paradise Island.** Do not head here expecting to see the rare bird of paradise; although the place was stocked several years ago, sighting the birds today is rare. The island seems to have its own lure for people who like tromping around remote places.

■■

SPORTS ON TOBAGO range from very professional golf at the Mount Irvine course, to tennis (also at that hotel) and some scuba facilities, but there's not much in the way of organized sailing. Check with the Johnson brothers at Buccoo Village about going out in a boat; they can make arrangements if anyone can.

Golf at Mount Irvine was pushed into prominence by television, with part of a tournament filmed on *Wide World of Sports.* A few people are still talking about it as a claim to fame, but most visitors are content to register at the nicely appointed clubhouse to set out on the 18-hole, 6780-yard, par 72 course. (The Bermuda grass on the greens was "imported from Georgia" and takes constant attention in the Caribbean sun.) Winter months, when the homeowners around Mount Irvine Estates are in residence and the hotel is full, sometimes require sign-up times, but most days you can have the place pretty much to yourself—paying a premium if you are a guest at other than Mount Irvine (about $15 greens fees).

Tennis has not taken hold on Tobago. There's a court at Mount Irvine, but not much else.

Scuba is centered at Crown Reef and Mt. Irvine, where arrangements can be made. With the start of *Evecar Travel*'s special scuba

holidays, operated through Ray and Jim Young's *Dive Tobago Shop,*
Tobago got some top-quality professional advice and teaching for
scuba. Inquire from the Trinidad & Tobago Tourist Office about
details for scuba holidays, if your local travel agent doesn't have the
facts. Count on about TT$40 per dive, plus TT$8 for regulator, vest,
mask, and fins. Five dives run about TT$180. Experienced divers
who bring their own equipment can find challenging sites, but
don't count on the last word in high-powered organization anywhere but Dive Tobago headquarters.

■■■

TREASURES AND TRIFLES ON TOBAGO are limited to what's
available at the market and a few small shops in Scarborough plus
whatever items have been brought in for tourists to the shops at
Mount Irvine and Crown Point area hotels. Check the stock at the
small shop at Buccoo Village where the person I talked with said
she could sew up dresses and other clothes for anyone who bought
fabric, knew what they wanted, and had the time (and inclination)
to wait for the work to be done. Shopping is not a main attraction
for Tobago.

Index

NOTES

NOTES

NOTES

NOTES

NOTES

NOTES

NOTES

NOTES

NOTES

NOTES